The A-Z of Contract Clauses

Sixth Edition

The A-Z of Contract Clauses

Sixth Edition

Deborah Fosbrook, BA (Hons)
Barrister of the Honourable Society of Gray's Inn

and

Adrian C Laing, LLB (Exon)
Solicitor Advocate, Laing & Co
Barrister of the Honourable Society of Inner Temple

Bloomsbury Professional

Bloomsbury Professional, Maxwelton House, 41–43 Boltro Road, Haywards Heath, West Sussex, RH16 1BJ

First Edition 1996

Second Edition 2003

Third Edition 2006

Fourth Edition 2008

Fifth Edition 2010

Sixth Edition published by Bloomsbury Professional 2014

© Deborah Fosbrook and Adrian C Laing 1996–2014

A CIP catalogue number for this book is available from the British Library.

ISBN   978 1 78043 196 3

Typeset by Phoenix Photosetting, Chatham, Kent
Printed in the UK by CPI Group (UK) Ltd, Croydon, CR0 4YY

With love to our children Katie, David, William, George and Peter.

Preface

Benefits of The A-Z of Contract Clauses Sixth Edition

This book and CD-Rom is an essential and invaluable commercial reference resource which provides quick, convenient and easy access to thousands of individual contract clauses; rights; definitions and terms to enable you to draft agreements that are clear, concise and comprehensive.

The authors are leading experts in copyright, contract and intellectual property and have extensive experience across many industries, thus enabling them to combine business and trade knowledge with the legal and practical aspects of concluding an agreement.

This book has been used and recommended by leading lawyers, law societies, universities, international film, TV and distribution companies, literary, media and advertising agencies, authors, publishers, sports bodies, government and trade organisations as well as other successful manufacturers, merchandising and online businesses in Europe, India, Australia and worldwide.

The main clause headings are sub-divided into broad areas: DVD, Videos and Discs; Film and Television; General Business and Commercial; Internet and Websites; Purchase and Supply of Products; Services; Merchandising; Publishing; Sponsorship; University, Library and Educational.

This book allows you to grasp the essence of the contents of agreements and to understand how clauses may be changed in order to achieve a completely different outcome and purpose.

It will assist as a reference resource checklist to identify topics which have not been covered in a contract. It will enable you to negotiate with greater confidence and enhance your drafting skills. The wide selection of clauses across industries encourages you to consider how to improve the terms that you may agree.

The clauses will act as building blocks and you will be able to vary and adapt them to suit your project which will save time and money. It will enable you to create a draft document for discussion rather than just raise an idea and so you can establish the initial parameters of the terms to your advantage.

It will help you in revising your existing contracts and ensure that you are not assigning ownership of new technology or rights or data which do not exist now but may be created in the future to a third party.

When required to review an agreement provided by a potential supplier or distributor you will be able to draw up your own list of key points and clauses to be added and so have the ability to effectively propose amendments.

The New Edition

The aim with every new edition is to create new contract clauses across a broad spectrum of subjects to take account of new legislation, case law, technology, gadgets, trends, trade practices and codes and also to develop new drafting concepts dealing with issues for the future. Account has been taken of the increasing demands of an interactive and multi-layered media environment which most organisations now encompass in their strategies.

There has been an increase in cross-promotion, collaborations and endorsements as well as sponsorship of events, festivals, products, services and exploitation through apps, mobiles, competitions, social media and more specific campaigns within a timeframe and target market. This has resulted in an increasing necessity to be clear as to who owns material; who has final editorial control; the processes of consultation that may be required for any changes and how gross and net receipts are defined; whether there is a licence or an assignment; and the format; rights and territory that have been cleared for use. The failure to acquire and control images related to a brand may result in a company not being able to register as a trade mark artwork which was commissioned for a product label. It is important to clarify and avoid disputes relating to ownership and to have control of domain names, titles, character names, logos, text, films, photographs, images, sound recordings or computer-generated adaptations, games or websites. Where rights are to be licensed to a third party for a new project then the ownership and extent of use of any new versions should be established at an early stage.

There are also increasing demands for parties to meet quality control provisions as to the source, methods of production and supply of services, products and material. There are clauses relating to environment, fair trading, compliance and policies in order to meet a corporate, charitable or personal ethical approach.

There are new clauses throughout the book including those relating to competitions, copyright clearance, due diligence, exclusivity, disclaimers, option, royalties, moral rights, originality, confidentiality, data protection, credits and copyright notices, waiver and third party transfer. There are new terms for force majeure and jurisdiction, as well as clauses which reduce or confirm liability or set out to extend or limit indemnity provisions, manage risk or transfer of ownership or confirm the scope of product liability. There are clauses to develop, option, produce, acquire, commission, licence, sub-licence and exploit rights, services, products and work supplied by an individual or company on the internet, via mobiles and apps, in print or in other formats.

In addition there are two new background articles and an extended legal, commercial and business development directory.

The CD-Rom allows you to access clauses under individual alphabetical letters; so that you can scroll through to find suitable clauses to copy, paste and edit. There is also a word search facility which can be used to assist you in your endeavours to find the perfect terms and conditions; and also to search the background articles and directory. You will also find the index in the book provides assistance as you will be referred to other main clause headings that may be relevant.

Throughout the book the main clause headings are on the top of the left page and the sub-headings are on the top of the right.

Jurisdiction: UK, EU, US, Commonwealth and worldwide.

Deborah Fosbrook BA (Hons), Barrister of Gray's Inn.

Her work has included Business Affairs in BBC Programme Acquisition and Head of Legal and Business Affairs and Company Secretary, TV-am plc. Co-author of The Media and Business Contracts Handbook (5th Edition).

Adrian C Laing LLB (Exon) Solicitor Advocate, Laing & Co. www.laingandco.co.uk

Previous roles as Director of Legal Affairs and Company Secretary HarperCollins Publishers; Assistant Head of Licensing Independent Television Commission and Consultant Thames Television plc. Co-author of The Media and Business Contracts Handbook (5th Edition). Also author of Rehab Blues and RD Laing: A Life.

Deborah Fosbrook and Adrian C Laing

January 2014

no valid explanation is provided which is accepted by the [Company]. The [Company] may decide at its absolute discretion that the [person] be sent a written warning notice from an authorised officer of the [Company]. The warning letter shall set out the full detailed grounds, provide the conditions which the [Company] wishes to be fulfilled and suggest a meeting to resolve the matter with the [human resources department]. In the event that the attendance of the [person] shall not improve as specified by the [Company] in order to fulfil the [person's] contract of employment. Then the [Company] shall be entitled to summarily dismiss the [person] without further notice provided that the [person] shall have been engaged or employed by the [Company] for less than [–]. In such event the [Company] shall pay all sums due or owing up to the date that the [person] ceases to work for the [Company].

A.005

The [Company] accepts and agrees that there may be occasions when the [Employee] may be absent due to domestic, family, dental, health, transport, weather conditions or due to some unforeseen emergency. The [Company] agrees that failure to give advance notice shall not in those circumstances be sufficient grounds to give a written warning regarding absence. Provided that the [Employee] contacts the [Company] as soon as reasonably possible to advise them of the position and unless the whole [Company] is affected and closed the [Employee] shall either substitute alternative hours at a later date or allocate the absence as part of their annual leave.

A.006

If the [Employee] is absent from work due to sickness, ill-health or incapacity for [specify days] in any [12-month] period (whether continuous or not). The [Company] shall have the right to decide that it can no longer continue to make the position available to the [Employee] and shall have the right to terminate the contract by notice in writing. The [Company] shall only be liable to pay any salary due to the date of termination of the contract. The [Employee] agrees that there shall be no sums due as compensation for loss of the position, damage to reputation or other financial loss which may arise. The [Company] shall provide a reference to the [Employee] which shall explain that the contract ended due to [health/other] reasons and was not connected to their standard of work in that position.

A.007

The [Company] reserves the right to set off against payment made to the [Executive] any statutory sick pay benefits received by it.

A.008

The [Executive] shall provide his/her exclusive services to the best of their skill and ability on a full-time basis and normal working days shall be [specify days/hours/breaks]. The [Executive] shall perform all his/her duties in a professional and diligent manner and shall not supply services of the same or similar nature to the job description under this Agreement to any third party without the prior written consent of the [Company].

A.009

In the event of absence from work the [Executive] may notify the [Company] as soon as possible, in person wherever possible or by the best available means at his/her disposal in the circumstances. In any event the [Executive] agrees to provide the [Company] with as much notice as possible in the event that the [Executive] is unable whether as a result of sickness or general circumstances beyond the control of the [Executive] to perform any of his/her obligations under this Agreement.

A.010

If the [Executive] is absent from duty without permission and without a reason acceptable to the [Company]. The [Company] reserves the right to withhold payment or deduct from the [Executive's] salary a day's pay for each day of unauthorised absence. Disciplinary action may also be taken in accordance with the Disciplinary Procedure in Schedule [–].

A.011

In the event that there is repeated unauthorised absence for all or part of the day when the [Employee] is expected to be at the office of the [Company]. Then the [Company] shall arrange for a meeting to discuss the matter with the [Employee]. Where the situation does not improve and the absences continue then the [Company] shall be entitled to give written notice of the termination of the contract of employment.

A.012

If the event that a temporary person or someone who is on a fixed term contract is unable for any reason (whether through illness, family problems, loss of a close relative, and/or a hospital, dentist, eye or other appointment relating to their health or an immediate family member which they are required to attend) does not attend work to fulfil their duties under this agreement for more than [–] days in any week of the agreement. Then the [Enterprise] shall be entitled but no obliged to give written notice of termination of the agreement which shall have immediate effect. No compensation for loss of any nature shall be due and the liability of the [Enterprise] shall only be for those days of work completed to the date of termination.

A.013

The Company agrees that the [Employee] shall be able to take such leave for dental, hospital, school and such other personal and family commitments which may be required during normal working hours provided that the [Employee] as far as possible notifies the Line Manager in advance by email exceptions are made for emergencies. Provided that the [Employee] ensures that the time is recompensed by either working additional hours and/or deducted from any holiday and/or bank leave due.

A.014

It is agreed by both parties that any unnotified leave of absence shall not be deemed a breach of this agreement where it is due to a genuine emergency, delay and/or failure to attend arising from a matter relating to the [Employee], his/her family, immediate grandparents and/or brothers and/or sisters which does not relate to ill health or death of the [Employee]. Provided that upon return to work the [Employee] provides an explanation in writing and agrees not to be paid for those dates where the [Employee] is absent. In the event that the period of absence on any one occasion is more than [number] days then the parties agree that the [Company] shall be entitled to notify the [Employee] of a date by which the [Employee] must return to work as per the agreement otherwise it will be terminated on that date.

General Business and Commercial

A.015

The [Company] shall have the right to terminate this Agreement immediately by notice in writing to the [Contractor] in the event that the [Contractor] is unable or unwilling in any period of [six months] to perform the Agreement as required for more than [twenty days] in total whether consecutive or not.

A.016

The [Specialist] agrees that he shall attend and appear as an [expert] in the case on the following dates and times at the specified location [[–] for the purpose of providing written and oral evidence of [[–]. The [Specialist] accepts that it is vital that he is not absent for any reason unless prevented by an emergency, serious medical grounds, death or an Act of God.

A.017

The [person] undertakes that they shall be required to attend the [Exhibition] from [date] to [date] and that they be obliged to work from [–] to [–] hours with only short breaks. In consideration of your agreement not to be absent for any reason and to recompense you for the longer hours you shall receive the additional fee of [–].

A.018

Any absence of any nature must be notified to [name] by email or telephone by you personally on the actual day itself specifying the reason and when you expect to be able to attend. Any absence will result in no payment for that day and a continuous absence of [five working days] will mean that the position is no longer available to you and you will be sent in the post any sums that may be due.

A.019
The [Company] agrees that in any one-year period the [person] shall be entitled to take [five days'] unpaid leave of absence in additional to their annual holiday to carry out public duties, union work, academic research and training.

A.020
The [Client] agrees that once the [booking/appointment] has been confirmed and a date and time agreed. That the [Company] shall be entitled to be paid whether or not the [Client] attends the [booking/appointment] unless at least [three days] prior notice is given to the [Company].

A.021
Absence or failure to attend all or any part of the [seminars/workshops] at the specified dates and times agreed between the [Company] and the [Client] shall not entitle the [Client] to any refund, reimbursement or otherwise of the fees paid.

A.022
Any absence or failure to attend on the dates specified in the Agreement shall not automatically entitle the [Company] to terminate the Agreement and/or to withhold any sums which may be due for other work which has been completed. The [Company] agrees that the [Person] shall be provided with the opportunity to rectify the matter within an additional period of [specify] days. Failure to do so shall mean that the [Company] shall have the right to take such steps as it thinks fit in the circumstances.

A.023
Where the [Consultant] is absent and/or out of [country] for more than [number] days for any reason whether due to holidays, health or otherwise. He/she shall ensure that there is a nominated contact at the [Consultant Company] at all times who has the same level of expertise and knowledge who is able to advise the [Enterprise]. Failure to provide this alternative shall be deemed a breach of this agreement.

A.024
It is a specific requirement of this Agreement that the following persons are involved in this [Project] and fulfil the following roles [[specify name/role/ job description]. The funding for the [Project] is provided solely upon that

5

basis and no substitution and/or absence may be covered by a third party and/or any other personnel. The [Company] agrees and undertakes that all the persons specified are available and shall not be absent and have been engages by the [Company] for the [Project].

Merchandising

A.025
The [Company] shall be obliged to notify the [Agent/Author] in the event that there is to be a change of management and/or the [Managing Director] of the [Company] is or will be absent for more than [specify] months. It is an important condition of this Agreement that the [Managing Director] be available and involved with the production, distribution and marketing of the [Product]. Where there is a change of management and/or the [Managing Director] is no longer employed by the [Company] and/or is to be absent for long periods. Then the [Author/Agent] shall have the right to terminate the Agreement and to ensure that all rights under the Agreement shall revert to the [Author/Agent].

A.026
The absence of any key personnel involved in the development, production, marketing and distribution of the [Product] shall not entitle the [Licensor] to cancel, terminate and/or amend the Agreement. Provided that the [Licensee] can ensure and is able to establish that the quality, content, promotion and sales of the [Product] shall not be damaged, harmed and/or diminished in any way.

A.027
Where the [Author/Assignor] is unable to attend any of the [dates/events] under the Agreement and/or is absent for any reason such as ill health, bereavement, transport delays, and prior commitments to their employee and/or publisher. Then such failure to attend shall not be considered reasonable grounds for reducing and/or delaying any payments and/or termination of the Agreement. Where feasible both parties shall endeavour to agree alternative [dates/events] upon the same and/or similar terms. Further no sums shall be due in compensation for any such absence and/or failure to attend at any time by the [Author/Assignor] to the [Assignee].

A.028
Where the [Licensor] is unable to fulfil all and/or any substantial part (namely more than [number] per cent of the appearances, promotions and marketing) of the terms of the licence granted to the [Licensee] due to the absence and/or failure of [name] to attend for any reason whatsoever. Then the [Licensor] agrees that, for each date and/or event, the [Licensee] shall

possible either before and/or on the day of the absence. Please provide a brief reason for the absence and a contact number and/or email so that you can be subsequently contacted if required by the [College/School/other].

ACCEPTANCE

DVD, Video and Discs

A.051
The [Licensee] agrees to reject or accept the [Master Material/other] within [one month] of delivery. In the event that the material is not acceptable then the reasons shall be set out by email or letter and the [Licensor] provided with the opportunity to provide a substitute. Material which is not accepted shall be collected by the [Licensor] or returned at the [Licensor's] expense.

A.052
The [Company] shall deliver the [DVD/Disc] subject to receipt and clearance of the payment. The [Client] shall be deemed to have accepted the [DVD/Disc] once it is delivered and shall not be entitled to return the [DVD/Disc] once opened from the packaging unless there is a defect or damage to the [DVD/Disc]. Where the wrong order has been delivered then the [DVD/Disc] should be returned unopened and unused to the [Supplier]. [None of these conditions are considered by the [Company] to supersede your statutory legal rights as a consumer.]

A.053
Delivery of the [Software/Disc] to the address of the [Company] shall not be deemed to be acceptance of the material. The [Company] shall have [number] days to assess, test and review the content of the [Software/Disc] from the date of delivery. The [Company] agrees that within [number] days of delivery it shall notify the [Supplier] as to whether it has accepted or rejected the [Software/Disc]. In the event that the [Software/Disc] is accepted then the [Company] shall authorise the payment under clause [–] and arrange payment within [number] days. Where the [Software/Disc] is rejected then the [Company] shall return the [Software/Disc] and all copies to the [Supplier]. Where the parties do not intend to pursue the matter further in order to resolve the problems which resulted in the rejection. The [Company] shall arrange for all reproductions of any nature in any medium to be deleted, destroyed and/or erased which are in its possession and/or control which are derived from the [Software/Disc].

A.054

The [Company] agrees to supply the [Client] with [Discs/other] which shall contain copies of all the images and filming which the [Company] shall arrange to be taken at the [Event] on behalf of the [Client].The material shall not be edited and/or adapted by the [Company]. In addition the [Company agrees to provide all the original master material and any copies which is in its possession and/or control and that of any person involved to take such images and/or film. Further the [Company] agrees that neither it nor the persons it engages to make the images and/or film shall retain, store and/or supply any part of any of the material in any format and/or medium except to the [Client].

Film and Television

A.055

This offer may be cancelled if your signed acceptance is not received in good time before the hour fixed for the broadcast and the [Broadcaster] considers that cancellation is necessary on account of scheduling requirements.

A.056

The [Company] shall endeavour to ensure that all subjects that may require approval and/or acceptance shall be carried out as quickly as possible and shall not delay the [Project]. The parties shall operate by allowing each other at least [–] working days to respond to any request. All requests of any nature shall be sent for the attention of [–] and copied to [–].

A.057

There is no acceptance of responsibility for the damage to, loss of or return of unsolicited material of any nature which is sent to the [Company].

A.058

The [Distributor] shall be deemed to have accepted the [Material] if no notice of rejection on quality and/or technical grounds is received by the [Licensor] within [number] days of delivery. The ownership of the physical material shall not be transferred to the [Distributor] until payment in full has been received by the [Licensor]. All risks shall pass to the [Distributor] upon delivery in respect of the loss, damage and/or destruction of the [Material] and the [Distributor] agrees to reimburse the [Licensor] in respect of the full cost of any replacement that may be necessary.

A.059

The delivery of a [Script/Proposal] to the [Company] by any member of the public in any format shall not be deemed to mean that the material can be treated as confidential and/or private by the [Company]. Nor can the acceptance of delivery of the material by the [Company] entitle the [Author] to seek to prohibit the [Company] creating its own independent and original programme based on the generic topic submitted.

A.060
Where [Material] is submitted to any department of the [Company] then it shall not be deemed to be accepted at the point of delivery. The [Company] shall have a period of [number] days within which to view and assess the [Material] and to decide whether it is suitable for exploitation and use by the [Company]. The [Company] shall notify the [Agency] that all and/or part of the [Material] has been accepted and offer the terms of use required and the fee proposed. The [Agency] may then accept and/or decline the offer by the [Company] which shall be in accordance with [specify document] of the [Company].

General Business and Commercial

A.061
If for any reason you wish to cancel acceptance of a place before entry or [name] does not join the course after the start date then a full terms fees shall still be due and paid less any deposit. No discounts, deductions or refunds shall be made for any reason.

A.062
The [Client] is deemed to have accepted the [quote/written offer/brochure details] when they agree to pay the sums specified by the [Company]. In the event that for any reason the contract cannot be fulfilled by the [Company] then an alternative equivalent standard booking shall be offered or where this is not accepted by the [Client] a full refund shall be made by the [Company].

A.063
Completion of the work, delivery of the goods or signature of a receipt form shall not constitute acceptance under this Agreement. The [Client] shall have a period of [28 days] in which to inspect the [Goods/Services/Work] and to provide written confirmation by email, fax or letter of acceptance or where material is not accepted to advise the [Company] to arrange collection or post it at the [Company's] cost.

A.064
Any tender, quotation or exchange of letters setting out the proposed terms in respect of [Goods/Work/Services/other] to be provided to the [Company/Government Department] shall not be deemed and should not be considered a contractual acceptance by the [Company/Government Department]. All proposals must be approved by the [Board of Directors/Chief Executive]

and adhere to the [Company's] policies and practices. Any letter, email or other document is an acceptance in principle and as such is subject to contract and conditional upon the signature and conclusion of a formal document setting out in detail all the rights and obligations of the parties.

A.065
Acceptance of the [Work/Article] shall take place when the full fee is paid by the [Client]. The [Client] shall have been provided with the opportunity to view the [Work/Article] in the exact form and content in which it is to be sold to the [Client] by the [Distributor]. The [Client] shall not be entitled after acceptance to seek a refund based on artistic, design and/or colour grounds.

Internet and Websites

A.066
Any person who would like to use this [Website] must agree to be bound by the terms and conditions of the [Company] and you are deemed to have accepted such terms when you access and use the [Website].

A.067
I agree that by ticking the box [and logging my details] that I have confirmed my acceptance that I will access, order products and use the [Website] in accordance with those terms and conditions specified in the [Terms and Conditions] pdf set out below. That I agree that I shall not be entitled to continue to use the [Website] if I no longer wish to be bound by such terms and conditions. Provided that I shall still be obliged to pay any sums that may be due or owing to the [Company] and the [Company] shall deliver any products that may have been ordered.

A.068
Important – please read this document carefully before [using this website/ breaking the seal to release the disc] as by doing so you are agreeing to be bound by the following conditions [–].

A.069
By breaking the seal you agree in full to the terms and conditions for the use of the [Disc] set out in the Licence Agreement which is contained in the Package.

A.070
When you access and use this [Website] whether for browsing, research, placing orders, playing games, or using any forum for exchanges between

individuals you are bound by the terms and conditions for access and use which you accept by either confirming your acceptance of the terms or by going beyond the first front page of the [Website] to other pages and links.

A.071

When you enter this [Website] you must accept the access and use contract which is displayed by the [Owner] and [Operator]. You are not authorised to use any of the material including text, data, images, banners, logos or databases other than for your own personal use at home. Any supply of material to a third party which is to be placed on another website or used for commercial purposes requires the prior consent of the [Owner] and [Operator] [specify contact details].

A.072

By installing the software which is on the [Disc/USB] into your computer you accept that you will be required to fulfil and be bound by the terms and conditions of the Licence Agreement which sets out the terms of trading and supply of the [Company]. If you do not wish to accept these terms then do not install or load the [Disc/USB/other].

A.073

There are no contractual terms and conditions which you must accept to use this [Website]. However we expect you to recognise and respect that material is displayed which is owned by other people. if you wish to use any of it for private home use and/or educational research and reports then you must provide a proper credit of their name and our [Website] as the source on which you found it. No authorisation is provided for any commercial use of any nature and prior written consent of the copyright owner is required in each case. Any person who acts in an unreasonable manner and/ or is defamatory and/or is in breach of the rights of any nature of a third party and/or the [Company] may be excluded by the [Company] from the [Website]. The [Company] may also seek to be indemnified for all costs and expenses incurred and/or sums paid in settlement and/or as a result of legal proceedings. Further the [Company] shall have the right to recover all its own legal, in-house management and other professional experts' costs and legal expenses that may be incurred as well as a claim for damages, interest, and to recover all sums incurred.

A.074

The use and access to the software is subject to the [User] agreeing to the terms and conditions displayed on this [Website] [reference] and the [User] will be deemed to have accepted and entered into agreement with the [Company] by downloading the software from the [Website].

A.075

If you proceed further than the first page of this [Website], then you accept and agree that any information, data, images, music, recordings, text, film, directory, databases, trade marks, logos, banners, advertisements and products may only be viewed and stored on your computer, hardware, software, discs, USB or any other device or equipment on a temporary basis for no more than [specify duration] and for your own private and non-commercial purposes. There is no implied or express licence granted to use any part of this [Website] or anything on it for commercial, educational or any other purpose. In the event that you wish to do so then please email [contact] setting out the details of your request. Failure to adhere to the terms of the use of the [Website] could result in the issue of legal proceedings against you without further notice.

A.076

This is a commercial [Website] which is owned and controlled by [Company]. All trademarks, logos, videos, films, images, text, databases, photographs, graphics, audio material, blogs, downloads, uploads, podcasts, music and any other material in any other format whether television, radio, DVDs, mobile phone content, and/or interactive games on this [Website] are owned, controlled and/or licensed from the copyright owner by the [Company]. You accept by your use and access to this [Website] that you agree to be bound by the following terms and conditions;

1.1 That as a visitor to this [Website] you have no right to copy, store, and retrieve, reproduce, supply, transfer and/or authorise the use of any such material by a third party.

1.2 That any copies made by you on your laptop, computer, and/or any storage and/or retrieval and/or interactive device such as a USB, mobile phone, gadget, disc or otherwise shall be temporary and only for your own personal use for no more than [number] hours.

1.3 That you agree after that period to delete all copies of any material. You agree that failure to do so could result in the threat of legal proceedings and/or a claim by the [Company] against you personally for damages and costs and/or any other remedy and/or any other copyright owner of any material at any time.

A.077

Access and use of this website is subject to the laws of the country in which you are living as well as where this site is used. Acceptance by the [Company] of your use of this site does not absolve you from a personal legal liability for the material and content that you submit and/or display and/or supply to third parties. The [Company] does not accept any responsibility for any costs, damages, fines, expenses and/or otherwise that you may incur through a criminal and/or civil action against you by any person, body or other local, government and/or national entity.

A.078

The acceptance by you of any email, image, download, advertisement and marketing, product, links, newsletter, cookies, software or otherwise through this site shall not mean that the [Company] which owns and controls this site and/or the [Enterprise] who operate it on their behalf shall be able to provide any reassurance as to whether it is genuine and/or a scam.

Merchandising

A.079

The [Retailer] shall be deemed to have accepted all [Articles] which are not returned within [7 days] of delivery.

A.080

The [Distributor] shall endeavour to ensure that all the agents, retailers and wholesalers agree to be bound by and accept the terms and conditions relating to the marketing and sales of the [Product] set out in this Agreement.

A.081

The [Author] shall not be bound to accept or agree to the marketing of any [Products] which would:

1.1 Not be suitable in style and/or content for the [children's/other] market.

1.2 The sample or prototype is not of an acceptable quality and/or standard and/or does not accurately reflect the artwork and/or text in the [Books].

1.3 There is no additional advance to be paid to the [Author] and/or the estimated revenue is less than [figure/currency] per year.

1.4 The proposed licensee and/or manufacturer is not an established business and has no market presence in [country].

A.082

There shall be no obligation on the [Illustrator/Creator] of the [Artwork/Material] who has collaborated with the [Author/Company] to create the [Book] to accept any of the terms for the merchandising and commercial exploitation in any other media except in [hardback, paperback and audiotape]. The financial arrangements proposed by the [Author/Company] for any such agreement must ensure that the [Illustrator] receives no less sums than the [Author] and equal prominence as regards credits in all products and marketing material.

A.083

The [Author/Artist] accept and agree that the [Distributor] shall be entitled to develop, adapt, produce, distribute and market toys, food related products, clothes, stationery, audiotapes, computer games, DVDs, a programme or series for television, and any other item or product based on the [Book/Script]. The [Author/Artist] accept and agree that the artwork, text, names, and storylines may be different and not necessarily an accurate reflection of the [Book/Script].

A.084

The [Company] agrees that it shall be deemed to have accepted the [Products] if they have not notified the [Distributor] by [email/letter/order form] within [three days of the delivery of the [Products] in accordance with the confirmed [email/letter/order form].

A.085

Provided that the merchandising material supplied by the [Company] is in exact accordance with the sample products. Then the merchandising material shall be accepted by the [Client] on the day of delivery and the fee paid for the balance on the same day. Where there is an error or omission in the design, quality, number and/or any other reason why the merchandising material fails to match the sample and order. Then the [Client] may reject all the order and request a full refund to be paid immediately.

A.086

The parties agree that there may be colour, technical, material and layout variations between the samples provided before manufacture and the finished product. The [Manufacturer] agrees to notify the [Company] of any discrepancies and to provide a new sample on each occasion so that the [Company] can decide whether to proceed with the production. The [Company] shall not be bound to accept delivery of the order unless it is in accordance with any such agreed samples.

Publishing

A.087

The [Publisher] agrees to either accept or provide written reasons for the rejection of the [Manuscript] of the [Book] within [one calendar month] of delivery. The [Publisher] agrees that it shall only use valid substantial reasons relating to the writing, content and style which an independent third party would find to be relevant criticism. Minor additions, deletions and changes required for less than [number] pages shall not be considered sufficient grounds not to accept the [Manuscript].

A.088

The [Publisher] agrees to accept or provide written reasons for its rejection of the [Work] within [–] of delivery. The [Publisher] agrees that any rejection of the [Work] shall be limited to the following grounds namely failure by the [Author] to meet the required professional writing standards agreed and/or failure to comply with the specifics of the summary synopsis.

A.089

In the event that the [Author] shall deliver the [Work] by the specified delivery date [and in the form and content agreed between the parties] the [Publisher] shall be allowed [–] days to provide written confirmation of the acceptance or rejection of the [Work]. In the event that there is no such confirmation then [–] days after the specified delivery date the [Work] shall be deemed to have been accepted by the [Publisher].

A.090

The [Publisher] agrees that it shall accept the [Book] for publication provided it is delivered in complete form by the [date] and is a true reflection of the agreed summary in both content and style.

A.091

The [Publisher] shall not be entitled to refuse to accept the [Book] if the reason for the delay in delivering the manuscript is due to ill-health or injury of the [Author]. Provided that the delivery date shall only be extended by a maximum of [three calendar months], after that date the [Publishers] may terminate the agreement by notice in writing at any time. It is agreed that the parties shall resolve the issue of repayment of the sums due by negotiation and that in any event the [Author] shall be entitled to a repayment period scheduled over at least [–] years.

A.092

The disc and all the data included thereon is supplied to you the [Purchaser] by the [Publisher] based entirely on the [Book]. If you do not wish to be bound by the terms and conditions of the use of the disc and data please do not remove the seal from the wallet. The following terms set out in the attached Licence shall apply to the use of the book, disc and data whilst it is in the possession or control of the [Purchaser].

A.093

The approval by the [Publisher] of one chapter or section of the [Book] does not constitute acceptance of the manuscript under clause [–].

A.094

After the complete manuscript has been delivered to the [Publisher] in the agreed format. The [Publishers] agree that within [ten days] excluding weekends that they shall notify the [Author] as to whether they accept or reject the [Work]. If the [Work] is accepted then the [Publisher] shall immediately arrange for payment of any sums due on delivery without delay.

A.095

In the event that the [Work] is not accepted then the [Publisher] shall specify the reasons in writing by letter. The [Publisher] agrees that it shall enter into negotiations with the [Author] to permit the [Author] to have the opportunity to resubmit the manuscript after it has been amended based on the grounds of rejection specified by the [Publisher]. In the event that the [Work] is not accepted after it is resubmitted. The [Publisher] agrees to ensure that all rights in the [Work] of any nature shall revert to the [Author] and that the [Author] shall not be obliged to repay any sums paid prior to delivery of the manuscript.

A.096

The [Publisher] agrees that it shall accept the [Work] provided that it is written to the standard and in accordance with the original synopsis and chapter outline and is factually accurate and true and does not make any allegations and/or statements which are misleading and/or inaccurate.

A.097

The [Publisher] shall not be bound to accept any delivery of the [Manuscript] of the [Book] and/or pay any further sums to the [Author] where since signature of the agreement the [Publisher] has discovered that the [Author] has deliberately and actively misled the [Publisher] as to their true identity and/or background.

Purchase and Supply of Products

A.098

The acceptance shall be deemed by the execution and return of the Acknowledgement Copy of the Purchase Order by the [Seller] or the [Seller's] execution or commencement of work or commencement of delivery pursuant to the Purchase Order on the terms hereof by the [Seller].

A.099

The [Purchaser] shall have the right to conduct at its sole expense an incoming inspection of the products at the destination specified in the Bill of Lading in accordance with the inspection procedures set forth in Appendix [–] attached hereto and made an integral part hereof. The [Purchaser] shall notify the [Company] of the result of the inspection judgment (acceptance or rejection) in accordance with the said inspection procedures by [method] within [one month] after the date of arrival of the products at the destination. In the event that the [Purchaser] fails to notify the [Company] within the [one-month] period, then the [Purchaser's] right of rejection of the products shall lapse and the said products shall be deemed to have been accepted by the [Purchaser].

A.100
The [Company] agrees to accept or reject the [Goods] and pay the sum due in full provided that they are delivered as follows:

1.1 Delivery date [–].

1.2 Type of Goods [–].

1.3 Quantity [–].

1.4 All [Goods] shall be of premium quality in accordance with the [Sample Prototype] and shall not be damaged or otherwise not fit or suited to the specified purpose.

1.5 Specified purpose of the [Goods] [–].

1.6 All [Goods] are to bear the words, logo or image specified in the [Sample/Prototype] and packaging as set out in the attached Schedule [–].

A.101
We accept no liability for any [Goods] delivered and/or services provided to the [Company] unless the Order has been authorised by a senior executive of the [Company].

A.102
Signature of the invoice by the [Purchaser] shall be acceptance of the [Product] [and the terms and conditions of the invoice].

A.103
The [Customer] accepts the quotation and agrees to pay the sums specified by signing the Order Form setting out the terms and conditions and the Delivery and Completion dates.

A.104
The delivery of the [Products] to the [Company] shall constitute acceptance unless upon receipt of the [Products] the [Company] specifies the grounds of rejection or dissatisfaction.

A.105

The [Company] shall be given a period of [number] [weeks/months] from receipt of the [Goods] in which to inspect the products and associated packaging. During that period the [Company] shall be entitled to accept or reject the [Goods] for any reason which is due to the quality and/or content and/or fitness for purpose. At the end of that review period unless the [Supplier] has received a written response in any form rejecting the [Goods] then they shall have been accepted by the [Company] and subject to payment of the sums due become the property of the [Company].

A.106

The [Agent] shall at all times adhere to and follow the [Principal's] price lists, sale instructions and conditions and terms of business. The [Agent] shall not have the right under any circumstances to change or otherwise vary or alter the terms of business or prices of the [Products] specified by the [Principal]. The [Agent] shall not accept or agree to discounts, allowances, deferments in payment, issue receipts, accept or transfer [Products] or agree to adopt any other similar exchange or reduction without the prior [written] consent of the [Principal].

A.107

The [Agent] agrees that the [Principal] shall at its sole discretion be entitled to accept or reject any Order obtained by the [Agent] for any reason including poor credit rating of the client, bad payment record, unavailability of materials or textiles, conflict of interest with existing clients. The [Agent] shall not be entitled to receive any payment for any Order so rejected.

A.108

Any catalogue, advertisement, leaflets, flyers and website information, quotes, promotional offers and prices are purely for guidance only and may be amended, updated and varied at any time by the [Company]. The [Customer] may make an offer to the [Company] to order the [Goods/Services] and the [Company] will then decide whether to accept the order or not and enter into an agreement for delivery.

A.109

The submission of the order, or request to purchase the [Goods/Services] displayed in the brochure, catalogue, flyer or website whether by telephone, email, in writing or otherwise shall be considered an offer by the [Customer]. The contract shall be accepted by the [Company] when a purchase invoice is raised setting out the terms agreed and payment has been received in full.

A.110

The [Company] agrees that the Order and/or [Products] shall be considered to have been accepted when one of the following events has taken place:

1.1 The payment for the [Products] has been received and the funds transferred to the [Company].

1.2 The [Company] has issued a confirmation form allocating a reference and details of the contract.

1.3 The Order has been fulfilled and the [Products] delivered as specified.

A.111

The [Customer] shall be deemed to have accepted the terms and conditions of trading of the business set out in the [catalogue/brochure/flyer] when an order is placed and payment is made for the [Products/Services].

A.112

Without affecting your statutory rights the [Company] agrees to accept returns of any [Product] within [twenty-eight days] of purchase provided that there is a receipt as proof of purchase and the [Product] and packaging is undamaged and has not been used or worn. You shall be entitled to a full refund or to substitute another item. There are a number of exceptions for hygiene and safety reasons which will not be exchanged or refunded unless they are faulty or defective namely [specify]. Where there is no receipt and some other proof of purchase is provided then the item can only be exchanged or payment for the refund made in [vouchers].

A.113

There shall be no obligation on the [Company] to accept the alteration, cancellation, postponement or other modifications to this Agreement whether or not arising from circumstances which could not be reasonably foreseen at the time of negotiation and conclusion of the Agreement. An increase in demand, conflict of orders or work is not sufficient and the [Company] reserves the right to claim any losses, costs and/or expenses from the [Supplier] which arise as a direct and/or indirect result where the contract has to be transferred to a third party, and/or delays occur and/or the [Company] has to cancel work or orders and/or the [Supplier] cannot fulfil the work required.

A.114

The [Client] shall not be deemed to have accepted delivery where the actual delivery is not to the address specified in the [agreement/invoice].

A.115

Where the [Product] packaging has clearly been opened and/or damaged prior to delivery to the [Client]. Then delivery shall not have taken place and

A.126

The [Institute/Company] agrees and accepts that it has approved the samples of the [Sponsor's] [Product/Services] and the proposed [Sponsorship Plan] in advance of the signature of this Agreement. That copies are attached as [Schedule A] and form part of this Agreement and accepted and agreed to by both parties as forming the basis of this Agreement. That neither party shall change and/or amend anything in [Schedule A] without the written consent of the other party. That all copies of the [Products/Services] to be distributed and/or marketed by the [Sponsor] under this Agreement shall be exact copies of the samples.

A.127

he [Company] accepts that it is not the sole sponsor and that it has no right to act on behalf of the [Owner] and/or hold itself out as having the authority to grant access to and/or any rights to third parties in respect of the [Event/ Programme/Festival] except those specified as follows [specify].

University, Library and Educational

A.128

The [Institute/Library] shall be entitled to accept and/or reject the [Product/ Service] within [number] [days/months] of [delivery/connection/supply] by the [Company] without any liability to pay any sums due provided that all the [Product/Service] is returned to the [Company]. The [Institute/Library] may reject the [Product/Service] on any reasonable grounds including but not limited to:

1.1 That the [Product/Service] does not comply with the description, quality, content, fitness for purpose that was ordered and/or offered.

1.2 That the [Product/Service] is incompatible with the existing and/or proposed system, process, schedule, plans and/or development by the [Institute/Library].

1.3 That [delivery/connection/supply] was delayed, incomplete and/or not carried out by suitably qualified personnel and/or did not fulfil the function which was expected.

A.129

Delivery of the [Manuscript/Painting/Work] to the [Institute] shall not be deemed acceptance of the authenticity of the authorship of the [Manuscript/ Painting/Work] nor confirmation that the [Fee] shall be paid to the [Agent]. The [Institute] shall be allowed [number] [days] to carry out a full review and to engage an expert to verify the authorship. The expert shall, subject to the prior written approval of the [Agent], be authorised to examine the

[Manuscript/Painting/Work] and to carry out such sample tests as are normal practice in order to test the veracity of the authorship. In the event that the [Institute] has not accepted and/or rejected the [Manuscript/Painting/Work] by [date]. Then the [Agent] shall be entitled to serve written notice either that the [Manuscript/Painting/Work] has been deemed accepted and/or that the Agreement is terminated and that all rights to buy the [Manuscript/Painting/Work] by the [Institute] have ceased.

A.130
The [Institute] agrees that where the [Consultant] carries out the work and performs the services required in accordance with the terms of this Agreement. That unless the [Consultant] has received written notice that the work is unsatisfactory and/or incomplete by [date]. That the [Institute] shall pay the sums due in Clause [–] within [number] days of invoice by the [Consultant].

ACCESS

Employment

A.131
There is no automatic right of access to the premises and land owned or controlled by the [Company]. You are only entitled to enter the building specified in your contract of employment during your normal hours of work. No access is permitted at other times without the prior consent of [Name]. The [Company] reserves the right to deny access at any time for any reason. The [Company] reserves the right to request that you leave the building, premises or land whether during your normal working day or not and may require that you be escorted by a representative from security.

A.132
Your terms of employment require that you accept and adhere to the health, safety and security measures in force at the premises, buildings and land of the [Company]

A.133
The [Employee] shall have access at any time to the premises of the [Company] for the sole purpose of fulfilling the duties and responsibilities set out in the job description. There is no right to use the facilities, premises and/or resources for any other purpose, nor to enter the premises outside the hours of [specify].

A.134

The [Executive] shall be entitled to gain access to any part of the premises of the [Company] at any time without restriction provided that they show their [security pass/code] and to use the facilities, resources and organise their office staff as may be required in the circumstances. The [Executive] shall be entitled to send and receive personal emails using the equipment owned by the [Company] and to use the facilities, resources and staff to organise his/her personal and family matters.

A.135

Access to the site is restricted to authorised personnel of the [Company] who have been vetted and provided with security passwords and codes. Any such personnel who facilitate access of a third party of any nature without following the proper procedure for access in accordance with [Company] [specify document/policy] shall be escorted off the premises and dismissed with immediate effect as such conduct is deemed to constitute a flagrant breach of the security protocol for the site.

A.136

There are no restrictions and/or limitations on access to any part of the [Land/Building] provided that you do not cause any damage to the wildlife, buildings and/or use any equipment and/or products which will cause contamination of the soil, water and/or air. Photography is permitted but not filming without prior arrangement and consent with the [Owner].

DVD, Video and Discs

A.137

The [Licensor] agrees that it shall not have an automatic right of access and entry to the [Premises/Factory] where the [DVDs/Discs] are produced. The [Licensor] and its professional advisors shall no more than [twice] in each year be entitled upon written request to the [Distributor] to have a tour of all the [Premises/Factory]; to inspect the warehouse and storage facilities and to be shown all certificates and/or records to confirm compliance with current health and safety legislation.

A.138

The [Author] of the [Disc] shall have no right of access and/or entry to the [Company's] premises and offices at any time. The [Author] shall only be entitled to attend if invited to do so by the [Company].

A.139

In the event that the [Distributor]:

1.1   Fails to account for any royalties and/or make payments for any sums due to the [Company] for the exploitation of the rights in the [Film/Game] granted under this Agreement.

1.2   Operates where financially insolvent and/or is likely to be placed in receivership, administration and/or is unable to meet its financial commitments.

Then the [Distributor] agrees that the [Company] shall have the right to enter the premises, offices and warehouses [without prior written notice/with [number] hours prior written notice] and to recover and remove all master material relating to the [Film/Game], all packaging, marketing and stock which either belong to the [Company] and/or compensate for the value of the sums which are due and have not been paid to the [Company].

A.140
Where the [Company] fails to return the [Master Material] to the [Owner]. Then the [Company] agrees that the [Client] shall have the right to make an appointment and/or to have access without prior consent to the [warehouse/offices] at any address where the [Company] may be located in order to collect the [Master Material] and any copies.

Film and Television

A.141
The [Company] shall not be allowed unlimited access to the [Premises] and shall have no automatic right of entry. The [Company] shall only be permitted to use the locations marked in red specified on the attached Site Map in [Appendix A] and in accordance with the Time and Date Schedule in [Appendix B]. In addition to the Licence Fee charged for access from [date] to [date] the [Company] shall also be liable to pay to the [Licensor] additional electricity, gas, water, rates, drainage, sewer and other charges and expenses that arise and/or become due as a result of the [Companys'] access to and/or use of the [Premises] and any loss and/or damage. The [Licensor] shall be entitled to reinstate the [Premises] to the condition it was in prior to the access and/or use by the [Company]. Where it is necessary to replace old with new as the old version cannot be repaired then [Company] shall be responsible for the additional cost.

A.142
The [Company] shall be allowed non-exclusive access for the production of the [Film/Programme/Series] in accordance with the agreed [Schedule A] and the [Land/Premises] marked out on the map in [Schedule B]. Copies of both Schedules are attached to and form part of this Agreement. The

[Owner] agrees that there shall be no obstruction and/or restriction of the access required by the [Company] at any time.

A.143

The [Company] shall be permitted unlimited access to and use of the [Premises] at any time and may store, park, film and use the [Premises] in such manner as it thinks fit for the purpose of making the [Film]. The [Company] agrees that it shall be obliged to pay the [Owner] for any damages, costs, expenses, fees and liability that may arise as a direct and/ or indirect result of its access to and use of the [Premises].

A.144

Access to the location by the crew, actors, transport, lighting, catering and other personnel engaged in the [Film] shall be in accordance with the route/ markings in Schedule [-]. The [Company] agree that they shall ensure that noise levels do not exceed [number] decibels after [time] each day and that no access route shall be blocked and/or obstructed at any time.

General Business and Commercial

A.145

The [Company] reserves the right to withdraw the right of entry, exclude, expel, remove and/or suspend any person who in their reasonable opinion is using offensive or threatening language, acts and/or behaves in a manner which is unacceptable and/or is believed to be drunk, on illegal drugs or other substances or carrying an offensive weapon or an item which is considered a danger to the safety of others and/or who has been warned that their conduct on previous occasions is unacceptable. The decision of the [Company] is final. There shall be no obligation to refund any sums paid for membership, or in fees, to carry out any further investigations or to disclose confidential sources. The [Company] reserve the right to report any matter to the [police/other].

A.146

Access to and use of this [location/activity] is entirely at your own risk and we expect you to take all reasonable precautions to protect your property and to act in a reasonable manner. There are health and safety signs and warnings displayed for your guidance which relate to age, height, equipment and conduct which you are advised to follow.

A.147

The [Customer] must allow access at any reasonable time which is agreed in advance in order for the [system/equipment/other] to be installed, repaired, inspected or removed at [address]. Access shall include the use of all necessary land, buildings and facilities including water, electricity, gas, and light at the [Customer's] expense as may be necessary to carry out and complete the work required. After the completion of the work all rights to such material shall be owned by the [Customer/Company].

A.148
There is no right of access at any time to the [Premises] and the [Company] may refuse entry or vary the terms or restrict access to all or any parts without notice.

A.149
There is only limited access to the [Land/Premises] and where an area have been excluded, fenced off and/or locked then you are not permitted to enter. There is no automatic right of entry to all areas of this site.

Internet and Websites

A.150
Access to and use of the services on the [Website] are based on your agreement to the following terms with the [Company] which is the [Owner/ Host Packager] of the [Website] [specify]

A.151
You agree to be bound by the terms and conditions of access to and use of the [Website] and all data, information, text, images, logos, sound, music, graphics, slogans, banners, links, chatrooms, games, databases and any other material at any time.

A.152
You agree that you will not use any material derived from or based on this site for any purpose without providing a full credit to the copyright owner of the material and a credit to the [Website] as the reference source.

A.153
You agree that where any material is to be used for commercial purposes or any other purpose other than your own personal use that you will not use any such material without first contacting [specify] at [–] for confirmation of the copyright position and prior written consent together with such financial arrangement as may be appropriate.

A.154
That you may not edit, adapt, alter, modify, or otherwise interfere with the [Website] and its contents and nor may you exploit, license, supply, or distribute copies in any form to third parties whether for commercial gain or

of the material in any format which may be displayed. The copyright in the content of this [Website], the trade marks, the computer software and the databases are owned or controlled by the [Company]. There is no consent provided to store, print, download, reproduce, quote, supply, distribute and/or exploit any part of this [Website] whether for private use at home, for research or educational purposes, for publication or other media purposes, or exploitation in any form whether commercial or not.

A.165

Access and use of any of the material on this [Website] is entirely at your own discretion, cost and liability. You may at your own discretion reproduce, store, supply and/or distribute any material provided that you acknowledge the [Website] as the source as follows [Name of Company/website reference]. All copyright ownership, trade marks or other rights which are specified on the [Website] should be reproduced with the relevant material in the exact form. The absence of a copyright notice in respect of any material does not mean that the copyright or any other intellectual property is not held by a third party or the [Company]. You use any material entirely at your own risk and no indemnity is provided or liability accepted by the [Company].

A.166

If you are registering details on the [Website] on behalf of a business and/or company. You undertake and agree that:

1.1 You have the authority to do so from an officer of the business and/or company.

1.2 That if so requested by the [Website] that confirmation in writing of this authorisation could be provided.

1.3 That the information provided is accurate and that in the event that it should change then updated details will be provided.

1.4 That the business and/or company is a bona fide operation and adheres to all applicable legal requirements in its country of origin.

A.167

The [Company] reserves the right as its sole discretion to refuse access to the [Website] and any part without any reason at any time whether before and/or after registration and/or during the operation of the [Website]. This may take place as a result of a direct email, notice on the [Website], a press release, shut down of the whole and/or part of the [Website] and/or by any other means that the [Company] deems fit in the circumstances. Any such refusal, cancellation, interruption, delay or denial of access shall not incur any liability on the part of the [Company] and/or any other third parties connected with the [Website] for any direct and/or indirect losses, financial commitments, damages, or consequences of any nature that may arise whether reasonably foreseeable or not. The [Website] is used entirely at your own risk and cost and no reliance should be placed on continuous access and/or service. [Where a subscription fee has been paid then the total liability of the [Company] shall be limited to the repayment of the total subscription cost of the period for which access has been denied.]

A.168

This [Disc] is supplied to you the [Purchaser] by the [Distributor/Company] based on the following terms and conditions which you must agree to before you remove the seal and install the [Disc] [and load the software].

1.1   That the [Purchaser] is granted a non-exclusive and non-transferable licence by the [Distributor/Company] to use the [Disc] for the purpose which it is intended in conjunction with the [Work] namely [specify purpose, the method and the type of use]. This right is personal to you the [Purchaser] and shall also permit you to make a copy of the files on the hard drive of your computer/laptop and one back up copy of the [Disc].

1.2   There is no right granted to copy the [Disc] whether directly and/or indirectly in any format and/or medium for supply to third parties in whole and/or part at any time. All such third parties should be advised to purchase their own disc as a licence is required.

1.3   There is no right to make additional copies and/or to reproduce the [Work] for any other reason and/or to add the [Disc] and/or [Work] to any centralised database, library and/or storage and retrieval system.

1.4   You shall not have the right to develop further works based upon the [Work] and/or [Disc]. Nor to display, supply, transmit, reproduce, licence, exploit, adapt, translate, create a new format and/or other version for use on the internet,

A.169

The use and access to the sealed software package is subject to the [Purchaser] agreeing to the following terms and conditions and the [Purchaser] will be deemed to have accepted the agreement by opening and installing the software:

1.1   That the [Company] granted the [Purchaser] the non-exclusive license in respect of this software package to install and use the software on a [number workstations/single PC] for [home/residential/office/business] use only.

1.2   That you may make one backup hard copy for your own use.

A.177

Where the [Company] notifies the [Manufacturer/Distributor] that they have concerns as to the source of the materials and/or water and/or energy, content, packaging, employee health and safety and/or any part of any of the [Products] and/or any associated person and /or factor of any nature. Then the [Manufacturer/Distributor] shall be obliged to provide unlimited access to any professional and expert advisors and/or executives of the [Company] that the [Company] may stipulate in order to investigate any concerns and/or allegations which may arise at any time. Whether this shall arise before, during and/or after delivery of any [Products] and/or completion of any order by the [Company] up to a period of [number/months/years] thereafter.

Sponsorship

A.178

The [Sponsor] shall not be entitled to authorise and/or grant access to the [Event/Festival] to any third parties unless it is through the use and/or purchase of valid tickets specified in clause [–]. Where the [Sponsor] is setting up a stand to give away and/or sell its products then the [Sponsor] must abide by the same rules of access as any other vendor. The [Company] reserves the right to withdraw the right of entry, exclude, expel, remove or suspend any person who in their opinion behaves in a manner which is unacceptable. The decision of the [Company] is final. There shall be no obligation to refund any sums paid for sponsorship.

A.179

Sponsorship of [Name] does not permit the [Company] and/or its directors and/or employees and/or consultants to have any direct access by telephone, email and/or letter to [Name]. All requests, payments and/or other matters must be directed to and/or made to the [Agent].

A.180

The [Sponsor] shall be permitted unlimited access subject to requesting permission in advance to film, photograph, interview and visit the following locations, persons and material of the [Club/Association] whether to advertise the [Sponsor's] products and/or in association with any marketing and/or to publish any book:

1.1 Training ground, gym, track, stage, hospitality venue, award ceremonies and [–].

1.2 Corporate brochures, promotional material, designs of the brand name and logo.

1.3 Management [specify names].

1.4   Sports Personnel/Athletes [–].

A.181

Where the [Athlete/other] fails to attend any requested medical, drug and/ or other tests by the governing national and/or international body known as [specify]. Where this results in the [Athlete/other] being disqualified after an event and/or having an award withdrawn. Then the [Sponsor] shall not be entitled to have access to any such medical records, proceedings and/ or test results which may arise at any time except those disclosed in formal public documents. The [Sponsor] shall however have the right to terminate the sponsorship with immediate effect and shall not be liable to pay any further sums under the Agreement.

A.182

[Name] agrees that for the purposes of promotion and marketing the [Product] on behalf of the [Sponsor] that Name] shall allow access by any film crews and photographers nominated by the [Sponsor] and agreed with [Name] to their family home at [address] for a maximum total of [number/ hours] between [date and [date]. Provided that no filming and photographs shall be of any of the children of [Name] and it shall be limited to the following locations in the house and garden [specify].

University, Library and Educational

A.183

1.1   Access to the [Collection/Archive] shall be entirely at the sole discretion of the [Institute] and there shall be no automatic right of entry and/or use of all and/or any part any of the material in the [Collection/Archive].

1.2   The [Institute] reserves the right to deny, withdraw and/or refuse entry and/or to request that any person leave the premises for any reason and without providing any grounds and/or justification for doing so. Whilst the [Institute] has terms and conditions for access that must be adhered to by any visitors, researchers and/or any other person.

1.3   The [Institute] reserves the right to amend and/or alter these terms and conditions at any time without notice. No liability is accepted by the [Institute] for any losses, damages, costs, expenses and/or any other sums that may arise directly and/or indirectly as a consequence of there being no access to the [Collection/Archive] at any time for any commercial, academic and/or other projects.

1.4   Access to the [Collection/Archive] shall be entirely at the person and/ or companies own risk except where any personal injury and/or death is directly caused by the negligence of the [Institute].

A.184

Access to the [Library] shall be subject to the production of a current [readership/student] identity pass. The [Library] shall be entitled to refuse access to the use of the facilities, services and/or books and/or other material based on any grounds including:

1.1 A health and safety risk to the building and/or its contents and/or that a person and/or their belongings are a threat to the safety of the public and/or that a person is under the influence of drink and/or drugs.

1.2 That there are staff shortages and/or that the premises are not open for business.

1.3 That a public disturbance and/or alleged crime has been committed and/or that any person has failed to comply with the terms and condition of the [Right of Access Policy].

A.185

1.1 The [Company] shall not have any automatic right of access to the [Premises/Land] specified in [Schedule A]. The [Institute] grants the [Company] a non-exclusive licence to use the [Premises/Land] from [date] to [date] for the purpose of the [Event] described in [Schedule B].

1.2 The [Company] agrees that it shall not be entitled to make any permanent alterations and/or additions to the [Premises/Land]. That the [Company] shall pay all the cost and expenses of any damages, losses and/or expenses incurred by the [Institute] as a direct result of the [Company's] use of the [Premises/Land] up to a maximum of [currency/figure].

ACCURACY

General Business and Commercial

A.186

The measurements, fabric, sizes and colours of the [Products] may vary from both the catalogue, website and samples. The [Company] cannot provide any assurances as to the accuracy of these factors as there is considerable variability.

A.187
It is important that all the information, data and material supplied is accurate and correct and exactly fits all the specifications required for the [Project]. Where the [Company] becomes aware that any part is inaccurate, or not as specified or defective then they undertake to alert the [Customer] to this fact as a matter of urgency.

A.188
It is agreed that the [Proposal] is in its early stages of development, and that therefore the sales projections and revenue are not accurate, but merely an estimate. The products, figures and details may change, but at this time are provided on the basis as being correct to the best of the knowledge and belief of [Name].

A.189
The data and information provided in this [Website/brochure/other] are for guidance and are not intended to be accurate and may be amended, varied or updated at any time.

A.190
The [Manufacturer] agrees to produce and supply the [Products] in accordance with the sample and specifications agreed in advance with the [Customer]. In the event that there are to be any variations, alterations or change of materials, text, images, packaging, style, content or otherwise of any nature however minor. Then the [Manufacturer] agrees that the [Customer] shall be consulted in advance and that the production shall not proceed unless prior approval has been provided by the [Customer].

A.191
[Name] agrees and undertakes that the information you have supplied regarding your personal and financial details are true and accurate. That you have not been deceptive, fraudulent or dishonest and that the information does not relate to a third party. That you are over the age of [18/21 years] and that there is no consent required from any third party [whether parent, guardian, bank, court or otherwise] for you to disclose or obtain prior to entering into this contract.

A.192
[Name] agrees that the personal information and qualifications which you have provided to the [Company] are true, accurate and up to date and that you are qualified to carry out the tasks and duties for this type of employment.

A.193
The [Institute] reserves the right to change, amend or vary any part of the [course/seminar] and/or the [lecturers/speakers] at any time without notice.

The [brochure/catalogue] are for guidance only and may not be a true reflection of the total [course/seminar]. The qualification to be attained at the end of the [course/seminar] shall not be affected.

A.194
The Agreement was entered into by the [Purchaser] due to the disclosure of the following documents [specify and list]. The facts and figures disclosed in the documents determined the price paid for the assets of the [Company] by the [Purchaser]. In the event that within a period of [number] years the documents are discovered to contain information, data, facts and/or figures which have material and significant errors [of more than [number] per cent overall] in favour of the [Company]. Then the [Company] shall be obliged to repay such proportion of the price paid for the assets of the [Company] as may be deemed by an independent expert to be appropriate in the circumstances. The cost of the appointment of any such expert shall be paid for by agreement in advance between the parties. This clause does not affect any rights and remedies of either party to take legal action and/or seek costs, damages and/or interest.

A.195
It is recognised by both parties that the accuracy of the financial information, sales figures, assets and liabilities are an important part of the consideration for the acquisition of the [Business/Products]. In the event that it becomes clear at a later date that the [Company] failed to disclose information which would have resulted in a lower price being negotiated then the [Company] shall be obliged to repay the sum which was overpaid due to their non-disclosure of material facts.

A.196
Both parties agree that they are each expected to take due care and attention before entering into this Agreement and shall seek such legal advice as may be necessary and engage such professional experts as may be required to protect their interests. Where any corporate documents, data, financial reports, audit reports, staff lists, stock reports, sales figures, expenditure, and/or other facts are later found to be wrong. Then it is agreed that no sums shall be repaid to either party under this Agreement provided that the error and/or inaccuracies did not arise as a result of dishonesty, fraud, and/or were deliberately altered, changed and/or amended with the intention of misleading the other party.

A.197
The [Accountant/Bank/Agent/other] agrees and undertakes that it shall keep accurate computer software data records and back-up copies of all sums received and paid from any source in any part of the world for and on behalf of [Name/Business]. That no sums shall be paid to any third party which

exceed [number/currency] without the written authority and signature of [Name] as authorisation. Further that no more than [number/currency] shall be held in any one bank and that upon request full details of all accounts together with all statements shall be supplied to [Name] at the expense of the [Accountant/Bank/Agent/other].

A.198

It is agreed between the parties that it is the [Purchaser's] responsibility and liability to assess and investigate the accuracy and reliability of all the data, information and disclosures, maps, charts and other material being sold by the [Seller]. That the [Purchaser] agrees that the acquisition is entirely at his/her own risk and that no reliance can be made in respect of any aspect of any part of the [Project].

A.199

The information, accounts and background supplied by the [Professional Advisor] is entirely based on the current financial data and disclosures supplied by [Name] in respect of their work. No undertakings can be provided in respect of the accuracy of the content.

A.200

The [Company] agrees that it shall use its reasonable endeavours to produce accurate and detailed data and market research which can be verified if required by supplying copies of the original material and responses whether in the form of telephone marketing, online surveys, street interviews and/or otherwise. The [Company] shall retain and make available such original material to the [Distributor] for a period of up to [number/months/years] after the final date of completion of the market research.

ACCOUNTING PERIOD

General Business and Commercial

A.201

'The Accounting Period' shall mean each period of a calendar month for the full duration of the Licence Term. Provided that the first Accounting Period shall commence on [date] and end on the final day of that calendar month.

A.202

'The Accounting Period' shall mean each calendar year from [date] until [date] and shall be treated as comprising of four quarterly three month

43

periods ending with 31 March, 30 June, 30 September and 31 December and shall continue until the expiry, or termination of the Agreement or the date upon which all manufacture, sale, rental, disposal or otherwise of the [Units] is accounted for to the [Licensor] whichever is the later.

A.203
'The Accounting Period' shall be as follows:

1.1   Start date [–].

1.2   End date [–] or such earlier or later date that shall be agreed between the parties in writing, but in any event until all units and sums due have been reported and paid.

1.3   Regular weekly period of accounts beginning Monday and ending Sunday. Statement to be provided at the end of each seven-day period.

1.4   Payment to be made every four weeks to the [Licensee].

A.204
'Accounting Period' shall mean [number/days/weeks] following the receipt by the [Seller] of an invoice for the [Product].

A.205
The [Distributor] shall be entitled to vary, alter or change the accounting period by providing the [Company] with [six months] written notice. Where the new accounting period will result in delays in payments to the [Company] by more than [two months] then the prior written consent of the [Company] shall be required.

A.206
'The Accounting Periods' shall mean the following three consecutive four months in each year during the term of this Agreement: 1 January to 30 April, 1 May to 31 August and 1 September to 31 December. By the last day of each such period the [Company] shall provide a full and comprehensive statement of all the sums or benefits received, credited to and/or due to the [Company], any parent or associated company or any third party of any nature from the exploitation of the [Services/Content/Product] licensed under this Agreement.

A.207
The [Company] agrees that it shall provide a statement to the [Creator] of the [App/Product] and pay any sums due in full by direct debit on a regular basis which shall be not less than once every [number/weeks/months]. Where there have been no sums received then the [Company] shall still provide a statement to that effect. Where the [App/Product] is very successful and

the [App/Product] sells more than [number] then the [Company] agrees to account to the [Creator] more frequently namely once every [number/weeks/months].

A.208

The [Distributor] shall provide at its own cost to [Name] at any time upon request by [Name] a copy of the latest advertising, marketing, promotion, production, distribution, sales and other sums received and/or credited in any currency in any part of the world whether through the [Distributor] and any other entity and/or person through which it has exploited any part of the [Work/Article/Product/other].

A.209

Where the [Company] does not intend to adhere to the accounting period and/or wishes to amend the dates. Then the [Company] must notify [Name] in advance and obtain their prior written consent.

ACCOUNTING PROVISIONS

DVD, Video and Discs

A.210

The [Licensee] undertakes that it and its sub-agents, and sub-licensees shall keep full and accurate books of account, records, contracts and stock showing the Gross Receipts and the calculation of the [Licensor's] Royalties.

A.211

The [Licensee] undertakes that it shall pay the [Licensor's] Royalties on [dates] in each year during the term of this Agreement and thereafter within [–] of receipt of payment until all sums due or owing are accounted for to the [Licensor].

A.212

The [Licensee] shall at all times maintain true and accurate books, records and accounts with respect to all [DVDs/Videos/Discs] which are produced, manufactured, sold, leased, licensed, lost, damaged, stolen, rented or otherwise exploited within the terms of this Agreement. The [Licensee] will render to the [Licensor] [twice a year] in accordance with the Accounting Period a true and accurate statement of all sums due to the [Licensor] under the terms of this Agreement. Such statement shall be accompanied by remittance of such amount shown to be due thereon.

A.213

The [Licensee] may withhold from amounts otherwise due reasonable reserves against anticipated returns. No monies paid to the [Licensee] and thereafter refunded or credited shall be included in the Gross Receipts or if included the amount thereof shall be deducted from subsequent Gross Receipts.

A.214

Any statement submitted by the [Licensee] shall be deemed true and correct and binding upon the [Licensor] unless the [Licensor] submits to the [Licensee] in writing specific grounds of dispute as to the statement within [three months] of the date upon which any such statement is received by the [Licensor].

A.215

The [Licensor] shall have the right to examine the books and records of the [Licensee] to the extent they specifically relate to the [Units/Discs] for the purpose of determining the accuracy of Accounting Statements supplied by the [Licensee]. Such examination shall be made during reasonable business hours upon reasonable advance notice at the regular place of business of the [Licensee] where such books and records are maintained and shall be conducted on the [Licensor's] behalf and at the [Licensor's expense] by a [certified public accountant/finance director/professional accountants and legal advisors]. Such examination shall not be made more frequently than annually and no more than once with respect to any quarter annual period or Accounting Statement.

A.216

Each statement and the accompanying remittance will be made to a nominated account specified by the [Licensor] at [bank] in [country]. If any foreign receipts are frozen or cannot be transferred to the country where the [Licensee] has its main business. Then the [Licensee] shall open an account in the name of the [Licensee] in such foreign country and notify the [Licensor]. Upon the [Licensor's] written request and upon condition that the same shall be permitted by the authorities of such foreign country the [Licensee] shall transfer to the [Licensor] in such foreign country and in the currency thereof at the [Licensor's] cost and expense such part of such foreign receipts to which the [Licensor] would be entitled if the sums were transmitted and paid in [country] in accordance with the terms hereof. Such notice and transfer shall discharge the [Licensee] of its obligation in respect only of those specific sums.

A.217

On the first day of [March, June, September, and December] in each year the [Assignee] undertakes that it shall pay the [Assignor's] Royalties due from the Gross Receipts to the [Assignor] by [method] in [currency].

A.218

On the first day of [March, June, September and December] in each year the [Assignee] shall provide a detailed report to the [Assignor] with a full breakdown of the exploitation of the [Series of Discs/DVDs] setting out the Gross Receipts and the [Assignor's] Royalties together with copies of all significant documentation to support the accounts. Where any sum is withheld or converted or otherwise not received when due then a side letter should set out the background information and reasons.

A.219

The [Licensee] agrees that it shall not be entitled to recover more than [–] costs under Distribution Expenses in any one accounting period. Any excess shall not be carried forward to the next period but shall be at the cost and expense of the [Licensee].

A.220

The [Licensee] agrees that it shall not fail to disclose to the [Licensor] any sums in any currency received by the [Licensee] which relate to the licensing, distribution, sale and exploitation of the [Film/Game] and [Units]. In the event that in any accounting period the [Licensee] fails to disclose any sums and this results in the [Licensor] not receiving a related payment. Then the [Licensee] shall pay an additional penalty of [number] per cent of that sum to the [Licensor] when the late payment made.

A.221

The [Licensee] agrees that the accounting report shall provide copies of supporting documents and records to substantiate the figures for any payment or expense in excess of [figure/currency].

A.222

The cost and expense of all currency conversions shall be stated in full and any charges itemised and the exchange rates and the date stipulated.

A.223

The [Licensee] shall not be liable in any way for any losses caused by fluctuation in the rate of exchange because of any failure to convert or remit any particular funds to the [country] at any particular time or at a more favourable cost or rate of exchange than the cost or rate of exchange at which such conversion and remittance was accomplished. It is agreed that the [Licensor] shall be bound by whatever arrangements the [Licensee] may make for the conversion and remittance of foreign funds and by whatever cost or rate of exchange is incurred or used for such conversion and remittance. If the laws of any jurisdiction require that taxes on such remittance be withheld at the source then remittance hereunder to the [Licensor] shall be reduced accordingly. The [Licensor] shall be entitled to receive full details of the calculation of the exchange rate, the costs and expenses and the reason for withholding any sums for taxes.

A.224

The [Distributor] shall pay all the sums due to the [Licensor] under this Agreement by the dates set out at the latest and where there is any delay or failure to pay at any time the [Distributor] shall pay an additional payment in compensation and as a penalty of [figure/currency] per [day/month] to the [Licensor].

A.225

The [Company] shall provide a summary royalty statement to [Name] by the end of [December/March] in each year during the continuation of this Agreement which shall set out the sums received from the sales and rental of the [DVDs and Videos] and the calculation of the royalty payments due to [Name]. The statement shall be accompanied by a cheque for the full sum due to [Name] [or the funds shall be electronically transferred to an account specified and authorised by [Name] whichever has been agreed in advance.] The [Company] shall not be obliged to account for any sums which fall within the following circumstances until such sums have been received, cleared and retained by the [Company]:

1.1 The sums have been received or credited, but have not been cleared by the bank.

1.2 The sums were paid, but then subsequently returned to a purchaser, wholesaler or other third party as a refund.

1.3 The sums have been received, but then offset or discounted for lost and damaged DVDs and Videos.

1.4 The sums have been credited in a foreign country, but have not been actually received and cleared to the [Company's] main office at [address].

1.5 The acts, omissions, fraud or dishonesty of a third party has resulted in the sums not being paid to or received by the [Company] including but not limited to accountants, licensees, distributors, wholesalers, retailers, but not the officers or employees of the [Company].

1.6   The sums have been reduced by the costs, charges and expenses incurred relating to the exchange of currencies.

1.7   That no interest or benefits arising from the sums shall be due to be added to the royalty payments.

1.8   That stock has been destroyed or sold at below cost price.

A.226

The [Licensee] agrees that it shall be obliged to report, account, verify and pay to the [Licensor] all the sums which may be due which have been received by, credited to and/or benefited the [Licensee] in any form from the exploitation of the [Film] by the [Licensee], and any persons or third parties which they have appointed or requested to exploit the [Film] at any time. This obligation shall continue after the expiry, or termination of this Agreement until such time as all sums due have been reported, accounted for and paid by the [Licensee]. The [Licensee] agrees to comply with the following conditions:

1.1   That all royalty and advance statements shall be full and comprehensive and disclose all relevant information including the contract reference, the date the sums were received by the [Licensee], any exchange rates which were applied and how they were calculated. Together with the calculation of the royalties or advances due to the [Licensor].

1.2   That the [Licensee] shall include in the accounting statement details of all sums of any nature which have been withheld, discounted, set off or written off or deducted and the specific reasons.

1.3   That the [Licensor] shall be entitled to receive copies of all contracts, agreements and terms of engagement, order forms, invoices, computer and manual records, bank statements, stock and other assets of the [Licensee] at the [Licensees] expense for each such period for up to [three/six years] after the date of receipt of the accounting statement by the [Licensor] relating to the [Film] in any form.

1.4   That the [Licensee] shall ensure that all third parties to be appointed or engaged by the [Licensee] to supply, produce, distribute, market or otherwise be involved in the exploitation of the [Film] under this Agreement shall be of good financial standing and shall agree to pay, account and report to the [Licensee] in sufficient detail for the [Licensee] to fulfil its obligations to the [Licensor].

A.227

That where sums are not accounted for or paid to the [Company] due to the error, omission, fraud, dishonesty, financial difficulties, bankruptcy or collapse of a third party or the [Distributor] for any reason. Then the [Parent

Company] agrees to pay all such sums as may be due to the [Company] together with such legal and accountancy fees which may be incurred in verifying and claiming the sums due [up to a maximum limit of [figure/currency] [in any one calendar year].

A.228

The [Company] agrees that all sums relating to the exploitation of the [DVD/Video/Disc] of the [Film] under this Agreement whether as funds, income, receipts, payments, expenses or costs must be kept in a separate business account in the name of [specify] with the following authorised signatories [specify]. The following parties shall be sent a bank statement relating to the account each calendar month [specify].

A.229

The [Licensee/Distributor] shall not be obliged to pay any royalties and/or other sums to the [Licensor] where any copies of the [Work/Film] has been provided to a third party for promotional, marketing and advertising purposes provided that the [Licensee/Distributor] has not received any payment and no more than [number] have been used for such purposes in any [calendar month]. Where that figure is exceeded then the [Licensee/Distributor] shall pay the [Licensor] a fixed sum of [number/currency] per copy. The [Licensee/Distributor] shall ensure that they keep a full and accurate records of all such copies supplied to third parties for any reason.

Film and Television

A.230

The [Licensee] agrees and undertakes that it and its sub-agents and sub-licensees shall keep full and accurate accounting records, statements, costs and contracts which shall clearly establish and identify the Gross Receipts, the Distribution Expenses, the Net Receipts, any taxes, exchange rate conversions, and government levies and set out the calculation and final figures of the [Licensee's] Commission and the [Licensor's] Royalties in respect of the exploitation of the [Series] under this Agreement.

A.231

The [Licensee] agrees that it shall pay the [Licensor's] Royalties on [dates] every year until all sums due to the [Licensee] have been paid [during the term of this Agreement/until the expiry or termination of this Agreement].

A.232

The [Licensee] shall provide a detailed report to the [Licensor] by [date] and [date] in each year with a full breakdown of the exploitation of the [Series] together with copies of all relevant documents and records for any sum in excess of [figure/currency]. The [Licensee] agrees that the [Licensor] shall be entitled to arrange for an audit at any time to inspect and make copies of the accounts records in any format, stock and any other material in order to verify the sums due to the [Licensor] within [–] of receipt of each report. Such audit to be at the [Licensor's] cost and by such reputable advisor as the [Licensor] may decide.

A.233
Prior to any audit the [Licensor] may be required to provide a written confidentiality undertaking to the [Licensee].

A.234
The [Licensee] agrees that all sums relating to the Gross Receipts for the [Series] shall be kept in a separate bank account and not mixed with any other monies of the [Licensee]. Nor shall a charge, lien, or other security be given in respect of the Agreement or the Gross Receipts or the bank account by the [Licensee].

A.235
The [Assignee] shall provide the [Assignor] with a statement within [one month] of the end of every financial year by [date] which specifies the full details of the exploitation of the [Film] in each country, and the sums received and the costs, expenses, commission, agents fees or other sums incurred and deducted.

A.236
The [Distributor] will provide an account in writing to the [Company] so that there shall be one account in each period of [three months] starting with the date of delivery of the first complete master copy of the [Programme] to the [Distributor]. Such account shall show particulars of all sums paid or payable by any person, company or third party who have or shall acquire any rights in any media in the [Programme] and/or any parts and all commission, remuneration and Distribution Expenses. Each such account shall be conclusive as between the [Distributor] and the [Company] as to:

1.1　The amounts of commission and any other sums due, paid or deducted by the [Distributor].

1.2　The sums due to be paid by the [Distributor] to the [Company].

1.3　Details of all sums due to the [Company] which have not been transferred by the [Distributor] to the [United Kingdom]. If for any reason monies due from any person, company or third party cannot be transferred by the [Distributor] to the [United Kingdom]. Then any such money shall be paid by the [Distributor] into a separate bank account in such country and held in the joint names of the [Company] and the [Distributor] and full details of the bank account shall be provided to the [Company].

1.4   Details of all sums due to the [Company] which have not been paid due to the default of a third party which has failed to pay the [Distributor] shall not be obliged to make any payment on sums not received provided that it shall use all reasonable endeavours to recover such sums.

A.237

The [Licensee] undertakes that it shall agree to the following terms in respect of the [Film] in respect of the accounts, audits and reports to the [Licensor]:

1.1   That the [Licensee] shall open a separate bank account and keep professional and accurate financial records, data, contracts, invoices and receipts both in paper form, and on computer software. No such material shall be destroyed, deleted, erased and/or disposed of without the prior written consent of the [Licensor] for a period of [seven] years.

1.2   That funds, production costs, advances or royalty payments from the [Licensor] or any third parties which may be received or credited to the [Licensee] shall not be used, mixed or offset in any way whatsoever with the account of any other film at any time for any reason.

1.3   The [Licensor] may carry out up to [four] audits of all financial, contractual and business records in any one calendar year during office hours provided that [fourteen days] written notice is given to the [Licensee]. In the event such audits reveal errors prejudicial to the [Licensor] all the sums which may be due to the [Licensor] as a result of such errors will be paid immediately and the cost of any such audit shall be paid for in full by the [Licensee].

1.4   The [Licensee] shall undertake immediately or whenever necessary to obtain permission for remittance of any sums due to the [Licensor]. Upon the [Licensor's] request and particularly in the event of difficulties in remitting the sums due the [Licensor] shall open an account in that territory in which the [Licensee] shall pay any sums due to the [Licensor]. The [Licensor] shall then bear sole responsibility for accounting and remitting the sums to the [United Kingdom].

A.238

The [Assignee] undertakes that it and its sub-agents and sub-licensees shall keep full and accurate books of account, records and contracts showing the Gross Receipts, the Distribution Expenses, the Sales Tax, the Net Receipts and the Assignor's Royalties in respect of the exploitation of the [Film].

A.239

The [Assignee] shall provide a detailed report to the [Assignor] with a full breakdown of the exploitation of the [Film] showing the Gross Receipts, the Distribution Expenses, the Sales Tax, the Net Receipts and the [Assignors] Royalties by [date] and [date] in each year. The report shall include details of all units sold, licensed, lost, stolen, damaged or given away, currency conversion costs and documentation to support any deduction of Distribution Expenses. No documentation shall be shredded or disposed of without first offering to make it available to the [Assignor].

A.240

The [Assignee] undertakes that it shall pay the [Assignor's] Royalties to the [Assignor] by [cheque/direct debit/other] by [date] and [date] in each year [during the continuance of this Agreement/until the expiry or termination of this Agreement/until such time whether after the end of the term of this Agreement or not all sums due to the [Assignor] under this Agreement shall have been reported, accounted for and paid].

A.241

The cost and expense of all currency conversions shall be stated in full and any charges itemised and the exchange rate, source and date stipulated.

A.242

The [Licensee] confirms that all sums received, credited to, or any other benefits or sums paid or benefits provided to a third party by the [Licensee] or any sub-agent, sub-licensee or any other person or company acting on behalf of the [Licensee] relating to the exploitation of the [Film] or any part in any media shall be disclosed to the [Licensor] in full in the [annual financial statement] including any content, music, products, books, CD-Roms, CDs, DVDs, mobile phones, subscription, pay per view or free broadband internet service, wireless, digital, cable or terrestrial television, merchandising:

1.1   Receipts, advances, royalties, and any other sums.

1.2   All expenses, costs, collecting society fees, copyright clearance, reproduction and supply of material, all discounts, losses, credits, refunds or setoffs.

A.243

Where an error or omission is found or later disclosed whether by the [Licensor] or the [Licensee] the [Licensee] shall not be entitled to a refund of any overpayment to the [Licensor]. Nor shall the [Licensor] be entitled to any interest, compensation, or damages for an error by the [Licensee] provided that the error was not deliberate or fraudulent and payment is made immediately it is clear that it is due. An error arising from an audit by the

[Licensor] shall result in the [Licensee] paying all costs of the accountants and legal advisors up to a maximum of [figure/currency] for each such audit.

A.244
The [Licensee] shall pay all sums due to the [Licensor] by [cheque/electronic transfer to a notified bank account/in cash] in [currency].

A.245
Nothing contained herein shall create or impose upon the [Company] any fiduciary obligations to the [Writer] or be deemed to mean that any monies due or payable to the [Writer] shall be held in trust by the [Company] for the [Writer]. It is the intention of the parties that the [Company] shall have the right to mix the monies or any portion of the sums payable to the [Writer] out of or on account of the Gross Receipts received in respect of the [Film] with any other such receipts or sums received in respect thereof provided that all such receipts or sums received shall be held in a separate account at the bank designated for the [Film] only.

A.246
The [Company] agrees to ensure the provision to the [Writer] of statements relating to the receipts or other sums received in respect of the [Film] and showing the relevant details. Such statements shall be rendered not less frequently than quarterly for a period of twelve months from and after the date of first public release of the [Film] and thereafter twice a year. At the same time as the delivery of such statements the [Company] shall deliver the remittance to the [Writer] of any sums to which it may be entitled. The public release of the [Film] shall be when the earliest of one of the following events takes place:

1.1 The [Film] is released in cinemas whether at a premier or to the public in [country/any part of the world].

1.2 The [Film] is broadcast or transmitted on terrestrial, cable, satellite or digital television in [country/any part of the world].

1.3 The [Film] is released, sold, rented or supplied on DVD, video to the public in [country/any part of the world].

A.247
The [Writer] shall have the right to employ a firm of chartered accountants to examine the books of account of the [Company] relevant to the [Film] but neither the [Writer] nor the said chartered accountants shall be entitled to enquire into or challenge any cumulative statement or any other statement which was despatched by the [Company] to the [Writer] more than [two years] previously. It is agreed between the parties that after each such period of [two years] all such statements shall be final and conclusive accounts

unless written objections shall have been made within the [two year] period setting out the grounds of complaint.

A.248

The [Company] shall not be bound to pay or cause to be paid to the [Writer] any sum to which it may become entitled pursuant to any clause under this Agreement if by reason of a moratorium, embargo, banking or other restriction such sums are not actually received into the account by the [Company] but in this event the [Writer] may (subject to the laws of the country or territory concerned) request that they be paid into another account at the [Writer's] expense.

A.249

The [Company] agrees and undertakes that:

1.1　There shall be an obligation to keep professional, complete and accurate books of account, records, contracts, computer data and other material showing all the Gross Receipts, the Distribution Expenses and the Authors Royalties in respect of the commercial exploitation of the [Film] or parts anywhere in the world [at any time/for [number] years/until no further sums are due to the [Author].

1.2　In all its contracts with its sub-agents, sub-licensees, distributors and any third parties involved in the exploitation of the [Film] or any part in any media that the same obligation in 1.1 above shall apply.

1.3　That the [Author] may serve notice to carry out an audit [once] in any financial year of the [Company] and shall be allowed access to all such material to verify the sums due to the [Author].

1.4　That in the event in any audit there is a deficit to the [Author] of [figure/currency] then the [Company] shall pay to the [Author] [twice the total] of the deficit and all costs of such audit.

A.250

The [Company] shall not be obliged to keep contracts, books of account, computer records or other material relating to the exploitation of the [Film] more than [ten years] unless there are sums still due to the [Agent] or there are legal proceedings or any dispute relating to the [Film]. If the [Company] decides to destroy the material then the [Company] agrees that it shall first notify the [Agent] of their intention to destroy such material and offer them the opportunity of making copies or purchasing such material.

A.251

The [Distributor] shall send to the [Company] an accounting statement and payments for the sums due under this Agreement by [date] in each year during the term of this Agreement. The statement shall specify how the sums due are calculated, but there shall be no obligation to provide further details in the statement. In the event that the [Company] wishes to dispute the statement or payment and believes for any reason that it has been underpaid. Then the [Company] shall notify the [Distributor] as soon as reasonably possible, but in any event within [six months] of receipt of the statement. The [Distributor] shall disclose such evidence and documents as may be relevant to satisfy the [Company] that the statement is accurate. There shall be no obligation to permit the [Company] to carry out an internal audit of the [Distributor]. The parties shall agree a suitable venue for all the documents and records that are relevant to be displayed and inspected. In the event that the matter cannot be resolved then no part of this clause is intended to prejudice the [Company's] right to take legal action for breach of contract and non-payment and to request a full audit nor to apply where there is fraud, false accounting by the [Distributor] or any of its sub-agents or sub-licensees or other third parties.

A.252
There shall be [no obligation/an obligation] for the [Company] to bear the cost of any errors, omissions, fraud, dishonesty, non-disclosure or failure to transfer or pay any sums of any sub-agent, sub-licensee or any third parties which effect or reduce the sums due to [Name] under the terms of this Agreement.

A.253
The [Company] shall be liable for the acts, omissions, errors, failure to account and report and/or allow inspection, and/or non-payment of any sums due to the [Artist] which any agent, representative, manufacturer, distributor or other third party engaged or authorised by the [Company] is required to fulfil in respect of the exploitation of the services and product of the work of the [Artist]. The [Company] shall be responsible for the adherence to the accounting provisions whether the work is sub-contracted out to professional accountants or not or any other advisor. In the event that there are errors, withholding of information, non-disclosure, failure to pay and/or any other defect. Then the [Company] agrees that the [Artist] shall be entitled to be paid the following sums in addition to the sum of more than [figure] [words and currency]:

1.1   Interest at [–]% [figure] per cent from the date the sum was due.

1.2   All the costs of professional legal and accountancy advisors, including court fees, counsel, administration, telephone, travel and accommodation.

A.254

The [Production Company] agrees and undertakes to holds all funds and sums of any nature received by them in respect of and/or relating to the [Film/Project] at [Name Bank] in [country] and that the signatories to the account shall be [specify]. Further that all sums received from the exploitation of the rights associated with the [Film/Work] by the [Production Company] shall be deposited in that account in [currency].That no third party shall be entitled to withdraw and/or charge and/or hold any lien over that account. That no additional bank account and/or deposit account shall be set up at any time. That the [Production Company] shall ensure that no payments and/or direct debits are made from that bank account which do not directly arise from the production of the [Film/Project]. That the [Production Company] shall not be entitled to use the account to pay any office, administration costs and salaries and/or other liabilities relating to the normal business of the [Production Company].

A.255

Both parties agree that they shall appoint [Advisor] as the [Accountant/Legal/other] for the [Project] and that all such costs and expenses shall be paid for out of the existing Budget in Schedule [–] up to a maximum of [figure/currency]. That the [Advisor] shall act for both parties and keep them both informed of the progress of the [Project]. Further that the parties shall take out joint insurance with a reputable company to cover [specify] and any legal action that may be necessary. The cost of such insurance shall also be paid for out of the Budget.

General Business and Commercial

A.256

The [Assignor] shall provide a full report to the [Company] of the costs and expenses incurred in respect of the [Commissioned Work] upon request. The [Assignor] shall keep full and accurate records and accounts of all costs and expenses incurred in respect of the [Commissioned Work] and agrees that the [Company] shall be entitled to inspect such records and material upon request. The [Assignor] shall not be obliged to keep any such financial records beyond [date].

A.257

The [Company] shall provide a full and detailed financial record and statement to the [Copyright Owner] of all sums received directly and/or indirectly by the [Company] and/or any associated business and/or enterprise from the exploitation of the [Product/Service/Work] at any time in any part of the universe in any medium. All records, documents, accounts, contracts, invoices, receipts and bank statements whether paper, software or some other medium shall be retained and not destroyed by the [Company] for a minimum of [six] years. The [Copyright Owner] and/or its professional advisors shall upon written notice be able to inspect all such material [once] in each year during the Term of this Agreement.

A.258
The [Company] shall employ a professional accountant to verify and audit the accounts at a maximum cost of [figure/currency] in each year.

A.259
The [Company] shall make any payments due to [Name] within [14 days] of receipt of any sums in excess of [figure/currency]. All other sums shall be allowed to accrue until they reach that same level at which point payment shall be made. In any event all sums shall be accounted for in a statement every [three months] from the start date of the contract to the end of that accounting period. The accounting statement shall include sums due and not yet received which shall be marked accordingly.

A.260
The [Company] shall ensure that any person who is engaged to work on this [Project] is suitably qualified and will be able to provide [national insurance, tax references/other] which may be required for accounting purposes and to comply with the legal requirements of [country].

A.261
No expense or cost or other sum shall be deducted from the accounts which cannot be verified by a receipt or other supporting documentation.

A.262
Any error by the [Company] in the final accounts which is later revealed to the detriment of [Name] shall result in a penalty payment of [figure/currency] for each such mistake and be paid immediately it is confirmed together with all directly-related accountant and legal costs which [name] incurred in order to prove the error.

A.263
The [Licensee] agrees and undertakes to the [Licensor] to:

1.1   Act in good faith and disclose any errors and/or omissions in the accounts and/or payments as soon as they are noticed.

1.2   To ensure that professional accounting practices according to [specify institute] are followed by the [Licensee] in respect of the calculation of any sums due to the [Licensor] under this Agreement.

1.3 To ensure prompt payment of any sums due to the [Licensor] and agree that failure to do so shall be considered a breach of this Agreement.

A.264
Both parties shall be entitled to full disclosure of all facts whether financial, stock, audit reports, company records, third party contracts and records relating to the business. Together with any material of any nature that may be required to establish the costs incurred, the sums expended and the sums due to be paid to each party.

A.265
All calculations shall be in [currency] and where conversion is necessary the date and exchange rate and costs clearly stated. Each party shall bear the costs of its own bank charges and commissions.

A.266
All payments and records shall be kept and made in [currency] by [Name].

A.267
Any payment which is made to either party on the basis of error or omission shall be repaid to the [Company] as and when it is identified. No penalty, surcharge or interest shall be due on such sums or any claim for costs, expenses or legal or accountants' fees.

A.268
In the event that the [Company] decides to take legal proceedings or institute any action or claim against the [Licensee] because of the failure of the [Licensee] to provide accounts, royalty statements and/or make payment of the sums due under this Agreement. The [Licensee] agrees to indemnify the [Company] in respect of the cost and expense of legal and accountants fees up to a maximum of [figure/currency] in total for the duration of this Agreement. [This clause shall apply where the fault lies with a third party and not the [Licensee].

A.269
It is agreed that the [Company] shall preserve and safeguard all relevant invoices, records, letters, accounts, contracts, licences, software, discs, microfilm, sales brochures, publicity and marketing material and any other material or medium on which information about [specify project] is held for a period of not less than [number/years] after the expiry or termination of the Agreement. The material shall be offered to [Name] before destruction or shredding at any time.

A.270

It is agreed between the parties that any inspection of the material relating to the exploitation of the [Product] or any part shall require:

1.1 That the [Company] give [–] written notice to [Name] at the [Distributor].

1.2 That the material be made available in normal business hours from [–] to [–] on [days] at [premises] with the use of a telephone and photocopier machine at the [Distributor's] cost.

1.3 That there is a time limit on each occasion of no more than [–] days unless for any reason documents or material are not available.

1.4 That senior executives of the [Distributor] will agree to meet to answer any outstanding questions that may arise.

1.5 That the [Distributor] will co-operate fully to make available any material in its possession or control relating directly or indirectly to the [Product].

A.271

The [Company] shall not be obliged to disclose the names, addresses and personal details of clients and customers, nor any confidential business information relating to third parties or the parent company as part of the accounting process.

A.272

The [Company] agrees to pay the sums due to [Name] as follows:

1.1 within [28 days] of the last days of [March, June, September and December] in each year for the first two years;

1.2 within [28 days] of the last days of [June and December] for the third, fourth and fifth year; and

1.3 thereafter within [28 days] of the last day of [December].

A.273

Where an audit is being carried out there shall be no obligation to release the confidential and private details of a parent company, associated company or any third parties who have not provided their consent to the disclosure of the information, data, financial records, documents or otherwise. The [Company] may arrange for portions of documents, files and software to be copied to only disclose the relevant parts.

Internet and Websites

A.274
The [Company] shall provide an annual report to [Name] which sets out details of the amount of [users/subscribers] in that period and who clicked on or accessed the pages on the [Website] relating to [Name]. The [Company] shall pay [Name] the sum of [figure/currency] if more than [number] click on or access the pages. Where the [Company] has ceased to display the webpages relating to [Name] then no report or payment shall be due to [Name].

A.275
The [Company] shall not be obliged to provide any report or pay any sums in respect of copying, transfer, exploitation or reproduction of material which may arise relating to the webpages of [Name] by third parties.

A.276
The [Company] shall provide a full and detailed disclosure of the subscriptions, payments, fees and other sums received by the [Company] or any third party engaged to process payments in respect of the display, use, sale and exploitation of the [Work] of [Name] on the [Website]. Whilst the [Company] shall not be obliged to provide personal customer details and financial records the [Company] should provide a list of numbers, country, type of payment, reason for payment and where refunds, cancellations or returns of any nature are made the reason. The [Company] agrees that the statement shall be accompanied by payment of all sums due to that date to [Name].

A.277
The [Company] agrees to pay the [Copyright Owner] the sum of [number] [words/currency] for each download by the public of the [Film/Music/Text/ Photograph] described as follows [brief description].

The [Company] shall provide a statement to the [Copyright Owner] at the end of each period of [three months] specifying the dates, times, duration, country of origin of the [equipment/device/internet connection] used to access the download, and number of downloads, but not any personal data which identify the user.

A.278
The [Company] agrees to pay to [Name] a fee of [number/currency] for every transaction which is completed (except where the sum received by the [Company] is not refunded and/or not credited) when the [Client] has followed the link from the [Affiliate] to the [Company] to place the order for

the [Product/Holiday/Service]. The [Company] agrees to credit the account of the [Affiliate] by direct debit with any sums due at the end of each [number/week/month] period.

A.279

The [Company] shall supply a simple statement of account of total sales, licence and/or exploitation of the [Work] in any format whether as a download, app, hard and/or paper copy, adaptation and/or otherwise. The same fee shall be paid to the [Contributor] for each completed transaction [number/currency] for each format. All sums due to the [Contributor] shall be paid within [number/days] by direct debit to [account] in the name of [specify] at [Bank]. No bank charges and/or costs shall be attributed and/or made to the [Contributor] by the [Company] in respect of such payment method.

A.280

The [Company] shall provide at its own cost and expense to the [Licensor] full and detailed statements and records by email and in paper form of all exploitation of the [Work/Logo] by the [Company] to any third party of any nature in any part of the world in every [three month] period starting [date]. The [Company] shall ensure that all statements and records are supported by any documents, invoices, bank records and/or other material no matter how it is stored and/or processed by the [Company] so that it is easily verified by the [Licensor]. Any additional documents and/or data and/or detail that the [Licensor] may request in order to assess the validity of the reports shall be supplied by the [Company]. Failure to comply with any request by the [Licensor] shall be deemed to be a breach of this Agreement and entitled the [Licensor] to terminate the Agreement with immediate effect.

Merchandising

A.281

The [Agent] acknowledges that the [Company] shall be entitled upon request to be provided with a copy of any record, document or other material in the possession or under the control of the [Agent] relating to the [Company], [prototype, samples, garments, logo, trade mark or other signature, slogan or image].

A.282

You shall within [30 days] after [31 March, 30 June, 30 September and 31 December] in each year provide accounts for each month showing the [Units/Products] which have been installed and with such accounts you will on each occasion make the appropriate payment to us. We shall have the right to reasonable access during ordinary business hours to inspect such of your books of account and other records as are relevant.

A.283

The [Distributor] shall endeavour to prepare accurate and complete records relating to the number of [Units] sold during each Accounting Period. The [Company] (or its duly authorised representative) may during the period of this Agreement and for up to [six] months thereafter upon giving notice of not less than [14 days] to the [Distributor] to visit the premises of that [Distributor] during normal business hours to carry out an inspection.

Inspection shall not be more frequently than once in any [twelve-month] period. The [Company] shall be entitled to inspect and make copies but shall not be entitled to make copies of any records containing names and addresses of [Purchasers] or former [Purchasers]. The [Company] shall cause as little disruption as possible during any such inspection to [Distributor's] business. The [Company's] rights of inspection shall be exercised by the [Company] at its own expense and cost.

A.284

The [Distributor] and the [Company] agree that the following terms shall apply in respect of payment and accounting:

1.1 In the event that any inspection discloses that the total amount which should have been accounted for by the [Distributor] exceeds by [10 per cent] or more the total amount that was so accounted for by during such period. Then if the [Distributor's] auditor will certify that such error or omission exists then the [Distributor] shall upon invoice reimburse the [Company] for the reasonable costs of the [Company's] inspection as well as paying the sum due [plus interest at [number] per cent].

1.2 If the [Company] shall not have disputed the accuracy or completeness of any accounts or payment within [one year] from the date of receipt by the [Company] then it shall be deemed complete and accurate.

1.3 If any inspection reveals that the [Distributor] has underreported the amount payable to the [Company] the [Distributor] agrees to make immediate payment to the [Company] of the proper amount due. If any inspection reveals that the [Distributor] has miscalculated and paid more than the amount due to the [Company] then the [Company] shall make an immediate refund of such sum to the [Distributor].

A.285

The [Licensee] shall send to the [Licensor] a statement on or before the [30th] day of the month following each of the quarterly periods ending on respectively the [last] days of June, September, December and March ('Accounting Statement') with full details of the computation of Royalties for the preceding quarter including without limitation the Gross Receipts received from the distribution and exploitation of the [Product(s)] during the relevant period the Distribution Expenses incurred or expended and the amount of Royalties payable. At the same time as a statement is sent to the [Licensor] the [Licensee] shall also make payment of the Royalties shown to be due. A final and conclusive payment shall be made at the expiration of [nine months] from the end of the Licence Period or the date of determination of the Agreement if earlier. The first Accounting Statement will be sent by the [Licensee] in respect of the period from the beginning of the Licence Period to the last days of June, September, December or March thereafter whether or not a payment is due in respect of such period and shall continue until such time as the Licensee is not dealing in or exploiting any rights under this Agreement and shall have accounted for all sums due.

A.286

The [Licensee] undertakes to the [Licensor] that it shall keep at its main place of business proper books of account, records and any other material, software, data or stock as may be reasonably necessary for the purpose of verifying the Accounting Statements. The [Licensee] agrees not more than twice per year during the Licence Period and for a period of one (1) year after the expiry of the Licence Period to allow the [Licensor] or its duly authorised officer, agent or representative upon reasonable notice during normal business hours and at the [Licensor's/Licensee's] expense to inspect and take copies of such books of account, records, documents and any other material software data or stock whether located at the main premises or elsewhere under the control or possession of the [Licensee].

A.287

The [Licensor] agrees that any information and records in any form supplied to the [Licensor] are provided only for the purposes of verifying Accounting Statements and is confidential and is imparted on that basis to the [Licensor] and may not be disclosed by the [Licensor] to any third party in any circumstances or used for any other purpose without the prior written approval of the [Licensee] except to the [Licensor's] professional legal and accounting advisors. This clause shall apply until such time as any such information is released publicly by the [Licensee].

A.288

The Statement of Accounts rendered to the [Company] by the [Licensee] shall be in the form of a statement stipulated from time to time during the Term by the [Company] by notice in writing and shall give the details requested which shall include details of opening stock numbers, [Licensed Articles] manufactured, number of sales of [Licensed Articles], closing stock, sale price of each category of [Licensed Articles] sold and a calculation of all royalties due to the [Company].

A.289

In respect of the production, manufacture, distribution, sale and disposal of the [Licensed Articles] the [Licensee] undertakes and agrees:

1.1 To keep professional, comprehensive and complete records and books of account relating to all dealings of any nature, disposal or transfer with the [Licensed Articles] as may be necessary to enable the amount of the royalties and any other sums due to the [Company] to be accurately stated, accounted and audited.

1.2 To permit the [Company] or their duly authorised accountant or other professional advisors upon written notice to inspect and audit and take copies or extracts from the relevant records and accounts in any form required to enable the amount of the Royalties and any other sums to be verified whether during the term of the Agreement or not and up to [six years] thereafter. In the event of any inspection revealing an error in excess of [five per cent] [5%] of the Royalties or other sums accrued due during the period for which such inspection and audit was made. The [Licensee] shall (subject to verification of the claim by their own professional or legal advisors) reimburse the [Company] with the full [accountancy/legal/administration] costs of such inspection and audit. The [Licensee] will pay to the [Company] any sums shown to be due by such inspection and audit together with interest thereon at [four per cent] [4%] per annum above the base lending rate from time to time of [Bank] from the dates on which any such sums should have been paid to the [Company].

1.3 To preserve all relevant invoices, records, contracts, licences, accounts and computer software, discs, microfilm and any other material or medium on which relevant information is held for a period of not less than [six years] after the expiry or end of the Agreement if earlier.

A.290

The [Designer] agrees to be responsible for the collection and safeguarding of the Gross Receipts and to pay the [Licensee's] Royalties within [two calendar months] of receipt of all such money to the [Licensee]. The Designer agrees to open a bank account at [Bank] for the specific purpose of depositing and dealing in all monies received from the commercial exploitation, supply, distribution and sale of the [Licensed Articles] and the payment of any third party remunerations. The [Designer] agrees that the signature of both the [Designer] and the [Licensee] shall be required for the payment of any monies out of the account.

A.291

The [Designer] undertakes that it and its sub-agents, sub-licensees and distributors shall keep full and accurate books of account, records, contracts and prices showing all dealings of the [Licensed Articles] including the number of units manufactured, supplied, distributed and sold whether by wholesale, retail or distributed without charge for promotional purposes and all units lost, damaged or stolen and the calculation of the [Designer's] Royalties and the [Licensee's] Royalties in respect of the [Licensed Articles].

A.292

The [Designer] agrees that the [Licensee] shall be entitled to arrange for an audit to inspect and make copies of the [Designer's] books of account, records, contracts and any other material in any form or medium in order to verify the sums due to the [Licensee]. In the event that in any audit there is a discrepancy of more than [figure/currency] in any one year to the detriment of the [Licensee] then the [Designer] shall be responsible for the reasonable costs incurred in respect of such audit up to maximum of [figure/currency].

A.293

The [Licensee] confirms that the minimum [retail selling] price for the [Product] shall be not less than [figure/currency] in [country].

A.294

The [Licensee] agrees to pay the [Licensor's] Royalties as follows:

1.1 Within [28 days] of the last days of [March, June, September and December] in each year for the first two years.

1.2 Within [28 days] of the last days of [June and December] for the third, fourth and fifth year and

1.3 Thereafter within [28 days] of the last day of [the last day of December].

A.295

The [Licensee] shall keep competent, accurate and complete books of account, records, contracts and prices showing all dealings of the [Licensed Article] manufactured, supplied, distributed and sold whether by wholesale or retail prices and details of units distributed without charge for promotional purposes and all units lost, damaged or stolen or any other reason why no royalty is paid to the [Licensor] and the calculation of the [Licensor's] Royalties in respect of the [Licensed Articles], together with copies of supporting documents to verify these figures.

A.296

By [dates] of each year the [Licensee] shall provide a written report to the [Licensor] showing all dealings and exploitation of the [Licensed Article] including the total number of units of the [Licensed Article] manufactured, distributed and sold and the wholesale and retail prices and the sums received or credited whether the [Licensee], any sub-agent or sub-licensee or other third party engaged by the [Licensees]. Details of units distributed without charge for promotional purposes, and all units lost, damaged, stolen, returned, destroyed or any other reason as to why no royalty is paid to the [Licensor]. The calculation of the [Licensor's] Royalty in respect of the [Licensed Articles] together with a copy of every document which refers to any sum in excess of [figure/currency] in the report. A cheque shall be sent, payable to the [Licensor], which pays in full the sums shown to be due in the report.

A.297
In the event it is established by the [Licensor] that there are errors in excess of [figure/currency] in any accounting period, then for each such period the [Licensee] shall pay the sum due in full plus [twice the error sum in compensation/other]. The fact that there is an overpayment shall not result in a refund, but a correction on the next accounting period that falls due, but with no interest.

A.298
In the event in any audit an error is found to the detriment of the [Licensor] in respect of the amount to be paid by the [Company] which is in excess of [number] per cent the [Company] shall be obliged to repay the sum due and where the error is more than [figure/currency] pay all the fees of the [Licensor] for its accountants up to a limit of [–] for any audit, but not for legal advisors or other administration costs incurred.

A.299
Each statement shall be rendered within [ninety (90) days] following the end of each accounting period. Any statement submitted by the [Licensee] hereunder shall conclusively be deemed true and correct and binding upon the [Company] unless the [Company] provides to the [Licensee] within [twelve (12) months] from the date any such statement has been received by the [Company] specific written grounds for disputing any such statement.

A.300
The [Company] shall have the right to examine the books and records of the [Licensee] to the extent they pertain to the [Units] containing the [Project/Character] for the purpose of determining the accuracy of any statements supplied by the [Licensee]. The [Company] may at its sole discretion appoint an independent chartered accountant at the [Company's] expense and upon at least [thirty days] written notice to examine the [Licensee's] books and records. The [Company] shall not be entitled to examine any books or records of the [Licensee] which do not relate to the production, manufacture, distribution and exploitation of the [Units] containing the

[Project/Character]. If the [Company's] examination has not been completed within [twenty days], then the [Licensee] may require the [Company] to end the examination at any time upon [seven days] written notice to the [Company]. The [Licensee] shall not be required to permit the [Company] to continue the examination after the end of that [seven day period] unless documents or records have been unavailable for inspection or access has been restricted for any reason.

A.301

The [Licensee] shall supply to the [Licensor] a quarterly written royalty statement no later than [sixty days] following the end of each quarter. Such quarters shall end on [31 March, 30 June, 30 September and 31 December] of each year. Each statement shall show the latest information received by the [Licensee] during each such period as to:

1.1   The number of [Units] rented supplied and sold by the [Licensee].

1.2   Full details of all royalties due and/or payable to the [Licensor].

1.3   Full details of all receipts from the [Units].

The statement shall be accompanied by a remittance for the full amount shown to be due to the [Licensor]. In the event that in any one quarter there are no receipts the [Licensee] shall not be under any obligation to supply a full statement to the [Licensor], but shall merely confirm this fact by letter. The [Licensee] shall continue to provide such statements during the Licence Period and thereafter until such time as all [Units] rented, supplied and sold whether for free or for a charge are accounted for by the [Licensee] to the [Licensor].

A.302

The [Licensee] shall maintain in its office, at its main business address [specify details] in [country] accurate books of account and records of the distribution and exploitation of the [Units] together with all relevant agreements, contracts, permissions, software, records and other material which shall be available at all reasonable times during business hours to a duly authorised representative of the [Licensor]. The [Licensor] may examine, inspect and request copies of or take excerpts from any such material and may request further information from senior executives or officers of the [Licensee] who deal or have dealt with such matters in any field either in meetings or in the form of written questions.

A.303

The [Licensor] shall also have the right to examine and take copies of the financial records, software and agreements of any sub-licensees, sub-distributors, agents or other third parties appointed by the [Licensee] to exploit, promote or market the [Units]. The [Licensee] shall ensure that all third parties engaged in respect of the [Units] in any capacity have a contractual obligation in such agreements and contracts to allow access to all relevant business dealings by the [Licensor] at the [Licensor's] cost.

A.304

The [Licensee] shall deliver to the [Licensor] at [address] commencing with the month in which the [Units] are first manufactured, a duplicate written statement in respect of the Gross Receipts. Such statements shall be supplied at the end of each period of [three calendar months] until the expiry or end of the Agreement or the [Licensee] ceases permanently manufacturing the [Units], whichever is the later. In any event the [Licensee] shall be obliged to account for the manufacture, distribution, exploitation and destruction of all [Units] whether sold for the full value or not or otherwise. Each such statement shall show reasonable details relating to the period to which it refers including the specific sources, description and breakdown of the Gross Receipts.

A.305

The [Licensee] shall accompany each such statement with a remittance to the [Licensor] or its assignees of such sums as may be due to the [Licensor] under the terms of this Agreement. The delivery to the [Licensor] of such remittance at the time stipulated by this Agreement is to be adhered to and is of the essence of this Agreement.

A.306

Each statement shall also include a complete recent list month by month of the number of [Units] manufactured or produced by the [Licensee] or its sub-licensees since the start of the Agreement, and the number lost, destroyed or given away, and the number sold or marketed together with all the sums received or credited as due.

A.307

Upon the written request of the [Licensor], the Licensee shall pay the amount to which the Licensor is entitled to any other third party designated by the [Licensor]. The payment by the [Licensee] to such third party in accordance with such written request shall be deemed payment to the [Licensor] and the [Licensee] shall be under no further liability to the [Licensor] in respect of such amount.

A.308

The [Licensee] shall use its best efforts to obtain the remittance to the [Licensor's] agents of all monies due to the [Licensor] pursuant to the terms of this Agreement at the then prevailing rate of exchange. If for any reason the [Licensee] finds it impossible to have such monies transmitted to the [Licensor] or the [Licensor's] agent as agreed then the [Licensor] shall have the right at any time by giving written notice to the [Licensee] to require the [Licensee] to deposit such monies in the [Licensor's] name in any bank or other depository designated by the [Licensor] in any country of the Territory in which such monies are located.

A.309

The [Licensor] may at its own expense use its own staff and officers and/ or appoint a [qualified accountant/lawyer/professional advisor/agent] to inspect and examine the financial and business records in any form of the [Licensee], its directors and any associated company in its possession or control which contain information, data or accounts relating directly or indirectly to the exploitation of the [Units/Character/Logo] under this Agreement, the calculation of the costs and expenses, the total sums received and therefore the sums due or paid to the [Licensor].

A.310

Such inspection shall be made at the main premises of the [Licensee] on a minimum of [thirty days] written notice and during normal business hours on such dates to be agreed with the [Licensee]. The [Licensor] shall not be entitled to take any copies without the prior consent of the [Licensee] and all copies shall be charged for at [amount per copy].

A.311

The right to inspect may not be exercised more than once in any period of [twelve months] and shall not extend beyond a period of [one year] from the end of the accounting period to which such inspection relates.

A.312

If the [Licensee] shall be found as a result of such inspection to have withheld for any reason save as provided for in this Agreement sums due to the [Licensor] then the [Licensee] shall forthwith pay the sums to the [Licensor]. In the event that such inspection reveals an error or omission to the detriment of the [Licensor] in excess of [figure/currency] in any one inspection the [Licensee] shall pay all reasonable costs directly incurred by the [Licensor] up to a maximum of [figure/currency]. The [Licensor] shall be entitled to reserve the right to pursue any other rights and/or remedies available to the [Licensor] arising out of such error or omission.

A.313

The [Licensee] shall not be obliged to provide any business, commercial or other details relating to the distribution and sales of the [Product/Character/ Logo] except those set out below which shall be shown in each accounting statement and supplied to the [Licensee] together with payment for any sums due:

1.1 The number of items sold at full retail price in each [country/market].

1.2 The number of items sold at a discount, less commission and/or agents fees in each [country/market] together with the reduced price.

1.3 The number of items destroyed, lost, given away, loaned, damaged, rejected as below standard, refunded or disposed of below manufacture cost price.

1.4 The value of total expenditure on marketing and promotion to that date.

1.5 Copies of all reviews, criticisms, marketing material, promotions, items sold in any country, and packaging.

1.6 Business and marketing plans for exploitation and sales the following year.

A.314
The [Distributor] agrees that it shall pay the [Assignor] an annual fee of [number/currency] per [number] of copies of the [Logo/Artwork] that the [Distributor] supplies, sells and/or licenses to any third party for any reason whether at no cost, cost price, full price and/or otherwise at any time. No pro rata payment shall be made and any such balance of copies shall be carried to the next period. All sums received from the exploitation of the [Logo/Artwork] shall belong to the [Distributor] including any right of resale, and sums due from any collecting society and/or any other form of exploitation in the future.

Publishing

A.315
The [Publishing Company] shall pay to [Television Company] the consideration set out in Schedule [–] hereto. Any royalty payable shall be calculated on any sale or disposal when payment for such sale or disposal becomes due to the [Publishing Company] and shall be made whether or not payment is actually received by the [Publishing Company]. Similarly the [Television Company] shall be obliged to pay the [Publishing Company] any payment still outstanding one year after the date of broadcast of the last [programme in the Series] which may be due from the [Series] whether or not the sums have been received.

A.316
By [dates] in each year of this Agreement the [Publishing Company] shall deliver to the [Television Company] a six-month report showing full details

of all matters necessary to enable the [Television Company] to calculate the royalty due (including but not limited to the number and type of copies of the Work sold and disposed of, the [Gross Price], the date payment fell due and when it was actually received, together with a [cheque/bank transfer] in respect of the royalty due to the [Television Company] for such period. The [Publishing Company] shall also deliver a copy of the auditor's certificate for the annual accounts confirming that the statements delivered by the [Publishing Company] for each such year are true and accurate.

A.317
Any royalty payable to the [Television Company] shall be paid in [sterling] without deduction of any bank commission, charges, currency conversion costs or otherwise.

A.318
The [Publishing Company] shall keep proper books of account and records in a form intelligible to the [Television Company] and its authorised agent showing all matters connected with the sales and disposals of the [Work] and the calculation of royalties due under this Agreement. The [Publishing Company] shall keep such books of accounts and records available to the [Television Company] or its authorised agent upon application during normal business hours and permit an inspection to be made and copies to be taken.

A.319
The [Publishing Company] shall keep and preserve such books of account and records for a period of [three years] after the termination or expiry of the Licence for whatever reason or for so long as a dispute shall in the opinion of either party exist between the parties in respect of this Agreement. In the event of any inspection carried out by or on behalf of the [Television Company] showing any royalty statement issued by the [Publishing Company] to be in error to the detriment of the [Television Company] by more than [5%] [five per cent] then the costs of such inspection shall be paid for by the [Publishing Company].

A.320
No royalties shall be payable by the [Publishing Company] to the [Television Company] in respect of the following:

1.1 Copies of the [Work] presented to the [Television Company] or any third party for promotional purposes either without charge or at cost.

1.2 Copies of the Work destroyed by fire, water, enemy action, in transit or otherwise. Provided that if any such copies shall have a salvage value other than as paper pulp which is realised in whole or in part whether by the [Publishing Company] or by any other person or body then the [Television Company] shall receive the royalty which would have been payable on the sums actually received by the [Publishing Company].

A.321

Accounts shall be made up every six months to [30 June and 31 December] respectively and the account provided and the sums due paid [3 calendar months/28 days] after each of those dates. No account shall be sent or payment made to the [Author] (unless specifically requested) in any period in which the sum due is [ten pounds] or less in which case that sum shall be carried forward to the next accounting date. When the [Publishers] receive a lump sum out of which [fifty pounds] or more is due to the [Author] under Clause [–] in respect of the subsidiary rights, then the sum due shall be paid to the [Author] within [28 days] of receipt of such sums by the [Publisher]. Any smaller sums shall be retained and paid in the next accounting period unless specifically requested by the [Author].

A.322

The [Author] or his/her authorised representative or agent shall have the right upon written request to examine the accounting records of the [Publishers] in respect of the sales, receipts and disposals of the [Work]. Any such inspection shall be at the [Author's] sole cost unless it is established that errors of [figure per cent/amount] or more of such sums are found to be to the detriment of the [Author] in [the last accounting period/in any accounting period] in which case the cost of any such inspection and audit shall be paid for [in full by the Publishers/50% by the Publishers.]

A.323

Any overpayments made by the [Publishers] to the [Author] in respect of the [Work] shall be deducted from any sums subsequently due to the [Author] from the [Publishers] in respect of the [Work/all works by the Author under any agreement with the Publisher].

A.324

The [Publisher] undertakes that it shall make accounts [twice yearly] as at [30 June and 31 December] and shall pay the [Author's] royalties within [90 days] of the last day of [June and December] in each year. The [Publisher] shall not be obliged to make any royalty payments to the [Author] if the amount due in any accounting period is less than [five pounds sterling] in which case such sums shall be carried forward to the next accounting period.

A.325

The Publishers shall create, keep and store for [specify period] the following material which may be relevant to the verification of the sums due to [Name]:

1.1　Financial records, accounts, contracts, invoices, sales, refunds, or sales documents in printed form, tabulated, stored on a computer or disc or by any other method.

1.2　Supply, manufacturing, artwork, cover and illustration costs, commissions, agent's fees, legal, copyright and intellectual property costs, expenses and clearance documents. Fees and documents relating to any collecting, performance or mechanical reproduction society.

1.3　Packaging and marketing material in respect of the [Book] in any form and any image, text, logo, character or music and any associated exploitation of the subsidiary rights, or merchandising whether based on the [Book] directly or derived or adopted from it. Together with two samples of any actual item.

A.326

By [dates] in each year the [Publisher] shall provide a detailed report to the [Author] with a full breakdown of the exploitation of the [Work] setting out the total sales including the number of copies of the [Work] used for publicity, promotional or review purposes and copies lost, damaged, destroyed, pulped or remaindered or any other reason for which there has been no royalty payment to the [Author].

A.327

The [Publisher] agrees that the [Author] shall be entitled to arrange or personally carry out an annual audit to inspect and make copies of the [Publisher's] books of account, records, contracts and any other relevant material in order to verify the sums due to the [Author]. The [Publisher] shall only be obliged to provide access to material which is directly relevant to the sums calculated to be due to the [Author]. The [Author] shall be obliged to undertake not to disclose any business plans of the [Company] that may be confidential which are revealed as a result of the audit. In the event that in any audit there is an error to the detriment of the [Author] in respect of the amount paid by the [Publisher] which is in excess of [figure/currency] then the [Publisher] shall pay the [Author] [figure/currency] as a contribution to the cost and as compensation for the error of each such audit.

A.328

The [Publisher] agrees to open a bank account in [country] at [specify] bank with [specify] for the specific purpose of depositing and dealing with all money relating to the exploitation of the [Work].

A.329

The [Publisher] and its sub-agents, sub-licensees and distributors shall keep for a minimum of [specify period] all material on which information is held relating to the [Work], books of account, records, invoices, discs, microfilm, computer software, letters and contracts showing the development, production, distribution and sale of the [Work] and all dealings of any nature, disposal, or transfer and all sums received by the [Publisher] in respect of the [Work].

A.330

The [Publisher] undertakes to the [Author] that a professional, comprehensive and complete history of the [Work] being exploited by the [Publisher] will be kept and recorded so that an accurate audit can be carried out by all the parties.

A.331

By [dates] the [Publisher] shall provide a detailed, accurate and complete report to the [Author] with a full breakdown of the exploitation of the [Work] including the number of copies lost through damage, theft or any other reason. The report shall be accompanied by a [method of payment] payable to [Name] for the full amount in [currency] shown to be due to the [Author].

A.332

The [Publisher] undertakes that it shall make accounts [twice yearly] as at [31 March and 30 September] and shall pay the [Author's] Royalties within [28 days] of the last day of [March and September] in each year. The [Publisher] shall not be obliged to make any royalty payments to the [Author] if the amount due in any accounting period is less than [ten pounds] in which case the sum shall be carried forward to the next period.

A.333

The [Publisher] undertakes and agrees in respect of the [Work] and/or any part and/or any form of exploitation in any media in any part of the world at any time:

1.1 That the [Publisher] shall keep full and accurate financial records and accounting statements in a manner which complies with the standards of [specify organisation]. Together with all receipts, invoices, contracts, letter agreements, bank statements and other material in any format which shows and/or can verify the sums received by or credited to the [Publisher] and/or its parent company and/or subsidiaries and any sub-agents, sub-licensees, distributors and/or joint venture partners.

1.2 This material shall be preserved and kept secure by the [Publisher] for a minimum of [three] years after the expiry or termination of the agreement or in the event there is a dispute between the parties for such longer period as may be necessary until it is resolved. [In any event any such material shall not be destroyed without prior written notice to the [Author] of the [Publisher's] intention to do so and the opportunity for the [Author] to collect and retain the material.]

1.3   That the [Publisher] shall provide copies of and/or access to inspect such background details, contracts, receipts, currency conversion records and other information, data, software and documents that the [Author] may request in order to verify whether the [Publisher] has complied with all the terms of this Agreement in respect of the publication and exploitation of the [Work] and the accounting statements to the [Author] and the sums paid.

A.334

In the event that any sums which are in fact due under this Agreement are deducted, withheld, credited but not cleared, have not been transferred by a third party, are delayed, inaccurate or omitted then the [Publisher] agrees to provide satisfactory evidence of the reason to the [Author] as soon as reasonably possible and make immediate payment where appropriate.

A.335

The [Publisher] will only account in respect of sums received from the publication and exploitation of the [Book] and is not responsible for the acts, omissions, breach of contract by or failure to pay of third parties whether agents, distributors, wholesalers, retailers or otherwise.

A.336

The [Distributor] shall only be obliged to account for and pay for each unit of the [Book] in the following [format] to the [Author] according to the accounting sample attached as Appendix [–] and forming part of this Agreement.

A.337

The [Company] agrees to provide regular updates to the [Author/Artist] as to the pre-publication marketing and actual terms of exploitation and licensing and sales of all formats of the [Work] throughout the world. The [Company] shall advise the [Author/Artist] of the name and nature of the role of any third parties including sub-agents, distributors, publicity companies, printers, suppliers, merchandising, music, food and drink, and other product companies and manufacturers who may be licensed and/or engaged for their services. The [Company] shall endeavour to ensure at all times that no third party is authorised who may bring the reputation of the [Author/Artist] and/or any of their brands and/or work into disrepute by association due to the failure of that third party to adhere to basic health and safety protection and testing, living wage employment conditions and/or their business does not have an account with a reputable bank.

Purchase and Supply of Products

A.338

The [Supplier] agrees that it shall provide the [Seller] with a full list of:

1.1   The Product and Value including wholesale and retail price;

1.2   Number, dimensions, weight content and description;

1.3   Method of transport together with shipment, carriage and storage costs;

1.4   Import/export taxes and duties; and

1.5   Insurance policy cost.

A.339

The [Supplier] shall provide a delivery statement with each assignment of the [Products] which shall be agreed by the [Seller] and returned to the [Supplier] on each occasion.

A.340

The [Seller] warrants and confirms that it will keep true and accurate records of all orders from the public and shall meet such requests promptly and will pay the [Supplier] for all the [Products] delivered.

A.341

The [Seller] agrees that its orders for the [Products] shall be in the quantity, specification and dates set out in Schedule [–]. That all repeat or additional orders shall be in writing to the [Supplier] in the agreed format.

A.342

The [Seller] agrees that the dates specified in this agreement are an important part of the terms which have to be fulfilled. The [Seller] agrees to provide detailed statements for any request for the [Product] and shall sign and retain a copy of the delivery statement with each consignment.

A.343

The [Factory] shall only reproduce and manufacture the exact number of the [Articles] requested by [name] in accordance with the written instructions on each occasion. The [Factory] shall ensure that full details are kept of all units produced, manufactured, distributed, destroyed, lost, or otherwise disposed of or returned to the [Factory]. The records kept shall include the dates, the codes and any other method of identification, the suppliers of the materials used of any nature however small, full details of the packaging together with an example of each type of item complete with all packaging to be kept for reference purposes.

A.344

The [Supplier] shall only engage, order supplies from or enter into a contract with any business or third party which have been in operation for at least [three years], has provided evidence of compliance with government health and safety regulations, has filed company accounts for at least [two years] and whose quality of work is of a suitable standard.

A.345

There shall be no obligation on the [Company/Distributor/Manufacturer] to produce, supply or allow access to any accounting or financial records of the business, health and safety documents and records or any other material relating to the provision supply or distribution of the [Products/Services/ Material under this Agreement] at any time. Where there is an allegation of piracy and copying, fraud, failure to pay or non-compliance with health and safety regulations and policies or failure to provide all the information required under the Agreement. Then the [Company/Distributor/Manufacturer] agrees to cooperate and provide copies of all directly relevant documents, material stored on computer and discs, accounts and other material which is in its possession or control provided that the cost of such administration is agreed in advance and will be paid by the [Purchaser].

A.346

The [Company/Distributor/Manufacturer] shall retain the following records, documents, contracts, letters, discs, data, receipts, invoices, bank records and any other material directly relevant to the creation, supply, distribution and exploitation of the [Product] under this Agreement for up to [six years] after the expiry or end of this Agreement:

1.1 All production sources, payments, costs and expenses, freight, customs and import and export duties and any taxes or levies.

1.2 All manufacture procedures, costs and expenses, payments, methods, compliance with health and safety legislation, regulations and policies, trials, samples, testing, and codes.

1.3 All distribution, supply, marketing and promotion costs and expenses and payments, lists, databases, packaging.

The [Company/Distributor/Manufacturer] agrees to provide a summary list of all such material and to allow access to and copies to be taken upon reasonable request by the [Name] at [Name's] sole cost.

A.347

The brochure, website and terms and conditions of trading may be varied and amended at any time without notice. The prices, costs and charges may be different when a product is ordered and all may be varied. The samples and products delivered may be different from the images portrayed in the brochure and on the website. The [Company] may only be able to partially complete an order for products. The [Company] may not keep any customer order details longer than [one week] if the payment has not been made in full.

A.348

The [Company] shall not be entitled to deduct from any payment due to the [Licensor] any cost of currency conversions, bank charges, commission, expenses, marketing material, travel, insurance, mobile phone, administration, office, staff, photography, filming, hotel, clothes, freight and/ or the cost of any professional and/or legal and/or health advisors and/or publicity agents and/or distributors and/or any other third party and/or any other matter of any nature which the [Company] may incur at any time.

A.349

The [Company] shall ensure that the manufacturer of the [Products] maintains full and accurate records of the production of the [Articles] so that the date and time of production can be verified and the source of the material from which it has been derived can be effectively traced if required. The [Company] agrees to provide such copies of all such records as may be kept by the manufacturer in any format and/or medium to the [Licensor] if so requested at any time.

Services

A.350

The [Manager] shall as far as possible keep the [Sportsperson] fully informed on a regular basis as regards any negotiations with any third party and agrees that the [Manager] shall not be entitled to conclude any agreement or sign any document or other record or conclude any financial, business or other arrangement on behalf of the [Sportsperson] without their prior [written] consent.

A.351

The [Manager] agrees that:

1.1 The [Sportsperson] shall be entitled upon request at the [Managers] cost to be provided with a copy of any contract, licence, document, list, copyright and intellectual property clearance and payment record, database, photographs, logos, artwork, recordings, receipts, sales and income figures and statements, financial records, bank statements, marketing and publicity reports or other material in the possession or under the control of the [Manager] directly [or indirectly] relating to the [Sportsperson] in any country.

79

1.2 The [Manager] shall retain and keep in a secure and safe manner all the material set out in 1.1 until [date].

1.3 The [Manager] shall not destroy, deliberately damage or shred any such material in 1.1 without the prior written consent of the [Sportsperson].

A.352

The [Manager] agrees that he shall not be entitled to any interest in or commission in respect of any work done or agreed to be done by the [Sportsperson] in respect of any work carried out or already agreed to be done by the [Sportsperson] prior to the date of this Agreement whether that work is performed during the term of this Agreement or not. A brief summary of the engagements is listed below [–].

A.353

The [Manager] shall keep full, accurate and separate financial, business and accounting records both in paper form and on computer [discs] showing the Gross Receipts, the Manager's Commission, the Authorised Expenses, the Net Receipts and the [Name] Fees and any other sums under this Agreement. Together with all original contracts, licences, letter agreements, and other documents, receipts, invoices, statements and databases. The [Manager] agrees that he/she shall not destroy any such material during the term of this Agreement which may be needed for tax purposes or to verify the sums paid and due by the authorised professional advisors of the [Name]. No charges or administration costs shall be made by the [Manager] unless agreed in advance for access to and to copy such material.

A.354

The [Manager] agrees to pay the [Sports Celebrity] Fees on the last day of each calendar month in the first two years and thereafter on a quarterly basis during the term of this Agreement. Any sums still outstanding which are not received until after the end or termination of the Agreement by the [Manager] shall be paid to the [Sports Celebrity] within [seven days] of receipt.

A.355

By [date] and [date] in each year the [Manager] agrees to provide the [Sportsperson] with a detailed written report containing a full breakdown of the Gross Receipts, the Authorised Expenses, the Manager's Commission, the Net Receipts and the [Sportsperson's] Fees [and any other sums credited or received from the exploitation of the [Sportsperson].

A.356

The [Manager] agrees that the [Sportsperson] shall be entitled to arrange for an audit for each accounting period to inspect and take copies of the

[Managers] and any associated companies or businesses' financial and accounting records, contracts, licences and other relevant material in order to verify the sums due under this Agreement. In the event that in any audit there is an error or omission to the [Sportsperson] in excess of [figure/currency] then the [Manager] shall pay all reasonable legal and accountancy costs and fees in respect of such audit and immediately pay the sums due together with interest at [figure per cent] for late payment.

A.357

The [Manager] agrees to assist the [Sportsperson] in general with the financial management of all the [Sportsperson's] Fees and their financial affairs generally including tax, value added tax, national insurance, pension health contributions, and personal insurance. The [Sportsperson] shall seek the benefit of independent specialist advice where appropriate and shall not seek to rely on the [Manager] to arrange and pay for the cost of such matters.

A.358

The [Manager] agrees to open a bank account at [bank] for the specific purpose of depositing and dealing in all monies received from the commercial exploitation of the product of the services of the [Sportsperson]. The following person [name] shall be the sole signatory for the withdrawal or transfer of any funds. This arrangement shall not be changed without the prior written consent of the [Sportsperson]. The [Manager] shall not be entitled to use the account to create a charge, lien or in any effect the claim to the sums by the [Sportsperson].

A.359

The [Agent] shall keep full and accurate books of account, records and contracts showing the Gross Receipts, the [Agent's] Commission, the Net Receipts under this Agreement. All sums relating to the [Artiste] shall be kept separate and apart from all other monies received by the [Agent]. The sums received shall be deposited at [bank] within one working day of payment. There shall be two signatories to the account and no sums may be withdrawn for any reason except with the required signature of the [Artiste] and the [Agent]. Both parties shall be entitled to receive statements and other transaction records and documents from the [bank].

A.360

The [Agent] agrees to pay the Net Receipts to the [Artiste] on the last day of each calendar month in each year during the term of this Agreement and thereafter on a quarterly basis. On the last day of [dates] the [Agent] agrees to provide a detailed report containing the breakdown of all sums received or credited together with all expenses and costs incurred, due or paid, the calculation and the sum received in commission by the [Agent] and the Net Receipts.

A.361

The [Author] authorises the [Agent] to collect all sums due to the [Author] in respect of the [Work] from any source throughout the Territory during the term of this Agreement and at any time thereafter relating to any agreement negotiated [and concluded] by the [Agent] during the term of the Agreement.

A.362

The [Record Company] shall send to the [Artiste] within [ninety days] after [March 31, June 30, September 30 and December 31] in each year a statement showing any royalties which have become due in the preceding quarterly period together with the amount shown therein to be due. The [Record Company] shall, however, be entitled to deduct from royalty payments any sums which may be demanded by any government in respect of such payments. The [Record Company's] liability to remit to the [Artiste] in the [United Kingdom] any royalty which has fallen due in countries where currency restrictions are in force shall be limited to the amounts actually received by the [Record Company] in the [United Kingdom]. Should such currency restrictions in any countries (including the United Kingdom) prevent the remittance of the whole or part of any royalty due then any part of the royalty not paid shall be held in an account to be nominated by the [Artiste] in the country concerned if legally possible.

A.363

The [Company] shall not be entitled to:

1.1 Withhold any sums due to the [Artiste] for any reason.

1.2 Withhold any sums as a reserve against returns.

1.3 Withhold any sums against existing and/or future liability whether or not legal proceedings have been instituted by a third party.

1.4 Withhold any sums to meet the claim and/or demand for payment to any agent and/or manager who has been and/or is engaged by the [Artiste].

1.5 Withhold any sums due to the delay of the transfer of funds between connected and/or associated companies and/or businesses whether parent, subsidiary or otherwise of the [Company].

A.364

The [Agent] and the [Company] both undertake and agree that all accounts, records, contracts, letters, computer records, software and electronic storage and retrieval systems and any other material in any medium and/or controlled by the [Agent] and/or the [Company] relating to the exploitation of [Name/Work/Product/Rights] shall be kept and retained in a secure and safe environment in [country] for no less than [number] years from [date]. That no such material of any nature shall be destroyed and/or erased and/or deleted before [date] in any event.

A.365

That the [Company/Distributor] agrees and undertakes that it shall follow and adhere to the recommended accounting and financial practices and policies of the [specify institute] in respect of the maintenance, reporting, auditing and accounting for the sums received in respect of this Agreement and the supply of reports and the payment of the sums due to [Name] under this Agreement.

A.366

The [Consultant] may claim a monthly expenses fee from the [Company] of up to [number/currency] without production of any receipts and/or invoices based on a written invoice by the [Consultant].

A.367

The [Consultant] shall be paid a total fee of [number/currency] for completion of the [Work/Project] and shall not be obliged to provide a detailed account of the dates, times and nature of the work that he/she has completed. Provided that the [Work/Project] is carried out in accordance with the agreed Schedule [–] attached.

Sponsorship

A.368

1.1 The [Company] shall at the end of every [three calendar months] for the duration of the Term of this Agreement and thereafter send an accounting statement and business report to [Name] showing any sums due, expenses deducted or commission charged together with a copy of the contract, licence or letter agreement that has been concluded and payment. Disclosure shall be as specific and full as known to the [Company] itself and no information shall be withheld for any reason.

1.2 The [Company] agrees that upon request it shall provide a copy of any record, document, accounts or other material which may assist the [Celebrity] in establishing the validity and accuracy of the information provided in the accounts and the sums due.

A.369

The [Sponsor] confirms that the [Organisers/Association] shall be entitled to retain all sums received from the exploitation of the [Festival/Event] including ticket and programme sales, advertising, merchandising, sound recordings, DVD, video, television and film, the internet or telecommunications including mobiles and any other medium and/or format and any associated logo, graphics, music, lyrics and/or products.

A.370

The [Licensor] acknowledges that the [Licensee] shall be entitled to retain all sums received from the exploitation of the [Licensee's] Product and the Product Package.

A.371

The [Promoter] undertakes that it and its sub-agents, sub-licenses and distributors shall keep full and accurate books of account, records, contracts, software and other material showing all sums received and spent in respect of the [Promoter's] Budget. That the material may be destroyed after [date] if there are no further details and copies required by the [Company].

A.372

The [Promoter] agrees that the [Organisers] shall be entitled to retain all sums received from the commercial and non-commercial exploitation of the [Event] and any associated activities, rights, material, revenue and payments received including but not limited to admission charges, sales from the official programme, advertising, sponsorship, merchandising, recordings, licensing, sales and receipts for exploitation on radio, television, mobiles, DVDs, CDs, CD-Roms, discs, and/or any trade marks, logos, music, and sound recordings. The [Promoter] agrees and undertakes that it shall not be entitled to any sums of any nature at any time from the [Organisers] except those specified for its services in Clause [–].

A.373

The parties agree to disclose to each other all sums received in the form of payment, benefits, expenses or goods for the sponsorship, promotion, endorsement of any person, company, goods or services at any time in any form. All parties shall however be entitled to retain whatever they have received and/or are due.

A.374

In the event that the number of tickets sold and/or the attendance of the public at the [Sports Event/Music Festival] do not reach the figures which the parties predicted prior to this Agreement and/or the event is cancelled due to circumstances beyond the reasonable control of the [Association].

The [Sponsor] shall not be entitled to a reduction of the [Sponsorship Fees] due to the [Association] and shall still be obliged to pay all such sums in full.

A.375

The [Association/Company] shall provide details of the [public attendance figures and admission tickets] of the [Event] to the [Sponsor] within [twenty-eight] days of the [Event]. Where the figures are [fifty] per cent lower than predicted in Clause [–] then the [Sponsor] shall not be obliged to pay the final payment under Clause [–] due to the [Association/Company].

A.376

The [Company] undertakes to the [Sponsor] that it shall comply with the following procedures in respect of the [Sponsorship Payment] by the [Sponsor] for the [Event/Festival/Film]:

1.1 That the [Company] shall open a new bank account for the purpose of holding the [Sponsorship Payment] to which only the following persons shall be designated signatories [specify].

1.2 That the [Sponsorship Payment] shall only be spent and allocated in accordance with the agreed [Budget] which is attached in Schedule A.

1.3 That no part of the [Sponsorship Payment] shall be used to reduce any debts and/or liability of the [Company] in respect of any matter and no funds shall be transferred outside [country].

1.4 That by [date] the [Company] shall provide to the [Sponsor] a full breakdown of all sums paid from the new bank account together with copies of the bank statements and supporting invoices and/or receipts in respect of the payments.

A.377

The [Sponsor] shall not be entitled to any accounts, press reports, admission details and/or any other data, records and/or marketing and/or any other material in any medium and/or format in respect of the [Event] from [Name/Association]. The [Sponsor] shall be obliged to use its own resources to analyse, assess, and/or gather marketing, ratings, admission and/or other details which would enable the [Sponsor] to reach a conclusion as to the value and extent of the advertising, television, press and media exposure.

A.378

The [Sponsor] shall not be entitled to copies of and/or access to any documents and any other material which are not already available to the public at any time including but not limited to the draft and audited accounts, financial records, projected forecasts and budgets, data, sales figures, losses, expenses, advertising and marketing costs, donations, personal data and payment records.

A.379

The [Club] shall as far as reasonably possible provide the [Sponsor] with details of the estimated number of people who took part in the [Event] together with details of any marketing, local and national press and media coverage whether on television, radio or personal blogs.

University, Library and Educational

A.380

1.1 The [Company] shall ensure that comprehensive and professional accounts are created and recorded in each [six month] period from 1 January to 30 June and from 1 July to 31 December. That within [28 days] after each of those dates the accounts shall be supplied to the [Institute] and any sum due shall be paid which is over [ten pounds sterling]. If it is less, then that sum shall be carried forward to the next accounting date unless specifically requested by the [Institute].

1.2 The [Institute] shall be entitled to appoint a representative from the management, board and/or legal and/or financial advisors to examine the accounting records in any medium of the [Company] in respect of the exploitation of the [Work]. Any such inspection shall be at the [Institute's] sole cost upon written notice to the [Company] and shall take place no more than twice a year. Where an error is established the [Company] shall be obliged to pay the interest on the sum from the date it should have been paid at [figure] per cent above base rate.

A.381

The [Licensee] undertakes that:

1.1 It shall provide the [Institute] with thorough and accurate financial reports and accounts audited by an accredited professional firm of accountants once in each calendar year during the Term of this Agreement and thereafter at the end of each three month period until all sums are received and verified.

1.2 It shall keep full and accurate financial records, receipts, invoices, contracts, letter agreements, databases, data, and storage and retrieval systems on computers, hardware, software, discs and gadgets and any other method of recording showing all sums received by or credited to the [Licensee] and/or its parent company and/or subsidiaries and/or any associated companies and any sub-agents, sub-licensees, distributors or joint venture partners. That all such material shall be preserved and kept secure by the [Licensee] for a minimum of [six years] after the expiry or termination of the Agreement or in the event there is a dispute between the parties for such longer period as may be necessary until it is resolved. In any event any such material shall not be destroyed without prior written notice to the [Institute] of the [Licensee's] intention to do so and the opportunity for the [Institute] to collect and retain the material.

A.382

1.1 The [Distributor] undertakes and agrees during the Term of this Agreement to keep and provide to the [Licensor] detailed accounts and records in respect of all exploitation of the [Work/Product].

1.2 The [Distributor] shall provide a detailed written report containing a full breakdown and a complete statement of accounts to the [Licensor] at the end of each [three-month] calendar period which shall set out all sums received and/or credited, and any sums paid out and/or material distributed. The [Distributor] shall pay the [Licensor] all sums that may be due at the same time in [currency] by [cheque/direct debit] at the [Distributors] cost and expense. Any sums still outstanding which are not received until after the end or termination of the Agreement by the [Distributor] shall be paid to the [Licensor] within [seven days] of receipt.

1.3 Where requested by the [Licensor] to do so, the [Distributor] shall provide copies of all and/or any contracts, licences, letter agreements, and other documents, receipts, invoices, databases, bank statements, computer related records, samples of the [Work/Product], and any other the material that the [Licensor] may require to verify the accounts, financial records, licences granted to third parties and the sums claimed as commission, or expenses and sums due to the [Licensor].

1.4 The [Distributor] agrees that it shall not destroy any of the material relating to the [Work/Product] in paragraph 1.1 to 1.3 above without the prior written consent of the [Licensor].

1.5 The [Distributor] agrees that all sums relating to the [Work/Product] shall be kept separate and apart from all other monies received by the [Distributor].

A.383

1.1 The [Institute] undertakes that it [and its sub-agents, and sub-licensees] shall keep full and accurate books of account, records and contracts showing the [Gross Receipts/sums received] and the calculation of the [Licensor's] Royalties.

1.2 The [Institute] agrees to account to the [Licensor] and pay the [Licensor's] Royalties by [date] in each year during the Term of this Agreement and thereafter within [–] of receipt of payment until all sums due or owing are accounted for to the [Licensor].

1.3 The [Institute] may withhold from amounts otherwise due reasonable reserves against anticipated returns. No monies paid to the [Institute] and thereafter refunded or credited shall be included in the Gross Receipts or if included the amount thereof shall be deducted from subsequent Gross Receipts. No payments shall be due for any lost, damaged, stolen, and/or for which the monies due are not received from a third party.

A.384

The [Institute] shall not be obliged to provide any accounts, financial information, costs and/or budget details to the [Company] at any time. Nor shall the [Company] be entitled to any control over and/or right of approval in respect of any matter relating to any sums to be spent and/or received in respect of the [Project] by the [Institute]. The [Company] shall not have any right of approval over whether a third party is to be accepted to participate in the cost of the [Project] and/or to provide sponsorship and/or some other contribution at any time.

A.385

The [Distributor] acknowledges and agrees that [Name] shall have the right to be provided with a full and frank disclosure regarding the exploitation of the [Work/Product] by the Distributor. The [Distributor] shall ensure that a written report is sent to [Name] by email at the end of each month from [date]. Details shall include the nature of all agreements concluded with a third party in respect of the [Work/Product] and where an agreement has been signed then a copy shall be supplied. As well as full details of any sums received from third parties and the date of payment and currency conversion costs if any incurred by the [Distributor].

ACT OF GOD

General Business and Commercial

A.386

In the event that this Agreement cannot be performed or its obligations fulfilled for any reason beyond the reasonable control of either party to this

Agreement, then such failure to perform or fulfil the obligations required under this Agreement by any such party shall accordingly be deemed not to be a breach of this Agreement. The reasons may include, but are not limited to, such events as war, industrial action, floods or Acts of God.

A.387

For the purpose of this Agreement, references to 'Act of God' shall include all uncontrollable natural forces and natural disasters whether flood, avalanche, storms, unforeseeable accidents or equipment failure which are not the fault of the party relying upon such circumstances, but shall specifically exclude acts of terrorism, war, industrial action and any acts or omissions of any employees in the course of their employment or consultants or other third parties.

A.388

This Agreement shall not be considered binding on either party in the event that an Act of God shall mean that the terms of the agreement cannot be properly fulfilled and carried out whether in whole or part. Both parties agree that in such event they shall as far as possible reach an amicable settlement to resolve the matter. Each party shall bear its own losses and costs and all the terms of the agreement shall end immediately except for payment relating to work which has already been fulfilled or concluded and transfer of ownership of material which shall only be concluded subject to receipt of payment.

A.389

The term 'Act of God' shall be defined as those acts or circumstances which could not reasonably have been predicted or guarded against which are beyond the control of the parties. Examples include, but are not limited, to lightning, floods, extreme weather conditions, defects in equipment, accidents, terrorism, war, violent outbursts, nation-wide power failures.
The following types of acts or omissions are not applicable:

1.1 negligent acts or omissions by employees, consultants or sub-contractors or other third parties engaged to carry out work.

1.2 industrial action.

1.3 wanton acts by trespassers or visitors.

A.390

Neither party shall be responsible to the other party in circumstances where the obligations under this Agreement cannot be completed due to circumstances outside the foreseeable reasonable control of the [Assignor] or the [Assignee]. In the event that this Agreement is not completed by

[date] then it will terminate with immediate effect and the following shall apply [payment/costs/ownership/return of material/other].

A.391

In the event that the [Service/Website] is unable to function, is interrupted or is scrambled or lost or otherwise at any time. Then the [Advertiser/Sponsor] shall not be entitled to reclaim any sum due under this Agreement which is due to a technical fault, some unforeseen energy failure or otherwise which is for less than [one week].

A.392

The [Designer] acknowledges that the [Company] shall not be obliged to set up and/or exploit and/or use the [Website] in the event of an Act of God which materially effects the supplies, operation or services of the [Company] or any distributor, bank or joint venture partner associated with it.

A.393

Any party which is unable in whole or part to carry out its obligations under this Agreement shall promptly give written notice to that effect to the other party stating in detail the circumstances and the estimated time it is believed will be needed to remedy the situation.

A.394

There shall be no obligation to fulfil the terms of this Agreement in the event that any of the following unforeseen circumstances shall occur in respect of the [Company], its suppliers, distributors and packagers:

1.1 A war is declared, or a state of national emergency, the national energy supplies are not functioning for more than [one week] in [country].

1.2 The Website is not functioning due to technical problems, viruses, hackers or spam for more than [one month].

1.3 Floods, hurricanes, storms, or other extreme weather conditions in [country/Europe/other].

1.4 The suspension of the [Company] on the [Stock Market/other].

1.5 A major product recall of its goods and services for health and safety reasons.

The Agreement shall either be suspended indefinitely until the conditions or problems cease or shall be ended on terms to be agreed between the parties.

A.395

Where the [Institute] is unable to fulfil the terms and conditions of all and/or any part of this Agreement due to circumstances beyond its control which were not reasonably foreseeable and are due to an Act of God including, but not limited to, lightning, floods, hurricanes, extreme weather conditions, defects in equipment, accidents, acts of terrorism, war, national power failures and/or has the effect of interrupting the supplies, services and/ or work of any third party associated with the [Institute] in respect of this Agreement. Then the Agreement shall be suspended until such time as it can be fulfilled by the [Institute] provided that it shall be for no more than a period of [one year]. Thereafter either party shall be entitled to serve notice to terminate the Agreement and for the parties to negotiate a settlement to resolve any outstanding matters.

A.396

Both parties agree that the following acts, failures, defects and matters are specifically excluded and are not an Act of God:

1.1 Defects in any equipment provided by either party.

1.2 A major product recall of its goods and services for health and safety reasons.

1.3 Technical failure of the [Work/Website/Product].

1.4 The suspension of the [Company] on the [Stock Market/other].

1.5 Hackers, spam, viruses and computer hardware and software failures and problems unless due to a national power failure.

1.6 Malicious, deliberate, negligent acts, omissions and errors by employees, consultants, sub-contractors, agents, licensees, directors, trustees or other third parties engaged to carry out work and/or who provide services.

1.7 Strike, industrial action and protests.

1.8 Malicious, deliberate, negligent acts, omissions and errors by trespassers and/or visitors.

A.397

Where the [Event/Programme] is cancelled by the [Institute] due to circumstances which are beyond its reasonable control and could not reasonably have been foreseen. Then the [Sponsor] agrees that it shall not withdraw its funding, but shall agree to the [Event/Festival] being rescheduled as soon as possible. Where the [Event/Programme] cannot be rescheduled, then the [Institute] shall not be obliged to return the [Sponsorship Fees] paid to the date of cancellation. The [Sponsor] shall not pay any further sums that may be due under the Agreement. In such event the [Sponsor] shall not have any further rights and the agreement shall be terminated. The

[Association] shall then be entitled to enter into a sponsorship agreement with a third party for the same [Event/Programme].

A.398

The [Sponsor] and the [Company] agree that the following matters shall constitute grounds for a claim of force majeure by either party where it has a direct impact on the provision of their services and/or fulfilment of the terms of this Agreement in respect of the [Film/Event].

1.1 Interruption and/or suspension of national and/or local and/or failure to work due to a defect including electricity, gas, water, sewage, air conditioning, computer hardware and/or software relating to ticket sales and/or processing of payments.

1.2 A national and/or local situation including war, threat of invasion, attacks, terrorism, strike, industrial action, blockades, protests, marches, threats of criminal action which would pose a serious threat, explosions, riot, suspension of public transport, a public announcement by the government that there is a state of crisis and/or a severe health risk to the public.

1.3 Major defects and/or health and safety problems with any building, equipment, stage and/or any major product recall of the [Products/ Services] of the Sponsor and/or Company and/or any suppliers.

1.4 Political, financial, and/or personnel problems at the [Sponsor/ Company] which would have a severe and detrimental effect on the marketing and/or sales figures.

1.5 Extreme weather including lightning, floods, hurricanes, snow, strong winds.

Where a valid assertion of force majeure is made by either and/or both parties which prevents the terms of this Agreement being fulfilled in any significant manner. Both parties agree that the defaulting party who is relying on an assertion of force majeure shall be allowed a period of [three] months to remedy the situation and/or to allow the situation to change. In the event that the Agreement cannot be fulfilled then the parties agree to enter into negotiations to reach an amicable settlement in respect of the matter. In any event neither party shall be obliged to pay any further sums to the other which may fall due under this Agreement as soon as a reliance on force majeure is made by either party.

A.399

Where the [Licensee] is unable to fulfil any of the terms of this Agreement due to force majeure which is beyond its reasonable control and/or for any other reason and this continues for a period of [number] months. Then the

[Licensor] shall have the right to terminate the Agreement immediately by notice in writing and all rights granted to the [Licensee] shall revert to the [Licensor]. The [Licensee] shall be obliged to return all material provided under this Agreement and to account to and pay any sums due under Clause [–].

A.400

Where any situation arises which relates to this Agreement which prevents the main terms being fulfilled due to circumstances beyond the control of either party. Then as soon as that situation becomes clear and/or either party has received notice to that effect from the other party. Then either party shall have the right to terminate the Agreement without any further liability and/or payments to the other party.

A.401

Where the [Licensee] is unable to fulfil and/or perform any and/or all of [Clauses/specify] for [number] [days/months] due to circumstances beyond the [Licensee's] reasonable control which are due to force majeure. Then the [Licensee] shall be obliged to notify the [Licensor] of the nature of the force majeure and the terms which the [Licensee] is unable to perform and/or fulfil. At the same time the [Licensee] must provide an estimated date by which the matter is expected to be remedied. In any event upon receipt of any such notification from the [Licensee] the [Licensor] shall have the right to terminate the Agreement by notice is writing. It shall be entirely at the [Licensor's] discretion as to whether the [Licensee] is permitted the opportunity to remedy the situation. In the event that the Agreement is terminated by the [Licensor] then the termination provisions in Clause [–] shall apply.

A.402

The [Licensor] and the [Licensee] agree that the following circumstances shall be accepted as grounds for force majeure. Provided that the force majeure occurs in the country in which the head office of the [Licensee] is situated namely [specify] and/or in which the manufacture and/or production of the [Product/Services] take place namely [specify]. Force majeure shall include war, threat of invasion, attacks, terrorism, strike, blockades, explosions, riot, fire, industrial action, floods, hurricanes, interruption and/or suspension of national but not local electricity, gas, and water supplies; a declaration of a state of national crisis and the suspension of any of the major services upon which the [Licensee] relies whether airlines, shipping, postal service, freight and/or other transport.

A.403

The [Licensor] and the [Licensee] agree that the following circumstances shall not be deemed and/or accepted as grounds for force majeure:

93

1.1   Snow, strong winds.

1.2   Defects in any equipment, material and/or packaging.

1.3   Technical failure of the website of the [Licensee].

1.4   Suspension and/or exclusion of the [Licensee] from the [Stock Market/ Institute].

1.5   Computer hardware and software failures.

1.6   Malicious, deliberate, negligent acts, omissions and errors by employees, consultants, sub-contractors, agents, directors and/or other third parties engaged to carry out work and/or to provide services by the [Licensee].

1.7   Protests, marches, arson, and/or criminal acts.

1.8   Malicious, deliberate, negligent acts, omissions and errors by trespassers and/or visitors.

A.404

Both parties agree that where one party to this Agreement is unable and/or unwilling to fulfil its terms due to circumstances which could not have been predicted at the time of the original signature of the Agreement. That the party who wishes to default may terminate the Agreement with immediate effect provided that it pays the sum of [currency/number] to the other party at the same time that it sends notice of termination.

A.405

The parties agree that the following circumstances shall constitute force majeure under this Agreement:

1.1   A local protest, riot, fire and/or explosion in the vicinity of the manufacturer who produces the [Article/other] for the [Distributor].

1.2   A political uprising, declaration of war, and/or an assassination of a major political figure either in that [country] and/or a neighbouring country.

1.3   A police and/or military lock down of an area in [country] which restricts movement of the public and./or transport.

1.4   Delays and cancellation of aeroplanes, ships and/or trains due to extreme weather conditions, rising water and floods, high temperatures and drought, wind, falling objects, tremors, earthquakes, volcanoes, tsunamis, obstruction of roads, power failures or lightning.

1.5   The above list is not intended to be exhaustive and any circumstance where there is violence, fear, distress and/or the threat of loss of life and/or a severe reduction in services may constitute a relevant factor and be deemed a situation covered by force majeure.

A.406
Neither party shall be entitled to rely on a force majeure circumstance which relates to a third party. Where a third party manufacturer and/or distributor is effected for more than [period] then the [Licensee] shall be obliged to find an effective alternative who can take over the work at the [Licensees'] cost. Failure to do so with a period of [number/months] from the first date of the force majeure shall be deemed a breach of this Agreement.

A.407
Both parties agree that where it is clear that this Agreement cannot be performed and/or carried out in the terms stated due the same circumstances which affects both parties. That the parties may either agree to delay the start of the Agreement and/or cancel the arrangement Provided that all sums paid by one party to the other prior to the date of cancellation [are refunded in full/shall not be returned].

A.408
Both parties agree and accept that in the event that either should seek to rely upon any reason of circumstances which they submit constitutes force majeure and provides notice to that effect to the other non-defaulting party. That the non-defaulting party shall have the absolute discretion to refuse to accept the delay and/or non-performance and as a direct result serve notice to the defaulting party that the agreement is terminated with immediate effect. Provided that in such circumstances the non-defaulting party shall not be entitled to seek any refund and/or repayment of any advance payment from the defaulting party.

A.409
Both parties agree that where a circumstance arises which is due to the actions, omission, delay, fault, negligence or otherwise of a third party, or arises from the weather, air, sea or land conditions and/or changes which impedes or delays the performance of this Agreement within the dates specified in clause [–]. That, whether or not the circumstances constitute force majeure, the parties agree to resolve the matter by discussions between the parties to as far as possible extend the Agreement. Where this matter cannot be resolved then the parties agree to appoint a mutually acceptable person to endeavour to assist the parties reaching a resolution. The cost of such person shall be paid for [equally by both parties/by the defaulting party].

ADAPTATION

General Business and Commercial

A.410

The [Company] shall without limitation be entitled to edit, adapt, alter, vary, change, translate, develop, add to and/or delete from the [Work/Product] and all the text, images, film, sound recordings, logos, graphics, music, slogans and any other content together with all packaging, advertising and marketing material which may be supplied by [Name]. All copyright, intellectual property and trade marks rights in any such new versions, adaptations, sequels, translations, and/or associated merchandising shall belong to [specify].

A.411

1.1 [Name] has not provided any authority to the [Company] and the [Company] agrees and undertakes that it shall not be entitled to adapt, edit, amend, add to, delete from, change, and/or alter the [Work/Artwork/Product] and/or to combine any part of the [Work/Artwork/Product] with any other material of any nature.

1.2 The [Company] must on each occasion make a written request for the prior written approval and consent of [Name] before any work and/or changes are carried out. The failure by the [Company] to fulfil the terms of this clause shall be a serious breach of this Agreement. [Name] shall not be obliged to consent to any request that may be made. Where [Name] agrees to provide written consent then this may be subject to further terms and conditions that may be imposed including additional payments and/or the condition that there be a new agreement where there is a different work, product and/or format of any nature which the [Company] wishes to be exploit.

A.412

The [Company/Distributor] agrees and undertakes that it shall not develop, adapt, revise, edit, delete from and/or add to, translate and/or otherwise change the title, layout, content, format, text, images, graphics, credits, copyright notices, trade marks, logos, moral rights assertions and/or any part of the [Work] at any time without the prior written approval in each case of the [Licensor]. The [Company/Distributor] agrees and undertakes not to licence and/or authorise any third party to change the [Work] and/or any material associated with it including the cover, index, packaging and marketing without the prior written consent of the [Author].

A.413

The [Company/Distributor] agrees and undertakes that it does not have any right of first refusal and/or any option and/or any other rights over the [Work] and/or any part and/or any variation to develop, reproduce and/or exploit any material in any medium and/or format which is a new edition, adaptation, sequel and/or similar and/or based upon the same concept, characters, format, layout and/or title.

A.414

The [Company] shall be entitled to edit and adapt the [Work/Artwork/Film] and all the text and images, for the purpose of developing a format which is suitable to be downloaded and stored on a [mobile phone/gadget/ computer]. The [Company] shall be able to reduce the size of the trade marks, logos and graphics, but not their location nor their colour and/ or shape. All copyright, intellectual property and trade marks rights in any such new versions and/or adaptations, sequels, translations, and/ or associated merchandising shall be assigned to and belong to the [Licensor]. The [Company] agrees that it shall not hold and/or control any rights in any such new material and shall execute all such documents as may be requested by the [Licensor] to ensure the assignment of all such rights to the [Licensor].

A.415

The [Licensee] shall be entitled to edit, delete from and add to the [Sound Recordings/Audio File/Music] licensed by the [Company] under this Agreement. Provided that the [Licensee] shall provide a complete copy of the final version of the proposed [Work/Product] derived from the [Sound Recordings/Audio File/Music] for the written approval of the [Company] prior to any commercial and/or non-commercial distribution to any third party. Where the final version is rejected by the [Company] for any reason. Then the [Licensee] shall be obliged to incorporate the proposed changes requested by the [Company] at the [Licensee's] sole cost.

Where the parties are unable and/or unwilling to reach agreement then the [Licensee] and/or the [Licensor] shall be entitled to terminate this Agreement by notice in writing provided that the party who serves notice of termination agrees to return all sums paid under the agreement to the other party.

A.416

The [Institute] shall not be entitled to adapt, develop and/or alter the credit, slogan, name, logo and/or trade mark of the [Sponsor/Company] in respect of any material, packaging, advertising and/or marketing which is created, reproduced, supplied, distributed, displayed and/or posted on any website for the purposes of this Agreement.

A.417

The [Author] accepts and agrees that the [Distributor] and/or any sub-licensee may need to adapt the title, images, text, credits, acknowledgements, index and the cover for the purpose of marketing the [Work] outside [country]. Wherever possible the [Distributor] and/or any sub-licensee shall consult with the [Author] in order to seek their views and advice so that integrity of the [Work] is maintained. The [Distributor] and/or sub-licensee shall not be entitled to engage a third party to re-write the [Work] and any adaptation must be as far as possible a strict translation of the original [Work]. Any rights in any development and/or adaptation shall be assigned by the [Distributor] and/or sub-licensee to the [Author]. The [Distributor] shall be responsible for the cost of any expenses that may be incurred to ensure the assignment of all such rights in all material in any format to the [Author].

A.418

The [Creator] agrees that the [Company] may be edit, adapt, add to and/or delete from the prototype software and concept of the [Work] for the [App] provided that the [Company] accepts that this does not entitle the [Company] to seek to claim any joint ownership and/or copyright, design, patent, trade mark, image and or other rights of any nature in any medium at any time in the [Work] and/or any part.

A.419

The [Author] has not authorised the [Company] to make any changes, deletions from and/or add to the [Work] whether in the form of a preface, index, cover, footnotes, maps, photographs and/or otherwise. Every part of the finished product shall be written and/or created and/or decided upon by the [Author]. Nor shall any name of any third party except [specify] be present on any part of the finished product.

A.420

Any adaptations and/or new versions must be authorised by the [Licensor] and there is no implied and/or express consent provided to permit any other [Products/Work] to be produced based on the [Logo/Image] except those specifically authorised in Schedule [–] attached.

A.421

The [Licensor] permits the public to download this free [App] to store on their own personal device and any other gadget they may personally own for use at home but not as a business and/or free service. There is no authority granted to edit, adapt, change and/or delete any part of the [App] and to use it in another format and/or medium in whole and/or in part. Nor is there any right granted for you to supply it and/or promote it use for any unauthorised purpose.

A.422

Where you are granted a licence by the [Licensor] to add the [Logo/Image] to your [Product/Website/Marketing] as part of a joint collaboration and partnership. Any adaptation and/or changes which may be made by a third party at your request must be assigned by that third party and you the [Licensee] to the [Licensor]. No commission, request for services, work and/or creating software, photographs, films, logos, text and/or otherwise should allow a third party to seek to claim any copyright and/or intellectual property rights of any nature in any format and/or medium at a later date. It is an condition of the grant of any rights that all adaptations, developments, changes, alterations and variations must be assigned to the [Licensor] by any party whether a company, person, employee, consultant or otherwise.

A.423

The [Consultant] is engaged to create a translation of the [Work] in [language] in which shall be delivered to the [Company] in the following form:[specify]. The Consultant agrees and undertakes that:

1.1 He/she shall transfer all copyright and any other rights of any nature to the [Company] and shall complete a comprehensive and detailed assignment of all rights in the adaptation and translation of the [Work] for a fee of [one/currency].

1.2 That where the translation differs from the original text due to adaptation and changes requested by the author of the [Work] and/or the [Company] due to cultural, religious, interpretation and/or other issues. Whether or not the [Consultant] is the originator he/she agrees not to make any claim to be the author of those changes, variations and/or adaptations. Further that where necessary the [Consultant] shall assign all rights including copyright and any other intellectual property rights to the [Company] so that absolutely none are held by the [Consultant].

1.3 That the [Consultant] shall not at any time hold himself as the author, originator and/or copyright owner and/or assert any moral rights to be identified. That the [Consultant] accepts that he shall not be entitled to any copyright notice at any time and only the words [translated by Consultant].

1.4 The [Consultant] agrees that at later date the [Company] shall be entitled to engage and/or use any other third person that it should wish to choose at its sole discretion for any additions, changes and/or alterations. That there is no obligation to use the [Consultant].

1.5 Further that after a period of [number] years from the date of this Agreement. The [Company] shall not be obliged to make any credit of any nature to the [Consultant] provided that the [Consultant] is paid an additional sum of [number/currency] by the [Company].

1.6 That the [Consultant] shall not be entitled to any additional fee, royalty and/or payment where the translation is used by the [Company] in any other format and/or medium than [specify].

1.7 The [Consultant] shall not seek to register any name, word, title, image and/or other material directly and/or indirectly associated with the [Work] and/or the translation and/or any parts in any part of the world.

ADVERSE CHANGE

General Business and Commercial

A.424

In the event that the world market in [subject] should fall in value dramatically in the next [period] then the [Company] shall be able to terminate the contract with immediate effect by written notice provided that it is willing to undertake to pay [figure/currency] in full immediately.

A.425

If in the first year of sales of [Product] it is clear that there is no real demand in any one or more of the [countries], or there are adverse conditions due to weather, strife, war, energy shortages, political unrest or financial instability of the economic market, purchasers or suppliers. Then the [Company] may cease to sell in that country, suspend the contract for up to [duration] or terminate the contract on the grounds of adverse conditions and only be liable to pay the sums due [in advances/in the first two years/other].

A.426

In the event that the [Institute] decides in its absolute discretion that the circumstances and/or budget and/or the criteria as to the value of the [Project] have changed to such an extent that the [Project] is no longer financially viable and/or the key personnel are no longer available and/or the [Project] is no longer agreed to be of value to the [Institute]. Then the [Institute] shall have the right to terminate the [Project] at any time by notice in writing to the [Company]. All rights granted by the [Institute] to the [Company] shall revert to the [Institute], and the [Institute] shall only be obliged to pay such sums as are due to the date of termination.

A.427

Where for any reason the [Film/Work] is not produced and/or distributed before [date] by the [Company] in [country] for any reason. Then the [Licensee] shall have the right to choose to either agree to an extension of the licence period or to serve notice of the termination of the Agreement. In the event that the Agreement is terminated then the [Licensor] shall be obliged to repay to the [Licensee] all the sums received under Clause [specify].

ADVERTISING

DVD, Video and Discs

A.428

The [Assignee] shall be entitled to use and permit the use of the [DVDs/Videos/CDs of the music] for trade exhibitions, in-store demonstrations, conferences for the purpose of advertisement, promotions and publicity.

A.429

The [Assignee] shall be entitled to include short extracts of the [Film] of less than [duration] in total of the same section in images, text, sound or vision or both in all media for the purpose of advertisement, promotion and publicity including but not limited to radio, television, other videos, DVDs, CD-Roms, discs, telephones and related gadgets, cinemas, shops and businesses, posters, billboards, computers, software and the internet.

A.430

The [Licensee] agrees to provide copies and samples of any publicity, promotional, advertising and packaging material in respect of the [Video/DVD/Discs at the [Licensee's] cost upon request by the [Licensor].

A.431

The [Licensee] shall not advertise the availability of the [Units] in any format in the [Territory] earlier than [date].

A.432

The [Company] shall not be under any obligation to use the [Work] and/or exploit it in any format at any time and the failure of the [Company] to do shall not give rise to any claim by the [Writer] for loss of publicity or reputation or loss of opportunity to enhance his/her reputation.

A.433

The [Licensee] shall not use the name of the [Distributor] for any purpose in connection with the distribution, advertising or publicising of the [specify] without the prior written consent of the [Distributor].

A.434

The [Licensor] shall from time to time promptly after receipt of the [Licensee's] written request send to the [Licensee] a press book and advertising accessories with respect to the [specify] but only to the extent that the [Licensor] shall have the foregoing available and only for use in direct connection with the exploitation of the [Videos/DVDs/Discs] under this Agreement. The [Licensee] shall pay the [Licensor] for all such material in advance together with the freight or postage costs.

A.435

The [Licensee] may design, create and manufacture solely at its own expense advertising material with respect to the [Videos/DVDs/Discs] for use in connection with the rights granted under this Agreement. The [Licensee] agrees to adhere to all contractual obligations, moral rights and legal obligations of the [Licensor] of which the [Licensee] has received notice. The [Licensee] shall make all such material manufactured by the [Licensee] available to the [Licensor] upon request at no charge to the [Licensor] except for the cost of postage, packaging and insurance.

A.436

The [Licensee] shall have sole, full and complete discretion concerning the production, manufacture, distribution, supply, advertising, marketing and other exploitation of all [Videos/DVDs/Discs] of the [Film] and/or any associated packaging. The [Company] agrees that it shall rely on the judgment of the [Licensee] and its sub-distributors in regard to any matter affecting the production manufacture, distribution or marketing including the quantity to be released. The [Licensee] shall have the right for the purpose of increasing the sales, rental or exposure of the [Videos/DVDs/Discs] to permit the same [short extract of less than two minutes in sound, vision, images and text] of the [Film] to be used on other DVDs, mobiles, the internet, television, radio or any other media but not to authorise any other part of the [Film] for such release and use.

A.437

The [Licensor] shall provide the [Licensee] with a full and detailed list of all contractual, moral and legal requirements that must be adhered to in any advertising, marketing and packaging material. This list shall include credits for the actors and all other relevant personnel, copyright notices, moral rights, legal disclaimer, trade marks and logos. The [Licensee] agrees to adhere to all such terms and shall only use the description of the content of the [Film], storyline, biographical details, images, text, logos, copyright notices and packaging provided by or approved by the [Licensor].

A.438

The [Company] agrees to be bound by any prohibitions, conditions or other requirements of any advertising or sponsorship codes, standards, policies, practices or rules, European directives, legislation, insurance, liability or other considerations which affect or concern the [Distributor] and in particular those relating to [specify].

A.439

The [Licensee] shall be entitled to promote the [Film] in the form of [DVDs/Discs] by banner advertisements and promotions on the internet, in newspapers and magazines, by text to mobile phones, recorded advertisements on the radio and television, by competitions and through arrangements with reputable food companies and/or supermarkets. Provided that no costs incurred are attributed to the [Licensor] and none take place before [date] or after [date].

A.440

The [Licensee] shall not be entitled to use and/or promote, market, exploit and/or authorise and/or permit the [Film] and/or any parts and/or the [Dvd/Disc] to be used and/or connected with and/or association with any product, game, business, person or otherwise which supplies, sells, markets and/or promotes [specify] at any time. Any failure to adhere to this requirement shall be a breach of this agreement by the [Licensee].

Film and Television

A.441

For the purposes of enabling the [Licensee] to exercise effectively the rights granted under this Agreement and to promote the [Licensee's] business the [Licensee] shall be entitled to:

1.1 Disseminate, reproduce, print and publish the name, likeness and biography of the performers, directors, producers, editors, writers, composers, musicians [and any other persons] who supplied or provided services in, or in connection with the development and production of the [Film] for the sole purpose of advertising, marketing and exploiting the [Film]. Such arrangement is subject to the crucial term that the [Licensee] strictly adheres to all conditions, restrictions and requirements notified in writing by the [Licensor] to the [Licensee] at any time relating to any persons contract and/or agreement with the [Licensor].

103

1.2 Advertise, market and promote the [Film]. The [Licensee] and any sub-licensee, sub-agent or other authorised person shall have the sole discretion as to the manner and method to be employed in the publicity, advertising, marketing and promotion of the [Film] and the amount to be expended thereon and the choice of advertising agencies, consultants, directors and material.

1.3 Produce and distribute promotional short trailers for the [Film] which shall be approximately [–] in length and shall not use in total extracts of the [Film] of not more than [–] in duration. The [Licensee] shall be entitled to use or arrange for the exhibition, transmission, display or otherwise of the trailer in order to promote or advertise the [Film] for use on television in any format, theatres, other programmes, DVDs, CD-Roms, exhibitions, conferences, websites, telephones in any format or otherwise. Provided that at all times the intended purpose is to promote and advertise the [Film] whether for criticism, review or promotional purposes.

1.4 The [Licensee] may at its discretion choose to use any trailers supplied by the [Licensor] but shall be under no obligation to do so.

1.5 The [Licensor] shall not be entitled to any prior approval of the content of any such promotional material, but nothing shall be done by the [Licensee] which is offensive or derogatory to the [Film] or any persons that appeared or contributed to the making of the [Film] or the [Author] or [specify].

A.442

The [Licensee] shall provide the [Licensor] at the [Licensee's] sole cost with one copy of all advertising, promotional or marketing material by [specify].

A.443

In the event that there is an error or omission in any advertising or promotional material, whether or not it has already been used or distributed by the [Licensee], then the [Licensee] shall agree to amend or change any material mistakes at its sole cost.

A.444

This Agreement shall not permit or allow the [Licensee] to license, arrange or otherwise deal in any form of sponsorship, product placement or cross promotion in respect of the [Film] and/or parts or any form of licensing or commercial exploitation of the [Film] in relation to any other products, services or companies.

A.445

The parties agree that all the press releases, statements, interviews, marketing, advertising, publicity and promotion of the [Film] and/or parts and/or the contents and/or any other related issue shall be the sole responsibility of the [Company]. Any matter relating thereto shall be passed to [specify title/name] to deal with howsoever it may arise and whatever the issues. Failure to adhere to this clause shall be considered by both parties as a significant breach of this agreement. All advisors, financiers and other persons involved in the [Film] shall agree to this term as part of their terms of engagement and confirm their acceptance in writing.

A.446

The [Licensee] may use prior to the broadcast and/or transmission of each [Film] the names and likenesses of the performers and the title of such [Film] in advertising the transmission of such [Film] provided that such use shall be made in such a manner as not to constitute either an implied or direct endorsement of any product or services of any kind.

A.447

The [Licensor] shall make available to the [Licensee] without any extra charge any trailers, promotion and publicity material and stills that may be available which shall be retained by the [Licensee] for the duration of the Agreement. In the event that trailers for any of the [Films] shall not be available then the [Licensee] may transmit and/or broadcast short sequences of not more than [three minutes] in duration from each of the [Films] for which a trailer is not so available for the purpose of programme announcements and trailing and such use. The [Licensee] shall make good and bear the cost of any damage caused to any of the [Films] by reason of the extraction of short sequences for such purposes.

A.448

The [Television Company] shall be entitled to broadcast and/or transmit short extracts of the [Programme] and to authorise others to do so whether on its own channel [–] or on the internet, video or telephone [specify other methods]. The extracts shall not be for more than [five minutes] in total of the material of the [Programme] which shall not be accumulative. Any such use to promote, advertise and trail the [Programme] shall not be placed where the surrounding material is offensive, incompatible, derogatory or offensive with the [Programme]. A full and detailed report shall be supplied to the [Licensor] detailing the date, frequency, type and length of any such use to be delivered on written request by the [Licensor].

A.449

The [Licensee] agrees that no third party shall be entitled to sponsor, or include their advertisements or have its logo, trade mark, service mark, design, product or image associated with or incorporated in the introductory trailer or end credits or any other part of the [Film] or any video, DVD, CD-Rom or CD or otherwise without the prior written consent of the [Licensor] except [specify].

A.450

The [Licensee] agrees not to arrange or agree to any sponsorship, advertisements, product placement or endorsement of products, services, music, slogans, sounds or noises, logos, trade marks or images or text before or after or in any part of the [Film] without prior notification to and consent of the [Licensor].

A.451

The [Licensee] agrees and undertakes that it shall not use the [Film] and/ or any parts for the purpose of advertisement, sponsorship, endorsement, promotion, and/or marketing of any other product, service, person, company, business, charity and/or other third party except with the prior written approval of the [Licensor] in each case. The [Licensor] shall not be obliged to provide consent to any such use and the [Licensor] shall be entitled to conclude a separate agreement and payment terms with the [Licensee] in each case.

A.452

There shall be no limit as to the nature and extent of the marketing, promotion and advertising of the [Film] by the [Distributor] provided that it is intended to increase ratings; does not involve granting a licence to a third party and is not a misrepresentation of the [Film] and/or its content. Provided that where the [Licensor] requests the [Distributor] to withdraw and/or not use a particular method that the [Distributor] shall comply with all such requests within [number/hours/days].

A.453

The [Company] may market and promote the [Film] for Channel [specify] only by the use of the authorised and approved promotional advert supplied by the [Licensor]. The [Company] may not use any part of the [Film] in any other programme of any nature. The [Company] shall not be entitled to authorise any third party to use any title, character, still, name, logo, words, images, slogan or theme.

A.454

The [Company] shall be entitled to market and promote the [Programme] using its name, logo, music, slogan and content in any form of collaborations and/or partnerships that it may seek to use such as mobile telephone, text, scratch card and supermarket competitions, advertisement, articles and features, posters, merchandising, whether on radio, television, the internet and in print in any part of the world. Provided that no third party is granted any sub-licence to exploit the rights and the sole and primary purpose is to raise the ratings and viewing figures of the [Programme] by the [Company]. In addition where any sums are generated which result in payments to the [Company] by any such third parties, that all such sums shall be equally shared between the Company] and the [Licensor]. All payments to be made to the [Licensor] at the end of each calendar month.

General Business and Commercial

A.455
The [Assignor] acknowledges that the [Assignee] shall have the sole discretion as to the manner and method to be used in marketing, promoting and advertising the [Product/Service/Work] and any adaptation and/or development. That the [Assignor] shall not have rights of approval and/or editorial control at any time.

A.456

1.1 The [Distributor] shall endeavour to keep the [Company] regularly updated in respect of the marketing, advertising and exploitation of the [Units] in each of the markets in which the [Units] is made available.

1.2 The [Distributor] shall offer the [Company] the opportunity at the [Distributors] cost to attend publicity, promotional and trade events and fairs in [country].

1.3 The [Distributor] shall provide details of and where available copies and samples of all brochures, flyers, advertisements and other marketing material which are made available to the trade and/or general public in respect of the [Units].

A.457
The [Assignor] agrees that from the date of this Agreement it shall not have any rights or interest in the advertising, promotion, marketing, or exploitation of the [Work] of any nature provided that the Assignment Fee is paid in full and the name, logo and trade mark of the [Assignor] does not appear on any copies of the [Work] in any format in any media.

A.458
Your appearance in the [Exhibition/Show/other] shall not permit you to wear, discuss or promote any clothing, item or goods or services nor hold or display them which have been provided to you by a company or person for the purpose of advertising or promotion whether you have received payment

or not, received the items for free without written obligation or received a discount on their purchase.

A.459

No reference is to be made to the terms and conditions of this Agreement in any advertising, publicity, marketing or promotional material of any nature without the express agreement of all the parties hereto.

A.460

Subject to prior consultation the [Name] agrees that the [Company] shall be entitled to use his/her name, recent biography, a specially commissioned photograph and image and signature in the advertising, marketing and exploitation of the [specify] provided they shall not be used for any product endorsement or to promote or market any other [product/film/services]. The [Name] shall be provided at the [Company's] cost with a sample of each item of any nature which has any reference to the [Name] created pursuant to this agreement prior to any use or exploitation of such item. The [Name] shall therefore be provided with an opportunity to comment and make recommendations before it is marketed or distributed. The [Company] agrees to incorporate all reasonable changes requested within [–] days of receipt by the [Name].

A.461

It is a condition that no logos and/or images other than [specify Name/ Brand] in respect of [type of Product] may be displayed at this [Event] whilst filming of the [Programme] is in progress by the [Company].

A.462

It is agreed that no changes shall be made to the layout, design, colour, size, shape or otherwise of the range of marketing formats of the [Logo/Name/ Image] provided by the [Licensor] to the [Licensee]. That all proposed samples shall be first submitted to the [Licensor] prior to production and/ or distribution to any third party. That all requests and changes by the [Licensor] shall be adhered to and complied with by the [Licensee]. That the [Licensee] shall ensure strict quality control standards in respect of reproduction of the [Logo/Name/Image].

A.463

[Name] and the [Company] agree that the [Company] may use the [Photographs/Film] which were commissioned by the [Company] and taken at [location] of [Name] on [date] for the sole purpose of [specify].Where the [Company] seeks to use the material for any other reason and/or to grant a licence to a third party. Then the prior consent of [Name] shall be required and an additional fee to [Name] must be negotiated and agreed.

A.464

[Name] agrees that there are no limitations on how the material commissioned and created by the [Company] of [Name] (whether during filming or not which relates directly and/or indirectly to the making, production, editing, transmission and/or distribution of the [Film]) shall be used and/or adapted at any time for any purpose including marketing and sub-licensing. Provided that no such use shall at any time expose [Name] to ridicule, embarrassment and/or impugn their reputation unless their prior consent has been sought.

Internet and Websites

A.465

1.1　The [Advertiser/Promoter/Sponsor/Name] agrees that all advertisers, promoters, sponsors and other users of the [Website] including the public shall be informed in advance and be subject to conditions of access and use of the [Website] by the [Company].

1.2　The [Advertiser/Promoter/Sponsor/Name] agrees and undertakes that one of the conditions shall be that no product, services and/or any emails, films, sound recordings, graphics and/or any other material shall be permitted on the [Website] which is offensive, defamatory, obscene, derogatory and rude, dangerous, fraudulent, dishonest, misleading, harmful, evidence of allegation of a criminal act and/or an alleged breach of a civil action, is likely to be or constitutes a threat to children and/or health and safety of any person and/or is otherwise deemed unacceptable at the sole discretion of the [Company].

1.3　In any such circumstances without any notice whatsoever the [Company] shall be entitled to ensure that all such material is removed, deleted and/or otherwise erased from the [Website] and any associated marketing and advertising. The person, company or entity shall not be entitled to any further access to and/or use of the [Website] and shall not be entitled to be refunded under sums paid under this Agreement to the [Company]. The [Company] shall not be liable for any direct and/or indirect losses suffered and/or incurred of any nature to any such person, company or entity whose material has been deleted. Erased and/or removed from the [Website].

A.466

The [Advertiser] shall not be entitled to place material [in the Banner/on the Website] which in the view of the [Company]:

1.1　Contains subliminal advertising in text, words, images, music or any other medium; and/or

1.2 Refers to [service/goods] offered which are not available and/or are not supplied and/or are not of the same standard; and/or

1.3 Contains political, religious or controversial content which is not acceptable; and/or

1.4 Offers services such as gambling, bingo and/or other products and does not make it clear that there is an age requirement; and/or

1.5 Poses a risk to health and safety; and/or

1.6 Causes offence following the response from the users of the [Banner/ Website].

The [Advertiser] agrees that if it is no longer permitted to advertise on the [Banner/Website] the [Company] will refund any outstanding sums paid in advance by the [Advertiser], but that no sums shall be due or paid as compensation for removal, loss of reputation, sales or revenue.

A.467

The [Company] agrees that it shall advertise the [Products] of the [Distributor] on the [Website] of [Name] web reference [–] as follows:

1.1 Main display advertiser other than [Name's] own goods or services. Such [Products] to feature on all the main webpages specifically [identify] all other webpages to include the [Logo] set out in Schedule [–].

1.2 No other advertiser or associated company shall be entitled to be displayed or featured on any such webpage where there is a direct conflict of interest resulting from being the same type of business, goods or services.

1.3 In any associated publicity, advertising, promotional literature, emails, text messages or marketing material of the [Company]. Then where appropriate the [Distributor] shall be given due credit and recognition as the main advertiser on the [Website].

1.4 In any flotation of the [Company] on any stock market the [Distributor] shall similarly feature in the documentation and publicity as the main advertiser.

1.5 The [Company] shall have the final editorial decision in respect of the position and size of the [Products] and [Logo] of the [Distributor] on the [Website] and any updates and changes that may be necessary. Provide that the [Company] shall take account as far as possible of the notified details of the [Products] and the [Logo] so that they are a true image.

A.468

The [Company] agrees to display the [Animated Film] of the [Product] on the [Website] which is supplied by the [Distributor] at the [Distributor's] cost and expense provided that:

1.1 The master material and/or copy which is supplied of the [Animated Film] is of suitable quality and fit for its intended purpose. Where any new format and/or changes and/or deletions are required they shall be entirely at the [Distributors] cost.

1.2 The [Animated Film] and the [Product] does not contain anything which is offensive, defamatory, dangerous and/or poses a health and safety risk and/or is likely to be in breach of any criminal and/or civil law in any part of the world and/or in breach of any relevant Code of Practice and/or Regulation and/or Directive of the European Union.

1.3 The [Distributor] has cleared and/or obtained all rights in the [Animated Film] including any music and is able to provide supporting documentation if required.

1.4 The [Distributor] undertakes and agrees that there has been no threat of any legal proceedings and/or any legal action taken within the last [two years] against the [Distributor] in respect of the [Animated Film] which has not been settled.

1.5 The [Distributor] agrees and undertakes to indemnify the [Company] up to [figure/currency] in total for any losses, damages, expenses and/or costs which are incurred by the [Company] directly arising from the display of the [Animated Film] on the [Website] and a claim and/or allegation by any third party of any nature.

1.6 The [Distributor] agrees that it holds product liability insurance for the [Product] as follows [specify].

A.469

The [Distributor] agrees that it shall monitor the website [specify] on which it is intended that the [Material] shall be available on a pay per view basis and/or as a downloadable app and/or otherwise. In the event that other films, text, images, music, apps and/or otherwise are being displayed which are not suitable for [specify]. Then the [Distributor] agrees that the [Author] shall have the right to insist that the [Material] is no longer made available from that [website]. The parties shall agree which other websites may be used to promote, market and exploit the [Material].

A.470

The [Distributor] agrees that it shall only market and promote [Product/Name] in a manner which is compatible with the market at which it is aimed [specify]

111

for persons age [specify] and under. No promotions, advertisements, banner links or other marketing shall be placed and/or directed at the following markets [specify]. The [Distributor] agrees that it shall try to ensure that no unsuitable images and text are placed near and/or with the [Product/Name] and shall only use any companies and businesses for which the approval of the [Licensor] has been provided and the manner and format to be used agreed in each case.

Merchandising

A.471

The [Agent] agrees that he/she is not permitted to advertise, promote, market or exploit the [Character] outside the [Territory/country] unless specifically agreed in advance with the [Licensor] on each occasion.

A.472

The [Licensee] shall be entitled to use the [Licensor's] name, biography, photograph and image, but not signature in the promotion, advertising, packaging and marketing of the [Character]. The [Licensee] shall bear all the costs of the development, production, reproduction and supply of any such material. The [Licensee] agrees to consult with the [Licensor] as to the choice of photograph, text, and any associated graphics and/or slogan. The [Licensee] shall provide a draft final copy to the [Licensor] in the colour and layout in which it is proposed to use the material in each case prior to the production and distribution of the promotion, advertising, packaging and marketing of the [Character].

A.473

The [Licensee] agrees that the [Licensor] shall have the right to approve all publicity, promotional, advertising in all media and the packaging material in respect of the [Licensed Article]. The [Licensee] acknowledges that such approval must be obtained in writing prior to manufacture, production and distribution of any such material so that any changes or alterations requested by the [Licensor] can be incorporated.

A.474

The [Licensee] is not entitled to grant, agree to and/or authorise either by consent and/or by omission the right of any third party and/or any director, officer, employee, consultant and/or freight company and/or insurer and/or other associates to create and/or develop other items and/or any material of any nature which bears the [logo/Image], title, any associated characters or otherwise of the [Book] and/or the [Product] at any time.

A.475

The [Licensee] shall sell and market the [Product] from the website known as [specify] and not through any other website without the prior written approval of the [Licensor].

A.476

The [Licensee] shall not have the right to create and/or develop an app and/or any other software, article, text, image, trade mark, logo, game, betting, lottery, quiz, scratch card, competition, radio and/or television programmes and advertisements and sponsorship, cartoon, banner advertisements, posters, artwork, greetings cards, food and/or drink and/or any other household and/or business products using any part of the [Image/Logo/Material] for which a licence is granted under this Agreement. All promotion, marketing and authorised exploitation is limited to the [Licensee's] website, packaging of the [Product] , direct marketing by the [Licensee] and all material of any nature that is to be distributed must be submitted to the [Licensor] in advance for approval.

Publishing

A.477

The [Company] shall not insert within the [Work] or on its cover or dust jackets [or any brochure, flyer or poster] any advertisement, promotion, sponsorship or endorsement other than for the [Author's] own work without the prior consent of the [Author].

A.478

The [Author] agrees that the [Agent/Company] shall be entitled to use and authorise the use of his/her name, photograph, image, biographical details, signature and any other material supplied by the [Author] or organised by the [Agent/Company] in respect of the advertising, promotion and commercial exploitation of the [Work] subject to:

1.1   The prior written approval of the [Author] of an exact copy of the draft and final proof or sample in each case.

1.2   No use of any material shall be made which would be offensive, and/or derogate from the reputation of the [Author] and/or would offend the [Author's] religion and/or beliefs and/or cause distress to the [Author's] family and/or effect the [Author's] career in a negative way.

1.3   Where an independently appointed [adjudicator/expert] agrees that sub-clause 1.2 has been breached. Then the [Agent/Company] shall pay the [Author] [figure/currency] as a fixed agreed form of compensation and damages in full and final settlement of any claim under sub-clause 1.2.

A.479

In the event that the [Satellite Company] or any subsidiary or associated company launches its own magazine for subscribers then the [Satellite Company] agrees to provide the [Company] with promotional space in such magazine for the purposes of advertising the [specify] at the [Satellite Company's] cost to the value of [figure/currency] at the commercial rates.

A.480

The [Company] agrees that it shall provide a budget of [–] for the advertising, promotion and publicity of the [first edition of the Work in hardback and paperback] in [country].

A.481

The [Company] agrees that all advertising, publicity, packaging and promotional material shall be provided to the [Presenter] in the exact form in which it is intended that it should be used by the [Company] and that the prior written approval of the [Presenter] shall be required prior to the use of any such advertising, publicity, packaging and promotional material. In the event that the approval of the [Presenter] is refused then such material shall not be used by the [Company].

A.482

The [Company] undertakes that it shall use its best endeavours to advertise, publicise and promote the [Work] and that on all occasions that the agreed credit and copyright notice to the [Author] shall be used.

A.483

Where the [Author] is required to attend any event in respect of the advertising, promotion or publicity of the [Work] in any form, then the [Company] agrees that it shall arrange for and bear the full cost and expense of all [first-class] accommodation, travel and meals and reimburse any other reasonable expenses incurred by the [Author] arising directly as a result of any such event. On each occasion an advance against the expected costs shall be made to the [Author].

A.484

The [Author] shall be available as reasonably required by the [Publisher] for the promotion and advertising of the [Work] for the following periods provided that the [Publisher] pays all the costs and expenses [number] appearances and interviews up to [number] months after the date of publication in [country] of [hardback/paperback/other].

A.485

The [Licensor] agrees to arrange one photographic session [duration/ date] with the [Licensee] at the [Licensee's] sole cost for the purpose of photographs to be used in the [periodical] in association with the [Extracts] and one interview [duration/date]. Provided that the [Licensee] agrees to assign the copyright and all other rights in the photographs and the interview and any material in any medium which is created or produced arising from such sessions to the [Licensor].

A.486

The [Company] shall have the right to use extracts of the [Author's Work] in other books and publications up to a limit of [specify] words without payment to the [Author]. Provide that the extracts are used for the purposes of advertising, promotion and publicity and no payment is received by the [Company]. This shall not apply to use of any such extract on the internet which shall require the prior written consent of the [Author].

A.487

The [Company] shall as far as possible send the [Author] regular copies of all publicity, advertising and promotional material for the [Book]. Where the [Author] reports an inaccuracy or error then the [Company] agrees that it shall try to make sure that the error or omission is not repeated. Further the [Company] agrees to consider all relevant marketing and advertising recommendations by the [Author].

A.488

The [Company] shall advise the [Author] of the advertising and marketing budget for the [Project] and shall fully disclose all intended expenditure. The [Author] shall be given the opportunity to comment and recommend other factors to be considered. The [Company] shall however make the final decision on the matter.

A.489

The [Distributor] shall provide a short marketing report to the [Author] before [date] listing the release dates, and the different methods of marketing which are proposed. The [Distributor] agrees to consult with the [Author] in each case and to provide a draft copy of each format and/or item upon which the [Author] can comment and make a contribution in respect of all forms of packaging, advertising, marketing and/or promotion including but not limited to catalogues, brochures, flyers, inserts, websites, films, emails, and texts.

A.490

The [Author] shall not be obliged to promote, market and/or advertise the [Product/Film/DVD] and/or to attend any launch, parties, readings, television and/or radio programmes and/or make any sound recordings and/or go to any other event and/or create any additional material. All such matters shall be entirely at the personal discretion of the [Author] and there shall be no contractual requirement to make any contribution of any nature to that effect. Where the [Author] is requested to attend any event and/or create any new material then the terms and conditions of the attendance and/or contribution of the [Author] shall be subject to separate contract.

A.491

The [Publisher] shall be entitled to promote, market and advertise the [Work] by means of listings of a brief summary of the content on its own and third party websites, printed catalogues, posters, flyers, email attachments and in any other format provided that the primary purpose is to increase prepublication and post publication sales of the [Work].

A.492

In the event that the [Publisher] wishes to display more than a brief summary of the [Work] on its own and/or any other website then it agrees not to exceed more than [number] of the same identical pages on all websites which can be viewed on line by the public prior to purchase of the [Work] as an [eBook/App/other]. That any additional requirement must be approved on each occasion with the [Author] and that the [Author] shall have the right to refuse consent.

A.493

The [Author] agrees that the [Publisher] and any distributor, sub-licensee and marketing company shall be authorised to reproduce, supply and distribute all images and film of the [Author] which the [Author] may supply to the [Publisher] during the term of this Agreement. That when this Agreement shall be terminated and/or expires that no further right shall exist. The [Author] may notify the [Publisher] and any distributor, sub-licensee and marketing company to confirm that they no longer hold any master copies on any computer system and/or hard drive and/or in any storage device.

A.494

The [Distributor] agrees and undertakes that it shall not acquire any copyright and/or any other intellectual property rights in any format of any nature in any material, text, artwork, photographs, logos, trade marks, music, maps, charts, articles and/or otherwise which the [Publisher] may supply for any purpose during the course of this Agreement. That where in the course of creating marketing, advertising and promotional material the [Distributor] develops any new material of any nature which results in a copyright or other intellectual property of any nature belonging to the [Distributor]. That the [Distributor] shall transfer any such rights back to the [Publisher] for a nominal fee of [£1] for each such transfer and sign any assignment that may be requested.

Purchase and Supply of Products

A.495

The [Agent] confirms that the [Advertising Copy] complies with all rules, guidelines, regulations, directives and codes in force which apply to the [Company] at any time including [list] prior to or at the time of use of the Advertisement for [specify].

A.496

The [Company] confirms that it shall ensure that the [Advertisement] will conform to all statutes, rules, directives, guidelines, practices and codes of advertising and sponsorship in relation to the exercise and exploitation by the [Distributor] of the [specify rights] in the [Product].

A.497

'The Company's Products' shall mean the [Products/Services] of the [Company] which are briefly described as follows [–]. A two-dimensional copy of the Company's Products is attached to and forms a part of this Agreement in Schedule [–] setting out all intellectual property rights including copyright, trade marks, service marks, logos, designs, slogans, text, title, recordings, scripts, music, photographs, artwork, products, artistes, graphics, computer generated material, all consents, releases, moral rights, contractual obligations obtained, paid for or due.

A.498

The [Promoter] confirms that the principle aims of this Agreement are to:

1.1 Promote and increase the sales of the [Company's Products].

1.2 Raise public awareness of the [Company's] existence throughout the Territory.

1.3 Inform the general public of the [Company's] positive track record within its industry.

1.4 Improve the consumer image of the [Company] throughout the Territory.

1.5 Create a favourable image of the [Company] to the public in general and in particular for the purpose of recruiting potential future employees.

1.6 Increase and improve the [Company's] goodwill and understanding amongst its present customers and increase significantly the number of purchasers of its products in general.

A.499

The [Licensee] agrees that the [Licensor] shall be entitled to approve the appointment of any sub-agent, sub-licensee or other third party in respect of the manufacture, distribution, supply, marketing and advertising or other exploitation of the [Units] under this Agreement.

A.500

The [Licensor] agrees to attend such meetings, exhibitions and promotional events including [specify] as may reasonably be required by the [Licensee] subject to the agreement to pay in advance all cost and expenses and to provide sufficient notice.

A.501

The [Purchaser] agrees that this agreement relates solely to the purchase and sale of the [Garment] for personal use and that the [Designs] and the [Garment] are not to be commercially exploited by the [Purchaser] in any form or used to endorse, advertise or promote any goods, products or services or otherwise without the prior written consent of the [Designer] and subject to the payment of an agreed consideration.

A.502

The [Company] agrees that the [Assignee] shall be entitled to commercially exploit the [Commissioned Work] in all media at any time in the world and shall be able to organise associated sponsorship, product placement or advertising and the [Company] shall not receive any further payment in respect of any such use.

A.503

The [Company] agrees that it shall arrange a major launch of the [Product] with a budget of not less than [specify]. That it shall arrange television and national press coverage, organise a publicity brochure, and a national advertising campaign of not less than [duration] in a leading magazine or newspaper. That in addition there will be promotion on [the internet/ text messages/advertising on CD-Roms free give-aways/billboards/other]. A review report of the promotion and advertising of the [Product] shall be provided by the [Company] within by [date]. All costs and expenses shall be entirely at [specify] sole cost.

A.504

The [Supplier] agrees that the [Seller] may engage any persons to endorse and/or advertise and/or promote the [Product] on the [Seller's] website. The [Supplier] agrees that the appointment is entirely at the discretion and cost of the [Seller] provided that the persons behave in a professional manner in their public life and do not bring the [Supplier] and/or its [Products] in to disrepute or tarnish or detrimentally affect their reputation and goodwill.

A.505

The [Artist] agrees that the [Distributor] shall be entitled to use the [Work/ Image] in any manner it thinks fit and in any format and/or medium for the purpose of increasing sales and revenue and marketing including but not limited to postcards, greetings cards, T shirts, wristbands, posters, reproduction on articles and/or collaborations and partnerships with other products and brands, in books, on film, on websites, in the form of licensed software, for exhibitions, festivals and events and performances in any location.

A.506

The [Distributor] agrees that the [Product/Article] is a limited edition and that it is not authorised to make, supply and/or authorise any copies of any nature for any purpose at any time in any form. That the only material which can be used by the [Distributor] are the agreed details [Name/Logo/Title/ Description] set out in Schedule [–] which may only be used on its website and in one marketing catalogue for the event.

A.507

There are no limitations placed by the [Licensor] as to how the [Licensee] may market and raise awareness of the [Work/Product] provided that:

1.1   It does not damage the reputation of the [Licensor] in any way.

1.2   It does not seek to associate the [Work/Product] with any other material which is offensive, of poor quality, does not comply with any legal requirements, the business and/or any person has recently been the subject of unfavourable media coverage.

1.3   At all times the [Licensee] shall withdraw and/or cancel any proposed plan where the [Licensor] raises objections and requests that it not proceed.

Services

A.508

The [Company] agrees to appoint the [Promoter] as the sole and exclusive advertising, marketing and promotions agent for the purpose of [specify] throughout the Territory for the Term of the Agreement in accordance with the terms of this Agreement.

A.509

In consideration of the [Fees and Expenses] the [Promoter] agrees to provide its non-exclusive services to the [Company] to act as agent to [specify] the [Company] and the [Company's Products] throughout the [specify countries] for the duration of start date [date] and until the end date [date] in accordance with the conditions set out in this contract.

A.510

The [Company] agrees that the use of the name, photograph, image or other material relating to [Name] supplied or created under this Agreement shall require her specific consent and approval of each and every example to be used in each case for any advertising, promotional or marketing purposes or any other commercial exploitation.

A.511

The [Promoter] undertakes to endeavour to ensure that as far as reasonably possible that all third parties engaged to produce material by the [Promoter] shall agree to assign the product of their services in all media throughout the world for the full period of copyright and any extensions or renewals to the [Company] so that the third parties retain no intellectual property, domain names or other rights whatsoever.

A.512

The [Agent] agrees to consult with the [Actor] in respect of any artwork, stills, photographs, film, biography, press releases and statements and any other material in any medium which may be used to advertise, market and promote the [Actor].

A.513

The [Agent] acknowledges that he shall be solely responsible for all costs incurred by him in respect of his services under this agreement including the advertising, promotion and marketing of [name] and shall not be able to recoup such sums from those due to [name].

A.514

[Name] gives all necessary consents to the [Company]:

1.1　To take or make directly or indirectly, by any means any photographs or other images, films, sound or other recordings whether for terrestrial, cable, satellite or digital television, radio, DVDs, the internet websites and for downloads of material, CD-Roms, games, publishers, newspapers, magazines or periodicals.

1.2　To use or authorise the use of the full name of [Name] and their stage name, image, caricatures, photographs, films, sound or other recordings, signature, biography and other [specify] in connection with the advertisement, publicity, exhibition and commercial exploitation of the [Programme].

1.3   To use all such material specified in 1.1 and 1.2 above in, or in connection with any endorsement, advertisements, publicity or promotion for any other goods or services marketed by the [Company].

A.515

The [Company] agrees that [Name] shall be the sole and exclusive personality to endorse, present, promote and advertise the [Product] throughout the Territory from [date] to [date].

A.516

The [Celebrity] undertakes that she shall not provide her services to any third party for the endorsement, advertisement or promotion of any other product or service of any type whether it directly competes with the [Company's] Product or not other than services of a charitable nature throughout the Term of this Agreement without the prior written consent of the [Company]. The following services which the [Celebrity] provides to [name] as part of their existing career shall be excluded from this clause [specify].

A.517

In consideration of the [Celebrity's] Fee and the Repeat Fees the [Celebrity] agrees to provide his exclusive services to the [Company] to endorse, promote, and advertise the [Company's] Product by personal appearances, performances, and recordings, film, software, images, photographs or otherwise of material of the [Celebrity] for advertisements for use in all media in accordance with the [Work Schedule] and on such other occasions as may be agreed between the parties.

A.518

The [Company] acknowledges that the [Celebrity] is already committed and entered into prior agreements for the following [goods/services/work] [specify].

A.519

The [Company] agrees that it shall not be entitled to use, exploit or license any of the material produced or created for the purpose of this Agreement in which the [Celebrity] appears in sound or vision or by any other reference for any purpose other than the endorsement, promotion, or advertising of the [Company's] Product during the existence of this Agreement. Where the [Company] wishes to use any such material at any time for any purpose not permitted or to license a third party then the prior written consent of the [Celebrity] is required and the settlement of a new agreement for each such permission.

A.520

The [Company] agrees that the [Agent] shall be entitled upon request to be provided at the [Company's] cost with a copy of any material in any medium produced under this Agreement which it is intended or has been released to the public which is in the possession or under the control of the [Company] or any sub-agents or sub-licensees, or any third parties engaged by the [Company] featuring or including any reference to the [Artiste].

A.521

In accordance with the [Work Schedule] the [Celebrity] agrees to provide the following specific services:

1.1 Presentation and performance in [number] advertisements described as follows [specify].

1.2 Presentation and performance in corporate video of no more than [–] minutes in duration and no more than [number] production days in [country].

1.3 Attendance at not less than [–] official functions and promotional events organised by the [Company] in [country].

1.4 Other/photographic sessions/sound recordings.

A.522

The [Company] shall not have the right to use the benefit of the [Presenter's] association and participation in the [Programme] to endorse or promote or advertise any other products, services or programmes sold or exploited by the [Company] without the prior written consent of the [Presenter] and the payment of an additional sum to be agreed in each case.

A.523

The [Company] shall engage the services of [Name] who agrees to be available on the following terms and conditions in consideration of the payment terms set out in clause [–]:

1.1 [Name] shall appear in [number] advertisements to be transmitted on regional and national television in [country] no later than [date].

1.2 The number of recording days shall be [specify] and include appearances in the studio for filming and recording in sound and vision. Additional days shall be paid at [specify].

1.3 [Name] shall not be required to perform any words or act in any manner which could be deemed prejudicial to their career or image.

1.4 The [Company] shall only be entitled to use and repeat the advertisements within the [first three years] from [date]. Thereafter additional payment and a new agreement are required for any use.

1.5 The use of the advertisements in any medium outside the Territory shall be subject to the payments set out in Schedule [–].

A.524

The [Company] shall not license, reproduce, permit, transfer, sell, supply, distribute or exploit any material which is created in the production of the [Advertisement] except the final approved Advertisement. All other material not used shall be destroyed.

A.525

[Name] agrees that his/her name, image and company email shall be exhibited on the [Company] website during the term of this Agreement. That the [Company] shall have the right to reproduce that image in any marketing and promotional material, on any security card and in internal personnel records for that period. The [Company] shall not have the right to supply any images and/or data of [Name] to any third party at any time without the prior written consent of [Name][except for compliance with legislation and/or a court order].

A.526

Where [Name] has provided services to the [Company] which has resulted in the creation of new material which mentions and/or features [Name] in any format including photographs, film, DVD, blu-ray, app, book, article, radio and television programme and/or interview. Then the [Company] agrees to supply to [Name] a copy of the material that it uses in the final work at the [Company's] cost but not all the original master material that is taken.

A.527

Where a photographer and/or any third party is commissioned by the [Distributor] to work with [Name] as part of his/her service to the [Distributor] to market and/or promote the business. [Name] agrees that he/she shall not have the right to approve that person. [Name] agrees that he/she may decide to terminate the Agreement with the [Distributor] and in such event that [Name] shall not be entitled to claim any further sums which may be due after the date of termination.

Sponsorship

A.528

The [Manager] agrees to ensure that the following [credit/copyright notice/trade mark/logo] of the [Company] appears on the [item] of the [Sportsperson] in any arrangements with a third party and as far as possible in all publicity, advertising, promotional and packaging material [detailed description, order and position].

A.529

The [Sportsperson] agrees to wear and/or display and/or endorse any item or service including clothing, equipment or other products provided by the [Manager] under this Agreement where a contract has been concluded with a third party to do so at all exhibitions, sports events, promotional and television appearances, press calls during the Term of this Agreement. The [Sportsperson] shall not be obliged to do so where in his own judgement it would not be appropriate for health and safety reasons, weather conditions, rules of the event or otherwise not suitable.

A.530

[Name] agrees to provide her exclusive services in a professional and competent manner in order to achieve the best she is capable of in the [sport/project]. [Name] agrees to provide the following services at the events set out below [List type of appearance and precisely the contribution to be made at each event. Competitions/promotions/appearances/press conferences/exhibitions].

A.531

The [Sponsor] agrees to provide the [Sportsperson] with reasonable notice of all promotional events and other meetings which they are required to attend. It is accepted by the [Sponsor] that no attendance shall be definite if there is less than [one calendar months] notice or there is a sporting or family matter which conflicts.

A.532

The [Sponsor] acknowledges that this Agreement does not oblige the [Sportsperson] to make any personal appearances in corporate events, in any film, DVD, or sound recording, on radio or television for the [Sponsor] in respect of the [Sponsor's] Product. Any additional work shall require a separate fee and agreement to be concluded in each case.

A.533

The [Company] agrees that no sponsorship, logo or product shall be used to endorse the [Unit] without the prior written consent of the [Licensor] which shall not be unreasonably withheld or delayed.

A.534

The [Sponsor] agrees that the [Radio Company] shall be entitled to advertise, promote and endorse any third party products in the [Programme] or in conjunction with it whether or not it directly competes with the [Sponsor's] business or products.

A.535

In consideration of the Sponsorship Fee the [Radio Station] grants to the [Sponsor] the non-exclusive right to sponsor the [Programme] and to promote the [Sponsor's Product] and to have the [Sponsor's] copy incorporated into the [Programme] throughout the Territory for the duration of the Sponsorship Period.

A.536

The [Sponsor] agrees that the [Radio Company] shall have the right to advertise promote and endorse any third-party products in the [Programme] or in conjunction with it whether or not it directly competes with the [Sponsor's] business or products.

A.537

The [Sponsor] acknowledges that the [Organisers] in accordance with and subject to the terms of this Agreement are entitled to license or authorise third parties to advertise at or sponsor or supply gifts, prizes or products or services in conjunction the [Festival].

A.538

The [Sponsor] agrees that the [Radio Station] shall have the sole discretion as to the manner and method to be used concerning:

1.1   The content of the advertising, sponsorship and other material before, after or in the [Programme].

1.2   The title of the [Programme], the presenter and the scheduling.

1.3   The marketing, promotion and advertising of the [Programme].

1.4   Any personnel, content, script, guests, music, endorsements, prizes, phone-ins, merchandising or otherwise.

1.5   Any cross promotion or advertising with respect to any event, exhibition, advertisement in any media, products, publishing, internet, telephones in sound, vision, text or music.

A.539

The [Sponsor] agrees to be bound by any sponsorship, advertising or other rules, directives, legislation, standards, practices and codes which apply to the [Radio Station] in respect of the use and transmission of the [Company's Product] and the [Company's Logo] in the [Programme] and any other material in [country].

A.540

The [Company] agrees that it shall not be entitled to use, exploit or promote the title of the [Programme] or any script, artist, music, slogan or any other parts of any nature in conjunction with the [Company's Product] on the [Programme] or any other products or services of the [Company] under any circumstances. This Agreement is not a sub-licence or any other authority for any use of material in or associated with the [Programme] by the [Company].

A.541

The [Association] accepts that the [Sponsor] shall be entitled to promote, advertise, display, publicise and otherwise commercially exploit to its own advantage the [Sponsor's] involvement in the [Event] in respect of its own products, goodwill, merchandise, advertisements, marketing material or otherwise for the duration of the [License Period].

A.542

The [Company] agrees that the [Organisers] have granted to the [Sponsor] the right to veto the advertising at the [Event] and in any tickets, brochures, advertising, equipment, uniforms, flags, banners and marketing material of any third party whose business or products directly compete or conflict with the following products or business of the [Sponsor] [specify].

A.543

The [Licensee] will ensure that the use of the [Licensor's Logo] will not infringe any sponsorship, advertising, promotional, gambling, religious, political, health and safety or marketing laws, regulations, codes and practices in force at the time of production of [country] which may apply.

A.544

The [Company] agree and undertake that the [Sponsor] shall be the main and primary sponsor of the [Event/Film] and that shall be made clear at the [Event/Film] and in all radio, film and media coverage; on the [Company's] website; in any reports and in all advertising, marketing, packaging and merchandising which is directly and indirectly associated with the [Event/Film].

A.545

The [Sponsor] shall not be entitled to advertise, promote and/or market the [Event/Film] either to promote the [Sponsors'] business and/or in association with any of its products without the written approval of the [Company] in each case. The [Sponsor] shall supply the [Company] with a sample copy of the material for approval in advance. The [Sponsor] shall be obliged to make such changes and/or alterations as the [Company] may require in order to give approval.

A.546

The [Sponsor] of the [Event/Festival] shall be entitled to market and promote its funding and support provided that it does not mislead anyone as to the extent of its sponsorship and that the images, logos, names, products, performers and any other material of any third party in any medium associated with the [Event/Festival] is not used by the [Sponsor] in anyway.

A.547
The [Agency] shall not be entitled to disclose the value of the funding by any of the [Sponsors] in any marketing and/or advertising relating directly and/or indirectly to the [Programme]. Nor shall the [Agency] have the right to reproduce any logo, trade marks, images, slogans, products and/or any other material associated with the [Sponsor] in any press release, blog, website content and/or otherwise in any medium at any time.

A.548
The [Sponsor] agrees that there is no obligation by the [Company] to ensure that the name, image, logo of the [Sponsor] is listed in all marketing and promotional material distributed and/or supplied by the [Company] and/or in any television, radio, newspaper, magazine, media and on line coverage at any time.

University, Library and Educational

A.549
The [Company] agrees that it shall be solely responsible for all costs and expenses incurred in respect of the advertising, promotion and marketing of the [Work/Service/Product] under this Agreement and shall not be able to recoup such sums from those due to the [Institute] nor shall the [Institute] be liable for any such costs and expenses.

A.550
The [Company] agrees and undertakes to ensure that the following [credit/copyright notice/trade mark/logo] of the [Institute] shall appear on all products, publicity, advertising, promotional, packaging and other material which is supplied, reproduced, distributed and/or licensed in respect of the [Project] [detailed description, order and position]. A copy of which is attached in Appendix [–].

A.551
The [Company] shall not have the right to use the name and logo of the [Institute] in the [Project/Work/Product] to endorse or promote or advertise any other products, services or work sold, licensed and/or exploited by the [Company] without the prior written consent of the [Institute] and any such arrangement shall be the subject of a separate contract.

A.552

The [Company] agrees and undertakes to follow and adhere to the rules, directives, legislation, standards, practices and codes which apply to the [Institute] in respect of the advertising, marketing, promotion, packaging and exploitation of the [Work/Service/Product] and the use of the [Institutes'] name, logo, material and premises. The [Company] agrees to provide an exact sample and/or draft of all material for prior written approval by the [Institute] in each case.

A.553

The parties agree that no material shall be distributed, displayed on a website and or supplied to a third party concerning the [Project] unless a draft has been circulated for approval by a nominated person on behalf of each party.

A.554

The [Licensee] agrees that the [Author] shall be consulted in respect of the content of any marketing and promotional material in printed form, by email in electronic form and on any website and/or app, and/or any other material in any format and/or medium. The [Licensee] shall provide the [Author] with a draft copy and take reasonable account of the requests for any changes by the [Author].

AFFILIATES

General Business and Commercial

A.555

'Affiliates' of the [Company] shall mean any legal entity or other business organisation anywhere in the world in which the [Company's] main holding company [specify] holds a [twenty-five per cent] or higher equity interest whether directly or indirectly, and whether the interest is shares, debentures or otherwise, voting or non-voting.

A.556

For the avoidance of doubt, the term 'Affiliate' shall have the same meaning as 'Subsidiary' throughout this Agreement.

A.557

The term 'Affiliate' shall not mean 'Subsidiary' but shall mean any company, organisation or other body to which the Company is legally connected to or associated with whether directly or not in the family tree to form part of the structure of an international or national corporate organisation or by duplication of the named directors although not linked in a corporate legal structure.

A.558

The [Affiliate] agrees that it shall have no claim and/or rights over any part of the business and/or interests and/or rights of any nature of the [Company]. That the arrangement is solely an agreement for payments in return for sending customers to purchase [Products/Services] at the website known as [specify].

A.559

The [Company] shall be entitled to cancel and/or terminate the agreement with [Name] that they may be affiliated to the [Company] as a source of customers. In the event that the [Company] cancels and/or terminates the agreement then no additional sums shall be due and/or paid to [Name] for expenses, losses, compensation and/or otherwise except those due to the date of cancellation and/or termination.

A.560

The [Affiliate] shall bear all its own costs and expenses which it may incur and ensure that it has suitable insurance cover for third party public liability. At no time shall the [Affiliate] be entitled to claim and/or seek to recover any of its costs of administration of its business from the [Company].

AGENCY

DVD, Video and Discs

A.561

In consideration of the Advance and the [Licensor's] Royalties the [Licensor] grants to the [Licensee] the sole and exclusive DVD and Videogram Rights and Non-Theatric Rights in the [Film] and parts and the right to authorise any third party to exercise such rights throughout the Territory for the duration of the Licence Period.

A.562

The [Licensee] agrees and undertakes that all other rights not specifically specified in clause [–] are retained by the [Licensor] and are specifically excluded from this Agreement.

A.563

[Name] appoints [Company] to act as his/her exclusive agent to market, distribute and exploit the [Film/Work] in the following formats of [DVD/VHS Videos/CDs/CD-Roms/Discs/Audiotapes] in the countries listed in Appendix A from [date] to [date]. No other formats and/or rights are granted to the [Company] and all rights shall revert to [Name] on [date].

A.564

1.1   The [Copyright Owner] appoints the [Consultant] to represent his interests and to advise on the best business strategy to market, distribute and exploit the [Film/Work] in respect of the following formats [specify] in the countries listed in Appendix A from [date] to [date].

1.2   The [Copyright owner] shall have the sole and absolute discretion as to whether any agreement is concluded with any third parties at any time.

1.3   The [Consultant] agrees that he/she has have no right and/or authority to conclude and/or sign any agreement, contract and/or letter which may be legally binding upon the [Copyright Owner].

1.4   The [Consultant] agrees that he/she shall not be entitled to any present and/or future payments, royalties and/or other sums from any agreement concluded by the [Copyright Owner] in respect of the [Film/Work] and shall only be entitled to the fixed fees set out in Clause [–].

A.565

The [Trustee] appoints the [Agent] to seek to negotiate the best agreements it can to exploit all the [Material] listed in the attached Schedule [-]. The [Agent] shall be appointed for a period of [one year] from [date] but shall not have the authority to conclude and sign any agreements on behalf of the [Trustee]. The [Agent] shall not acquire any rights and/or interest in any of the [Material] and/or seek to enter into any arrangement at any time to benefit from his/her access to the [Material].

A.566

The [Agent Company] shall be entitled to store, reproduce, supply and/or distribute copies of the [Images] for use in any format including as artwork for book covers, DVDs, CDs, and for use in software for mobile phones, apps, websites, games and any other format and/or medium. Provided that no third party shall be authorised to use and/or adapt any of the [Images] without a minimum fee of [number/currency] in each case and the conclusion of a licence agreement a copy of which can be supplied to the [Author/Artist].

A.567

The [Agent] agrees that it does not have sole and exclusive rights and that the [Licensor] may also grant the exact same rights to a third party at any time. That the [Agent] is only authorised to act as the administrator for the [Company] from [date] to [date] and that no transfer of any copyright and/ or other intellectual property and/or any other rights of any type whether known now and/or developed at a later date are granted and/or assigned to the [Agent] either now and/or during the course of this Agreement. That the [Agent] shall not be able to insist upon any credit and/or copyright notice and/or seek to grant and/or licence and/or assign any part of the [Work/Film/ other] to any third party.

Film and Television

A.568

In consideration of the payment of the non-returnable Advance and the [Licensor's] Royalties the [Licensor] grants to the [Licensee] the sole and exclusive [Television Rights/DVD Rights/Videogram Rights/Non-Theatric Rights] throughout the Territory for the duration of the Licence Period and the right to authorise third parties to exploit and/or exercise such rights.

A.569

The [Licensee] agrees that all other rights are specifically excluded from this Agreement and are retained by the [Licensor] including the Merchandising Rights and the Publication Rights.

A.570

The [Copyright Owner] appoints the [Company] to act and represent the [Copyright Owner] solely in relation to the exploitation of the following rights in the [Work] in the [Territory] from [date] to [date]:

1.1   All forms of television including terrestrial, digital, cable, satellite but excluding film and/or video through mobiles, small gadgets, PCs and laptops and/or other similar equipment.

1.2   All forms of radio including terrestrial, analogue, digital, cable, satellite but excluding film and/or video through mobiles, small gadgets, PCs and laptops and/or other similar equipment.

A.571

The [Agent] shall not have any right to any sums of any nature from the exploitation of the rights in Clause [–] which have not been received by the [Agent] before [End Date]. The [Agent] shall not be entitled to any sums from any agreements after [End Date] whether or not any such agreement was signed during the [Agency Period] and/or the sums were due but not received.

A.572

The [Agent] agrees and acknowledges that it shall not be entitled to any royalties, payments, commission and/or other sums from any new work by the [Copyright Owner] and/or any sequel of the [Work] and/or part at any time.

A.573

The [Agent] agrees and acknowledges that it shall not be entitled to register and/or claim the rights to and/or ownership of any title, characters, logos, trade marks, design rights, graphics, computer generated material, music, slogan, format and/or any other rights of any nature in any media at any time.

A.574

The [Distributor] is acting as an authorised agent of [Name] with respect to the [Programme/Film] from [date] to [date]. During that period the [Distributor] may enter into discussions, negotiations and agreements on behalf of [Name] to licence, sell supply copies of the [Programme/Film] for satellite, cable, WiFi, terrestrial, pay per view, video on demand, DVDs, and in the form of transmissions for play back at a later date, viewing on a computer, mobile and/or other gadget, and in the form of viewings at exhibitions, aeroplanes, cinemas, theatres, clubs, festivals. The rights are limited to the original version in [specify] language and not any translation and/or sub-titled version. Nor does the [Distributor[acquire any right to edit, adapt and/or alter the [Programme/Film] and/or to licence and/or grant any rights and/or option relating to any of the characters, music, costumes, script, content and/or otherwise.

A.575

The [Agent] may market the [Author] and their [Work] and any associated material in which the [Author] owns the rights provided that the [Author] has the final right to either consent or refuse to finalise the agreement proposed by the [Agent]. That the [Agent] shall not seek to negotiate with any business and/or enterprise and/or individual which does not have a sound financial record.

General Business and Commercial

A.576

The [Agent] shall mean the following [Company/individual] whose address is at [address] who is authorised to act on behalf of [Name] in respect of the following areas [list] in [country] from [date] to [date].

A.577

The [Agent] shall not be entitled and is not authorised to sign any agreement, consent or other release or document or to commit the attendance of [Name]. The [Agent] is merely permitted to negotiate and agree proposed terms, but the consent for appearances, signature and conclusion of any contracts or otherwise requires the signature of [Name] in each case.

A.578

The [Agent] shall keep [Name] at the [Company] fully informed on a regular basis as regards any negotiations with any third party and agrees that he shall not have the right to conclude any agreement or provide any release or consent relating to [specify] or the [Company] without the prior verbal consent of [Name].

A.579

The [Agent] undertakes that she does not have the right to negotiate or promote in any manner the commercial interests of the [Company] outside the [country] unless specifically agreed in advance on each occasion. Any consent given does not mean that there is a waiver of consent for any subsequent matter.

A.580

It is the intention of both parties that all products of the business services of the [Name] should be dealt with by the [Agent] whether performances, appearances, recordings, endorsements, publishing or otherwise and whether for financial gain or not from [date] to [date].

A.581

[Name] agrees that [Company] shall be his exclusive agent for all business work in any media for the Term of the Agreement throughout the Territory. The [Company] agrees to provide its first-class services as far as reasonably possible and attend at such locations, dates and times as agreed in advance with [Name].

A.582

[Name] confirms that he shall regularly advise the [Agent] in advance in writing of dates when he shall not be available and confirms now that he is available [specify] days a week except [specify] each month until the end of the contract.

A.583

[Name] shall ensure at all times that he keeps the [Company] informed of his landline and mobile telephone number, address, and email and agrees to notify any changes.

133

A.584

In consideration of the payment of [figure/currency] by [date], the [Company] grants the [Agent] the sole and exclusive [specify rights] and the right to authorise any third party to exercise such rights throughout the [country] from [start date] to [end date].

A.585

The [Company] shall not be entitled to use the name of the [Agent] in any marketing, promotional material or in any programme, conference, products or corporate documents without the prior approval of the [Agent] in each case.

A.586

The [Agent] shall be entitled to receive payment in accordance with the Agreement in respect of all contracts negotiated by her during the term of the Agreement, but not signed until after the expiry of the Agreement.

A.587

The [Agent] shall only be entitled to receive its commission in respect of any sums which are received by the [Agent] and/or the [Copyright Owner] for agreements relating to the exploitation of the rights in Clause [–] signed and concluded between [start date] and [end date]. The [Agent] shall be entitled to be paid commission on all such agreements even if the payments are received after the [end date]. The [Agent] shall not however be entitled to commission on any period for which an agreement is renewed and/or extended beyond the original term of the agreement.

A.588

The [Agent] agrees that it shall not be entitled to any commission on any advance, royalties, payments, commission and/or other sums from any new work by the [Copyright Owner] whether or not derived from and/or based on the [Work]. Further the [Agent] agrees that it shall not be entitled to any commission on any advance, royalties, payments, commission and/or other sums from any sequel and/or later adaptation of the [Work] and/or part at any time.

A.589

The [Agent] agrees that it shall not be entitled to register and/or claim the rights to and/or ownership of any title, characters, logos, trade marks, domain names, design rights, graphics, computer generated material, typography, music, slogan, map, table, data, software, invention, patent and/or any other rights of any nature in any media at any time. That all rights in the [Work] and any development drafts, prototypes and/or variations, translations, adaptations and/or rights which can be registered with any collecting society shall be held in the name of the [Copyright Owner/Other].

A.590

The [Agent] shall not seek to hold the [Author] responsible for any expense, cost and/or other sum which is in excess of [number/currency] which has not been specifically authorised in advance by the [Author].

A.591

The [Agent] agrees that the [Authors'] professional accountancy and legal advisors shall be entitled to have access to and to inspect and make copies of all records, data, agreements, documents, invoices, expenses, costs whether on computer, paper, in a storage device and/or gadget, at a bank and/or other financial institution and/or at one of the residential homes of the staff and/or a personal laptop and/or gadget in order to seek to verify the accuracy of the statements from the [Agent] and the sums due and/or paid.

Internet and Websites

A.592

The [Agent] shall act for and on behalf of the [Company] in relation to all matters relating to the internet and websites whether accessed or received on computers, television or mobiles or some other gadget in consideration of the sums set out in Clause [–]. The [Agent] shall only be on a short term contract of [specify] months and during that period shall advise and be involved in the setting up of:

1.1 The budget, development, creation, legal protection of and marketing for a website and the domain name.

1.2 The promotion and establishment of the website in [country] through a major advertising campaign.

1.3 To carry out a comprehensive survey and report on competing companies worldwide which exist or are setting up on the internet and to analyse their operations and marketing.

1.4 To carry out a detailed evaluation of the website to examine the benefits and negative factors and its effect on the [Company]. To look at this development in conjunction with the overall strategy of the [Company].

A.593

The [Agent] shall act on behalf of the [Company] solely and exclusively in relation to enhance the [Company's] websites, and the registration of domain names, and to develop an internet strategy.

A.594

In consideration of the mutual promises and representations made by one party to the other under this Agreement including payments agreed to be made by the [Company] to the [Designer]. The [Company] agrees to engage the non-exclusive services of the [Designer] to design, develop, integrate and support the [Company's] Website in accordance with the terms of this Agreement.

A.595

The [Designer] shall perform its obligations under this Agreement to the best of its skill and ability and shall maintain such high standards as are reasonably expected by the [Company] to create a fully functional website for the [Company's] commercial and marketing purposes on or before the Launch Date.

A.596

The [Designer] acknowledges that the [Company] shall not be obliged to set up, exploit or use the [Website].

A.597

The [Designer] agrees that the [Company] may at any time engage any other third party at its sole discretion to carry out work on the [Website] or any other internet project for the [Company]. This shall include the right of the [Company] to use any third party to provide support services at any time.

A.598

The [Designer] agrees that the [Company] may decide at any time not to use the services of the [Designer] and shall give notice of the end of the Agreement and shall pay in full on receipt of all material to be returned the sums set out in Schedule [–].

A.599

All work, expenses costs and developments shall at all times be subject to the prior written approval of [Name] at the [Company]. The decision of the [Company] in any matter shall be final.

A.600

The [Software Company] are not authorised to act as agents for the [Supplier] nor can they authorise the purchase of any material, services and/or market and/or hold themselves out as being entitled to do so for any reason.

A.601

The [Software Company] may as required engage such other persons and companies for the [Project] as may be needed in order to meet the delivery date and cost and content targets set out in Schedule [–]. The [Software Company] is acting as agent for the [Supplier] and all terms of engagement shall require that the invoice for payment is sent to [specify].

A.602

The [Company] agrees to promote and market the club known as [specify] and its website [specify] as non-exclusive agents for a period of [number] months from [date]. The [Company] shall charge of fee of [number/currency] per calendar month and in addition additional charges set out in Appendix [A] for printed flyers, wristbands, telephone marketing, online articles and content display and otherwise up to a maximum of [number/currency] per month.

Merchandising

A.603

In consideration of the [Agent's] Commission the [Agent] agrees to provide her non-exclusive services to the [Licensor] for the Licence Period throughout the Territory and to fulfil the following role [specify].

A.604

In consideration of the Net Receipts the [Licensor] agrees to engage the exclusive services of the [Agent] for the Licence Period throughout the Territory and grants to the [Agent] the sole and exclusive right to negotiate agreements on behalf of the [Licensor] for the production, manufacture, distribution, sale, exploitation and marketing of the [Licensed Articles] for the Licence Period throughout the Territory.

A.605

The [Agent] acknowledges and agrees that there is only a non-exclusive right granted in respect of the negotiation of agreements for the associated trade marks and logos which are on the packaging or marketing material of the [Licensed Articles].

A.606

The [Agent] agrees that she shall not have the right to commit the [Licensor] to any agreement whether in writing or not without the prior written consent of the [Licensor] and that all licence agreements must be in writing and signed by or authorised by the [Licensor].

A.607

The [Agent] shall provide a professional and efficient service during normal working hours to ensure that as far as reasonably possible the [Character] is commercially exploited and released in the following format [specify] in [country] by [date].

A.608

The [Agent] shall disclose to the [Licensor] any other business relationship and/or client which may exist or be created at any time which conflicts with or competes with the interests of the [Licensor] under this Agreement. In the event that as a result of the disclosure the [Licensor] considers that the reputation of the [Licensor] and/or its business is likely to be damaged, harmed and/or to suffer losses. Then the [Licensor] shall have the right to serve written notice of the termination of the Agreement without further liability to the [Agent].

A.609

The [Agent] agrees that she shall be responsible for all costs and expenses which she may incur in respect of the provision of her services under this Agreement.

A.610

The [Agent] agrees and undertakes that she shall not have the right to negotiate, conclude, promote or market the commercial interests of the [Character] in any form outside the Territory unless specifically agreed in advance with the [Licensor].

A.611

The [Agent] agrees that it shall only be entitled to receive sums from contracts which are negotiated, concluded and signed in full during the continuance of the Agreement. The right to receive commission shall be for the duration of the licence agreement which relates to the exploitation of the rights. Where any agreement is not signed until later, then the [Agent] shall not be entitled to any sums despite having developed and prepared the project.

A.612

The [Agent] agrees that the [Copyright Owner] shall be entitled to terminate the Agreement for the services of the [Agent] at any time at the [Copyright Owners'] sole discretion. The [Agent] shall only be entitled to receive commission on any sums received to the date of termination. The [Agent] shall not be entitled to receive commission on any sums which accrue but are not paid before the date of termination. The [Agent] shall not be entitled to be paid any commission after the date of termination which has not been received whether or not the agreement was signed for that date of termination.

A.613

he [Agent] shall be obliged to take out insurance cover and policy for the benefit of [Name] for public liability and/or loss of funds due to [Name] which may be due but not paid by the [Agent] for any reason whether due to management failures, theft, fire, and/or any other reason. So that in the event that [name] is not paid by the [Agent] then [Name] can make a claim against the insurance policy. The [Agent] shall provide a copy of the policy to [Name] and proof that all premiums have been paid.

A.614
The [Agent] shall not seek to withhold from [Name] any sums which he/she receives from any [Licensee] into an account outside [country]. The [Agent] agrees to advise [Name] of the receipt of the funds and the method and date by which it is intended it shall be transferred to [country] and paid to [Name].

A.615
The [Agent] may appoint sub-agents in other countries to carry out duties and arrangements in respect of the [Work] but the [Agent] shall not be entitled to recoup the cost of any commission, charges, fees and/or other costs from the sums due to the [Company].

Publishing

A.616
In consideration of the [Agent's] Commission the [Agent] agrees to provide his non-exclusive services to the [Author] as a literary agent for the [Work] from [date] to [date] in [country] and shall fulfil the following services [specify].

A.617
In consideration of the Net Receipts the [Author] agrees to engage the exclusive services of the [Agent] as a literary agent for the [Work] for the following period [start date] to [end date] throughout the Territory for the purpose of the commercial exploitation of the [Work] in all media.

A.618
The [Agent] shall provide his services to the [Author] and use his skill and knowledge to perform his duties to endeavour to ensure that an agreement is negotiated with a reputable publisher in respect of the [Work] for the publication by [year] in hardback and [year] in paperback in [specify countries].

A.619
The [Agent] shall use his expertise to exploit commercially and promote the [Author] and his writing and manuscripts in all forms of the media throughout [specify countries] including hardback and paperback books, radio and

television appearances and adaptations of any written work, serialisations in newspapers and magazines, promotional articles, readings and reviews, translations, software, DVDs and websites.

A.620

The [Agent] as far as possible should keep the [Author] fully informed on a regular basis as regards any negotiations concerning the [Author], his published and unpublished writing and manuscripts or other material. The [Agent] agrees that he shall not have the right to commit the [Author] or conclude any agreement or provide any consent without the prior approval of the [Author] based on full disclosure of the facts.

A.621

This Agreement does not appoint the [Agent] as an agent or partner or otherwise with the [Company] at any time. The services of the [Agent] are only engaged to advise, negotiate and act on behalf of the [Company] in respect of [subject] from [date] to [date] for the agreed fixed sum of [specify]. The [Agent] shall not be entitled to royalty, commission, or other sums in respect of the exploitation of the [subject].

A.622

All monies payable under this Agreement to the [Author] shall be paid to [Name/Company] of [address] who is authorised by the [Author] to collect and receive such monies as his [Agent]. The [Author] agrees that the receipt by the [Agent] shall be a good and valid discharge of the sums due under this Agreement.

A.623

The [Authors] confirm that neither party has entered into or is bound by any agreement with an agent in respect of their [Work]. The [Authors] agree that an agent shall not be appointed for the purpose of negotiating a publishing agreement or any other form of exploiting the [Work] without the knowledge and consent of both parties.

A.624

The [Author] agrees that the [Agent] shall not be bound to find the [Author] a publisher as a term of this Agreement. The [Author] agrees that the [Work] may not be considered of suitable quality and/or may be rejected by the publishing companies.

A.625

[Name] agrees that the [Company] shall have the right to negotiate, conclude and exploit the [Work/Product] in any media in order to achieve the most financial return and profit to [Name]. Provided that no agreement shall assign any rights and all licences concluded are limited to a maximum of [number] years for each licence.

A.626
The [Publisher] agrees and undertakes that no sub-agents, sub-licensees and/or distributors shall be entitled to edit, adapt, revise and translate the [Work]. That all such proposals are subject to the prior agreement of [Name] in writing and/or his/her agent.

A.627
The [Agent] agrees that [Name] has not appointed the [Agent] to act on his/her behalf in any form whether in relation to the [work] or not outside [country]. That [Name] may appoint any person he/she thinks fit to exploit any rights in the [Work] and/or his services outside [country] and that the [Agent] shall not be entitled to any part of any sums received from such exploitation.

Purchase and Supply of Products

A.628
The [Distributor] shall be the [Agent] and not the principal in any negotiations, agreements, consents or contract under this Agreement.

A.629
The [Distributor] shall be permitted to appoint sub-agents or sub-licensees to carry out all or any of its responsibilities under this contract. The [Distributor] shall forward to the [Company] a copy of any such contract within [one month] of the date of conclusion of a signed agreement.

A.630
Each [Licensee] undertakes that it is not the agent acting on behalf of any undisclosed company or third party whose business or products compete with or conflict with the business interests of the [Licensor].

A.631
The [Supplier] agrees to deliver the [Product] to the [Seller] for sale on the [Seller's] website on a non-exclusive basis for the Duration of the Agreement in consideration of the payments to be made hereunder.

A.632
The [Supplier] confirms that it has not and shall not enter into any arrangement which has or might conflict with this Agreement.

A.633

The [Seller] agrees that the [Product] shall only be sold from [specify] and not from any other website or premises unless the [Supplier's] prior [verbal/written] approval has been obtained, such approval not to be unreasonably withheld or delayed.

A.634

The [Seller] agrees that no other product or advertisement or service shall be displayed on or featured on the [Seller's] Website where there is a direct conflict of interest which would directly compete with any product supplied under this Agreement.

A.635

The [Seller] agrees that it shall not be entitled to adapt and/or alter the [Product] including the packaging in any way without the prior consent of the [Supplier].

A.636

The [Seller] agrees that the [Supplier] shall be entitled to supply the [Product] to any third party whether on the internet or otherwise. Provided that where the [Supplier] intends to supply the [Product] to any of the following businesses [specify]. Then the [Supplier] shall notify the [Seller] of its intentions.

A.637

Both parties agree that this Agreement is not intended to restrict, prohibit, prevent or effect the supply, distribution, use, endorsement or acting on behalf of any other goods, services or material by either of the parties.

A.638

There is no authority provided to any agent, distributor, supplier and/or otherwise to alter, add to change, vary, adapt any part of the [Product/Article] and/or packaging as submitted to the [Company] in its final form prior to production.

A.639

There is no form of agency, partnership, joint venture and/or other legal arrangement created by the agreement of the [Organisers] to include the [products/articles/work] in its [festival/on line shop/event]. The [Organisers] reserve the right at any time to withdraw their agreement and to remove the [Company] and the [products/articles/work] from the [festival/online shop/event]. In such circumstances the [Company] agree that the [Organisers] will not have to provide a reason and shall not be liable for any resulting losses, damages and/or consequences. The [Company] agrees that it accepts this risk and potential cost.

Services

A.640
In consideration of the [Manager's] Commission the [Manager] agrees to provide his non-exclusive services to the [Sportsperson] to act as agent and manager in the following areas of the media [specify] from [date] to [date] in [country].

A.641
In consideration of the [Sportsperson's] Fees the [Sportsperson] agrees to engage the non-exclusive services of the [Manager] from [date] to [date] in [country] in the following [television, radio, DVDs, film, the internet, computer games and software, newspapers, periodicals, books and publishing including a biography, music, professional and public appearances, sponsorship, endorsements, promotions, competitions, events, exhibitions and other commercial exploitation].

A.642
The [Manager] agrees to provide the [Sportsperson] with reasonable notice of meetings, events, recordings, interviews or otherwise that she is required to attend in a written format at least [one month] in advance.

A.643
The [Agent] shall provide her services to the best of her skill and ability and shall perform all services diligently to ensure that the [Artiste] is regularly engaged by third parties on the best possible terms.

A.644
The [Agent] shall use his knowledge and expertise to promote and publicise the [Artiste] in the following areas of the media [television, radio, video and DVDs, film, newspapers, magazines, books, records, public appearances].

A.645
In consideration of the [Agent's] Commission, the [Agent] agrees to provide his non-exclusive services to the [Actor] for the Term of this Agreement throughout the Territory. In consideration of the Net Receipts the [Actor] agrees to engage the exclusive services of the Agent for the Term of this Agreement throughout the Territory in all media including but not limited to appearances, performances, recordings in sound and vision in all forms of television, film, theatre, radio, videos, DVDs, corporate videos, advertisements, internet, telephone and mobile phones, promotional events and exhibitions, features and articles in newspapers and magazines, publishing in any format, sponsorship, and merchandising, promotional, conference and exhibition appearances and endorsements.

143

A.646

In consideration of the Net Receipts the [Artiste] agrees to engage the exclusive services of the [Agent] for the Term of the Agreement throughout the Territory. The [Agent] shall use his reasonable endeavours to arrange for the engagement and commercial exploitation of the [Artiste] in all media in any format whether in existence now or created during the existence of this Agreement including but not limited to all forms of films, video, DVD, television, CD-Roms and other computer software, merchandising, publications, advertising, promotional appearances, exhibitions and endorsements, theatric and non-theatric in sound, images, text or otherwise both on the internet, websites, mobile phones and other interactive multi-media.

A.647

The [Agent] agrees that the [Actor] shall not be obliged to provide his services to any third party or the [Agent] and that prior to any detailed negotiations the prior approval of the [Actor] shall be required by the [Agent] which may be refused for any reason whether reasonable or not.

A.648

The [Agent] agrees that any form of exploitation of the product of the [Artiste's] services shall require the prior consent of the [Artiste]. The [Artiste] shall be entitled to refuse to carry out any work for any reason whether or not the [Agent] will suffer a financial or other loss. The [Agent] shall not be entitled to seek any compensation, loss or damages which arises from the failure or refusal of the [Artiste] to provide consent or to perform any work.

A.649

1.1 The [Author] appoints the [Agent] to represent him/her and to endeavour to conclude agreements with third parties for the exploitation of works proposed and/or written by the [Author] during the Term of the Agreement in the Territory in respect of the following rights: All forms of publications in print form whether hardback or paperback books, magazines, digests, periodicals, brochures, newspapers, pull-outs. All forms of television, cable, satellite, digital, pay on demand, subscription, film via landline telephone or mobile, DVD, discs, software and gambling, betting and lotteries in any format and games sold for use on computers and laptops and other gadgets.

1.2 The [Agent] shall be entitled to receive commission in respect of all agreements concluded and signed by the [Author] with the third parties before the termination and/or expiry of this Agreement in respect of the rights and countries stated in 1.1 above. The [Agent] shall be entitled to receive the commission for the duration of each such agreement.

144

A.650

The [Agent] agrees to act in the best interests of the [Author] at all times and to provide the [Author] with details of any conflict of interest that may arise at any time due to the appointment of another client and/or other business interests. The [Agent] shall also provide advice and guidance on the commercial aspects of the agreements, liaise with any collecting societies and organise registration for the [Author] and collect any sums due in respect of the rights and territory granted under this Agreement.

A.651

Until the expiry and/or termination of this Agreement the [Agent] is entitled to collect and be paid any sums due under any agreement with any third party provided that the sums are held in a separate and clearly identifiable account to which both parties are joint signatories and both must sign to issue any payments.

After the expiry and/or termination of the Agreement then the [Author] shall be responsible for collecting all sums due and shall ensure that the [Agent] is paid any commission that may be due.

A.652

Where the [Agent] owes any sums which are outstanding to the [Author]. The [Agent] agrees that the [Author] may setoff and claim any such sums from those due to the [Agent] from the sums received.

A.653

The [Agent] shall not be entitled to exploit rights not specifically set out above and agrees and undertakes to do any of the following without the prior written consent of the [Author].

1.1 Set up a fan website and/or any other website relating to the [Writer].

1.2 To register the name of the [Author] as a domain name.

1.3 To sign any documents, agreements and/other apply for any trade mark and/or other rights which are owned and/or controlled by the [Author] and/or relate to the [Author's] work in any media.

A.654

The [Agent] is engaged to represent [Name] to book music venues for performances and not with any rights as regards the content of any music and/or lyrics which may be performed and/or created by [Name].

A.655

The [Author/Artist] may cease to engage the services of the [Agent] at any time and the [Agent] shall have no right to seek to claim and rights, interests and/or payment from after the date of termination whether created and/or developed and/or booked during the contract or not.

A.656

[Name] agrees that the [Agent] may engage the services of third parties to create new material and/or develop and market the services of [Name]. Provided that all proposals are discussed and agreed with [Name] in advance and that the [Agent] agrees to pay [number] per cent of the costs and expenses.

Sponsorship

A.657

The [Company] agrees to appoint the [Promoter] as the sole and exclusive sponsorship, advertising and promotion agent for the purpose of promoting and advertising and arranging sponsorship for the [Company] and the [Company's] Products throughout the Territory for the duration of the Term of this Agreement.

A.658

1.1 In consideration of the Promotion Fee and the Promotion Expenses the [Promoter] agrees to provide its non-exclusive services to the [Company] to act as agent to promote, advertise and arrange sponsorship for the [Company] and the [Company's] Products throughout the Territory from [date] to date].

1.2 The [Promoter] acknowledges and agrees that the [Company] may appoint any other person and/or company to work with the [Promoter] at any time and the [Promoter] agrees to assist and cooperate where necessary.

A.659

The [Promoter] acknowledges and confirms that the principal aims of this Agreement are to:

1.1 Promote and increase the sales of the [Company's] Products.

1.2 Raise public awareness of the [Company] and the [Company's] Products throughout the Territory.

1.3 Arrange sponsorship and endorsement of events, exhibitions, conferences and individuals which will improve and develop the image, press coverage, or sales of the [Company].

1.4 Any other specific aims [–].

A.660

The [Sponsor] agrees that the sponsorship of [–] does not give it the right to use the [Company's] name, logo, programme title, slogan or other material owned or controlled by the [Company] in any advertising, promotion, marketing or product owned or controlled by the [Sponsor].

A.661

The [Agency] confirms that it has not and shall not enter into any arrangement with any person, enterprise and/or business and/or for any service and/ or product which has or might conflict with this Agreement. The [Agency] agrees to provide the [Company] with details of any conflict of interest that may arise at any time due to the appointment of other clients and/or other business interests. The [Agency] agrees and undertakes to provide written notice of any conflict within [seven] days of the conclusion of any agreement. Where a conflict arises which the [Company] finds unacceptable then the [Agency] agrees that the [Company] may at its sole discretion serve written notice of the termination of the Agreement. In such event the [Company] shall only owe and/or pay to the [Agency] such sums as are due to the date of termination. The [Agency] agrees that no sums and/or commission shall be paid to the [Agency] in respect of any agreement which exists after the termination date.

A.662

The [Company] agrees that the [Sponsor] shall have the [final decision/right to be consulted] in respect of the content, operation and organisation of the [Event/Programme]. The [Company] agrees to seek the prior approval of the [Sponsor] at all stages of the development, production, marketing and advertising of the [Event/Programme] prior to any final commitments and/or agreements being concluded.

A.663

The [Company] shall not the right to sign any agreement which requires the use of the [Sponsors] trade mark, logo and/or slogan by any third party whether for any commercial and/or non-commercial purpose. The prior written consent of the [Sponsor] shall be requested by the [Company] in each case. Any such company and/or person shall be required by the [Sponsor] to sign a trade mark user licence agreement and to assign all rights in all media throughout the universe to the [Sponsor] in any such new development and/or variation.

A.664

Neither the [Sponsor] nor the [Company] shall delegate responsibility for any work and/or contribution to this [Film/Festival] to any agent and/or third party unless both parties have agreed that is the best course of action and have both approved the action.

A.665

Where the [Sponsor] appoints an agent and/or other third party to carry out its duties under this Agreement and the [Company] agrees. Such consent by the [Company] does not mean that the [Sponsor] is not directly responsible and it has not transferred any liability and/or obligations under this Agreement.

University, Library and Educational

A.666

1.1 In consideration of the [Commission] the [Agent] agrees to provide his non-exclusive services to the [Institute] from [date to [date] for the following purpose [specify Project].

1.2 The [Institute] agrees to engage the services of the [Agent] as set out in 1.1 above.

1.3 The [Agent] acknowledges that the [Institute] shall have the right to appoint another agent and/or third party in respect of any matter including the [Project] and that this is not an exclusive agreement.

1.4 The [Agent] agrees that there is no right granted to the [Agent] to commit the [Institute] to any agreement whether in writing or not without the prior written consent of the [Institute] and that all agreements must be in writing and signed by the [Institute].

1.5 The [Agent] agrees that he shall be responsible for all costs and expenses which may be incurred in respect of the provision of his services under this Agreement.

A.667

1.1 The [Agent] agrees and undertakes to keep the [Institute] fully informed on a regular basis as regards any negotiations concerning the [Project] and shall provide copies of all correspondence, emails, proposals, samples and any other material to the [Institute] on a regular basis.

1.2 The services of the [Agent] are only engaged to advise and negotiate but not to conclude any agreement on behalf of the [Institute] in respect of the [Project] from [date] to [date] for the agreed fixed sum of [figure/currency] [words].

1.3 The [Agent] agrees that he shall not be entitled to any additional sums and/or royalties from the exploitation of the [Project] during the

Agreement nor after it has ended and/or any costs and expenses of any nature.

A.668
The [Agency] shall perform its obligations under this Agreement to the best of its skill and ability and shall ensure that its personnel, contractors and consultants are professionally qualified and shall maintain high standards in accordance with the requirements specified by the [Company/Institute] for the following purpose and aim [specify Project]. A summary of which is attached to, and forms part of, this Agreement.

A.669
The [Enterprise] acts as a non-exclusive agent to promote, market and distribute via its website, short films, photographs, events, exhibitions and online marketing details of the [Students] and their [Projects].

A.670
The [Charity] does not act as a representative of any third party person and/or business associated with its organisations. Nor is any such third party person and/or business entitled to represent directly and/or indirectly that they are authorised to make statements, press releases, and/or authorise work and/or services. The use of the[Charity] name, logo and image is only authorised through organised events.

AMENDMENTS

General Business and Commercial

A.671
This Agreement contains the full understanding of the parties with respect to the subject matter hereof and supersedes any previous agreements between the parties regarding such subject matter. This Agreement may not be amended nor any of its provisions waived except in writing executed by the party against which such amendment or waiver is sought to be enforced.

A.672
This Agreement supersedes all prior agreements and arrangements and embodies the entire understanding and all the terms agreed between the parties relating to the Licence and no oral representations, warranties or promises shall be implied as terms of this Agreement.

A.673

This Agreement may be amended only by instrument in writing signed on behalf of both parties and the terms of this Agreement shall include any amendments contained in any such instruction.

A.674

The General Terms and the Special Conditions constitutes the whole agreement between the parties and neither party relies on any representation other than any reduced to writing herein and no variation or waiver of any term hereof shall be effective unless committed to writing.

A.675

This Agreement sets out the entire and complete agreement between the parties hereto and any amendment or discharge must be in writing and signed by an authorised signatory of both the [Company] and the [Agent].

A.676

This Agreement contains the full and complete understanding between the parties and supersedes all prior arrangements and understandings whether written or oral, appertaining to the subject matter of this Agreement and may not be varied except by an instrument in writing signed by all of the parties to this Agreement.

A.677

Each Licensee acknowledges that no representations or promises not expressly contained in this Agreement have been made by the [Company] or any of its officers, servants, agents, employees, members or representatives.

A.678

The contractual terms between the [Company] and the [Purchaser] are contained exclusively within this document and in no circumstances will the [Company] be bound by any purported addition to, or other variation of these terms whether oral or in writing unless any such written addition or variation by reference to these terms is signed on behalf of the [Company]. The parties agree that any representation made by any person before or at the time the contract is entered into whether oral or in writing is expressly excluded.

A.679

This Agreement may not be changed, modified, amended or supplemented except in a written document signed by both parties. Each of the parties acknowledges and agrees that the other has not made any representations, warranties or agreements of any kind except as may be expressly set forth herein. This Agreement constitutes and contains the entire agreement between the parties with respect to the subject matter hereof and supersedes any prior or contemporaneous agreements oral or in writing. Nothing herein contained shall be binding upon the parties until a copy of this Agreement has been executed by an officer of each party and has been delivered to the other party. This Agreement may be executed in counterparts each of which shall be deemed an original but all of which shall together be one and the same instrument. Paragraph headings are inserted herein for convenience only and do not constitute a part of this Agreement.

A.680

This Agreement may not be altered, changed or modified except by written instrument duly executed by both the [Licensor] and the [Licensee] and this provision may not be waived except by written instrument duly executed by both the [Licensor] and the [Licensee]. This Agreement is complete and embraces the entire understanding between the parties, all prior understandings whether oral or written having been incorporated as far as agreed herein. No representations or warranties of any kind or nature have been made by either of the parties to the other to induce the making of this Agreement except as specifically set out in this Agreement and each of the parties hereto agrees not to assert to the contrary.

A.681

This Agreement which has been signed by all parties is the final and absolute statement of the terms and conditions to which everyone has agreed to be bound. All matters discussed, written, offered, waivered, inducements or otherwise in negotiations or prior to the signature of this Agreement of any nature are only relevant to the extent that they are specified in this Agreement. Neither party shall seek to imply additional terms and conditions at a later date nor seek to imply additional terms, facts or other matters which have not been specified in the Agreement.

A.682

This Agreement sets out the entire terms agreed between the parties hereto and supersedes all previous representations, warranties and terms (whether in writing or not) previously made between the parties. Any amendments, additions or alterations to this Agreement shall not be made except in writing and signed by a duly authorised representative of both parties.

A.683

This document constitutes the entire agreement between the parties relating to the [service] and supersedes and operates to the exclusion of all previous arrangements, representations, practices or otherwise made by on behalf of the [Company]. No amendments shall be binding and valid unless in writing and signed by both parties.

A.684

This Agreement represents the entire agreement between the parties and supersedes all previous agreements, promises, and representations made by either party to the other. Any amendment or alteration to this Agreement shall be in writing and signed by an authorised senior executive from each of the parties.

A.685

This Agreement sets out the full and complete terms agreed between the parties. No prior promise written or oral shall be taken into account unless specified in this Agreement. Any amendment or variation must be in writing on a document signed by the [Agent] and the [Actor].

A.686

This Agreement supersedes all previous agreements, representations, undertakings and assurances given prior to this Agreement and sets out all the terms agreed between the parties. Any amendment or alteration to this Agreement must be in writing and signed by the [Company] and the [Individual].

A.687

Any amendment or alteration to this Agreement must be in writing and signed by both parties.

A.688

Any amendment or alteration to this Agreement must be in writing and signed by an authorised signatory of each of the parties.

A.689

This Agreement sets out all matters agreed between the parties relating to the [subject] and no earlier documents, records or conversations shall be relied upon at a later date to supersede these terms. All future amendments to this Agreement must be in writing and the document signed by both parties.

A.690

This Agreement sets out the entire and complete understanding of the terms agreed between the parties and may not be changed or superseded except in a written document signed by both parties.

A.691

This Agreement sets out the entire and complete agreement between the parties and all previous arrangements written or oral relating to [subject] between the parties have been or are now terminated so that they no longer apply. This Agreement may be altered, amended or changed by an exchange of written signed documents in which the terms agreed are specified. There can be no oral binding amendment or signature by only one party.

A.692

This Agreement must not be changed, modified, amended or supplemented except in a written document signed by both parties in each case.

A.693

Amendment, alteration or changes to this document may be in writing or oral provided that it is agreed in advance by both parties.

A.694

Any representations, facts, inducements, promises or other matters which were raised by either party in order for the agreement to be entered into by the other party shall still be binding whether specified in this Agreement or not.

A.695

All the representations, documents, statements and material supplied and put forward as [fact/background material/projected figures] by both parties shall form part of this Agreement.

A.696

This Agreement can be amended by any one of the following methods:

1.1 An exchange of emails confirming agreement on new terms and conditions.

1.2 A side letter which is signed by one party and agreed to in a responding letter.

1.3 A formal new amending document which both parties sign and date.

A.697

The [Institute] and the [Company] agree that this Agreement cannot be amended by emails, invoices, receipts and/or verbal exchanges. That the formal notification of any amendment must be agreed between parties and authorised by the [Chief Executive] of both parties and/or a delegated authority.

A.698

The following documents and representations made by the [Company] which are attached in Appendix [–] form part of this Agreement. No other information, data, representations and/or disclosures shall be deemed and/or are intended to be part of this Agreement. Both parties agree and undertake that any prior exchanges of nature not in Appendix [–] are specifically excluded. No amendments and/or additions to this Agreement can be made by email, telephone, text, voicemail and/or other medium of any nature except in writing on paper and signed by authorised representatives of both parties.

A.699

1.1   Both parties agree that this document is intended to be updated, amended and varied as required to suit the circumstances and the business requirements of the parties. Either party may send the other proposed amendments by email, fax, letter and any other written form except text message.

1.2   All proposed amendments should be sent to [Name] on behalf of the [Distributor] and [Name] on behalf of the [Company]. Either the [Distributor] and/or the [Company] shall be entitled to reject any such proposed amendments as not feasible on cost grounds and/or for any other reason. There shall be no time limit for the rejection and/or acceptance of any proposed amendment unless specified in the proposal.

1.3   All additions and/or amendments to the Agreement shall be bound by all the terms of the existing Agreement. Where any term of the existing Agreement is to be deleted then both parties agree to specify the exact clause in the proposed amendment.

A.700

The [Sponsor] agrees that if for any reason the terms of the Agreement are to be amended then the amendment must be in the form of a written document signed by the [Managing Director] of each party. The [Sponsor] agrees and undertakes that clauses [–] relating to the [Sponsorship Fee] and the [Payment Schedule] shall not be amended at any time.

A.701

The [Sub-Licensee] shall not have any right and/or authority to amend, delete from, vary and/or deviate from the terms of this Agreement. No attempt by the [Sub-Licensee] whether by letter, email, fax, text and/or by representations to third parties outside the agreed terms and/or otherwise shall be legally binding upon the [Licensor] and/or the [Licensee]. Where the [Sub-Licensee] is found to be acting outside its authority and/or on the basis by its actions that the Agreement has been changed, amended and/or varied. Then in such event the [Sub-Licensee] shall be in breach of the terms of this Agreement and the [Licensor] and/or the [Licensee] shall have the right to give written notice of the termination of the Agreement with immediate effect.

A.702

No amendment, change, variation and/or deletion from the Agreement between the [Licensee] and the [Sub-Licensee] shall be outside the rights and or terms granted by the [Copyright Owner/Licensor] to the [Licensee]. The [Licensee] shall have the final decision as to whether to agree to any amendment of the Agreement with the [Sub-Licensee]. Any amendment must be in writing signed by a director of both parties, dated and subject to the laws of [specify].

A.703

Both parties agree that any part of this agreement can be amended, changed, altered and/or cancelled and/or terminated. This can be by any choice of method that either party should so choose including advertisements in the press, email to the account, by letter and/or marketing flyer and/or without any prior notice and/or warning. This shall include price increases and additional costs and charges except that the party due to pay the additional sums shall have the right to refuse to do so and may cancel and/or terminate the agreement.

A.704

It is agreed between the parties that the terms and conditions shall not be altered and/or amended for any reason during each [number] period of [month/years].

A.705

Where one of the parties is in unable and/or unwilling to fulfil the terms of this Agreement then the terms may be varied to permit another third party to assume some and/or all of the liabilities and/or responsibilities provided that [Project/Work] is still completed to the same standard and delivery date is not altered and/or varied.

A.706

The [Company] is unable to provide a consistent service and/or supply of the personnel at times due to reasons which it cannot control and so reserves the right to amend and/or alter this agreement subject to adjustments in the total price. Where the [Company] is obliged to make amendments and/or changes which effect more than [number] per cent of the service and/or personnel. Then the [Distributor] shall have the right to terminate the

Agreement and shall have the right to go to a third party to complete the [Project].

A.707

It is agreed that no documents relating to this [Work/Service] upon which either party would seek to rely in a court of law shall be capable of being amended by email, text and/or any other method which is not in written form on paper and signed by a person who has the authority and capacity to bind that party.

ANTIQUITIES

Building

A.708

All fossils, antiquities and other objects of interest or value which may be found on the site or in excavating the same during the progress of the [Project] shall become the property of the [Employer] and upon discovery of such an object the [Management Contractor] shall forthwith:

1.1　Use his best endeavours not to disturb the objects and shall cease work if the continuance of the work would endanger the objects or prevent or impede its excavation or its removal.

1.2　Take all steps which may be necessary to preserve the objects in the exact position and condition in which they are found.

1.3　Inform the Architect/Contract Administrator or the clerk of works of the discovery and precise location of the objects.

A.709

The [Architect/Contract Administrator] shall issue instructions in regard to the steps to be taken concerning an object reported by the [Management Contractor] under Clause [–] and may require the [Management Contractor] to permit the examination, excavation or removal of the object by a third party. Any such third party shall for the purposes of Clauses [–] be deemed to be a person for whom the Management Contractor is not responsible.

ARBITRATION

Building

A.710

In the event that any dispute or difference between the [Contractor] and the [Sub-Contractor] which arises at any time before the issue of the Final Certificate of Payment under the Main Contract and the subject matter of such dispute thereof is substantially the same as a matter which is in dispute between the [Contractor] and the [Purchaser] and/or the Engineer which has been submitted to arbitration under the Main Contract. Then in such event the [Contractor] shall be entitled to require the [Sub-Contractor] to be joined as a party to such arbitration. The [Sub-Contractor] undertakes to agree to be joined to such arbitration and the costs to be paid by [specify].

A.711

Either party may at its own cost request access to third-party agreements held, owned, controlled or possessed by the other party who is believed or it is alleged to have failed to account, disclose information or acted in accordance with the terms of this Agreement. The party seeking access shall send a written request to the other party stating that within [fourteen days including weekends] of the date of receipt of the request that the other defaulting party shall permit an expert who shall be a nominated independent accountant, auditor or economist which is acceptable to both parties access to such third party agreements of the alleged defaulting party for the purpose of resolving the dispute.

A.712

The [Expert's] decision shall be final and binding on the parties and both parties agree to be bound by and to carry out the decision. The party who has been found by the [Expert] to be at fault shall within [seven days] of receipt of the [Expert's] decision pay to the other party the amount due together with interest at [number per cent] per annum above the base rate of [Bank plc] from the date on which such sums according to the decision of the [Expert] should have been paid.

A.713

The costs and expenses of the [Expert] shall be apportioned between both parties in such proportions as the [Expert] shall in her decision consider appropriate and the [Expert's] allocation of the costs shall be binding.

A.714

If at any time any question, dispute or difference shall arise between the [Purchaser] and the [Contractor] in relation to the contract or in any way

157

connected with the work proposed or to be carried out which cannot be settled by negotiation. Then either party shall as soon as reasonably practicable give to the other notice of the existence of such question, dispute or difference specifying its nature and the point at issue and the matter shall be referred to the arbitration of a person with suitable qualifications. The arbitrator who will consider evidence from both parties and then provide a decision to which both parties agree to be bound and to fulfil.

A.715

In the event that the parties cannot reach agreement upon the person with suitable qualifications and expertise to act as an [Expert] to consider the facts and reach a decision. Then within [specify period] after the date of such notice either party may apply for the arbitration to be conducted by some professional and suitably qualified person appointed by the President of the Institution of [Name] or by his deputy appointed by such President for the purpose. A question, dispute or difference relating to a decision, instruction or order of the [Expert] shall not be referred to arbitration unless the performance of the Contract is suspended. The performance of the Contract shall continue during arbitration proceedings unless the [Expert] shall order the Contract be suspended. If such suspension is to be ordered the additional costs to the [Contractor] occasioned by such suspension shall be [added to the Contract Price/ be subject to further agreement between the parties]. No payment due or payable by the [Purchaser] shall be withheld on account of a pending reference to arbitration.

General Business and Commercial

A.716

All questions or differences whatsoever arising from or relating to this Agreement shall be referred to a single Arbitrator to be agreed upon by the parties hereto or failing agreement to be appointed by the then [President of the Law Society] such Arbitrator to have all the powers conferred on arbitrators by any law, legislation, statute, directive, or regulation for the time being in force in [country].

A.717

If any dispute or difference shall arise between the parties hereto on any matter touching this Agreement or any matter arising therefrom the same shall be referred to the arbitration of a single Arbitrator to be agreed between the parties or in the case of failure to be nominated by [person] of [Company].

A.718

In the event of any dispute between the parties concerning the interpretation or application of this Agreement then both parties agree to refer the dispute to the following parties whose joint decision shall be binding on both parties:

1.1   [specify individual/body/company]; and

1.2   [specify individual/body/company].

A.719

Either party to this Agreement may elect for any reason not to resolve any difference or dispute through the arbitration procedure set out in this Agreement. In such event either party shall not be bound to accept the decision and either party may try to resolve the matter by any other method that they should so decide including mediation, alternative dispute resolution and litigation.

A.720

I agree to act as arbitrator to this Agreement if requested to do so by both the above named parties subject to agreement as to my costs. Signed by [Arbitrator] [Name] [Title] [date].

A.721

In the event of any dispute, disagreement or other claim or damage arising by either party from this Agreement then it is agreed that:

1.1   Each party shall specify the grounds of its complaint or defence in writing to the other to provide them with an opportunity of resolving the matter.

1.2   In the event that if after [specify period] any matter is still outstanding then either party may refer the issue to [–] of [–] provided that they agree to pay the cost of the arbitration. That [Company/person] shall act as arbitrator to offer a settlement of the issue and the costs to the satisfaction of both parties.

1.3   In the event that this system of settlement fails then either party may choose to exercise their legal rights and remedies.

A.722

Any dispute, disagreement, claim or inability to resolve differences of opinion regarding the terms, meaning or consequences of this Agreement arising directly or indirectly shall be submitted to the arbitration rules and procedures of [specify name of organisation]. All documents and proceedings shall be in [specify] language.

A.723

The parties agree that the decision of the Arbitrator shall [not] be final and binding on both the parties.

A.724

There shall be no obligation or right of either party to insist that any dispute or problem or interpretation of the contract shall be referred to arbitration or any other form of process. If any matter is referred however both parties agree that the decision of the arbitrator shall be final and binding and the allocation and payment of costs shall be as follows [specify].

A.725

In the event of any dispute and/or any disagreement in respect of the interpretation of the clauses and/or any allegation of breach of contract and/or some other allegation which is unresolved between the parties which relates to the Agreement. Then both parties agree to refer the dispute to an independent arbitrator whose cost shall be paid for by [specify]. The arbitrator shall be appointed by arrangement with [specify organisation]. The parties agree that the decision shall not be considered binding. Both parties agree not to commence legal proceedings during the arbitration process and until after it has ended. Either party shall have the option after completion of the arbitration process and/or within [one year] whichever is the earliest to commence legal proceedings.

A.726

Where there is any dispute of any nature regarding this Agreement then the [Licensor] shall have the right to notify the [Licensee] in writing that it wishes to enter into arbitration or mediation prior to taking any legal action against the [Licensee]. The written notification shall specify the reason for the request and the steps required to remedy the matter. The [Licensee] agrees to enter into arbitration or mediation if so notified in writing provided that the Licensor bears the cost for the appointment of the arbitrator or mediator.

A.727

There shall be no obligation on either party to agree and enter into any mediation, arbitration and/or alternative dispute resolution at any time. Where the [Licensor] has grounds for complaint and/or alleges breach of contract on any grounds including failure to pay any advance and/or royalties and/or produce and/or market the [DVD/Disc]. Then the [Distributor] agrees to arrange to meet with the [Licensor] and its legal representatives to discuss the complaint and/or the allegations in each case. The [Distributor] agrees to provide a written response within [one week] of any such complaint and/or allegations.

A.728

In the event of any dispute and/or allegation of breach of contract by either party arising from the terms of this Agreement. Then it is agreed that each party shall specify the grounds of its complaint and/or the allegations in writing to the other and shall set out the proposed terms upon which the matter could be resolved. Within [twenty-one days] the other party shall provide a detailed response in writing addressing each of the allegations. In the event that the parties cannot resolve any dispute they both agree that prior to any legal proceedings being issued that they shall consider the option of arbitration in order to save costs. In the event that both parties agree to pursue the option of arbitration then they agree that the cost of the arbitrator shall be paid for [equally between the parties/as ordered by the arbitrator]. The arbitrator shall be chosen by the parties from a recommended list issued by [specify institute]. The parties agree and undertake that if they enter into arbitration at any time that the decision of the arbitrator shall not be a full and final settlement of the dispute and the costs unless a formal settlement document has been drawn up by the relevant legal advisors and is signed by a director of each party. In the event that this system of settlement fails then either party may choose to exercise their legal rights and remedies.

A.729

Where there are more than [number] parties involved in this [Project] it is agreed that where more than [number] per cent wish to refer the matter to arbitration. That all the parties shall endeavour to agree the terms of arbitration and shall bear the costs in equal proportions. Provided that the arbitration shall take place in the [specify] language in [country] and be held within [number/months] of the dispute arising and be subject to the following legislation and policy [specify].

A.730

Where any disputes, errors, omissions, claims and/or damages, expenses, costs and/or other issues shall arise between the [Company] and [Name]. Then the parties agree that they shall be entitled to try to reach agreement through any method including mediation, arbitration, dispute resolution but there is no obligation to do so. The parties agree that they shall disclose all relevant data, plans, invoices and other information and material which may support their case and shall set out a statement in detail of the facts prior to taking any legal action.

A.731

Where a serious dispute arises between the parties which involves a claim for more than [number/currency] by one and/or more parties. Then it is agreed that the [Licensor/Licensee] shall try to settle the matter through arbitration and/or mediation using [specify method/institute] at which each party shall bear its own initial costs until a final decision is reached by the person appointed to act as arbitrator.

A.732

The parties agree that where the total sum in dispute is less than [number/currency] that there shall be no obligation to take the matter to arbitration. Further than any legal action by either party shall be in the [name] courts under the [quick claims process] in [country].

Merchandising

A.733

There shall be no obligation to enter any form of mediation, arbitration and/or alternative dispute resolution prior to the start of any legal proceedings. Any such agreement shall be subject to the terms of a separate document agreed between and signed by both parties.

A.734

Where there is a dispute between the parties and/or disagreement as to the terms, the rights and/or any payments made and/or due. Then the parties agree to negotiate and conclude an arbitration procedure with an independent third party who can review that facts and make a recommendation as to the settlement of any such matter.

A.735

Both the [Licensor] and the [Licensee] shall be bound by the rules, terms and conditions of [specify institute] in respect of any process in place to resolve disputes and/or disagreements as to interpretation. Both parties agree that they shall endeavour to follow the dispute settlement process subject to the cost of administration and legal representation.

A.736

The [Supplier] agrees that where the [Client] is in dispute with the [Supplier] regarding the source and/or content of any [Product/Article] that the [Supplier] has manufactured and/or supplied. That the [Supplier] accepts and agrees that a written report which identifies and specifies failures by the [Supplier] to adhere to [international] health and safety standards and/or content supported by scientific tests, site visits and recommendations by a recognised government department in [country] known as [specify] and/or a private inspector engaged by the [Client] shall be regarded as conclusive evidence against the [Supplier].

A.737

Where the [Supplier] is based outside [country] which is the main office of the [Client]. In the event that the parties agree to enter into arbitration to resolve a matter. Then the [Supplier] agrees that the arbitration shall take place in [country] in [city] in [specify] language according to the procedure and process set out by [specify organisation] as at the time of the dispute. Failure to reach terms of arbitration within a period of [number] months of the dispute arising and/or being notified to the other party shall mean that either party may take legal action as they think fit in any country of the world.

Publishing

A.738
Both the [Author] and the [Publisher] agree to resolve any disputes concerning this Agreement either through referral to arbitration under the rules of [specify institute or other body] or to the Informal Disputes Settlement Procedure of the [body] in [country].

A.739
If any difference shall arise between the [Publishers] and the [Author] regarding the interpretation of this Agreement including the rights and liabilities of the parties such matters shall be referred to the arbitration of two persons one named by either party and the cost to be paid for by [specify].

A.740
Any dispute arising in respect of this contract shall be settled in accordance with the procedure for the settlement of disputes set forth in the Agreement between [–] and the Company.

A.741
Any disputes arising from the interpretation and/or execution of this contract shall be settled through negotiations by both parties and if that shall fail the conciliation process and if that shall fail arbitration by an agreed organisation or individual. The parties reserve the right to issue legal proceedings unless a matter has been finally resolved to the satisfaction of both parties.

A.742
All disputes which may at any time arise between the [Author] and the [Publishing Company] in respect of the Agreement or the subject matter thereof and whether as to construction or otherwise shall be referred to a joint committee composed of a nominee of the [Author] and a nominee of the [Publishing Company] whose unanimous decision shall be binding. Failing unanimous agreement the disputes shall be referred to a sole arbitrator to be agreed upon by the parties to the contract and in default of such agreement to a sole arbitrator to be nominated by [specify institute or body] and shall act in accordance with the existing law relating to arbitration at that time.

A.743

If any difference shall arise between the [Publisher] and the [Company] concerning any part of this Agreement, and its meaning or the rights, obligations and liabilities of the parties. The case shall be referred to alternative dispute resolution, mediation, conciliation or arbitration or such other method as shall be agreed in writing between the parties in order to minimise the costs of the dispute and resolve the matter quickly.

A.744

The parties agree that arbitration, mediation and formal dispute resolution may be considered and proposed prior to taking legal action but there is no obligation to do so. The parties agree that the [Work] supplied by the [Licensor] has been made available worldwide by the [Company] and that the business and premises of the [Company] are international. The [Company] agrees that any legal action, arbitration, mediation and/or formal dispute resolution shall be limited to the legislation of [country] and take place in [City].

Services

A.745

The [Manager] and the [Sportsperson] agree that prior to the commencement of any legal proceedings in the event of a dispute, difference or other problems which arise pursuant to this Agreement which cannot be resolved by negotiation between the parties. That without prejudice to any legal rights of either party the parties agree to refer the matter to the [body] for their advice and guidance, but which shall not be binding, in order to try to resolve the matter.

A.746

If any dispute or difference of any nature shall occur which is not resolved within [specify period] of the issue arising between the parties then both parties agree that in order to try to void litigation the parties agree to appoint an [arbitrator] from the [body] at the cost of [–] to resolve the matter. The decision shall not be binding on either party, but the parties must agree in advance and be bound by the allocation and liability of the cost.

A.747

In the event that there is a dispute arising from the operation of the Agreement covered by this document the following procedures shall apply:

1.1 There shall be a meeting between a representative of the [Company] and a Union Representative of the [Person], at which the member shall also be present if he so wishes.

1.2   In the event of a failure to agree at the above meeting a further meeting shall be held between the [Union] and the [Company] to seek to resolve the dispute.

1.3   In the event of a further failure to agree consideration shall be given to conciliation or arbitration in a form mutually to be agreed or to a reference to [institute or body] in [country].

1.4   It is expressly agreed and understood that this disputes procedure does not constitute a contractual obligation for parties to this Agreement to follow and that it is included to help regulate and settle any difficulties and dispute that may arise in the spirit and intention of maintaining good relations between the parties to the Agreement.

A.748

There is no obligation on the [person] or the [Company] to refer any dispute, alleged breach or otherwise under this Agreement to arbitration, mediation or dispute resolution. All proposals to resolve any matter by any of these methods will need the prior written consent of both parties in a document which states the procedure, the time-scale, the cost and the effect of the decision.

A.749

The [Company] agrees to act in a reasonable manner in the event of a dispute or other inability to resolve an important issue in respect of the contract which has or will arise. The parties agree to meet with a fixed agenda with a list of issues set out by each party at a suitable venue with [person] whose role will be to act as unofficial arbitrator.

A.750

All disputes, complaints or otherwise shall be referred to [body/person] whether related to the fulfilment of the terms of this Agreement or the quality of the [goods/services].

A.751

As far as possible the parties agree not to take legal action without exploring all other avenues of settlement including discussions, alternative dispute resolution, mediation, arbitration, set off and other methods reasonably available. The appointment and allocation of cost shall be agreed in advance by the parties, but may reimbursed as part of a final settlement.

A.752

Where services have been and/or are provided by any person through the [Supplier] who has failed to provide a reasonable quality of work according to the order placed by the [Company]. Then the [Supplier] agrees to substitute an alternative person to complete the work at no extra cost to the [Company]. Where the work is still not completed and/or fulfilled then the [Company] may engage a third party and seek to recover all the cost from the [Supplier] for such work as may be required. Provided that the [Supplier] is given the opportunity before the third party starts the work to complete the work on the exact same terms at the [Suppliers]' cost.

Sponsorship

A.753

The [Sponsor] agrees and undertakes that in the event there is any allegation by the [Sponsor] against the [Company] for any reason. That the [Sponsor] will not automatically issue legal proceedings, but will explore all available non-litigious avenues to resolve the matter. That prior to the issue of any writ the [Sponsor] will consider and attempt all the following methods:

1.1   Amicable discussions.

1.2   A written exchange of the basis of the allegations and the defence.

1.3   Arbitration and/or the appointment of an independent expert approved by both parties by [specify institute].

A.754

The [Sponsor] and the [Distributor] agree and undertake to resolve all disputes, complaints, allegations of breach of contract and/or non-payment of any sums by means of arbitration. Both parties agree that the arbitrator should be a member of [specify institute] and qualified as [specify profession]. The appointment of the arbitrator shall be subject to the prior written approval of both parties. The arbitrator shall decide who shall bear the cost and expenses of the arbitration based on the facts of the case. Both parties agree and undertake to be bound by the final decision of the arbitrator.

A.755

In the event that the parties cannot agree upon any matter concerning the interpretation, exercise and/or performance of the obligations, liability and/or any other issue concerning this Agreement. Then the parties shall endeavour to reach heads of agreement as to how to resolve the problem. Both parties reserve the right unless otherwise agreed in writing at any stage to take such legal steps as may be necessary to protect their interests.

A.756

The parties agree that any arbitration, legal proceedings and/or other procedures shall be taken in [country] by either party. Both agree and waive the right to do so in any other part of the world at any time in respect of this Agreement and any matter that may arise either directly and/or indirectly.

University, Library and Educational

A.757

The [Institute] and the [Contributor] agree that in the event that there are any disputes, complaints, and/or allegations made by one party against the other arising from the interpretation, performance, fulfilment, rights and/or any other matter relating to this Agreement. That in the first instance the parties shall try to resolve the matter through negotiations by both parties. If that shall fail then the parties agree to consider the option of entering into arbitration prior to any litigation. There shall be no obligation on either party to enter into arbitration and both parties reserve the right to commence legal proceedings at any time.

A.758

The [Institute] and the [Author] agree to resolve any disputes, allegations, complaints, and other problems of any nature arising under this Agreement which cannot be resolved between the parties by one of the following procedures either arbitration, mediation, or informal disputes settlement. Both parties agree that they shall endeavour to resolve any matter through one of these procedures prior to the commencement of any legal proceedings.

A.759

The [Institute] and the [Company] agree that where there is any dispute, and/or difference of opinion as to interpretation of the terms and/or there are allegations that one party has failed to perform their part of the Agreement and/or other problems which arise pursuant to this Agreement. That in the first instance both parties agree that they shall endeavour to resolve the problems by negotiation between the parties. In any event the parties shall not be obliged to do this for more than [one calendar month] from the date on which one party has notified the other of the problem in each case. That without prejudice to any legal rights of either party the parties agree to then refer the matter to an independent [arbitrator/mediator] in [country] in accordance with the rules and regulations of [specify Organisation] governed by [specify country] law. The parties agree that the decision of the [arbitrator/mediator] shall not be binding unless agreed in advance between the parties in writing.

A.760

In the event that the parties cannot agree upon the interpretation, rights, performance, obligations, liability and/or any other issue concerning this Agreement. Then both parties agree to refer the dispute to the following [organisations/body/person] [specify detail]. The parties shall reach agreement as to the terms of reference, whether the decision is to be binding and the allocation of costs. Both parties reserve the right unless otherwise agreed in writing at any stage to take legal action against the other at any stage.

A.761

The [Consortium] and each party to it agree that where there is a dispute relating to this [Project] between the parties and/or between the [Consortium] and any third party. That the legal advice of [firm] shall be sought for a total budget of no more than [number/currency] which shall be paid for out of the sums held by [Name] under this Agreement. There shall be no obligation on any party to pay additional legal costs and/or to make a contribution to any arbitration and/or mediation costs and/or to taking legal action where any such party does not wish to proceed either due to the legal advice and/or because of the financial cost and risk involved.

ASSIGNMENT

Employment

A.762

The [Executive] acknowledges and agrees that all intellectual property rights, domain names, inventions and patents, copyright, design rights, property rights, rights to data, and databases, trade marks, service marks, community marks and any other rights in the services or any work at any time of the [Executive] in the course of or in connection with her employment shall remain and be the sole and exclusive property of the [Company]. This Agreement does not purport to assign, grant, or transfer any such rights to the [Executive].

A.763

The [Executive] may not reproduce or otherwise exploit any material or work created in the course of her employment or at the [Company's] request without the prior written consent of the [position] of the [Company] in each case.

A.764

Without prejudice to the statutory or legal rights and remedies of the [Executive], the [Executive] shall during the course of his employment (or after the end of the Agreement or if there is a dispute or litigation), at the request and cost of the [Company] execute and assist in the assignment to the [Company] of any right, domain name, discovery, invention, patent, or otherwise that may be required to protect the intellectual and proprietary rights of the [Company]. The [Company] shall pay the full cost and expense of an independent legal advisor for the [Executive] in such circumstances, and an agreed sum for the [Executive] for his services when the Agreement has ended.

A.765

It is agreed between the [Company] and the [Employee]:

1.1   That the [Employee] shall not acquire, obtain, register in his name, own, exploit or transfer any intellectual property rights, patents, inventions, copyright, computer software, trade marks, logos, service marks, community marks, design rights, database rights, domain name, music, lyrics, slogan in any material, text, images, artwork, maps, diagrams, computer generated material, film, recordings, sound, development, concept, format or product created during the course of their employment at any time in any media or on any subject.

1.2   That the [Employee] undertakes to assign and authorise any documentation required by the [Company] which may be necessary to transfer, register or confirm the position set out in 1.1 above to a third party in any [country]. Provided that where personal expenses, costs and legal fees are to be incurred by the [Employee] for that purpose then the [Company] agrees to pay.

A.766

The [Employee] assigns to the [Company] all rights, copyright, intellectual property rights, interest, claims and or title of any nature in all media in any format and/or medium which may exist now or be developed at any time in the planning, production, and completion of any work and/or services that he/she may fulfil as part of their existing and/or future duties at the [Company] [whether at the premises of the [Company], at the offices of a [Client] and/or at home.] for the full period of copyright in any country of the world and for infinity and beyond.

A.767

[Name] agrees and accepts that there shall be no right to any sums from the exploitation and/or licensing and/or assignment and/or registration of any ideas, concepts, formats, proposals, development projects, research, surveys, data, images, text, sound and/or film, index, music, logo, artwork, photographs, maps, website material, apps, mobile phone content and texts, games, quizzes, competitions, gambling, books, DVDs and/or any other material originated and/or contributed to by [Name] during office hours and/or at home while in the employment of the [Company] which arise directly and/or indirectly from the employment of [Name] by the [Company].

DVD, Video and Discs

A.768

In consideration of the Budget for the production of the [Series] by the [Assignor] based on a project created by [Name]. The [Assignor] agrees to assign to the [Assignee] the sole and exclusive DVD and Video Rights and Non-Theatric Rights in the [Series] and parts throughout the Territory for [specify period]. Upon expiry of that period then the rights shall revert back to joint copyright ownership between the parties. The [Assignee] agrees that it shall pay and the [Assignor] shall be entitled to the [Assignor's] Royalties in respect of the exploitation of the DVD and Video Rights and the Non-Theatric Rights.

A.769

Subject to the above Clause [–] the [Assignor] and the [Assignee] both agree that they shall hold joint present and future copyright and all other rights in the [Series] and parts in all media whether in existence now or created in the future throughout the Territory for the full period of copyright and any extensions and renewals. Further that the consent of both parties shall be required to exploit such rights which shall be the subject of separate agreements in each case.

A.770

In consideration of the payment of the Budget and the Assignment Fee the [Assignor] assigns to the [Assignee] All Media Rights in the [DVD/Video/Disc/Work] and parts throughout the [countries] for the full period of copyright and any extensions and renewals [which shall continue in perpetuity].

A.771

In consideration of the payment of the Assignment Fee the [Company] assigns to the [Distributor] the sole and exclusive DVD Rights in the [Film] including any parts throughout the [country] for the [full period of copyright and any extensions and renewals] from [date] to [date].

A.772

1.1   In consideration of the [Fee] the [Author] assigns the right to reproduce and/or exploit the [Work] in the following formats to the [Distributor] in [country] from [date] to [date] [DVD/VHS/Audiotapes/Discs] to be played on computer and/or laptop and/or other gadget] specified as follows [–].

1.2 All other formats and methods not specifically mentioned above are excluded. No rights are granted and/or assigned in respect of any rights owned and/or controlled by the [Author] in respect of the exploitation of rights on the internet and/or by means of any telecommunication system including mobile phones and/or any storage and retrieval and download system. Nor is any right granted and/or assigned by the [Author] which permits and/or allows the [Distributor] to register any copyright, domain name, business name and/or company based on and/or derived from any character, title, slogan and/or any other content and/or new material directly and/or indirectly arising from the [Work].

A.773

In consideration of the [fee] which shall be due on [date] that [Name] shall pay the [Assignor] in full by electronic transfer direct to their notified bank account. The [Assignor] assigns to [Name] all copyright and intellectual property rights and interest and any other rights which may exist at any time in any part of the world either now and/or later in the [Material/Recordings/other] and any associated title, logo, image, slogan and documents listed in Schedule [–] attached to this Agreement.

A.774

The [Assignor] agrees and accepts that this assignment shall prohibit any future claim by the estate of the [Assignor] and/or any trustees and/or beneficiaries. That the [assignor] shall specifically not mention any such [Material] in their will and/or inheritance documents once it has been assigned to [Name].

A.775

That the [Assignor] agrees that [Name] may register the title, logo, personal name, signature, image and other material listed in Appendix [–] in the name of the [Assignee] with any type of body to record and register their interest and ownership in any part of the world.

Film and Television

A.776

1.1 In consideration of the payment of the Advance and the [Assignor's] Royalties the [Assignor] assigns to the [Company] the sole and exclusive rights to the [Work] in all media except [specify formats/rights/countries] throughout the Territory for the full period of copyright and any extensions and renewals and forever without any limit on the duration of time.

1.2 The [Assignor] agrees and undertakes to assist the [Company] in respect of the transfer of any copyright ownership to the [Company] and/or the collection of any sums due in respect of the rights assigned to the [Company]. The [Assignor] and/or an authorised representative shall sign and/or complete such affidavits, documents, registration forms and collecting society forms that may be necessary.

1.3 In the event that the [Company] fails to pay the Advance and/or the [Assignor's] Royalties by the dates set out in this Agreement. Then the [Assignor] shall have the right to serve written notice on the [Company] to terminate the Agreement with immediate effect and all rights in the [Work] and any new developments including ownership of any material shall revert to the [Assignor].

A.777

In consideration of the [Presenter's] Fee the [Presenter] assigns to the [Company] all present and future copyright, and all trade marks, domain names and any other intellectual property rights in all media throughout the world and universe in the product of her services and any other material created hereunder for the purpose of this Agreement for the full period of copyright and any extensions and renewals and in perpetuity including but not limited to films, formats, books, brochures, catalogues and publications, advertisements, scripts, website and newsfeed material, programme and slot titles, slogans, jingles, music, photographs, sound or other recordings, DVDs, CDs, marketing material, scripts, interactive and/or website and internet material, computer software, discs, CD-Roms.

A.778

The [Presenter] agrees that any intellectual property, trade marks, patents, property rights of any kind, domain names and computer software including but not limited to copyright, design rights, service marks, trade marks, logos, inventions, titles, slogans, and any other rights or material held by the [Company] or which are created or developed in conjunction with the services of the [Presenter] shall be the sole and exclusive property of the [Company]. The [Presenter] shall not acquire any rights or interest nor does this Agreement purport to grant, assign or transfer such rights in the product of the services to the [Presenter] in any form.

A.779

In consideration of the Fee and the Repeat Fees the [Name] assigns to the [Company] all present and future copyright and any other rights in all media throughout the Territory in the product of his services and any other material created for the purpose of this Agreement for the full period of copyright and any extensions and renewals. This assignment is subject to the clause set out below.

A.780

The [Company] agrees that it shall not be entitled to use, exploit or license any of the material produced or created for the purposes of this Agreement in which the Celebrity appears in sound or vision or by any other reference for any purpose at any time other than the endorsement, promotion or advertising of the [Company] or the [Company's Product] during the Term of the Agreement. Where the [Company] wishes to use any such material at any time for any purpose or to license a third party then it is clear that the prior written consent of the [Name] is required and the terms agreed in writing for such use including payment in writing by both parties.

A.781

In consideration of the fees the [Contributor] assigns to the [Company] the sole and exclusive rights in all media whether now known or hereinafter invented in the [Film] and/or parts including the soundtrack and in any other product of the services of the [Contributor] under this Agreement throughout the [Territory/world/universe] for the full period of copyright and any extensions and renewals including but not limited to: all forms of television, satellite, cable, digital terrestrial; all forms of video, DVD, CD, CD Rom, games and computer software; merchandising, publishing, interactive multi-media in any text, sound, vision or otherwise; the storage, retrieval or dissemination of information; websites and the internet; mobile phones and any other device for telecommunication systems; and the right to authorise, reproduce, licence and transfer any such rights to third parties and to exploit any such rights at any time in any format and in any form in whole or in part.

A.782

The [Contributor] agrees on request to execute and sign any other documents which may be required at a later date to effect the assignment to the [Company].

A.783

In consideration of the Assignment Fee the [Director] assigns all present and future copyright and any other rights in all media throughout the world in the product of his services and in the [Programme] and any other material created during the existence of this Agreement to the [Company] for the full period of copyright and any extensions or renewals. For the avoidance of doubt all media shall include but not be limited to television, internet, radio, video, DVD, CD-Rom, computer software and games, publishing and merchandising.

A.784

In consideration of the [Presenter's] Fee and the [Presenter's] Royalties the [Presenter] assigns to the [Company] the Television Rights, the DVD and Video Rights, the Theatric Rights and the Non-Theatric Rights in the product of her services in the [Series] (including the scripts and sound recordings) under this Agreement throughout the Territory for the full period of copyright and any extensions and renewals. The [Company] agrees that all rights not specifically assigned to the [Company] in this clause [–] are reserved by the [Presenter].

A.785

The [Assignor] and the [Company] agree that in consideration of the [Company] funding the full cost of the [Pilot] the [Company] shall become the joint copyright owner of the [Pilot] with the [Assignor]. The [Assignor] assigns to the [Company] the joint copyright ownership with the [Assignor] in the [Pilot] whether in existence now or created in the future in all the Media Rights throughout the [world/country] for the full period of copyright and any extensions and renewals [except for any rights in the Format]. The [Company] acknowledges and agrees that all copyright and any rights in the Format shall remain vested in the [Assignor].

A.786

In consideration of the provision of the Budget by the [Assignee] to the [Assignor] to make the [Film], the [Assignor] assigns all present and future copyright in respect of the Television Rights, the DVD and Video Rights, the Non-Theatric Rights and the Theatric Rights in the [Film] and parts throughout the Territory for the duration of the Assignment Period which shall commence on the date of this Agreement and continue until [date].

A.787

The [Assignee] agrees that all other rights in the [Film] not specifically assigned under this agreement shall remain the property of the [Assignor] including but not limited to any merchandising, publication rights, computer software and games.

A.788

The [Assignee] undertakes that at the end of the Assignment Period it will execute any document or do anything required by the [Assignor] to confirm the reversion of rights to the [Assignor]. So that no rights in the [Film] are held by the [Assignee] after that time.

A.789

In consideration of the payment of the Approved Budget by the [Distributor] and the payment of the [Producer's] Royalties, the [Producer] assigns to

174

the [Distributor] the sole and exclusive All Media Rights which are defined in clause [–] in the [Series] and/or parts throughout the [world] for the full period of copyright and any extensions, renewals or variations in perpetuity and without limitation.

A.790

[Name] assigns to the [Company] all copyright and other rights of ownership, interest and/.or control of any nature which may exist now and/or be created by law, technological developments and/or otherwise in the future. [Name] agrees that the assignment shall be for the full period of copyright and any extensions and/or renewals and continue indefinitely without limitation in respect of all rights regardless of when those rights may arise. [Name] agrees that the consideration shall be limited to a payment of [number/currency] by the [Company] to [Name] by [date]. No delay in payment shall effect the transfer of this assignment unless payment is not received by [Name] by [date].

A.791

In consideration of the payments under this agreement the [Marketing Company] assigns to the [Distributor] all copyright rights and any other intellectual property rights in all media throughout the universe in the following material which it has been commissioned to develop and create and promote and shall retain no right whatsoever to exploit any such material at any time:

1.1   Surveys and data.

1.2   Advertisements and poster campaigns.

1.3   Apps and mobile text and image messages.

1.4   Call centre responses.

1.5   Competition rules and terms of entry.

1.6   Jingles, music and sound recordings.

1.7   Stills, photographs, films, sketches, caricatures, cartoons.

1.8   Press releases, rights documents, and any other material stored in any form and/or medium.

A.792

The [Agent] agrees and undertakes that they are authorised by [Name] to assign all the copyright and any other intellectual property rights to the [Company] in respect of the performance of [Name] in the [Programme] and any associated promotional material for the full period of copyright and in perpetuity throughout the universe. That where at a later date the signature of [Name] is required for any reason to effect such transfer to the [Company] that the [Agent] shall arrange for [Name] to sign any such documents provided that the [Company] agrees to pay any expenses and costs that [Name] may incur.

General Business and Commercial

A.793

In consideration of the payment of the Assignment Fee by the [Assignee] to the [Assignor] the [Assignor] assigns All Media Rights which are in existence now or may be created in the future in the [Work] or parts to be assigned to the [Assignee] for the Assignment Period throughout the Territory. 'All Media Rights' shall mean all intellectual property rights of whatever nature including without limitation all copyright, trade marks, service marks, community marks, design rights, trade secrets, moral rights and confidential information and domain names. The sole and exclusive right to adapt, vary, delete from and add to, use, copy, license, authorise, print, transmit, disseminate, store retrieve, display, process, record, playback, rent, lend, supply or sale, distribute, market, use for sponsorship or for endorsement of any material, services, or person, promote or otherwise exploit by any method, medium or process whether created in the future or in existence now of any nature and any developments or variations or adaptations whether text, visual images, photographs, drawings, plans, sketches, electronically generated, video, computer or other method for creating art, graphics, and other material, sounds, sound effects, music, software, interactive, information, logos, background, banner, bookmark, border table, caption, character, clip art, cartoons, computer generated art, map image, map link, data, domain name, footnotes, titles, headings including but not limited to:

1.1   All forms of television including standard, cable, digital, satellite;

1.2   All forms of radio including cable, digital and satellite;

1.3   All forms of telecommunication systems including telephones, mobile phones, pagers;

1.4   All forms of mechanical reproduction including videograms, lasers, discs, cassettes, DVDs;

1.5   All forms of non-theatric audiences whether for business or commercial use, educational, cultural, religious or social, schools, colleges, universities, museums, readings, plays, addresses, speeches, lectures, seminars, conferences, or discussions;

1.6   All forms of theatric exploitation including cinemas;

1.7   All forms of publishing in printed form, hardback, paperback, digests, serialisation, newspapers, magazines, comics, periodicals, quotations, anthologies or translations in any such format in any language;

1.8   All forms of publishing and/or dissemination of information and/or deposit scheme by any electronic method and process including but not limited to the internet, worldwide web, intranet, downloads, eBooks, blogs, podcasts, newsfeeds and emails;

1.9   All forms of computer software and interactive multi-media such as compact discs, CD-Roms, computer games including all circumstances where there is an element of interactivity and/or there is a combination of sound, text, vision, graphics, or otherwise;

1.10 All forms of merchandising, toys, clothing, mugs, stationery, games, posters, shoes, games, and any other two or three dimensional representation;

1.11 Theatre, stage plays;

1.12 Films, advertisements, banner advertisements;

1.13 All rights in any title, chapter heading, format, character, storyline, rules, entry conditions, equipment and layout.

1.14 All forms of storage and retrieval in any form in any medium and all database rights, rights in any index and/or taxonomy.

1.15 All forms of reproduction and/or methods of delivery of all and/or any part in any medium including photocopying, scanning, and document delivery.

1.16 All forms of exploitation of the sound, music, lyrics, words, titles whether as audio files, ringtones, downloads, CDs, audiotapes, sheet music or any other form.

A.794

In consideration of the [Assignment Fee] the [Assignor] assigns to the [Assignee] all intellectual property rights and any other rights in the [Work] and the [Work Material] which are owned or controlled by the [Assignor] for the full period of copyright including any extensions and renewals to continue indefinitely in perpetuity throughout the [Territory/world/universe].

A.795

In consideration of the [Assignment Fee] the [Assignor] assigns to the [Assignee] all intellectual property rights and any other rights in the [Work] and the [Work Material] which are owned or controlled by the [Assignor] from [start date] to [end date] in [country]. After the [end date] all the intellectual property rights and any other rights in the [Work Material] and any development and/or variation shall be assigned by the [Assignee] to the [Assignor].

A.796

'The Work Material' shall mean all material of the [Work] in the possession or under the control of the [Assignor] [excluding accounts, or financial records relating to sums received but not expenses incurred for creating and exploiting material] including:

1.1 All copies of any master material in any form;

1.2 A list of locations at which any material is held together with access letters giving irrevocable authority for the [Assignee] to remove such material; and

1.3 All documents, records, data in any form and other material of any nature including contracts, licences, invoices relating to material expenses, consents, waivers, lists, proofs, scripts, publicity, advertising material, computer software, photographs, negatives, posters, catalogues, drawings, plans, sketches, electronically generated material, sounds, sound effects, music, computer generated art, video, DVDs, film, data, and databases.

The [Assignor] agrees that it shall not retain any rights or interest in the [Work] and/or the [Work Material].

A.797

The [Assignor] also transfers and grants to the [Assignee] All Media Rights in the [Work] and the [Work Material] in respect of the following matters [except those owned or controlled by a third party] including any associated goodwill:

1.1 Trade Marks and Community Marks.

1.2 Design rights.

1.3 Service Marks.

1.4 Logos.

1.5 Domain Names.

1.6 Trade secrets and confidential information.

1.7 Music and Sound Recordings associated with any of the material in 1.1 to 1.5 above.

A.798

The [Assignor] undertakes and agrees that he is the original creator and the sole owner of all copyright and any other rights in the [Work] which are assigned under this Agreement. That the [Assignor] has not exploited the [Work] in any form except those listed in Schedule [–].

A.799

That the [Assignor] undertakes and agrees that he is the sole owner of all intellectual property rights including copyright and any other rights in the [Work Material] which are bound by the following obligations, payments, credits and moral rights a complete list of which is set out in Schedule [–] to this Agreement. The [Assignor] shall be responsible for all sums due and other obligations up to the day before this Agreement and the [Assignee] shall bear all cost and expenses owed and obligations to any third party from the date of this Agreement.

A.800

In consideration of the payment of the Assignment Fee in full by the agreed date the [Assignor] assigns to the [Assignee] all present and future copyright and all other rights in all media whether in existence now or developed by new technology or by changes in the law in the [Work] including any parts and the [Work Material Package] throughout the Territory for the full period of copyright and any extensions and renewals including but not limited to:

1.1 All forms of exploitation through the medium of television and radio whether the transmission is terrestrial, by cable, digital, satellite, microwave, over the air; whether free, pay per view, encrypted or not or otherwise;

1.2 All forms of exploitation through telecommunication systems, computer software and hardware, DVDs, CD Roms, telephones, mobile phones, pagers, electronic merchandise or the internet;

1.3 All forms of exploitation through videos, cassettes, lasers, discs, merchandising, cinemas, non-paying audiences in educational, cultural, religious and social establishments, clubs, universities, and/ or commercial use by businesses;

1.4 All forms of publishing whether in printed or electronic form; and/or

1.5 All forms of exploitation not covered above in any medium.

A.801

The [Assignor] and the [Assignee] agree that the assignment in Clause [–] is subject to the following existing agreements [list documents]. Copies of the existing agreements are attached to and form part of this Agreement as Schedule [–].

A.802

The [Company] acknowledges and agrees that this Agreement is not intended and does not constitute an assignment of the rights in the [Work] and/or any part to the [Company]. Where for any reason new material is created in the future by any third party commissioned by the [Company] and/or the [Company] creates and/or develops any new material based on and/or derived from the [Work]. Then the [Company] agrees and undertakes to assign and/or to ensure the assignment of all rights in all media in the [Work] and/or parts throughout the world to the [Author] so that the [Author] owns and/or controls such rights.

A.803

No rights of any nature are intended to be transferred by virtue of this letter of [Confidentiality] by the [Seller] to the [Buyer] except as expressly stated.

A.804

The [Name] agrees that on request by the [Company] at the [Company's] sole cost and expense he shall execute and sign such other documents as may reasonably be required by their professional legal advisors to vest the [intellectual property rights/copyright/other rights] assigned under this Agreement in the [Company].

A.805

1.1   The [Distributor] agrees and undertakes that it shall assign all the copyright and any other rights in any new material based on and/or derived from and/or associated with the [Work] of any nature in any medium to the [Author/Copyright Owner] (whether the new material is commissioned from a third party and/or created by an employee and/or consultant).

1.2   The [Distributor] agrees and undertakes that the assignment in clause [–] above shall include but not be limited to translations, packaging, marketing, newspaper, television and radio advertisements, banner ads, links, logos, slogans, images, text and trade marks.

1.3   That the [Distributor] agrees and undertakes to bear all the legal and administrative expenses that may be incurred by both parties in order to ensure the effective transfer of all such rights to the [Author/Copyright Owner].

A.806

The parties agree that this assignment is intended to be a full and effective transfer to the [Company] of all rights in all media in all formats throughout the universe in the [Work] and any parts and all associated material listed in Schedule [–]. If for any reason a new right is created by the development of new technology and/or new legislation and/or an existing right has to be registered. Then the [Author/Contributor] agrees and undertakes to sign and execute any additional legal documents that may be required to ensure that all rights are held, owned and controlled by the [Company]. Provided that the [Company] agrees and undertakes to pay for all legal, administrative and other costs that may be incurred by both parties [and also pays the [Author/Contributor] an additional fee of [figure/currency] in each such case].

A.807
The [Consortium] agree and undertake that where is order to effect an assignment and/or registration of any rights and/or interest of any [Material] created and/or developed and/or designed and/or which can be registered and/or for which application can be made to protect the rights. Then it is agreed between the parties that the owner shall be [specify] of [address] in which each party to the [Consortium] shall hold equal shares and the directors of which shall be [specify].

A.808
Where the [Company] fails and/or delays more than [specify period] to pay the Fee and/or any royalties due to [Name] under this Agreement at any time. Then [Name] shall be entitled to serve notice that the consideration under this Agreement has not been complied with in full and that the assignment clause fails to take effect due to such circumstances. [Name] may therefore also serve notice that the Agreement is terminated with immediate effect and that all copyright and any other rights in the [Work] shall revert to [Name].

A.809
It agreed that [name] shall assign to the [Company] all copyright and intellectual property rights in the [Script/Work] which may exist in any media including but not limited to television, film, animation and cartoons, blu-ray, DVD, publishing, online business, advertising and marketing, mobiles phones and computers, games, food and drink and other household and commercial products and merchandising, audio, radio, wireless and other forms of communication and exploitation, development and adaptation of any nature which exist in [year] and/or thereafter in any time and/or space.

Internet and Websites

A.810
1.1   You shall not acquire and you are not granted the right to use, assign, licence, exploit and/or adapt any copyright, intellectual property rights, trade marks, logos, slogans, artwork, text, emails, film, video, podcasts,

blogs, news feeds, television, radio, sound recordings, audio material, domain names, databases, computer software, taxonomy, sitemap and/or any other rights and/or material of any nature.

1.2 All rights in all media of any nature belong to [Company] unless stated otherwise.

1.3 It is a condition of your use of this [Website] that any person and/or company that registers to gain access must agree to assign to the [Company] all copyright and other intellectual property rights which they may own and/or control in any email, film, video, advertisement, photograph and/or other material which is sent by them to be displayed on the [Website] for the full period of copyright including any extensions and renewals to continue indefinitely in perpetuity throughout the world and universe.

A.811

The [Company] shall not acquire any copyright and/or any other rights in any emails, text, film, video, advertisement, photographs, images and/or any other material which is submitted, sent, displayed, sold and/or supplied by any member of the public and/or any business and/or charity and/or educational establishment to any section of this [Website]. There shall be no obligation to assign any rights to the [Company] and/or to pay any percentage of any sums received.

A.812

The [Artist] agrees and undertakes:

1.1 That he/she is the sole and original creator of the [Artwork/Design].

1.2 That the [Artwork/Design] is owned by the [Artist].

1.3 That the [Artwork/Design] has not been licensed, exploited and/or adapted in any format in any medium by the [Artist] and/or any third party.

1.4 In consideration of the payment of the Assignment Fee the [Artist] assigns to the [Website Company] all present and future copyright and all other intellectual property rights in all media and in all [formats/medium] whether in existence now or developed by new technology or by changes in the law or otherwise in the [Artwork/Design] throughout the [world/universe] for the full period of copyright and any extensions and renewals and forever without limit of time. For the avoidance of doubt it is agreed that 'all media' shall include but not be limited to terrestrial, cable, digital and satellite television and radio; whether free, pay per view, encrypted or not. All methods of telecommunication systems, computer software and hardware, laptops, DVDs, CD Roms, discs, telephones, mobile phones, pagers, the internet, websites and downloads, gadgets, videos, audiocassettes, lasers, discs and sound recordings. All forms of publishing whether in printed or electronic form, and the right to supply and distribute copies in any format by any means and merchandising, gambling, betting and lotteries.

1.5 The [Artist] agrees and acknowledges that the [Website Company] shall be entitled to register ownership of the copyright with any collecting society and/or other organisation and shall have the right to reproduce, licence, and exploit the [Artwork/Design] in any manner that it thinks fit. The [Website Company] shall not be obliged to consult with and/or seek the approval of the [Artist]. Nor shall the [Artist] be entitled to receive any additional payment and/or other sums.

1.6 The [Artist] agrees and acknowledges that the [Website Company] shall be entitled to adapt, translate, vary, develop, add to and delete from the [Artwork/Design] at any time. Further the [Website Company] shall be entitled to sell, dispose of, assign and/or create a charge over the [Artwork/Design]. The [Artist] waives all rights to any additional royalties, payments and/or other sums that may become due at any time including resale and any other form of reproduction.

1.7 The [Artist] agrees that the [Website Company] shall have the right to register the [Artwork/Design] as part of a trade mark, community mark, design right, service mark, and/or domain name and which is to be registered as owned and/or controlled by the [Website Company].

A.813

There shall be no transfer of rights and/or assignment in the [Music] and/or the [Sound Recordings] to any person who may have access to and/or use this [Website] and listen to and/or download and/or store any material which is available. Any person who reproduces, stores and retrieves, exploits, supplies and/or the distributes the [Music] and/or the [Sound Recordings] to a third party whether for commercial, educational and/or non-commercial purposes shall be in breach of copyright and legal proceedings may be taken against them.

A.814

The [Company] has engaged the [Consultant/Supplier] to carry out the [Work] set out in [Schedule A] to develop, design and create suitable computer software and other material for the [Website]. The [Consultant/Supplier] agrees and undertakes to assign to the [Company] all intellectual property rights and copyright, computer software rights, design rights, future design rights, patents, trade marks, service marks, domain names and any other rights in the [Work] and any other material created under this Agreement throughout the world and universe for the full period of all such rights and without limit of time in perpetuity. The [Consultant/Supplier] agrees that it shall not be entitled to register any claim and/or interest and/or to receive any additional payment of any nature from the exploitation and/or or reproduction of any copies in any format and/or medium at any time. The [Company] shall be entitled to use, licence, exploit and adapt the [Work] and the material as it thinks fit and to engage such third parties as it shall decide shall be required at any time.

A.815

The [Contractor] has been engaged by the [Company's] to design, create and develop a name, logo and image known as the [Project] for the [Company's] Website in accordance with the specifications in [Appendix A]. The [Contractor] agrees and undertakes:

1.1 To ensure that all persons who contribute to the [Project] at any time are employees and copyright is acquired by the [Company] and/or freelance and their terms of engagement assign all the rights to the [Company].

1.2 That no person requested to contribute to any part of the [Project] by the [Company] shall acquire any rights and/or interest and/or be entitled to receive any payments, royalties and/or other benefits from the assignment, registration and exploitation of their contribution and/or or work of any nature whether original or not.

1.3 That all rights to any acknowledgement, credit, copyright notice and/or moral rights are and/or will be waived.

1.4 To assign to the [Company] all intellectual property rights and copyright, computer software rights and source code, design rights, future design rights, patents, trade marks, service marks, domain names and any other rights in the [Project] and/or any other material created under this Agreement in all [media/medium/methods] and formats throughout the universe for the full period of copyright and any extensions and renewals and for the full period of all other rights and forever without limitation of time.

1.5 That it shall not be entitled to register any claim and/or interest and/or to receive any additional payments of any nature from the exploitation and/or reproduction of any copies in any format and/or medium at any time.

1.6 That the [Company] shall be entitled to use, licence, exploit and adapt the [Project] and/or any other material as it thinks fit and to engage such third parties as it shall decide shall be required at any time.

A.816

1.1 The [Designer] has and/or will design, develop, create and deliver a prototype and finished [App/Banner Link/other] based on all the [Logo/Image/Brand/Products] of the [Company] which are listed in Appendix [–] and on the proposed target outcomes in terms of achievable targets in Appendix [–] and the budget in Appendix [–].

1.2 The [Designer] agrees to and does assign in this document any future copyright and/or intellectual property rights, design rights, software rights, patents, music, sounds, shapes, images, text, characters, codes and any other material and/or data and/or charts that he/she may acquire and/or bring into existence as a direct result of this [Project] to the [Company] for the full period of copyright and any extensions and renewals and for the full period of the life of any other rights without limit. At no time shall the assignment period end so that any rights of any nature revert to the [Designer].

1.3 The [Designer] agrees to retain and deliver to the [Company] all development material of any nature and any copies of the final version together with any documents and records held and/or controlled by them in any format and/or medium which can be held by the [Company] for use as archive material. The [Company] agrees to pay the cost of such delivery.

A.817

[Name] does not grant any assignment to the [Company] of any of the rights in the [Image/Text/Banner] where it is displayed and/or exhibited on the website. Nor does [Name] grant the [Company] any right to authorise any third party to use and/or adapt any part of the [Image/Text/Banner] whether or not it is for the purpose of marketing, promotion and/or review. The prior consent of [Name] must be sought in each case and may be refused.

A.818

In consideration of the payment for their services the [Company] assigns all copyright and any other rights and/or interest in the [Material] which may exist during production and the final version of the [App] which has been developed and adapted to the [Distributor] for the full period of copyright and any such rights which shall continue indefinitely without limit. The [Company] does not assign any rights in any software which are owned by a third party.

Merchandising

A.819

The [Licensee] acknowledges that it is not acquiring any copyright, or any other intellectual property rights in the [Work/Character] and/or any Licensed Articles and/or any sequel and/or any logo, trade mark, title, name, character or otherwise which shall remain with and belong solely to the [Licensor].

A.820

In consideration of the payment of the Assignment Fee the [Company] assigns to the [Distributor] all present and future copyright and all other rights in all media in the [Work/Film/Project] and/or parts whether in existence now or created in the future throughout the [Territory/world/universe] for the full period of copyright and any extensions or renewals to continue in perpetuity including but not limited to:

1.1 All forms of exploitation through the medium of television and radio including reception and transmission by standard terrestrial, cable, satellite, digital television, regardless of the method of payment or not or the technical method whether encrypted or otherwise;

1.2 All forms of exploitation through the medium of a machine, television or other product whether capable of being recorded stored or played by cassette, disc, laser, DVD whether by any method of payment, sales, rental, and lease to the public;

1.3 All forms of television and video and non-theatric audiences including, but not limited to, businesses and commercial use, educational, cultural, religious and social establishments, schools, churches, prisons, hospitals, camps, garages, workshops, film groups, professional and trade bodies, private and public libraries, colleges, universities, hotels, airlines and airports, clubs, shops, ships;

1.4 ll forms of theatric exploitation including cinemas;

1.5 All forms of publishing whether in printed or electronic form of text or words or music;

1.6 All forms of telecommunication, electronic, internet, intranet and multimedia exploitation and interactive scenarios including CD-Roms and any other methods of combining the use of sound, text, music, graphics and vision;

1.7 All forms of merchandising whether based on character, logo, images, rules or otherwise including commercial exploitation of any item of any nature, toys, clothing, accessories, cutlery, badges, sweets, stationery or otherwise;

1.8 All forms of exploitation of the sound, music, lyrics, words, titles whether as audio files, ringtones, downloads, CDs, audiotapes, sheet music or any other form;

1.9 All forms of adaptation, translation, variation or development. Together with the right to assign, sub-licence, sell, supply, reproduce, distribute and exploit in any market and in any format and/or medium whether for the educational, charitable, commercial and/or non-commercial purpose.

A.821

The [Distributor] agrees and undertakes that this Agreement does not transfer and/or assign any intellectual property rights, copyright, computer software rights, design rights and future design rights, trade marks, service marks, community marks or any other rights in the [Work/Character] and/or in any [Licensed Articles] and/or in any development, variation and/or adaptation to the [Distributor] and all rights shall remain with and belong to the [Licensor].

A.822

The [Distributor] agrees and undertakes to assign to the [Licensor] all present and future copyright and any other rights in the product of the services of the [Distributor] and/or any third party relating to the development, production, supply and sale of the [Licensed Articles] and/or the [Work/Character] and/or any associated packaging, marketing and promotional material in all media throughout the world for the full period of copyright and any extensions and renewal.

A.823

The [Distributor] agrees and undertakes that the name of the [Work/Character] and any goodwill and reputation created in respect of any trade mark, service mark, community mark, business name or logo whether existing and/or developed for the [Licensed Articles] shall remain the sole and exclusive property of the [Licensor] and/or assigned to the [Licensor]. That no part of this Agreement is intended to assign, transfer or vest any such rights in the [Work/Character] and/or the [Licensed Articles] and/or any associated packaging, marketing and promotional material to the [Distributor].

A.824

The [Distributor] agrees and undertakes that it is not the intention of this Agreement that the [Distributor] and/or any of its designers, employees and/or consultants should acquire any copyright and/or any other rights in any of the products, articles and/or other material commissioned and/

or developed through the [Distributor]. Where any new rights of any nature and/or medium are created and held by the [Distributor] and/or any of its designers, employees and/or consultants. Then the [Distributor] agrees that they shall be bound to sign and authorise the assignment of all such rights to the [Company] in consideration of a nominal sum of less than [number/currency] in each case.

A.825

The [Artist] assigns all copyright, intellectual property rights and any other rights and/or interest in any media and/or format and/or medium and in any adaptation and/or development to the [Company] which may exist now and/or be created at any time in the [Image/Logo/Work] in consideration of the payment of [number/currency] on [date] each year for a period of [number] years. In the event that the fee is not aid in any year then the [Artist] shall have the right to serve notice that unless the fee is paid within [number] days that the [Company] shall be obliged to pay the [Artist] an additional sum of [number/currency] for that period.

Publishing

A.826

The [Company] agrees that it shall not acquire any rights or interest in the [Work] or any part at any time save as set out in the short form permission and that any developments or variation of the [Work], title, text, artwork and of any other material relating to the [Work] and/or the [Author] shall be vested in, transferred to and belong to the [Author]. No rights of any nature shall be acquired by or belong to the [Company] and the [Company] shall transfer and assign all rights, interest and copyright in all media to the [Author] at the end of this Agreement any which may have been created or acquired relating to the [Author] and the [Work].

A.827

The [Researcher] agrees to assign to the [Company] all present and future copyright and any other rights in the product of his services relating to [Project] throughout the world for the full period of copyright and any extensions and renewals.

A.828

In consideration of the payment of the [Ghost-writer's] Fee the [Ghost-writer] assigns to the [Name] all present and future copyright and all other rights in the product of his services including all scripts, drafts, notes, photographs or other material which is created by him under this Agreement and in the [Work] in all media whether in existence now or created in the future including but not limited to the title, publication, anthology, quotations, mechanical reproductions, serialisations, translations, dramatic and non-dramatic adaptations for radio, television, film, theatre or DVD or videos, sound and audio recordings and any merchandising throughout the Territory for the full period of copyright and any extensions and renewals.

A.829

In consideration of the Assignment Fee the [Author] assigns to the [Assignee] all present and future copyright and All Media Rights and any other rights of any nature whether in existence now or created later either by technology or changes and developments in the law in the [Work] and parts including the [Artwork] and the material in Schedule [–] throughout the Territory for the full period of any copyright and any extensions and renewals and in perpetuity.

The [Artwork] shall mean any photograph, drawing, sketch, picture, diagram, map, chart plan and any other illustration or any engraving, lithograph, image or other material listed which forms part of this [Work] [–].

'All Media Rights' shall mean the sole and exclusive right to produce, manufacture, supply, rent, sell, distribute, license, market and exploit the [Work] and any parts in all forms of the media whether in existence now or created in the future either by developments in the law or technology including but not limited to: all forms of publication; hardback, paperback; all forms of radio, television and video; cable, digital, satellite, terrestrial, cassette, disc, any technical method of delivery; any method of payment, charging, subscription, rental, lease and for free; all forms of telecommunication systems; sound, vision, graphics, text, icons, images; all forms of theatric and non-theatric exploitation; all forms of mechanical and electronic reproduction, dissemination or otherwise, internet, intranet and multimedia exploitation; CD-Roms, all methods of music and merchandising and any other developments, variations or adaptations of any nature.

A.830

In consideration of the Fee the [Name] agrees, undertakes and shall assign all rights so that the [Publisher] owns all present and future intellectual property rights including copyright and all other rights in the [Articles] and the [Recordings] and the [Photographs] in all media whether in existence now or created in the future throughout the Territory for the full period of copyright and any extensions or renewals [and thereafter].

A.831

The [Publisher] and the [Interviewee] agree and undertake not to commercially exploit the [Articles], the [Recordings] and/or the [Photographs] or the [Artwork] in any media other than the publication in the Periodical on the publication dates without the prior consent of and additional payment to the [Name] on such terms as shall be agreed on each occasion.

A.832

The [Author] assigns all copyright in the [Work/Review] to the [Company] for the full period of copyright and any extensions and renewals throughout the world and universe for use on the website [specify] and in any associated online service, newspapers, periodicals and subscription and/or news feed of the [Company] and by any other manner the [Company] should decide at its sole discretion. Provided that the [Company] pays the fee due promptly by [date] and provides a credit to the [Author] as follows [specify].

A.833

The [Author] assigns all copyright, intellectual property rights and any other rights in the [Work] including the title, headings, index and preface to the [Company] for the full period of copyright and any other period in which ownership of rights of any nature may exist at any time throughout the [world/country] subject to the following conditions:

1.1 That the [Company] credits the [Author] as the creator as follows [specify]

1.2 That all sums due under this Agreement are paid in full.

1.3 That the [Company] does not go into insolvency and/or administration and/or does not publish and/or exploit the [Work] in any form by [date].

Where the [Company] fails to fulfil any of the above conditions then the [Company] agrees that the consideration for the assignment has not been fulfilled.

Purchase and Supply of Products

A.834

The [Supplier] agrees that it shall not acquire any rights or interest in the [Seller's] Website except those which relate to the development or variation of the [Supplier's] existing [Product] and/or [Trade Mark, logo, slogans, text, image, sound, music].

A.835

The [Seller] agrees that it shall not acquire any patent, copyright, design rights, trade mark, service mark or logo, slogan, text, image, music or other intellectual property rights in the [Product] and/or any other marketing material and it shall be the sole and exclusive property of the [Supplier] together with any goodwill. The [Seller] shall not acquire any rights therein including any developments, variations or otherwise. Further, the [Seller] shall provide to the [Supplier] any necessary documentation to support or transfer any such rights or interest to the [Supplier] at the [Supplier's] cost and expense.

A.836

The [Promoter] assigns to the [Company] all present and future intellectual property rights including copyright and any other rights which may exist or be created by itself or any third party engaged by them to assist in respect of the [Company] and the [Company's] Products within its possession or control throughout the [universe] for the full period of copyright and any extensions or renewals in perpetuity.

A.837

The [Distributor] agrees that all present and future copyright, design rights and intellectual property rights and patents in the [Designs], the [Licensed Articles], the [Prototypes] and the [Complete Set] are and shall remain the sole property of the [Company] and this Agreement does not purport to transfer or assign any rights to the [Licensee].

A.838

The [Purchaser] confirms and agrees that this Agreement relates solely to the sale and purchase of the [Garment] based on the [Designs] for personal use and does not assign any copyright, design rights or otherwise nor permit the [Purchaser] to commercially exploit the [Garment] or [Designs] in any form.

A.839

The [Production Company] agrees to ensure that anyone engaged in developing, creating, designing, developing, testing, modelling, producing any part of the [Product] and/or any associated packaging shall be required to assign all such copyright , intellectual property rights, design rights, trade marks, patents, sounds, text, images and processes, mechanisms and/or discoveries and inventions to [Name].

Services

A.840

The [Agent] agrees that the name of the [Actor] and any goodwill and reputation created in respect of any trade mark, business name or logo shall remain the sole and exclusive property of the [Actor] whether in existence now or created in the future during the term of this Agreement and that no part of this Agreement is intended to assign, transfer or vest any rights in the [Actor] in the [Agent].

A.841

The [Designer] in consideration of the payment of the sums set out in Clause [–] assigns to the [Company] the sole and exclusive rights in all media including internet, website password and source code rights in any rights owned or controlled by the [Designer] in the Product Specification, Domain Name, website and computer software and any other documents, programs, formats or material of any nature which may arise in pursuance of this Agreement, whether in existence now or created in the future, throughout the universe for the full period of copyright and any other rights and any other extensions renewals or otherwise.

A.842

The [Designer] shall not acquire any rights or interest in the Website except the [source code]. Nor shall the [Designer] be entitled at any time to review, register and/or claim any rights, interest or equity in the Domain Name, or any logo, service mark, trade mark or other image, text, or slogan which has been created or developed for the purpose of the [Company's] website and/or any advertising, marketing or promotion and/or which is to be used generally in the [Company's] business.

A.843

The [Contributor] agrees that present and future copyright as may exist in the product of the [Contributor's] Work provided to the [Owner] during the course of this Agreement is assigned solely and exclusively to the [Owner] for the full period of copyright including any extensions and renewals throughout the Territory and that the [Contributor] shall not acquire any rights or interest of any nature whether originated by the [Contributor] or not.

A.844

The [Contributor] acknowledges that such copyright and any other rights of any nature as may exist now or be created in the future with respect to any element of the [Website] and any associated material to which she is providing her skill, services and work shall belong absolutely to the [Owner].

A.845

In consideration of the [Basic Fee] the [Company] agrees to provide the services of [Name] and both parties agree to assign to the [Owner] all products of the services under this Agreement, whether in existence now or created in the future in all media throughout the Territory for the full period of copyright and any extensions and renewals including but not limited to documents, recordings, photographs, and interactive responses. The [Owner] shall not however acquire any rights or interest in any material in which the copyright already exists which is owned or controlled by the [Contributor] which is supplied under this Agreement including books, documents, photographs, biography, slogans, name, business names, programme titles, and music.

A.846

The [Owner] agrees that it shall not be entitled to exploit any product of the services of the [Contributor] outside the [Engagement Period] or in any media without the negotiation and settlement of additional payments to the [Contributor] for each different type and method and length of exploitation. Both parties shall use their endeavours to reach agreement in good faith based on full disclosure of the facts. In the event that there is no exploitation of the material within [specify period] by the [Owner] then the [Contributor] may acquire a full assignment of all rights subject to an agreement of the terms.

A.847

The [Consultant] assigns all copyright and any other rights in the [Work] and all material to the [Company] whether in existence now or created in the future in the product of her service under this Agreement in all media throughout the world, universe and outer space for the full period of copyright and any extensions and renewals.

A.848

In consideration of the [Photographer's] Fee and the [Authorised Expenses] the [Photographer] assigns to the [Company] all rights in the [Commissioned Work] whether in existence now or created in the future [either by changes in the law or developments in new technology] including but not limited to film, television, video, merchandising, publishing, and the internet throughout the [world] for the full period of copyright and any extensions and renewals.

A.849

The [Supplier] agrees and undertakes that it has developed, created and delivered the computer software, computer hardware, data, source code and any other material set out in Appendix [–] the specification for the [Project]. The [Supplier] agrees and acknowledges that all work and contributions by the [Supplier] to the [Project] shall be original except to the extent specified in Appendix [–]. The [Supplier] agrees it is the sole owner of All Intellectual Property, Patent, Computer Software and other Rights of all the [Computer software/Data/Source Code/Computer hardware] and any other material set out in Appendix [–] the specification for the [Project] which are assigned to the [Company]. That the [Supplier] has not exploited any such material in any form and/or licensed the rights to any third party.

A.850

The [Company] has engaged the services of the [Supplier] to develop, create and deliver the computer software, computer hardware, data, source code and any other material set out in Appendix [–] the specification for the [Project]. The [Supplier] agrees and acknowledges that it is a key term and condition of this Agreement that All Intellectual Property, Patent, Computer Software and other Rights of all the [Computer software/Data/Source Code/Computer hardware] and any other material set out in Appendix [–] the specification for the [Project] which are owned, controlled and/or come into existence in the future should belong to and/or be assigned to the [Company].

A.851

In consideration of the payment of the [Assignment Fee] and the [Project Fee] by the [Company] to the [Supplier] the [Supplier] assigns to the [Company] All Intellectual Property, Patent, Computer Software and other Rights of all the [Computer software/Data/Source Code/Computer hardware] and any other material set out in Appendix [–] the specification for the [Project] which are owned, controlled and/or come into existence in the future in all media and by all medium, means and processes whether in existence now and/or created in the future throughout the world and the universe for the full period of copyright and any extensions and renewals and in perpetuity.

'All Intellectual Property, Patent, Computer Software and other Rights' shall mean without limitation all intellectual property rights, copyright, patents, inventions, database rights, trade marks, service marks, community marks, design rights, future design rights, computer software rights, trade secrets, moral rights, confidential information, and domain names.

The sole and exclusive right to register any interest and/or rights as the owner and/or to adapt, vary, delete from and add to, use, copy, license, authorise, print, transmit, disseminate, store, retrieve, display, process, record, playback, rent, lend, supply, sell, distribute, market and/or otherwise exploit. Together with the right to do so for any developments, variations and/or adaptations.

Whether text, images, source code, tables, computer generated material, software, drawings, plans, sketches, graphics, film, video, a two dimensional and/or three dimensional representation, prototype, electronically generated material of any nature and/or medium, sound effects, music, interactive, data, logos, caption, characters, maps, links, site map, search words, taxonomy, index including but not limited to:

1.1 All forms of film, video, radio and television including terrestrial, cable, digital, satellite whether direct to a television set, by means of a computer and/or some other gadget and/or other means. All forms of non-theatric, theatric exploitation, and publishing in printed and/or electronic form.

1.2 All forms of telecommunication systems and mechanical reproduction including telephones, mobile phones, pagers, videograms, lasers, discs, cassettes, DVDs.

1.3   Translations and/or adaptations in any such format by any means and process in any language.

1.4   All forms of exploitation and/or dissemination of material by any electronic method and process, and/or all forms of storage and/or retrieval system through the use of computer hardware and/or software and/or interactive multi-media including but not limited to the internet, worldwide web, intranet, downloads, e-books, blogs, podcasts, apps, newsfeeds, emails, compact discs, CD-Roms, computer games, audio files, ringtones, downloads.

1.5   All forms of reproduction and/or exploitation and/or methods and/or processes of delivery of all and/or any part in any medium.

A.852

Any assignment of any rights under this Agreement is solely limited to the appearance and performance of [Name] at [Event] and any filming and photographs that may be taken and/or commissioned by the [Company] from third parties. It shall not include the right to develop and/or adapt and/or distort, and/or alter and/or licence the material to another third party in a different medium.

Sponsorship

A.853

1.1   The [Sponsor] agrees and undertakes that this Agreement does not transfer and/or assign any intellectual property rights, copyright, computer software rights, design rights and future design rights, trade marks, service marks, community marks, patents, know how or any other rights in anything owned and/or controlled by the [Company] to the [Sponsor] whether in existence at the time of this Agreement and/or developed in the future.

1.2   The [Sponsor] agrees and undertakes that all rights shall remain with and belong to the [Company] in any adaptations, merchandising, films, sound recordings, and/or any other material designed in house and/or commissioned and/or developed under this Agreement by the [Company] whether or not the [Sponsor] has been consulted and/or has made any contribution to the development and/or final version.

A.854

Where the [Company] engages the services of third parties for the purposes of the [Event] which may include but not be limited the following activities:

(a)   To develop and print brochures, posters, flyers, and other printed and photographic material.

(b) To design and develop an operational website.

(c) To produce edited highlights for a promotional DVD.

(d) To provide public relations advice and access to the media and television companies.

The [Company] agrees and undertakes to ensure that such third parties shall not be entitled to exploit and/or sub-licence any product of their services to the [Company] and/or [Sponsor] to any third party in any media at any time.

A.855

The [Company] agrees and undertakes to ensure that such third parties shall not be entitled to acquire any rights in any patents, know how, copyright, design rights, trade marks, service marks, logos, slogan, text, image, music and/or any other intellectual property rights in the products and/or services and/or marketing and/or any other material and/or contribution of the [Sponsor]. That the [Sponsor] shall be the sole and exclusive owner of all such rights including any developments, variations or otherwise.

A.856

The [Company] agrees and undertakes to ensure that such third parties shall provide to the [Sponsor] any necessary documentation to support or transfer any such rights or interest to the [Sponsor] at the [Sponsor's/ Company's] cost and expense.

A.857

The [Company] agrees that all trade marks, business names, domain names, community marks, service marks, logos, design rights, copyright and all other intellectual property rights in respect of the [Sponsor's] business and/ or its products and/or services and/or any other material provided by the [Sponsor] under this Agreement shall remain the sole and exclusive property of the [Sponsor] whether in existence now and/or developed in the future. That it is not the intention of either party to transfer, assign and/or create any interest of any nature in any rights in the [Sponsor's] business and/or its products and/or services to the [Company].

A.858

1.1 The [Agent] and the [Sportsperson] agree and undertake that they shall not acquire any rights and/or interest and/or attempt to register any right and/or interest in the trade marks, business names, domain names, community marks, service marks, logos, design rights, copyright and all other intellectual property rights owned and/or controlled by the [Sponsors] and/or any development and/or adaptation whether in existence now and/or developed in the future. This shall include but not be limited to any of its businesses and/or its products and/or services and/or any marketing, packaging, advertising and/or other material owned and/or controlled by the [Sponsor] and/or provided by the [Sponsor] under this Agreement.

1.2 The [Agent] and the [Sportsperson] agree that the trade marks, business names, domain names, community marks, service marks, logos, design rights, copyright and all other intellectual property rights owned and/or controlled by the [Sponsors'] and/or any development and/or adaptation whether in existence now and/or developed in the future shall be the sole and exclusive property of the [Sponsor]. That no part of this Agreement is intended to assign, transfer or vest any such rights in the [Agent] and the [Sportsperson].

A.859
The [Sponsor] agrees that where a new and original logo, design, trade mark, domain name and/or other material is created and developed as a direct result of the joint collaboration of the [Sponsor] and the [Sportsperson]. That the parties shall hold the new and original material as joint owners of all such rights and shall each receive an equal credit, recognition in any copyright notice and make any registration of the rights in the names of both parties. The [Sponsor] agrees to bear the total cost of any such legal, administrative and registration costs. The signature of both parties shall be required to assign any rights and to grant any sub-licence.

A.860
The [Sponsor] agrees that it has not acquired and/or been assigned and/or granted any right and/or option by the [Organiser] to attend, sponsor and/or take part in any future [Festivals/Events]. Nor has the [Sponsor] been assigned and/or granted any right to use and/or adapt the name of the [Organiser] [Festival/Event] in any future product development, marketing and/or promotions.

A.861
Neither the [Sponsor] nor the [Company] shall be entitled to assign, transfer and/or exploit the [Logo/name/Image] which they have jointly created for this [Project] without the written consent and agreement of the managing director of both parties.

University, Library and Educational

A.862
The [Author/Contributor] agrees and undertakes that she has created and developed the original [Work/Product] and is the sole owner of all copyright, computer software, and any other intellectual property rights in the [Work/

197

Product] which are assigned under this Agreement to the [Institute]. That the [Author/Contributor] has not exploited the [Work/Product] in any form and/or licensed the rights to any third party.

A.863

In consideration of the payment of the Assignment Fee in full by the agreed date the [Author/Contributor] assigns to the [Institute] all present and future copyright and all other rights, interest in all media whether in existence now or developed by new technology or by changes in the law in the [Work/Product] including any parts and the [Material] throughout the world, universe and outer space for the full period of copyright and any extensions and renewals and forever without limit of time including but not limited to: all forms of television, computer, gadgets and radio whether the transmission is terrestrial, by cable, digital, satellite, microwave, over the air, or wireless; whether free, pay per view, encrypted or not or otherwise. All forms of exploitation through telecommunication systems, computers, DVDs, CD-Roms, software, telephones, mobile phones, pagers, the internet and other equipment and devices. All forms of exploitation through videos, audiocassettes, lasers, discs, merchandising, cinemas, educational, cultural, religious and social establishments, clubs, universities, commercial use by businesses. All forms of publishing whether in printed or electronic form. All forms of exploitation not already covered above in any medium. The right to register any computer software, trade mark, community mark, design right, service mark, logo, domain name, and any associated goodwill, trade secret and confidential information. All forms of adaptation, translation, variation or development of any nature.

A.864

The [Company] agrees that the name of the [Institute] and the [Work] and any goodwill and reputation created in respect of any trade mark, business name, domain name, and logo shall remain the sole and exclusive property of the [Institute] whether in existence now or created in the course of the Agreement. That no part of this Agreement is intended to assign, transfer or vest any rights in the [Company].

A.865

In consideration of the [Fee] the [Company] agrees to assign to the [Institute] all copyright, intellectual property rights, and all other interests and material which is created and developed in respect of this [Project] which are created, developed, owned and/or controlled by the [Company] whether in existence now or created in the future in all media throughout the [Territory/world/country/universe] for the full period of copyright and any extensions and renewals and in perpetuity. No rights and/or interest of any nature shall remain vested in the [Company] and/or any employee.

A.866

he [Institute] agrees that the [Student] shall not be obliged to assign any copyright in the [Work/theses] to the [Institute] and that all rights of any nature in any medium including copyright and intellectual property rights are retained and owned by the [Student] the original creator and writer. That where the [Institute] wishes to use, display and/or archive the [Work/theses] for any reason they shall be obliged to seek the prior written approval of the [Student].

ASSIGNMENT FEE

General Business and Commercial

A.867

'The Assignment Fee' shall be the sum of [figure/words/currency].

A.868

'The Assignment Fee' means the fee of [figure/currency/words] payable by the [Assignee] to the [Company] in respect of the Rights to be assigned by the [Company] to the [Assignee].

A.869

The Assignment Fee shall be payable:

1.1 [figure] [words and currency] paid on [date] (receipt of which is hereby acknowledged).

1.2 [figure] [words and currency] payable on [date] subject to acceptance of the Delivery items.

A.870

'The Assignment Fee' means the fee of [–] payable by the [Satellite Company] to the [Distribution Company] in respect of the [Television Rights, the Theatric and Non-Theatric Rights] to be assigned under this Agreement.

A.871

The Assignment Fee shall be paid as follows:

1.1 [figure/words/currency] payable within [specify period] of acceptance of the delivery items in respect of the [Film].

1.2 [figure/words/currency] payable on [date] [subject to acceptance of the delivery items].

1.3 [figure/words/currency] payable on [date] subject to acceptance of the delivery items in respect of the [Mini-Series].

1.4 [figure/words/currency] payable on [date] subject to compliance with sub- clauses [–] and [–] herein.

A.872

'The Assignment Fee' shall be the sum of [[figure/words/currency]. In consideration of the rights assigned by the [Author] the [Assignee] shall pay to the [Author] the Assignment Fee as follows:

1.1 [figure/words/currency] upon signature of this Agreement by both parties.

1.2 [figure/words/currency] upon [deliver/acceptance] of the material under Clause [–].

1.3 [figure/words/currency] on or before [[date].

A.873

'The [Contributor's] Fee' shall mean the hourly sum of [figure/currency].

A.874

You will be paid in the following manner [direct debit/cheque] in accordance with your agreed monthly fees.

A.875

The [Company] shall pay the [Name] Fees as follows:

1.1 [–] upon signature of this Agreement.

1.2 [–] on or before [date] subject to the completion and delivery of [specify work and material].

A.876

In consideration of the work by [Name] the [Company] is to pay the fee of [figure/currency] by [date] in [form] to [Name] which shall be in full and final settlement. No further sums of any nature for any reason shall be due to [Name] for the provision of his/her services and/or the exploitation of the material provided by [Name] in any media at any time.

A.877

'The Serialisation Fee' shall be the sum of [figure/currency].

A.878

'The Payment Schedule' shall be the details of the payment of [sum] by the [Assignee] to the [Assignor]. A copy of the Payment Schedule is attached to and forms part of this Agreement as [–].

A.879

'The Presenter's Fee' shall be the following sums to be paid by [Company] to [Name]:

1.1   [figure/currency] for the first twelve calendar months;

1.2   [figure/currency] for the following twelve calendar months;

1.3   [–] thereafter.

A.880

1.1   The Novation Price shall be the sum of [–].

1.2   The [Company] shall pay the Novation Price to the [Publisher] in the following manner [specify method of payment] on or before [date].

1.3   In the event that the [Company] fails to make payment as specified in 1.1 and 1.2 above then this Agreement shall have no effect whatsoever and no assignment of rights shall take effect.

A.881

'The Fee' of [number] shall be in [currency] and paid by [direct debit] to the nominated account of [Name] within [number] hours of acceptance and delivery of the [Work].

A.882

The Assignment Fee shall be paid in instalments on the following dates [specify] in equal instalments subject to the delivery of [specify amount] of the [Material] by date and the balance by [date]. Where there is a delay in delivery the payments shall also be delayed accordingly.

ASSIGNMENT PERIOD

General Business and Commercial

A.883

'The Assignment Period' shall be for a fixed period of [five years] which shall commence from the date of full execution of this Agreement.

A.884

'The Assignment Period' shall commence on [date] and shall continue until [date] unless extended under the option provisions contained within Clause

[–] of this Agreement or as subsequently varied by the parties hereto in writing.

A.885

'The Assignment Period' shall commence on the date of this Agreement and shall be for the full period of copyright including any extensions or renewals as far as possible in perpetuity.

A.886

'The Assignment Period' shall mean the full period of copyright including any extensions or renewals to continue indefinitely in perpetuity.

A.887

'The Term of this Agreement' shall commence on the [date] of this Agreement and shall continue until [date].

A.888

'The Assignment Period' shall commence on full execution of this Agreement by both parties and shall continue forever without limitation of time including but not limited to the full period of copyright and any extensions, renewals, adaptations, developments or revisions thereof at any time in any territory.

A.889

'The Assignment Period' shall commence on acceptance of the [Work] by the [Company] which shall be confirmed in writing and shall continue for a period of [ten] years thereafter provided that the [Company] shall be promoting, selling and exploiting the [Work] and payments shall be received by the [Name].

A.890

'The Assignment Period' shall start on [date] and shall for the full period of copyright and any extensions and renewals and for the full period of all other rights and forever without limitation of time.

A.891

'The Term' shall mean for the full period of copyright and any extensions, renewals and/or extensions in perpetuity and without limitation.

A.892

The assignment period shall start on [date] and end on [date]. At the end of the assignment period the [Company] may either negotiate a new annual assignment fee or all the rights which were assigned will revert to [Name] and/or any beneficiaries of their estate and/or the control of any trustees.

AUDIO FILES

General Business and Commercial

A.893

'The Audio File' shall mean the storage of the sound recording of the [Work] and/or any part in any medium by electronic means [regardless of the medium on which the sound recording is made and/or the method by which the sounds are produced and/or reproduced] and to make it available to the public by means of an electronic retrieval system.

A.894

'The Audio File' shall mean to store by any electronic means and to make available to the public by means of an electronic retrieval system the reproduction of the recording of the whole and/or any part of a literary, dramatic and/or musical work from which sounds reproducing the work may be produced. This shall include but not be limited to the spoken version of the text of a book, music, singing, interviews, discussions, and other sounds. Regardless of the medium upon which the recording is made and/or the method by which the sounds are produced and/or reproduced.

A.895

'The Audio File' shall mean the digital electronic files created and developed by the [Company] which are in the following format [specify] which are held by and/or stored in a system known as [specify] which has been reproduced from the following work and/or material [List name of material, source and copyright owner]. The files are to be used as part of database and a storage and retrieval system and supplied as reproductions of the digital electronic files on the following websites [[specify name/web reference].

A.896

'The Exclusive Audio File and Publication Rights' shall mean

1.1 The exclusive right to store the sound recording of the [Work] and/ or any part in any medium by electronic means [regardless of the medium on which the sound recording is made and/or the method by which the sounds are produced and/or reproduced] and to make it available to the public by means of an electronic retrieval system and/ or as reproductions of the digital electronic files.

1.2 The sole and exclusive right to the exclusion of all third parties and the copyright owner to control, exploit, licence, reproduce, supply, distribute, and/or authorise the reproduction by a third party of all and/ or any part of the [Work] by means of a sound recording in electronic form which is stored as a file and made available to the public [by means of an electronic retrieval system].

1.3 The right to the sole and exclusive publication rights as the first publisher of a previously unpublished work when copies of that work are made available by means of an electronic retrieval system and/or in electronic form by some other method.

AUTHORISATION

General Business and Commercial

A.897
We accept no liability for any Goods delivered or services provided unless the Order has been placed or amended on our behalf by a duly authorised officer.

A.898
The [Company] warrants that it has good title and full right and authority to grant the rights set out in this Agreement and undertakes that it is and it will remain fully entitled to give the warranties and undertakings and make the representations concerning the [Product] and/or part(s) in this Agreement.

A.899
Nothing contained herein shall grant the [Agent] or his employees the power to bind the [Principal], to transact any business in the [Principal's] name or make any representations or incur any obligations on the [Principal's] behalf and the [Agent] may only represent itself as an independent contractor who has been engaged as Sales Agent in the Territory subject to the terms of this Agreement.

A.900
The [Author] authorises the [Agent] to collect all sums due to the [Author] in respect of the [Work] from any source throughout the Territory during the Term of the Agreement and at any time thereafter relating to any agreement negotiated and concluded by the [Agent] during the Term of the Agreement.

A.901
The [Artist] provides his consent to the [Agent] collecting all monies due to the [Artist] under the following [[agreements/categories or types of work] for

the period starting [[date] and ending [[date]. The [Agent] is not permitted to collect monies from any other agreements or work concerning the [Artist] at any time. Nor shall the [Agent] be entitled to collect monies direct outside the specified dates whether or not the [Agent] negotiated or concluded the contract. Further, all sums so collected shall be held in a separate account for the benefit of the [Artist] and shall not be mixed with or offset against or charged in any manner.

A.902

The [Company] authorises the [Web Company] to act on its behalf in respect of all matters relating to the internet including the collection of sums due, registration of domain manes, development of international strategy, creation of websites, and associated advertising. Provided that all work shall be agreed in detail in Nothing contained herein shall grant the [Agent] or his employees the power to bind the [Principal], to transact any business in the [Principal's] name or make any representations or incur any obligations on the [Principal's] behalf and the [Agent] may only represent itself as an independent contractor who has been engaged as Sales Agent in the Territory subject to the terms of this Agreement.

A.903

[Name] shall be entitled to rely on the authorisation of the [Company] where an instruction, request, agreement or consent is provided by any method in writing or verbally by an officer and/or director of the [Company].

A.904

Nothing contained in this document shall grant the [Agent] and/or his employees the power to bind the [Principal], to transact any business in the [Principal's] name or make any representations and/or to incur and/or to agree to any obligations on the [Principal's] behalf. The [Agent] may only represent itself as an independent contractor who has been engaged as Sales Agent in the Territory subject to the terms of this Agreement.

A.905

The [Sponsor] agrees and undertakes that it shall not have any power, authority and/or right to authorise, make representations to third parties and/or to commit to and/or to incur any expense, cost and/or liability in respect of any work, material, publicity, contracts, rights, commissions, facilities, marketing, tickets and/or otherwise for any reason in respect of the [Company] and/or the [Event/Name]. The [Sponsor] agree and undertake that where they have acted outside the terms of Agreement that the [Sponsor] shall bear all the costs of both parties that may be incurred whether directly and/or indirectly which relate to the authorisation outside the Agreement.

A.906

The [Distributor] shall not have any authority, right and/or power to delegate the development, production, distribution and/or exploitation of the [Character] to any third party. Where the [Distributor] is found and/or alleged by the [Licensor] to have acted, committed and/or made representations outside the terms of this Agreement to third parties. Then the [Licensor] shall have the right to serve notice of termination of the Agreement upon such terms as may be determined by the [Licensor].

A.907

The [Consultant] is authorised by the [Company] to act upon behalf of the [Company] for the purpose of preparing, writing and delivering a report on the subject of [--]. The [Consultant] may contact and interview an agreed list of businesses, persons and contacts which are agreed in advance with the [Managing Director]. The [Consultant] shall keep a full record and log of all emails, letters and discussions which shall be made available to the [Company] upon request. No authority is provided to the [Consultant] to make any representations, commitments, disclosures and/or sign any agreement which may bind the [Company] at any time.

A.908

The parties agree that any approvals, amendments and/or authorisations which may be required under this Agreement require the written and/or verbal approval of [specify] at the [Company] and [Name] not his/her agent. Where there is likely to be a delay and/or loss incurred there is no authority granted to proceed without the necessary approval.

A.909

[Name] will permit and allow the [Agent] to make such decisions and expend such funds as may be required during each calendar month up to a maximum of [number/currency] in total. Provided that the proposal has already been discussed in detail with [Name] and all relevant information disclosed.

B

BANK HOLIDAYS

General Business and Commercial

B.001
'Bank Holidays' shall mean all recognised public holidays which are observed by banks, businesses and services each year in [England and Wales/Northern Ireland/the United Kingdom excluding Scotland and Northern Ireland/country].

B.002
'Bank Holidays' shall mean those days recognised as public holidays by the [government/law courts] whether at the conclusion of and/or subsequently during the existence of this Agreement.

B.003
[Name] shall be entitled to take off as [paid/unpaid] leave any days which are bank and/or public holidays which may be applicable in the [Territory] whether recognised at the time of the Agreement or created at a later date by royal proclamation, legislation or otherwise.

B.004
[Name] shall be entitled to take as paid leave the following bank holidays [specify dates and names] in [country] which shall be in addition to any holiday entitlement specified in clause [–]. Any other religious festivals, celebrations or otherwise shall be arranged to be taken as part of annual leave or as unpaid absence subject to advance consent.

B.005
Where a bank holiday falls on a day upon which the [Name] is not normally working, there shall be no entitlement to an additional day off in lieu.

B.006
In the [United Kingdom and the Republic of Ireland] the following bank holidays shall apply in [year] and in any subsequent year of this Agreement, subject to variation in date in each year:

1.1   New Year's Day (UK and Republic of Ireland) [date]

1.2   St David's Day (Wales) [date]

1.3   St Patrick's Day (Northern Ireland and Republic of Ireland) [date]

1.4   Good Friday (UK) [date]

1.5   Easter Monday (UK and Republic of Ireland) [date]

1.6   St George's Day (England) [date]

1.7   May Day (UK and Republic of Ireland) [date]

1.8   Spring Bank Holiday (UK) [date]

1.9   St Stephen's Day (Republic of Ireland) [date]

1.10 Bank Holiday (Northern Ireland) [date]

1.11 Summer Holiday (UK) [date]

1.12 Orangemen's Day Holiday (Northern Ireland) [date]

1.13 St Andrew's Day (Scotland) [date]

1.14 Christmas Day [date]

1.15 Boxing Day Bank Holiday [date]

1.16 New Year's Day Bank Holiday [date].

B.007

'Bank Holidays' shall mean all recognised bank and public holidays in [country] as specified according to [government department] but shall not include any other days which are celebrated as part of any other religious body, belief or political organisation. It is however acceptable to substitute alternative dates off in lieu provided that [Name] is able to carry out their duties at the [Company] on the recognised bank or public holidays or other suitable arrangements can be made in advance.

B.008

The [Company] acknowledges that the [Person] shall be entitled to the Executive's Holidays in addition to Bank Holidays. The [Company] agrees that the [Executive] shall be entitled to be paid at the full rate whilst on leave for any day which is either part of the Bank Holidays and/or the Executive's Holidays.

B.009

The [Company] confirms that in the event that the [Executive] is requested to work on Bank Holidays or on those days which have been agreed as the

Executive's Holidays. Then such work shall be paid for on an ad hoc basis on terms to be agreed between the parties as to the additional remuneration, but at no less than the existing rate of payment.

B.010
This position does not entitle you to receive any payments for public or national holidays and all sums shall only be paid for and subject to completion of the required work. Nor shall there be any additional leave or absence in lieu of work on any of such days.

B.011
Your entitlement to bank, public or other extra days shall be as follows [specify] and you shall be paid in full for each such day. Any such paid leave shall be in addition to your annual leave allowance in paragraph [–].

B.012
The [Consultant] shall not be obliged to provide his/her services and shall not be paid any sums by the [Company] for any period where the [Consultant] is absent due to public holidays, religious festivals, weekends, or other occasions which arise due to family, medical or other emergencies. Where the absence continues for [–] consecutive days which were scheduled to be work days then the [Company] shall be entitled to terminate the contract by written notice and shall not be liable to pay any further sums due under the contract.

B.013
There shall be no obligation under this Agreement to be available to provide the services of the [Agency] and/or [Name] on any weekend and/or bank holidays and/or annual leave during the Term of this Agreement.

B.014
In the calculation of the days of notification and/or payment under this Agreement it is agreed that all weekends and Bank Holidays shall [not] be included in the number of days.

B.015
For the purpose of this Agreement it is irrelevant whether or not any day is a bank holiday and/or weekend and/or other festival, celebration and/or religious day for any faith. All days of the week shall be treated as the same and any notice period and/or calculation shall include all the days in sequence regardless of whether it is a bank holiday or not.

BANK RATE

General Business and Commercial

B.016
Unless both parties agree to the contrary in writing all references in this Agreement to 'Bank Rate' shall mean [three per cent above] [3%] above the prevailing bank rate of [Bank] in [country] on the relevant date of the transaction.

B.017
In determining the Interest Rate the parties agree to use the rate specified by the London Inter-Bank Offered Rate (LIBOR) at 11 am on the [Payment Date] and such rate shall apply for [three months] and shall be renewable for [three-monthly] intervals thereafter.

B.018
The [Company] shall be entitled to charge a varied bank rate depending upon the circumstances at any time and shall not be bound to continue to charge the existing rate. Further where applicable an additional sum may be charged by way of penalty or accumulative interest if when served with notice to remedy a serious breach or default the other party does not rectify the matter within [one calendar month] of receipt of a notice setting out all the details.

B.019
'Bank Rate' shall be such percentage figure as shall be published by the Bank of [England/other] on the relevant date it is to be used to calculate the sum due. Where there is a discrepancy as to which figure is to be used then the lower percentage figure shall apply.

B.020
'The Bank Rate' shall be fixed at [number] per cent [–] % on [figure/sum] from [start date] to [end date]. It shall not be varied and there shall be no accumulation or imposition of a penalty or additional charges, costs or other sums which would result in a higher bank rate being applied or any additional sum becoming due.

B.021
There shall be no interest, penalties, charges, or other additional sums due under the terms of this Agreement at any time where any payment or undertaking is delayed for a period of [three months]. Thereafter there shall be a fixed sum charged as a penalty each [day/month] for failure to comply

with the following main clauses of this Agreement [specify clauses] [specify sum/currency for each clause]. The position shall be reviewed at the end of each calendar month and an invoice issued for the penalty payments due to be paid immediately upon receipt of an invoice.

B.022

The [Bank] shall loan the [Customer] the following sum [figure/currency] for the following purpose [specify]. The [Bank] shall not be entitled to any charge, lien or control over the assets or interests of the [Customer] or its business or property and shall only be entitled to charge the following rate of interest [number] per cent [–] % on [sum/currency] from [date] to [date]. Thereafter the [Bank] may charge the following [higher/lower] rate of [specify].

No additional sums may be added for administration, currency conversion, legal costs or otherwise unless the [Customer] defaults on the loan for a period of [three months].

B.023

The [Consultant] shall be entitled to charge the [Company] an additional sum of [figure/currency] for each occasion on which the sums due under this agreement are not paid according to the specified dates. These sums shall be in lieu of charging interest, or imposing a penalty, but shall without prejudice to the [Consultants] right to take legal action.

B.024

The [Company] of [specify] shall be entitled to charge interest at [number] per cent [figure] % above the Bank base rate. The [Company] can calculate and charge the interest from the day after any sum has not been received until the sum due has been paid in full. The [Company] shall notify the [Client] that interest is payable, and the [Client] is in default. Where payment is received within [seven days] of the default the [Company] may decide to waive the interest at its absolute discretion.

B.025

The [Company] agrees and undertakes that the maximum that it shall be entitled to claim in interest on any default in payment by the [Distributor] shall be limited to the sum of [figure] [words/currency].

B.026

The parties both agree that neither shall be entitled to claim any interest, penalty or additional charges in respect of any sums due under the terms of this Agreement which may be delayed and unpaid by the due date, not accounted for or some other error. Provided that the matter is resolved within [two months] of the default. Thereafter either party may claim interest, penalty charges, administration and legal and accountants costs against the other. Any interest claimed by either party shall be at the fixed rate of [figure] % [words] per cent from the first date the default or error arose.

B.027
The [Company] agrees the interest rate that it shall be entitled to charge in respect of the sums owed under this Agreement shall not exceed [number] per cent [figure] % at any time. This shall be the case whether or not the bank rate set by the [specify] bank exceeds this rate or not.

B.028
The rate of interest shall be fixed from [date] to [date] and shall not be dependent and/or adjusted by any changes in the bank rate; economy and/or other variations in the financial sector in any part of the world. The rate of interest cannot be increased and/or decreased by either party. The rate of interest shall be charged on the sum of [number/currency/words] and/or any increase and/or decrease in that figure that may be authorised during the period by the [Company].

B.029
After the expiry of a period of [two years] from the date of issue of the [sum/payment] to [Name] by the [Company]. The [Company] shall be entitled to issue a new rate of interest applicable to the repayment terms based on any criteria which the [Company] may in its sole discretion decide provided that the [Company] agrees that it shall not exceed [figure] % [words] per cent and the rate of interest will not vary more than [once/twice] in any [six-month] period.

BANNER ADVERTISEMENTS

Internet and Websites

B.030
'Banner' shall mean the advertisement [specify size/shape/position] on the web page and site [reference]. The banner shall contain the following content supplied by the [Licensee] [specify] which shall have the purpose of encouraging any user of the website to click to another site linked through the banner. No other advertisements or web pages or links shall be covered by this expression.

B.031

The [Website Company] shall not acquire any rights or interest or attempt to register or licence or agree to transfer to any third party anything of any nature relating to the [Product Company] or any of its products, goods or services or business at any time. Nor shall the [Website Company] seek to register or seek to acquire any interest and/or rights through usage and the establishment of reputation and goodwill and agrees that all such rights and interest shall belong entirely to the [Product Company].

B.032

The [Website Company] shall not acquire any intellectual property rights, interest or patent or the right to licence third parties or any rights of exploitation in any media [except those set out in this document] in any material supplied under this Agreement to appear in the banner or associated site and links, meta tags or advertisements. This shall apply to all the original material and any variations, adaptations and developments of the [Product Company] and its products, goods or services including but not limited to any characters, trade marks, service marks, community marks, both registered and unregistered, logos, words, phrases, letters or artwork, images, sounds, sound recordings, music, film, computer hardware and software or any other material in any media of any nature which are supplied by or arranged for or created for or for which use is consented to by the [Product Company] at any time.

B.033

'Banner' shall mean the advertisement created by the [Website Company] on website [reference] [position/size] and linked to promote the goods and services of the [Product Company] on website [reference].

B.034

The [Company] agrees that the [Supplier] shall be able to place its banner advertisement on the [Website] reference [www.] which is owned and controlled by the [Company] on the following terms and conditions:

1.1   That the banner advertisement shall be in the form and style described as follows [specify] and a representational copy with all the content, words, slogans, artwork, computer-generated material, music, sound recordings, links and any other material of any nature which is to be displayed, appear or be connected in any form is attached and forms part of this Agreement.

1.2   That the [Supplier] shall own or control all the material set out in 1.1 and accepts full responsibility for any loss, damage, or other direct or indirect consequences financial or otherwise arising from the placement of the banner advertising on the Website of the [Company].

213

1.3 That the [Supplier] shall indemnify the [Company] against any claim, action or loss made or incurred by the [Company] or by a third party which arises as a direct or indirect result of the banner advertisement on the Website or any link.

1.4 The [Supplier] agrees that it shall not be entitled to use the name, logo, trade marks, community marks, products, services or any artwork, text, slogan or information or data from the [Company's] Website or business to promote, market or advertise the [Supplier] or any of its goods or services or to provide or supply any such material to third parties in any form without the prior written consent of the [Company].

1.5 That the [Company] shall be entitled to nominate the jurisdiction to which this Agreement shall be bound at a later date depending on the facts of the case on each occasion. Prior to any legal proceedings being issued by either party both parties agree that they shall endeavour to resolve any dispute by the appointment of an agreed mediator the cost of which shall be shared equally between both parties.

B.035

There shall be no obligation to provide banner advertisement, or additional display details of any nature in respect of products or services which the [Company] agrees that it shall sell, distribute or supply on its [Website].

B.036

In consideration of the banner advertisement the [Company] shall be paid the following sums by the [Distributor]:

1.1 The [Company] shall be paid a fixed fee of [figure/currency] for the display of the banner advertisement on its website reference [–] from [date] to [date]. The fee shall be paid in full by the [Supplier] by [date].

1.2 The [Company] shall also be entitled to be paid a click through fee of [figure/currency] for every mouse click on the banner advertisement whether or not the persons purchased any goods or services. These sums shall be paid in full to the [Company] at the end of each [three month] period.

1.3 The [Company] shall also be entitled to be paid a royalty of [number] % of the total value of all sales or orders or other business directly arising from the click through of any person or company through the banner advertisement which is coded by the [Distributor] quote [code number]. This sum shall be paid in full at the end of each [six month] period.

B.037

The [Company] shall not be entitled or have the right to receive any payments, royalty, click through fee or other sums of any nature including any percentage of sales or other business income from the [Distributor] which arises as a result of the placement of the banner advertisements on the [Company] [Website]. The [Distributor] shall only be obliged to pay the placement fee specified in clause [–].

B.038

The [Company] shall not be obliged to display the banner advertisement and/ or any related promotion on the [Website] in the event that the [Distributor] and/or the [Products/Services] which the business promotes are the subject of a product recall, health and safety investigation and/or any other matter which may prejudice the business of the [Company]. In such case the [Company] shall be entitled to remove the banner advertisement without further notice. The [Company] shall be entitled to retain all sums paid by the [Distributor] which are due to the [Company] until the date the banner advertisement is removed from the [Website].

B.039

In order for the banner advertisement to adhere to the advertising and promotional policy of the [Website Company] which may be different depending on the primary language of the market or be changed from time to time. The [Advertising Company] shall be obliged to adapt, develop, change or edit any part of the banner advertisement at its own cost and expense which may be required by the [Website Company].

B.040

All copyright and any other rights in the [Products/Services] shall belong to the [Supplier]. The banner advertisements and any associated sound recordings and links which are created, developed and produced by the [Website Company/Supplier] shall belong to the [Website Company/ Supplier].

B.041

The [Supplier] shall have the option to purchase the copyright and other rights in the banner advertisement created by the [Website Company] for the [Supplier]. Provided that the [Supplier] pays all the costs and expenses which have been incurred and/or are due in respect of the creation, development, production, clearance and acquisition of rights, staff costs and any other sums which arise directly and/or indirectly which have and/or are due to be paid by the [Company].

B.042

The [Supplier] agrees and undertakes that no banner advertisement and/or the content of any links and/or references to and/or the content of any text services, mobile services, premium rate line services and/or otherwise of

215

any nature which are referred to in the banner advertisement shall contain any material which is defamatory, pornographic, offensive, [unsuitable for children] and/or is contrary to any existing laws and/or code of practice and/or policy in [country]. The [Supplier] agrees and undertakes that every effort shall be made at the first opportunity to delete, amend, erase, correct and/or remove any material from the banner advertisement and/or any associated service which is requested by the [Company] on the grounds that its content is not acceptable and is contrary to its [Company's] policy as to the suitability of the content.

B.043

The [Advertiser] agrees and undertakes that:

1.1 It has cleared and owns and/or controls all copyright, music, logos, trademarks, text, film, sound recordings, videos, blogs, text messages and mobile services, photographs, images, links, competitions, promotions, products and/or services and any other intellectual property rights and/or material which is contained within and/or associated with the [Banner Advert] on the [Website] and the associated service to send text messages to a premium rate phone line and/or any associated link and/or other website.

1.2 That the [Company] that operates and/or owns the [Website] shall not be responsible and/or liable for any sums due for the use and/or or exploitation of such rights and/or material in sub-clause 1.1 above to any copyright owner, collecting society and/or any other third party for the display of the [Banner Advert] on the [Website] and/or the associated text message and/or any link and/or any other form of exploitation that may arise.

1.3 The [Advertiser] shall indemnify the [Company] in respect of any direct claim, costs and/or expenses that may be due and/or paid to any third party by the [Company] to settle any matter where in the opinion of the [Company] sufficient evidence has been produced to justify the payment of the sum claimed and/or where as a result of legal action by a third party an award of damages and/or costs is made against the [Company]. In addition the [Advertiser] shall pay to the [Company] all legal and administrative costs that may be incurred as a result of seeking legal advice from a solicitor and/or barrister and/or other expert outside the [Company] in order to seek an opinion and/or to defend a claim made against the [Company].

B.044

The [Licensee] agrees that it shall not be entitled to authorise, licence, supply, adapt and/or reproduce and/or alter, distort and/or make a caricature of any

216

part of the [Licensors'] names, images, logos, films, and associated products which may be in any banner links, advertisements, blogs, newsfeeds and/or any other material supplied by the [Licensor] to the [Licensee] at any time. The [Licensee] agrees that all material must be used in the exact media and form it is delivered by the [Licensor] for display, broadcast, transmission and use on the [Licensees] website known as [specify].

B.045

The [Company] reserves the right not to display any banner links, advertisements, promotions, marketing newsfeed and/or any other material supplied by the [Advertiser] which in the opinion of the [Company] will result in the threat of a legal action, have a negative effect on the main business of the [Company] and/or may give rise to involvement in adverse publicity and/or news reports in any part of the world. In such event where the [Company] on any grounds does not display any material as previously agreed and expected. The total liability of the [Company] shall be limited to [number/currency] and the Advertiser agrees to this limitation and agrees that it shall have no claim for loss of sales and/or defamation and/or any effect on it business.

B.046

The [Company] agrees to display the banner links of the [Licensor] in respect of the [Product] on the website [specify] from [date] to [date]. Together with an editorial review by [Name] on page [number] of the site. The [Company] agrees that the banner links shall not appear next to any material on the site associated with [specify subjects].

B.047

There is no agreement by the parties which places any restriction and/or prohibition on the display, promotion, marketing, editorial and/or features of any competing and/or rival products, brands, names, logos, images, text or otherwise of any type of material in any medium directly next to, before, after and/or with any material and/or banner link supplied by the [Licensor] for the website.

B.048

Where the display, use, broadcast, transmission and/or promotion of the banner links and any associated content, logo, text, image, film and music results in a claim and/or legal action and/or liability against the parent company owner of the website and/or any associated company and/or distributor by a collecting society, copyright owner and/or any other third party who has a valid claim and provides evidence in support to that effect. Then the [Supplier] of all such material agrees that the claim may be settled without any legal proceedings having been started. In addition that the [Supplier] shall be obliged to pay to the parent company owner and/or associated company and/or distributor all such sums, administrative costs, expenses, legal fees and costs and other sums that they may have to pay to resolve the matter up to a maximum of [number/currency] in total.

BEST ENDEAVOURS

General Business and Commercial

B.049
'Best Endeavours' shall mean taking every step which a [government institution/company/partnership] would be expected to take in achieving the objectives as if it were acting in its own best interests and taking into account its size, resources, financial position and the seriousness and consequences of the obligations.

B.050
The parties hereto agree that where the expression 'Best Endeavours' is used throughout this Agreement the onus on such party shall be to use all endeavours to achieve the specified aim within legal, financial and ethical restraints at that time.

B.051
'Best Endeavours' shall mean taking every step that could be taken even at considerable expense and cost which a large public company would take to achieve its stated objectives and aims based on sound and informed legal, financial and corporate advice.

B.052
The [Person] shall perform their obligations under this Agreement to the best of their skill and ability and shall supply such standards of work as may be reasonably required by the [Company] in accordance with the terms of this Agreement. Provided that the [Company] shall ensure that the [Person] shall be supplied with such technical material and facilities as may be necessary for that purpose at the [Company's] sole cost.

B.053
The [Company] agrees and undertakes that it shall provide its services to the best of its professional skill and ability providing highly qualified and specialist

experienced persons to carry out the work and provide advice, guidance, research and recommendations to the [Enterprise]. The [Company] shall not supply trainees, unqualified or inexperienced personnel. The [Enterprise] shall be entitled to request copies of the professional qualifications and curriculum vitae of each of the persons proposed for any work and shall be entitled to reject them on the grounds that they lack the necessary expertise, knowledge or experience.

B.054
Neither party shall be obliged to use their best endeavours to fulfil the terms of this Agreement and shall instead act in a commercially prudent and reasonable manner in accordance with the circumstances. Where any part cannot be performed due to the high costs involved or where the performance of the contract would be delayed and therefore be too late. Then a financial settlement in compensation shall be agreed between the parties which shall be by negotiation or alternative dispute resolution prior to any legal proceedings.

B.055
Both parties agree that they shall act in good faith and shall be bound by the following undertakings:

1.1 To carry out the performance of the work to be undertaken to a professional and competent standard until such time as the Agreement is ended, suspended or terminated for any reason.

1.2 That where due to unforeseen circumstances additional costs and expenses arise which directly relate to the completion of the work. That no additional costs or expenses shall be incurred or committed without the written consent of both parties.

1.3 Both parties agree to obtain and bear the cost of such consents, clearances, materials, facilities, documentation, personnel, or other matters which are being relied upon by the other party based on the terms of this Agreement provided that some unforeseen expense, cost, defect or restriction shall not arise which would fundamentally effect the economic viability of the [Project].

1.4 That where defects, errors, accounting or financial irregularities or any other material changes arise in relation to either party, or the work or their financial stability which effect the fulfilment of the terms of this Agreement. That the party who becomes aware of such matters should notify the other in writing of such problems as soon as reasonably possible.

B.056

There shall be no obligation on either party to provide the services and work under this contract to the best of their endeavours. In the event that the details specified in Schedule [–] cannot be fulfilled, then either party shall have the right to cancel the contract by notice in writing with immediate effect. In such event the party who has cancelled the contract shall not have any further liability to the other of any nature whether as to costs already incurred or in respect of payments under the contract.

B.057

The [Licensee] shall use its best endeavours to ensure that the [Product] is promoted and advertised in the following manner [specify catalogue/ newspaper/magazine/trade fair/website] in [country] by [date]. In the event that this clause is not fulfilled then the [Licensee] agrees to pay the [Licensor] the additional sum of [figure/currency] in the next accounting period.

B.058

The [Licensee] shall use its reasonable endeavours to make not less than [number] of the [Product] available in the following countries [specify] by [date] at the following [retail outlets/distributors/trade shows]. The [Licensee] shall provide the [Licensor] with a report of the wholesale and trade availability of the [Product] in each country together with details and samples copies of the [Product], packaging, marketing, and advertising.

B.059

The [Sponsor] agrees to use its best endeavours to ensure that the [Company] is provided with all the items listed in Schedule [A] for the [Sports Event/ Festival] by [date]. In the event that the [Sponsor] is unable to provide any items by that date then the [Sponsor] agrees to provide a suitable alternative substitute at its own cost.

B.060

The [Company] agrees that it shall endeavour to ensure that no product and/ or service is made available to [Athletes/Public] at the [Sports Event] within the confines of the official grounds specified in [Appendix A] which would directly conflict with and/or compete with the products and/or services of the [Sponsor] and specifically not the following companies and/or types of products and services [specify].

B.061

Each party agrees and undertakes that subject to the financial constraints of the need by the business to make a profit for this [Project]. That each party shall use its best endeavours to ensure that the best people within its business who are available are allocated as far as possible to work on the [Project].

B.062
Each party agrees and undertakes that it shall use its best endeavours to ensure the management, content and delivery of the [Project] shall be in accordance with the attached Schedules [–] and that no changes and/or variations of any nature, however minor, will made without the prior consent of all the parties.

BILL OF LADING

General Business and Commercial

B.063
'Bill of Lading' shall mean the written evidence in whatever form of the contract for the carriage and delivery of goods sent under the terms of this Agreement by [sea/other] whether such contract is referred to as a Contract for Bailment or any other term.

B.064
'The Bill of Lading' shall be the terms and conditions specified in writing between the parties between the [Owner] of the [Products] and the [Merchant Company] as to the liability, insurance, risk, indemnities, rights, responsibilities and cost of transport and delivery of the [Products] and their container from [the port of loading on to a vessel/address of receipt] to [the port of discharge when they are discharged/delivery address when they are delivered].

B.065
The 'Bill of Lading' may be made up of one and/or more printed documents, email attachments, texts and/or other written material which set out the basis upon which the parties have agreed terms and conditions for the movement of the [Material/Goods] from one location to another in any part of the world. In the event that any terms and conditions are incomplete, inaccurate and/ or not finalised. Then it is agreed between the parties that the presumption shall be that the person and/or company who has ordered the [Material/ Goods] shall not attain full ownership until all sums due for the purchase price of full title to the [Material/Goods] and freight, insurance, taxes, imports and export duties and any other associated costs have been paid in full to the other party.

BLOG

Internet and Websites

B.066
'The Blog' shall be defined as the text, images, films, sound recordings, photographs, designs, logos, music, slogans, trade marks, quotes, links, copyright notices and credits and other material which is provided by the [Contributor] to the [Company] to host and display the contents on the Website [Name] [web reference].

B.067
The [Website] is monitored regularly by the [Company], but the [Company] does not accept any responsibility and/or liability for any material and content that is placed on the [Website] on the [Blog] which may be in breach of copyright, trade marks, intellectual property, contract, confidentiality, defamatory and/or offensive and/or for any other reason an infringement and/or breach of a third parties rights and/or contrary to any legislation in any country in any part of the world. You are strongly advised not to supply, upload, reproduce, exploit and/or distribute any material and/or content on the [Blog] in which you have not acquired permission from the copyright owner and/or cleared the material and/or rights and/or which is likely to result in a legal action and/or claim for damages and/or costs.

B.068
I am the copyright owner of the following work [title/pages/ISBN reference]. I consent to the following extract of my work being displayed on the Website [specify web reference] on [Blog] [Name]. The duration of my consent is [specify period] and is subject to the written withdrawal of my consent at any time by notice in writing or email to the [Contributor].

B.069
The [Company] undertakes and agrees that it shall not acquire any rights or interest in the [Blog] and/or any part at any time. Except that the [Contributor] grants the [Company] the non-exclusive right to display, promote and exploit the [Blog] in association with the [Website] by means of marketing, but not any form of commercial exploitation which shall be subject to the terms of a separate agreement.

B.070
The [Contributor] shall own and/or control all copyright, intellectual property rights, trade marks, interest and goodwill in all media in the [Blog] and/or parts which are supplied and/or uploaded by the [Contributor].

B.071

The [Company] agrees that it shall not acquire any rights or interest in the [Blog] by the [Contributor] of any nature except [specify].

B.072

The [Contributor] agrees and undertakes that it shall not be entitled to be entitled to register and/or claim any rights, interest and/or equity in the domain name of the [Website] and/or any trade mark, logo, slogan, and/or any content which is owned and/or controlled by the [Company] in respect of the [Website] and/or any content except the [Blog].

B.073

The [Contributor] shall either be the original copyright owner or shall be responsible for the clearance and payment for the use of all content for the [Blog] on the [Website] and any associated exploitation and/or marketing. The [Contributor] shall be liable for the clearance and payment in respect of all intellectual property rights, copyright, trade marks, logos, databases, quotes, film, text, text messages, images, graphics, photographs, music, contracts and any other rights in respect of the [Blog] and any parts.

B.074

The [Contributor] agrees and undertakes that it shall be responsible for all intellectual property rights, copyright, consent, contract and other fees due to third parties arising from the posting, supply, display, marketing and distribution of the content and any updates of the [Blog] on the [Company's Website] [from [date] to [date]].

B.075

The [Company] disclaims any responsibility and/or liability for any consequences arising from your access to or use of this [Website] or any links in order to upload, display, amend, edit, update and/or delete the [Blog]. All content of the [Blog] may be reviewed, amended, deleted, erased, and/or edited at any time entirely at the sole discretion of the [Company]. In the event that permission to display and/or upload the [Blog] is denied for any reason. Then no compensation and/or costs and/or other sums shall be due to the [Contributor] at any time.

B.076

You use this [Website] and view, access, respond and download the contents of any [Blogs] and/or link entirely at your own discretion and risk. The [Company] is not responsible for and does not originate and/or contribute to the contents of the [Blogs] and/or any links, premium rate phone lines, and/or other services, products and/or other material. No reliance can be placed on the accuracy, truth, advice, information, opinions, and/or contents of the [Blogs]. The [Company] does not recommend, endorse, agree with and/or support the views, opinions and/or contents of the [Blogs]. Listing should not be taken as an endorsement of any kind nor as a recommendation as to the reliability, quality, or otherwise of the [Blogs] and/or any links.

B.077

The [Company] relies on the [Contributors] to the [Blogs] on this [Website] to act in good faith and to provide accurate up-to-date information, data, images, text and records. All dates, prices, special offers, and other details are subject to availability and may be changed at any time. No responsibility or liability can be accepted for any errors, omissions, damages, losses, and/or expenses and/or any other sums that may arise from your use of, reliance on and/or connected to in anyway with any [Blog]. The [Company] only permits access to browse, order goods and services and access information for private and personal use. The [Website] and/or the [Blogs] and content may not be reproduced, published and/or commercially exploited without the prior written consent of the [Company].

B.078

The [Parent Company], the [Subsidiary], the [Distributor] cannot accept liability for your reliance on any [Blog] on this [Website] of any nature and this site must be used for guidance only and may not accurate, complete or up to date. You are advised to take independent advice from a third party to review and advise on your particular circumstances and facts. You accept as a condition of your access to and use of any [Blogs] on this [Website] that you do so at your own risk and cost and [Parent Company], the [Subsidiary], and/or the [Distributor] shall not be responsible and/or liable for:

1.1 Any loss, damage or other consequent direct or indirect cost, expense or liability that may arise from your use or reliance on any material.

1.2 Any content which is misleading or an error, failure of any operation or function, virus, destruction or interference with software or equipment, security lapse or breach or failure to deliver goods or services.

1.3 Any defamatory, offensive, derogatory material or statements on any part of the site whether temporary or permanent.

1.4 Any trade descriptions, quality of goods or services, fitness for purpose, prices, payment, delivery, delay or failure to deliver.

1.5 Any infringement or breach of copyright, design rights, moral rights, trade marks, service marks or any other intellectual property rights, or any contractual or other rights of any nature.

1.6   Any links, banner advertisements, promotions, competitions, lotteries, premium rate phone lines and/or other advertising, marketing and promotional material.

B.079

The [Blogs] on this [Website] rely on users to act in good faith and in a reasonable manner. Where material is displayed or accessible which has been provided by such third party users for [Blogs] then the [Company] does not accept responsibility for any material which is defamatory, offensive, inaccurate, unavailable, unlawful or misleading. The [Company] have a policy of dealing with complaints. In the first instance email [specify] stating in detail the reasons. The [Company] shall then decide whether the complaint is justified and if so arrange for the deletion of any material which it concludes should be removed for any reason.

B.080

The Blog shall mean the text, images, photographs, films, logos and products and all other material in draft and final form created, developed, supplied and/or edited by [Name] and displayed, promoted, transmitted and reproduced on the website [specify] under the heading, slogan, image and logo as follows [specify].

B.081

The [Writer] agrees that he/she shall try to ensure that no material which is owned and/or controlled by a third party is included in the [blog/article] without an acknowledgement of copyright and/or other form of ownership. That the [Writer] shall not seek to represent that any material is original to him/her which is directly derived from the work of someone else. Nor shall the [Writer] seek to review and/or support any work of a third party who is a close business associate and/or member of their family and/or friend without proper disclosure of that fact in the [blog/article].

B.082

The [Company] agrees that it shall bear all the risk and liability of the costs, expenses, damages and sums which may be due in any form from any allegations, claims, legal actions, writs, summons, orders for contempt of court and/or any other matter which may arise directly and/or indirectly from the display, use, adaptation and/or dissemination of the [Blog/article] by the [Writer] in any part of the world at any time. This shall include any steps taken against the [Writer] and/or the Company] and/or any associated licensee, distributor and/or otherwise. The [Company] agrees to use its own in house legal team and/or any other third party legal services that may be necessary to defend, settle and/or set aside any such matters at its sole cost and expense and no liability of any nature shall be attributed and/or due to the [Writer].

Further the [Company] agrees to pay to the [Writer] any loss, expenses, costs and/or other sums which he/she may incur which arise due to such matters.

B.083

The [Writer] has created, designed and developed the blog known as [specify] which comprises regular [sport/fashion/political] comment and features. In consideration of the payment of a monthly fee of [specify] on the first day of each month by direct debit. The [Writer] grants a non-exclusive worldwide licence to the [Company] to use and adapt up to [number] articles of no more than [number] words from the blog for their website [specify]. Provided that there is a credit to the [Writer] as follows [specify] and the [Company] agrees that it uses the material from the blog entirely at its own risk and that there are no undertakings by the [Writer] of any nature.

B.084

The [Company] commissions [Name] to prepare, create and develop a new blog for its websites and as part of its online marketing. [Name] shall create an original and innovative name for the blog together with a logo, slogan and image which [Name] shall assign to the [Company] for the sum of [number/currency] so that [Name] has no control, ownership, rights and/or interest in any media and/or medium at any time. [Name] shall sign all such documents and registration forms as may be required to effect the assignment of all intellectual property rights and any other rights including trade marks to the [Company] of any material created by [Name] associated with the new blog in any format.

B.085

1.1 The [Company] agrees that the [Contributor] may deliver such material and articles, photographs and films as she/he would like to offer to the [Company] to be considered for the column and blog known as [specify].

1.2 The [Contributor] agrees that no payment shall be due to the [Contributor] unless the [Company] decides to use any part and/or all of the material, articles, photographs and film and/or any concept, idea and/or theme which arises from any of the proposals.

1.3 The [Company] agrees to pay the [Contributor] in accordance with the payment rates set put in Schedule [–] which is dependent on the type of use by the [Company]. All payments shall be made within [number] days of invoice by the [Contributor] direct to a notified bank account by electronic transfer at no cost to the [Contributor].

1.4 Where the [Contributor] creates and develops a new slogan, title, name, logo, image and/or any other material in any medium and/

or format which is original to the [Contributor] and then used by the [Company]. Then the [Company] and the [Contributor] agree that both parties shall be joint copyright owners of any such new rights that may be created and/or developed. Further that the [Contributor] and [Company] shall share equally all sums received from the exploitation of such new rights and both shall be registered equally as the joint owners.

1.5 Either party may assign and/or transfer their share to a third party at any time provided that the other party is notified in advance and provided with [number] days to make a better offer.

B.086

1.1 The [Artist] has not granted any rights and/or agreement to any use by any person who views these [Images].

1.2 You are specifically advised that you are not permitted to use the [Images] for reviews, for educational purposes and/or to reproduce, copy, supply and/or distribute copies of the [Images] displayed and available for viewing on [specify] website without the prior written consent of [Name].

1.3 The [Artist] is the copyright owner and owns and controls all copyright, intellectual property rights, trade marks, rights of resale, design rights and all rights to reproduce, adapt, licence, distort the [Images] and any associated titles, words, slogans and marketing in any format and any medium whether it exists now and/or is discovered, created, developed and/or brought into existence in the future.

B.087

In consideration of access to and use of the website and any associated material for posting and linking a blog by [Name]. Name agrees and assigns to the [Company]:

1.1 All copyright, intellectual property rights and the right to register and/or to receive any revenue from the exploitation of any title, name, domain name, trade mark, slogan, image, logo, sound recordings, sound, film, text, sub-title, photograph and any other material supplied and/or displayed on the blog known as [specify].

1.2 The assignment shall include the right by the [Company] to permit, authorise and develop any adaptation and/or variation in any medium and/or format including the right to sub-licence to a third party and/or to transfer all rights owned and/or controlled by the [Company] in full to a third party.

227

1.3 Provided that the [Company] agrees that [Name] shall be entitled to be paid [number] per cent of all the gross sums received and retained by the [Company] at any time from the exploitation and/or assignment of the blog and/or any part and/or any associated adaptation and/or variation of any part.

B.088

The parent company and the subsidiary company which controls the website on which the blog by [Name] is to be supplied, posted and distributed and promoted accept all legal and financial risk and liability arising from the use and exploitation of all material in and/or associated with the blog. The parent company and the subsidiary company agree that they shall not seek to take any civil and/or criminal proceedings and/or action against [Name] and/or his estate at any time nor to recover and/or be reimbursed in respect of any sums which they have lost, expended and/or paid to a third party for any reason.

BOARD

General Business and Commercial

B.089

'The Board' means the Board of [Directors/Trustees] for the time being of the [Company/Trust] formally appointed by resolution and notified to [Companies House/other] in the [United Kingdom/other].

B.090

'The Board' means the Board of [Directors/other] for the time being of the [Company] appointed under the current legislation of [country].

B.091

'The Board of Directors' shall be:

1.1 The Non-Executive Directors and the employed Executive Directors of the [Company].

1.2 These persons are all jointly and severally liable for the acts, omissions and errors of the [Company].

1.3 This is the current list [specify] at the date of this Agreement of those who have the status of Directors of the Board who have been appointed by formal resolution and completed the formal statutory returns required by law to [Companies House/other].

1.4   Any resignation, dismissal or change shall take effect from the date of such action or receipt by the Board and not the time at which it is formally notified to the authorities.

1.5   Each Director shall continue to be liable after departure from the [Company] for any consequences arising from his/her period of office and shall be entitled to the benefit of such insurance cover as have may have been arranged to cover such liability for the benefit of the Board.

B.092

'The Directors of the Board' shall mean all formally appointed Executives and Non-Executives of the main board of the parent company who approve and adopt by resolution the annual report and accounts of the [Company] at any time during the existence of this Agreement.

B.093

'The Board of Trustees' shall mean such individuals as may be appointed from time to time for periods of office to operate, administer and fulfil the terms and conditions of the charity registration number [specify name/ number].

B.094

The [Executive] shall only be obliged to report to and follow the management directions of the main Board of the [Company] and shall fulfil the following duties and areas of responsibility [specify description]. The [Executive] shall not be obliged to carry out any instruction which would be derogatory, offensive, or prejudicial to his/her standing or reputation nor be detrimental to or in breach of any of their professional qualifications, is potentially in breach of the laws of any country in which the [Executive] resides or works or is against their religion.

B.095

'The Directors of the Companies' shall mean all Executive and Non-Executive Directors of the main board of the Parent Company [specify] and any subsidiary, associate, holding or directly or indirectly related company whether due to a connection by shares, management, control, joint venture contract, the provision of financial support or bank guarantees [whether in existence at the time of this agreement or purchased or created thereafter] including the following companies [–].

B.096

'The Directors of the Companies' shall mean all Directors of the Group known as [specify] which shall include the Parent Company [specify] and any subsidiary, associate, holding or directly related company and shall include all the following companies [list].

B.097

'The Board of Directors of the Company' shall be [name/status/title] [together with such other names as may be added at a later date.] All appointed Directors of the Board shall be jointly and severally liable until such time as they shall resign or be removed. Thereafter they shall only be liable for matters which may have arisen during their term as Director but shall not include [specify].

B.098

'The Board' shall mean the trustees of the [Trust] and not any employees, volunteers and/or any other professional advisors who may attend regular meetings.

B.099

The parties agree that the board of the [Consortium] shall comprise the following persons [specify]. That in the event that any person is unable and/or unwilling to continue to fulfil that role. Then it is agreed that new members shall be appointed by agreement between [Name] and [Name] in the capacity of a sub-committee of the board. All proposed persons shall be subject to final approval of the [Chair] of the board prior to any offer being made at any time.

B.100

The Board agrees that they shall all be jointly and severally liable for all decisions that are taken at any time by the Board whether they took part in any decision or not and whether they have an executive and/or non-executive role provided that they are in office and have not retired and/or resigned and/or are no longer with the Board. All persons shall remain responsible and liable for all such decisions for a period of [number] years after their departure from the Board.

B.101

[Name] is appointed on [date] to the Board of [Company] and not any associated and/or related business. The [Company] agrees to indemnify [Name] in full from any claim, action, allegation, threat, loss, expense, cost, which may arise at any time directly and/or indirectly related to the work and decisions of the Board and any material, products, information and data which the Board and its directors, and officers, employees, consultants and advisors may distribute, supply, reproduce, market either whilst [Name] is on the Board or thereafter. The [Company] shall arrange and pay comprehensive insurance cover for [Name] for such purpose at the [Company's] sole cost with [Name] specified as the sole beneficiary.

BONA FIDE

General Business and Commercial

B.102

'Bona Fide' shall mean that the parties shall act in good faith, with due regard to accuracy, honesty, and disclosure of material facts to fulfil the terms of this Agreement.

B.103

'Bona Fide' shall mean that the parties shall:

1.1   Act in good faith.

1.2   Disclose all material facts accurately.

1.3   Not omit crucial information.

1.4   Not fail to disclose that they are acting act in concert with third parties.

1.5   Intend to fulfil and perform the terms of the Agreement.

1.6   Be solvent and financially sound and able to meet the commitments required.

B.104

The [Licensee] shall carry out sufficient due diligence on any manufacturer, wholesaler, distributor, freight company, publicity, promotions or other business, company or person who is to be engaged to produce, supply, distribute, promote or otherwise assist in the exploitation of the [Product/services/other]. The [Licensee] shall endeavour to ensure that they are satisfied that the company or person will act in a bona fide manner and meet all the necessary criteria which may be stipulated and deliver as required and is capable of handling the finances in a fit and proper manner and to account and make payments on time.

B.105

The parties shall both act in a bone fide manner and use their reasonable endeavours to fulfil the terms of this Agreement. There is however no obligation to reveal corporate, financial and/or marketing details except as set out in the marketing and accounting provisions in paragraphs [–].

B.106

There is no bona fide provision and it is agreed:

1.1   That each party is responsible for carrying out its own background research as to the viability of the proposed [Project].

1.2 That each party shall be entitled to act in its own best interests in all the circumstances.

1.3 Each party must carry out its own investigation as to the financial stability, reliability as to deliveries, and the status, conduct and credit worthiness of the business of the other party to this Agreement.

1.4 Both parties accept that there is no obligation on either party to disclose facts, information, data or business plans to the other of any nature whether or not any such material may subsequently be shown to be relevant to the conclusion of this Agreement.

B.107

The [Licensee] agrees to ensure that all persons connected with the production, distribution, and marketing of the [Product] are bona fide and genuine businesses which have operated for a minimum of [number] years and are based in [country].

B.108

The [Company] shall endeavour to ensure that any other company, person and/or business associated with the [Event/Programme] shall:

1.1 Act in good faith.

1.2 Be solvent and have three years of audited accounts.

1.3 Be capable and have appropriate professional expertise for the work required.

B.109

Where the [Company] at a later date discovers and/or finds out that it has been [actively] misled by one or more parties to this Agreement in respect of sales projections, historic data and/or the financial stability and/or who owns and/or controls any products, services and/or other material relating to this Agreement.. Then the [Company] reserves the right to terminate the Agreement with immediate effect without notice and to seek to be repaid all sums which have been paid to date to any party under this Agreement.

B.110

It is agreed and accepted by all parties that no responsibility can be accepted for the failure to act and/or conduct themselves and/or to supply any material including data in a professional honest and bone fide manner by any third party including consultants, legal and financial advisors, auditors, software suppliers, publicity and marketing agents and/or otherwise. That where a problem is later identified which has an effect on the terms and conditions of the Agreement that all the parties agree to enter into mediation to resolve the matter.

BONUS

DVD, Video and Discs

B.111

In the event that the [DVD] achieves any of the following target levels of sales, rental or awards then the corresponding bonus shall be payable within [in the next accounting period/within one calendar month of such event in each case] to the [Artist]:

1.1   For sales of [figure] copies of the [DVD] in [world/Country]. Bonus [figure/currency] and thereafter a bonus of [figure/currency] for every [figure] copies sold.

1.2   For rental of [figure] copies of the [DVD] in [world/Country]. Bonus [figure/currency] and thereafter a bonus of [figure/currency] for every [figure] copies sold.

1.3   For [Country] platinum best-selling [DVD] list. Bonus [figure/currency].

1.4   For [Amazon/other website] best-selling [DVD] list. Bonus [figure/currency].

1.5   For the [magazine/newspaper] best-selling [DVD] list. Bonus [figure/currency].

B.112

In the event that the total sales figures of the [DVD] in [specify Territory] exceed [figure] then for every additional [figure] copies sold thereafter the [Artists] shall each receive an additional sum as a bonus of [figure/currency] on each occasion from the [Distributor]. There shall be no upper limit on these bonuses and such sums shall be due to be paid in respect of the accounting period in which they arise and fall due.

B.113

There shall be no performance related, bonus or other additional payments to the [Artist] and the [Company] shall only be responsible for the payment to the [Artist] of such royalties as may arise from the [sales and rental/all exploitation] of the DVDs and videos under this Agreement.

B.114

The [Presenter/Agent] shall only be entitled to be paid those payments set in Clause [–] and shall not be entitled to receive any additional sums under this Agreement of any nature for any of the following:

1.1   Performance-related bonus related to achieved sales, gross receipts or net receipts.

1.2   Exploitation of any nature in any media at any time.

1.3   Licensing, assignment or transfer of rights to third parties.

1.4   Cancellation, termination or delay of the [DVD/project].

1.5   Change of material, personnel, production, technical details, or content of the [DVD/project].

B.115

The [Distributor] agrees that the [Artist/Choreographer/Performer] shall be entitled to the following bonuses or additional payments in respect of the exploitation of the [DVD/film] if any or all of the following matters occur:

1.1   The [DVD/Film] wins the following award [specify] Then the payment shall be [figure] [words/currency].

1.2   The [DVD/Film] reaches number [one] in the DVD chart on [specify]. Then the payment shall be [figure/currency] [words].

1.3   The [DVD/Film] is distributed as a free copy in any newspaper, magazine or other article or product for distribution to the public or at any trade fair or exhibition. Then the payment shall be [figure/currency] [words].

B.116

The [Company] shall be entitled to the following additional payments as a bonus, performance or target related payment, or in consideration of the acceptance of alterations to the agreed project details and completion dates set out in Schedule [–]. All the sums set out below shall be paid by the [Distributor] to the [Company] within [28 days] of any such event.

1.1   Achieved sales of Disc by [Distributor] in excess of [figure] in [country] by [date] one off payment due [figure/currency] to the [Company].

1.2   [specify internet company] achieves sales (excluding returns, and those lost and damaged) of Disc at any time one off payment to [Company] of [figure/currency].

1.3   In the event that any rights including the Disc rights are sub-licensed to a third party, then on each occasion a one off payment shall be paid to the [Company] of [figure/currency] in respect of each license.

B.117

It is agreed between the [Company] and the [Distributor] that in the event that more than [number] copies of the [Work] are sold and supplied to the public for more than [figure/currency] in any [one/three-] month period. That the [Distributor] agrees that it shall pay the [Company] a royalty at the rate of [number] % on all copies sold to the public in excess of [number] for that period.

B.118
The [Writer/Company] agree and accept that even where sales exceed projections in any market and/or the [Distributor] is awarded a financial prize linked to sales as an industry award in any country and/or for any other reasons exceeds expectations. No additional sums and/or payments shall be due and/or owed to the [Writer] except those set out in this Agreement.

B.119
It is agreed that in the event that the sums received by the [Distributor] exceed the figures set out in column [–] of the attached Schedule [–] for each of the countries specified [at any time during the term of this Agreement/ from [date] to [date].] That the [Presenter] shall be entitled to be paid the additional sums set out in column [–] of the Schedule and all such sums shall be paid within [specify period] of the achievement of the target by the [Distributor] whether or not the accounts have been audited or not.

B.120
Where more than [number] copies of the [Work/Disc] are sold, supplied and/ or licensed to any third party at any time by the [Company]. The [Company] agrees to pay [Name] an additional payment of [figure/currency] in arrears each calendar month by direct debit as an additional advance against future royalties. This additional payment is not a bonus.

Employment

B.121
'Bonus' shall mean a discretionary gratuity which is over and above the [Employee's] agreed remuneration under the terms of this Agreement and shall be treated as a goodwill payment on behalf of the [Employer] and no rights of enforcement shall arise against the [Employer] in the event of non-payment of the Bonus.

B.122
'Bonus' shall mean those sums to which the [Employee] is entitled as of right under the terms of the Bonus Scheme and payment of such Bonus shall be treated as an enforceable contractual term.

B.123
'Additional Remuneration' shall mean such financial rewards, options or benefits in kind or payments by the [Company] to which the [Executive]

shall be or shall become entitled or be awarded during the course of his/her employment including but not limited to:

1.1 Any annual bonus which may be payable in the event the Executive achieves either personal targets and/or the [Company] achieves specified turnover, profit and/or cash flow targets as specified in the Executive Bonus Scheme attached as Schedule [–].

1.2 Any Executive Share Option Schemes details of which are attached as Schedule [–] which may be granted or exercised.

B.124

The [Executive] shall only be entitled to receive any bonus payments or other sums from the exercise of an option or bonus scheme or performance related targets or other benefits during the existence of this Agreement. When the Agreement has been terminated or expired, then the [Executive] shall not have any further rights in respect thereof, except where a sum should have been paid and was not received by the [Executive].

B.125

The [Employee] shall not have any right to any bonus, performance-related pay, additional sums, remuneration, options, benefits or rewards other than those set out under the terms of this Agreement. This shall be the case whether or not someone else at a comparable level or job description in the [Company] receives or is awarded any additional sums, shares, rewards or otherwise at the discretion of the [Company].

B.126

The [Company] undertakes and agrees that it shall ensure that the [Employee] is awarded or is entitled to receive share options, bonuses, performance related pay, expenses, relocation costs, executive benefits and any other sums or privileges on the same scale and level as any other person employed in a comparative position or salary in the company at any time provided that the [Employee] shall fulfil the stipulated criteria.

B.127

The [Company] agrees that the bonuses which are to be provided to the [Executive] under this Agreement form an important part of the agreed financial package and are not discretionary and shall not lapse upon the expiry or termination of this Agreement unless it can be shown that the [Executive] was dismissed for gross misconduct.

B.128

The award of a bonus, additional payment, additional leave, an all-expenses-paid holiday, car, sporting event tickets or other products or items at any time by the [Company] to an [Employee] shall not incorporate this into the contract nor place any obligation on the [Company] to continue to provide at a later date other similar or equal in value rewards and bonuses.

B.129

The [Company] agrees and undertakes that it shall be obliged to provide to the [Executive] the same standard of benefits, rights and payments as would be available to any other person at the same level in the [Company] either before or after the [Executive] joined the [Company]. This shall apply in respect of the salary, bonuses, performance-related pay, share options, pension rights, health care and dental cover, life insurance, expenses, travel, accommodation, car, telephone, relocation costs and any other sums. Although the position of the [Executive] may be improved due to this clause, the [Company] shall not have the right to use it to reduce payments or otherwise to the [Executive].

B.130

The [Company] agrees and undertakes that every year the [Executive] shall be set an agreed Budget for their department which shall be the maximum expenditure for the year. In the event that the [Executive] delivers the target set. The [Company] shall pay to the [Executive] the additional sum of [figure/currency] for each year that the target is attained. The payment shall be made within [two months] of the end of each financial year.

B.131

The [Company] agrees that it shall pay the [Executive] the bonus set out in this Agreement provided that:

1.1 He/she achieves the performance targets which have been set in appendix [–]; and/or

1.2 He/she is not the subject of a disciplinary proceeding for misconduct by the [Company] and/or a regulatory body which oversees the business of the [Company]; and/or

1.3 He/she has not brought the [Company] into disrepute; and/or

1.4 He/she is not the subject of criminal proceedings which could result in a prison sentence.

B.132

The payment of the bonus under this agreement to the [Executive] is not based on the [Company] being in profit overall as a business but merely the achievement of the targets set for the [Executive].

B.133

The [Company] agrees that where it fails to comply and pay the bonus to the [Executive] as required by the terms of this Agreement and the [Executive] has to take legal action to obtain payment. That the [Company] shall in addition be obliged to pay an additional fee of [number/currency] for each calendar month and/or part pro rata that it fails to fulfil the terms of this Agreement if the [Executive] succeeds in obtaining an order for payment of all of the bonus claimed.

Film and Television

B.134

The following specified individuals shall receive an additional payment of a bonus in the event that the [Film] is completed by [date] in accordance with the Production Schedule and Budget [Name/figure/currency/due date].

B.135

In the event that the [Film] achieves Gross Receipts worldwide within [two years] from the date of first distribution to the paying public anywhere in the world. Then the [Name] shall be entitled to receive a bonus of [figure/ currency] for each sum of [figure/currency] achieved over the total of [figure/ currency] of Gross Receipts. All such bonus payment sums shall be paid within [three calendar months] of the achievement and financial verification of the targets. The payments shall not be delayed to follow the usual accounting procedures under clauses [–].

B.136

The following additional sums shall be paid by the [Company] to [Agent] in respect of the [Artist] which shall be due in the accounting period in which they shall arise:

1.1   The [Film] achieves rating viewing figures of [number] on [channel/ country] [specify]. Bonus [figure/currency].

1.2   In excess of [number] people use the premium rate line phone. Bonus [figure/currency] for every [figure] in excess of [figure] in each country.

1.3   In excess of [figure] copies of the DVD are sold in [world/country]. Bonus payment [figure/currency].

1.4   In excess of the Target figures as gross revenue is achieved by the [Company] in each of the following merchandising categories:

    1.4.1   Toys and Board Games: Target figure [–] Bonus [–].

    1.4.2   Books, magazines, comics: Target figure [–] Bonus [–].

1.4.3   Computer Games and software: Target Figure [–] Bonus [–].

1.4.4   Clothes, lunchboxes, household, stationery: Target Figure [–] Bonus [–].

1.4.5   Sales, rental and supply of DVDs and Videos: Target Figure [–] by [date] Bonus [–].

1.4.6   Music downloads only from an authorised website on the internet (whether for PCs, mobiles, televisions, radio or some other device): Target Figure [–] Bonus [–].

1.4.7   Sales, rental and supply of CDs, tapes:

1.4.8   Target Figure [–] by date. Target Figure [–] by [date] Bonus [–].

1.4.9   Premium rate phone line or text message service: Target figure [–] Bonus [–].

1.4.10 Sports, promotional and corporate events: Target Figure [–] Bonus [–].

1.4.11 All other forms and methods of licensing and/or exploitation in any other material, use or rights not specified above: Target figure [–] Bonus [–].

B.137

If the [Distributor] successfully concludes contracts with the following companies [–] in respect of [Film/Programme/Series] then [Name] shall be entitled to an additional payment of [figure/currency] as a bonus.

B.138

In the event that the [DVD] achieves any of the following target levels of sales, rental or awards then the corresponding bonus shall be payable within [in the next accounting period/within one calendar month of such event in each case] to the [Artist]:

1.1   For sales of [figure] copies of the [DVD] in [world/Country]. Bonus [figure/currency] and thereafter a bonus of [figure/currency] for every [figure] copies sold.

1.2   For rental of [figure] copies of the [DVD] in [world/Country]. Bonus [figure/currency] and thereafter a bonus of [figure/currency] for every [figure] copies sold.

1.3   For [Country] platinum best-selling [DVD] list. Bonus [figure/currency].

1.4   For [Amazon/other website] best-selling [DVD] list. Bonus [figure/currency].

1.5 For the [magazine/newspaper] best-selling [DVD] list. Bonus [figure/currency].

B.139

In the event that the total sales figures of the [DVD] in [specify Territory] exceed [figure] then for every additional [figure] copies sold thereafter the [Artists] shall each receive an additional sum as a bonus of [figure/currency] on each occasion from the [Distributor]. There shall be no upper limit on these bonuses and such sums shall be due to be paid in respect of the accounting period in which they arise and fall due.

B.140

There shall be no performance related, bonus or other additional payments to the [Artist] and the [Company] shall only be responsible for the payment to the [Artist] of such royalties as may arise from the [sales and rental/all exploitation] of the DVDs and videos under this Agreement.

B.141

The [Presenter/Agent] shall only be entitled to be paid those payments set in Clause [–] and shall not be entitled to receive any additional sums under this Agreement of any nature for any of the following:

1.1 performance-related bonus related to achieved sales, gross receipts or net receipts;

1.2 exploitation of any nature in any media at any time;

1.3 licensing, assignment or transfer of rights to third parties;

1.4 cancellation, termination or delay of the [DVD/Project];

1.5 change of material, personnel, production, technical details, or content of the [DVD/Project].

B.142

The [Distributor] agrees that the [Artist/Choreographer/Performer] shall be entitled to the following bonuses or additional payments in respect of the exploitation of the [DVD/Film] if any or all of the following matters occur:

1.1 The [DVD/Film] wins the following award [specify]. Then the payment shall be [figure] [words/currency].

1.2 The [DVD/Film] reaches number [one] in the DVD chart on [specify]. Then the payment shall be [figure] [words/currency].

1.3 The [DVD/Film] is distributed as a free copy in any newspaper, magazine or other article or product for distribution to the public or at any trade fair or exhibition. Then the payment shall be [figure] [words/currency].

B.143

The [Artist] shall be entitled to the following additional payments as a bonus if the [Film/DVD] achieves commercial success and/or wins any awards. All the sums set out below shall be paid by the [Company] to the [Artist] within [two months] of any such event.

1.1 The total number of sales of the [Film/DVD] worldwide by the [Company/Distributor] are in excess of [figure/words]. The [Company/Distributor] shall be obliged to notify the [Artist] that this target has been achieved. The [Artist] shall be entitled to be paid the sum of [figure/currency] [words].

1.2 In the event that the total advertising, merchandising, music and sub-licensing gross receipts received by the [Company/Distributor] are in excess of [figure/currency] [words]. The [Company/Distributor] shall be obliged to notify the [Artist] that this target has been achieved. The [Artist] shall be entitled to be paid the sum of [figure] [words/currency].

1.3 The [DVD/Film] wins the following award [specify] Then the payment shall be [figure/currency] [words] to the [Artist].

B.144

In the event that the [Series] is nominated for and/or wins any of the following awards [specify] whilst [Name] is the main presenter during the term of this Agreement. Then the [Distributor] agrees to pay [Name] an additional fee of [specify] within [one month] that the nomination and/or award is made to any of the parties involved in the [Series] including the [Distributor], production company [specify] and/or the parent company [specify].

B.145

There shall be no obligation for the [Company] to pay any additional sums, bonuses and/or an increased royalty and/or advance at any time to any persons and/or company involved in any capacity in respect of the [Film]. All parties agree that any award, prize, article, sums and/or other benefits may be retained by the [Company] and that there is no obligation to share and/or allocate any part to any other person and/or company whether based on and/or arising from the work and/or performance of an individual or not.

B.146

The [Presenter] shall be entitled to be paid an additional fixed fee of [figure/currency] within [one month] of transmission on each occasion where the viewing figures for the public in [country] on any form of delivery by television exceed [number]. The fixed fee relates to each separate transmission [but not archive television on demand].

General Business and Commercial

B.147

The [Company] shall not be entitled to receive any additional sums, bonuses, performance related, contingency, residual or repeat fees or other benefits, shares, or stock or interest of any nature under the terms of this Agreement under any circumstances.

B.148

The [Executive] agrees and undertakes that he/she has freely negotiated this Agreement and shall not be entitled to claim that he/she should receive the same standard of benefits, rights and payments as would be available to any other person at the same level in the [Company] either before or after the [Executive] joined the [Company]. This shall apply in respect of the salary, bonuses, performance related pay, share options, pension rights, health care and dental cover, life insurance, expenses, travel, accommodation, car, telephone, relocation costs and any other sums. The [Executive] agrees that such matters are entirely at the sole discretion of the [Company].

B.149

The [Company] may at its absolute discretion decide at any time to award bonuses or other additional benefits to its employees by way of a reward for hard work, recognised effort and dedication or a particular achievement for the [Company]. However there no legal obligation to do so and this reward system may be discontinued at any time, and is not related to status in the [Company] or any other particular criteria.

B.150

Sums which are not expended as set out in the Agreement and the Budget shall not be retained and all such sums must be repaid to the [Company].

B.151

The award of a bonus, additional payment, or products or items at any time to any person, business or company shall not incorporate this into a term of any contract nor place any obligation on the [Company] to continue to provide at a later date other payments or rewards of a similar nature or equal in value.

B.152

Where in any part of this Agreement the [Company] agrees to pay a bonus and/or performance related fee. This shall only be due and/or payable to [Name] where the parent company [specify] and the subsidiary who is party to this Agreement is financially solvent and able to pay any sums due to [Name]. In the event that it is unable to pay the sums due then [Name] agrees that he/she shall not be entitled to place any lien and/or charge over the parent company only the subsidiary.

B.153

The [Company] agrees that where any bonus is due to [Name] due to the financial success of the [Project]:

1.1 That any such sums shall be kept in a separate bank account which is clearly identifiable and not mixed with other funds of the [Company].

1.2 That no lien, charge and/or other claim shall be made over these funds which are due to be paid as a bonus.

1.3 That [Name] shall be provided with confirmation as to where the funds are held and the date and method by which they are to be transferred to [Name].

Internet and Websites

B.154

The [Artist/Consultant] has been paid a fee for the supply of their services and any material for the [Website]. No additional sums shall be due at any time for any reason for any exploitation, licensing, sale, reproduction, distribution or otherwise of all or any part of the Website. There shall be no bonus, performance related fees, share options, stock or additional sums due of any nature.

B.155

The [Company] shall not be entitled to any additional payment or bonus from the [Advertiser] in the event that the [Website] receives in excess of the target [hits/subscribers/banner links]. Nor shall the [Advertiser] be entitled to reduce the fee, withhold payment or request a refund of any nature if the target is not achieved.

B.156

In the event that the [Website] is successful and achieves in excess of [figure] [hits/subscribers/gross turnover] in the period from [date] to [date]. Then thereafter the [Advertiser] agrees to pay an additional bonus payment of [figure/currency] at the end of each [six month] period thereafter starting [date] whilst those figures are maintained or exceeded.

B.157

The [Artist/Presenter] shall be entitled to the following additional sums under this Agreement in respect of the provision of their services and the use of such material on the [Company] Website under this Agreement as follows:

1.1 Annual [gross/net receipts] is equal to or more than [figure/currency] in any period from [specify start and end date] then a payment of [figure/currency] shall be due for each such period.

1.2 Banner advertising receipts exceed [figure/currency] then a one off payment of [figure/currency] shall be paid.

1.3 A [Film/DVD/Book/other] is produced by the [Company] or sub-licensed by the [Company] to a third party based on the [Website]. Then a percentage royalty of [number] per cent of the sums received by the [Company] shall be due to the [Artist/Presenter] which shall be paid within [one] calendar month.

B.158

The parties both agree that where the [Company] and website is valued by a reputable bank and/or other financial institution of international recognition at a figure of no less than [number/currency] and/or is listed on the [specify] market. That the following parties set out in Schedule [–] shall be entitled to be paid a one off bonus payment set out in that document. Provided that at the time of the achievement of either of those targets any such person is still employed in the role specified by their name and/or is a director, shareholder and/or consultant to the [Company].

B.159

No additional fees, expenses, costs, royalties, bonuses and/or other payments shall be made to the [Consultant] for any work and/or contribution to any of the websites, business plans, projects, brands and marketing, products and/or otherwise for any new ideas, concepts, ventures, partnerships, sales and/or any other additional material and/or working hours that may be incurred at any time.

B.160

1.1 In consideration of the [Project Fee] the [Design Company] shall be obliged to assign all copyright, intellectual property rights and all other rights of any nature in any media and/or any adaptation to the [Distributor] which arise directly and/or indirectly as a result of the work on the [Project] including any ideas, concepts, formats, logos, images, software and hardware developments, codes, patents and inventions, film and sound recordings, apps, music, characters, games and merchandising whether recognised by any law in any country at the time of the [Project] or not, including all prototypes, samples and any supporting documents, information and data stored on any device and/or gadget and/or computer and/or other electronic form of reproduction or telecommunication.

1.2　The [Distributor] agrees and undertakes that where they receive in total in excess of [number/currency] from the exploitation of any of the rights set out in 1.1 by [date] then the [Design Company] shall be entitled a single additional payment of [number/currency] as a bonus [but not a royalty] which shall be paid to them by the end of the year in which such sum is received and/or achieved by the [Distributor].

Merchandising

B.161
The [Licensor/Distributor] shall not be entitled to any additional payment and/or bonus from the [Licensee] in the event that the [Product] wins an award, exceeds the projected sales, is sold out in any country and/or exceeds [figure/currency] in total retail sales in any year.

B.162
In the event that the [Product/Book/Series] and/or any sequel is adapted and/or exploited in any form. The [Contributor] agrees that he/she shall not be entitled to receive any additional payments, royalties, bonuses, expenses, or other benefits or interest of any nature under the terms of this Agreement at any time.

B.163
The [Licensee] shall pay the [Licensor] the following bonus payments in the event that the [Work] achieves any of the following targets. All sums shall be paid by the [Licensee] to the [Licensor] within [two months] of achievement of the target:

1.1　[Figure/currency] in the event that the [first/any edition] of the [Work] sells [number] [hardback/paperback] copies in [country] in the first year of publication.

1.2　[Figure/currency] if the [Work] wins any of the following awards [specify].

1.3　[Figure/currency] in the event that an agreement is concluded for an option for the [Work] to be made into a [Film/DVD].

1.4　[Figure/currency] where the Gross Receipts received by the [Licensee] exceed [figure/currency] in any financial accounting year.

B.164
Where the [Licensee] receives more than [number/currency] in any one accounting period from the sales and exploitation of the [Product/Work]. Then the [Licensee] agrees to pay the [Author] an additional bonus of [number/currency] for that accounting period which shall not be considered an

advance against royalties. The [Licensee] agrees that such bonus sum could be due to the [Author] for each accounting period if the target is achieved.

B.165
The [Licensor] agrees and accepts that no additional fees, bonus and/or other sums shall be due even if the sales and/or exploitation of the [Work] exceeds the projections and/or the [Distributor] negotiates and/or receives additional fees from a form of exploitation which was not predicted at the time of the conclusion of the agreement.

B.166
The [Distributor] agrees to pay additional fees to the [Author] in the form of bonuses set out in Schedule [–] which are not an advance. The [Distributor] agrees to pay the sums within [number] days of when the target specified is achieved.

Publishing

B.167
The [Publisher] shall pay the [Author] the following additional sums as a bonus in the event that the [Novel] achieves any of the following targets. All sums shall be paid by the [Company] within [14 days] of invoice upon completion of the target:

1.1 [Figure/currency] in the event that the [first edition] of the [Novel] sells [number] [hardback/paperback] copies worldwide in the first year of publication.

1.2 [Figure/currency] if the [Novel] is nominated for the [Award].

1.3 [Figure/currency] in the event that the [Author] is announced the winner of the [Award].

1.4 [Figure/currency] in the event that the [Publisher] achieves gross sales in [country] of [format] within [number] years of first publication of the [hardback/paperback] in [country].

1.5 [Figure/currency] in the event that an agreement is concluded for the [Novel] to be made into a [Film/DVD].

1.6 [Figure/currency] in the event that the [Author] agrees to a repackaging deal to collate two novels in one paperback for distribution primarily in supermarkets.

1.7 [Figure/currency] in the event that the [Novel] achieves any top ten bestselling list from the following sources [specify Website/Newspaper/Magazine].

B.168

The [Distributor] shall pay the [Author] the following performance related sums in the event that the [Work] achieves any of the following targets. These sums shall not be an advance against royalties nor shall they be set off against other agreements or sums. The obligation shall be on the [Distributor] to notify the [Author] that the target has been met and all sums shall be paid by the [Distributor] in the next accounting period following achievement of the target:

1.1   [Figure/currency] in the event that the [first edition] of the [Work] sells [number] [hardback/paperback] copies in [country] by [date] or within [six months] of publication whichever is the later.

1.2   [Figure/currency] if the [Work] wins the award [specify].

1.3   [Figure/currency] in the event that the [Work] is translated into more than [number] languages worldwide.

1.4   [Figure/currency] if the gross receipts received or credited to the [Distributor] exceed [figure/currency] from exploitation of the [Work] in any form.

1.5   [Figure/currency] in the event that an agreement is concluded for an option for the [Work] to be made into a [Film/DVD].

1.6   [Figure/currency] in the event that the [Author] agrees to a repackaging deal to collate the [Work] with another work by the same author into one paperback for distribution primarily in supermarkets.

1.7   [Figure/currency] in the event that the [Work] is number [figure] or higher in the top ten best-selling list from one of the following sources [Website/ Newspaper/Magazine] for a period of a minimum of [specify duration].

B.169

The [Publisher] and the [Distributor] or any sub-agent or sub-licensee shall not be under obligation to pay the [Author] any bonus, performance related payment, or additional sums in the event that the [Book] appears in any bestsellers list, wins or is nominated for any award, or is reprinted more frequently than predicted, or the sales of the [Book] exceed projected targets discussed prior to or after conclusion of the Agreement.

B.170

For every financial year of the [Publisher] during the term of this Agreement in which the total receipts from the exploitation of the [Work] exceeds [figure/ currency] the [Publisher] agrees to pay the [Author] [figure/currency]. Any sum due shall be paid within [one calendar month] of the end of each such financial year.

B.171

The [Company] agrees that where it concludes a serialisation agreement with one or more national newspapers in [country] and/or any part of the world. Where the [Company] receives [number/currency] or more for each such serialisation. That the [Author] shall be entitled to an additional bonus fee of [number/currency] in respect of each such serialisation which shall not be offset against future royalties. All sums due to the [Author] shall be paid within [one] calendar month of invoice by the [Author]. The [Company] agrees that it shall be obliged to notify the [Author] of the achievement of any of the proposed targets in any country in each case.

B.172

The [Publisher] agrees that where the [Artwork] for the cover and marketing is licensed by the [Publisher] for reproduction and commercial exploitation in any form at any time. That the [Artist] shall be entitle to an additional payment of [number/currency] as a bonus. Provided that the [Artist] does not seek to have any right to any royalty and/or other claim in respect of the [Artwork].

B.173

The [Distributor] agrees that where in the first [two] calendar months from the first date of publication the [Work] is in one and/or all of the bestseller lists of [specify]. That the [Distributor] shall pay the [Author] a one-off bonus of [number/currency] regardless of the volume of sales at that time. The bonus shall be set off against future royalties by the [Distributor] and shall be paid to the [Author] within [number] days of the event.

Purchase and Supply of Products

B.174

The [Supplier/Contractor] shall not be entitled to any bonus and shall not have the right to retain any sums which are under spent on the [Budget/Cost] at any time. All sums which cannot be verified by supporting documentation as to their allocation and use must be returned to the [Company].

B.175

The [Supplier] and any third parties engaged by them to [complete this Project/supply the Products] shall not be entitled to withhold the repayment of any unused funds, or to receive any bonus, additional sums or to otherwise claim any benefit or interest in their exploitation, rights or financial or other benefits that may arise or become due to the [Company] at any time.

B.176

In the event that the [Contractor] delivers all the [Products/Services] on time and in accordance with the requirements and costs set out in this contract.

Then the [Contractor] shall be awarded a bonus/satisfactory service reward of [figure/currency] by the [Company] payable within [one calendar month] of the final completion of the contract and compliance with all the terms and conditions.

B.177
It is agreed between the parties that where the [Supplier] meets all the delivery dates and has fully complied with all requirements in respect of the [Articles] ordered by the [Company] from [date] to [date]. That the [Company] may at its entire discretion decide to pay an additional one-off payment to the [Supplier] as a form of bonus of [number/currency] within [three months] of the end of that period. The [Supplier] acknowledges that the [Company] is under no obligation to pay the bonus to the [Supplier].

B.178
The [Distributor] may from time to time add additional content to the [Products] by way of a bonus and/or promotional offer for a limited period. The [Distributor] shall not be obliged to continue to supply the additional content after the expiry of any such period.

B.179
Where the [Distributor] requires the [Supplier] to fulfil an order and/or increase production which incurs additional unforeseen costs in any month to the [Supplier] in excess of [number/currency]. Then the [Distributor] agrees that it shall pay the [Supplier] an additional fixed bonus of [number/currency] for that month.

Services

B.180
'Bonus Fee' shall mean a one-off fee of [figure/currency] which is separate and additional to the Basic Fee and Contributors Expenses which shall be payable to the [Contributor] by the [Company] in the next accounting period in the event that the [Contributor] meets all the targets set out below:

1.1 adheres to all the time schedules stipulated for the completion and delivery of material;

1.2 completes and supplies all the documentation requested; and

1.3 attends all meetings, production and filming dates.

B.181
There shall be no additional sums of any nature shall be due to the [Contributor] at any time. The [Company] shall be entitled to exploit the material created

under this Agreement at any time in any media and to assign, transfer and sub-licence the material provided the [Fee] has been paid.

B.182

In the event that the [licence/research project] known as [reference] is awarded to the [Company] by [Name] [for the next five years]. Then the [Company] agrees to pay the [Consultant] the sum of [figure/currency] as a bonus. Payment to be made within [three months] of [receipt of confirmation of award/conclusion of the agreement].

B.183

The award of the tender, licence, research project, or government contract, renewal, sale or transfer of any interest in the business shall not result in any additional sums, benefits, products, stock or shares being due to [Name] as a bonus, reward, percentage, or otherwise.

B.184

There shall be no entitlement under this Agreement to any additional form of payment by way of a bonus, royalty and/or performance related fee at any time to the [Consultant] and/or any other party whom he/she may engage for the purpose of this Agreement.

B.185

Where any application for funding by the [Consortium] is approved and paid to them by a third party and the [Consultant] has played an integral part in the preparation of the documentation, presentation and application. Then the [Consortium] agree in respect of each such successful application where the funds awarded exceed [number/currency]. That the [Consortium] shall pay the [Consultant] an additional fixed bonus of [number/currency] for each such receipt of funds from each application.

Sponsorship

B.186

'The Performance-related Fee' shall be the sums to be paid by the [Sponsor] to the [Sportsperson] in the event that the [Sportsperson] wins or achieves any of the events, records or other matters which are set out in the [Performance-related Schedule: specify target achievement/payment/date due] which is attached to and forms part of this Agreement.

B.187

In addition to the Sponsorship Fee the [Sponsor] agrees to pay to the [Sportsperson] any sums set out in the [Performance-related Schedule] within [specify period] of the event or occasion upon which the [Sportsperson] becomes entitled to any such payment.

B.188
In the event that the [Athlete/Sportsperson] achieves any of the events, records or other matters set out in the Performance-related Schedule, but is subsequently found to be disqualified and/or tests positive for drugs and/or is found to be using illegal and/or banned products which enhance performance. Then the [Sponsor] shall be entitled to refuse payment of any sum to which the allegation and/or proof relates to the [Athlete/Sportsperson]. Where the [Athlete/Sportsperson] is banned by its [athletics/sports] organisation and/or suspended then the [Sponsor] shall also be entitled to terminate the agreement. In such event no payments under the Performance Related Schedule which have not already been paid shall be due.

B.189
The [Sponsor] agrees that where the viewing ratings for any programme in the [Series] achieve [number] in [country] whether through broadcast, transmission, play back television and /or viewing on a computer and/or other gadget in any one week from [date] to [date]. That the [Sponsor] shall pay the [Company] and each of the following members of the cast [specify] a one-off fee as a bonus each of [number/currency]. Total payment of [number/currency] which cannot be recouped by the [Sponsor] under any other agreement with the [Company].

B.190
In the event that the [Sponsor's] name of [specify] and product [specify] appear in the [Programme] in full shot and are used by one of the main characters in the cast. Then an additional bonus fee of [number/currency] shall be paid to the [Company] for each different character that uses the product. The [Company] agrees that payment shall not be due for more than [number] characters in the [Programme].

B.191
No bonus, additional sum, advance, royalty, assignment fee and/or other sum shall be due to be paid by the [Licensee] under this Agreement.

University, Library and Educational

B.192
The [Supplier/Contractor] shall not be entitled to any bonus, performance related payments, products, stock, shares, rights, interest or otherwise. Nor shall the [Supplier/Contractor] be entitled to save costs and retain any

sums which are under spent on the [Budget/Cost/Price] at any time as an additional benefit.

B.193

In the event that the [Contractor] delivers all the [Products/Services] exactly in accordance with the delivery dates, costs and quality set out in this contract and complies with all the other terms and conditions. Then the [Institute] agrees that the [Contractor] shall be supplied with a letter of recommendation that it may use as a reference for future customers. The [Institute] also agrees that the [Contractor] may use a quote from the [Institute] which shall be agreed between the parties on its website and in its promotional material.

B.194

The [Company] shall only be entitled to those payments specified under clause [–]. There shall be no additional sums, benefits, products, stock shares, rights, royalties, bonuses or other interest due to the [Company]. The [University] shall be entitled to exploit the material, products, data, patents, copyright and any other rights or interest created or developed by the [Company] under this Agreement relating to the [Project] at any time in any media and to assign, transfer and sub-licence any part of the [Project]. In the event that there is a subsequent project, licence, or government contract or the [Project] or any part is sold or transferred no additional sum shall be due to the [Company] and no right to be involved or kept informed.

B.195

The [Enterprise] shall pay the [Consultant] the following performance-related sums as a bonus in the event that the [Work/Project] achieves any of the following targets. The sums shall be due within [twenty eight days] upon invoice by the [Consultant] provided that the target has been completed:

1.1 [Figure/currency] in the event that the first research and report to the [Enterprise] is completed, delivered and accepted by [date].

1.2 [Figure/currency] if the [Work/Project] results in the award of the tender for [specify] to the [Enterprise] by [date].

1.3 [Figure/currency] if the [Work/Project] is to be developed into a second phase and the [Consultant] is not to be engaged as a main contributor under a new agreement.

1.4 [Figure/currency] in the event that the contribution of the [Consultant] to the [Work/Project] results in the creation of new computer software, patent, or other intellectual property which the [Enterprise] is able to register as the owner anywhere in the world. In return for the payment the [Consultant] agrees to sign and execute any documents that may be required at the [Enterprise's] sole cost.

B.196

'Bonus Fee' shall mean a single one-off fee of [figure/currency] which shall be payable to the [Contributor] by the [Library] if the [Library] concludes an agreement for the commercial exploitation of the [Work] with a third party.

B.197

Where the [Institute] seeks to commercially exploit the [Concept] with a third party as a joint venture. Then the [Institute] agrees that [Name] shall be entitled to be party to that Agreement as the original creator of the [Concept] and to receive both his/her own advance and percentage royalty of any sums that may be negotiated and/or due. As well as [number] per cent of all sums due and/or paid to the [Institute] as an additional bonus payment for continued work on the [Concept] at the [Institute].

BOOKS

General Business and Commercial

B.198

'Books' shall be defined to mean any form of material comprising title, text and/or images which is produced by printing or other form of reproduction which forms a collection of pages and has a main cover whether hardback or paperback. A copy of which is required to be lodged with the [British Library] and which is allocated an ISBN for the purposes of reference. The pages may be made of paper, plastic or fabric or other material. There may also be some interactive or other component, but it shall not form the main part of the book. The following types of books shall fall within this definition:

1.1　Hardback.

1.2　Paperback.

1.3　Anthology.

1.4　Children's annuals, plastic and fabric books; books with interactive buttons or other gadgets.

1.5　Educational editions.

1.6　Translations in any language.

1.7　Quotations from the text.

1.8　Straight radio, television, festival, promotional and exhibition readings.

1.9   Large prints, Braille.

1.10 Book Club editions.

1.11 The right to sub-licence any of the above rights shall be [included/ excluded].

B.199

The following shall not be covered by and is specifically excluded from the definition of 'Books' in Clause [–] above in this Agreement:

1.1   Serialisation, one-shot digest, publication in newspapers, magazines and other periodicals and/or downloads of any text or images on mobiles, gadgets and websites whether in written or audio form.

1.2   Mechanical reproductions, computer software, PC and game consoles including audiocassettes, DVD, audio CD, CD-Rom, CD, cartridges and other gadgets.

1.3   Adaptation or reproduction for film, cable, satellite, digital or terrestrial television or other visual image of viewing material.

1.4   The internet or world wide web in any form.

1.5   Telecommunication and wireless systems in any form including mobile phones, screensavers, clips, images, games, gaming, ringtones and animations.

1.6   National and local sound broadcasting and digital radio, theatre and cinema and any form of exhibition or performance.

1.7   Merchandising and formats which are not set out as permitted. Sponsorship, product placement, endorsement, cross-promotion, banner advertisements, text advertising.

1.8   Photographs, images, strip cartoons or picture forms.

1.9   Storage, retrieval, supply, database, library or system of electronic, mechanical or transmission or conveyance of text, images, data or other material in any media.

1.10 Adaptation or reproduction as any form of disc, software, gadget or method to be used to listen to, view or record including DVD, CD, and CD-Rom and any other medium of any nature except those set out in 1.1 to 1.10 above.

B.200

'Books' shall be defined as printed paper hardback and paperback only; all other formats, methods of reproduction or exploitation are specifically reserved by the [Company] and excluded from this Agreement.

B.201

'The Book' shall mean the Front cover, Preface, Contents and Index described as follows:

ISBN [–] Title [–] Author [–]
[–] Pages [–] Photographs [–]

[excluding/including] any packaging, disc, free gift, advertising, vouchers, or promotional inserts.

B.202

'The Work' shall mean the [original] work to be produced and delivered by the [Author] based on the [Synopsis and Summary] provisionally entitled [–] which is attached to and forms part of this Agreement. This shall [include/exclude] the front cover, preface, introduction, artwork, graphics, index and any associated material.

B.203

'The E Book' shall mean a reproduction of a digital file of an exact copy of the original first edition of the [Work] [including the cover, front pages, and index] by [Author] which has the ISBN reference [number] and which is in the [English/other] language in [hardback/paperback]. [Together with any illustrations, photographs, images, and trade marks].

B.204

'The Audiobook' shall mean a reproduction of a sound recording of a person reading in the [specify languages] the text of the original first edition of the [Work] by [Author] which has the ISBN reference [number].

B.205

'The Digital Book' shall mean the reproduction in electronic form for the purpose of supply and /or reproduction by a telecommunication system to a third party in whole and/or in part of the cover, content and index of the [Work] by [Author] which has a printed ISBN of [number]. Such form of reproduction to include pdf, email attachment, download onto a machine or portable gadget for reading online but shall not include a mobile telephone, text service, television, film, games, betting or any other type of service or any method not currently created and/or developed in [year].

B.206

The 'Work' shall mean the project entitled [specify] written by [specify names] as joint contributors and which it is proposed shall consist of [number] A4 pages, [number] images in [format] together with a cover, index and preface all to be supplied to the [Company] by [Name].

University, Library and Educational

B.207

'The Book' shall mean the first edition of the work [title] written by the Author [full name] which consists of [number] pages and [number] [photographs/plates/engravings]. The copyright owner is [name] and the work was published in [date]. A copy of the cover and the first pages of the work are attached to and form part of this Agreement.

B.208

'The Book' shall mean the loose cover, the binding, copyright notices, preface, text, images, drawings, photographs, index, footnotes, disclaimer and any associated CD-Rom or attached CD which is sold or supplied with the work which is described as follows:

> Author [full professional name] otherwise known as [personal name]
> Title [–] ISBN [–] Language [specify]

B.209

'The Manuscript' shall be the final proof copy submitted by the [Student] to the [Institute] for the [Dissertation] which is based on a research title supplied by the [Institute] as follows [specify].

B.210

'The Book' is the work of facts and information originated, developed, written and delivered by [Name] on the subject of [specify] which comprises approximately [number] draft pages in [specify] font. Together with approximately [numbers] images designed and created by [Name] to support and enhance the text.

BRAND

General Business and Commercial

B.211

The [Company] manufactures, develops, markets and supplies types of [generic product] and [owns/controls] the rights in the following brands and styles [specify in detail], [photographs/images] of which are attached in [Schedule 1] and form part of this Agreement.

In the event that the [Advertising Agency] is required to arrange or commission any new logos, words, phrases, slogans, images, sounds, smells, music or any other material of any nature by the [Company] or deriving from their work for the [Company]. The [Advertising Company] shall ensure that neither themselves nor their employees nor any third party shall acquire any rights or interest in any such new material in any form or medium and that all copyright, design rights, trade marks, community marks or any other rights, patents, inventions and computer software shall be transferred entirely to the [Company]. Further that the [Advertising Company] shall assist in the arrangements for the signature of all such legal documents as the [Company] may reasonably request in order to transfer, assign or register any rights or interest at the [Company's] cost.

B.212

'The Brand' shall mean the following [Products/Services] which are owned or controlled by the [Company] described as follows [specify product type/colour/shape/images/noise/sounds/music/smell/words/phrases/logo/trade marks/design rights/packaging/advertising/marketing].

A complete set of [images/text/other] of which is attached to and forms part of this Agreement.

B.213

The [Website Company] agrees that it shall not acquire any interest in any part of the brand of the [Advertiser] or any part of its business whether in existence now or created in the future including trade names, slogans, text, characters, images, music, packaging, products or other material in any medium. All original artwork, computer-generated material, and any other material supplied by the [Advertiser] or created by an employee, consultant or third party engaged by the [Website Company] shall be returned to and owned by the [Advertiser]. The [Website Company] and any other person or business shall not be entitled to acquire any rights and the [Website Company] shall co-operate in ensuring that all intellectual property and other rights are transferred to the [Advertiser] at the [Advertiser's] cost.

1.1 Where in the course of the [Project] the [Consultant] is required to arrange, commission and/or contribute to the research, development, packaging, reproduction and/or any other use and/or exploitation in any format or media of any nature of any material including but not limited to any new logos, words, phrases, slogans, text, film, recordings, computer software, music, trials, tests, prototypes.

1.2 The [Consultant] shall ensure that they shall not and neither shall their employees, agents or representatives nor any third party acquire any rights or interest in any material whether supplied by the [Institute] or another third party or is new and original.

1.3   The [Consultant] undertakes and agrees that any rights or interest in any material whether supplied by the [Institute] or another third party or is new and original in any form or medium which is arranged by the [Consultant] shall be entirely owned by the [Institute] and/or transferred or assigned to them including all copyright, design rights, trade marks, community marks, patents, inventions and computer software and any other intellectual property rights and ownership of any material. Provided that the [Institute] agrees to bear the reasonable cost of the legal expense of any such documents, applications and registrations that may be required.

B.214

The [Consultant/Contractor] shall not be responsible for the protection, registration and/or monitoring of the trade marks, logos, slogans, copyright, patents, inventions, computer software or other intellectual property rights or any other interests of the [Enterprise] under this Agreement. The [Consultant/Contractor] agrees and undertakes to assign to the [Enterprise] all rights of any nature in any media in any material which may be created or commissioned by the [Enterprise] for the purposes of this Agreement.

B.215

'The Brand' shall mean the following [Products/Services] which are owned or controlled by the [Institute] a reproduction and sample of which is set out in Schedule [–] which is attached to and forms part of this Agreement.

B.216

The [Website Company] agrees that it shall not acquire any interest or rights in any part of the [Institute] or any part of the [Website/podcasts/downloads] and/or any other material of any nature which is in existence now or created in the future. All original artwork, computer-generated material, and any other material supplied by the [Institute] or created by an employee, consultant or third party engaged by the [Website Company] shall be returned to and owned by the [Institute]. Neither the [Website Company] nor any third party engaged by them shall be entitled to acquire any rights or interest without the prior written consent of the [Institute]. The [Website Company] shall co-operate in ensuring that all intellectual property and other rights including trade names, slogans, text, characters, images, music, packaging, products or other material in any medium are assigned and transferred to the [Institute] at the [Institutes'] cost prior to the payment of the final fee under clause [–].

B.217

The [Licensee] agrees and undertakes that:

1.1 It shall not acquire any copyright, intellectual property rights, trade marks, computer software rights, images, characters, music, computer-generated material, patents, design rights or any other rights and/or interest in the [Product/Programme/Work] of any nature which is in existence now or created in the future.

1.2 That all original artwork, prototypes, sample material and any other material supplied by the [Licensor] shall be owned and controlled by the [Licensor].

1.3 It shall not acquire any copyright or intellectual property rights in any drawings, sketches, maps, databases which are created and/or developed for the manufacture and reproduction of the final product and/or any subsequent model.

B.218

The [Author] is not assigning any copyright, intellectual property rights, trade marks and/or any other right to register an interest and/or collect funds from a collecting society to the [Distributor] in respect of the [Work]. The [Author] shall at all times own and control the title, logo, format and content of the [Work] and the right to licence and/or exploit a sequel based on the same main characters. No right to own and/or control any part of the [Work] and/or the title and/or content is assigned to the [Distributor].

B.219

The [Distributor] agrees and undertakes:

1.1 Not to register and/or attempt to register any copyright, intellectual property rights, trade marks and/or any other right as an interest and/or with any collecting society in the name of the [Distributor] in respect of the [Work] and/or any adaptation.

1.2 That the [Author] shall at all times own and control the title, logo, format and content of the [Work] and have the right to licence and/or exploit a sequel whether based on the same main characters and/or any other part of the [Work].

B.220

The [Sponsor] shall not acquire any rights in respect of the copyright and intellectual property rights in the title of the [Event] and any associated logo, trade mark, slogan, image, and/or music and/or lyrics that may be developed, produced and/or distributed by the [Company] and/or the [Sponsor]. If for any reason the [Sponsor] inadvertently acquires any such rights then the [Sponsor] agrees to assign all such rights to the [Company] at the [Company's] cost.

B.221

The [Licensee] agrees that it shall have no right and/or authority to use, reproduce and/or adapt any other product, article, logo, trade mark, image and/or brand owned and/or controlled by the [Licensor] and/or any associated companies, suppliers and/or manufacturers at any time. That the licence granted under this agreement is limited solely to the logo and image and product listed and reproduced in Appendix [–] for the period from [date] to [date].

B.222

After the end of this Agreement provided that there is no dispute and/or legal proceedings pending and/or in action. The [Licensee] shall ensure that all master copies of the [Licensors'] logos and image held by the [Licensee] in any form shall be returned to the [Licensor] at the [Licensee's] cost. That the [Licensee] shall offer the [Licensor] the opportunity to acquire any further material which it has within its possession and/control which bears the logo and/or image of the [Licensor] prior to any plan to destroy such material.

B.223

Where a new brand image, name and/or logo arises through the licence to the [Licensee] which is developed from and/or adapted from the original [Logo/Image] for which rights are granted under this Agreement. Then the [Licensee] agrees that all copyright, trade marks, service marks, and any other intellectual property rights and any other rights and interest shall belong to and be assigned by the [Licensee] and/or any third party from whom work has been commissioned to the [Licensor]. That the [Licensee] shall not have any claim to any funds from any exploitation except under this Agreement and/or any right to register any image, name, logo and/or use in the [Licensee's] name in any country or part of the world.

B.224

1.1   [Name] agrees to pay the [Artist] the sum of [number/currency] for the creation, design and supply of a draft and final logo, image and layout for the new business of [Name].

1.2   In consideration of an additional fee of [number/currency] the [Artist] agrees to waive all moral rights of any nature and agrees that [Name] shall be entitled to put a copyright notice in the following form [specify] and/or in any other manner next to the logo, image and layout.

1.3   That the [Artist] agrees that he/she shall not in future be entitled to reproduce, use and/or adapt the logo, image and/or layout and/or authorise others to do so for any reasons including review, articles, merchandising and/or for display on the internet to provide examples of past work.

1.4   That the [Artist] agrees to assign all copyright and the sole rights of ownership including but not limited to trade marks, service marks, intellectual property rights, rights of reproduction on film, television, radio, in computer software and on any hardware and/or gadgets, as merchandising and in the form of sponsorship and in any other form to [Name] in all media and in any format and for any purpose which exists at the time of the creation of the logo, image and layout and/ or may come into existence at some future date and/or due to a new format of the work being created throughout time and space and in all countries, languages, forms of representation, reproduction and rights of registration and/or ownership and/or control at any time without further payment to the [Artist].

BREAK CLAUSES

General Business and Commercial

B.225

The [Company] shall have the right at its sole discretion to end the contract by [one month's] notice any time during the term of this contract. Payments shall only be due for services provided to that end date. No sums shall be due as a penalty, charge, for disconnection, early termination or for any period after the end date.

B.226

If the [Company] repays the sums due under this Agreement at an earlier date than set out and the contract or the scheme is brought to an end. There shall be no additional payments to be made by the [Company] to compensate for the loss of interest, fees or commission or imposed as an early redemption charge, cost or penalty.

B.227

The Agreement shall not automatically continue and be renewed on a rolling basis, and every period of a calendar year shall be a separate Agreement. The Agreement shall only continue if the [Supplier/Contractor] receives written confirmation from the [Company] or payment is made for work for the next period.

B.228

This Agreement may be ended by [Name] by [method] on or by the following dates [specify]. No reason is required and no sums are due to the

[Distributor] after the end date either as compensation for early termination, or for any losses or expenses which may arise either directly or indirectly as a result.

B.229
Either party shall have the right to terminate this Agreement after the expiry of a period of [six months] from the [start date] of the Agreement. Written notice to that effect must be received within [seven days] of the expiry of the [six month] period. No reason for the termination is required and no sums shall be due in compensation and/or as damages for any losses. The only payments which shall be made are those which are still due to the date of termination. No sums shall be paid for any agreements and/or other arrangements which exist and/or were due to be signed after the date of termination.

B.230
Where the [Agent] for the [Company] acts in such a manner and/or makes such allegations which are untrue, in accurate and likely to effect the reputation of [Name]. Then [Name] shall be entitled to terminate this Agreement with immediate effect and shall not be liable to pay any further sums due to the [Company] under this Agreement which may fall due for work after that date.

B.231
Where in the first [three-month] period of this Agreement either party shall fail to fulfil and perform the terms in accordance with the Agreement. Then the party who has not complied with all the terms may be served notice by the other party that the Agreement will end on any date that they shall decide to notify and there shall be no obligation to continue with any part of the Agreement after that end date.

BUDGET

DVD, Video and Discs

B.232
'The Budget' shall mean the Budget for the [Film] which shall set out in detail all the fees, costs, charges, copyright clearance payments, mechanical reproduction and performing rights payments for any music, insurance costs, expenses, reproduction costs, and contractual obligations and liabilities connected with the development, production, completion,

distribution and exploitation of the [Film] in accordance with the Production Schedule. A copy of the following documents are attached to and form part of this Agreement [Budget/Production Schedule/Marketing Report].

B.233

In consideration of the production of the [Film] by the [Production Company] and the supply, assignment to and exploitation by the [Distributor] primarily in the [DVD/Video] market. The Distributor agrees to pay the total sum set out in the attached Budget to the [Production Company] in accordance with the payment dates specified subject to completion of work. The Budget is attached and forms part of this Agreement. Where the Budget is exceeded the [Production Company] shall not be entitled to any additional sums without verification as to the reason an audit as to the sums expended and the written consent of the [Distributor].

B.234

Without prejudice to the [Production Company's] entitlement to receive a share of the proceeds of exploitation of the [Film]. The Budget shall be accepted as consideration by the [Production Company] and shall be paid by the [Distributor] in full satisfaction of the amounts due to the [Production Company] in respect of all costs incurred by the [Production Company] in making, completing and supplying a technically acceptable first class quality master copy of the [Film]. The Budget shall include but not be limited to the following matters:

1.1 Directors', actors', musicians', writers', performers', composers' and contributors' fees, expenses and costs to the date of completion and a schedule for any sums due thereafter.

1.2 All intellectual property rights and copyright clearances and payments, consents, scriptwriters, directors and producers fees.

1.3 All costs and expenses for development, reproduction, editing, front titles and credits

1.4 Legal, administrative, insurance, location access, accommodation, meals, travel, freight, stationery, packaging, telephone and mobile costs.

1.5 Music clearance and payments, any sums due to any collecting societies or union members or any other person or company for recordings, reproduction, performances, distribution and exploitation.

B.235

The [Production Company] shall deliver to the [Television Company] by [the end of each month] from the date of this Agreement a written statement of the pre-production, production and post-production costs of the [Series] on an accrued cost basis. Each statement shall show the final estimated cost of the production of the [Series] against the Budget and shall contain a full and proper explanation of any variances from the Budget.

B.236

The [Production Company] shall deliver to the [Distributor] within [three calendar months] of the [delivery/acceptance] of the Master Copy of the [Film] a report which provides a detailed statement of expenditure of all costs and expenses incurred and due. Wherever possible, copies of supporting receipts and invoices will be provided. If there is a dispute between the parties as to the validity of all the sums then there shall be an audit carried out by an independent firm of chartered accountants approved by both the parties at the [Distributors] cost and expense. The [Production Company] shall not be entitled to retain any sums not expended and shall only be entitled to receive any sums in excess of the Budget if there has been written authorisation in advance by the [Distributor].

B.237

'The Approved Budget' shall be the agreed cost of making the [DVD] whether direct or indirect inclusive of all locations, facilities, technical and skilled consultants, companies and personnel, products, insurance, music, artwork, computer-generated material, permissions and consents, licences, agency fees, transport, hotel and telephone costs and expenses necessary for the development, pre-production, production, editing and supply of the [DVD]. A copy of which is attached and forms part of this Agreement.

B.238

[Name] agrees that he/she is not entitled to order any goods or services or to pledge, commit or authorise any payment, credit or other matter without the prior consent of [specify] in the [Company].

B.239

The [Assignor] undertakes that it shall produce the [DVD/other] using the Key Personnel in accordance with the Artistic Concept, the Approved Budget and the Production Schedule.

In the event of the Approved Budget being exceeded by up to [figure/currency/percentage] the [Assignor] agrees to inform the [Assignee] in advance and provide the [Assignee] with a statement of costs incurred to date and details of the additional costs.

B.240

In the event of the Approved Budget being exceeded by more than [specify amount] the [Assignor] agrees that the prior written approval of the

[Assignee] shall be required in an order to authorise any further expenditure and any further payment shall be at the [Assignee's] sole discretion.

B.241

The [Assignor] undertakes that all sums due in respect of the production of the [Series] will be paid as set out in the Budget. That in the event that it is expected that the Budget will be exceeded, the [Assignee] shall be notified immediately in writing. That no additional costs or expenses shall be incurred without the prior written consent of the [Assignee]. That the Budget only sets out the cost of clearance and payments for the following rights [–] in [country] and not all other media.

B.242

'The Budget' shall be the total cost of making the [Film] or the [DVD] whether direct or indirect, inclusive of all locations, facilities and other items necessary for the development, pre-production, post-production, comprehensive personal injury insurance and product liability and delivery. The [DVD] shall only be cleared for use in the following countries [–]. A copy of the Budget is attached to and forms part of this Agreement as Schedule [–].

B.243

The [Assignor] undertakes that all sums due in respect of the production and exploitation of the [Film] for the [DVD/Video] will be paid as set out in the Budget and that the [Assignee] is not and will not be liable for any such payments except in respect of the [person] and the Musical Work which are not included in the Budget.

B.244

The parties agree that [DVD] of the [Film] is only intended to be sold and exploited in [country] at first for [market] so the Budget does not cover the cost of clearance and payments for the exploitation of any other countries or rights. These may be cleared and acquired by the [Company] at their own cost at a later date.

B.245

'The Budget' shall be no more than [figure/currency] in total. This sum shall be used for the preparation, development and production of the master sound recordings for the [Disc] prior to manufacture, distribution and exploitation. The Budget shall be used to arrange clearance of and payment of any the music and/or lyrics, payment and buyout of any session and other background musicians, and/or the conclusion of any relevant contracts with musicians, artists and performers and any advance, use of any studios and/ or location, and/or facilities and all relevant technical support to produce the master sound recordings.

B.246

'The Mini-Film Pilot Budget' shall be the sum of [number/currency] to be paid by the [Trust] to [Name] to film and edit a short film of no more than [duration] minutes based on the topic of [subject] in the form of the synopsis attached to this Agreement to be delivered by [date] in [format].

B.247

[Name] is not authorised by the [Company] to exceed the budget allocated to the [Project/Film] at any time. The [Company] will not and does not accept any liability in respect of any commitment to pay and/or expenditure incurred in excess of the agreed budget of [number/currency].

B.248

It is accepted by both parties that the sums specified is a provisional and estimated budget and may be exceeded due to additional costs and expenses which may arise directly and/or indirectly from the development, production, reproduction and distribution of the [Film] in different formats including artwork, advertising, packaging, music, promotions and in store online marketing. The [Company] and the [Distributor] agree that the [specify] shall pay all the cost of the budget up to a maximum of [number/currency].

Film and Television

B.249

'The Approved Budget' shall mean the agreed direct and indirect costs of making the [Advertisement], inclusive of all location facilities and other items necessary for the development, pre-production, production, post-production and delivery of the [Advertisement] and shall include any contingency allowance, completion guarantee and full insurance cover for personnel, artistes and delivery of the Advertisement Material. A copy of the Approved Budget is attached to and forms part of this Agreement.

B.250

'The Approved Budget' shall be the agreed cost of making the [Pilot], whether direct or indirect, necessary for the development, pre-production, production, post-production, completion and delivery of the [Pilot] including but not limited to facilities, location costs, insurance, personnel, copyright clearance, consents, music, artistes, equipment, technical material or contingency allowance, any completion guarantee and the producer's fee. A copy of the Approved Budget is set out in Appendix [–] which is attached to and forms part of this Agreement.

B.251

In the event of the Approved Budget being exceeded the [Assignor] agrees to inform the [Company] in advance and provide a statement of costs incurred to date and details of the proposed additional costs. The [Assignor] agrees that the prior written authorisation by [Name] at the [Company] shall be required before incurring any further costs.

B.252

'The Programme Budget' shall be the aggregate of the sums paid by the [Television Company] (other than to the Television Company's employees or consultants) in relation to the production of the [Programme] which shall include (by way of example and not limitation) the following fees for the rights and/or services acquired or provided for the production of the [Programme] and which are not included in the [Producer's] Budget: any levy charge by any film, television, video or entertainment agency, contributions towards the costs of the blanket agreements with the [Mechanical Copyright Protection Society/Phonographic Performance Limited/Video Performance Limited/ Performing Rights Society] to the extent agreed between the parties, insurance premiums, audit fees and the [Television Company] executive's travel costs, interest on the [Producer's] Budget calculated from the date of the [Television Company's] payment of the relevant sum until the repayment thereof to the [Television Company] out of the Net Receipts at [two per cent] per annum above [Bank] plc's base rate prevailing at that time.

The production costs shall also include a sum for contingency as monies available for expenditure only with the [Television Company's] prior agreement and upon a particular item contingent upon requirements of the production of the [Programme] not otherwise anticipated by the Budget. The production costs shall also include a sum for any literary, dramatic, artistic or musical material and any library or other film or sound recordings incorporated into or synchronised with or otherwise forming part of the [Programme] which has neither been commissioned for the [Programme] nor produced at the expense of the [Producer] out of the Production Account, but has been created by third parties or by the [Producer] for purposes other than production of the [Programme].

The final total sum for the Programme Budget shall be the aggregate cost of production of the [Programme] as shown by the final cost statement delivered in accordance with Schedule [reference] drawn up by the [Producer] and the actual production costs of the [Television Company] applicable to the [Programme] as set out in the final statement by the [Television Company].

B.253

'The Budget' shall mean the fixed price sum of [figure/currency] (exclusive of VAT) which both parties to this Agreement acknowledge and agree to be the entire cost of development, pre-production, production, post-production and delivery of the Programme in accordance with the terms of this Agreement. For the avoidance of doubt the Budget shall include in particular but not by way of limitation provision for:

1.1   The fees and exploitation fees to be paid to performers and all other contributors to the Programme in accordance with the terms of this Agreement.

1.2   The cost of any film and/or video studio hire (if any) and the services to be provided by the studio proprietors and the cost processing, editing, credits, title, copies and storage for the completion and delivery of the Programme.

1.3   The fees payable for the services of all the persons specified in this Agreement as being involved in the Programme including [specify names] and all other persons, firms and companies contracted, engaged or who in some form provide a contribution whether artistic, photographic, graphic, creative, computer-generated, technical, and legal services and facilities for the production and delivery of the Programme.

1.4   The cost of location, production, including the transport costs, meals, telephone, mobile internet, postage, freight and accommodation of all personnel.

1.5   All costs of acquiring the [non] exclusive rights in the Third Party Material for the duration of the Licensed Period and such other rights in All Media throughout the Territory where such rights can be obtained. No material is to be incorporated which cannot be cleared for the intended purpose of this Agreement.

1.6   The cost of the Completion Guarantee referred to under this Agreement.

B.254

'The Budget' shall mean the fixed sum of [figure/currency] (exclusive of value added tax) which shall be the entire cost of the development, pre-production, production, post-production and delivery of the [Film] in accordance with the terms of this Agreement. A copy of the Budget is attached to and forms part of this Agreement as Schedule [–]. For the avoidance of doubt the Budget shall include:

1.1   The fees and exploitation fees to be paid to all performers, artists, contributors or other persons who appear in sound/or vision;

1.2   The cost of film and/or studio, location, equipment, set costs such as costumes, lighting, furniture, development, processing, editing, reproduction, credits and titles, freight and storage costs;

1.3   The cost of any personnel, director, crew, support staff, legal, accounting, graphics or other artwork, computer and software, photographic, music, technical, insurance cover and completion guarantee;

1.4   The cost of all materials such as telephone, stationery, internet use, transport and travel accommodation, food and drink, clothing, makeup, props.

1.5   The arrangement of and obtaining of all necessary consents, clearances, releases, moral rights, contracts, copyright, software, trademarks, logos, images, formats in any material or of any person or company.

B.255
The [Assignee] agrees that it shall not be entitled to offset the Budget from the Gross Receipts which shall be limited to the defined Distribution Expenses.

B.256
The [Assignor] shall set up a separate bank account for the Budget and the administration of the production, marketing, distribution and sales of the [Film].

B.257
The [Consortium] agrees to release [number/currency] to be held in a bank account at [bank] opened for the purpose of funding the pilot development of the [Film] in the name of a limited company where the two directors and signatories to the bank account are [specify]. Subject to the provision that the funds must only be used for the purpose of developing a script and pilot film as set out in the attached documents in Schedule [–].

B.258
It is agreed by both parties that where the budget is exceeded and the additional costs cannot be met by either party. That subject to the consent of both parties a third person and/or company may contribute to the cost in return for the allocation of rights to exploit the [Film].

B.259
The [Artist] agrees that the [Company] has awarded a budget of [number/currency] as the total budget to produce, direct and collaborate on a creative film on the subject of [specify]. That any additional costs and expenses shall be the responsibility of the [Artist] and not the [Company] including any sums due for music, collecting societies, copyright and rights clearance and payments, technical and manufacturing costs and venue hire.

General Business and Commercial

B.260

The [Company] agrees that it shall bear its own costs in respect of [specify] and these are not intended to be recouped as part of the allocated Budget.

B.261

In the event that it is anticipated that the Budget is to be or is exceeded then the prior written consent of the [Parent Company] is required before the [Distributor] incurs any additional costs. In the event that there is consent provided to such costs then the [Distributor] shall be liable to pay such sums.

B.262

The [Company] agrees that the Budget is a statement of the total cost of the [Project] and is not for guidance, but the maximum price agreed between the parties.

B.263

The [Company] agrees and undertakes that it shall only use and pay for items for the [Project] set out in the Approved Budget and that no such sums shall be used to fund other projects. That the [Company] shall pay for all of the [Project] out of the Approved Budget and that the [Fund Provider/ Government Body] shall not be liable for any additional payments or costs once the Approved Budget has been paid to the [Company].

B.264

In the event of the Budget being exceeded up to [specify figure or percentage] the [Company] agrees to inform the [Client] in advance and to provide the [Client] with a statement of costs incurred to date and details of the additional costs.

B.265

In the event of the Budget being exceeded by more than [figure/currency] then the [Company] agrees that the prior written approval of the [Client] shall be required in order to authorise any further expenditure which shall be at the [Client's] sole discretion.

B.266

'The Promotion Budget' shall be the combined costs of the Promotion Fee and the Promotion Expenses which shall not exceed [figure/currency].

B.267

The parties have agreed that the total budget for the [Installation] shall be [number/currency] in accordance with the attached budget plan and the deadlines for the delivery. Both parties accept and agree that where any cost is expected to increase at any time that provided that it falls within the additional [ten] per cent contingency that it shall be permitted without prior authorisation.

B.268

The [Company] has provided a quote of [number/currency] as the proposed budget for the work to [specify purpose] and create and deliver [specify] to [Name]. The [Company reserves the right to adjust and increase the cost due to additional changes requested by [Name], delay in placing the order and/or any other matter resulting from variations and changes to the order at any time and/or increase in supply costs of materials.

Internet and Websites

B.269

The [Design Company] shall not be entitled to any additional sums of any nature from [Name] unless agreed in writing in advance. The total liability and budget for designing, creating and setting up the [Website] shall be limited to [figure/currency]. The sums due shall be paid in stages according to the development and completion of the [Website] as follows [specify].

B.270

Authorisation for additional expenditure for the budget may be by email exchanges, letters or phone call and the [Client] agrees to pay all such sums subject to completion of the authorised additional work.

B.271

'The Budget' shall be the total cost of creating, developing and delivering a functioning [Website] for the [Company]. The Budget shall only include the costs specified in the attached Schedule which is attached to and forms part of this Agreement.

B.272

'The Budget' shall be the total cost of creating, developing, marketing, setting up and delivering a functioning [Website] for the [Company]. The budget shall include all the costs which directly relate to the design, development, testing, functioning, consumer and market research and establishment of the [Website] on the internet which operates in the manner specified by the [Company]. The costs shall be inclusive: of all locations, facilities, personnel, third party presenters or contributors and insurance, computer software, computer hardware, source codes and licences; acquisition and clearance of any text, artwork, photographs, images, trade marks, logos, music, sound recordings, film, DVDs; the cost of any registrations with any organisations;

271

the cost of all sponsored links, listings, banner advertisements. The Budget specified in the attached Schedule [–] is for guidance only and may be amended due to changes in the requirements specified by the [Company]. In any event the Budget shall not exceed [figure/currency] unless the prior written approval of the [Company] has been obtained in advance.

B.273

The [Development Company] has agreed and undertaken to design, create, develop and deliver a finished [Website] in accordance with the description in Appendix [A] and the Budget in Appendix [B]. The Budget shall also include all the costs, expenses and payments that may be necessary to host the [Website] for [three years] on the internet, to register the domain name, and for the [Website] to fulfil the functions and operate in the manner set out in the objectives and targets in Appendix [C].

B.274

The [Designer] confirms that the price quoted for the production of the website for the [Company] may be increased due to additional work and changes requested by the [Company]. That where the production and/ or development is stopped due to the [Company] being unwilling and/or unable to pay any further costs to finish the website. That the [Designer] agrees that the [Company] shall have the right to develop, adapt and finish the website on its own and/or with a third party. Provided that the [Designer] has been paid in full for all work up to the date of termination of the project by the [Company].

B.275

The [Designer] agrees that the [Company] may at its sole discretion decide not to further engage the services of the [Designer] to work on and/or complete the [Project] at any time. The [Company] shall have the right to end the agreement with the [Designer] whether or not all of the budget has been spent and whether or not any work is not completed. The [Company] may appoint a third party to work on the [Project] with the [Designer] and no approval and/or consent of that person and/or company being required.

B.276

Where the original budget has been exceeded and the [Design Company] and the [Trust] cannot agree terms regarding the additional costs to complete the [Project/Website/App]. Then provided that the [Design Company] has been paid for all their work under the original budget and any other work authorised by the [Trust]. Then the [Design Company] agrees that it shall have no right to refuse to permit the [Trust] to arrange for the collection of all the original material, copies of all software related to the [Project/Website/App], development plans and work and any associated material in any format and/or medium required by the [Trust] in order for them to transfer the work to a third party. Provided that where copies have to be made for any reason that the [Trust] shall pay the cost provided it has authorised the reproduction in each case.

B.277
[Name] acknowledges and agrees that the [Designer] has only provided a rough quotation for the purposes of guidance of the cost of development of the [App/Download]. That additional costs and expenses may be required to complete the project so that it functions as requested by [Name]. [Name] agrees that all changes, variations and adaptations requested by [Name] at any stage of development will incur additional costs and charges by the [Designer].

B.278
The [Designer] agrees to keep [Name] regularly informed as to the costs and expenses and charges which may be incurred beyond the original quotation for the work. That authorisation shall be sought in advance for any sum in excess of [number/currency]. That in any event the [Designer] agrees that the maximum liability of [Name] to the [Designer] for the [Project] shall not exceed [number/currency]. That any sum in excess of that figure shall be at the [Designer's] sole cost.

Merchandising

B.279
The [Company] agrees that it shall provide at its sole cost a Budget of [figure/currency] for the purpose of promoting, marketing and publicising the [Product].

B.280
The [Company] confirms that the proposed Budget for the [Product] is not less than [figure/currency].

B.281
The [Company] agrees that it shall allocate and spend an annual budget of [figure/currency] in [country] for each year for the duration of the first [three] years of the Agreement in order to advertise, promote and market the [Product] in the following medium [specify].

B.282
The [Distributor] agrees and undertakes that the following sums shall be spent by the [Distributor] in developing, testing, marketing and advertising the [Service/Product/Work]:

1.1   Development budget [figure/currency] from [date] to [date].

1.2   Testing of prototypes for health, safety and quality [figure/currency] before [date].

1.3   Marketing and advertising budget [figure/currency] from [date] to [date].

B.283

The [Licensee] agrees and undertakes that it shall not be entitled to deduct any costs, expenses and/or any liability arising from the development, production, manufacture, exploitation and/or marketing of any products which are based on the [Work] from the Gross Receipts and/or the Net Receipts. That the cost of all such payments shall be entirely the responsibility of the [Licensee].

B.284

The [Distributor] agrees to advise the [Licensor] of the marketing and advertising budget which is being allocated to the [Project]. The [Distributor] agrees to consult with the [Licensor] as to the potential and most effective use of the funds for the purpose of reaching the target market. The [Licensor] agrees that any use of such budget is at the [Distributors] sole discretion and choice, and that it may be withdrawn without any reason being provided.

B.285

The [Licensee] agrees and undertakes to provide a total budget of no less than [figure/currency] in the first two calendar years from [date] for the purpose of advertising, marketing, selling and raising the profile and the brand of the [Products].

B.286

The [Company] agrees and undertakes:

1.1   To design, develop, make and produce a fully functional [Prototype Product] using the key personnel in accordance with the Approved Budget agreed with the [Author]. A copy of the Approved Budget which specifies the key personnel is attached to and forms part of this Agreement in Schedule [–].

1.2   That no authority and/or consent is provided by the [Author] to exceed the Approved Budget and that any additional costs and/or expenses incurred shall be the responsibility and liability of the [Company].

1.3   Upon delivery of the completed [Prototype product] the [Company] shall supply an itemised breakdown of the Approved Budget which confirms which sums have been spent. Where not all the sums have been spent then the [Author] shall pay the lower sum rather than the agreed Approved Budget.

B.287
The [Market Consultants] agree and undertake that they shall not have any right under this Agreement to authorise and/or commit the [Company] and reach agreement by email, verbally and/or in any written form with any other person and/or business in respect of the brand [specify] unless the exact terms and conditions have specifically been agreed with the [Executive] of the [Company] in advance in each case. This shall include but not be limited to any advertising and/or sponsorship campaign whether in print, on line and/or through events, product placement and films, radio, television and computer software and hardware in all forms including archive access, blu-ray and DVDs, photographs, and any associated venue hire, catering, music and/or other expenditure and/or obligations.

B.288
The [Distributor] agrees and undertakes that they shall develop and produce the [Article/Product] in the exact from and content as the [sample/ prototype] and with all the material and packaging sourced by the means and method specified details of which are attached in Schedule [–] and form part of this Agreement. That if at any time there is any proposal to change, vary and/or adapt any part however small that the [Distributor] will notify the [Company] immediately and not commence any production with such changes, variations and/or adaptation until it has been approved by [Name] at the [Company] or his/her delegated officer.

B.289
The [Distributor] reserves the right to:

1.1 Increase the cost of development, production, supply and delivery due to the [Company] at any time for any reason.

1.2 Change the content and source of any ingredient and material.

1.3 Cancel and/or terminate any order and/or part for any reason including the fact that production has ended.

1.4 Change the packaging, text, image, logo, shape, weight, language and instructions.

1.5 Change the health and safety guidelines, test procedures and warning notices.

1.6 Be unable to supply spare parts and/or replacements due to discontinuance of the [Product/Article].

B.290

The [Company] agrees that it has provided a fixed quote of [number/currency] for [order] provided that it is confirmed by [Name] by [date] and [time] and the price quoted is paid in advance in full together with all costs of secure and registered delivery to the notified address.

Purchase and Supply of Products

B.291

'The Authorised Budget' shall be the agreed cost of producing and supplying the [Commissioned Work] which shall include:

1.1 Material which shall be of the following quality and description [specify in detail].

1.2 Travel and accommodation costs incurred in making the Commissioned Work up to a limit of [figure/currency] in total/or for a fixed period.

1.3 The costs of insurance and delivery of the Commissioned Work.

1.4 Other [specify].

B.292

'The Budget' shall be the maximum total payment to be made by the [Company] to the [Assignor] in respect of the [Commissioned Work] which shall not exceed [figure/currency] and shall include:

1.1 The cost of all preparatory artwork and designs.

1.2 The cost of all raw materials [including the hiring of locations].

1.3 The cost of development, production, manufacture or supply.

1.4 Any travel and accommodation costs.

1.5 The cost of any [computer-generated] graphics.

1.6 The costs of insurance and delivery.

1.7 All necessary copyright and other clearance payments.

1.8 Labour costs of the [Assignor].

1.9 Any other agreed costs [–].

B.293

The [Assignor] undertakes that it will produce the [Commissioned Work] in accordance with the Budget. In the event that the Budget is to be exceeded, the [Assignor] agrees that the prior written approval of the [Company] shall be required in order to authorise any further expenditure and that any further payment shall be at the [Company's] sole discretion.

B.294

The [Assignor] shall provide a full report to the [Company] of the costs incurred in respect of the [Commissioned Work] upon request. In the event that the costs incurred in respect of the [Commissioned Work] are less than the Budget, then the [Assignor] agrees that the [Company] shall only be obliged to pay the lesser sum. In the event that the Budget is exceeded, the [Company] agrees to pay such additional costs provided that it has given prior written approval of the expenditure to the [Assignor].

B.295

The [Company] agrees that the Budget of [Name and Title] a copy of which is attached hereto and forms part of this Agreement is a statement of the total cost for the supply of the [Product] by the Delivery Date to the [Purchaser]. The Budget is not for guidance, but the final agreed price between the parties. Any additional costs to be incurred in order to fulfil this Agreement shall be the sole responsibility of the [Company].

B.296

The prices quoted on this website are for guidance only and may be varied at any time. Please contact the [Company] and obtain a quote for the [wholesale/retail] supply of the products. All prices are quoted exclusive of any taxes, custom duties, currency conversion costs and bank charges, freight and insurance costs which may be due to be paid by the [Client]. All costs, charges and sums due must be paid in full in advance before any products will be sent to the designated delivery address.

B.297

'The Budget' shall be the estimated cost of all the source materials, tools and machinery, transport, insurance, staff and artist fee for the production of the [Article/Work] by [Name] and delivery of the completed form of the [Article/Work] to the [Company] at [address] by [date].

B.298

The [Company] agrees to pay all the costs, expenses and fees which may arise for any reason as a result of late delivery, changes in content, design, material, production schedule, location, compliance with health and safety and/or security and/or planning controls which may be necessary in respect of the installation of the [Article/Work].

B.299

'The Budget 'shall set out the fixed costs for the [Project] of [number/ currency] which may not be exceeded for any reason and shall be paid by the [Company] to [Name]. The costs shall include:

1.1 Reproduction and preparation of artwork, logos and material together with all editing, changes and amendments.

1.2 Supplying a sample proof copy and/or prototype (together with packaging) which is in the exact form it is proposed to reproduce it.

1.3 Adding changes to and varying the sample and/or prototype (and any packaging) prior to reproduction.

1.4 Supplying [number] of [format] of the final sample and/or prototype (and any packaging) in boxes of [number] in each.

1.5 All costs of delivery, freight, insurance, taxes, custom duties and any other charges and costs.

Services

B.300
There shall be a [monthly/annual] agreed budget for the services of [Name] which shall be paid in regular instalments on [dates] subject to completion of work.

B.301
The budget shall not be amended, increased, varied or reduced at any time without agreement in writing in a formal document signed by both parties.

B.302
The [Company] agrees that the [Consultant] shall be entitled to be repaid by the [Company] for the following sums [without receipts and/or itemised bills] which will be allocated in the budget for his/her expenditure each calendar month as follows:

1.1 Car hire and associated costs, travel by bus, train, rail, plane and helicopter at a maximum of [number/currency].

1.2 Landline, mobile, WiFi and internet charges and costs at a maximum of [number/currency].

1.3 Hotels, accommodation, clothes, magazines and newspaper subscriptions, marketing and print costs, entertainment and hospitality at a maximum of [number/currency].

B.303
The [Company] shall not be liable for any administration, telephone, travel, marketing and/or any other costs and/or expenses and/or commitments of the [Consultant] at any time. Nor shall the [Consultant] have the authority to agree any budget and/or expenditure on behalf of the [Company] to a third

party and/or to represent that he/she has the power to authorise any such agreement.

B.304

Where either party makes such changes to the terms of the services supplied and/or paid for under this Agreement that there are changes to any costs, payments, prices and/or fees. Then it is agreed that this Agreement shall be terminated automatically and a new Agreement shall be negotiated and new terms and conditions agreed. That there is no right by either party to make such changes and insist that the present Agreement continues.

Sponsorship

B.305

The [Sponsor] agrees and undertakes that it shall bear the cost of and pay for the Sponsorship Budget set out in Appendix [–] for the [Project]. Provided that none of the sums paid to the [Club/Company] shall be used for any other purpose. Nor shall the [Sponsor] shall be liable for any additional payments or costs which may be incurred and/or due arising from the [Project].

B.306

In the event of the Sponsorship Budget being insufficient for the completion of the [Project/Programme]. Then in the event that the [Official Sponsor] decides not to pay such additional costs and expenses that may need to be incurred and/or which will arise in order to complete the [Project]. Then the [Official Sponsor] agrees that the [Club/Company] may seek and appoint a second and/or additional persons and/or businesses as secondary level supporters of the [Project/Programme]. Provided that the [Club/Company] agrees not to appoint any supporter who business directly conflicts with that of the [Official Sponsor] in the [specify] industry.

B.307

'The Budget' shall be the maximum total payment to be made by the [Sponsor] to the [Club/Company/Charity] which shall not exceed [figure/currency] and shall include the completion and delivery of the following work for the [Event/Project/Race]:

1.1   The cost of all preparatory artwork, design, development, production, manufacture or supply of the [T-shirts, bottles, balloons, posters, banners, stalls, free gifts and bags].

1.2   The cost of hiring of and access to the location.

1.3   The cost of any [computer-generated] graphics and the creation, development and supply of the relevant webpages for the website [reference].

279

1.4 The cost of all health and safety risk assessments for the [Event/Project/Race], and the supply of relevant personnel, first aid provision, and insurance cover.

1.5 Any other agreed costs [–].

B.308

In the event that it is likely that the Budget is to be exceeded the [Club/Company/Charity] agrees to contact the [Sponsor] at the earliest opportunity and to provide them with a revised costing. The prior written approval of the [Sponsor] shall be required in order to authorise any further expenditure and any such further payment shall be at the [Sponsor's] sole discretion.

B.309

The [Club/Company/Charity] shall [not] be obliged to set up a separate bank account for deposit and expenditure of the Budget which shall require the signature of [two Directors] to authorise expenditure in relation to the [Event/Project/Race].

B.310

The [Sponsor] agrees that it shall provide the following budget and pay for the costs and expenses for the [Event] as set out below:

1.1 Flags, banners, tents, stands and displays and products [specify layout/number/name].

1.2 Freelance qualified catering staff, security and employees in the following roles [–].

1.3 Rubbish removal and waste disposal, support equipment, generators, transport and lighting [–].

1.4 Security and identity tags and safety barriers.

1.5 Health and safety liability and risk assessment together with comprehensive public liability insurance of not less than [number/currency] for [cover].

1.6 Training and procedures for emergencies and first aid cover.

1.7 All other costs and expenses that may arise directly and/or indirectly to reinstate the land, access route and use of the venue allocated to and/or used by the [Sponsor] back to the state it was in prior to its use by the [Sponsor] before, during and/after the [Event].

B.311

The [Company] may at its absolute discretion increase the cost of sponsorship of any particular part programme in the [Event] at any time and the current prices displayed on the website are for guidance only and not binding.

University, Library and Educational

B.312
The [Company] agrees that it shall bear its own costs, expenses and insurance in respect of the [Project/Work] and these sums are not intended to be recouped as part of the allocated Budget. Nor shall the [Institute] bear any responsibility or liability in respect of the inability for any reason for the [Company] to pay its own costs and expenses in respect of the [Project/Work].

B.313
In the event that it is anticipated that the Budget is to be exceeded then the prior written consent of the [Institute] is required before the [Distributor] incurs any additional costs. In the event that there is no consent or approval provided by the [Institute] then the [Distributor] shall be liable to pay such sums.

B.314
The [Company] agrees that the Budget is a statement of the total fixed cost of the [Project]. That the [Company] shall be obliged to adhere to the Budget and shall only be permitted to authorise expenditure in respect of those items in the Budget. The [Company] agrees and undertakes that it shall not be able to incur or commit the [Institute] to any additional cost or expense.

B.315
In the event that the [Company] expects that the [Budget] will be exceeded then prior to any additional costs and/or expenses being incurred or committed, the [Company] agrees to inform the [Institute] in advance in writing specifying in detail the reasons. At the same time the [Company] shall provide the [Institute] with a statement of costs incurred and details of the work which has been carried out.

B.316
'The Budget' shall be the estimated costs of the [Project] a copy of which is attached in Schedule [–] and forms part of this Agreement. The Budget costs shall in any event not exceed [figure/currency] [words] which be shared equally between the [Company] and the [Institute].

B.317
'The Budget' shall be the agreed cost of [number/currency] in total to be paid by [Company] to [Name] for completion of the [Work] in [format] by [date] and delivery in full to the [Company].

B.318

The [Consortium] agree that until the budget for the [Project] is finalised and approved by the sub-committee comprising [specify]. That no steps and/or action and/or commitment shall be made by any party in respect of the work to be completed and/or the expenditure of the budget.

BUSINESS DAY

General Business and Commercial

B.319

'Business Day' means a day (other than a Saturday or Sunday) on which banks are generally open for business in [city/country].

B.320

'Business Day' shall mean any day from Monday to Friday which is not a bank or public holiday of [country].

B.321

'Business Day' shall mean any day on which banks are authorised to close in the city of [specify].

B.322

All days of the week including weekends and bank holidays shall be counted as a day for the purposes of the calculation of any delay and/or notice and/or for any other reason.

BUY-OUT

General Business and Commercial

B.323

'Buy-out of all rights' shall mean the complete assignment and transfer of all ownership of the physical material and all copyright, trade marks patents and any other intellectual property rights and computer software rights which are held or controlled by the [Owner] in the [Product] and/or parts in all media whether in existence now or created in the future throughout the world [and universe] for the full period of copyright and any extensions or renewals and in perpetuity to the [Company]. Thereafter the [Owner] shall not hold or control any rights or interest whatsoever in the [Product] and/or parts and shall not be entitled to receive any payments, sums or royalties from any exploitation in any form.

B.324

In consideration of the payment of the [Assignment Fee] by the [Company] to the [Assignor]. The [Assignor] assigns all media rights which are in existence now or which may be created in the future in the [Work] and/or parts [and all the Material] to the [Company] from [date] for the full period of copyright and any extensions and renewals throughout the [country/world/ universe].

B.325

'All Media Rights' shall mean:

1.1   All copyright, intellectual property rights, computer software and any other rights or interest of any nature in [Product/Work/Service] and in the physical property throughout the [country/world/universe] whether in existence now or developed in the future in any language, format or medium.

1.2   The sole and exclusive right to licence, assign, transfer, copy, reproduce, lend, supply, adapt, translate, authorise, hire, sell, record, store in any form, recreate or develop in another format, disseminate or otherwise exploit by any method or medium whether it exists in technology and/or law at the time of the acquisition of the rights or is created in the future which shall include but not be limited to all matters set out in 1.1 to 1.12.

1.3   All trade marks, service marks, logos, characters, and all words, phrases, colour, shape, noise and smell associated with or part of them, design rights and future design rights.

1.4   All database rights, trade secrets, moral rights and waivers, confidential information, and patents.

1.5   All forms of film, television, radio and interactive material including analogue, digital, terrestrial, cable or satellite received by television or transmitted or received via the internet on a PC, mobile phone or other gadgets or devices or methods.

1.6   All mechanical forms of reproduction including DVD, VHS, audiocassettes, CDs and all methods of performance and performing rights, together with the right to retain all sums due from any collecting society in any country at any time.

1.7 All text, data, index, titles, rules, images, photographs, drawings, plans, maps, sketches, marketing, packaging, posters, flyers.

1.8 All computer-generated material whether on screen or software and any material created for use with computers, pocket PCs, CD-Rom, discs or any other devices or gadgets.

1.9 All music, sound recordings, sounds and effects, noises.

1.10 All printed forms including books, magazines, brochures, serialisations.

1.11 All forms of merchandising, and exploitation of any kind, including toys, games, clothes, household products.

1.12 All forms of wireless and telecommunication services in respect of any part of the electromagnetic spectrum whether national, local, private or commercial and reception or transmission or broadband, ultra wide band or otherwise which shall include but not be limited to mobile phones, two way radios, paging, data networks, public access radio, private business radio, common base stations, fixed wireless access, scanning telemetry, fixed terrestrial links, broadcasting, satellite, space science.

B.326

The [Assignor] assigns to the [Assignee] all copyright, trade marks, computer software, domain names and intellectual property rights of any nature in any media in any format whether in existence now or created in the future in the [Work] and any part and any other form of reproduction and/or adaptation for the full period of copyright and any other rights and without limit of time indefinitely including but not limited to the following:

1.1 All scripts, title, text, content, formats, codes and passwords.

1.2 All material, labels, packaging, sales, marketing and distribution material, data, records, agreements, licences, consents, documents, databases, invoices, sales reports, accounts and financial records whether in print form, stored in a computer or other gadget and/or stored in another format.

1.3 All drawings, designs, logos, artwork, graphics, maps, computer-generated material, formulae, processes, inventions, patents and technological developments.

1.4 All radio, television, film, sound recordings, recordings, advertisements, music, lyrics, jingles, telephone, internet, website, sponsorship, endorsement, product placement, merchandising, performing rights and mechanical reproduction rights.

1.5 The right to retain all royalties and other sums received at any time from the exploitation, reproduction, performance, transmission, broadcast and/or any other type of use in any country of the world on land, sea and/or in the air and/or any part of the universe.

1.6 The right to adapt, vary, amend, alter, add to and/or delete from the [Work] at any time at the [Assignee's] sole discretion.

1.7 The right to represent that the [Assignee] owns and controls the copyright and all other rights and to register any claim and/or interest.

B.327

In consideration of the Contributors Fee the [Contributor] assigns to the [Company] all copyright, intellectual property rights, and any other rights in the [Contributor's] work and the product of the [Contributor's] services and the Podcast to the [Company] in all medium and in any media whether in existence now and/or created in the future for the full period of copyright and any extensions and/or renewals and in perpetuity throughout the world and universe. This shall include the right to transmit, broadcast, display, licence, supply, distribute and/or exploit the [Contributor's] work and/or the podcast and/or any parts on the internet, television, radio, in print, mobiles or any other format whether by text, images, sound and/or any adaptation.

B.328

The [Contributor] shall not be entitled to receive any additional payments of any nature from any exploitation of the [Contributor's] work and the product of the [Contributor's] services and the Podcast by the [Company] and/or any third party in all medium and/or in any media whether in existence now and/or created in the future.

B.329

In consideration of the payment of the Assignment Fee, the [Assignor] assigns to the [Assignee] all present and future copyright and all intellectual property rights, trade marks, domain names, computer software rights and any other rights in all media in any medium in the Artwork [and the Artwork Material] and/or any part(s) and/or any adaptation and/or development whether in existence now or created in the future throughout the [territory/world, universe, land, sea, air and sub-terrain] for the full period of copyright and any extensions and renewals as far as possible in perpetuity, including but not limited to:

(a) All forms of exploitation through the medium of television and radio including but not limit to terrestrial television, cable, satellite, and digital television.

(b) All forms of exploitation through the medium of videograms, cassettes, disc laser, DVDs, and CDs.

(c) All forms of television, video and non-theatric audiences including but not limited to businesses and commercial use, educational, cultural, religious and social establishments, schools, churches, prisons, hospitals, camps, workshops, film societies, professional and trade bodies, private and public libraries, colleges, universities, hotels, clubs, shops, airlines.

(d) All forms of theatric exploitation including cinemas.

(e) All forms of publishing whether in printed or electronic form, hardback, paperback, e books, downloads and interactive material.

(f) All forms of electronic dissemination and/or storage and/or retrieval whether over the Internet, any website, banners, links, downloads, intranet and all systems involving multi-media exploitation including CD-Roms, USBs and any other gadget and all other methods of interactivity, sound, noise, text, data, artwork or graphics.

(g) All forms of merchandising including commercial exploitation of any item of any nature, cards, posters, clothing, accessories, badges, sweets, stickers, stationery or otherwise.

(h) All forms of telecommunication systems including telephones, mobiles and/or other gadgets and/or devices to transmit, store and/or retrieve any sort of content.

(i) All other forms of adaptation, variation or development of the Artwork and/or any sequel and any other rights.

B.330

The [Assignor] agrees that he/she shall only be entitled to be paid the Assignment Fee and shall not be entitled to receive any additional sums, royalties and/or otherwise that may arise directly and/or indirectly at any time from the exploitation of the Artwork and/or the Artwork Material and/or development and/or variation by the [Assignee] and/or any third party.

B.331

The [Assignor] agrees that all developments, variations, changes, marketing and exploitation of the Artwork and the Artwork Material shall be at the [Assignee's] sole discretion and cost.

B.332

The [Assignor] agrees that the [Assignee] shall be entitled to be registered as the copyright owner of the Artwork and/or the Artwork Material and to apply and register for any trade mark, service mark, community mark and/or other right and/or interest associated with any part.

B.333

The [Assignee] agrees and undertakes that it shall be responsible for any sums due in respect of the development, distribution, marketing and exploitation of the Artwork and/or the Artwork Material in any media at any time and that the Assignor shall not be liable for any such sums.

B.334

In consideration of the payment of the [Assignment Fee] by the [Company] to the [Assignor]. The [Assignor] assigns all copyright, intellectual property rights, computer software and any other rights or interest of any nature in the [Music/Lyrics/Sound Recordings] and all original and master material [specified in Schedule [–] which is attached to and forms part of this Agreement] and/or parts to the [Company] from [date] for the full period of copyright and any extensions and renewals throughout the [country/world/universe] whether in existence now or developed in the future in any language, format or medium.

For the avoidance of doubt this shall include but not be limited to:

1.1 The sole and exclusive right to licence, assign, transfer, copy, reproduce, lend, supply, adapt, translate, authorise, hire, sell, record, store in any form, recreate or develop in another format, disseminate or otherwise exploit by any method or medium whether it exists in technology and/or law at the time of the acquisition of the rights or is created in the future.

1.2 All forms of text, film, television, radio and interactive material including analogue, digital, terrestrial, cable or satellite received by television or transmitted or received via the internet to download and/or store and retrieve on a PC, mobile phone or other gadgets or devices or methods.

1.3 All mechanical forms of reproduction including DVDs, VHS, audiocassettes, CDs and all methods of performance and performing rights, together with the right to retain all sums due from any collecting society in any country at any time.

1.4 All computer-generated material whether on screen or software and any material created for use with computers, pocket PCs, CD-Rom, discs or any other devices or gadgets.

1.5 All printed forms including music and song sheets, music books, and/or compilations with other works.

1.6 All forms of merchandising, endorsement, sponsorship, advertising, promotion and commercial and non-commercial exploitation of any kind.

1.7 All forms of wireless and telecommunication services in respect of any part of the electromagnetic spectrum whether national, local, private or commercial and reception or transmission or broadband, ultra wide band or otherwise which shall include but not be limited to mobile phones, two way radios, paging, data networks, public access radio, private business radio, common base stations, fixed wireless access, scanning telemetry, fixed terrestrial links, broadcasting, satellite, space science.

B.335

In consideration of the payment of the [Budget] by the [Enterprise] to the [Development Company]. The [Development Company] agrees and assigns all copyright, intellectual property rights, computer software rights, database rights and any other rights or interest of any nature whether in existence now or developed in the future in any language, format, process, system and/or method in all media and medium in the [Computer Software and the Source Code] and the physical material specified in Appendix [–] which is attached to and forms part of this Agreement] and/or parts to the [Enterprise] for the full period of copyright and any extensions and renewals and in perpetuity throughout the [country/world/universe]. For the avoidance of doubt this shall include:

1.1 The sole and exclusive right for the [Enterprise] to licence, assign, transfer, copy, reproduce, lend, supply, adapt, translate, authorise, hire, sell, record, store in any form, recreate or develop in another format, disseminate or otherwise exploit by any method or medium whether it exists in technology and/or law at the time of the acquisition of the rights or is created in the future.

1.2 The right to retain all royalties and other sums received at any time from the reproduction, supply, transmission, download, distribution and/or any other type of use.

1.3 The right to adapt, vary, amend, alter, add to and/or delete and/or sub-licence and/or assign any part at any time at the [Enterprise's] sole discretion.

1.4 The right to represent that the [Enterprise] owns and controls the copyright and all other rights and to register any claim and/or interest.

B.336

In consideration of the payment of the [Fee] the [Contributor] assigns to the [Company] all present and future copyright and all intellectual property rights, trade marks, domain names, computer software rights, database rights and any other rights in all media in any medium in the [Database/Taxonomy/Index] [and the development and master material and any copies] and/or any part(s) specified in Appendix [–] whether in existence now or created in the future (either in law and/or technology) throughout the world and universe for the full period of copyright and any extensions and renewals and to continue throughout time in perpetuity. The [Contributor] shall not have the right to receive any further sums received at any time from the reproduction, supply, transmission, download, distribution and/or any other type of use. The [Company] shall have the right to adapt, vary, amend, alter, add to and/or delete and/or sub-licence and/or assign any part at any time at the [Company's] sole discretion. The [Company] shall have the right to represent that the [Company] owns and controls the copyright and all other rights and to register any rights and/or interest in the name of the [Company] and/or any other third party.

B.337

In consideration of the payment of the [Fee] the [Author] assigns to the [Company] the right to exploit the [Work/Film] and/or any parts such as the title, characters and storyline in the form of merchandising by the following methods and formats from [date] until [date]: Cards, posters, clothing for adults and children, accessories, badges, playing cards, sweets, stickers, games, stationery, hardback and paperback books, audiobooks, and other formats of children's books, toys, food products which are marketed to children, household items and bedding used for children's bedrooms.

The assignment of rights in 1.1 shall not include:

1.1 Film, television, DVDs, videos, CDs, radio, analogue, digital, terrestrial, cable or satellite, the internet, the right to download, store and/or retrieve on a PC, mobile phone or other gadgets or devices or methods.

1.2 The right to register with any collecting society and to receive any sums from the broadcast, transmission, performing rights, and/or other form of exploitation from any collecting society in any country at any time.

1.3 All computer generated material whether on screen or software and any material created for use with computers, pocket PCs, CD-Rom and interactive games, discs or any other devices or gadgets.

1.4 All printed forms including music and song sheets, music books, and/or compilations with other works.

1.5 All forms of endorsement, sponsorship, advertising, promotion and commercial and non-commercial exploitation of any kind.

1.6   All forms of wireless and telecommunication services in respect of any part of the electromagnetic spectrum whether national, local, private or commercial and reception or transmission or broad band, ultra wide band or otherwise which shall include but not be limited to mobile phones, two-way radios, paging, data networks, public access radio, private business radio, common base stations, fixed wireless access, scanning telemetry, fixed terrestrial links, broadcasting, satellite.

B.338

In consideration of the payment of the [Advance and the Royalties] the [Author] assigns to the [Distributor] all present and future copyright and all intellectual property rights in the [Work] [and the Work Material] throughout the [territory] in the [English/other] language for the full period of copyright and any extensions in all printed forms of publishing whether hardback, paperback, co-editions and packaging, large print, serialisation in newspapers or magazines and/or children's plastic books.

B.339

The assignment in Clause [–] by the [Company] shall not include:

1.1   Television, radio whether terrestrial, cable, satellite, and/or digital.

1.2   Videograms, cassettes, disc laser, DVDs, CDs.

1.3   Electronic dissemination and/or storage and/or retrieval whether over the internet, any website, banners, links, downloads, intranet and all systems involving multi-media exploitation including e books, downloads, CD-Roms and any other gadget.

1.4   Telecommunication systems including telephones, mobiles and/or other gadgets and/or devices to transmit, store and/or retrieve any sort of content.

1.5   All other forms of adaptation, variation and/or development and/or any sequel and/or any other rights.

B.340

In consideration of the payment of the [Assignment Fee] by the [Institute] to the [Contributor]. The [Contributor] assigns all rights, interest and ownership, and the right to licence, supply, distribute and/or exploit the [Work/Service/Product] and any parts or subsequent developments of any nature in any material and/or format whether they are in existence now or created in the future for the full period of copyright and any extensions and renewals throughout the [world/universe]. This assignment shall include, but not be limited to copyright, intellectual property rights, computer software, patents, trade marks, service marks, logos, characters, design rights, future design rights. database rights, moral rights, all printed forms including hardback and paperback books, text, index, titles, rules, images, photographs, engravings, drawings, plans, maps, sketches, marketing, packaging, posters, flyers, brochures, toys, games, household products, music, sound recordings, wireless and telecommunication services, mobile phones, two way radios, analogue, digital, terrestrial, cable and satellite television, film, radio, the internet and any electronic, digital or electromagnetic form, computers, CD-Rom, DVDs, videos, CDs, and any other form of mechanical reproduction or performance. The sole and exclusive right to licence, assign, transfer, copy, reproduce, lend, supply, adapt, translate, authorise, hire, sell, record, store and retrieve in any form, or otherwise exploit by any method or medium.

B.341

The [Consultant] assigns to the [Institute] all copyright, trade marks, computer software, domain names and intellectual property rights of any nature in any media in any format whether in existence now or created in the future in the [Work/Project] and any part and any other form of reproduction and/or adaptation and any technological developments for the full period of copyright and any extensions or renewals including but not limited to the following:

1.1 The completed report, drafts, questionnaires and responses, correspondence, any material stored on discs, or USB or hard drive relating to the [Project] which shall be copied for supply to the [Institute].

1.2 All research, marketing, financial, scientific, and distribution material, data, records, agreements, licences, consents, documents, databases, invoices, sales reports, accounts and financial records whether in print form, stored in a computer or other gadget and/or stored in another format.

1.3 All images, photographs, drawings, designs, logos, artwork, graphics, maps, computer-generated material, formulae, processes, inventions, patents, codes, passwords or access data or information.

B.342

The [Institute] shall have the right to:

1.1 Retain all sums or benefits received including royalties received at any time from the exploitation, reproduction, performance, transmission, sale or supply of the [Work/Project] or any part. No further sums or payments shall be due to the [Consultant].

1.2 The right to develop, adapt, vary, amend, alter, exploit, add to and/or delete from the [Work/Project] and/or register any right and/or interest at any time at the [Institute's] sole discretion. No consent or approval shall be required from the [Consultant].

B.343

1.1 The [Artist] agrees to supply to [Name] at [Names'] cost all original draft and final sketches, drawings, software and any other reproductions and/or copies of the artwork, images, photographs, recordings, text, words and logos which have been created and developed for [Name] for the [Project]. The [Artist] agrees that no material shall be retained by the [Artist].

1.2 That the [Artist] agrees to assign all copyright and all intellectual property rights and the right to copy, licence, sell, supply, distribute and to register any rights and/or receive any sums from the exploitation in any of the material in 1.1 above to [Name] for the full period of copyright and any period thereafter indefinitely without limit throughout the universe, galaxy, world in any form and/or medium. Provided that the [Artist] has been paid the [Fee] and [Budget] in full by [Name].

1.3 The [Artist] agrees that any part of the material in 1.1 may be adapted, edited, changed and/or credited to a third party and/or name. That the [Artist] agrees that he/she has waived all moral rights and/or any right to have a copyright notice, credit and/or be attributed as the creator of the material.

B.344

[Name] has agreed to carry out filming for the [Distributor] on various dates to be agreed between the parties. [Name] agrees and assigns to the [Distributor] all copyright, intellectual property rights throughout the land, sea and air of the planet Earth in the [films] and [sound recordings] to be made by [Name] including feature and documentary film, DVD, blu-ray and footage rights, satellite, cable, on demand and archive and playback and terrestrial television, together with viewing, downloads, games, blogs, banner links, posts and other material for computers, websites and gadgets, publishing and merchandising and any other exploitation of any adaptation which may exist now or be invented, created and/or developed in the future.

B.345

1.1 [Name] has agreed to be interviewed by [specify] for [specify medium/ publication]. In return for a fee of [number/currency] [Name] assigns to the [Company] the copyright in the words spoken and in all sound and other recordings made in the interview on [date] and the photograph taken on [date] by [specify] for the purpose of publication and reproduction as an article in [country] and to use and/or adapt the material on the online website of the [Company] and to supply to third parties as part of their news service.

1.2 The [Company] agrees that where a third party wishes to use and adapt the material in any form that [Name] shall be notified and an additional fee negotiated for [Name] for any such use.

B.346

[Name] is the designer and creator of an original concept and format and prototype for an [App] which he/she has developed using the following [materials/software] [specify].

In consideration of a non-returnable fee of [number/currency], a royalty on all sales of not less than [number] per cent and [number] shares in [specify]. [Name] agrees that he/she shall assign to the [Company] all copyright, software, design rights, trade marks, service marks, film, sound recordings, music and lyrics, noises, animation, characters, logos and any intellectual property rights and interest and/or to reproduce, exploit and/or licence which may exist now or be created at some time in the future throughout the universe and for all periods of such rights of nay nature whenever they may start and/or end including any renewals and extensions.

B.347

[Name] agrees that the [Company] can buy the asset [specify] for a fixed fee of [number/currency] and that subject to payment in full to [Name]. [Name] agrees and undertakes to transfer, assign, execute any document and provide support in the form of an affidavit if required that all title, ownership and control of the asset has passed and been assigned to the [Company]. That [Name] has no rights and/or interest and/or claim and/or any right to licence, exploit, sell and/or receive any money from the asset.

B.348

Where the [Company] has paid a fee for rights and/or an assignment which it later discovers cannot be granted and/or assigned by [Name]. Then the [Company] shall be entitled to a full refund by [Name] of all sums paid together with interest at [number] per cent and to enter on the premises of the business of [Name] and to seek to recover the sum by removing any items of value which can be sold to recoup the sum due plus any additional costs that may be incurred.

B.349

1.1 [Name] has developed a [script/manuscript] for a [play/film/DVD] which has been commissioned by the [Company] on the subject of [specify]. [Name] acknowledges and agrees that he/she was not the originator of the idea, concept, format and/or project.

1.2 [Name] agrees that except for the payment of the fee for the preparation and development of the [script/manuscript], meetings, travel, editing and delivery of a final draft. That [Name] shall have no right to any further sums from the exploitation of the [script/manuscript] in any form, medium and/or adaptation at any time by the [Company].

1.3 Further, [Name] agrees and waives all rights to any form of moral rights and/or credit except as [specify] and accepts that the [Company] may omit this credit at its sole discretion where circumstances require it to do so.

1.4 [Name] assigns all present and future copyright and intellectual property rights in [script/manuscript] and all drafts and the final version to the [Company] throughout the world and universe for the full period of copyright and any additional periods that may be permitted and/or created and for all other rights for the full duration of any such rights which shall be in all forms of commercial, charitable, educational and/or non-paying forms of production, exploitation and marketing in all media in any manner and/or format at any time through technology which exists now or becomes available at a later date.

CANCELLATION

General Business and Commercial

C.001
The [Company] retains the right to cancel the contract without reason provided that the [Customer] is given at least [two calendar months'] written notice prior to [date]. This shall not be the same as ending the contract under the termination provisions due to failure to carry out the terms of the contract.

C.002
The [Contractor] agrees that the [Governing Body/Company] shall have the right at its sole discretion to cancel this Agreement at any time without any reason or explanation or any grounds of complaint in respect of the Agreement or the quality of the service or work. The [Governing Body/Company] shall only be obliged to give [28 days'] notice of cancellation of the Agreement. This clause shall be in addition to any other rights under this Agreement including termination, rejection, or force majeure.

C.003
There shall be no right of cancellation under this Agreement and the parties agree that the terms shall be fulfilled and the expenditure and payments made by the [Company] for the duration of the Agreement.

C.004
It may be necessary for the [Client] to cancel the [booking/break/activity] due to injury, medical reasons, accident, family bereavement, and other unexpected circumstances. In such cases the [Company] should be contacted by [telephone/email/fax] as soon as possible. The [Client] shall not be entitled to a refund of any sums already incurred in respect of the ordering of goods or services from third parties which have already been ordered, invoiced or performed where payments are due or have been made by the [Company] on behalf of the [Client]. The following sums shall be refunded and shall be dependent on the period of notice given in each case less the deposit and insurance premium and any third party costs:

1.1 More than [60 days] [full refund less deductible costs].

1.2 Between [40–59 days] [refund of 60 per cent less deductible costs].

1.3 Between [39–15 days] [refund of 30 per cent less deductible costs].

1.4 Between [Less than 14 days] [no refund].

C.005
There may be a cancellation of the Order by the [Client] at any time until payment has been made in full for the [Products] to the [Company].

C.006
There shall be no cancellation fees, charges or costs and no additional sums shall be invoiced as a penalty, for any direct or indirect loss or damage to reputation arising from the cancellation.

C.007
The parties have agreed that the booking, dates, arrangements and details of the [Event] shall not be released, supplied or disclosed by the [Company] or any of its employees, sub-contractors, or other individuals or businesses engaged to provide their services to any third party at any time until [date]. That if it is established that information, photographs, or details were disclosed to newspapers, magazines, television companies or news or media organisations from such a source without permission from the [Client] before [date] that the [Client] may cancel the booking. If the [Client] cancels the booking for that reason then the [Client] shall only be obliged to pay [figure/currency] by [date].

C.008
If you should fail to pay your annual registration fee [or such other sums as advised] before the date on which your registration of your [Domain Name/ Membership/other] is due to lapse or end each year. Then the registration shall be cancelled by the [Company] and shall end on the final date. The [Company] shall not be responsible for, or liable to you for any reason for, any loss, damage, costs or other consequences which may arise as a result of your failure to renew or extend the registration.

C.009
If you wish to cancel the service at any time then you must give at least [one month's notice] to the [Company]. You shall only be obliged to pay any subscription fee to the end of that period. Any payments made for any period after the cancellation date shall be refunded.

C.010
The [Client] shall not be entitled to cancel the Order unless the [Company] advises that it cannot deliver the quantity requested, is unable to meet the

delivery date or the specifications of the Products are different. If the Order is cancelled for any of these reasons a full refund shall be provided to the [Client] of all sums paid on account in respect of the Order.

C.011

The [Customer] may cancel the [service/subscription] within [seven days] of the start of the [service/subscription] and shall be entitled to be paid a refund of all sums paid for the [service/subscription]. The refund shall be paid by the [Company] within [30 days] of the receipt of notice of cancellation.

C.012

Where an Order is cancelled then no deposits or other advance payments shall be refunded. Where an Order is available for collection, but is unclaimed for more than [three months], then the goods or products may be destroyed or sold off. No sums shall be due to the [Customer] in such circumstances as a refund, compensation or otherwise.

C.013

The [Governing Body/Company] may cancel the [Participants/Exhibitors/other] right of access to the [premises] for any of the following reasons:

1.1　There has been a failure to comply with rules relating to health and safety, and installation or repair of electrical equipment, or permitted products or goods.

1.2　The behaviour, language, gestures, and appearance of employees, agents or others invited by them to the [premises] has resulted in complaints.

1.3　There has been a failure to pay the sums due under the Agreement by the specified deadlines.

C.014

In the event the [Company] is required to cancel the [Event/Holiday/Concert] for any reason then the [Client] shall be entitled to a full refund of the cost of the [Event/Holiday/Concert]. Where possible the [Company] shall try to offer an alternative arrangement for the [Client] to consider, but which it shall not be obliged to accept. The [Company] shall not be liable for any additional costs, expenses, losses, damages and/or other sums that may and/or have been incurred as a result of the cancellation.

C.015

The [Agent] acknowledges that the [Artist] is under [eighteen] years of age at the time of the signature and conclusion of this Agreement. That the [parents/guardian] have signed on behalf of the [Artist] who will be bound until the [Artist] is [eighteen] years old provided that the [Agent] performs the terms of the Agreement and the Agreement is not terminated or ended for any reason. When the [Artist] reaches the age of [eighteen] years, the [Artist] shall in that year from [date] to [date] be entitled to exercise the right to end the Agreement by notice in writing to the [Agent] to end the Agreement on the [Artist's] [nineteenth birthday]. After that end date all sums, advances and royalties arising from any agreement, contract or other work by the [Agent] for or on behalf of the [Artist] shall be paid direct to the [Artist] and the [Agent] shall not be entitled to any further commission, expenses or fees.

C.016
The [Company] reserves the right to cancel the [Service/Order/Right of Entry] at any time and for any reason. The total liability shall be limited to refund the payment made if any for the [Service/Order/Right of Entry] which has not been fulfilled by the [Company] for any period after the date of cancellation.

C.017
Where the [Client] is unable and/or unwilling to use the [Tickets/Service/Order] and/or changes their decision and cancels the [booking/purchase] for any reason which is not due to the fault of the [Company]. Then the [Company] shall not be obliged to refund and/or repayment any sums paid up to and including the date of cancellation.

C.018
Where the [Company] is obliged to substitute another product and/or colour to fulfil any order under this Agreement. Then the [Client] shall be entitled to cancel such part of the order and purchase as relates to such proposed substitution. The [Client] agrees that any such cancellation of one part of any order shall not affect those which the [Company] is able to fulfil according to the specification and delivery date.

C.019
Where in any circumstances the [Client] has waived his and/or her rights to any cancellation of any part of this Agreement. The [Company] agrees that any such waiver shall only relate to the specific part of the [Service/Order] and shall not prevent the [Client] from exercising their rights of cancellation in respect of another matter at a later date.

Internet and Websites

C.020
In the event that the [Client/Subscriber/Customer] does not adhere to the agreed terms and conditions of use and access to the [Website]. Then the

[Company] may at any time cancel the service and/or block access and/or refuse to permit access to and/or use of the [Website] without providing any advance notice and/or reasons for taking such action. The [Company] shall not be obliged to justify the cancellation nor shall the [Client/Subscriber/Customer] be entitled to any compensation, damages, losses, damage to reputation and/or other sums which arise as a direct and/or indirect result of such action by the [Company].

C.021

The [Client/Subscriber/Customer] accepts and agrees that its use and access to the [Website] is entirely at its own risk and cost and agrees that no responsibility and/or liability shall be attached to and be accepted by the [Company] which arise from the [Client/Subscriber/Customer's] reliance on the supply, accuracy, reliability and/or otherwise of the [Website] and/or any service. The [Client/Subscriber/Customer] accepts and agrees that the [Company] may at any time cancel, interrupt, alter, adapt, add to, delete from and/or otherwise change the service and/or block access and/or refuse to permit access to and/or use of the [Website] without providing any advance notice and/or reasons for taking such action. The [Client/Subscriber/Customer] accepts and agrees that it shall not be entitled to any compensation, damages, losses and/or other sums which arise as a direct and/or indirect result of such action by the [Company].

C.022

The [Customer] may cancel their access and use of the [Service/Newsletter] by sending an email to [specify]. The [Company] agrees and undertakes to delete the [Customer] from their database records and to cease providing the [Service/Newsletter].

C.023

Where the [Company] decides that the email address and [User/Supplier] which is uploading images, film, text, and/or any other material to the [Website] is supplying material which in the opinion of the [Company] is in breach of contract, an infringement of copyright, in breach of a third party's trade marks, services marks, name and/or logo, defamatory, offensive, inaccurate, dangerous, and/or in any other manner unacceptable and not in keeping with the theme and/or spirit and/or operation of the [Website]. Then the [Company] may without notice cancel, terminate and/or block the email address and/or the supply of any further material to the [Website]. The [Company] shall also delete and erase all material supplied and/or uploaded to the [Website] and/or all references to the email address and [User/Supplier].

C.024

The [Company] reserves the right to cancel your right to use any account opened at any time on any grounds without notice if it discovers and/or receives reports that the [Account holder] is using the account for any illegal and/or immoral purpose by the laws of any country in the world which the [Company] may decide at its absolute discretion are appropriate.

C.025

The [Company] reserves the right, if it should cancel your right to access the account, to hold the account and permit access to it by any international and national authorities such as the police and intelligence which may exist to prevent crime, money laundering and any other unlawful purpose.

C.026

Where the [Client] fails to pay the fees for the account by the due date on any occasion. Then the [Company] shall have the absolute right without further notice to cancel the subscription service with effect from the actual date for which no sums have been received.

C.027

Where any party to this Agreement cancels all and/or any part of their contribution to the [Site/Project] for any reason. Then it is agreed that the non-defaulting party shall have the right to cancel the whole of the Agreement in its entirety with immediate effect by notice by email to the [Managing Director] of the party who has cancelled. Where the non-defaulting party has incurred expenses and costs in reliance on the contribution to be made by the other party. Then the party which has cancelled shall be liable for all such sums.

Merchandising

C.028

The [Company] shall have the right to cancel the order to manufacture the [Product] where the [Sample/First Delivery] supplied by the [Manufacturer] does not adhere to and/or is in breach of any and/or all of the following criteria:

1.1   The health and safety standards and product quality controls required in the [United Kingdom/country].

1.2   The size, colour, content and function specifications supplied by the [Company].

1.3   The name, logo, packaging, labels, inserts and additional material is inaccurate, offensive, and/or misleading quality.

C.029

The [Licensor] may cancel the non-exclusive Licence at any time by [one month's] written notice to the [Licensee]. The [Licensee] shall cease to arrange the manufacture of any new stock and shall have the right to sell off existing stock for a period of [three months] from the date of cancellation.

C.030

Where the payment under clause [–] is not received by the [Company] by [date] then the [Company] shall have the right to cancel the Agreement which shall take immediate effect by the [Company] sending a [email/letter/written notice] to the [Distributor]. The [Distributor] shall then have no right to reproduce, distribute and/or supply any products and/or services with the [Name/Logo/Trade Mark] at any time. The [Distributor] agrees that the contract shall be ended immediately and the [Distributor] shall have no right of action and/or claim against the [Company] for any sums, losses and/or damages which may arise and/or are due as a result of the cancellation at any time. Nor shall the [Distributor] be entitled to pay the sum due as a late payment and be entitled to then rely on the continuance of the contract.

C.031

The [Licensor] agrees that where he/she has approved samples of the products he/she shall not be entitled to delay and/or cancel the production of the [Articles/Products] unless there have been significant changes in the quality of the materials to be used and/or colour and/or design and/or name and/or packaging.

C.032

The [Client] agrees that the manufacturer shall not be required to make any further changes to the sample and/or artwork for production once it has been agreed within the original price quote. That all additional changes and/or alterations shall be subject to a further cost and expense to be paid by the [Client].

C.033

Both parties agree that they shall not have the right to cancel the Agreement once the following stages of the [Project] have been completed [specify]. The parties shall however have the right to reach an arrangement for the substitution of a third party to carry out the agreement on their behalf and with their authority. Provided that the main party remains obliged to fulfil all the duties, obligations and undertakings and continues to monitor and comply with the terms of the Agreement for the [Project].

Sponsorship

C.034

The [Sponsor] shall not be entitled to cancel funding for the [Project] and shall be obliged to pay all the sums due in Clause [–]. Where the [Project] is delayed and/or behind schedule and/or altered in any material form for any reason. The [Company] may agree to delay the payment of the funding by the [Sponsor]. Any such changes shall not entitle the [Sponsor] to cancel and/or withdraw the funds at any time.

C.035

The [Sponsor] reserves the right to cancel the funding of the [Event/Project/Film] in the event that the [Company] commits any act and/or takes any action and/or associates with any person and/or organisation which the [Sponsor] considers would affect the reputation of the [Sponsor] and/or any of its products. The [Sponsor] shall be entitled to cancel the [Event/Project/Film] with immediate effect by written notice to [Name] at [address]. The [Sponsor] shall not be obliged to specify in detail the nature of the reason for the cancellation.

C.036

In the event that the [Sponsor] cancels the funding, the [Sponsor] shall not be entitled to a refund of any sums due to the date of cancellation. The [Company] shall be entitled to retain all such sums, but shall not be paid any further sums by the [Sponsor] whether the costs and/or expenses have already been incurred by the [Company] or not.

C.037

The [Sponsor] may cancel the use of their name and products in connection with [Name] but shall not be entitled to withdraw from funding of [Name] for any reason after [date] regardless of their conduct, media reports and/or any other matter until all the sums due under the terms of this Agreement have been paid in full.

C.038

The [Sponsor] may cancel the Agreement by notice by email to [specify] at [specify] or text to [specify] at [number] at any time where:

1.1   The [Company] has not acquired a licence for the use of the [Site].

1.2   The [Site] has been made unusable due to weather conditions, floods, contamination and/or otherwise.

1.3   Health and safety, security and/or waste disposal and access to water have not been resolved to comply with the minimum standards required by any relevant authority.

C.039

Where the [Sponsor] decides to cancel the Agreement it agrees that it shall not be entitled to seek to recover any sums paid to the date of cancellation and/or termination whether the [Event] has taken place or not.

University, Library and Educational

C.040

The [Institute] shall have the right to cancel the Agreement with the [Company/Consultant] at any time as it thinks fit provided that the [Company/Consultant] is either given [two calendar months] written notice or payment is made of [two calendar months] fee in lieu of notice. In either event the [Company/Consultant] shall not be entitled to any additional sums, costs or compensation from such termination.

C.041

Where the [Board/Chief Executive] of the [Institute] reaches the conclusion that the [Company/Consultant] is not fulfilling the terms of the Agreement to the standard and quality which was specified. Then the [Company/Consultant] shall be notified of the alleged breach of the Agreement and provided with the opportunity to remedy the situation by a particular date. Failure to comply with all the terms of the steps required to remedy the alleged breach shall entitle the [Institute] to cancel the Agreement by notice in writing with immediate effect. The [Institute] shall then only be liable to pay for such [Work/Services] as were completed to the satisfaction of the [Board/Chief Executive] prior to the date of cancellation. Any outstanding matters shall then either be resolved by negotiation between the parties or referred to an independent arbitrator at the equal cost of both parties.

C.042

Where the [Institute] due to a reduction in its annual budget decides that it no longer requires the [Service/Work] at any time. Then the [Institute] shall be entitled to cancel the Agreement with [number] months' written notice to the [Company] at [address]. The [Company] agrees that no further sums shall be due to the [Company] for any reason after the expiry of the cancellation period.

C.043

Where the [Company] has not carried out the quality and consistency of service and work represented to the [Institute] at the time of the Agreement. The [Institute] shall not be obliged to permit the [Company] to remedy the situation but may cancel the Agreement at any time and all liability shall end and no further sums shall be due to the [Company] from the [Institute].

CAPACITY

DVD, Video and Discs

C.044

The [Licensor] confirms that it has and will continue to have the authority and right to conclude this Agreement and fulfil its terms and that no previous agreement of any nature has been signed or existed which concerns any part of the [specify rights] in the [Film].

C.045

The [Author] undertakes to the [Distributor] that he/she owns and controls the [DVD/Video Rights] in the [Book] entitled [title] ISBN reference [–] and these have not been granted or assigned to the [Publishers/specify name] at any time.

C.046

That the [Artist] is age [specify] and has taken the advice of his/her agent, parents and professional advisors before concluding and signing this Agreement. That there is no medical, physical or mental reason or inability to read and write which would impair the [Artist's] ability to understand the terms or the consequences of carrying out the terms of this Agreement.

C.047

That there is no undertaking, confirmation or otherwise regarding the background, status, finances or experience of [Name/Company] and/or previous agreements which they may have entered into which may conflict with this Agreement.

C.048

The [Company] agrees that it shall not permit and/or encourage through marketing and promotional material the use of the [VOD Service] by anyone under [age] years.

C.049

The [Licensor] warrants and undertakes that it holds all the rights granted to the [Licensee] under this Agreement and that it is not aware of any legal proceedings and/or claim which would affect the grant of those rights in any part of the world. Further that the [Licensor] has not entered into and/or committed any part of those rights to a third party which would prevent them being exercised and/or exploited by the [Licensee].

Employment

C.050
The [Executive] confirms that he/she has correctly and accurately disclosed his/her [qualifications/references/education/business experience] and has the authority to enter into this Agreement and is not bound by any previous agreements, undertakings or otherwise which would adversely affect this Agreement.

C.051
The [Executive] agrees that there are no existing agreements, undertakings, or court orders which would prevent them from entering into or being available to carry out the duties required under this Agreement.

C.052
That the [Employee] is a national of [country] and is aged [–] and holds a valid passport for [country] [reference] and holds a [work/other] permit to work as [specify] until [date] issued on [date] by [government body]. That the [Employee] holds a valid national insurance number [reference]. That the [Employer] shall be entitled to view all original documents and to retain a copy for their own personnel records and for compliance with any legal requirements.

C.053
The [Employee] holds the following qualifications and membership of professional bodies [list]. That by the start date of this Agreement the [Employee] shall be available to carry out the duties of [position] at the [Company] and there shall be no restrictions from a previous employee or other business which would interfere with or prevent the [Employee] entering into this Agreement.

C.054
That the [Employee] is over [age] and is available to work the days and hours required by the [Company] in the general position of [specify] at [premises] from [date] to [date].

C.055
The [Company] agrees that it shall not engage anyone under the age of [number] years to work on any part of the [Article/Project].

C.056
[Name] confirms that he/she is a qualified [specify] and comply with all the conditions specified by their professional body [specify] as at [date].

Film and Television

C.057
The [Licensor] confirms that he/she possesses full power and authority to enter into and perform this Agreement and that there are not nor will there be any liens, encumbrances or other restrictions against the [Work] or any part or the exploitation thereof which would derogate from or be inconsistent with the rights granted to the [Distributor] in this Agreement.

C.058
The [Assignor] agrees that he/she has full power and authority to enter into this Agreement and that the [Assignor] has not exploited the [Work] in any form except those matters specified in Schedule [–].

C.059
[Name] confirms that they are a full, current and paid up (where appropriate) member of [union/organisation].

C.060
The [Licensor] confirms that it has good title and authority to enter into this Agreement and that it is not bound by any conflicting or prior agreement which would jeopardise or be detrimental to this Agreement.

C.061
The [Company] confirms that the following rights have [not] been exploited [in country/worldwide] [list].

C.062
The [Distributor] undertakes that the following rights have not been granted in [Europe/Asia/other] to any third party [specify].

C.063
[Name] agrees that they shall not have any right and/or authority to represent to any third party that he/she is the agent for the [Actor] at any time. [Name] agrees and accepts that their role is limited to [specify] and that this does not include negotiating and/or concluding any type of agreement and/or receiving payments and/or gifts on behalf of and/or for the [Actor].

General Business and Commercial

C.064
All members of the [Group] confirm that they are [eighteen] years of age or older at the date of signing this Agreement. Any member who is not [eighteen] years of age at the date of this Agreement must have this document signed

on his/her behalf by a parent or guardian who is responsible for their welfare, and with whom they live.

C.065
[Name] confirms that he/she has been advised to take separate legal advice in respect of this Agreement and [has taken specialist legal advice/or decided of his/her own free will not to do so] and fully comprehends the consequences of signing this Agreement and agrees to be bound by its terms.

C.066
Both parties to this Agreement confirm that they are aged [eighteen/twenty-one] years or over at the date of signing this Agreement.

C.067
Unless the parties agree to the contrary in writing the term 'Full Age' shall mean the age of [twenty-one] years or over.

C.068
That the [Company] is a legal entity registered in [country] as [type/reference] and is able to meet the terms and obligations set out in this Agreement.

C.069
There are no representations, undertakings or verification provided as to the capacity of either party to enter into this Agreement. Each party must carry out is own background research as to the authority, reliability and financial stability of the other party.

C.070
Upon request the [Company] agrees to provide copies of legal documents and agreements and other material connecting the [Company] to any licensee with which it may conclude terms relating to the [Work] under the terms of this Agreement with the [Consortium].

C.071
Where the [Company] is not able to recruit the quality of personnel needed to fulfil the terms of this Agreement by [date]. Then the [Company] shall be obliged to notify the [Consortium] of that fact and set out the reasons and the date by which they expect the situation to be remedied.

Internet and Websites

C.072
You are granted access and use of this [Website] upon the condition that you are over [eighteen] years of age, and have the authority of the person who:

1.1   Owns or controls the [computer/mobile/television/gadget] that you are using and

1.2   The person who pays the cost of the internet access service online and

1.3   The person who pays for the cost of telephone charges and calls that may be incurred.

C.073

The [Company] does not wish persons under [number] years of age to use this [Website] and any person who permits or allows these facilities and service to be used in any manner by someone who is not over the legal age limit shall be served immediate notice to end their access to and use of the [Website]. The service shall be cancelled and any such person shall lose all right to any repayment, refunds or compensation and all future access by that person or from that [company/address] shall be denied.

C.074

This [Service/Website] may only be used and/or accessed by any persons over [number] years of age with the consent of the parent and/or guardian in each case. Together with the approval and/or consent of the person and/or company that is paying the phone, WiFi, broadband and/or other access point for the [Service/Website].

C.075

Where an adult who holds the account authorises a person under [age] years to have access to the code for the account and to use any part of the service and/or games. Then the adult shall be liable for all costs, charges and expenses that may be incurred by the young person whether the young person acted without their knowledge or not in agreeing to any additional sums.

Merchandising

C.076

The [Licensor] agrees and undertakes that it has the full title and authority to enter into this Agreement and is not bound by any previous agreement which adversely affects this Agreement.

C.077

The [Author] undertakes that he/she has owns or controls the [specify] rights in [country/Europe/other] and that the publishing agreement with [Company] does not contain any clauses or undertaking which would prevent or conflict with the terms of this Agreement.

C.078

The [Licensor] confirms that he/she possesses full power and authority to enter into and perform this Agreement and that there are not nor will there be any liens, encumbrances or other restrictions against the [Work] or any part or the exploitation thereof which would derogate from or be inconsistent with the rights granted to the [Distributor] in this Agreement.

C.079

The [Distributor] confirms and undertakes that it has an agreement with [specify copyright owner] for the exclusive licence for the exploitation of the [Film/Work/Product] in [format] in [country]. That the [Distributor] has not licenced and/or exploited the [Film/Work/Product] in [format] in [country] at any time prior to [date].

C.080

The [Distributor] confirms and undertakes that to the best of its knowledge and belief the [Distributor] is not bound by any conflicting or prior agreement in respect of the [Film/Work/Product] in [format] in [country] which would jeopardise or be detrimental to the rights granted under this Agreement to the [Sub-Licensee].

C.081

There are no undertaking and/or warranties provided by [Name] in respect of this [Work] and [Name] does not purport to be the copyright owner of the [Work] and/or a licensee. [Name] owns a physical copy of the [Work] which he/she is willing to make available to the [Company] at the [Company's] risk and expense for the purpose of this Agreement.

C.082

The [Licensee] agrees to verify the financial stability, work practices and compliance with health and safety procedures of any proposed distributor and/or third party to be engaged by the [Licensee] to exploit the [Work].

Publishing

C.083

The [Company] hereby warrants and represents that [Name] is under no disability, restriction or prohibition, contractually or otherwise with respect to the rights granted and obligations entered into under this Agreement.

C.084

The [Owner] is a private limited liability company incorporated in [country] with the following identification [reference number]. The [Owner] has the full power, legal capacity and authority to enter into this Agreement to fulfil its terms and grant the rights set out herein. The [Owner] is a company with an established quality reputation, with a good trading record and financially sound.

C.085
The [Company] will not on behalf of the [Publisher] enter into any commitment, contract or arrangement with any other person, body or company.

C.086
The [Sub-Publisher] warrants, undertakes, confirms and agrees with the [Publisher] that:

1.1 It is free to enter into this Agreement.

1.2 It is not under any disability, restriction or prohibition which might prevent the [Sub-Publisher] from performing or observing any of the [Sub-Publisher's] obligations under this Agreement.

1.3 It has not entered into and shall not enter into any arrangement which has or might conflict with this Agreement.

C.087
The [Author] warrants that he/she has full authority to enter into this Agreement and that he/she is not bound by any previous agreement which adversely affects this Agreement.

C.088
The [Artist] warrants that he has not concealed another name or withheld details of his professional career and that at the time of signing this contract he is not and will not be bound by any other commitment, contract or memorandum which would prevent him fulfilling this Agreement.

C.089
The [Author] warrants to the [Publisher] that the [Author] has the right and power to enter this Agreement.

C.090
The [Author] confirms that the [specify] Rights in the [Work] have not been previously licensed or otherwise exploited in any form throughout the [country] except as previously disclosed in writing to the [Publisher], a copy of which is attached to and forms part of this Agreement.

C.091
The [Proprietor] warrants that it has and will retain good title and authority to enter into this Agreement.

310

C.092

The [Author] and the [Illustrator] undertake that they jointly and severally have created, developed, written and illustrated the [Work] and that they have not granted, assigned or licensed any part of the rights at any time to any third party. That there is no document or contract in existence to their knowledge which would affect their ability to enter in to this Agreement.

C.093

That the [Publisher] has not concluded any agreement with another author or artist which is on the same subject of [specify] in the last [two years] which is due to be published at the same time as the [Author's] [Book] which has not been disclosed.

C.094

The [Author] confirms that no agreement which has been signed by or on behalf of the [Author] concerning the publication of the [Author's] Work throughout the Territory prohibits the [Author] from granting the rights in the [Author's] Work granted under this Agreement.

C.095

The [Authors] confirm that neither party has entered into or is bound by an agreement with an agent in respect of the [Work].

C.096

[Name] is the authorised representative of the estate of the late [specify] and agrees that he/she has full authority of the estate to enter into and bind the estate to this Agreement with the [Company].

C.097

That [Name] agrees to supply at his/her sole cost a letter of confirmation of that authority to grant such rights under this Agreement from the following members [specify] of the family of the late author [specify].

Services

C.098

The [Manager] shall keep the [Group] informed on a regular basis as regards any negotiations with any third party and agrees that he shall not commit the [Group] or its members to any agreement or recording contract without the prior written consent of each member of the [Group] based on full disclosure of all the relevant facts.

C.099

The [Company] warrants that it has the power and authority to execute and perform this Agreement and to grant to the [Distributor] all of its rights herein granted and agreed to be granted. That there is no contract with any other person, firm, corporation or body which will in any way interfere with or infringe upon any such rights.

C.100

The [Artist] warrants that where a previous contract prejudices his right to enter into this Agreement the necessary permission has been obtained from the other party or parties and that the [Artist] undertakes to produce the written consent document for inspection by the [Company] upon request.

C.101

The [Agent] agrees that the [Agent] shall not be entitled to commit the [Author] or agree final terms with any third party at any time without the express consent of the [Author]. The [Agent] agrees that the [Author] shall have the final decision in respect of all agreements of any nature (whether as to the terms or whether to sign or not) relating to the exploitation of the [Work]. No authority is granted to the [Agent] under this Agreement to sign any document on behalf of the [Author].

C.102

The [Sportsperson] confirms that he has full title and authority to enter into this Agreement and is not bound by any previous agreement, professional rules, codes of conduct and/or decisions of a governing body which adversely affect this Agreement.

C.103

The [Agent] confirms that he has good title and authority to enter into and perform this Agreement and is not bound by any other agreement which adversely affects this Agreement. The [Agent] confirms that in particular there is an agreement between the [Agent] and [Advertiser] which fully authorises the [Agent] to act on the [Advertiser's] behalf in respect of this Agreement.

C.104

The [Agent] confirms that the [Author] shall have the final decision to conclude and sign any contract or other document with any third party relating to the exploitation of the [Work] and that no authority is granted under this Agreement for the [Agent] to sign or contract with third parties on behalf of the [Author].

C.105

The [Author] authorises the [Agent] to collect all sums due to the [Author] in respect of the [Work] from any source throughout the Territory during the Term of the Agreement and any time thereafter relating to any agreement negotiated by the [Agent] during the Term of the Agreement.

C.106

The [Designer] shall perform its obligations under this Agreement to the best of its skill and ability and shall maintain standards as are reasonably expected by the [Company] to create a fully functional website for the [Company's] commercial and marketing purposes on or before [date].

C.107

The [Designer] shall at all times have suitably qualified and experienced [staff/consultants/freelancers] who are able to effectively contribute to the successful completion of the [project] and are willing to sign and be bound by the terms of the confidentiality agreement.

C.108

The [Contributor] has expertise and experience in [website design and creation] and wishes to be engaged on a freelance basis [specify task].

C.109

The [Actor] agrees to provide his services and perform his duties at such times, dates and locations and in such manner as may reasonably be agreed with the [Agent] and any third party.

C.110

The [Actor] confirms that he/she shall make himself/herself available for all work arranged by the [Agent] except for the following dates [–].

C.111

The [Company] confirms that [Name] and the [Company] have the full authority and power to enter in this Agreement and that neither is bound by any prior contract, undertaking or restriction which has not been disclosed except for the following commitments [specify].

C.112

The [Consultant] is a professional [specify] and a member of the following bodies [specify]. The [Consultant's] professional qualifications are [–] and he is an expert in the field of [–].

C.113

[Name] agrees and undertakes that he/she has no physical and/or mental impairment and/or ill health and/or symptoms which would prevent and/or increase the premiums significantly for any insurance cover for the [Project].

C.114

[Name] agrees and undertakes not to drink alcohol for the duration of the [Project] and/or to take any prescribed medication except in an emergency which would affect his/her capacity to safely perform the tasks set out in this Agreement.

Sponsorship

C.115
The [Sportsperson] confirms that he/she is a full member of the following sports organisation [–] and is not banned, prohibited or restricted from practising his/her profession by any body or organisation in any part of the world.

C.116
The [Sportsperson] agrees to conduct himself/herself in a fit, proper and professional manner at all times during the Term of the Agreement.

C.117
[Name] confirms that she has full title and authority to enter into this Agreement and is not bound by any previous agreement or professional rules or codes of conduct which would affect, prohibit or restrict the performance of this Agreement.

C.118
The [Sponsor] confirms that it has and will retain authority to enter into this Agreement and is not bound by any agreement with any third party which will have or might have any adverse effect on this Agreement.

C.119
The [Athlete] and [Agent] confirm that there is no arrangement, agreement, contract or commitment to any advertiser, manufacturer, television company, radio company, news organisation, newspaper or magazine or other third party for the services of the athlete, endorsements of products or services, or use of products by the athlete or display of logos, or slogans which would prevent the [Athlete] carrying out or being bound by the terms or granting the rights or promoting the [services/products] of the [Company].

C.120
The [Athlete] is a [amateur/professional] and bound by the governing body [specify] which permits the [Athlete] to enter into [sponsorship/endorsement/promotional] agreements. The [Athlete] already has agreements with the companies listed in Appendix [–], but they do not prevent the [Athlete] entering into this Agreement.

C.121
The [Charity] is registered with the [Charities Commission/other] number [specify] and its Board of Trustees have and will comply with all the legal

314

requirements and codes of practice which exist in [country] at any time from [date] to [date].

C.122

The [Company] agrees to sponsor the [Event] provided that the following individuals will appear in the programme [specify]. In the event that more than two of these persons decide at a later date not to appear then the [Sponsor] shall have the right to nominate who the [Enterprise] should consider as an alternative.

University, Library and Educational

C.123

The [Consultant/Company] agrees and undertakes that:

1.1   There is no conflict of interest of which they are aware which if known to the [Institute] would affect their decision to enter into this Agreement.

1.2   That there is no arrangement, agreement, contract or commitment to any other university, library, business, advertiser, manufacturer, television company, radio company, news organisation, newspaper or magazine or other third party for the services of the [Consultant/Company] or use of products which would prevent or conflict with or have an adverse effect upon the obligations to the [Institute] and/or the [Institute's] reputation.

C.124

[Name] [Title] of [Institute] agrees and undertakes that they have been authorised to sign this Agreement on behalf of the [Institute]. That the [Institute] is permitted by its [Charter/Trust Deed/Terms of Reference] and has the full authority and power to enter in this Agreement.

C.125

The [Company] and the [Institute] both agree and undertake that they have the power and authority to enter into this Agreement. That neither is bound by any prior contract, undertaking or restriction which has not been disclosed except for the following commitments [specify].

C.126

The [Company] confirms that it is currently solvent, and that its accounts are audited by [name] and that it is not expected to make a loss in the next [two years].

C.127

The [Company] agrees that it shall only use suitably qualified and professional personnel for this [Project] who have the following skills [specify]. That all such personnel shall be current members of one of the following [unions/ trade/professional organisations] [–].

C.128
Where the [Consortium] have set up a new company for the [Project] which is independent from the [Institute]. Then the [Consortium] agrees that the [Institute] shall hold not less than [number] per cent of the [shares] and control [51]% of the new company. In addition it shall be entitled to [number] [non-executive] directors.

CARRIAGE COSTS

General Business and Commercial

C.129
The method of carriage shall be determined by the [Company] at its sole discretion and the [Customer] shall pay and be responsible for all carriage costs. In the event that the material is ordered less than [five days] (exclusive of Saturday, Sunday and Bank Holidays) prior to the Dispatch Date the [Customer] shall pay the [Company's] express surcharge then in force and any additional carriage costs incurred.

C.130
The cost of post, packaging and insurance shall be agreed with and paid for by the [Client] in advance of delivery.

C.131
The [Company] and the [Client] shall agree the method of sending and/ or delivering any goods and/or products in advance and the cost of any insurance cover and additional charges. However as a minimum charge the cost payable by the [Client] shall be:

1.1 Recorded delivery post in [country] shall be not less than [figure/ currency].

1.2 Recorded airmail and postage outside the [country] shall be not less than [figure/currency].

1.3 [Other].

C.132
The cost of delivery, insurance, and additional packaging are not included in the quoted price and will be an additional charge which may vary according to the destination and the order required.

C.133
The [Client] shall be required to pay in advance all the costs for the delivery of the [Articles] to the nominated address on the order form as confirmed by the [Client]. The actual choice of the form of delivery shall be at the discretion of the [Company] in accordance with their usual business practices. After the order has been confirmed no other address may then be nominated for delivery unless the [Client] agrees to an additional administration charge.

COLLECTING SOCIETIES

General Business and Commercial

C.134
The [Company] shall be responsible for registration with, clearance of all material, reporting to and payment of any sums due to the following organisations and bodies [list names and countries] for the use and exploitation of the [material].

C.135
Both parties agree that they shall register the [Book/Music/DVD/other] with the [collecting/trade organisation] [name] in the following manner:

1.1 Copyright owner to be listed as [Names].

1.2 Allocation and payment of sums received to be [split between the parties equally/other]. All sums to be paid directly to [specify].

1.3 No authorisation is to be permitted from only one person to grant a sub-license, transfer of rights or adaptation at any time except [specify].

C.136
The [Company] agrees that [Name] shall have the sole right to register with any [collecting societies/trade bodies/other] and to receive payment of all the sums received by them at any time for any exploitation, reproduction, performance, transmission, broadcast or any other type of use of the [Work/Music/Film/DVD/lyrics/other] and/or any parts in any country in the world on

land, sea, or in the air in any format of any nature whether in existence now or developed in the future.

C.137

The [Company] and the [Author] agree that the [Work/other] shall not be registered with [organisation] [or any other trade or collecting body] but shall be listed as an excluded work. All requests for permission to copy, reproduce, adapt, transmit, perform, sub-license, or otherwise exploit the [Work] in any form shall be referred for the approval and written consent of the [Author]. That the [Company] shall only be entitled to exercise the specific rights granted under this Agreement and that this does not include the right to grant consents or permission or transfer or sub-license rights to any third party at any time.

C.138

[Name] and [Name] agree that they shall register as joint owners of the [Film/Music/Work] with the following any copyright, trade mark, computer software, database and any other trade, industry, commercial and/or collecting societies in [country] and also with any other organisations or companies worldwide. The following registration details shall be provided to all such organisations [specify in detail].

Both parties agree that all sums received by any such organisations or companies shall be equally split between the parties on the basis of fifty per cent each.

C.139

The [Licensee] shall be solely responsible for the clearance of the rights and the payment of any sums due to any collecting societies, trade organisation, copyright organisation, and/or any other person and/or company which may arise from the exercise of the rights granted under this Agreement. The [licensor] shall not be liable for any such sums.

C.140

Where there are collecting societies for which the parties may register rights for any part and/or all of the rights in the [Work] in any format, medium whether text, sounds, images, designs, sound recordings, film, music scores, lyrics or any other material. It is agreed that both parties shall be registered as joint owners and that both shall share the sums received and/or due equally. That where one has to be nominated that the other party shall account immediately for any sums received and hold any funds so received for the other.

C.141

The parties agree that they shall seek to exclude the [Work/Project] form any control and/or registration with the following collecting societies. That all sub-licensing and exploitation shall be subject to the prior written approval and agreement of the [Company] and [Name]. That where both parties fail to agree that there shall be no obligation to provide consent to any proposal even where this results in loss of future revenue.

C.142
The [Assignor] agrees that the [Company] shall have the right to register with any collecting societies and/or in any legal system and with any other authority and with any other third parties as the copyright owner and the holder of all other rights in the [Work] including the name, title, logo, trade mark and any adaptation and exploitation that may be derived from the [Work] in any form. The [Assignor] agrees that they shall have no right to objection and/or to register a complaint in respect of any such registration in any part of the world from [date].

C.143
Where a new collecting society is created in the future which does not exist at the time of this Agreement which creates a new source of revenue to the [Company] form the exploitation of the [Work]. Then the [Company] agrees that any sums so received shall be include in the accounts and reports to [Name] and/or their estate and/or beneficiaries and/or heirs.

COLLECTIVE WORKS

General Business and Commercial

C.144
'Collective Work' shall mean any encyclopaedia, dictionary, yearbook or similar work, a newspaper, review, magazine or similar periodical and any work written in distinct parts by different authors or in which works or part of works of different authors are incorporated.

C.145
'Collective Work' shall mean a work of joint authorship or a work in which there are distinct contributions by different authors or in which works or parts of works of different authors are incorporated.

C.146
'The Collective Work' shall mean the periodical entitled [–] in the [specify language] published in [countries] by the [Company].

C.147

'Collective Work' shall include any original research papers, articles, talks, or works of the authors which already exist in a separate and independent form (whether or not they have been published) and which are collated and published together as a single periodical, hardback or paperback book [and/or CD-Rom] with the original text, images, data, and references.

C.148

In consideration of the payment of the [Advance Fee] and the additional [unit/royalty] fees. The [Author] grants the [Company] the non-exclusive right to incorporate the [Paper/article/talk] in the [periodical/on the website] known as [title/reference] from [date] to [date] on the following conditions:

1.1   The name of the [Author] shall be displayed in the contents list with the title, and at the beginning and end of the [article/paper/talk] with a copyright notice and the year [–]. That the following contact details shall be included so that any third party may seek permission for any further use [specify] at the end of the article.

1.2   That the [Company] agrees and undertakes not to authorise any third party to exploit, reproduce or adapt the [article/paper/talk] and the [Company] shall be limited to allowing [sales and marketing of the periodical/access and use of its website].

1.3   That the [Company] shall not be entitled to delete, add to, change, amend, or alter any part of the title and content of the [article/paper/talk] unless submitted to the [Author] for approval and agreed by the [Author] in advance.

1.4   No part of this Agreement is intended to transfer, assign or vest any intellectual property rights, including copyright, software, trade marks, logos or format, formulae, data, patents, inventions, technological developments, or other rights of any nature in the [Company] nor in any adaptation, variation or amended version. Nor shall the [Company] seek to register, represent to third parties or display any trade mark, copyright notice or warning which states that the [Company] owns any of these rights.

C.149

The [Author] does not grant nor authorise the [Company] the right to sub-licence the [Work] to third parties in any form whether part of the [Collective Work] or not. The prior written approval of the [Author], an additional fee and a separate agreement shall be required in the event that the [Company] which to sub-licence and/or assign the whole of the [Collective Work] to a third party. The [author] shall not be under any obligation to provide any consent and may request the exclusion of the [Work] from any such form of exploitation.

C.150

Where the [Company] uses sections and/or parts of the [Work] of less than [number] pages and includes these with material from other authors in a compilation work which is under a different title. Then the [Author] accepts that he/she shall not be entitled to the royalty payments set out in clause [–]. The [Company] agrees that it shall be obliged and the [Author] agrees to negotiate either a complete buyout fee or a royalty fee based on the new project. The parties agree that where they fail to agree terms for any such use that they shall engage a mediator at the [Company's] sole cost to resolve the matter.

COMMISSION

General Business and Commercial

C.151

There shall be no commission, agency fees, expenses, charges or costs deducted from the [Sale Price] and all sums due to [Name] by the [Company] shall be paid in full within [seven days] of receipt. The [Company] acknowledges that [Name] has already paid an advanced fixed fee of [specify] for their services.

C.152

Where the transaction is arranged, negotiated or agreed, but no final document is signed and/or no payment is received by the [Seller] then no commission shall be paid to the [Company].

C.153

The [Company] shall have the right to deduct the commission, expenses and costs due to the [Company] by [Name] under this Agreement prior to the payment of any sums due to [Name].

C.154

[Name] shall be obliged to pay commission to the [Company] where any person, or company is introduced to [Name] and that person or third party subsequently concludes an agreement with [Name] in respect of [specific type of transaction/rights] directly. This clause shall apply [at any time/for duration of this Agreement/from [date] to [date]].

C.155

The [Company] shall only be entitled to receive commission on any sums actually received and paid to [Name] and retained by [Name]. Any commission paid to the [Company] may be claimed back by [Name] within [two years] of payment where the sum on which the commission is calculated is repaid to a third party by [Name] due to an error, omission, refund, overpayment, breach of contract, legal action or any other reason.

C.156

When commission has been paid to the [Company] then no sum can be reclaimed, refunded or returned to [Name] unless due to an error or omission, negligence or fraud of the [Company].

C.157

The commission payments due to [Name] shall be subject to a maximum annual limit of [figure/currency] from [date] to [date].

C.158

'The Commission' shall be paid to [Name] on the actually sums received from the [purchasers/customers/retailers/others] and paid to the [Company] for acquisition of the following [Services/Products/Benefits] [detailed description]. Payment to [Name] shall be in accordance with the rates set out below:

1.1 From [0] to [figure] [currency] [number] per cent payable at the end of each six month period.

1.2 From [50,000] to [100,000] [currency] [number] per cent payable at the end of each year by [date].

C.159

[Name] shall be paid commission for the number of [tickets/products] which are sold by [Name] through their recommendation, links, website, articles and blogs and purchased by the public from the [Company] for which payment is received in [country] and not refunded at any time using the [code number/reference] [specify] from [date] to [date].

C.160

No commission shall be due to [Name] after [date] even if sums are received by the [Company] from the work and/or contribution of [Name] of any nature on or after that date. [Name] agrees that he/she shall not be entitled to any commission after [date] even if it relates to work completed by [Name] before that date which has not yet been received by the [Company].

C.161

Commission payable to [Name] shall be based on the net sums received by the [Company] after the deduction of marketing and administration costs, agency fees, telephone and mobile phones costs, bank charges, currency conversion costs, travel and accommodation costs, cost of supply of equipment, insurance cover and staff costs.

Internet and Websites

C.162
There shall be no agency fees, commission, royalties, fees, costs, expenses or other payments due to any third party who links to, accesses, downloads from, supplies material to or promotes this [Website].

C.163
The [Service Company] agrees to pay the [Website Company] commission of [10 per cent] of the [Subscription Fees] for the first three years for any person, body or company that enters into a [Service Contract] with the [Service Company] as a direct result of a referral, link or article on the [Website] and who uses the quote reference [specify].

C.164
The [Advertiser/Distributor] shall pay the [Website Company] a fixed unit commission of [figure/currency] for every [number] customers which follow the banner link and provide their personal details to the [Advertiser/ Distributor] and purchase [products/services].

C.165
The [Supplier] agrees that the [Seller] may market, promote and sell the [Product] at any price it deems fit on the [Seller's] website. Provided that the [Dealer Price] shall be paid for each unit of the [Product] to the [Supplier] in each case whether or not sums have been received by the [Seller].

C.166
This [Website] does not pay commission in money but allocates vouchers which can be redeemed against other products, services and benefits on the [Website]. There is no cash alternative available at any time and failure to redeem and/or use the commission and the vouchers within the allocated period and expiry date will not entitle you to make a claim for any financial and/or other loss. It is a condition of your participation in this [Scheme] that you agree and accept this term and condition. In the event that it is not acceptable then do not proceed and sign up to the [Scheme].

C.167
The [Company] does not pay a percentage fee based on sales and/or sums received. All payments in respect of commission for our agents are calculated on the number of customers who have [specify] and completed

323

a purchase of more than [value/currency/number] on our [Site] in each three month calendar period. Where you have reached your target of [specify] you will receive a one off fee of [currency/number] which will be paid direct to your nominated bank account by direct debit within one calendar month of your successful completion of the target by you and the customers.

Merchandising

C.168
The [Licensor] agrees that the [Licensee] shall be entitled to receive commission of [number] per cent [figure] % on any sums actually received by the [Licensee] in respect of the exploitation of the [Product/Work/Film] for the duration of this Agreement.

C.169
The [Licensee] shall not be entitled to receive commission on any sums received by the [Licensee] and/or the [Licensor] after the termination and/ or expiry of this Agreement for any contracts concluded by the [Licensee] during the term of this Agreement Any sums received by the [Licensee] after the expiry and/or termination of the Agreement shall belong entirely to the [Licensor] and shall be paid to the [Licensor].

C.170
The [Licensee] shall be entitled to be paid and calculate their commission at the end of [calendar month/accounting period]. The [Licensee] shall disclose all commission deducted and received by the [Licensee] in the relevant accounting statements to the [Licensor].

C.171
All commission shall be paid in [sterling/dollars/other] and shall be calculated after conversion from another currency. All payments to the [Licensee] shall be directly to a bank account in [country] and no additional bank charges shall be deducted and/or claimed by the [Licensee].

C.172
The [Licensee] shall not be entitled to commission on sums which are due and/or owing where the sums are not paid by the third parties. No payments shall be made by the [Licensor] for any loss of commission.

C.173
The [Company] shall be entitled to receive commission on all agreements which it negotiates and concludes which are signed by [Name] in respect of the exploitation of the rights specified in clause [–] of this Agreement. The [Company] shall be entitled to receive commission from those agreements

even after the expiry of this Agreement on all sums which are received by [Name] from those agreements. The right of the [Company] to receive commission shall cease either on the expiry and/or termination of the agreements in each case and/or by [date] whichever is the earliest.

C.174

The [Licensee] agrees and undertakes that it shall not agree and commit to pay any commission and/or agency fees which are in excess of [number] per cent and/or [figure/currency] in any country at any time. That it shall seek the approval and advice of the [Licensor] in any case where it would like to conclude and/or commit to any arrangement which is in excess of these levels. Failure to seek approval will mean that in any accounts and sums received the [Licensee] shall bear all the cost of the excess levels and shall not share the costs and/or recoup them before payment to the [Licensor].

C.175

The [Licensee] shall ensure that all agents, distributors and third parties that receive commission to promote and sell the [Work/Product] do not acquire any copyright and/or any other rights of any nature in any medium in the original [Work] and/or in any adaptation and/or variation. That where new material is to be created that the [Licensee] shall ensure that before any such parties are paid any commission they shall assign all rights in any new material created to the [Licensor].

Purchase and Supply of Products

C.176

The [Company] shall be paid a commission of [number] per cent in respect of the total value of each order placed by a wholesaler, retail outlet, website business or other purchaser at the end of each six month period starting [date]. Subject to payment for any such order being received and no refund, discount or returns being made where the lower value will be applied.

C.177

The [Company] shall be paid a fixed sum of [figure/currency] for each unit of [Products] which are purchased by members of the public, retailers and distributors at above [price] from [date] to [date] in [country] from the [Company].

C.178

The [Sales Representative] shall be entitled to retain [fifteen per cent] of the [Retail/Wholesale Price] of each of the items sold provided that the [Retail/Wholesale Price] in any event shall not with respect to each item be less than [figure/currency].

C.179

Commission for the purposes of this Agreement shall only be paid to [Name] for their work in promoting and marketing the products, services and name of the [Company] from [date] to [date]. Commission shall only be due and paid to [Name] where a person and/or other business purchases and pays for in full for any of the following products and/or services [specify] and at the time of purchase and payment either provides a [voucher/code/other] which has been supplied by [Name] and/or they have followed a link from a blog and/or article written by [Name] which refers to the [Company] and some of its products.

C.180

Commission shall be calculated by the [Company] on the total [retail/wholesale/other] monetary value of the orders made and paid full in full in each calendar month. The [Company] shall pay [Name] as follows:

1.1   Sums received by the [Company] up to [figure/currency] – [number] per cent of the sums received.

1.2   From [figure/number] to [figure/currency] – [number] per cent of the sums received.

1.3   Where payments have not been made in full and no ownership has passed to the [Customer] then no commission shall be due.

1.4   Where the [Company] incurs legal and/or administrative costs which arise from a dispute relating to any order then the [Company] shall be entitled to set aside a reasonable sum and not pay any commission until the matter has been resolved.

1.5   Payment to [Name] shall be within [one] calendar month of any [six] month accounting period of the [Company].

1.6   The commission payable to [Name] shall not exceed [number/currency] in any event in anyone accounting period and shall be capped at that figure.

Services

C.181

'The [Agent's] Commission' shall be the following percentage of the Gross Receipts by the [Agent] [number] per cent.

C.182

The [Agent] shall be entitled to a commission of [number] per cent of the [Author's] Gross Receipts as defined under Clause [–] subject to the terms of this Agreement.

C.183

In consideration of the [Agent's] Commission the [Agent] agrees to provide his non-exclusive services to the [Artiste] for the Term of the Agreement throughout the Territory.

C.184

The [Company] hereby commissions the [Photographer] to take portrait photographs of [Individual] Work and the [Photographer] hereby accepts the commission.

C.185

The [Company] agrees to pay the [Agent's] Commission to the [Agent] on a quarterly basis throughout the Term of the Agreement. Such payment to be made in [currency] after conversion from [currency] of the sum due and deduction of currency exchange costs by such method as the [Company] decides.

C.186

'The [Licensee's] Commission' shall be the following percentage of the Net Receipts [figures and words].

C.187

'The [Manager's] Commission' shall be the following percentage of the Gross Receipts after deduction of the Authorised Expenses [number] per cent.

C.188

'The [Agent's] Commission' shall mean the following percentage of the Gross Receipts in respect of the following forms of the [Work] [and any appearances, interviews with [Name] in conjunction with the [Work] in [Territory/Europe/countries]:

1.1   [number] per cent [–]% in respect of all hardback and paperback copies including discounted, reduced price, overstock, remainder, premium offer, book clubs, educational editions, anthologies, quotations, translations.

1.2   [number] per cent [–]% for any serialisation of the [Work] in any newspaper, magazine or periodical.

1.3   [number] per cent [–]% in respect of DVDs, videos, CDs, audiotapes and other forms of mechanical reproduction and any sums due from collecting societies. [Excluding uses on mobile phones, computers, other gadgets and the internet.]

1.4   [number] per cent [–]% in respect of any option for or exercise of any form of film, television, radio or stage rights including digital, cable, terrestrial and satellite, theatric or non-theatric and any sums due from collecting societies. [Excluding uses on mobile phones, computers, other gadgets and the internet.]

1.5 [number] per cent [–]% in respect of merchandising, the internet and multi-media and any other method or format of exploitation [whether in existence now or developed in the future] including comic cartoons, computer games, CD-Roms, mobile phone adaptations by text, images or recordings, other uses on mobile phones and other gadgets.

C.189

'The Agent's Commission' shall be the following percentage of the Gross Receipts in respect of the following forms of exploitation of the [Work] [received by the Agent/other]:

1.1 number] per cent [–]% of all hardback and paperback copies of the [Work] sold in the United Kingdom of Great Britain and Northern Ireland, the Republic of Ireland, the Channel Islands, the Isle of Man.

1.2 [number] per cent [–]% of all hardback and paperback copies of the [Work] sold throughout the Territory excluding the United Kingdom of Great Britain, Northern Ireland, the Republic of Ireland, the Channel Islands, the Isle of Man, the United States of America and Canada.

1.3 [number] per cent [–]% of all hardback and paperback copies of the [Work] sold in the United States of America and Canada.

1.4 [number] per cent [–]% of all copies of the [Work] which are disposed of by a third party throughout the Territory at a discount, reduced price, remainder or overstock.

1.5 [number] per cent [–]% of all copies of the [Work] which are disposed of throughout the Territory as a premium offer, book club or educational editions.

1.6 [number] per cent [–]% of all copies of any anthologies and quotations.

1.7 [number] per cent [–]% of all translations.

1.8 [number] per cent [–]% of all straight non-dramatic radio and television reading.

1.9 [number] per cent [–]% of first serialisation of the [Work] in any newspaper, magazine or periodical.

1.10 [number] per cent [–]% of second and subsequent serialisations of the [Work] in any newspaper, magazine and periodical.

1.11 [number] per cent [–] % of strip cartoon or other similar representation.

1.12 [number] per cent [–]% Merchandising excluding the image and name rights of [Name].

1.13 Non-theatric rights [–].

1.14 [number] per cent [–]% of all adaptations, developments associated with or derived from and/or any exploitation from all forms of film, television, radio, video, DVD, audiotapes, computer discs, CD-Roms, computer software, internet, mobile phones and interactive multi-media, music, CDs, collecting societies or other medium not listed above whether invented now or created in the future.

C.190
'The Agent's Commission' shall be the following percentage of the Gross Receipts [number] per cent [–]%.

C.191
'The Manager's Commission' shall be the following percentage of the Net Receipts [number] per cent [–]%.

C.192
The [Sportsperson] agrees to refer all requests of a commercial nature to the [Manager] and agrees that the [Manager] shall have the sole and exclusive right to negotiate with third parties for the commercial services of the [Sportsperson] during the Term of the Agreement.

C.193
The [Agent] confirms that the [Author] shall not be responsible for any costs or expenses incurred by the [Agent] and that the [Agent] shall only be entitled to receive the [Agent's Commission].

C.194
The [Manager] acknowledges that he/she shall not be entitled to any commission in respect of any work done or agreed to be done by the [Sportsperson] prior to the date of this Agreement whether that work is performed during the Term of the Agreement or not.

C.195
The [Manager] acknowledges that she shall be solely responsible for her own expenses and costs in providing her services to the [Sportsperson] under this Agreement and shall only be entitled to receive the [Manager's Commission]. The [Sportsperson] shall not be liable for any expenses or costs of the [Manager] or incurred on behalf of the [Sportsperson] by the [Manager].

C.196

The [Sportsperson] acknowledges that the [Manager] shall be entitled to the [Manager's Commission] after the expiry of this Agreement in respect of all agreements negotiated by the [Manager] and concluded during the Term of this Agreement.

C.197

In consideration of the mutual promises and representations made by one party to the other under this Agreement including the payments to be made by the [Company] to the [Designer]. The [Company] agrees to engage the non-exclusive services of the [Designer] to design, develop, integrate and support the [Company's] website in accordance with the Term of this Agreement.

C.198

The [Company] confirms that all rights in any [material] supplied to the [Designer] under this Agreement shall be owned or controlled by the [Company] unless expressly stated to belong to a third party.

C.199

The [Designer] shall at all times employ suitably qualified and experienced [staff/artists/others] who are able to contribute to the successful completion of the [Project] and the proper fulfilment of the obligations under this Agreement.

C.200

That the [Company] may at any time decide not to use or continue to use the services of the [Designer] and shall only be obliged to pay in full the sums set out in Schedule [–].

C.201

The [Designer] agrees that the [Company] may at any time engage any third party at its sole discretion to carry out work on the website or any other internet related project for the [Company].

C.202

The [Agent] agrees that any form of exploitation of the product of the [Artiste's] services shall require the prior consent of the [Artiste]. The [Artiste] shall be entitled to refuse to carry out any work for any reason whether or not the [Agent] will suffer a financial or other loss. The [Agent] shall not be entitled to seek any compensation, loss or damages from the [Artiste] which arises from such failure to provide consent.

C.203

The [Agent] confirms that the [Author] shall have the final decision to conclude and sign any agreement, contract or other document relating to the exploitation of the [Work] and that no authority is granted under this Agreement for the [Agent] to do so.

C.204
'The Commissioned Work' shall be the [specify] to be prepared, produced and delivered by the [Assignor] to the [Company] which is briefly described as follows [title/duration/format].

C.205
'The Commissioned Work' shall be the following series of photographs based on the summary [A copy of which is attached setting out locations, persons, themes, colours, items and words] to be created, produced, developed, printed and delivered by the [Photographer] to the [Company].

C.206
The [Assignor] undertakes that it shall produce the [Commissioned Work] in accordance with the Budget, in the following format [–] by [date].

C.207
The [Photographer] agrees that he/she shall produce the [Commissioned Work] in accordance with the summary and deliver the following material [detail] by [date].

C.208

1.1 The [Company] engages and commissions the [Consultant] to carry out a market survey, and to analyse and assess and report back on the topic of [specify] with the following aims [specify].

1.2 The [Consultant] agrees to provide [number] copies of an A4 bound report written in [language] of no less than [number] pages together with [number] copies in [form] at the [Consultants'] sole cost by [date].

1.3 The [Consultant] agrees to also provide copies of all the market survey material, supporting material, research and data to the [Company] upon request.

1.4 The [Consultant] agrees that the [Fee] shall be the total limit of the liability of the [Company] and there shall be no additional charges, costs and expenses attributed and/or claimed by the [Consultant] for any part of the work under this Agreement.

1.5 The [Consultant] agrees to ensure that in any market survey the contributors have the option to agree that can be contacted at a later date by the [Company].

1.6 The [Consultant] agrees to assign any and all rights including copyright, database rights and any other rights in any part of the world

331

to the [Company] in consideration of the [Fee] and also waives all moral rights and right to be attributed as the copyright owner of the report. The [Consultant] agrees and accepts that the [Company] may edit, adapt and revise the report in any manner and also engage a third party to do so. That in any such circumstance the prior approval and/or consent of the [Consultant] shall not be required. Nor shall the [Consultant] have any claim for loss of reputation and/or otherwise.

C.209

The [Company] agrees that where [Name] has commissioned design work and development for a website from the [Company] based on an original quote and that sum has now been exceeded whether caused by [Name] or not. That [Name] shall have the right to terminate the agreement with the [Company] and to be delivered and have ownership transferred of all originals and copies of all material including drawings, software and codes and passwords, animation, film, video, images, text, music and underlying technology in any state developed to date which relate to the website commissioned by [Name] provided that the [Company has received [figure/currency] from [Name] in payment.

Sponsorship

C.210

[Name] agrees to the following terms in respect of sponsorship and/or other commercial funding of [Project/Event/other]:

1.1 To refer all matters relating to sponsorship and/or other commercial funding of [Project/Event/other] to the [Company].

1.2 That the [Company] shall have the sole and exclusive right to negotiate with third parties for the sponsorship and/or other commercial funding of [Project/Event/other] from [date] to [date].

1.3 That [Name] shall not be responsible for any costs, expenses and/or other sums incurred by the [Company] at any time.

1.4 That the [Company] shall only be entitled to receive the [number] per cent [figure] % of all sums received by [Name] in respect of all sums received from sponsorship and/or other commercial funding of [Project/Event/other] from [date] to [date].

1.5 That the [Company] shall not be entitled to any commission in respect of any sum received from sponsorship and/or other commercial funding of [Project/Event/other] before [date] and/or after [date] whether or not negotiations and/or agreements were made and/or concluded during the continuance of this Agreement.

C.211

It is agreed that no agency fees and/or commission, and/or other payments and/or deductions shall be made to any third party in respect of the Sponsorship Fees being provided by the [Sponsor] for the [Event]. All the sums paid by the [Sponsor] shall be used by the [Company] for the sole purpose of the [Project] as specified in the Budget in Schedule [1].

C.212

The [Company] agrees that any form of sponsorship of the [Event] which involves the commissioned [Work/Services] of the [Artists/Author] shall be notified in the [Artist/Author] either before it is concluded and/or as soon as possible thereafter. The [Company] shall provide a list of sponsors and the method by which they are using and/or promoting their products and/or services. The [Artist/Author] shall have the right to refuse to be involved with the [Event] and/or to attend and/or provide any additional work and/or services if the [Artist/Author] does not agree with the choice of sponsorship and/or the method. The [Artist/Author] shall be entitled to notify the [Company] to that effect without any liability as to the losses, damages, costs, expenses and/or any other sums that may be incurred as a result.

C.213

The [Company] agrees that where any new artwork, text, logo, name and/or other material is commissioned by them which relates to the [Sponsor], the [Event] and/or any of the services, products and/or marketing relating to the [Sponsor]. That the [Company] shall ensure that any new material shall be assigned to the [Company] and then to the [Sponsor] so that no such rights are owned and/or controlled by a third party. Where the [Company] fails to do so and the [Sponsor] is at a later date required to take legal action then the [Company] shall be obliged to bear [number] per cent of the costs incurred by the [Sponsor] and their legal and other professional advisors engaged for that purpose.

C.214

The [Company] agrees that after the [Event] it shall conduct market research and gain feedback from the public, performers and others involved in order to assess how to improve and develop. The [Company] agrees to provide the [Sponsor] with a copy of any such report that may be completed and/or any new related commissioned report.

C.215

The [Sponsor] acknowledges and agrees that it shall not have any rights in any material in any medium including but not limited to names, titles, logo, images, music, sound recordings, films, photographs, apps, promotional games, and/or merchandising commissioned and/or developed by the

[Company] which relates to the [Event]. That the [Sponsor] shall not have the right to use and/or exploit and/or authorise others to reproduce, adapt, supply and/or licence any part at any time and that there is no licence granted either express or implied to do so.

University, Library and Educational

C.216
'The Commissioned [Work/Project]' is called [title] to be prepared, produced and delivered by the [Institute]. A summary is attached as Appendix [–] and forms part of this Agreement.

C.217
The [Company] agrees that the [Institute] may at its sole discretion cancel the Agreement for the use of the [Company's] services and/or engage a third party to carry out work on the [Website/Project/Service].

C.218
The [Institute] shall be entitled to refuse to carry out or collaborate with the [Company] where to do so would seriously affect the reputation of the [Institute] or is likely to result in legal proceedings by a third party. The [Company] shall not be entitled to seek any compensation, loss or damages from the [Institute] which arises from such refusal.

C.219
The [Consultant] agrees that the [Institute] shall have the final decision in respect of all matters and that there is no consent, authority or implication under this commission that the [Consultant] is entitled to represent the [Institute] or to act as their agent or to sign any document or to commit to any agreement.

C.220
That the [Institute] may at any time decide to cease engaging the services of the [Company] whether the [Project] has been completed or not. The [institute] shall only be required to provide [seven days] written notice to the [Company] and to pay such sums as may be due for work completed to that date.

C.221
There shall be no commission, agency fees, expenses, charges or costs due to the [Company]. The [Company] acknowledges that the [Institute] has already agreed a fixed fee of [figure/currency] [words] for their services.

C.222
Where the [Institute] commissions a report, photograph, data analysis and any other work from [Name] during the course of their unpaid internship at

the [Institute]. It is a condition of that internship that all copyright and any other rights of any nature shall belong to the [Institute]. [Name] agrees to sign and execute for [one/currency] any documents that may be required at a later date to effect transfer provided that no rights shall be sought to be transferred by the [Institute] that [Name] was already working on and/or developing in any form prior to the internship.

C.223

The [Institute] authorises the [Consortium] to commission work and engage consultants, researchers and such as persons as may be required for the [Project] provided that:

1.1 The agreed budget is not exceeded.

1.2 The [Project] terms of reference are adhered to at all times.

1.3 Regular monthly reports detailing progress; completion of tasks and expenditure are provided to [Name] at the [Institute] by the [Consortium].

1.4 That where there are to be any variations from the original proposal for the [Project]; terms of reference and/or costs that no commitment may be made without obtaining the prior written approval of [Name] at the [Institute] based on a full disclosure of the facts.

COMPANY

General Business and Commercial

C.224

'The Company' shall be [full name/registered address/company reference/ trading name] [and shall include any parent, associated or other company whether related directly or indirectly through directors, companies, bodies or shareholdings or otherwise] and shall under this Agreement include its assigns licensees and successors in title.

C.225

'The Company' shall mean [Name Ltd/plc] whose main place of business is at [address] and shall not include any associated holding or other person or corporation whether connected directly or indirectly with the [Company]. Nor shall it include any assigns, licensees, or successors in title.

C.226
'Person' shall mean an individual, corporation, limited or unlimited liability company, general or limited partnership, trust, unincorporated association, joint venture, joint-stock company, government, governmental authority or agency or any other entity.

C.227
'Director' in relation to a body corporate whose affairs are managed by its members shall mean any member of that body corporate.

C.228
'The Agent' shall mean the following [Company] which is authorised to act on behalf of the following Celebrity [–] whose registered office is at [–].

C.229
'The Company' shall be [registered company name/trading name] of [registered address/business address].

C.230
[Name] registered in [country/address] whose principal place of business is at [address] (to be known as) [–].

C.231
'Consumer' means any individual, body corporate or otherwise which accesses the ISP's website and references throughout this Agreement to the singular shall include all references to the plural.

C.232
This Agreement is purely between [specify parties] and does not transfer, provide or make over any rights or obligations to any other person, body or company.

C.233
'The Publisher' shall mean the following company with which the [Licensor] has entered into a written agreement for the publication of the [Work] in [format] [–].

C.234
'The Company' shall be the company which has signed this Agreement together with any other directly related entity or body whether a parent company by lineage or part of a group structure or acting together or trading under a group name.

C.235
'The Companies' shall be as follows:

1.1 The subsidiary known as [trading name] incorporated in the name of [–] in [country] registration reference [–] who registered office is at [address] and

1.2 The parent company known as [trading name] incorporated in the name of [–] in [country] registration reference [–] who registered office is at [address].

C.236
'The Company' shall mean [specify] which is a [limited company/partnership/plc/other] trading as [specify] with a main business address of [–] [including/excluding] any parent company, subsidiary, affiliate, joint venture partner, consortium, associate, distributor, sub-licensee, assignees and successors in business in whole or part.

C.237
'The Company' the limited liability company [specify] owned by the directors [name] and any assets, contracts, intellectual property rights and domain names, databases and documents and computer records held at the its business address at [specify].

C.238
'The Company' shall be [Name] of [Address] which is a [sole trader] which provides the [subject] services of [Name].

C.239
'The Parent Company' is [Name] of [Address] trading as [specify trading name].

C.240
All references to the [Company] in this Agreement shall not include any parent company, associated company, subsidiary, partnership, business associates, agents, distributors, trusts, and/or any other entity.

C.241
The Parent Company of the [Sponsor] in this Agreement agrees and undertakes to be bound by any clauses which the [Sponsor] is unable to fulfil where the [Sponsor] would be breach of this Agreement. In particular the payment clauses in [specify] and the indemnity clause [specify].

C.242
This Agreement has been reached with you the [Licensee] as a specific company and there is no right and/or permission provided that allows and/or permits the [Licensee] to assign, transfer and/or delegate any part of this

Agreement to a third party whether or not that other company is associated with and/or connected to the [Licensee]. Any attempt and/or evidence that you intend to do so shall entitle [Name] to terminate this agreement with immediate effect by notice by [email].

C.243
The [Company] trades under the name [specify] in [country].

C.244
The [Company] is registered in [country] as [specify] and is authorised to trade in the field of [specify].

C.245
All health and safety and premises licences and authorisation and insurance for the [Company] are held and registered in the name of [specify] at [address] in [country].

C.246
The [Company] has the following parent company, associated companies, business partners, associates, distributors, suppliers and agents as at [date] [specify].

COMPETITIONS

General Business and Commercial

C.247
You the entrant [Name] of [address] age [specify] and date of birth [specify] contact details [telephone/email/mobile] agree and undertake that you shall be bound by and comply with the terms and conditions for entry to the [Competition]. That in the event that you fail to comply with the terms and conditions of entry for any reason that your entry shall not be eligible and shall be disqualified from the Competition.

C.248
In order to be able to enter the Competition and to be eligible to comply with the terms and conditions of entry. It is a condition that any person who enters the Competition must be a resident of the [United Kingdom/Channel Islands/ Isle of Man] and [eighteen/other] years of age or older.

C.249

Any person who is an employee of any of the following companies [specify names] and/or any other agent, promoter and/or other person connected with the Competition and/or a member of their [immediate/extended/other] family shall not be allowed to enter the Competition and shall be ineligible to participate. If any such person should enter then they will be automatically disqualified and not entitled to claim and/or be awarded any prize.

C.250

The [Company] shall be entitled at its sole discretion to declare that any entry is not to be entered for the [Competition] and is disqualified (whether or not the answer is correct). In such event the [Company] shall not be obliged to notify the person who has entered of their disqualification nor shall it be obliged to provide a reason for its decision.

C.251

The [Company] shall be entitled at its sole discretion to decide that any entry is disqualified from the Competition due to the fact that it is in breach of the terms and conditions of entry. Where an entrant is disqualified the [Company] shall provide a written reason for the disqualification if so requested by the entrant.

C.252

All decisions of any nature made by the Directors and/or officers of the [Company] and/or other authorised third parties shall be final and not subject to any appeal process. The [Company] shall not enter into any correspondence, dialogue and/or otherwise with any person and/or entrant regarding any aspect of the Competition.

C.253

All parts of the procedure of the Competition, the decisions as to eligibility and the correctness of any answers and the award of prizes and any other matter of any nature shall be entirely at the sole discretion of the [Company] whose decision shall be final. The results of the Competition shall be available from [address] by sending a stamped address envelope marked [specify].

C.254

All entries must be original and the work of the person named as the entrant. No entry should be abusive, defamatory, offensive, derogatory, degrading and/or otherwise not acceptable due to the nature of the material submitted. The [Company] may at its sole discretion decide that any entry is not eligible due to the nature of the content of the entry and may disqualify a person from the Competition [and any such future competitions].

C.255

The prize(s) shall consist of [specify in detail]. The prize(s) shall not include [specify in detail].

The following costs and expenses shall not be part of the prize(s) and shall be the responsibility of the person who is selected to be awarded a prize [specify in detail]. [Where a specific prize is not available for any reason then the prize winner shall be awarded a prize which is similar in value and of a similar type.]

C.256

The Competition starts on [date] and ends on [date]. All entries must be received by [time] on [date]. All entries received and/or made after that time shall not be eligible to be entered into the Competition and shall be disqualified. There may be a charge incurred even though the entry is not accepted as valid.

C.257

All costs of entry are the responsibility of the person entering the Competition. There are no refunds for any entries which are received by the [Company] which are ineligible, illegible, damaged, lost, delayed and/or received after the deadline. Only the following methods of entry to the Competition will be accepted by the [Company] [specify].

C.258

All entries by post shall be on an original official entry form from the [Product] accompanied by [number] of original official vouchers which have been collected from the [Product] together with a receipt and/or other proof of purchase. No photocopies are accepted. No more than [number] entries will be accepted by the [Company] from each [household/address]. All entries must have arrived at the [address] post paid by the deadline. No acknowledgement of the entry will be provided by the [Company]. A charge may still be incurred for an entry which is ineligible and disqualified.

C.259

All entries by telephone and mobiles shall be by telephone call to [telephone number] and then follow the instructions provided which will be in the [English] language and to leave your answer and personal details. No more than [number] entries will be accepted by the [Company] from each mobile and/or landline. All entries must be completed by the deadline [specify]. Each call shall be charged at [figure/currency] from a [specify] landline from the [United Kingdom]. Calls from mobile phones and/or other networks and/or by any other method may be charged at a much higher level. All persons who enter by telephone and/or mobile must have the permission of the person in whose name the telephone and/or mobile is held and/or who pays the bill. No acknowledgement of the entry will be provided by the [Company].

C.260
All entries by text messages from mobile phones and/or other gadgets shall be in [English/other] to [telephone number] and send your answer and [specify details]. No more than [number] entries will be accepted by the [Company] from each mobile and/or gadget. All entries must be completed by the deadline. Each text will be charged at [figure/currency] from a mobile in the [United Kingdom] plus the network rate which is charged by their network for sending a text message. Texts by any other method may be charged at a much higher level. All persons who enter by text must have the permission of the person in whose name the mobile is held and/or who pays the bill. All entries by text before the deadline will receive a text confirming their entry.

C.261
All entries online on the website [name/reference] shall be made by filling in all the details required in the entry form online in [English/other] and confirming your acceptance of the terms and conditions of entry and completing the answer and sending it to the [Company]. No more than [number] entries will be accepted by the [Company] from each person. All entries must be completed by the deadline. All persons who enter by this method must have the permission of the person in whose name the computer is held and/or who pays the bill. An acknowledgement of entry will be provided by the [Company], but no reference provided.

C.262
No responsibility can be accepted by the [Company] for any entries which are lost, incomplete, are delayed beyond the deadlines, fail to arrive, are damaged, are illegible, inaudible, are not transmitted, do not arrive and/or for any other reason are not received by the deadline and/or are ineligible. Proof of posting is not accepted as proof of delivery to the [Company]. Proof of submitting an email and/or sending a text message is not accepted as proof of delivery to the [Company]. If the details of entry are not received by the [Company] for any reason then the entry is ineligible.

C.263
No responsibility can be accepted by the [Company] for any costs, expenses and/or charges incurred in respect of any entries by any method. The [Company] shall not be liable for any reason to any person who may enter the Competition and/or any third party whose facilities and/or equipment may be used and each person enters at their own risk and cost.

C.264

The prizes will be awarded in the order that they are drawn. The winning entries will be drawn at random [in order from first to last] selected by [method] by [date] from all eligible entrants who have provided the correct answer.

C.265

The prizes will be awarded in order of merit. The winning entries shall be selected by a panel of judges appointed by the [Company] by [date]. The [Company] may at any time appoint, withdraw and/or substitute any of the judges on the panel.

C.266

Independent supervision of all valid entries received shall be made by [specify].

C.267

There shall be no independent supervision of the Competition and all decisions are at the sole discretion of the [Company].

C.268

The decision of the [Company] as to the winners of the Competition shall be final.

C.269

No entrant can be awarded more than one prize per competition.

C.270

Entrants can be awarded more than one prize in the Competition.

C.271

The winners will be notified by [specify method] within the timescale specified below unless the [Company] decides at its sole discretion that the timescale for notification needs to be extended for any reason.

C.272

Notification to the winners shall be by first class post by letter to the address provided by the person when they entered the Competition [within number days of the date of/after] the close of the Competition.

C.273

Notification of the winners shall be by email to the email address provided by the person when they entered the Competition [within number days of the date of/after] the close of the Competition.

C.274

Notification of the winners shall be by text to the mobile number provided by the person when they entered the Competition [within number days of the date of/after] the close of the Competition.

C.275

Any prize has to be accepted and taken by the person who is awarded the prize before [date]. After that date no prize shall be available to that person and at the [Company's] sole discretion another eligible person may be selected for the prize.

C.276

The prize can only be awarded and/or taken by the person whose name is provided at the time of entry to the Competition. There is no cash available as an alternative to any prize, nor is the [Company] obliged to exchange and/or transfer any prize to another person.

C.277

The list of winners is available by [specify] until [date]. The results of the Competition shall be available from [address] by sending a stamped addressed envelope marked [specify].

C.278

The [Company] reserves the right at its sole discretion to withdraw and/or substitute any prize at any time for any reason. The [Company] may replace and/or substitute any prize with any products, goods, services and/or cash which the [Company] decides [is appropriate/of equal value/similar] in the circumstances.

C.279

The [Company] may at any time decide to change, cancel, amend, vary, delete, add to and/or otherwise alter the terms and conditions of entry, the prizes, the criteria by which winners are chosen and/or selected and/or any other part of the Competition. The [Company] shall not be required to send separate notification to each person who has and/or may enter the Competition. It shall be sufficient that details shall be available on the [Company's] website at [specify].

C.280

It is a condition of entry that the person entering the Competition agrees and undertakes to assign to the [Company] the sole and exclusive intellectual property rights including copyright whether in existence now and/or created in the future and any other rights in all media throughout the world and universe in all the material entered for the Competition (except their personal details) [including but limited to any text, film, photograph, and/or otherwise] for the full period of copyright and any extensions and/or renewals and in perpetuity. The [Company] shall have the right to assign, licence and/or commercially exploit the material in any form and the person shall not be entitled to receive any sums. No rights of any nature shall be retained by the person who entered the Competition.

C.281

The entrant grants the [Company] the exclusive right to reproduce, distribute, supply and otherwise exploit the material submitted for the Competition for a period of [ten/other] years from [date/the date of entry] in all intellectual property rights including copyright, trade marks, computer software rights, database rights, design rights, patents and/or any other rights and/or interest which may exist and/or be created in the future in all media [throughout the world and universe/in country] (except their personal details) including but not limited to film, television, merchandising, publishing, the internet and downloads, mobiles, marketing and advertising. The [Company] shall also have the right to sub-licence, add to, delete from, adapt and/or otherwise exploit the material without the payment of any advance, royalty and/or other sum to the entrant.

C.282

The person who entered the Competition waives the right to be identified as the author of the material submitted for the Competition. It is agreed that the [Company] may be credited as the copyright owner and may assign, licence and/or commercially exploit the material in any form and the person shall not be entitled to receive any sums.

C.283

The person who entered the Competition shall have the right to be identified as the author of the material submitted for the Competition and credited as the copyright owner on all copies of the material used and/or exploited by the Company] in the following form wherever possible: © [year] [name of entrant].

C.284

The personal details which have been submitted for the Competition will be held by the [Company/other]. This information will only be shared with third parties involved with the Competition for the administration of the Competition and/or the supply and delivery of the prizes. The personal details will only be held for the earlier of [number/months] and the period necessary to complete the administration of the Competition. All personal details will then be destroyed and/or deleted.

C.285

Where for any reason beyond the reasonable control of the [Company] the Competition cannot be carried out and/or completed as planned and/or advertised. Then the [Company] reserve the right to cancel the [Competition] at any time and in such event shall not be liable to any person who, for any reason, may have entered the Competition. The total liability if any shall be the cost of the postage, email, and/or text which in any event shall not exceed [figure/currency].

C.286

The terms and conditions of this Competition shall be subject to the Laws of [England/other].

C.287

All winners shall have their name and answer [announced/displayed/printed] on [specify].

C.288

All winners agree to the following publicity and marketing [specify].

C.289

All winners agree to participate in such reasonable marketing and photographic shoots as may reasonably be requested by the [Company [subject to the payment of travel costs].

C.290

You agree that you enter this [race/competition/event] at your own risk and that the [Organisers] cannot accept any responsibility for any loss of any equipment, injury to any part of your body, death and/or permanent disability. You have been advised that this [race/competition/event is very dangerous and that the [Organisers] do not hold any insurance cover nor is any provided by any governing body associated with the sport. You waive all claims against the [Organisers] and the volunteers and the support services which arise from your own errors, judgement and actions. You agree that the only exception is where injury or death is caused by the negligence and/or material failure of the [Organisers] to take sufficient precautions which are within a reasonable cost with respect to any material adverse conditions.

C.291

Only one entry is permitted per person. If at a later date any person is found to have entered more than once then the [Company] reserves the right to exclude them from any further participation in the competition and they shall not be entitled to be considered in any process and/or decision to assess the winners and award prizes.

C.292

This competition is only open to those age [number] and under who live in [country] and have purchased a promotional copy of [specify product] from [store] between [date and [date].

C.293

The [Company] shall announce the winners of the competition of its website [reference] on [date]. All winners are obliged agree to have a promotional photograph taken and to agree that it may be used by the [Company] to promote and market the [Product] in any media at any time. The [Company] agrees to provide each winner with a copy of their promotional photograph in a frame. The [Company] agrees that where additional photographs, filming and/or appearances may be required that the [Company] shall pay the winners a reasonable fee and expenses for their services on each occasion.

COMPLETION GUARANTEE

General Business and Commercial

C.294

The [Producer] confirms that he has entered into a completion agreement with [Name] referred to as the [Completion Guarantor]. The [Producer] acknowledges that the completion guarantee effective between the [Completion Guarantor] and the [Commissioning Company] referred to in Clause [–] below covers any sums due to be paid to any third party for the successful completion of the terms of this Agreement and that such costs shall not be less than the total production costs.

C.295

The [Producer] acknowledges that the [Commissioning Company] has entered into a Completion Guarantee arrangement with the [Completion Guarantor]. A copy of the fully executed Completion Guarantee is attached to and forms part of this Agreement as Schedule [–] to this Agreement. For the avoidance of doubt the fee due to be paid by the [Commissioning Company] for the Completion Guarantee and the completion agreement shall, in accordance with Clause [–] above, be an agreed item of the Fixed Price Budget notwithstanding the payment of such fee directly to the Completion Guarantor by the [Commissioning Company].

C.296
The [Company] shall take out a completion guarantee or such other underwriting, or insurance policy as may be applicable to cover the consequences of delay or the failure to complete or deliver the [Film/project/ other]. The terms of and exclusions under the cover, the value and the cost of the premiums and other payments shall be entirely at the [Company's] expense and shall not be recoverable under the [Budget] or from [Name]. The sole beneficiary of any sums paid under such completion guarantee or policy shall be the [Company/other].

C.297
The [Company] agrees to arrange suitable insurance cover for the [Project] so that in the event there are any losses, accidents, deaths, failures of equipment and/or power, cancellation of flights and other travel and accommodation arrangements, booking of venues and hire of locations, damage to and loss of costumes and sets, fire, riots, explosions and/ or withdrawal of services by any party and/or the failure to complete the [Project] that any sums which may fall due will be covered.

C.298
The [Enterprise] agrees and accepts that no insurance and/or completion guarantee is to be arranged by the [Producer] for the [Project]. That the [Budget] will be released in stages subject to the completion of the target tasks set out in Schedule [–].

COMPLIANCE

Building

C.299
The [Management Contractor] shall immediately comply or secure compliance with all instructions. In the event that any instruction requires a Works Contract to be altered the [Management Contractor] before compliance shall submit to the [Architect] any written objection, consent or otherwise. The [Management Contractor] need not comply or secure compliance with such instruction to the extent that the instruction is unreasonable, unsafe, or not competent.

C.300
The [Contractor] agrees and undertakes that it shall comply and ensure the continual compliance with all legislation, directives, codes of practice,

policies and regulation that may be relevant to all aspects of the [Project]. In particular any requirements of the [Trade organisation/Health and Safety Executive/Trade Union/other] and the following documents [specify].

DVD, Video and Discs

C.301
The [Assignor] confirms that the [DVD] shall not contain any music, text or sound effects other than the [Musical Work] unless there is prior written consent in advance by the [Assignee].

C.302
The [Company] undertakes that the [film] for the [DVD] shall adhere to all the following criteria set out in Appendix [–] [specify title, duration, artistes, scenes, locations, music, products, script, production crew, director].

C.303
That the production, manufacture, reproduction and distribution of the [DVD/other] shall be in accordance with any legal, censorship, programming, health and safety or union requirements or practices of [country/other] in existence at the time of signing this Agreement or which may come in to effect during the term of the agreement.

C.304
Both parties agree and undertake that they shall endeavour to comply with all legislation, regulations, directives, codes, policies and guidelines which may exist and/or be created in respect of the production, reproduction, supply, licensing and distribution of the [Material] in the [Territory] during the Term of this Agreement.

C.305
The [Licensee] agrees and undertakes to ensure that the following terms and conditions are fulfilled in respect of the reproduction, distribution and/or supply of the [Discs] of the [Work]:

1.1   That the [Discs] shall not contain any other material except the [Work] without the prior written consent in advance of the [Licensor].

1.2   That the [Discs] shall only be an exact reproduction of the [Work] from the original format of [specify] and no additional text, word, lyrics, music, film, trade marks, products and/or other material shall be added in anyway.

1.3   That the [Licensee] shall ensure compliance at all times with all product liability, health and safety and/or legal requirements, regulations, directives, government and trade organisations codes of practice, policies and guidelines [in country/worldwide].

C.306
That the [Licensee] shall ensure that the [Discs] do not breach and/or infringe any codes of practices, standards and/or policies relating to advertisement, sponsorship, promotion, marketing and commercial exploitation [in country/worldwide].

C.307
The [Licensee] shall be ensure that the manufacturer, packaging, marketing and advertising companies involved in the reproduction, distribution, supply and promotion of the [Discs] are financially viable and able to fulfil the work required according to the proposed schedule and to the professional standard necessary.

C.308
The [Licensee] agrees not to distribute, market and/or promote the [DVD/Disc/CD] on any website, in any printed material and/or in any manner and/or form which is not suitable for the [children's] market and shall endeavour to ensure that

C.309
The [Licensee] agrees and undertakes that it shall not alter, adapt and/or change any part of the [Film/Work] in respect of the reproduction of the [Film/Work] for the exploitation of the rights granted under this Agreement. Further the [Licensee] agrees and undertakes that the where the [Licensor] requests that the [Licensee] use any different title, sound recordings and/or sub-titles in any country that the [Licensee] shall comply with all such requests.

C.310
The [Licensor] agrees that where due to legal requirements, codes of practice and/or policies of any government and/or governing body and/or institute which regulates any relevant industry the [Licensee] is required to exclude and/or add material to the final version of any [DVD/Disc/other]. That the [Licensor] shall not object provided that such alterations and/or additions are notified in advance to the [Licensor] and supported by evidence of the need for such exclusions and/or additions in each case and are made at the [Licensee's] sole cost.

Employment

C.311
The [Employee] agrees to abide by the [Staff Handbook/Code of Conduct/other] supplied by the [Company] which is included as part of the main

Agreement. This shall include the right of the [Company] to refuse access to any premises to an employee who is believed in the reasonable opinion of the [security staff/other] to be under the influence of drink and/or drugs.

C.312

The [Employee] agrees to be abide by all existing procedures and practices relating to the operation of the business and any future company policies and directions relating to clothing, conduct and behaviour, how to deal with clients, use of equipment, personal telephone calls and emails, use of the internet or otherwise.

C.313

The [Executive] shall not be bound by any practices, directions, policies or rules of the [Company] which have not been raised in negotiations and incorporated as a term of this Agreement.

C.314

The [Company] agrees that failure to comply with the [policies/rules] relating to the following issues shall not be a ground to suspend or terminate this Agreement [specify].

C.315

The [Employee] acknowledges that in the event the [Employee] breaches any of the following [policies/rules] of the [Company]. That the [Company] shall have the right to terminate the employment of the [Employee] by notice in writing with immediate effect.

C.316

The [Employee] agrees and undertakes to comply with [Staff Handbook] and such additional policies and guidelines as may be issued by the [Parent Company], the subsidiary, and/or any associated company for which the [Employee] may from time to time carry out work and/or fulfil functions.

C.317

The [Company] agrees to supply the [Employee] with a copy of any new policies and guidelines. The [Employee] will not be expected to be bound by any policies and/or guidelines which have not been drawn to the attention of the [Employee].

C.318

The [Employee] agrees and undertakes to wear and/or carry out and/or fulfil such health and safety measures and/or precautions as the [Company] may require in order to comply with all existing and/or future legislation, directives, regulations, codes of practice, guidelines and/or other stipulations that may be required as a result of a government and/or trade health and/or safety warning.

C.319

The [Company] agrees and undertakes to ensure that the conditions of work for the [Employee] comply with any existing and/or future legislation, directives, regulations, codes of practice, guidelines and/or otherwise and in particular that all health and safety procedures are of a sufficiently high standard to ensure that there is no health risk to the [Employee].

C.320

The [Employee] agrees and undertakes to ensure that he/she will not make any commitment on behalf of the [Company] which exceeds his and/or her authority and/or job designation without the prior consent of an officer and/or director of the [Company].

C.321

The [Employee] agrees and undertakes to ensure that he/she will not exceed the [Budget/Expenditure] which he/she may from time to time be allocated by the [Company] to meet as a total target without the prior consent of an officer and/or director of the [Company].

C.322

The [Employee] agrees to attend such training sessions, conferences, trade shows and other events that the [Company] may from time to time specify as part of the professional development of the [Employee] and/or the [Company]. Provided that the [Company] agrees to ensure that the [Employee] is paid for such attendance and also paid in advance for any additional costs and expenses.

C.323

[Name] agrees that he/she shall adhere to all reasonable requests, policies, codes of conduct and guidelines issued by the [Company] and/or its parent company which relates to:

1.1 Use of the [Company] name and products in private emails and blogs outside of business hours.

1.2 The purchase of discounted goods and products for friends and family.

1.3 Wearing of jewellery and other body adornments such as earrings and piercings.

1.4 The use of [Company] laptops, telephones, mobiles and other resources during business hours which are for private use and not related to the [Company] and/or your position as [specify]

C.324

Where the [Employee] has breached and/or not complied with a policy of the [Company] then the [Company] agrees that it shall not have any right to subject the [Employee] to a disciplinary hearing and/or dismiss them where it can be shown that the [Employee] was not personally supplied with a copy of any such policy either at the time of their original engagement and the conclusion of their terms of employment and/or within [number] months thereafter. The [Company] agrees that it cannot enforce a new policy which it has introduced against an employee who has been with the [Company] before the date of the new policy.

C.325

The [Company] shall from time to time create and develop new policies, practices and systems including but not limited to new rosters, hours and days of work, security access and codes, fire and health and safety, absences and ill health, disposal of damaged products and waste, purchase of products by employees, uniforms, appearance and protective clothing, religion and ethical issues. All such details shall be displayed on the [Company] HR resources section; notified by email to all individuals and a printed copy may be supplied upon request. All such material as amended form time to time shall be applicable to all staff and must be complied with as part of your terms and conditions of employment with the [Company].

Film and Television

C.326

The [Television Company] agrees to ensure that the [Programme] shall not infringe or breach any rules, codes, standards, practices, directives or statutes which apply to the [Television Company] in [specify countries] in respect of sponsorship, endorsements, advertising, product placement, prizes, children, or any other relevant issues which apply now or may come into existence.

C.327

Where a [Television Company] is to broadcast or transmit a [Film] it will fulfil the duty of ensuring that the [Film] complies with the Regulations and Codes of Practices of [Name] and any guidelines of the [Network] and is not libellous or defamatory and these matters shall not be the responsibility of the [Production Company]. The [Production Company] shall still be bound by the terms set out in its Agreement with the [Television Company] despite the compliance role of the [Television Company].

C.328

The [Company] confirms that the [Work] shall comply fully at all times with all laws, regulations, European Union Directives, existing contractual relationships and obligations, Codes of Practice and Regulations in particular but not limited to [–] and all rules and guidelines issued by all relevant regulatory and trade bodies.

C.329
The [Production Company] confirms that it shall ensure that the [Advertisement] will conform to all statutes, rules, directives and advertising Codes of Standards and Practice in relation to the exercise of the [digital, cable, satellite and terrestrial television rights] in [country].

C.330
The [Assignor] shall not without the prior written approval of the [Assignee] inform any person except those absolutely necessary for the production of the [Film] of any content of the Scripts and/or Film except to agents of those involved in the Film, advisors and production personnel. Nor shall the [Assignor] issue any press releases or statements regarding the development, production, marketing, sales or otherwise of the [Film] without the prior consent of the [Assignee].

C.331
The [Production Company] undertakes as far as reasonably possible that all production personnel, artistes and musicians involved in the production of the [Advertisement] shall be members of recognised trade or craft unions.

C.332
The [Licensee] is permitted to edit, adapt and change the [Film/Work] subject to the prior approval of the [Licensee] by [email] where it is necessary in order to comply with any policies, standards and codes by [specify] in respect of the broadcast and/or transmission in [country] for the purposes of the exercise of the rights granted in this Agreement.

C.333
The [Licensee] agrees that the burden shall be on the [Licensee] to take advice and consider whether any changes, edits and/or deletions shall be necessary in any part of the world where the [Film/Work] is to be exploited in order not to be subject to any complaint, claim, fine and/or investigation by a regulatory and/or government body and/or any civil and/or criminal proceedings. The [Licensee] shall only be authorised by the [Licensor] to the extent that any changes, edits and/or deletions are absolutely necessary and exceed no more than [number] minutes in duration in total of the [Work/Film].

C.334
The [Licensee] agrees that it shall not have any right to authorise and/or grant any rights to third parties for an use and/or exploitation of the [Film/

Work] including but not limited to an archive and/or subscription service and/or one off payment playback and/or online internet, mobile, app and/or any other method and/or medium of reproduction of all and/or part of the [Film/Work] and/or any sound recordings at any time. The [Licensee] agrees and undertakes that it shall only be entitled to licence the [Film/Work] for exhibition at the following festivals; [specify] cinemas [specify] and university film clubs:[specify] and other members of [specify] body in its entirety as it is supplied by the [Licensor] in [country] from [date] to [date].

General Business and Commercial

C.335
The [Company] confirms that it shall not make nor authorise or permit copies of the [Work] to be made at any time for any purpose whilst the [Work] is in its possession or control.

C.336
The [Company] will use reasonable endeavours to ensure that the [Work] is at all times kept in a safe and secure manner and all reasonable steps will be taken to ensure that no unauthorised person may gain access to the [Work].

C.337
The [Buyer] will return at the [Buyer's] cost as soon as is reasonably practicable to the [Seller] all original documentation and copies as may be specified under this letter relating to [specify subject] in accordance with the [Seller's] instructions. The [Seller] acknowledges that the [Buyer] will be entitled to keep and retain correspondence between the parties provided that no part is to be used for publication or for any commercial purpose and is for personal reference only.

C.338
The [Company] undertakes that its employees, agents and contractors will be suitably qualified, be currently registered with a recognised trade body and experienced to carry out the work required under this Agreement. That they will be able to produce any necessary documentation required by the [Customer] to verify these facts and satisfy any [government agency/local authority/other].

C.339
The [Consortium] agrees that all arrangements with [Name] are subject to the recognition that [Name] is obliged to comply with the governing body [specify] and cannot carry out any performances, work and/or marketing which would lead to his/her removal from the listed of members of that organisation. That where such an issue would arise then [Name] shall be

entitled not to agree to the request from the [Consortium] and that such refusal would not be deemed to be a breach of this Agreement.

C.340

The [Assignor] does not provide any confirmation and/or agreement that any part of the [Work/Project] complies with any codes, regulations, policies and/or industry practise which may either now and/or at a later date be considered relevant. The [Company] agrees that they accept the [Work/Project] at their own risk and cost and that any failure, deficiency and/or non-compliance which is revealed shall be the sole responsibility and liability of the [Company].

C.341

You are hereby notified that you are expected to comply with all the following policies of the [Company] which are not only for guidance but form part of your terms of engagement [specify list of policies]. Copies of the policies are attached and form part of this Agreement. The [Company] reserves the right to revise and update the policies and will ensure that you will be sent a copy of any new policy. The [Company] recognises that there may be personal circumstances where the [Company] may need to agree to minor adjustments to any policy. You are asked to notify [Name] by [email] or by appointment to discuss any such requests.

Internet and Websites

C.342

The [Company] agrees that the [Contributor's] name, image and endorsement of the [Owner's] Website shall not be used for any other purpose than the promotion and marketing of the [Contributors] [interactive response service] to the public.

C.343

The [Designer] agrees and undertakes that the [Website] shall be consistent with and to the standard and functionality specified in [Website Plan and Operation Document] in Schedule [–].

C.344

The [Designer] shall use its best endeavours to ensure that the [Website] is completed to a high standard and is fully operational by the [Company] in accordance with the proposal costing no more than the Maximum Fee consistent with the time scale stated in the Payment Schedule [–].

C.345

The [Development Company] shall not without the prior written approval of [Name] inform any person except those absolutely necessary for the

355

production of the [Website] employed and/or engaged by the [Development Company] of any content of the proposed [Website], the launch date, and/or any other confidential information. The [Development] shall ensure that all personnel are aware of the need not to supply and/or distribute any information regarding the project to third parties, any competitor and/or the media and/or newspapers.

C.346

The [Development Company] shall not be responsible for ensuring that the [Website], the domain name and/or any content which is delivered to [Name] shall not infringe and/or breach any legislation, rules, codes of practices and guidelines, directives or otherwise which apply to and/or regulate the internet and websites, premium phone services, downloads and/or any other services and/or supply of images, text, music, film, photographs, sponsorship, advertising, and/or competitions which may apply now or may come into existence. All such matters shall be the responsibility of [Name] and the [Development Company] shall not be liable for any reason.

C.347

The [Development Company] agrees and undertakes that:

1.1 It will only use and/or employ suitably qualified personnel to create, design, build and deliver the [Website] for [Name].

1.2 That all the technical content of the [Website] shall comply with the latest technology so that it able to fulfil all the requirements specified in the [Website Summary] in Appendix [–].

1.3 That all the software which is to be used is the latest current version and that in the opinion of the [Development Company] is the best available on the market for the allocated budget.

1.4 That all the required source codes and any other data, master copies, computer software and/or information will be provided at no additional cost so that the [Website] can easily be updated and amended by [Name] and/or a third party.

C.348

The [Company] agrees that it shall not enter into any agreement, arrangement and/or partnership and/or permit the use of the [Website] for banner advertising and/or other promotions by any third party connected and/or associated with [specify].

C.349

The [Company] shall have the right and authority to remove, delete and/or pass to any international enforcement agency, police and/or regulatory and/or compliance body any data, images, text, sound recordings, film, video, passwords and codes which in its opinion show that the person who opened the account and/or who is using it poses a risk to children under [age] years.

C.350
The [Company] reserves the right to delete any material from this [Website] which is posted by any person and/or company at any time. No notice shall be required and no reason shall need to be provided. The total limit of the liability of the [Company] to any such person and/or company shall be [number/currency].

Merchandising

C.351
That the [Licensee] shall ensure that each [Licensed Product] shall conform in all respects to the quality, design, packaging and materials of the sample submitted to and approved by the [Licensor]. That the workmanship or materials shall not be defective, of a different standard or quality or in any way different in shape, size, format or content.

C.352
The [Licensor] agrees to attend such meetings, exhibitions and promotional events as may reasonably be required by the [Company] subject to sufficient prior notice at the [Company's] cost and expense.

C.353
In the event that the [Products] manufactured and distributed by the [Distributor] do not comply with all the product liability, health, safety, packaging and any other legislation, regulations, directives, codes, guidelines, policies and/or industry practices which may exist at the date of this Agreement or which may come into effect thereafter. Then the [Distributor] shall be solely liable for any loss, damage, expense, cost and charges that may be incurred as a result of a product recall, replacement and/or refunds in respect of any products.

C.354
That the [Distributor] shall ensure that the [Product/Service/Work] shall comply with the description and purpose set out in the attached Schedule [–] and the sample prototype approved by the [Licensor]. The [Distributor] shall not be entitled to alter, add to, delete from or amend the quality, design, content, colours, packaging and materials approved by the [Licensor] without the prior written consent of the [Licensor].

C.355

The [Distributor] agrees and undertakes that the [Product/Service/Work] shall comply with all the product liability, health, safety, packaging and any other legislation, regulations, directives, codes, guidelines, policies and/or industry practices which may exist at the date of this Agreement or which may come into effect thereafter.

C.356

That the [Distributor] shall ensure that testing takes place of the prototype or sample to ensure that it is not defective, is fit for the purpose and does not contain any materials which are toxic or unsuitable for use by [specify]. That there shall be regular reviews of the quality and content of the [Product] to ensure that the standard has not fallen and that no new substances or other material has been added. The results of all such tests and reviews shall be made available on request to the [Licensee] at the [Distributors] cost.

C.357

Where after a product is available to the public it is subsequently discovered that the content is not as represented on the label and packaging. Then the [Supplier] agrees that it shall be responsible for all the costs that the [Distributor] may incur in recalling all products sold to the public including online and print advertisements, posters and other marketing. As well, as laboratory tests and analysis, legal and other professional costs but excluding the internal administrative costs of the [Distributor].

C.358

The [Manufacturer] does not accept any responsibility for compliance with any codes, guidelines, policies and/or legal requirements in any part of the world relating to the [Products]. The [Products] have been made to the specification, design and content requested by the [Company]. The [Company] agrees that it shall be solely liable to ensure that the [Products] are safe, of suitable quality for their intended use and do not pose a danger to the public.

Publishing

C.359

The [Agent] agrees that the artistic and editorial control of the [Work] shall be at the sole discretion and decision of the [Author] and/or [Publisher].

C.360

The [Ghostwriter] agrees to provide regular reports to the [Company] and to make available all material which he/she has obtained, recorded or has access to so that copies can be made and/or inspected.

C.361

The [Distributor] shall endeavour to ensure that:

1.1 All sub-licensees comply with the contractual obligations to the [Author] set out in this Agreement in clauses [–] and that they are incorporated in their contracts.

1.2 That the [Author] shall have a right of inspection and auditing of their accounts.

1.3 That no such sub-licence shall extend beyond the Term of this Agreement.

1.4 That no sub-licensee shall acquire any copyright, title, character, format, plot, packaging, domain name or any other rights or interest in the [Work] or any part or any associated material at any time which is supplied to or adapted, developed or translated from the [Work].

C.362

The [Author] agrees that the cover, layout, typography and index shall be required to adhere to the [Publishers] standard policies which may be in existence at any time.

C.363

The [Author] agrees that where any content in the [Work] and in any associated marketing, promotions and appearances he/she makes recommendations and/or provides advice to the public. That the [Author] shall ensure that the public is made aware in that the [Author] is not a [specify] and that guidance should be sought from a professional [specify] before they follow any proposals.

C.364

The [Publisher] agrees that the [Author] shall not be obliged to register either themselves and/or the [Work] with the following trade organisations and that the [Author] and the [Work] may be listed as excluded.

C.365

The [Publisher] agrees that the [Author] shall not be obliged to use the house style for the [Publisher] for the [Work] and that the cover, font, layout, index and content shall be entirely at the [Authors'] choice and discretion.

Purchase and Supply of Products

C.366

The [Licensor] accepts and agrees that it shall be responsible for ensuring that the [Product] complies with all relevant statutes, authorities, guidelines, directives, regulations, standards, practices, codes or any other material issued by any authority or body in the [Territory/Europe/other] at any time in which the [Product] is delivered or supplied to the [Licensee]. In the event that after delivery the [Licensor] becomes aware of any matter which affects the [Product] and its compliance with any such material then the [Licensor] shall immediately notify the [Licensee] and any changes to future [Products] that may be required shall be at the [Licensee's] cost.

C.367
The [Supplier] agrees that the [Product] shall comply and continue to comply with all the provisions relating to design, content and material, manufacture, supply, use, and packaging of any unit of the [Product] relating to any statute, regulation, order, directive, standards, practices, code or guidelines or governing law in force at the time of delivery to the [Seller] in the [country].

C.368
The [Seller] agrees that no other product or advertisement, banner, logo, trade mark, domain name, slogan, music, text, image, review, criticism, praise or comparison shall be displayed or featured in [specify] where there is a direct conflict of interest with any [Product/Service] supplied under this Agreement.

C.369
That the [Product] will be of first class technical quality and comply with the standards, guidelines and safety tests of [specify body/code].

C.370
The [Distributor] shall be obliged to arrange it own insurance cover to protect itself against any claims, fines, actions, losses and/or other consequences including the temporary closure and/or the end of trading of the [Distributor] that may arise directly and/or indirectly as a result of the failure of the [Licensee] to have ensured that the [Products/Services] adhere to any minimum standards, tests, criteria, quality control, health and safety and/or other requirements in any country at any time.

C.371
The parties agree they must both comply and ensure compliance by any third party that they may appoint with any regulations and codes of practice issued by the following organisations [specify].

Services

C.372
That the [Artiste] agrees to keep the [Agent] informed of his/her mobile and home telephone number, address, business and work schedule and holidays at all reasonable times during the Term of this Agreement.

C.373

The [Artiste] agrees that to the best of her knowledge and belief that she is not now nor has at any time been subject to or suffered from any injury or illness which would prevent her from providing her services. The [Artiste] will at all times do all that is reasonably necessary to attain and maintain a good state of health, physical fitness and appearance as will enable her to fully fulfil the terms of this contract.

C.374

The [Actor] confirms that she is a full current member of [specify union] and will continue to be so until [date].

C.375

All information, advice and material provided by the [Consultant] to the [Company] shall to the best of his knowledge and belief be true and accurate and based on factual evidence unless otherwise stated.

C.376

The [Consultant] is a professional [specify] and a member of the following bodies [–]. The [Consultant's] qualifications are [–] and she is an expert in the field of [–].

C.377

The [Researcher] agrees to observe all rules and regulations in force at any location at which she is required to work by the [Company] and shall adhere to any instructions or requests in respect of her work.

C.378

[Name] acknowledges and agrees that the licence issued to the [Company] by [specify] for the operation of their business as a [specify] at [address] has the following conditions attached [specify]. [Name] agrees and undertakes to take account of and not breach these conditions in their [Programme]. Nor shall [Name] promote and/or market the [Programme] and/or themselves in any manner which would affect the reputation of the [Company] in a detrimental manner.

C.379

The independent [Consultant] shall not be bound by any regulations, codes, guidance and/or other rules which may affect the [Consortium] by [specify]. The [Consultant] is not responsible for taking account of [specify] in his/her report and these facts are to be covered by a third party.

Sponsorship

C.380

The [Licensee] agrees that no sponsorship, logo, image, music, text, product or person shall be used to endorse, appear in or be used in any way in conjunction with the [Series] without the prior written approval of the [Licensor] which shall not be unreasonably withheld or delayed.

C.381

The [Sponsor] agrees to ensure that the size, shape, nature and use of the [Sponsor's Logo] and the [Sponsor's Product] will not infringe any statutes, rules, directives, standards or practices currently in existence with regard to the [specify television authority/other] and the following sports organisation [specify] or any other relevant regulatory body in [country].

C.382

The [Association] shall ensure that the use of the [Promotional Logo] and the [Sponsor's Logo] will not infringe any sponsorship, advertising or promotional standards, practices and policies currently in existence with regard to the [specify governing bodies and government agencies] in [country/Europe/other].

C.383

The [Television Company] agrees to ensure that the broadcast and/or transmission of the [Sponsor's] name, trade mark, logo, images, product, music and premium rate number telephone and text line will not infringe any sponsorship, advertising or product placement rules, directives or statutes which apply to the [Television Company] or have been issued by [Ofcom] whether relating to size, colour, words, position or general nature.

C.384

The [Sponsor] agrees to be bound by the requirements of the [Company] in respect of any sponsorship or advertising standards, practices, codes, directives, statutes, or otherwise which apply to the [Film] and the exploitation of the any rights relating to it.

C.385

The [Promoter] will ensure that all material produced under this Agreement will not infringe any sponsorship, advertising, product placement, product safety standards and rules, statutes or directives currently in existence issued by the European Union, Ofcom, Oftel, the Advertising Standards Authority or Trading Standards.

C.386

The [Agent] confirms that the [Advertising Copy] complies with the rules and guidelines, regulations or otherwise issued by any committee or body which regulates advertisements which apply to the [Television Company] or television franchise holders in general at that time or any other regulations, directives or policies which may be in force.

C.387

The [Sportsperson] confirms that he is a bona fide and current member of the following sports organisations [–].

C.388

The [Sportsperson] agrees to conduct himself in a fit proper and professional manner at all times during the Term of the Agreement at sports events and in public appearances.

C.389

The [Sponsor] acknowledges that the sponsorship of the [Programme] does not give the [Sponsor] the right to use the [Television Company's] name, logo, programme title, or any other material owned or controlled by the [Television Company] in any promotion, advertising, marketing, product or otherwise owned or controlled by the [Sponsor].

C.390

The [Sponsor] agrees that the [Radio Station] shall be entitled at its sole discretion to replace the [Presenter] with a person of [similar quality/reputation/ratings].

C.391

The [Radio Station] confirms that the [Presenter] is contractually bound to the [Radio Station] to be the on-air host of the [Series] for the duration of this Agreement until [date].

C.392

The [Sponsor] undertakes that the specific products or services being promoted under this Agreement together with all other products and services owned or controlled by the [Sponsor] which the public would reasonably associate with the [Sponsor's] [trade mark, logo, images, product, music, slogans, ringtones, and premium rate number telephone and text line] shall be safe and fit for their intended use and comply with all statutes, regulations, directives, standards and codes in force in [country].

C.393

The [Company] agrees and undertakes to ensure that all third parties involved with the [Event] and any sub-licensees shall comply with the contractual obligations to the [Sponsor] set out in clauses [–] of this Agreement and that such clauses are incorporated as a condition in their letters of engagement and/or agreements.

C.394

The [Company] agrees and undertakes that:

1.1 No sub-licence shall extend beyond [date].

1.2 No sub-licensee shall be assigned any rights in respect of the [Event] and/or any material and/or rights owned and/or controlled by the [Sponsor].

1.3 That no person who enters the [Event], any business partner, sub-licensee, advertising agent, publicity agency and/or any other third party shall acquire any copyright in the title of the [Event], the domain name for the website and/or any other rights or interest in the sponsorship of the [Event].

1.4 That no other person, business, licensee, distributor, product, advertisement, banner, logo, trade mark, domain name, slogan, music, text, image, film, photograph or otherwise shall be displayed or featured on the website, on any merchandising material, in any film, on any participant, on any marketing and publicity and/or other material of any nature which appears to give the impression and/or is credited as the [main] sponsor, promoter and/or source of funding for the [Event].

1.5 That no products and/or services shall be used at the [Event] which are not supplied by the [Sponsor] in the following categories [specify].

C.395

The [Sponsor] agrees that the all health and safety compliance, insurance, fire regulations, police, stewards, sanitation, artistic and editorial control of the [Event], the programme, the schedule, the layout and location, marketing, publicity, and merchandising shall be at the sole discretion and cost of the [Company]. There shall be no obligation to consult with and/or seek the prior approval of the [Sponsor] for any changes, amendments and/or delays that may be necessary.

C.396

Where in the sole opinion of the [Company] the [Sponsor] and/or it business and/or its presence at the [Event] pose such a threat due to recent adverse publicity associated with them. The [Company] shall be entitled to take the view and reach the conclusion that all reference to the [Sponsor] and/or its' business and/or its involvement in the [Event] may be deleted without notice. Provided that the [Company] agrees to refund to the [Sponsor] [number] per cent of the sums paid by the [Sponsor] to date. The [Sponsor] agrees in such instance that such action shall be accepted by the [Sponsor] and that all rights to any legal claim and/or action are waived.

C.397
The [Sponsor] agrees and accepts that all staff, officers and other agents associated with the [Sponsor] at [location] from [date] to [date] must accept the instruction, orders and directions of [Name] at the [Festival]. This shall be the case whether or not it is contrary to the prior arrangements with the [Sponsor] in this Agreement. Where despite a request the [Sponsor] and its staff, officers and agents fail to comply then [Name] may at his/her sole discretion use of the services of the security staff at the [location] to ensure compliance as a last resort and remove all such persons from the [location].

C.398
The [Sponsor] agrees and accepts that the [Company] may due to unforeseen circumstances and/or excessive crowds and/or lack of facilities and/or resources and/or any accident and/or other reason alter the duration of the booking for the [Sponsor] and/or the display of their signs and banners, and/or location of their tents and stalls. The [Sponsor] agrees to comply with all directions made by authorised employees of the [Company] and to make such changes as may be required at no additional cost to the [Company].

University, Library and Educational

C.399
The [Company] recognises that the [Charter/Terms of Reference] of the [Institute] must be adhered to and its integrity, reputation and rights not derogated from or effected by a third party. The [Company] agrees that no other business, company, person, product, advertisement, banner, logo, trade mark, domain name, slogan, music, text, image, review, criticism, praise or comparison shall be displayed or featured in, on or near the [Work/Project/Webpage] without the prior written consent of the [Institute].

C.400
The [Consultant/Company] agrees and undertakes to comply with all instructions, standards, codes, procedures and practices which the [Institute] may require to be followed during the Term of this Agreement.

C.401
Where the [Company] fails to comply with the terms and conditions of the attached [Handbook/Code of Practice/Professional Standards] when fulfilling the terms of this Agreement. Then the [Institute] shall have the right to terminate the Agreement without providing any notice or the opportunity

to remedy the situation. The [Institute] shall not be responsible for any loss, cost or expense that may arise as a result of the termination.

C.402

The [Researcher] acknowledges and agrees that the [Institute] and the [Researcher] shall be obliged to comply with all the protocols, regulations, codes and guidelines laid down by [specify organisation] in the [Project] including [specify]. The [Researcher] agrees to notify the [Institute] in the event that there is any proposal not to follow these procedures in any part of the [Project]. In such event the [Institute] shall have the right to either insist that the procedures be followed and/or to agree that they be waived. The [Researcher] agrees that the decision shall be at the sole discretion of the [Institute] and shall be final.

C.403

The [Institute] may from time to time issue new policies and guidelines for [specify] which shall be posted and displayed on its website [reference] under [section]. There shall be no obligation on the [Institute] to notify each person individually and you are expected to review the terms and conditions at the start of each new academic term. Where you have a problem with any of the policies and guidelines then please contact [Name] at [specify].

COMPUTER-GENERATED

General Business and Commercial

C.404

'Computer-Generated' in relation to a work shall mean that the work is generated by computer in circumstances such that there is no human author of the work [in accordance with the Copyright Designs and Patents Act 1988 as amended].

C.405

'Computer-Generated' in relation to a design means that the design is generated by computer in circumstances such that there is no human designer [as defined in the Copyright Designs and Patents Act 1988 as subsequently amended].

C.406

All work and designs generated by computer under this Agreement shall belong to the [Distributor] and not the [Company] which owns or controls the computer. The [Company] agrees and undertakes to sign and assign any rights in the work and designs which it does or will hold under this Agreement to the [Distributor] at the [Distributors'] cost.

C.407
Where any material is created, developed, designed and/or produced by [Name] in relation to this [Project] whether it is used in the final version or not including but not limited to the websites, links, banners, images, text, titles, apps, blogs, film, video, sound recordings, music, lyrics, photographs, mobile telephones and other telecommunications, ringtones, software programmes and hardware, supply and use of data, messaging, and/ or any other means at any time. [Name] agrees and undertakes that the [Consortium] shall hold [number] per cent of any interest and/or rights of any nature without limitation. This shall not apply to anything owned and/or controlled by [Name] prior to [date].

CONFIDENTIALITY

Employment

C.408
The [Executive] shall not divulge nor communicate to any person (other than those who need to know or with proper authority) any of the business plans or trade secrets or other confidential information relating to the [Company] which he may have received or obtained while in the service of the [Company]. This restriction shall continue to apply after the termination of his engagement for a period of [specify duration] but shall cease to apply to information or knowledge which may come into the public domain otherwise than through the default of the [Executive] or which has been received by the [Executive] from a third party not entitled to disclose the material.

C.409
The [Executive] is not permitted to publish any letters or articles purporting to represent the views of the [Company] unless prior permission is obtained from the [Company].

C.410
The [Executive] must not contact or communicate with any member of the press or media or anyone so connected on behalf of the [Company] without the prior [verbal/written] consent of [position/name].

C.411

When the [Executive] ceases to be employed by the [Company] for any reason then the [Executive] shall only be obliged to keep confidential information which was not already or does not become placed in the public domain by the [Company], by its reports, marketing or other employees. Any restriction as to the use of confidential information shall only apply for [three years] thereafter it is presumed to be out of date and no longer relevant to the business circumstances of the [Company].

C.412

The [Employee] agrees not to disclose at any time in the future any formula, content, recipe, data, manufacturing process or other confidential information relating to the [Product] which is not on the label, packaging or available to distributors or the public by the [Company].

C.413

The [Company] agrees that there are no confidentiality restrictions imposed on [Name] by virtue of this Agreement. That [Name] shall not be prohibited from sharing and/or distributing any information which relates to the [Company] and/or its business at any time.

C.414

The [Company] agrees that the [Employee] will be notified in each case if any information and/or data is confidential to the [Company]. Further the [Company] agrees to also provide the [Employee] with a notified expiry date where it is no longer confidential and the [Employee] will be released from the obligation.

C.415

The [Employee] agrees that where he/she is informed that any material to which the [Company] has access and/or which is supplied by a third party is under an embargo and/or likely to prejudice civil and/or criminal proceedings and/or the subject of a legal action. Then the [Employee] agrees and undertakes not to distribute, supply, reproduce and/or disseminate any such material to any person except their immediate family members.

DVD, Video and Discs

C.416

Each party undertakes to keep confidential and not disclose to any third party confidential information supplied by the other under this Agreement. Unless both parties agree that the information is necessary as an aid to sales, marketing, or distribution of the [DVDs/Discs].

C.417

Both parties shall not and shall procure that their employees, agents and associated companies shall not, except in the performance of their duties for their respective businesses, disclose to any third party any information relating to the other party or its business or trade secrets, records, agreements or data which are not or do not become available to the public and which have been acquired during the course of this Agreement in circumstances which inferred or were made clear it was confidential.

C.418

The [written/verbal] consent of both parties shall be required in the event that a statement, press release or conference or other material is to be distributed to the media or the public which is not consistent with the agreed marketing material or which in any way affects either of the parties' businesses whether beneficial or detrimental.

C.419

The [Assignor] and the [Assignee] shall not disclose or communicate to any third party any confidential information of the other party at any time except professional advisors or those who need to know for the purpose of fulfilling the terms of this agreement. All publicity, advertising and promotional material as well as press releases shall be agreed between the parties in each case. The production details of the [DVD/Discs], the work and private life and performance of the [Artiste] and the release date are all considered confidential by the [Assignee].

C.420

The parties agree to keep confidential except for the purpose of their agents, legal and other professional advisors and government bodies to whom they must report all the details of the cost of production, exploitation and marketing of the [Project]. No disclosure shall be made to any media, newspaper, magazine and/or any other third party without the prior approval and consent of all parties.

C.421

Prior to development, production and exploitation of the [Project] in the [DVD/other] market in [country]. It is agreed by [Name] who appears as the main performer that he/she shall not inform, reproduce and/or discuss and/or post on any website and/or blog any part of the detailed plans in respect of the [Project] at any time before [date] except the following agreed details [specify].

Film and Television

C.422

The [Assignor] and the [Company] shall not disclose to any third party except professional legal advisors, accountants or companies or persons involved in the [Pilot] any confidential information regarding [specify] acquired before or during the course of this Agreement except strictly on a need to know basis and an understanding that it is confidential and must remain so.

C.423

The [Licensor] and the [Licensee] agree that any information which either may disclose to the other in circumstances in which it is made clear that the information is confidential shall not be disclosed to any third party except any professional legal advisors, directors, officers, statutory and/or government bodies who have the right to request such information. Where either party releases and/or authorises the disclosure of such confidential information into the public domain then the other party shall no longer be bound to treat the information as confidential.

C.424

Any script, pilot, film, document and/or email circulated by the [Company] relating to its programmes, schedules, content and exploitation of any material on Channel [–] prior to broadcast and/or transmission and/or release to the press, media and/or public is to be treated as confidential and is not to be supplied, reproduced and/or distributed by any person without the prior consent of the [Company] except to legal advisors, personal agents and managers and/or such third parties directly involved in the completion of any necessary arrangements who may be informed of a limited amount of information to fulfil their task.

C.425

The [Company] will consider and review any programme idea submitted by a member of the public by the following process [specify]. However no assurance can be provided that any matter is confidential, and/or will not be supplied to third parties. Any submission is entirely at your own risk. The [Company] may already be working and/or have drawn up a list of ideas and projects which may be similar and/or exactly the same prior to receipt of your idea. There is no commitment and/or agreement by the [Company] to reach an agreement for the use and/or exploitation of any idea submitted.

C.426

No information, idea, project, pilot, game and/or merchandising, developed, created and/or proposed by any employee, researcher, consultant, agent and/or any other third party will be considered and/or deemed confidential by the [Company]. There shall be no restriction and/or prohibition which prevents by the [Company] from creating, developing and exploiting a television and/or radio and/or any other type of programme and/or project based on the same generic topic.

C.427

The parties agree that the attached synopsis supplied by the [Company] is confidential and shall remain so until [date]. Thereafter the confidentiality restriction shall not apply.

General Business and Commercial

C.428

No reference is to be made to the terms of this Agreement by either party in any media at any time without the prior written consent of the other party in each case.

C.429

Each party undertakes to keep confidential and not disclose to any third party any confidential information supplied by the other under this Agreement including but not limited to any reference to the terms and conditions in any advertising or publicity material without the prior written approval of the other party.

C.430

Both parties to this Agreement agree that they shall maintain the following matters in the utmost secrecy and confidence:

1.1   The terms of this Agreement.

1.2   All oral communications, representations and information of any nature made by the parties and/or their advisors pursuant to the conclusion and fulfilment of this Agreement.

1.3   All documents, data, reports, recordings, records, software, formula, processes, inventions or information or any material or facts of any nature in any media which were supplied or conveyed prior to or after the conclusion of this Agreement and/or pursuant to this Agreement.

1.4   Further that all such matters shall be restricted to the knowledge of [the Board of Directors/other] of either party, and any statutory body which may have the right to request any details, including any professional advisers. In such cases all persons shall be required to abide by a request of confidentiality.

1.5   No further disclosures shall be made without the prior written consent of both parties.

1.6 This clause shall survive the termination and/or expiry of this Agreement and shall continue until matters are in public domain or until such time as the parties mutually agree to release each other from the undertaking.

C.431

The [Company] and [specify party] shall not disclose to any third party any confidential business or future plans of the other party at any time acquired during the existence of this Agreement. No reference is to be made to the terms of this Agreement by either party in any advertising, or marketing or any other material of any nature (except to professional legal and accountancy advisors) without the prior consent of the party. In the event that both parties agree to hold a press conference and/or issue a press release then the following statement shall be included [specify].

C.432

The [Licensor] and the [Licensee] shall not disclose to any third party (except professional legal advisors, consultants and accountants) any confidential information, business, future plans of the other party at any time which is acquired from the other party either prior to the conclusion or pursuant to this Agreement. Both parties agree that no reference is to be made to the terms, or discussions relating to this Agreement in any advertising, promotional, publicity or other material in any media for distribution to the general public, or any media companies without the prior written approval of the [Managing Director] of the other party.

C.433

I acknowledge receipt of [document] supplied to me by [Name] and confirm that the sole purpose of being granted access is [specify].

C.434

I confirm that I shall not make nor authorise nor permit any copies of the [Work] to be made at any time for any purpose whilst it is in my possession. I shall keep the [Work] in a safe and secure manner and take all reasonable steps to ensure that no unauthorised party gains access to the [Work].

C.435

I shall keep the existence and content of the [Work] strictly confidential and will only disclose the existence and content of the [Work] to [specify]. In the event that the existence and contents of the [Work] are disclosed for some unexpected reason to other senior executives of the [Company] then I shall advise [Name] immediately and I shall ensure that any such persons are made fully aware of this Agreement and undertake to maintain strict confidentiality.

C.436

I will immediately return the [Work] to [Name] upon request and in any event shall deliver it in a safe and secure manner no later than [date]. I shall confirm in writing that no further copies or reproductions of any part of the [Work] are in my possession or control and that were made or supplied to other persons.

C.437

1.1 The [Company] agrees to release copies of the following documents to [name] of [firm] who act as [specify] for the [Consortium] for the purpose of due diligence on the sole basis that all the content is confidential and private to the [Company] [specify documents].

1.2 The [Consortium] agrees and undertakes not to release, reproduce, distribute and/or supply copies of any part of the documents in 1.1 in any medium and/or form at any time to any person and/or third party except [specify].

1.3 The [Consortium] agrees that where for any reason they are at a later date shown to be in breach of 1.2 that the [Company] shall be entitled to financial compensation of [number/currency] regardless of whether any loss and/or damage can be shown to have been suffered.

C.438

No material shall be deemed to be confidential where it is already available on the [Company] website and in its marketing material and/or that of any parent and/or associated business and/or it is available upon request and supplied to any member of the public and/or has been reproduced in a report and/or statement by the [Company] and/or a third party in any part of the world

Internet and Websites

C.439

You are permitted access to any confidential information or data on this [Website] by using your personal identity code and password on the condition that you agree that you are bound by the terms and conditions of access, and will not attempt to interfere with, reproduce, supply, distribute or use any such material without the prior written consent of the [Owner] of any such material and the [Company] which controls this [Website].

C.440

You will be denied access to any material, data or information which is deemed confidential on this [website] unless you have signed a confidentiality document and been allocated a password and user name.

C.441

The [Contributor] agrees and undertakes not to disclose, supply, reproduce and/or distribute (except to his/her own professional legal advisors, agent and/or accountant) any verbal communications, representations, emails, documents, data, reports, recordings, film, images, records, business plans, marketing strategy, databases, computer software, inventions, technology and/or any material or facts of any nature in any media which is supplied in circumstances where it is made clear by the [Company] and/or its directors, officers, consultants and/or professional advisors that it is confidential. Both parties agree that no reference is to be made to the terms of this Agreement to any third party without the prior written approval of both parties.

C.442

There shall be no requirement that either party is bound to treat as confidential any information and/or other material which is disclosed at any time during the conclusion of this Agreement and/or thereafter by either party.

C.443

No information which is supplied to this [Website] can be treated as confidential except for your personal details and password which will not be disclosed to any third party except under a Court Order. All other material which you submit and/or disclose on any blog, forum, chatroom and/or other section of this [Website] is at your own risk and no assurance can be provided that it cannot be read by third parties who are not registered as friends and/or contacts.

C.444

Where the [Company] inadvertently releases confidential personal details due to theft, hacking, fraud, failure of the technological systems and/or for any other reason. Then you agree that the total liability of the [Company] to you shall be limited to [number/currency].

C.445

Data, personal details, passwords and other information which is entered by you on this [Website] shall be treated as confidential provided that it is not later released by you to the public and/or found to be associated with an intention to commit and/or you have committed a criminal act using this [Website] and/or any of its facilities to arrange, commission and/or convey details to other third parties. In any such cases there shall be no duty of confidentiality and the [Company] may at its sole discretion supply all such material to [the police] and/or any other law enforcement agency in any part of the world.

Merchandising

C.446
The [Licensor] and the [Licensee] shall not disclose to any third party any confidential information or future business plans of the other party at any time acquired pursuant to the conclusion of or during the existence of this agreement. Where access is required to confidential information a separate confidentiality agreement for that purpose may be requested to be signed.

C.447
The [Company] agrees not to disclose any script, text, title, content, format, music, artiste or other [Programme] production or scheduling details or any other matter which relates to the [Programme] or the [Company's Product] or the [Company's Logo] in the [Programme] prior to the transmission of the [Programme] without the prior written consent of the [Television Company]. Failure to adhere to this clause shall result in the removal of the [Company's Product] and the [Company's Logo] from the [Programme] and the right of the [Television Company] to keep all sums paid.

C.448
Both parties shall maintain the following issues in the utmost secrecy and confidence:

1.1   The terms of this Agreement.

1.2   All representations, documents, emails and recordings viewed or made or exchanged prior to or after this Agreement relating to the [Company's Product], the [Company's Logo] and the [Programme]. Disclosure shall only be made on the agreed basis of this Agreement or with the prior approval of the other party.

C.449
The [Licensee] agrees that it and/or its agents and/or distributors shall not disclose and/or reproduce, supply, distribute and/or release to the public and/or the media any business plans, launch dates, financial data, contract details, management policies, audit reports, verbal representations made in private meetings and/or any other material and/or information which is made available to the [Licensor] under this Agreement to the [Licensee] regardless of whether it is confidential. That where the [Licensee] and/or its agents and/or distributors are considered by the [Licensor] to be in breach of this clause [–] that they shall be provided with the opportunity to refute the allegations and resolve the matter. Where the [Licensees] failure to adhere to this clause is not resolved and has resulted in a financial loss and/or damage to the reputation of the [Licensor]. The [Licensor] shall have the

right to terminate this Agreement by [one] month's notice by written notice to that effect.

C.450

Where the [Company] provides proposals for new products, recipes, business plans, samples and /or any other material and/or data and/or information in meetings and/or by email and/or any other form of exchanges and supply to the [Distributor] and its executives, management and employees and consultants. Then the [Distributor] agrees that it shall be assumed that it is confidential and not for public release and/or reproduction and/or use by the [Distributor] in any manner and/or form at any time without the prior written approval of [Name] at the [Company].

C.451

The [Licensee] shall not be entitled to have access and/or use of any film, sound recordings, scripts, drawings, photographs, posters, manuscripts and/or other material held by [Name] in respect of the [subject] except for [specify] copies of which are to be reproduced by the [Licensor] and delivered by [date] to the [Licensee]. The [Licensee] shall pay all costs of any reproduction, insurance and delivery.

Publishing

C.452

The [Ghostwriter] undertakes not to disclose any material of any nature to any third party nor make any statement (whether true or not) concerning the private, sexual, personal and public life or views of [Individual] to any third party acquired directly or indirectly during the course of the preparation of the [Work] or from any other source of any nature. The [Ghostwriter] further agrees that such non-disclosure shall operate during the course of the Term of this Agreement and any time thereafter [indefinitely/until such material and/or information is in the public domain].

C.453

The [Company] acknowledges and agrees that the [Originator] shall be entitled to exploit any material created by him under this Agreement. Provided that all references to and any confidential information and material supplied by the [Company] shall be deleted or the prior written approval of the [Company] obtained in each case.

C.454

The [Author] and the [Publisher] agree that they shall not:

1.1 Disclose to any third party except their respective professional agents, legal, audit, insurance and accounting advisors any confidential, business or future plans of the other party at any time acquired before or during the existence of this Agreement.

1.2 No reference is to be made to any part of this Agreement except those agreed for the credits, moral rights and marketing of the [Work] in any advertising, promotional publicity or corporate material without the prior [written] consent of the other party.

1.3 The parties shall agree a press release to announce this Agreement.

1.4 That the [Publisher] shall not release, inform or disclose any details of the [Work] or its contents to another writer or third party prior to the publication date where the purpose is to create a competing or similar work.

1.5 That this clause shall not be applicable where the information or contents are available to the public in general.

1.6 That this clause shall only apply until one year after the termination or expiry of this Agreement.

C.455
The [Contributor] shall not disclose or release at any stage to any third party any confidential business, future plans, information, data, software, artwork or other material of the [Company] or the commercial terms of this Agreement except to [specify].

C.456
In the event that a press statement is to be released by either the [Author] or the [Agent] it shall be limited to the following personal descriptions of the parties and their backgrounds [–].

C.457
After the expiry or termination of this Agreement all parties undertake not to disclose to the press or any other media company, publisher or otherwise information relating to events, conversations, finance, documents or general behaviour of the other party which arose from private meetings and were not intended for public knowledge.

C.458
The [Trustees] of the estate of [name] agree that where access to diaries, documents, photographs, sound recordings, film, video and/or any other material in any form is requested by the [Publisher] in order to defend and/or refute an allegation by a third party of defamation in respect of the [Work]. That the [Trustees] shall provide copies of such original confidential material as may be necessary in order to support the allegations and also

377

provide an affidavit in support to the legal advisors of the [Publishers] at the [Publishers'] sole cost.

C.459

No unsolicited submission in any format by an author to the [Company] shall be treated at any time as confidential whether marked to that effect or not. The only circumstances where the [Company] agrees to treat material as confidential will be where an author, agent and/or other person has agreed terms and conditions of confidentiality in advance prior to the submission of any such material and the [Company] has signed a confidentiality agreement authorised by the [Managing Director] of the [Company].

Purchase and Supply of Products

C.460

The [Company] and the [Supplier] shall be required, save in the event of written and prior authorisation of the other party, to maintain secrecy and not to disclose any confidential information, facts, knowledge, documents, prices, data, software or computer records or other material which the [Company] or the [Supplier] have communicated or provided to the other as confidential. This obligation shall remain binding on both parties until the consent of the relevant party. The [Company] and the [Supplier] shall request their agents and sub-contractors to also be bound by this clause of confidentiality.

C.461

The [Supplier] and the [Seller] shall not disclose at any stage to any third party (except their respective professional legal advisors, accountants and banks) any confidential business or future plans, information, data or material of the other party including but not limited to disclosures made during the course of negotiations of this Agreement and the terms concluded. This clause does not apply to anything already in or subsequently released into the public domain by a third party not acting in concert with the [Supplier] or [Seller].

C.462

The [Buyer] will act in good faith at all times and shall only use the [specify and refer to as confidential information] for the purpose for which it is intended namely [specify] and for no other purpose. Nor will the [Buyer] under any circumstances seek to take commercial advantage over the [Seller] by virtue of acquiring the confidential information. The [Seller] agrees that this does not apply once the material is released by a third party or the [Seller] into the public domain.

C.463

The [Buyer] will only disclose the confidential information to such employees, professional and financial advisors or consultants on a need to know basis. Every person permitted access shall be shown this letter of confidentiality and each person shall provide a written undertaking to be bound by the terms to the [Buyer]. The list of names shall be provided to the [Seller] when the material is returned.

C.464

The [Buyer] agrees to be bound by the following terms:

1.1 Not to make any copies in any medium unless specifically authorised to do so.

1.2 To keep the material secure and safe at [address].

1.3 To return at the [Buyer's] cost by courier all the material by [date].

1.4 That no rights of any nature are intended to be transferred to or vested on the [Buyer].

1.5 Not to use the material to entice, poach, or solicit employees, customers or suppliers of the [Seller].

1.6 To indemnify the [Seller] for any damages, losses, costs and expenses suffered or arising as a [direct/indirect] breach and/or alleged breach of this Agreement.

C.465

1.1 The [Manufacturer] agrees that all the work to be completed for the [Company] shall be treated by the [Manufacturer] and its employees and others engaged by them involved in the process of production, packaging and delivery of any products as confidential and private as far as possible.

1.2 That in event that any third party should contact the [Manufacturer] at any time requesting any information, data, documents, samples and/ or any other material of any nature. That the [Manufacturer] shall refer any such request to [name] at the [Company] and also notify [name] to that effect.

1.3 That the [Manufacturer] shall ensure that all business plans, product proposals, samples, test results, final products, details of processes and any other material are held in a secure location and that where any material is held on a hard drive that access is restricted.

C.466

Where in the course of developing and/or producing any product and/ or method of packaging and/or manufacturing process the [Company] specifies the use of a system, method, mechanism, technique and/or other new advance which is not already carried out by the [Manufacturer] which is innovative, original and new. Than the [Manufacturer] agrees that all rights including inventions, copyright, design rights and any other rights in any such creation, material and/or development shall belong entirely to the [Company] who shall be the sole owners and shall have the right to insist that it be kept confidential by the [Manufacturer].

Services

C.467
The [Designer] and the [Company] shall not disclose at any stage to any third party any confidential, business or future plans of the other party including but not limited to the commercial terms of this Agreement unless a public disclosure, press statement or similar release or any advertising, publicity, promotional or corporate document or other material has been specifically agreed by a duly authorised representative of both parties.

C.468
Where the [Designer] is approaching third parties for contributions or assistance in respect of the [Website] then the information to be disclosed shall be kept to a minimum and a representative of the [Company] shall attend all such meetings with the [Designer].

C.469
The [Designer] shall keep a proper record of all discussions with all third parties relating to the [Project].

C.470
The [Contributor] shall not issue any statement in public or to the media including press, radio, television or internet concerning any confidential business or future plans of the [Company] or its website without the prior consent of [Name] or any subsequent [Director of Corporate Communications].

C.471
[Name] shall not disclose to any third party any confidential business of the [Company], its employees, consultants, advisors, or presenters or any detail concerning the scheduling acquisitions or other sensitive information of the [Company] acquired in pursuance of or during the existence of this Agreement. No reference is to be made to the terms of this Agreement by either party in any advertising, press releases, recordings or promotional material.

C.472

After the expiry or termination of this Agreement all parties undertake not to seek to get published or transmitted or make any disclosure to the press, radio, television, publishers, or any other media or otherwise put in the public domain, details of any events, conversations, documents, financial details, private family or professional details of the other party without the consent of that person except on a strictly client to personal advisor basis to their own professional legal advisors, accountants, or agent.

C.473

The [Presenter] shall not, except in the provision of the services in this Agreement either during or after the termination of this Agreement, use or divulge to any person and shall use his reasonable endeavours to prevent the publication or disclosure of:

1.1 Any confidential information concerning the business or finances of the [Company] or its subsidiaries or any of their affairs.

1.2 Any script, text, rules, pictures, design, arrangement, title, format, music, programme idea or theme, film, DVD, book in whole or any part based on or derived from any material owned, controlled or used by the [Company] or any subsidiary.

1.3 All records and other materials made or received by the [Presenter] in the course of the provision of his/her services hereunder shall be the property of the [Company] and shall be returned to the [Company] upon termination or expiry of this Agreement or at the request of a Director of the [Company] at any time during the Term of this Agreement.

C.474

The [Artist] shall not issue any statement in public or display any logo, sign or message or communicate or supply to the media including newspapers, magazines, news organisations, radio, television, mobile phone companies or users or the internet any confidential business or future plans of the [Record Company] acquired under this Agreement and this clause shall apply until [date].

C.475

The [Group] agrees not to issue any statement to the press, media or on the internet during the Term of this Agreement concerning the future plans of the [Group] or the [Manager] without the prior consent of the [Manager].

C.476

The [Group] and the [Manager] shall not disclose to any third party any confidential business or future plans of the other party at any time acquired during the existence of this Agreement. No reference is to be made to the terms of this Agreement by either party in any advertising publicity or promotional material without the prior consent of the other party on each occasion. After the expiry or termination of this Agreement all parties undertake not to make any disclosure to the press or any other media company, publisher, or on the internet or otherwise relating to events, conversations, documents, financial arrangements or general behaviour of any party to this Agreement without the specific consent of that person (except professional legal and financial advisers).

C.477

The [Contributor] undertakes that he shall not disclose any confidential information, data, marketing, advertising or financial plans concerning the [Company] to any third party from the date of this Agreement until [date] which is originally acquired in the course of his/her engagement under this Agreement.

C.478

The [Artist] agrees not to issue any statement to the media, newspapers, or on the internet or to supply to any third party any confidential business or future plans of the [Agent] or details of any negotiations or terms of any agreements in progress or concluded by the [Agent] whether relating to the [Artist] or relating to the [Agents] other clients.

C.479

The [Designer] agrees that she shall enter into an escrow agreement which shall entitle the [Company] to access the source code of the website if the [Designer] goes into liquidation or receivership or administrative receivership or when there is a breach of the agreement by the [Designer].

C.480

This Agreement acknowledges and accepts the full terms of the Escrow Agreement signed by the [Owner], the [Agent] and the [Licensee] which sets out:

1.1 The circumstances in which the [Agent] shall be obliged to disclose the data, information, source code, software listings and specifications to the [Licensee] necessary for the maintaining, modifying and enhancing the software.

1.2 The terms of duty of confidentiality between the [Owner] and the [Agent] prior to the circumstances coming into effect which require the release of the information by the [Agent] to the [Licensee].

C.481

The [Promoter] agrees not to use, release, exploit or use to their advantage or to the detriment of the [Company] any commercially sensitive information, data, documents, software, photographs or any other material in any medium during the Term of this Agreement without the prior express approval of [Name] at the [Company].

C.482

The [Agent] and the [Artist] mutually agree that each of them shall not during the Term of this Agreement publish in writing or otherwise or make known to the public or act in any way likely to result in publication of any matter concerning the business affairs of the other without their prior consent. This shall not apply after the expiry of this Agreement nor in the event of legal proceedings being instituted by either party.

C.483

No reference is to be made to the terms of this Agreement by either party in public, to any newspaper, publisher, news organisation, magazine, on the internet, in any film or recording for television or radio without the prior consent of the other party.

C.484

The [Consultant] agrees that he/she shall not:

1.1 Disclose to any third party any confidential information which is provided by the [Company] at any time of any nature and/or in any medium and/or format from the date of this Agreement until [date]. This shall not apply to any information which is released by the [Company] into the public domain and/or to the media and/or a significant sector of an industry.

1.2 No reference is to be made to any part of this Agreement except with the prior approval and/or written consent of a director and/or officer the [Company]. The parties shall agree a press release to announce this Agreement.

1.3 The [Consultant] shall not be entitled to advertise and/or promote that the [Consultant] has worked for the [Company] on any website and/or any marketing and/or advertising material except with the prior approval and/or written consent of a director and/or officer the [Company].

1.4 This clause shall no longer apply after [date] and all restrictions shall cease.

C.485

[Name] and their [Agent] agree that where future programme ideas and projects are discussed at meetings with the [Company] prior to the

383

conclusion of any agreement for the services of [Name]. That [Name] and their [Agent] agree not to supply, distribute and/or reproduce any part of such information and/or any associated material to any national and/or local media and/or other third party including but not limited to newspapers, magazines, radio, television and/or in any personal blog, press release and/or statement without the prior approval of the [Company] before [date].

C.486

The [Company] agrees and accepts that no part of this Agreement and/or any future information, data and/or material released and/or supplied to [Name] shall at any time be treated as confidential. That [Name] shall not be placed under any restrictions, prohibitions and/or obligations and may market and promote his appearances, contribution and work at the [Company].

Sponsorship

C.487

In the event that [Name] shall decide to write a biography and/or engage a ghostwriter to do so and/or be commissioned by a publisher to do so and/or agree to a film and/or other recording of his/her life. Then prior to the supply of the proofs to the publisher and/or completion of the script. [Name] agrees to disclose and supply extracts of any references to the [Sponsor] and/or its directors and/or officers to the [Sponsor].

C.488

The [Sponsor] and [Name] both agree and undertake that they shall not disclose to any third party (except professional legal advisors, agents and accountants) any confidential information and/or future plans of the other party at any time acquired as a result of the existence of this Agreement. No reference is to be made to the terms of this Agreement by either party in any advertising, publicity, promotional material and/or any website without the prior approval of the other party. After the expiry and/or termination of this Agreement all parties agree that this clause [–] shall apply until [date].

C.489

Both parties agree that none of the information and/or any other material released and/or supplied under this Agreement shall be considered and/or deemed confidential and/or commercially sensitive. Neither the [Sponsor] nor the [Company] shall be bound by any rules of confidentiality in respect of this [Project]. Both parties agree that they shall be entitled to reproduce, supply, distribute and display on their website any part of the information provided by either party in respect of the [Project] for the purpose of marketing, advertising and fundraising for the [Project]. Provided that a suitable acknowledgment of copyright ownership and/or trade marks is made in a reasonably prominent and clear position in each case.

C.490
The [Company] agrees and undertakes that it shall not either during the Term of this Agreement until [date] reproduce, supply, distribute and/or disclose to any third party [except consultants, agents, public relations and professional advisors] any information, business plans, inventions, computer software, financial information, reports, assessments and/or other material which is disclosed and/or supplied to the [Company] where at the time of disclosure it is made clear by the [Sponsor] that it is confidential.

C.491
No confidentiality shall be applicable by the [Company] to the [Sponsor] and where information is inadvertently released and/or any statement made by any person at the [Company] and/or third person which is derogatory and/or likely to adversely affect the sales of the [Sponsor's] services and/ products. The [Sponsor] agrees that the [Company] shall not be held responsible and/or liable and that all rights are waived by the [Sponsor] in respect of any claim, action, loss and/or damage which may be created and/or suffered. That the [Sponsor] agrees to bear the cost of all such risk and consequences of its participation in the [Festival/Event/Programme].

C.492
Both parties agree and confirm that there are no confidentiality provisions in this Agreement and neither shall they be applied at any time in the future and that they have waived any right to rely on any terms of confidentiality.

University, Library and Educational

C.493
The [Institute] and the [Company] both agree and undertake that [as far as reasonably possible] they shall not disclose during the Term of this Agreement and thereafter until [date] any confidential, business or future plans of the other party to a third party including but not limited to the commercial terms of this Agreement without the prior [written] consent of the other party. This clause shall not apply to the disclosure to legal and professional advisors, government departments or any person engaged by the [Institute] who is a [Consultant] on the [Project]. Both parties agree and undertake they will both approve any press or media statement or interviews, and any advertising, publicity, promotional, corporate or registration documents.

C.494
The [Consultant] agrees and undertakes that he shall not, either during the Term of this Agreement or thereafter at any time, use or divulge to any

person any confidential information, business plans, data, patents, financial information, reports or assessments relating to the [Institute], its employees and/or students which are provided either in confidence or on the basis that they are not for publication and/or distribution to a third party. This clause shall not apply where the disclosure is made by a third party or the material is put in the public domain by the [Institute] or is available as a matter of public record at a later date.

C.495

All material including text, images, photographs, computer software, discs, hard drive, sound recordings, film, DVD, videos, reports, catalogues, financial data and directories supplied to, created by and/or commissioned by the [Company] in respect of the [Project] for the [Institute] shall remain and/or be assigned to the [Institute] as the legal owner of all rights in all media at any time. All material of any nature in the possession and/or under the control of the [Company] shall be returned to the [Institute] upon termination or expiry of this Agreement at the [Company's] cost. The [Institute] may, at any time, request a full list of all material held and/or controlled by the [Company].

C.496

The [Institute] agrees not to use, release, exploit or use to their advantage or to the detriment of the [Author] any commercially sensitive information, data, documents, software, photographs or any other material in any medium during the Term of this Agreement without the prior express approval of [Author].

C.497

Neither party shall provide any undertaking as to confidentiality either of the [Project], or of any information disclosed in any presentation, report, interview and/or any other material unless it is specifically stated to be so at the time. Both parties agree that they shall be entitled to make any press statement, use any data, information, concepts, film, sound recordings, DVDs, reports, business knowledge and plans, and develop any new material without any approval or consent being necessary from the other.

C.498

Both parties undertake to agree a press and media statement relating to the media which will be co-ordinated by the [Institute]. There shall be no further disclosure or release into the public domain until both parties agree the method and terms of reference. Both parties agree to endeavour not to release or disclose confidential information, but accept neither responsibility nor liability for any release or disclosure.

C.499

The [Consortium] agree that any information distributed and/or supplied by one party to any other party involved in this [Project] shall not be treated as confidential and/or restricted in anyway and may be released to professional legal and tax advisors, employees, consultants and form part of any report, press release and may be distributed, supplied and/or reproduced by a third party.

CONFLICT OF INTEREST

General Business and Commercial

C.500

The [Promoter] confirms that this Agreement will not cause any conflict of interest with any of its existing clients and undertakes not to enter into any agreement with any third party during the duration of this Agreement which would result in a conflict of interests with the [Company].

C.501

Where either party becomes aware of any order, information, customer, product or other factor which could potentially create a conflict of interest between the parties under this Agreement. Then that party shall be obliged to disclose such material facts to allow the other party to decide whether they wish to cancel or withdraw from the Agreement on terms to be agreed between the parties.

C.502

There shall be no duty by either party to report to or inform the other party of a potential or actual conflict of interest. Either party may engage in business or provide services or goods to any person, company or organisation at any time whether or not they are in competition with the other party.

C.503

The [Consultant] agrees and undertakes that he/she is not engaged and/or involved with any existing business, person and/or company which is a direct competitor of the [Web Company] and/or involved in the [specify] market. In the event that after the conclusion of this Agreement the [Consultant] decides to work for a competitor then the [Consultant] shall notify the [Web Company] of the conflict of interest and agree to terminate this Agreement in terms to be agreed between the parties.

C.504

The [Sponsor] agrees that the existence of this Agreement and the funding of the [Event] does not permit and/or allow the [Sponsor] to promote, advertise and/or use in anyway their association with the [Institute] and/or the [Event] in a manner and/or form which would damage the reputation and/or conflict with the interests of the [Institute].

C.505

The [Licensee] shall be entitled to enter into licensing arrangements and agreements with any third party that it thinks fit including a direct competitor of the [Licensor] and/or the [Product/Services] which are referred to in this Agreement.

C.506

Where at a later date the agent, advisor and/or consultant is engaged to provide services to a company which is a direct competitor of the [Distributor]. Then the [Distributor] shall be entitled to terminate the agreement with immediate effect and shall only be liable to pay for the services of the agent, advisor and/or consultant to the date of termination.

CONSORTIUM

General Business and Commercial

C.507

'The Consortium' shall consist of the following members [Company Name, address and status] who shall each work as equal partners and be jointly and severally party to and responsible for this Agreement.

C.508

Each member of the [Consortium] shall only be bound by their own individual undertakings, responsibilities and liabilities to each other and in respect of the performance and completion of this [Project].

C.509

The [Institute] shall not be liable for any acts, omissions, errors, responsibilities and liabilities of the other members of the [Consortium] and/or the [Consortium] as a whole. There is no partnership, agency, subsidiary, associate or parent company relationship between the parties. There is no right on the part of any other member to authorise, commit, pledge, waive, sign and/or agree to any changes, variations and/or deletions for any reason on behalf of the [Institute].

C.510

The [Sponsor] acknowledges that other third parties shall fund the [Event] and acquire other rights/and interests. The [Sponsor] agrees that the [Company] shall be entitled to disclose the following terms and conditions of this Agreement [specify clauses] to ensure that such third parties are also bound by the undertakings in their agreement to the [Sponsor].

C.511

Each member of the [Consortium] agrees and authorises [Name] to negotiate, conclude and sign all agreements relating to the exploitation of the following rights [merchandising/other] in respect of the [Film/Website/Work] from [date] to [date]. No agreement shall be signed by [Name] which relates to any other rights and/or which is an assignment and/or which grants any rights after [date].

C.512

In the event that two or more members of the [Consortium] wish to withdraw and/or terminate their arrangements with the other parties due to lack of funding and/or a change in the nature of the [Project] which is contrary to their terms of reference and/or is in conflict with their moral, ethical and/or legal position. Then it is agreed that the [Consortium] shall be brought to an end and the agreement terminated and/or cancelled. Provided that the remaining parties may seek to create a new organisation and agreement and transfer the work of the [Consortium] to the new enterprise.

C.513

'The Consortium' shall comprise the following names who shall each hold the same rights and interest in the [Project] and also be jointly and severally liable for any losses that may be incurred [specify].

CONSULTATION

DVD, Video and Discs

C.514

The [Distributor] agrees to consult with the [Artist/Company] in respect of the content of the editing of the [Film] for the [DVD], but shall not be bound to incorporate the deletions or additions requested.

C.515

The [Distributor] shall be bound to adhere to all instructions, directions, and orders regarding the editing, production, manufacture, addition or deletion of any material, packaging, distribution and release of the [DVD/other] of the [Film]. The [Company] shall not be obliged to consult with the [Distributor] nor seek their approval.

C.516

The [Licensee] shall make available and deliver to the [Licensor] at the [Licensee's] cost a sample copy of the [Disc], the cover and any labels, packaging and marketing material for [the views and opinion/written approval] of the [Licensor] before it is manufactured, printed and/or distributed.

C.517

The [Company] agrees and accepts that all editorial decisions, arrangements, licences and agreements in respect of the production, manufacture, distribution, marketing and promotion of the [Work] by the [Licensee] shall not require any prior consultation and/or approval by the [Company] in respect of the [Disc].

C.518

[Name] shall be entitled to be consulted on the production and editing of the final version of the sound recording, film, cover, marketing, advertising and content of any part of any material relating to the [DVD/Disc/other] at the [Licensee's] cost.

C.519

The [Licensee] shall consult with and seek the views and opinions of [Name] as regarding:

1.1 The production schedule; use of third parties; locations; product placement and layout of any sets; use of background music and lighting; choice of editor and production company for manufacture of the [Product].

1.2 Marketing and advertising strategy in print, on radio and television and online as banner links, blogs and on websites.

1.3 That in any event the [Licensee] shall supply [Name] with a copy of all such material as may be available at the [Licensees] sole and expense which shall not be deducted from any sums due to [Name].

Film and Television

C.520

The [Executive Producer] appointed by the [Company] and such representatives as may be nominated shall, without making any disruption to the making of the [Film] or any material or sound recording, be entitled to attend during any shoot or recording to view [Film] and the preparatory materials and listen to any sound recording at any reasonable time during the production of the [Film] as may be necessary. Such costs and expenses of the representatives shall be agreed in advance by the parties and the reasonable and proper expenses of the personnel shall be attributed to the Budget as part of the production costs.

C.521

The [Production Company] shall not permit the [Author] any editorial control in respect of the [Film], but agree that the [Author] may [be consulted/ approve] the [draft and final script/the main characters/any product placement/any music/locations/other].

C.522

The [Company] agrees to arrange for the [Author] and his representatives a private viewing of the completed final version of the [Series] before it is made available to third parties.

C.523

The [Company] agrees to keep the [Author] advised on a regular basis as regards the production, licensing and exploitation of the [Series] and any associated merchandising. The [Company] agrees to consult with the [Author] and [Agent] to listen to and consider their proposals to change, amend or exploit any material in the [Film], any rights in any format, and any associated packaging or marketing. The [Company] shall not be obliged to carry out the requests unless it relates to the contract terms relating to the title of the book, or images based on artwork, slogans, logos or trademarks supplied or licensed by the [Author].

C.524

The [Licensee] agrees to keep the [Licensor] informed of proposed transmission dates and to provide the [Licensor] with copies of any associated merchandising, publicity and advertising material that may be created at the [Licensee's] cost.

C.525

This Agreement shall not grant and/or assign any rights and/or option and/ or interest in any sequel of the [Work] and/or any subsequent series in any form in any medium to the [Licensee]. There shall be no obligation to notify and/or consult with the [Licensee] in the event that the [Licensor] intends to exercise any such rights and/or grant them to a third party. This Agreement is solely for the production, distribution and exploitation of the [Film/Product/Book].

C.526
The [Distributor] shall not be obliged to consult with [Name] in respect of any exploitation and/or marketing of the [Film] and/or parts provided that no use shall be made of any part of the [Film] which features [Name] which would be deemed offensive and/or would give the impression and/or represent that [Name] supported a political campaign and/or was linked to the promotion and/or marketing of a product, service and/or charity.

C.527
The [Company] agrees to consult with the [Agent] and [Name] in respect of the proposal to market, promote and broadcast and/or transmit the [Programme] in association with any sponsor, service and/or product at any time. In any event the [Company] agrees not to enter into any such agreement with the following types of businesses [specify].

General Business and Commercial

C.528
The [Company] agrees that [Name] shall have the right to be consulted with respect to the [Work] but such right of consultation, for the avoidance of doubt, shall not be deemed to be a right of approval or confer any right of veto.

C.529
The [Company] shall consult with any interested parties who are involved in the [Project] and [the local community/the public/consumers] to endeavour to take into account all reasonable requests to change, develop or alter the [draft plan] based on demand, supply, use, availability of resources, costs, health and safety and environmental issues. Where there is shown to be strong objections which raise issues relating to health and safety, environment, cost or other reasons. Then the [Company] accept that it shall be the final decision of [specify] as to whether the [Project] proceeds or is cancelled.

C.530
The [Company] agrees and undertakes to carry a detailed and comprehensive consultation with the following specified persons and companies [public/trade/other] in order to ascertain their views and opinions on the proposed [Project] by the [Enterprise]. A copy of the [Project] is attached to and forms part of this Agreement.

C.531

The [Company] shall agree in advance and seek the prior written approval of [Name] of the [Enterprise] as to:

1.1   The method and content of the consultation and the languages in which it is to be made available.

1.2   The amount of advertising and promotion required.

1.3   The formalities for compliance with any legislation including data protection, privacy, freedom of information.

1.4   The layout and structure of the report of the consultancy and the analysis of the results.

1.5   The final proposed budget for the consultation.

C.532

The [Company] agrees and undertakes to carry out such public consultations, surveys and assessments and to engage such qualified experts as may be required to provide valid evidence in respect of the [Project] and the proposed expenditure. That the [Company] shall not withhold and/or destroy any results which conflict and/or are to the detriment of the local community and/or the [Company] and/or the [Project] which are raised at any time.

C.533

[Name] shall not be obliged to consult with the [Company] to seek approval and/or to make them aware of any activity, work and/or other marketing, blog, articles or otherwise that [Name] may write, create, develop and/or participate in. Provided it is does not involve services, premises and/or equipment owned and/or controlled by the [Company] and any such work is not done by [Name] within the exclusive hours allocated to the [Company].

Internet and Websites

C.534

Any consultation process shall not be binding on the [Company] and shall be purely for background information and assistance. There shall be no obligation on the [Company] to disclose any further information, data, or material nor to pay any participant in the consultation for their suggestions, ideas or proposals whether used and adopted by the [Company] or not.

C.535

There [Company] shall be entitled to sell the [Product/Work] and to discount, reduce, increase and/or cross promote and market the [Work/Product] at its sole discretion without any prior consultation and/or approval by the

[Supplier/Author]. Provided that the [Product/Work] is not altered and/or adapted in any manner and the payments due to the [Supplier/Author] in clause [–] are not affected.

C.536
The [Company] operates and runs this [Website] entirely at its own cost and discretion. There is no obligation on the [Company] to consult with, seek the approval and/or obtain permission from any person and/or business and/or other third party who uses this [Website] in any manner. The [Company] may at any time delete, adapt, change, vary, add to, suspend operation of, transfer all the business to another website and/or assign and sell rights and obligations to a third party. This clause shall not apply to the supply of any goods and/or services where there has been a payment made. In such instance where the [Company] is unable and/or unwilling to fulfil the terms of the Agreement the [Company] shall repay the total sum paid for any such incomplete work and/or obligations. The [Company] shall not be under any further liability to pay any additional sums.

C.537
The [Company] agrees that the [Contributor] shall be consulted in respect of the final version of the [Podcast] and any photographs, biography, image, likeness, quotes and/or other material relating to the [Contributor], his/her work and/or services on the [Website] and in any links, banners, promotional, publicity, advertising, and marketing owned and/or controlled by the [Company].

C.538
The [Company] shall not be obliged to consult with you prior to the deletion, removal, and/or changes to your name, title, content and display of your comment on the [Website].

C.539
The [Company] agrees not to edit, adapt and/or add any banner links, images, text and/or other material to your [Blog] on the website without prior consultation. In the event that [Name] objects to any material, then the [Company] agrees that it shall not insist on such changes, provided that the [Company] will not incur any direct financial losses as a result. In the event that the [Company] will lose advertising and promotional revenue from a third party, then [Name] accepts that the decision of the [Company] shall be final and may make such changes as may be needed in the circumstances.

Merchandising

C.540

The [Licensee] shall keep the [Licensor] regularly informed regarding all developments in respect of the production and exploitation of the [Work]. The [Licensee] shall at its own cost supply the [Licensor] with samples copies of all material, items, budgets, advertising and marketing proposals prior to any final decision, production and/or distribution to a third party. The [Licensee] shall be obliged to follow the decision of the [Licensor] in all matters subject to the criteria that the preferred option is not within the [Licensee's] budget. This shall include but not be limited to any prototypes, artwork and designs, covers, promotional, publicity, packaging, brochures, flyers, advertising, website details and marketing.

C.541

The [Company] agrees and undertakes that all sub-licensing of the [Work] shall be subject to the prior written approval of [Name] which may be withheld for any reason. There is no obligation on [Name] to agree to any sub-licence proposals nor does the [Company] have the authority to sign and/or authorise any such agreements which must be signed by [Name]. The [Company] shall consult with [Name] as to which businesses may be suitable and shall ensure that they are financially secure and solvent prior to entering any negotiations.

C.542

The [Distributor] shall sell, supply, market and exploit the [Work] to the best of its ability and shall not be obliged to consult and/or seek the prior approval of [Name] for any adaptation, translation, modification, addition to, and/or deletion from the [Work].

C.543

1.1   The [Sub-Licensee] agrees and undertakes not to alter, adapt, amend and/or add to any material relating to the [Work/Film/Image] and/or [Name] supplied by the [Licensee] at any time.

1.2   The [Sub-Licensee] agrees that it shall be in breach of this Agreement if it does not consult with and obtain the prior written approval of the [Licensee] in respect of any new material that the [Sub-Licensee] may wish to develop for production, packaging, marketing or any other purpose in respect of the rights granted under this Agreement.

C.544

The [Licensor] agrees that the [Licensee] shall have absolute discretion as to the exploitation and marketing of the [Work/Product] and that there shall be no obligation to consult with the [Licensor] and/or seek approval of any kind during the development, production, manufacture and distribution of the [Work/Product]. That the [Licensee] may make any such decisions as regard the content, packaging and promotion as it thinks fit.

C.545
The [Licensee] agrees:

1.1 Not to change the title and/or words of any text and/or any images in the [Work] and/or any part of any translation of the [Work] into another language and/or sub-titling without the prior approval of the [Licensor] of the draft proposal.

1.2 That the [Licensor] shall be provided with a minimum of [one] calendar month to consider any such proposal in each case.

1.3 That where the [Licensor] authorises any new title and text in any translation it shall be the responsibility of the [Licensee] to check that this does not conflict with an existing title in the market for such the translation of the [Work] is intended to be supplied, sold and distributed.

Publishing

C.546
That the [Company] shall allow the [Author] to be consulted on the detail of the display of the [Author's] [Book] on the [Company's] Website.

C.547
The [Publisher] shall keep the [Author] reasonably informed regarding all developments in respect of the exploitation of the [Work] including the samples, packaging, posters, covers publication and release dates.

C.548
The [Publisher] agrees that the [Author] shall be consulted in relation to material in respect of the [Work] which shall be of a high professional standard: including but not limited to photographs, illustrations, artwork, typography, design, blurb on jacket, layout of the website material, biography, image, likeness and representations of the [Author] and any signature, summaries of the text, use of third parties to promote or endorse the [Work], promotional, publicity, packaging, brochures, flyers, advertising, website details and marketing.

C.549
The [Licensee] agrees that the [Licensor] shall be consulted in relation to any artwork and designs to be created by the [Licensee] in respect of the [Extracts].

C.550

[Name] and the [Company] agree that [Name] shall be consulted regarding the accuracy and detail of the [Articles] prior to publication in the form in which it is intended to be published in the [magazine]. In the event that [Name] is not satisfied that the [Article] is accurate and that the detail is correct and the [Company] are not willing or able to change the [Article] then the [Company] agrees that the [Article] shall not be published by them and this Agreement shall be terminated and all sums that have already been paid shall be returned.

C.551

The [Company] agrees after consultation with the [Author] to revise, amend, correct, delete or change any material of any nature and in any format which is created under this Agreement which it proposes to market and exploit so that it meets the stipulations of the [Author].

C.552

The [Author] acknowledges that there shall be no right of approval, consultation, or to be advised of any matter relating to the exploitation of the [Work] and any variation or development at any time.

C.553

Where the [Publisher] has reached a decision that it is considering the option that it should cease printing copies of the [Work] and only to supply the [Work] as an online ebook via the internet as a download and/or in some other digital and/or electronic form but not in hardback and/or paperback. Then the [Publisher] agrees to notify the [Author] of their proposed plan to take such action and to provide the [Author] with an opportunity to have a meeting and to be consulted before any final decision by the [Publisher].

C.554

The [Publisher] agrees that where after any consultation the [Author] decides that he/she does not wish to remain with the [Publisher] if there are to be less than [number] copies of the printed version of the [Work] available for sale at any time during this Agreement. Then the [Author] may provide the [Publisher] with [three/six] months written notice of the termination of the Agreement. In such event the [Publisher] agrees to release the [Author] from any contractual obligations and to sign and execute any document requested by a third party to confirm such release.

Purchase and Supply of Products

C.555

The [Designer] agrees to consult with the [Licensee] with respect to the prices at which the [Licensed Articles] are to be sold whether by retail, wholesale or at a discounted price.

C.556

The [Distributor] shall consult with the [Supplier] in respect of any images, photographs, reviews, price comparisons, price changes or special offers of the [Products] on the website, in its catalogues or to customers and any marketing, packaging or promotional material.

C.557

There shall be no obligation or requirement to consult, advise or contact the [Company] regarding any price changes, discount, reduction, images, slogans, text or cross promotion regarding the [Products] by the [Distributor]. Provided that all the packaging, labels, copyright and trade mark notices and warnings are not removed, covered over or interfered with by the [Distributor]. That any representation of the [Product] shall be a true image and no derogatory, offensive or inappropriate comments shall be displayed with or close to the [Products].

C.558

The [Distributor] agrees that there shall be no consultation and/or approval process to make any changes to any part of the [Article/Product] and any associated material including but not limited to:

1.1   The source of supply of materials for the content;

1.2   The process and methods used to create the [Article/Product];

1.3   The name and logo and image, labels, leaflets and/or brochures and/ or any packaging;

1.4   The copyright and trade mark notices; and the warning and safety advice for use.

C.559

That where the [Distributor] is unable and/or unwilling to follow the strict guidelines and/or directions and/or conditions set by the [Licensor] as a condition of this Agreement. That production by the [Distributor] must cease until such time as the [Licensor] instructs otherwise. That where the matter is unresolved for more than [number] [days] including weekends and public holidays. That the [Licensor] may terminate and/or cancel the remainder of the Agreement. That the [Distributor] agrees that in such event the total liability of the [Licensor] shall be limited to [number/currency].

Services

C.560

The [Company] agrees to consult with the [Celebrity] and the [Agent] in respect of any material or form of exploitation relating to the [Celebrity] or

398

the [Series] in which the [Celebrity] features including press packs, photo sessions, competitions, packaging, prototypes and samples, merchandising, advertising, promotional, publicity and marketing material prior to the production, manufacture, release or marketing of any such material.

C.561

The [Manager] shall keep the [Athlete] fully informed on a regular basis as regards any negotiations with any third party and agrees that he shall not be entitled to conclude any agreement or sign any document or other record on behalf of the [Sportsperson] without the prior [written] consent of and consultation with the [Sportsperson].

C.562

The [Agent] acknowledges that it shall not be entitled to carry out or authorise any third party to adapt, alter, edit, add to or delete from or in any way change the [Work] without the prior [written] consent of the [Author].

C.563

The [Agent] agrees to consult with the [Author] in respect of any proposed translation of the [Work] in a foreign language, or subtitling in any other form. The [Agent] shall endeavour to ensure that all related costs are paid by the third party, but that copyright is assigned to the [Author].

C.564

Subject to prior consultation the [Actor] agrees that the [Agent] shall be entitled to use his name, signature, biography, photograph, image and stage name in the promotion, advertising and marketing of the [Actor], provided that a copy of any such material shall be supplied to the [Actor] when so requested.

C.565

The [Agent] shall not be obliged to consult with [Name] in respect of accepting bookings or signing contracts which have been broadly discussed and agreed in advance. Where [Name] has advised the [Agent] that they specifically wish to review the terms of a proposed deal personally prior to signature, then the [Agent] shall not proceed without the prior consent of [Name]. The [Agent] acknowledges that [Name] will not carry out the following types of work [specify].

C.566

The [Company] shall not be obliged to seek the approval and/or provide any details to the [Consultant] in respect of the [Project/Report] once it has been delivered to the [Company]. No reference shall be made to the contribution and/or work of the [Consultant] and all copyright in the [Project/Report] shall belong to the [Company] in accordance with the assignment under clause [–].

C.567
The [Agent] agrees to consult with [Name] in respect of all proposed work and shall not commit [Name] as their agent unless [Name] has agreed to proceed with any work and/or project and has agreed to the fees and expenses.

C.568
The [Company] agrees that it shall not authorise and/or permit anyone at the [Company] to include the name, title, image and details of the services provided by the [Consultant] including their fees and expenses to be included in any annual and/or corporate report and/or any marketing material and/or advertising and/or to post any film, photographs, text and/or other work and/or material on any website and/or database without prior consultation with the [Consultant] in each case.

University, Library and Educational

C.569
The [Institute] agrees to consult with [Name] in respect of the final version of the [Work] but such right of consultation, for the avoidance of doubt, shall not be deemed to be a right of approval or the right to prevent publication and/or distribution.

C.570
The [Author] shall not have any editorial control in respect of the [Project] once it has been delivered to the [Institute]. The [Institute] agrees to provide details of any significant amendments, deletions and/or changes in respect of the final report to [Name] but the [Institute] shall not be obliged to act on any recommendation or complaint.

C.571
The [Institute] agrees that [Name] shall be provided with a complete copy of the final version and have the right to be consulted regarding the accuracy and detail of the [Article/Report/Research] prior to publication and/or distribution.

C.572
The [Institute] agrees and undertakes that the [Author] shall have the right to be consulted in relation to all material and forms of exploitation in respect of the [Work] by the [Institute] including but not limited to photographs, illustrations, artwork, typography, index, design, blurb on jacket, biography, image, likeness and representations of the [Author], summaries of the

text, use of third parties to promote or endorse the [Work], samples, and merchandising promotional, publicity, packaging, brochures, flyers, advertising, website details and marketing.

A copy of any such material shall be provided as soon as it is available in draft form or as a prototype and sent to the [Author]. As far as reasonably possible the [Institute] shall incorporate any changes, amendments, deletions, proposals and objections the [Author] may have to any material at any time.

C.573
The [Enterprise] shall keep the [Institute] fully informed on a regular basis as regards any negotiations with any third party and agrees that it shall not be entitled to conclude any agreement or sign any document or other record on behalf of the [Institute] without the prior [written] consent of and consultation with the [Institute].

C.574
The [Joint Venture/Consortium] all undertake and agree that unless any steps, expenditure and/or work has been authorised by the [committee/ other]. Then any new proposals may not be developed and/or progressed so that any costs are incurred without consultation with all the members of the [Joint Venture/Consortium]. Failure to do so shall mean that the individual and/or institute that independently incurred costs and expenses shall be personally liable and not the [Joint Venture/Consortium].

C.575
The [Joint Venture/Consortium] shall be obliged to consult with its members, legal advisors and trustees at each stage of the [Project]. In the event at any stage a decision is reached by any of them that they should cease funding the [Project] based on the fact that the costs and expenses have escalated beyond the original budget. Then that representative of the [Joint Venture/Consortium] may serve notice to the others that they terminate the Agreement and will not supply any funds in excess of the original budget.

CONTINUOUS EMPLOYMENT

General Business and Commercial

C.576
'Continuous Employment' for the purpose of the existing legal requirements shall mean that the period shall start on [date].

C.577

Where a person ceases employment with the parent company and starts a new position at an associated company and/or subsidiary. That shall not be deemed a period of continuous employment.

CONTROL

General Business and Commercial

C.578

'Change of Control' shall mean circumstances when any person, company, body or entity acquires (whether by a series of transactions pursuant to a scheme or otherwise), shares [or stock] in the [Company] which if taken together with all the other shares [or stock held] by the acquirer and persons acting in concert with it would result in the acquirer gaining an overall controlling interest in the [Company].

C.579

'Control' shall be defined in accordance with the following [statute/policy document] issued by the [government department/other].

C.580

'Controlling Company' shall mean any company or other body or individual which holds or is beneficially entitled to [fifty per cent] or more of the shares or voting power of the [Company].

C.581

'Control' shall be defined on a de facto basis which shall in any event include an interest of [thirty per cent] or more.

C.582

'Control' shall mean any interest in the [Company] which enables any third party by virtue of any interest of any nature whether through shares, voting power or by virtue of the [Company's] Articles of Association to secure that the affairs of the Company are conducted in accordance with the wishes of the third party or any company or body associated with the company or third party.

C.583

In the event that there is a change of control of the [Company] because it is sold, placed in administration, declared insolvent and/or there is a majority shareholding acquired by another company and/or it no longer exists as it is incorporated into another company. Then the [Company] agrees and undertakes that all rights in the [Work] and all rights to ownership of all the master material which may be owned or controlled by the [Company] shall revert to the [Author].

C.584

There shall not have been a change of control where the transfer of the ownership of the [Company] is to an existing associate, or parent company. In the event that there is a change of control to a third party whether by the acquisition of the majority of the shares by one or more persons acting in concert, a sale, disposal and/or transfer. Then the following sums shall be paid to the following persons [–].

C.585

Where more than [number] of the voting shares of the [Company] are transferred and/or disposed of to a third party whether for money and/or other some other benefit by any person and/or company at any time. That transfer and/or disposal shall be considered and agreed as a change of control of the [Company].

C.586

[Name] agrees that where he/she intends to dispose of any shares and/ or interest and/or enter into any charge and/or lien in and/or over the [Enterprise] and its assets to a third party. That [Name] shall provide written notice in writing to the other parties to this Agreement of that proposal in each case at least [one] month prior to any such steps and/or action being taken.

COOKIES

Internet and Websites

C.587

The [Client/User] agrees that:

1.1 The [Enterprise] [and/or any parent, subsidiary, and/or associated third party, agent, market and/or research company] may send, transmit, place, deposit, store, retrieve, reproduce, alter, adapt, change, move, and/or otherwise vary the number, location, function, purpose, method, process, and/or otherwise of the Cookies on the hard drive on the

[Clients'/Users] computer, mobile phone, gadget, and/or other system and/or device which the [Client] may own and/or control and through which you have gained access to the [Website] known as [specify] which is [owned/controlled/other] by the [Enterprise].

1.2   That all and/or some of the Cookies may remain indefinitely on the hard drive until such time as they may be deleted and/or modified and/or otherwise changed by the [Enterprise] and/or the [Client/User].

1.3   That there is no transfer and/or assignment of any copyright, database rights, computer software rights and/or any other intellectual property rights in the Cookies by the [Enterprise]. That the [Client/User] shall not acquire any rights and/or interest of any nature in any medium at any time.

1.4   That where the [Client/User] are under [number] years of age, that a parent and/or guardian is aware of your use and/or access to the [Website] and has provided consent.

1.5   That the [Enterprise] shall have the right to allocate the [Client/User] a unique identifier code which shall be linked to all the data and/or other information retrieved from the Cookies.

1.6   That the [Enterprise] shall have the right to use the unique identifier code to retrieve, collate, analyse and/or store all the data and/or other information which can be derived from the Cookies regarding the [Clients'/Users'] use of sectors of and access to the [Website], pattern of behaviour over a period of one or more visits, personal profile and online preferences, use of [subject] resources, use of any links and/or banners and/or any other material whether text, images, film, sound recordings, and/or otherwise.

C.588

The [Enterprise] agree and undertake that there shall be no obligation on the [Client/User] to accept the Cookies from the [Enterprise] [and/or any parent, subsidiary, and/or associated third party, agent, market and/or research company] that the [Enterprise] may wish to store and/or retrieve to and from the hard drive of the computer, mobile phone, gadget, and/or other system and/or device of the [Client/User] through which the [Client/User] has gained access to the [Website] known as [specify] which is [owned/controlled/other] by the [Enterprise].

C.589

The [Enterprise] agrees that the [Client/User] may delete, block and/or deny access and/or the supply of the Cookies by the [Enterprise]. The [Enterprise] is obliged to inform the [Client/User] as to how to delete and/or block access by any Cookies. The following methods are advised [specify].

C.590

The [Client/User] agrees that the [Enterprise] may obtain and use the data and information in the form of log file data, codes and identifier codes obtained from the Cookies which are placed on the hard drive to carry out the following functions:

1.1　Track online traffic flows and preferences.

1.2　Analyse profiles of visitors.

1.3　Assess how to make the website more user-friendly.

1.4　Aid the playing of any online game.

1.5　Supply the cookies, log file data and unique identifier code to measurement and research companies to analyse and report back on how the service could be improved.

1.6　Save the [Client/User] repeating different functions they have already completed when they visit the [Website] including auto-resume, customised elements, layout of page, animation, audio material preferences, preferences based on geographic location and subject, news, weather, sport, colours.

1.7　Attach a unique identifier number for each hard drive on any computer and/or other gadget and/or mobile.

1.8　Track and record the journey through the [Website] by any [Client/User].

1.9　Assist in the downloading of forms.

C.591

The [Enterprise] has the following main Cookies embedded in the [Website] [specify name/type/function].

C.592

The [Enterprise] agrees and undertakes that none of the data and information obtained from the Cookies shall be supplied to any third parties except [specify names and addresses] who will analyse the data only in relation to a code and not with any personal details of the [Client/User].

C.593

The [Company] shall not be entitled to load and/or use cookies in respect of your data, searches and/or other use of the [Company] email newsletters, websites and banner links and other advertising unless you have provided your explicit prior consent. Failure to provide consent may mean that the [Company] will be obliged to restrict access.

C.594

Where data is collected through the use of cookies and/or any other analysis and/or storage and/or tracking device by the [Company], its distributors, payment agents, banks advertisers and delivery agents. The [Company] shall not treat all such information as confidential nor can it undertake that it can prevent access by all unauthorised third parties. The [Company] shall however ensure that all bank account details and passwords and codes are classified as private and confidential. A delivery name and address shall not be confidential nor shall the details of the products purchased.

COPYRIGHT CLEARANCE

DVD, Video and Discs

C.595

The [Company] shall be solely responsible for all arranging, obtaining and bearing the costs of all clearances, consents, permissions, contracts, copyright and intellectual property, artists, performers, contributors, employees, locations, musicians, music, lyrics, products and collecting societies or trade organisations, for production or post-production required, due or arising to third parties arising out of or in connection with the [Work] produced, recorded or reproduced on the [DVDs/Videos] or any part created, manufactured, distributed, sold, rented or supplied under this Agreement.

C.596

The [Owner] warrants that neither the [Owner] nor anyone with any rights in the [Programme] or parts has any contract with any third party including any agency, distribution, or license in respect of [DVDs/Videos/other] of the [Programme] which might conflict or interfere with any of the terms of this Agreement or the exercise by the [Licensee] of the rights granted in this Agreement.

C.597

The [Owner] warrants that:

1.1 The [Owner] has obtained and will continue to own or control all rights throughout the [Territory] for the Term of the Agreement and the Sell Off Period in the [Programme].

1.2 The [Owner] has (or third parties have) paid and will pay all the development, production, copyright, contract and reproduction costs

406

of the [Film/Recording] and/or any part due and/or owing and all taxes, costs, salaries, fees, residuals, advances, royalties or other sums due to performers, artists, writers, composers, musicians, (whether under contract or not) and the clearance, cost and use of all content of the [Film/Recording] including images, stills, archive footage, graphics, artwork, music, products, ringtones, sounds, computer generated material, and any other material of any nature which may become due as a result of the reproduction and exploitation of the [DVD/Videos/ Discs] of the [Programme] by the [Licensee] except payments due to collecting societies for the reproduction, transmission or performance of the [DVD/Videos/Discs] which shall be at the [Licensee's] cost.

1.3   That [Owner] undertakes that the [Licensee] shall not be liable for any such sums set out in 1.1 and 1.2 and in the event that they are paid for any reason by the [Licensee] the [Licensee] shall be reimbursed by the [Owner] upon receipt of an invoice.

C.598

The [Owner] warrants that to the best of its knowledge and belief the [Film/ Recording], its title and content including any music, lyrics, performances, products, and services and the exploitation in the [Territory/country] by means of [DVDs/Videos/Discs] does not and will not infringe, breach or encroach upon the trade mark, trade name, service marks, domain name, trading name, copyright, literary, dramatic, musical, artistic, reproduction, performance, contractual or legal rights of any third party in [country] from [date] to [date].

C.599

The [Licensee] warrants and undertakes that it shall be solely responsible for the payments of any sums which arise through the exploitation of the [DVD/Video] Rights under this Agreement which are due to the collecting societies [Performing Rights Society and/or the Mechanical Copyright Protection Society or any society affiliated to them] in the [Territory].

C.600

The [Licensor] shall be solely responsible for the consents, clearances, waivers, licences and payment in respect of all copyright, intellectual property, contract, and other rights and obligations due or owed to third parties arising directly or indirectly from any material reproduced in the [DVDs] of the [Film] in respect of the exercise of the rights granted hereunder including but not limited to artistic, musical, literary works, sound recordings, films. The [Licensor] shall supply to the [Licensee] at the [Licensor's] cost and expense upon request by the [Licensee] copies of all consents, clearances, waivers, licenses and details of contract obligations.

In the event that the [Licensee] shall be required to make any payment to any third party for any reason due to the failure of the [Licensor] to obtain clearance or consents then the [Licensor] agrees to reimburse in full the Licensee together with an additional fee of [ten per cent] of such amount which shall be paid within [28 (twenty eight) days] of receipt of any invoice by the [Licensor]. In the event that the [Licensor] should fail to pay any such sums then the [Licensee] shall be entitled to deduct them from any sums due to the [Licensor] under this Agreement.

C.601

The [Assignee] agrees that it shall be responsible for all payments which are or may become due in respect of the Artiste and/or the [Musical Work] and any sums due in respect of the distribution and exploitation of the [DVD/Video/Disc] in any media throughout the [specify countries] [not set out in the Budget].

C.602

In respect of the [Film/Recording] to be used in the form of a [DVD] the [Assignor] undertakes that all copyright and any other rights [except for the Artiste and the Musical Work] including consents required under the [Copyright, Designs and Patents Act 1988 as amended] shall be cleared and paid for in respect of the rights assigned under this Agreement for use by the Assignee] of the [Film/Recording] in the form of a [DVD] for promotional purposes. Provided that the [Assignor] shall only be responsible for such clearance payments as are set out in the [Budget].

C.603

The [Assignee] confirms that it shall be responsible for any payments in respect of the [Artiste] and the [Musical Work] and any sums due in respect of the distribution and exploitation of the [DVD/Video/Disc] in any media throughout the [Territory] which are not set out in the Budget. The [Assignee] confirms that it shall be responsible for any payments due in respect of any performing rights in any music and the mechanical reproduction of the [DVD/Video/Disc].

C.604

The [Assignee] undertakes and agrees that it shall be entirely responsible for all payments due or which may become due in respect of the performing rights in any music and the mechanical reproduction of the [Film/Recording/DVD].

C.605

The [Company] represents and warrants that it will be the owner of or will control all rights in the [Film/Programme/Recording] which are granted to the

[Distributor] hereunder. The [Company] will secure and pay for the consent in writing of all artists, musicians and other contributors whose appearances or performances are reproduced in the [Film/Programme/Recording] and all other consents necessary for the reproduction, distribution, sale, rental and supply and promotion of the [DVDs] hereunder and for the use and publication by [Distributor] of the promotional artwork supplied by the [Company] and of the legal and professional names photographs, biographies and likenesses of the artists, characters and other persons concerned in the [Film/Recording/Programme] which may be supplied to the [Distributor] by the [Company] hereunder. The [Company] shall provide the [Distributor] with a list of any additional payments that may become due as a result of the exploitation of the rights by the [Distributor] and that such sums shall be the responsibility of the [Distributor] and/or any third party who may acquire any rights herein.

C.606

The [Licensor] warrants that it will be the owner of or control all rights in the [Film/Recording/other] which are granted to the [Licensee] hereunder. The [Licensor] will pay for and secure the consent in writing of all Artists (including all musicians) whose performances are reproduced in the [Film/Recording/other] and obtain and pay for all other consents necessary for the production, manufacture, distribution, sale and rental of [DVDs/other] hereunder and for the use, publication and reproduction by the [Licensee] of the promotional material and artwork and of artists and any other persons concerned in the making of the [Film/Recording/other] which may be supplied to the [Licensee] by the [Licensor] hereunder. The [Licensee] shall be responsible for any payments in respect of the performing rights in any music [as are controlled by the Performing Rights Society or any society affiliated to it] and the mechanical reproduction of any music [controlled by the Mechanical Copyright Protection Society or a society affiliated to it] and [specify other organisations/bodies] in respect of the exercise of the rights granted to the [Licensee].

C.607

The [Assignee] agrees that it shall be responsible for any payments due in respect of the [Artiste] and the [Musical Work] and any other sums due in respect of the reproduction, distribution, performance, transmission and exploitation of the [DVD/Video/Recording] in any format or media not set out in the [Budget/Production Costs].

C.608

The [Assignee] undertakes that it shall pay all sums due in respect of the performing rights in any music and the mechanical reproduction of the [DVD].

C.609

The [Promoter] agrees to provide the [Company] with the following details in respect of the production of any promotional material for the [Company's] prior approval. A full breakdown of the copyright clearances and any other consents and payments required for use by the [Company] of the [Non-Theatric Rights] in any promotional [Film/Recording/DVD/Video] including those concerning artistes, performers, musicians, lyrics and music [under the Copyright, Designs and Patents Act 1988 as amended] together with details of all payments that will be required to any royalty collecting society in respect of the mechanical reproduction, performance or other exploitation of the [music/other] in [countries].

C.610

The [Assignor] warrants that it is the sole owner of or controls all copyright, intellectual property rights and any other rights in the [Film/DVD/Video] which are assigned under this Agreement except [the Artiste/Musical Work/products/other].

C.611

The [Assignor] undertakes that all copyrights and any other rights (except for the Artiste and the Musical Work) including consents required under the [Copyright, Designs and Patents Act 1988 as amended] shall be cleared and paid for in respect of the rights assigned under this Agreement for the use by the [Assignee] of the [Recording/Promotional Video] for promotional purposes. Provided the [Assignor] shall only be responsible for such clearance, consents and contractual payments as are set out in the [Production Costs].

C.612

The [Assignor] undertakes that all sums due in respect of the production of the [specify title] of [Film/Recording/DVD] shall be paid as set out in the [Budget]. That in the event that it is expected that the [Budget] will be exceeded the [Assignee] shall be notified immediately in writing. That no additional costs or expenses shall be incurred without the prior consent of the [Assignee]. That the [Budget] only sets out the cost of clearance and payments for the [DVD Rights and the Non-Theatric Rights] and not all other media, nor the performing rights in any music or the mechanical reproduction of recordings by any third party.

C.613

The [Licensor] confirms that all sums due to produce the [Film] have or will be paid for and that no such costs are the responsibility of the [Licensee]. The [Licensor] confirms that it has arranged for clearances, consents, waivers, releases and all necessary copyright, moral right, intellectual property, and contractual matters for the exploitation of the [Television Rights, DVD and Video Rights] in the [Film]. The [Licensee] shall bear the cost of all such payments including sums due for transmission, mechanical reproduction or other exploitation which may arise.

C.614

The [Assignee] agrees and undertakes that it shall be responsible for and bear the cost of providing the services of and attendance of the [Artiste] and the [Musical Works] as required by the [Assignor] for the purpose of producing the [Recording/Film/other] for [specify purpose].

C.615

In respect of the [Film/Recording] the [Licensor] confirms that all copyright and any other rights of any nature including music, stills, footage and consents under the [Copyright, Designs and Patents Act 1988 as amended] have been obtained in respect of the rights granted under this Agreement. The [Licensee] shall not be responsible for any payments except for any sums that arise through the exploitation of the [DVD] Rights and the associated promotional uses under this Agreement in relation to the performing rights or the mechanical reproduction in respect of any music.

C.616

The [Licensee] confirms that it shall be responsible for payment of any sums which arise through the exploitation of the [DVD/Video/Disc] Rights under this Agreement due to the [Performing Rights Society or the Mechanical Copyright Protection Society] or any society affiliated to them outside the [United Kingdom].

C.617

The [Assignor] confirms in respect of the [Film] that all copyright and any other rights (musical or otherwise) including consents required under the [Copyright, Designs and Patents Act 1988 as amended] have been obtained in respect of the rights assigned under this Agreement. Save that the [Assignee] shall be responsible for all copyright payments and any other sums that may arise due to any third party in any country in respect of the exploitation of the [DVD/Video/Disc] Rights in the [Film] and any permitted promotion and marketing by the [Assignee].

C.618

The [Assignee] undertakes and agrees that it shall be solely responsible for any sums due in respect of the manufacture, reproduction, distribution, marketing and exploitation of the [DVD/Video/Disc] Rights in the [Film] and any parts including any payments due for the performing rights in any music and the mechanical reproduction of the [Film].

411

C.619

The [Assignor] undertakes in respect of the [Series] that all copyright, consents, releases, waivers, licences and other rights and clearances including performers, musicians, appearances, format, script, text, quotes, rules, music, artwork, logos, trade marks, service marks, stills, footage, computer-generated material, ringtones, sounds, slogans, title and credits, products and any other material or content of any nature shall be cleared in respect of the [specify rights] assigned under this Agreement provided that the [Assignor] shall only be liable to make such payments [as are set out in the Budget] [already due and paid].

C.620

The [Assignee] confirms that it shall be responsible for any sums which arise through the exploitation of the rights which are not set out in the [Approved Budget] including but not limited to any payments due to the [Performing Rights Society or the Mechanical Copyright Protection Society] or any other organisation in respect of the performing rights and/or the mechanical reproduction of any music in the [Series].

C.621

In respect of the [Film/DVD/Video] the [Assignor] undertakes and agrees that all copyright and any further rights including music and consents under the [Copyright, Designs and Patents Act 1988 as amended] shall be cleared in respect of the [Non-Theatric Rights] assigned under this Agreement provided that the [Assignor] shall only be responsible for such clearance payments as follows [–].

C.622

The [Assignor] confirms that it shall be responsible for the clearance, acquisition of rights, consents, releases, permissions, waivers, contracts, and payments of all costs, fees, royalties and other sums due in respect of the following matters in the [Film/Recording/Pilot] in respect of the use, reproduction, performance, mechanical reproduction, performing rights, transmission, distribution and licensing of the [specify] Rights in [country] from [date] to [date]:

1.1 Artistes, musicians, production, technical and editing personnel and companies, consultants, services, promotional and marketing persons and companies.

1.2 Music, lyrics, stills, films, products, ringtones, sounds, computer generated material, images, graphics, text, slogans, service marks, trade marks, domain names, artwork, sound recordings, internet material and [other].

C.623

The [Assignee] agrees that from the date of full signature of this assignment it shall be liable to bear the cost and expense of clearing and paying for all copyright, consents, releases and any sums due for the use and exploitation of the [Work] and the [Work Material] of any nature. The [Assignor] shall not be liable whether or not the matter was disclosed to the [Assignee] at any time or not.

C.624

[Name] shall not be obliged to have cleared, obtained any consents, copyright or any other rights in any part of the [Material] which is being acquired and assigned to the [Company] nor does [Name] purport to know who owns or controls any such rights. It is the responsibility of the [Company] to obtain and pay for any rights which it intends to or does exploit at any time and no sums shall be claimed from or due to be paid by [Name].

C.625

The [Presenter] agrees and accepts that the [Distributor] shall be entitled to recoup all costs, expenses, fees, charges and copyright clearances, mechanical reproduction and/or any other sums due to any collecting society and/or other third parties for the development, production, reproduction, manufacture and exploitation of the [format] of the [Film/Recording] from the payments received before the calculation of the Net Receipts to the [Presenter].

C.626

All sums which may arise and/or be due which relate to the payment of copyright clearance and/or other fees for the use, reproduction and exploitation of any photographs, films, videos, manuscripts and diaries and/or any other material involved in the [Project] shall be the entirely at the cost and expense of the [Production Company] and not [Name].

C.627

It is agreed by the parties that [Name] shall not be liable to pay and/or contribute to any costs, sums and/or expenses that may be incurred and/or fall due at any time in respect of any third party contract, licence and/or copyright clearance and/or the acquisition of any intellectual property rights and/or any other material and/or contribution and/or performance and/or product and/or any other medium of any nature and/or images, text and/or music and/or sound recording and/or lyrics that appear in and/or reproduced in the [Film] and/or any other recording and/or exploitation of the [DVD/Disc/other] and/or any associated marketing, promotion and/or merchandising material in any part of the world at any time. The sums shall

413

be the sole responsibility and liability of the [Company] and the [Company] waives all rights to make any such claim against [Name].

Employment

C.628
The [Executive] acknowledges that all intellectual property rights including copyright, design rights, property rights, rights to data and databases, trademarks, service marks and any other rights created or developed in the course of the provision of the services of the [Executive] shall be and remain the sole and exclusive property of the [Company]. This Agreement does not purport to grant, assign or transfer any rights of any nature that may be created to the [Executive]. For the avoidance of doubt all rights including copyright in any work or invention created at any time by the [Executive] in the course of or in connection with his employment will belong by law to the [Company].

C.629
The [Company] agrees and undertakes that it shall not acquire any rights or interest or be entitled to register any claim to any of the following owned or controlled by the [Executive] [Books/Work/subject/other].

C.630
The [Company] agrees and undertakes that the [Company] shall not at any time be entitled to make a claim and/or take any legal and/or other action against [Name] for failure to consent to the use and/or exploitation by the [Company] of any material, copyright and/or other intellectual property rights held by [Name] prior to the date of this Agreement.

C.631
[Name] agrees and provides consent to the fact that the [Company] shall own and control all material of any nature which may be created by [Name] during the course of his /her employment with the [Company] which is created and/or developed in the course of their position as [specify]. That [Name] agrees that the [Company] and/or any third party distributor, sub-licensee may use and exploit any such material including titles, text, images, film, music, photographs, software, databases, sound recordings, codes, passwords, articles and products. That [Name] shall agree to sign any further agreements and documents that the [Company] may require relating to any work and creations of [Name] in order to effect any transfer and/or assignment to the [Company] after the termination of the employment provided that the [Company] shall agree to pay an additional fee to [Name] of [number/currency].

C.632

Where the cost of copyright clearances, payments in respect of performing and broadcast rights and/or mechanical reproduction, appearance and performance fees, insurance and other sums have not been decided and the budget for the [Project] finalised. Then it is agreed between the parties that no costs and expenses shall be incurred by any party to the development and production of this [DVD/Disc/other] unless all parties have provided prior approval to the expenditure. Where for any reason sums are due which are not covered by the funding achieved and/or budget then all parties shall bear the cost equally.

Film and Television

C.633

'Copyright' shall include all copyright and all other underlying intellectual property rights in the [Film] including the soundtrack and music and shall further include for contractual purposes all Format Rights as defined under Clause [–] in this Agreement.

C.634

The [Producer] confirms that all necessary copyright and other underlying intellectual property rights in the [Programme] and soundtrack have been cleared for the intended commercial purposes of the [Programme] as specified under Clauses [–] of this Agreement for the Term of this Agreement throughout the Territory.

C.635

The [Company] confirms that all clearances and consents have been obtained from all performers, musicians, actors, writers, directors, producers and any other contributors to the [Programme] and all relevant copyright related collecting agencies including but not limited to the [specify] and that any payments which may arise as a result of the commercial exploitation of the [Programme] throughout the Territory during the term of this Agreement whether referred to as advances, residuals, royalties or fees have been fully specified in the attached Schedule [–].

C.636

The [Television Company] confirms and undertakes that all clearances, consents and payments which shall arise as a result of the exploitation of the [Programme] by the [Television Company] including but not limited to all transmissions in the [Territory] with respect to all relevant copyright, performance or recording related collecting agencies and trade bodies including but not limited to the [specify] shall be the sole responsibility of the [Television Company] and not the [Producer].

415

C.637

The [Producer] confirms that all contractual arrangements with third parties have been entered into on a complete buy-out basis and that no fees of any nature to any third parties will arise as a result of the fulfilment of the terms of this Agreement with the exception of any sums due to the [Performing Rights Society/other] which sums shall be paid for by the [Company].

C.638

The [Licensor] confirms that it is the sole owner of or controls all copyright and any other rights in the [Film] which are granted to the [Licensee] under this Agreement.

C.639

The [Licensor] confirms that it is the sole owner of or controls all copyright and any further rights in this [Format].

C.640

The [Assignor] confirms that it is the sole owner of or controls all copyright and any other rights in the [Series/Film] which are assigned under this Agreement.

C.641

In respect of the [Series] the [Assignor] undertakes that all copyright and any other rights including footage, stills, music, and performances and consents required shall as far as reasonably possible be obtained and cleared for use in all media. The [Assignor] confirms that it shall be responsible for any payments in respect of the exploitation of the [Series] including any sums due in respect of the performing rights in any music as are controlled by the Performing Rights Society or a society affiliated to it and any sum due in respect of the mechanical reproduction of the [Series].

C.642

In respect of the [Film] the [Assignor] undertakes that all copyright and any other rights musical or otherwise, including consents required under the [Copyright, Designs and Patents Act 1988 as amended] shall be obtained and cleared in respect of the rights assigned under this Agreement. Provided that the [Assignor] shall only be responsible for such clearance payments as are set out in the Budget. That the [Assignee] shall be responsible for all other sums that may be due from the exploitation of the [Film].

C.643

The [Assignee] confirms that it shall be solely responsible for any sums due in respect of the exploitation of the [Film] and that the [Assignor] shall not be liable for any such payments. The [Assignee] shall also be responsible for any sums in respect of the performing rights in any music and the mechanical reproduction of the [Film].

C.644

The [Licensor] confirms that it has obtained all such consents as are required under [Copyright, Designs and Patents Act 1988 as amended] in [country] from [date] to [date].

C.645

The [Licensor] confirms that all sums due in respect of the development and production of the [Film] have been paid including options, writers, artists, director, musicians, all technical and production crews, location fees, copyright, consents, waivers, contractual obligations and any other rights in the [Film] granted to the [Licensee]. The [Licensee] is and will not be liable for any such payments and shall only be responsible for the following payments [specify].

C.646

The [Television Company] undertakes that all sums due in respect of the development, production, reproduction, distribution and exploitation of the [Programme] will be paid by the [Television Company] or its distributors or sub-licenses and that the [Sponsor] is not and will not be liable for any such payments.

C.647

The [Producer] shall be responsible for ensuring that any Artist, Musician, and/or other Contributors required by the [Company] shall, subject to the terms of the applicable trade agreements, be available to make trailers and that all necessary copyright and/or other clearances are obtained for the use of trailers by the [Company] in promoting any [Programme] hereunder. Any additional cost incurred by the [Producer] in securing the availability of any Artists, Musicians or other Contributors or in obtaining any necessary clearances shall be paid for by the [Company].

C.648

The [Company] warrants that it is the sole and absolute owner of, or to the extent that the [Film] has not yet been made, the prospective owner of the entire copyright and all other rights in all material incorporated or to be incorporated in the [Film] including all rights of copyright as are or may be required to permit the [Film] to be produced and exploited by all means and in all media save such as are administered by the [Performing Rights Societies or a society affiliated to it] throughout the world. Such rights are or will prior to the start of the Option Period be vested in the [Company] or it successors free from encumbrances.

417

C.649

The [Company] warrants that it is the person by whom the arrangements necessary for the making of the [Film] are being and will continue to be undertaken.

C.650

The Licensor undertakes, represents and warrants:

1.1 That it will be the owner of or will control all rights in the [Series] which are granted to the [Broadcaster] in this Agreement and that [Licensor] has or will secure the consent in writing of all artists (including all musicians) whose performances are reproduced in the [Series] (including the soundtrack) and all writers and all other consents necessary for the television broadcast and transmission of the [Series] hereunder and for the use by the [Broadcaster] of the publicity material and artwork supplied by the [Licensor] and of the legal and professional names, photographs, biographies and likenesses of the Artists and characters whose performances are reproduced in the [Series] and any other persons concerned in the making of the [Series] which may be supplied to the [Broadcaster] by the [Licensor] hereunder. With the exception of such performing rights in any music as are controlled by the [Performing Rights Society] or a society affiliated to it in which case it is agreed that the [Broadcaster] shall be responsible for any payment to such society in respect of the performance of any music.

1.2 That it possesses full power and authority to enter into and perform this Agreement and that at the date of execution hereof there are not and during the full period of time during which the [Broadcaster] retains rights of television broadcast and transmission hereunder there will not be any liens or encumbrances against the [Series] which will or might impair the fullest exercise by the [Broadcaster] of its rights hereunder and further the [Licensor] has not granted and will not grant any rights the exercise of which would derogate from or be inconsistent with the rights granted to the [Broadcaster] hereunder.

C.651

The [Assignor] agrees and undertakes:

1.1 It will ensure that all such consents as are necessary under [Copyright, Designs and Patents Act 1988 as amended] to make and exploit and authorise the exploitation of the Film(s) and/or part(s) have been obtained.

1.2 It has paid or will pay all sums due in order to enable it to make the Film(s) and acquire the rights in the Film(s) and/or part(s) assigned to the [Assignee] hereunder and that no sums (other than those payable under Clause [–] of this Agreement and any value added tax thereon) shall be payable by the [Assignee] in respect of the exercise of the rights acquired by it hereunder except music performing fees to the relevant [Performing Rights Society] in any part of the world.

C.652

The [Company] warrants that it was the maker of the [Film] and the person by whom the arrangements necessary for the making of the [Film] were undertaken and the first owner of the copyright in the [Film] and acquired all rights in all material on which the [Film] was based and is incorporated in it as are necessary for its exploitation hereunder.

C.653

The [Company] warrants that none of the rights hereby granted to the [Licensee] have been assigned or licensed or charged in any way dealt with by the [Company].

C.654

The [Company] warrants that it is the exclusive licensee of the rights granted to the [Licensee] and is fully entitled to give the warranties and make the representations concerning the [Film] which are set out in the Agreement.

C.655

The [Company] warrants that all consents necessary under [Copyright, Designs and Patents Act 1988 as amended] to make, exploit and authorise the exploitation of the [Film] have been obtained and paid for by the [Company].

C.656

The [Company] warrants that all sums due to make the [Film] and acquire the [Television Rights/DVD Rights/Internet Rights/Telephone Rights] for [countries] during the Licence Period have been paid and that no sums other than those payable under Clause [–] and any value added tax shall be payable by the [Licensee] in respect of the rights acquired by it hereunder except performing rights payments to the relevant [Performing Rights Society] or any society affiliated to it and the mechanical reproduction payments due to the [Mechanical Copyright Protection Society].

C.657

The [Company] warrants that neither the Film nor any matter included in it infringes the copyright or any other rights of any person or company in the Territory [in respect of the rights granted under this Agreement.

C.658

The [Licensee] undertakes that it shall be responsible for all payments due in respect of the performing rights in any music as controlled by the [Performing Rights Society] or a society affiliated to it in respect of the exercise of the rights in the [specify] granted under this Agreement.

C.659

The [Licensor] confirms that all copyright and any other rights (musical or otherwise) including consents required under the [Copyright, Designs and Patents Act 1988 as amended] have been or will be obtained in respect of the rights granted under this Agreement and that the Licensee shall be responsible for such payments as may arise and become due as a result of the exploitation of the [Film].

C.660

The [Licensee] warrants that it shall be responsible for all payments which may arise in respect of the exploitation of the [Film] including any sums due in respect of the performing rights in any music and the mechanical reproduction of the [Film] in respect of the exercise of the rights granted under this Agreement.

C.661

The [Licensee] warrants that it is or shall be the owner of or will control all rights in the [Programme] which are granted to the [Distributor] hereunder. The [Licensee] has or shall secure the consent in writing of all performers (including musicians) whose performances are reproduced in the [Programme] and all other consents necessary for the exploitation of the [Programme] by all means and by all media whether now known or discovered hereafter and for the use and publication by the [Distributor] of photographs, biographies and likenesses of all those persons whose performances are reproduced in the [Programme] or who were concerned in the making thereof which may be supplied by the [Licensor] to the Distributor hereunder.

C.662

The [Assignor] warrants to the [Assignee]:

1.1 That the [Film(s)] be vested in the [Assignor] absolutely free from encumbrances save that the [Assignee] shall be responsible for any payments in respect of the performing rights in any music as are controlled by the [Performing Rights Society] or a society affiliated thereto in respect of the exercises of the rights assigned hereunder to the [Assignee].

1.2 It has ensured that the person by whom the arrangements necessary for the making of the [Film(s)] have been made has assigned all the rights to the [Assignor] and is able to provide signed written documents to that effect.

C.663

'Residuals' shall mean those sums due to any artist, actor, director, performer, producer, musician, writer or any other contributor of any nature to the [Programme] who by virtue of any written agreement is entitled to further remuneration by reference to the original payment made to such contributor for his or her original contribution to the [Programme] (and not by reference to any royalty arrangement) in consequence of the re-transmission, subsequent broadcast or further commercial exploitation of the [Programme] throughout the territory during the Term of this Agreement. A definite list of all individuals who are entitled to Residuals and the amount due to each individual by virtue of the exercise of the rights granted under this Agreement is attached to and forms part of this Agreement.

C.664

The [Licensor] confirms and agrees that all obligations of any nature with respect to the [Film] and the production, distribution and exploitation including, but not limited to, salaries, royalties, residuals, deferments, licence fees, service charges, laboratories processing and editing costs, union or trade organisations payments have or will be fully paid by the [Licensor]. Except for those costs and expenses which the [Licensee] or sub-licensee is contracted to pay for or are subsequently incurred by them in respect of the exercise of the rights hereunder and payments due in respect of the performance or broadcast of the music in the [Film] and in respect of mechanical reproduction of the [Film].

C.665

The [Licensee] acknowledges and accepts that the [Licensor] is only licensing the right to use the [Film Clip] itself and is not providing any rights in respect of the performances of the actors, performers, musicians and/or the music soundtrack or otherwise. The [Licensee] shall not use the [Film Clip] without obtaining all the necessary consents, releases, authorisations, clearances and licences from any person, company or entity as may be necessary, and the [Licensee] shall be responsible for the payment of all sums that are paid or become due as a result of the exercise of the rights granted in this Agreement.

C.666

The fee includes payment for original performers, repeat performances, mechanical reproduction, assignment of copyright, and all other rights granted therein.

C.667

The [Licensor] confirms that it has or will obtain and bear the cost of all necessary third party consents and rights required for the performance of this Agreement including the performers consents under the [Copyright, Designs and Patents Act 1988 as amended by any subsequent legislation].

C.668

The [Company] shall use their reasonable endeavours at the [Company's] sole cost to engage all performers (including actors, artists, composers, musicians, directors, writers and any other contributors) performing or taking part in or contributing to the production of the [Programme] on the basis of a complete buy-out subject to any restrictions or trade agreements or relevant societies that may prevent such action.

C.669

The [Licensor] agrees and undertakes that it is the sole owner of or controls all copyright and any other rights in the [Footage]. That all copyright and any other rights (musical or otherwise) including consents under the [Copyright, Designs and Patents Act 1988 as subsequently amended] have been obtained and the [Licensee] is not liable for any payments other than those specified under this Agreement.

C.670

The [Licensee] agrees and undertakes that it shall be responsible for any payment in respect of the performing rights in any music as are controlled by the [Performing Rights Society] or a society affiliated to it in respect of the rights in the [Footage] granted under this Agreement.

C.671

The [Sponsor] and the [Association] agree to the following:

1.1   That all copyright and any other rights including but not limited to the Satellite, Cable, Digital, Terrestrial Television Rights, the Theatric Rights, the Non- Theatric Rights, the internet, Computer, Television and Gadget Games, Merchandising and Telecommunication and Telephone Rights] in the [Recordings] shall be the sole exclusive property of the [Association].

1.2   The [Association] shall be entitled to retain all sums received at any time from the exploitation in any nature, format, process or method in whole or part or derived directly or indirectly from the [Recordings].

1.3   That the [Sponsor] agrees it is the sole owner of or controls all copyright and any other rights in the [Sponsor's Logo] and the use of the [Sponsor's Logo] by the [Association] and the [Television Company] under this Agreement will not expose the [Association] and/or the [Television Company] to any criminal or civil proceedings.

1.4 That the [Association] agrees it is the sole owner of or controls all copyright and any other rights in the [Promotional Logo] and that the use of the [Promotional Logo] under this Agreement will not expose the [Sponsor] to any criminal or civil proceedings.

C.672

The [Company] confirms that it is the sole owner of or controls all present and future copyright and any other rights in the [Advertisement] which are assigned under this Agreement except for the [Product] and any other material supplied by the [Commissioning Company].

C.673

In respect of the [Advertisement] the [Company] undertakes that all copyright and any other rights (musical or otherwise) and consents required under the [Copyright, Designs and Patents Act 1988 as amended] shall be cleared in respect of the [specify rights/countries] for exploitation by the [Commissioning Company]. Provided that the [Company] shall only be liable for such payments as are set out in the Approved Budget.

C.674

The [Commissioning Company] agrees and undertakes that it shall bear the cost of obtaining and paying for all copyright, consents, clearance, waiver and contract payments set out in the [Approved Budget] including any sums due in respect of the distribution, exploitation, performance and/or mechanical reproduction of any music in respect of the [Advertisement] in any media throughout the Territory.

C.675

The [Agent] undertakes that all copyright, consents, music and any other rights required under the [Copyright, Designs and Patents Act 1988 as amended] have or will be cleared and paid for in respect of the transmission and/or broadcast by the [Television Company] of the [Advertisement] including the soundtrack including any sums due in respect of the mechanical reproduction due to the [MCPS] or a society affiliated to it. The [Television Company] will not be liable for any such payments except for such sums due in respect of the performance of the music to the [Performing Rights Society] or a society affiliated to it.

C.676

The [Production Company] confirms that it shall be the sole owner of or control all copyright or any other rights in the [Film] except for the [Author's

Work]. The [Production Company] shall be entirely responsible for all costs incurred and sums due in respect of the development, production, distribution, marketing and exploitation of the [Film] and parts in any form and that the [Author] is not and shall not be liable for any such payments and that the [Production Company] shall not be entitled to deduct any such sums from the Gross Receipts.

C.677

The [Production Company] agrees that it shall be solely responsible for obtaining and paying for all copyright clearances, consents, waivers, licences, contractual obligations and any other rights which are due or owed to any third parties arising directly or indirectly in respect of any material in the [Film] and parts. The [Production Company] shall also be solely responsible for the cost of any exploitation of any of the rights in any media granted under this Agreement including but not limited to, artistic, musical, literary works, sound recordings, films, performing rights in any music, mechanical reproduction of any recordings, actors, writers, stills, footage, computer generated material, and products. None of these costs shall be the responsibility of the [Author] and they shall not be deducted from the Gross Receipts.

C.678

The [Author] confirms that the [Author's Work] is the original work of the [Author] and does not infringe the copyright or any other rights of any third party throughout the Territory in respect of the rights granted to the [Production Company] under this Agreement.

C.679

The [Company] undertakes that it was the maker of the [Film] and the person by whom the arrangements necessary for the making of the [Film] were made and the first owner of copyright in the [Film] and has acquired all rights in all material on which the [Film] is based as are necessary for the exercise of the rights granted under this Agreement.

C.680

In respect of the [Pilot] the [Assignor] undertakes that all sums due in respect of the production of the [Pilot] will be paid and that the [Company] is not and will not be liable for any such payments. In respect of the [Pilot] the [Assignor] undertakes that all copyright and any other rights, consents, clearances, music or otherwise shall be cleared for private viewing only and for such clearance payments as are set out in the [Budget].

C.681

The [Assignor] agrees and undertakes that all copyright, consents, releases, moral rights, contractual obligations, music and any other rights of any nature shall be cleared in respect of all rights granted under this Agreement but shall only be paid for to the extent that such payment is provided for in the [Budget]. The [Assignee] shall bear any additional costs of clearance payments which shall be included in the Distribution Expenses. Payments due in respect of the performing rights in any music or the mechanical reproduction of the recordings shall as far as possible be at the cost of any third party who is authorised to exploit the [Film].

C.682

The [Company] shall set out a clear statement of all material to be cleared and acquired for the [Advertisement] and the cost of clearance for:

1.1 All forms of satellite, digital, terrestrial, cable television on [specify].

1.2 Banners on websites, CDs and CD-Roms, ringtones, images, sound and text on mobile phones, computers, televisions and other gadgets or devices.

1.3 Billboards, posters, newspapers, magazines, comics, food products, clothing and other forms of merchandising.

The [Company] shall use the budget to clear and pay for such rights. Where possible the [Company] shall acquire all media rights but where this would result in the Budget being exceeded they should merely advise the [Commissioning Company] of this fact and not acquire additional rights. The [Company] shall only be responsible for clearance and payment for material to the limit of the Budget.

C.683

The [Commissioning Company] confirms that it shall be responsible at its sole cost for all copyright and other clearance payments not set out in the Budget including any sums due in respect of the distribution and exploitation of the [Advertisement] in any media throughout the Territory including any sums due for the performing rights in any music and the mechanical reproduction of any music of the [Advertisement].

C.684

The [Company] confirms and undertakes that all rights necessary for the use of [Work] on [Channel/Film/other] have been acquired and paid for by the [Company] except the [Fees] to the [Company] set out in Clause [–] and any sums due to the following organisations [specify] and that the [Licensee] shall be entitled to exercise the following rights without any additional payments in [countries] from [date] to [date]:

1.1 Cable, satellite, terrestrial and digital television.

1.2 Premium text message and phone lines.

425

1.3   Extracts of images, text, music for promotion on websites, telephones, CD-Roms, DVDs, publications, advertisements and [other] [description].

C.685

1.1   In consideration of the [Interview Fee] [Name] agrees to be interviewed by [Presenter] and filmed by the [Company] for the [Film/Series] to be broadcast, transmitted and exploited by [Distributor]. Further [Name] also agrees to assign to the [Company] all present and future copyright and intellectual property rights in any film and/or sound recordings that may be created in the interview by [Name] on [date] at [location] throughout the world and universe for the full period of copyright and/or any other terms of any other rights and any extensions and forever without limit of time and/or space.

1.2   The Interview Fee shall not include payment for access to his/her home for the purposes of filming which shall be a separate [Location Access Fee] of [number/currency] and subject to a separate agreement.

1.3   In addition a separate copyright and usage fee and agreement shall be agreed between [Name] and the [Company] for any reproduction, filming and/or exploitation of any documents, manuscripts, books, photographs, videos and other film and/or any other material which may belong to [Name] and/or any other member of his/her family and/or any third party. There shall be no presumption that because the [Company] has been permitted access to view any material that there is an automatic right by the [Company] to use such material. No implied and/or express licence is granted by this Agreement. That no authority has been granted by [Name] and/or any third party until a new licence which shall link payments to [Name] and/or any third party to each and every form of exploitation and not a one single payment.

C.686

1.1   [Name] agrees to be in the audience of the programme entitled [specify] and may be selected to take part as a contestant.

1.2   In the event that [Name] is selected to be a contestant then the [Company] shall pay [Name] a single payment of [number/currency] in order to buy out all copyright and rights that [Name] may have in their contribution to the programme in any form including performance, singing, dance, acrobatics and other material but not lyrics and/or music and/or [specify]. [Name] agrees and assigns to the [Company] all future copyright and any other intellectual property rights in his/her future contribution and/or appearance in all media and in all formats and forms of exploitation including new forms developed at a later date which do not exist now throughout the world for the full period of copyright and any other period where it extended and in perpetuity for all the contribution of [Name] except any music, lyrics and [specify].

General Business and Commercial

C.687
'Copyright' shall have the same meaning as set out under the [Copyright, Designs and Patents Act 1988 as amended].

C.688
'Future Copyright' shall mean copyright which will or may come into existence in respect of a future work or class of works or on the occurrence of a future event and shall be defined in accordance with [section 91 of the Copyright, Designs and Patents Act 1988 as amended].

C.689
The [Licensor] confirms that all copyright, music and any other rights have been obtained and that the [Licensee] is not liable for any payments other than those specified as follows [–].

C.690
The [Company] agrees that all copyright and any other rights necessary for the use by [Name] of the [item] from [date] to [date] at [address] in the following manner [specify use] has been obtained and paid for by the [Company].

C.691
In respect of the [Commissioned Work] the [Company] warrants that all copyright and any other rights including consents required under the [Copyright, Designs and Patents Act 1988 as subsequently amended] shall be obtained and paid for in respect of the rights assigned under this Agreement for use by the [Assignee].

C.692
The [Licensor] agrees and undertakes that all copyright and any other rights in the [Work/drawings/other] including consents required under the [Copyright, Designs and Patents Act 1988 as subsequently amended] have been obtained and that the [Licensee] is not and shall not be liable for any payments other than those specified under this Agreement.

C.693
The [Originator] confirms that he/she shall bear the cost of any copyright clearance and consent payments for the use of any material for the [Work] including artwork which is owned or controlled by a third party.

C.694

The [Artist/other] agrees and undertakes that he is the sole owner of or controls all copyright and any other right in the [Commissioned Work] which are assigned under this Agreement. The [Artist/other] undertakes that all copyright and any other right including consents required under the [Copyright, Designs and Patents Act 1988 as amended] shall be cleared and paid for in respect of the rights assigned under this Agreement to the [Assignee].

C.695

The [Company] agrees and undertakes that as far as reasonably possible it shall clear and pay for all copyright, intellectual property rights, consents, releases, waivers, trade marks, logos, service marks, or any other rights of any nature in the [Work] or parts necessary for the exploitation of the [Work] by the [Distributor] in [countries] in the following formats [–].

C.696

The [Company] shall obtain and pay for the clearance and acquisition of rights in respect of any artist, musician, contributor, stills, footage, music, product, trade marks, logos, service mark, product, title, artwork, computer generated material, graphics, documents, books, and any other material of any nature incorporated in the [Work]. All such material shall be cleared for use by the [Distributor] subject to any notified restrictions or additional costs, which shall be the responsibility of the [Distributor] for the duration of this Agreement.

C.697

The [Assignor] agrees that it is the sole owner of all property rights and any other rights in the [Work Material] except for the obligations, credits and moral rights, a complete list of which is set out in Appendix [–] to this Agreement. The [Assignor] shall be responsible for all sums due up to the date of this Agreement and the [Assignee] shall bear all costs and expenses owed to any third party from [date].

C.698

The [Company] undertakes that it shall be responsible for all sums due for the production, reproduction and exploitation of the [Work] to any third party whether for consents, copyright licences, waivers or otherwise of any material or rights which are not owned or controlled by [Name].

C.699

The [Licensor] agrees and undertakes that it controls and is an exclusive distributor of the rights in [specify item] which are granted to the [Licensee] under this Agreement and that there is no third party except the copyright owner [specify name] who has a claim to own or control the rights which have been granted. The copyright owner is aware of this Agreement and has provided written consent that it may be concluded.

C.700
The [Distributor] agrees that the [Company] shall only pay such clearance costs as may be set out in the [Budget]. Any sums due from the exploitation of the [specify item] to any third party by the [Distributor] shall be paid by the [Distributor] and recouped under the Distribution Expenses.

C.701
There is no undertaking, confirmation or statement in relation to any part of the [Service/unit/other] as to whether material is available for use in a particular country, complies with legislation, has the consent of all parties who may claim ownership of any part or otherwise. It is the responsibility of the [Purchaser] to arrange for and pay any sums that may be due to third parties for the use of [Service/Unit/other] and any additional costs and charges.

C.702

1.1 It shall be the responsibility of the [Marketing Agency] to ensure that no material is distributed and/or released to the public in any form in print, television and/or on the internet in respect of the promotion campaign for the [Distributor] in which the performance fees, location fees, music, stills and images, logos and brand names, reproduction of any music, lyrics, sound recordings, mechanical reproduction, broadcast and/or transmission fees, copyright and/or other rights have not been cleared and a licence agreement obtained for such authorised use in each case.

1.2 That the verbal agreement of a third party shall not be sufficient for the purpose of clearance of any rights and that the [Marketing Company] shall ensure that full and accurate complete records and documents are kept both in print form and on a hard drive. That upon request at any time the [Marketing Company] shall provide copies to the [Distributor].

C.703

1.1 The [Company] agrees and accepts that [Name] is not supplying any agreement and/or undertakings as to the clearance of any rights including copyright and/or payment of fees due to any third parties from the exploitation of the [Film/Photograph/Work] by the [Company].

1.2 That the [Company] is paying a fee to [Name] solely for the purpose of physical access to the [Film/Photograph/Work] in order to [make a copy/film/display in an exhibition].

1.3   That in the event that any use and/or adaptation and/or reproduction by the [Company] results in a claim and/or allegation against [Name] and/or the [Company] for breach of contract, copyright infringement and/or otherwise relating to the [Film/Photograph/Work] that the [Company] shall be liable to deal with the matter on behalf of [Name] and shall bear all costs, expenses and legal cost and payments to any third party that may arise. [Name] shall not make a contribution to and/or be liable for any sums that may be due for any reason.

Internet and Websites

C.704

The material on this [Website] cannot be assumed to have been cleared for use by you except for viewing the site without printing, downloading or reproducing any material. There is no licence granted, permission given or any claims made as to the copyright, intellectual property or ownership of material unless specifically stated or a copyright notice or person or company's name is displayed. In such cases you should contact the copyright owner direct for permission or [company contact].

C.705

The [Website] is monitored regularly, but material and content is placed on the [Website] which may be in breach of copyright, contract or confidential. You are advised not to reproduce, exploit, supply or distribute any content without first establishing the legal position as to who owns and controls the material and the rights. The [Company] will not assist you or reimburse you or be responsible for any claim against you for infringement of copyright, legal costs, breach of contract or otherwise which may arise from your use of any material.

C.706

I am the sole author and copyright owner of the following work; [title/pages/ISBN reference]. I consent to the following extract of my work being displayed on the internet at the website location and address [specify] under the domain name [specify] whose main place of business is at [specify]. The duration of my consent is [specify period] and is subject to the written withdrawal of my consent at any time by notice in writing or email to the [Company].

C.707

The [Company] agrees that it shall not acquire any rights or interest in the [Work] or any part at any time save as set out in the short form permission and that any new material created which directly relates to the [Work] shall be transferred to and belong to the [Author] at the end of this Agreement and no rights shall belong to the [Company].

430

C.708

The [Designer] in consideration of the sums paid under the Payment Schedule assigns to the [Company] all copyright, intellectual property rights, interest and goodwill in all media including the internet, telecommunication and computer software rights in any material and any format, process or method in whole or part owned or controlled by the [Designer] in the [Product Specification, Proposal, Material, Domain Name and website] which may arise in pursuance of this Agreement whether in existence now or created in the future throughout the universe for the full period of copyright and any extensions, renewals or other developments that may arise.

C.709

The [Designer] and the [Company] agree that:

1.1 The [Designer] shall not acquire any rights or interest in the [Website] of any nature except [specify]. Nor shall the [Designer] be entitled to review, register and/or claim any rights, interest or equity in the Domain Name or any Material which has been created or developed for the purpose of the [Company's] [Website] under the terms of this Agreement.

1.2 The [Company] confirms that any and all rights in any resource material supplied to the [Designer] under this Agreement shall be owned or controlled by the [Company] unless expressly stated to belong to a third party.

C.710

The [Licensor] shall be responsible for the clearance of all contractual, copyright and any other rights in respect of the [Work] and any parts and any associated copyright notices, credits, moral rights, trade marks, service marks, logos, text, images, graphics, sounds and music. The [Internet Service Provider] shall bear the cost of all payments relating to all material for use on its [website] except for the [text] which shall be the responsibility of the [Licensor].

C.711

The [Company] agrees that it shall be responsible for all copyright, consent, and other fees due to third parties arising from the operation of the [website] from [date/launch date] for all the materials of any nature whether comprising of text, images, whether visual or subliminal internal or external, whether graphics which are static, interactive or moving, photographs, drawings, plans, sketches, electronically generated material, sounds, sound effects, music, logos, trade marks, design rights, background, banners, bookmarks, borders, tables, captions, characters, clip art, cartoons, computer generated art, maps, image map links, common gateway interface script, date, domain names, footnotes, headings, hypertext, video, DVD, CD-Rom, material for telephone, mobile, telecommunication system or other device for transferring, downloading supplying or distributing sound, vision, text and icons or any other development and any and all combination of such elements, software and information. Prior to that date all such costs shall have been included in the report of the [Designer] and paid under the Payment Schedule.

C.712

[Name] agrees not to:

1.1 Post any material on the [Blog/website] which has not been cleared and paid for so it can legitimately and legally be used in that manner.

1.2 Use any material in a way which would bring a claim of copyright infringement and/or any other breach of any other intellectual property rights against the [Company] by any person and/or business in any country in any part of the world.

1.3 Post any material which he/she knows to belong to a third party without a suitable credit and/or copyright notice to that third party.

1.4 Distort, vary, change and adapt any material from a third party and represent it as the original work and effort of [Name].

C.713

Where you use and post material on this [Website] you must ensure not to infringe and/or breach any copyright and/or other rights of any other person and/company. Where the [Webmaster/Distributor] are notified by a third party of any allegation of infringement and/or breach it is our policy to act swiftly to remove, delete and cancel both the material in question and the account of the person involved. No responsibility is accepted by the [Webmaster/Distributor] for your posting and/or actions and you remain at all times liable for a claim against you by such third party. Your personal details will be supplied to such third party in the event that they obtain either a court order.

Merchandising

C.714

The [Licensor] confirms that he is the original creator and sole owner or controls all copyright, trade marks, logos, name and any other rights in the [Character] which are granted under this Agreement.

C.715

The [Designer] confirms that he is the original creator and sole owner of or controls all copyright, design rights and any other rights in the [Designs] and the [Garments].

C.716

The [Licensor] confirms that he is the original creator and sole owner of all copyright, design rights and any other rights in the [Board Game] and [Prototype] which are granted to the [Company] under this Agreement and do not infringe the copyright, design rights or any other rights of any third party in [country].

C.717

The [Assignor] agrees that it has fully disclosed any rights or interests of third parties in the [Work] and the [Material] [specify].

C.718

The [Assignee] agrees that from the date of this Agreement it shall be liable to bear the cost and expense for clearing and paying for all copyright, consents and any other rights in the [Work] and the [Material] of any nature and the fulfilment of any obligations. The [Assignor] shall not be liable for such sums whether such matter was disclosed and/or known by the [Assignee] at the time of the date of this Agreement.

C.719

The [Company] agrees that it shall not be entitled to use, exploit or license any of the material produced or created for the purposes of this Agreement in which the [Celebrity] appears in sound, vision or any other form or reference other than the endorsement, promotion or advertising of the [Company's Product] during the Term of the Agreement. Where the [Company] wishes to use any such material for any purpose or to license a third party then it is clear that the prior written agreement of the [Celebrity] is required and the negotiation and settlement of an agreement or consent form on each occasion.

C.720

The [Agent] agrees that she is not entitled to negotiate or promote in any manner or form the commercial interests of the [Character/Work] outside [countries] unless specifically agreed in advance with the [Licensor].

C.721

The [Agent] agrees that he is not acquiring nor shall he represent that he owns, controls or attempt to register any copyright or any other rights or interest in the [Character/Work] and/or any [Licensed Articles] and/or any slogan, logo, trade mark, domain name or in any other medium or format in whole or in part whether directly or indirectly derived from or based on the [Character/Work] and/or any [Licensed Articles] which shall remain with and belong solely to the [Licensor].

C.722

That the [Company] will have cleared and paid for all copyright and any other rights, consents, waivers, releases, clearances or otherwise necessary for the [Company] to grant the [Distributor] and for the [Distributor] to be able to exercise the rights granted under this Agreement.

C.723

The [Licensee] acknowledges that it is solely responsible for all costs incurred in the commercial exploitation of the [Licensed Articles] including development, production, manufacturing, packaging, storage, distribution, supply, selling, advertising, promotion whether incurred as a direct cost or owed to a third party for clearance of any rights of any nature or for services or otherwise.

C.724

The [Purchaser] agrees that the [Designer] shall be entitled to sell, license or exploit the [specify material] and any reproduction in any form at any time throughout the world and no sums or rights shall be due to or acquired by the [Purchaser].

C.725

The [Licensor] shall have obtained an assignment, licence, and/or contractual clearance and/or own all the copyright, computer software rights, database rights, design rights, intellectual property rights, music, lyrics, sound recordings, mechanical and performing rights, and/or other sums to collecting societies, waivers, trade marks, service marks and any other rights and/or interest that may be required for the exploitation of the [Work] by the [Licensee] for the Term of the Agreement. The [Licensor] agrees and undertakes that to date it has paid the sums set out in Schedule [–]. The [Licensee] shall be responsible to pay such additional costs as are set out in Schedule [–].

C.726

Where the [Licensee] grants any sub-licence to a third party then the [Licensee] shall bear the cost of any sums that may fall due arising from the exercise of the rights which have been granted where such sub-licensee fails and/or is unable to pay. The [Licensee] shall ensure that any such sub-licensee is solvent and capable of paying any sums due prior to the conclusion of the Agreement. The [Licensee] shall be responsible for all sums due to the [Licensor] which any sub-licensee fails to pay.

C.727

The [Distributor] agrees and accepts that where new material is created and/or developed in order to produce a new licensed article bearing the [Logo/

434

Name]. That the cost of all copyright clearances and any other intellectual property and/or contractual payments and/or royalties and fees that may be due and/or arise shall be at the [Distributors] cost and expense. That the [Distributor] shall not be entitled to seek to offset, claim and/or recover any sums from [Name] and/or the [Company] and/or to seek to reduce the royalty payments and/or any sums due at any time.

C.728
Where at a later date an additional fee and/or royalty becomes due to a third party which arises from the clearance of any copyright, intellectual property rights, rights of performance, reproduction, resale, mechanical reproduction, transmission and/or broadcast and/or any other form of exploitation in the [Project]. Then it is agreed that the [Licensee] may use up to [number/currency] for that purpose to resolve the matter and set any such sum off against any payments due to the [Licensor]. Provided that any such offset is supported by the supply of documents supporting the sums paid and the reason.

Publishing

C.729
The [Authors] agree that notwithstanding the nature of their individual contributions to the [Work] the copyright and any other rights in all media in the [Work] and the [Artwork] shall belong to the [Authors] jointly and equally during the existence of this Agreement and at any time thereafter.

C.730
The [Author] confirms that the [Work] and the [Photographs] are the sole and original creation of the [Author] and that she is the sole owner of all copyright and any other rights which are assigned under this Agreement to the [Company].

C.731
The [Licensee] agrees to be responsible for the cost of any additional material or photographs that may be required for the [Article/Book/other] and in the event of the creation of any new material shall provide a copy to the [Licensor].

C.732
The [Licensor] confirms that all copyright clearances and consents necessary for the publication of the [Article/Book/Work] have been obtained and have and/or will be paid for by the [Licensor].

C.733

The [Author] warrants that the [Work] will in no way whatsoever give rise to a breach of an existing copyright of a third party or breach of an existing agreement between the [Author] and a third party.

C.734

The [Author] undertakes to obtain and pay for all copyright clearances and consents necessary for the publication of the [Work] including the [Artwork] throughout the [specify countries]. The [Author] agrees to obtain all such clearances and consents in writing and to provide the [Company] with such copies as may be requested.

C.735

The [Ghostwriter] shall keep full and accurate records of all interviews, information and documents relied upon in the [Work] and shall keep film and sound recordings of all meetings and interviews. The [Ghostwriter] shall provide a detailed bibliography of press cuttings, sound recordings, film, video or DVD material, photographs, stills, footage, websites, books and any other archive, family, estates, museums or other sources relied upon or quoted. Together with a report on ownership of copyright, copyright notices, contractual obligations, moral rights, credits, trade marks and the cost of clearance and use of any such material and details of the terms on which it is available.

C.736

The [Publisher] shall pay any copyright fees for the illustrations and/or quotations up to [figure/currency]. Any further sum shall be repaid by the [Author] but deducted by agreement between the parties. In default of such agreement the [Publisher] shall at its discretion be entitled to recoup the additional sum from the advance and/or royalties due to the [Author].

C.737

The [Author] confirms that he has good title and authority to enter into this Agreement and is not bound by any previous agreement which adversely affects this Agreement.

C.738

The [Proprietor] shall use its reasonable endeavours to clear and pay for the exploitation of the [Work] in all media throughout the Territory. In the event that any material cannot be cleared for such use then it shall not be included in the [Work].

C.739

The [Author] agrees that he shall ensure that the [Work] is cleared for publication in respect of the following rights granted to the [Publisher] under this Agreement throughout the world:

1.1   Hardback and paperback books.

1.2   Anthologies and quotations.

1.3   Cassettes or talking books.

1.4   Straight non-dramatic radio and television readings.

1.5   Dramatic adaptations for all forms of television, radio, film, theatre, excluding video.

1.6   Dramatic or non-dramatic adaptations for radio.

1.7   Serialisation in magazines, periodicals or newspapers.

1.8   Hardback and paperback reprints rights and to sub-licence to a third party in that format including large print and educational editions.

1.9   Digest book rights in volume form.

1.10 One shot digest rights to publish an abridgement in a magazine, periodical or newspaper.

1.11 Book club editions licensed or sold to another publisher.

1.12 Merchandising, picture cartoons, electronic or mechanical reproduction in any form.

The [Author] shall only be responsible for the administration of obtaining clearance of any copyright or consents in respect of the publication of the [Work] in the [specify countries] and shall bear the cost of the payments for those uses in Clause [–] listed above. Whilst the [Author] shall use his best endeavours to arrange for the clearance of all such material for any other use the payment for any costs that may be incurred or become due shall be the sole responsibility of the [Publisher] and the [Author] shall not be liable for any such sums. All such clearances, consents and payments shall be limited to the period of the duration in which the rights in the [Work] are granted to the [Publisher].

C.740

The [Author] agrees that he/she shall bear the cost and responsibility of obtaining all consents, clearances and copyright in any material included in the [Work] including, but not limited to, quotations, photographs, references, drawings, tables, index and titles in respect of the rights granted to the [Publisher] in this Agreement for the publication of the [Work] in hardback and paperback in the United Kingdom, and the serialisation of [Work] in a magazine or newspaper. The [Author] shall not be under any obligation to clear any other rights in the [Work]. In the event that any further additional rights in the [Work] are granted to the [Publisher] at a later date then it is agreed that the obtaining of and payment for any further clearances, consents and copyright shall be the responsibility of the [Publisher] and that the [Author] shall not be liable or have any such sums deducted from his royalties.

C.741

The [Interviewee] confirms that he owns or controls all copyright and any other rights in the [Photographs] and that the supply by the [Interviewee] and the publication of the [Photographs] in the [newspaper/magazine/other] throughout the Territory will not infringe the copyright of any other rights of any third party and will not expose the [Publisher] to any civil or criminal proceedings.

C.742

The [Publisher] confirms that it shall bear the cost of any copyright or other consent payments for the use of any material which is owned or controlled by a third party which is incorporated in the [Article] and the [Interviewee] shall not be liable for any such payments.

C.743

The [Author] confirms that the [Work] and the [Artwork] are the sole and original creation of the [Author] and that he/she is the sole owner of all copyright and any other rights in the [Work] and the [Artwork] which are granted under this Agreement.

C.744

The [Author] undertakes to obtain all copyright clearances and other consents necessary for the publication of the [Work] including artwork and photographs throughout the Territory in respect of the rights granted in this Agreement. All such clearances and consents shall be obtained in writing and provided to the [Publisher]. The [Publisher] agrees that all sums to be paid in respect of such clearances and consents shall be at the [Publisher's] cost up to a maximum of [figure/currency].

C.745

The [Author] confirms that the [specify rights] have not been previously licensed or otherwise exploited in any form throughout the [specify countries] except as disclosed in writing to the [Publisher], a copy of which is attached to and forms part of this Agreement.

C.746

The [Author] undertakes to obtain and pay for all copyright clearances and consents necessary for the publication of the [Work] including the Artwork throughout the Territory for the duration of the Licence Period. The [Author] agrees to obtain all such clearances and consents in writing and to provide the [Publisher] with such copies as may be requested. The [Publisher] shall reimburse the [Author] upon receipt of an invoice for all sums due in respect of obtaining by the [Author] and the grant by third parties of the cost and expense of all such clearances and consents in respect of the rights granted under this Agreement.

C.747

The [Publisher] confirms that it shall be solely responsible for and bear the cost of all intellectual property rights including copyright, trade marks, service marks, logos, designs, slogans, text, artwork, title, graphics, computer generated material and all other consents, moral rights, endorsements, sponsorship, contractual obligations due and/or arising to any third party on or in respect of the [Articles] and/or any packaging, promotions, advertising or marketing.

C.748

The [Author] provides no undertaking as to the originality, copyright and intellectual property position, any claims by any third party or the legal position in any country as regards the [Work/Article]. Any publication, reproduction, distribution and exploitation shall be entirely at the [Publishers] own risk and expense and no claim for any sums due shall be made by the [Publisher] against the [Author] at any time.

C.749

1.1   The [Author] agrees that he/she shall not supply to the [Publisher] any work in any form which he/she represents as the original work of the [Author] which in fact is derived from and/or and/ or is sourced from a third parties book, website, article and/or other material.

1.2   The [Author] agrees that he/she shall provide a credit and/or copyright notice to any such third party where a story, the chronology of a series of events and/or any descriptive words and/or extracts of any length are copied, reproduced used and/or adapted.

C.750

Where the majority of the material supplied by the [Author] to the [Company] is later found to be attributed to another person and/or the [Author] has not provided their true name. Then the [Company] reserves the right to terminate this Agreement and no further sums shall be due to the [Author] and/or his/her agent including those sums which may be due and/or owed. The [Company] shall be entitled to seek to be repaid all sums paid to the [Author] up to the date of termination together with interest and legal costs.

439

Purchase and Supply of Products

C.751
The [Company] does not warrant that the importation, sales or distribution or use of [Products] will not infringe any patent rights, design rights or any other intellectual property rights of any third party. The [Company] shall not be responsible for or under any liability to the [Purchaser] in respect thereof.

C.752
It shall be the [Customers] responsibility to obtain and pay for a licence from [collecting society] or a society connected with it for the use of the [Film/DVD/Video] on their business premises.

C.753
The [Company] confirms that it is the sole owner of or controls all copyright, design rights, trade marks and logos and any other rights and/or interest in the [Company] and the [Company's] Products throughout the world.

C.754
The [Company] confirms that the [Company] and the [Company's] Products including any trade marks, logo, title, artwork, discs, packaging and any developments or variations provided by the [Company] under this Agreement do not and will not contain any material which infringes the copyright, design rights, intellectual property rights or any other rights of any third party in the [Territory].

C.755
The [Supplier] confirms that it is the sole owner of or controls all copyright, design rights, trade marks, service marks, and any other rights in the [Product], the [Supplier's Logo] and any associated packaging, advertising or other material throughout the [specify countries] except as disclosed in writing to the [Seller].

C.756
The [Seller] agrees and undertakes that the following details are true and accurate and that it is the owner and/or controls all rights and interest in:

1.1   The Domain Name [specify].

1.2   The Seller's Website [specify].

1.3   The main business address [specify].

C.757
The [Seller] confirms that the selling process and dealings with the public will conform in all material respects with all relevant legislation, regulations,

directives, standards, practices and codes of conduct (voluntary or otherwise) in [United Kingdom/European Union], or otherwise in the [world/ Territory].

C.758
The [Seller] agrees that any modification, variation, adaptation or development of the [Product] and/or the [Supplier's Logo] and/or any logo, service mark, trade mark or similar image, text, icon, slogan, sound or sound effects, music, graphics or otherwise identifying, associated with or otherwise developed directly relating to the [Supplier] on the [Seller's website] and/or any other material of any nature created or commissioned by the [Seller]. All such material shall be the property of the [Supplier] and the [Seller] shall use its best endeavours to ensure that any necessary documentation is concluded by the [Seller] to confirm or transfer ownership to the [Supplier] at the [Supplier's] cost and expense.

C.759
In respect of the [Commissioned Work] the [Assignor] undertakes that all copyright and any other rights including consents and moral rights shall be cleared and paid for in respect of the rights assigned under this Agreement.

C.760
The [Assignee] shall be entirely liable for and pay the costs of the [specify work] and the [Assignor] shall not be responsible for any such costs or sums.

C.761
The [Product/Service/other] is supplied to the [Customer] with labels, packaging and leaflets which explains the ownership of the intellectual property rights in any material. There is no permission, licence or rights given by the [Company] or its representatives which seeks to give you consent to reproduce, interfere with, supply, distribute or exploit the material in any manner except for your own [personal/commercial] use at in [residential/ business] premises.

C.762

1.1 The [Artist] agrees supply an original and new logo for [Name] for his/ her new business for a fee of [number/currency] by [date] subject to delivery of the artwork by [date] to [Name].

1.2 The [Artist] shall deliver the artwork of the logo in [format] together with all draft drawings, reproductions and other copies. The [Artist] shall only keep one copy for personal and archive reasons and not for commercial use and/or exploitation.

1.3   In consideration of the fee in 1.1 the [Artist] assigns to [Name] all copyright and intellectual property rights and the right to register the logo as a trade mark throughout the world in all media and in all mediums and to use, exploit, adapt and reproduce the logo and to sub-licence others to do so at any time and for the full period of copyright and in perpetuity without limit.

1.4   The [Artist] agrees that he/she shall not be entitled to any additional fee, royalty, payment and/or sum for any exploitation, registration and/or use whether known now and/or created at a later date.

1.5   The [Artist] waives all rights to be identified either by a copyright notice, credit and/or any moral rights and agrees and accepts that the logo may be distorted, adapted and varied entirely as [Name] thinks fit and no consent and/or approval of the [Artist] shall be required nor shall any additional payments and/or sums be due.

C.763

1.1   The [Supplier] shall be responsible for all clearances, consents, design, patent, copyright and performance and reproduction payments and any other fees that may be due to any third party and/or collecting society for the design, development, production, manufacture, distribution, sale, supply and marketing and promotion of the [Product] and its packaging by the [Company] in [country] from [date] during the term of this Agreement.

1.2   The [Company] agrees to notify the [Supplier] in the event of any allegation and/or claim being brought to its attention in respect of 1.1 above.

1.3   The [Company] agrees that where the [Supplier] decides to change, adapt, alter and/or delete any part of any material as a result of a decision by the [Supplier]. That the [Company] shall assist the [Supplier] and at the [Suppliers'] cost add, remove and/or delete material provided that such actions would not create a threat of criminal and/or civil proceedings against the [Company] for any reason.

Services

C.764

The [Contributor] assigns to the [Company] all present and future copyright and any other rights in all media in the product of his services and any material created under this Agreement throughout the world, outer space and the universe for the full period of copyright and any extensions or renewals. All media shall include, but not be limited to television, DVD, video, radio, publishing, telephones and telecommunications, internet, merchandising and computer software.

C.765
The [Company] agrees that all rights not specifically assigned to the [Company] are reserved by [Name].

C.766
The [Record Company] acknowledges that the [Artist] shall retain all copyright in any original [Musical Work] including any associated lyrics or arrangement owned or controlled or created by the [Artist] whether in existence or created during the Term of this Agreement and whether incorporated in the [Sound Recordings] or not.

C.767
The [Presenter] hereby gives all necessary consents to the [Company] as follows:

1.1 To take or make directly or indirectly by any means any photographs, images, films, sound or other recordings of the [Presenter].

1.2 To use or authorise the use of the [Presenter's] name, photographs and other reproductions of the [Presenter] and the autograph and biography of the [Presenter] either in whole or part in direct relation to the advertisement, publicity, exhibition and commercial exploitation of the product of the [Presenter's] services. The [Company] shall whenever practicable and reasonable consult with the [Presenter] prior to such use and authorisation. The [Company] shall not without the approval of the [Presenter] use or authorise the use of the [Presenter's] name, photograph, film, sound or other recordings of the [Presenter] for the endorsement of any product and/or other company.

C.768
In consideration of the [Presenter's Fee] the [Presenter] assigns to the [Company] all present and future copyright and any other rights in all media throughout the world [and universe] in the product of her services and any other material created for the purpose of this Agreement for the full period of copyright and any extensions and/or renewals and/or other developments including, but not limited to photographs, films, sound or other recordings, advertisements, scripts, computer generated material, articles, interviews, slogans, icons, graphics, DVDs, website and internet related material, merchandising, telephone competitions, messaging or promotions, advertising and marketing material.

443

C.769

The [Presenter] agrees that any intellectual property of any kind including, but not limited to copyright, design rights, service marks, trade marks, logos, inventions, titles, formats, slogans, property rights and any other rights held by the [Company] or which are created or developed in conjunction with the services of the [Presenter] under this Agreement, shall be the sole and exclusive property of the [Company]. The [Presenter] shall not acquire any rights or interest nor does this Agreement purport to grant, transfer or assign any rights in the product of the services to the [Presenter].

C.770

The [Contributor] agrees that the [Company] shall be entitled to assign, transfer, sub-license or otherwise exploit any product of the services of the [Contributor] created under this Agreement. The [Contributor] agrees on request to execute and sign any other documents which may be required at a later date to effect the assignment to the [Company] or third party provided that the [Company] pays all reasonable expenses incurred by the [Contributor].

C.771

The [Artist] agrees that his consent as may be required under the [Copyright, Designs and Patents Act 1988] is provided by this Agreement for the purpose of the exercise of the rights [assigned/granted] to the [Company] and any sub-licensee or distributor under this Agreement.

C.772

The [Manager] acknowledges that he is not acquiring any copyright, intellectual property rights or domain names or any other rights in any material, work or services owned or controlled by the [Group] or any of its members individually including any rights in any musical works, lyrics, or arrangement, manuscript, book, article, photographs, images, logo, trade mark, ringtone or otherwise whether in existence prior to this Agreement or created at any time during the Term of this Agreement.

C.773

The [Agent] acknowledges that he is not acquiring any copyright or any other rights in any material owned or controlled by the [Artiste] or in the name of the [Artiste] and any goodwill and reputation created in respect of any trade mark, business name, logo, slogan, or image or otherwise which shall remain the sole property of the [Artiste]. No part of this Agreement is intended to transfer, grant or vest any such rights in the [Agent] whether in existence prior to this Agreement or created at any time thereafter.

C.774
At the end of the agreement the [Agent] agrees to transfer any copyright in the advertising, marketing and promotional material relating to the [Artiste] under the Agreement provided that the [Artiste] shall pay the sum of [figure/currency].

C.775
Subject to the [Performing Rights] in the [Work] being held by the [Performing Rights Society] the [Author] confirms that the [Work] is the original creation of the [Author] and that he is the sole owner of or controls all copyright and any other rights in the [Work] which are assigned under this Agreement.

C.776
The [Contributor] agrees that such present and future copyright as may exist in the product of the [Contributor's Work] provided to the [Company] during the course of this Agreement is hereby assigned solely and exclusively to the [Company] for the full period of copyright and any extensions and renewals throughout the [Territory]. The [Contributor] shall not acquire any rights or interest of any nature whether originated by the [Contributor] or not.

C.777
The [Contributor] acknowledges that such copyright and any other rights of any nature as may exist now or in the future with respect to any element of the [website/business/product/other] shall belong absolutely to the [Company].

C.778
The [Licensor] confirms that the [Musical Work] shall be his original creation and that he shall be the sole owner of or control all copyright and any other rights in the [Musical work] which are granted under this Agreement.

C.779
The [Originator] confirms that he is the original creator and sole owner of or controls all copyright, design rights, computer software, domain names, logos, trade marks, service, marks, formats and any other rights or interest in the product of his services to the [Company] under this Agreement excluding any information or material supplied by or included at the request of the [Company].

C.780
In consideration of the [fee] the [Name] agrees to assign to the [Company] all the product which is created arising out of his services under this Agreement whether in existence now or created in the future in all media throughout the [Territory] for the full period of copyright and any extensions or renewals and ownership and control shall pass entirely to the [Company] including but not

limited to documents, films, sound recordings, photographs, images, logos, slogans, music, advertising, marketing, merchandising, website banners and other material, icons, text, messaging, sounds, ringtones, computer software, formats, inventions and innovative ideas. The [Company] shall not acquire any rights or interest in any material, goodwill, products, trade marks or any other rights or interest in which copyright or other rights are already owned or controlled by the [Name] prior to [date] which is supplied under this Agreement including photographs, documents, biography and books, slogans, name and business names including [specify].

C.781

The [Company] agrees that it shall not be entitled to exploit any of the product of the services of the [Name] outside the [Engagement Period] or in any other media without the negotiation and settlement of additional payments to [Name] for each type, method and length of exploitation. Both parties shall use their reasonable endeavours to reach agreement in good faith. Failure to do so shall result in the material not being exploited at any time and destroyed by the [Company] within [one year].

C.782

The [Company] agrees that this Agreement only relates to the provision of the services by [Name] for the [Engagement Period]. The [Company] does not acquire any rights, interest, option or other right to exploit any other works of the [Name].

C.783

The [Agent] agrees that all copyright and any other rights in the [Work] in all media throughout the world whether in existence now or created in the future and any associated title, artwork, developments or adaptations are and shall remain the sole property of the [Name] and the [Agent] shall not acquire any rights, nor represent that he owns such rights nor attempt to register any ownership. That any advice, guidance, contribution or otherwise by the [Agent] shall be in the role of adviser and shall not give rise to any claim for joint authorship with [Name] and any such rights are waived by the [Agent] and shall be transferred to [Name].

C.784

The [Agent] shall ensure that all third parties who are licensed, appointed, engaged or involved in the exploitation of the [Work] shall not acquire any rights or interest in the [Work] other than those specifically set out in the Agreement. The [Agent] shall at his cost ensure that any necessary documentation is executed to ensure an assignment to the [Name] by third parties of any rights that may be created in any reproductions, developments, adaptations or associated packaging, products, marketing and advertising.

C.785

The [Manager] acknowledges that he is not acquiring any copyright or any other rights in any name, logos, trade mark, image, photographs, or slogan or any other material owned or controlled by the [Name].

C.786

The [Company] agrees that all copyright, design rights and any other rights in the product of the services provided by the [Creator] excluding any material provided by the [Company] shall remain the sole and exclusive property of the [Creator] and this Agreement does not purport to assign, grant or transfer any rights to the [Company].

C.787

The [Company] and the [Creator] agree that any material arising from the services of the [Creator] shall only be used by the [Company] for the following specific purposes [–].

In the event that the [Company] wishes to use any material for any other purpose then the prior written consent of the [Creator] shall be required and an additional fee paid in each case on terms to be agreed between the parties.

C.788

The [Company] agrees that the [Creator] shall be able to [use/refer to] the material created under this Agreement as follows [specify] provided that all confidential information is deleted and all material supplied by the [Company].

C.789

There is no agreement or consent provided by either party to this Agreement to assign, transfer or vest any rights in the other party. Each party shall continue to own and control all material, rights and interest it held prior to entering into this Agreement and any others which it may create, develop or invent in the future at any time.

C.790

1.1 [Name] agrees to provide his services to the [Distributor] for the purpose of developing, creating and writing new [financial/marketing/ promotional] content for the website, blog, app and corporate material of the [Distributor].

1.2 The [Distributor] agrees that all the products, data, information and background material for the work is being supplied by the [Distributor] and/or obtained from third parties who are suppliers, customers, advisors, employees and/or consultants of the [Distributor].

1.3 The [Distributor] agrees and undertakes that it shall not be the responsibility of [Name] to verify the accuracy of any such material in 1.1 and 1.2 nor to seek any documents to be signed for the purpose of copyright and/or other consents prior to publication and/or reproduction by the [Distributor]. Nor shall the [Distributor] seek to hold [Name] liable at any time and the [Distributor] agrees that it shall use any such material at its own risk and cost. That the [Distributor] shall have the sole discretion whether to use any such material and to decide whether to have a legal assessment and report conducted on any material.

C.791

The [Consultant] agrees that where he/she provides a written report to the [Company] in respect of any [Project]. That where in any part of a report the material is not the original work of the [Consultant] and has been derived from and/or adapted from any work of a third party in any medium whether it is out of copyright and/or not attributed to a known person . In any such case the [Consultant] shall provide such detailed information as to permit the [Company] to view and access that other third party source directly.

Sponsorship

C.792

The [Sponsor] confirms that it is the sole owner of or controls all copyright and any other rights in the [Sponsor's Logo] and the [Sponsor's Product] and that any use of them by [Name] under this Agreement will not expose it to criminal or civil proceedings in [country].

C.793

[Name] acknowledges and undertakes that all copyright and any other rights in the [Sponsor's Logo] and the [Sponsor's Product] together with any goodwill shall belong to and remain the sole property of the [Sponsor]. [Name] shall not acquire any rights or interests in the [Sponsor's Logo] or the [Sponsor's Product] including any trade mark, service mark, design, logo, title, artwork, banner advertisement, links, icons, text messaging, invention, computer software and any developments, variations or representations of any nature.

C.794

The [Sponsor] confirms that it is the sole owner of or controls and will have paid for and cleared all copyright, consents, releases, trade marks, logos, service marks, designs, slogans, title, artwork, music, graphics, computer generated material throughout the Territory in the [Sponsor's Logo] and any other material supplied by the [Sponsor] under this Agreement.

C.795

The [Company] agrees that all rights, copyright, consents, releases, waivers, insurance, music or other material or costs of any nature [except the Sponsor's Product] and the [Sponsor's Logo] in respect of the [Event/ Festival/other] shall be arranged, cleared and paid for by the [Company].

C.796

The [Licensee] agrees that it shall be solely responsible for all costs and expenses incurred in reproducing and incorporating the [Licensor's Logo] in the [Product Package].

C.797

The [Sponsor] agrees to bear the cost all clearances, consents, waivers, releases, trading, alcohol, licences, agreement, reproduction, marketing, advertising, health and safety compliance and certificates, administration and legal costs and expenses that may be incurred by the [Company] or any third party appointed by them in using the [Sponsors Logo] and [Products] for the [Film/Event/other] whether this involves trade or government bodies, local authorities, television companies, owners of premises, other sponsors or advertisers or any other person, body or company.

C.798

The [Sponsor] shall not be liable for any cost and/or expenses incurred by the [Company] in respect of the clearance, acquisition, buyout, agreement and/or insurance for any music, artists, presenters, locations, facilities, and/ or any other third parties and/or services and/or any payments due to any collecting societies for [Event] and/or the exploitation of the rights in any part of the world at any time.

C.799

The [Sponsor] shall ensure that any copyright, intellectual property rights, design rights, trademarks, service marks, titles, slogans, products, clothes, and other material supplied by the [Sponsor] to [Name] are owned and/or controlled by the [Sponsor] for use by [Name]. That [Name] shall not be responsible and/or liable for any sums which have not been and/or may be due in respect of any such rights, material and/or other interests which shall be at the [Sponsors'] cost.

C.800

1.1 Where the [Sponsor] uses a specific sound recording, music and/ or lyrics and/or jingle with their products, logos, names and brands which they intend to use and perform at the [Event] and to authorise third parties and the [Distributor] to reproduce and broadcast and/

449

or transmit and/or exploit. It shall be the sole responsibility of the [Sponsor] to ensure that the [Sponsor] is legally entitled to do so and has the authority and consent of all parties who have created, played, contributed to, performed and written and/or who control and/or own such copyright and other intellectual property rights in any format including any licences required and/or payments to any collecting societies.

1.2   The [Sponsor] shall provide such evidence as may be required and requested by the [Distributor] and their legal advisors to establish any such matters in 1.1 have been dealt with and that there is no risk of legal action against the [Distributor] and/or any associated partner for the [Event].

1.3   The [Sponsor] agrees that where it fails to justify any use of any material at any time then the [Distributor] may insist that any part of any material in 1.1 may be omitted and/or deleted and/or adapted in any manner the [Distributor] thinks fit in the circumstances.

University, Library and Educational

C.801
The [Company/Author] confirms that it is the original creator and sole owner of or controls all copyright, design rights, computer software, domain names, logos, trade marks, service marks, formats and any other intellectual property rights or interest in the product of its services to the [Institute] under this Agreement excluding any information or material supplied by or included at the request of the [Institute].

C.802
The [Author] acknowledges and undertakes that he is not acquiring any copyright or any other intellectual property rights in any copyright, design rights, patent, computer software, image, text, film, sound recordings, data, name, logos, trade mark, photographs, or slogan or any other material owned or controlled by the [Institute] or any third party. Further that where the [Author] makes any contribution, development or other adaptation of any material to any work as part of any project and any rights are created to the [Author]. The [Author] agrees and undertakes to assign all rights in all media to the [Institute] without any additional payment and to sign such documents as the [Institute] may require in order to establish ownership.

C.803
The [Company] agrees that this Agreement does not purport to assign, grant or transfer any rights to the [Company] whether based on original material which exists prior to the date of this Agreement held by the [Institute] and/

or created under this Agreement. Nor shall the [Company] be authorised to exploit, license, supply and/or distribute any information, data and/or material without the prior written consent of the [Institute] under a separate licence.

C.804

In consideration of the [Consultant's Fee] the [Consultant] assigns to the [Institute] all present and future copyright and any other rights in all media throughout the world and universe in the product of her services and any other material created for the purpose of this Agreement for the full period of copyright and any extensions and/or renewals and/or other developments including, but not limited to all reports, text, data, photographs, films, sound or other recordings, advertisements, computer generated material, computer software, slogans, logos, icons, graphics, merchandising, databases, promotional and marketing material.

C.805

The [Consultant] agrees to draw up a list of material in her possession or under her control which relates to the [Project] at any time when requested to do so by the [Institute]. The [Consultant] shall itemise and describe each type of material and specify the contact details of the parties who own the copyright and other intellectual property rights of any such material.

C.806

The [Researcher] shall not be expected to identify and report on the ownership of any material where no original author can be attributed to a work and any such work shall be listed as an unknown and/or orphan work.

C.807

1.1 The [Consultant] shall not be liable for the accuracy and/or contents of those parts of the [Report] which are based on information, data, records, documents, translations, tests and/or computer analysis and statistics supplied by the [Institute] and/or commissioned by them from a third party and/or interviews and/or market surveys and/or any other material of any nature which is not the original work of the [Consultant].

1.2 The [Consultant] agrees to highlight material where 1.1 shall be relevant, but cannot ensure that this is done in every case. Where in the opinion of the [Consultant] the [Report] cannot in any sense be approved by him/her then the [Consultant] reserves the right to remove his/her name but shall still be paid for the production of the [Report].

451

COPYRIGHT NOTICE

DVD, Video and Discs

C.808

The [Sub-Licensee] agrees and undertakes that all [DVDs/Videos/other] of the [Film] and all artwork, labels, packaging, advertising, and marketing material relating thereto shall be subject to the following terms:

1.1 That all such products and material shall be produced, manufactured, supplied, sold, rented, made available and distributed in accordance with all applicable international, EU and national legislation, directives, regulations, policies and practices.

1.2 That all products and material shall include on every copy all intellectual property, trade mark, and copyright symbols and/or words necessary to protect the rights of the [Licensor] [and the Copyright Owner] shall be included on any such products and material. That the [Sub-Licensee] will agree in advance with the [Licensor] on each occasion which copyright notices, trade marks, logos, text and warnings should be used. So that the ownership of any material, trade marks and content is asserted in a clear and prominent position, the contractual obligations of the [Licensor] to third parties are complied with and there is a warning that the public is not allowed to copy, transfer, to download or send or arrange transmission by any means.

C.809

The [Distributor] confirms that it will own, control or will obtain such consents, licences and clearances from any third party in respect of any trade mark, service mark, copyright notice, logos, images, text, credits, film, recordings, music, lyrics, computer generated material, persons or material that the [Distributor] shall decide to include in the [DVD/Video/other] and any packaging, extracts, promotional or marketing material at the [Distributors] cost. That [Name] shall not be liable for any such sums or the costs of any disputes or legal proceedings that may arise. The [Distributor] shall not be entitled to deduct any such sums from the advances, royalties or other sums due to [Name] and that it shall be the sole responsibility of the [Distributor] to organise, comply with and bear the cost of all such sums, expenses and legal fees.

C.810

The [Licensee] agrees and undertakes to ensure that:

1.1 All copyright notices, credits, trade marks, service marks, designs, logos and moral rights in the [Film] and in any packaging, advertising, publicity or promotional material notified by the [Licensor] with the [Film Material] shall be transmitted or incorporated as required by the [Licensor].

1.2   That it shall not delete, change, or alter the position, size, order or fail to transmit any of the matters in 1.1 in the exploitation of the [Television Rights/DVD/other] Rights in the [Film] or parts or any associated material.

1.3   That where an error, omission, or other failure to comply arises that the [Licensee] shall use its [best/reasonable] endeavours to comply with the requests of the [Licensor] to remedy the position.

C.811

The parties agree that they shall follow the [Universal Copyright Convention] in respect of the notification of claim to copyright and ownership of the [Work]. From the time of first publication all copies of the [Work] published with the authority of the [Author] or copyright owner shall bear the symbol © accompanied by the name of the copyright owner, the year of first publication placed in such manner as to give reasonable notice of claim of copyright. The parties agree that the copyright notice shall be as follows [specify].

C.812

[Name] agrees that the position, size, prominence, order and whether to include any credit, copyright notice, logo, trade mark, service mark, disclaimer, warning or otherwise in the [Film], [DVD/other] and any extracts, packaging, marketing, advertisements, CD Rom, CD, or internet or website material or otherwise of any nature shall be entirely at the discretion of the [Company]. That [Name] shall not have the right to any recognition or acknowledgement and has waived all such claims in respect of the exercise of the rights by the [Company] under this Agreement.

C.813

Copyright © [Company] [year]. Manufactured and distributed by [Name] under license from [Company]. All rights reserved.

C.814

Produced by [specify] [website reference] [year] [Company] under exclusive licence to [specify name] of [specify name] Group.

All rights of the manufacturer and the owner of the work produced are reserved.

Unauthorised reproduction, copying, hiring, lending, public performance, broadcasting, transmission, and uploading to the internet and/or other files is prohibited.

C.815

All rights reserved [and may not be reproduced and/or duplicated in any format]

Made in [country]

Software [year-year] [specify name] [trade mark name] are trade marks or registered trade marks of [–]

Published and distributed by [specify name and logo]

Software exclusively licensed to [specify name and logo]

C.816

© [year] [Company] All rights reserved

© [year] layout and design [name] All rights reserved

For home use only. Do not duplicate

C.817

Film © [year] [Company] All rights reserved

Label Design and Artwork © [year] [Name] All rights reserved

[DVD/Disc] Logo is a trade mark of [name]

Not for rental this [DVD/Disc] is for retail sale to the public for private use only

Copyright warning [specify].

C.818

© [year] [Company] Licensed and distributed by [Name].

All rights reserved. For promotional use only not for sale. Copyright Warning [specify].

C.819

The [Licensee] undertakes to ensure that:

1.1   A copyright notice and registered trade mark notice, logo image and title to the [Licensor] and any other third party requested by the [Licensor] shall be as follows [specify] which is to be reproduced on all copies of the [Licensed Product] in the size, manner and form and position set out in Appendix A.

1.2   No other copyright notice, trade mark notice, logo, image and title and/or claim of ownership and/or any interest is to be permitted and/or reproduced except for the [Licensee] as follows [specify] which is to be reproduced on all copies of the [Licensed Product] in the size, manner and form and position set out in Appendix B.

1.3 That all labels, packaging sleeves and boxes, posters, banners, catalogues, online images and text on any website and/or the internet, any printed promotional and/or marketing material and associated merchandise, all advertisements and any other material in any medium and/or form used to exploit the rights granted under this Agreement shall bear the copyright notice and registered trade mark notice and any logo, image and title specified in 1.1.

1.4 That neither the [Licensee] nor any unauthorised third party shall be entitled and/or permitted to add to, delete from, adapt and/or vary any part of the copyright notice and registered trade mark notice and any logo, image and title specified in 1.1.

1.5 Where the [Licensor] discovers that there has been a breach of any of the above terms and conditions. That the [Licensee] shall withdraw all such material as the [Licensor] may request immediately and take such steps as the [Licensor] may stipulate to resolve the matter at the [Licensee's] cost.

C.820

[Name] agrees and accepts to waive all copyright and intellectual property rights and all rights to any copyright notice and/or other credit and all moral rights in any country in the world in the [Film] and/or any part and/or any sound recording, performance, interview and/or any packaging, marketing and/or other material which may be created, developed, produced and/or distributed by the [Company] at any time whether such rights exist now and/or come into existence by new technology and/or laws.

Film and Television

C.821

The [Licensee] agrees to provide the following copyright notice, credit, trade mark, service mark, logo and image to the [Licensor] in any advertising, publicity, promotional and packaging material in respect of the marketing and distribution of the [Film]. The [Licensee] agrees to provide the [Licensor] with copies and samples of any advertising, publicity, promotional and packaging material in respect of the exploitation of the [Film] at the [Licensee's] cost.

C.822

Both parties agree that the following copyright notice shall be used in respect of the [Film] and in respect of all material in any media directly arising from the exploitation of any rights therein [specify and attach sample].

C.823

The [Distributor] agrees to acknowledge by suitable legend the ownership of any copyrights in any such material they may use provided that the [Licensor] shall have so advised the [Distributor] in writing.

C.824

The [Consultant] shall not be entitled to any credit or acknowledgement unless he appears in sound or vision in which case the following credit shall appear in the [Series] [name] [on screen/at the end of each film]. The [Consultant] agrees that the position, size, order and whether it is included in any marketing and promotional material shall be entirely the [Company's] decision.

C.825

The [Company] agrees to provide the following on screen credit and copyright notice, [trade mark/logo/image] to the [Author] in the [Film] and in any packaging, publicity, promotional, advertising and any other material of any nature in respect of any marketing and exploitation of the [Film] in any media [–]. A copy of which is attached and forms part of this Agreement.

C.826

The [Licensee] agrees and acknowledges that it shall use and shall not delete the credits, copyright notices, moral rights, trade marks, service marks, logos, titles or otherwise set out in Schedule [–] which is attached and forms part of this Agreement. Except that the failure to broadcast or transmit any item listed due to unexpected lack of air time, failure of facilities or other unforeseen circumstances shall not be a breach of this Agreement provided that reasonable endeavours had been made to comply.

C.827

© [Name] and [Name] [year]. All rights reserved

The copyright [Owner/Company] has licensed the [Picture/Film] [including the soundtrack] contained in this [DVD/VHS/Disc] to [Distributor]

[Cover/label/package design] © [year] [Distributor/other]

C.828

© [Company] [year]. All rights reserved

Manufactured, sold and distributed by [Distributor]

C.829

© [Name] and [Name] in the [Book/Character] [year of publication]

[Company] in the [Film] © [year of release/other]

Manufactured and distributed under License by [Distributor] in [language] in [countries]

© [Name] in the label, cover, packaging and marketing material [year]

C.830

© Copyright [specify copyright owner] [year]

C.831

The parties agree the following credits and copyright notice for the [Series]:

1.1   Based on a book entitled [specify] by [Author]

1.2   Adapted by [Writer] in collaboration with [specify]

1.3   Translated by [specify]

1.4   Music and lyrics by [specify]

1.5   Orchestration and sound recording by [specify]

1.6   Produced by [specify]

1.7   Director [specify]

1.8   Special effects and animation by [specify]

1.9   Costumes [specify]

1.10 Equipment [specify]

1.11 Performance of songs and singing [specify]

1.12 Cast [specify]

1.13 Locations [specify]

1.14 Editing [specify]

1.15 Lighting [specify]

1.16 Animals and livestock [specify]

1.17 Production Company [specify]

1.18 Television Company [specify]

1.19 Distribution Company [specify]

1.20 [other].

C.832

1.1   It is agreed that the parties shall agree at a later the exact details of the copyright notices, credits, trademarks, logos and images that shall be reproduced at the end of the [Film] and/or any other material in any medium. The parties agree that as far as possible they shall all receive an equal and proportionate allocation of space and duration in each case.

1.2   That as a minimum no material shall be released in any form unless it bears the following copyright notice and credit to [Name] and the [Company] as follows [specify].

1.3   That where the parties disagree as to the exact form of any copyright notices, credits, trade marks, logos and images to be used and/or reproduced that any dispute shall be resolved by mediation at the [Company's] cost.

General Business and Commercial

C.833
The [Licensee] agrees to acknowledge by suitable words, credit or copyright notice the ownership of any copyright in any material in the [Work] provided that the [Licensor] shall advise the [Licensee] in writing of the conditions required to be fulfilled.

C.834
The [Company] requests the following copyright notice in the following form and style [–] on all copies of any material based on the [specify material].

C.835
All copyright in [item] is owned or controlled by [full company name/ individual] [contact details]. You are permitted to use the material for [private research/specify] but any other use requires written permission and payment of a [fee] and agreement to provide the following copyright notice: © [year of first publication] [name of copyright owner].

C.836
The [Assignee] agrees to provide and observe the copyright notices, credits, moral rights and contractual obligations regarding, size, order, position and prominence and any applicable other conditions to third parties in respect of the [Work] and the [Material] notified to the [Assignee] by the [Assignor].

C.837
The [Researcher] agrees that he/she shall not be entitled to any credit, copyright notice or other acknowledgment in respect of the work provided under this Agreement whether original material created by the [Researcher] or not.

C.838
© [Name] [year]

C.839
© [Name] of the [Title/text/slogans/quotes] [year]–[year]

© [Name] of the [Artwork/graphics/images/photographs] [year]

© [Name] of the [Film/computer generated material/sound recordings/format] [year]

Manufactured under License from [specify] by [Name] Distributed by [Name] under the Brand [specify]

C.840
It shall not be a justifiable reason for the termination of this Agreement in the event that a copyright notice and/or trade mark and/or logo is not reproduced in the exact form stipulated and agreed and/or is omitted and/or altered in some way in the course of the exploitation of the [Work/Product]. Provided that the [Licensee] takes all reasonable steps to mitigate the damage and agrees to pay the [Licensor] a reasonable sum in compensation.

C.841

1.1 The [Company] agrees and undertakes that it shall not represent and/or convey the impression in any way in any marketing, promotion and/or advertising that it holds and/or controls the copyright, intellectual property rights and/or any other rights in the [Work/Service].

1.2 The [Company] agrees and undertakes that where it makes reference to the [Work/Service] in any manner that the following words and statement shall appear [specify]. Further that where an extract of the [Work/Service] is used that the following copyright notice, credit, trade mark notice, slogan, logo and image shall also be positioned with that extract:[specify].

Internet and Websites

C.842
This [Website/Material] was originally created and exploited in [year] by [name of business] the copyright owner. The contents are regularly updated and revised and the copyright owner remains the same. You are permitted to use this material for your own personal [non-commercial] use and to copy and print the information. In the event that you wish to commercially exploit any material of any nature then contact [email/address] for clearance and details of copyright fees that may be due.

C.843

© [Name] [year of release/publication/other] [Name] All Rights Reserved.

C.844

Copyright [Company] is a wholly owned subsidiary of [Parent Company] © [year] – [year] held by [Company].

C.845

Copyright Database and Index © [Name] [year].

C.846

Index and Taxonomy © [Company/Author] [year-year]

C.847

Copyright Notice. The contents of these pages are © [name] [year – year].

C.848

Copyright © [year] [Company] a division of [specify]. All Rights Reserved.

C.849

All contents are protected by copyright and owned, controlled or licensed to the [Company] © [year-year] [Company]. This notice applies to the whole site and where material is owned by third parties a separate notice or warning will appear.

C.850

All contents are the property of [Name] unless otherwise stated or represented. © [Name] [year].

C.851

Copyright, intellectual property rights, computer software, databases, codes, passwords and any other material which is on this [Website] known as [Trading Name] is owned, controlled and distributed by [Name] under the [Trading Name]. Overall copyright ownership of the [Website] is held by [Name] in [country]. There is material which is owned by third parties who may or may not display a copyright notice, failure to do so does not imply a right to copy or reproduce or supply any such material.

C.852

[Email/Letter] © [Author] [year]

C.853

© [Company] [year] All rights are reserved in all emails, letters, orders and other records or documents sent by any employee or officer of the [Company] and there is no right granted to reproduce, supply, licence, distribute and/ or exploit any part to any third party and/or on any website and/or in any newspaper and/or by mobile phone.

C.854

Database, index and taxonomy [year-year] © [Company]

C.855

Word entries on search engine on [Website] © [year-year] [Company]

C.856

Podcast on [subject] Copyright © [year] [Name]

C.857

[Video/Film/Mobile] clip © [year] All rights reserved.

C.858

[Newsfeed/Subscription Service] © [year] [Company] under licence from [Distributor].

C.859

[Blog title] © [year] [Name/Writer/Company]

[Blog Image] © [year] [Name/Artist]

[Blog Slogan] © [year] [Name/Writer]

[Blog Photograph] © [year] [Name/Artist]

[Blog Database] © [year] [Name/Writer]

[Blog Film] © [year] [Name/Company]

[Blog Sound recordings] © [year] [Name/Company]

[Work] sourced and reproduced under [non-exclusive/exclusive] licence from [Company/Collecting Society] written by [Author] © [year] [Company/ Author]

[Blog Website] owned and controlled by [Name/Company] and hosted by [Name/Company].

C.860

[App title, logo, image and slogan] © [specify]

[App hardware] [specify]

[App Software] [specify]

[App Programme and Animation] [specify]

[App Maps/Games/Prizes] [specify]

[App Data] held by [specify]

Merchandising

C.861

The [Agent] agrees to ensure that any third party shall agree to provide the following credit, copyright notice, trade mark and logo to the [Licensor] in respect of the [Licensed Articles] and in all publicity, advertising, promotional and packaging material in respect of the marketing, distribution and exploitation of the [Licensed Articles] [–].

C.862

The [Licensee] shall ensure that the following words are set out on each and every item of the Product and the [Product Package] [trade mark/trade mark registration/copyright notice/warning/other/text/slogan/position/size/order] [specify] and an example of each is attached to and forms part of this Agreement.

'The Product Package' shall mean all material associated with the [Licensee's Product] including any packaging, labels, advertising, promotion and publicity material, films, videos, television and radio commercials and any other visual or sound recordings, photographs, computer generated graphics, scripts, artwork, music, DVDs, CD-Roms, CDs, internet, or mobile phones.

C.863

'The Company's Products' shall mean the products and services of the [Company] which are briefly described as follows [–]. A two-dimensional copy of the Company's Products is attached to and forms part of this Agreement setting out all intellectual property rights and where they should be displayed or put including copyright, trade marks, service marks, logos, designs, slogans, text, artwork, title, recordings, scripts, music, photographs, computer software, patents, products, artistes, graphics, computer generated material, all consents, releases, moral rights, contractual obligations obtained, paid for and/or due.

C.864

© [year – year] [Company] and parent company [specify]. All Rights Reserved.

C.865

Game Code © [year – year] [Company]. All rights reserved.

C.866
Distributed by [Distributor] under License from [Company].

C.867
Copyright © [Company] [year of release/publication/other]

C.868
[year] [Original characters/book/film/other] [Company] © [year]

[year] [Product] [Licensee]. Exclusive Distributor [Name]

C.869
The [Licensee] agrees and undertakes to ensure that the [Licensee] and any distributor, sub-licensee, consultant and/or marketing company and/or may be engaged by and/or under contract to the [Licensee] shall ensure that no reference shall be made to the [Work] in any material and/or a copy made in any format in any medium without a copyright notice, credit, trade mark, and logo] in the following manner to the [Licensee] to appear in a prominent position on each and every copy [specify] in any advertising, publicity, marketing Samples of which are described and exhibited and form part of this Agreement in Appendix [–].

C.870
The [Licensee] agrees and undertakes to ensure that the [Licensee] and any distributor, sub-licensee, consultant and/or marketing company and/or may be engaged by and/or under contract to the [Licensee] shall:

1.1 Ensure that the following copyright notice will be incorporated on every copy of the [Product] which is based on the [Work] [name] [year] and

1.2 Not at any time delete and/or authorise the removal and/or omission of such copyright notice. The copyright notice shall be placed in such manner and position as to give reasonable notice to the public of the claim of copyright.

1.3 Send to the [Licensor] for the prior written approval of the [Licensor]

   (a) All proposed drafts and copies of any advertising, marketing, and press releases and promotional material before it is issued to the press and/or public including email, website material, banners, trade exhibition material, catalogues, brochures, flyers, display stands and point of sale material.

   (b) Drawings and samples of any prototype and the final version of the [Product] before any tools for manufacture are created and/or the production, distribution and/or sale to the public.

(c)   Drawings and samples of any prototype and the final version of the [Product] before production, distribution and/or sale to the public of all packaging.

C.871

The [Licensee] agrees and undertakes to ensure that it shall not allow any third party to be involved in the production, distribution and/or sales and/or act as agent and/or otherwise who is not bound by a contractual obligation to the [Licensee] as follows:

1.1   To act in good faith and ensure that the copyright notice and credit, and trade mark in Appendix [–] to the [Licensor] and the [Author] appear on all copies of the [Work/Film/Product/Disc].

1.2   To agree and undertake that they shall not acquire any copyright, intellectual property rights, computer software rights, design rights, and/or any other rights in any trade mark, service mark, logos or images, names, words and titles and shall not attempt to register any rights.

1.3   To ensure that the copyright notice and credit, and trade mark are not deleted, removed and/or omitted from any copy of the [Work/Film/Product/Disc] and/or any packaging, marketing, publicity and/or promotional material.

C.872

© [year – year] [Copyright Owner] Based on [Work] by [Author]

Artwork/Cover © [year] [Name]

Computer generated material © [year] [Name]

Software © [year] [Name]

Lyrics © [year] [Name]

Music © [year] [Name]

Film © [Title] [year] [Name]

DVD/Disc Distributed by [Name]

C.873

1.1   The [Licensor] may notify and insist that the [Licensee] [at any stage during the agreement up to one year before the expiry date] make such changes, adaptations, deletions and/or variations of any copyright notices, credits, trademarks, logos and disclaimers and/or the terms and conditions of use of the [Work/Product/Service] and/or any other part and/or of any packaging, marketing and promotional material.

1.2 The [Licensee] agrees and undertakes to comply with 1.1 and to carry out such work at its sole cost and expense. Where any material is withdrawn from the market of the [Work/Product/Service] then the [Licensee] shall be entitled to dispose of such material in the remainder market and use any such sums received to recoup the costs of complying with 1.1. The [Licensee] shall be obliged to account for any sums received and any set off by the [Licensee] to recoup costs.

Publishing

C.874
The [Assignee] agrees and undertakes that all copies of the [Work] published pursuant to this publishing agreement shall bear a copyright notice reading [the year of publication] [the Assignor's full corporate name] on each item and comply with the [Universal Copyright Convention].

C.875
The [Company] shall ensure that any copyright notices, credits, moral rights, trade marks, service marks and logos included in the publication of the [Work] in [form] shall appear in the same form on the [Company's] website. The [Licensor] shall also be provided with the following [copyright notice, credit, trade mark, logo] in respect of the reference to or the use of the [Work] in any advertising, publicity, marketing and distribution material as set out in Appendix [–] and samples of which are described and exhibited and form part of this Agreement.

C.876
The [Company] agrees as far as reasonably possible that it will ensure that a copyright notice shall be displayed showing that the copyright of the [extracts] and the [Work] belong to [Name] and are only displayed for the following purpose [specify].

C.877
The [Publisher] undertakes that the following copyright notice will be incorporated on every copy of the [Work] © [name] [year of first publication] and on any material based on or derived from it including discs, tapes, advertising, brochures, flyers, websites, posters and in any other media created, developed, commissioned, licensed, sold or supplied by the [Publisher]. The [Publisher] shall not at any time delete or authorise the removal or omission of such copyright notice. The copyright notice shall be placed in such manner and position as to give reasonable notice to the public of the claim of copyright.

C.878

The [Publisher] agrees to impose a contractual obligation on any sub-licensee, agent, parent company, subsidiary, or any other third party with whom it enters an arrangement, agreement or license in respect any copy of the [Work] in any media that:

1.1 They will incorporate the copyright notice in clause [–] to the [Author].

1.2 They shall not acquire any copyright, or any other intellectual property rights or computer software rights or interest or trade mark, service mark, logos or images, names, words and titles and shall not attempt to register any rights.

1.3 Where there is an error or omission in the copyright notice they shall withdraw all the material as soon as possible and rectify the position.

C.879

The [Ghostwriter] agrees that he shall not have any copyright notice, credit or acknowledgment and waives all such rights in respect of the exploitation of the [Work] by the [Author] or any third party in any media at any time. The [Ghostwriter] agrees that the [Author] shall receive sole credit for researching, writing and the copyright notice shall be as follows [–].

C.880

The [Author] waives all right to a copyright notice in respect of the [Work] and any parts and the artwork and material in Schedule [–] in all media at any time in the [Territory]. The [Author] agrees that the copyright notice shall be as follows [–].

C.881

The [Company] agrees and undertakes that:

1.1 The following copyright notice and words shall be displayed in the precise manner and order set out [–] and printed at the end of the [Extract] in each and every copy of the [Periodical] together with the name of the Publisher and the title of the [Work] as follows [–].

1.2 That any reference to the [Extract] in the periodical on the front cover, advertising, marketing and other promotional material shall be limited to the following [words/images/statement] and that the copyright notice in 1.1 does [not] apply.

C.882

The [Licensee] agrees that it shall not at any time delete or authorise the removal or omission of such copyright notice which shall be legible and in such a size and position as to give reasonable notice of the copyright owner's rights.

C.883

A copyright notice in the form of a letter C enclosed by a circle followed by the name of the [Copyright Owner] and the first year of publication shall be displayed in the precise manner and order under Clause [–] and printed on all copies of the [Work] on one of the first four pages. The [Copyright Owners] shall appear prominently on the jacket binding and the title page of the [Work] and in all publicity material. The [Company] shall use its reasonable endeavours to ensure that an identical copyright notice appears in all sub-licensed editions of the [Work]. The [Company] agrees to ensure that any third party or successor in business in title shall agree to provide the conditions set out in Clause [–] to the [Author].

C.884

The Publisher agrees that it is an important term of the Agreement:

1.1 That a copyright notice to the [Authors] as follows [first/last year of publication] [names] appears to the [Authors] on each and every copy of the hardback and paperback book on the front inside pages. The [Publisher] agrees to supply a copy for approval at the same time as the proofs.

1.2 That no copies of the [Work] or any part in any media should be distributed, supplied, released, licensed or otherwise exploited by the [Publisher] or any wholesalers, retailers, websites, agent, sub-licensee or any third party engaged, appointed or who has an arrangement or agreement with the [Publisher] without the copyright notice to the [Authors] and that this will be imposed by the [Publishers] as a pre-condition. Further that samples for approval should be sent for the prior approval of the [Authors] in each case.

C.885

The [Publisher] shall not authorise or permit third parties who are engaged, licensed or have an agreement with the [Publisher] to impose their own copyright notice on any part of the [Work] or any reproduction, development, adaptation, merchandising, packaging, labels, advertising, marketing in any format in any media. The [Authors] shall be the only persons entitled to a copyright notice, claim of authorship or other credit as authors of the [Work].

C.886

The [Authors] accept that there is a practice not to display a copyright notice on the following material which markets and advertises the material on which only a summary of the [Work] will be included and no actual extracts of the [Work] [specify].

C.887

The [Author] agrees that where [the cover/illustrations/other] have been designed, commissioned and developed by the [Publisher] that the [Publisher] shall be entitled to a copyright notice in respect of that material.

C.888

The [Author] agrees that where third parties are appointed to create and develop new formats of the [Work] as manufacturers, sub-licensees and/or distributors. Then the [Publisher] shall submit to the [Author] a draft of any proposed form of copyright notice and acknowledgements on samples of the label, packaging, products, advertising and marketing material in each case. The [Publisher] shall require the prior written approval of the [Author] before any manufacturer, sub-licensee or distributor can proceed to produce, manufacture or release any products.

C.889

Title, preface, text and index © [Name] [year]

Illustrations © [Name] [year]

Front Cover [photograph/computer generated design] [year] © [Name]

C.890

© [Copyright Owner] [year]

C.891

Copyright © [Name] [year] All rights reserved

C.892

[Title of Work] Hardback © [year to year] [Company/Distributor]

[Title of Work] Paperback © [year to year] [Company/Distributor]

[Title of Work] [E book/Download/electronic form] © [year to year] [Company/Distributor]

[Artwork/Photograph] for the [cover/online image] created by [name] © [year] [Company]

[Index/databases] created by [name] © [year] [Company]

[Interactive content/Article] supplied by [name] © [year] [Company]

Product Placement [name] [product] [logo] [image] trade mark of [Company]

C.893

[Work/extract] author unknown [ownership of physical copy] [Institute]. No licence is granted and/or implied to reproduce this work for commercial purposes without the prior consent and licence of the [Institute].

Purchase and Supply of Products

C.894

The [Seller] agrees that in any associated publicity, advertising, promotional material, emails, webpages or other marketing material by the [Seller] of the [Seller's] Website that the [Supplier's Logo] and the [Product] shall be given reasonable prominence, recognition and a copyright notice, trade mark notice and credit given in respect of the [Supplier's Logo] and [Product].

C.895

The [Seller] agrees to provide the following copyright notice, credit, service mark, trade mark or logo to the [Supplier] in respect of the [Product] as is specified in Schedule [–] in the [Seller's] website and any advertising, marketing, publicity promotional and packaging material. The [Seller] shall provide the [Supplier] with copies and samples at the [Seller's] cost on a regular basis.

C.896

The [Distributor] agrees to provide the following [copyright notice, credit, trade mark, logo, design, statement, other] to the [Company] in the following circumstances:

1.1   [–] on all packaging, labels, jackets, sleeves;

1.2   [–] on all posters, brochures, catalogues, advertisements;

1.3   [–] on all press releases;

1.4   [–] on display stands at exhibitions.

C.897

Produced in [country] for [Retailer] [year] [Company].

C.898

The [Distributor] agrees not to supply, release or market [Products] which do not bear the copyright notice to the [Licensor] and all such items shall be destroyed and the matter reported to the [Licensor].

C.899

The manufacturer, supplier and distributor appointed by [Name] under this Agreement shall not produce, release or distribute any copies of the [Work] in any country at any time unless it bears the following copyright notice to [Name] on each and every copy and in every style, format and media in which anything based or derived from the [Work/Character/Service/other] or any part.

C.900

[Logo/Shape] © [year] [Company]

[Slogan] © [year] [Company]

[Product Name] © [year] [Company]

[specify] registered trade mark of [Company]

[specify] registered community mark of [Company]

[specify] registered service mark of [Company].

C.901

Manufactured by [specify].

Distributed by [specify].

Licensed by [specify].

Made in [country] by [specify]

© [year] [Company] part of the [specify] brand.

Services

C.902

The [Record Company] agrees that:

1.1 It shall provide the following copyright notice, logo, and trade mark to the [Artiste] in respect of the [Musical Works] on each and every copy produced, manufactured, released, distributed, supplied, sold or downloaded as follows [specify] [both in words and sound].

1.2 It shall not at any time reproduce, release, distribute, supply, market, promote, and/or exploit the [Musical Work] in any media or manner or authorise others to do so without providing the copyright notice to the [Artiste] for such [Musical Works].

C.903

The [Manager] agrees to ensure that the following [credit/copyright notice/ trade mark/logo/compliance mark] of the [Artist] shall be prominently placed and displayed on all materials of any nature to be used or exploited by third parties in connection with the [Artist] including, but not limited to CDs, labels, packaging, publicity, advertising, websites and downloading.

C.904

The [Distributor] agrees to provide the following copyright notice, credit, trade mark and logo to the [Company] in all publicity, advertising, promotional and packaging material in respect of the marketing, distribution and exploitation of the product of the [Company's] services under this Agreement [specify] [attach examples].

C.905

The [Consultant] agrees that when preparing, compiling and writing the Report that he/she shall ensure that all third party ownership of the copyright and/or intellectual property rights and/or any material shall be suitably acknowledged and highlighted in the Report in the form of a copyright notice and/or other relevant credit. The [Consultant] shall provide a complete separate list of the title of the work, the source used and any reference, the contact details, confirmation as to whether there are any copyright and/or contract issues outstanding and/or whether the material is cleared for use by the [Company] and if so the payments that may be required.

C.906

The [Sub-Licensee] agrees and undertakes that all copyright notices, logos, trade marks and other credits and/or copyright warnings which the [Licensee] notifies the [Sub-Licensee] shall be on each and every copy of the [Work/Product] shall be adhered to and not deleted, amended and/or removed. That the [Sub-licensee] shall ensure that no copy is produced, manufactured, released, distributed, supplied, and/or otherwise exploited by the [Sub-Licensee] and/or anyone else authorised to act on its behalf. The [Sub-Licensee] acknowledges that failure to carry out this important requirement may result in the immediate termination of this Agreement by the [Licensee].

C.907

The [Consultant] and the [Company] agree that the [Company] shall own all the copyright and intellectual property rights to the [Report], the title and any draft copies and/other material created and/or supplied by the [Consultant].

The [Company] and the [Consultant] agree that the following copyright notice and credit shall be reproduced on the front page of all copies:

[Title of Report] [Company] [year]

© Copyright all content: except where stated otherwise

Report prepared and compiled by [Consultant] [Business name/website reference]

C.908

Product [year] [Company] [Trade Mark/Logo]

Website [year] [Company] [Trade Mark/Logo]

471

Software [year] [Name]

Newsletter [year] [Name]

Photographs/Images [year] [Name]

DVD/Video/Film [year] [Name]

Audio material/Radio [year] [Name]

Banner Advert [year] [Name]

Links [year] [Name]

Music [year] [Name]

C.909

The [Contributor] agrees and undertakes that he shall not represent to any third party that he/she is the copyright owner of any work and/or services provided to the [Company] under this Agreement. The [Contributor] agrees and undertakes that all his/her work is based on material and/or other directions, ideas and projects proposed by the [Company] and is not original to the [Contributor]. That the [Contributor] agrees that he/she shall not be entitled to any copyright notice for any of his/her work at any time for the [Company].

C.910

1.1   [Name] shall be attributed as the author of the [Project] in the following manner [specify] in any printed material, website content, download, film and/or marketing material by the [Company] and/or any agent and/or consultant authorised by them.

1.2   [Name] shall be attributed as the author of the [Project] in the following manner [specify] in any audio and/or sound recording and/or radio and/or any licensed recording and/or interview by the [Company] and/or or any agent and/or consultant authorised by them.

Sponsorship

C.911

The [Promoter] agrees to provide the following copyright notice, words, and image to the [Company] in any publicity, promotional, advertising, merchandising and packaging material concerning the [Company] and/or the [Event] [specify]. A copy of which is attached to, and forms part of, this Agreement.

C.912

That no copies of the [Sponsors] [Product/Services/Logo] and/or any part should be distributed, supplied or otherwise exploited in any media by the [Promoter] and/or placed on any websites, and/or used by any agent, sub-licensee or any third party engaged, appointed and/or who has an arrangement or agreement with the [Promoter] without the copyright notice to the [Sponsors] and that this will be imposed by the [Promoters] as a pre-condition. [That samples for approval should be sent for the prior written approval of the [Sponsors] in each case.]

C.913

The [Company] agrees that the [Sponsor's] copyright notice, credit, trade mark, logo and slogan set out in attached Appendix [–] shall be exactly reproduced in any medium and/or format and shall not be adapted and/or changed and/or anything added at any time.

C.914

That in the event that in the course of the development, production, staging, marketing, promotion, and/or exploitation of the [Event] a new version of any material, trade mark, logo of the [Sponsors'] shall be adapted, designed, created and/or used then the [Company] shall ensure that the employee, person or other third party shall assign and transfer all rights to the [Sponsor].

C.915

The [Sponsor] agrees that where for any reason the [Company] omits, deletes, and/or fails to provide a copyright notice, trade mark, logo and/or credit to the [Sponsor] for any reason. That provided the [Company] acknowledges the failure and remedies the position as soon as possible it shall not be deemed a breach of this Agreement.

C.916

[Company] [address] [web reference]

[Title of Event] [Company] © [year]

This Guide is produced by [Company]

Publisher [Name]

Editor [Name]

Layout [Name]

Printed by [Name]

[Specify Logos] are the registered trademarks of [Company]

Copyright Warning [specify]

C.917

The [Sponsor] shall not be entitled to any copyright notices, trademark and/or other attributions of ownership and/or control on any material at the [Event] which in the opinion of the [Organisers] would not be suitable due to lack of space; design and artistic issues; delays in creating material; failure to deliver master copies for reproduction within the time limits set and/or otherwise. The [Sponsor] agrees that in such event they shall not be entitled to paid any sums for any reason for any loss and/or otherwise and/or to seek a repayment of any sums paid to date.

C.918

Where for any reason copyright notices and credits do not appear and/or are not reproduced and/or are deleted, removed, edited out and/or altered and/or amended without the prior written approval and the consent of [Name]. Then [Name] shall have a valid claim for breach of this Agreement and shall be entitled to a payment of [number/currency] for each and every case where the [Company] fails to comply. Any such sums due shall be paid within [number] days of invoice by [Name] specifying the failure by the [Company].

University, Library and Educational

C.919

The parties agree to use the following copyright notices to provide notice of ownership and title of any text, images and other material in respect of the [Project]:

[Title of text] and the index and taxonomy [Institute] © [year – year]

[Title of Illustrations/Photographs] [Name] © [year]

[Artwork/Design/Computer generated design] [Institute] © [year – year]

All rights reserved.

Exclusive Distributor [Enterprise] under License from the [Institute].

C.920

The [Institute] agrees to provide the following copyright notice, credit, service mark, trade mark or logo to the [Author] in respect of the [Work/Product] and in all advertising, marketing, publicity promotional and packaging material. The [Institute] shall provide the [Author] with copies and samples at the [Institute's] cost on a regular basis.

C.921

1.1   The [Distributor/Licensee] agrees to provide the following copyright notice; [name] [year of first publication], credit, and logo and slogan to the [Company/Author] which shall be displayed in a prominent position on each and every copy and in every style, format and media on anything based or derived from the [Work/Service/Products] or any part so that it can be clearly read by any member of the public and/or purchaser. A copy of which is attached in Schedule [–] and forms part of this Agreement.

1.2 The [Distributor/Licensee] agrees not to reproduce, supply, release, and/or market [Work/Service/Products] which do not bear the copyright notice to any third party. The [Distributor/Licensee] shall not at any time delete or authorise the removal and/or omission of such copyright notice.

1.3 The [Distributor/Licensee] undertakes that the following copyright notice, credit, and logo and slogan to the [Company/Author] in 1.1 above shall also be incorporated on any material based on or derived from the [Work/Service/Products] including discs, tapes, brochures, flyers, on all packaging, labels, jackets, sleeves, posters, catalogues, advertisements, press releases, display stands at exhibitions, websites, posters and in any other media created, developed, commissioned, licensed, sold or supplied by the [Distributor/Licensee].

1.4 The [Distributor/Licensee] agrees and undertakes that it shall not acquire any copyright, trade mark, service marks, design rights, logo or any other intellectual property rights and/or computer software rights, names, words and titles in respect of the [Work/Service/Products] and/ or the [institute] and shall not attempt to register any rights and/or interest and/or authorise others to do so.

C.922

The [Distributor/Licensee] agrees to impose a contractual obligation on any sub-licensee, agent, parent company, subsidiary, or any other third party with whom it enters an arrangement, agreement or license in respect any copy of the [Work/Service/Products] in any media:

1.1 To provide the following copyright notice; [name] [year of first publication], credit, and logo and slogan to the [Institute/Author] on each and every copy of the [Work/Service/Products] or any part so that it can be clearly read by any member of the public and/or purchaser. A copy of which is attached in Schedule [–] and forms part of this Agreement.

1.2 An undertaking that they shall not acquire any copyright, trade mark, service marks, design rights, logo or any other intellectual property rights and/or computer software rights, names, words and titles and shall not attempt to register any rights and/or interest.

C.923

The [Institute] may at its sole discretion credit the [Contributor] as [specify] in the [Work/Product] in a similar manner and form as the other contributors at any time. The [Contributor] agrees that he/she shall have not right to a copyright notice in any form nor shall there be any obligation on the [Institute] to use the work of the [Contributor] and that it may be omitted in its entirety either now and/or at a later date from the [Work/Product].

COPYRIGHT WARNINGS

General Business and Commercial

C.924

The copyright and intellectual property rights, trade marks, logos and images are owned by [specify] and distributed under license. You are not authorised to make any copy, alter, adapt, supply, distribute, release, market or otherwise exploit this [Product/Service] in any media at any time. Requests for permission for any such uses should be sent to [–].

C.925

You are only authorised to use this [Work] for residential and domestic purposes and any commercial use shall require the prior written consent of [Name].

C.926

All copyright, intellectual property rights and all other rights are held or controlled by [Name]. There is no authority provided to you either directly or implied to permit you to acquire any rights in any material on this [specify] or to attempt to register any interest in any material based on or derived from it at any time.

C.927

The following uses of this [Work/other] as a whole are permitted, but all others require the prior consent of the [Company]:

1.1 Criticism, review or comparisons.

1.2 Educational resource in schools, colleges and universities.

1.3 Advertising, promotion and marketing by [retailers and wholesalers].

C.928
The [Company] has a strong policy of copyright enforcement and will issue a charge and take action against any person and/or business who in any part of the world is discovered to have illegally reproduced and/or exploited this [Work/Project] whether they have made money from it or not.

Internet and Websites

C.929
You may only download [all/extracts of] these web pages to your computer, telephone or other gadget for your own personal use at home on residential premises and not for any commercial project, your own website or any other educational or business purpose.

C.930
You are not permitted to supply, transfer, distribute, or copy all or large extracts of these webpages to any third party at any time. You may keep copies at your personal address for your own use and research, but any commercial work, regular exchanges with others of text, pictures, data or other parts or any contribution to another website, book, film, or other adaptation using any of the material on this [Website] will require our prior written consent. Failure to obtain permission could create a risk of being sued for copyright infringement and a claim for all the legal costs. In any event all material sourced from this [Website] should be credited as follows [–].

C.931
This [Website] is owned and controlled by [Name] trading as [Name]. Users are allowed to view the material to read the contents. There is no consent provided to permit copies to be made of any part in any form or to supply any such material to third parties whether for commercial gain or not. If you wish to store a copy at home, include material in a commercial project or send copies of extracts to others then complete the licensing application form and receive advance authorisation.

C.932
No reproductions, copies, translations, adaptations, edited versions, quotes, extracts, films, CD-Roms, CDs, advertisements, marketing, DVDs, products, services, databases, or other material or uses may be made or derived from any part of the material on this [Website].

C.933
You are only authorised to make [one copy] of all the pages on the [Website] for use at home by you to read in printed form or to store on a disc.

C.934

There is no right to supply, transfer, edit, alter, change or interfere or reproduce the material or any parts on [specify] without prior written consent from [specify].

C.935

You are not authorised to use the material on this [Website] or any part for the purpose of advertising or promoting a product, service, book, CD, CD-Rom, film or other subject or item nor to give the impression that it is endorsed, supported by or associated with the [Website].

C.936

All the text, images, logos, data, advertisements, games, titles, trade names, formats, recordings, film, sounds, ringtones and other material belong to a company or person who owns the copyright and who may or may not have displayed a copyright notice depending on the circumstances. You will need to ask for permission and prior written consent if you wish to make any use of their material or supply it to others and the [Website] [Company] has not provided any authorisation to you for any purpose except to view this [Website] and read it directly on your [computer/television/telephone/other].

C.937

All the contributors on this [Website] have provided their work on the basis that it shall be made freely available to others on the internet for their own use at [home/business/commercial] premises. That any persons or company who read, download, make extracts or reproduce the material in any format will acknowledge copyright ownership as displayed on the webpages and not attempt to hide or delete authorship of any person or substitute another and that where the material is to be used for a commercial project will obtain the prior written consent of the copyright owner.

C.938

All the content of this [Website/App/Blog] are owned and controlled by [Name/Company] and/or third parties. There is no express and/or implied licence that you may supply others, make copies, use any of the material on another website and/or reproduce any images, data, text, photographs, films, sound recordings, comments and posts and/or any exploit anything in any other medium regardless of whether you do so for your own personal use, for charity, an educational purpose and/or a commercial reason. You require a licence and must follow the stated procedure at [reference].

Merchandising

C.939
The copyright and intellectual property rights in this [Work/Film/Disc/other] are owned by [specify] and distributed under licence by [specify]. The public have no right to copy, reproduce and/or in any way exploit any part and to do so will be an infringement of the rights of both these parties who may issue legal proceedings at any time.

C.940
You are not permitted to reproduce, hire, supply, distribute, broadcast, transmit, upload to the internet and/or any website, store and/or retrieve on any hard drive of your computer, and/or any disc, mobile phone and/or any other gadget, and/or telecommunication system, film, record, edit and/or adapt this [Work/Film/Disc/other]. The purchase of this [Work/Film/Disc/other] only permits you to play the [Work/Film/Disc/other] at residential premises in private without making any charge for viewing the [Work/Film/Disc/other] to others.

C.941
This copy is supplied for personal and private home use only. Do not make any copies, edit, adapt, change, add to, delete from and/or join this [Work/Product/Disc] with any other at any time.

C.942
Reproduction of any part of this [Work] is strictly forbidden.

C.943
The [title], [logo], [image] [characters] in the [Work] and the [Articles] belong to [Name]. (©) [year] [specify] trade mark [specify] . No reproduction is authorised and all rights are reserved.

Publishing

C.944
No licence is granted to sell and/or supply [extracts] or copies from or of this [Book] for any legal, business or advisory website or otherwise on the internet. Please apply to the [Publishers/Authors] for any reproductions in whole or part of this [Book]. All acknowledgements in respect of the [Authors] and [Publishers] must state the source and be clearly and prominently displayed.

C.945
No part of this [Book/Work] and/or [disc/tape/CD-Rom] may be reproduced, transmitted or exploited in any media by any means and/or stored in

any retrieval system of any nature without the prior written consent of the [Publishers] and the [authors] except for:

1.1 Authorised use of the [Book/Work] and/or [disc/tape/CD-Rom] set out in the Software End User Licence.

1.2 Permitted fair dealing under the Copyright Designs and Patents Act as amended.

1.3 Any use in accordance with the terms of a licence issued by the [Copyright Licensing Agency] in respect of photocopying and/or reprographic reproduction.

1.4 Where a person or business uses the [Book/Work] and/or [disc/tape/ CD-Rom] during the normal course of their business provided such is not intended for publication or other commercial exploitation.

C.946
All rights reserved. No part of this publication may be reproduced, stored in a retrieval system, or transmitted in any form or by any means without the prior written consent of the [Publisher], nor be otherwise circulated in any form of binding or cover other than that in which it is published and without a similar condition being imposed on the subsequent purchaser.

C.947
No part of this publication shall be reproduced, adapted, translated, used or exploited in any media without the prior written consent of the [Author] and the [Publisher].

C.948
There is no right granted for any person and/or third party to display, reproduce, edit, adapt, change and/or translate any part of this [Work/ Project] on any website, the internet and/or any form of mobile, app, blog and/or telecommunication system at any time. Such prohibition shall apply to quotations, reviews, criticisms and/or otherwise to all text, logos, images, titles and headings, recipes, taxonomy, data, maps, charts, statistics, formulae and other material in any form which is contained in the [Work/ Project] and/or associated with it in anyway.

Sponsorship

C.949
The [Sponsor] of the [Project] agrees that the [Schools/other] that register with the [Company] shall be granted a non-exclusive licence to reproduce the [specify material] at their own cost for the duration of the [Project]. Provided that a suitable [copyright/trade mark/logo] acknowledgement to

the [Sponsor] is provided on all copies. Failure to do so may result in the withdrawal of the right to participate in the [Project].

C.950
Do not duplicate, hire, rent, adapt, edit, transmit, broadcast, film, record, store on a computer or mobile phone or other storage device any copies of this [specify] which is strictly prohibited. All rights are reserved and the copyright is owned by [Name].

C.951
All rights are reserved. No part of this publication and/or the [Event] may be filmed, recorded, broadcast, transmitted, stored in a retrieval system, reproduced, adapted, distributed, sold, or otherwise exploited by any person who attends and/or has a stand at the [Event].

C.952
There is no authority provided by the [Sponsor] or the [Company] to copy, reproduce, alter, adapt, supply, distribute, release, market, film, record, broadcast, transmit, upload to the internet and/or otherwise exploit this [Product/Service/Event] in any format and/or in any media at any time. Requests for permission for any such uses should be sent to [–].

C.953
The [Company] shall ensure that any sub-licensees and/or distributors and/or agents are made aware and informed of and provided with a copy the corporate policy of the [Sponsor] regarding the use of its [Brand] and products a copy of which is attached in [–] and forms part of this Agreement.

University, Library and Educational

C.954
All copyright and intellectual property rights are owned and/or controlled by the [Institute]. There is no right to reproduce, supply, distribute, license and/or exploit whether for non-commercial, academic, educational, the internet, translation, and/or commercial purposes and/or any adaptation of any of the content, title, text, images, and/or any associated material of any part of this [Work/Service/Product]. Please contact [specify details] to enquire about any possible use of any material.

C.955
It is permitted to make a short quotation from the [Work/Service] provided that it is for the purpose of review and/or criticism in an article and/or educational purposes for private study provided that it is limited to no more than [number] words in total and there is a credit to the [Institute] and the

correct title, author and ISBN details quoted together with the website address of the [Institute].

C.956
Where the [Institute] owns the physical copy of a [document] but has no record of the [author] and/or attribution of any credit. Any person licenced by the [Institute] must not claim and/or represent that either they are and/or are aware of the name of the [author] and/or otherwise.

CORRUPTION

General Business and Commercial

C.957
Where at a later date after the signature of this Agreement there is evidence to show that the [Contractor] offered inducements, rewards, money or goods to any person involved in the award of the [Tender/Contract] which were not disclosed or discovered prior to signature of the contract. Then the [Company] shall have the right to terminate the contract at once and shall be under no further liability to pay any sums due after that date or outstanding and shall be entitled to a full refund of all sums paid to the [Contractor].

C.958
The [Company] undertakes that it shall not offer any inducements, rewards, benefits or act in any manner which could be construed as corrupt, dishonest, or in breach of any rules, policies or legislation governing applications for [subject] contracts in [country].

C.959
That the [Company] shall not seek to spread information, data or stories regarding other applicants for the [contract/subject] which would affect the value of their company assets, share price, reputation or products in order to effect the award of the [contract/subject] except where based on verifiable facts and evidence.

C.960
No offers, inducements, money, goods or shares shall be offered to any person, company, associate, officer or agents involved in the procurement, tender and award process at any time by any applicant. If there is any alleged evidence of such behaviour or acts by an applicant or someone acting on

their behalf the [Company] reserves the right to refuse them permission to continue in the contract application procedure.

C.961
The [Contractor] shall not act in collusion or concert with another party or authorise someone else to do with the intention to misrepresent facts or distort the market in [subject] or to affect the [bidding] or lower the price of the [Products].

C.962
No information, data, contract, agreement, partnership, agency, copyright ownership, costs, expenses, financial records, registration details, sales and marketing or other material facts shall have been withheld, amended, altered or projected which would significantly affect the terms or award of this Agreement to the [Company].

C.963
The [Consultant] shall disclose any shares, business interest, contracts and any other [personal and/or] business matters which may conflict with the work he/she is to carry out for the [Company]. The [Consultant] shall not offer any cash, goods and/or other inducement to any person and/or company involved in the allocation of the tenders to which the [Enterprise] has and/or will apply and in which the [Consultant] has and/or will assist.

C.964
In the event that an agent, advisor and/or other person who received funds on behalf of [Name] with the permission and authority from [Name] to the [Company]. Then where [Name] is the subject of fraud and/or negligence by any such agent, advisor and/or other person the [Company] shall not be liable and [Name] shall not be entitled to make any claim against the [Company] as the liability of the [Company] ceased once the sums were paid.

COSTS

DVD, Video and Discs

C.965
The [Licensee] warrants and undertakes that it shall be solely responsible for any sums due in respect of the manufacture, distribution, marketing and

exploitation of [DVD/video/other] Rights in the [Film] and that the [Licensor] shall not be liable for any such payments.

C.966

It is agreed that all packaging, marketing, administration, storage and distribution will be carried out under the control of the [Licensee] and at the Licensee's expense.

C.967

The [Assignee] agrees and undertakes that it shall be solely responsible for any sums due in respect of the production, manufacture, distribution, marketing, copyright clearance and fees, mechanical reproduction or performance of any music and any sums due of any nature arising from the exploitation of the [DVD Rights in the [Compilation] and that the [Assignor] shall not be liable for any such payments.

C.968

The [Company] acknowledges and undertakes that it shall bear sole liability for any sums due for the development, manufacture, distribution, marketing and exploitation of the [DVD and Non-Theatric Rights in the [Programme] and that the [Sponsors] shall not be liable for any such sums.

C.969

The [Assignee] agrees to bear the cost of all sums due for the exploitation of the [DVD Rights] in the [Film] including the performing rights in any music, mechanical reproduction of the recordings of the music and any union members.

C.970

The [Licensee] confirms that it shall be responsible for payment of any sums which arise through the exploitation of the [DVD/video] Rights under this Agreement due to [Performing Rights Society and Mechanical Copyright Protection Society and [other]. All other sums shall have been cleared and shall be paid for by the [Licensor].

C.971

The [Work] is provided by the [Company] and supplied to the public by the [Distributor] as a promotional [Disc] to be supplied with [specify product/goods/services]. The [Company] agrees that it is solely responsible for all costs due and/or to be incurred for any payment arising from assignment, licence, contract and/or any royalty and/or clearance of any copyright, intellectual property rights, photographs, images, music, lyrics, sound recordings, mechanical and performing rights, and/or other sums due to any collecting societies, and/or for any waivers, trademarks and any other rights and/or interest that may be required for the supply, reproduction and distribution exploitation of the [Work] and any use on any packaging, marketing, advertising and/or supply to the public for private home use only.

C.972

The [Distributor] agrees and undertakes that the total budget for the cost of the reproduction, supply and distribution of the [Work] as a promotional [Disc] shall not exceed [figure/currency] in total. The [Distributor] agrees to pay [number] per cent of the final cost and the balance shall be paid by the [Company] within [one month] of receipt of invoice. The [Distributor] shall be paid an advance deposit of [figure/currency] by the [Company] to be set off against the final sums due. The deposit shall be paid as the same time as the delivery of the master of the [Disc].

C.973

The costs of any marketing, advertising and promotion including any associated banner links, advertisements on television, radio, in cinemas and on the internet in the form of banner links, paid search words and/or free associated apps for the [DVD/Disc] shall be at the sole cost of the [Licensee]. The [Licensee] shall not be entitled to recoup any of these sums from the gross receipts from the exploitation of the [DVD/Disc] and/or to offset them against any advance and/or royalty due to the [Licensor] at any time.

C.974

Where [Name] provides any additional personal material for the [DVD/Disc] which is then used by the [Company]. It is agreed that no additional payment and/or fees shall be due to [Name] for the use and exploitation of such material including but limited to photographs, film, diaries, objects and other material.

Film and Television

C.975

'The Production Costs' shall mean the actual cost of making the [Programme] inclusive of the Producer's Fee. In the event that the Production Costs are less than the agreed Budget then the [Producer] shall return any excess sums paid by the [Broadcaster] upon request.

C.976

'Production Cost' shall mean the actual cost of production of the [Film] including all interest on borrowed money banking and finance charges as shall be certified by the [Company's] auditors and agreed between the [Company] and its principle distributors.

485

C.977

'Production Costs' means the total actual certified cost of the production of the [Film] including all finance and banking charges and interest and the overhead expenses of the [Company] attributable to the [Film] and all sums payable to the Completion Guarantor.

C.978

'The Production Costs' shall be the total costs whether direct or indirect of making the [Series] including all items necessary for the development, pre-production, production, post-production and delivery of the [Series] (including the Licensor's Fee) which are not recovered from any third party.

C.979

The [Licensor] confirms that all sums due in respect of the production of the [Film/Pilot] have been paid and that the [Licensee] is not and will not be liable for any such payments.

C.980

The [Production Company] undertakes that it shall be responsible for any sums due in respect of the production, reproduction, distribution, marketing and exploitation of the rights in the [Series] and any associated material including any sums due in respect of any third party from the clearance, consent or otherwise of any material which is in the [Work] which is not owned or controlled by the [Author].

C.981

The [Television Company] confirms that it shall be solely responsible for all costs incurred in the production, broadcast, transmission, distribution and exploitation of the [Programme] and that the [Sponsor] shall not be liable for any such sums.

C.982

The [Production Company] undertakes that all sums due in respect of the production of the [Programme] will be paid and that the [Sponsor] is not and will not be liable for any such payments.

C.983

The [Company] agrees that it shall be entirely responsible for all costs incurred and sums due for the development, production, distribution, marketing and exploitation of the [Film] and soundtrack in any form. The [Author] is not liable for any such payments and the [Company] shall not be entitled to deduct such sums from the Gross Receipts.

C.984
The [Production Company] confirms and undertakes that all copyright and any other rights, consents, releases or licenses including consents under the [Copyright, Designs and Patents Act 1988 as amended] in respect of all material of any nature in the [Film] has been or shall be cleared and paid for. This undertaking includes, but is not limited to, stills, music, footage, performers, artists, products, text, recordings, images, crew, editing and the [Licensee] shall not be liable for any such payments. The [Licensee] shall only be liable to pay sums due from the recording and transmission of music in the [Film] namely the mechanical reproduction and performing rights payments.

C.985
The [Licensee] shall be responsible for such costs as are incurred in the conversion of the [Film] to [specify].

C.986
The [Assignor] confirms that all sums due in respect of the production of the [Film] have been paid and that the [Assignee] is not and shall not be liable for any such payments.

C.987
[Name] agrees that he/she shall be paid a fee of [number/currency] for his/her contribution to the [Work/Script] in full and final settlement. That the [Company] shall not be due to pay any additional sum as a royalty and/or other fee for any form of exploitation of any part of the [Work/Script] in any media. [Name] agrees that he/she has no right to make a claim of originality as the [Work/Script] is based on a book entitled [specify] by [specify] and [Name] has only contributed to a draft manuscript which was already developed by [specify]. [Name] agrees that no additional costs, sums and/or expenses are due to [Name].

C.988
Both parties agree that for the purposes of this Agreement the budget is in draft form and that where it is increased and/or adjusted at a later date that both parties shall be equally liable up to a maximum of [number/currency] in total for each party. Neither party authorises any costs beyond that limit and/or accepts any liability.

General Business and Commercial

C.989
'Costs' shall mean all costs including expenses.

C.990

There shall be no costs paid by [name] of any nature except [specify amount]. All other sums shall be paid by [Name].

C.991

The [Cost] of [specify subject] shall be limited to a maximum of [figure/currency] under this Contract and shall not be exceeded for any reason.

C.992

There may be additional costs and sums due for taxes, import and export, freight or conversion of currency which shall all be at the [Company's/other] cost.

C.993

It is agreed between the parties that where the costs are exceeded. The [Company] shall not be liable for more than a [ten per cent] increase unless the additional costs over [ten per cent] were authorised in advance.

C.994

The [Company] shall be entitled to request a deposit of [figure/currency] as an advance against the total final costs of the [Work/Event]. This sum shall not be mixed with the other funds of the [Company], but shall be held separately until such time as the [Company] has completed the agreed duties and tasks to a satisfactory level that are required according to Schedule [–] which forms part of this Agreement.

C.995

The cost of each product shall be the wholesale price quoted at the time of the order by the [Company] less any discount for the size of the order in each case.

C.996

All prices displayed are for guidance only and may be adjusted by the [Company] and are not confirmed until a quote has been issued to you and accepted within the time limit specified. All prices are exclusive of any taxes, freight and transport, insurance, currency conversion and bank charges.

Internet and Websites

C.997

The cost of any [item/product/service/freight] may be varied at any time without notice prior to the acceptance of any order and the costs and prices and other details are for guidance only.

C.998

The [Client/User] shall be responsible for all costs that may be incurred to obtain access to and/or use of and/or reliance upon the [Website] and any content and/or any links, competitions, chatrooms and/or other material. The [Client/User] shall be responsible for all the costs and charges that may arise and/or fall due including landline rental costs, and telephone charges, connection charges, broadband costs, premium rate phone lines or otherwise and the [Company] shall not be liable and/or responsible for any such costs and charges.

C.999

The [Client/User] obtains access to, uses and relies upon this [Website] entirely at their own risk and cost. Where access to and/or use of and/or reliance upon the [Website] and any content and/or any links, competitions, chatrooms and/or other material is interrupted, delayed, slow, inaccurate, withdrawn, amended, deleted and/or otherwise altered and/or varied. The [Company] shall not be liable for any costs and charges that may be arise at any time.

C.1000

Where [Products/Services] are ordered and/or obtained from a third party through the use of this [Website]. Then all such transactions are at the [Purchasers'] own risk and expense and no costs, charges and/or liability can be accepted by the [Company]. We advise you to follow the following [safety procedures].

C.1001

The [Service] is at present provided for free on this [Website] and no subscription or other charges will be incurred by completing the application form to receive the [marketing] email from the [Company]. You may unsubscribe at any time by taking the following steps [specify]. The marketing emails will contain special offers, competitions and the latest products. Any order and/or commitment to purchase any goods and services from a third party as a result of such emails shall be entirely at your own risk and not the responsibility of the [Company].

C.1002

No costs are charged for accessing and/or downloading this [App] to use the [Basic App]. Charges, costs and subscription fees will be incurred for the [Premium App].

C.1003

1.1 Use of any premium rate phone line listed here [specify] will incur an increased charge to your [mobile and/or landline telephone] at the rate of approximately [number/currency] per minute which will immediately be charged to that account.

1.2   We adhere to the Code of Practice and guidelines issued by [specify] in respect of premium rate telephone lines.

Merchandising

C.1004

The [Licensee] agrees that it shall be solely responsible for all costs and expenses incurred in respect of reproducing and incorporating the [Licensor's Logo] in the [Product Package].

C.1005

The [Licensee] agrees that it shall be solely responsible for all costs incurred [authorised by the Licensee] in respect of the development, production, manufacture, distribution, marketing and any other commercial exploitation of the [Licensee's Product] and the [Product Package].

C.1006

The [Licensee] agrees that all sums due and paid for in respect of the marketing and exploitation of the [specify format/goods/other] shall be at the [Licensee's] sole cost and may be deducted as Distribution Expenses from the Gross Receipts prior to the payment of the [Licensor's Royalties] of the Net Receipts.

C.1007

The [Assignee] confirms that it shall be responsible for any sums due in respect of the development, production, distribution, marketing and exploitation of the [Format] in any media at any time and that the [Assignor] shall not be liable for any such sums.

C.1008

The [Licensee] acknowledges that it shall pay for all costs incurred in the commercial exploitation of the [Licensed Article] including the development, manufacture, distribution, selling, advertising and promotion. Such sums shall [not] be set off against the [Licensor's Royalties].

C.1009

The [Company] confirms that it shall be solely responsible for all costs incurred in the development, production, manufacture, distribution, marketing, promotion, advertising and exploitation of the [Licensed Articles] and that such sums shall not be offset against the [Licensor's] Royalties.

C.1010

The [Distributor] shall not be obliged to pay for any sums in respect of the manufacture or packaging of the [Products] supplied by the [Licensee]. The

[Distributor] shall bear all costs relating to its own business, website and the taxes, import and exports charges, currency exchanges, freight and insurance costs or any other sums arising from the sale, supply and distribution to retailers, wholesalers and other customers under this Agreement.

C.1011

The [Licensor] agrees and undertakes to be responsible for the clearance of any copyright and intellectual property rights in the [Work/Artwork/Sound Recordings/Film] supplied to the [Licensee]. The [Licensor] shall pay all the costs, fees, royalties and expenses incurred to the date upon which the [Licensee] acquires the rights under this Agreement. Thereafter the [Licensee] shall pay all the sums that may be due for the exercise of the rights by the [Licensee] and the [Licensor] shall not be liable for any payments. The [Licensee] shall therefore any licence and/or contract royalty payments and under sums due to any collecting society for the broadcast, performance, transmission, mechanical reproduction or otherwise that may become due.

C.1012

The [Licensee] agrees and undertakes that it shall be solely responsible for all corporate, administrative, legal, production, insurance, product liability, and other costs incurred and/or which may arise directly and/or indirectly from the development, manufacture, supply, distribution, sub-licensing, marketing and exploitation of the [Product] in any part of the [world/country]. The [Licensor] shall not pay the cost of any of these sums.

C.1013

The [Licensee] shall not be paid any costs and/or expenses for supplying and supporting any trade mark and/or other registration which the [Licensor] wishes to file and/or make in any part of the world during the term of this Agreement.

C.1014

[Name] agrees to attend and contribute to [number] promotional events for no more than [duration] organised by the [Company] in [country] at no additional cost and expense. Where the [Company] wishes [Name] to attend additional events then it is agreed that the [Company] must pay all costs of expenses of travel, hotels, meals, travel insurance and mobile and laptop costs plus a fee of no less than [number/currency].

Publishing

C.1015

The [Assignee] confirms that it shall be solely responsible for all costs incurred or due in respect of the reproduction, manufacture, supply, distribution, marketing and exploitation of the [Work] and the [Artwork] and the material in Schedule [–] in any media at any time throughout the Territory and that the [Author] shall not be liable for any such sums.

C.1016

The [Licensee] agrees that it shall bear all costs in respect of the production, publication, distribution, marketing and advertising of the [Article] and the [Magazine].

C.1017

The [Publisher] agrees that it shall be solely responsible for all costs incurred in the developing, printing, reproducing, publishing, distributing, marketing and exploiting the [Work] throughout the [Territory] and that no such sums shall be deducted from payments due to the [Author] under this Agreement.

C.1018

The [Licensee] agrees to be responsible for the cost of any additional material or photographs that may be required for the [Article] and in the event of the creation of any new material shall provide a copy to the [Licensor].

C.1019

The [Ghostwriter] shall not be responsible for or liable to pay any fees, sums, royalties or costs arising in connection with the publication of the [Work] including but not limited to all copyright clearances of archive material, stills, recordings, film, websites, or other consents, moral rights, contractual and other legal obligations, legal costs which will be paid for entirely at [Names] cost and expense.

C.1020

The [Agent] confirms that the [Author] shall not be responsible for any costs or expenses incurred by the [Agent] pursuant to this Agreement including but not limited to telephone bills, freight, accommodation, travel, advertising, marketing and that the [Agent] shall only be entitled to the [Agent's Commission].

C.1021

The [Writer] shall not incur any liabilities on behalf of the [Company] or pledge the [Company's] credit.

C.1022

The [Publisher] agrees that it shall bear the entire cost of producing, publishing, distributing, marketing and exploiting the [Work] throughout the Territory.

C.1023
The Licensor agrees that it shall be solely responsible for the cost including the Extracts and the Periodical and the production, distribution, marketing and publicity.

C.1024
The [Assignee] confirms that it shall be solely responsible for all costs incurred in respect of the distribution, marketing and exploitation of the [Work] and the [Artwork] in any media throughout the Territory and that the [Author] shall not be liable for such sums.

C.1025
No sums of any nature shall be due to be paid by the [Author] or deducted from the advance or royalties unless prior written consent is provided by the [Author].

C.1026
The [Publisher] shall not be responsible for any research and/or access, costs, charges and/or expenses of [Name] incurred in developing, editing, writing and/or collaborating with any third parties in respect of the [Work].

C.1027
The [Writer] shall not incur any costs and/or expenses and/or fees on behalf of the [Publisher] at any time and/or represent that he/she has the right and/or authority to do so.

Purchase and Supply of Products

C.1028
The [Designer] agrees to bear the cost of creating the [Designs] and all labour, material and freight costs necessary for the purpose of producing and supplying the [Garment].

C.1029
The [Supplier] agrees that it shall be responsible for any and all [export duties, custom and excise charges and fees, taxes/other] and shall continue to be responsible until the [Product] is delivered to the [destination address] all property rights, risks, liabilities and costs shall remain with the [Supplier].

C.1030
The packaging of the [Product] shall be at the sole cost of the [Supplier]. Delivery and any freight costs shall be paid for by the [Sellers].

C.1031

The [Seller] confirms that it shall be solely responsible for all costs in respect of the exploitation and sale of the [Product].

C.1032

The [Purchaser] agrees that it shall be personally liable for any costs and expenses that may arise from any use of the [Product].

C.1033

The [Assignee] confirms that it shall be solely responsible for all sums due in respect of the reproduction, distribution, marketing and exploitation of the [Commissioned Work] in any media in [specify countries].

C.1034

The [Supplier] shall be held liable for any direct or indirect loss and additional costs which may be incurred under this order for [goods/services] which are not specified as to be paid by the [Purchaser].

C.1035

In the event that the cost of each [Unit] is to be increased by more than [figure/currency] then the [Supplier] shall notify the [Purchaser] and the [Purchaser] may cancel the [Units] at the increased price.

C.1036

Where after an order has been agreed the value of the source material of the content of the [Product] increases to such an extent that the [Supplier] is unable to deliver the order as agreed. Then the [Supplier] shall have the right to terminate the order provided that all sums paid for any part of the order not delivered is returned to the [Company].

Services

C.1037

It is agreed that the [Company] shall pay all production, manufacture, distribution, advertising, marketing and exploitation] costs in respect of the [Recordings/Film/Stills/Work] of the [Artist] made under the terms of this Agreement. The [Artist] agrees that all such costs shall be recoupable by the [Company] prior to the payment of any royalties to the [Artist].

C.1038

The [Company] agrees to pay for all costs incurred of any nature which relate to the production, manufacture, distribution, marketing, advertising, and exploitation of the product of the services of the [Artist]. That the [company] shall not be entitled to recoup, offset or claim the right to a contribution to any such costs from the [Artist].

C.1039

The [Lender] warrants that the [Presenter] will not pledge the [Company's] credit or enter into any commitments or negotiate contracts or incur any costs on its behalf without written authority.

C.1040

The [Agent] confirms that he shall be solely responsible for any costs or expenses incurred by the [Agent] pursuant to this Agreement and that the Agent shall only be entitled to receive the Agent's Commission.

C.1041

The [Agent] acknowledges and agrees that he is solely responsible for all costs and expenses that he may incur in respect of the provision of his services under this Agreement and that the [Agent] shall not be entitled to recoup or reimbursement any other sums expended by him in respect of his services unless specifically agreed in advance by the [Licensor].

C.1042

The [Record Company] agrees and undertakes that it shall be solely responsible for any sums due in respect of the productions, manufacture, distribution, marketing and exploitation of the Sound Recordings and the Records and that the [Artist] shall not be liable for any such payments.

C.1043

The [Licensee] confirms that it shall be responsible for all costs incurred in producing any sound recordings of the [Musical Work].

C.1044

The [Agent] agrees that it shall be totally responsible for all costs incurred of any nature by it in respect of the [Agent's] services and the exploitation of the [Artist].

C.1045

The [Designer] agrees to incur no additional expenses nor to exceed the maximum cost agreed without the [Company's] prior approval.

C.1046

The [Agent] undertakes that he shall not seek to be reimbursed by the [Artist] in respect of any costs and expenses incurred by the [Agent] in respect of the performance of his duties under this Agreement unless specifically agreed in detail in advance with the [Artiste].

C.1047

The [Artiste] agrees that he/she shall bear the cost and expense of all his own hotel, telephone, stationery, travel, tax, personal insurance and national insurance. That the [Agent] shall only bear the cost of such expenditure which is specifically authorised within the allocated monthly budget of [–] or is agreed in advance.

C.1048

The [Manager] agrees to assist the [Sportsperson] in general with the financial management of all the [Sportsperson's] Fees and financial affairs generally including tax, value added tax, national insurance, pension and health contributions and personal insurance. Provided that the [Sportsperson] shall seek specialist professional advice where appropriate and shall not seek to rely on the [Manager] to be liable for any errors or losses or the cost.

C.1049

The [Sportsperson] accepts that though the [Manager] may assist in his financial affairs he shall not be liable for any loss or error, nor shall he bear the cost of seeking professional expert advice. The [Sportsperson] shall be liable for his own tax, national insurance, value added tax and other costs and expenses not specified under this Agreement.

C.1050

The [Company] agrees that all costs and expenses incurred in the development, production, distribution and exploitation of the [Company's Product] and any advertisements, promotional events and any other material shall be at the [Company's] sole cost and the [Celebrity] shall not be liable to pay any such sums, costs, or losses that may arise.

C.1051

The [Company] agrees that it shall be solely responsible for any sums due in respect of the production and exploitation of the [specify project] and that [Name] shall not be liable for any such payments whether authorised by him/her or not provided that it is in pursuance of the specified terms of this Agreement.

C.1052

The [Agent] acknowledges that he/she is solely responsible for all costs he/she may incur in respect of his/her services under this Agreement.

C.1053

The [Consultant] shall be entitled to charge no more than [figure/currency] as additional costs and expenses under this Agreement. This allowance may not be exceeded and may only be claimed for [specify] and must be supported by itemised receipts.

C.1054
Where after the conclusion and delivery of the [Report] the [Consortium] require additional work, information and/or data from the [Consultant]. Then the [Consultant] shall be entitled to be paid at the rate of [specify] by the [Consortium] for any such work and payment shall be made on a [weekly basis] by direct debit subject to invoice.

Sponsorship

C.1055
The [Sponsor] confirms that it shall be solely responsible for all costs incurred in respect of the production, distribution, promotion and exploitation of the [Sponsor's Product] and the [Sponsor's Logo] and that the [Sportsperson] shall not be liable for any such sums.

C.1056
The [Sponsor] agrees to bear all costs of creating the [Sponsor's Copy] and of supplying the [Sponsor's Copy] in a technical medium acceptable to the [Radio Station] for its incorporation in the [Programme] on or before [date].

C.1057
The [Company] agrees it shall pay all the costs of producing and incorporating the [Company's Product] and the [Company's Logo] in [specify details] subject to the supply of the original material to the [Company].

C.1058
The [Company] agrees that all sums incurred or due in respect of the production and exploitation of the [specify programme/event/other] will be paid by the [Company] and that the [Sponsor] is not and will not be liable for any payments.

C.1059
The [Sponsor] shall not be responsible for any costs arising from the hospitality suite and other facilities provided by the [Association].

C.1060
The [Sponsor] shall not be entitled to authorise third parties to assist in the funding of the [Event] without the prior written consent of the [Association]. Nor shall the [Sponsor] authorise, pledge or commit the [Authority] to any third party.

C.1061

The [Association] agrees that the [Sponsor] shall not be responsible for any direct or indirect costs relating to the [Event] other than those specifically set out in this Agreement in Clauses [–].

C.1062

The parties agree that the total cost of all expenditure shall be limited to [figure/currency] to be paid for by [specify]. In the event that this is exceeded for any reason then the person or company that incurred, authorised or agreed to the extra cost will be liable to pay and shall be entitled to seek a contribution from the other parties.

C.1063

The cost of the commissioning of the articles, photographs, artwork, production, editing, and printing of the [Brochure/Guide] shall be at the [Sponsor's/Company's] expense.

C.1064

The [Sponsor] agrees and undertakes to pay to the [Company] the cost of all the facilities, supplies, materials, electricity, gas, telephone charges, broadband access, food and drink, stationery, equipment and any other additional expenses which arise at the [Event] which not specified in advance in the Budget under this Agreement which are incurred by the [Sponsor].

C.1065

The [Company] agrees and undertakes that the [Sponsor] shall not be liable for any sums and/or payments except those set out in clauses [specify]. That the [Company] is liable for any costs and/or payments that may be due either before, during and/or after the [Event].

C.1066

Where due to cancellation of the [Event] the [Sponsor] incurs additional costs and expenses. The [Sponsor] agrees that it shall not seek to recover any such sums from the [Organisers] for any reason.

C.1067

Where through the actions and/or omissions and/or errors and/or negligence and/or failure of the [Sponsors] to use suitably qualified employees, casual staff and/or any other third parties and/or that their equipment, displays, stalls and tents and/or products are and/or were unsafe and not fit for purpose. That in the event that there is an allegation that any person has suffered injury, damage and/or loss. Then the [Company] shall be entitled to seek an advance payment towards legal costs from the [Sponsor] to instruct a legal advisor to review and advise on any claim. Where the legal advisor recommends the matter be settled then the [Sponsor] shall pay all the costs, expenses and damages of all the parties involved in each case.

University, Library and Educational

C.1068

1.1 The [Institute] agrees and undertakes that it shall bear all the costs and expenses in respect of the development, production, printing, publication, distribution, marketing, advertising, all copyright clearances or other consents, moral rights, contractual and other legal obligations, payments to collecting societies, any adaptation, translation, and/or sequel, telephone bills, freight, accommodation, travel and any exploitation of the [Work/Service/Artwork] in any media throughout the world.

1.2 That the [Contributor/Company shall not be liable for any such sums [except for those rights and undertakings provided in clauses [specify].] nor shall the [Contributor/Company] be entitled to claim or be paid any sums except those set out in clause [–].

C.1069

The [Institute] agrees that it shall be solely responsible for all costs and expenses incurred in respect of the [Project] and that no such sums shall be deducted from any payments due to the [Company] under this Agreement.

C.1070

The [Author/Contributor] agrees and undertakes that he/she shall bear the cost and expense of all his/her own hotel, telephone and mobile phone bills and charges, stationery, postage and freight, travel, tax, personal insurance, national insurance, value added tax, pension and health contributions and any other costs and expenses incurred in respect of the performance of the services and/or supply of material under this Agreement. The [Author/Contributor] agrees that the [Institute] shall not be liable for any such costs and expenses.

C.1071

The [Researcher] shall only be entitled to be paid such costs and expenses as may be authorised in advance by the [Institute] which relate directly to the [Project]. No sums will be authorised at any time for [specify].

CREDITS

DVD, Video and Discs

C.1072

The [Licensee] agrees to adhere to all credit, copyright notice, moral right, contractual and legal obligations, trade mark, service mark, logo or other rights notified by the [Licensor] in the written statement with the [Film Package]. The [Licensee] shall add its own distribution name as: Distributed by [–] with the following logo/mark [–] in all exploitation of the rights and any associated packaging, brochures, catalogues, websites, publicity, advertising or otherwise whether by the [Licensee] or any authorised third party.

C.1073

The [Licensee] shall ensure that the [Film] and any credits, copyright or other contractual obligations and rights are accurately and adequately described and set out in the packaging, catalogues, brochures and other marketing material. That the packaging and all text and artwork shall be of a high professional standard.

C.1074

The [Licensee] agrees to provide the following copyright notice, trade mark, logo and credit to the [Licensor] in any publicity, promotional, advertising and packaging material in any medium in respect of the exercise of the [DVD/Disc] Rights in the [Film] granted under this Agreement as follows [–].

C.1075

The [Licensor] shall not be accorded a credit in any case in which the [Licensee] is also not credited which may be due to the type of promotion, lack of time and/or space. In any event the [Licensor] shall at all times be credited in the manner above on all copies of the [Film] and on all packaging of the [DVD/Videos].

C.1076

The [Assignee] agrees to abide by any credit obligations provided by the [Assignor].

C.1077

The [Company] agrees to provide the following trade mark, logo and credit to the [Sponsor] in any publicity, promotional, advertising and packaging material in respect of the exploitation of the [DVD and Non-Theatric Rights] in the [Film/Recordings] as follows [specify and attach a copy]. The position on the front and back of the label and packaging of the [DVD] shall be as follows [specify and attach a copy]. The [Company] agrees to provide the [Sponsor] with copies of all such material in which a credit appears to the [Sponsor] upon request by the [Sponsor] at the [Company's] expense.

C.1078
Neither the [Sub-licensee] nor any agent and/or distributor shall not delete, amend and/or vary any copyright notice, credits, trade marks, or copyright warning which the [Licensee] has specified should be on the [Disc] and any copies, all packaging, marketing and advertising material.

C.1079
[Name] original author of [specify]

Adapted and translated by [specify]

Distributed in [country] by [specify]

Film and Television

C.1080
The [Television Company] agrees and acknowledges where appropriate by suitable legend to broadcast, transmit and display on all copies and material the ownership of any copyrights in any material they may use and shall not delete any credits or titles from the [Film] material supplied under this Agreement. The failure to broadcast, transmit or display credits and/ or titles due to any reason beyond the control of the [Television Company] including, but not limited to, lack of time, failure of facilities or otherwise shall not be a breach of this Agreement.

C.1081
The [Television Company] shall not delete from the [Film(s)] any copyright notice, credits, acknowledgement, trade mark, service mark, logo, text or images accorded to any person, author, director, actor, company or distributor in the [Film] or any material supplied under this Agreement.

C.1082
The [Television Company] agrees that no other third party shall be entitled to sponsor the [Programme] or have its logo, trade mark, service mark, design, product, image or slogan or ringtone or music incorporated in the [Programme] or in the introduction, trailer, or end credits whether for the purpose of corporate promotion, advertising or other publicity purposes at any time during the Term of this Agreement in the Territory.

C.1083

The [Distributor] shall comply with all reasonable copyright notice, credits, acknowledgement, trade mark, service mark, logo, text or images notified to the [Distributor] in writing by the [Licensor] and in all advertising and publicity relating thereto. The [Distributor] shall first submit all such material to the [Licensor] for approval (such approval not to be unreasonably withheld). Approval shall be deemed to have been given if the [Licensor] shall not express written objection within [one calendar month] of having received proof copies from the [Distributor].

C.1084

The [Television Company] confirms that the [Sponsor's] Logo will be reasonably, prominently and clearly identifiable in the [Programme] and shall not be obscured or otherwise positioned so that it is not easily recognisable. The [Television Company] agrees that the [Sponsor's] logo shall appear as follows [description: duration/position/background].

C.1085

The [Television Company] agrees that it is its responsibility to ensure that the broadcast, transmission, premium rate phone line and website exploitation of the [Sponsor's] name, product, music, slogan and images will not infringe any sponsorship, endorsement or advertising standards and practices, directives or legislation which apply to the [Television Company] or have been issued by the [Ofcom/other].

C.1086

The [Television Company] confirms and agrees that the [Sponsor] shall be entitled to the following [credit/words/text/image/product] in all publicity, promotion, advertising and marketing material distributed in written form by the [Television Company] [specify format and attach copy]. Provided that the [Television Company] shall not be liable for the failure of any third party to credit the [Sponsor].

C.1087

The [Television Company] agrees to broadcast and/or transmit the [Programme] incorporating the [Sponsor's Logo] in the following on-screen position [–].

C.1088

The [Television Company] confirms that the [Sponsor's] Logo will be reasonably and prominently and clearly identifiable in the [Programme] and in any event will not be less than the following relative on-screen dimensions: Horizontally [–]% Vertically [–]%. During the duration of the [Programme] the

[Television Company] undertakes that the [Sponsor's] Logo will appear on screen for not less than [–] seconds on not less than [–] separate occasions.

C.1089

The [Television Company] confirms that the [Sponsor's] Logo will appear on-screen during the [Programme] with the following background in view [specify].

C.1090

The [Production Company] agrees and shall ensure that the following trade mark, logo and credit to the [Sponsor] shall appear in any publicity, promotional, advertising, website and packaging material in respect of the marketing and distribution of the Programme [specify].

C.1091

The [Licensee] agrees to provide the following copyright notice, credits, trade marks and/or logos to the [Licensor] in any advertising publicity, promotional and packaging material in respect of the exploitation of the [Film] by the [Licensee] as follows [–].

The [Licensee] shall provide the [Licensor] with copies and samples of all such material upon request at the expense of the [Licensee].

C.1092

The [Licensee] agrees to provide the following copyright notice and on-screen credit to the [Licensor] in respect of the [Musical Work] in the [Series] and in all copies of the Series, and in all publicity promotional and associated material [specify].

C.1093

The [Company] undertakes that the [Contributor] shall be entitled to the following on-screen credit at the end of the [Film] [specify] and where applicable in any associated advertising, publicity and promotional material.

C.1094

The [Contributor] agrees that the failure to transmit, broadcast or include the credit in any material shall not be considered a breach of this Agreement where it occurs inadvertently, due to lack of space or time or some other justifiable reason.

C.1095

The [Assignor] agrees that he shall not be entitled to any credit or acknowledgment in respect of the exploitation of the [Format] in any media by the Assignee or any third party.

C.1096

The [Licensee] undertakes to provide the [Licensor] with the following on-screen credit in respect of the [Footage/Stills] [specify].

C.1097

There is no obligation on the part of the [Company] to provide an on-screen credit in the [Film/Recordings] of the material filmed on the [Owner's] premises.

C.1098

The [Radio Station] undertakes to include in any programme schedule, promotional advertising, publicity, website material issued or distributed by the [Radio Station] in respect of the [Programme] the following [credit/slogan/image] to the [Sponsor] for the Term of this Agreement. A sample of which is attached to and forms part of this Agreement.

C.1099

The [Consultant] agrees that he/she shall not be able to claim any right to a credit or acknowledgment unless he/she appears in sound or vision for more than [specify duration]. In such event the following credit shall appear [at the end of the Programme/on screen/on advertising] [–].

C.1100

The [Consultant] agrees to provide a true and honest biography, to allow photographs to be taken for a portrait and to allow the [Company] to use his name in any publicity or promotional material relating to the [Series] and/or the [Company] at any time.

C.1101

[Name] agrees and accepts that there is no right to a credit on the [Film/Programme/other] either when he/she appears and/or at the end and/or in any verbal and /or audio form and/or in any exploitation of any of the rights by the [Company] and/or any third party.

C.1102

The [Company] reserves the right to remove and/or delete the credit and/or performance of any person who in their opinion has been discredited and/or exposed as a fraud and/or is the subject of a serious criminal legal action at any time.

General Business and Commercial

C.1103

The [Company] agrees to ensure that any third party or successor in title shall agree to comply and be contractually bound to carry out the conditions set out in Clause [–].

C.1104
[Name] agrees that the [Company] shall be permitted to use his/her [name, image, photograph, signature, slogan, comments, recordings, film] for the marketing and exploitation of [specify purpose] provided that it is not used for any other reason or to endorse any products without prior written consent.

C.1105
[Name] shall be provided with an exact sample of each and every item of material of any nature which features, mentions or refers to the name, biography, image, signature or otherwise of [Name] produced or distributed or otherwise exploited by the [Company] under this Agreement.

C.1106
The [Company] agrees to allow the [Personality] to be given the opportunity to view in advance where possible any item, document or other material which it intends to distribute referring to or featuring the [Personality] in any form.

C.1107
The [Company] agrees not to permit or license any part of the material produced under this Agreement to endorse any product produced by a third party unless the prior written consent of the [Actor/Agent] has been obtained.

C.1108
The [Licensee] agrees that it shall not be allowed to make or authorise any cuts, changes, alterations or deletions to the credits, copyright notice, logos or trade marks which have been agreed under this Agreement.

C.1109
No third party shall be entitled or authorised to fund or sponsor the [Film/Product/other] or have its logo, trade mark, service mark, design, product or image associated with or in any part of the [Film/Product/other] without the written consent of both parties to this Agreement.

C.1110
The [Assignor] agrees to provide a detailed and complete list of credits, copyright notices, service marks, trade marks, logos, slogans to the [Assignee] by [date] in respect of all the [Film/Works/other] which have been assigned under this Agreement. The [Assignor] shall provide originals of all relevant documents, material and artwork that may be available at the [Assignor's] cost.

C.1111

The [Licensee] agrees to display prominently all copyright notices, credits, trade marks, service marks, designs and logos in the [specify item] in any advertising, publicity, promotional and packaging material requested by the [Licensor] when the [material] is delivered.

C.1112

The [Licensee] agrees that in all publicity, promotional and advertising material for [Film/Product/Services] no other [Artists] shall appear in sound or vision more frequently than [Name].

C.1113

The [Assignee] agrees to abide by any contractual, moral, copyright and credit obligations specified by the [Assignor] in Clause [–].

C.1114

The [Licensee] agrees that all quotes and use of statements from third parties to be used in packaging or marketing material shall be subject to the prior approval of the [Licensor].

C.1115

The [Name] agrees that where the [Company] fails to exhibit, display, print or include a credit for any reason to [Name] in any material that it shall not be deemed a breach of this Agreement. There shall be no obligation to withdraw, destroy or correct the omission, but any new material must include the correction.

C.1116

Where a credit is not included in any material due to lack of space, time, the type of material, a printing error, technical failure, or some other reason by the [Company, an agent or sub-licensee. This shall not give raise to a claim for compensation, damages, loss of reputation or breach of contract.

C.1117

Your participation in this [Event/Market Survey] is provided without any obligation to provide your personal details except [specify]. The [Company] agrees and undertakes not to attribute and/or credit any part so as to release and/or publish your identity.

Internet and Websites

C.1118

There shall be no obligation to provide a credit to any person who contributes to this [Website] unless it has been agreed in writing with the [Company].

C.1119
Any person who contributes to this [Website] who has been found to claim credit or copyright ownership of any material which is in fact incorrect or untrue shall have the worked removed, deleted and erased, and be denied access to the [Website].

C.1120
Where any material whether text, images, logo, sound recording, film, music, lyrics, or any other material of any type contains a copyright notice, credit or other acknowledgement. There is no right to delete, remove, alter and/or attribute the material to another person. There is no automatic right to reproduce, distribute, supply and/or exploit any such material. If you use any of this material for any reason than private residential use at home and without storing it on a hard drive then you may be at risk of a threat of legal action.

C.1121
Where any material on this [Website] is downloaded with the permission of the [Company] and in accordance with the terms and conditions. It is important that all copyright notices, credits, trade marks, logos and other references to distributors, licences and/or software are not deleted, removed, altered and/or changed. Where the [Website] and/or part is to be referred to in any article, research, and/or reproduced in any medium and/or format at any time. There should be a clear statement of the web reference [specify] together with all copyright notices, credits, trade marks, logos and any other acknowledgements.

C.1122
Where the [Company] decides in its absolute discretion that a credit is not to be attributed and/or made on their [Website] and/or in their programme catalogue. Then you shall have the right to withdraw the [Work] and cancel the Agreement.

C.1123
The [Company] shall only be able to use copyright notices and credits on the [Website/Blog/App] next to the material and/or other rights in which ownership and/or control is claimed where there is the space and it will not impair the functionality. It reserves the right to list copyright notices and credits in one allocated zone at the bottom of the [screen/page/other].

Merchandising

C.1124
The [Licensee] agrees to acknowledge by suitable legend the ownership of any copyrights in any such material they may use provided that the

[Licensor] shall have informed the [Licensee] in writing as to the required copyright notices, credits and logos at the time of delivery of the material.

C.1125
The [Licensee] and any sub-licensee may include in the [Product] the name and logo of the [Licensee] and/or any sub-licensee provided that neither the [Licensee] nor any sub-licensee shall alter or delete any credit, logo or copyright notice appearing on the [Product].

C.1126
The [Agent] agrees to ensure that any third party shall agree to provide the following credit, copyright notice, trade mark or logo to the [Licensor] in respect of the [Licensed Articles] and in all publicity, advertising, promotional, website and packaging material in respect of the marketing and distribution of the [Licensed Articles] [–].

C.1127
The [Agent] acknowledges and agrees to ensure that all third parties to be licensed by the [Licensor] under this Agreement shall agree that the copyright notice for the [Character] and any trade mark or logo, together with any credit, shall be incorporated on each item of the [Licensed Article] as far as possible and on all packaging, promotional advertising and other material relating to the [Licensed Article].

C.1128
The [Company] shall provide the following credit, copyright notice and logo or trade mark as follows [specify exact words, size, position and order] to the [Author] which shall be displayed in a prominent and visible position in every copy of any item produced under this Agreement and on all marketing, advertising or packaging material. The [Author] shall at all times be acknowledged as the copyright owner and no other party shall have their name listed first in order or in a more significant position.

C.1129
The [Assignor] agrees that he/she shall not be entitled to any credit or acknowledgment in respect of the exploitation of the [Format] in any media by the [Assignee].

C.1130
[Article] distributed by [specify]

Country of origin [specify]

© [year] [Name]

[Trade Mark/Logo/Image] [specify]

[address]

Publishing

C.1131
The [Ghostwriter] agrees that he shall not be entitled to any credit or acknowledgment in respect of the exploitation of the [Work] by the [Company] or any person or any media at any time. The [Ghostwriter] agrees that the [Company] shall be entitled to receive the sole credit and copyright notice for producing and writing the Work.

C.1132
The [Agent] confirms that in addition to the moral rights of the [Author] under this Agreement the [Agent] shall ensure that the [Author] is provided with the following copyright notice, trade mark, logo and credit in the [Work] in any form and in any publicity, promotional, advertising, website or packaging material in respect of any type of exploitation of the Work as follows [–].

C.1133
The [Agent] agrees to ensure that as far as reasonably possible the [Author] shall be entitled to approve all proposed copies, samples and other material of the [Work] or any adaptation, development or variation whether by a publisher, distributor, wholesaler, or licensee and any associated promotional or publicity material, including labels, packaging, catalogues, posters and websites in respect of the manufacture, distribution, exploitation and marketing of the [Work].

C.1134
The [Licensee] agrees to provide the following copyright notice, trade mark, logo and credit to the [Licensor] in the [Periodical] in relation to the [Extracts] and in any publicity, promotional, advertising, website and packaging material in respect of the exercise of the Serialisation Rights [–].

C.1135
The [Publisher] shall use its reasonable endeavours to ensure that the [Work] is accurately described in any marketing and advertising material and that the [Author's] name is clearly displayed. Further the [Publisher] shall use its reasonable endeavours to ensure that any quotes or use of statements by third parties in relation to the [Work] which it intends to use shall be subject to the approval of the [Author].

C.1136

The [Publisher] agrees to identify the [Author] as the original creator of the [Work] as follows [Name/size/location] in a suitable and prominent position on the cover, the binding and the inside front pages of the [Work], on any packaging material, on all draft and printed copies, on any disks or other material, and in all media on every item and any associated parts together with any website, advertising, marketing or publicity material.

C.1137

The [Authors] agree that in all circumstances relating to the exploitation of the [Work] that the following credit shall apply [name of first author] [name of second author] which shall be [on the same level/which shall be parallel on separate lines] and in the same style, size and both appear on any occasion that one is credited. Both [Authors] shall also endeavour to ensure that in any commercial exploitation of the [Work] or any reference in public that they shall each acknowledge the co-authorship of the other and not give the impression that they are the main or sole contributor.

C.1138

The [Author] is entitled to the following credit in the following form and style [–] on all copies of any material based on the [Author's Work].

C.1139

[Name] agrees and accepts that he/she shall not receive any acknowledgement and/or credit for their contribution to the development, preparation and conclusion of the [Project]. That [Name] agrees that he/she has no legal and/or other moral right to a credit and/or copyright notice in any form and/or any sums from the exploitation of the [Project]. That [Name] has accepted and received the [Fee] in full and final settlement.

Purchase and Supply of Products

C.1140

The [Seller] agrees that in any associated publicity, advertising, promotional material, emails, text message, adverts, webpages or other marketing material by the [Seller] of the [Seller's] website that where appropriate the [Supplier's Logo] and the [Product] shall be given reasonable prominence, recognition and credit as follows [specify name/size/location/position].

C.1141

The [Seller] agrees to provide the following copyright notice, credit, service mark, trade mark or logo to the [Supplier] in respect of the [Product] as is specified in Schedule [–] in respect of the [Sellers] Website and any advertising, marketing, publicity, promotional and packaging material and shall provide the [Supplier] with copies and samples at the [Seller's] cost on a regular basis.

C.1142
The [Seller] agrees that the [Supplier] shall be entitled to refer to the [Seller's] Website in its own marketing, publicity and advertising material in the form set out as follows [specify]. Such use shall be subject to the prior approval of the [Seller] in each case and the [Supplier] shall supply an exact copy of the use to the [Seller] for approval.

C.1143
The [Distributor] agrees that it shall not erase, remove, delete and/or in any way deface, alter and/or change and/or conceal any of the copyright notices, credits and trademarks of any of the parties on the [Product/Article/Work].

Services

C.1144
Subject to prior consultation the [Presenter] agrees that the [Company] shall be entitled to use her name, biography, photograph, signature, image and quotations in respect of the [Series] and any exploitation of the material and any advertising or promotion.

C.1145
The [Celebrity] shall be reasonably, prominently and clearly identified at all times in the following [style/manner/format] and in particular by the following; [Name] whether in any original material created and exploited under this Agreement supplied by the [Celebrity] or issued in press releases, set out on the website [reference] or otherwise.

C.1146
The [Celebrity] agrees that the [Company] shall be entitled to use and permit the use of the [Celebrity's] name, biography, photograph and image for the purpose of promoting and advertising [specify product/services/other] but not for any other reason during the Term of this Agreement. Provided that the [Agent] is notified in each case and is fully consulted as to the exact form and medium in which it is intended to be exploited.

C.1147
In the event that the [Film] is completed using the services of the [Director] then the [Director] shall be accorded a credit in the following manner [specify name, size, location] in all publicity, advertising and promotional material and in the end credits of the [Film]. The [Director] acknowledges that he shall not be provided with a credit in the following circumstances:

1.1 Short extracts of the [Film] to promote, advertise and/or exploit the [Film] in any media including television, radio, websites, DVDs, CD-Roms and mobile phones.

1.2 Where any advertising, publicity or other exploitation relates to the work on which the [Film] is based or the screenplay or any members of the cast, personnel, author or producer. Except when such material relates to the [Director] then a credit shall be provided.

1.3 Advertising, publicity and promotion in any media where due to lack of time or space no other artist or person involved in the production of the [Film] is credited.

1.4 All commercial tie-ins, merchandising or other related exploitation including publications, periodicals and other written form and sound recordings in any format.

1.5 Exploitation in the form of [DVDs/other] credit shall be on the [Film] but not the associated packaging.

1.6 Any other exploitation where no credits are provided to any other production personnel.

The [Company] shall not be responsible for failure by third parties to provide a credit to the [Director] which was unintentional. Provided that when the [Company] becomes aware of any such failure or default it shall use its endeavours to remedy the position as soon as possible.

C.1148

The [Director] shall be entitled to a credit on the negative and all positive copies of the [Film] made by or to the order of the [Company]. The [Director's] credit in the opening credits of the [Film] shall be in the last position of a size not less than 75% (seventy-five per cent) of the size of the title on a separate panel in the form: Directed by [–]. The [Director's] credit may at the [Company's] discretion be accompanied in small print by the [Company's] Logo and/or copyright notice.

C.1149

The [Record Company] agrees and undertakes that the [Artiste] shall be clearly, prominently and reasonably identifiable by the following credit and copyright notice [–] which shall be provided on the material of any nature in relation to the record, the musical work and/or the [Artiste] which is created, distributed and/or released in any media by the [Record Company] including in all packaging, labels, covers, websites, downloads, telecommunications systems and mobile phones, publicity, advertising and promotional material at any time.

C.1150

The [Publisher] agrees to ensure that the [Author] [shall be provided with the following credit in all copies of the [Work] and in any publicity, advertising, promotional and packaging material [–] in respect of any part of the [Work] whether the original musical work, any associated, lyrics and/or arrangement.

C.1151

The [Contributor] understands and agrees that the [Company] shall not be obliged to use the contribution in any form or to provide a credit or acknowledgment to the [Contributor].

C.1152

The [Company] agrees that the [Contributor's] name, image and endorsement shall not be used for any purpose other than the promotion and marketing of the [Contributor's] [specify subject] to the public.

C.1153

Subject to prior consultation the [Actor] agrees that the [Agent] shall be entitled to use his name, signature, biography, photograph, image and stage name in the promotion, advertising and marketing of the [Actor] and to authorise others to do so provided that a copy of any such material shall in due course be provided by the [Agent] to the [Actor] [upon request/each month].

C.1154

The [Manager] agrees to ensure that the following; [credit/copyright notice/trade mark/logo/slogan/image] of the [Sportsperson] shall appear prominently in any material distributed by the [Agent] or agreed with or licensed to third parties relating to the [Sportsperson] of any nature including all publicity, advertising, promotional and packaging material or any products [detailed description].

C.1155

The Company agrees that the [Actor] shall be provided with the following on screen credit [specify name, size, order, location] at the end of each programme of the [Series] and on any other occasion in which other lead actors receive additional on-screen credits. The [Company] shall ensure that no copy of any part of the [Series] shall distributed, exploited or marketed without adhering to the provision of the credit unless agreed in advance in writing with the [Actor]. Failure to provide credits on more than [number] occasions shall be deemed to be a breach and the [Actor] shall be paid an additional fee of [specify sum] in each such case.

C.1156

The [Company] agrees that the [Consultant] shall be entitled to the following credit in respect of the [Project] on the main report, any copies and any summary on the [Website] of the [Company] in respect of the [Consultants'] contribution to the [Project]. Where the [Consultants'] contribution is deleted from the main report and/or [Website] no credit shall be due. The [Consultant] shall not be entitled to a credit in any promotional, marketing, advertising and/or other material that may developed and/or created at any time.

C.1157

The [Consultant] agrees and undertakes that he/she shall not be entitled to any credit, recognition and/or acknowledgement in respect of their services and/or any work and material provided under this Agreement. The [Consultant] waives all moral rights to be identified and/or to object to derogatory treatment of his/her work. The [Consultant] agrees that the [Company] shall be entitled to edit, delete, add to, amend and/or translate the work and material provided by the [Consultant] as it thinks fit at its sole discretion.

C.1158

The [Agent] agrees to provide the [Company] with a list of credit and copyright and/or contractual obligations that must be fulfilled in respect of the [Project]. Where possible the [Agent] shall supply current contact details of the party to whom such obligations are owed and a provisional list of the cost of any payments that shall fall due.

Sponsorship

C.1159

The [Television Company] confirms that the [Company's Product] will be reasonably and clearly identifiable in the [Programme] and in any event will be seen on-screen on not less than [number] of separate [scenes/occasions] each time for not less than [duration] seconds.

C.1160

The [Sponsor] agrees to provide the [Sportsperson] with samples of all proposed promotional, advertising publicity, packaging and other material in which it is intended to use the name, image and endorsement of the [Sportsperson] under this Agreement.

C.1161

The [Sponsor] agrees that the name image and endorsement of the [Sportsperson] shall not be used for any purpose other than the promotion and endorsement of the [Sponsor's Product] for the duration of the Sponsorship Period.

C.1162

The [Company] agrees that the [Presenter's] name, image, signature and endorsement shall not be used for any other purpose other than the marketing and exploitation of the [Programme] and [Company] unless agreed in advance on each occasion with the [Presenter]. The [Company] agrees to provide the [Presenter] with exact samples of all materials in any medium in which it is intended to use the name, image, endorsement or otherwise of the [Presenter]. In the event that the [Presenter] requests alterations or changes in any form then the [Company] agrees to carry out the request provided that it is reasonable in the circumstances and the cost is not prohibitive.

C.1163
The [Sponsor] agrees to provide the [Agent] with samples of all proposed promotional, advertising, publicity, packaging and other material in which it is intended to use the name, image, endorsement or any other contribution in any form of the [Sportsperson] under this Agreement.

C.1164
The [Company] confirms that the [Sponsor] shall be entitled to the following text, slogan, trade mark, credit, image in all publicity, promotion and marketing material appearing in any [written] form; [–] distributed by the [Company] in respect of the [specify project]. The [Sponsor] shall be able to use the following corresponding details regarding the [Company] [specify] in its own promotional or advertising material.

C.1165
The [Company] undertakes to include in any programme schedule, promotional, advertising, publicity or other literature or in any film, recordings, group or corporate photographs, graphics or on the website [Name] or in any other material of any type released or published in respect of the [Programme] the following [credit/trade mark/slogan/statement] on behalf of the [Sponsor] [–].

C.1166
The [Sponsor] accepts that the script, programme schedule, presenters and other aspects of [Series] may be changed due to editorial, programme policy or legal reasons at the [Television Company's] own discretion. In the event that this results in less exposure of the [Company's Product] and [Company's Logo] then no sums shall be repaid or claimed by the [Sponsor] unless the duration of which the [Company's Product] is visible on screen is less than [specify length] [in total in the Series/or in any one Programme].

C.1167
The [Sponsor] accepts that any reference to the [Company's Product] and the [Company's Logo] in the [Programme] in any publicity, advertising

515

and promotional material may differ on occasions depending on the circumstances and may not be mentioned at all.

C.1168

The [Company] shall include the following mention, credit, photograph and statement on behalf of the [Sponsor] in any material that may be issued or released or created relating to the [Event/Series/Artist] so that fair recognition is attributed to the [Sponsor's] contribution under this Agreement.

C.1169

The [Company] agrees to provide the following [credit/trade mark/service mark/logo/image/copyright notice/statement/slogan] to the [Sponsor] in the following circumstances:

1.1 [–] on all packaging, labels, jackets or sleeves.

1.2 [–] on all posters, brochures, catalogues, and advertisements.

1.3 [–] on the first press release.

1.4 [–] on the display stand signs at any exhibition.

1.5 [–] in radio commercials.

1.6 [–] in television commercials.

1.7 [–] in commercials.

1.8 [–] on the website, internet or interactive gadgets or games.

1.9 [–] in any DVD, products or merchandising.

C.1170

The [Sponsor] shall not use the name of the [Association] or any trade mark, service mark, logo, slogan or otherwise of the [Event] [Promoter] or any third party in any manner including competitors in any manner or advertising or promotion of goods or services not specifically authorised under this Agreement.

C.1171

The [Company] agree that an official printed programme shall be made available to the general public during the [Festival] at a price within the discretion of the [Company]. The [Company] agree that the official programme shall bear the [Sponsor's Logo] on the front page, a half page statement from the [Sponsor] on page [–] and a full page advertisement for the [Sponsor's Product] on the back of the cover.

C.1172

The [Company] agree to display the [name, logo and image] of the [Sponsor] in a form to be agreed throughout the venue on flags, banners, seating, pitch and any other suitable locations. Provided that it shall not cause any health and safety issues and/or impede the primary focus of the [Company] to [specify] and the [Sponsor] shall pay all the costs of any such materials, work and/or planning applications, legal and consultants costs, administrative costs and any other costs and expenses that may be required to both install and maintain any such marketing and promotional material for the [Sponsor]. At no time shall the [Company] be expected to pay and/or incur any costs and/or charges.

University, Library and Educational

C.1173
The [Institute] confirms that the [Contributor/Consultant] shall be entitled to the following credit in respect of the [Project]. In the event that no credit appears in any copies then the [Contributor/Consultant] agrees that there shall be no liability by the [Institute] to the [Contributor/Consultant] for any loss of reputation and/or breach of moral rights. The [Contributor/Consultant] waives all rights to any claim for losses, damages and/or otherwise in respect of any failure to put a credit on any material at any time.

C.1174
The [Company/Distributor] agrees that it shall not use the name, logo, trade mark and/or appearance of the [Institute] and/or the [Work/Service/Project] and/or any other material associated with them for the purposes of advertising, and/or marketing the other goods, services and work of the [Company/Distributor] and/or for any purpose not specifically authorised under this Agreement.

C.1175
The [Institute] agrees and undertakes to use its reasonable endeavours to ensure that the following; [credit/copyright notice/trade mark/logo/slogan/image] of the [Company/Author] shall appear prominently on all copies of the [Project/Work] reproduced, supplied, distributed and exploited by the [Institute] and/or licensed to third parties relating to the [Company/Author] including any associated material such as publicity, advertising, promotional, packaging and merchandising.

C.1176
The [Institute] does not endorse and/or promote any commercial events and/or projects without a written agreement setting out the terms and conditions of support, use of the logo, image and name and liability. Where a third party uses and adapts the logo, image and/or name of the [Institute] without authority then the event and/or project may be cancelled without notice.

D

DAMAGES

General Business and Commercial

D.001
The [Contractor] shall be obliged to pay the [Company] such sums as set out in this Agreement as may be due for failure to complete the [Project] by the Completion Date. The [Company] shall provide written notice of the total sums and the details thereof after the Certificate has been issued to the [Contractor] by the [Individual]. The [Contractor] shall be obliged to pay such sums within [specify duration] of notice. In the event that the payment is not received by the [Company] within that period then the [Company] shall be entitled to seek to recover the debt together with interest at [specify percentage] above base rate of [Name Bank plc]. In addition the [Company] shall be entitled at its sole option to withhold and retain the total sums due from the [Contractor] from any monies that the [Company] is due to pay to the [Contractor] under this Agreement in settlement of the debt.

D.002
Nothing in this Agreement shall entitle the [Licensee] to any remuneration, payment, costs, expenses or damages from the [Licensor] if the failure to fulfil the terms of this Agreement and/or its performance shall arise due to the default of the [Licensee].

D.003
In the event of the [Company] being obliged to pay damages or compensation in respect of any problem of any nature caused directly or indirectly by the [Exhibitor] and/or its personnel and/or guests. Then the [Exhibitor] shall reimburse the [Company] for the total amount of the sum paid together with any legal costs.

D.004
The [Company] agrees and undertakes that it shall be liable for any physical damage, power failures, indirect and direct financial loss, interference with existing functions of software, machinery or devices, failure to supply, deliver or distribute any material or products, cancellation or termination of orders

or contracts or negotiations or any other consequence whether foreseeable or not which arises from the [Service/Product/other].

D.005
Where damage is caused of any nature to the [Customer's] personal belongings as a result of using these facilities. The [Company] shall not be liable to pay for any damage, to compensate the [Customer] or offer any refund.

D.006
In the event that the [Company] is prevented from exercising the rights granted to it under this Agreement by reason of a material breach by the [Licensor]. Then the [Licensor] shall pay to the [Company] the total sum of [currency/figure] in damages within [duration] of notice of the claim and the grounds on which it is based.

D.007
'The Damages' shall mean any sums to which the [Company] may become entitled as a result of any breach by the [Licensor] of any of its obligations under this Agreement.

D.008
Neither party shall be liable to the other for indirect consequential or punitive damages of any kind whether due to loss of profits and/or interruption of business.

D.009
In the event of non-performance of the conditions set out in Clause [–] of this Agreement then the party who has defaulted shall be liable to pay the [Company] the sum of [currency/figure] per [day/week/month] as liquidated damages. These sums are agreed by all parties to be a fair and accurate assessment of the damages due to the [Company]. The parties expressly agree that such sums are not to be construed as a penalty clause.

D.010
Any damage which arises to either of the parties' businesses or products or reputations as a result of this Agreement shall not be claimed against the other party. Each party agrees and undertakes to take out insurance cover to the value of [specify] for their own benefit and at their own cost to cover any such consequences.

D.011
All claims for damages, loss or other liability under this Agreement against the [Company] shall be limited to [figure/currency] in total [unless caused

by deliberate fraud, malice, negligence or results in death or serious injury.]

D.012

Where the [Company] supplies access to and/or use of any services, products and/or other material by [Name] while they are at the [Event]. That it is agreed that [Name] must take due care and consideration and not cause any loss, damage and/or injury at any time. Where [Name] causes any damage and/or loss and/or injury then the [Company] shall be paid in full for all sums which shall be due, claimed and/or settled including legal costs and expenses which shall have arisen due to [Name]. Provided that the [Company] can provide full details of any such sums and supporting evidence and it is not covered by any insurance policy of the [Company].

D.013

If any of the participants at the [Event] cause damage and/or loss for any reason then the [Company] shall hold [Name] liable for any sums which it may have to incur to remedy the situation and replace, repair and/or substitute any objects, decorations and fittings, furniture and/or to bring the accommodation and/or any part of the [Venue] up to the standard that it was before the [Event]. Where the impact has caused loss of other business for the [Company] then [Name] shall also be obliged to pay for that loss where other parties had booked.

D.014

The [Company] agrees to pay for the cost of a [surveyor/auditor/loss adjustor] to review and assess the facts and circumstances and to provide a written report and recommendation as to the best course of action and the likely costs that can be expected if alternative projects to remedy the damages are proceeded with by the parties.

D.015

It is agreed that in the event that any items are damaged for any reason that the maximum that [Name] will be liable to pay shall be [number/currency] per [specify]. That normal wear and tear and/or damage which is arises where there is no evidence of negligence and/or carelessness and/or malice and/or excessive force shall not be paid for by [Name] and the [Company] shall bear its own costs for such damages.

Internet and Websites

D.016

The [Company] shall not be responsible for any damage which may arise as a result of following the advice on this [Website] as to how to [specify]. This advice is for guidance only and you are expected to read the instructions which accompany the [Product] and use the item in accordance with those instructions issued by the [manufacturer/supplier]. In any event where any claim is made you agree that the total maximum claim for damages is limited to [figure/currency].

D.017

The [Website Company] may claim damages against any supplier, distributor, or manufacturer who provides goods or services to the [Website] which are found to be defective, not fit for their purpose, misleading as to their content or uses, pose a risk to health or are not produced in accordance with product safety standards or fail to comply with all necessary legislation, directives, standards and practices in [country/other]. The claim for damages is not fixed or limited in value and may include:

1.1 loss of profit;

1.2 administration, public relation and legal costs;

1.3 the costs of product recall from the public and other customers including freight and refund charges;

1.4 damage to and loss of reputation and goodwill;

1.5 fall in share price of the [Website Company];

1.6 cancellation or termination of existing contracts and agreements; or

1.7 cancellation of promotions, advertising or marketing.

D.018

The [Company] supplies the service, information and data to you and makes no recommendation as to the personal decisions that you make seek to make based on any such material. The [Company] does not accept any responsibility for any subsequent losses, damages, failures and/or expenses that may arise and you are advised to seek professional and expert advice. This service is for [entertainment] and is not based on verifiable sources that can be disclosed to you.

D.019

This [Blog] is a personal diary and not intended to be considered as a professional advice column by its readers. No losses, damages, actions, failures, expenses, costs and/or any other omissions, errors, delays and/or any other matter can or will be accepted by and/or paid for by [Name] from any third party at any time. You must make your own decisions and do your own research and there is no promotion and/or endorsement of any product, business and/or person in any form and/or recommendation to purchase, sell, contribute to and/or engage with any third party.

D.020

This [App] and its contents and use are provided to you to use for free as you think fit for your own purposes and to your own advantage. Provided that you agree to the following terms of use:

1.1 That you agree to waive all rights to make any claim and/or allegation and/or summons for any damages, losses, expenses and/or any other sum arising from such use including viruses, security failures and loss of data and/or other material.

1.2 That you will not reproduce and/or exploit any part of the [App] in any form and/or media at any time.

1.3 That where you intend to incur any costs and/or take any steps based on information derived from your use of the [App] that you agree that any such decision is at your own cost and risk.

1.4 That you agree that the [Company] and the [Distributor] have only granted you a non-exclusive licence to use the {App] and content and that there is no right to sub-licence and/or grant and/or exploit any part at any time.

Merchandising

D.021

There shall be no obligation to account for [Licensed Articles] which have been damaged in transit, destroyed, are lost or stolen or otherwise not delivered to the [Distributor] by the [Supplier].

D.022

The total liability for damages by the [Company] which can arise in respect of this [Order] and [Products/Services/other] shall be limited to the total value of the payment for that [Order].

D.023

Where no payment is made to the [Licensor] in respect of [Material/Products/Services] due to loss or damage of any nature for which the [Company] subsequently receives compensation under an insurance claim. Then the [Licensor] shall be entitled to receive payment upon terms to be agreed between the parties.

D.024

Where any claim and/or payment is made to any person and/or third party for damages, losses, expenses, interest, refunds, product liability and/any other liability and/or sum is made by the [Licensee] and/or any sub-licensee.

There shall be no automatic right to deduct any such payments from the royalties due to the [Licensor]. Unless the payment and/or sum is directly due to a breach and/or an alleged breach of a term of this Agreement by the [Licensor]. Then all such payments and/or sums shall be the responsibility of the [Licensee] and/or any sub-licensee and not the [Licensor].

D.025

The [Sub-Licensee] agrees and undertakes that where there is any failure and/or delay in any manufacturing process and/or service required to produce and/or distribute the [Articles]. That where any damages, losses and/or expenses are incurred that all such sums shall be at the [Sub-Licensees] sole cost and cannot be offset and/or recouped from the sums due to the [Company].

D.026

It is agreed between the parties that where [Products] are manufactured and/or distributed which are not of sufficient quality and/or are damaged in some form. That the [Licensee] may sell and dispose of these [Products] provided that:

1.1   The items are clearly marked as sub-standard and

1.2   The brand name and labels are removed and

1.3   The [Licensee] shall pay the [Licensor] a royalty of [number] per cent of all sums received.

D.027

Where any items are lost, damaged, destroyed, returned as faulty and/or for any other reason are unsuitable to be sold to the public as fit for purpose as [specify] under the brand [specify]. Than it is agreed between the parties that all such items shall be destroyed and not sold and/or disposed of as seconds and/or at a discount at any time. Further that no evidence shall be required as a record of destruction nor shall any such item need to be mentioned in the accounting reports to the [Company].

Publishing

D.028

No royalties shall be paid to the [Assignor] in respect of copies of the [Work/Products] and/or parts which are destroyed in transit, by fire, water, remaindered, sold at cost, or otherwise damaged or disposed of at cost price or below. Provided that no income or credit above cost, or other benefit is received from such disposal, loss or damage.

D.029

The [Distributor] undertakes that the [Work] shall be stored in a secure place and shall be packaged and sent by such method as to ensure that the [Work] shall not damaged in transit.

D.030

The [Publisher] shall not be liable for any loss and/or damage to the manuscript, USB and/or other device upon which the material is stored and/or for any photographs and/or other material supplied for the [Work] and/or as part of the packaging, marketing and/or advertising by the [Author]. The [Author] shall be obliged to keep a complete copy of all material and only to supply copies of photographs not originals. The [Author] accepts and agrees that all material is supplied at the [Author's] cost and risk.

D.031

Where the [Publisher] discounts and/or disposes of copies of the [Work] due to the fact that there are errors, damages and/or omissions to all and/or any part. Then the [Author] agrees that the [Publisher] may provide a figure for the sum received and the name of the party third party rather than the number of copies. That the [Author] shall be paid [number] per cent of all sums received and that payment shall be within [number] days of receipt of payment by the [Publisher].

D.032

Where damage to any [Work] is caused by fire, explosion, riot, war, flood, earthquake, tornado and/or any other extreme weather conditions, outbreaks of violence in any locality and/or country and the [Publisher] is unable to verify either the exact circumstances and/or the value of the stock damaged. Then the [Author] agrees that the best estimate shall be acceptable for the purposes of accounting provided that the [Publisher] shall not seek to offset any damages and losses against sums due to the [Author] at any time.

Purchase and Supply of Products

D.033

The [Supplier] shall not be liable for any loss or damage incurred or suffered by the [Customer] and/or any third party arising from the use and/or reproduction of the [Work].

D.034

In the event of delay by the [Purchaser] of taking delivery of the [Products] the [Purchaser] agrees to pay the [Seller] storage charges for the [Products] and any other expenses and damages that the [Seller] may sustain. Any such payment shall be without prejudice to any other rights and remedies of the [Seller].

D.035

If the [Product] is lost, stolen or damaged after it has been delivered and/or installed, then the [Customer] must pay the cost of repair or replacing it excluding fair wear and tear.

D.036

That the [Company] shall not responsible for any damage, loss or failure which may arise in a machine or gadget owned or controlled by the [Customer] in which the [Customer] installs or uses the [Product/DVD/other] which is not directly caused by a defect in the [Product/DVD/other].

D.037

1.1 This [Product] is not for general use and is only suitable for [specify] and not [specify]. You are advised not to use it in conjunction with any other [specify] and not to exceed [number] applications per [week]. Before general use you are advised to try a test sample on [specify]. In the event that you show any sensitivity do not use on any part of [specify] and/or anywhere else. Do not use on any person under age [specify]. Do not use after the expiry date on [specify]. Avoid contact with [specify].

1.2 No responsibility can be accepted for damage to the [Product] due to exposure to sunlight and/or use with other materials and/or any use which is not in accordance with the instructions.

D.038

No [Product] may be returned to the [Company] as faulty where the damage has arisen directly as a result of the fact that the consumer has used the [Product as follows:

1.1 the wrong tools have been used to operate it;

1.2 the instructions in the brochure were not followed;

1.3 the [Product] was used in conjunction with another product which was faulty which caused the damage;

1.4 there was a power failure and/or power surge; or

1.5 water, heat and/or pressure was applied to the [Product] and caused damage.

D.039

In the event that any party wishes to make a claim for damages arising from this Agreement. It is agreed that that such party shall provide a detailed statement of the damage and sum claimed and provide the other party with [number] days to respond prior to the issue of any legal action and/or summons.

Services

D.040
The [Company] acknowledges that the services of the [Individual] are of a personal nature which can only be compensated in damages. The [Company] agrees that the [Company] shall not be entitled to and shall not seek, if the circumstances arise, an injunction or other equitable remedy to prevent or curtail any actual or threatened breach by the [Individual] with respect to the provisions of his/her services under this Agreement.

D.041
The [Composer] acknowledges that the services of the [Composer] are of a unique nature and character, the loss of which cannot be reasonably or adequately compensated in damages in an action at law. The [Composer] agrees that the [Company] shall be entitled to seek equitable relief by way of an injunction to prevent or curtail any actual or threatened breach by the [Composer] of the provisions of this Agreement.

D.042
The [Organisers] and the [Promoter] agree that:

1.1 If the [Promoter] is given notice of the cancellation of the [Event] by the [Organisers] on or before [date] then the [Promoter] shall only be entitled to be paid [figure/currency] together with all sums incurred in respect of the Promotion Expenses.

1.2 If the [Event] is cancelled after [date] then the [Organisers] and the [Promoters] agree that the [Promoter] shall be entitled to be paid the [Promoter's] Fee in total in addition to all sums incurred in respect of the Promotion Expenses.

1.3 These clauses shall not apply where the event is cancelled due to force majeure under clause [–].

1.4 In the event that these clauses are relied upon there shall be no further claim by either party of any nature against each other relating to the [Event].

D.043
In the event that [Name] causes any damage to any property of the [Company] and/or any third party whilst at the [Event]. Than [Name] agrees that he/she shall be liable to pay to repair and/or replace any such damaged property

directly caused by his/her negligence and/or as a result of a deliberate act of malice. Where the damage arises due to the original state of the property and/or wear and tear then [Name] shall not be liable for any sum. In any event [Name] shall not be liable for more than [number/currency] in total.

D.044

Damages which may arise in respect of the [Company] relating to the services of [Name] shall not be the responsibility of [Name] at any time. The [Company] agrees to bear all risk, costs and damages however they may arise and for whatever reason even if based on the work of [Name] and/or indirectly related.

Sponsorship

D.045

The [Sponsor] confirms that it shall be entirely responsible and bear all costs, expenses and damages that may arise from:

1.1   A comprehensive insurance policy including product liability at the Venue [of not less than figure/currency for any claim] and subsequently during the course of the [Festival] in respect of the [Sponsor's] Product and any other material, goods, displays and advertising that may be owned, controlled or organised by the [Sponsor] or any agent or other third party authorised by them to act on their behalf at any time.

1.2   Loss, theft, damage to all material provided by the [Sponsor].

1.3   Loss, theft, damage or any other claim of any nature from the [Organisers] and/or the public directly or indirectly arising from the [Festival] and/or access to and/or use of any material provided by the [Sponsors] including all products, goods and services.

D.046

The [Sponsor] agrees that it shall not be entitled to make any claim against the [Company] nor seek repayment of any fees or offset any sum for any damages, costs, losses, expenses or any other reason arising under this Agreement including but not limited to:

1.1   Breach or alleged breach of contract by the [Company] or any of its agents, subcontractors or participants which is remedied.

1.2   Loss of reputation or goodwill by the [Sponsor].

1.3   Failure or delay in launching a new brand or product by the [Sponsor].

1.4   Advertising, marketing and promotional costs of the [Sponsor].

1.5   Fees and payments due to third parties engaged by the [Sponsor].

1.6   The [Event] is cancelled, delayed, reduced in size or capacity for health and safety reasons, or any [Artists/Athletes] do not appear.

1.7   The [Event] is not broadcast or transmitted as planned on radio, television and/or on a website and/or by any other means.

1.8   The [Event] does not achieve the anticipated exhibitors, public admission figures, projected sales of [specify] or the expected ratings on [television/radio/website].

D.047

If any agents, consultants, employees, casual staff and/or any other person and/or third party engaged and/or appointed by the [Sponsor] causes any damages and/or losses and/or incurs any costs and expenses which have to be paid by the [Company] which relate directly and/or indirectly to the [Sponsor] and it participation at the [Festival]. Then the [Sponsor] agrees that it shall pay the [Company] all such sums within [number] days of invoice by the [Company] subject to supporting evidence of any matter being made available to the [Sponsor].

D.048

Where there is any dispute between the [Sponsor] and the [Company] as to any claim for losses and/or damages made by either party. Then it is agreed that the party claiming the sum owed shall:

1.1   Send a detailed itemised report and list of the reason for the sum claimed and the cost of any replacement, substitution and/or repair supported by quotes from third parties.

1.2   Confirm that such losses and/or damages are not covered by an existing insurance policy they may hold and that no claim has been submitted and/or paid.

1.3   Where payment of any sum cannot be agreed that the parties shall appoint a person to act as a resolution negotiator between the two parties in order to avoid additional legal costs. The cost of such a person shall be paid by the person claiming the sum owed and added to the final total claimed.

University, Library and Educational

D.049

The [Institute] shall have the right to claim and be paid damages, costs and expenses against any [Consultant/Supplier/Distributor/third party] who provides goods and/or services to the [Institute] which the [Institute] decides:

1.1 Do not fit the agreed description and order;

1.2 Are defective;

1.3 Are not fit for their intended purpose;

1.4 Are misleading as to their content or uses;

1.5 Pose a risk to health;

1.6 Are not produced in accordance with product safety standards;

1.7 Fail to comply with all necessary legislation, directives, standards and practices in [country].

The claim for damages is not fixed or limited in value and may include:

1.1 Loss of profit,

1.2 Administration, public relation and legal costs,

1.3 The costs of product recall from the public and other customers including freight and refund charges,

1.4 Damage to and loss of reputation and goodwill,

1.5 Cancellation or termination of existing contracts and agreements,

1.6 Cancellation of promotions, advertising or marketing.

D.050

That the total liability of the [Institute] shall be limited to a maximum claim of [figure/currency] [words] in respect of any damage, loss, failure or defect due to the actions and/or failures of the [Institute] its employees, students and visitors. This limit shall not apply in the case of gross negligence or death.

D.051

The [Company/Consultant] agrees that in the event the [Institute] decides to cancel and/or terminate the Agreement at any time. That the [Company/Consultant] shall not be entitled to any additional sum in compensation, as damages, for loss of reputation or goodwill, costs, losses, expenses or any other reason. That the total liability of the [Institute] shall be limited to the fees due under Clause [–] to the date of termination or cancellation.

D.052

Where any member of the public removes temporarily and/or permanently and/or internally and/or externally damages and/or causes any other losses and/or reduction in value of any material exhibited by the [Institute] and supplied by [Name] including [specify]. Then the [Institute] agrees and undertakes that it shall bear all cost and responsibility for any sums due to repair, replace and/or compensate [Name] for any loss and/or damage. That the following sums shall be the minimum due for any of the following circumstances [specify event] [number/currency].

D.053

It is accepted by both parties that the condition of the [Manuscript/Work] is fragile and liable to deteriorate and/or suffer damage and/or fade and/or fall apart at any time. [Name] agrees and accepts that the [Institute] shall not be liable for any damages suffered by the [Manuscript/Work] and/or any subsequent losses, costs and expenses suffered by [Name] whether it occurred while the [Manuscript/Work] was in the possession and/or control of the [Institute] and/or in transit and/or being viewed by another third party.

DATA

General Business and Commercial

D.054

'Data' shall be the following databases, indexes, codes and records [specify].

D.055

'Data' shall mean the material, software and documents listed in Schedule [–].

D.056

'Data' shall mean any material and rights of any nature including but not limited to text, images, graphics, logos, names, titles, headings, computer-generated material, codes, source references, taxonomy, indexes, databases, algorithms, computer software, discs, CD Rom, storage, retrieval, supply and distribution method [which are in existence now and/or created in the future].

D.057

'Data' shall mean any material held by [Name] at [address] from [date] to [date] which directly relates to [specify].

D.058

'Data' shall mean any rights and/or any material of any nature owned, controlled by or in the possession of the [Company]:

1.1 All documents, records, text, rules, titles, procedures, slogans, formats, scripts, lyrics, contracts, licences, consents or undertakings.

1.2 Images, film, recordings, sound recordings, music, noises, ringtones and sounds, cartoons, characters, logos, drawing, maps, designs, photographs, plans, products and merchandising.

1.3 Computer software, computer generated material, discs, CD-Rom, website, internet material and domain names.

1.4 All patents, inventions, processes, applications and registrations.

1.5 All copyright, design rights, trade marks, service marks, musical, artistic, dramatic, literary works.

1.6 All trade secrets, moral rights, confidential information.

1.7 All board minutes, and reports, auditors reports, financial statements, projections and forecasts, tables, order forms, customer databases, wholesaler and supplier databases and any other list or compilation of information.

1.8 Marketing, advertising, publicity and promotional material.

1.9 All health, safety, security, compliance, product liability, legal actions or claims and any assessments, monitoring, reports, failures, criticism, warnings, fines, or estimated liability and forecasts.

1.10 All tax, insurance, telephone, water, gas, electricity, rates, material, staff, transport, freight, customs, and other costs, expenses and charges.

D.059

The [Contractor] agrees and undertakes that:

1.1 All rights in the Data supplied in any format under this Agreement shall remain the property of the [Company]. That this [tender/agreement/license] is not intended to transfer any copyright, trade marks, service marks, design rights, computer software, database or any other rights of any nature to the [Contractor].

1.2 That neither the [Contractor] nor any of its employees nor any third party engaged or appointed by it shall acquire any rights or interest of any nature in any variations, development or adaptations of the Data which shall remain the sole property of the [Company].

1.3 That the [Contractor] shall ensure that neither it nor any third party engaged or appointed by them shall copy, edit, adapt, alter or vary any Data except for the purpose of this Agreement.

1.4   That the [Contractor] shall ensure that neither it nor any third party engaged or appointed by them shall delete the copyright notice to the [Company] on any copies in any form.

1.5   That the [Contractor] shall ensure that both it and any third party engaged or appointed by them shall ensure that a copyright notice to the [Company] is put on any new material.

D.060

The [Contractor] shall take reasonable care of the [Company's] Data, and shall not authorise any person, firm or third party to copy or reproduce the material in any form without the prior knowledge and consent of the [Company].

D.061

That access by the [Contractor] to the [Company's] Data on the business premises of the [Company] does not permit or authorise the [Contractor] to send, remove, copy, supply or distribute any Data to any other source, site, person or company at any time.

D.062

That all Data collected, compiled and developed under this Agreement shall belong to the [Company]. The [Company] shall have the right to exploit, license, supply and distribute the Data in any manner its thinks fit without the prior consent of the [Enterprise].

D.063

The [Purchaser] shall not use the Disk and/or data in any manner inconsistent with the terms and conditions of this License. The [Purchaser] shall under no circumstances alter, remove, deface, erase or delete the copyright notice, trade marks or details regarding the [Publisher/Distributor] displayed on any part of this disk and/or its packaging.

D.064

The [Licensee] agrees and undertakes that the [Licensor] and/or any parent company shall be entitled to copies and/or access to all of the following data and material either directly from the [Licensee] and/or any sub-licensee in respect of the [Product/Work/Service]:

1.1   All contracts, licences, consents, waivers, copyright and intellectual property details in respect of any material; and

1.2   Invoices, receipts, bank statements, stock and in any form in any medium [on any premises].

D.065

The [Sponsor] shall not be entitled to access to and/or use of any data, databases, customer lists, bank account statements and/or any other financial, administrative and/or other details of the costs, income from and/or any other information and/or material regarding the operation of and/or visitors to the [Event]. The [Sponsor] shall only be entitled to a report of the total number of visitors for each day.

D.066

The [Consultant] undertakes and agrees that:

1.1 All Data which is supplied by the [Company] and/or any parent, subsidiary and/or associated business and/or any legal and/or professional advisors by the [Consultant] shall belong to the [Company] and not the [Consultant].

1.2 That any adaptation of the Data in any medium shall belong to the [Company] and not the [Consultant] and that the [Consultant] shall assign any rights that he/she may acquire to the [Company] at the [Company's] cost.

1.3 That the [Consultant] shall not have the right to release and/or disclose any content of the Data and/or any adaptation to any third party without the prior [written] consent of the [Managing Director/Name]. That to do shall constitute a breach of this Agreement and entitle the [Company] to terminate the Agreement with immediate effect and without any further liability to pay any further sums to the [Consultant].

D.067

Tables, data and statistics © [Name] [year] – [year]

Copyright and all other rights throughout the world owned by [Name].

No rights of reproduction in any form granted for any reason without prior consent and a licence from [Name].

D.068

1.1 [Name] grants a non-exclusive licence to the [Company] to use all the data provided to them in this [Market Survey] in any manner they shall think fit provided that the name, address and personal contact details of [Name] are deleted and a code allocated.

1.2 Provided that the [Company] shall not use any of the data provided to contact the businesses and persons mentioned using the name, address and personal details of [Name] at any time.

D.069

It is agreed that no party to this [Consortium] shall be entitled to release, supply, distribute and/or reproduce the data, information and other material recorded, collected and developed in respect of the [Project] to any third party at any time (whether in confidence or not) without the prior written approval of the others parties and agreement as to the terms and any copyright notice.

D.070

It is agreed that no party to this [Consortium] shall be entitled to authorise, commence and/or make any application for funding and/or development of a new project based on and/or derived from any data, information and/or conclusions from the current [Project] unless:

1.1 The current [Project] has already been released to the public and the data and research is generally available to everyone at no cost.

1.2 All the other parties have agreed and are part of the new funding application.

1.3 The applicant has bought out the rights of the other parties to the [Project].

DATABASE

General Business and Commercial

D.071

'The Database' shall be the names, addresses and [specify details] which were originally compiled and created by the [Company] and of which the [Company is the copyright owner in the form of an ordered structure which is stored in the following format [on computer/disc/other] at [address] in [country].

D.072

'The Databases' shall mean the lists, directories and reference material in any format or material held by [Company] or any subsidiary, affiliate or associate owned or controlled by the [Company] or any company with which it has an agreement or arrangement relating to [specify subject] including lists relating to customers, suppliers, manufacturers, retailers, wholesalers, returns and refunds.

D.073

The copyright in this database and index is owned by [Name] and you are only permitted to view the contents, make one copy for your own personal use and not for any educational, research or commercial purposes which requires the prior written consent of the copyright owner [Name].

D.074

The [Company] is an exclusive licensee of [Licensor] of the database entitled [title] which is used by the [Company] for the purpose of the promotion and marketing of [specify subject] and which it is authorised to do so from [date] to [date].

D.075

The copyright owners of this database are [Name] and there is no right to copy, reproduce, adapt, supply, to add as links on your website, reproduce in your business for distribution to colleagues, use for storage and retrieval in your library, or develop the title, headings or contents for any purpose whatsoever except as a research guide for your own personal use whether on residential or business premises. Any other type of use requires the prior permission of the copyright owners.

D.076

The [Company] agrees and undertakes that the [Author] is the copyright owner of the Database for the [Work]. That the [Company] shall only be entitled to use the Database in the manner and for the purpose stated in Clause [–] for the Term of this Agreement. The [Company] undertakes that it shall not use and/or exploit the Database to promote any other work or project without the prior written consent of the [Author] and the payment of an additional fee and/or royalty.

D.077

The [Licensee] agrees that the [Author] shall be entitled to a right of access to and to inspect and make copies of any data in any format and/or medium and any database whether recorded in printed form and/or on a computer and/or other storage and retrieval device of any nature which relates to the development, production, distribution and exploitation of the [Work] in order to verify the sums due to the [Author] under this Agreement.

D.078

The [Sponsor] shall not have the authority and/or right to exploit and/or use any database to which it is provided access by the [Company] except for the purpose of verifying the following criteria in respect of the [Event] [specify].

D.079

The [Company] agrees that [Name] the non-exclusive use to have access to and/or to inspect and/or make copies of the information and details on the Database entitled [specify]. In consideration of the Fee of [figure/currency] the [Company] grants [Name] the non-exclusive to copy, adapt and edit the Database and to use and/or display it in the following manner [provided that no charge is made to a third party for access to the Database] [Book/Website/mobile].

D.080

The [Company] shall retain all your personal details on a hard drive at the [Company] and be entitled to make copies and/or supply them to such professional financial, legal, and insurance advisors associated with the [Company] who may advise and/or assist in the business and/or a third party who needs to be informed for the purpose of fulfilling the terms of this Agreement for no more than [number] years.

D.081

No personal details and/or any data stored on any database at the [Company] shall be supplied to any third party who is not connected with the business, nor shall any such data be sold and/or disclosed to a third party for the purpose of marketing, promotion and/or any other purpose.

D.082

The [Company] owns and/or controls all copyright, intellectual property rights, taxonomy and database rights in the [List/Index/Compilation]. There is no right granted to exploit and/or adapt the [List/Index/Compilation] for any purpose and/or to make any copies. There is no automatic right of access, but it is agreed that you may inspect the [List/Index/Compilation] from [date] to [date] to use any information for your own personal use and not for any form of charitable, educational and/or commercial purpose.

D.083

In consideration of the payment of [figure/currency] the [Author/Company] grants the [Distributor] the non-exclusive right to use and display the [Database/Taxonomy/Index] on the Website reference [specify] from [date] to [date] and to grant a non-exclusive license to third parties for access to and/or the use of the [Database/Taxonomy/Index] for their own personal research.

D.084

Compilations, listings, indexes, themes, subject orders and any databases whether in the form of text, images, film and video, apps, sound recordings, downloads, tables, maps, charts and/or any other form on any page of this

[Website] and/or any associated material are owned and/or controlled by the [Company]. There is no permission and/or consent granted to use, adapt and/or exploit any part without prior consent and authorisation whether for commercial, educational, charitable and/or non-profit purposes. You are strongly advised to email [specify] and to seek permission.

D.085

Databases reproduced under licence from [Company] based on research by [Name].

D.086

It is agreed by the [Company] that where it creates databases and/or other information and/or material in any form including computer generated graphs, statistics, flow charts, presentations, maps and/or three dimensional projections. That all such data, databases and/or other material shall be assigned to and belong to the [Distributor] in all media and in all medium throughout the universe and world for the full period of any term of all rights including copyright, intellectual property and database rights and any extensions and/or renewals whether the technology and/or rights exist now and/or are created at a later date. That the [Company] shall not retain any rights, claim and/or ownership and/or control and/or have the right to any additional payment and/or other sums from any exploitation and/or transfer of rights.

DATA PROTECTION

General Business and Commercial

D.087

The personal information, data, and [password/access code] which is collected by the [Company] on this [Website] shall not be supplied, transferred or copied to any other third party for any purposes except with your prior written consent.

D.088

The [Company] shall be entitled to store, retain and disclose to their professional advisors my personal and financial details which I have provided on any software, documents or other records for the purpose of fulfilling the terms of this Agreement, drawing up their accounts, carrying out an audit, tax returns or compliance with statutory or other legal obligations.

Provided that any such advisors shall be obliged to keep my financial details confidential.

D.089

The [Applicant] agrees it is a pre-condition of the contract process that the [Company/Authority] be entitled as a [government/public] body which is accountable for its decisions and awards that it should be able to disclose and make available to the public all the content of the tender documents for the contract which have been completed and submitted by the [Applicant] except those parts which are clearly marked [confidential/exempt/not to be disclosed] by the [Company/Authority]. This clause shall apply whether or not the [Applicant] is awarded the contract for [specify].

D.090

The [Company] shall abide fully with all relevant data protection legislation, directives standards, and policies that may be in force during the existence of the Agreement in [country].

D.091

The [Company] shall not disclose any personal information submitted by the [Executive], created by the [Company] or its officers whether in the form of annual reviews, personnel assessments, disciplinary proceedings, management courses, complaints by the [Executive] relating to the actions or words of other employees at the [Company], matters relating to pension, national insurance, tax, benefits or other financial matters, the terms of employment or contract for services of the [Executive] or any other report, record, computer software, agreement, or any other material relating to the [Executive] which may exist prior to or during the Term of this Agreement or after termination to any third party without the prior written consent of the [Employee]. This restriction shall apply to any parent, subsidiary, associate, affiliate or partner of the [Company], and all advisors, consultants except the [Company's] professional legal and accounting advisors and any disclosure required by law to a government agency or under a court order.

D.092

The [Company] shall abide by its data protection policy in force from time to time and shall not disclose to any third party such information which is personal and private whether sensitive or not without the [Executive's] prior approval.

D.093

That the [Contractor] shall comply with the requirements of any legislation, regulation, directive or guidelines relating to the collection, storage, supply and release of any personal data in [country].

D.094
That the use, disclosure or access to any personal data permitted or granted by the [Company] shall be in accordance with the [specify] and shall only be provided in confidence and not for public disclosure.

D.095
You confirm and agree that the Data collected by the [Company] may be stored, retrieved, transferred and verified to and by any third party for the following purposes:

1.1 Compliance with laws, directives, regulations, or codes of practice whether in relation to identity, address, nationality, residence, tax, national insurance, data protection, national security, money laundering, financial and credit status or otherwise.

1.2 For the exchange and supply of information with and to parent, subsidiary, associate, and affiliate companies and agents, underwriters, insurers, accountants, legal advisors, human resources, corporate affairs and public relations, the police, regulatory bodies, government agencies.

D.096
This clause shall apply from [date] to [date] in [country].

D.097
This clause shall apply at any time and be applicable to any part of the world in which the [Company] trades, operates or does business.

D.098
The [Company] and its associated companies, and agents shall be entitled to use, supply, store and retrieve the personal data and information you supply for any of the following purposes:

1.1 To carry out an identity, credit and financial background check whether against public records, by using a private investigator, or otherwise to prevent fraud, or money laundering or to verify the statements and details of the application.

1.2 To verify your medical history and current medical condition.

1.3 To add to or amend the records with the results of 1.1 and 1.2 including where fraud or dishonesty is suspected.

1.4 To supply material to others for statistical research, analysis, provided that personal sensitive information is deleted.

D.099
The [Company] agrees and undertakes that the personal information, medical records or reports, contract or any data relating to [Name] will only

be disclosed at the [Company] to the [Managing Director]. The [Company] undertakes not to supply, inform, reproduce or distribute any personal information, medical records or reports or data to any other person, employee, director, agent, insurer, underwriter, government agency or authority, or third party at any time without the prior written consent of [Name].

D.100

The [Company] shall abide by any law, judgement, directive, statutory instrument or legislation, that imposes upon it restrictions, methods and/ or obligations regarding the use of any personal data obtained from an individual and/or company. This may include personal name, address, passwords and codes, username, bank details, credit card details, age, blood group, DNA, medical history.

D.101

All personal, family, financial, medical, and/or other material of any nature supplied under and/or pursuant to this Agreement to the [Company] shall be deemed to be confidential and private data whether or not it is covered by the legislation relating to data protection except for [specify]. The [Company] shall not supply, release, distribute, licence and/exploit any of this material to a third party without the prior written consent of [Name].

D.102

The [Company] shall abide with all relevant data protection legislation, directives or government guidelines. The [Company] shall abide by its data protection policy which may be in force at the time and shall not disclose to any third party such information personal and private relating to the [Executive] without the [Executives'] prior approval whether that information is deemed sensitive or not.

D.103

[Company] is registered as a Data Controller under the [Data Protection Act 1998 as amended and/or revised]. The information collected by the [Company] must be processed fairly and lawfully. The [Customer] is entitled to know how the [Company] intend to use any information provided by the [Customer]. The [Company] will use the personal information provided by you and/or your agent acting on your behalf to the [Company] to process your [Order/Booking/other] and to deliver the [Products/Service/other]. The [Company] may need to pass your information to the [Company's] agents, distributors and third party services engaged by the [Company]. We may also pass your information to [government authorities] as required by law. The [Company] and its agents and third party representatives will also the information for statistical analysis, market research, and keeping records. This information may be shared between the parties.

D.104

The [Company] may monitor and record telephone calls made to the [Company] for quality control and staff training purposes.

D.105

Where the [Customer] provides personal and financial details including but not limited to the [Customers'] name, address, landline, mobile, email, passwords and codes, username, bank details, credit card and other personal data for the purpose of ordering [Goods/Services] on the [Company's] [Website]. The [Company] agrees and undertakes to the [Customer]:

1.1 That the [Website] is secure and protected by [specify].

1.2 To ensure that the [Company] complies with all legislation, directives and codes of practice relating to data protection.

1.3 To ensure that the [Company] complies with all legislation, directives and codes of practice relating to payments, banking and finance.

1.4 That no third party [except professional advisors] shall be supplied and/or authorised access to any such data.

1.5 That a copy of the [Company's] Data Protection Policy is available at [specify].

D.106

It is agreed by the [Client] that the [Sponsor/Company] and/or parent, associated and/or any subsidiary, agent, consultant and other persons and/or businesses engaged by the [Sponsor] and/or with whom the [Sponsor] works as a joint venture and/or partnership and/or otherwise may store, retrieve, use, supply and/or edit the personal information which you have provided for the purposes of this [Survey/Competition] in order to [specify procedures].

D.107

The [Institute/University] stores on a hard drive of its computers and in paper form details of all those who complete the application form(s) [specify] and apply to the [Institute/University].

The [Institute/University] uses the information and data from the application form to process your application, and to compile statistics in order to report to government agencies. If you are offered on a course and accept the offer then the information and data will be used to verify your place on the course if it is accepted for the purposes of grants and bursaries, to administer and process your course, monitor attendance and performance and to provide a range of support. In addition the information and Data you provide to the [Institute/University] may be used for the purpose of credit assessment and review, the collection of debts, to comply with money laundering legislation and guidelines, and to prevent crime and/or fraud. For any of these purposes there may be disclosure to third party agents, legal and professional advisors and/or government bodies. The Data Protection Officer for the [Institute/University] can be contacted on [specify].

D.108

It is agreed that the [Institute] shall not be entitled to release and/or supply any personal information and details which you may provide in the course of your application for [specify post].

Except the following matters for which you provide your consent and agreement:

1.1 Your name, address, age, date of birth, passport number and photograph and application to verify the terms of your residency and your right to work in [country] with any government agency.

1.2 Your name, address, age, date of birth and photograph with your [university] to verify your qualifications.

1.3 Your name, address, age, date of birth, photograph and application with all the references that have been supplied.

1.4 Your name, address, age, date of birth and photograph and application with our medical advisor if your application is successful in order to arrange insurance cover.

1.5 Your name, address, age, date of birth and photograph and application with the national body [specify] to carry out a criminal record assessment and/or review.

D.109

You agree that the [Company] may use your name, gender and email address for the purpose of sending you newsletters and updates and promotional events. That the [Company] may also use such information to sell and/or supply such data and information to third parties who promote products and services through its website [specify] so that they may contact ytu directly with offers and discounts.

D.110

The [Company] agrees and undertakes that it shall not as a matter of policy collect and/or store email addresses, date of birth, names and/or other details and information in respect of children age [16/18] years and under. That it is the policy of the [Company] to contact and liaise with parents and carers and to obtain their prior consent and authorisation. That the

[Company] accepts and agrees that a child age [16/18] years and under cannot enter into a legally binding agreement without the consent of the parent and/or carer. Further that any costs and expenses incurred and/or attributed without such consent cannot be claimed by and/.or are not owed by the parents and/or carers to the [Company].

DEATH

General Business and Commercial

D.111

If before making his final award the [Arbitrator] dies or ceases to act as the arbitrator the parties shall immediately appoint a further arbitrator. No such further arbitrator shall be entitled to disregard any direction of the previous arbitrator or to vary or revise any award of the previous arbitrator except to the extent that the previous arbitrator had power to do so under the relevant Arbitration Rules at that time and/or with the agreement of both parties to this Agreement.

D.112

The [Authors] agree that in the event of the death of one of the [Authors] to this Agreement after the delivery of the [Work] for publication then the estate of the deceased [Author] shall be entitled to any monies which would have been due to the [Author] had he/she not died.

D.113

In the event of the death of the [Author] before the delivery of the [Work] then all further payments under this Agreement shall cease unless sufficient material exists for the completion of the [Work] by a writer to be jointly selected by the [Publisher] and the appointed representative of the deceased's estate. In the event that the [Publisher] and the appointed representative agree not to appoint a writer to complete the [Work] then this Agreement shall be terminated and the [Publisher] shall [not] be entitled to be repaid any sums previously paid to the [Author] under this Agreement.

D.114

In the event that the [Licensor] should die during the Term of this Agreement the [Licensee] agrees that all sums which would have been due to the [Licensor] shall be paid to an appointed representative of the [Licensor's] estate or such other person who has been assigned copyright either by the estate or inherited from the [Licensor].

D.115

In the event of the death of [Name] the rights and obligations under this Agreement shall be terminated forthwith by notice in writing by the [Company] to the estate. Save that the [Company] shall be obliged to pay such sums as may be due for any work completed by [Name] up to the date of termination.

D.116

In the event of the death of [Name] then the [Company] may terminate this Agreement by notice in writing to the [Name's] estate provided that the [Work] has not been delivered in draft and/or completed form. In such case all rights in the [Work] shall revert in full to the estate of [Name] but the [Company] shall be entitled to reclaim any sums which have already been paid to the [Name] and/or his agent(s) and/or representatives. In the event that a draft and/or the completed [Work] has been delivered then the [Company] shall be obliged to fulfil all its obligations set out in this Agreement and to pay all sums that fall due to the estate of the deceased [Name]. The estate shall be entitled to assume the rights of [Name] in respect of approval, editorial control, audit, inspection and all other undertakings set out in this Agreement. In the event that another person is required to contribute to the [Work] prior to its commercial exploitation then such person shall be subject to the prior approval of the estate, and shall not be entitled to a credit as author of the [Work] and all costs incurred in respect of their contribution shall be paid for entirely by the [Company]. The [Company] shall not be entitled to deduct any such sums from the monies due to the estate of [Name] for any reason. The [Company] shall in addition submit any material revised, edited or contributed to by that person to the estate for their written approval prior to the exploitation of the [Work] in any form.

D.117

The [Agent] confirms that in the event of the death of the [Author] after the conclusion of a written agreement with a publisher for the publication of the [Work], the [Agent] agrees to ensure that all sums which are due to the [Author] are paid to the [Author's] estate.

D.118

The [Publisher] confirms that in the event of the death of the [Author] after the acceptance of the manuscript of the [Work] then all sums due to the [Author] under this Agreement shall be payable to the [Author's] estate.

D.119

In the event that the [Author] dies prior to the delivery of the manuscript the [Publisher] agrees to negotiate in good faith with the executors and/ or administrators of the [Author's] estate concerning the publication or otherwise of the [Work].

D.120

In the event of the death, severe incapacity or degenerative illness of the [Name] so that they are unable to fulfil the terms of this Agreement then it is agreed that the Agreement shall be terminated by [specify method] so that it shall [specify expiry/end period]. All sums paid to the [date of termination] shall be retained by [Name] and no sums shall be due thereafter of any nature.

D.121

Where as a result of the death or serious injury of any personnel involved in this [Project] the [Project] is to be delayed, cannot be fulfilled by the same persons specified in the contract or for which there is no possibility of an alternative substitute being agreed. Then the parties agree to enter into negotiations to agree the terms upon which the contract for the [Project] is to terminated, who is to bear the costs and pay for the outstanding commitments and who is to own the rights. Where no agreement can be reached the parties agree to enter into alternative dispute resolution, mediation or arbitration and shall only resort to legal proceedings if they have first tried one of those processes.

D.122

Where [Name] dies during the course of this Agreement for some reason unconnected with the [Company]. Then the [Company] shall be liable to pay all sums due until the date of death. Thereafter no further sums shall be due to [Name] or his/her estate and the [Company] shall be entitled to substitute another person to complete the work set out under the Agreement and there is no requirement to provide any credit or reference to [Name] in any completed work of any nature.

D.123

If [Name] dies or is seriously ill and unable to fulfil the terms of this Agreement the [Company] shall not be entitled to continue with this Agreement without the prior written consent of an authorised representative of [Name] or the estate of [Name]. Where [Name] has delivered or completed all the required work, then the [Company] shall be entitled to proceed as set out in the [Agreement] provide that it fulfils all the undertakings, credit obligations and payments to an authorised representative of [Name] or [Name's] estate.

D.124

Where [Name] the subject of the [Work] by the [Ghostwriter] dies and/or severely mentally incapacitated prior to the approval and/or delivery of the [Work]. Then a nominated member of the family of [Name] and/or the [Executors] of the Estate may fulfil the role of providing authority to approve and/or reject the draft manuscript prior to delivery to the publishers.

D.125

Where [Name] is unable through death, illness, incapacity and/or otherwise to attend and/or participate in the [Event]. The [Sponsor] shall not have the right to withdraw the sponsorship funds and agrees that the [Enterprise] shall be entitled to substitute and/or replace the person with someone of equal stature and reputation. Where this does not happen and the person is not as well-known and/or successful then the [Sponsors'] shall be entitled to be repaid [figure/currency] within [one month] of the end of the [Event].

D.126

In the event that one of the [Contributors] suffers ill health which results in severe incapacity for more than [number] months and/or dies during the course of this Agreement before his/her work is started, developed and/or completed. Then all the [Contributors] agree that the [Company] shall have the right to substitute a new person to commence, continue with and/or finish the work required of that person. Provided a reasonable settlement is negotiated and agreed with a nominated representative of any such person to buy out all rights to their contribution and interest in this Agreement by the [Company]. Where a settlement cannot be agreed then the [Project] will be held in suspension until the matter is resolved. In such instance all the parties agree that the timescales under this Agreement may be adjusted to take account of the period of delay due to such suspension. Where the suspension continues for more than [number] years. Then any party may serve notice of termination of the Agreement to the others by notice in writing and/or by email and the [Project] shall cease immediately.

D.127

In the event of the death of [Name] the creator, developer and writer of the [Blog] then all ownership, control and interest in the copyright, intellectual property rights and assets in the domain name, title of the blog and any trade mark and content shall be transferred and assigned to his/her nominated successor in title [specify person] who shall have access and permission to use such codes, passwords and accounts as have may been used and/or accessed by [Name].

D.128

The [Company] agrees to arrange at its sole cost suitable insurance cover for the benefit of the family and children of [Name] to cover his/her position as [specify title of post] which involves considerable risk and danger at different times. The [Company] agrees to pay all the premiums and to ensure that they are kept up to date and that a copy of the policy is provided to [Name] and the stated beneficiaries listed on that document. That the [Company] shall ensure that the policy is not invalidated and/or does not exclude any area of work and/or travel and/or ill health and/or death in any country for any reason. That the [Company] agrees and accepts that cover shall be for a minimum of [specify figure/currency] for the following [illness/death/other]. That in any event the [Company] shall in addition provide its own personal additional cover which shall be paid to the family and estate of [Name] of [figure/currency] if he/she should die during the course of his/her work, and/or any assignment and/or travel requested by the [Company] at any time. Such sum to be paid within [number] days of death of [Name] in such circumstances which shall not be delayed due to the inquest and/or establishment of the final facts in such case.

DEBENTURE

General Business and Commercial

D.129

For the purpose of this Agreement 'Debenture' and 'Debenture Stock' shall be construed synonymously and shall [exclude/include] without limitation:

1.1   All charges on property whether mortgage debentures or otherwise.

1.2   The benefit of all documents referred to as Bonds.

1.3   All written acknowledgments of debts whether under seal or not.

1.4   Any restrictions of the [Company] from giving a prior charge.

1.5   Any document signed by one or more appointed Directors of the [Company] acknowledging a lawful debt of any nature.

1.6   Any special debt of the [Company] whether accompanied by any security of any nature or not.

1.7   Any document referred to as a 'Unit Certificate' whether such obligations refer to the payment of premiums on a policy or otherwise.

1.8   Any other specific matters listed under the attached Schedule [–] to this Agreement.

D.130

1.1   The debentures are held by [specify] in the [Company].

1.2   The debentures hold the following rights [specify].

1.3   In the event that there is a change in control of the [Company] then the debentures may be changed, altered and/or varied by the following method:[specify].

1.4 In order to transfer, assign and/or dispose of, charge and/or sell any debenture the following method must be complied with [specify].

DECLARATION

General Business and Commercial

D.131

The [Company] hereby declares that it has disclosed:

1.1 All particulars of its registered shareholders.

1.2 All options (conditional or otherwise) entitling any party to acquire any share or loan capital of the [Company].

1.3 The full names, addresses, occupation(s), nationality and country of residence of all Directors of the [Company].

1.4 Copies of its up-to-date Memorandum and Articles of Association and any deeds affecting control of the [Company] including full details of all Resolutions adopted by the [Company] in the previous [twelve months].

D.132

We the undersigned, hereby declare that the contents of our [Application] are true to the best of our knowledge and belief and that all relevant information has been disclosed to [specify body/company] as required under Clause [–] of the [Application Form].

D.133

The Declaration by the [Company] concerning its affairs and the representations contained therein are not false or inaccurate in any material particular.

D.134

The signature by [Name] on behalf of [Company] of [specify document] is a declaration that the facts, information, statements, figures and representations which have been made are true and accurate and can be verified by the [Company]. That no facts, information, data or material has been withheld, misrepresented, distorted, altered or omitted.

D.135

1.1 [Name] of [address] who holds post of [specify] at the company known as [specify].

1.2 [Name] confirms and agrees that [he/she has taken an oath that] these facts are true and that there is no information and/or documents which they are aware of which either may contradict and/or show this statement to be false as at [date].

1.3 [Name] confirms and declares that he/she is making this statement in good faith and without malice.

1.4 [Name] agrees that if after the date of this declaration he/she becomes aware of any facts which would show this statement to be misleading, inaccurate and/or false that he/she shall disclose such information to [specify].

1.5 That [Name] acknowledges and agrees that the supply of false information could constitute a civil and/or criminal offence.

DEED

General Business and Commercial

D.136

IN WITNESS whereof the parties hereto have executed and delivered this Agreement as a Deed the day, month and year first hereinbefore written:

1.1 Executed and Delivered as a Deed by the [Assignee] and signed by two Directors or one Director and the Company Secretary.

1.2 Executed and Delivered as a Deed by [Name] and witnessed by [Name].

D.137

This Deed shall cease to have effect [twelve years] after the full completion of the development under the [Management Contract] provided that no legal proceedings shall have been commenced against the [Management Contractor] prior to the expiry of the said period by the [Company].

D.138

This deed shall not negate or diminish any duty or liability otherwise owed by the [Contractor] to the [Developer].

D.139

No approval, inspection, testing or otherwise of the [Development] or of any designs or specifications of any work or materials by or on behalf of the [Developer] shall diminish and/or bring to an end and/or be deemed a waiver any duty or liability of the [Contractor] arising under Deed. The [Contractor] shall remain at all times entirely responsible and liable for all the designs, work and/or materials carried out by and/or provided by the [Contractor] in respect of the [Development] at any time.

D.140

By a Deed of charge dated [–] the [Company] charged its rights under the lease in favour of certain investors in the [Work] as security for the performance of certain obligations owed by the [Company] to them.

D.141

This Deed dated [–] in respect of the property known as [address] in county in country [–] is evidence in writing of the freehold ownership of the house and land set out in Schedule [–] which forms part of this Deed. The freehold ownership is held by [name]. Any transfer and/or assignment and/or lien and/or charge must be in writing and registered with [specify body] at [address].

D.142

By a deed dated [–] [Name] owned the [Asset/Property] during his/her lifetime and there were no outstanding mortgages, charges, liens and/or other control and/or ownership by any third party as at [date]. [Name] died on [date] and left a will for which probate was obtained on [date] by executors of the will. By a deed dated [–] the [Asset/Property] and all control and ownership is assigned and conveyed to [specify beneficiary] free from any encumbrances so that [beneficiary] may sell, exploit and/or charge the [Asset/Property] as he/she thinks fit.

DEFAMATION

DVD, Video and Discs

D.143

The [Assignee] agrees that it shall be responsible and/or liable for any damages, losses, costs and expenses arising from the content of the [DVD/Disc]. The [Assignee] undertakes to the [Assignor] that the [DVD/Disc] will not contain any material whether film, text, title, images, designs, music, lyrics and/or otherwise which are offensive, obscene, racially prejudiced, likely to incite violence and/or is likely to cause a danger and/or could affect the health and/or safety of children and/or could be defamatory and/

or expose the [Assignor] and/or the [Assignee] and/or any sub-licensee, distributor and/or agent to criminal and/or civil proceedings.

D.144

The [Assignor] undertakes that the [DVDs/Discs], packaging and any associated advertising, marketing and promotional material will not contain any material, text, images, words, lyrics, gestures, innuendos or any other material in sound and/or vision which may be considered obscene, give rise to an allegation of contempt of court, is and/or may be deemed defamatory or which is likely to lead to a criminal and/or civil action.

D.145

This clause shall to any material for which approval has been provided or has been agreed in advance in writing between the parties.

D.146

The [Licensee] agrees that it has viewed the [Film] and does not rely on any undertaking by the [Licensor] as to its content in respect of obscenity, defamation or whether there is a real risk of civil or criminal proceedings and will seek its own legal advice.

D.147

The [Licensor] confirms that the [Film] does not contain any obscene, defamatory or other material and will not expose the [Licensee] to civil or criminal proceedings in [country]. Provided that the liability of the [Licensor] shall be a maximum of [figure/currency] in total and no further sums shall be paid once this limit has been reached.

D.148

This [Film] and the right to exploit it in the form of a [DVD/Disc] is provided to the [Licensee] without any undertaking or commitment as to the suitability of the title or content for any country as to whether the material will be considered by the laws of any country to be obscene, offensive, defamatory, derogatory, in contempt of court, an infringement of copyright, or otherwise in breach of any laws, regulations, directives, codes or practices. The [Licensee] shall not seek to recover any sums, costs or legal expenses from the [Licensor] in respect of any allegation or claim at any time or to seek an indemnity and agrees that it shall reproduce, supply and distribute the [Film] at its own risk and cost.

D.149

The [Licensee] shall not be under any obligation to include any material from the [Film] and/or any sound recording on any [DVD/CD/Disc] to be reproduced and distributed under this Agreement which would prevent and/

or restrict and/or increase the risk of legal proceedings in any country. That the [Licensee] may edit, delete and remove material which in its view is objectionable and/or may result in a claim and/or allegation of defamation, copyright infringement and/or other matter. The [Licensee] may not add any film and/or sound recordings and/or other material except music authorised in advance for the purposes of continuity.

D.150

Where at any stage the [Licensor] receives an allegation and/or claim of defamation in respect of the [Film] and/or any sound recording and/or parts. Then the [Licensor] may decide to withdraw the [Film] from this Agreement and may serve notice on the [Licensee] to that effect at any time prior to the commencement of reproduction of [DVDs/CDs/Discs]. The [Licensor] shall offer the [Licensee] the same terms for another film which the [Licensee] shall not be obliged to accept. If the [Licensee] does not accept the alternative then all sums paid to the [Licensor] in respect of the withdrawn {film] shall be repaid plus an additional sum of [number/currency] in the form of fixed compensation. These sums shall be paid within [number] days of the rejection of the proposal by the [Licensee].

Film and Television

D.151

The [Production Company] hereby warrants to the [Television Company] that the [Programme] does not and will not contain any material which is obscene, libellous, defamatory, scandalous, blasphemous, improper or otherwise unlawful including but not limited to, any possible actions for contempt of court and that all material contained in the [Programme] whether visual images, graphics, film, recordings, interviews, voice-overs, text, lyrics, music, documents and source references and/or of any other nature purporting to be facts are true and accurate.

D.152

The [Licensee] undertakes not to use or permit the [Film] and/or parts to be used in any manner which is likely to bring the [Licensor] into disrepute and/or which is defamatory of any person.

D.153

The [Artist] warrants that his performances shall not contain anything defamatory or which is likely to bring the [Company] into disrepute. Further that his performances shall not endorse any products and/or contain any advertisements and/or promotions and/or trademarks, logos or other images, text or representations of any third party of any nature [not authorised by the Company].

D.154

The [Licensee] undertakes not to edit the [Material] in anyway likely to impair its quality meaning or integrity and not to use or permit to be used any [Work] in any manner which is likely to bring the [Licensor] into disrepute or which is defamatory of any person, company or business.

D.155

The [Company] shall not knowingly include in any [Film] or part which is transmitted or broadcast and/or exploited by it whether by way of visual images, sounds, music, text, photographs or otherwise, any material which is defamatory, seditious, blasphemous or obscene, or which constitutes falsehood or slander or any infringement of copyright, trademark, intellectual property, design rights or which is a contravention of the [Official Secrets Act] or contempt of court or may, or is likely to, or does result in any civil and/or criminal proceedings.

D.156

The [Licensor] confirms that the [Film] does not and will not contain any material of any nature which is obscene or defamatory or will expose the [Licensee] to criminal proceedings in [specify countries]. The [Licensor] confirms that the version of the [Film] to be supplied under the Agreement will be that which has been rated by the [censorship body in country] as [state code].

D.157

The [Licensor] agrees and undertakes that the [Film] is not obscene, defamatory and/or contravenes any code of practice in any of the following countries [–] and will not expose the [Licensee] to criminal or civil proceedings in those countries.

D.158

The [Licensor] agrees and undertakes that to the best of its knowledge and belief the [Film] does not contain any material which is obscene, defamatory, libellous, offensive or likely to incite violence or [specify] in the jurisdiction of [country]. The parties to the Agreement acknowledge that the [Film] has not been cleared for every country in the world, only for those specified.

D.159

The [Assignee] agrees that it has viewed the [Film] and does not rely on any undertaking by the [Assignor] as to its content in respect of obscenity, defamation, or incitement and shall seek its own legal advice for use of the [Film].

D.160

The [Licensor] confirms that its own legal advisors do not believe the [Film] to be defamatory, offensive or likely to lead to criminal or civil proceedings in [countries]. However no such assurance or undertaking is given to the [Licensee] who has viewed the [Film] and must take their own independent advice. The [Licensee] must also arrange suitable insurance cover for the benefit of [Licensor] and the [Licensee] in respect of the threat of any legal action arising from the exploitation of the [Film] by the [Licensee].

D.161

The [Licensor] shall be entitled to insist that the [Licensee] delete, edit, add or alter any part of the [Film] which for legal reasons the [Licensor] has been advised should be changed and any such changes shall be at the [Licensors] cost.

D.162

The [Licensee] agrees and undertakes that it shall only be entitled to exploit the [Film] in the form, shape and content as it is delivered by the [Licensor].

D.163

The [Licensor] shall not be entitled to add, delete, amend, change or alter any part of the [Film], the sound recording, the credits, copyright and trade mark notices or the duration of the [Film].

D.164

The [Licensor] agrees and undertakes that it shall not:

1.1 Add any distributor's credit, logo, text or sound, or market and promote any other films, products or persons without the prior written approval of the [Licensor].

1.2 Market or exploit the [Film] or any part or use any packaging or any other material or person in association with the [Film] or parts which may cause the [Licensor] to be in breach of contract with a third party, may result in a claim for defamation, or any other criminal or civil proceedings at any time.

D.165

The [Licensor] undertakes that the [Series] or [Parts] are or will not be defamatory and that in the event that there is any claim or allegation the [Licensor] has an insurance policy to cover all such legal costs and expenses and damages. That the [Licensee] shall not be responsible for any such sums and shall be entitled to recoup all sums expended from the [Licensor].

D.166

The [Company/Distributor] agrees and undertakes that it [and/or its successors in business and/or title] shall be responsible and bear all administrative, travel and hotel, legal and other advice and any other costs of any nature that may be incurred and/or arise from the use and/or adaptation of the interviews, filming and sound recordings of [Name] [and/or any other third party] which is made and/or reproduced and/or included in the [Programme] and any associated exploitation in any form at any time.

D.167

Where any presenter and/or artist deliberately and maliciously seeks to use any programme and/or recording in which he/she appears to defame any person, company, sponsor and/or business. Then the [Company] reserves the right to take legal action against such presenter/artist in respect of any sums which the [Company] may incur in order to resolve and settle the matter as swiftly as possible including but limited to legal costs, corporate and staff expenses.

D.168

1.1   The [Company] agrees and accepts all the risk, responsibility and liability for ensuring that the [Films] and/or any part of the [Series] are free from and/or are at minimal risk of exposure to the threat of a legal action in any country in which it will be exploited due to its title, sound recording, content and/or marketing.

1.2   The [Company] shall not be entitled to seek any sum in payment from [Name] and/or his/her agent in respect of any civil and/or criminal proceedings and/or legal claim, action, summons and/or allegation that may occur at any time due to the promotion, marketing, transmission and exploitation of the [Films] and/or any part in the [Series] [in which [Name] appears, contributes and/or has his/her name mentioned and/or any other reference in any form.]

General Business and Commercial

D.169

The [Assignee] undertakes not to reproduce or misrepresent the commissioned [Work] in any way which is likely to bring the [Individual] into disrepute or which is obscene or offensive in nature.

D.170

In the event that the [Exhibitor], his representative or employees shall conduct themselves on the premises in a manner and/or verbally and/or in writing which is considered by the [Organisers] to be objectionable, offensive, defamatory and/or likely to cause obstruction, then the [Organisers] shall be entitled to request that the [Exhibitor] and his personnel vacate the premises immediately.

D.171
The [Company] reserves the right in its absolute discretion to cancel the [Contract] and not to fulfil its obligations hereunder for any good reason. This shall include, but not be limited to the following reasons in respect of the [Work] where the [Company] considers that it is defamatory, pornographic, obscene, socially unacceptable, or otherwise against [Company] policy. The [Client] shall not be entitled to be repaid any sums already paid in the event that the contract is so cancelled.

D.172
To the best of the knowledge and belief of [Company] the [Work] contains no defamatory matter under the [laws of England].

D.173
The [Assignor] makes no warranty or undertaking as to whether any part of the [Work] and/or the [Work Material] is obscene, offensive or defamatory or likely to lead to criminal or civil proceedings. The [Assignee] accepts full responsibility from the date of this Agreement for any subsequent consequences arising from its exploitation by the [Assignee] under this Agreement.

D.174
The [Company] shall be entitled to edit, delete, erase, remove, change or alter any material which on the advice of its professional legal advisors is considered defamatory, in contempt of court, obscene, is an incitement to political unrest, war, or acts of terrorism, offensive, dangerous, misleading, factually incorrect, an infringement of copyright, trade marks, domain names or is otherwise considered to be prejudicial to the commercial interests of the [Company].

D.175
The [Company] shall be under no obligation to reproduce, display, exhibit, publish, distribute or otherwise use or exploit any material which in the view of the [Company] is defamatory, obscene, offensive or which could bring the [Company] into disrepute or prejudice its business.

D.176
The [Company] shall be obliged to take out an annual policy in respect of the threat of any allegation of defamation in any one case for a minimum of [number/currency] at its sole cost. In the event that the [Company] is

unable to obtain defamation insurance then it must develop a robust and effective policy to deal with allegations and/or complaints at an early stage to minimise the risk and costs. The [Company] must appoint an adjudicator to deal with such matters who has the authority to initiate removal of material from the [Website/Blog/other].

D.177

All [Exhibitors] are warned and advised not to make any defamatory statements and/or allegations and/or representations and/or actions concerning the products, business practices and/or marketing of any other company and/or third party and/or any member of the public. The [Organisers] do not accept any liability and/or responsibility for any summons, claims, complaints and/or legal action that may be made against you and/or any member of your staff on your stand and/or elsewhere at any time. The [Exhibitors] reserve the right to provide any assistance and/or information and/or security films they think fit to any third party without a court order.

Internet and Websites

D.178

You agree that you shall not submit, send, or enter any material whether words, images, graphics, logos, lyrics, films, sound recordings, or otherwise which could be construed as defamatory, derogatory, insulting, rude, obscene, violent or an incitement to violence, offensive, or reveal personal details of a third person which they would not want disclosed. Where there is any breach of this clause the [Company] shall remove, delete and erase all such material and shall seek to be indemnified by you for any claim that may arise from the material you submitted.

D.179

The [Company] has made it a requirement that all contributors to this [Website] read and abide by the conditions of clause [–]. The [Company] monitors the [Website] and deletes any inappropriate material and allows users to report incidents to the [Company]. The [Company] advises any person or business who wishes to complain about any content to inform the [Company] as soon as possible. We will then correct or delete the material. Where you institute legal proceedings and you lose the action we will seek to reclaim all our legal costs from you.

D.180

The [Contributor] agrees and undertakes not to supply and/or to upload to the [Website] and/or any part any material of any nature whether words, images, graphics, logos, lyrics, films, sound recordings, photographs, drawings, music and/or otherwise which is contrary to the policy of the

[Company]. That the [Company] shall be entitled to remove, delete, bar, block and/or to refuse access to the [Website] by the [Contributor] whether free and/or as part of a paid for service where the [Contributor] is in breach of the policy of the [Company] as follows:

1.1 All and/or any part of the material is likely to be defamatory, obscene, offensive, may incite violence, is derogatory, insulting, rude, violent and/or an incitement to violence, political unrest, riots, and/or acts of terrorism.

1.2 The material and/or any part reveals personal data regarding a child who is under [number] years of age without parental consent.

1.3 The material and/or any part reveals personal data of a third party without consent of that person.

1.4 The material and/or any part has been disclosed in breach of contract, and/or licence and/or is in contempt of court.

1.5 The material and/or any part infringes the copyright, trade marks, database rights, domain name, computer software rights and/or intellectual property rights of a third party.

1.6 The material and/or any part has, and/or may, damage[d] the reputation of the [Company] and/or any customer and/or bring the [Company] into disrepute.

1.7 The material and/or any part is misleading, factually inaccurate and/or against the commercial interest of the [Company] and/or any customers.

D.181
[Name] agrees and undertakes not to make any comment, statement, innuendo and/or contribute any material in any form as text, words, sounds, images, photographs, film, videos, caricatures, gestures and/or otherwise to the [Blog/Column/Programme] which is likely to be and/or is in fact defamatory, offensive, derogatory and/or demeaning of any person whether or not [Name] know and/or believes such material to be true or not.

D.182
[Name] agrees that he/she must abide by the [Company] policy of clearing in advance all programme material for use with [specify] in the event that he/she expects that it may be defamatory, controversial and/or cause a strong political reaction from any party and/or campaigning group. [Name] agrees that he/she shall not be entitled to seek legal and/or other advice on matters relating to programme material from any third party without permission. That where [specify person] at the [Company] indicates that

there should be a delay and/or further verification of the veracity of the source that this should be adhered to until formal authorisation is provided. Failure to comply with the policy will be considered a matter of gross misconduct.

Merchandising

D.183
The [Licensor] confirms that the [Characters] do not contain any obscene or defamatory [or offensive] material and will not expose the [Licensee] to criminal or civil proceedings [in the country].

D.184
The [Licensor] has only provided a limited undertaking in respect of the actual [Character] and the associated material which is supplied by the [Licensor] under this Agreement. As the products to be produced under this Agreement are intended for the [children's] market no text, slogan, title, images, graphics, music, logos, trademarks or otherwise are to be included in the product, packaging, advertising, marketing and promotional material which are or could be construed as unsuitable for children, misleading, defamatory, obscene, likely to corrupt, or be offensive in any of the following countries [specify].

D.185
The [Licensee] agrees and undertakes to arrange and pay for insurance cover for the exploitation of the [Product] based on the [Work] which shall cover product liability, and any claim for personal injury including death, defamation, and/or any criminal and/or civil proceedings.

D.186
The [Distributor] agrees and undertakes not that the [Work/Product] and/or any packaging, marketing and advertising shall only be reproduced in the exact from agreed with the [Licensor] prior to supply to the retailers and/or the public. In the event there are any changes, additions and/or deletions which result in an allegation of defamation, infringement of copyright and/or trade mark and/or any other intellectual property rights. Then any sums due as costs and/or expense and/or as payment for any damages shall be the responsibility of the [Distributor] and not the [Licensor].

D.187
The [Licensee] and any distributor, sub-licensee and agent agree not to make any allegations against any third party and/or competitor regarding a competing product and/or work. The [Licensee] shall not have the right to include the name of the [Licensor] in any press release which has not

been approved by the [Licensor]. Where defamatory allegations against the [Work/Product] are made by a third party of which the [Licensee] and any distributor, sub-licensee and agent becomes aware at any time. The [Licensee] shall notify the details to the [Licensor]. The [Licensee] agrees that it shall not take any legal action and/or release any press statement regarding the allegations without prior consultation with the [Licensor]. All the administrative and legal costs of dealing with any such allegation shall be paid by the party that incurred the cost. All damages and costs in settlement to a third party shall be split between exactly between the parties.

D.188

All the title, text, photographs and other contents of the [Work] have been reviewed and cleared of any legal problems for defamation, copyright clearances and payments, trade mark infringement, passing off and other potential threats of legal actions and/or claims. The [Licensor] provides an assurance and agreement that it shall deal with any matters which arise from the exact reproduction of all the material supplied by the [Licensor] at any time. Provided that the [Licensee] passes all such matters directly to the [Licensor] to deal with as they think fit and the [Licensor] is not required to consult with the [Licensee] regarding any settlement. The [Licensee] agrees that it shall not seek to be paid any legal costs by the [Licensor] that it may incur at any time.

D.189

Any sub-licensee and/or distributor shall be liable for any action and/or claim that may be made against it arising from this Agreement at its own risk and cost. Any sub-licensee and/or distributor must agree to waive all claims against the [Licensor] and [Licensee] arising from the distribution, supply, sale and exploitation of the [Material] and/or any promotion and/or marketing.

Publishing

D.190

The [Author] warrants to the [Publisher] that the [Work] does not and will not contain any material which is obscene, defamatory, scandalous, blasphemous, improper or otherwise unlawful and that all statements contained therein purporting to be facts are true and accurate.

D.191

The [Author] undertakes that the synopsis and the [Work] do not and will not contain any obscene, offensive or defamatory material and will not expose the [Agent] to civil or criminal proceedings.

D.192

The [Author] confirms that the [Work] does not and will not contain any obscene, offensive, defamatory, blasphemous, sexual or racially prejudiced material which is against the law. Nor will the [Work] incite violence, riot and/or other unlawful activity. The [Author] agrees and undertakes that the [Work] does not and will not contain any statements, photographs, drawings, formulae or other material which is likely to or will threaten or expose the [Publisher] to any criminal, civil and/or other proceedings of any nature whether in the licensed Territory and/or elsewhere in the world at any time. The [Author] shall not be responsible for any material of any nature contributed by the [Publisher] whether text, drawings, cover, photographs, index or otherwise. The [Publishers] shall be solely liable for any civil or criminal proceedings threatened or which may arise as a result of their editing, translation or other contribution to the [Work] at any stage in any part of the world whether by themselves directly or as a result of the actions of any sub-agent, sub-licensee and/or sub-distributor and/or any further third party engaged by the [Publisher].

D.193

The [Author] confirms that the [Work] does not and will not contain any material which is obscene, offensive, and/or defamatory, and/or will commit any breach of privacy, contract and/or duty of confidence and/or be in contempt of court and/or violate any laws and/or expose the [Publisher] to civil and/or criminal proceedings throughout the Territory during the Licence Period.

D.194

The [Author] has reasonable knowledge to believe that the [Work] does not contain any text, image or other material which is likely to result in legal action by any third party. However no assurances are given as to the content of any type and it is for the [Publisher] to take its own legal advice as to defamation, obscenity, contempt of court, breach of confidence, contract or privacy and any other threatened claim or action that may arise whether civil or criminal. The [Publisher] shall bear all the risk, cost, expenses and damages and shall not be entitled to seek to recover any sums or contribution from the [Author].

D.195

The [Author] confirms and undertakes that to the best of his/her knowledge and belief the facts and information contained in the [Work] will be and are true and accurate except where material is supplied or included at the request of the [Publisher].

D.196

The [Assignee] undertakes that the [Work] and the [Artwork] and the material in Schedule [–] will not be used in any manner or form which is obscene, offensive, defamatory or derogatory and will not expose the [Author] to civil or criminal proceedings.

D.197

The [Licensor] confirms that the [Extracts] have been reviewed by their legal advisors for legal problems prior to the proposed publication of the [Work] in hardback. The [Licensor] does not accept responsibility for any legal action that may arise from the publication of the [Extracts] by the [Licensee] and the [Licensee] must seek its own specialist advice in respect of the threat of potential claims or actions by the public or any third party.

D.198

The [Authors] shall not be liable for any sums due in respect of any civil or criminal legal actions, claims, allegations or consequences that may arise from the publication and exploitation of the [Work] and any associated material by the [Publishers] including but not limited to defamation, infringement of copyright, trade marks and any other rights, breach of contract and confidentiality.

D.199

1.1 The [Publisher] agrees and undertakes to the [Contributor] that the [Publisher] and not the [Contributor] shall bear all liability, risk and cost of any allegations of defamation and/or any civil and/or criminal proceedings in respect of any material of any nature submitted by the [Contributor] and then published, used and/or adapted and/or distributed by the [Publisher].

1.2 That where the [Contributor] is also made the subject of any allegations, action and/or claim that the [Publisher] agrees that it shall fund directly in advance all the costs and expenses that may be incurred in respect of the administration, investigation and provision of legal and professional advice and reports. Provided that this obligation shall cease after [date].

1.3 The [Contributor] agrees that where further evidence is required by the [Publisher] in any form including but not limited to emails, telephone and mobile records, documents, images and other medium. That the [Contributor] shall assist at the [Publishers'] cost and provided he/she is paid an additional fee for their services.

D.200

No responsibility and/or liability is accepted by the [Publisher] and/or any parent company, distributor, sub-licensee and/or other third party for any information which is distorted, misrepresented and/or defamatory of any person and/or business which is included in any [Work] and/or posted and/or reproduced as an extract. The [Publisher] will without notice exercise the right to delete, amend, alter and/or remove any material including text and images which it has decided in its opinion are likely to result in an allegation and/or claim [whether this is based on the advice of a legally qualified person or not.]

Purchase and Supply of Products

D.201

The [Supplier] agrees that it shall be the decision of the [Seller] as to the nature of the image, display, text and method of marketing and exploiting the [Product] in their [Website/shop/other]. Provided that the combined effect shall not be:

1.1　Defamatory, offensive, demeaning or derogatory of the [Supplier] and/or its products and/or any third party.

1.2　Expose the [Supplier] to any allegation of breach of industry standards and practice by a government agency or authority.

1.3　Expose the [Supplier] to any civil or criminal legal actions, claims or allegations.

D.202

The supply of the [Product] by the [Company] to [Name] on loan for the purpose of [specify] shall be on the basis that [Name] agrees not to use, display, exhibit, adapt or present the [Product] in any media in a manner which is offensive, defamatory, derogatory, misleading, violent, dangerous, or damaging to the sales of the [Product], the business interests of the [Company] or its brands.

D.203

The [Supplier] agrees and undertakes to advise the [Distributor] of any serious allegations that may be made concerning the [Work/Product/Service] where the advice of professional legal advisors have been sought and they have reached the conclusion that there is a real risk that the allegations may result in adverse publicity and/or withdrawal and/or cancellation of production of the [Work/Product/Service] and/or identify a serious health and safety risk to the public.

D.204

The [Distributor] agrees that where it becomes aware of any negative, defamatory and/or other statements from the public including any customers which concern any aspect of the [Product/Work] and its packaging and marketing which may affect sales, result in features on television and/or radio and/or on the internet and/or create an impact on any of the brands owned and/or controlled by the [Supplier]. That the [Distributor] agrees and undertakes to inform the [Supplier] in each case and shall co-operate with them in respect of any strategy which may be developed to deal with the matter. Provided that all costs and expenses in each case shall be paid for by the [Supplier] and not the [Distributor].

Services

D.205

The [Actor] confirms that the product of his/her services will not contain any obscene, offensive or defamatory material and will not expose the [Agent] and/or his employees and/or representatives to any criminal or civil proceedings except where any material is included at the request of the [Agent] and/or a third party for whom the [Agent] has agreed the work on behalf of the [Author].

D.206

The [Originator] confirms that the services will not contain any obscene, offensive or defamatory material and will not expose the [Company] to any civil or criminal proceedings except for any information or material supplied by or included at the request of the [Company].

D.207

The [Company] agrees that the [Presenter] shall only be responsible for any costs, loss or damage arising directly from a breach of this Agreement by the [Presenter] during the Term of this Agreement. The [Presenter] shall not be liable nor be under any obligation to indemnify the [Company] in relation to any matter concerning the transmission, broadcast or exploitation of the [Programme] whether on television, the internet, merchandising, by telephone or otherwise which shall be entirely at the [Company's] cost and risk. The [Company] shall arrange public liability, defamation, obscenity, breach of confidence, infringement of copyright, trade marks, contract and other comprehensive insurance policies for the benefit of the [Company] and the [Presenter] at the [Company's] cost.

D.208

The [Presenter] undertakes that all the product of his/her services under this Agreement shall not contain any obscene or defamatory material or anything of an advertising or promotional nature for any organisation, person or body which would breach the codes of practice and standards of [specify] or expose the [Company] to civil or criminal proceedings except where work is based on or incorporates material at the [Company's] request. The total liability of the [Presenter] shall be limited to [figure/currency] and any other sums over this amount shall be paid for by the [Company].

D.209

The [Company] agrees that the [Celebrity] shall have the right not to be subject at any time under this Agreement to carry out or be subject to any material, words or actions which amount to derogatory treatment, are obscene, racist, offensive, defamatory, degrading or which impugn or demean the character, reputation or name of the [Celebrity].

D.210

[Name] has agreed to be interviewed and contribute to [specify]. The [Company] agrees and undertakes that:

1.1   The [Company] shall be responsible for and shall ensure that there are no legal problems prior to the use of the material.

1.2   That [Name] shall not be liable to the [Company] in respect of any claim for defamation, libel, obscenity, breach of any laws, codes or standards, or contract.

1.3   That the [Company] shall bear the cost and indemnify [Name] in respect of any costs, expenses, damages or legal fees that may arise from the use of the material by the [Company].

D.211

The [Contributor] agrees and undertakes that he/she shall not during the course of the [programme/interview/presentation]:

1.1   Make any statement, allegation, threat and/or incite violence, war and/or riot and/or any other public disorder.

1.2   Represent any facts as true which he/she knows to be false.

1.3   Claim ownership of any material of any nature which he/she knows to belong to another person.

1.4   Claim that he/she is the original creator of a work which is in fact based on the work of another person and/or company.

1.5   Attribute any material and/or work to another person and/or company which is incorrect and/or deliberately false.

D.212

The [Company] agrees that any legal problems which may arise from the use of the [films/sound recordings/images/service] supplied by [Name] shall be the sole responsibility of the [Company] and that [Name] shall not be liable for any use, exploitation and/or adaptation by the [Company] at any time. The [Company] acknowledges and agrees that no undertakings have been provided by [Name] as to the ownership and/or copyright clearances and/ or any other rights payments and/or sums that may be and/or become due.

Sponsorship

D.213

The [Sponsor] and the [Sportsperson] both undertake and agree that neither party shall do anything or authorise any third party to do so any act, words or material which might reasonably be expected to damage the reputation of that other party. If notified of an unacceptable matter then both parties agree that they shall work together in good faith to minimise the damage which shall include withdrawal and destruction of material if required and payment of compensation and costs.

D.214

The [Sportsperson] agrees to provide his/her services to the best of their skill and ability to ensure the fulfilment of this Agreement. The [Sportsperson] shall conduct his/her public and private life in such a manner that they are not damaging the reputation of the [Sponsor], its business or products. Nor shall the [Sportsperson] be defamatory, derogatory or criticize the [Sponsors] or any part of their business.

D.215

There are no undertakings provide in this Agreement as to the conduct, actions, publications, films, recordings, photographs, images, slogans, words or other behaviour or communications, interviews, work, or private life of [Name] and/or his/her family and none should be implied. This Agreement is not intended to provide any such undertakings or constraints or to provide any indemnity to the [Company] for any allegation of defamation against [Name] and/or the [Company] or any civil or criminal proceedings. Each party shall bear their own costs, expenses, loss, damages, penalties and legal costs in respect of any allegations, claims or proceedings including any prejudice to their business interests, and loss of reputation.

D.216

The [Sponsor] shall not be responsible for the conduct of [Name] and their agent nor any behaviour, acts, words or statements which are defamatory, offensive, obscene, threatening, or damages or loss caused directly or indirectly to any person, company or property. Whether at an event, conference, press launch, or other occasion organised by or on behalf of the [Sponsor].

D.217

The [Sponsor] shall be responsible and bear the cost of any allegation and/or settlement and/or claim in respect of any threat, abuse, violence, defamation and/or other misconduct caused by any officer of the [Sponsor], any employees, casual staff, consultants and/or other third party arranged by the [Sponsor] for the [Event]. The [Company] shall not be responsible for, nor required to make, any payment for any such matters.

D.218

The [Company] shall not be responsible for any legal problems whether defamation, obscenity, breach of any laws, breach of any codes of practice and/or guidelines, and/or any breach of contract and/or civil and/or criminal proceedings which may arise from the products, services and work provided by the [Sponsor] under this Agreement. The [Sponsor] shall be entitled to deal with all such matters without the approval of the [Company] at its own cost. The [Company] shall be entitled to be paid for any services and/or administrative support that may be requested by the [Company] together with any legal costs.

D.219

The [Sponsor] agrees and undertakes that neither it nor any of its employees, consultants and agents shall use the [Event] and/or any associated promotional and/or marketing material in any media to make any derogatory and/or defamatory reference and/or statement concerning any other person and/or business in competition with and/or with whom the [Sponsor] may have any dispute and/or legal action and/or otherwise. The [Sponsor] agrees that if for any reason it should breach this clause that the [Company] shall be entitled to terminate this agreement with the [Sponsor]. That in such event the [Sponsor] shall still be obliged to pay all the sums due in clause [–].

D.220

The [Sponsor] shall not be held liable for any acts, words, statements, allegations, threats and/or any claim for defamation and/or any civil and/or criminal proceedings and/or disciplinary actions against any member of the teams and/or management at the [Club]. Nor shall the [Club] be entitled to seek any contribution and/or payment by the [Sponsor] towards any such costs, expenses, losses, damages and/or legal costs that may arise in dealing with such matters.

University, Library and Educational

D.221

The [Institute] confirms that the [Work] will be reviewed by their legal advisors for legal and defamation problems prior to the proposed publication and/or distribution. The [Institute] accepts full responsibility for all costs and expenses from any legal action that may arise from the publication, distribution and/or any other exploitation of the [Work] by the [Institute]. The [Institute] shall not seek to recover any sums from the fees and/or royalties due to [Name].

D.222

The [Contributor] shall be liable for any sums due and/or paid to a third party by the [Institute] in respect of any civil and/or criminal legal actions, defamation, copyright infringement, claims, allegations or consequences that may arise from the publication and exploitation of the [Work] and any associated material by the [Institute]. The total liability of the [Contributor] shall be limited to [figure/currency] [words].

D.223

The [Institute] shall not be responsible for nor liable for [Enterprise] and their representative nor any behaviour, acts, words or statements which are defamatory, offensive, obscene, threatening, and/or any damages and/or loss and/or any civil and/or criminal legal action.

D.224

The [Contributor] undertakes that all the product of her services under this Agreement shall not contain any obscene or defamatory material or anything of an advertising or promotional nature for any organisation, person or body which would breach the codes of practice and standards of [specify] or expose the [Institute] to civil or criminal proceedings except where material is included at the [Institute's] request.

D.225

The [Consultant] confirms that the product of her services will not contain any obscene, offensive or defamatory material and will not expose the [Institute] and/or its employees and/or representatives to any criminal or civil proceedings in the [United kingdom]. The [Institute] shall not be under any obligation to reproduce, distribute or otherwise use or exploit any material which in the view of the [Institute] is likely to bring the [Institute] into disrepute, damage its reputation and/or is believed to be defamatory.

D.226

The [Contributor] agrees that he/she shall be personally liable for any presentation, statement and/or words and/or acts and/or text, images and/

or other material that he/she may use, distribute, supply, reproduce and/ or make available in any form at the [Event] and/or at any time thereafter. That no material has been approved and /or reviewed by the [Institute] and that no liability and/or responsibility is accepted by the [Institute] for any allegation of defamation and/or any other complaint, claim summons and/ or legal action that may directly arise. That the [Institute] shall in any case in which it is involved be entitled to settle the matter as it thinks fit and without any consultation with [Name].

DEFAULT

General Business and Commercial

D.227
Both parties agree that in the event of a material breach by either party, the non-defaulting party shall notify the defaulting party of details of the breach and give them an opportunity to rectify the position within [specify period] of the notice being required. In the event that the defaulting party does not so remedy the position then the non-defaulting party may terminate this Agreement immediately by service of a notice in writing to that effect. By way of example a material breach shall include, but not be limited to non-payment, failure to deliver, and failure to seek approval in accordance with the Terms of this Agreement.

D.228
Any defaulting party or a party terminated under Clause [–] shall pay all reasonable compensation for losses and damages incurred by the other party as a direct result of the default and/or termination of this Agreement.

D.229
Where one party is unable or unwilling to carry out or comply with the terms of the Agreement. Then that party shall be deemed to be in breach of the Agreement and shall have [one calendar month] from the date of the default to remedy the breach. Failure to correct the breach shall result in the Agreement being automatically terminated and does not require service of notice. The non-defaulting party shall then be entitled to reclaim all sums paid under the Agreement, but shall not be entitled to claim for any other costs, losses, expenses or damages that may arise whether directly or indirectly in consequence of the breach or termination.

D.230

The [Company] shall be in default of this Agreement in the event that it fails to comply with Clauses [–] under this Agreement. Such default shall entitle the [Licensor] to notify the [Company] that the Agreement shall terminate with immediate effect and that all rights shall revert to the [Licensor]. The [Company] shall not be entitled to any compensation, damages, expenses and costs for such termination unless the [Licensor] has acted unreasonably.

D.231

Where the [Licensor] defaults and fails to provide the [Master Material] for the reproduction of the [Work/Product] by the specified date. The [Licensee] shall be entitled to a full refund of all the sums paid in clause [–] and to terminate the Agreement with immediate effect. After the termination date both parties agree to enter into negotiations to settle the matter by arbitration, mediation and/or some other method prior the commencement of any legal proceedings. Where no conclusion can be reached within [number] [months] of termination then either party may issue legal proceedings at its own risk and cost.

D.232

Where the [Sponsor] fails to pay all and/or part of the sums due in clause [–] and/or to deliver the goods and/or services in clause [–]. Then the [Company] shall notify the [Sponsor] that they are in default and specify the reasons and allow them [number] [hours/days/weeks] to remedy the issue in the manner specified by the [Company]. Where there is a total and/or partial failure to complete the remedy the [Company] shall have the right to serve notice of termination on the [Sponsor] and/or to claim any direct and/or indirect damages, losses costs and expenses that may arise including all costs and/or payments from the cancellation of the [Event].

D.233

Where the [Service] is not available for any period of [number] days then the [Company] shall have defaulted and the [Distributor] shall be entitled to terminate the Agreement and claim a full refund for all days that the service was not available together with an additional sum of [number/currency] per day in compensation for the lack of service. The sum due shall be paid by the [Company] with [number] days of the demand from the [Distributor] by email which sets out the sums due and the reason.

D.234

Where one party defaults under this Agreement for any reason and the other party confirms that he/she shall agree to a delayed delivery date. That does not entitle the defaulting party to seek to delay the delivery date for a second time and the non-defaulting party may serve notice of termination of the Agreement and a full refund of all payments made to date for failure to deliver by the agreed date.

DELIVERY

Building

D.235

If the Completion Date is not likely to be or has not been achieved, the [Contractor] shall immediately advise the [Architect] of the cause of the delay in writing. The [Architect] may as soon as he is able to assess the length of the delay beyond the Completion Date give in writing an extension of time by fixing such later dates (the Extended Completion Date) which he considers to be fair and reasonable. If in the opinion of the [Architect] it is not fair and reasonable to fix a later date as the Extended Completion Date he shall so notify the [Contractor] and specify the reasons for the refusal of the extension.

D.236

If the [Contractor] fails to secure the completion of the [Project] by the Completion Date then the [Contract Administrator] shall issue a certificate to the effect. In the event of an extension of time being made after the issue of such a certificate the [Contract Administrator] shall cancel that certificate and shall issue such further certificates as may be necessary.

DVD, Video and Discs

D.237

The [Company] shall deliver to the [Customer] at such address in [England] as the [Customer] may specify [DVDs/Discs] as required as soon as practicable after receipt of a written order but within not more than [thirty] days of the order. The written order shall specify the [film/format/quantity/ delivery address/date/payment method/date/cost of delivery].

D.238

The risk in any [DVDs/Games/Disc] delivered to the [Customer] by the [Company] shall pass immediately upon delivery to the [Customer] but the property shall remain with the [Company] until all sums due to the Company have been paid by the [Customer].

D.239

The delivery date provided by the [Company] is for guidance only and may vary according to availability of the [DVD/Product], the delivery method, and the country of destination. The [Customer] agrees that they shall not have the right to make any claim against nor seek to be indemnified by the [Company] for any delay or default in delivery which results in losses, expenses, or costs to the [Customer] or a third party. The [Company's] liability shall be limited to a full refund of the payment made by the [Customer].

D.240

Prior to the reproduction of the final master copy of the [Disc] of the sound recordings which shall include any copyright notices, credits and other information on the label. The [Company] shall at its sole cost supply a complete copy to the [Author/Composer/Performer] at [address] and/or arrange for a suitable date and/or time for them to listen to and/or analyse the content, label and cover of the [Disc]. The prior written approval of the [Author/Composer/Performer] shall be needed before the [Company] has the authority and/or right to reproduce, distribute and/or supply the copies of the [Disc] to any third party.

D.241

The [Client] agrees that where delivery is not by registered and/or recorded delivery and paid for by the [Client] as an additional cost and is sent by normal post. That the [Company] shall not be liable for the failure of the order to arrive where the [Company] can produce evidence of posting the [Disc/other].

D.242

1.1 [Name] shall arrange and pay for delivery to the [Company] at [address] on [date] before [time] [number] copies of the [Film/Sound recording] in [format/size] which is suitable for use and reproduction in conjunction with [specify gadget].

1.2 [Name] agrees that no charge shall be made to the [Company] for delivery.

1.3 The [Company] agrees to pay [Name] the sum of [figure/currency] on [date] by direct debit to bank account [specify].

Film and Television

D.243

The [Licensor] shall at the [Licensor's] cost and risk deliver to the [Licensee's] offices at [address] or such other offices as the [Licensee] may at any time designate, the material described in Clause [–] by [date]. Within [specify period] after delivery the [Licensee] will review such materials and will also verify that a print of the [Film] satisfactory to the [Licensee] has been made. The [Licensee] shall notify the [Licensor] of any defect(s) and the [Licensor] shall promptly remedy such defect(s) at the [Licensors] cost and deliver a replacement as soon as possible.

D.244

Each of the parties shall keep the other fully informed as to the [Film] material which is available and shall promptly on demand supply original or copies of such prints, videotapes, films, DVDs, recordings, sound recordings, discs, scripts, credit and copyright notice lists, lyrics, advertisements, promotions, music, publicity material and music cue sheets as may be reasonably required for the exercise of the rights granted hereunder, provided that the party requesting such items shall:

1.1   Make its own arrangements for the collection, freight handling, customs duties, taxes and insurance of all such items at its own expense.

1.2   Reimburse the party supplying the items with all costs incurred in supplying such items including reproduction costs [provided that they have been agreed in advance].

D.245

The [Licensor] agrees to deliver to the [Licensee] by the date specified under Clause [–] an English language master of the [Series] together with the documents referred to in Schedule [–] and all video recordings, DVDs, and sound recordings created by the [Licensor] in making the Series which have not been incorporated in the master including, but not limited to, negatives, unused takes, off-cuts and any copies which shall correspond to the labels on the material. The material shall be accompanied by a thorough inventory list.

D.246

The [Company] shall have the right to approve the rough cut of the [Film] and for this purpose it is agreed that [specify format] shall be sent by the [Licensor] at its cost to the [Company's] representative on or by [date].

D.247

The [Licensor] shall deliver to the [Company] at the [Licensor's] sole cost and expense on or by [date] the following material of the [Film] to be held by the [Company] for the Term of the Agreement:

1.1   Technically acceptable master material in [format].

1.2   Associated sound recordings, music, photographs, graphics, computer generated material, rules, questions and answers, slogans and catchphrases.

1.3 Lists of credits, copyright notices, moral rights, contractual obligations.

1.4 Advertising, promotional, posters, telephone line and website marketing and catalogues.

D.248

It is agreed that within [fourteen days] of full signature of this Agreement the [Company] shall arrange for the provision of [specify items to be delivered] at the [Company's] cost to the [Licensor]. The [Licensor] shall arrange for the [format] to be delivered to the [Company's] representative at [address]. The [Company] shall arrange and bear the cost of [specify process or work]. The [Licensor] shall then collect the [format] which shall be [specify work] at the [Licensor's] cost.

D.249

All tapes and material supplied hereunder shall be in first class condition and shall be to the technical standard required by the [Company] with all commercial breaks removed. In the event that the [Company] rejects any material on the grounds of unsatisfactory technical quality the [Licensor] shall use its best endeavours to provide acceptable replacement material as required by the [Company]. The [Licensor] shall use its best endeavours to provide copies of the full length version of the [Series]. In the event that the [Licensor] is unable to supply acceptable material of any of the [Series] as required by the [Company] and/or the [Licensor] is unable to provide any full length version of an acceptable substitute then the [Company] shall be entitled to repayment of all the sums paid to the [Licensor] for the [Series] together with any additional costs and expenses already incurred by the [Company] in respect of the [Series].

D.250

The [Production Company] shall deliver the scripts and storyboard of the [Advertisement] to the [Company] for approval on or before the following dates:

The draft scripts [date]. The final script [date]. The storyboard [date]

D.251

The [Production Company] shall deliver the [Advertisement Package] to the [Commissioning Company] on or before [date].

D.252

The [Company] agrees that the [Author] shall be entitled to approve the [Scripts/other] and shall deliver the [Scripts] to the [Author] for approval on or before the following dates:

Draft Script [date]. Final Script [date].

D.253

The [Assignor] shall deliver the rough cut of the [Series] for approval to the [Assignee] at the [Assignor's] cost as follows: Format [specify material] on or before [date] to [address].

D.254

Unless the [Licensee] advises the [Company] that the material delivered is incomplete, technically unacceptable, or incorrect within [three calendar months]. Then the material shall be deemed to have been accepted.

D.255

The [Company] shall deliver one new and clean copy of the [Programme] in [specify format] in the [specify] language to [address] in [country] together with a list of the cast and all credits, copyright notices, trademarks, music, sponsors and other third parties and specify how and when they must be acknowledged in any marketing and promotion. Together with a statement as to any restrictions and/or prohibitions as to the form of use of any content in any media which may apply.

D.256

Where the [Programme] is cancelled due to the failure of the [Company] to deliver in accordance with the specified dates in clause [–]. Then it is agreed that the [Distributor] shall have the right to terminate the Agreement and refuse to arrange further dates for transmission. The Company] must then return all of the sums paid by the [Distributor] to date to fund the [Programme] within [number] months of any demand.

General Business and Commercial

D.257

Notwithstanding any other provision contained within this Agreement both parties expressly agree that all relevant dates including, but not limited to those dates referred to under Clauses [–] shall be of the essence of this Agreement.

D.258

Both parties agree that all the delivery, completion, payment and other dates set out in this Agreement are not merely for guidance but are an important and material part of this Agreement. Further that failure by either party to comply with the dates shall be a fundamental breach of this Agreement. In the event that for any reason either party should agree to a later date, then this shall not entitle the defaulting party to consider that all subsequent dates may also be delayed, and such dates shall remain the essence of this Agreement.

D.259

The [Company] agrees to supply at its cost copies of such artwork and other material in its possession or control including any goods, packaging, music, film and copies of any trademarks, logos, credits, copyright notices which may be required by the [Promoter] for the purposes of this Agreement.

D.260

'The Delivery Date' shall be the date by which the [Agent] agrees to deliver the [Work] to the [Company] [date].

D.261

The [Company] agrees that the [Work] shall remain the property of the [Agent] and that at the end or within [21 days] of the completion of this Agreement the [Work] shall be returned to the [Agent] at the [Company's] expense.

D.262

[Goods] may not be delivered to and/or removed from the exhibition during the hours that it is open to the general public without the prior consent of the [Organisers]. All [Exhibitors] shall be responsible for the supply and removal of their own [Goods].

D.263

All delivery dates are approximate only but every effort will be made to avoid delay. In the event that the [Goods] are not delivered within [specify duration] of the delivery dates it is accepted that the [Goods] shall not have been delivered in accordance with the terms of this Agreement.

D.264

All [Goods] must be delivered carriage paid and display full details of the [Company].

D.265

The [Seller] confirms that the selling process and dealings with the public will conform in all material respects with all relevant legislation, regulations, directives, codes of conduct, and standards voluntary or otherwise, in the United Kingdom, European Union and the following countries [–].

D.266

The [Seller] agrees that the [Supplier] shall not be responsible for the delay in delivery, damage to or failure of the [Product] to arrive at its destination for any reason once the [Product] is dispatched from the [Suppliers] premises including but not limited to theft, loss in transit, delivery to wrong address, acceptance of delivery by a third party.

D.267
Shipments shall be made to the delivery address unless notice in writing is received by the [Supplier] from the [Seller].

D.268
The [Seller] agrees that the [Supplier] shall be entitled to deal with, sell, loan, hire, distribute or otherwise exploit the [Product] at any time to any third parties whether on the internet or otherwise. Provided that the [Seller] shall not alter, adapt, vary, change or interfere with the [Product] including any packaging after receipt from the [Supplier] and before delivery to the third party.

D.269
Where the [Distributor] is unable to supply the [Product/Service] to the [Company] and delivery is to be delayed for more than [number] days. Then the [Company] shall have the right to terminate and/or cancel the delivery and to receive a full refund of all the payments made to date.

D.270
Both parties agree that where delivery and/or payment is delayed for any reason due to force majeure and/or any other reason. That they shall as far as reasonably possible without incurring any additional costs endeavour to mitigate the impact of the delay. Where the delay continues for more than [specify period]. Then the party who is not in default shall have the right to take such steps as may be necessary to terminate the agreement with immediate effect without prejudice to any outstanding claim under this Agreement.

D.271
It is accepted that delivery may be delayed and the delivery dates adjusted at any time due to lack of ingredients and/or other production issues. The [Company] agrees that no failure to deliver by a specific date shall be grounds for termination unless there has been a complete failure to deliver [number] [weight] by [date].

D.272
All the delivery dates specified are for guidance only and may be changed by the [Company] at any time. In the event that delivery is changed then you will be allocated a new date as soon as possible. No sums are paid in compensation for failure to deliver unless the delay extends beyond [number] weeks from the date of the order of the [Articles].

Internet and Websites

D.273
Delivery is only made within the following area [specify] at [fixed price]. All other deliveries shall be made in accordance with the quoted charge according to the circumstances which shall be agreed in advance.

D.274
The person or company which placed the [Order] or an authorised representative will be requested to produce the [Reference/Order form] and shall be asked to check the condition of the [Products] on delivery and to sign an acknowledgement receipt of delivery.

D.275
No date, time or method of delivery can be guaranteed by the [Company] nor any advance notice. As far as possible we will contact you if the initial delivery date is to be changed. If the [Products] are returned due to non-delivery then an additional charge will be made for any further dates if the [Customer] was unavailable.

D.276
The [Company] agrees to deliver or supply the [Goods/services] at the dates and times agreed with the [Customer] and any failure by the [Company] to comply with these terms shall result in the right of the [Customer] to cancel the contract and be repaid a full refund of all sums paid to the [Company] within [ten days]. In the event that the [Customer] does not cancel the contract and another date and time is substituted the [Company] agrees to provide the [Customer] with [voucher/benefit].

D.277

1.1 The delivery dates for the supply of [Products/Services] are subject to variation and are only provided as guidance. The [Company] can only guarantee delivery next day and/or within [number] days if one of the following additional sums is paid to be provided with a recorded and/or registered delivery and/or courier delivery to the specified address in the [country]. [List price and type of delivery.]

1.2 Any delivery outside [country] will be by [freight/airmail/other] and the following choices are available at an additional cost. [List price and type of delivery.]

1.3 Insurance cover may be provided to cover the risk of loss and/or damage of the [Products/Services] whilst in transit at an additional cost. [List price and type of cover.]

D.278

Where the [Company] has been unable to deliver the [Order] due to an incorrect address and/or post code. Then an additional fee shall be paid to deliver the [Order] to any new address.

D.279

Delivery shall be at your own risk and cost unless you pay an additional fee for secure and signed for delivery. Where delivery is made to an address and signed for by any person who lives at that address and/or is employed by you in some capacity. Then delivery shall have been completed. Where there is any dispute regarding delivery then you must provide contact [specify] and provide details within [number] days of the agreed delivery date.

Merchandising

D.280

The [Company] undertakes to deliver to the [Licensee] a representation of the [Character] in two-dimensional form as an artistic work, in colour with such colour shades and dimensions as it may specify together with [specify material/script/format] on or by [date] at the [Company's] cost.

D.281

'The Delivery Date' shall be the following date by which the [Delivery Package] is to be delivered by the [Photographer] to the [Assignee] [date].

D.282

The [Assignor] confirms that it shall deliver the commissioned [Work] to the [Company] on or before the Delivery Date.

D.283

In the event that the [Distributor] fails to release and deliver the [Licensed Articles] to the wholesalers, retailers and public by [date] to coincide with the transmission of the [Series] then the [Distributor] shall pay the [Licensor] fixed compensation of [figure/currency] for every [day/month] that the delivery is delayed and the [Distributor] has delivered less than [number] copies of the [Licensed Articles] in [country].

D.284

The delivery by the [Author/Company] of the [Work/Film/Sound Recordings/ Photographs] to the [Distributor] by [date] is crucial to the performance of this Agreement for the [season] market. Where the material is delayed, not delivered and/or partially delivered for any reason. The [Author/Company] shall have a period of [specify] to fulfil and complete the obligation beyond the delivery date. In the event that this is not complied with and there is no satisfactory delivery then the [Distributor] shall be entitled, at its sole discretion, to terminate the Agreement and to seek a full refund of any advance paid to date.

D.285
All the costs and expenses of delivery of any material of any nature under this Agreement shall be paid for by the [Distributor]. Where the [Author/ Company] has incurred any such sums then the full cost shall be reimbursed subject to the prior production of receipts.

D.286
The [Licensee] agrees that it shall ensure that:

1.1 The [Products] of the [Character] are manufactured and ready for distribution and delivery by [date] in [country].

1.2 That where there is a problem with production, manufacture, packaging and/or distribution of the [Products] of the [Character] that the [Licensor] shall be informed and provided with details of the reasons.

1.3 That where the [Products] are not available before [date] then the [Licensor] shall have the right to terminate the Agreement and seek to appoint a new licensee for the same rights.

Publishing

D.287
The [Author] and the [Company] agree the following schedule for the delivery of the material:

1.1 Delivery of Synopsis by [date]. Acceptance or rejection within [specify duration] of receipt.

1.2 Delivery of the Draft Manuscript [date]. Acceptance or rejection within [specify duration] of receipt.

1.3 Delivery of the Final Manuscript by [date]. Acceptance or rejection within [specify duration] of receipt.

D.288
The [Author] shall deliver not later than the Delivery Date [two] legible copies of the manuscript of the [Work]. The [Work] shall comply in every way with the specifications outlined below and shall be of a standard, in both style and content, that is of a sufficient quality for the [Work] to be published.

D.289

The [Author] shall deliver [two] complete typescripts of the [Work] finally revised and ready for printing to the [Publisher] together with [two] [CD-Roms/Discs/other] on or before [date]. The [Author] shall ensure that the Work shall contain approximately [number] words, [number] [stills/photographs], index, preface, disclaimers, copyright notices and list of copyright acknowledgements of source material.

D.290

The [Author] shall at his/her sole cost supply the following material for inclusion in the Work]: Index, quotations, photographs, pictures, maps, diagrams, illustrations, bibliography.

The [Author] shall ensure that the necessary permissions and consents have been obtained by him/her in writing for the publication of the [Work] by the [Publisher] in the Territory in respect of the following rights [specify rights to be obtained].

D.291

The [Author] undertakes to deliver to the [Publisher] at the [Author's] cost not later than [date] two complete typescripts of the text of the [Work] ready for the printer which shall consist of approximately [number] words together with approximately [fifty] colour photographs sufficient to make [sixteen] pages of illustration. The [Publisher] undertakes to return an additional copy of the typescript at the [Publisher's] cost.

D.292

The [Author] shall provide the [Publisher] with an index, tables, bibliography and such other additional material as may be requested by the [Publisher] for this [Work] at the [Author's] sole cost and expense subject to Clause [–] which sets out the responsibility for payment for the cost of consents and permissions.

D.293

The [Author] shall deliver to the [Publisher] two sets of the complete manuscript acceptable to the [Publisher] and ready for the printer the original [Work] of the [Author] entitled [title] of approximately [number] words in length, as well as any illustrations or additional material agreed with the [Publisher].

D.294

'The Delivery Date' shall be the following date by which the manuscript of the [Work] is to be completed for publication purposes [date] and delivered to the [Publisher]. The Author understands that time is of the essence.

D.295

The [Author] agrees to write and deliver two copies of the [Work] to the [Agent] based on the synopsis on or before the delivery date [date].

D.296

The [Author] undertakes to prepare an index for the [Work] which shall be delivered with the proofs to the [Publisher].

D.297

'The Delivery Date' shall be the following date by which the [Work] is to be delivered to the [Publisher] by the [Author] [date].

D.298

'The Target Date' shall be the following date by which the work is intended to be completed and delivered to a publisher [date].

D.299

The [Writer] shall deliver the [Treatment] to the [Company] not later than [three months] after the date of full execution of this Agreement. The [Writer] shall deliver the [Scripts] to the [Company] within [twelve months] after receipt of the [Company's] written approval of the [Treatment].

D.300

In the event that the delivery of the [Work] is delayed for any reason the advance payments linked to delivery shall not be made until the [Work] has been delivered to and accepted by the [Publishers].

D.301

Where there is a new delivery date substituted in the contract whether due to the [Author] or [Publisher] and a new publication date. There shall not be any alteration to the duration of the Agreement or any other terms.

D.302

The [Publisher] agrees that it may at its discretion at the request of the [Author] adjust and delay delivery of the [Work] for a period of [number] months. Provided that the [Author] agrees that where delivery is delayed beyond [number] months from the original date without consent. Then the [Publisher] shall be entitled to terminate the Agreement and seek to arrange an agreement with a third party to write a book on the generic subject of [specify]. The [Publisher] agrees that it shall not have any right and/or claim to use and/or adapt any synopsis and/or part of the [Work] already received from the [Author].

D.303

The [Contributor] agrees and undertakes to deliver [number] written typed pages of each chapter of the [Work] by the following dates [specify].

Purchase and Supply of Products

D.304

In the event that the [Supplier] fails to deliver the [Goods] in accordance with the terms of this Agreement and/or in accordance with Schedule [–] to this Agreement and/or by the Delivery Date specified under Clause [–] (time being of the essence). The [Purchaser] shall have the right to terminate this Agreement forthwith in writing and no further obligations shall apply to the [Purchaser] unless the force majeure provisions apply. In the event that this Agreement is terminated on the grounds of non-delivery of the [Goods] in accordance with Clause [–] of this Agreement the [Supplier] shall be liable to the [Purchaser] for all direct and indirect loss incurred by the [Purchaser]. The [Supplier] shall repay all monies paid by the [Purchaser] to the [Supplier] and all reasonable costs incurred in obtaining alternative [Goods] and for any increase in the cost of acquiring the [Goods] on the same or similar terms as contained in this Agreement.

D.305

The carriage and transport of the [Goods] shall be free on board [f.o.b.] which shall mean that all costs of whatever nature incurred in placing the [Goods] upon [name of vessel] shall be borne by the [Seller]. The [Seller] acknowledges that the [Seller] shall be responsible for any and all export duty. Until the [Goods] are actually on board all property rights, risks and liabilities with respect to the [Goods] shall remain with the [Seller].

D.306

The [Seller] will replace free of charge any [Material] proved to the [Seller's] satisfaction to have been damaged in transit provided that within [three days] after delivery both the [Seller] and the carriers have received from the [Purchaser] notification in writing of the damage.

D.307

The [Seller] shall only accept responsibility for non-delivery of any item on the delivery note and/or damage to the [Products] caused in transit if within [seven days] of receipt of the [Products] by the [Customer] written notice is provided to the [Seller]. Where the [Seller] accepts responsibility under this clause, it shall at its sole option, repair or replace (as the case may be) the items concerned which are proved to the [Seller's] satisfaction to have been lost or damaged prior to the delivery to the [Customer].

D.308

The [Company] shall promptly make shipment of the [Products] after manufacture in each production month as agreed. Delivery terms shall be on the basis of f.o.b. [Country].

D.309

The [Company] shall not be responsible for the delay in production and/or shipment of the [Products] or any other consequences arising from the late arrivals of a Purchase Order or similar document.

D.310

Shipments shall be made to the addresses stated in the contract. The [Company] nevertheless reserves the right to change such addresses in which case the cost of carriage shall be paid by mutual agreement between the parties.

D.311

The [Supplier] shall arrange and pay for all formalities involved in shipping, transfer, import or export as appropriate including packaging, storage, freight costs, customs duties, import and export taxes, product content verification, security checks, and any other matter required to comply with the laws, regulations, directives, codes, practices and standards of any country. Any documents required by the [Company] and confirmation of payment shall be provided by the [Supplier] upon request by the [Company].

D.312

The [Supplier] shall provide the [Company] at least [specify duration] before the [Products] are despatched ex-factory and in any event not later than the date of shipment with the following details of the products:

1.1 Number, dimensions, net weight, gross weight, with content and description. Together with a sample label on the product and packaging.

1.2 Date and place of shipment and method, with reference.

1.3 Date, method of importation, transportation and delivery address.

1.4 Value (pro forma invoice), setting out the ex-factory price of the unpackaged goods, packaging, carriage, duties, taxes and insurance costs in [currency] together with the reference numbers of the [items/ products].

D.313

Each delivery order shall be in triplicate, one attached to the package, the second sent to the receiving agent, and the third sent to the [Company]. If the delivery order is missing and/or delivery is delayed for any reason then all the consequential additional [expenses/costs/losses/other] of any kind shall be at the [Supplier's] sole cost and expense.

D.314

The packaging, shipping, duties, taxes, carriage and insurance of the [Supplies] shall be the sole responsibility of and entirely at the expense and risk of the [Contractor].

D.315

The delivery dates and times quoted are for guidance only and are subject to further confirmation by the [Company]. Delivery times and dates shall not be of the essence of the contract. The [Company] shall not be liable for any loss or damage to the [Customer] arising from the failure to deliver. Delivery shall be to the name and address in the order form unless the [Customer] otherwise confirms in writing. The [Customer] shall be obliged to notify in writing within [twenty-eight days] any claims in respect of defects, damage and/or deficit in respect of any part of the [Order]. Unless it has been stated on the [Order] that the order shall be fulfilled in one instalment the [Company] shall be entitled to make deliveries by instalments.

D.316

Time is of the essence in the performance of the Purchase Order. If delivery dates cannot be met the [Seller] shall promptly notify the [Company] of the earliest possible date for delivery. Notwithstanding such notice and unless a substitute delivery date has been expressly agreed by the [Company] in writing, the [Seller's] failure to effect delivery on the date specified shall entitle the [Company] to cancel this order without liability to the [Seller] to purchase substitute items elsewhere. The [Company] shall be entitled to request a full refund of all sums paid and to hold the [Seller] liable for any loss and/or additional costs that the [Company] may incur.

D.317

A detailed Delivery Statement must accompany each consignment of goods and materials. A Delivery Statement signed by a duly authorised representative of the [Company] shall include an acknowledgment of the delivery subject to the terms of this contract. A copy shall be retained by the [Company].

D.318

The [Supplier] shall provide a detailed delivery statement with each consignment of the [Product] which shall be agreed or otherwise by the [Seller] and returned to the [Supplier] on each occasion.

D.319

Time shall be of the essence of this order. Delivery of the [Goods] shall be effected at your own risk and expense including deterioration, loss and/ or damage to the [Goods] in transit. In the event that the [Goods] are not delivered in accordance with this Order and/or by the specified dates then the [Company] shall be entitled to cancel the Order.

D.320

The [Supplier] shall deliver the [Product] in accordance with the delivery dates and quantities specified in accordance with Schedule [–]. Thereafter the [Supplier] shall provide each unit of the [Product] upon written request in accordance with an agreed format.

D.321

The [Supplier] will replace free of charge any product proved to the [Supplier's] reasonable satisfaction to have been lost or damaged in transit. Provided that within [ten days] after acceptance of the delivery statement the [Supplier] has received notification in writing of the loss or damage.

D.322

It is agreed that any requested delivery date cannot be confirmed until the order is accepted and paid for by the customer. That delivery dates may be varied due to weather conditions, transport problems, unexpected manufacture and/or packaging issues and/or any other reason. Where delivery is delayed more than [number] days you may cancel the order and be provided with a full refund. No sums are paid for any reason for any damages, losses and/or costs you may have incurred. The [Company] may offer at its discretion a voucher and/or discount against a future purchase.

D.323

If the delivery date relates to a purchase for a special occasion such as a wedding and/or birthday. Then you must make this clear on the order and request [specify delivery] and pay an additional sum of [figure/currency] to have the delivery date and time of delivery confirmed as guaranteed by the [Distributor].

Services

D.324

Where the nominated personnel of the [Consultancy] is unavailable and cannot deliver the services and/or report required for the purposes of this Agreement. Then the [Company] agrees that a suitably required substitute may be provided by the [Consultancy] to complete the [Project].

D.325

Where the delivery of material, products and/or services by and/or actions of a third party engaged by the [Company] has impacted and/or delayed the completion and delivery of this Agreement by [Name]. Then the [Company] agrees and undertakes that [Name] will not be deemed and/or construed as in breach of this Agreement where the delay and/or failure is due to such third party.

D.326

Where the supply of the services and/or the delivery of the required materials by the [Company] to the [Enterprise] cannot be provided in accordance with the agreed Schedule [–] which is attached to and forms part of this Agreement. Then the [Enterprise] shall have the option at its sole discretion to either agree to a delay or to cancel this Agreement and to be paid a full refund of all payments made under this Agreement.

D.327

The delivery of an uninterrupted [Service] by the [Company] under this Agreement is a major reason for entering into this Agreement. Where delivery is delayed, irregular, intermittent and/or otherwise unreliable. Then the [Enterprise] shall be entitled to terminate the [Service] and this Agreement and shall not be liable to pay any further sums to the [Company] from the date of termination.

Sponsorship

D.328

The [Sponsor] shall arrange delivery of the agreed number of [Products] specified in Schedule [–] which forms part of this Agreement to the [Company] at [address] at its sole risk, cost and expense. Where [Products] are damaged and/or lost in transit and/or lave lost their labels then additional copies shall be supplied upon request.

D.329

The [Sponsor] shall supply to the [Company] a delivery [invoice/statement] specifying the number and detail of the [Products] and the fact that it is supplied at no cost.

D.330

Where the delivery by the [Company] to the [Sponsor] of any marketing, advertising material, samples of goods and/or attendance figures and/or any other data is delayed for any reason. Both parties agree that the [Company] shall not be deemed to be in breach of this Agreement.

D.331

The [Sponsor] agrees that failure to deliver the materials necessary for the reproduction of the [Sponsors'] name and logo on any marketing and event banners by the delivery date agreed with the [Company] may result in the absence of the [Sponsors] details on such material.

University, Library and Educational

D.332

The [Contractor] shall arrange and pay for all formalities involved in shipping, transfer, import or export as appropriate including packaging, storage, freight and delivery costs, customs duties, import and export taxes, product content verification, security checks, insurance and any other matter required to comply with the laws, regulations, directives, codes, practices and standards of any country in respect of all [Services/Documents/Products] delivered to the [Institute] under this Agreement. The [Contractor] will when requested to do so by the [Institute] provide a copy of any such documentation and proof of payments of the costs and expenses. The [Institute] shall not be liable for nor bear the cost and expense of any such matters.

D.333

The [delivery/availability] dates and times quoted are for guidance only and may be changed without any notice and shall not be of the essence of this Agreement. The [Institute] shall not be liable for any loss and/or damage and/or any costs and expenses which arise directly and/or indirectly from the failure to deliver and/or non-availability of any [Service/Product/Article].

D.334

Time shall be of the essence of this order. The [Contractor] shall deliver the [Goods/Services/Material] at its own risk and expense. The [Institute] shall not be liable for the deterioration, loss and/or damage to the [Goods/Services/Material] at any time prior to delivery and acceptance by the [Institute]. In the event that the [Goods/Services/Material] are not delivered in accordance with the specifications as to quantity, content, quality, use, colour, and/or by the delivery dates. Then the [Institute] shall be entitled to refuse to accept delivery and shall not be liable for any of the sums due for the [Goods/Services/Material] which did not adhere to the terms and conditions of the Agreement.

D.335

The [Institute] shall not be obliged to accept delivery of the [Product/Services/other] until the [Product/Services/other] have been tested, assessed, analysed, counted, verified and audited. The [Institute] reserves the right to refuse acceptance up to [seven days] after delivery on the grounds that all and/or any part of the delivery of the [Product/Services/other] fails to be in accordance with the agreed specifications and terms agreed between the parties.

D.336
All delivery deadlines specified for any coursework, dissertations and projects by any tutor, exam board and/or department must be adhered to by all students. Where for any reason these are not met then you must provide a certified medical certificate to show that your condition was examined and reviewed by a medical practitioner and a justifiable reason put forward and a detailed explanation as to the impact, effect and consequences. There is no automatic right to have any deadline delayed and/or extended.

DEPOSIT

General Business and Commercial

D.337
The [Purchaser] acknowledges that the deposit shall be treated as part payment for the [Goods]. In the event that the [Goods] are not paid for in full within the time specified the [Seller] shall be entitled to retain the deposit and shall not be liable to return the deposit for any reason, and shall be entitled to take legal proceedings to reclaim the outstanding sum (plus interest) due or to seek the immediate return of the [Goods]. Title in the [Goods] shall not pass to the [Purchaser] until such time as the [Goods] have been paid for in full.

D.338
[Packages] on which a deposit is charged shall be paid at the same time as payment for the [Company's] [Products] is made by the [Buyer]. If [Packages] are returned to the [Company] and reach the [Company] in a condition fit for use then the amount of deposit paid shall be credited to the [Buyer] in full. The [Company's] decision as to the condition of the package upon receipt shall be final and conclusive. In the event that the [Packages] are not fit for use then the payment if any to be made by the [Company] shall be subject to agreement between parties.

D.339
It is agreed that where [Client] is placing a firm order for [Goods] to be ordered from the manufacturer then a deposit of [twenty per cent of the

retail price] will be required by the [Company]. Where [Goods] are being purchased from existing stock then a minimum deposit of [fifty per cent] shall be required. The [Goods] shall not be delivered until the balance has been paid, and any payment by has been cleared by a bank. In any event no deposit shall be refunded and/or transferred or offset against other [Goods]. In the event the [Company] agrees to provide a credit note or refund, no other additional sums shall be paid for any reason. The [Company] shall be entitled to retain [ten per cent] of the total value of the [Goods] to cover expenses. The refund shall only be made payable in the name of the [Client] that appears on the invoice.

D.340
'Legal Deposit' shall mean the act of depositing published material (which includes all printed publications) in designated libraries and/or archives. Publishers (defined as anyone who issues or distributes publications to the public) and distributors in the United Kingdom and in Ireland have the legal obligation to deposit published material in the six legal deposit libraries which collectively maintain the national published archive of the United Kingdom:

1.1   The British Library; the Bodleian Library, Oxford; the University Library, Cambridge; the National Library of Scotland, Edinburgh; the Library of Trinity College, Dublin; the National Library of Wales, Aberystwyth.

1.2   Publishers are obliged to send one copy of each of their publications to the British Library within one month of publication. The other five libraries have a right to claim those publications from the publishers or distributors.

1.3   This covers material published and distributed in the United Kingdom or published elsewhere, but distributed in the United Kingdom. The print run, size of material, subject, location of printing or publication is not relevant.

D.341
'The Deposit' shall be [ten] per cent of the [Price] exclusive of [Value Added Tax/other].

D.342
The deposit must be paid to the [Company] by the [Customer] by [method] from an approved bank on the day of the [Order/Purchase] and any interest on the deposit may be retained by the [Company]. The payment shall be supported by two documents which verify your identity.

D.343

In the event that the [Customer] does not comply with the payment terms and conditions in [document] then the deposit shall be forfeited and shall be retained by the [Company].

D.344

The [Distributor] agrees to deposit a copy of the [Work/Book/] in each of the main national libraries in the following countries [–]. These copies shall be deposited at the [Distributors'] cost and expense.

D.345

Where a deposit is paid on account as a contribution to the cost of any work and/or service to be provided by the [Company]. Then this shall not be returned under any circumstances where the [Client] subsequently decides to cancel and/or not proceed with the work and/or service at any time.

D.346

The [Company] shall hold your deposit in good faith as security against damage and/or loss of any [Articles] provided on loan. This sum shall be refunded to you in full in the event that the [Articles] are returned to the [Company] by the agreed date [specify] and in the same condition without losses and/or damages.

DERIVATIVES

General Business and Commercial

D.347

'Derivatives' shall mean glass masters, metal parts or copy master tapes manufactured by or for the [Licensee] from the Master.

D.348

'Derivatives' shall mean any adaptations, developments, variations, translations, new versions, new editions, merchandising or other forms of exploitation in any format and media directly and/or indirectly based on the whole and/or part of the [item] whether inside, outside and/or a process, right, mechanism, and/or on the packaging whether in existence now and/or developed in the future in any country at any time in any part of the world.

DESIGNS

General Business and Commercial

D.349

The [Company] acknowledges that all present and future Design Rights in the Design Documents, the Approved Designs, the Prototype Designs and the Complete Set are and will remain the sole property of [Name]. This Agreement does not in any way purport to vest or transfer any copyright, intellectual property rights and/or Design Rights [and/or Future Design Rights] to the [Company].

D.350

In consideration of the sum of [fee/currency] receipt of which is hereby acknowledged the [Company] hereby sells assigns and transfers in perpetuity all intellectual property rights including patents, copyright, registered design rights, future design rights and associated designs in the Design Documents, the Approved Designs, the Prototype Designs, and the Complete Set to [Name]. The [Company] shall not have further claim, right, ownership or interest.

D.351

The [Contractor] warrants and undertakes to the [Developer] that it has and shall supply originals or copies in its possession or control of any designs, drawings, details or other information relating to the [Works] to the [Developer] upon request so as not to delay or disrupt the execution and completion of this Agreement.

D.352

The [Developer] shall be entitled on written request and upon paying a reasonable copying charge thereof to be supplied by the [Contractor] with complete copies of all drawings, designs, details, specifications, calculations, documents, records, computer generated material, models or other material prepared by or on behalf of the [Contractor] relating to the [Development]. The [Contractor] grants to the [Developer] a [non] exclusive, royalty free licence to use, reproduce and permit third parties to do so any material provided that it is for the construction of the [Development] and/or the maintenance, repair, reinstatement, reconstruction and extension thereof at any time whether now or in the future. The copyright in the designs, documents or other material relating to the [Development] shall be the property of the [Contractor] who shall be entitled to exhibit and display a copyright notice on all material and a credit for the design.

D.353

'Design' shall mean the novel shape, configuration, pattern or surface decoration of an [article/item] which has aesthetic appeal and can be manufactured and sold separately and is not an integral part of another article or item or purely functional in nature.

D.354

'Design document' shall mean any record of a design whether in the form of a drawing, a written description, photograph, data stored in a computer or otherwise.

D.355

'Design' shall mean the original design of any aspect of the shape or configuration (whether internal or external) of the whole or any substantial part of an article and/or any reproduction in the form of a prototype.

D.356

'Design Right' shall be defined as a property right which subsists in an original design. The design shall mean any aspect of the shape or configuration (whether internal or external) of the whole or any substantial part of an article. The design right shall not subsist until the design has been recorded in a design document or an article has been made to the design which was made or recorded after that part of the [Copyright, Designs and Patents Act 1988 as amended] had commenced. The design right does not exist in a method or principle of construction, or the features of shape or configuration of an article (which enable the article to be connected to or placed in around or against another article so that the article may perform its function or are dependent upon appearance of another article of which the article is intended by the designer to form an integral part) or which is surface decoration. Design right shall only subsist if the design qualifies for protection in [country/other].

D.357

'Designer' in relation to a design shall be defined in accordance with [the Copyright, Designs and Patents Act 1988 as subsequently amended] and shall mean the person who creates the design. Where the design is computer generated it shall mean the person by whom the arrangements necessary for the creation of the design are undertaken.

D.358

The [Designer] agrees and acknowledges that as the design is created in pursuance of a commission that the [Company] commissioning the [Design] shall be the first owner of any design rights.

D.359

The [Employee] agrees and undertakes that where in the course of his employment he creates a design or article that the [Employer] shall be the owner of any design rights or future design rights in the [Design] and/or [Article] and that the [Employee] shall not be entitled to claim any interest in or benefit thereto at any time or any sums in respect of the exploitation of any articles based on or derived from the [Design] and/or [Article].

D.360

'Future Design Right' shall [be defined in accordance the Copyright, Designs and Patents Act 1988 as amended and/or revised] and shall mean the design right which will or may come into existence in respect of future design or class of designs or on the occurrence of a future event.

D.361

'Joint Design' shall mean a design produced by the collaboration of two or more designers in which the contribution of each is not distinct from that of the other(s) [in accordance with the Copyright, Designs and Patents Act 1988 as amended].

D.362

'British Design' shall mean a design which qualifies for design right protection by reason of a connection with the United Kingdom of the designer or by the person by whom the design is commissioned or the designer is employed [in accordance with the Copyright, Designs and Patents Act 1988 as amended].

D.363

'The Designs' shall be the original concept and two-dimensional designs for a range of [specify items] and other products to be created and provided by the [Designer]. The designs shall include all such designs which are set out in the attached schedule and form part of this Agreement together with such other designs as are created by the [Designer] in accordance with the Terms of this Agreement.

D.364

'The Licensed Articles' shall be the three-dimensional reproduction and adaptations of the designs to be manufactured by the [Licensee] based on the [Prototype].

D.365

'The Designs' shall be the original concept and two-dimensional designs, sketches, drawings and patterns for an individual piece of clothing described as follows [description].

D.366

The [Employee] acknowledges and agrees that all patents, inventions, trade marks, copyright, design rights, future design rights, property rights and any other rights of any nature in the product of his services during the normal course of his employment shall remain the sole and exclusive property of the [Company]. The [Employee] shall not acquire any rights or interest or be entitled to receive any payments, royalties or other benefits in respect of any form of registration, licensing or exploitation by the [Company].

D.367

The [Employee] undertakes and agrees to sign any documents or forms which may be required by the [Company] to assign, transfer or confirm ownership of any of the material created in Clause [–] above. Provided that where any costs and expenses have to be incurred by the [Employee] the [Company] will agree and pay in advance a sum agreed between the parties.

D.368

'Designs' shall include all two-dimensional representations of the [Character] in whatever form and shall also include all three-dimensional objects of any nature derived from or based on two-dimensional design and vice versa.

D.369

'Design' shall mean all two-dimensional artistic designs created by or for or licensed to the [Company] for the purpose of developing the [Character].

D.370

Design, drawings, specifications and other work developed under this Agreement shall be the exclusive property of the [Company]. The [Company] may use and/or exploit such material in any way that it may decide. No such material may be released exploited and/or published and/or used by the [Contractor] except for the purposes of this Agreement without the prior written consent of the [Company]. All originals, copies and any other reproductions in any medium shall be delivered to the [Company] by the [Contractor] upon completion of this Agreement or at the [Company's] request.

D.371

There shall be no transfer, assignment, license or other grant of rights in the [Designs] and/or the [Article] under this Agreement and all design rights, future design rights, patents, copyright, trademarks, computer software, domain name and any other rights and the right to reproduce copies in any form or media and to license others to do so shall be retained by the [Designer]. No other party shall be entitled to display or exhibit or distribute any material which claims ownership of any material at any time or to register any interest.

D.372

The [Company] shall not be entitled to claim any intellectual property rights, copyright, design rights and future design rights, patent rights, computer software rights, trade mark, domain name or other rights, interest or assignment of any of the following work, material or activities by the [Employee/Consultant] to the [Company] which are specifically excluded from the terms of this Agreement and shall be retained by the [Employee/ Consultant].

D.373

The [Company] agrees and undertakes that it shall not engage and/ or appoint any other third party to work on and/or advise on the [Design/ Project/Product] without the prior consent of the [Designer].

D.374

The [Designer] shall have the right as all times to be acknowledged as the original artist for the [Project] and in all artwork, reports, marketing and any form of reproduction and/or exploitation in any media at any time as follows [–]. The [Designer] shall have the right to specify to the [Company] that that their name and acknowledgement does not appear in any particular case.

D.375

The [Designer] shall retain all copyright, design rights and future design rights and intellectual property rights and the right to register any trade mark, domain name, patent and/or any other rights and/or interest of any nature in the [Design Work] in any format and/or medium whether in existence now and/or in the future. The [Designer] shall have the sole right to retain all royalties, fees and/other sums received from the reproduction, licensing and/or exploitation of the [Design Work]. The [Designer] shall have the right to assign and/or transfer any and/or all of the rights to a third party at any time.

D.376

Where the [Company] commissions a designer to develop, and create a new [design/logo/symbol] for the [Event] whether computer generated, by drawing and/or any use of any other means. The [Company] shall ensure that such person and/or any business and/or the [Company] shall assign all copyright, intellectual property rights, design rights, future design rights, trade marks, service marks, community marks, rights in any computer generated material, the right to any domain name and any other rights of any nature (whether in existence now and/or created in the future) to the [Sponsor/Name]. Further that such person and/or business and/or the [Company] shall not be entitled to received and/or be paid any royalties and/or other sums of any nature from the use and/or exploitation of the [design/logo/symbol] by the [Sponsor/Name] at any time.

D.377

1.1 The [Artist] has created, developed and supplied the shape, design, logo, name and domain name for [Individual] for the total sum of [figure/currency] for his/her business which currently trades under the name of [specify].

1.2 In consideration of the additional payment of [figure/currency] the [Artist] agrees and undertakes to assign all present and future copyright, intellectual property rights, domain names and any variations, trade marks and any other rights to [Individual] in all media and in all medium throughout the planet earth and on land, sea and air and throughout the universe for the full period of all such copyright, intellectual property rights and any other rights and any extensions and for any new rights which may be created at a later date which do not exist now. No additional payments and/or royalties shall be due to the [Artist] from [Individual] and/or any collecting society and/or from any exploitation and/or reproduction in any form.

D.378

[Name] has created and produced a three dimensional object entitled [specify]. [Name] sells the original object to [specify] for the sum of [figure/currency] to the [Company]. [Name] does not grant and/or authorise any reproduction of the original object in the form of posters, statues and/or in any other form and/or medium unless [Name] enters into a merchandising agreement with the [Company] upon terms to be agreed.

D.379

The [Artist] has designed, produced and made a series of original [Objects] on the theme of [subject] in [material] by [specify method]. In consideration of the payment of the sum of [figure/currency] the [Artist] authorises the [Purchaser] to reproduce, use and adapt and exploit the [Objects] as they think fit and at their sole discretion and no additional sums shall be due and/or owed.

DIRECTOR

General Business and Commercial

D.380

The duties of the [Executive] as a [Director] of the [Company] if appointed, shall be subject to the Articles of Association and Memorandum of the Company for the time being in effect and shall be separate from and additional to her duties as Executive. The [Executive's] remuneration is inclusive of any remuneration to which the [Executive] may be entitled as a [Director] of the [Company] or any associated company.

D.381

Upon termination of the position of the [Executive] for whatever reason at any time the [Executive] shall at the request of the [Company] forthwith in writing resign his/her position of the office of Director of the [Company]. The [Company] shall not be liable to pay any compensation for loss of office as Director by the [Executive].

D.382

The [Director] shall notify the [Company] of any material changes at the [Company] which may affect the ability of the [Company] to fulfil the terms of this Agreement.

D.383

Where a [Director] has been and/or is disqualified from and/or is the subject to an investigation which may result in disqualification from holding the office of a director of a company. Then the [Director] shall be obliged to notify this fact to the [Company Secretary] in writing with [seven days] of the event.

D.384

Where for any reason the [Director] decides not to proceed with the [Project] then he/she shall be obliged to repay all sums paid by the [Company] under this Agreement for any work not completed to the date of notification by the [Director].

D.385

The final decision as to the appointment and/or replacement and/or removal for any reason of any Director shall be with [specify] and his/her decision shall be final. There shall be no requirement to consult with any shareholders, management and/or funders of the [Project] before any decision is reached and/or any action taken.

DISASTER RECOVERY

General Business and Commercial

D.386

The [Company] confirms that it has entered into a fully comprehensive Disaster Recovery Service Agreement (a copy of which is attached to and forms part of this Agreement). In the event of a breakdown, interruption or failure to obtain access to the data processing centre, the [Company] shall have access to and use of immediate alternative data processing back-up after receipt by the [Supplier] of notice to that effect.

D.387

Where a sub-licensee, distributor and/or other third party who is due and/or liable to account to the [Licensor] has failed to put in place a recovery system and/or data storage policy. In the event that records are not available and destroyed then it shall be deemed a breach of this Agreement.

DISCHARGE

General Business and Commercial

D.388

The rights and obligations of [Name] shall be formally discharged and end upon full and final payment of all sums due under Clause [–] of this Agreement except in respect of Clauses [–] provisions relating to warranties, indemnities and confidentiality which shall continue in full force and effect until [date].

D.389

All rights, obligations and undertakings of any nature by either party shall be brought to an end on the date that the following conditions in Clauses [–] have been carried out and fulfilled. After that date the Agreement shall have been discharged so that neither party is bound by any contractual condition of any nature to the other.

D.390

Provided that the [Seller] shall have provided the [Goods] and the [Purchaser] shall have paid the full price stipulated then all rights and obligations of either party shall be discharged. Except that there shall be a surviving obligation by the [Seller] for [one] year in relation to Clauses [–] of this Agreement relating to the description, use, condition and function of the [Goods].

D.391
Where an invoice shall have been paid in full to the [Agent] then it shall have been discharged and there is no further liability by the [Company] in the event the [Agent] fails to pay [Name].

DISCLAIMER

General Business and Commercial

D.392
The reference to any products, articles, packaging, advertising, method, process, trade mark, distributor, supplier or manufacturer does not constitute or imply an endorsement, recommendation or preference by the [Company]. The views and opinions of [specify] shall not be used for advertising or product endorsement or any other purposes without the prior written consent of the [Company].

D.393
All rights are reserved. You are specifically prohibited and not allowed to reproduce, copy, duplicate, manufacture, supply, sell, hire, distribute or adapt all or any part of this [Article] including any packaging.

D.394
The [Service] and any associated [material/software] is supplied to and used by you on the on the following basis that you have agreed that:

1.1 That there are no undertakings, warranties, terms of agreement between the parties or guarantees by the [Company] as to the quality, standard and function of the content and the direct and indirect consequences arising from the use of the [Service] and any associated [material/software].

1.2 That there is no assurance that the [Service] and any associated [material/ software] is free from defects, errors, or omissions, or is accurate or not flawed in any way or does not contain viruses or other corruptions, is undamaged, fit for any particular purpose, or suitable to be used in conjunction with any other particular products or systems, or will operate without interruption, delay or will be available or will not be suspended, cancelled or terminated.

1.3 That the [Company] shall not be liable for any consequences which arise as a result of the use of the [Service] and any associated [material/software] by you or any third party to whom you supply, copy, send, or distribute the [Service] and any associated [material/ software] including but not limited to loss of profit, loss of data and information, business, revenue, contracts, reputation or goodwill or any other expenses, costs and damages whether direct or indirect and whether reasonably foreseeable or not.

1.4 There is no assurance as to whether any content is in breach or infringes any copyright, patents, trade marks, service marks, computer software, film, sound recording, music, lyrics, photographs, DVDs, domain name, confidential information, designs or contract or any other rights in any country or of any person, business or organisation.

1.5 That all the risk, liability and choice of using the [Service] and any associated [material/software] is with you and you shall not seek to claim any sums from the [Company] unless the death, or serious injury of a person is directly linked to and arises from their use of this [Service] and any associated [material/software] on your behalf and was directly caused by the negligence of the [Company].

D.395

This information and summary is for background material and may not be up to date or fully state all the relevant facts. There is no recommendation, endorsement or promotion of any person or company in preference to another or any commercial assessment or financial forecast which you may use to promote a product or business or which you should rely upon to make a decision regarding investment, or other commitment. The [Company] shall not be liable for any use of this material and you must make your own judgement and seek professional advice.

D.396

The [Agency/other] shall not be liable for any sums incurred by, or for any loss, damages, expenses or contractual obligations or penalties or other consequences which may be alleged or may arise directly or indirectly to any person or company who applies for or completes the tender process whether they are awarded the contract or not. It is a pre-condition of any application that the applicants do so at their own risk and that there is no obligation by or claim against the [Agency] in respect of the application or any direct or indirect consequences.

D.397

[Name] and/or the [Company] are and will not be responsible for any use of the [Work] and any [disc/gadget/gift/other] and/or any content, data, information or packaging by any person, company or business which has not acquired the material directly from an authorised source and used the material exactly in accordance with the instructions and/or the intended purpose and/or which is outside [country].

D.398

Any recommendation by the [Company] and/or any employee as to the [Footwear] that the customer should purchase is for guidance only. No responsibility can be taken for any personal injuries, stress fractures and/or any loss and/or damage arising from the use of any [Footwear] and/or the purchase of any item which is unsuitable for its intended use due to the type of terrain and/or sport for which it has been used.

D.399

[Name] does not recommend that:

1.1   This [Product] be used by anyone under age [specify].

1.2   Follow the installation instructions exactly and do not use with other equipment and/or electrical connections which are out of date and/or have not been verified as of suitable standard.

D.400

Data, charts and statistics in this report including those which show projections for the future are based on sample surveys and current usage. They are theoretical projections and not to be relied upon to be accurate and/or may be subject to change at any time. No financial investment should be made based on these figures without seeking professional independent advice from an expert.

Internet and Websites

D.401

We disclaim responsibility for any consequences arising from your access to or use of this website or any links. All content which is included is entirely at the sole discretion of the [Editor/Webmaster] and may be altered or deleted at any time. Any material which you add to the site by way of postings or otherwise shall not be defamatory, in breach of copyright and shall either be cleared for use in this manner or shall be your own original material. You agree that we shall have the right to use any such material in our publicity, advertising, newspapers and magazines.

D.402

The [Company] are not responsible for the contents or reliability of the linked websites and does not [necessarily] endorse the views expressed in them.

Listing shall not be taken as an endorsement of any kind. We have no control over the access to and content of the links.

D.403

The data, information, records, images, text, slogans, graphics, trademarks, service marks or any other material on this site and/or any links may not be accurate and there may be other more recent material available elsewhere. This site is intended only to be used for research and is not intended to replace specialist advice from a [medical/scientific/other].

D.404

You use this site and any material and download any of its contents at your own discretion and risk. The [Company] [and its associates/affiliates/sponsors/suppliers] do not accept responsibility for any consequences that may arise from your reliance on any material and/or the downloading of any contents.

D.405

The [Company] and any content providers on this [Website] and/or any links in any part of the world or in any associated publicity, advertising and marketing and/or software and/or material of any nature which is stored, displayed or downloaded from and/or in conjunction with this [Website] shall not be liable to [you the user] for any consequence that may arise from your access to, use of and/or actions based on or derived from anything on this [Website]. This shall include the supply of your personal and financial details whether for ordering goods and/or services and/or research information and data. You agree that you have accepted that no representations, undertakings or warranties have been made as to the content and that you are advised to seek specialist professional advice and that this site is intended for guidance only.

D.406

The [Website Owners] rely on the suppliers of the information on this site to act in good faith and to provide accurate up-to-date data and records. All dates, prices, special offers, and other details are subject to availability and may be changed at any time. No responsibility or liability can be accepted for any errors, omissions or losses that may arise from your use, order or reliance on this site. The [Website Owners] and the copyright owners of this site permit access to browse, order goods and services and access information for private and personal use. The site, data, information and content may not be reproduced, published or commercially exploited without the prior written consent of the [Website Owner].

D.407

We endeavour to provide accurate, quality, detailed information, data and services on this site which is owned by [Company], operated by [Name] and trades as [Website]. However we cannot accept liability for your reliance on this site and you are advised to take independent legal advice. You accept as a condition of your use of the site that you will make no claim for any loss, damage or expenses that may arise. There is no undertaking by us that any part of the site is accurate, complete or up to date and this site must be used for guidance only to highlight possible issues.

D.408

The [Website Owners] rely on the suppliers of the information on this site to act in good faith and to provide accurate up-to-date data and records. All dates, prices, special offers, and other details are subject to availability and may be changed at any time. No responsibility and/or liability can be accepted for any errors, omissions and/or losses that may arise from your use, order or reliance on this site. The [Website Owners] and the copyright owners of this site permit access to browse, order goods and services and access information for private and personal use. The site, data, information, content, good and services and banner advertisements may not be reproduced, published or commercially exploited without the prior written consent of the [Website Owner] and any copyright owner.

D.409

The [Parent Company], the [Subsidiary], the [Distributor] and [other] cannot accept liability for your reliance on this [Website] of any nature whether commercial, financial, legal, medical, scientific or property and you are advised to take independent advice from a third party to review and advise on your particular circumstances and facts. Do not carry out any action, commitment, or undertaking based on this [Website] alone or you may suffer some loss, damage, expense or other consequences which could have been avoided. You accept as a condition of your use of the [Website] that you will make no claim or seek to be indemnified for any loss, damage, expenses or other consequences that may arise. There is no undertaking by us that any part of the site is accurate, complete or up to date and this site must be used for guidance only to highlight possible issues.

D.410

You must only use this site if you agree that the [Owners], service providers, sponsors and any other third parties associated with the [Website] shall not be responsible and/or liable for:

1.1   Any loss, damage or other consequent direct or indirect cost, expense or liability that may arise from your use or reliance on material.

1.2 Any content which is misleading or an error, failure of any operation or function, virus, destruction or interference with software or equipment, security lapse or breach or failure to deliver goods or services.

1.3 Any defamatory, offensive, derogatory material or statements on any part of the site whether temporary or permanent.

1.4 Any trade descriptions, quality of goods or services, fitness for purpose, prices, payment, delivery, delay or failure to deliver.

1.5 Any infringement or breach of copyright, design rights, moral rights, trademarks, service marks or any other intellectual property rights, or any contractual or other rights of any nature.

D.411

The [links/banner advertisements/offers/other] on this [Website] are used by you at your own risk, cost and liability and shall not be the responsibility of the [Company] for any reason. The website details, terms and conditions of use and content of the links are not owned or controlled by the [Company] and there is no consent, endorsement or recommendation provided by the [Company] express or implied that you should use the [links/banner advertisements/offers/other] or otherwise.

D.412

There are sections of this site that rely on the users to provide information and data in good faith. Where material is displayed or accessible which has been provided by third party users then we do not accept responsibility for any material which is defamatory, offensive, inaccurate, unavailable, unlawful or misleading. We do however have a policy of receiving any complaints at [specify] and will delete any material which we conclude should be removed for any reason.

D.413

Any guidance, advice, recommendations and/or promotions on this [Website] may be followed at your own risk and cost. The [Website Company] cannot accept any responsibility for any payments you may make to a third party and/or any actions that you may take as a direct and/or indirect result of viewing and/or having access to any content, advertisements, links, databases and/or any other material. You are strongly advised where you are paying significant sums of money to ensure that you take independent advice and to check that the company and/or person is a legitimate operation and registered with an appropriate [trade/commercial] organisation and that your money is secure if you are paying over the internet.

D.414

This [Company] permits you to upload material to the [Website] upon the following terms and conditions:

1.1 That all the personal information is true and verifiable and is not inaccurate and/or dishonest.

1.2 That you will only upload material in which you are the copyright owner and which is your original work and not copied and/or adapted from the work of a third party.

1.3 That the content of the material which you upload is not and/or is not alleged to be offensive, illegal, defamatory, obscene, violent, an incitement to violence, evidence of a civil and/or criminal act against a person and/or property, encouraging any act which is potentially harmful to any person, in breach of any agreement, an infringement of the rights of a third party who owns and/or controls the material.

1.4 That the material uploaded by you is free from defects, errors, omissions, is accurate, and not misleading, does not contain viruses and/or other corruptions.

1.5 You will be entirely responsible for any legal action and/or other consequences taken against you whether by the [Company] and/or a third party for damages, costs, expenses and/or otherwise which may arise as a result of uploading the material to the [Website]. The [Company] shall not be liable for any consequences including but not limited to costs and damages whether direct or indirect and whether reasonably foreseeable or not.

1.6 The [Company] will assist and/or supply material and/or data to any third party who has a Court Order who has taken legal action against the [Company] in order to obtain details of the person who has uploaded any material to the [Website].

D.415

Images may be edited, distorted, adapted and changed. The [Company] cannot verify that any images have not altered and/or varied prior to being posted on the [Website]. The [Company] does not accept responsibility and/or liability for any damages and/or loss that may be suffered by any person by such actions by a third party but undertakes to remove and/or delete all images reported to them as defamatory, offensive, false and/or posted without authority of the owner of the image.

D.416

Where the [Company] sends free samples of any product to any person at its own cost. Then that person shall not be entitled to any refund and/or other sum and/or any other product as a substitute in the event that they should return any such sample. Liability of the [Company] is limited to [figure/currency] and any claim for personal injury can only relate to a claim for gross negligence and/or death directly caused by the [Company] and its samples in the country in which the sample was supplied to the person and used in accordance with the instructions.

Merchandising

D.417

The [Licensor] does not accept any responsibility for any legal action, losses, costs and/or liability for the [Product] manufactured and distributed by the [Distributor] at any time. The [Distributor] shall ensure that the [Product] is tested and sampled regularly so that it complies with all legislation, regulations, directives and policies in any part of the world in which the [Product] is to be sold, supplied and/or distributed. The [Distributor] shall arrange insurance cover to meet any potential liabilities from such exploitation.

D.418

Neither the [Company], nor its agents and representatives accept any responsibility for any use of this [Product/Article] in a manner and/or for a purpose which it was not intended to be used and which could not be reasonably be foreseen. There shall be no liability for any direct and/or indirect consequences, damages, losses, costs, expenses, and/or any other matter unless caused by the negligence of the [Company] and/or a death has occurred.

D.419

Neither the [Licensor] nor the [Licensee] shall accept any responsibility for any legal or other consequences that may arise directly or indirectly as a result of the use and/or adaptation of any of the contents of the [Product/Work/Service] and/or any accompanying [packaging/disc/equipment].

D.420

Neither the [Company] nor the [Distributor] shall accept any responsibility for any costs, expenses, losses, damages and/or any legal or other consequences that may arise directly or indirectly as a result of the use and/or adaptation of any of the contents of the [Product/Work] and/or any accompanying [packaging/disc/equipment]. You are at all times advised to seek specialist [subject] advice.

D.421

If any disc and/or data is incompatible with the [Purchasers] hardware and there is no alternative product available. Then there is no liability and/or responsibility on the part of the [Company] to provide another disc and/or data and/or any refund and/or reimbursement of any nature to the [Purchaser].

D.422

The [Company] and/or [Distributor] will only accept responsibility for any injury and/or death arising from the use of this [Product] where it is used in accordance with the [Instruction Manual] and the injury is caused as a direct result of the negligence of the [Company] and/or [Distributor]. No liability for any consequences is accepted where the [Product] in used in an unauthorised manner and/or in any way in which the [Product] was not intended to be used. This [Product] is not a toy and should not be used by any person under [number] age.

D.423

The [Distributor] supplies corporate information, data, maps, financial, insurance and analytical reports, podcasts, films, reviews and archive service to any third party at their own risk and provides no undertakings and/or confirmation as to the reliability, accuracy and/or impact of any of the material and/or any recommendations. Any decisions, investment, strategies and development proposal cannot rely on this material and all losses, damages, expenses and costs will not be paid for [Distributor] who disclaims all liability of any kind at any time which may arise whether it is directly and/or indirectly related to any material obtained from the [Distributor]. That in any event the total liability of [Distributor] to any third party is fixed at a maximum of [figure/currency].

D.424

The [Company] seeks to provide regular reports, updates and references for use by third parties in the [subject] market. It must be acknowledged that there may be variations in the quality of the service in different countries due to differences in translations of terminology, technology both software and hardware and the location. Fluctuations in the number of reports, variations in content and power failures will all affect the level of service. No refunds, compensation and/or other costs and expenses will be paid at any time unless there has been a complete failure of the service for a continuous period of [number] days and then the payment shall be fixed at [number/currency] per day in total per company.

Publishing

D.425

This [Novel] is a work of fiction. Names and characters are the product of the [Author's] imagination and creation and any resemblance to actual persons living or dead is entirely coincidental.

D.426

This book is a work of fiction. Names, characters, places and incidents are either products of the [Author's] imagination or used fictitiously. Any resemblance to actual people living or dead, events, locations or business establishments is entirely coincidental.

D.427

This book is a work of fiction and any person, character, name, business or other enterprise, locations and incidents or plots are the result of the original work of the [Author].

D.428

Neither the [Publishers] nor the [Authors] can accept any responsibility for any losses, damages costs, expenses and/or legal or other consequences that may arise directly or indirectly as a result of the use or adaptation of this book and/or any associated disc and/or material. You are advised to seek independent legal advice before entering into any agreement whether based on a contract from this book or not.

D.429

The [Author] and/or the [Publishers] are and will not be responsible for any use of the [Book] and any [disc/gadget/gift/other] and/or any content, data, information or packaging by any person, company or business at any time in any manner.

D.430

Any advice, recommendations, exercises and proposals made in this [Work] are the opinion of [Name] who is not a qualified practitioner of [subject]. You must take advice from an expert who can advise on your personal circumstances. If you decide to proceed without expert advice then you do so at your own risk and any consequences shall be at your own cost and no liability can be attributed to [Name]. If you have any of the following conditions you are advised not to follow any part of this [Work]: specify].

Sponsorship

D.431

The [Company] agrees and undertakes that:

1.1 The [Company] shall be responsible for and bear the cost of all claims, losses, damages, legal action and/or otherwise which arise as a direct result of the [Event].

1.2 That the [Sponsor] shall not be liable to make any contribution and/or bear any costs and/or expenses unless caused by the actions, negligence, omission and/or error of the [Sponsor] and/or a third party engaged by the [Sponsor].

1.3 That the [Company] shall arrange and pay for the cost of insurance cover of [figure/currency] which shall cover the following scenarios [specify].

D.432

The [Parent Company], the [Sponsor], the [Distributor] and [Organiser] cannot accept liability for your entry into and/or taking part in the [Event]. You are advised to take medical advice as to your health before making any payment for your entry. No responsibility cannot be accepted for any travel, accommodation, food, insurance, telephone and mobile costs and charges that may arise as a result of your entry and participation in the [Event] which you do at your own cost and risk. There is no undertaking by the [Parent Company], the [Sponsor], the [Distributor] and/or the [Organiser] that any part of the [Website] is accurate, complete or up to date and this site must be used for guidance only. Data, information times and dates may be changed and amended and/or the location and/or dates changed at short notice due to unforeseen circumstances and/or weather conditions. No liability is accepted by Parent Company], the [Sponsor], the [Distributor] and [Organiser] for any damages, losses, costs and/or expenses which arise as a result. You accept as a condition of your use of the [Website] and entry to the [Event] that you will make no claim or seek to be indemnified for any loss, damage, expenses or other consequences that may arise unless it is for personal injury caused by the negligence of the [Parent Company], the [Sponsor], the [Distributor] and/or the [Organiser].

D.433

The [Sponsor] agrees and undertakes that it shall not be entitled to disclaim any responsibility and/or liability for any products, services, equipment, staff, marketing, advertising and other material and/or persons which is has and/or will supply for the [Event]. That the [Sponsor] shall ensure that it has arranged and paid for suitable insurance cover of [figure/currency] for any one claim and shall provide a copy of such policy to the [Company] upon request.

D.434

The [Sponsor] is not responsible for the acts, omissions, errors and/or views of any third party associated with the [Event]. No assurance as to the ownership of, reliability, accuracy and/or otherwise is provided by the [Sponsor]. The [Sponsor] does not endorse, agree with and/or monitor the content relating to any third party. The [Sponsor] does not have any editorial control over and/or power to delete, change and/or amend any material either on this [Website] and/or in relation to the [Event].

D.435

1.1   The [Sponsor] does not agree to be liable for the failures and/or omissions of the [Company] at the [Event] in respect of any third parties including performers, visitors and/or caterers.

1.2   The [Company] must not represent to third parties that the [Sponsors'] are joint partners in the [Event] and/or responsible for any planning, organisation, insurance and/or marketing.

1.3   The total liability of the [Sponsor] is fixed at [number/currency] to the [Company] to make a funding contribution in return for product placement promotion at the [Event].

1.4   Any additional liability by the [Sponsor] to any third party for personal injury and/or death and/or any other reason shall be covered by the [Sponsors'] own public liability insurance taken out for its own benefit for that [Event].

University, Library and Educational

D.436

The [Institute] does accept liability for your reliance on any information, data, products, advice, prices, availability or other matters of any nature provided by its employees, representatives, on its website and/or in its catalogues, emails and/or correspondence. All details may change without notice, may contain errors and/or inaccuracies and are intended for guidance only. No responsibility can be accepted by the [Institute] for any loss, damage, expense or other consequences which may arise as a direct and/or indirect reliance on anything provided by the [Institute].

D.437

No responsibility or liability can be accepted for any errors, omissions or losses that may arise from your reliance on any information, recommendations, data, software, databases, prices, services and/or access to information and products whether for private and personal use and/or commercial exploitation. No consent, licence, permission and/or agreement is provided for any reproduction, supply, distribution and/or commercial exploitation.

D.438

The [Institute] shall not be responsible for the use by you of any information, data, articles, databases, film, DVDs, sound recordings, books, computer software and/or any other media to which you are granted access and use of at the [Institute]. It is your responsibility to clear and pay for a licence for the exploitation of the copyright and other intellectual property rights in any material. You must abide by the photocopying and reproduction policy of the [Institute]. The [Institute] reserves the right to seek to make a claim for loss, damages and expenses against you in the event that the [Institute] is joined in any legal action with you and/or legal action is threatened as a result of the use of material obtained by you through the [Institute].

D.439

The [Institute] cannot and does not accept full liability for any scientific data and statements that it releases and/or distributes to any third party at any time. There is no authority provided to any third party to use and/or adapt and/or develop and/or rely on this resource as more than an archive library. Material is out of date at the time of release and new data may be withheld due to legal, confidential and/or other reasons.

DISCOUNT

General Business and Commercial

D.440

The [Company] shall receive not less than [specify] per cent of the highest [retail/subscription] price of the [Work/Service] received by the [Distributor] whether or not the [Work/Service] is sold, supplied or promoted at a lower price.

D.441

Where a discount has been made to a [Customer] for [Products] which have a fault or are seconds and the price is reduced for that reason and the [Customer] is made aware of the fault or condition of the seconds at the time of purchase then there shall be no obligation to provide a refund and the [Products] cannot be returned.

D.442

The [Licensee] shall have the right to reduce the price to zero and/or to make such arrangements for two products for the price of one and/or such other cross promotions as it thinks fit in the circumstances in respect of the [Product]. Provided that the [Licensee] shall pay the [Licensor] no less than [figure/currency] in each accounting period.

D.443

The [Company] shall only be entitled to discount and/or reduce the price for the [Product/Work] by [figure/currency] from the price of [figure/currency] for each item. Any further reduction shall require the prior written agreement and consent of the [Licensor].

D.444

There shall be no discount and/or reduction offered by the [Company] unless the value of the order made and paid for by the [Customer] exceeds [number/currency] for any one order. Then a discount of [number] per cent on the total value paid for the [Products] will be made and a voucher provided which can be offset against the next purchase by the [Customer]. No sums are paid in cash and/or refunded. The voucher will expire within [six months] of the date it is issued.

D.445

Where any [Materials/Products] are advertised and/or promoted at a discount, reduced price and/or as factory seconds and/or clearance stock and/or otherwise at any lower value than either the [retail/wholesale] price. The total liability of the [Company] shall be limited to the figure for which the [Materials/Products] are sold to the [Client] and no refunds and/or returns of any nature shall be made and/or are permitted. The [Company] is selling the [Materials/Products] to any [Client] subject to this condition.

D.446

The offer of this discount and reduction on the value of the purchase of [Work/Service] commences [date/time] and ends [date/time]. The discount and reduction is only available to those persons who complete the following registration for the [Company] newsletter [specify] and live and/or reside in [country] and are over [age] years.

DISCRIMINATION

General Business and Commercial

D.447

The [Company] agrees and undertakes that it shall not discriminate against any [person/company] who complies with all the criteria and undertakings set out in the application, meets all the deadlines and is able to verify the facts with supporting documentation. All applicants will be treated fairly and provided with the same information and assistance.

D.448

There shall be no discrimination on the grounds of age, status, gender, religion, racial group, family background, political beliefs, or disability.

D.449

There shall be no discrimination in favour of any particular race, educational background, or social group. All applicants will be judged on their personal ability, skills and experience.

D.450

The [Company] requires persons with fluency in the following languages [specify] and the following qualifications [specify].

D.451

The [Company] will only consider applications for [work experience/ internship/roles/jobs] for the position of [specify] from persons over age [number] for the fixed term contract who have one or more of the following disabilities; hearing which is impaired; deaf; visually impaired; blind and/ or physical and/or mobility disability. The [Company] shall as part of the position put in place a disability access and support programme to facilitate the role by any person appointed.

D.452

It shall not be deemed discrimination to reject any candidates and/or applications in any part of the process either before and/or after appointment for a position at the [Company] who are found to have provided incorrect and/ false details in respect of any references; residence and/or home addresses; medical record and/or state of health; criminal record and pending legal and/or disciplinary actions; qualifications and work experience; holding of a valid passport and/or visa for the right to work. The [Company] reserves and shall have the right to terminate any agreement immediately and to withdraw all benefits and obligations which have been agreed with any such persons.

D.453

The [Agent/Distributor] agree and undertake that they shall ensure that both they and/or any sub-agent, sub-licensee and/or any other third party shall comply with any legislation and policies that may exist in any country in which they operate and/or do business including but not limited to those relating to discrimination, health and safety, product liability, transport, pay and conditions for employees.

DISMISSAL

General Business and Commercial

D.454

The [Company] agrees to abide by procedures and processes set out in the [Staff Handbook] subject to any existing legislation.

D.455

The [Company] agrees that it shall not be entitled to rely on the [Employees'] personal use of the [Company's] telephone, mobile, internet, postage and/or refreshments as grounds for dismissal.

D.456

The [Company] shall be entitled to dismiss the [Executive/Presenter] without notice and with immediate effect in the event:

1.1 That the [Executive/Presenter] fails a random drug test and/or fails the annual medical.

1.2 That the [Company] has evidence that the [Executive/Presenter] has provided information and data to a rival business or competitor.

1.3 That the [Company] has evidence that the [Executive/Presenter] committed a serious crime and been charged.

1.4 That the [Executive/Presenter] has failed to attend meetings and/or engagements for more than [two weeks] without a medical note and/or authorised absence.

1.5 That the [Executive/Presenter] has been dishonest and obtained money, goods and/or services from the [Company]; not been truthful about his qualifications and/or acted in such a manner that his behaviour was a threat to other staff.

D.457

In the event that the [Company] believes that it has reasonable grounds for dismissing the [Executive] from his position at the [Company]. Then the [Company] agrees to advise the [Executive] in writing of the grounds and to allow the [Executive] the opportunity to refute the allegations.

D.458

The [Executive] agrees to be bound by the terms of the [Grievance Procedure] which is attached to and forms part of this Agreement as Schedule [–].

D.459

In the event that there are concerns regarding the work, timekeeping and/or failure to wear the uniform required of any casual employee. The [Company] agrees to hold a meeting with the person to discuss the issues and to agree a resolution of the problem. Where after that meeting the casual employee still does not comply as requested then the [Company] reserves the right to terminate the Agreement with them and shall pay them to the end of that calendar month in which the Agreement is terminated.

D.460

The [Company] must comply with the highest standards relating to hygiene and health and safety at its premises and all employees are required to comply with the policy attached in Appendix [–] which form part of your terms and conditions of employment. Failure to comply with any part of the policy which is not due to the fault of the [Company] and/or a member of the management team will result in a written warning stating how you have failed to comply and an opportunity to respond. Then dismissal and/or termination of your employment and/or temporary suspension on [paid] leave depending on the severity of the matter.

DISPUTES

General Business and Commercial

D.461

The [Distributor] agrees that in the event of any dispute between the parties under Clause [–] of this Agreement. The [Licensor] shall be entitled to receive copies of all documents, papers, contracts, correspondence (both internal and external), computer records and discs and all other material relevant to the dispute and the cost of providing such materials shall be borne by the [Licensor].

D.462

The acceptance of the [Company] of any sums paid under this Agreement shall not prevent the [Company] at a later date disputing or demanding detail of the sums due at any time. Nor shall such acceptance constitute a waiver of any breach of any terms by the [Licensee] that may occur.

D.463

The parties agree that a dispute relating to the contract should be determined by an expert. Any party may request that an expert be appointed. The parties shall try to agree a single expert by whom the matter shall be adjudicated. If the parties fail to agree the expert within [specify duration] of request then the parties agree that the following body shall nominate the expert [name/address]. The expert once appointed shall specify a reasonable time and date for submissions, and information by each party. The parties shall co-operate with the expert and with such enquiries that he/she may deem necessary. No confidential information supplied to the expert shall be disclosed to any third party. The expert shall not be an arbitrator but an expert permitted to set out his/her own procedure and be entitled to award financial damages in [currency] or to order the performance or prohibition of any act as he/she deems fit or otherwise. Both parties agree to abide by the decision of the expert in any such matter.

D.464

Any dispute arising in respect of this Contract shall be settled in accordance with the procedure for settlement of disputes in the Agreement between [Name] and the [Company].

D.465

The parties agree that before taking any legal proceedings that they shall try to agree to go through the process of either mediation, alternative disputes resolution or arbitration in [country]. This clause shall not apply if one party is unable, unwilling or fails to attend in which case either party shall be entitled to take any legal action and seek any remedy.

D.466

Both parties agree that this Agreement shall as far as possible be first resolved by mediation through [specify] and legal proceedings shall only be instituted as a final resort after both parties have used their reasonable endeavours to resolve the dispute.

D.467

Both parties agree that they will use all reasonable endeavours to resolve such disputes as may arise between them in a professional and efficient manner. That they shall both co-operate and provide such documents as may reasonably be required from the other party to verify the facts of the dispute.

D.468

In the event that any dispute of any nature under this Agreement cannot be resolved by the reasonable endeavours of both parties. Then the [Author] and the [Distributor] agree to resolve any disputes concerning this agreement using the following forum and means [Alternative Dispute Resolution].

D.469

Where the [Licensor] and/or the [Licensee] are in dispute as to the sums owed to the [Licensor] under this Agreement. Then the [Licensee] agrees o a full disclosure of all relevant bank statements, accounts, invoices, receipts and otherwise of the [Licensee] and any sub-licensee and/or agent to the [Licensor] at the offices of the [Licensee] by the [Finance Director]. The [Licensee] shall not be able to take copies, but shall be entitled to inspect all records.

D.470

Where the [Sponsor] and/or the [Company] and/or any third party are in dispute. Then the [Sponsor] and/or the [Company] agree that prior to the issue of any legal proceedings the parties shall try to arrange to meet to discuss and try to resolve the matter amicably without incurring any additional legal costs on a without prejudice basis. That the next step shall be an attempt to agree a form of mediation, arbitration and/or other informal resolution of the matter. Neither party shall be bound to take any of these steps prior to the issue of legal proceedings.

D.471

The [Consultant] agrees that where there is a dispute between the [Company] and the [Consultant] that the matter shall be resolved by the following method [specify] and that both parties agree to participate and the decision of that person shall be binding on both parties.

D.472

It is agreed between the parties to the [Consortium] that where there is any dispute that the parties shall endeavour to avoid legal proceedings and shall adopt a policy of negotiation and resolution of any matter by the appointment of an expert in the field to review and assess the facts and to make a recommendation as to how it may best be resolved to the satisfaction of all parties. The cost of the expert shall be paid for out of the [Consortium] funds for the [Project] and authorised by all parties. Any such review and recommendation shall not be binding and any of the parties shall have the right to take such legal proceedings as they think fit at any time.

D.473

Where there are any disputes between the [Agent] and the [Author] regarding fees, royalties and/or any other sums which may be due and/or owing to the [Author]. The [Agent] shall not be entitled to withhold and/or retain any sums against future costs and expenses and/or sums due to the [Agent]. The [Agent] shall supply copies of all bank statements, invoices, documents, agreements, royalty statements, emails and attachments that may be requested by the [Author] and/or any consultant, accountant and/or legal advisor who may be assisting him and/or her. No charge shall be made by the [Agent] for this service to the [Author].

D.474

Disputes between any [Club] and its members shall be resolved by the procedure and process set out in its [Constitution/Memorandum and Articles of Association]. In the event that it cannot be resolved by this process then any member may make a resolution at the [Annual General Meeting] for consideration by all members provided it is supported by [number] members and submitted [number] days prior to the date of the meeting. Where the [Club] is subject to the rules and guidelines of a national governing body then account shall be taken in the resolution of the dispute of any rules, policies and guidelines that they may have issued which are applicable at the time.

DISQUALIFICATION

General Business and Commercial

D.475

Any applicant who cannot provide supporting evidence in the form required by the [Agency] or by the notified deadline may be disqualified at the total discretion of the [Agency].

D.476

In the event that any participant or their families, or their agents attempt to offer inducements, bribes, benefits or other rewards to any official, officer, or Director of the [Company/Agency/other] then that participant shall be disqualified.

D.477

The [Sponsor] shall not be entitled to withdraw the funds under clause [–] in the event that [Name] is not in the team for any reason and/or the team [specify] is disqualified from participating in the [Event].

D.478

1.1 Where an entry form is not submitted by the deadline of [date] to [address]. Then any person shall not be permitted to enter the [Event/ Race].

1.2   The application will be rejected if the fee payment is not made according to the deadline whether or not the form has been submitted.

1.3   Where you have provided misleading and/or false information and/or data and/or represented that you have attained a standard and/or level which is inaccurate and/or false. Then the [Company] shall have the right to cancel your right to enter the [Event/Race] at any time.

1.4   You will not be permitted to take part where at a later date you are discovered to have used and/or failed a banned drug test in any country at any time. In such event your entry fee will be refunded and your place cancelled. There will be no right of appeal.

1.5   Failure to wear the required safety [equipment/other] will automatically disqualify you from participation on the day. The judgement of the [Company] is final and there is no right of appeal.

1.6   Any behaviour which is deemed inappropriate and/or offensive either before, during and/or after the [Event/Race] may result in you being banned from all future [Events/Races] for up [one year].

DISTRIBUTION EXPENSES

General Business and Commercial

D.479
'Distribution Expenses' shall mean all sums reasonably and properly incurred or charged by the [Television Company] in connection with the clearance, acquisition, licensing and administration of any intellectual property rights including distribution, commissions, repeat fees and residuals, editing, legal fees and any other sums of any nature that may arise which are not covered in the Budget.

D.480
'Distribution Expenses' shall mean all costs and expenses properly and reasonably incurred by or on behalf of the [Co-Producer] in connection with the exercise of the rights granted to the [Co-Producer] under Clause [–], including, but not limited to, all advertising costs, promotion costs, collection costs, legal and accounting costs, all residual, clearance, consent and copyright fees and other rights payments (save for those already provided for in the Budget), all costs associated with prints, films, and materials, the costs of foreign language versions, costs of insurance, shipping, packaging,

storage, inspection, duties and imports, the protection of any rights against the third parties, cost of commissions due to and expenses incurred by sub-licensees and sub-distributors of the [Programme] throughout the Territory.

D.481

'The Distribution Expenses' shall be the following costs reasonably and properly incurred in respect of the exploitation of the [Film] by the [Licensee] which are not recouped from any third party:

1.1 Duplication such as prints, duplicate negatives, cassettes, repairs and replacements.

1.2 Delivery, storage, shipping, custom duties, freight, handling charges and insurance.

1.3 Trailers and promotional material.

1.4 Publicity and advertising material.

1.5 Copyright, permissions and consents, clearance and performing right payments and other fees and expenses to individuals, companies and/or collecting societies for any material relating to the exploitation of the [Film].

1.6 Distributors', sub-distributors' and sub-licensees' commission.

1.7 Dubbing, editing, sub-titling, translation and other costs for foreign versions.

1.8 Accounting and legal fees whether for debt collection and/or protection of any legal rights of the parties and/or auditing.

D.482

'The Promotion Expenses' shall mean all costs reasonably and properly expended by the [Promoter] in furtherance of this Agreement which have not been recouped from any third party:

1.1 Survey and marketing reports.

1.2 Creation, supply and placement of advertisements in newspapers, periodicals and other publications.

1.3 Development, production, exhibition and distribution of marketing DVD, and website material.

1.4 Cost of all artwork, designs, photographs, text and any other material for publicity, advertising and/or promotions.

1.5 All delivery, storage, shipping, customs duties, freight, handling charges and insurance.

1.6   All fees, and expenses to obtain any rights in any material, or consent to the use of any work.

1.7   [Any other costs].

D.483
The [Organisers] confirm that it shall be solely responsible for all sums incurred in respect of the [Event]. The [Promoter] shall not be responsible for any sums except for any unauthorised expenditure and costs incurred by the [Promoter] which are not within the Promotion Expenses and which are not agreed in advance with the [Organisers].

D.484
The [Agent] confirms that the [Author] shall not be responsible for any costs or expenses incurred by the [Agent] pursuant to this Agreement. The [Agent] shall only be entitled to receive the [Agent's Commission].

D.485
The [Publisher] agrees that it shall be solely responsible for all costs incurred in printing, publishing, distributing, marketing and exploiting the [Work] throughout the Territory.

D.486
The [Assignee] confirms that it shall be solely responsible for all sums due in respect of the production, distribution, marketing and exploitation of the Commissioned [Work] in any media throughout the Territory.

D.487
The [Company] confirms that it shall be solely responsible for all costs incurred in the development, production, manufacture, distribution, marketing, promotion, advertising and exploitation of the [Products] and that such sums shall not be deducted and/or set off prior to the calculation and payment of the Licensor's Royalties under this Agreement. The [Company] shall be entirely liable for all such costs and no contribution of any nature shall be due from and/or made against the [Licensor].

D.488
The [Assignee] acknowledges that it shall be solely responsible for any sums due in respect of the manufacture, distribution, marketing and exploitation of the [DVD Rights] in the [Film]. The [Assignor] shall not be liable for any such payments.

D.489
The [Record Company] agrees that the [Artiste] shall not be liable for any payments that may be incurred by the [Record Company] for any reason

unless specifically authorised in writing by the [Artiste]. Nor shall the [Record Company] be entitled to deduct any sums from the Royalties due to the [Artiste] at any time. The [Record Company] shall solely be responsible and liable for all costs that may be incurred by them including, but not limited to, production, manufacture, distribution, marketing and exploitation of the Sound Recordings, the Records, the DVD and/or any other material created and/or exploited pursuant to this Agreement.

D.490

The [Distributor] agrees and undertakes that it shall provide a full breakdown of all the Distribution Expenses that may and/or have been deducted from the Gross Receipts pursuant to this Agreement. Further that upon request by the [Licensor] the [Distributor] shall provide the [Licensor] with the opportunity to inspect the original documents and/or shall provide copies thereof. The [Distributor] agrees that in any event the [Distributor] shall not be entitled to deduct more than [figure/currency] in respect of the aggregate Distribution Expenses during the Term of this Agreement. Any further sums in excess of that total shall be the sole responsibility of the [Distributor] and the sums shall not be deducted from the Gross Receipts prior to the payment of Royalties due to the [Licensor].

D.491

'The Distribution Expenses' shall be the aggregate total maximum of [figure/currency] being such sums which the [Licensee] shall be entitled to deduct in respect of all costs reasonably and properly paid to third parties (which are not recouped) in respect of the commercial distribution and exploitation of the [Product].

D.492

'Distribution Expenses' shall mean the expenses by the [Company] in respect of the distribution of the [Film] and shall include, but not be limited to:

1.1 The cost of making and/or repairing all material that may be required such as cassettes, videos, DVDs, films, prints, tapes.

1.2 The cost of all dubbing, sub-titling, editing, adaptation, trailers, banners, and clips of the [Film].

1.3 The cost of all delivery, storage, publicity and marketing material in any medium, customs duties, packaging, labels, freight, shipment, importation taxes and/or duties, fees and costs incurred in respect of obtaining approval from any third party, governmental or other bodies that may arise.

1.4   The cost of obtaining clearance, consent, waiver, and/or authority to exploit any material in the [Film] whether copyright, trademarks, design rights, and/or any other rights in the [Film] and/or soundtrack. All costs and payments in respect of the use and performance of any music whether to an individual, union and/or collecting society. All costs and payments in respect of consents for material which has already been obtained, but for which further sums are due.

1.5   The cost of all accountant fees, legal fees, professional agencies, technical and computer software companies in respect of the production, distribution and exploitation of the [Film], and/or the institution of legal proceedings and/or the collection of any payment and/or the registration of any rights.

1.6   The cost of insurance cover for the [Film] and any material at any time including indemnity provisions.

D.493
The [Company] shall be entitled to deduct all costs and expenses of and relating to the distribution, sale and/or other exploitation of the [Work] including, but not limited to, all other distributors, agents and representatives charges, commission expenses which they may suffer or incur or under any indemnity by their agreements with the [Company].

D.494
'Distribution Expenses' means all sums reasonably and properly incurred or expended by the [Licensee] and/or any sub-licensee in respect of the distribution, exhibition, and exploitation of the [Work] in the Territory.

D.495
'Maximum Fee' shall mean the sum of [figure/currency] which shall for the avoidance of doubt be the combined total costs of the [Fee and Expenses] as may be paid by the [Company] to the [Designer].

D.496
The [Distributor] shall be entirely responsible for all the cost of distributing, supplying and marketing the [Product] including but not limited to insurance, freight, advertisements, packaging, telephone charges, custom duties and taxes, compliance with trading standards and other legal requirements. The [Distributor] agrees and undertakes that it shall not seek to recoup any sums from [Name] even if the projected sales of the [Product] are not achieved.

D.497
The [Licensee] and/or any sub-licensee and/agent shall not have the right to deduct any distribution charges, costs, expenses, commission, freight and

transport, insurance and product liability, packaging, marketing, legal costs, damages, losses and/or any other sums from the percentage of the Gross Receipts due to the [Licensor] under this Agreement.

D.498

The [Sponsor] shall reimburse the [Company/Institute] subject to the production of invoices and/or an itemised statement of the full cost of reproducing, supplying, packaging, distributing and marketing the [Sponsor's] logo, slogan and products as set out in Schedule [–] which is attached to and forms part of this Agreement. The [Company/Institute] agrees that the total cost shall not exceed [figure/currency] without the prior written consent of the [Sponsor] which it shall not be obliged to provide. That any additional costs not authorised by the [Sponsor] shall be the responsibility of the [Company/Institute].

D.499

Distribution expenses does not include any office and management expenses, travel, accommodation, mobile and landline telephone costs and charges, stationary, marketing and publicity on line, catalogues, flyers and/or any social events, entertainment, promotional and exhibition events of the [Agent] and/or any sub-licensee, distributor and/or other third party.

D.500

Distribution expenses which can be deducted prior to payment to [Name] under this Agreement shall be limited to [number] per cent of the reasonable reproduction costs of the [Work] and [number] per cent of the reasonable freight, postage and insurance costs. No other sums may be deducted from any sums due to [Name] and the [Company] shall bear all other costs and expenses. Where any sums are deducted then full details of the cost and original documents must be provided.

D.501

The [Company] and any sub-agent, sub-licensee agree and undertake that they must bear all the costs and expenses and liability of all sums that may be due and/or arise from the exploitation of the [Work] including but not limited sums due to develop, manufacture, reproduce, market, promote, exhibit and distribute the [Work]. [Name] shall not be obliged to make any contribution and/or pay any such sums at any time. Nor shall the [Company] seek to withhold any sums due to [Name] for that reason. No such costs and expenses may be set off and/or recouped from the Gross Receipts and any sums due to [Name]. The [Company] will remain and continue to be responsible for all the obligations and liabilities to [Name] of any sub-licensee and/or sub-agent. The [Company] and all such parties must pay all such sums at their own risk and cost.

DIVIDEND

General Business and Commercial

D.502

'Dividend' shall mean throughout this Agreement all payments due from the profits of the [Company] to the registered shareholders in accordance with the [Company's] Memorandum and Articles of Association as amended from time to time by Special Resolution.

D.503

The parties to this Agreement hereby agree that any dividends due to [Name] shall be enforceable as a contractual right and shall not be treated as a gift or bonus.

D.504

Where the [Company/Group] fail to make a profit in any one year then the [Board] may decide not to pay any dividend.

DOMAIN NAME

Internet and Websites

D.505

The [Designer] shall not acquire any rights or interest in the Domain Name and/or [Website] specified as follows [–]. The [Designer] shall not be entitled to register, apply, claim or otherwise represent that she owns or controls any right, interest or equity in the Domain Name and/or [Website] and/or any other material created or developed for the [Company] under this Agreement.

D.506

Unless there is an agreement in writing to the contrary the [Company] confirms that the [Designer] shall not be responsible for any exploitation, use, error, defamation or otherwise by the [Company] of the [Website] or the [Domain Name] at any time.

D.507

The [Company] agrees that it has or will register the Domain Name [specify]. A copy of which is attached to and forms part of this Agreement. The

[Company] undertakes that it shall be entirely responsible for all registration, trade mark, legal costs and expenses and any third party liability incurred or arising in respect of the Domain Name.

D.508

The [Designer] agrees and undertakes that it will not directly or indirectly seek to register or exploit the Domain Name [specify] or any other name which could be reasonably construed as derived from, similar to or prejudicial to the Domain Name held by the [Company].

D.509

The [Seller] undertakes that the following details are true and accurate:

1.1 That the [Seller] is the original creator of and owns all rights and interest in the Domain Name [specify] and the [Seller's] Website [specify]. That to the best of the knowledge and belief of the [Seller] there is no claim, legal action, complaint or interest in the Domain Name which has been made or threatened by a third party at any time.

1.2 That the Domain Name is registered with [specify] in the name of [specify] and that all fees have been paid to [date].

1.3 That the domain was not based on, derived from or copied from any third party and/or any other material owned and/or controlled by a third party by the [Seller].

D.510

The Domain Name [specify] together with the accompanying images, logo and sound recordings on this [Website] are owned and controlled by [Name] and may not be used, copied, adapted, displayed or reproduced on any article, book, magazine, newspaper, merchandising, telephone, film or any other medium without the prior written consent of [Name] unless for sole personal non-commercial use at home.

D.511

Both parties agree that the Domain Names, Trade Marks and any other names, logos and or intellectual property rights relating to the [Joint Venture] shall be registered in the name of both parties as the equal joint legal owners.

D.512

Both parties agree and undertake that they shall be jointly liable for the payment of any registration fees, renewals, and any other sums in respect of the Domain Names, Trade Marks and any other names, logos and or intellectual property rights relating to the [Joint Venture] which the parties agree must be registered to protect their interests.

D.513

Neither party shall be entitled to assign, transfer, licence, exploit and/or agree to any variation in respect of the Domain Names, Trade Marks and any other names, logos and or intellectual property rights relating to the [Joint Venture] without the prior written consent of either party.

D.514

'Domain Name' shall mean [specify] which is owned by [Name] and is registered with [specify] reference [–] and shall not include any associated artwork, logo and/or trademark.

D.515

The [Licensee] agrees that it shall not register and/or attempt to register any domain name, trade mark, service mark, community mark and/or any other words, image and/or shape which is the same and/or similar to the [title/ name] of the [Work] and/or [Product]. The [Licensee] shall ensure that any sub-licensee, agent and/or any consultant that the [Licensee] shall engage and/or have an agreement with regarding the sales and/or marketing of the [Product] shall also agree to this condition.

D.516

The [Sponsor] shall have the right to register the following domain names [specify] in respect of the [Event]. The [Company/Institute] agrees that the [Sponsor] shall own and/or control all rights in respect of the domain names and that the [Company/Institute] shall not have any rights and/or interest.

D.517

The [Consultant] agrees that where he/she has worked on the [Project] to develop, create and design a corporate name, logo, design, domain name, banner links and other promotional material that he/she shall not have right and/or authority to attempt and/or to register, exploit and/or benefit from any such material and that all rights are held and/or owned and/or controlled by the [Company] and are assets of that [Company].

D.518

1.1   [Name] confirms that he/she has registered the domain name [specify] with [specify] with the web reference [specify]. That the domain name and web reference are used in conjunction with the slogan and logo and all the material set out in Schedule [–].

1.2   In consideration of [number/currency] [Name] assigns and transfers all control and ownership of all rights and interest in 1.1 and Schedule [–] to the [Club/Company] for the full term of any ownership and also the right to renew and extend any period of interest.

1.3 In consideration of [number/currency] [Name] assigns all the rights and interest in 1.1 to the [Club/Company] together with any copyright, intellectual property rights, trade marks, service marks and domain name rights of any text, image, logo and/or other material in 1.1 and/or the Schedule [–].

DOWNLOADING

Internet and Websites

D.519

Any downloading of material from this [Website] must be done subject to the terms and conditions set out in [specify location] on this [Website] and all material should be credited with the following acknowledgement and copyright notices must not be erased or deleted, nor should material be edited or adapted:

[Website Name] [website reference]

[Name of Website Copyright Owner] © [year]

[Specify Material] is owned by [Copyright Owner of Material]

[Name of Material Copyright Owner] [year]

[Specify Material] is distributed under licence by [Distributor of Material]

All rights reserved

D.520

Downloading, storage and retrieval of any material on any system, gadget or by any method or process or means whether in existence now or created in the future is strictly forbidden unless you have registered and agreed to abide by the terms and conditions of the [Subscription Service/Access/other].

D.521

There is not a general right to download material of any nature from the internet, and you are expected to respect the copyright notices, trade marks and domain names of others which are displayed and to seek their permission for the use of any material you may wish to exploit. You are allowed to make copies of all the pages on this site for personal and non-commercial and educational purposes only for your own use.

D.522

Material on this [Website] may be downloaded, copied, stored for personal use and educational purposes, review, criticism, quotes, and research. No licence and/or permission is provided and/or granted to supply any material to a third party for the use and/or the commercial exploitation in any form of any part of the [Website] and/or any content.

D.523

You download material form this [Website] at your own risk and expense. No liability is accepted by the owners of the [Website] and/or the copyright owner of any material for any consequences that may arise as a result of your downloading the material. There is no undertaking and/or assurance that the material is free from viruses and/or other defects and you are advised to carry out your own scan of any material.

D.524

The free [Downloads/Royalty Free Material] on this [Website] may be downloaded, stored, retrieved, distributed, copied and/or adapted and/or developed without charge at your sole discretion. There is no obligation to credit this [Website] as the source nor to pay any sums for the use and/or exploitation of any material.

D.525

The material on this [Website] is owned and/or controlled by [Copyright Owner] and [Licensee] and [Distributor]. You are only entitled to view the [Website] and no authority is given to store, retrieve, print, download, reproduce, transmit, supply, distribute and/or adapt any material and/or any part of the content. Where material and/or content is stored and/or downloaded temporarily for personal use only and subsequently deleted and/or destroyed then no legal action will be taken for infringement and/or breach of any rights. Please apply to [specify] for any application for a license for any other use for which a fee and/or royalties will be charged.

D.526

There is a non-exclusive license granted to the [Customer] to:

1.1 Make a maximum [number] copies of no more than [number] pages of this [Website] for private, non-commercial, residential purposes only in [country] at any time. This shall not include [specify areas].

1.2 Provided that where the pages are stored on the hard drive before printing they are subsequently deleted.

1.3 Provided that each page has a copyright notice as follows [specify].

D.527

Where any part of this website permits and/or offers you the choice of downloading and/or accessing any material for free then any use and/or reproduction is limited to non-commercial purposes by you and your friends and/or gadgets. You are not permitted to edit, adapt, change and/or vary the content in the course of reproduction and/or supply to another person and you are not permitted to add any logos, images and/or other material belonging to a third party. The [Company] reserves the right to request at any time that you delete copies of the material that you have downloaded as you have used the material in a manner which they believe is derogatory, damaging and/or not in keeping with the reputation and policies of the [Company] in any part of the world.

D.528

There is no automatic right granted by the [Institute] to any person who accesses and/or enters this [Website] to reproduce, download, copy, adapt, edit and/or use any part of this [Website] and/or any material on it and/or linked to it and/or any archive except for non-commercial and educational research purposes only for their sole and personal use in the course of their education at a school, college and/or university. Provided that a full title, credit and copyright notice is provided as follows [specify] to the [Institute] and the author. Any references must not exceed [number] words including any to be used for criticism and/or review. There is no authority and/or permission to exceed that limit and no defence of fair dealing and/or public domain will be considered and/or accepted as a valid excuse for failure to comply. All other persons must seek a written licence and authority from [specify] contact [specify].

DRAMATIC WORK

General Business and Commercial

D.529

'Dramatic Work' under this Agreement shall have the same meaning as afforded under the Copyright, Designs and Patents Act 1988 and/or any subsequent legislation and/or European Directive that may be in force in the [United Kingdom] at the time of this Agreement.

D.530

The parties agree that the [Work] does [not] include a dramatic work for the purpose of the [Copyright, Designs and Patents Act 1988 as subsequently amended].

D.531

The performance of the [Work] will require permission from the copyright owner and all necessary rights, clearances, licenses and consents will be obtained and paid for by [Name].

D.532

'Dramatic Work' shall be construed in accordance with the [Copyright, Designs and Patents Act 1988 as subsequently amended] and shall include a work of dance or mime. Copyright shall not subsist in a dramatic work until it is recorded in writing or otherwise. The time at which such a work is made is the time at which it is so recorded (whether or not it is recorded by or with the permission of the [Author]).

D.533

The [Author] authorises and grants the [Company] the right to film, record and reproduce a [Programme/Disc] based on filming and recording of the [Play] at [theatre] from [date] to [date]. The [Company] shall produce an edited version and then consult with the [Author] as to the final version to be reproduced. The parties agree that no additional material shall be added at any time except a new sound track, music and credits and/or sub-titles.

DUE DILIGENCE

General Business and Commercial

D.534

The [Assignee] warrants that all representations as to good title in this Agreement are made on the basis of the [Assignee] having instructed their duly qualified solicitors to conduct a full exercise of due diligence at the [Assignee's] sole cost.

D.535

The [Company] confirms that it will use all due diligence to ensure conformity with all laws, rules and regulations whether under [specify legislation] and/or any EU directive and/or any other relevant law in force in [country] at the time of the performance of this Agreement.

D.536

Both parties shall have the opportunity to carry out due diligence at their own costs and expense in respect of [Project] from [date] to [date]. Both parties shall make available any material which is requested by the other side which is directly relevant to the [Project] and shall arrange inspection of original material. All exchanges of material, information and data under due diligence shall be deemed confidential and not for release to any third party and shall be strictly contained within a named list of personnel on both sides.

D.537
Both parties agree that neither shall be entitled to rely on any representations, disclosures or material made available under due diligence which are not incorporated as terms and condition of the final agreement signed by both parties.

D.538
Each party shall be responsible for arranging and bearing the cost of its own due diligence in respect of the [Joint Venture]. There shall be no liability to the other party for failure to disclose information, facts, data, financial records, stock, and/or corporate details which one party acquires. The parties shall be limited to the undertakings and terms which are set out in the final agreement for the [Joint Venture].

D.539
Where in the process of due diligence the [Company] has deliberately misled, misrepresented and/or withheld vital and significant information, facts, financial records, corporate reports and projections, information relating to shareholders and stock and/or the terms and conditions of its agreements with its directors, employees and/or third parties. Then the [Company] shall have the right either to seek to claim compensation, damages, losses, costs and expenses plus interest and/or to be paid the fixed sum of [figure/currency] [words] upon demand and the provision of supporting evidence.

D.540
The [Licensee] agrees to carry out due diligence on all sub-licensees, agents and distributors who are and/or will be engaged to market the [Product/Work/Film] to ensure that they comply with the following criteria:

1.1   That they are established and experienced in the field and have been in operation for no less than [number] years.

1.2   That audited accounts are available to verify their solvency and ability to fulfil their contractual obligations.

1.3   That there are no pending legal actions, investigations and/or claims against them which would effect and/or damage the reputation of the [Product/Work/Film] and/or the [Licensor].

D.541

The [Sponsor] shall not have the right to carry out due diligence on any third party that the [Company] may wish to use for the [Event]. All such decisions are entirely at the sole discretion of the [Company]. There shall be no obligation to notify the [Sponsor] of the names and details relating to any third party.

D.542

Where the [Licensee] would like to obtain the prior consent of the [Licensor] to sub-licence the [Product/Work/Film]. Then the [Licensee] shall provide a comprehensive and thorough due diligence report which shall include the last three years of audited accounts, summary of the directors, staff and premises, health and safety compliance assessment, examples of products, marketing and advertising.

D.543

Where after the completion of this Agreement the [Purchaser] considers and/or has evidence that the [Seller] over valued any part of the [Assets]. Then it is agreed that the [Purchaser] shall not be entitled to seek a refund and/or rebate and/or damages and/or any losses and agrees and accepts that it had the right to investigate and assess and review all the [Assets] prior to purchase with an independent company and has therefore no claim and/or legal and/or equitable action against the [Seller] and/or any of its advisors.

D.544

The [Company] agrees to provide access to [Name] view [and make copies of] all reports, surveys, statistics and other assessments made by the [Company] and its consultants and agents from [date] to [date] on the subject of [specify]. Provided that [Name] agrees that no undertakings and/or any confirmation is provided by the [Company] that all the content is accurate, true and/or up to date and that [Name] cannot rely on it in order to take any steps and/or action and/or enter into any agreement which may result in any financial and/or other losses and/or damages at any time. Further that [Name] waives the right to make any claim and/or take any action against the [Company].

D.545

Where at any time documents, data, information and/or any other materials in any medium are withheld and/or destroyed during the course of the due diligence by the [Seller] which would materially affect the value of the [Asset] being transferred and/or sold. Then the [Seller] shall only be liable to reimburse the [Purchaser] for the difference in the value if it can be shown that it would have caused the [Purchaser] to withdraw from the Agreement and/or make a substantially lower offer.

E

EDITORIAL CONTROL

DVD, Video and Discs

E.001

The [Licensee] shall record the [Film] in its entirety on each [DVD/Disc], including titles and credits, without cuts, deletions, alterations, modifications, additions or editing of any kind without written authorisation from the [Licensor]. The [Licensee] shall have the right to incorporate on to the [DVDs/Discs] preceding the main titles and/or following the end titles of the [Film] and in all advertising and publicity relating thereto the words [Distributed by Licensee].

E.002

The [Assignee] shall be entitled, at its sole discretion and cost, to make minor changes, deletions, alterations, interruptions or additions to the [Film] as may be reasonably required of not less than [period] in duration. In the event that significant or major changes are envisaged the prior approval of the [Assignor] shall be required in advance.

E.003

The [Assignor] accepts that all editorial decisions in respect of the [DVD/Disc] are at the [Assignee's] sole discretion and agrees to carry out all such requests as may be made provided that the [Assignee] shall bear the cost whether included in the Budget or not. The [Assignee] agrees that where editorial changes are requested by the [Assignee] that affect the Budget and will result in additional costs, the [Assignee] shall be responsible for the cost of the additional work.

E.004

The [Assignor] acknowledges that the [Assignee] shall have the right entirely at its sole cost and discretion to:

1.1   Edit, adapt, alter or amend any part of the [Film] including any soundtrack, music, images, graphics, words, text and/or computer generated material.

1.2   Add or delete any product placement, advertisements, sponsors, endorsements of products or services.

1.3   This right shall not include the material, credits and products of any of the following actors, companies or distributors [specify].

E.005

There is no right whatsoever to alter, amend, adapt, develop or edit any part of the [Film] and/or any other material provided under this Agreement. Any changes whether of size, length, colour, style, content, credits, or any other type of any nature must be notified in advance to the [Company] for their consideration and may only be proceeded with if written consent is provided. In the event that this procedure is not followed then the [Company] shall have the right to order the destruction of all material not so approved.

E.006

The [Distributor] agrees that it shall not distort or significantly change the [Film] in the event that any editing, dubbing or other alterations are required to exploit the [Film] and shall not add any additional material nor change the credits, copyright notices and trade marks. The [Distributor] shall, however, be able to change any material which its legal advisors have recommended be removed in order to avoid the likelihood of criminal or civil proceedings against the [Distributor] in any country to which it markets the [Film].

E.007

The [Licensee] shall not be entitled to edit, adapt or alter the [Film] nor to authorise any third party to do so without the prior written consent of the [Licensor]. The [Licensor] agrees that subject to prior written consent the [Licensee] may carry out minor edits of up to [period] in duration of the [Film] provided that it does not interfere with the integrity or continuity of the [Film].

E.008

The [Company] agrees that the [Distributor] may edit, alter, delete and change parts of the [Film], the sound track and the title in order to adapt the [Film] for different countries, markets, formats and languages. Provided that the [Distributor] shall consult with the [Company] in advance and provide a copy of each different version which may be created at the [Distributor's] cost.

E.009

[Name] agrees that the [Company] may make such changes, additions, variations and distortions, caricatures and/or arrangement of all and/or any part of the [Film], sound recordings, name, image and representation of [Name] as it wishes in order to develop, enhance and/or increase sales and revenue. Provided that at no time shall any material be used in a form and/or manner which is likely to result in [Name] being depicted as associated with any act, words and/or other material which may be a civil and/or criminal offence in any country.

E.010

The [Company] acknowledges and agrees that the signature, name, image, representation and personal name and performance name of [Name] are owned and controlled by [Name]. That at no time before, during and/or after this Agreement shall the [Company] be entitled to claim ownership, control and/or the right to authorise any changes, additions and/or any variations of any nature either in the [Film] and/or credits and/or in any marketing and/or promotion and/or merchandising in any medium and/or format. Nor shall the [Company] seek to register any interest, rights and/or trade mark associated with [Name] and/or any signature, name, image, representation and/or personal name and/or performance name and/or associated slogan, music and/or sound.

Film and Television

E.011

Prior to the online edit of the [Programme] and the final sound mix the [Producer] shall screen the off-line edit of the [Programme] together with all rushes of the [Programme]. The [Broadcaster] shall be entitled to make any editorial changes deemed necessary for the purposes of conforming with any regulatory codes, standards, directives and contractual obligations.

E.012

The [Company] shall notify the [Author] of any changes required in the script and where possible shall do so within [thirty days] of delivery. Later alterations to the radio or television programme may require the [Company] to request changes necessary to reflect the content of the associated programme. In such case the [Company] shall have the right (subject to prior consultation with the [Author] or his duly authorised representative) to edit the [Work].

E.013

The [Television Company] may at its sole discretion make any changes, alterations and amendments to the [Script] in order to conform with all rules, regulations, standards and Codes of Practice in force from time to time with respect to any regulatory bodies including but not limited to [Ofcom/other].

E.014

The [Television Company] may at its sole discretion and cost, edit, adapt and make such changes and deletions in respect of the [Series] as may be required in pursuance of its programme policy governing suitability of material contained therein and/or demands of accurate timing or presentation. The [Television Company] shall not exercise this right unreasonably or unnecessarily and any editing or deletions shall be of a minor nature and not impair continuity.

E.015

The [Broadcaster] may at its discretion, edit and adapt the [Films(s)] at its sole cost in order to comply with its programme requirements and for the purpose of exploitation of the [Film(s)].

E.016

The [Author] acknowledges that the [Production Company] shall be entitled to make alterations to the scripts during the production of the [Film] provided that such amendments are minor and not substantial, and do not amount to unjustified modifications or derogatory treatment of the [Author's] work.

E.017

The [Company] acknowledges that it shall not be entitled to arrange or permit the development and writing of any treatment, script or other material relating to the [Author's] work unless it has exercised the option granted under Clause [–] and an agreement has been concluded between the parties relating to the transmission and exploitation of the [Author's] work.

E.018

The [Company] shall be entitled at its sole discretion to make such changes additions, deletions and/or interruptions to any [Film] required by the [Company]. Prior to making any material alterations of any nature the [Company] shall consult with the [Producer] and take into account the requests of the [Producer] as far as reasonably possible. In the event of any disagreement or failure to reach a solution that the decision of the [Company] shall prevail and be final.

E.019

The [Company] may at its sole discretion edit and/or adapt the [Film] for the purpose of interposing advertising material, or public or political broadcasts, and/or to assist in the transmission schedules for the [Company], and/or to meet the requirements of any statutes, codes, policies, and/or other guidelines, and/or laws relating to the content of the material transmitted by the [Company].

E.020

The cost of all editing carried out by the [Company] under this Agreement shall be paid to the [Company] by the [Producer]. The [Company] shall provide full details of the reasons for the work and the rates charged. The sum shall be payable by the [Producer] within [ninety days] of receipt of an invoice.

E.021
The [Company] shall have the right to edit the [Film] and also to adapt the [Film] at a later date by adding an interview with [Individual] which shall be at the [Company's] sole cost and discretion.

E.022
The [Company] may at its discretion undertake minor editing of and deletions from any of the [Films] in pursuance of its programme policy governing the suitability of material and/or the requirement of accurate timing of its schedules. The [Company] shall not exercise this right unreasonably or unnecessarily and any editing or deletions shall be of a minor nature and not impair continuity.

E.023
The [Company's] representative shall be entitled to attend the production and post-production of the [Film] at any time and to view and examine the rushes and/or the [Film] and/or part(s). Provided that such attendance shall be in such a manner as to not interfere with the completion of the [Film]. The [Production Company] shall consider the verbal and written comments of the representative. The [Production Company] shall have the final decision in respect of all editorial matters relating to the [Film].

E.024
The [Company] may produce and/or authorise the production of an edited or otherwise amended version of the [Films] including the use of outtakes for the purpose of exercising the rights granted in this Agreement. Prior to making any such changes the [Company] shall advise the [Executive Producer] and shall obtain consent for any other intended purposes. If the [Company] authorises a third party to carry out the work it shall still continue to observe the terms of this Agreement. The [Company] undertakes to ensure that any such work shall not misrepresent or distort the views of [Individual] in the [Films].

E.025
The [Licensee] shall use all reasonable means to ensure that the [Film] is exhibited in its entirety in its original form in which it was delivered by the [Licensee] without any changes, alterations, additions and/or deletions.

E.026
For the avoidance of doubt all programming, editorial and scheduling decisions shall be at the sole cost and discretion of the [Company].

E.027

The [Series] shall follow the [Scripts] except for such minor alterations as may be necessary as a result of unforeseeable production or management changes. The [Company] shall not unreasonably withhold its consent to any other alterations required by the [Producer] unless in the opinion of the [Company] the alterations would render the [Series] unsuitable for its programme purposes.

E.028

The final decision on editorial matters will rest solely with the [Company]. However, the [Company] agrees to allow a representative of the [Production Company] to view [the rough cut/other] of the final version of the [Films] and to make available the Executive Producer to discuss with and take note of the representative's comments in respect of the [Films].

E.029

Either party may edit the [Programme Material] licensed to it under this Agreement to meet its broadcast requirements provided that editorial integrity of such material is maintained.

E.030

The editing of such material shall be subject to periodic review. If on any such review the party whose material has been edited is not satisfied that the editorial integrity of such material has been maintained. Then such party may by notice in writing require the other party to observe the criteria specified in editing such material. Failure to comply shall result in the party who has served notice having the right to cancel or terminate the Agreement.

E.031

The [Licensee] shall not be entitled to edit, adapt or alter the [Film] except for minor editing or deletions for the purpose of complying with the [Licensee's] programme policy and scheduling.

E.032

The [Assignee] shall be entitled at its sole discretion and cost to make such changes, deletions, alterations, interruptions or additions to the [Series] as may reasonably be required. Provided that as far as reasonably possible the [Assignee] shall be consulted in advance.

E.033

The [Company] shall be entitled to edit, adapt, alter, change, delete from, add to, translate, and exercise whatever editorial control is required in order to transmit, exhibit, reproduce, promote, supply, manufacture, distribute and exploit the [Film], the soundtrack and title in any format under this Agreement and to engage third parties to carry out such work.

E.034

It is agreed by [Name] that the [Company] may make the following alterations in respect of his/her appearance and/or performance in any recording, sound recording, and/or films for the [Programmes] and any form of exploitation:

1.1 Change the character's name and/or add a different person's voice and/or computer generated version for the sound recording.

1.2 Change the words spoken for the purpose of sub-titles and/or translation.

1.3 Edit, change and/or delete any part in order to meet transmission schedules and/or create shorter programmes and/or to develop the [Programmes] in other media and/or formats.

Provided that no more than [number] per cent of the total length shall be deleted of the whole performance in any programme.

E.035

Neither the [Company] nor any sub-licensee nor any other third party engaged to market, promote, distribute and/or exhibit the [Film] at any time shall be entitled to make any changes, alterations and/or add any material and/or music and/or sounds to the [Footage] supplied by the [Licensor]. No copies of the [Footage] shall be reproduced and/or supplied to any third party which has not been specifically approved and authorised by the [Licensor] in advance. Failure to adhere to this procedure shall entitle the [Licensor] to terminate the Agreement by notice by email to [Name] with immediate effect.

General Business and Commercial

E.036

The [Company] shall give due consideration in good faith to any representations made by the [Organisation/Name] with respect to the content of the [Work]. Provided that the [Company] adheres to the approved outline of the [Work] the [Company] shall not be obliged to make any changes except where the [Organisation/Name] requests changes for reasons beyond their control and/or because of the threat of legal proceedings. Then the [Company] shall as far as possible incorporate such changes and/or alterations.

E.037

If after viewing and/or examining the [Work] the [Organisation/Name] requests further changes, then the [Company] shall comply with such requests. All costs incurred in respect of such further changes which are not covered by the agreed Budget shall be at the expense of the [Organisation/ Name]. However, where such additional changes were due entirely to the failure of the [Company] to fulfil the terms of this Agreement and to adhere to the conditions and outline of the [Work], the [Company] shall bear the cost.

E.038
No addition to, deletion from, alteration to or adaptation of the [Work] may be made without the prior written permission of the [Company/Licensor/Supplier].

E.039
The [Company] undertakes not to edit the [Work] in any way which is likely to impair its quality, meaning and/or integrity.

E.040
The [Company] agrees to obtain the prior [written] consent of [Name] before any major editing of the [Work] is undertaken.

E.041
The final decision on all editorial matters rests solely with the [Company].

E.042
The [Company] has the right to [use/reproduce/distribute] the [Work] in the form and version herein licensed and supplied by the [Licensor]. The [Company] is not authorised to make any changes in the [Work] whatsoever.

E.043
The [Company] may not in any manner or for any purpose alter, modify or change the [Work] and/or authorise any such acts except with the prior written consent of [Name] during his lifetime and a representative of his estate thereafter.

E.044
The editorial decisions in respect of all material are entirely at the [Company's] sole discretion.

E.045
The [Company] shall be entitled to modify, revise, enhance, improve, adapt, alter, amend, translate, vary and/or develop the [Work] and/or any related material whether contained in instructions, brochures or packaging.

E.046
For the avoidance of doubt the [Company] agrees and confirms that by virtue of the assignment of the intellectual property rights and the transfer of the ownership and control of the material under this Agreement, the [Assignee] or

its assigns or any person or company licensed, authorised or permitted by it shall be entitled to edit, adapt, modify, change and/or develop the [Work] in all formats, in any media and in any language throughout the [Territory/country] for the Term of the Agreement subject to the restrictions and limitations specified in Schedule [–] which set out the copyright, trade mark, contract, credit, moral rights and other obligations in respect of the [Work].

E.047
The [Company] acknowledges that all such adaptations, variations, edits or developments of the [Work] as are permitted have the effect of creating a new copyright or any other intellectual property rights, patents, computer software, trade marks or domain names shall belong to the [Assignee].

E.048
The [Company] shall be entitled to modify, revise, enhance, improve, adapt and/or develop the [Work] or any related documentation or material in any manner the [Company] may decide. The [Company] shall be the owner of any such modifications, revisions, enhancements, improvements, adaptations and developments and may use and exploit any of them at the [Company's] sole discretion.

E.049
The [Company] shall be entitled to make use of the [Works] in such manner as it shall in its sole discretion think fit including the making of changes, alterations and/or substitutions.

E.050
The artistic and editorial control of the [Work] shall be at the sole discretion and decision of the [Company]. The [Company] shall in good faith consider the requests and suggestions of [Name] in respect of content, interpretation and presentation.

E.051
The [Licensee] shall not be entitled to edit, adapt or alter the [Work] without the prior consent of the [Licensor].

E.052
The [Licensee] shall not be entitled itself or to authorise any third party to edit, adapt or alter the [Work] without the prior written consent of the [Licensor].

E.053
The final editorial decisions in respect of the [Work] shall be at the [Licensee's] sole discretion. The [Licensee] agrees to consult fully with the [Licensor] and to take due consideration of any editorial views expressed by the [Licensor].

E.054

The [Company] agrees that no alteration shall be made to the Work Plan or the Work Schedule without the prior approval of the [Originator].

E.055

The decision of [Name/Company] shall be final in respect of all production, manufacture, editorial, scheduling, release dates, marketing, advertising, licensing, distribution, prices and fees, the appointment of third parties, the adaptation, alteration, variation and development of the [Work] and any packaging and the use of any other goods or services in conjunction with it, or the endorsement, sponsorship of or reviews by any person or company.

E.056

The [Company] shall not have the right to instruct, permit or allow any third party to contribute to the [Work] or to publish, produce, distribute or market the [Work] together with other works or for any material in any format in any medium to be added to, appear with or be attached to the [Work] unless in each case the prior written consent of [Name] have been provided for such purpose.

E.057

No authority is provided and/or granted to reproduce and/or adapt and/or supply and/or edit any part of the material, products and/or services which is provided at any time under this Agreement.

E.058

The [Company] agrees that it shall not make any editorial changes to the [Work] without prior consultation with [Name] as to the alterations, amendments and/or additions that it would like [Name] to make to the [Work]. That where after consultation the parties cannot agree that [Name] shall be provided with an opportunity to make an alternative proposal within [one] calendar month for the [Company] to consider. If thereafter the parties have still failed to reach agreement then the [Company] and/or [Name] shall have the right to terminate the Agreement provided that all funds paid to date are repaid.

Internet and Websites

E.059

The [Company] shall have the final editorial decision in respect of the content of and links to this [Website]. The [Company] shall be entitled to edit, delete, comment upon, endorse, or develop the subject matter of any material which is displayed or posted on this [Website].

E.060

The [Webmaster] and the [Company] have the right to control all material of any nature on this [Website] and at their sole discretion either of them may without notice to you delete, edit, adapt, vary, reproduce in another section, license, distribute to another third party, or amend, translate, publish, issue as part of a press release any material in any format or medium which is contributed to, displayed on, communicated to or added to this [Website] by any person, company or organisation.

E.061

The [Company] is in charge of this [Website] and shall have the final decision in respect of anything on or connected to it of any nature. Therefore the [Company] will able to do anything it decides is in its best interests subject to any laws, rights and contractual obligations which may exist which may be relevant at the time.

E.062

The [Company] agrees and undertakes that:

1.1   The [Company] shall not change, alter, adapt, amend, edit, translate, revise, interfere with or reproduce in another format or medium the [Article/Work], the title or any part which has or will be supplied by [Name]. Nor shall the [Company] permit, authorise, license or agree with any other person or company that they may do so without the prior written consent of [Name] in case and the agreement of additional terms and payment.

1.2   The [Company] shall not delete, erase or remove the copyright notice to [Name] or credit any other person or company with ownership of the [Article/Work] or give them permission to make any contribution to the [Article/Work] whatsoever.

E.063

You the [Client] must accept full responsibility for any consequences arising from your access to and/or use of this [Website] and/or any content and/or links. You use this [Website] and any content and download any of its contents at your own discretion and risk. All content may be altered, deleted, added to and/or adapted at any time by the [Company] without notice. The [Company] are not responsible for the contents and/or reliability of the linked websites. Listing should not be taken as an endorsement of any kind. All dates, prices, special offers, products, services. Premium rate services and other content are subject to availability and may be changed at any time. There is no assurance provided that there are no inaccuracies, errors, viruses, false attributions, misleading or illegal content. We will delete any material which we conclude should be removed for any reason and make any changes we may decide are necessary to update, maintain and improve the [Website] whether or not this causes interruptions, delays and/or a suspension of the [Website].

E.064
Where the [Company] decides that any person has uploaded text, images, music, lyrics, sound recordings, film and/or other material to the [Website] which amounts to advertising, promotion and/or is malicious, and/or not acceptable for any reason. Then the [Company] may delete any such material without notice and block the persons use and/or access to the [Website].

E.065
You may post, display and distribute [images/photographs/other] which you own, control and/or have taken on this [Website]. You are not entitled to falsely attribute any name to any identity and/or misrepresent their association with any person and/or group. You are not entitled to add any slogan, comment, images, words, text and/or other material which alters, degrades, defames, humiliates, offends and/or makes any derogatory implication regarding that persons' appearance, relationships, employment, religion, school, university, family life and/or career and/or otherwise whether false, malicious and/or true.

E.066
This [Website] is owned by [specify] and the material is monitored and controlled by [Name] who acts as the webmaster. You are advised to email [specify] with any concerns as to any content whether regarding copyright ownership, offensive material and/or errors.

E.067
Material is posted at your own risk and no liability is accepted by the [Company] for any defamatory material which you submit and/or any claims and/or actions against you which may be made at any time by any third party. The [Company] reserves the right to remove, delete and/or destroy all material which poses a threat to the [Company] on any grounds whatsoever whether an allegation has been made or not including but not limited to security, obscenity, a breach of any criminal and/or civil legislation and/or any international policies.

Merchandising

E.068
No translations of the [Work] shall be made without the prior written approval of the [Licensor].

E.069

The [Company] shall allow the [Distributor] to have full and complete control over the manner and extent of the exploitation, advertisement of the [Work] throughout the Territory. The [Company] authorises the [Distributor] to make and authorise the making of alterations in adaptations of and additions to the [Work] at the [Distributor's] discretion and to provide translations of new words or lyrics in other languages.

E.070

The [Company] shall provide a [style guide presentation layout pack] for the [Products/Service] for the [Distributor], sub-agents and retailers. The [Distributor] shall monitor the displays and catalogues to ensure that the standards are maintained and that the brand and quality of presentations and displays is high and in prominent locations.

E.071

The [Distributor] confirms that it will not edit, adapt, alter or add to the [Material/Article] without the prior approval of the [Licensor] and that any such changes shall be at the [Distributor's] sole cost and shall not be offset against any sums due to the [Licensor].

E.072

The [Licensor] acknowledges that the [Distributor] shall have the sole discretion as to the manner and method to be used in the production, manufacture, distribution, marketing and promotion of the [Work].

E.073

The decision of [Name/Company] shall be final in respect of the [Work/ Character]:

1.1 Production, manufacture, and approval of the final prototype of the Article, packaging and labels, and release dates to the public.

1.2 Appointment of all third parties including artwork, graphics, computer generated material, agents, distributors, printers, suppliers.

1.3 Promotion, marketing, advertising, editorial, sponsorship, endorsements, and cross promotion.

1.4 The adaptation, alteration, variation, translation, and development.

E.074

The [Licensor] agrees that the [Licensee] and any sub-licensee shall be entitled to edit, adapt, change, translate and/or otherwise develop the [Work] provided that all rights in all new material which is created are assigned to the [Licensor] without the payment of any additional sums.

E.075

1.1   The [Licensor] does not grant the [Licensee] any right to adapt, change, alter and/or vary the colour of the [Name/Logo/image] which is set out in Schedule [–].

1.2   The [Licensee] agrees that it must reproduce, distribute and supply the [Name/Logo/Image] which is set out in Schedule [–] in the exact shape, form and size and without any changes however minor.

1.3   The [Licensee] agrees that it has no authority to permit, allow and/or represent to any third party that they may use, reproduce and/or supply the [Name/Logo/image] which is set out in Schedule [–] for any reason. That all third parties including agents, marketing and publicity companies and distributors must be authorised directly and personally by the [Licensor].

E.076

The [Author] agrees that the [Agent] and/or the [Distributor] may make changes, alterations and/or adaptations to the storylines, characters, book titles, chapter titles, images and illustrations and/or backgrounds and locations and/or equipment and/or products mentioned and/or words and/or language and/or translations which may be needed to take account of local market cultures, religions and/or to form product placement partnerships and/or to create and/or develop the [Work] in other forms and/or media including but not limited to film, television, radio, discs and/or as a download and/or for educational material and/or licensing for associated products.

Publishing

E.077

The [Author] acknowledges that the [Company] shall be entitled to make alterations to the [Scripts] provided that such amendments are not substantial and do not amount to unjustified modifications or derogatory treatment of the [Author's] Work.

E.078

The [Publisher] shall at its sole discretion be entitled to edit and revise the [Work] either before the [Work] is ready for first publication or thereafter before a new edition is issued. The [Publisher] shall notify the [Author] in writing specifying the editing, revision and new material required and shall stipulate a reasonable date for completion of such work. In the event that the [Author] shall neglect or be unable for any reason to edit or revise the Work or supply new material to the satisfaction of the [Publisher] the [Publisher] shall be entitled to procure some other competent person to carry out such work and any fee or other payment made to such person shall be payable by the [Author] and deducted from the Royalties due under this Agreement. The choice of such person and the fee to be paid to such person shall be subject to the [Author's] prior approval and such approval is not to be unreasonably withheld or delayed.

E.079

The [Publisher] shall not be entitled to edit, revise, change, alter, add to, delete from or amend any part of the [Work] of the [Author] or any material derived therefrom at any time in any media without the prior written approval of the [Author]. The [Publisher] agrees to provide full details of any proposed changes and to negotiate with the [Author] an additional fee for the cost of such editing, revision, or other changes by the [Author]. The [Publisher] shall not be entitled to deduct the additional fee from any sums due to the [Author] under this Agreement.

E.080

The [Publisher] shall make no changes in the title or text of the [Work] without the [Author's] written consent except that the [Publisher] shall be entitled to correct factual errors and to delete any material which would render the [Publisher] or its sub-licensees liable to legal action or which it considers would bring the [Publisher] into disrepute.

E.081

The [Publisher] agrees that it will not allow any alteration in the title or text of the [Work] to be made in sub-licensed editions without the prior written consent of the [Author] except for those alterations which have been made for the publication of the [hardback/paperback] volume in the [United Kingdom/country] by the [Publisher].

E.082

The [Publisher] acknowledges that it shall not be entitled itself or to authorise any third party to adapt, alter, edit, add to, delete from or in any way change the [Work] including any words, lyrics or arrangement without the prior written consent of the [Author].

E.083

The [Publisher] undertakes to consult with the [Author] in respect of any proposed translation of the [Work] into a foreign language and such translations shall be at the [Publisher's] sole cost and expense. The [Publisher] shall not be entitled to deduct such translation costs from any sums due to the [Author] under this Agreement.

E.084

If the [Publisher] considers it necessary to modify the layout, and/or alter the date and/or position of the advertisement, and/or to make any other alteration the [Publisher] shall as soon as reasonably possible notify the [Advertiser]. The [Advertiser] shall have the right to cancel the insertion of that advertisement if the alterations requested are unacceptable (unless for reasons beyond the reasonable control of the [Publisher] the [Advertiser] cannot be contacted prior to the production of the [Periodical]).

E.085

The [Publishers] shall consult with the [Authors] as to the cover, copyright notices, disclaimer, print size, font, format, layout, design, binding and marketing of the [Work]. The [Authors] shall be provided with an opportunity to meet the marketing team and to provide information, summaries of key selling points, quotes and shall be entitled to comment on the draft cover and marketing material that is produced in all formats and for all markets whether for the website, catalogues, shops, posters or bookmarks. The general management of the editorial process the choice of editor, proofreader and the production, publication, promotion, pricing, the size of any print run, reprinting, sale and distribution of the [Work] shall be entirely at the [Publisher's] cost and discretion.

E.086

The [Author] shall discuss with the [Company] the content of the [Work] and shall implement the [Company's] reasonable requests with regard to its contents. When the first draft of the [Work] has been written the [Author] shall submit a copy to the [Company] and shall implement the [Company's] reasonable requests with regard to the manner in which it shall be revised. If the [Author] is unwilling to implement the [Company's] reasonable requests with regard to the writing or the revision of the [Work] then the [Company] shall have no obligation to pay the [Author] any further sums hereunder.

E.087

The [Journalist] and the [Publisher] agree that the [Individual] shall be entitled to approve the [Article] prior to publication in the form in which it is intended to be published in the [Magazine]. In the event that the [Article] is not approved by the [Individual]. Then the [Journalist] and the [Publisher] agree that the [Article] and the Photographs shall not be published at any time, in which case the [Individual] shall repay [figure/currency] to the [Publisher]. Any copyright and other rights in the unpublished [Article], any recordings, film, notes or photographs or any other material created under this Agreement shall belong to [specify].

E.088

The [Author] agrees to amend, alter or edit such parts of the [Work] as the [Publisher] may request in the event that its legal advisors consider that the Work contains material which is likely to result in legal proceedings against the [Publisher].

E.089

The [Publisher] agrees that the [Author] shall be entitled to be consulted in relation to the artwork and design of the cover of the [Work] and in relation to the marketing of the [Work].

E.090

The [Licensee] undertakes not to edit, adjust, alter or amend or in any way change the [Extracts] without the prior written consent of the [Licensor].

E.091

The [Ghostwriter] agrees that [Name/Company] shall have the sole and exclusive discretion as to the research, interviews and content of the [Work] and any title, acknowledgements, copyright notices, cover, photographs, artwork or other material and any production, printing, licensing, distribution and exploitation of the [Work] and any associated material which is created by the [Ghostwriter] pursuant to this Agreement.

E.092

The [Ghostwriter] agrees to redraft, alter, adapt, edit and amend the [Work] as requested by the [Originator] during the Term of the Agreement and prior to the acceptance of the [Work] by the [Publisher].

E.093

The [Authors] agree that no material is to be included in the [Work] or the [Artwork] or added, deleted or changed or adapted unless both parties provide their consent.

E.094

The [Author] acknowledges that the [Assignee] shall be entitled to edit, adapt, translate, alter or amend the [Work] entirely at its sole cost and discretion.

E.095

The [Publisher] accepts that no alteration, amendment, deletion, addition, translation, adaptation or variation or development of the [Work] shall be made, agreed or licensed without the [Author's] prior written consent. Further, the [Author] shall then be entitled to approve any such [Work] or any sample article or product prior to production, printing or manufacture.

In the event that approval is withheld by the [Author] for any reason then the [Work] in that form shall not be produced by the [Publisher] at any time.

E.096

The [Author] agrees that where any alteration in the text or title is required prior to exploitation in the Territory, due to factual errors or the serious threat of legal action, then the [Author] shall not unreasonably withhold or delay his/her consent to such changes.

E.097

The [Publishers] shall not have the right to instruct, permit or allow any third party to contribute to the [Work] or to publish the [Work] together with other works or for any material in any format in any medium to be added to, appear with or be attached to the [Work].

E.098

The [Publisher] shall be entitled to exploit, reproduce, adapt, develop or distribute the [Work] or any article, product or right based on or derived from it in any manner, shape, form or method that it decides and shall not be required to inform, advise, consult or obtain consent from [Name] at any time. Nor shall there be any restriction or limit on the length of time, countries, associated products, services, companies or persons that may be used by the [Publisher].

E.099

The [Publisher] agrees that the [Author] shall not be obliged to make any edits, changes and/or alterations to the [Work] prior to publication which he/she does not wish to consider. That the [Author] shall have the final decision in respect of the content of the [Work] and any cover, index, preface, marketing, promotion, exploitation and translation and/or adaptation at any time.

E.100

The [Contributor] agrees that the [Publisher] shall be entitled to edit, change, adapt and/or translate the [Work] as it thinks fit and shall not be obliged to consult with the [Contributor]. That in addition the [Publisher] may appoint a third party to add, change, alter and amend material to the [Work] and that such person may also be credited as the writer in respect of the later version as well as the [Contributor].

Purchase and Supply of Products

E.101

The [Product] shall not be changed, altered, added to, adapted or varied in any way by the [Distributor] and shall be kept in the exact same form, content and packaging in which it is delivered by the [Supplier].

E.102

The [Manufacturer] acknowledges that the [Distributor] shall have the sole discretion as to the manner and method to be used in the production, supply of source materials, manufacture, labels, packaging, delivery, distribution, marketing and promotion of the [Work]. No changes, additions, variations, deletions or otherwise of any nature shall be made or authorised by the [Manufacturer] without the prior consent of [Name] at the [Company].

E.103

It is agreed that minor variations, in colour, content, appearance, labels and packaging may occur due to the source of the materials, the production process, the length of storage and the delivery method. No major changes, alterations or variations will be made to the [Product/Article] or any packaging or storage or delivery method without the advance approval and written consent of the [Company].

E.104

The [Distributor] agrees that any labels, brochures and/or packaging supplied by the [Company] in respect of each of the [Products] shall not be removed, covered, hidden, damaged and/or altered by the [Distributor] at any time during the course of this Agreement.

E.105

[Name] agrees that the [Distributor] shall not be restricted as to the reproduction, manufacture and form of exploitation of the [Products]. That the [Distributor] shall have the choice at any time to develop, change and/or adapt and/or alter the name, colour, layout, design and/or packaging of the [Products] and/or any parts in order to promote, market and achieve more sales of the [Products].

Services

E.106

The [Director] shall not alter, amend or deviate from the Production Schedule, the Budget, or the Final Script provided by the [Company] without the prior consent of the [Company] in each case.

E.107

The [Artist] acknowledges that the Company's decision shall be final in respect of all matters of any nature regarding the content, editing, other changes, exploitation or marketing of the [Film].

E.108

The [Agent] shall not be entitled to alter, amend, adapt or edit the synopsis of the [Work] without the prior written consent of the [Author].

E.109

The [Agent] agrees not to promote, advertise or market the [Artist] in any way which might impugn the reputation or embarrass the [Artist]. As far as possible the [Agent] shall provide copies of all proposed material and agrees to adhere to all changes requested by the [Artist]. The [Agent] agrees that it shall be entirely responsible for the cost of all such material and changes and no sums shall be paid by the [Artist].

E.110

The [Agent] agrees that:

1.1 It shall not authorise or carry out any alterations, amendments, adaptations or editing of the synopsis or the [Work] without the prior written consent of the [Author].

1.2 That the artistic and editorial control of the [Work] shall be at the sole discretion and decision of the [Author].

1.3 That the [Agent] shall use reasonable endeavours to ensure that any third party will not have the right to edit, adapt or alter the [Work] without the prior written consent of the [Author].

1.4 That the [Agent] does not have the right itself to carry out or to authorise others to edit, adapt, add to, delete or in any way change the [Work] without the prior written consent of the [Author].

1.5 That as far as possible all authorised changes shall be at the sole cost of the third party and that all copyright and other rights shall be assigned to the [Author] including any proposed translation.

E.111

The [Manager] accepts that the [Sportsperson] shall be entitled to refuse to carry out any work which he/she deems to be in conflict with his/her image, religious beliefs and reputation or which is offensive, demeaning, hazardous or conflicts with any code of conduct of any [professional body] of which he/she is a member or other work or family commitments or contracts.

E.112

The [Company] agrees to consult with and to seriously consider the recommendations and requests of [Name] and the [Agent] in respect of all proposed scripts, titles, slogans, logos, music, lyrics, photographs, films, videos, DVDs, sound recordings, CD-Roms and computer generated material, website material, telephone material, any material which is to be downloaded in any format, packaging, advertising, promotional, publicity and marketing material in all media prior to production, manufacture, supply and distribution of such material.

E.113

The [Celebrity] acknowledges that all final editorial decisions in respect of all content, material, services and exploitation under this agreement shall be at the sole discretion of the [Company] subject to the clause to consult in Clause [–]. The [Company] shall have the right to edit, adapt, add or delete material and other persons as it thinks fit and shall not be obliged to include the services of the [Celebrity].

E.114

The [Company] agrees that the name, image and endorsement of the [Sportsperson] shall not be used for any other purpose other than [specify] for the duration of the Sponsorship Period.

E.115

The [Name] agrees that the [Company] shall have the sole discretion as to the manner and method and content to be used in the production, distribution and exploitation of the [Work/Film/other] and that no further sums shall be due to the [Name] except those set out under this Agreement. The [Company] shall have the final editorial decision in all matters and shall be entitled to edit, amend, adapt and delete and authorise others to do so. The [Company] shall not be obliged to include the product of the services and it may be left out entirely provided that all sums due under Clause [–] are paid.

E.116

In the event that the parties shall fail to agree on the choice of material to be recorded under this Agreement then the decision of the [Artist/Company] shall be final.

E.117

The [Licensee] acknowledges that it shall not be entitled to exploit in any manner any [Sound Recordings] of the [Musical Work] without the prior written consent of the [Licensor].

E.118

The [Agent/Company] agree that [Name] must be consulted and provide prior authorisation to any proposed to any changes to any part the content of the [Event/Work/Project] set out in Schedule [–] which is attached to and forms part of this Agreement. That the decision of [Name] shall be final and that where [Name] refuses consent any liability and/or consequences that arise shall be at the [Agent's/Company's] sole cost and not attributed to [Name].

E.119

Where the services of [Name] are no longer required for any reason and/or are not included in the final version of the [Work] which is produced and/

or developed by the [Company]. Then there shall be no obligation by the [Company] to use and/or include any part of the contribution, performance and/or product of the services of [Name] and/or to add any credit and/or acknowledgement of their participation at any time.

Sponsorship

E.120
The [Sponsor] acknowledges that the [Association] has no editorial control in respect of the times, dates, duration and content of the broadcast, transmission or other exploitation of the [Recordings] and/or any [Film] and cannot be responsible for any technical failures, cancellation, or other delays or interruptions that may occur of any intended coverage on television, radio, websites or otherwise.

E.121
The [Sponsor] acknowledges that all editorial, scheduling and programming decisions concerning the [Programme] are entirely at the sole discretion of the [Television Company].

E.122
The [Television Company] shall be entitled at its sole discretion and cost to make such changes, deletions, alterations, interruptions, adjustments or additions to the content of the [Series/Film/Recordings] as may be required for any reason including but not limited to artists, music, script, products, locations, and title.

E.123
The [Television Company] shall have final editorial control of the [Series] but in the event that the [Series] is to be substantially changed, altered or the content no longer uses the services of [Artist], music by [Name] or script by [Name]. The [Television Company] shall inform the [Sponsor] in writing and provide them with the opportunity to cancel the Agreement upon terms to be agreed between the parties. The [Sponsor] accepts that in any agreement to cancel the sponsorship there shall be no additional repayments by the [Television Company] as compensation, damages or otherwise.

E.124
The [Sponsor] agrees that it shall have no editorial control over any part of the [Event], the content, agreements with third parties, the brochure and/or any media coverage arranged and/or organised by the [Company]. Nor shall the [Sponsor] have any right of approval and/or to be consulted.

E.125

The [Sponsor] agrees that it shall have no control and/or rights to be consulted and/or approve any part of the [Project/Work/Film]. That the [Company] may change the title, content, dates and means of exploitation and/or distribution and/or the use of third parties as the executives and management of the [Company] chooses for any reason. That the [Sponsor] agrees that such variations and changes shall not be provide grounds for withdrawal and/or termination of this Agreement provided that the [Company] completes the obligations in clause [–] before [date].

E.126

The [Company] agrees that the [Sponsor] has agreed to provide the funds in clause [–] due to the proposed appearance and performance by [Name] at the [Event/Programme]. In the event that [Name] should cancel and/or terminate their appearance and/or performance and/or contribution. Then the [Company] agrees to notify the [Sponsor] and to agree alternative individuals who could be approached which would be acceptable to both parties. Where the substitute is not of a comparable status then the payment by the [Sponsor] under clause [–] shall be reduced by [number] per cent.

University, Library and Educational

E.127

The [Contributor] agrees that the [Institute] shall have:

1.1   The sole discretion as to the manner and method and content to be used in the production, distribution and exploitation of the [Work/Film/Text].

1.2   No obligation to pay any additional royalties and/or other sums to the [Contributor] for any form of exploitation in any media and shall only pay those set out under this Agreement in Clause [–].

1.3   The final editorial control in respect of all material produced under this Agreement.

1.4   The right to edit, amend, adapt, add to and/or delete all material produced under this Agreement and/or authorise others to do so in such manner and method as the [Institute] in its absolute discretion thinks fit.

1.5   The right not to include the product of the services provided by the [Contributor] in any final [Work/Film/Text] but shall still be obliged to pay all sums due under Clause [–].

E.128

The [Company/Contributor] agree and undertakes that in the event that the [Institute] requests deletions, amendments, alterations and/or changes to

659

the title, characters, text, images, photographs, cover, products, packaging, publicity, marketing and/or any other material at any time due to errors, omissions, and/or the threat of civil and/or criminal actions. Then the [Company/Contributor] agrees to consent to such deletions, amendments, alterations and/or changes as may be necessary provided that the additional costs are met by the [Institute].

E.129

The [Licensee] undertakes not to edit, alter, delete, amend, alter, add to and/or change in any way the [Work/Film/Article] without the prior written approval and consent of the [Institute].

E.130

The [Licensee] agrees and undertakes that the [Work/Film/Article] shall only be reproduced, distributed, supplied and sold in the exact form and with the same content, packaging, marketing and promotional material as approved by the [Institute].

E.131

The [Company] acknowledges and undertakes that the decisions and requirements of the [Institute] shall be paramount in respect of the creation of the [Service/Website/Project]. That it shall be the [Institute] and not the [Company] which has all final decision in respect of all matters relating to the [Service/Website/Project].

E.132

After the [Company/Contributor] have delivered the [Project] and been paid in full for the provision of their services. The [Institute] shall have the absolute right to engage such third parties as it thinks fit to develop, adapt, exploit, vary, amend and edit the [Project] as its sole discretion. No consent and/or agreement shall be required from the [Company/Contributor] nor shall any additional sums be due.

E.133

The [Institute] agrees that:

1.1 Neither the [Trustees/Directors] nor any employees, representatives, nor agents shall carry out any alterations, amendments, adaptations or editing of the [Work/Film/Article/Image] without the prior written consent of the [Copyright Owner].

1.2 That the artistic and editorial control of the [Work/Film/Article/Image] shall be at the sole discretion and decision of the [Copyright Owner].

1.3 That the [Institute] shall use reasonable endeavours to ensure that any third party shall be informed in writing that they do not have the right to edit, adapt or alter the [Work/Film/Article/Image] without the prior written consent of the [Copyright Owner].

E.134
The [Institute] shall at the [Institute's] cost and expense:

1.1 Consult with the [Company] as to the cover, copyright notices, disclaimer, print size, font, format, layout, design, binding and marketing of the [Work/Film/Product].

1.2 Provide the [Company] with draft copies and samples of all proposed material including the [Work/Film/Product], packaging, flyers, brochures, posters, website banners, advertisements, bookmarks, website details and listings, promotional and marketing material. The Company shall be consulted as to the accuracy, artistic and editorial content.

1.3 Provide the [Company] with two examples of any finished version of all material for the [Company] to keep as a record.

E.135
[Name] agrees that the [Institute] and/or any publisher and/or distributor shall have the right to edit, adapt, change, alter, add to, delete and/or distort and/or mutilate any part of the [Work] which he/she has written, contributed to and/or appeared in voice and/or film as part of the [Project]. That [Name] agrees and accepts that he/she has no claim any/or rights and/or interest and/or moral rights over any such product of his/her services and/or [Work]. That the [Fee] paid by the [Institute] included a sum to include this fact.

E.136
The [Author] agrees that the [Institute] may use and/or adapt up to [number] words as an extract of the [Work] for the purpose of promoting and marketing the [Institute] and/or the [Event] and/or for reproduction in the distribution material of a sponsor. Provided that a credit and acknowledgement is provided to the [Author] and a link to [specify].

ELECTRONIC

General Business and Commercial

E.137
'Electronic' shall mean words, texts, sounds, music, images, logos, graphics, film recordings, and sound recordings conveyed, transferred, supplied, or

distributed by electric, magnetic, electro-magnetic, electro-chemical or electro-mechanical means through any method or material.

E.138

'Electronic Rights' shall mean the sole and exclusive right to use, display, exhibit, supply, license, reproduce, distribute and exploit any form of rights and material whether in existence now or developed in the future in relation to the internet, websites, computers, telephones or any form of telecommunication system and the exclusive right to download any such material whether, text, sound, or images or other format to any other gadget, device or machine whether by subscription, free or pay per use on land, sea and air in any part of the world and throughout the universe [from [date] to [date]/for the full period of copyright and any extensions, renewals without limit of time or duration].

E.139

'Electronic Rights' shall mean the right to be the sole owner of and have the sole and exclusive right to exploit in any form any words, texts, sounds, music, images, logos, graphics, film recordings, and sound recordings stored, conveyed, transferred, supplied, or distributed by electric, magnetic, electro-magnetic, electro-chemical or electro-mechanical means through any method or material. That shall include but not be limited to the sole and exclusive right to use, display, exhibit, supply, license, reproduce, distribute and exploit any form of rights and material whether in existence now or developed in the future in relation to the internet, websites, computers, telephones, mobiles, or any form of telecommunications system and the exclusive right to download any such material whether, text, sound, or images or other format to any other gadget, device or machine whether by subscription, free or pay per use on land, sea and air in any part of the world and throughout the universe for the full period of copyright and any extensions, renewals and thereafter in perpetuity.

E.140

'Electronic Form' shall mean in a form usable only by electronic means.

E.141

'Electronic communication' shall mean a communication transmitted from one person to another or one device to another or vice versa by means of a telecommunication system or by any other means which is in electronic form [as defined by the Electronic Communications Act 2000 as amended].

E.142

'Communication' shall include a communication comprising sounds or images or both and a communication effecting payment.

E.143

The [Company] agrees and undertakes that:

1.1   The [Copyright Owner] is and shall remain the sole and exclusive of all rights in the [Work/Film/Image/Project].

1.2   That it shall not acquire any rights and/or interest in any material which already exists which is owned and/or controlled by the [Copyright Owner] nor in any new material which may be created by either party which is derived from and/or based on such material.

1.3   The [Company] also agrees that any new material created which is entirely original which relates to the [Work/Film/Image/Project] shall also be assigned by the [Company] to the [Copyright Owner] including the electronic rights so that no rights are retained by the [Company].

E.144

'The Electronic Digital Files' shall mean all the words, texts, sounds, music, images, logos, graphics, film recordings, and sound recordings stored, conveyed, transferred, supplied, or distributed by electric, magnetic, electro-magnetic, electro-chemical or electro-mechanical means through any method or material whether in existence now or developed in the future including the internet, websites, computers, telephones, mobiles, or any form of telecommunication system.

E.145

'The Electronic Digital Files' shall mean the [format] files held by the [Company] reproduced from the [Material] which are to be used to [specify purpose].

E.146

'The Telecommunication and Transmission Rights' shall mean all forms of telecommunication and/or transmission through sound, air, land and/or water and/or any chemical, substance, wireless telegraphy and WiFi and/or method and/or material and/or by intermediary gadgets and/or equipment by any means whether known now as at [date] and/or developed in the future including images, text, film, recordings, photographs, music, sound recordings, animation and/or any computer generated creations and/or otherwise including but not limited to by television, radio, landline and mobile phones, laptops, computers, websites and the internet, portable devices for downloading and accessing any material and/or storage systems in any medium.

EMBARGO

General Business and Commercial

E.147

[Name] the recipient of this news release hereby confirms and accepts that the content of the document shall not be placed into the public domain until after [time] on [date]. That in the event that the embargo is not complied with as requested that the following conditions shall apply [specify].

E.148

For the purposes of this Agreement, Embargo shall mean an arrest laid on [name of vessel] or any merchandise contained therein by any public authority, or an order prohibiting [name of vessel] from putting to sea and/or entering a port. In the event of such Embargo Clause [–] shall apply.

E.149

The [Company] agrees and undertakes not to make available, release, sell, distribute, and/or otherwise supply the [Product/Service/Work] to the public before [time] on [date]. That the [Product/Service/Work] shall be kept under maximum security at the head office and only the following agreed personnel shall be allowed access and/or to be made aware of the launch [specify personnel]. The [Company] shall not respond to any press and/or media enquiries and shall refer all such matters to [specify].

E.150

This [Work] must not be reproduced and/or distributed to any third party before [time] [date] without the prior written consent of [Name].

E.151

Where in any part of the preparation of the [Work] any material is and/or has been provided to [Name] by a third party which is confidential and private and/or is the subject of legal proceedings concerning two persons who are the subject of a court order regarding their identity. Then [Name] shall not be under any obligation to the [Company] to supply details and may withhold such information.

ENDORSEMENT

General Business and Commercial

E.152
In consideration of the payments agreed to be made hereunder [Name] agrees to endorse the following product [specify] [manufactured/distributed/ sub-licensed] by or to the [Company] in [country].

E.153
[Name] shall during the course of this Agreement behave himself in a fit, proper and professional manner and shall do no act by omission or commission which would bring the [Company] or its products (whether the subject-matter of this Agreement or not) into disrepute.

E.154
The [Company] agrees and undertakes that the [Company] is financially stable and will continue to be able to make the payment commitments in Clause [–] to [Name] and the [Company] is not under threat of any kind and likely to stop production of the [Product] during the Term of this Agreement.

E.155
The [Company] agrees and undertakes that the entire range of all its products and in particular the [Product] together with any packaging are entirely safe and fit for their intended purpose and function, and comply with all standards, legal requirements and tests that are or may be applicable.

E.156
The [Company] agrees and undertakes that neither [Name], nor their business, nor their agent shall be in anyway responsible for or liable to pay any sums of any nature if there is any allegation, any claim, action, or otherwise against the [Company] arising from the provision of the services and work of [Name] under this Agreement at any time.

E.157
References to endorsement in the Agreement shall be construed as meaning the act of signing any relevant document including, but not limited to, any deed, bill of exchange or promissory note.

E.158
The [Company] agrees to provide the non-exclusive services of the [Name] who has agreed to endorse and promote the [Distributor's] [Product/ Services] upon the following terms:

665

1.1 The [Company] shall pay [Name] as follows [specify advance/fees/ repeat fees/additional uses/expenses]. Payment shall be by the following method [specify] by [date] subject to completion of work in each case. Together with a fully comprehensive insurance cover in the name of and for the benefit of [Name] for any claim relating to provision of their services in the sum of [figure] paid for by the [Company].

1.2 [Name] shall carry out the following work [Number, duration and detail of recordings in sound, film, advertisements, personal appearances, newspapers, magazines and trade journals, website material, mobile telephone material, written statements, logos, and any associated material].

E.159

The product of the work of the services of [Name] shall only be exploited by the [Company] from [date] to [date] thereafter the [Company] must either destroy all the material or store it and undertake not to use it without the prior written consent [Name].

E.160

The [Company] shall not have the right to use, transmit, supply or distribute the material produced under this Agreement in any form except in [country/ Europe/other] in [the English language] from [date] to [date].

E.161

The [Company] shall not have the right to sub-license or authorise others to copy, supply, distribute or exploit the material created under this Agreement unless it is specifically to promote, market and advertise the [Product] in the manner, means and style agreed with [Name]. All other such uses shall require the prior written consent of [Name], a further agreement and additional payments. Failure to comply with this clause shall entitle [Name] to [specify].

E.162

The [Company] agrees that it shall not be entitled to use, exploit or license any of the material produced or created for the purposes of this Agreement in which the [Celebrity] appears in sound, vision for any purpose at any time other than for the endorsement, promotion or advertising of the [Company's] Product during the Term of the Agreement. Where the [Company] wishes to use any such material at any time for any purpose or to license a third party then a new agreement setting out the terms of the written consent of the [Celebrity] and payment of additional sums.

E.163

[Name] and their agent [specify] agree that the [Company] shall be entitled to exploit, sub-license, distribute, market, transfer, assign, and reproduce the material created under this Agreement including the name of the person at any time and in any format and there shall be no restrictions or prohibitions on its use. Provided that the [Company] undertakes to ensure that the material shall be acknowledged as being originally related to an endorsement of the [Product] and that no use shall be derogatory, defamatory or prejudicial to the career of [Name] or their business.

E.164

In the event that the [Product/Magazine/Advertisement] is withdrawn from the market and/or is nor reproduced and/or distributed for any reason the [Company] shall still be entitled to receive all the sums specified in Clause [–] for the endorsement by [Name].

E.165

The products, articles, links, blogs, and all other material on this [Website] are displayed, reproduced and used at your own risk and cost. There is no recommendation and/or endorsement by the [Company] nor any acceptance of any liability for any consequences that may arise. If there are any inaccuracies, omissions, and/or offensive material please email us with the details so that we can try to delete and/or amend them accordingly.

E.166

[Name] agrees that the [Company] shall be entitled to edit, adapt, add to and/or delete the [Film/Work/Images/Photographs] of [Name] endorsing the [Product/services] of the [Company] provided that the final version is not offensive, derogatory and/or likely to damage the reputation of [Name].

E.167

The [Company] shall be entitled to add other products, services, images, text and any other material as it thinks fit to the final [Film/Work/Project] which [Name] is not endorsing. Providing that the [Company] ensures that:

1.1 it is clear that there is no such endorsement by [Name]; and

1.2 it is not a competing product of [specify]; and

1.3 [Name] is not in close proximity to and/or seen to be wearing, using and/or in any way associated with this other material.

E.168

[Name] reserves the right to withdraw his/her support of the [Company] and/ or its work and/or products where any senior executive and/or management make a political statement against [specify] which would be contrary to the existing views o f [Name]. In such circumstances [Name] may terminate this Agreement and retain all the sums paid to date for all work which has been completed.

E.169
[Name] agrees to be used in a short term marketing campaign from [date] to [date] for the new app on the subject of [specify] for the [Distributor]. [Name] agrees that the [Distributor] may use his/her name, image and logo for that sole purpose but not for marketing and promoting the other products of the [Distributor]. [Name] shall not be obliged to do any photo shoot and/ or filming and shall supply his/her own images that he/she agrees can be used. Provided that the [Company] agrees that they are not authorised to use those images after [date].

E.170
[Name] shall have the right to seek sponsors and/or third parties to endorse and/or sponsor and/or enter into product placement and/or affiliation programmes with [Name] for the [Blog] at any time. [Name] shall be entitled to retain all sums and benefits received and shall not be obliged to account and/or share any sums with the [Company].

E.171
The [Company] agrees and undertakes not to become involved in any controversy, campaign and/or legal proceedings which would lead to association with [Name] who endorses their products. The [Company] agrees to inform [Name] of any such proposal and to allow them the opportunity to withdraw their support before any public announcement of the [Company's] involvement in any controversy, campaign and/or legal proceedings.

ENVIRONMENTAL

General Business and Commercial

E.172
The [Company] undertakes that it shall use its reasonable endeavours to ensure that the following policies are adopted, maintained, and monitored as part of its planning, purchase and operational requirements of the business:

1.1   That it will try to source materials from verifiable sustainable resources and use and give preference to other services and goods which are rated as better for the environment.

1.2   That it will reduce and phase out the use of toxic or dangerous substances, chemicals and solvents, or those gases or emissions which damage the ozone layer or pollute the air.

1.3   That it will reduce and prevent discharges into land, sea and rivers and will conserve water, energy and resources; reduce waste and recycle.

1.4   That transport methods are considered not only by the cost, but also the effect on the environment.

E.173

The [Company] confirms and undertakes that it has and will maintain the following environmental policies in relation to all its [Products] and packaging:

1.1   All sources of material come from sustainable resources.

1.2   No additional chemicals, salt, additives, preservatives or other substances or ingredients are added which have not been declared on the label even in very small amounts whether required by law or not.

1.3   No genetically modified material is present in any form or any substance combined with or derived from it.

1.4   There is a set target to reduce packaging, and packaging is kept to a minimum and is capable of being recycled.

1.5   That preference is given environmentally friendly products, services and transport and other companies and businesses that adopt environmentally aware practices.

1.6   That there are regular reviews and records, documents and evidence can be supplied to support their compliance and procedures.

1.7   That there is use and support of fair trade for self-supporting communities and that it is a condition of their contracts with suppliers or other businesses that working practices must comply with certain minimum standards.

E.174

The [Company] agrees that it shall not and undertakes that it shall not allow any person and/or company and/or agent to enter on, gain access to and/or use in any way, and/or pass over, under, or through any part of any structure, building, article, lighting, utility, whether on the land, above or below the surface or in the sea, the air or any part of [address] [land registry reference] anything related to the following subjects [mobile phone masts/transmitters/

pesticides/toxic or poisonous substances/quarry/factory/other] at any time. The [Company] acknowledges that this is an important clause without which this Agreement would not have been entered into by [–].

E.175
The [Company] agrees and undertakes that it shall have a policy for sustainable development and shall its [best/reasonable] endeavours to reduce all packaging and to source all materials to ensure that the contents of the [Product] and all the packaging can be recycled as far as possible.

E.176
The [Company] agrees that it must operate a energy and environmental conservation, resource and sustainability policy in line with the targets of [specify]. That the [Company] shall reduce use of paper and encourage recycling of materials; that where equipment and/or other fittings are replaced they will be disposed of for re-use by a charity and/or other community use and not added to landfill. That use of public transport and walking shall be encouraged to all staff and no costs incurred for personal cars and/or other private transport within [distance] of [location].

E.177
The [Enterprise] shall operate a policy of effective use of resources in accordance with the guidelines laid down by [specify]. The [Enterprise] shall monitor and report on its use of water, paper, light, heat, petrol, equipment, ink cartridges, furniture and other resources and waste disposal and recycling. The [Enterprise] agrees and undertakes to have an active plan to reduce costs and adopt as far as possible a sustainable green policy.

EQUAL OPPORTUNITIES

General Business and Commercial

E.178
The [Company] shall make arrangements for promoting in relation to employment, equality of opportunity between men and women and between persons of different racial groups and people of disabilities and review those arrangements from time to time.

E.179
The [Company] undertakes that it shall endeavour to ensure that there is compliance with all equal opportunity requirements in [country] from [date]

670

to [date] and that all applicants for positions at the [Company] shall be treated in a fair manner based on their qualifications and experience and not race, disability, gender, religion or otherwise.

E.180
The parties agree to treat all candidates equally regardless of gender, race, disability, religion, type of education, socio-economic group, political views and/or age.

E.181
The policy of equal opportunities applies to all candidates, but it is a requirement of the position that in the application form each person who applies agrees to be subject to a full [DRB/Criminal Record] check.

E.182
The [Company] agrees that all applicants shall be considered on their merits and based on their qualifications and work experience. No preference is provided to any person except that it is a requirement of all positions that you be entitled to work in [country] and can speak and write fluent [language].

E.183
The [Contractor] agrees and undertakes to at all times operate and adhere to:

1.1 An equal opportunities policy in accordance with any legislation and policies of [country] which may exist and/or may be brought into existence and

1.2 To provide a minimum of [number] training apprenticeships for candidates [age 18–24] years for not less than [number] weeks for not less than [payment] per person.

ERROR

General Business and Commercial

E.184
References to errors, incorrect statements, mistakes or omissions in this Agreement shall not include those which are of a minor or inconsequential nature.

E.185

The [Company] undertakes to minimise disruption that may be caused by technical errors, viruses or any other phenomenon which affects the function of the [Website]. There can be no assurance that the data, information and any material whether text, images, graphics, music, sounds or sound effects or recordings, chatrooms, icons, links or otherwise are free of errors. Nor can the [Company] accept responsibility for any impact or loss or damage that the failure of this [Website] to function effectively may have on you personally and/or your business.

E.186

Where an error is found or later disclosed whether by the [Licensor] or the [Licensee] the [Licensee] shall not be entitled to a refund of any overpayment to the [Licensor]. Nor shall the [Licensor] be entitled to any interest, compensation, or damages for an error provided that the error was not deliberate or fraudulent and payment is made immediately. An error arising from an audit by the [Licensor] shall result in the [Licensee] paying all cost and expenses in respect of the accountants and the legal advisors for such audit where the error is more than [–].

E.187

Errors, inaccuracies, mistakes, incorrect advice, formulae, contents, faulty connections, system failures, viruses, bugs, hackers, loss, damage, theft, or identity disclosures of email addresses by mistake, or the failure to encrypt information are possible when using this [Website] and the [Company] is not and will not be responsible. [Name] accepts and agrees that they use this [Website] at their own risk.

E.188

The [Institute] cannot accept any responsibility for the consequences and/or liabilities arising from any errors, omissions, misrepresentations, prices and/or dates on the [Brochure/Website/Work]. All details may be changed and/or amended without notice by the [Institute].

E.189

Where there has been an error, omission and/or default at any time which is caused by the [Company] has and/or will result in losses and/or damages being suffered and/or incurred directly and/or indirectly by the [Licensor]. Then the [Company] shall be obliged to pay the full cost and expense of all such losses and /or damages to the [Licensor] together with interest at [number] per cent from the date of the error, omission and/or default.

E.190
It is accepted by all parties that there shall be no claim and/or action and/or demand against any of the others in the [Consortium] for any errors, omissions, mistakes, deletions and/or fraud and/or negligence by any of the persons involved in the development, creation and delivery of the [Project]. That all parties shall bear their own losses, damages, costs and expenses and are party to this Agreement at their own risk.

ESCALATOR

General Business and Commercial

E.191
In the event the [Distributor] receives in excess of [figure/currency] as the annual total revenue from the exploitation of the [Film/Product] in any calendar year during the Term of the Agreement (or thereafter until all sums due have been received and the [Distributor] has no right to receive payment.) Then the additional sum of [figure/currency] shall be paid to the [Licensor] on each and every occasion that such an event takes place. There is no limitation on the number of times that this additional payment may be made.

E.192
The [Company] shall pay [Name] at the following rates in respect of the [Total Revenue/Gross Receipts/Net Receipts]:

1.1 [Figure] per cent up to [figure/currency].

1.2 [Figure] per cent from [figure/currency] up to [figure/currency].

1.3 [Figure] per cent from [figure/currency] up to [figure/currency].

1.4 Thereafter at an increased rate of [figure] per cent for any amount over [figure/currency].

E.193
The [Author/Licensor] shall receive the fixed sum of [figure/currency] for each unit of each type of [Product/Article/Book] in [country] as follows:

1.1 [Figure] per cent up to [number of units].

1.2 [Figure] per cent from [number of units] up to [number of units].

1.3 [Figure] per cent from [number of units] up to [number of units].

E.194

In the event that the total sales of the tickets for the [Event] exceed [number] by [date] then the [Company] agrees to pay an additional advance fee to the [Agent] of [number/currency] which shall be paid within [number] days of conclusion of the provisional [accounts/financial report] at the end of each calendar month.

E.195

There shall be no additional fees, royalties and/or other sums paid to [Name] in the event that the [Distributor] exceeds the projected sales of the [Work/Product] set out in this Agreement unless the total gross receipts exceed [number/currency]. In such event [Name] shall be entitled to be paid an additional payment of [figure/currency] for every additional [number/currency] which is received by the [Distributor]. These additional payments shall be paid to [Name] by the [Distributor] within [number] days of the verification of the achievement of the targets and subject to invoice by [Name].

ESTATE

General Business and Commercial

E.196

For the purposes of this Agreement the term 'Estate' shall only mean real property.

E.197

For the purposes of this Agreement the term 'Estate' shall include all property belonging to [Name] including without limitation, all land howsoever held, chattels, money, choses in action and all other goods of any nature including [excluding] all debts and lawful liabilities of [Individual].

E.198

'The Estate' shall include all the following matters:

1.1   Property, land, freehold, leasehold, rental agreements, rights of occupation, rights of way and access, fishing rights, sea and coastal areas owned, controlled or held in the name of [specify] or for the benefit of [Name] known as [address/reference/deposited at/charges/liens/other].

1.2   All intellectual property rights, copyright, patents, trade marks, service marks, design rights, future design rights, computer software, trade secrets, domain names, registrations, contracts, licences, confidential information or other rights in any media of any nature whether in existence now or created in the future owned, controlled or held in the name of [Name] or for the benefit of [Name].

E.199

The estate of [Name] shall include the following Books, Films, Articles, DVDs, Websites, Products, Diaries, drafts, letters, accounts, bank records, medical records and other material in any media and property owned and/ or controlled by [Name] [specify in detail]. Together with all intellectual property rights, copyright, patents, trade marks, service marks, design rights, future design rights, computer software, trade secrets, domain names, registrations, contracts, licences, confidential information or other rights in any text, image, logo, photograph, sound recordings, films, and in any other media of any nature whether in existence now or created in the future owned, controlled or held in the name of [Name] or for the benefit of [Name] by any person, company and/or other entity.

E.200

'The Literary Estate' shall comprise all the material by [Name] which are owned and/or controlled by Name] from [date] to his/her death. This material shall include all text, manuscripts, drafts and notes, correspondence with agents, publishers, television companies, and any other third party, images, film, video, photographs, negatives, sound recordings, material stored on any hard drive of a computer, gadget and/or some other device, drawings, sketches, paintings which directly relates to the work of [Name] during that period. It shall not include material which relates solely to immediate family members [specify] and/or for any material prior to [date].

E.201

1.1 The Estate of [Name] of [address] who was born on [date] and died on [date] in [country] shall be referred to as [specify].

1.2 [Probate/other] was granted on [date] by [specify]. A copy of which is attached and forms part of this Agreement.

1.3 The [Executors/Trustees] of the Estate are [specify] who have the following authority [specify].

1.4 The beneficiaries and their guardians of the Estate are as follows [specify].

1.5 The assets of the Estate as at [date] are as follows [specify].

1.6 The liabilities of the Estate as at [date] are as follows [specify].

EUROPEAN UNION

General Business and Commercial

E.202

The [Supplier] warrants that all goods and services shall comply with all relevant European Union Directives, regulations, standards, policies and codes which are and may come into existence during the Term of this Agreement which may be applicable including, but not limited to [specify].

E.203

The [Company] undertakes that the [Work/Services/Products] shall comply with all the existing and future European directives, regulations and cases. That the [Company] shall regularly review whether they are fulfilling all the terms required and update accordingly.

E.204

The [Product/Article/Service] and the [Company] shall comply with all legal requirements, directives, regulations and practices required by the European Union which are displayed on its websites, published in its journals, or are applicable as binding decisions, judgements, or notified to member states and/or incorporated in the legislation of any member state.

E.205

The [Consultant] agrees and undertakes that he/she is willing to travel and work throughout the European Union in order to carry out the requirements of the [Project]. That there is no reason and/or restriction which would prevent and/or hinder and/or delay the [Consultant] from fulfilling and/or completing the [Project].

E.206

The [Company] agrees that there shall be no restrictions as to supply of the [Product/Service] imposed in respect of any member state of the [European Union] and/or any third party which does not apply to all purchasers of the [Product/Service].

EXCLUSIVITY

DVD, Video and Discs

E.207

1.1 In consideration of the payment of the Non-returnable Advance and the Licensor's Royalties, the [Licensor] grants to [Licensee] the sole and exclusive [DVD/Video/Disc] rights in the Territory for the duration of the Licence Period and the right to authorise third parties to exercise such rights.

1.2 The [Licensee] agrees that all rights not specifically granted are excluded from this Agreement including [television, format, mobile and landline telephone use, merchandising and publishing.]

1.3 That after the end of the Licence Period the [Licensee] shall not have any rights in the [Film] and/or any material developed or created pursuant to this Agreement and that all rights shall revert to the [Licensor].

1.4 That the [Licensor] shall not assign, grant or otherwise exploit the rights granted to the [Licensee] nor shall it do anything in derogation from such Licence.

E.208

That the [Licensee] shall be permitted to use and permit the use of extracts of the [Film] to be shown at trade exhibitions and fairs for the purpose of the promotion of the [DVDs/Videos/Discs].

E.209

The [Licensee] shall be permitted to incorporate parts of the [Film] on other suitable [DVDs/Discs] provided that the subject matter of the other films is not violent, offensive or [specify] and no more than [duration] is used of the [Extract] and the purpose is the promotion and advertising of the [DVD/Disc] of the [Film].

E.210

The [Licensee] acknowledges that all other rights including terrestrial, satellite, cable, digital television, merchandising, clip, archive and library rights, advertising, CD-Roms, internet and website material and any other use in connection with computers, and/or telephones and any electronic or telecommunication system of any nature except those in clause [–] for [DVDs/Discs] is reserved by and to the [Licensor] who will retain and own all such rights.

E.211

The [Distributor] grants the [Sub-Licensee] the exclusive right to obtain orders for, advertise, market and sell copies of the [DVD/Disc] in [country] from [date] to [date]. The [Sub-licensee] shall not be entitled to produce, reproduce, or translate, sub-title or create its own version or packaging for the [DVD/Disc] and all requests for copies of the [DVD/Disc] shall be forwarded to the [Distributor] who shall provide the stock.

E.212

In consideration of the [Fee] the [Licensor] grants the [Licensee] the non-exclusive right to exhibit and show the [Work] on the [Disc] at the [specify venue and address] to a non-paying audience on [date]. Provided that the copyright notice and credit is not omitted and/or deleted at the time of the exhibition and the exhibition is to promote and advertise [specify reason]. There is no right to exhibit and/or use the [Work] and/or [Disc] at any other time and/or to make copies and/or to add and/or change any part of the [Work] and/or [Disc] supplied by the [Licensor].

E.213

1.1 The [Copyright Owner] grants the [Licensee] the non-exclusive right to include the [Image/Text] known as [specify/reference] in the [Work] and [Film] to be reproduced in the form of a printed [Report] and [Disc] in [country] from [date] to [date].

1.2 The [Licensee] shall only be entitled to make copies and/or reproduce the [Image/Text] for the purpose of producing the [Report] and [Disc] which shall only be used to submit for [specify reason] purposes to [specify organisation].

1.3 No right is granted to create an electronic and/or digital version and/or to licence and/or authorise any third party to make copies for any reason. Nor is any right granted to add to, vary, change and/or delete from the [Image/Text] which should remain unchanged, in content, colour and layout. Nor is any translation and/or adaptation authorised and all other rights are reserved to the [Copyright Owner].

E.214

1.1 In consideration of the [Fee] and the royalties due in clause [–] [Name] grants to the [Distributor] the exclusive right to reproduce, exploit and sub-licence the performance and appearances of [Name] in all films, sound recordings, photographs, computer generated images and any other associated material created and/or developed under this Agreement which features [Name] throughout the world. [Name] grants such exclusive rights to the [Distributor] for a period of [number] years from [date].

1.2   There after the [Distributor] shall have the right and/or option to renew the exclusive period of rights for an additional period of [number] years subject to a further non-returnable fee which cannot be offset against royalties of [number/currency].

1.3   In the event that the exclusive period is not extended then neither party shall be entitled to exploit any of the material created under this Agreement and/or the rights set out in 1.1 unless both parties agree terms and conditions.

E.215

1.1   [Name] has agreed to be recorded on [date] at [location] to appear and contribute to a [film] provisionally entitled [specify] which is to be sold and marketed as a [subject] for the [DVD/disc/other] market.

1.2   In consideration of the payment of a fee of [number/currency] [Name] grants an exclusive licence to the [Company] in all his/her contribution, performance and product of his/her work for the [Film] in any form throughout the world and universe which he/she may and/or will make including all present and future copyright and intellectual property rights and any other rights and/or interest in any media and/or format for the [DVD/Disc/other] and any associated packaging , marketing and promotion.

Employment

E.216
The [Employee] shall provide his/her services to the best of his/her skill and ability on a full-time and exclusive basis and shall perform all services diligently to ensure that the obligations under this Agreement are satisfactorily performed.

E.217
The [Employee] warrants that he/she will not undertake any other employment outside his/her working hours whether remunerated by payment or benefits in kind or otherwise, nor will he/she have any interest in any business or project which directly or indirectly competes with the business interests of the [Company], its subsidiaries or associates without the prior written consent of the [Managing Director].

E.218
The [Employee] confirms that he/she shall not during the course of his/her Agreement supply services of the same or similar nature to any third party without the prior consent of the [Company].

E.219

'The Services' shall mean the product of the services of the [Executive] to be provided to the [Company] under this Agreement which are described in the [Executive Job Description] attached in Schedule [–].

E.220

During the continuance of the appointment the [Executive] shall provide his/her services to the [Company]:

1.1 In a professional manner, on a full-time and exclusive basis and shall perform his/her duties diligently and in good faith so that his/her services are satisfactorily performed under this Agreement.

1.2 Carry out the duties described in the [Executive Job Description] in Schedule [–].

1.3 Undertake such other duties and exercise such powers in relation to the conduct and management of the [Company] and its associated businesses as the [Board of Directors] may request, direct and resolve provided that the additional matters are not major changes and effectively a new job description.

E.221

The [Executive] agrees that he/she shall not at any time during the course of this Agreement supply services to any third party without the prior written consent of the [Company] for duties which would be either prejudicial to the interest of the [Company] and/or be performed during working hours.

E.222

The [Company] agrees that this is not an exclusive agreement for the provision of the [Name] services and is only a limited contract of employment which is not long term and/or full time. The [Name] may enter into an agreement and/or be employed by any third party that he/she thinks fit whether or not it is a direct rival of the [Company] or not.

E.223

The [Company] agrees that the writing, books, contributions, publications, speeches, talks and any other matters which the [Executive] performs or does outside his scheduled work at the [Company] are not a matter which is relevant to this contract and are entirely at the discretion of the [Executive] and his choice and responsibility.

E.224

The [Company] agrees and acknowledges that there is no exclusive arrangement for the services of [Name]. That [Name] is at liberty to work with, endorse, promote and/or advertise any other company, service and/ or product at any time. The [Company] agrees that there are no verbal and/ or written restrictions, and/or codes of practice and/or guidelines to which [Name] must adhere. Nor is there any requirement by the [Company] that [Name] should notify and/or seek the approval of the [Company] at any time prior to any commitment to a third party.

E.225
[Name] agrees that all reports, blogs, articles and contributions made by him/her during the course of his/her employment with the [Company] including any title, image and logo associated with him/her shall belong to the [Company] but not the actual first and surname of [Name].

E.226
The [Company] acknowledges and agrees that [Name] is entitled during his/ her working day at the [Company] to access and send personal emails; use social media and operate and write his/her own blog and website. That any such use shall not be grounds for termination of this Agreement provided that [Name] completes the work and services required by the [Company].

E.227
The [Company] agrees that [Name] shall be employed and work at the main head office at [address]. In the event that this is relocated for any reason then [Name] shall be provided with the option of moving with the [Company] and/ or taking voluntary redundancy on terms to be agreed between the parties

Film and Television

E.228
The [Company] shall have the non-exclusive rights in the Territory during the Term of this Agreement to use and broadcast excerpts of the [Film] of not more than [three minutes] each for the purposes of any advertising, publicity, promotion or review.

E.229
The [Company] will not from the date of this Agreement until the expiry of the Licence Period and/or the termination of the Agreement exercise and/ or authorise, and/or procure, and/or suffer the exercise in the Territory the exploitation by any means of the [Film] and/or parts and/or any characters and/or storylines including, but not limited to satellite, terrestrial, cable, digital and television, radio, videos, DVDs, discs, internet and website material, mobile and/or landline telephones and/or by some other gadget or device and/or by any adaptation and/or merchandising and/or theme parks, gambling and/or betting and/or lotteries in any form.

E.230

During the period of this Agreement and with immediate effect the [Name] undertakes and warrants to the [Consortium] that the [Name] will not exercise and/or authorise the use by any third party of any of the rights granted to the [Consortium] under this Agreement. Except that [Name] shall be permitted to use the [Film] for illustration purposes during the course of any public lectures in [country].

E.231

The [Company] undertakes that it will not from the date of the Agreement until the expiry and/or termination of the Agreement exercise and/or license, and/or authorise, and/or procure, and/or suffer the exercise in the Territory the exploitation in any media of the [Film] and/or part(s).

E.232

In consideration of the Distribution Income under Clause [–] the [Company] grants to the [Licensee] the sole and exclusive licence in the Territory throughout the Licence Period to exploit the [Theatric Rights, Non-Theatric Rights, DVD and Video Rights and Cable Rights] in the [Film].

E.233

In consideration of the Licence Fee the [Company] grants to the [Television Company] the sole and exclusive rights in all media whether now known or hereafter discovered in the [Film] and/or part(s) (including the soundtracks) throughout the Territory for the Term of this Agreement. For the avoidance of doubt it is agreed that such rights shall include, but not be limited to the [Television Rights, DVD Rights, Theatric and Non-Theatric Rights, Library Rights, Publication Rights, Merchandising Rights].

E.234

In consideration of the Licence Fee and the Author's Royalties the [Author] grants to the [Company] the sole and exclusive right to produce the [Series] based on the [Author's Work] and to exploit the Standard Television Rights, the Cable Television Rights, the Satellite Television Rights in the [Series] for the duration of the Licence Period throughout the Territory.

E.235

The [Company] acknowledges that it shall not be entitled to exploit any other rights in the [Author's] Work not specifically granted under this Agreement including, but not limited to the right to exploit extracts of the Series, merchandising, publication rights, the right to transmit, display or download the [Series] on the internet, by any telecommunication system or to use the Series to endorse any person, company or product.

E.236

In consideration of the [Fee] and the [Additional Fees] the [Copyright Owner] grants the [Licensee] the non-exclusive right to broadcast and/or transmit the [Film/Image/Text] in the [Programme] and appoint an authorised distributor to sell, supply and reproduce the [Film/Image/Text] in the [Programme] to third parties in order to exploit the following rights [specify] in [specify countries] from [date] to [date].

E.237

The grant of the non-exclusive right in clause [–] to the [Licensee] shall not entitle the [Licensee] to exploit any other rights which are reserved by the [Copyright Owner]. Where the rights have not been created and/or the technology developed at the time of this Agreement. Then any such rights shall belong to the [Copyright Owner] and not the [Licensee].

E.238

In consideration of the payment of a fee of [number/currency] by [date] then the [Owner] grants the [Company] the exclusive right to occupy and film at the location set out in Schedule [–] from [date] to [date].

E.239

In consideration of the [Advance Fee] and the future royalties from the exploitation of the [Programme]. The [Licensor] grants the [Licensee] the non-exclusive right to include the [Sound Recordings] and the extracts of the [Films] in the [Programme] and to sub-licence and to appoint a distributor to exploit and market such non-exclusive rights in the [Programme] throughout the [Territory] from [date] to [date]. Provided that all the [Advance fee] and royalties which fall due are paid and accounted for to the [Licensor]. Further that the [Licensor] is provided with the following credit at the end of the [Programme] [specify].

General Business and Commercial

E.240

During the continuance of this Agreement the [Contractor] is not required to make its services available exclusively to the [Company] but at all times the interests of the [Company] shall prevail. The [Contractor] shall not undertake any engagement or activity which is liable to detract from its ability to render its services hereunder or impair its efficiency to do so or which would conflict with or be detrimental to the interests and operation of the [Company].

E.241

[Name] will perform the role and exercise the powers and functions which may be reasonably given to him/her by the [Company]. [Name] undertakes that he/she will not enter into any agreement or perform any act or do anything which may derogate from or interfere with the [Company's] exercise or use of the rights granted pursuant to this Agreement.

E.242

'Exclusive Licence' in respect of copyright works shall mean a licence in writing signed by or on behalf of the [Copyright Owner] authorising the [Licensee] to the exclusion of all other persons including the person granting the Licence to exercise a right which would be exercisable exclusively by the [Copyright Owner]. The parties accept that the [Licensee] under an exclusive Licence has the same rights against a successor in title who is bound by the Licence as he/she has against the person granting the Licence [under the Copyright, Designs and Patents Act 1988 as amended].

E.243

'Exclusive Licence' shall [be defined in accordance with the Copyright, Designs and Patents Act 1988 as amended in respect of dealings with design right] and shall mean a licence in writing signed by or on behalf of the [Design Right Owner] authorising the [Licensee] to the exclusion of all other persons including the person granting the Licence to exercise a right which would otherwise be exercisable exclusively by the [Design Right Owner].

E.244

This Agreement shall take effect to grant to the [Company] the exclusive rights to do all the acts authorised under Clause [–] to the exclusion of all others for the Term of the Agreement.

E.245

During the period of this Agreement and with immediate effect the [Company] hereby warrants that the [Company] will not grant access to the [Material/Work/Services] to any third party. Neither will the [Company] exercise or authorise the use or exploitation by any third party of the rights granted exclusively to the [Licensee].

E.246

The [Company] warrants and undertakes to the [Distributor] that it has not and will not grant to any third party any rights, licences, permissions or authorisations which will or might conflict with or derogate from the rights granted to the [Distributor] under this Agreement.

E.247

[Name] reserves all rights not specifically [granted/assigned] under this Agreement.

E.248

'A Non-Exclusive Licence' shall mean a licence in writing in respect of copyright works signed by or on behalf of the [Copyright Owner] which grants the [Licensee] the right to exercise a non-exclusive right. The [Copyright Owner] can also grant this right to as many other third parties as it decides without any regard to the [Licensee].

E.249

The [Company] reserves the right to use any third party that it shall decide may be required to change, develop, improve, add to, maintain, repair, and/or for any other reason. Both parties agree that the exclusivity of this Agreement shall not prevent, restrict and/or prohibit the [Company] from exercising this right and the [Enterprise] agrees to cooperate and assist such third party as may be required by the [Company].

E.250

No authority, licence and/or consent is given and/or granted (either directly and/or implied) by the supply of and/or access to any material provided by the [Company]. You have no right of any nature to copy, reproduce, distribute and/or otherwise replicate and/or adapt any part of any material for any reason.

E.251

[Name] grants the [Company] the sole and exclusive rights to market, promote and exploit the [Event] on [date] at [location]. Such an exclusive arrangement shall be for a fixed period of [number] months starting on [date]. Provided that [Name] receives and is paid [number] per cent of all gross sums which are received by and/or accrued by the [Company] at any time without the deduction of any expenses, costs, discounts and/or any other sums incurred by the [Company]. The [Company] agrees that it shall have no rights and/or other interest and/or claim to any part of the [Event] and/or its name, image, logo and/or any sums received after [date].

Internet and Websites

E.252

I am the sole author and copyright owner of [Work/title/length/reference]. I consent to the following extract of my Work being used and displayed as follows [specify length/name and address of business/domain name/exact use]. The consent is to be for a minimum period of [three months] and is subject to withdrawal at any time thereafter by notice in writing or email to the [Company]. The fee to be paid shall be [figure/currency] for each period of [three months] payable in advance.

E.253

The [Company] shall not authorise, permit, allow or encourage others to reproduce or display the [Work] on other websites or in any other format in any medium without the prior written consent of [Name].

E.254

The [Company] recognises that there is no exclusivity over the [Work] submitted to the [Website] by [Name] and that no rights have been granted except to display the [Work] in full without deletions, editing or additions with the full title and the copyright notice to [Name]. There is no right to reproduce the [Work] elsewhere for any purpose, or to authorise or licence others to do so whether for educational, promotional, review, non-commercial or commercial reasons at any time.

E.255

The parties agree as follows:

1.1   [Name] grants the [Company] the sole and exclusive right to display the [Material/Work] on the [Website] known as [specify] [reference] owned and controlled by the [Company] trading under the name of [specify] from [date] to [date].

1.2   The [Company] shall be entitled to authorise users of the [Website] to view the [Material], but not to make copies or to reproduce or exploit the [Material].

1.3   [Name] shall not from [date] to [date] authorise, permit, license or agree that any other person, company or organisation may display the [Material] on their website, on the internet or download the [Material] to a television, telephone, gadget or other machine, article or receiving device.

1.4   The [Company] shall be liable to [Name] for the actions of any user of the [Website] who may reproduce, distribute or supply the [Material] elsewhere or in another format at any time.

E.256

In consideration of the Licence Fee the [Licensor] grants to [Company] the non-exclusive Internet Rights in the [Work] for the duration of the Licence Period throughout the Territory for exploitation on the [Company's] Website and to make copies for security purposes.

E.257

1.1   The [Copyright Owner] grants the [Company] the non-exclusive right to include and display the [Text/Image] on the [Website] in the following format and manner [specify].

1.2   The [Company] shall have the right to display the [Text/Image] on the [Website] for the purpose of viewing by the public over the internet and/or supplied over any telecommunication system, and/or accessed by any television, mobile, or other gadget in any part of the world from [date] until [date].

1.3   The [Company] shall not have the right to authorise and/or facilitate the [Text/Image] on the [Website] to be downloaded, stored, and/or retrieved.

1.4   The [Company] shall not have the right to sub-licence the [Text/Image] to any third party at any time nor to authorise any adaptation, merchandising and/or endorsement.

E.258

All other rights are retained by the [Copyright Owner]. The [Copyright Owner] shall be entitled to grant another licence on any terms in respect of the [Text/Image] to any other website and/or third party whether or not it is a competing business.

E.259

1.1   In consideration of the payment of [figure/currency] by [date]. The [Author] grants a non-exclusive licence for the [Music/Lyrics] and the Sound Recordings to the [Company] to use for a banner advertisement for the [Company] on the [Website] on the internet in any part of the world from [date] until [date].

1.2   The [Company] shall only be entitled edit the [Music/Lyrics] and the Sound Recordings and shall not be entitled to add any new material without the prior written consent of the [Author].

1.3   All other rights are reserved. No right is granted to make advertisement for television and/or radio and/or to grants any rights to third parties at any time. Nor is there any right to substitute another person for the [Music/Lyrics] and the Sound Recordings and/or to make any translation.

E.260

In consideration of the [Fee] the [Author/Company] grants the [Distributor] the sole and exclusive right to reproduce, display and exploit the product of the services under this Agreement summarised in Appendix [–] which may be created and/or developed and/or delivered which are owned by the [Author/Company] in all media and in any format throughout the world, on land, sea and in the sky and into outer space and any other planets including, but not limited to, on any website, over the internet, downloads, mobiles, DVDs, discs, television, radio, theatre, merchandising and publishing.

E.261

Clause [–] shall include the right to authorise a third party to exercise such rights and/or to adapt, edit and/or translate the [Work]. No sub-licence shall extend beyond the period of the original grant of rights by the [Copyright Owner].

E.262

[Name] provides a non-exclusive agreement for the [Distributor] to market, promote and sell their [Products/Articles] in their stores, catalogue and on line at their website [specify]. [Name] agrees that the [Distributor] shall be supplied with the [Products/Articles] on loan by [Name] and that the [Distributor] shall hold the [Products/Articles] on behalf of [Name]. That no ownership and/or risk shall pass until the [Distributor] has received funds from the [Client] and paid [Name] all the sums received less a commission of [number] per cent.

E.263

1.1   The [Designer] grants the [Company] an exclusive licence to display, reproduce, supply, adapt and exploit in all media and medium of any nature from [date] to [date] the image and logo and the three dimensional copy in Schedule [–] which forms part of this Agreement.

1.2   The [Designer] agrees that both the [Designer] and the [Company] shall be registered as holding a joint and equal interest in respect of the image and logo and the three dimensional copy in Schedule [–] which forms part of this Agreement. Provided that the [Company] shall pay all costs and expenses of any applications and registration fees and charges.

Merchandising

E.264

In consideration of the [Agent's Commission] the [Agent] agrees to provide his/her non-exclusive services to the [Licensor] for the Licence Period throughout [countries].

E.265

In consideration of the Net Receipts the [Licensor] agrees to engage the non-exclusive services of the [Agent] for the Licence Period throughout the [countries] and grants the [Agent] the non-exclusive right to negotiate agreements for the manufacture, distribution and sale of the [Licensed Articles] and the associated trademark or logo.

The [Agent] agrees that he/she shall not be permitted or authorised to commit the [Licensor] or to sign, authorise or provide consent to any third party on behalf of the [Licensor]. That all licences must be in writing and may only be signed and authorised by the [Licensor]. That the [Licensor] shall have the right to refuse to conclude any agreement at its sole discretion.

E.266
The [Company] agrees that after [date] and/or the expiry and/or termination of this Agreement, whichever is the earlier, the [Company] shall not be entitled to exploit the [Licensed Articles] and shall have no right or interest.

E.267

1.1 In consideration of the [Agent's Commission] the [Agent] agrees to provide his non-exclusive services to the [Licensor] for the Term of the Agreement throughout the Territory.

1.2 In consideration of the Net Receipts the [Licensor] engages the exclusive services of the [Agent] for the Term of the Agreement throughout the Territory and grants to the [Agent] the sole and exclusive right to instigate and negotiate agreements for the production, manufacture, distribution, sale and supply of the [Licensed Articles] for the Term of the Agreement throughout the Territory.

E.268
In consideration of the Non-Returnable Advance and the Licensor's Royalties the [Licensor] grants to the [Company] the sole and exclusive right to develop, produce, manufacture, distribute, supply, and sell the [Licensed Articles] based on the Prototype throughout the Territory for the duration of the Licence Period.

E.269
The [Company] shall also be entitled to appoint third parties as sub-agents to distribute, supply and sell the [Licensed Articles] provided that they comply with the terms of this Agreement, but the [Company] shall not be entitled to appoint any other as manufacturer except [specify].

E.270
The [Licensor] undertakes that it will not license, permit or grant any third party to produce, manufacture, supply, reproduce, distribute, adapt or translate the [Board Game] or the Prototype including any developments or variations throughout the Territory for the duration of the Licence Period.

E.271
The [Designer] undertakes that he will not license or grant any right to any third party to produce, make, manufacture, copy, supply, or distribute the [Designs] or the [Licensed Articles] or any development or variation thereof

throughout the Territory during the Licence Period [and until the expiry of a period [1] (one) year from the end of the Licence Period].

E.272

The [Company] grants the [Distributor] a non-exclusive licence to reproduce the [Trade Mark/Logo] on all copies of the packaging for the [Products] and associated advertising which are approved by the [Company] for the [specify] campaign. The [Distributor] shall be entitled to sell, supply, distribute and promote the [Products] with the [Trade Mark/Logo] on all copies of the packaging in [country] from [date] to [date].

E.273

No right is granted by the [Company] to authorise and/or use the [Trade Mark/Logo] in any other manner and/or by any third party. No right to register any version of the [Trade Mark/Logo] are granted to and/or acquired by the Distributor] and all rights are retained by the [Company]. Where any new material is created and/or developed the [Distributor] agrees and undertakes that any such rights shall be assigned to the [Company] the [Trade Mark/Logo] on all copies of the packaging.

E.274

In consideration of the Advance and the [Royalties/Unit Payments] the [Author] grants to the [Company] the sole and exclusive right to reproduce, supply and sell a toy product in the form of a [specify] based on the character called [name] from the [Book/Film] entitled [specify]. The licence shall be exclusive from [date] to [date] and thereafter the licence shall be non-exclusive until expiry on [date]. The licence shall be for the Territory.

E.275

The licence granted in respect of the [Articles] by [Name] does not entitle the [Company] to use, exploit, register and/or market the name, logo and brand of [Name] in conjunction with the [Articles] at any time.

E.276

1.1 The [Distributor] grants the non-exclusive licence to the [Supplier] to create, develop, reproduce, supply, sell and distribute a [specify] [toy/book/product] based on the character [specify] with the name [specify] from the [Programme] subject to the approval of the sample prior to manufacture.

1.2 The licence shall commence on the date of this Agreement and continue until [date].

1.3 The licence is limited to the following countries and languages [specify]

1.4 The licence will only start if the [Fee] has been paid to the [Distributor] and the [Supplier] continues to pay the sums due and provides regular accounts, statements and payments as set out in clauses [–].

1.5 At the end of the licence period all rights granted shall revert to the [Distributor] and all production, reproduction and exploitation in any form shall cease and all remaining stock shall be destroyed by the [Supplier].

Publishing

E.277
In consideration of the Author's Royalties and the Advance Royalty Payment(s) the [Author] grants to the [Publisher] the sole and exclusive right to publish and exploit the [Work] and any parts in All Media throughout the Territory for the duration of the Licence Period.

E.278
The [Author] confirms that the [Work] has not been previously licensed to any third party and has not been exploited in any form at any time throughout the Territory.

E.279
In consideration of the fee [Name] agrees to be [exclusively] interviewed by the [Journalist] on behalf of the [Publisher] for the purpose of the [Journalist] preparing and writing the [Article] to be published in the [Periodical] on the publication dates throughout the Territory.

E.280
[Name] agrees that from [date] until [date] she will not give any interviews or information to the media including, but not limited to, newspapers, magazines, television, radio, news agencies, telephone companies and/or their agents or grant permission for or consent to the reproduction, supply or distribution of the [photographs/other] by any third party in [country].

E.281
The [Publisher] and [Journalist] acknowledge that after [date] [Name] shall be entitled to divulge the same or similar information provided under this Agreement to any third party.

E.282
The [Journalist] and the [Publisher] agree that they shall not be entitled to exploit in any media the Article, any recordings or notes and/or the photographs and/or images for any purpose other than for publication in

the [Periodical] on the publication dates without the prior written consent of [Name]. In such event [Name] shall be entitled to receive such additional sums as may be agreed between the parties.

E.283

In consideration of the Author's Royalties and the Advance Royalty Payment the [Author] grants to the [Publisher] the sole and exclusive right to publish and exploit the [Work] and any parts in all media including, but not limited to, all methods of publication and reproduction including hardback, paperback, serialisation, translations, anthologies, quotations, mechanical reproduction, radio, theatre, film, television, telephone, games and merchandising throughout the Territory for the duration of the Licence Period.

E.284

The [Author] acknowledges that the [Publisher] shall be entitled to permit Braille and charitable recordings to be made of the [Work] for the sole use of the blind and handicapped free of charge during the Licence Period.

E.285

In consideration of the fee the [Ghostwriter] agrees to provide his non-exclusive services to the [Company] for the Term of the Agreement to write, research and produce the [Work] in accordance with the terms of this Agreement.

E.286

The [Originator] agrees to engage the services of the [Writer] to write, research and produce the [Work] for the Term of the Agreement in accordance with the terms of this Agreement.

E.287

The [Originator] agrees not to engage or enter into any agreement with any third party to write, research or produce any other book or publication based on the synopsis or any development or variation at any time during the Term of the Agreement throughout the Territory.

E.288

The [Author] undertakes that during the continuance of this Agreement he/she have not and will not, other than for the [Publisher], authorise publication or reproduction of the [Work] or any expansion or abridgement or part [in Volume Form] in the [Publisher's] exclusive Territory nor shall the [Author] prepare anything of a nature which is likely to affect prejudicially the sales of the [Publisher] in respect of the [Work].

E.289

The [Licensor] agrees that for the duration of the Licence Period the [Licensor] shall not directly or indirectly license, sub-license, authorise, promote, distribute or make available the [Work] or any parts or any adaptation, translation, development or variation in any of the following rights [specify] within the Territory during the Licence Period to any other third party.

E.290

That the [Licensor] has not granted any licence or other authorisation to any third party to make the [Work] in whole or part available over the [internet or any website], to be downloaded, stored, retrieved or supplied over any telecommunication system, or to any television, radio, telephone, or any other machine, gadget or reception, delivery system or otherwise.

E.291

The [Author] reserves and the [Publisher] shall not have the right to:

1.1 Appoint, employ or engage any third party to contribute in any form to the [Work] or any adaptation or development without the prior written approval of the [Author].

1.2 To publish, supply and distribute the [Work] in any form except as a separate book and it shall not be packaged, combined with or added together with any other article, work or book.

1.3 To use the [Work] in any form to endorse, promote or sponsor any event, article, item, book, person or other matter.

E.292

1.1 The [Author] grants the [Publisher] the sole and exclusive right to publish, distribute and supply the [Work] in [hardback/paperback] in country from [date to [date] using the following printer [specify].

1.2 All other rights are specifically not granted and are retained by the [Author].

1.3 The [Company] shall be entitled to market, sell and promote the [Work] on their Website reference [specify]. The company shall not have the right to supply to or appoint another internet or website company to sell and distribute the [Work].

E.293

In consideration of the [Fee] the [Author] grants the [Company/Name] the non-exclusive right to reproduce [number] copies of [number] pages of the [Work] in printed form on paper by means of photocopying in [country] during the period from [date] to [date]. The [Company/Name] agrees and undertakes that the correct copyright notice and title shall be on the front of all copies together with the words 'All rights reserved. No right to copy and/ or reproduce in any form.'

E.294

In consideration of the [Fee] the [Author] grants the [Company/Name] the non-exclusive right to scan [number] copies of [number] pages of the [Work] onto the hard drive of the computer temporarily and to supply and distribute by means of an email attachment the same material to [number] persons over the internet during the licence period from [date] to the completion of the task but no late than [date]. The [Company/Name] agrees and undertakes to ensure that the correct copyright notice and title shall be on the front of all copies in any email attachment together with the words 'All rights reserved. No permission is granted to store permanently on your hard drive and/or to supply copies to others. Please print only one copy.'

E.295

In consideration of the [Fee] the [Company] grants the [Publisher] the exclusive rights to the [Image/Photograph] for the [Magazine/Book] cover and any associated website, advertising and marketing from [date] to [date]. The [Publisher] shall not have the right to sub-licence and/or assign the rights to any third party. The [Publisher] shall at all times acknowledge the copyright ownership of the [Company] as follows [specify] and credit the photographer as follows [specify] in respect of all copies of the [Image/ Photograph] in a prominent position on the edge of the [Image/Photograph].

E.296

1.1 In consideration of the [Fee] the [Author] grants the [Publisher/ Distributor] the non-exclusive licence to use [number] words on pages [specify] as a quote from the [Work] reference ISBN [specify] to be included in the Book entitled [specify] in the [specify] language which is to be sold in printed form in hardback, paperback and as an audio disc throughout the [world/Territory] from [date] until the expiry of a period of [number] years.

1.2 All other rights are reserved by the [Author] and no rights are granted to sub-licence, and/or assign the extract from the [Work] and/or to exploit the [Work] in any other media at any time. Nor is any right granted to register any right and/or interest in any part of the [Work] and/or the title and/or any character.

E.297

1.1 In consideration of the payment of the Licence Fee the [Licensor] grants to the [Licensee] the non-exclusive right to reproduce the [Licensors'] Logo on each copy of the [Product] and any associated packaging, marketing and advertising in accordance with Schedule [–] throughout the Territory for the duration of the Licence Period.

1.2 The [Licensee] agrees and undertakes to ensure that on all copies of the [Licensors'] Logo which are reproduced shall appear the words. 'The trade mark is reproduced under licence from [Licensor] and is the registered trade mark of [Licensor].'

E.298

In consideration of payments per [Unit] the [Author] grants to the [Company] the non-exclusive right to reproduce, supply, sell and distribute copies of the [Work] and/or part as part of a documentary delivery service whether over the internet by means of scanning and an email attachment, by fax and/or by post and/or some other delivery method. The [Author] acknowledges that copies may be stored, and retrieved by the [Company] and/or any third party by means of a hard drive on a computer and/or any other gadget and may make one and/or more copies. This licence shall apply throughout the world and shall commence on [date] and expire on [date].

E.299

1.1 In consideration of the sum of [number/currency] [Name] grants an exclusive licence to the [Distributor] for the reproduction, distribution and exploitation of his/her [Article/Project] in whole and/or in part on one and/or more of the websites owned and/or controlled by the [Distributor] and/or any sub-licensee, sub-distributor and/or other third party in any country of the world and in any medium at any time.

1.2 This licence in 1.1 shall include the right to reproduce the [Article/ Project] in hardback and paperback form, and/or as part of another work with other contributors and/or as an electronic and/or ebook and/ or to adapt the contents for radio, television and/or film and/or to create any translation and/or subtitled work.

E.300

The [Title] and [Slogan] and [Image] are owned by [Name] and no licence is granted to use, adapt, register and/or exploit the [Title] [Slogan] and/ or [Image] except in the form of a book cover and online marketing and promotion directly related to the work of [Name].

Purchase and Supply of Products

E.301

The [Supplier] agrees to deliver the [Product] to the [Seller] for sale on the [Seller's] website on a non-exclusive basis for the duration of this Agreement in consideration of the payments to be made hereunder.

E.302

That the [Supplier] has not entered into and shall not enter into an agreement with any of the following [companies/website owners/other].

E.303

The [Seller] agrees:

1.1 That the [Product] will only be sold from the [Seller's] website and not from any other unless agreed in advance.

1.2 That the [Seller] has fully disclosed and shall continue to disclose details of any links to other sites.

1.3 That no other product, advertisement, sponsorship, banner or icon shall be displayed or featured on the website where there is a direct conflict of interest with any product supplied under this Agreement and in particular the following products [–].

E.304

The [Company] agrees to appoint the [Distributor] as the sole and exclusive supplier of [Product] and any other products in the category of [specify] to the [Company] from [date] to [date].

E.305

This clause shall not apply to any parent, subsidiary, affiliated or associated company of the [Group].

E.306

This Agreement shall only apply to the following countries [–], formats [–] websites [–].

E.307

The [Distributor] shall not be entitled to authorise and/or supply the master material of the [Products] to another manufacturer at any time during the term of this Agreement unless the prior written approval of [Name] has been provided in advance.

E.308

The exclusive licence shall cease with immediate effect in the event that the [Distributor] should fail at any time during the term of this Agreement to pay the royalties by the due date. No delay, error, omission and/or other reason including force majeure shall be considered relevant criteria for such failure.

Services

E.309

1.1 In consideration of the [Agent's] Commission the [Agent] agrees to provide his non-exclusive services to the [Author] as Literary Agent for the [Work] for the Term of the Agreement throughout the Territory.

1.2 In consideration of the Net Receipts the [Author] agrees to engage the exclusive services of the [Agent] as Literary Agent for the [Work] for the Term of the Agreement for the purpose of the commercial exploitation of the [Work] in all media.

1.3 The [Agent] confirms that the [Author] shall have the final decision to conclude and sign any agreement, contract or other document relating to the exploitation of the [Work] and that no authority is granted under this Agreement for the [Agent] to sign on behalf of the [Author].

1.4 The [Agent] acknowledges that this Agreement related solely to the [Work] and that the [Agent] is not entitled to exploit any other material including any books created by the [Author] without the prior written consent of the [Author] and the conclusion of a further agreement.

E.310

It is expressly agreed between the parties hereto that this Agreement shall be exclusive to the Agent for the duration of the Term of this Agreement throughout the [United Kingdom and Northern Ireland] but non-exclusive for all other territories throughout the world.

E.311

The [Artist] agrees that the [Manager] shall have the sole and exclusive right to represent the [Artist] throughout the Territory for the Term of the Agreement only in respect of those activities specified under Schedule [–] to this Agreement.

E.312

The [Artist] agrees that the [Manager] shall have the non-exclusive right to represent the [Artist] throughout the Territory for the Term of the Agreement in respect of the product of the [Artist's] services in the field of [acting/

filming/advertisements] but not [writing/singing/dancing/painting/computer-generated material/music/other].

E.313

The [Artist] agrees that the [Manager] shall have the sole and exclusive right to represent the [Artist] throughout the Territory for the Term of the Agreement and thereafter on a non-exclusive basis unless otherwise agreed between the parties in writing.

E.314

1.1 In consideration of the [Agent's Commission] the [Agent] agrees to provide his/her non-exclusive services to the [Artist] for the Term of the Agreement throughout [country].

1.2 In consideration of the Net Receipts the [Artist] engages the exclusive services of the [Agent] for the Term of the Agreement throughout the Territory to engage and commercially exploit the [Artist] their name, image, services and work in all media including, but not limited to, all forms of sound, vision, interactive, image, text, icons, film, video, DVD, television, radio, theatre, telephones, merchandising, publishing, biography, endorsements, advertising, commercials, promotional work and on the internet and websites.

1.3 The [Agent] agrees that any form of exploitation of the [Artist's] services, name or work shall require the prior consent of the [Artist]. The [Artist] shall be entitled to refuse to agree to any work or to carry it out or for the use of his/her name for any reason and the [Agent] shall not be entitled to seek any compensation, loss or damages or otherwise which arises from the failure of the [Artist] to provide consent and/or provide his/her services.

E.315

1.1 In consideration of the [Guaranteed Fees] and the [Group's Fees] the [Group] agrees to engage the services of the [Manager] and the [Group] shall provide its exclusive services to the Manager for the Term of the Agreement throughout the Territory.

1.2 In consideration of the [Manager's Commission] the [Manager] agrees to provide his [non-]exclusive services to the [Group] for the Term of the Agreement throughout the Territory.

E.316

The [Company] agrees to appoint the [Promoter] as the sole and exclusive agent to market, advertise and promote the [Product] on behalf of the [Company] throughout the [country] from [date] until [date].

E.317

The [Company] agrees to engage the non-exclusive services of the [Name] on an hourly basis and to pay the [Name] the fee in accordance with this Agreement.

E.318

1.1   The [Company] agrees to engage the services of the [Contributor] throughout the Engagement Period and to pay the Basic Fee, the Expenses and the Bonus Fee in accordance with this Agreement.

1.2   The [Contributor] agrees that for the duration of the Engagement Period the [Contributor] agrees to provide his/her professional services exclusively to the [Company] and not to any other website or online service on the worldwide web, text messaging or any landline or mobile service.

1.3   The [Company] acknowledges that the [Contributor] shall be permitted to offer his/her services in any other media not specified in 1.2 above during the Engagement Period to third parties. Where for reasons beyond the control of the [Contributor] such material should appear on the worldwide web the [Contributor] shall not be held to be in breach or liable in any manner under this Agreement.

E.319

In consideration of the Promotion Fee and the Promotion Expenses the [Promoter] agrees to provide its non-exclusive services to the [Company] to act as agent to promote, market and advertise the [Company] and the [Services/Products] throughout the [country] for the duration of this Agreement. The [Promoter] agrees that the principal aim and objective of its services to the [Company] shall be to: promote and increase the sale of the [Company's] [Services/Products]; to increase the public profile of the [Company] and to improve the consumer image of the [Company].

E.320

The [Promoter] confirms that this Agreement shall not cause any conflict of interest with any of its existing clients and undertakes not to enter into any agreement with any third party during the Term of this Agreement which would conflict with or be prejudicial to the interests of the [Company], and/or whose products or services compete directly or indirectly with the [Company] and/or whose consumer image or reputation could be harmful to, damage or cause loss to the [Company].

E.321

The [Company] and the [Presenter] agree that in consideration of the Presenter's Fee and the Presenter's Royalties the [Presenter] shall provide

699

his exclusive services as principal presenter for the [specify] and provide such other contributions as specified under this Agreement for the Term of the Engagement.

E.322

The [Presenter] agrees to provide the following exclusive services to the [Company]:

1.1 To attend at such times, dates, locations and premises in [location/country] as the [Company] may reasonably require subject to sufficient prior notice which shall not be less than [specify period of notice].

1.2 To comply with all rules in force at such locations.

1.3 To observe all reasonable directions given by [specify person] on behalf of the [Company].

1.4 To assist in such background research as may be required.

1.5 To be available for the post-production, synchronisation, editing, dubbing or promotional work which may be necessary for a period of [specify period] maximum of [specify length of time] and thereafter upon agreement in respect of an additional fee.

E.323

1.1 The [Company] and the [Presenter] agree that in consideration of the [Presenter's] Fee the [Presenter] shall provide his/her exclusive services to the [Company] as presenter of the [Series] and provide such other contributions as may reasonably be required by the [Company] in respect of recordings, films, photographs, appearances, meetings and other work directly related to presenting and promoting the [Series] for the Term of the Agreement throughout the Territory.

1.2 The [Presenter] agrees not to provide his/her services for any other [television/radio/telephone/internet and website/publisher/other] whether educational, non-commercial or commercial business and specifically not [–] during the Term of this Agreement without the prior written consent of the [Company].

E.324

The [Company] hereby engages and the [Lender] agrees to make available the freelance non-exclusive services of [Name] on first call to the Company or any associated company in the capacity of [Position] as and when required by the [Company] for a period of [one year] from [date].

E.325

[Name] shall be free to provide his services to other companies in the [media/technical/other] industry in the [United Kingdom/country/area] subject to obtaining prior confirmation from the [Company] that its interests are not prejudiced thereby [such confirmation not to be reasonably withheld or delayed].

E.326

The [Company] agrees to engage the services of the [Artist] to be the principal person to promote and advertise the [Company's] products in all advertisements for television, radio, newspapers and magazines, promotional films, and events for the Term of the Agreement throughout the Territory.

E.327

The [Presenter] undertakes to the [Company] that during the continuance of this Agreement the [Company] shall be entitled to the exclusive services of the [Presenter] in respect of radio and television journalism in the [United Kingdom/country/area]. The [Presenter] shall not during such period without the previous written consent of the [Company] either directly or indirectly:

1.1 Contribute in any way to news and current affairs television in any form (including closed circuit television and/or pay television) or radio by any method in [specify country/area] for any party other than the [Company] or be associated in any capacity whatsoever with any radio or television organisation other than the [Company].

1.2 Undertake any activity which associates or is liable to associate the [Presenter] in any way with commercial advertising on television or radio in [specify country/area] nor permit himself/herself to be so associated.

E.328

1.1 In consideration of the [Agent's Commission] the [Agent] agrees to provide his non-exclusive services to the [Artiste] for the Term of the Agreement throughout the Territory.

1.2 In consideration of the Net Receipts the [Artiste] agrees to engage the exclusive services of the [Agent] for the Term of the Agreement throughout the Territory in all media including television, radio, videos, DVDs, CD-Roms, film, newspapers and periodicals, books, CDs, tapes, merchandising, public appearances and any other commercial exploitation of the [Artiste] under this Agreement.

E.329

The [Agent] acknowledges that he/she shall not be entitled to negotiate or promote in any manner or form the commercial interests of the [Artiste] outside the Territory unless specifically agreed in advance with the [Artiste].

E.330

The [Actor] agrees that the [Agent] shall be his exclusive agent in respect of all work in respect of appearances and performances in satellite, cable, digital and standard television programmes, theatre, national and local radio, commercials on radio and television, feature films, corporate and educational DVDs, voice-overs, and merchandising for the Term of the Agreement throughout the Territory.

E.331

The [Agent] agrees and undertakes that this Agreement does not give any rights or permit the [Agent] to act on behalf of or commit the [Actor] in any of the following areas: any image rights, and any registration and exploitation of the name or signature of the [Actor], biography, publishing, internet and website material, music, sponsorship, endorsements or agreements for images, text or promoting telephone or telecommunication systems.]

E.332

The [Company] and the [Name] agree the following terms:

1.1 The [Company] agrees to engage [Name] for the purpose of providing his non-exclusive services to the [Company] throughout the Territory for the Term of this Agreement in accordance with the Work Plan and Schedule.

1.2 In consideration of the Fee and Expenses the [Name] agrees to provide his non-exclusive services to the [Company] throughout the Territory for the Term of the Agreement as set out in the Work Plan and Schedule.

1.3 That any material arising from the services of [Name] shall only be used by the [Company] for the following specific purposes [–]. In the event that the [Company] wishes to use the material for any other purpose then the prior consent of [Name] shall be required together with an additional payment to be agreed between the parties.

E.333

The [Company] acknowledges that the [Originator] shall be entitled to exploit any material created by the [Originator] under this Agreement provided that all references to and any confidential information and material provided by the [Company] are deleted.

E.334

The [Company] acknowledges that the [Originator] is already committed and entitled to carry out the following work for third parties during the Term of the Agreement [specify parties and work].

E.335

In consideration of the Fee and Repeat Fees the [Artist] agrees to provide his non-exclusive services to the [Company] to promote and advertise the [Company's] Products by personal appearances, performances, voice-overs, for advertisements, for television, radio, newspapers, magazines, promotional films and events in accordance with the Work Schedule attached to this Agreement and on such other occasions as may be agreed for the Term of this Agreement throughout the Territory.

E.336

The [Artist] agrees not to promote or advertise or otherwise endorse any commercial product or service of any type whether it competes with the [Company's] Product or not throughout the Term of the Agreement without the prior written consent of the [Company] except for those contributions of an entirely charitable purpose.

E.337

1.1 The [Company] and the [Director] agree that in consideration of the [Director's] Fee the [Director] shall provide his exclusive services as Director and such other contributions as specified under this Agreement in respect of the [Film] for the Production Period.

1.2 The [Director] agrees to provide his exclusive services to the [Company] as the [title] for the Production Period, and in accordance with the Production Schedule and to assist in such other matters including script revisions and pre-shooting arrangements as may be required for the completion of the [Film].

E.338

1.1 In consideration of the [Manager's Commission] the [Manager] agrees to provide his non-exclusive services to the [Sportsperson] to act as agent and manager in all media for the Term of the Agreement throughout the Territory.

1.2 In consideration of the [Sportsperson's Fees] the [Sportsperson] agrees to engage the exclusive services of the [Manager] for the Term of the Agreement throughout the Territory in all media including radio, television, DVD, magazines and newspapers, public and professional appearances, sponsorship, promotions, endorsements and any other exploitation of the [Sportsperson], his name and image.

1.3 The [Sportsperson] agrees to refer all requests for his services and any rights or consents to the [Manager] and agrees that the [Manager] shall have the sole and exclusive right to negotiate with third parties for the commercial services (but not the sports appearances) of the [Sportsperson] during the Term of this Agreement.

E.339

1.1 The [Company] agrees that [Name] shall be the sole and exclusive personality to be engaged by the [Company] for the Term of this Agreement in the Territory to endorse, promote and advertise the [Company's Products].

1.2 In consideration of the Fee, [the Repeat Fees and the Expenses and the Products], [Name] agrees to provide his/her exclusive services to the [Company] to endorse, promote and advertise the [Company's Products] by personal appearances, performances, recordings, films, images, photographs, text messages or otherwise of material of or associated with the [Name] for advertisements and promotions in all media in accordance with the Work Schedule and on such other occasions as may be agreed for the Term of the Agreement in [country] in accordance with the terms of this Agreement.

1.3 [Name] undertakes not to provide his/her services to any third party for the endorsement, advertisement or promotion of any other product or service of any type whether it directly competes with the [Company's Product] or not without the prior written consent of the [Company] except in the following services or work to which there is a prior commitment [specify].

E.340

'Exclusive Recording Contract' shall [be defined in accordance with the Copyright Designs and Patents Act 1988 as amended] and shall mean a contract between a performer and another person under which that person is entitled to the exclusion of all other persons (including the performer) to make recordings of one or more of his/her performances with a view to their commercial exploitation namely with a view to the recordings being sold or let for hire or shown or played in public.

E.341

1.1 The [Company] agrees to engage the non-exclusive services of the [Consultant] promote, market and advertise the [Company] and the

[Website] throughout the Territory for the Term of this Agreement in accordance with Marketing and Advertising Strategy Plan in Appendix [–].

1.2   In consideration of the Fee and Expenses the [Consultant] agrees and undertakes to provide his/her non-exclusive services to the [Company] throughout the Territory for the Term of the Agreement in accordance with Marketing and Advertising Strategy Plan in Appendix [–].

1.3   The [Consultant] agrees and undertakes not to provide any services and/or to work for the following companies during the Term of this Agreement [specify companies].

E.342

The [Consortium] agrees that the [Consultant] may provide his/her services to any third party during the term of this Agreement including the competitors of any members of the [Consortium].

E.343

The [Agent] agrees and undertakes that he/she shall not engage any person as a client for his/her agency whose political and/or personal life would conflict with and/or create problems by association through the agency with the reputation of [Name]. That in such event then [Name] shall have the right to terminate the Agreement and provide [number] months notice. That thereafter the [Agent] shall have no right to any sums derived from the work, services and/or exploitation of any copyright and/or intellectual property rights and/or trademarks owned and/or controlled by [Name] in any form at any time.

Purchase and Supply of Products

E.344

In consideration of the Agent's Fee the [Agent] agrees to provide its non-exclusive services to the [Company] for the Term of the Agreement throughout the Territory for the purpose of promoting, marketing and obtaining orders for the purchase of the [Goods] from retail stores and other trade outlets.

E.345

The [Company] shall be the sole and exclusive agent and representative for [Name] for the [Work/Product/Service] for the zone specified as [area detail] a copy of which is reproduced on the map which is attached to and forms part of this Agreement. The period of exclusivity shall start on [date] and end on [date]. Thereafter the [Company] shall only act on a non-exclusive until [date].

E.346

The [Company] agrees that it does not have any exclusive rights to the [Product] and undertakes not to represent in any marketing, advertising and/or on its website that it has any sort of exclusive arrangement with [Name].

E.347

The [Supplier] acknowledges and agrees that the [Company] shall have the right to use and/or engage any other person and/or business that it thinks fit to work on the [Project] and/or with the [Supplier] and/or to maintain, repair and/or develop the equipment.

E.348

No appointment of any supplier, distributor and/or any other third party by the [Company] is on an exclusive basis and all agreements are non-exclusive and for a maximum period of [one] [day/month/year] at any time. The [Company] reserves the right to use whoever they think fit dependent on the circumstances and to cancel, terminate and alter the terms and conditions.

Sponsorship

E.349

In consideration of the [Sponsorship Fee] and the Performance Related Fee the [Sportsperson] agrees to provide his/her non-exclusive services to the [Sponsor] to promote and endorse the [Sponsor's Product] for the duration of the Sponsorship Period throughout the Territory in accordance with the terms of this Agreement.

E.350

The [Sponsor] agrees to engage the non-exclusive services of the [Sportsperson] to promote and endorse the [Sponsor's Product] throughout the Territory for the duration of the Sponsorship Period.

E.351

The [Sportsperson] undertakes not to enter into any other sponsorship agreement with any third party concerning the same or similar items in respect of the [Sponsor's Product] namely [–] for the duration of the Sponsorship Period.

E.352

The [Sportsperson] undertakes not to enter an agreement to promote or endorse the products of the following companies for the duration of the Sponsorship Period [–].

706

E.353

The [Sponsor] agrees that it does not have any exclusive rights in respect of the [Event/Programme] and the [Company] shall be entitled to receive and/ or arrange such other forms of funding, endorsement, product placement and sponsorship with any third party it thinks fit. That no consultation with and/or approval by the [Sponsor] is required prior to the conclusion of any agreement.

E.354

The [Company] agrees and undertakes not to enter any arrangement and/or agreement with a third party in respect of the [Event/Programme] which will be detrimental and/or damaging to the reputation of the [Sponsor]. Nor shall the [Company] make arrangements and/or enter into agreements with any organisations, persons and/or third parties whose products, services and/or business are not suitable for [specify market/children].

E.355

The [Company] agrees that the [Sponsor] shall always be ranked first and be prominent in the brochure for the programme, at the [Event], on the website and in any packaging, advertising, marketing and promotional material.

E.356

The [Company] reserves the right to appoint additional sponsors and/or contributors and/or third parties for product placement, advertising and/or promotion and/or include material associated with political campaigns and lobbying in connection with the [Event/Programme/Film].

E.357

Where any other sponsor is to be appointed by the [Company] to either contribute sums and/or products to the [Event/Programme]. Then the [Company] agrees that it shall not include a manufacturer and/or distributor of [articles] in [country].

University, Library and Educational

E.358

The [Company] and the [Contributor/Author/Artist] agree that in consideration of the Fee and Expenses the [Contributor/Author/Artist] shall provide her exclusive services as [specific title/role] for the [Work/Project] from [date] to [date] to carry out the following duties and deliver the following material [specify in detail].

707

E.359

1.1 The [Consultant] agrees and undertakes to provide his non-exclusive services to the [Institute] in respect of the [Project].

1.2 The [Consultant] shall attend at such hours and for such meetings as specified in the Work Schedule [A]. The [Consultant] shall be available at such other times and dates as may be mutually agreed between the parties.

1.3 In the event that the [Consultant] is regularly unavailable to attend meetings and/or respond to the [Institute's] requests. The [Institute] shall have the right to terminate the Agreement with immediate effect by notice in writing to the [Consultant]. In such event no sums shall be due for work which has not been completed and/or delivered prior to the date of termination.

1.4 The [Consultant] shall complete and deliver the documents, reports and assessments specified below to the [Institute] by the relevant dates:

[Name of document]; [Delivery Format/A4 typed] Delivery Date [–]

[Name of report]; [Delivery Format/A4 typed] Delivery Date [–]

E.360
The [Agent/Consultant] agrees and undertakes that this Agreement does not give any rights and/or interests to the [Agent/Consultant] in any intellectual property rights, domain names, patents and/or computer software and/or any material owned and/or controlled by the [Institute]. The [Agent/Consultant] agrees and undertakes not to authorise any exploitation in any media, and/or licence, and/or enter into any contract of any nature whether for rights, goods, and/or services and/or to authorise any work on behalf of the [Institute].

E.361
In consideration of the [Author's] Royalties and the Advance the [Author] grants to the [Institute] the sole and exclusive right to publish and exploit the [Work] and any parts in All Media throughout the Territory for the duration of the Licence Period.

E.362
The [Author] confirms that the [Work] has not been previously licensed to any third party and has not been exploited in any form at any time throughout the Territory.

E.363
In consideration of the Royalties and the Advance the [Author] grants to the [Institute] the sole and exclusive right to print, reproduce, supply, distribute, licence, publish and exploit the [Work] and any parts in all media including, but not limited to, all methods of publication and reproduction including

hardback, paperback, serialisation, translations, anthologies, quotations, mechanical reproduction, radio, theatre, film, terrestrial, cable, satellite and digital television, the internet, worldwide web and downloads, telephones, mobiles and all forms of telecommunication and electronic means and any gadgets and devices, games and merchandising and lottery, gambling, betting, theme parks, advertising and promotional event or material derived from and/or based upon any title, name, character, word or sound or music, words or text whether in existence now and/or created in the future throughout the world and universe for the duration of the full period of copyright and all intellectual property rights and thereafter to continue without an end date and indefinitely.

E.364
The [Contributor] agrees not to enter into any arrangement, and/or agreement with any third party to write, research or produce any other book or publication which is on the same topic and/or has a similar title, subject matter and/or theme before [date].

E.365
All rights not specifically granted to the [Licensee] are reserved and are retained by the [Licensor]. That the [Licensor] has not granted any licence or other authorisation to the [Licensee] and/or any third party to make the [Work] in whole or part available over the [internet or any website], to be downloaded, stored, retrieved or supplied over any telecommunication system, or to any television, radio, telephone, or any other machine, gadget or reception, delivery system or otherwise.

E.366

1.1   The [Institute] grants the [Distributor] the exclusive rights to exploit the [Work] in the following format [specify] in the following countries [list] from [date] to [date].

1.2   The [Distributor] shall not have the right to sub-licence the [Work] to any third party at any time.

1.3   The reproduction, manufacture, distribution and sales of the [Work] must be carried out by the [Distributor] in accordance with the samples, drafts and to the quality agreed and approved with the [Institute].

E.367
The [Author] grants the [Institute] the non-exclusive right to store, retrieve, reproduce and make available the [Report including the copyright notice and credits] to other students of the [Institute] at no charge and to staff and personnel from [date] to [date] in [country]. There is no right granted to supply copies to other third parties and/or to charge any fees for the supply

of a copy except photocopying costs. The [Institute] shall not register and/ or attempt to register an interest as the copyright owner and the [Institute] agrees that the copyright is owned by the [Author].

E.368
The [Institute] agrees that it shall only have exclusive rights to the [Work] from [date] to [date]. After [date] then the [Institute] agrees that any licence granted to it by [Name] shall be non-exclusive and that [Name] may appoint other parties to reproduce and exploit the [Work] in any form.

EXECUTOR

General Business and Commercial

E.369
In the event of the death of the [Author] the following person shall be treated as the literary executor of the work [Name] of [Address].

E.370
In the event of the death of [Name] or a power of attorney being made to another person then all rights, interest, benefits and sums due under this Agreement shall be transferred to the estate or authorised power of attorney of [Name]. The obligations of the [Company] shall continue under the terms of the Agreement.

E.371
Where the [Executor] is unable and/or unwilling due to ill health and/or other personal reasons to administer the [Estate] for [Name]. Then the following person may be substituted to act in their place [specify]. Provided that all the beneficiaries agree and no additional costs are required.

EXPENSES

Employment

E.372
In addition to the remuneration specified under Clause [–] the [Executive] shall be reimbursed by the [Company] for all costs incurred with his/her

duties under this contract including all travelling, hotel and other expenses properly and reasonably incurred by him/her in the discharge of his/her duties and in accordance with the rules and practices of the Company for the time being in force.

E.373

Any credit and charge cards supplied to the [Executive] by the Company shall be returned to the [Company] on leaving the [Company's] employment. Any money paid to the [Executive] to meet expenses incurred on a [Company] credit or charge card shall be used for that purpose and no other. The [Executive] shall be liable for the discharge of any personal expenses incurred by him/her using the [Company] credit or charge card.

E.374

The [Company] shall pay the [Manager] during the continuance of his/her employment such reasonable train, aeroplane, car, travel insurance, hotel, entertainment, telephone (both landline and mobile), and computer or laptop, and other expenses incurred by the [Manager] wholly necessarily and exclusively in connection with the rendering of services hereunder. All such expenses must be subsequently supported by receipts and not exceed the allocated monthly budget allocated for this purpose.

E.375

All expenses shall be paid in accordance with the provisions of the agreement between the [Company] and the [Union] of which [Name] is a member.

E.376

The [Employee] agrees not to pledge either during the Term of this Agreement or any time thereafter the [Company's] credit or enter into any commitments or negotiate contracts on the [Company's] behalf except within the limits and authority set out by the [Company].

E.377

[Name] agrees that he/she is not permitted to order any goods, services or otherwise or to commit the credit of the [Company] nor make any payment or agree to make any payment to any person whatsoever on behalf of the [Company].

E.378

The [Company] shall provide comprehensive personal and life insurance cover for the [Executive] and his family and the benefit of his estate for [the term of the provision of his services/during the period of service at the [Company] and any period of illness] at the [Company's] cost. The

[Executive] shall be provided with a complete copy of the policy which shall be for not less than [figure/currency].

E.379
The [Employee] is not entitled to any additional payments and/or expenses in respect of their work and no sums shall be paid unless authorised in advance by [specify] and supported by receipts and/or invoice as requested.

E.380
Mobile telephone and WiFi charges and costs, clothes and uniform washing and dry cleaning, petrol and travel costs and any other expenses incurred by you are not paid for by the [Company] and remain your responsibility.

Film and Television

E.381
The [Company] agrees to supply the services of the [Executive Producer] without charge to the [Consortium]. It is agreed that the actual personal expenses of the [Executive Producer] in respect of the provision of his services to the [Consortium] shall be paid for by the [Consortium] under Clause [–].

E.382
The actual costs and expenses incurred by the [Company] in respect of the operation of the [Service] shall be reimbursed to the [Company] by the [Consortium] under Clause [–]. The [Company] shall make no charge to the [Consortium] for the provision of staff, equipment and/or premises in connection with the [Service].

E.383
The [Licensee] agrees to reimburse the [Licensor] in respect of all the reproduction, insurance, delivery, import and export duties, taxes and costs incurred in providing an acceptable [Film Package] subject to satisfactory receipts being provided upon request.

E.384
Where an expense and/or cost is not covered by the provisional budget allocated for the [Project] if it exceeds [number/currency]. Then it must be authorised in advance by [Name] and failure to adhere to this corporate policy may be considered a disciplinary matter.

E.385
The [Company] agrees to provide [Name] with the following costs and expenses:

1.1 Relocation costs from [place] to [place] of [number/currency].

1.2 Business class travel for [Name] and a partner on all travel in [country] and elsewhere on [Company] business.

1.3 Technology at work and home as follows [specify] with all costs of installation, maintenance and any payments due paid for by the [Company].

1.4 Life insurance for [Name] of not less than [number/currency] for death and [number/currency] for any other disability during the course of the Agreement and up to [number] years thereafter. The cost of all premiums to be paid for by the [Company].

1.5 Mortgage and/or rental payments of [number/currency] per month direct to [Name] for the first [twelve] months of the Agreement.

General Business and Commercial

E.386
The cost and expense of all currency conversions and commissions shall be paid by [–] and the items clearly set out and the rate and date specified.

E.387
Each party to this Agreement shall bear all their own expenses and disbursements incurred or made in pursuance of this Agreement unless it is expressly specified as a term of this Agreement to be the responsibility of a particular party or it is otherwise agreed in writing.

E.388
The [Company] agrees to reimburse [Name] in respect of subsistence and reasonable travelling expenses incurred by [Name] in carrying out his obligations hereunder and/or authorised by the [Company]. The [Company] may require any such expenses to be supported by receipts or other evidence of the expenditure.

E.389
The [Licensee] agrees to reimburse the [Licensor] in respect of all reasonable expenses incurred by the [Licensor] for the purpose of this Agreement subject to satisfactory receipts or other records being produced upon request.

E.390
[Name] confirms that he shall be responsible for his own expenses, value added tax, personal insurance, national insurance and personal tax arising under this Agreement.

E.391

[Name] agrees to obtain the prior consent of the [Company] in respect of all costs and expenses to be incurred in excess of [figure/currency] in any one working week. The [Company] agrees to pay [Name's] expenses reasonably and properly incurred for the purpose of this Agreement subject to satisfactory receipts or records being produced upon request.

E.392

[Name] shall not order any goods or services, provide consent or make payment on behalf of the [Company] without the prior consent of the [Company].

E.393

The [Company] agrees to provide the following items and benefits to [Name] at the [Company's] sole cost and expense for the duration of the Agreement:

1.1   The Product [–]

1.2   Clothing [–]

1.3   Equipment [–]

1.4   Facilities [–]

1.5   Medical Benefits [–]

1.6   Insurance [–]

E.394

The [Company] agrees that it shall provide [Name] with a new car bearing the [Company's] Logo described below for his/her personal and professional use which shall be comprehensively insured, taxed, serviced and any road charges, tolls, parking fines and charges shall be at the [Company's] expense and shall remain the property of the [Company]. The car shall be [specify make/age/value].

E.395

'The Authorised Expenses' shall be the agreed costs of producing, supplying and distributing the [Work] which shall include [specify] and shall not exceed [figure/currency].

E.396

In addition to the Fee the Assignee agrees to reimburse [Name] in respect of the Authorised Expenses within [seven] days of the presentation of an invoice or other record of expenditure.

E.397

[Name] shall not without the prior written consent of the [Publisher] incur any expenditure or costs on behalf of the [Publisher].

E.398

No costs, expenses, obligations, commitments or pledges shall be made by or on behalf of the [Company] and the total sums to be paid by the [Company] shall be limited to those set out in Clause [–].

E.399

Attached is a copy of the [Company] policy regarding any claims for expenses and costs. The [Company] reserves the right to amend and/or remove any authorised expenditure at any time and shall notify all relevant parties by a display on [specify]. There is no automatic right to be paid any costs and expenses under any agreement and payment is made at the discretion of the [Company].

E.400

The [Company] agrees to pay all expenses and costs incurred by the [Consultant] directly related to their work for the [Company] including but not limited to mobile telephone costs; cost of design, reproduction and supply of marketing and promotional material; travel by bus, train, coach but not taxi in [city]. No claim shall be paid for food and drink and/or accommodation. All sums shall be paid upon invoice by the [Consultant] which itemises the costs and sums due and dates incurred.

Internet and Websites

E.401

There shall be no responsibility for any costs, charges, expenses, loss, damage, telephone bills and connection charges, replacement costs, copyright, performing, music, trade mark or other rights fees and payments incurred or arising directly or indirectly or any other sums that may be incurred or owed to any person, company or business as a result of the use of any material or any content on this [Website] at any time.

E.402

The [Company] shall not be liable for any costs, expenses, charges, penalties, damages, losses, connection charges, telephone bills, viruses, defects, cookies, legal fees, replacement costs, credit card and bank charges, interest and/or any other sums incurred by the [Customer] from the use of this [Website] and any downloads, software and/or products.

E.403

The [Customer] is responsible for payment of all the costs and expenses relating to delivery of the [Work/Product] including freight, customs duties, taxes, insurance and packaging costs and any associated administration expenses.

Merchandising

E.404

The [Distributor] shall not be responsible for any personal and/or custom and excise taxes, national insurance, costs and/or expenses incurred by the [Licensor] at any time in respect of the performance of this Agreement. Each party agrees to bear its own costs and expenses for travel, accommodation, insurance, telephone bills, freight, administrative costs and other charges which may occur and shall not seek to be reimbursed and/or deduct any such expenses from any sums due under this Agreement.

E.405

The [Distributor] agrees and undertakes that it shall be responsible for and bear the cost of all sums incurred in respect of the development, tests, production, manufacture, distribution, agents, freight, packaging, product recall, product liability, insurance, [legal proceedings], marketing, advertising and promotion of the [Product] based on the [Work]. That the [Author] shall not be liable for any such sums and no such sums shall be deducted from any payments due to the [Author] under this Agreement.

E.406

The [Distributor] agrees and undertakes that all sub-licensees shall in any agreement be required to pay the following costs and expenses in respect of the [Product] based on the [Work] [specify].

E.407

The [Company] agrees that any additional costs and/or expenses not included in the quote must be sent to the [Client] for approval in advance. That the [Client] shall have the right to cancel the order due to the additional sums requested and shall be entitled to a full refund of any sums paid to date.

Publishing

E.408

The [Author] shall not be responsible for any costs and expenses of the [Agent] and the [Agent] shall only have the right to claim the [Agent's Commission].

716

E.409

The [Publisher] agrees to pay or reimburse [Name] in respect of all expenses reasonably and properly incurred in providing his/her services under this Agreement including travel and accommodation subject to satisfactory receipts or records being produced upon request.

E.410

The [Agent] agrees to pay or reimburse the [Ghostwriter] in respect of all expenses incurred in providing his/her services during the Term of the Agreement subject to satisfactory receipts or records being produced upon request up to a calendar monthly maximum of [figure/currency] which shall include all telephone, photocopying and archive access fees, travel, and accommodation, but exclude [insurance/stationery/other]. There shall be a maximum limit of [specify amount and period].

E.411

The [Originator] agrees to pay for any travel and accommodation costs specifically agreed in advance with the [Ghostwriter] for the purpose of fulfilling his/her obligations under this Agreement. The [Originator] agrees that as far as possible all accommodation shall be a minimum of [three star] hotel and all forms of travel shall be business class.

E.412

The [Authors] agree to be personally responsible for their own expenses incurred in respect of the preparation, research, writing required for the satisfactory completion and delivery of the [Work].

E.413

The [Publishers] agree to pay the [Authors] for the following sum in advance for the costs and expenses incurred in researching, writing, supplying and marketing the [Work] [figure/currency]. No receipts or evidence shall be required at a later date and the [Author] shall be entitled to retain this sum which shall not be deducted from or offset against any other sum under this Agreement or any other.

E.414

The [Publisher] agrees to pay for the cost of a photographer to take suitable images for its website and marketing material and other promotions of the [Author] and the [Work]. Such sums shall not be offset and/or recouped from any sums due to the [Author].

Purchase and Supply of Goods

E.415
The [Agent/Distributor] agrees that it shall be solely responsible and the [Company] shall not be liable for the costs and expenses incurred by the [Agent/Distributor] in respect of the provision of its services under this Agreement including, but not limited to travel, accommodation, entertainment, meals, equipment, telephone, publicity and promotional material, freight and cost of premises and staff. If the [Agent/Distributor] should visit the premises of the [Design Company] at any time the [Agent/Distributor] shall be solely responsible for any costs and expenses it may incur unless the [Company] has provided written specific consent to reimburse or contribute to authorised costs in advance.

E.416
Each party shall bear its own costs and expenses for its business, staff, telephone, freight, transport, health and safety, compliance, copyright and intellectual property and any other subject of any nature which it incurs whether related to a service or product under this Agreement or not unless specified in clauses [–].

E.417
Where additional equipment and/or other items are purchased to develop, produce and/or reproduce the [Articles/Work]. Then the [Supplier] shall receive a contribution of up to a maximum of [number/currency] from the [Company] as an additional payment towards costs. Provided that valid receipts can be supplied with the relevant invoices to the [Company]. The [Company] agrees that the [Supplier] shall own such material not the [Company].

Services

E.418
The [Agent] shall be entitled to deduct all reasonable expenses properly incurred in furtherance of this Agreement from the Gross Receipts provided that the [Agent] shall at all times whenever possible and practicable keep all relevant receipts and documents confirming such expenses.

E.419
The [Company] shall pay for or provide the [Director] with chauffeur-driven transport to and from the location where the [Film] is being made, and all entertainment or hospitality expenses which are reasonably consistent with his duties as [Director] hereunder subject to the [Director] keeping receipts whenever possible.

E.420

If the [Composer] shall at the request of the [Company] attend at any place more than [distance] from [town] in order to render the services the [Company] shall pay to or reimburse the [Composer] with the reasonable cost of return travel to such location (by air where appropriate and with the prior consent of the [Company]) together with the cost of meals (excluding drinks) except to the extent that meals are provided to the [Composer] by or on behalf of or at the request of the [Company].

E.421

If the [Composer] shall at the request of the [Company] be required to stay in any place referred to in Clause [–] for one or more nights the [Company] shall provide suitable hotel or other accommodation for the [Composer] or pay or reimburse the [Composer] for the reasonable pre-approved cost of such accommodation subject to the production and delivery to the [Company] of all appropriate receipts and vouchers.

E.422

In respect of all copying charges relating to the production by the [Composer] of the score and orchestral and/or vocal parts of the [Music] the [Company] shall pay the cost of such copying at the [Standard Guild or Union scale rate] for the time being in force subject to the production and delivery to the [Company] of full and correct invoices for such amount from third parties addressed to the [Company].

E.423

The [Company] shall reimburse the [Presenter] on the presentation of appropriate invoices for reasonable wardrobe expenses incurred by the [Presenter] subject to an overall maximum of [figure/currency] per calendar month which shall become the property of [specify].

E.424

The [Company] agrees to pay or reimburse the [Presenter] in respect of all expenses reasonably and properly incurred in the provision of the services including [taxis, clothes, beauty and hairdressing] subject to satisfactory receipts or records.

E.425

The [Agent] agrees that it shall only be entitled to the [Agent's] Commission for the Term of the Agreement subject to the provision of the services by the [Agent] and the continuance of this Agreement. The [Agent] shall not be entitled to any other sums, garments, compensation, cancellation fee, expenses, costs or otherwise from the [Company].

E.426

The [Company] shall pay such reasonable expenses incurred by [Name] wholly necessarily and exclusively in connection with the provision of his/her freelance services in this Agreement. Provided that such expenses are authorised in advance and are subsequently supported by receipts.

E.427

The [Company] agree to pay or reimburse the [Artist] in respect of all fees, charges, costs and expenses reasonably and properly incurred by the [Artist] in the provision of his services under this Agreement [without any limit on the sum] including:

1.1 Travel, car, taxis, air including ticket, travel insurance, surcharges, excess baggage costs and upgrades.

1.2 Accommodation whether hotel, rental, temporary or long term.

1.3 Beauty treatments, cosmetics, hair, clothes, personal trainer, cosmetic dentistry, BUPA and other health related matters.

1.4 Internet connection, telephone, both landline and mobile, fax, email.

1.5 Medical and health reviews.

1.6 Equipment [laptop/mobile/other specify make and model] [and any updates] to be owned by [specify].

E.428

The [Company] agrees to pay the [Presenter] throughout the Term of the Agreement a monthly clothing and hairdressing allowance of [figure/currency].

E.429

In addition to the [Presenter's] Fee and the hairdressing and clothing allowance, the [Company] agrees to reimburse the [Presenter] in respect of all expenses reasonably and properly incurred for the purpose of fulfilling his obligations under this Agreement including taxis, petrol, telephone charges and business lunches subject to satisfactory receipts or other records being produced upon request.

E.430

The [Company] agrees that it shall provide the [Presenter] with:

1.1 A new executive car for his/her personal use for the Term of the Agreement which shall be comprehensively insured, tested, taxed and serviced entirely at the [Company's] expense and shall remain the property of the [Company] or its leasing agents [specify].

1.2   A new company charge card to be used for all the authorised expenses [specify].

1.3   Private health care with [Name] for the [Presenter] and their family with the following benefits [specify].

1.4   Life Assurance for the benefit of [specify] in the sum of [amount].

1.5   Pension benefits [specify].

E.431

The [Company] shall ensure that suitable insurance cover is arranged for the [Presenter] and her personal property and shall provide her with a copy of the policy upon request. The [Company] confirms that the [Presenter's] life insurance for the benefit of her estate shall not be less than [sum].

E.432

The [Company] agrees to arrange and pay for any travel and accommodation required of the [Presenter] by the [Company] under this Agreement. The [Company] undertakes that as far as possible all accommodation shall be a minimum of four-star hotel and all forms of travel will be business or first class.

E.433

The [Agent] acknowledges that he/she is solely responsible for all costs he/she may incur in respect of the provision of his/her services under this Agreement including the promotion, advertising and marketing of the [Actor] in [specify].

E.434

'The Authorised Expenses' shall be the following sums reasonably and properly expended by the [Manager] for and behalf of the [Sportsperson] which are not recovered through any third party:

1.1   The first class travelling costs and the cost of all accommodation. Provided that the [Sportperson] is attending competitions, events or other business matters under the terms of this Agreement or at the request of the [Manager].

1.2   The following credit and charge card shall be supplied by the [Manager] to the [Sportsperson] which shall be used by them only and not family members for the purpose of settling his expenses under this Agreement which shall be the responsibility of the [Company] to pay [–] which shall be returned at the end of the agreement.

1.3   The following goods or equipment shall be supplied for the [Sportsperson] to retain and own [specify items/value].

1.4   A clothing allowance for the [Sportsperson] up to a monthly limit of [–] of which the money or goods shall be the property of the [Sportsperson].

1.5   The cost of a comprehensive insurance policy in respect of the [Sportsperson, his sports equipment and family [specify] items/persons/value].

1.6   Specialist medical benefits [–].

1.7   Training facilities [–].

1.8   Other [–].

E.435

'The Promotion Expenses' shall be all the costs and expenses reasonably and properly expended by the [Promoter] in furtherance of this Agreement which are not recouped from any third party:

1.1   Survey and marketing reports.

1.2   The creation, supply and cost of advertising in local and national newspapers including photographs.

1.3   The development, production and distribution of a promotional [DVD/CD-Rom/CD].

1.4   The development, production and distribution of a radio advertisement.

1.5   The development, production and distribution of webpages, banners and/or other advertising for the internet.

1.6   The commissioning of any artwork, graphics, music, text, merchandising or any other material for publicity, advertising and promotional material.

1.7   Delivery, storage, shipping custom duties, insurance and handling charges, mobile and landline telephone costs and internet charges.

1.8   Clearance costs, fees and expenses for the negotiation and acquisition of any material.

E.436

'The Authorised Expenses' shall be the following sums reasonably and properly expended by the [Manager] solely on behalf of the [Group] which are not recovered through any third party: travel costs, accommodation, clothing, publicity, advertising and promotion, equipment, telephone, stationery, insurance cover.

E.437

The [Manager] acknowledges that any materials provided as part of the Authorised Expenses shall be the property of the member of the [Group] for whom it was originally purchased.

E.438

There shall be no obligation to pay any additional sums for costs and/or expenses incurred by the [Company/Agent/Artist] in providing their services under the Agreement. The total sum to be paid by the [Distributor] shall be limited to the [Fees].

E.439

Where [Name] requires additional costs and expenses to be paid for any reason in order to fulfil the terms of this Agreement. Then the [Distributor] agrees to pay a maximum of [number/currency] in each calendar month subject to invoice by [Name] for a period of [three] months.

E.440

[Name] shall not be entitled to any costs, expenses and/or other sums except the [Fee] for the [Internship/Work]. In the event for any reason [Name] is requested to commit and/or incur any cost and expense on behalf of the [Company] by any person. Then [Name] shall be entitled to refuse and shall seek the advice and permission of [Executive] to provide authority for such expenditure.

Sponsorship

E.441

The [Sponsor] agrees to bear all costs and expenses of developing, creating and producing the [Sponsors'] Logo and supplying the [Sponsors'] Logo in a format which is suitable and accepted by the [Company] for its incorporation in any material for the [Programme/Event]. The [Company] shall not bear any such costs. In the event that the material is to be developed and/or created by a third party who is already engaged in the [Programme/Event]. The a budget shall be agreed in advance with the [Sponsor] who shall pay such sums in advance subject to the conclusion of a full assignment of all rights in the new material to the [Sponsor].

E.442

The [Company] agrees that it shall bear all the cost and expense of the preparation, design, development, production, distribution, marketing and exploitation of the [Event/Programme] and that [Name] shall not have any liability whatsoever that may arise at any time.

E.443

The [Sponsor] shall pay all the agreed expenses set out in Appendix [–] subject to the production of receipts, bank statements and/or other supporting evidence before [date]. After that [date] no further sums shall be paid by the [Sponsor].

E.444

The [Sponsor] agrees that where due to unforeseen circumstances, error and/or some other reason insufficient quantities of the [Sponsors'] product are available for the [Competitors]. That the [Sponsor] shall reimburse the [Company] with the full cost of purchasing and/or arranging for the supply of alternative products at short notice which may be incurred by the [Company].

E.445

Where the [Company] have to incur costs and expenses due to the acts, negligence, errors, omissions and/or fault of the [Sponsor] and/or any of their agents, employees, casual staff and/or other persons associated and/or engaged by them. Then the [Company] shall be entitled to incur such sums on their behalf as may be necessary to remedy and/or resolve a matter and the [Sponsor] shall be liable for and pay all the costs and expenses upon demand by the [Company]. Together with such administrative and damage fee as the [Company] may decide to charge dependent on the circumstances.

University, Library and Educational

E.446

The [Contributor] agrees that she shall be bear the cost of all her own travel, accommodation, telephone charges, photocopying, computer software and hardware costs, and other expenses incurred in respect of the preparation, research, and writing required for the satisfactory completion and delivery of the [Work] to the [Institute].

E.447

The [Institute] agrees to pay or reimburse the [Contributor] in respect of all expenses reasonably and properly incurred in the provision of the services under this Agreement subject to satisfactory receipts or records up to a maximum of [figure/currency] [words].

E.448

The [Institute] and the [Company] both agree that they shall bear own costs and expenses incurred in respect of this Agreement and shall not seek to reclaim and/or deduct any such sums from any sums due to the other party. Each party shall be responsible for the administration and provision of employees and consultants in its own business and any telephone and mobile charges, payments, freight, and transport that each party shall be responsible for its own health and safety, and compliance with legislation, directives, regulations and policies, and the cost of any insurance.

E.449

The [Consultant] acknowledges and agrees that she shall be responsible for all costs and expenses that she may incur in respect of the provision of her services under this Agreement. The [Consultant] shall ensure that the [Consultant] has suitable personal insurance cover for herself and her equipment.

E.450

The [Institute] shall pay the [Executive] during the continuance of his employment such reasonable train, air, car, travel insurance, hotel, entertainment, telephone (both landline and mobile), and computer or laptop, and other expenses and costs incurred by the [Executive] directly in order to carry out his duties under this Agreement. All expenses over [figure/currency] [words] must be agreed and authorised in advance in each case and supported by receipts.

E.451

The [Institute] shall during the Term of this Agreement provide comprehensive life, personal and health insurance cover for the [Executive] and family and for the benefit of his estate at the [Institute's] cost for not less than [figure/currency] [words].

E.452

Where the [Institute] requires a [Researcher/Student] to attend a conference and/or to make any presentation and/or wishes to exploit their [Thesis]. Then it is agreed that the [Institute] shall pay them a fee of [number/currency] per [day/month] in arrears at the end of each calendar month. Together with all travel, accommodation, telephone and mobile and WiFi, meals and other costs of not less than [number/currency].

FACILITY ACCESS

DVD, Video and Discs

F.001

1.1 The [Company] agrees to provide access to [specify space] of the premises at [address] at such times and dates of [number] days from [date] to [date] to be agreed in order for the [Distributor] to record, film and take such images as may be required for the [Project] and/or any associated marketing.

1.2 This arrangement in 1.1 shall include the use of electricity, gas, water, lights and heating by the [Distributor] and the supply of security and additional staff and also any necessary insurance cover. No charge shall be made to the [Distributor] and all costs shall be met by the [Company].

1.3 The [Distributor] agrees that it shall not use and/or access any areas which are closed and/or blocked off and shall provide a deposit to the [Company] of [number/currency] against any loss and/or damages which may be incurred which are not covered by insurance cover held by the [Company].

1.4 Where the [Company] is unable and/or unwilling to permit access, then the [Distributor] agrees that it shall not have any action, claim and/or legal action against the [Company] and that the [Company] has the right to refuse access and/or use of their facilities at any time.

F.002

1.1 [Name] consents to access by the [Company] and any associated personnel to their home for the purpose of filming and interviewing [Name] on [date] in their [specify space]. This shall not include the right to film and/or record other members of the family and/or other locations within the house.

1.2   Where at any time [Name] decides that he/she wishes to cancel, terminate and/or reschedule the filming and/or interview then [Name] shall be entitled to do so for any reason. Provided that in the event that no filming and/or interview of [Name] takes place then non-payment shall be due and any sums paid shall be refunded to the [Company].

F.003

1.1   The [Distributor] agrees to provide access to and use of the following facilities [specify] to the [Company] and its personnel at the [Distributors'] cost to produce, edit, reproduce and to supply copies of the [Film] for the [Disc/Project].

1.2   The [Company] agrees that it shall not be entitled to incur any additional cost and expenses and/or to commit the [Distributor] in any manner to pay for and/or be liable for any person, service and/or other material required by the [Company] at any time.

Film and Television

F.004

The [Producer] agrees to provide to the [Television Company] a Facility Access Letter signed by a Director of the [Facilities House] and the [Producer] which shall apply [specify duration] which sets out the following terms:

1.1   An undertaking that the [Facilities House] will retain possession of the [Master of the Series] and any part or parts thereof and not to part with or destroy any such material without the prior written consent of the [Television Company].

1.2   An undertaking by the [Facilities House] not to accept orders from the [Producer] or any other person for any material in connection with the [Series] or any parts.

1.3   An undertaking to fulfil all orders for copies and any other materials relating to the [Series] and any parts received from the [Television Company] at the [Television Company's] cost.

1.4   The [Facilities House] shall not claim any right, interest, liens or charge of any nature against the [Master of the Series] or other materials at any time or refuse to release the material.

1.5   An undertaking by the [Facilities House] that the product of the services provided will result in material of the highest quality and will in any event at all times comply with all technical standard and transmission requirements of [Ofcom/other].

F.005

The [Company] may offer some or all of its internal facilities for the production of any [Programme] subject to their availability. There should be no obligation to use the facilities or for them to be provided. In the event that the [Production Company] does use the facilities of the [Company] then the cost to be charged shall be the actual cost to the [Company] without any profit or additional charge. Both parties shall enter into a separate facilities agreement for that purpose.

F.006

This Agreement does permit and/or authorise the [Company] and/or any executives and/or third parties engaged by them to use and/or have access to any premises, equipment and/or other facilities of the [Distributor] at any time. The normal procedures for bookings at the [Distributor] must be adhered to at all times and the [Company] shall be liable to pay hire costs and other relevant charges at the usual rate for any arrangement that may be agreed. There are no reduced rates, discounts and/or waiver of any cost and/or expenses by the [Distributor] to the [Company].

F.007

The [Company] agrees that:

1.1   Name] shall be allocated his/her own [space/room] from [date] to [date] with its own personal facilities as follows [specify] and

1.2   There shall in addition be sufficient security paid for by the [Company] to prevent access by unauthorised visitors.

1.3   The [Company] shall also ensure that there are no hidden bugs and/or cameras prior to access and/or use of the [space/room] by [Name].

1.4   [Name] shall be provided with sole use of the [space/room] for the period and shall be entitled to make his/her own arrangements for cleaning and servicing the [space/room] as he/she thinks fit.

1.5   No claim and/or action shall be made for any costs, expenses and/or loss and/or damage that [Name] may incur provided it is less than [number/currency]. [Name] shall be obliged to pay any sum due to the [Company] in excess of that figure.

General Business and Commercial

F.008

The [Company] undertakes that it will not authorise or consent to the removal, destruction or reduction of any material relating to the [Film/Work/Products] from any [laboratory/designer/warehouse/manufacturer] in [country] without complying with the following conditions:

1.1 The [company] shall notify [Name] of the intention to move, destroy or reduce the [Film/Work/Products] and provide [Name] with an opportunity of not less than [28 days] to express view on the matter and provide objections.

1.2 The [Company] shall provide a new access letter which is transferred to another address for storage and the terms and cost of access shall be no less favourable. Any additional cost shall be met by the [Company].

F.009

The [Assignor] shall provide all material of any nature and in any format which exists or is created in the future in the [Work] in the possession or under the control of the [Assignor] or any director, officer, or representative or agent, licensee or other third party known by the [Assignor] to be in possession of material to the [Assignee] including but not limited to:

1.1 All copies of any master material in any form.

1.2 A list of locations in any country whether residential or business addresses at which any material is held together with access letters giving irrevocable authority for the [Assignee] to remove such material and confirming that the [Assignee] now have all rights of ownership and possession.

1.3 All documents, records, contracts, copyright clearances and fees, consents, proofs, scripts, publicity, advertising material and any other data in any form whether printed, stored on computer or computer software, advertising and marketing material, posters, catalogues, labels, articles, drawings, plans, sketches, sound recordings, music, computer generated material, graphics, artwork, videos, films, CDs, DVDs or otherwise.

1.4 All material relating to any name, character name, image, trading name, associated trade marks, design rights, service marks, logos, domain names, trade secrets, or any slogan, text, icon, image, jingle, ringtone or otherwise.

F.010

[Name] provides supervised access to [Name] of [Company] for the purpose of [specify] to the following material [list] at [address] during normal business hours on [date] provided that the sum of [fee] is paid in advance and the [Company] accepts full liability for any damage or loss that arises directly as a result of their access. There shall be no use of the telephone, photocopying or other facilities at the site.

F.011

The [Company] shall not be obliged to provide use of their facilities, equipment or materials to any person or business who they appoint as an agent, service provider or in any other capacity to act on their behalf or to produce any material. The decision shall be entirely at the discretion of the [Company] at any time. Where facilities, equipment or materials are not made available the [Agent/Service Business/other] shall make their own arrangements at their own cost and agree that there is no right to seek to reclaim any such sum from the [Company] as an additional or unforeseen expense.

F.012

The [Institute] shall not be obliged to provide use of its facilities and/or access to the premises for the purposes of this Agreement. Where permission is granted the [Company] shall obey all the policies and instructions given by the representatives of the [Institute] and shall use any such facilities and premises at the [Company's] own risk and cost. The [Company] shall indemnify the [Institute] in respect of all direct and indirect damages, losses, expenses, legal costs and for any temporary relocation costs that may be needed that may be incurred. This shall apply to any property, products, services and/or other matter owned and/or under the control of the [Institute] and/or any personnel, staff and/or those of a third party.

F.013

Where facilities are made available to the [Company] at the premises of [Name]. The [Company] agrees to abide by and adhere to all the following policies [specify] which are applicable. The [Company] agrees that any persons from the [Company] shall be required to follow any instructions of authorised personnel of [Name] who may be in charge of and operating the [equipment/systems]. The [Company] shall be obliged to pay for any additional costs that may be incurred which may arise as a result of the access to and/or use of the facilities. The [Company] [shall be obliged to provide a schedule [one month] in advance to the [Name] which specifies in detail the proposed use of the facilities, the persons who will attend and the material which will be used.

F.014

The [Agent] shall not have any access to and/or use of the facilities and/or premises of [Name] at any time as part of this Agreement. The [Agent] shall be obliged to pay for all administration, reproduction, development and marketing costs and expenses at his/her sole cost. There shall be no obligation on [Name] to supply and/or deliver any material including archive photographs and/or other recordings and/or films which he/she may own and/or control.

FAIR DEALING

General Business and Commercial

F.015

'Fair Dealing' shall mean the quotation, small sample or agreed extract of the [Work] which shall be acknowledged with the relevant title, copyright notice and credit to the [Copyright Owner], and/or [Exclusive Licensee/ Distributor] and source reference for the [Work] for the purpose of review or criticism in [country]. This shall not include any educational, charitable and/ or commercial enterprise, databases and/or storage and retrieval system and/or any adaptation and/or any right to license third parties which shall require the prior written consent of the [Copyright Owner].

F.016

'Fair Dealing' in the context of this Agreement shall mean to deal with fairly and reasonably but in any event the [Licensee] shall use no more than [ten per cent] of the [Licensor's] material for promotional purposes.

F.017

There is no right to quote from, extract sample words, data or images from this [Work] or any part. For review or criticism purposes you may only refer to the title, copyright owner and source of reference and a maximum of [number words] in [country] for a non-commercial purpose. Any other direct use of material out of the [Work] requires the prior written consent of [specify]. This clause shall apply for all purposes whether educational, charitable, commercial, or as a non-fee paying contribution to a website, magazine and/or enterprise.

F.018

1.1 The [Licensor] grants the [Licensee] the non-exclusive right to use the following [Text/Images/Data] [Title] [Description] [Words/pages/ copy of image] A copy of which is attached to and forms part of this Agreement.

1.2 The [Licensee] shall only be entitled to use the [Text/Images/Data] in the following manner [specify purpose in detail].

In the following countries [specify]

For the Licence Period from [date] to [date].

1.3 The [Licensee] agrees that at all times the following credit and copyright notice shall be provided to the [Licensor] on all copies and all associated packaging and marketing material [specify].

F.019

It is acknowledged by all parties to the [Consortium]:

1.1　That all the products of any contribution to the [Project] should as far as possible be assigned to the [Consortium] as [specify name]. To be held as joint owners by all the parties.

1.2　That this [Project] is a commercial enterprise and that no reliance must be placed on clearing and/or acquiring material and/or services on any concept of fair dealing, public domain and/or review, criticism and/or otherwise.

1.3　That as a matter of policy rights should be acquired by assignment and/or exclusive licence for the most extensive use worldwide within the constraints of the [Budget]. That if possible payments should be agreed for future use so that projected costs can be fixed.

1.4　That proper records of clearance of all copyright, intellectual property rights, credits, copyright notices, trade marks and any other rights should be maintained and held by [specify] and not destroyed at any time. That these details shall be supplied to any party to the [Consortium] upon request provided that they meet all costs required to fulfil such task.

F.020

1.1　[Name] agrees that the [Author] may use the following lyrics, words, sound recording and film [specify] from the song entitled [specify] on their blog called [specify].

1.2　Provided that the [Author] agrees that a link is provided from the blog as follows [specify link web reference] and a copyright notice and credit is displayed as follows at all times next to the lyrics, words, sound recording and film as follows [–].

1.3　That the [Author] agrees not to post and/or display and/or use and/or adapt the material in 1.1 on any other website and/or in any other format and/or medium at any time without the prior written consent of [Name].

FAIR TRADING

General Business and Commercial

F.021

The [Company/Distributor] agrees and undertake not to abuse any dominant market position which it may have or achieve in respect of the [Product] and/

or to enter into any agreements which would or might restrict or distort the market and/or competition in [countries].

F.022

The [Company/Distributor] agrees and undertake not to abuse any dominant market position which it may have or achieve in respect of [any of its products or services] and/or to enter into any agreements which would or might restrict or distort the market and/or competition in any part of the world.

F.023

The [Company] agrees not to source material or enter into agreements with suppliers, manufacturers, agents or other third parties who do not follow the fair trade principles of [specify organisation] during the Term of this Agreement.

F.024

The [Manufacturer] agrees and undertakes to comply with all the following principles in its working practices for its business and in its dealings with the [Company]:

1.1 Not to employ child labour and/or any person under the age of [specify].

1.2 To adopt health and safety practices which comply with [specify body].

1.3 To source all materials as far as possible from sustainable resources and from a source which can be identified through the chain at all times.

1.4 To pay [workers/staff/others] no less than [specify rate] in [country].

1.5 To provide a health care programme, medical cover and insurance as follows [specify].

1.6 To provide the [Company] access to the premises, offices and warehouses of the [Manufacturer] at any time without prior notice to verify compliance with any of the above and to make it a condition that any suppliers or any third parties agree to comply and provide access on the same terms.

1.7 To comply with all the following policy documents [specify].

F.025

1.1 The [Supplier] agrees and undertakes to develop, produce, manufacture, package and deliver all [Products] ordered by the [Company] in accordance with the [subject] policy of [organisation] in [country].

1.2   That the [Supplier] agrees that where for any reason there is a failure and/or discrepancy and/or departure from these principles for any reason in respect of any order that the [Company] shall be advised before the delivery is despatched and provided with the opportunity to cancel the order.

F.026

It is not a requirement of this Agreement that any part of the [Products/Services/Work] comply with and/or are subject to any fair trade, green, recycling, carbon neutral and/or any other environmental and/or international development policy.

FILMS

General Business and Commercial

F.027

'The Film' means a feature-length film [and the accompanying soundtrack and musical score] complying with the following particulars:

Title [specify]

Running Time [specify] minutes

Based on [book/idea/script/synopsis] created by [name]

Individual Producer [name]

Director [name]

Composer [name]

Principal Artists [name]

Technical description of material [–]

Budget cost of production [specify]

F.028

'The Film' means a film of approximately [duration] minutes entitled [title] based on the [novel by name] and the expression shall include the sounds and/or music embodied in any soundtrack relating thereto.

F.029

'The Film' shall mean the film entitled [title] with a running time of not less than [duration]. Based on a screenplay to be written by [Writer] which is based on an original published book entitled [name of publishers] in [country] and a treatment by the original creator and writer [Author].

F.030

'The Films' shall mean the feature-length films complying with the particulars given in Schedule [–] which is attached to and forms part of this Agreement.

F.031

'The Film' shall mean a feature film provisionally entitled [title] based on a novel entitled [title] by the Author [Name] which is published by [Company] and ISBN reference [–].

F.032

'Film' shall [have the same meaning as defined in the Copyright, Designs and Patents Act 1988 as subsequently amended] in [country] namely a recording on any medium from which a moving image may by any means be produced.

F.033

'The Series' shall mean the Series provisionally entitled [title] of [number] Programmes each of approximately between [length in minutes] duration on the subject of [specify topic] based upon the books on such subject entitled [Title] written by the [Author] and prior to the date hereof published by the [Publisher]. The Programmes shall be in accordance with the Script which is agreed and approved by the [Licensee] and attached in Schedule [–].

F.034

'The Series' shall be the series of films and any associated sound recording based on the treatment and the script entitled [title] consisting of [number] episodes each of which shall be [length in minutes] in duration.

F.035

'Programme' includes any advertisement in relation to any service and any item included in that service.

F.036

'Television Programme' includes a teletext transmission.

F.037

'Programme Material' includes a film [within the meaning of the Copyright, Designs and Patents Act 1988 as amended] and any other recording and any advertisement or other advertising material.

F.038

'Programme' shall mean the live or recorded television programme and shall include all underlying works whether literary, dramatic, artistic, musical and/ or sound and/or commentary which form part of the Programme.

F.039

'Cable Programme' shall [be defined in accordance with the Copyright, Designs and Patents Act 1988 as amended] and shall mean any item included in a cable programme service.

F.040

'Feature Film Material' shall mean all pre-existing film material as specified under Schedule [–] to this Agreement including all accompanying soundtrack which it is intended to be incorporated in the [Programmes] to be produced by the [Company].

F.041

'The Programme' shall be the following film and any associated sound recordings and/or music with a running time of not less than [length] which is described as follows [name/number of episodes/language/sponsorship details/other].

F.042

'The Film' shall be the feature-length cinematic film and associated sound recordings to be produced by the [Production Company] based on and adapted from the [Author's Work] which is an original work by the Author including [title/artwork/characters/quotes/other] [title/publishers/ISBN/ distributors/countries/languages]. The Film is briefly described as follows [length/language/format].

F.043

'The Series' shall be the series of films and any associated sound recordings based on the [Pilot] which both parties may agree to produce, develop and exploit following satisfactory completion of the [Pilot].

F.044

'The [Video/DVD/Disc]' shall be the promotional film and any associated sound recording for the [Musical Work] to be performed by the [Artist].

F.045

'The Film' shall be the following film in which 'The Commissioned Work' is to be incorporated entitled [–]. 'The Commissioned Work' shall be the title sequences and end copyright notices, trade marks, service marks, domain names, credits, disclaimers and copyright warnings to be prepared, produced and delivered by the [Assignor] to the [Production Company] which is briefly described as follows [duration/design/colour/list].

F.046
'The Footage' shall be the following parts of the [Film] including sound recordings called [Name] [Reference Code/duration/format/specify extract].

F.047
'The Corporate Video' shall be the following film and any associated sound recordings and musical works in which the footage is to be included [title/duration/description/company].

F.048
'The Film' shall be the film called [title] of [length] [brief description] together with any appearances, contributions or material of any nature which may be incorporated including sound recordings, ringtones, voice and sound effects, music, computer generated material, stills, advertisements, product placement, articles, merchandising, sponsorship, sculptures, paintings, buildings, transport, footage, artists, persons, animals, or gadgets.

F.049
'The Archive Film' shall be film material entitled [specify title/reference] which is [number] minutes in duration which is controlled by the [Institute] but for which the copyright owner is either unknown and/or unconfirmed.

F.050
'The Banner Advertisement' shall be the film and sound recording known as [specify title] which can run for up to [number] minutes and be repeated indefinitely on the web page. It is linked to the website [reference] and when a person clicks on the film the connection opens to the linked website.

F.051
'The Training Film' shall mean the reproduction and final edited version of the filming of the participants completing the requested tasks and the interviews which followed at a training day. The specific purpose of the training film is to illustrate and highlight the methods and techniques to be used to [specify].

F.052
'The Advertiser Funded Film' shall mean a film including sound recording entitled; [specify] which shall be [number] minutes in duration which is produced, edited and supplied to the [Product Distributor] by the [Production Company] which is in accordance with the Project Specifications and Budget set out in Appendix [–].

F.053
'The Sponsored Film' shall mean the film and the sound recording which is [number] minutes in length to promote and market the [Charity] and their work with [subject] produced by [specify] in which the following parties jointly hold the copyright [specify].

F.054
'The Short Film' shall mean the video, film and/or moving images of [number] minutes recorded by [Name] on [gadget] of the participants at the [Event] on [date] in [format] with the [slogan/title] [specify] in which the copyright and all other rights in [country] are owned by [Name].

F.055

1.1 The [Agent] agrees that there shall be no right to edit, adapt, add to and/or delete from any part of the [Film] and/or sound recording and/or to add any additional credits, acknowledgements, sounds, images, sub-titles, music, text, products, logos and/or recordings. The [Company] shall use and exhibit the [Film] at [location] in the exact form and sequence in which it is delivered by the [Artist].

1.2 The [Agent] agrees and undertakes not to authorise and/or permit any person and/or third party to take any photographs and/or film and/or other images of the [Film] during the exhibition.

F.056
'The Films' shall be the series of films to be transmitted by the [Company] on channel [number] in [country] under the theme [subject] supplied by the [Distributor] as set out in Schedule [–] which forms part of this Agreement.

FIRST REFUSAL

General Business and Commercial

F.057
In consideration of the payments made under this Agreement the [Author] hereby grants to [Agent/Publisher] the exclusive right of first refusal with respect to [any subsequent literary work including his next novel].

F.058
'First Refusal' shall mean the obligation of the [Author] to provide an opportunity to the [Agent] to acquire the same or similar rights as those granted under

this Agreement with respect to the [Work] prior to the subsequent work being offered to any third party. For the avoidance of doubt, the [Agent] shall be under no obligation to acquire the subsequent work whether on the same or similar terms as contained within this Agreement or not. The right of First Refusal shall continue until such time as the parties hereto agree final terms for the exploitation of the subsequent work or [six weeks] from the time the Agent is first offered the work, whichever is the sooner.

F.059

The [Author] agrees to provide the [Publisher] with a limited right of first refusal with respect to his next literary work provisionally entitled [title] [the New Work] which is due to be completed in [draft form] by [date]. In consideration of the payment of [figure/currency] [which is a separate sum from the advance against royalties] upon full signature of this Agreement the [Author] grants to the [Publisher] the following rights of first refusal in respect of the [New Work]:

1.1 That the [Author] shall provide the [Publisher] with a copy of the finished manuscript by [date] or by such later date that the [New Work] is completed.

1.2 That the [Publisher] shall have [14 days] from the date of delivery of the finished manuscript to express interest in the [New Work] and to confirm that they wish to make an offer to publish the [New Work].

1.3 That the [Publisher] shall have [four weeks] from the date of delivery of the manuscript to make an offer to the [Author] of proposed advance, royalties and terms for the publication of the [New Work] in [country].

1.4 The [Author] shall not be bound to accept any offer by the [Publisher] nor shall he/she be obliged to give any reasons for any rejection. The [Author] shall be entitled to agree any terms which he/she so decides are in his/her interests, and shall not be obliged to accept the same terms as this Agreement.

1.5 The [Publisher] agrees that all material and representations provided or made by the [Author] are in confidence and are not for distribution or reproduction to any parties or person other than [specify] without the prior written approval of the [Author].

F.060

The [Organisation] grants to the [Sponsor] the right of first refusal to sponsor the [Event]. The right of first refusal shall commence on [date] and expire on [date]. In the event that the [Organisation] and the [Sponsor] have not agreed in writing the principal terms of an agreement for the sponsorship of the [Event] in that period then the right of first refusal shall end. The

[Organisation] shall then be entitled to negotiate an agreement for the sponsorship of the [Event] with any third party. Save in the event that any more favourable terms for agreement are negotiated with a third party that was not offered to the [Sponsor]. Then the [Organisation] shall offer such terms to the [Sponsor] who shall have [seven days] to accept or reject such terms. In the event that the [Sponsor] does not reply within the [seven days] it shall be deemed to have rejected the terms. Unless the terms are accepted by the [Sponsor] within that period then the [Organisation] shall be entitled to conclude a sponsorship agreement with the third party.

F.061
Before disposing of the [Rights] or any part thereof the [Company] shall offer the rights which it proposes to dispose of to the [Distributor] by notice in writing. The [Distributor] shall have [one month] from the date of such written offer to accept the terms offered by notice in writing to the [Company]. If the [Distributor] shall reject or fail to accept such offer in writing within [one month] then the [Company] shall be free to dispose of such rights to any third party on terms no less favourable to the [Company] than the terms offered to the [Distributor]. Before disposal of any rights on less favourable terms than offered by the [Company] to the [Distributor] the [Distributor] shall be given first refusal of such terms and will have [one month] to reject or accept the offer by notice in writing.

F.062
The [Licensor] agrees and undertakes to provide the [Licensee] with a right of first refusal in respect of the [specify rights] in [Product/Work] in [country] in the event that the [Licensor] decides at any time before [date] to dispose of, license, assign or transfer any such rights.

F.063
[Name] agrees to provide the [Distributor] with the right of first refusal to make a satisfactory offer to market and exploit the next sequel of the [Book/Work/Product/Services] created, developed and written by [Name] which [Name] intends to make commercially available through a third party. [Name] shall notify the [Distributor] of the rights and material available and set a deadline of not less than [seven days] for a written response and offer. If there is not an offer within the period specified or the offer by the [Distributor] is less than [figure/currency/terms] then the first refusal clause shall cease to apply and [Name] may offer the rights and material elsewhere.

F.064
This clause shall only apply from [date] to [date] and shall be limited to the subject of [specify] and shall not apply to [specify].

F.065

This first right of refusal shall only apply to the next [Film/Work/other] and not any other subsequent work, rights or material.

F.066

This clause shall only apply to the [Company] and not any parent company, subsidiary or associated company.

F.067

The [Company] shall not acquire any option, first right of refusal and/or any right of renewal and/or other rights and/or interest under this Agreement.

F.068

Where a [Sponsor] has been the sole and exclusive company and/or person to pay for the cost of the [Project] and to be acknowledged as the only source of funding. Then the [Sponsor] shall be provided with the opportunity to increase the funding in the event that additional funds are required at a later date by the [Company]. The [Sponsor] shall be permitted [one month] to refuse and/or to confirm that they will make the additional payments. In the event that the [Sponsor] refuses the request. Then the [Company] shall be allowed to seek funds elsewhere and to have an additional sponsor who is ranked below the first party in any promotional displays.

F.069

The [Distributor] shall not have any first right of refusal, option and/or any right, interest and/or claim over any rights which are reserved and/or any sequel and/or adaptation of the [Work] at any time.

F.070

1.1 In consideration of the sum of [number/currency] to the [Agent] of [Name] by [date]. [Name] agrees to grant the [Company] the right of first refusal to acquire and purchase the right to exploit the [Work] in the form of [specify] in [country] from [date].

1.2 After payment of the fee in 1.1 the [Agent] and [Name] agrees to provide the [Company] with the detail of the rights offered and the payments and sums which they want to achieve. The [Agent] and [Name] agree to permit the [Company] a period of [number] months to negotiate and conclude an agreement from the date of notification of the proposal by the [Agent] and [Name].

1.3 if the parties cannot conclude and sign an agreement within the period of [three] months in 1.2. Then the [Agent] and [Name] shall be entitled to retain the fee in 1.1 and also offer the rights to any other third party.

In the event that they change the rights and/or term of the offer there shall be no obligations to provide another right of first refusal to the [Company] even if the sum required is lower.

FIXTURES

General Business and Commercial

F.071
For the purposes of this Agreement the term 'Fixtures' shall mean all property of any nature which is affixed to but does not form part of the property [and shall include without limitation all items listed in the attached Inventory under the heading 'Fixtures'].

F.072
'The Stand' shall mean the space or area allotted to the [Exhibitor] by the [Company] including any fixtures, fittings, or furniture provided.

F.073
The fixtures and fittings shall for the purpose of this Agreement include all the following materials:[specify].

FORCE MAJEURE

DVD, Video and Discs

F.074
In the event the Agreement cannot be performed or its obligations fulfilled for any reason beyond the reasonable control of either party including war, industrial action, floods for a period of [duration] [which need not be continuous] then either party may at its discretion terminate this Agreement by notice in writing at the end of that period provided no payments have been made and no master material delivered.

F.075
Neither party shall be liable to the other for any loss or damage arising from its failure to perform its obligations under this Agreement for any reason whatsoever beyond its reasonable control.

F.076

In the event that this Agreement cannot be performed or its obligations fulfilled in whole or part for any reason beyond the reasonable control of either party including war, industrial action, floods, Act of God then such non-performance or failure to fulfil its obligations shall be deemed not to be a breach of this Agreement. In the event that this Agreement cannot be performed or its obligations fulfilled for any reason beyond either parties reasonable control for a continuous period of [specify duration]. Then the other party who is not in default may at its sole discretion terminate this Agreement by notice in writing at the end of that period.

F.077

Where the [Licensee] is prevented from fulfilling the terms of this Agreement and is unable to produce, manufacture, distribute and supply [DVDs] of the [Film] for any reason beyond the control of the [Licensee]. Whether caused or due to an Act of God or other force majeure such as war, fire, earthquake, strike, lockout, death or incapacity of the artist(s), labour controversy, civil commotion, act of any government, its agencies or officers, or any order, regulation or ruling thereof, or action by any union or trade association of artists, musicians, composers or employees or by delays in the delivery of materials and supplies The [Licensee] shall have the right by written notice to the [Licensor] and without liability to suspend the obligations of both parties and the terms of this Agreement until such time as the circumstances have changed and the parties can perform and carry out this Agreement. The parties agree that the Licence Period shall be extended by the period for which the Agreement was suspended and not fulfilled.

F.078

Notwithstanding anything contained in this Agreement, in the event that it is rendered impossible to perform by either party for any reason beyond its reasonable control which reasons may include, but are not be limited to, war, invasion, act of foreign enemy, hostilities (whether war be declared or not) civil war or strike, rebellion, lockouts or other industrial disputes or actions, Acts of God, acts of government or other prevailing authorities or defaults of third parties, then such non-performance shall be deemed not to constitute a breach of this Agreement. If such an event occurs to the extent that the Agreement cannot be performed for a period of [three months] or more then the [Company] shall have the right at its discretion to terminate this Agreement by notice in writing at the end of such period. If any of the events occurs in part of the Territory only then the [Company] may decide at its discretion to terminate the Agreement in respect of those countries but not the rest of the unaffected countries.

F.079

The [Company] shall use its reasonable endeavours to fulfil orders accepted by it for the manufacture of videos and DVDs of the [Film] within a reasonable time of receipt thereof. Provided that the [Company] shall not be liable for any failure or delay in the fulfilment of any order or any part(s) resulting from any cause beyond the [Company's] reasonable control.

F.080

There shall be no right by either party to claim for damages, losses or expense where the Agreement is suspended, terminated or not fulfilled due to any Act of God caused by storm, lightning, flooding, hurricane, snow, temperatures, earthquake, landslides or other extreme catastrophes, fire, or failure of supply of power, energy resources or water.

F.081

The parties both agree that the following matters shall not be considered force majeure under this Agreement:

1.1 The failure to clear and/or pay for the necessary copyright, moral rights, waivers, licences and/or any other contracts and/or consents required from third parties.

1.2 Any failure due to poor maintenance, lack of security, non-compliance with any legislation and/or inadequate planning.

1.3 Postal strikes, slow and/or suspended internet service, failure of the telephone system and/or heavy snow.

F.082

The [Licensee] agrees and undertakes that the following circumstances shall not constitute force majeure under this Agreement:

1.1 A suspension and/or failure of electricity, gas and/or water for less than [number] days.

1.2 A declaration of emergency measures by the government relating to water conservation.

1.3 Suspension of transport by air, sea and/or rail for less than [number] days.

1.4 Any extreme weather conditions storm, lightning, flooding, hurricane, snow, temperatures which last for less than [number] days.

1.5 Any fire and/or smoke damage which is not at the main premises of the [Company].

F.083

The [Company] shall not be entitled to rely on the force majeure term in this Agreement where any delays, errors, omissions, losses and/or damages have been and/or are caused by the fact that the [Company] failed to engage, use and enter into agreements with reputable and financially secure third parties and should have known and/or been aware that the third parties which have caused the problems were at risk of entering into administration and/or bankruptcy at the time. In such cases the [Company] agrees that it shall be liable for all the payments due to [Name] from such third parties and that the [Company] may not recoup such sums from any other payments due to [Name].

F.084

Force majeure shall not apply under this Agreement where there is a reasonable cost effective alternative for the [Licensee] to follow which would resolve the issue. Provided that any changes shall be approved in advance by the [Licensor] and shall not involve the grant of additional rights and/or reduce the sums due to the [Licensor].

Film and Television

F.085

No party shall be liable for its inability or delay in performing any of its obligations hereunder if such delay is caused by circumstances beyond the reasonable control of the party including, but not limited to, delay caused through industrial action, fire, flood, riot, governmental or other regulation, Act of God, lightning, aircraft impact, explosion, civil commotion, malicious damage, storm, tempest, earthquake, legal enactment, satellite transmission failure or lack of stability, failure of terrestrial facilities or regular interruption of image or sound or any other circumstances beyond the reasonable control of the affected party.

F.086

The [Company] shall use all reasonable endeavours to transmit the [Customer Material] at the times agreed with the [Customer] and otherwise comply with the terms of this Agreement. The [Company] shall be under no liability to the [Customer] and/or any third party with regard to:

1.1 Any failure to make any transmission whether at the time specified and/or otherwise. Any interruptions, delays inaccuracies errors or omissions in the transmission of the [Customer Material] if the [Company] is prevented for any reason from making that transmission by reason of the termination of any agreements it may have with [–] and/or any government and/or statutory body for any reason.

1.2 Any failure to provide the [Service] in accordance with this Agreement where such failure is caused by Acts of God, equipment failure, or any laws, order, regulation, or directive of any government, authority, international body or statutory body, or any emergency, war, strike, lockout, work stoppage, labour difficulty and/or any matter which is not with the reasonable control of the [Company].

1.3 Any failure to provide the [Service] in accordance with this Agreement which results in whole or part from any fault or negligence of the [Customer] and/or its equipment and/or facilities.

F.087

In the event that the production or delivery of the [Film] shall be prevented, interrupted or otherwise delayed by reason of fire, flood, casualty, lockout, strikes, labour problems, unavoidable accident, natural disaster, mechanical or other breakdown of electrical or sound equipment, failure or delay by a supplier, unforeseen problems with export or transport, Act of God, impact of any statutory provision, any cause arising out of or attributed to war or by any other cause of any nature beyond the control of the [Licensor] then the obligations of the [Licensor] in respect of the [Film] shall be suspended for such period as may be necessary. In such circumstances the [Licensee] shall not be entitled to claim damages from the [Licensor] nor to cancel the Agreement.

F.088

If either party is unable to observe or perform any obligations under this Agreement due to an event or circumstance which is beyond that parties' reasonable control. Then that party shall be entitled by notice in writing to the other to suspend performance of its obligations in relation to the [Films]. The suspension shall start on the date of the notice and end at the time at which the party notifies the other that the event or circumstance is has ceased or has been resolved. During the suspension the parties shall both mitigate all costs and expenses in respect of the [Films]. If the suspension continues for [three calendar months] or more then the [Television Company] shall be entitled to terminate the Agreement by notice in working. Upon such termination there shall be no further obligation on the [Production Company] to produce and deliver the [Films]. The [Company] shall not be obliged to pay any further sums other than those necessary to settle the sums owed up to the date of termination. Upon such termination all rights in the [Films] (whether completed or not) shall revert to the [Company] and the [Production Company] shall not be entitled to any interest or claim.

F.089

If the [Company's] transmission and business activities are effected, restricted, prevented or changed by any legislation, statute, directive, regulation, code, standard or any other act or thing beyond the [Company's] reasonable control. The [Company] shall have the choice as to whether to terminate this contract and any such termination shall be without prejudice to the [Company's] right to be paid by the [Agency/Advertiser] any sums which are due and/or owing at the date of termination.

F.090

In the event that the [Company] decides that due to unforeseen or unusual circumstances it is necessary to change the [Film] arrangements and/or the performances under this Agreement and/or there is some reason of force majeure which prevents the Agreement being fulfilled and/or any other cause beyond the reasonable control of the [Company] then the [Company] may immediately or at any time thereafter terminate this Agreement. Upon such termination the [Artist] shall not be entitled to any sums from the [Company] except for the payment of the fees in respect of the work carried out up to the date of termination.

F.091

Neither of the parties shall be liable to the other for any loss or damage whatsoever arising from its failure to perform any of its obligations in this Agreement by reason of any cause whatsoever beyond its reasonable control. If the [Company] is unable to broadcast and/or transmit any of the [Films] due to force majeure. Then the Licence Period shall be extended for such period of time as may be necessary to enable all the [Films] to be broadcast and/or transmitted in accordance with the terms of this Agreement.

F.092

If the [Company] is prevented from starting the production of the [Programmes] or the production, or delivery is delayed or interrupted at any time due to an event or circumstances beyond the reasonable control of the [Company] then the [Company] shall not be liable for any loss, damage, (either direct or indirect) or otherwise that the [Contractor] may incur or suffer on account of the [Company's] failure to fulfil the terms of this Agreement. This shall include, but not be limited to, fire, or other disaster, withdrawal of labour or other services (overtime ban, work to rule) industrial dispute, withdrawal or interruption of public or power services, illness, incapacity or death of key personnel, provided that such event was not due to the neglect of the [Company] and/or was not reasonably foreseeable at the date of this Agreement.

F.093

Notwithstanding any other term of this Agreement if either party for any cause beyond its reasonable control cannot perform this Agreement then such non-performance shall be deemed not to be a breach of this Agreement. If any such event occurs to prevent the performance of this Agreement for a period in excess of [four] months this Agreement may then be terminated at the end of such period by notice in writing by the [Company]. If the [Company] is unable to broadcast/transmit the [Film] for any reason beyond its reasonable control then the Licence Period shall be extended for such period as may be necessary to enable it to be broadcast/transmitted but in any event the Licence Period shall not be extended beyond [date].

F.094
The parties both agree that the following circumstances shall not be considered force majeure under this Agreement:

1.1 A fire which is contained and which does not prevent the operation of the main business of the [Company] from the premises.

1.2 An industrial dispute which is in arbitration and/or mediation.

1.3 Failure and/or suspension of gas, electricity, water for less than [one week].

1.4 The removal and/or suspension of [Name].

1.5 Breakdown and/or maintenance of equipment.

1.6 Failure to comply with health and safety legislation.

F.095
Where the parties cannot agree whether the circumstances constitute force majeure or not. It is agreed that the parties will put all the facts to an independent person whom both parties agree to share the cost of in order to reach a non-binding view of the issue. This shall be without prejudice of the right of either party to issue legal proceedings for breach of contract.

F.096
It is agreed between the parties that it shall be deemed that the Agreement has been subject to force majeure where filming cannot take place due to riots, threats of outbreaks of violence and/or terrorist attacks and/or war, military occupation, fires, kidnaps of civilians, looting and/or political campaigns and/or other threats and/or lack of resources which would pose a risk to health and/or safety of any person associated with the [Project] at any time. It is agreed that the [Project] may be delayed for up to [number] months and thereafter any party shall have the right to serve notice that the [Project] must either go ahead as planned and/or be ended by terms to be agreed between the parties.

F.097
It is agreed that the [Licensee] shall not be entitled to rely on force majeure of any kind in order to delay payment and/or transfer of any sums to the [Licensor] under this Agreement.

General Business and Commercial

F.098
Force majeure shall mean any circumstances beyond the reasonable control of either of the parties including but not limited to:

1.1 War, acts of warfare, hostilities (whether war be declared or not) invasion, incursion by armed forces, act of hostile army, nation or enemy.

1.2 Riot, uprising against constituted authority, civil commotion, disorder, rebellion, organised armed resistance to the government, insurrection, revolt, military or usurped power, civil war.

1.3 Acts which hinder the course of or stop, hinder, prevent, interrupt or breach the supply and/or provision and/or distribution of any material and/or power and/or resource which is required under this Agreement.

1.4 Any hazardous, dangerous, perilous, unsafe chemical, substance, material, property, use or adaptation which threatens or poses a risk to the health, safety or liability of either party or the general public.

1.5 Flood, fire, arson, storm, lightning, tempest, hurricane, accident, or other Acts of God.

1.6 Epidemic, disease, earthquake, landslides, avalanches, acts of terrorism, hijacking, sabotage, vandalism, and other criminal acts which cause destruction.

1.7 Damage of equipment, machinery, master material or property.

1.8 Chemical, nuclear or other warfare, insurgence, attack and/or accident.

1.9 Death, injury or illness of key personnel.

F.099
In the event that this Agreement cannot be performed or its obligations fulfilled for any reason beyond the reasonable control of either party to this Agreement as a result of such events as war, industrial action, floods or Acts of God. Then such non-performance or failure to fulfil its obligations by any such party shall be deemed not to be a breach of this Agreement.

F.100
No party to this Agreement shall be held in any way responsible for any failure to fulfil its obligations under this Agreement if such failure has been caused (directly or indirectly) by circumstances beyond the control of the defaulting party. This shall include accident or equipment failure, war, riot, industrial action or act of terrorism (except where such accident or equipment failure

has been caused by the negligence of the defaulting party, its employees, sub-licensees, sub-contractors, agents or otherwise).

F.101

In the event that this Agreement cannot be performed or its obligations fulfilled for any reason beyond the reasonable control of either party to this Agreement for a continuous period of [three months]. Then the non-defaulting party may at its discretion terminate this Agreement by notice in writing at the end of that period. If this Agreement is so terminated then both parties shall agree a fair and reasonable payment for the work completed up to the date of termination taking into account any prior contractual commitments entered into in reliance on the performance of this Agreement.

F.102

Irrespective of any rights or remedies provided by law, both parties to this Agreement agree that this Agreement will be dissolved by frustration only if unforeseen supervening circumstances render this Agreement impossible to perform but shall not apply in favour of a party which is responsible wholly, mainly or partly for the circumstances giving rise to the frustration.

F.103

Neither party shall be liable to the other for failure to perform any of its obligations under this contract, other than obligations to make payments due under this contract when performance is hindered or prevented due to force majeure. For the purposes of this contract force majeure shall mean causes which are unpredictable and beyond the reasonable control of the party claiming force majeure which could not have been avoided or prevented by reasonable foresight, planning and implementation.

F.104

Notwithstanding anything contained in this Agreement, in the event of this Agreement being rendered impossible of performance by either party for any reason beyond its reasonable control (including, but not limited to, war, invasion, act of foreign enemy, hostilities, whether war be declared or not, civil war or strife, rebellion, strikes, lockout or other industrial dispute or actions, Acts of God, acts of government or other prevailing authorities or defaults of third parties), then such non-performance shall be deemed not to constitute a breach of this Agreement.

F.105

If in the opinion of the [Licensor] the performance of this Agreement shall for reasons arising from state of war, civil commotion, lockout, strike, industrial action, breakdown of equipment, natural disaster or other abnormal circumstances become impractical or if the complete performance of the

Agreement shall be prevented by force majeure or any other cause beyond the reasonable control of the [Licensor] or the [Licensee] the [Licensor] may terminate the Agreement immediately. In this event the [Licensee] shall have no claim on the [Licensor] for remuneration, expenses, costs, damages or otherwise except for such proportion of the total fees as may already have been paid to the [Licensor] by the [Licensee] under the terms of this Agreement.

F.106

No responsibility will be taken by the [Organisers] in the event of the postponement, abandonment or restriction of any [Exhibition] as a result of the premises becoming entirely or partly unavailable for any reason beyond the reasonable control of the [Organisers].

F.107

None of the parties to this Agreement shall be under any liability to the others or any other party in respect of anything which may constitute a breach of this Agreement arising by reason of force majeure. Force majeure shall include all circumstances beyond the control of the parties including, but not limited to, the following events: Acts of God, perils of the sea or air, fire, flood, drought, explosion, sabotage, accident, embargo, riot, civil commotion, acts of local or natural government bodies or authorities.

F.108

Notwithstanding any other provision of this Agreement to the contrary neither party shall be liable to the other for any failure to perform this Agreement which is due to an Act of God, accident, fire, lockout, strike, labour dispute, riot, civil commotion, failure of technical facilities, act of public enemy, statutory provisions, rule, order or directive (whether national or local), the failure of electricity, gas or other power facilities or any other acts of any nature beyond the reasonable control of either party. Any such occurrence shall be deemed an event of force majeure.

F.109

If either the [Company] or the [Distributor] is prevented or delayed in the performance of any of its obligations under this Agreement by force majeure then such party shall have written notice to the other party specifying the detail of the reasons for force majeure and provide such evidence as may be available. In addition it shall estimate the period for which it is expected that the delay or otherwise shall continue. In these circumstances the party shall not be liable for the performance by the stipulated date from the date of such notice for such period as the delay or otherwise shall continue.

F.110

The [Company] shall not be under any liability if by reason of abnormal circumstances beyond its control it is unable to hold the [Conference]. These circumstances shall include, but not be limited to, strikes, lockout, labour troubles, fire, explosions, civil disturbances, riots, political unrest, electrical or other power breakdowns.

F.111

In the event that this Agreement cannot be performed or its obligations fulfilled for any reason beyond the reasonable control of the [Licensor] or the [Licensee] including such events as war, industrial action or Acts of God, then such non-performance or failure to fulfil its obligations shall be deemed not to be a breach of this Agreement. In the event that this Agreement cannot be performed or its obligations fulfilled for any reason beyond the reasonable control of the defaulting party for a continuous period of [two] months then the other party may at its discretion terminate this Agreement by notice in writing at the end of that period.

F.112

Neither party shall be responsible to the other party in circumstances where the obligations under this Agreement cannot be performed or carried out due to matters or conditions outside the control of the [Assignee] or the [Assignor]. In the event that this Agreement is not fulfilled or performed by [date] then this Agreement shall automatically end on that date.

F.113

In the event that this Agreement cannot be fulfilled by either party due to force majeure which is beyond their reasonable control both parties agree that the whole but not part of the agreement can be suspended for one continuous period of [duration] by written notice by either party who is so effected. If after that period of suspension the situation continues so that the agreement is still prevented from being fulfilled then both parties agree to bring the agreement to an end as soon as possible by negotiating a settlement.

F.114

Where circumstances are such that a party to this Agreement is prevented from fulfilling their obligations and responsibilities due to force majeure which are beyond their reasonable control and which could not have been reasonably expected and/or predicted. Then it is agreed that such party shall be provided with an additional period of [number] days to comply. If the matter cannot be resolved within that period then the other parties shall have the right to terminate, cancel and/or amend the Agreement as they think fit in order to resolve the matter and this shall include the right to demand a repayment of all and/or some of the sums paid to date.

Internet and Websites

F.115

Where the [Company] is unable to provide the [Service/Work/Products] for any reason due to circumstances beyond its reasonable control. Then the [Company] at its sole discretion decide to suspend, delay, or cancel the delivery of the [Service/Work/ Products] by the [Company]. In such event the [Company] shall not be liable to pay any additional sums in compensation or as damages or for expenses which may be incurred and the total liability of the [Company] shall be to return the payment for that part of the [Service/Work/Products] which have not been delivered to the [Customer].

F.116

The [Website Company] shall not be liable to the [Customer] and/or any associated business and/or equipment and/or software for any sums, costs, expenses, charges, penalties, interest, damages, losses, and/or other claims that may arise as a result of force majeure. Force majeure shall include but not be limited to power failure, equipment failure, accident, fire, lockout, strike, labour dispute, riot, civil commotion, failure of technical and payment facilities, state of war, lockout, strike, industrial action, natural disaster, perils of the sea or air, fire, flood, drought, explosion, sabotage, accident, an order or directive of a national government or local authority, and embargo. The [Website Company] shall have the right to terminate the Agreement without notice and to only be liable to pay back to the [Customer] the sums received for any delivery which has not been made.

F.117

The [Company] shall not be liable to the [Client] in the event that this Agreement cannot be performed or its obligations fulfilled for any reason beyond the reasonable control of the [Company]. This shall mean force majeure and shall include but not be limited to war, hostilities, strikes, Acts of God, breakdown of equipment, fire, flood, earthquake, storm or other natural disaster, invasion, act of foreign enemies (whether war be declared or not), civil war, rebellion, labour dispute, strike, lockout, boycott, interruption or failure of electricity, gas, water or telephone service; Failure of the supply of any equipment, machinery or material required by the [Company].

F.118

The parties agree that the following situations shall not be force majeure under this Agreement:

1.1 Power failure for less than [number] days.

1.2 Equipment failure where another can be hired and/or bought and/or is available on another premises.

1.3 An accident, and/or any failure to complete a risk assessment and/or any legal proceedings by a government body.

1.4 Failure to comply with any legislation, regulation and/or directive.

F.119

The parties agree that no reliance shall be placed by either party on force majeure without strong evidence that the fact disclosed is the reason for the failure to perform and fulfil the terms of this Agreement. The parties agree that the following situations shall not constitute force majeure:

1.1 Street riots, protests and/or disorder which last for less than [number] days.

1.2 The suspension and/or interruption of electricity, gas, water and/or the internet for less than [number] days.

1.3 The non-delivery of the materials required from a third party due to an embargo, blockade and/or other interruption to the ports and/or airports for less than [number] days.

F.120

Where a situation arises where one party seeks to rely on force majeure as the reason for the delay and/or failure to fulfil all and/or part of the Agreement. The parties agree that the defaulting party shall specify the reason in writing and offer the other party the right to accept the terms offered and/or receive a full refund of all payments which relate to the unfulfilled work.

F.121

Force Majeure shall not include:

1.1 Viruses, hacks and security breaches by third parties.

1.2 Failure to renew and/or register any domain name, copyright, trade mark and/or other rights held by [Name].

1.3 Failures and/or delays due to failure to comply with custom, border control and other duty, taxes and government legislation, regulation and policies.

Merchandising

F.122

No party shall be held in any way responsible for any failure to fulfil the obligations if such failure has been caused directly by circumstances beyond the reasonable control of the defaulting party. This shall include accident, equipment failures, war, riot, industrial action, terrorism. The defaulting party shall notify the other party as soon as possible and propose a cause of action and delay which the other party must accept if the situation is to be remedied within [duration] or may reject if a longer period is envisaged.

F.123

No party shall be liable to the other for any loss or damage arising from the failure to carry out all or part of the terms that it is required to fulfil under this Agreement for any cause whatsoever which is beyond the reasonable control of that party.

F.124

In the event that this Agreement cannot be performed or its obligations fulfilled for any reason beyond the reasonable control of either party including war, hostilities, strikes, Acts of God, natural disasters, fire, breakdown of equipment not caused by negligence or neglect then this Agreement shall be suspended [in whole/part] up to a period of [duration]. Thereafter either party may terminate this Agreement by notice in writing subject to the agreement of an equitable settlement giving due regard to the circumstances.

F.125

In the event that either party cannot perform or fulfil the obligations under this Agreement due to conditions which are outside their control then the following terms shall apply:

1.1 The party which is unable to perform and/or fulfil the terms shall promptly give notice to that effect to the other party stating in detail the circumstances for such force majeure and the estimated time to remedy such event.

1.2 Then the party who has not defaulted shall have the right to serve notice to terminate the Agreement if the problem is not remedied within [one calendar month] of receipt of the notice in 1.1.

1.3 Both parties agree that they shall endeavour to reach an amicable settlement to resolve the matter.

F.126

The [Licensee] shall not be entitled to rely on a matter of force majeure for the failure to pay the [Licensor] any payments which have accrued under this Agreement. The [Licensee] agrees that where funds cannot be transferred for any reason from a third party from which the [Licensor] is due a royalty. That the [Licensee] shall bear the cost and pay the [Licensor] the sum owed and then seek to recover the sums from the third party.

F.127

The parties agree that the following facts shall not be deemed force majeure and shall be excluded [specify].

F.128

Where the [Licensee] and/or any sub-agent, sub-distributor and/or other third party seeks to rely on grounds of force majeure for any reason. Then it is agreed by the [Licensee] that the [Licensor] shall not be obliged to permit any delay to extend beyond [number] months from the date of the first notification of the issue. That thereafter the [Licensee] agrees that the [Licensor] may take such steps as it thinks fit to remedy and/or resolve the matter including but not limited to terminating the licence to the [Licensee] and any such sub-agent, sub-distributor and/or third party.

F.129

It is agreed between the parties that force majeure shall include:

1.1 Failure to pass the health and safety and product tests for [subject].

1.2 Delays in processing applications and authorisations by [organisation].

1.3 Fire, flood, war, riots, earthquake, tornados, heat wave and/or any other extreme condition which effects the operation of any of the resources and/or the premises of the factory where the [Products/Work] are produced and/or made.

Publishing

F.130

'Force Majeure' shall mean any Act of God including, but not limited to, fire, flood, earthquake, storm or other natural disaster, war, invasion, act of foreign enemies, hostilities (whether war be declared or not), civil war, rebellion, revolution, insurrection, military or usurped power or confiscation, nationalisation, requisition, destruction or damage to property by or under the order of any government or public or local authority or imposition of government sanction, embargo or similar action: law, judgment, order, decree, embargo, blockade, labour dispute, strike, lockout, boycott, interruption or failure of electricity, gas, water or telephone service; Failure of the supply of any equipment, machinery or material required by the [Publisher] for publication of the [Work]; Breach of contract by any key personnel or any other matter or cause beyond the control of the [Publisher].

F.131

In the event that this Agreement cannot be performed or its obligations fulfilled for any reason beyond the reasonable control of the [Author] or the

[Publisher] including the ill health of the [Author], war, industrial action, floods or Acts of God, then such non-performance or failure to fulfil its obligations shall be deemed not to be a breach of this Agreement. In the event that this Agreement cannot be performed or its obligations fulfilled for any reason beyond the reasonable control of the defaulting party for a continuous period of [six months] then [the other/either] party may at its discretion terminate this Agreement by notice in writing at the end of that period provided that both parties agree to negotiate in good faith on equitable settlement of the work already performed to the date of termination.

F.132

Neither party shall be liable to the other for any loss, damage, compensation or expenses arising from its failure to perform its obligations under this Agreement for any cause whatsoever beyond its reasonable control.

F.133

Neither the [Author] nor the [Publisher] shall be liable for any loss or damage suffered or incurred by the other arising directly or indirectly from its failure to carry out, fulfil or perform any of its obligations under this Agreement of any nature, provided that such events or circumstances shall be due to matters which were not reasonably foreseeable at the date of this Agreement, and/or were not due to the neglect or deliberate act of such party and/or were due entirely to an event or circumstance of force majeure. The party affected shall use its best endeavours to immediately rectify the position and advise and write to the other party explaining the reason for the situation. The party shall provide an estimate of the delay or interruption and propose a date by which it is anticipated that the position will be rectified. In the event that the matter relates to the failure by the [Publisher] to publish the [Work] then this clause shall not relieve the [Publisher] of his obligation to pay the [Author] all the advance in full and to agree a settlement for the loss of royalties from the exploitation of the [Work] and the enhancement of the [Author's] reputation.

F.134

In the event that due to unforeseen or unusual circumstances it is necessary to delete, change or alter the interview arrangements, photographs, headline or advertising or the publication dates then it is agreed that the agreement may be entirely suspended for [duration] and the relevant dates adjusted accordingly to a later period up to a date no later than [date]. After that time either party may at its discretion terminate this Agreement without prejudice to any rights and remedies either may have in respect of the agreement.

F.135

In the event that the [Publisher] does not publish the [Work] of the [Author] for any reason due to force majeure. Then the [Author] shall have the right to serve notice on the [Publisher] at any time to terminate the Agreement and subject to the repayment of the [Advance] to have all rights and all material revert to, assigned to and be owned by the [Author] and for all rights held by the [Publisher] to be terminated without any additional payment.

F.136
Where the [Distributor] is unable to reproduce, publish, distribute and supply the [Work] for any reason beyond its control for a period of [three calendar months]. Then the [Author] shall have the right to serve notice on the [Distributor] that unless the [Work] is made available to the public within [two calendar months] and not less than [number] copies. Then all rights shall revert to the [Author] and shall be assigned back by the [Distributor]. The [Distributor] agrees that the [Author] shall not be obliged to pay any sums for such reversion of rights. The [Distributor] also agrees to provide at the [Distributors] cost any manuscript, printers ready copy and any other material held by and/or under the control of the [Distributor] relating to the [Work].

F.137
For the purpose of this agreement force majeure shall include:

1.1   The failure and/or destruction and/or damage to the laptop, computer, storage devices and/or other material of the [Author] which prevents and/or delays delivery of the [Work].

1.2   Ill health and/or disability which results in the [Author] being unable to write, edit and deliver the [Work] by the deadline.

1.3   The failure of the internet for more than [one] day.

1.4   Failure to deliver the [Work] in written form by freight and/or postal delivery due to strikes, power failures, crime and/or destruction of any building.

Purchase and Supply of Products

F.138
If the ability of the [Assignee] to accept the [Material] and/or the performance of the terms of this Agreement is delayed, hindered or prevented by circumstances beyond the reasonable control of the [Assignor] or [Assignee]. Then such delivery or performance shall be suspended and if it cannot be effected within a reasonable time after the due date then the Agreement may be cancelled by either party by notice in writing and an equitable settlement reached.

F.139

If the ability of the [Company] to accept delivery of the [Goods] and/or the provision or performance of services is delayed, hindered or prevented by circumstances beyond the reasonable control of the [Company]. Such delivery and/or provision or performance shall be suspended and if it cannot be carried out within a reasonable time after the due date then it shall be cancelled by notice in writing by the [Company] to the [Seller].

F.140

Neither party shall be liable for any consequential loss to the other for failure to perform any of their obligations under this Agreement for reasons outside their control. If for any such reason the [Supplier] ceases to be able to make available any further [Products] hereunder then the [Purchaser's] obligation to make further payments pursuant to this Agreement shall be suspended. The suspension shall continue until such time as the [Supplier] is able to supply the [Products] whereupon payments by the [Purchaser] shall be resumed. The amount due to the [Supplier] in the Contract shall be adjusted to reflect the period of suspension and the quantity of the [Product] affected.

F.141

The [Company] shall not be liable to the [Supplier] for failure to accept delivery of the [Goods] resulting from any breakdown of plant or apparatus, fire, explosion, accident, strike, lockout or any other event or cause beyond the control of the [Company]. If the [Supplier] shall fail to perform any part of this Order by reason of any event or cause specified above. Then in either case the [Company] may at its discretion suspend or cancel the delivery of the [Goods] and/or performance of this Order without any liability to the [Supplier] in respect of the payments and/or other sums due.

F.142

In the event that one or both parties cannot perform or fulfil the obligations under this Agreement due to conditions which are outside the control of one or both parties the following terms shall then become applicable:

1.1   One or both parties who are in default shall promptly give notice to that effect to the other party stating in detail the circumstances for such force majeure and the estimated time to remedy such event.

1.2   Then the defaulting party or both parties if relevant may only serve notice of the end of this Agreement specifying an end date if the situation continues for a period of [two months] from [the date on which the failure first occurred].

1.3   Both parties agree that in the event they reach an amicable settlement to resolve the matter. Each party shall bear its own losses and costs except that the [Seller] shall pay for all units of the [Product] which have already been delivered. The [Supplier] shall not be under any obligation to buy back products already supplied or to replace damaged or lost stock.

F.143

Neither party shall be liable to the other party for any loss and damage in circumstances where the obligations under this Agreement cannot be performed due to factors beyond the reasonable control of the defaulting party. If the factors prevent the Agreement being fulfilled for a period of [duration] then the non-defaulting party may terminate this Agreement by notice in writing and both parties agree to negotiate in good faith an equitable settlement.

F.144

In the event that this Agreement cannot be performed or its obligations fulfilled for any reason beyond the reasonable control of either party for a continuous period of [one month] then either party may at its discretion terminate this Agreement. Where notice is given by the [Company] the [Company] shall pay a fair and reasonable sum to the [Contributor] taking into account work completed and any financial loss suffered by the [Contributor] as a direct result which arises from the Agreement.

F.145

No party shall be liable for its inability or delay in performing any of its obligations if caused by circumstances beyond the reasonable control of the party including, but not limited to, industrial action, fire, flood, earthquake, bad weather conditions, explosion, war or a terrorist attack.

F.146

The parties agree that the following shall not be deemed and/or accepted as circumstances which constitute force majeure:

1.1   The temporary ill-health of the [Author] for less than [number] weeks.

1.2   The closure of the [Publishers] offices due to fire, flood and/or terrorist action.

1.3   The printers being placed in administration, receivership and/or unable to operate and/or delivery the finished product before any work of the [Author] is delivered.

1.4   The loss of the manuscript on the hard drive of the computer of the [Author].

1.5   The death and/or incapacity of the subject of the work where the interviews and material has already been concluded.

F.147

Where the parties are unable to agree as to whether a particular circumstance and/or event constitutes force majeure or not. It is agreed that an independent person shall be appointed who is a member of the [specify body] who shall review all of the written arguments of both sides. The parties both agree to share equally the cost of the independent person and to endeavour to reach a settlement based on their decision prior to the commencement of any legal proceedings.

F.148

The delivery date for the [Products] is not adjustable and where force majeure and/or any other circumstances delay delivery and/or result in the [Products] not being produced at all. The [Client] has the right to terminate the Agreement and to obtain a full refund of all payments made to date. The [Company] shall not be entitled to deduct and/or recoup and/or charge for any costs incurred.

Services

F.149

If a condition of force majeure is declared by either party and continues for a period of at least [ten consecutive days] then either party may cancel the provision of the services [but not necessarily terminate this Contract] on [ten days including weekends and bank holidays] written notice to the other party.

F.150

Force majeure shall include Acts of God, war (declared or undeclared), insurrections, hostilities, strikes (other than strikes by the parties' employees which shall be decreed not to be a force majeure event), lockouts (other than lockouts by parties of its employees which shall be decreed not to be a force majeure event) riots, fire, storm, government intervention.

F.151

Any party which is unable in whole or part to carry out its obligations under this contract shall promptly give written notice to that effect to the other party stating in detail the circumstances for such force majeure and the estimated time to remedy such event. Any party claiming force majeure shall diligently use all reasonable efforts to remove the cause of such force majeure, and shall give written notice to the other party when the force majeure has ended and shall resume performance of any suspended obligations as soon as possible.

F.152

In the event that this Agreement cannot be performed or its obligations fulfilled for any reason beyond the reasonable control of the [Licensor] or the [Licensee] including such events as war, industrial action, unforeseen technical failure, floods or Acts of God. Then such non-performance or failure of its obligations by any such party shall be deemed not to be a breach of this Agreement. In the event that this Agreement cannot be performed or its obligations fulfilled beyond the reasonable control of the [Licensor] or the [Licensee] for [a continuous period of three months]. Then the party who has not defaulted and/or both parties or if both are affected may terminate this Agreement by notice in writing at the end of that period. If this Agreement is so terminated then both parties shall agree a fair and reasonable payment for the work completed up to the date of termination. This payment shall take into account any prior contractual commitments entered into in reliance of the performance of this Agreement.

F.153

Neither party shall be responsible to the other party in circumstances where the obligations under this Agreement cannot be performed due to circumstances outside the reasonable control of the defaulting party. However if such circumstances persist for more than [five working days] the non-defaulting party [or either if both are affected] may terminate this Agreement in writing having made reasonable [compensation/damages/ return all products] to the other party for such work completed and/or products supplied to date.

F.154

In the event that this Agreement cannot be performed or fulfilled in respect of some significant or major part due to any reason beyond the control of either party including war, industrial action, floods, Acts of God, then the failure to carry out such work or deliver any material shall be deemed not to be a breach of this Agreement. Any party which is unable in whole or part shall, if reasonably possible, give written notice stating the problem to the other party and whether it is expected that issue will be resolved and the effect on the agreement. A failure for a period of [two months] whether continuous or interrupted shall entitle the non-defaulting party to notify the other that the Agreement is to end on a specified date. The parties shall then be obliged to agree a fair settlement.

F.155

In the event that this Agreement cannot be performed or its obligations fulfilled for any reason beyond the reasonable control of the [Agent] or the [Actor] including the ill-health of the [Actor], war, industrial action, floods, or other unforeseen circumstances. Then this shall not be considered a breach of this Agreement, but it shall be allowed to continue provided every effort is made to remedy the problem, and shall be treated as suspended temporarily. When it is clear after [duration] that the problem will continue indefinitely and will not be quickly resolved then the non-defaulting party may serve notice of a termination date together with a proposal for settlement.

F.156

Any party which is unable in whole or part to carry out its obligations under this Agreement shall promptly notify the other party. The reasons for such force majeure should be stated and the estimated time before the terms agreed can be performed. In the event that this is not possible and the situation cannot be remedied within a reasonable period then either party may terminate the agreement without prejudice to any legal rights and remedies

F.157

The parties agree and undertake that the following situations shall not be considered and shall be specifically excluded from force majeure under this Agreement:

1.1   Non-performance for any period which is caused by any reason for a period of less than [number] days.

1.2   A delay which is caused due the failure of one party to deliver and/or supply material and/data which is vital to the next stage of the [Project].

1.3   The withdrawal of funding and/or other professional support which arises as a result of a finding of a breach of health and safety legislation and/or directives and/or regulations by a court and/or government body in respect of any part of the [project] and/or one party.

F.158

Where the parties are not agreed as to whether a fact and/or circumstance constitutes force majeure under this Agreement. Then prior to the instigation of any legal proceedings both parties agree to meet for a conference to endeavour to resolve the situation with a third party acting as the independent mediator. The cost of the independent mediator shall be agreed in advance by both parties and shall be part of any settlement that shall be reached.

F.159

The [Distributor] shall not be entitled to rely on force majeure for any reason where it is unable and/or unwilling to supply the [Company] with the required level of personnel which it must of deliver set out in [–]. Failure by the [Distributor] to recruit and/or find relevant qualified personnel for the service shall not constitute a ground for force majeure.

F.160

The [Company] agrees that the [Supplier] may delay, adapt and/or provide an alternative service to the [Company] as it thinks fit where circumstances beyond its normal control have affected the quality and/or duration of the content of the service at any time. The [Company] agrees that no refund, compensation and/or other payments for any losses and/or damages shall be due and the [Company] waives any such claim and/or action against the [Supplier].

Sponsorship

F.161

No party shall be liable to the other for any loss or damage arising from the failure to perform any of its obligations in this Agreement or for any cause whatsoever beyond its control. The Agreement shall automatically terminate after a continuous [delay/failure] of force majeure of [duration]. The parties shall then enter into mediation to reach a settlement of the outstanding issues relating to the Agreement.

F.162

In the event that the terms of this Agreement cannot be completely or partially fulfilled due to any reason beyond the reasonable control of either party including war, terrorism, industrial action, floods, equipment failure, fire or any other failure, delay or interruption which was beyond the control of either or both parties be considered a breach of this Agreement. Where the situation continues for more than [duration] then either party if both are affected by force majeure or the party who has not defaulted if only one is effected may serve written notice to the other that they wish to terminate the agreement subject to payment for any work completed to the end date and return of any material.

F.163

In the event that this Agreement cannot be performed or its obligations fulfilled for any reason beyond the reasonable control of the [Sponsor] or the [Organisers] then either party may terminate or suspend this Agreement by notice in writing.

F.164

The parties both agree that the following facts and circumstances shall not be considered force majeure:

1.1 The suspension and/or failure of the electricity, gas, water, sewage, drainage, and/or heating for the [Venue] provided that it is for less than [number] hours.

1.2 The failure to obtain a licence from the local authority to sell and/or supply alcohol.

1.3 The disruption, suspension and/or blockade of the local roads, motorway, rail, airport and/or transport links.

1.4 The identification of a health and safety hazard at the [Venue] which is being investigated by the local authority and/or government agency.

F.165

The [Sponsor] agrees that the following circumstances shall constitute force majeure for the purposes of this Agreement:

1.1 The location and venue is not available due to adverse weather conditions, floods, fire, security and/or health and safety matters.

1.2 [Name] has withdrawn from the [Event] and a new performer is required.

1.3 There has been an outbreak of some disease and/or virus which has resulted in restrictions on people, animals, traffic in and/or near the location and/or venue.

1.4 Lack of sanitary and water facilities at the location and/or venue.

1.5 Failure to be granted any relevant licence, planning permission and/or insurance cover.

University, Library and Educational

F.166

The [Institute] [and its employees, sub-licensees, sub-contractors, agents or otherwise] shall not be liable for the failure to perform, deliver, pay, carry out work and/or provide a service and/or facilities and/or any other circumstances beyond the reasonable control of the [Institute] including but not limited to war, hostilities, invasion, terrorism, riot, civil war and/or any other uprising, takeover, or attack whether caused by the public, army, an enemy or military, chemical, nuclear or other warfare and/or accident; the failure, interruption, non-availability of water, gas, electricity, oil, light and any other material and resources; any health and safety issue; flood, fire, arson, storm, lightning, tempest, hurricane, accident, epidemic, disease, earthquake, landslides, avalanches, acts of terrorism, hijacking, sabotage, vandalism, and other criminal acts which cause destruction; damage of equipment, machinery, master material or property; death, injury or illness of key personnel.

F.167

No party to this Agreement shall be held in any way responsible for any failure to fulfil its obligations under this Agreement if such failure has been

766

caused by force majeure and is beyond the reasonable control of either the [Company] and/or the [Institute]. Force majeure shall include any Act of God, fire, flood, earthquake, storm, natural disaster, war, invasion, hostilities, civil war, military power, government, local authority or international imposition of government sanction, embargo or order, labour dispute, strike, boycott, interruption or failure of oil, electricity, gas, water or telecommunication and website service; failure of the supply of any equipment, machinery or material. In the event that the Agreement is suspended and/or cannot be fulfilled for [two months] then either party may terminate the Agreement by notice in writing. The parties agree to enter into negotiations to reach a settlement in relating to the outstanding issues and if they are unable to agree shall appoint an independent mediator and/or arbitrator prior to any litigation.

F.168

In the event that this Agreement cannot be performed, fulfilled and/or carried in respect of clauses [–] due to circumstances which are force majeure of that party. Then any such non-performance, failure and/or delay shall not be considered a breach of this Agreement. The defaulting party must immediately endeavour to notify and/or contact the other and to explain the circumstances and the expected date by which it should be resolved. Where the default shall and/or is likely to continue for a period of [three months]. The non-defaulting party shall have the opportunity at any time to notify the other party that the Agreement is to end on a specified date. The parties shall then be obliged to agree a fair settlement and a reversion of all rights granted under the Agreement.

F.169

The parties agree that the following situations and/or causes will not be deemed force majeure under this Agreement:

1.1   Fire, flood, storm, lightning and/or other condition which only affects part of the premises and the rest is still open to the public.

1.2   A failure of the light, electricity, gas, heating, water, drainage, air conditioning and/or any other part of the premises which can be remedied within [number] hours.

1.3   The ill-health of the main speaker where a suitably qualified substitute is available at short notice.

F.170

The [Institute] shall be entitled to rely on force majeure where it is obliged to restrict and/or limit and/or close any part of the venue to the public at any time due to any unexpected incident, crime, health and safety and/or security matter and/or any other reason which may arise at any time. There shall be no obligation to refund any part of any entrance fee to any person although the [Institute] may offer a voucher for an alternative later date.

FORMAT

General Business and Commercial

F.171

'The Format' of the [Film/Work] shall mean all copyright, design rights, future design rights, trade marks, service marks, domain names, and logos, and computer software and computer-generated and stored material, music, sound recordings in each and every part of the [Film/Work] including the title, the basic idea and concept set out in any treatment, the running order and sequence of items, the design and layout of the set, the content and presentation of the questions and answers, sound effects, score system and prizes, catchphrases, slogans, graphics, images, artwork, two and three dimensional representations of any person, article or product.

F.172

'The Format' shall mean in respect of the [Series] the following:

1.1 The goodwill and reputation.

1.2 The title, slogan, logo and image.

1.3 The basic idea.

1.4 The original manuscripts, drafts, scripts, characters, plots and storylines of the Series including the general location and dramatic sequences.

1.5 The music, sound recordings, advertisements and promotions, jingles or otherwise.

1.6 All intellectual property rights of whatever nature in any media at any time.

F.173

'The Format' shall mean the exclusive rights granted by the [Licensor] to the [Licensee] to produce, reproduce and distribute another [Series] based on the [Films] in the Territory for the Term of the Agreement and to appoint third parties to do so as sub-licensees and sub-distributors. The format shall include, but not be limited to:

1.1   The right to copy, reproduce and exploit the [Series] and any associated trailers, advertising, publicity and other material.

1.2   The right to use the title known as [specify] and the associated trade mark, logo and artwork.

1.3   The right to reproduce the design, layout, colour, signs, scoreboards, and equipment of the studio set.

1.4   The right to use and reproduce both in the studio and for distribution the rules, procedures, catchphrases, slogans, questions and answers.

1.5   The right to use and reproduce the costumes and outfits.

1.6   The right to reproduce and exploit copies of all running orders, scripts and other written material.

1.7   The right to exploit the goodwill and reputation.

1.8   The right to exploit the copyright, design rights, trade mark, logo, literary, musical, dramatic, artistic and all other intellectual property rights.

F.174

The [Licensor] grants the [Licensee] the non-exclusive right to reproduce, manufacture, sell and distribute the [Licensed Articles] based on the [Format] in the [Series] for the duration of the Licence Period throughout the Territory.

F.175

'The Format' shall be the original concept and novel idea for and structure of a [Television Programme] which is briefly described as follows [specify]. Full details of which are attached to and form part of this Agreement.

F.176

'The Format Material' shall be all material of the Format in the possession or under the control of the [Assignor] including copies of all documents, records and other data in any form together with a complete list of all material relating to the [Format] held by any third party.

F.177

The [Licensor] and the [Licensee] both acknowledge that although there is no recognised copyright in the Format of the [Game show] which is acknowledged in law in this country, they wish to transfer the right to exploit such elements of such rights as do exist or may be created in the future. The [Licensor] grants to the [Licensee] the exclusive right to produce, reproduce, distribute, sell and exploit the [Television Rights, the DVD Rights, the Merchandising Rights, the Publishing Rights] in the [Game show] throughout the [world] for the duration of the Term of this Agreement.

F.178
The [Licensee] agrees and undertakes that it shall not acquire any rights or interest in the concept or [Format] owned or controlled by the [Licensor] whether in existence now or created in the future. The [Licensee] shall be limited to the exploitation of the rights specifically granted in this Agreement for the Licence Period. Further, in the event that there are any adaptations, translations, variations or developments or alterations of the [Format] created or commissioned by the [Licensee] pursuant to the exercise of the rights granted the [Licensee] agrees to assign and transfer all such rights in any such adaptation, translation, development, variation or alteration back to the [Licensor] entirely and the Licensee shall have no claim or interest or rights and shall not seek to register any rights.

F.179
'The Programme Format' shall mean the Format of the [Programme] including the characters, storylines, scripts, structure, scenarios, slogans, title, set, graphics and costumes, music, sound effects, sound recordings and all appearances, contributions and artists.

F.180
'The Format' shall be the original concept and novel idea for and structure of a series of films which is briefly described as follows [specify] full details of which are attached and form part of this agreement in Appendix [–]. [Title, script, characters, plot, storyline, location, intellectual property rights, running order, sequence, design and layout of set, presentation of questions and answers, score system, prizes, slogans, graphics, costumes, advertising, publicity, trade marks, service marks, logos, icons, domain names, credits, copyright notices, music, photographs, stills, images, graphics, text, computer generated material, interactive website and telephone line material].

F.181
'The Format' shall mean the style, method, pattern, appearance and to be entitled to make other films which shall be derived from the original film of [Name] which shall include the right to use and benefit from the goodwill and reputation, the title, the basic idea and concept, the original script, character, plot, storyline, location, running order, design, layout, colour signs, scoreboards and studio equipment, the rules, procedures, catchphrases, questions and answers, slogans, costumes and outfits, all written material and artwork, computer generated graphics, all intellectual property rights, design rights, trade marks, service marks, logo, musical, literary, dramatic, artistic and other works which are described in detail in Appendix [–] and

shall form part of this Agreement. The format does not relate to any other material other than the original film [–] therefore advertising, publicity and merchandising are specifically excluded.

F.182
The [Licensee] agrees that all rights not specifically granted are reserved by the [Licensor] including but not limited to [specify].

F.183
There is no right granted to license, appoint, authorise or to engage any third party to exploit the [Format] at any time.

F.184
'The Quiz Format' shall mean the original concept and idea for a [Quiz]. The material shall include the title, logo, slogan, scripts, design and layout of the set structure, presentation of questions and answers, list of prizes, graphics, images and text, score system and charts, running order, music, sound effects, sound recordings, gadgets, advertising and publicity campaign and promotional material, [trade marks, service marks, icons, domain name] credits, copyright notices, computer generated material, [interactive website], premium rate telephone line questions and answers, [and call centre plan] and contributions by presenters. Full details of which are attached and form part of this Agreement in Appendix [A].

F.185
'The Premium Rate Line Format' shall be the original concept and idea for a phone in service on a premium rate line number to a call centre together with a newspaper, magazine and media advertising and publicity campaign and promotional material. Full details of which are attached and form part of this Agreement in Appendix [B].

F.186
The [Licensee] agrees and acknowledges that it shall not register and/or attempt to register the domain name, trade mark, service mark, community mark, logo, slogan, music, sound recordings, copyright and/or any intellectual property rights in respect of any part of the [Format] with any company, trade organisation, collecting society, copyright organisation and/or otherwise. The [Licensee] agrees that all such rights are owned and/or controlled by the [Licensor].

F.187
No format rights and/or right to adapt and/or distort and/or to authorise the reproduction and/or to licence any characters, logos, names, images and/or text in respect of this [Film/Work] are granted under this licence.

F.188

1.1 [Name] is the original writer and copyright owner of the [Work].

1.2 [Name] has licensed the [paperback and hardback and ebook] rights in [specify] language to the [Distributor].

1.3 [Name] owns and controls the title and logo and the content of the [Work] and the right to adapt, vary, change and distort the [Work] for exploitation by any means through television and film throughout the world and has not provided an option and/or granted any such rights to any third party except 1.2.

G

GARDENING LEAVE

General Business and Commercial

G.001

In the event that [Name] serves notice under this Agreement to cease to be employed by the [Company] at any time for whatever reason. Then the [Company] shall have the right at its sole discretion to decide that it shall continue to pay all the sums and benefits due under the Agreement to [Name] until the date of termination, but that [Name] shall no longer attend or carry out his duties and that access to the premises shall be denied. Provided that no false statement or claim shall be made by the [Company] relating to the reason and [Name] shall be entitled to arrange for the removal of his possessions without undue haste or pressure or in any way which creates an impression that there has been any wrongdoing.

G.002

In the event that the [Company] wishes to pursue the option that the [Executive] should be placed on gardening leave for all or part of the remaining term of notice or agreement. Then the parties shall enter into a settlement which sets out the following matters:

1.1 The payments of the sums due and benefits and the date upon which they should cease or be given up. Agreement in respect of the payment of any bonuses, rewards, options, reviews, increases or promotion which would arise in that period.

1.2 An agreed press statement and circular for staff.

1.3 A reference for future employers signed by [specify] which is the agreed wording for any future reference.

1.4 A statement of the pension benefits, insurance cover, and share options and how this is affected by the gardening leave. Where the benefits lapse then a financial payment shall be agreed.

1.5 An agreement by the [Company] as to the property and products to be owned and retained by the [Executive].

1.6   An agreement by the [company] to bear all legal costs and expenses of the [Executive] in relation to his tax, and legal costs and expenses in resolving the matters arising from the settlement up to a maximum limit of [specify].

G.003

The [Company] shall not have the right to place the [Executive] on gardening leave unless the [Executive] serves notice that he/she intends to leave and work for one of the competing companies or businesses set out in the following list [specify names].

G.004

The [Company] shall not have the right to place the [Executive] on gardening leave unless the [Executive] serves notice that he/she intends to leave and work for a company in one of the following markets in [country] [specify subject].

G.005

The [Company] agrees and undertakes that it shall not have the right to request or force the [Executive] to vacate the premises and not attend work as required under the terms of this Agreement. It is accepted that the [Company] can only terminate the Agreement by mutual consent, serve notice of dismissal with the grounds and/or offer the [Executive] the opportunity to resign.

G.006

The [Company] agrees and undertakes that it shall not have the right to insist that the [Executive] take paid leave of absence. Such action by the [Company] shall be deemed a breach of this Agreement. Nor shall the [Company] have the right to give the [Executive] no notice that his/her services are not required and to arrange an escort from the building. That any such action by the [Company] shall be deemed a breach of this Agreement. In either case the [Company] agrees to pay the [Executive] [figure/currency] for each such instance in addition and without prejudice to any claims the [Executive] may have for unfair dismissal or otherwise.

G.007

1.1   The [Company] may at any time notify the [Executive] that he/she is to commence from a specified date up to but no more than [number] [days/months] as a leave of absence which shall be subject to full salary payments but not bonuses for that period. During that leave of absence the [Executive] shall not be required to carry out his/her normal duties but may be asked to comply with any investigation.

1.2 The [Company] agrees that the [Executive] shall have the right to refuse the proposed leave of absence and may decide to treat such notification as breach and/or termination of the Agreement and/or to make an allegation of as unfair dismissal.

GIFTS

General Business and Commercial

G.008
For the purposes of this Agreement 'Gift' shall mean a transfer of property without consideration of a beneficial interest.

G.009
Shares settled on trust for the [Employees] shall be deemed not to be personal gifts.

G.010
No gifts, gratuities, benefits, rewards or financial payments shall be offered, promised, given or provided to any person, business or company at any time in order to secure favour or preference. Where it comes to light that any of these has taken place then the [Company] shall have the right to cancel the contract immediately and request all sums be repaid for work which has not be performed or carried out.

G.011
The employees, agents, representatives and licensee of the [Institute] may only accept gifts, gratuities and monies which are valued at less than [figure/currency] [words]. Any sum and/or benefit offered over that sum must be notified to and approved in advance with the [Chief Executive] prior to acceptance. The [Chief Executive] may decide at his absolute discretion that the gift, gratuity and/or money should become the property of the [Institute].

G.012
The [Institute] agrees that directors, trustees, employees, and agents shall be entitled to accept gifts and hospitality provided that it is declared and reported in accordance with the policy document referred to as [policy]. In the event that there is a significant delay and/or failure to report such matters then the [Institute] may decide in its absolute discretion dismiss, reprimand and/or terminate the agreement with person and/or company.

G.013

Any hospitality, benefit, gift and/or contribution which is valued below [figure/currency] shall not fall within the policy [specify] and shall not be deemed a breach of the contract with the [Company].

G.014

It is a policy of the [Institute/Company] that all directorships, non-executive positions, work, gifts, benefits, free tickets, free services, use of facilities, loans and/or financial arrangements, provision of transport by car, rail and/or air, accommodation and/or any other similar interest which is made with any third party as a result of your connections with the [Institute/Company] are declared in the [Register of Interests/Gifts].

G.015

The [Company] agrees that any employee, agent and/or consultant may accept money, gifts, gratuities, tickets, products and free meals and accommodation from any third party who may be interested in entering into agreements with the [Company]. Provided that no commitment and/or obligation is made to such third party by any employment, agent and/or employee that the [Company] will make any agreement.

G.016

Any gift made to any person who is part of the [Consortium] which relates to the [Project] and which is in excess of [number/currency] must be declared and reported to [Name].

GOODWILL

General Business and Commercial

G.017

'The Goodwill' of the [Company] shall mean the reputation, good standing, esteem, respectability, fame in general and high regard of the [Company] and its [Products] including the goodwill attached to but not the ownership of the names, style, premises, trademarks, service marks, logos, domain names, designs, goods and any other material of any nature attached to or in the possession or control of the [Company], and its relationship with its customers, and the list of its customers, which Goodwill is a separate element of the [Company].

G.018

All Goodwill generated as a result of the use by the [Licensee] arising out of its sub-licence of any trademark, logo, design or any other material provided by the [Licensor] under this Agreement shall vest in and belong entirely to the [Licensor].

G.019

The [Licensee] agrees and undertakes that all intellectual property rights including copyright, design rights, future design rights, computer generated material, computer software rights and patents and goodwill are reserved by and belong exclusively to the [Licensor] in the [Product] and any packaging, marketing and promotional material and merchandising and in the trademarks, logos, images, text, graphics and slogans. The [Licensee] shall not acquire any rights, interest, or goodwill as a result of the [Licensee's] use thereof pursuant to this Agreement and shall not attempt to register any rights or represent to others that the [Licensee] has the right to do so.

G.020

The [Licensee] agrees and undertakes that any goodwill and copyright and intellectual property rights and any other rights generated as a result of the use and exploitation by the [Licensee] of any trademark, domain name, title, slogan, name, text, image, logo, design or artwork, graphics, computer software or computer generated material shall belong to the [Licensor].

G.021

All goodwill arising as a result of the use by the [Licensee] of its sub-licence of any trademark, copyright, designs rights, logo, image, text, slogan, graphics or other material licensed and supplied by the [Licensor] shall belong entirely to the [Licensor]. The [Licensee] shall not acquire any interest or rights in any such goodwill at any time nor shall the [Licensee] be entitled to transfer or authorise any third party to exploit such goodwill.

G.022

The [Agent] acknowledges that it shall not acquire any title in the [Collection samples, the Garments or the Company Logo]. The [Agent] confirms that any goodwill and reputation created in the [Company Logo] shall remain the sole and exclusive property of the [Company] and that no part of this Agreement is intended to transfer any copyright, design rights or any other rights in the [Company Logo, the Collection Samples or the Garments] to the [Agent].

G.023

The [Company] agrees that all copyright, design rights, future design rights, computer software rights, trade marks, service marks, domain names, logos and any adaptations, variations, developments, translations and any other rights and goodwill in the [Celebrity's] birth name, business name, marketing name, image, profile, representations, slogan, catchphrase or any aspect of the [Celebrity] [and/or his family] shall remain the sole and exclusive property of the [Celebrity]. That there is no intention to assign or transfer any such rights and goodwill to the [Company] which undertakes to assign to the [Celebrity] any such rights and material created under this Agreement.

G.024

The [Assignor] agrees that from the date of this Agreement it shall not have any rights, goodwill or interest in the promotion, marketing or exploitation of the [Work] of any nature provided that the [Assignment Fee] is paid in full.

G.025

The [Assignor] agrees that it shall not at any time seek to undermine, prejudice or otherwise impugn the goodwill and reputation of the [Work/ Name] by making statements to the media which are intended to be critical, offensive or derogatory or would affect the sales, marketing and promotion of the [Work].

G.026

The [Manager] agrees and undertakes that the name of the [Sportsperson] and any copyright, goodwill and reputation and any other rights created in respect of the [Sportsperson] and his/her name, trademark, business name, logo, image, text, graphics, music, slogan or other material owned or controlled by the [Sportsperson] shall remain the sole and exclusive property of the [Sportsperson] including any developments or variations whether proposed by the [Manager] or not or some third party. That no part of this Agreement is intended to assign, transfer, grant or authorise the [Manager] to acquire these rights at any time. That the [Manager] shall cooperate fully in the documentation required for any assignment to the [Sportsperson].

G.027

The [Company] agrees and undertakes that any title, name, logo, trade mark, service mark, domain name, image, slogan, catchphrase [and music, ringtones, sound recordings, sounds] which is created or developed by [Name] in respect of their services under this Agreement which directly relates to them personally and is not based on or derived from the [Series] shall belong to [Name] together with any goodwill. The [Company] shall supply any requested copies of material at the [Company's] cost which may be necessary to support any application for any registration or the protection of any rights whether during the Term of this Agreement or for up to [three years] thereafter.

G.028
The [Distributor] agrees and undertakes that all intellectual property, copyright, design rights, future design rights, computer software rights, data and database rights, trade marks, service marks, domain names, logos and any adaptations, variations, developments, translations and any other rights and goodwill in the [Material/Website/Manuscripts/Film] supplied by the [Institute] and any developments, variations and/or any new material which is created relating to the [Project] shall be owned and controlled by the [Institute]. The [Distributor] shall not retain, own and/or control any such rights and/or interest and shall authorise transfer and assignment to the [Institute] without delay at the [Institute's] cost.

G.029
The [Company] agrees and acknowledges that any name, title, slogan, logo, image, trade mark, service mark, community mark, domain name, business name, trading name and/or otherwise either on and/or associated with the [Sponsors'] products and/or services and/or personnel and/or any adaptation together with any goodwill shall be the sole property of the [Sponsor]. The [Company] shall not have any claim and/or interest and shall not attempt to register any right with any third party at any time.

G.030
Where the [Distributor] creates and/or develops a new name, title, logo, trade mark and/or community mark and/or domain name which is used in respect of the [Product] and/or a series of [Products]. Then it is agreed that the [Licensor] and the [Distributor] shall be registered as joint owners of the copyright in the name, title, logo, trade mark and/or community mark and/or domain name and any goodwill. The parties agree that they shall share any benefits from such rights and interest equally.

G.031
All goodwill and reputation in respect of the [Project], title, logo, image and any trade mark, copyright, patent, invention and/or any other intellectual property rights which may exist in any material and/or be created and/or developed shall belong jointly and severally to all members of the [Consortium] equally and any interest shall be registered as such and any revenue shall be divided on that basis.

G.032
Goodwill shall not be quantified for the purpose of this Agreement and no sum shall be attributed. Goodwill generated and/or created by the [Licensee] shall not permit the [Licensee] to register and/or acquire any rights and/or interest in any part of the [Product/Work] which is owned by the [Licensor].

G.033

Goodwill in respect of [specify] has been valued by [specify] at [figure/currency] on the basis of the following documents set out in Schedule [–] supplied by the [Seller]. In the event that at a later date the documents are discovered to contain errors and/or omissions. Then it is agreed between the parties that the [Seller] shall not be liable for any losses, damages, costs and/or expenses. That the [Purchaser] was advised to take an independent valuation of the goodwill.

GROSS RECEIPTS

DVD, Video and Discs

G.034

The term 'Gross Receipts' shall mean the total of 1.1 and 1.2 set out below but excluding the items set out in 1.3:

1.1 All gross monies derived by the [Licensee], its subsidiaries, affiliates, sub- distributors, and agents from dealing in and the licensing, rental, distribution and exploitation of the [DVDs/Videos/Discs] and/or part(s) and all rights therein licensed by this Agreement in the Territory. There shall be no reduction allowed for subsidiaries', affiliates' or agents' fees or commissions of any kind.

1.2 All damages, benefits or payments which may be derived after deducting reasonable attorneys' or legal fees if any, expended by the [Licensee] from any claims, suits or proceedings against third parties for infringement of any of the [Licensee's] rights hereunder.

1.3 All monies required to be paid by the [Licensee] to its sub-distributors and agents as levies, taxes and other like charges, imposed by any government, or taxing authority based upon the Gross Receipts, but not including any income, gross receipts or company taxes of the [Licensee], its sub-distributors or agents.

G.035

'Gross Receipts' shall mean the gross amount of monies received by the [Licensee] in any quarter directly or indirectly in respect of the exploitation of the [DVDs/Videos/Discs] of the [Film] howsoever arising after the deduction of any value added taxes or similar taxes to be borne by the [Licensee].

G.036

'Gross Receipts' shall mean all monies actually received by the [Licensee] from [DVDs/Videos/Discs] containing the [Film] sold (and not returned) and all monies actually received by the [Licensee], its sub-licensees, sub-agents and distributors and any other third party from the supply, licences, rental, distribution or other exploitation of [DVDs/Videos/Discs] containing the [Film] at any time in the [Territory] including but not limited to advances, fees and other sums. In calculating the Royalties earned the [Licensee] shall be entitled to deduct from the Gross Receipts all the cost of the masters and a charge of [fifteen per cent] of the Gross Receipts, together with all taxes to be paid by the [Licensee], its sub-licensees, sub-agents and distributors [and any other third party] which are made by any government or other authority in respect of the Gross Receipts including, but not limited to sales taxes, value added tax, but excluding personal or corporate taxes which relate to turnover, income or profit.

G.037

'The Gross Receipts' shall be all the monies of any nature whether lending or rental income, sales whether retail or wholesale, or otherwise any sums or benefits which are credited to, paid to and/or received in respect of the [Series] by the [Assignee] and/or any sub-licensee and/or distributor and/or any other third party engaged by the [Assignee] in respect of the exploitation of the [Series] at any time from the rights granted under this Agreement.

G.038

'The Gross Receipts' shall mean all sums paid to the [Company] after deductions of any refunds, returns, discounts, and any setoffs, free and promotional material or other adjustments which result in the reduction or return of funds in respect of the exploitation of the [DVD/Video/Disc] Rights in the [Film] and any part in [country] from [date] to [date] whether sale, supply, distribution, rental, subscription.

G.039

'Gross Receipts' shall mean all sums and benefits paid to, received by or credited to the [Company] and any parent company, subsidiary, affiliate or associate, or any sub-agent, sub-licensee, sub-distributor or other third party in respect of the exploitation of the [DVD/Video/Disc] Rights in the [Film] and any parts of any nature at any time in any country whether sale, supply, distribution, rental, subscription or otherwise whether during the Term of this Agreement or thereafter.

G.040

'The Gross Receipts' shall be the total sums received by the [Company] [and any authorise agents, distributors and other third parties] from the exploitation of the [Discs] based on the [Sound Recordings] and any parts throughout the [country] from [date to [date] after the deduction of taxes, [commission, the cost of reproduction of material, and freight costs.] No deductions shall be made for administration, telephone charges, packaging, marketing and advertising.

G.041

'The Gross Receipts' shall mean all the sums received in [sterling] after conversion from any other currency in the [country] by the [Company] from the exploitation of the rights granted in respect of the [Images, Text and Music] on the [Disc]. No deductions shall be made of any nature except costs incurred in currency conversion and exchange, sums payable to governments for taxes for the supply, distribution and/or export and/or import of the [Discs].

G.042

'The Gross Receipts' in respect of the exploitation of the [CDs/Discs/Project] shall mean all sums received by the [Company] and/or any agent, sub-licensee and/or distributor and/or any other third party and/or associated and/or parent company at any time in any part of the world in the currency in which it is received whether or not it has been paid to the [Company] before the deduction of any commission, discounts, bank and/or currency charges, expenses and/or any other costs

G.043

'The Gross Receipts' shall mean the total sums received by the [Distributor] in respect of the sale and exploitation of the [CD/Disc/Work] during the continuance of this Agreement and thereafter until all sums have been accounted for by the [Distributor]. Without any deduction for development, production, manufacture, packaging, marketing, freight, administration and/or commission and/or any other costs and/or expenses.

Film and Television

G.044

'The Gross Receipts' shall be the total proceeds from the exploitation of the [Series] and any parts throughout the Territory at any time received by or credited to the [Company] and its authorised sub-agents, and other third parties acting on its behalf after the deduction of [taxes/commission/material costs/other].

G.045

'Gross Receipts' shall mean all sums actually received by the [Television Company/Distributor] from the exploitation of all rights in all media in the

782

[Programme] and all material therein including any advances, fees or royalties but excluding:

1.1   Any sums received by the [Television Company/Distributor] from the simultaneous relay by cable television (wherever occurring) of any broadcast programme service intended primarily for reception in the [United Kingdom] which includes the [Programme] [or any other person or business with which there is an annual agreement for access to material].

1.2   Any sums received in respect of advertising, product placement, sponsorship, or endorsement of any person, product or services or premium-rate telephone line service and any viewer information services or competitions or promotions which are or will be included at the beginning, in, during or after the [Programme] or any breaks.

G.046
'The Gross Receipts' means the aggregate proceeds of the exploitation of rights in the [Film] and/or part(s) in any media actually received by the [Licensor] and/or an appointed distributor or any other third party at any time.

G.047
The Gross Income arising from the exercise by the [Company] of the distribution rights granted to the [Company] under Clause [–] shall be shared between the [Company] and the [Production Company] in the proportions of [sixty per cent] to the [Company] and [forty per cent] to the [Production Company].

G.048
'Gross Receipts' shall mean the gross proceeds of the exploitation of the [specify rights] in the [Film] actually received by the [Company] in freely convertible currency after there shall have been deducted from such proceeds all costs and expenses of and relating to the reproduction, supply, distribution, sale or other exploitation of the [Film] including, but not limited to, commission, agency fees, reproduction costs, editing, translations, packaging and freight, advertising and promotional material, copyright clearance fees, royalties, recording, performance and transmission of any music, composition and lyrics, refunds, discounts and deductions, legal costs, and under other sums paid under indemnity or otherwise incurred relating to the exercise of the rights under this Agreement.

G.049
The Distribution Gross Receipts' shall mean the total receipts from the distribution, exhibition and exploitation of the [Film] actually received from

the [Distributors] by the [Company] in accordance with the terms of the Distribution Licences.

G.050

'Gross Receipts' shall mean all the monies, lending and rental income, compensation, advances, subsidies, grants and any other sums or payment of any kind in any currency which is credited to, paid to and/or received by the [Licensee] and/or any sub-licensee and/or any distributor in respect of the distribution, exhibition and/or exploitation of the [Film] in the Territory in respect of the rights granted in Clause [–].

G.051

'Gross Receipts' are defined as all actual sums invoiced and received from each theatre exhibiting the [Film] as well as any other sums collected by the [Licensee] on any account whatsoever in connection with the [Film]. The Gross Receipts are the exclusive property of the [Licensor] who authorises the [Licensee] to retain the sums due to it under Clause [–].

G.052

'Gross Receipts' shall mean all sums of money actually received by or credited to the [Distributor] or its sub-agents or sub-licensees arising from the distribution and exploitation of the [Series] during the Term of this Agreement.

G.053

'The Gross Receipts' shall be the total proceeds from the exploitation of the [Film] and any parts including any music throughout the Territory at any time received by or credited to the [Production Company] or its sub-agents, sub-licensees or distributors after the deduction of any sales tax, and value added tax.

G.054

'Gross Receipts' shall mean all monies in any currency received by and paid to the [Company] at any time from [date] to [date] in respect of the [specify rights/subject] after the deduction of any taxes, levies or charges which are added to the payment which must be reported to and repaid to any government.

G.055

'The Gross Receipts' shall be all the sums received from the sale, supply, licensing, distribution, exploitation and/or adaptation in any format and/or medium and/or derived from the [Footage] in any part of the world by the [Licensee] and/or any agent, sub-licensee and/or any other third party at any time whether during the term of this Agreement and/or thereafter.

G.056

'The Gross Receipts' shall mean all the sums received by the [Distributor] in respect of ticket sales, merchandising, exhibition, transmission and any other exploitation of the [Film] by the [Distributor] at any time after deduction of any venue hire costs, marketing costs up to [number/currency] and any taxes and/or costs of reproduction of any material costs of the [Film] up to [number/currency]. No other costs and/or charges shall be deducted. All administration and staff costs shall be paid for by the [Distributor].

G.057

'The Gross Receipts' shall be the total amount of all sums received by [Name] in [country] in [currency] between [date] and [date] from the exploitation and licensing of the [Film/Work] after deduction of commission, agents fees, freight, insurance, material, marketing legal and bank costs and charges that may be due and/or paid which directly arise from any agreement that may be concluded but which shall be limited to no more than [number/currency].

General Business and Commercial

G.058

'Gross Receipts' shall mean [one hundred per cent] [100%] of all gross sums arising directly or indirectly from the exploitation of the [Compositions/other] in the Territory during the Term excluding value added taxes, sales taxes or other similar taxes, standard commissions deducted by the [Performing Rights Society] and any other performing or mechanical collection societies or agencies but including all advances, credits, costs, fees, expenses and damages paid or awarded in settlement or as a result of any legal proceedings in connection with the [Compositions].

G.059

'Gross Receipts' shall mean [one hundred per cent] [100%] of all sums actually received by the [Company] in sterling in the [United Kingdom] arising directly and identifiably from the use and/or exploitation of the [Music/other] in the Territory by the [Company] at any time.

G.060

If one or more of the [Musical Compositions] is packaged together for marketing as a single unit with any other musical composition, the amount of Gross Receipts accrued to the [Owner's] account hereunder with respect to the [Musical Compositions] shall be the amount of Gross Receipts derived from such compilation, multiplied by a fraction, the numerator of which is the amount of time represented by the [Musical Composition] and the denominator of which is the total amount of time recorded on such compilation.

G.061

'Gross Receipts' shall mean [one hundred per cent] [100%] of all sums actually received by or credited to the [Company] in sterling in the [United Kingdom] arising directly and identifiably from the use and/or exploitation of the [Compositions/other] in the Territory during the Term after the deduction of the Excluded Items.

G.062

The [Company] shall retain all Gross Receipts until the expenses set out in Clause [–] have been fully recovered. Thereafter the [Company] shall be entitled to retain [fifty per cent] [50%] of the Gross Receipts.

G.063

The [Licensee] agrees to pay the [Licensor] royalties of:

1.1   in [countries] [eighty per cent] [80%] of the Gross Receipts after deduction of Distribution Expenses] from the exploitation of the [Rights]; and

1.2   in [countries] [sixty per cent] [60%] of the Gross Receipts after deduction of Distribution Expenses.

G.064

The [Licensee] makes no representation or warranty with respect to the amount of any Gross Receipts which may be derived from the exploitation of the [Property].

G.065

'The Gross Receipts' shall be the total proceeds from the exploitation of the [Property] throughout the Territory at any time received by or credited to the [Licensee] or its sub-agents or sub-licensees after the deduction of sales tax, and any value added tax paid by the [Licensee].

G.066

'Gross Receipts' shall mean all sums received from the commercial exploitation of the [Product] including all taxes of any nature.

G.067

'The Gross Receipts' shall be defined as all sums which the [Agent] is able to receive and retain and deposit in the nominated account and shall not include the following costs and expenses which may have to be deducted:

1.1   Any import, export and/or supply taxes, duties and payments.

1.2   Any sales tax or value added tax or any other government charge on goods or services [excluding personal and corporation tax].

1.3   Any currency conversion or exchange costs or losses.

1.4   Any insurance, bank or transfer costs or commissions.

1.5   Any agent, or third party commission, fees, expenses, royalty, consent or performance or mechanical reproduction payments or waiver.

1.6   Any damage, loss, error, legal proceedings, product liability, or fines.

1.7   Any discounts, returns, errors, replacement, remainder, packaging, and freight costs.

1.8   Any editing, translations, censorship, credits, copyright notices and copyright protection.

1.9   Marketing, promotional and advertising material, labels [including website material and mobile phone promotions].

G.068
'The Gross Receipts' from the [Project] shall be all sums and/or benefits and/or rights and/or interest which may be created, developed and/or arise directly and/or indirectly in respect of the [Project] and/or any part at any time including but not limited to all sums from registration of any copyright, patents, trade marks, computer software and database rights, licences, assignments, and/or other forms of exploitation which exist now and/or may be created at a later date in any part of the world and/or universe .

G.069
'The Gross Receipts' shall mean the total amount which is paid to [Name] from the sale of the [Work] excluding [government taxes on supply] without deduction of any expenses, costs and/or charges.

Internet and Websites

G.070
'Gross Receipts' shall mean all the sums received and paid to the [Website Company] from the [Financial Transaction Company] which collects and administers the payments for access and use of the [Website] less any commission, charges, rebates, refunds or other sums which are deducted or paid back at any time.

G.071
'Gross Receipts' shall mean the subscription fees and payments received and retained by the [Company] in respect of the supply and use of the [Service] on the Website [specify trading name and reference] [from date to date/at any time] and in any part of the world without any deductions for costs, expenses, charges or otherwise of any nature except taxes on the

supply or provision of any services which directly apply to the payments under this Agreement.

G.072

'Gross Receipts' shall be all sums paid to, received by or credited to the [Company] whether directly or indirectly and/or through a third party and/or a subsidiary, affiliate or associate or parent company which relate to the supply, sale, distribution, or licence of any [Work] on any website, or any part of the internet and/or any mobile phone or telecommunication system and/or any television, gadget or instrument at any time and to any country and whether free to the public and acquired through a blanket licence, subscription, pay per download, or any other payment or access method.

G.073

'Gross Receipts' shall mean the sums received and retained by the [Company] relating to the sale, supply, rental and distribution of the [Product/Service/Work] on the [Website] after the deduction of the following costs:

1.1   Commission.

1.2   Agency fees.

1.3   Currency exchange costs and losses.

1.4   Bank charges and fees.

1.5   Administration costs and charges.

1.6   Any import, export and/or supply taxes, duties and payments.

1.7   Any sales tax or value added tax or any other government charge on goods or services.

1.8   Any insurance costs and charges.

1.9   Copyright and consent fees and royalties; usage; performance; mechanical reproduction payments and/or waiver.

1.10 Any costs for damage, loss, error, legal proceedings, product liability, and/or fines.

1.11 Any discounts, returns, errors, replacement, remainder, packaging, and freight costs.

G.074

'The Gross Receipts' shall be the total sums from the exploitation of the [Product/Work/Service] throughout the [world/universe] at any time received by or credited to the [Licensee] or its sub-agents or sub-licensees and/or any authorised third party after the deduction of sales tax, and any value added tax paid. There shall be no right to deduct any other sums of any nature.

G.075
'The Gross Receipts' shall be all the sums received by the [Company] from the provision of a premium rate phone line and service to the public on the [Website] after the deduction of the cost of the supply of the service charged by [Name] which shall not exceed [figure/currency].

G.076
'Gross Receipts' shall be all the sums received by the [Company] and converted to [sterling/euros/dollars/other] and held in a nominated bank account in [country] after the deduction of currency conversion costs and bank charges [and before taxes.]

G.077
'Gross Receipts' shall be the sums paid to the [Company] by any third party in respect of the [Website/Blog/Work] which are received and not returned and/or cancelled after deduction of any [specify tax], delivery costs and an [agency/commission] fee of [number] per cent during the term of this Agreement and thereafter until expiry and/or termination of this Agreement.

Merchandising

G.078
The [Licensor] acknowledges that the amount of Gross Receipts which may be realised from the distribution of the [Licensed Articles] is speculative and that the [Licensee] makes no representation or warranty with respect to the amount of any Gross Receipts which may be achieved.

G.079
The [Distributor] shall be entitled to receive [number per cent] of the Gross Revenue which shall be received as a result of the exploitation of the Merchandising Rights in the [Territory] in consideration of their services.

G.080
'Gross Receipts' shall mean all revenue generated through the exploitation of the [Character] in any form at any time in any country under the terms of this Agreement less any value added tax or other tax on sales or supply of goods which is not retained and is repaid to a government body or agency under any legislation, policy or practice, but not corporate or personal tax.

G.081
'The Gross Receipts' shall be the total proceeds from the exploitation of the [Licensed Articles] throughout the Territory at any time directly or indirectly

received by or credited to the [Agent] or any sub-agent or sub-licensee after the deduction of any value added tax [or any other taxes on the proceeds of the Licensed Articles].

G.082

The [Agent] agrees that all sums received in respect of the exploitation of the [Character] under this Agreement shall be deposited in a separate bank account at a bank to be agreed with the [Licensor]. Further that the [Licensor] shall be permitted access at all times to statements of account directly with the bank. The [Agent] shall not be entitled to create any charge or lien over the sums nor to withdraw any sums without the prior authorisation to the bank by the [Licensor].

G.083

'The Gross Receipts' shall be all sums and the total proceeds actually received by or credited to the [Production Company] or any of its sub-agents, sub-licensees, or any other third party arising from the exploitation of the [Film] based on and adapted from the [Author's Work] and any parts and all media rights under this Agreement after the deduction of such commission, agency and distributor charges and expenses which shall be specified in the account in detail and the deduction of [sales tax, value added tax].

G.084

The [Company] agrees to deposit and keep all sums received in respect of the exploitation of the [Licensed Article/Product] in a separate bank account in the [specify country] to be administered by [specify accountant/lawyer] over which no lien, charge or undertaking to a third party shall be given by the [Company].

G.085

'The Gross Receipts' shall mean [one hundred per cent] of all sums received or credited to the [Company] in [sterling] in the [United Kingdom] arising directly, indirectly or otherwise from the use and exploitation of the [specify Work/other] in the Territory at any time after the deduction of any taxes and currency conversion charges.

G.086

'The Gross Receipts' shall be the sums received in [currency] by the [Company] from the sale, supply and distribution of the [Licensed Articles] under the terms of this Agreement after the deduction of any taxes, currency exchange charges, and bank costs.

G.087

Where a third party does not remit, pay or transfer the monies due to the [Company] at any time. There shall be no obligation on the [Company] to be liable for the failures of such third party or to pay the deficit to increase the Gross Receipts.

G.088

The [Sub-Licensee] agrees and undertakes:

1.1 To disclose and verify to the [Licensee] all sums received and/or credited and/or any benefits derived from the exploitation of the [Work/ Service] in the [Territory].

1.2 To not withhold any sums for currency conversion and/or bank charges, commission, freight and/or material costs without the prior agreement of the sums with the [Licensee] that it is an authorised deduction.

G.089

The [Sub-Licensee] agrees that it shall not be entitled to deduct any sum in excess of [figure/currency] from the Gross receipts in any one accounting period. Any sum which is not recouped must be delayed and included in the next accounting period.

G.090

'The Gross Receipts' shall mean all sums of any nature received by the [Distributor] and/or any parent and/or associated company from the exploitation of the [Work] and/or any part and/or any character, name, image, logo and/or text of the original and/or any adaptation which is owned and controlled by [Name] and/or developed by the [Distributor] and/or from any registration, licence, supply, sale, rental and/or reproduction subject only to a deduction of:

1.1 Agents fees of no more than [number] per cent.

1.2 Commission to the [Distributor].

1.3 No marketing costs.

1.4 No legal costs.

1.5 No costs of supplying material in any format.

1.6 Taxes which relate to supply and/or transfer of rights but not corporate and/or personal tax.

1.7 No costs of administration.

1.8 Custom duties.

1.9 No insurance costs.

Publishing

G.091

'The Gross Receipts' shall be the total proceeds from the exploitation of the [Work] in any form throughout the Territory at any time directly or indirectly received by or credited to the [Agent] in any form and/or any sub-agent after the deduction of [value added tax, sales tax].

G.092

'The Gross Receipts' shall be the total proceeds from the distribution and exploitation of the [Work] and/or parts throughout the [country/Territory] [at any time/during the Term of this Agreement] received by [and credited to] the [Publisher] and/or its [Distributor] its sub-agents, sub-licensees or any other person or body after the deduction of [sales tax/value added tax/ currency and conversion charges, but not additional bank charges.]

G.093

'The Gross Receipts' shall be all sums, credits, benefits or financial gains of any nature received by the [Company] and any parent company, subsidiary, affiliate, associate or business partner or consortium member relating directly or indirectly to the [Work] and any part and title, Character, format, name, image, logo, music, lyrics or any adaptation, translation and/or development and/or all rights in any media in any format including intellectual property rights, computer software, patents, trade marks, domain names and merchandising at any time whether during the Term of the Agreement or not and in any part of the world, air, sea or otherwise.

G.094

'The Gross Receipts' shall be all sums in [currency] (after conversion) actually received by the [Distributor] arising from the reproduction, sale, licence, supply, adaptation, exploitation of the [Work] and/or any part by the [Author] in any media and/or format at any time before the deduction of any of the authorised expenditure listed in Appendix [–] which is attached to and forms part of this Agreement.

G.095

'The Gross Receipts' shall be defined as the sums received and/or accrued from the sale, supply, licence, rental, hire, reproduction, distribution, use and/ or exploitation of the [Work] and/or part by the [Company], any subsidiary, associated company, parent company, partner, joint venture and/or any other third party at any time without any deductions except for such sums as are due under legislation to any government.

G.096

'Gross Receipts' shall mean the sums received in [sterling] by the [Publisher] in [country] and/or any other part of the world relating to exploitation of any of the rights granted under this Agreement in the [Work] after the following authorised deductions:

1.1   Commission which shall not exceed [number] %

1.2   Agency fees which shall not exceed [number] %

1.3   Currency exchange costs and charges.

1.4   Any import, export and/or supply taxes, duties and payments.

1.5   Any sales tax or value added tax or any other government charge.

G.097

For the avoidance of doubt all sums accrued and owed and/or paid to the [Distributor] in respect of the exploitation of the [Work] shall be used to calculate the gross receipts and the sums due to [Name]. The [Distributor] shall bear the liability and risk of any sums accrued and not yet paid.

G.098

'Gross Receipts' shall be the total sum of the payments which the [Consortium] receives through its distributor and/or sub-licensees from the supply of the [Work] as part of a subscription and/or educational service and/or directly to any person and/or company but not for any material supplied for free and/or for charitable purposes.

Purchase and Supply of Products

G.099

'The Gross Receipts' shall mean the total monies in sterling derived from the ex-factory prices quoted for the [Garments] actually received and paid to the [Company] at any time from the parties in the Territory during the Term of the Agreement [after deduction of any sums incurred due to exchanges of currency, alterations, rejections, discounts and any other reduction in the ex-factory price but excluding freight, and additional insurance not included in the ex-factory price] and any taxes or duties arising directly from orders obtained by the Agent under this Agreement.

G.100

'The Gross Receipts' shall mean the total monies in [currency] received by the [Company] in the [country] and not refunded, returned or claimed back in respect of the distribution, sale, supply, marketing, promotion and exploitation of the [Product]. The [Company] shall [not] be entitled to deduct:

1.1 Any custom duties, export and import taxes, taxes on the sale and supply of goods or services, [but not corporation tax].

1.2 Any currency conversion or exchange costs or bank charges, commissions.

1.3 Any insurance, loss, discounts, returns, errors, replacement, remainder, packaging, and freight costs.

1.4 Any agent, or third party commission, fees, expenses, royalty, consent or performance or mechanical reproduction payments or waiver.

1.5 Any editing, translations, censorship, credits, copyright notices and copyright protection, registrations of rights, product liability, product recall, legal costs and sums awarded in damages or compensation, or otherwise to third parties.

1.6 Marketing, promotional and advertising material, labels, including website material and mobile phone promotions and premium telephone line costs.

G.101

Where a distributor, agent, licensee and/or other third party ceases trading for any reason and/or does not pay the sums due to the [Company] which is all and/or part of the Gross Receipts. Then it is agreed by both parties that the [Company] shall not be held responsible and/or liable to pay any such sums which it has not received to the [Licensor].

G.102

Where any sub-licensee, agent, distributor and/or other third party is appointed and/or engaged to exploit the [Work] on behalf of the [Company]. Then where any such person and/or third party does not pay any sums due to the [Company]. The [Company] shall still be obliged to pay the [Licensor] any royalty which would have fallen due out of its own funds.

G.103

The [Company] agrees and undertakes that all the sums received in respect of the [Product] under this Agreement shall be held separately from the other funds of the [Company]. The [Company] shall arrange a new bank account for the deposit of the funds in a separate bank account at a bank to be agreed with the [Licensor]. Further that the [Licensor] shall be permitted access at all times to statements of account directly with the bank. The [Agent] shall not be entitled to create any charge or lien over the sums nor to withdraw any sums without the prior authorisation to the bank by the [Licensor].

G.104

'Gross Receipts' shall be the retail price paid and sums received for the [Product/Work] [without deduction of any costs, fees, commission and/or any other charges which may be incurred] and retained by the [Company] during the term of this Agreement and thereafter until all stock has been accounted for and the [Product/Work] is no longer supplied and/or sold by the [Company].

G.105

'Gross Receipts' shall be all sums received by the [Consortium] from the sale, supply and exploitation of the [Product/Work] after deduction of the following costs which can be supported by relevant original documents:

1.1 Development costs of the [Product/Work] which shall be no more than [number/currency].

1.2 Manufacturing costs of the [Product/Work] which shall be no more than [number/currency].

1.3 Marketing, promotion and advertising costs and expenses related to the [Consortium] and the [Product/Work] which shall be no more than [number/currency].

1.4 Any bank charges, commission, discounts, price reductions and returns, taxes, customs duties, product liability and other insurance premiums and excess claims.

Services

G.106

'Gross Receipts' shall mean the total proceeds from the exploitation in any form of the [Sportsperson] whether commercial or not throughout the Territory at any time received by or credited to the [Manager] or any sub-agent or sub-licensee after the deduction of any value added tax or sales tax whether received during the Term of this Agreement or any time thereafter including:

1.1 Sponsorship, endorsements and promotion advances, fees and royalties, payments for public appearances and performances, satellite, cable, digital, terrestrial television, DVDs, videos, radio, the internet, live and pre-recorded radio, recordings, films, biography, publications, articles.

1.2 Prize money and appearance fees for performances at professional sporting events.

1.3 The name of the [Sportsperson], and any associated logo, trade mark and/or brand whether registered or not.

G.107

'The Gross Receipts' shall be the total proceeds from the exploitation of the [Work] in any form throughout the Territory at any time directly or indirectly received by or credited to the [Agent] or any sub-agent after the deduction of any value added tax.

G.108

'The Gross Receipts' shall be the total sums derived from the exploitation of the performances, appearances, recordings or the commercial exploitation in any other form specified under this Agreement of the [Actor] throughout the Territory at any time directly or indirectly received by or credited to the Agent or any sub-agent after the deduction of any value added tax.

G.109

'The Gross Receipts' shall be the total proceeds from the exploitation of the performances, appearances, recordings, endorsements or the commercial exploitation in any form of the [Artiste] throughout the Territory at any time directly or indirectly received by or credited to the [Agent] after the deduction of any value added tax whether received during the Term of this Agreement or thereafter.

G.110

'The Gross Receipts' shall be the total proceeds from all events, competitions, promotions, sponsorship fees, public appearances and performances, television and radio appearances, recordings, endorsements, publications, merchandising or other sums from the commercial exploitation in any form in any media of the [Sportsperson] throughout the [specify countries/Territory] at any time directly or indirectly received by, credited to the [Manager] [or any third party acting for or on behalf of the Manager] after the deduction of [value added tax/other].

G.111

The [Sportsperson] authorises the [Manager] to receive and deposit the [Gross Receipts] in the following joint bank account [specify account details]. This account shall require the signature of both parties for the removal of any funds, and the [Manager] undertake to comply at all times with this procedure. The [Manager] agrees not to deposit any sums not relating to the [Sportsperson] nor to charge or create any lien over the funds for any reason.

G.112

The [Manager] agrees and undertakes not to deduct any sums from the Gross Receipts and shall disclose all sums received by or credited to the [Manager] to the [Sportsperson] prior to the deduction of any commission or sums due to the [Manager] under this Agreement. No sums shall be hidden, misrepresented or transferred to prevent payment to the [Sportsperson].

G.113

'The Gross Receipts' shall be all the sums received and/or credited to the [Company] for the services of [Name] and/or any associated licensing of rights, endorsement, merchandising and/or any other exploitation in any media and/or medium whether received during the term of this Agreement or thereafter.

G.114

The [Company] agrees and undertakes to keep the sums due which accrue from the Gross Receipts in respect of [Name] in a separate account which is clearly identifiable and held for [Name]. The [Company] agrees that no charge, lien and/or other right shall be given to any third party over the funds. In the event that the [Company] is to cease trading and/or is in receivership and/or administration the [Company] and/or any third party shall not have any rights to the sums in the separate account.

G.115

The [Consultant] agrees and undertakes that it shall have no right to receive payment and/or hold any sums on behalf of the [Company] from third parties. That the [Consultant] shall ensure that all payments are made direct to the [Company] for the duration of this Agreement.

G.116

The [Company] agrees to pay all fees due to the [Consultant] as a total gross payment as stated in the invoice submitted including expenses and shall not deduct any tax, national insurance and/or any other sum at any time.

Sponsorship

G.117

The [Sponsor] agrees that it shall not have any right to any part of the total proceeds from the ticket sales, merchandising, television coverage and/or any other exploitation in any media throughout the world at any time.

G.118

'Gross Receipts' shall be defined as all sums received by the [Company] from the [Event] which shall include ticket sales, advertising, sponsorship, merchandising, television, DVD and internet licences and sales, and any other exploitation in all and/or any part of the [Event] before [date].

G.119

'The Gross Receipts' shall be the total amount of money received by the [Company] from all the series of [Programmes] sponsored by [Name]. Together with any sums received from any associated premium rate phone lines, competitions, publications, merchandising, television, radio, DVD, the internet and/or any other exploitation in any media throughout the world.

G.120

The [Company] and/or any licensee and/or sub-licensee shall only be entitled to deduct any payments and/or taxes due to a government which must be paid and/or deducted at source. No other deductions and/or payments made be made.

G.121

'The Gross Sponsorship Fees' shall be all payments by any method which are received by and/or due under any binding agreement to the [Company] from any third party which relates to the [Event] at [location] in [year] and any filming and recording and exploitation through any media at any time in any part of the world and/or any products, services and/or merchandising and/or derived from any sub-licence, sub-agent and/or sub-distributor at any time. It shall not apply to any other annual event and/or after [date].

University, Library and Educational

G.122

The [Institute] provides no undertaking and/or commitment as to the level of revenue, income, and/or gross and/or net receipts and/or any royalties due under this Agreement.

G.123

'The Gross Receipts' shall mean all the monies received or credited to the [Institute] in [sterling] in the [United Kingdom] arising directly, indirectly or otherwise from the use and exploitation of the [Service/Work/Product] throughout the world at any time after the deduction of any taxes, exchange and bank conversion charges.

G.124

'Gross Receipts' shall mean all the sums received and retained by the [Institute/Company] relating to the sale, supply, rental, distribution and exploitation of the [Product/Service/Work] throughout the world in any format and/or by any means after the deduction of the following costs:

1.1   Commission to any third party.

1.2   Agency fees.

1.3 Currency exchange costs and losses.

1.4 Bank charges and fees.

1.5 Administration costs and charges.

1.6 Any import, export and/or supply taxes, duties and payments.

1.7 Any sales tax or value added tax or any other government charge on goods or services.

1.8 Any insurance costs and charges.

1.9 Copyright and consent fees and royalties; usage; performance; mechanical reproduction payments and/or waiver.

1.10 Any costs for damage, loss, error, legal proceedings, product liability, and/or fines.

1.11 Advances, fees and royalties.

1.12 Distributor charges and expenses.

1.13 Telephone, mobile, internet and fax costs.

1.14 Stationery, packaging and postage.

G.125

'The Gross Receipts' shall be the sums received and/or credited to the [Enterprise] at any time whether during the Term of the Agreement or thereafter by the [Enterprise] and/or any associated business, agent, representative from the exploitation of the [Work/Service/Product].

G.126

The [Institute] shall not be liable for the default and/or failure to pay and/or account and/or any damages and/or loss caused by a third party engaged by the [Institute] and/or the [Company] for the [Project].

G.127

'The Gross Receipts' shall be all sums, credits, and/or gains of any nature received by the [Enterprise] and any parent company, subsidiary, affiliate, associate or business partner or consortium member relating directly or indirectly to the [Work/Service/Product] form the exploitation in any form and any part and/or any adaptation, development and/or variation from [date] to [date] in the [Licensed Area].

G.128

'The Gross Receipts' shall be all the sums held in [sterling] by the [Enterprise] in [country] which are the payments received from third parties for the non-exclusive right to access, read and make one copy of [Project] which is owned by [Name].

G.129

No sum shall be attributed as within gross receipts if it has not been paid even if it is owed and/or due at that time. The [Institute] shall have the discretion to retain, withhold and/or accrue any sums which are in dispute and/or the subject of legal proceedings and/or where costs have been incurred to convert the payment into [sterling].

GROUP ACCOUNTS

General Business and Commercial

G.130

'Accounts' in this Agreement shall include all accounts relating to the [Company's] parent, subsidiaries, associates, affiliates, consortium partners, joint venture partners, and holding company and any other business, venture, or project in which it has an interest of stock, shares and/or a contractual arrangement which permits or allows control of the management and/or board and/or business plans.

G.131

Throughout this Agreement references to Accounts shall relate solely to the Accounts of the [Company] in [country] and not to any associated company, holding company or subsidiary of the [Company].

G.132

The [Company] may not rely on group accounts to support any statements as to the sums due to [Name]. The [Company] agrees and undertakes that [Name] shall be supplied with copies of a set of accounts for each individual parent, associate and/or licensee company at the [Company's] sole cost.

GUARANTEE

DVD, Video and Discs

G.133

In consideration of the rights granted to the [Licensee] by the [Licensor] hereunder. The [Licensee] hereby agrees to pay to the [Licensor] a non-returnable guarantee in the amount of [figure/currency] hereunder referred to as the 'Minimum Guarantee' plus the additional sums if any payable to the [Licensor] under Clause [–]. Such Minimum Guarantee shall be payable as follows:

1.1   [figure/currency] upon signature by both parties of this Agreement.

1.2   [figure/currency] upon delivery to and acceptance by the [Licensee] of the Delivery Materials.

1.3   [figure/currency] upon [first release to the general public] of the [DVD/Disc] of the [Film] in the Territory.

1.4   The [Licensee] shall recoup the full amount of the Minimum Guarantee from the [Licensor's] share of Gross Receipts.

1.5   All expenses and cost [specify] shall be borne solely by the [Licensee].

1.6   The Gross Receipts shall be deemed the property of the [Licensor] subject to the [Licensee's] rights to recoup and retain the amounts described in this Clause [–].

G.134
There are no undertakings, projections, or binding figures in respect of the revenue, income or sums due from the exploitation of the [DVD/Video/Disc] either as gross receipts or in royalty payments to the [Licensor].

G.135
There is no undertaking in respect of the release date, price, packaging, distributor and/or countries in which the [DVD/Video/Disc] will be exploited, sold or exploited. Except the [Company] agrees and undertakes that [number] copies of the [DVD/Video/Disc] will be released to the general public in [country] by [date] at the latest at [price/currency] by [Distributor] in the [specify] language.

G.136
The [Licensee] cannot guarantee the sales and/or royalty payments that may be made to the [Author] as a result of the exploitation of the [Disc] reproducing the [Sound Recording].

G.137
The [Sub-Licensee] agrees and undertakes to pay the [Licensee] not less than [figure/currency] in each accounting period in respect of the exploitation of the [Disc] reproducing the [Sound Recording] for the Term of this Agreement.

G.138

The [Company] agrees and undertakes to provide a guaranteed payment to [Name] of [figure/currency] in respect of the [Work/Project] by [date] which shall not be set off and/or recouped against any other sums due to [Name]. Provided that [Name] is available and capable of completing the [Work/Project] regardless of whether it goes ahead or not and/or is cancelled and/or delayed for any reason including grounds of force majeure.

Film and Television

G.139

The [Company] shall be entitled to stipulate the terms and conditions of the completion guarantee and to approve any such arrangements. In the event that the completion guarantor is a third party then the cost of such completion guarantee shall be set out in the [Budget]. In the event that there is any surplus of sums paid in respect of the completion guarantee by anyone at any time then it shall be repaid to the [Company]. The [Production Company] shall use its best endeavours to comply with all the terms of the Completion Guarantee.

G.140

'The Completion Guarantors Advance' shall mean all sums provided by the [Completion Guarantor] in respect of the [Film] to the [Company] and the [Co-Production Company] to produce, complete and deliver the [Film] together with all costs, charges and expenses or other sums which are advanced until recouped as set out in the document between the [Completion Guarantor] and the [Company] and the [Co-Production Company].

G.141

The [Company] confirms that it has taken out a Completion Guarantee with a reputable financial institution and that the beneficiary is the [Name]. The [Company] confirms that the Completion Guarantee covers any sums due to be paid to any third party for the successful completion of the terms of this Agreement and such costs shall not be less than the [Fixed Price Budget].

G.142

There are guarantees and/or undertakings provided by the [Distributor] that the [Film/Programme] will be transmitted and/or exploited and/or that any minimum payments will be made to [Name] in respect of the exercise of the rights granted in this Agreement.

Services

G.143

The [Contractor] guarantees to the [Company] that all work supplied by the [Contractor] in performance of this contract shall be supplied by personnel who are qualified, skilled, experienced and competent in their respective professions. The [Contractor] further guarantees to the [Company] that the work shall conform with recognised professional standards and principles and further that this Guarantee shall remain for a period of [20] years from the date hereon.

G.144

The [Supplier] agrees and undertakes that:

1.1 It shall comply with all the policies of the [Company] set out in Appendix [–] which form part of this Agreement and

1.2 It shall also comply with the Code of Practice and Guidelines reference [specify] of [Organisation].

G.145

The [Company] agrees and undertakes and guarantees that only suitably qualified personnel will be engaged for the [Project] with a minimum of [number] years as [specify post] with valid work permits and/or visas and who are fluent in the technical language [specify] and registered as [specify] with [governing body].

Sponsorship

G.146

The [Sponsor] agrees and undertakes that all personnel who attend the [Event] on behalf of the [Sponsor] shall be entitled to work in the [country], have no criminal record and be suitably qualified to fulfil the task they are allocated.

G.147

The [Sponsor] agrees and undertakes to the [Company] that it shall deliver all the material specified in Schedule [–] to the [Company] at its own cost and risk before [date]. That, where any items are damaged, lost and/or unsuitable, the [Company] guarantees to supply replacements with [number] hours.

G.148

The [Sponsor] agrees and acknowledges that there are no warranties, guarantees and/or undertakings as to the number of people who will attend the [Event] and/or any sums to received from the sales of the tickets.

G.149

The [Sponsor] agrees and undertakes to pay an additional fee of [figure/currency] where the [Company] is able to provide valid evidence that in excess of [number] persons attended at [location] at the [Event] on any day.

G.150

The [Company] agrees and undertakes to the [Sponsor] that a minimum of [number] members of the public will attend the [Event] on [dates] at [location] provided that the [Event] is not cancelled and/or delayed due to circumstances beyond the [Company's] control as set out in clause [–] relating to force majeure.

Purchase and Supply of Products

G.151

If within [12 months] after the [Goods] have been put into service any defect in the [Goods] shall be discovered or arise under normal use which is related to a design fault, materials or workmanship. Then the [Supplier] agrees that it shall remedy the defect either by replacement or repair at the [Supplier's] expense. The [Supplier] agrees that it shall not be entitled to reject any claim made in respect of any defect arising under this Guarantee within the [12-month] period on the basis that the complaint was not notified within that period. The [Supplier] agrees that this Clause shall apply for a further [12-month] period from the date of replacement or repair of the [Goods]. This Guarantee shall be without prejudice to any other rights or remedy that the [Purchaser] may be entitled to for any defect or otherwise. This guarantee shall only apply in [countries].

G.152

Your [Item] is guaranteed for [two years] from the date of purchase. In the event that the [Item] should become defective in that period then the defective part(s) will be repaired or at the [Supplier's] option replaced free of charge. This Guarantee shall not apply in the event that the [Item] is not used properly for its intended purpose in accordance with the instructions and/or there is no proof of purchase and/or the [Item] has not been previously repaired by unauthorised part(s) and/or personnel. Nor shall the Guarantee cover parts which are expected to be replaced due to normal wear and tear such as [–]. This Guarantee is not intended and does not in any way affect the [Purchaser's] legal and statutory rights in respect of the [Item].

G.153

All [Goods] purchased are guaranteed for [12 months] from the date of the till receipt or delivery whichever one is the later. [Goods] will only be accepted for repair or replacement upon proof of purchase from the [Company]. The [Company] shall not be liable for:

1.1 Any defects resulting from wear and tear, accident, neglect or improper use by the [Customer] other than in accordance with the instructions or advice of the [Company] and/or the manufacturer.

1.2 Any [Goods] which have been modified or repaired except by the [Company]. The [Customer's] legal rights are not affected in any way by this guarantee.

G.154

In the event of any manufacturing defect in materials or workmanship in any part of your [Product] which arises within [specify period] of the date of the original purchase [or hire purchase] of your [Product] then the [Customer] must return the [Product] to the [Company] at the [Customer's] risk and cost within that period. The [Company] shall repair or replace any defective part(s) covered by this guarantee at no cost to the [Customer]. When the [Product] is repaired the [Customer] will be responsible for collecting it at the [Customer's] cost and risk. The guarantee does not operate in the following circumstances:

1.1 Damage arising from work on the [Product] by a person who is not a qualified engineer.

1.2 The original purchase receipt cannot be produced, or some other evidence of date of purchase or there is no guarantee.

1.3 There is no compensation for any losses, expenses, costs or damage to any other item used by the [Customer] in conjunction with the [Product].

1.4 There is no compensation for any delay or otherwise in repairing the [Product].

G.155

The [Manufacturer] confirms that the [Product] is protected by a [five year] guarantee. This guarantee is in addition to your statutory rights at law. The guarantee excludes faults due to incorrect installation or misuse, accidental or wilful damage, repair or interference with the [Product] by a person not authorised by the [Company], non-domestic or commercial use of the [Product] or any country outside [specify].

G.156

The [Company] undertakes that if within [6 months] of the date of purchase the [Item] [or any part(s)] is proved to be defective by reason of faulty workmanship or materials the [Company] will repair or replace the [Item] free of any charge for labour materials or freight provided that the [Item] has only been used for [domestic purposes only] and in accordance with the instructions and the item has not been serviced, maintained, repaired or tampered with by any person not authorised by the [Company]. All service work must be carried out by [Name]. Any [Item] replaced shall become the [Company's] property. This guarantee is in addition to your statutory and other legal rights. The guarantee does not cover:

1.1 Damage from transportation, improper use or neglect, the replacement of part(s) deemed under Clause [–] to be the [Customer's] responsibility.

1.2 Commercial use except under licence.

1.3 Ancillary telephone or internet costs or damage to any associated or connected equipment or services.

G.157

The [Company] makes no guarantee as to the effectiveness of the [Goods] nor of the results of any [treatment] or [service] except as provided in Clause [–]. This provision shall in no way be construed as to relieve the [Company] of any warranty, obligation or liability the [Company] may have at law as the [Manufacturer/Distributor] of [Goods]/[Service/Treatment] either in the [United Kingdom/or Europe/world].

G.158

The guarantee will cease to apply in the following circumstances;

1.1 You and/or a third a party have deliberately and/or intentionally damaged the [Product].

1.2 You failed to use the [Product] in accordance with the instructions.

1.3 You used the [Product] in conjunction with another item which was faulty and caused the damage.

1.4 You exposed the [Product] to excessive water, heat, light.

1.5 The [Product] is more than [number] years old.

1.6 There is no evidence of proof of purchase, ownership and/or the level and/or type of damage is inconsistent with the details of the claim.

HALLMARK

General Business and Commercial

H.001
'Hallmark' shall mean any of the various official marks used at [Goldsmith's Hall and by the British Assay Offices] for marking the standard of gold, silver or platinum.

HANDSEL

General Business and Commercial

H.002
'Handsel' shall mean the first instalment and payment of such sum which shall be offset against the purchase price.

H.003
'Handsel' shall mean a goodwill deposit and shall not be treated in any way as part of the purchase price.

HEALTH

Employment

H.004
The [Employee] confirms that he/she is in good health and has disclosed all matters relating to his/her personal health on the enclosed [Private Health Declaration] to be returned to the Personnel officer marked 'strictly private

and confidential'. The [Employer] agrees that the document shall at all times be kept private and confidential and shall only be used for company insurance purposes and no other purposes under any circumstances.

H.005

The [Employee] is not required to participate in any medical examination or complete any report with regard to the specific or general nature of their health at any time. The [Employer] recognises that they have no inherent right to request private and confidential medical details from either the [Employee] or their medical advisor unless the written consent of the [Employee] is provided. A medical certificate from the [Employee's] General Practitioner will be regarded as sufficient for leave due to ill-health for any period in excess of [three days].

H.006

The [Company] shall have the right to request that the [Employee] provides a blood, urine or hair sample to a medically qualified practitioner engaged by the [Company] to test for drugs, alcohol or other substances in respect of [Name] where it is suspected and there is already evidence that [Name] is carrying out his duties whilst drunk, incapacitated or on drugs not prescribed by a doctor or available over the counter in a pharmacist.

H.007

There shall be no obligation on the [Name] to co-operate, assist or provide a blood, urine or hair sample to a medically qualified practitioner engaged by the [Company] or any other person to test for drugs, alcohol or other substances in respect of [Name] under any circumstances even where it is suspected and/or there is already evidence that [Name] is carrying out his duties whilst drunk, incapacitated or on drugs. Nor shall the [Company] be entitled to make a presumption of guilt due to any failure to provide a sample or co-operate nor to use this fact as a ground for alleging gross misconduct or otherwise.

H.008

It shall be sufficient that the [Employee] provide a letter from their personal [general practitioner/medical practice] that they are fit to work and capable of performing the tasks required for their fulfilment of this Agreement. It is agreed that no medical examination shall be requested by the [Company] for any reason.

General Business and Commercial

H.009

The [Company] agrees and undertakes that it shall at all times maintain a safe and healthy workplace and shall at all times comply with all laws, regulations and EU Directives with respect to health and safety matters in [country] at [premises].

H.010

The [Company] acknowledges its duties and undertakes that it will:

1.1 Take reasonable care to ensure that all equipment, premises, and systems of work used in the business are safe and to select and engage other employees who are in good health and competent for the job for which they are employed.

1.2 Make available to all employees and to keep up-to-date a statement of the [Company's] general policy with respect to the health and safety at work of its employees and of the arrangements for carrying out that policy.

1.3 Consult such representatives of the [Health and Safety Executive] with a view to making and maintaining effective arrangements for the health and safety of its employees.

H.011

The [Contractor] agrees to perform the work in accordance with the health, safety and quality control standards of the [Company] and strictly to comply with all standards and practices of the [specify organisation] in [country] which are in force at the time, and all legislation, directives, codes and professional trade guidelines.

H.012

The [Contractor] and its agents, officers and personnel will exercise all reasonable diligence to:

1.1 Prevent pollution in performing work under this contract. No rubbish, equipment, waste, oil, fuel, gases, lubricant, radioactive or hazardous substances or other pollutants will be discharged, or left by the [Contractor] or his equipment. The [Contractor] shall clean up, make good and remove any such pollution caused by the [Contractor], its personnel or agents in performance of this contract.

1.2 Comply with the [Operator's] safety, health and environmental policies and procedures including compliance with any prohibition, tests and searches for drugs, alcohol and weapons.

H.013

The [Company] shall at its sole cost and responsibility take all necessary steps so that the [Product] shall pass the health and safety standards set by [specify body] at all times during the Term of this Agreement. The [Company] shall monitor the production and distribution of all stages of the [Product] so that quality control is maintained and where any [Product] is recalled due to any reason shall bear all the administration and advertising costs.

H.014

In the event that after the date of this Agreement any of the health and safety standards set by [specify body/rules/other] should be changed or modified or any other standards applicable to the [Product] under any laws, regulations, directives, industry practice or otherwise in the Territory. Then the [Company] shall provide such information to the [Licensor] and the [Company/Licensor] agrees to bear all costs and expenses incurred in connection with or arising out of any modifications, changes, alterations to the tools, prototypes, samples and [Product] required to attain and pass new health and safety standards.

H.015

No [Product] shall be shipped unless and until the [Product] has passed the health and safety standards applicable at that time unless the [Licensor] so directs or provides consent and agrees to bear responsibility and liability for any consequence arising from such shipment.

H.016

If the [Goods] are perishable or have a life expectancy of a fixed duration or if there are any circumstances known to you which would adversely affect the life span of the [Goods] you will immediately advise us in writing of all such necessary and appropriate information relating thereto which shall form part of the description of the [Goods].

H.017

[Name] shall be responsible for ensuring that all equipment, or other item or material supplied by [Name] pursuant to this Agreement shall be safe, and complies with the health and safety policy of the [Company]. [Name] shall not supply or use any material of any kind which shall or might pose any risk to the health and safety of any employee or agent of the [Company] and/or the general public in any circumstances.

H.018

The [Artist] agrees that to the best of his knowledge and belief he is not now nor has at any time been subject to any illness, injury or medical condition which would in any way prevent him providing his services. The [Artist] will at all times do all that is reasonably necessary to attain and maintain such sound state of health as will enable him to perform fully his services under this Agreement and will not undertake any hazardous pursuits.

H.019

The [Sportsperson] agrees to conduct himself/herself in a fit, proper and professional manner at all times during the Term of the Agreement.

H.020

Irrespective of any holiday leave the [Company] agrees that the [Presenter's] fee shall not be affected by any leave due to ill-health provided that it does not exceed [ten days] in any one year and is supported by a medical certificate.

H.021

In the event that the [Director] is unable to perform his/her obligations under this Agreement for any reason including ill-health the [Company] shall be entitled to terminate the Agreement subject to making fair and reasonable payment to the [Director] in respect of the services already provided.

H.022

The [Company] shall have the right by notice in writing to terminate this Agreement if the [Presenter] is unavailable through ill-health or any other reason for more than [duration] to provide his/her services as agreed.

H.023

The [Company] agrees not to cancel this Agreement due to the illness, injury or death of a person listed as key personnel provided that a suitable substitute can be arranged within [one calendar month] from the date that the person is unavailable, incapacitated and/or has died.

H.024

In the event that all and/or any of the key personnel provided by the [Enterprise] for this [Project/Work] are not available for a continuous period of more than [seven days] [excluding weekends]. Then the [Company] shall have the right to terminate the Agreement with immediate effect and to only pay for such work as has been completed and/or approved prior to the date of termination. All work and material which has been created, developed and/or commissioned by the [Enterprise] for the [Company] shall be assigned to and owned by the [Company]. Where there are outstanding issues the parties agree to enter into mediation and/or dispute resolution and/or arbitration prior to commencing any litigation.

H.025

The [Company] agrees that [Name] shall be entitled to unpaid leave of absence of for up to [four days] on an annual basis for the purpose of completing an annual health check-up, medical and hospital treatment, dental appointments and treatment, eye tests, mental health and drug treatment and therapy, homeopathy, osteopathy, physiotherapy and related health and wellbeing matters.

H.026

Where any part of a [Product/Project] involves tests, materials and/or processes and/or packaging that pose a risk to human health. Then the [Company] agrees and undertakes to ensure that all necessary steps are taken to reduce risk and any potential liability to a level of safety that complies with the standards set out in [country] together with any guidelines, codes and legislation.

H.027

The [Company] agrees that where any person is absent on leave due to ill health and then returns but cannot fulfil their previous role. That the [Company] shall consult with them to offer alternative roles which may be available and/or agree a termination and compromise agreement.

HIRE PURCHASE

General Business and Commercial

H.028

The [Goods] have been lent for hire under the terms and conditions attached hereto and no title or proprietary right shall pass under any circumstances to the [Hirer].

H.029

This Agreement is a 'Hire Purchase Agreement' and accordingly is not a conditional sale. The [Goods] are bailed (or in Scotland hired) in return for periodical payments by the person to whom they are bailed or hired. The property in the [Goods] will pass to that person only once the terms of the Agreement are complied with in full.

HOLDING COMPANY

General Business and Commercial

H.030

'Holding Company' shall mean any company which directly or indirectly owns not less than [51%] [fifty-one per cent] of the voting share capital of another company and Subsidiary shall mean such other company in relation to any company. The expression Associated shall refer to its subsidiaries and Holding Companies and all other subsidiaries of such Holding Companies.

H.031

'Holding Company' in this Agreement shall mean a Holding Company as defined by [specify legislation] in [country] at the date of this Agreement.

H.032

'The Groups' shall mean the [Company] including any holding company or companies of the [Company] and any subsidiary or subsidiaries of, any such holding company. 'Holding Company' and 'Subsidiary' shall be defined according to [the Companies Act 1985 and as subsequently amended].

H.033

'The Holding Group' shall mean the following companies which are linked either indirectly through associated businesses, directly through shareholdings as subsidiaries [specify name/company registration/address].

H.034

1.1 The [Company] is the holding company for the receipt of funds and payments for the [Consortium] known as [specify name] which was created on [date] and funded by [specify].

1.2 The [Company] shall not pay, commit and/or transfer any funds out of the accounts relating to the [Consortium] unless authorised by [Name] on behalf of the [Consortium].

1.3 The [Company] shall hold any funds in [specify account] in the name of [specify] and shall provide copies of statements on a regular basis upon request.

HOLIDAYS

General Business and Commercial

H.035

The [Employee] shall be entitled to [25] [twenty-five] days leave on holiday per annum which shall include all recognised Bank Holidays but exclude Saturdays and Sundays.

H.036
The [Company] acknowledges that the [Executive] is entitled to the Executive's Holidays in addition to Bank Holidays. The [Company] agrees that Bank Holidays and the Executive's Holidays shall be subject to the agreed rates of payment in accordance with the Executive's Remuneration. In the event that the [Executive] is requested to work on Bank Holidays or on days which have been agreed as the Executive's Holiday then such work will be paid for on an ad hoc basis on terms to be agreed between the [Company] and [Executive] at a higher rate than normal. The [Executive] shall at all times provide proper and reasonable notice to [specify position] prior to taking any holiday entitlement. The [Company] shall not unreasonably refuse any request or provide unnecessary delay in providing their authorisation. Where no response is received within [seven days] then the [Executive] shall be entitled to presume and it shall be deemed that authorisation has been provided for any such leave.

H.037
The holiday year will be [1 January] to [31 December]. Holiday entitlement shall accrue at the rate of [2 days] for each four-weekly period worked up to a maximum of [25 days] in the holiday year. In addition the [Employee] shall be entitled to all public and Bank Holidays.

H.038
The [Employee] is not entitled to carry over holiday entitlement from one year to the next. In exceptional circumstances the [Company] may at its discretion allow the holiday entitlement to be carried over to the first [three] months of the following holiday year.

H.039
All holiday dates must be agreed in advance with the [Employee's manager].

H.040
[Employees] leaving the employment of the [Company] shall be entitled to payment in lieu of accrued holiday entitlement. For the purpose of calculating accrued holiday pay, a day's pay will be [1/30] of the [Employee's] basic four-weekly pay. If on leaving the [Company's] employment the [Employee] has received paid holiday in excess of his/her accrued holiday entitlement then the [Company] shall be entitled to deduct such excess holiday payment from any other sum(s) due to the [Employee].

H.041
The [Company and the [Employee] agree that following terms:

1.1 Holidays accrue pro rata during the period of employment. The [Company] shall be entitled to require the [Employee] to work on public and Bank Holidays if such holidays fall on a day on which the [Employee] would normally be required to work.

1.2   All holiday dates must be agreed with the [Director of Personnel] a minimum of four weeks in advance.

1.3   [Employees] leaving the [Company] shall be entitled to payment in lieu of accrued holiday entitlement. For the purpose of calculating the accrued holiday pay a day's pay shall be calculated at [1/28] of the [Employee's] basic four-weekly pay.

1.4   If on leaving the [Company's] employment the [Employee] has received paid holiday in excess of accrued holiday entitlement the [Company] may deduct such overpayment of any sums for holiday entitlement from any other sums(s) due to the [Employee] from the [Company] in respect of his employment [excluding person and share options].

H.042

In addition to the usual public holidays the [Manager] shall be entitled to [five weeks] paid holiday in each consecutive period of [twelve months] commencing on [1 April]. The holidays shall be taken at such times as may be agreed between the [Manager] and the [Company]. The [Manager] may not without the consent of the [Company] carry unused holiday leave over to the next yearly period.

H.043

In the event of the termination of the [Manager's] employment for any reason the [Manager] shall be entitled in respect of the holiday year in which termination occurs to a proportionate part of the period of paid holiday and shall be paid in respect of any holiday that remains outstanding and has not yet been taken. Any payment to the [Manager] in respect of holiday already taken by the [Manager] in excess of the paid holiday entitlement shall be deducted by the [Company] from the final salary payment to the [Manager].

H.044

The [Employee] accepts that the precise date relating to the [Employee's] holidays if not already specified in Clause [–] shall be agreed between the [Company] and the [Employee]. The [Employee] shall be required to give reasonable notice with respect to the taking of any holidays other than public or Bank Holidays. The [Company] shall be entitled to deduct from any sums (in respect of the fees or salary) due to the [Manager] any sums due to the [Company] for any holiday leave which is in excess of that to which the [Employee] is entitled.

H.045

'Employee's Holidays' shall be [number] working days in any calendar year in addition to Bank Holidays.

H.046

'Executive's Holidays' shall be [number] working week days in any calendar year in addition to Bank Holidays.

H.047

'The Holiday Schedule' shall mean the times and dates during which the [Sportsperson] shall not be obliged to provide his services under this Agreement. A copy of the Holiday Schedule is attached to and forms part of this Agreement.

The [Manager] agrees that the [Sportsperson] shall be entitled to such holidays and other leave as set out in the Holiday Schedule together with such other dates as may be agreed between the [Manager] and the [Sportsperson].

H.048

The [Company] confirms that in any event the [Presenter] shall be entitled to not less than [number] days' holiday leave per year excluding public and bank holidays and weekends.

H.049

The [Presenter] shall inform the [Company] at the earliest opportunity of all leave which he/she intends to take under the terms of this Agreement which are not in the attached Schedule [–] and in any event to give the [Company] not less than [number] days notification to [Name].

H.050

There shall be no obligation on the [Company] to pay for holiday leave or any other period of absence. All payments are subject to completion of work. Provided that [Name] fulfils the scheduled [appearances/contributions] there is no notice required of any leave of any nature.

H.051

The [Executive] shall be entitled to take up to [ten days] additional leave of absence which is unpaid during the year. Provided that at least [one calendar months] notice is provided to the [Company] and it is not during the following dates [specify dates].

H.052

Holiday entitlement does not apply until you have completed the [probationary/internship] period and have been notified that your agreement will continue thereafter. The holiday leave is [number] days in the first year from the date of the end of the probationary period. This period is in addition to bank and public holidays.

HOTEL

General Business and Commercial

H.053

For the purposes of determining the extent of the 'Non-Theatric Rights' granted under this Agreement 'Hotel' shall [include/exclude] any boarding house, hostel, inn, tavern, guest house and lodging house.

I

ILLEGALITY

General Business and Commercial

I.001
The [Licensor] shall not be responsible for any act, omission, illegality or conduct which comes within the doctrine of ultra vires or is against public policy by the [Licensee].

I.002
The [Purchaser] agrees that it shall not use and/or authorise any type of use of the [Work/Disc/Data/information] in any manner or nature which is inconsistent with the intended purpose of the licence in this document. Nor shall the [Purchaser] deface, erase, remove, delete, add to or alter any part of the [copyright notice, trademarks, service marks, disclaimer, serial codes] displayed and/or incorporated into the [Work/disc/other] and any packaging. Nor shall the [Purchaser] make more copies than permitted and shall not supply the [Work/Disc/Data/information] to a third party for their own use and exploitation without the consent of the [Licensor].

I.003
The [Licensee] shall not and shall not authorise others to carry any act, use any materials or display any image or text in relation to the [Product] which could be construed as in breach of any laws of [country]. In the event that it becomes apparent that there is an allegation of wrongdoing of any nature whether fraud, banned ingredients, or failure to comply with international standards or some other reason then the [Licensor] shall have the right to suspend and/or terminate the Agreement with immediate effect by notice in writing to the [Licensee] without prejudice to any claim for damages, losses, payments under the contract and/or loss of reputation.

I.004
In the event that there is any allegation of fraud, corruption, breach of copyright, infringement of trade marks and/or any logos, irregular accounting practices, failure to adhere to health and safety standards and control, or any other breaches or allegations which could or do result in criminal or civil

proceedings against the [Licensee]. Then the [Licensor] shall have the right to suspend and/or terminate and/or to serve notice to revert all rights back to the [Licensor].

I.005

Where the [Institute] becomes aware and/or is informed by any authority, police and/or government and/or regulating body that the [Company] and/or its directors:

1.1   Are being investigated and/or prosecuted for a breach of the following Codes [specify titles].

1.2   Are alleged and/or have breached health and safety regulations and legislation;

1.3   Are alleged and/or have failed to adhere to normal accounting practises and committed a fraud and/or misappropriated funds.

Then the [Institute] shall have the right to serve notice on the [Company] to terminate this Agreement and no further sums which may be due shall be paid to the [Company] and all rights shall revert to the [Institute].

I.006

Where the [Consultant] becomes aware that there is a conflict of interest between the interests of the [Company] and the [Consultant] and/or that there is an intention by a person at the [Company] and/or any contractor not to fully comply with all the required legislation, Codes of Practice and Guidelines. Then the [Consultant] agrees to advise the [Company] of the potential problems as soon as reasonably possible.

I.007

Where at any time during the continuance of this Agreement the [Consortium] discovers and/or becomes aware that one party and/or any of their employees, researchers, consultants and/or agents and/or any other third party engaged by them have obtained, supplied, distributed and/or reproduced any data, information , records and/other material of any nature for the [Project] without consent and/or in breach of the code of conduct and protocol of [specify body] and/or may have committed one and/or more breaches of copyright, data protection and/or an allegation has been made of a criminal offence and/or civil and/or criminal proceedings have started and are pending. Then it is agreed that the [Consortium] shall appoint a person to investigate the matter and to report on the circumstances. Provided that it is agreed that no steps shall be taken by the [Consortium] where an external and/or civil and/or criminal action is pending except to suspend any person from involvement in the [Project] until the matter has been decided.

I.008

The [Consortium] reserves the right to terminate and/or cancel this Agreement in the event that the identity of any person and/or the nature of the work of any company is found to be involved in criminal activity in any country of the world not just limited to [country].

IMPLIED TERMS

General Business and Commercial

I.009

For the avoidance of doubt all express terms contained herein shall prevail over any terms implied by law.

I.010

Nothing in this Agreement shall seek to prevail over any and all terms implied by law.

I.011

This Agreement set out the terms, conditions and undertakings which have been agreed between the parties in respect of [subject]. No terms should be implied which directly conflict with any of these clauses and/or which grant any rights which have not been specifically granted to the [Licensee].

I.012

The parties agree that any matters discussed, disclosed, planned and/or projected for the future whether in writing, email and/or in person shall not be applicable and an implied condition and/or term of this Agreement unless it has been specifically stated as such in this Agreement.

I.013

All discussions, disclosures, promises, representations, projections, plans, marketing proposals and any other matter made by the [Company] to the [Institute] in respect of this [Project] shall form a part of this Agreement and be in addition to this written Agreement.

I.014

There shall be no implied terms in respect of this Agreement. The standard, quality and condition of all material is as stated and there is no assurance of uniformity, that there will be no flaws and/or that the material will not deteriorate whilst in transit.

I.015

The parties both agree that all implied terms are specifically excluded from this contract and the terms are only those which are stated.

I.016

No representation by any person, officer, director, trustee and./or other trust, company and/or entity nor any data, records, documents, financial projections, software, emails, sound recordings, samples, prototypes, film, text, image and/or logo can be implied into this Agreement at any time. The parties agree that any disclosures were not intended to be part of this Agreement and that the [Purchaser] must base their decision on their own research and not on any facts and/or information supplied prior to the date of the Agreement.

INCOME

General Business and Commercial

I.017

'Income' shall be the aggregate of all sums and/or financial benefits of any nature received by and/or credited to the [Company] (or any connected body) including sums from advertisements, sponsorship, endorsements, product placement, licensing of material; any service on the internet and/or any telecommunications system.

I.018

'Income' shall include all income derived from the exploitation of the rights granted hereunder whether such income is received by the Company itself and/or the Company's sub-licensees, sub-agents, sub-distributors, assigns, assignees, licensees, successors in title, subsidiaries, associates and/or connected bodies.

I.019

'Income' shall mean all sums actually received by the [Licensee] from the exploitation of the rights granted under this Agreement after the deduction of the following costs, expenses, commission and fees [specify].

I.020

'Income' shall mean such income as is subject to taxation under the existing legislation in [country].

I.021

'Income' shall be the sums received by [person] in respect of the position [specify] for [Company] from [date] to [date] which is taxed by the government of [country], but excluding any [Share option/Bonus/expenses/ pension/insurance/car/allowances/other].

I.022

'Executives Basic Remuneration' shall mean the annual sum of [figure/ currency] which shall be the gross sum payable by the [Company] to the [Executive] in accordance with the terms of this Agreement.

I.023

The [Company] agrees to pay the [Executives] Remuneration by credit transfer to the [Executives] personal bank or building society account on the last [specify day] of each month. In the event that the payment date is a bank holiday then the payment shall be made the day before the due date.

I.024

'The Total Income' shall be all the sums received by the [Consortium] in respect of the [Project] after conversion to [currency] from any source for any purpose which are deposited in the main consortium bank account held at [bank] less all sums expended in accordance with the directions and approval of the [Finance Committee/Finance officer] and with the authority of the Board of the [Consortium].

I.025

The [Licensee/Agent] agrees that it shall be obliged to disclose all sums and benefits and gifts and free and/or discounted resources and/or material which are received, supplied and/or offered at any time whether or not directly attributable as income which relate to [Name], his/her image, logo and/or services and/or any related merchandise, promotion and/or marketing.

INDEMNITY

Building

I.026

The [Contractor] shall be liable for, and shall indemnify the [Company] against any expense, costs, damages, liability, loss, claim and/or proceedings whatsoever arising under any legislation, directive, regulation, codes, standards or policies of any government agency or the European Union in respect of personal injury and/or death of any person arising out of and/or in connection with the [Project] except to the extent that the matter is due to any act or neglect of the [Company] and/or of any person for whom the [Company] is responsible.

I.027

The [Contractor] shall, subject to Clause [–] be liable for, and shall indemnify the [Employer] against any costs, liability, damages, loss, claims or proceedings in respect of any injury or damage whatsoever to any property where such injury or damage arises out of or in the course of or by reason of the performance of the [Project]. Provided that it is due to the negligence, breach of statutory duty, or omission or default of the [Contractor], his servants or agents, or of any person employed or engaged in connection with the [Project], or of any other person employed, engaged or authorised by the [Contractor] or by any local authority or statutory body executing work solely in pursuance of its statutory rights or obligations but not the [Employer].

I.028

The [site/location] set out in Schedule [–] and which forms part of this Agreement is not safe and is not habitable and is used by your [Company] at your own risk. There are no indemnity provisions and/or undertakings as to suitability for any use. Prior to access you must agree to take out insurance cover at your own cost for all persons that may enter and/or use the [site/location] to provide protection for the [Owner] and your [Company].

Employment

I.029

The [Employee] undertakes to indemnify the [Company] against all liabilities, claims, demands, actions, costs, damages or loss arising out of any breach by the [Employee] of any of the terms of this Agreement including the [Employee's] negligence, recklessness, dishonesty and/or defamation.

I.030

The [Executive] does not provide any indemnity whatsoever to the [Company] in respect of any loss, claim or damage that may arise from this Agreement.

I.031

There is no indemnity provided to the [Company] under this Agreement by [Name] in respect of any act, conduct, words, work, documents, communications, damage, loss or claim which may be brought against the [Company] at any time due to [Name]. The [Company] agrees and undertakes that it shall not seek to be indemnified by [Name] under any circumstances and the [Company] shall be responsible for all the risk and costs and any other direct and indirect consequences that may arise.

I.032
The total liability of the [Executive/Company] under this Agreement shall be limited to [figure/currency].

I.033
The [Company] agrees and undertakes that it shall arrange suitable insurance cover at the [Company's] cost for the benefit of the [Company] [and the Executive] to cover any matters that may arise from the employment and/ or the ultra vires actions of the [Executive] and any claim by the [Company] and/or a third party and/or shareholder.

I.034
It is agreed by the [Company] that the [Employee] provides no indemnity to the [Company] of any nature in respect of his/her work and/or any use of any equipment, clothes and/or other materials they may be required to use and/ or wear under this Agreement.

I.035
The [Company] agrees and undertakes to indemnify [Name] for all sums which for any reason may result in the fact that [Name] does and/or will suffer losses, damages, costs, expenses, actions, claims, summons, investigations and/or other matters which arise as a direct result of his/ her work at the [Company] and/or their use of any property owned and/or controlled by the [Company] and/or as a result of following any instruction, direction and/or policy and/or arising from any statement, photographs, films, sound recordings, image and/or exploitation and/or adaptation of any material and/or premises relating to the [Company].

DVD, Video and Discs

I.036
The [Company] shall keep the [Distributor] indemnified against all liabilities, claims, actions, proceedings, damages and loss incurred by the [Distributor] or awarded against the [Distributor] and any sums agreed and paid by the [Distributor] on the advice of its legal advisors in consequence of any breach or alleged breach or non-performance of any of the terms on the [Company's] part set out in this Agreement.

I.037
The [Assignor] agrees to indemnify the [Assignee] against all claims, liabilities, demands, actions, costs, damages or reasonably foreseeable loss

arising directly out of any breach by the [Assignor] of any term, warranties, representations or inducements made under this Agreement which may arise before [date]. After that time the [Assignor] shall not be liable to pay the [Assignee] any sums whatsoever however they may arise. The [Assignee] agrees that the indemnity shall not continue after [date].

I.038

In the event of any claim, writ, dispute, action, summons or threatened legal proceedings of any nature in connection with Clause [–] above before the end of the indemnity. The parties agree that the party who may seek to rely on the indemnity shall notify the other party as soon as reasonably practicable. Neither party shall incur any costs of any nature in such circumstances without first obtaining the prior approval of the other party which shall not be unreasonably delayed or withheld. In any event no settlement shall be made to the claim of any third party unless the party from whom the indemnity is sought has had an opportunity to review the case and offer its opinion.

I.039

The [Company] shall indemnify the [Distributor] against any liability, loss, damage, expense or cost arising directly or indirectly from the rights in the [Film] and the [Film Material] under this Agreement and/or the failure by the [Company] to perform the terms of this Agreement.

I.040

The [Company] shall indemnify the [Distributor] against any liability, loss, damage, expense or other matter arising directly or indirectly from the breach or non-performance of this Agreement by the [Company] with the following limitation of liability in each country [–].

I.041

The [Producer] and the [Distributor] agree that they shall not provide indemnity provisions to each other but shall arrange insurance cover for such purpose in the sum of [figure/currency] for the benefit of both parties.

I.042

The [Company] shall indemnify the [Distributor] in respect of any claim, action, or other legal proceedings, loss, or damage which directly relates to any part of the [Film] including the artists, music, script, format, computer generated material, credits, trade marks, logos and sound recordings provided that the [Distributor] complies with the following procedures:

1.1 That the [Distributor] will notify the [Company] as soon as possible of any matter upon which it seeks to be indemnified by the [Company] and will disclose all facts and documents and access to any material that may be relevant.

1.2   That the [Distributor] shall not take any steps or make any offer to settle without the authority or approval of the [Company].

1.3   That all legal costs shall be kept to a minimum and the [Distributor] shall regularly keep the [Company] informed of any expenditure over [figure/currency] which it intends to incur.

1.4   That where any sums can be recouped or reimbursed under an insurance policy held by the [Distributor] then the [Distributor] shall not seek to be indemnified by the [Company].

I.043

The [Distributor] agrees to indemnify the [Licensor] in respect of any dispute, settlement, claim, action, and/or other legal proceedings, losses, damages, legal costs and expenses incurred by the [Licensor] as a direct result of the actions, omissions and/or errors of the [Distributor] in respect of the exploitation of the [Sound Recordings] on the [Disc] by the [Distributor] and/or any sub-licensee, agent and/or other third party engaged and/or authorised by the [Distributor].

I.044

The parties agree that the following matters are not covered by any indemnity from one party to the other:

1.1   Administrative and reproduction costs.

1.2   Costs of financial and accounting advice.

1.3   Telephone, accommodation and travel costs.

1.4   Fees for consultants, agents, and other experts except legal advisors.

1.5   Matters which arise as a result of the actions and/or failure to pay of any sub-licensee, agent and/or any other third party.

I.045

The [Licensor] and the [Licensee] agree that the total maximum liability of each party under this Agreement shall be limited to [figure/currency]. That no party shall be entitled to be indemnified for any reason beyond that sum whether or not the excess sum is claimed as a result of negligence, error, omission and/or for any other reason.

I.046

The [Distributor] agrees that no indemnity in respect of the [Film/Work] and/or any of the [CDs/Discs/other] has been provided to the [Distributor] either before this Agreement and/or as part of this Agreement. That the [Distributor] shall not be entitled at a later date to seek any sum in whole or part as a contribution from [Name]. The [Distributor] recognises that they have purchased the stock without verification as to clearance and/or payment for any rights and/or as to ownership in any form. The [Distributor] shall bear all the risk and shall be liable for all costs, expenses and any civil and/or criminal proceedings that arise and shall not seek to join [Name] as a party and/or institute any legal proceedings against [Name].

I.047

1.1 The total liability of any indemnity by [Name] to the [Distributor] shall be limited to [number/currency].

1.2 The [Distributor] agrees that they shall not be entitled to any sums in excess of that figure in 1.1.

1.3 The [Distributor] agrees that it shall bear the cost of any matter which is less than [number/currency] and that [Name] shall not be liable to pay such sums below that figure at any time.

1.4 Any indemnity between [Name] and the [Distributor] shall end on [date].

Film and Television

I.048

The [Licensor] will at its own expense, indemnify, save and hold harmless the [Licensee] and its successors, licensees, assigns and employees, from and against any and all liability, loss, damage, cost and expense (including without limitation reasonable attorneys' and legal fees) incurred by them by reason of or resulting from any alleged breach, actual breach or claim by a third party with respect to any of the warranties, undertakings or terms made by the [Licensor].

I.049

Any liability, loss, damage, cost or expense resulting from any such alleged breach and/or breach and/or claim may be recouped by the [Licensee] from the [Licensor's] share of the Gross Receipts. If the [Licensor's] share of Gross Receipts is not sufficient to satisfy any obligation hereunder then the [Licensor] shall still be obliged to pay the balance of the sums due.

I.050

In the event that any person shall make any claim or institute any suit or proceedings alleging any facts which, if true, would constitute a breach by the [Licensor]. The [Licensee] shall give prompt written notice to the [Licensor] and the [Licensor] shall undertake at its own cost and expense the defence thereof and shall supply competent and experienced [Counsel/

legal advisors] to defend any such suit or proceedings. If the [Licensor] shall fail to promptly appoint competent and experienced [Counsel/legal advisors], the [Licensee] may engage their own [Counsel/legal advisors] and the reasonable charges made in connection therewith shall be paid by the [Licensor]. Any settlement or compromise shall only be made with the [Licensor's] approval, which approval shall not be unreasonably withheld. The [Licensee] shall have the right to withhold and reserve from any monies whatsoever payable to the [Licensor] hereunder, sums reasonably sufficient to repay the [Licensee] any sums due under this indemnity.

I.051

The [Guest] agrees to indemnify the [Television Company] in respect of all actions, proceedings, claims, damages, expenses and liability whatsoever which may be made or brought against or suffered or incurred by the [Television Company] in consequence of any breach of any of the terms and conditions contained herein.

I.052

The [Guest] shall not be liable to the [Company] for any allegations, claims, defamation, civil or criminal offence, breach of contract, infringement of copyright, disclosure of confidential information, damages, losses, expenses, costs or otherwise arising from the provision of the [Guests] services and the appearance on [Programme]. Nor shall the [Company] seek to obtain any indemnity and the [Company] agrees that any direct or indirect consequences that may arise are entirely at the [Company's] risk and cost.

I.053

In consideration of permission being granted to allow filming facilities at your premises. The [Company] agree that we shall indemnify the [Owner] up to [figure/currency] for any liability, losses, claims or proceedings which may arise in respect of personal injury, death, loss or damage to property caused by the negligence, omission or acts of the [Company] or any person for whom the [Company] is responsible and/or has engaged and/or invited onto the premises.

I.054

The [Licensor] will indemnify the [Licensee] against any liability, loss, damage, expense or cost of the [Licensee] arising from the reproduction and/or transmission and/or broadcast of any music recorded on the soundtrack of the [Film].

I.055

The [Company] and the [Co-Producer] will each indemnify and keep indemnified each other against liabilities, claims, demands, actions, costs including reasonable legal fees and/or damages arising out of the performance and/or non-performance of any of the obligations undertakings, rights and/or terms set out in this Agreement.

I.056
The [Licensee] undertakes to keep the [Licensor] at all times indemnified against all costs, actions, proceedings, claims, demands and expenses which may be brought against, suffered or incurred by the [Licensor] in consequence of any breach of any undertaking or warranty by the [Licensee] in respect of this Agreement.

I.057
The [Licensor] indemnifies the [Licensee] against all liabilities, claims, demands, actions, costs or damages arising out of the warranties given in this Agreement and/or the infringement and/or the alleged infringement of any intellectual property rights and/or defamatory material in respect of the [Film] and/or part(s).

I.058
The [Company] shall indemnify the [Operator] and keep it indemnified and the [Operator] shall indemnify the [Company] and keep it indemnified against all liabilities, claims, costs, damages and expenses including reasonable legal costs which are reasonably incurred in respect of any alleged breach, default or other matter arising under this Agreement.

I.059
The [Operator] shall indemnify the [Company] against all liabilities, claims, costs, damages and expenses including all reasonable legal costs and expenses in respect of any subscriber to the service or by any third party in respect of the content of the service except any matter which arises out of a breach by the [Company] of its obligations under this Agreement. Provided that the [Operator] and/or the [Company] has promptly notified the other of any claim or legal proceedings upon which it shall seek to rely on the indemnity both parties agree that they shall allow the other party who shall have to pay the indemnity to take full control of the case and deal with it as they think fit.

I.060
The [Licensee] agrees to and shall indemnify the [Distributor] and hold the [Distributor] harmless from and against any and all claims, demands, causes of action, losses, judgments, legal fees, costs and expenses that may be made against or sustained or paid out or incurred by the [Distributor] on account of any breach or alleged breach by the [Licensee] of any term in this Agreement or on account of any agreement made by the [Distributor]

with any sub-distributor, sub-licensee, exhibitor or others with respect to the [Film] or any parts.

I.061

That the [Licensor] will keep the [Company] indemnified from and against all liabilities, claims, actions, proceedings, damages and loss suffered or incurred by the [Company] or awarded against the [Company] and any compensation agreed and paid by the [Company] on the advice of Counsel in consequence of or arising out of any breach or alleged breach or non-performance of all or any of the covenants, warranties, representations, obligations, undertakings or agreements on the [Licensor's] part contained in this Agreement.

I.062

The [Company] shall indemnify and keep indemnified the [Television Company] against all liabilities, claims, demands, actions, suits, costs, expenses (including reasonable legal fees and disbursements) and/or damages arising out of or in connection with any breach or alleged breach of any of the warranties contained in this Agreement.

I.063

The [Company] warrants and undertakes that it and its assignees, licensees and successors in title shall indemnify the [Contractor] for all costs and expenses the [Contractor] may incur due to any breach by the [Company] of the terms and undertakings set out in this Agreement including payment of all advances, copyright fees, residuals, royalties or contractual obligations or otherwise due to any third party in respect of the exploitation of the [Programmes] in all media.

I.064

Unless otherwise stated the [Company] warrants that it has all the necessary rights to enable it to enter into this Agreement. The [Company] will indemnify the [Licensee] against any claim arising out of the use of the [Material] which is in accordance with the terms of this Agreement.

I.065

If notified by the [Company] that permissions and clearances must be obtained by the [Licensee] from contributors, copyright owners and/or any other third party prior to the exercise of the rights granted by this Agreement. The [Licensee] agrees and undertakes that it will obtain at its sole expense all such permissions and clearances. The [Licensee] shall indemnify the [Company] against all actions, claims, costs, legal costs, damages and expenses incurred, awarded against or paid out by the [Company] in consequence of any breach and/or non-observance of this warranty and/or any other term of this Agreement.

I.066

The [Author] and the [Production Company] undertake to indemnify each other against all liabilities, claims, demands, actions, costs, damages and loss arising out of any breach by them to the other party of any of the terms of this Agreement.

I.067

In the event that the parties cannot agree the terms upon which to settle a claim, action, liability or demand. Then it is agreed that the advice of a suitably qualified legal expert in the subject shall be sought at the [Company's] cost, but shall not be considered binding.

I.068

The [Licensor] and the [Licensee] mutually undertake to indemnify the other against all liabilities, claims, demands, actions, costs, damages and loss arising out of any breach by the other party of any of the terms of this Agreement. Both parties agree that in such an event they shall provide full details to the other party at the earliest opportunity. If either party wishes to assert its right to be indemnified then it must promptly:

1.1   Notify the other party of any threat or claim which may arise and make no admission of settlement.

1.2   Provide the other party with the opportunity to be fully consulted in respect of the proposed course of action with the case.

1.3   The maximum liability of either party shall be limited to [figure/currency] in total for each party under this Agreement to the other party.

1.4   The indemnity shall only apply if the party seeking to rely on the indemnity has notified the full nature of the claim and co-operated fully with the other party.

I.069

The [Author] and the [Company] agree and undertake that:

1.1   In the event of any claim, dispute, action, writ or summons arising out of this Agreement, each party agrees to provide full details to the other party at the earliest opportunity and shall not settle any matter without first consulting the other party if they intend such matter to be indemnified.

1.2   No settlement shall be made of any allegation, claim or action of any third party unless such claim is settled on reasonable grounds and in good faith taking into account the advice of a legal advisor who is an expert in that field.

1.3   The [Author] agrees to indemnify the [Company] up to a maximum of [figure/currency] in respect of any loss, damage or costs arising from any breach of the undertakings by the [Author] in this Agreement subject to Clauses 1.1 and 1.2 above.

1.4   The [Production Company] indemnifies the [Author] in respect of any losses, damages or costs arising from any breach by the [Production Company] subject to Clauses 1.1 and1.2 above.

I.070

There are no undertakings and/or indemnity provided to the [Company] under this Agreement of any nature in respect of originality of the work, copyright ownership, infringement of copyright, or whether all the rights in the material have been acquired by or belong to [Name] and/or have been paid. The [Company] has been provided use of and access to the [Material] at its own risk and agrees to bear the cost of any allegations, claims, actions, legal proceedings, copyright clearance fees, legal costs and settlements that may arise from their use of the [Material].

I.071

The [Publisher] agrees that any material and/or content whether title, text, images, logo, graphics, maps, illustrations, sound recordings, computer generated material and/or otherwise shall be excluded from the indemnity by the [Author] in the event that:

1.1   The [Publisher] has decided to include the material and/or content despite the fact that the [Author] has indicated that there might be a legal problem and/or the [Publisher] has received legal advice that there is a risk of being sued by a third party.

1.2   The [Author] has advised the [Publisher] that the copyright owner is unknown and/or untraceable and/or the material has not been cleared in advance.

1.3   There has been an error, omission and/or negligence by the [Publisher] and/or printer.

1.4   The claim for any sum relates to an action and/or other matter outside [specify countries].

I.072

This indemnity by the [Author] to the [Publisher] shall end on [date] and after that date the [Publisher] shall not be entitled to make under claim and/or seek to be indemnified for any matter by the [Author] whether it is a legitimate claim or not. The [Publisher] agrees and undertakes not to take make any claim against and/or seek to be indemnified by the [Author] after [date].

I.073

1.1 [Name] agrees that he/she shall be interviewed and filmed by the [Company] on [date] for the purpose of a contribution to the [Programme] entitled [specify].

1.2 [Name] shall not be liable to the [Company] in respect of any matters which may arise in respect of the broadcast, transmission and/or exploitation the [Programme] which contains the material in 1.1 relating to [Name]. The [Company] agrees and accepts that [Name] provides no indemnity and/or undertaking and any claim which may arise for defamation and/or shall be at the [Company's] sole risk and cost.

1.3 [Name] agrees that where the [Company] requires additional information and/or interviews and/or documents and/or affidavits signed by [Name]. That [Name] will co-operate and assist provided additional fees and expenses are paid to [Name].

1.4 That the [Company] agrees and undertakes to waive all claims of any sums against [Name] of any nature arising from 1.1 and accepts that the information may be misleading, wrong and/or malicious as recollected by [Name].

I.074

The [Owner] of the [Film] supplies the material to the [Distributor] for display, use and supply on [Website] and app [specify] and to be adapted and edited as the [Distributor] thinks fit in the circumstances on a non-exclusive basis and without the provision of any undertakings and/or indemnity to the [Distributor]. The [Distributor] agrees that it has waived all undertakings by [Name] as to originality, ownership, liability and indemnity and that [Distributor] all exploitation is at its own risk and cost.

General Business and Commercial

I.075

The [Licensor] agrees to indemnify the [Licensee] in respect of any third party claim, loss, damage, settlement, legal cost and expenses against the [Licensee] which may be paid to such third party as a result of any matter relating to the [Work/Services/other] in respect of the [exercise of the rights granted/use of the Service] under this Agreement. Provided that in all cases the [Licensee] shall:

1.1 Notify the [Licensor] as soon as possible of the details of any claim, loss or damage.

1.2 Consult with the [Licensor] as to the best course of action in dealing with such matters.

1.3   Not agree to pay any third party any sum without the prior approval of the [Licensor] which shall not be unreasonably withheld or delayed.

I.076
The [Licensor] shall only indemnify the [Licensee] in respect of any breach of this Agreement where the [Licensee] has suffered a quantifiable loss or damage.

I.077
The [Company] shall indemnify and keep indemnified the [Licensee] including the [Licensee's] officers, directors, employees and agents against all liabilities, claims, costs, damages, expenses and legal fees reasonably and properly incurred arising out of any breach of any representation, warranty, undertaking or obligation on the part of the [Company] contained in this Agreement.

I.078
If the [Licensee] wishes to assert its rights to be indemnified as set forth in this Agreement it must:

1.1   Promptly notify the [Licensor] of any allegation, claim or legal proceedings which give rise to such right and make no admission or settlement without the prior written authority of the [Licensor].

1.2   Provide the [Licensor] with the opportunity to participate in and fully control any compromise, settlement or other resolution or disposition of such claim or proceedings (subject to being fully indemnified and secured by the [Licensor] to the [Licensees] satisfaction).

1.3   Fully co-operate with the reasonable requests of the [Licensor] and at the [Licensor's] reasonable expense in its participation and control of any compromise, settlement or resolution or other disposition of such claim or proceedings.

I.079
The [Licensor] warrants that the [Licensor] will keep the [Licensee] and the [Licensee's] associates indemnified from and against all liabilities, claims, actions, proceedings, damages and loss suffered or incurred by the [Licensee] or the [Licensee's] associates or awarded against the [Licensee] or the [Licensee's] associates and any compensation agreed and paid by the [Licensee] and/or the [Licensee's] associates on the advice of Counsel in consequence of or arising out of any breach or alleged breach or non-performance of all or any of the covenants, warranties, representations, obligations, undertakings or agreements on the [Licensor's] part set out in this Agreement.

I.080

The [Licensor] warrants that it will keep the [Licensee] indemnified from and against all liabilities, claims, actions, proceedings, damages and loss suffered or incurred by the [Licensee] or awarded against the [Licensee] and any compensation agreed and paid by the [Licensee] on the advice of Counsel (and agreed by the [Licensor]) in consequence of or arising out of any breach or non-performance of all or any of the covenants, warranties, representations, obligations, undertakings or agreements on the [Licensor's] part contained in this Agreement.

I.081

The [Licensee] will, at its own expense, indemnify, save and hold harmless the [Licensor] and its respective successors, assigns and employees from and against any and all liability, loss, damage, cost and expense (including without limitation reasonable attorneys' fees) incurred or sustained by the [Licensor] and others or resulting from any breach or claim by a third party with respect to any of the warranties or terms in this Agreement made by the [Licensee]. In the event that any person shall make any claim or institute any suit or proceedings alleging any facts which, if true, would constitute a breach by the [Licensee]. The [Licensor] shall give prompt written notice to the [Licensee] and the [Licensee] shall undertake, at its own cost and expense, the defence and shall supply competent and experienced [Counsel/legal advisers] to defend any such suit or proceedings. If the [Licensee] shall fail to promptly appoint [Counsel/legal advisers], the [Licensor] may instruct its own [Counsel/legal advisers] and the reasonable charges made in connection therewith shall be paid by and/or reimbursed by the [Licensee]. If the [Licensor] shall settle or compromise any such suit, claim or proceedings, the settlement amount shall be paid for by the [Licensee] [subject to the [Licensee's] prior written approval].

I.082

The [Company] will indemnify and hold harmless the [Licensee], its officers, directors and employees against any and all claims, damages, liabilities, losses and expenses (except for any consequential and/or indirect loss) including any reasonable lawyers' fees and costs arising out of any addition, deletion or other act of the [Company] in connection with the [Property]. The [Licensee] shall promptly notify the [Company] in writing of any litigation, claim, or threat of legal action to which this indemnity applies. The [Company] shall at its own expense assume the defence of or deal with any such matter. The [Company] shall not be obliged to indemnify the [Licensee] in respect of any settlement of any claim, threat or litigation which has not been approved by and/or authorised by the [Company].

1.083

If the [Company] is prevented from exercising the rights in respect of the [Work/Product/Service] by reason of any breach by the [Licensor] of the terms set out in this Agreement for a period of more than [specify duration]. The [Licensor] agrees and undertakes that it shall pay to the [Company] the total sum of [figure/currency] in respect of each such occasion. The [Company] may set off the sum due from the [Licensor] against payments due from the [Company] under Clause [–]. The [Licensor] shall not liable to indemnify the [Company] in respect of any loss of profit, business, stock or customers that may arise by reason of any breach by the [Licensor] of this Agreement.

1.084

The [Assignor] will keep the [Assignee] indemnified from and against all liabilities, actions, claims, proceedings, damages and loss suffered or incurred by the [Assignee] or awarded against the [Assignee] and any compensation agreed and paid by the [Assignee] in consequence of any breach and/or alleged breach of the terms of this Agreement by the [Assignor].

1.085

The [Company] shall for the Term of the Agreement indemnify the [Contractor] against all actions, claims, liabilities, costs, settlements, judgments, loss and expenses including legal fees in respect of any breach of any nature of any representation, warranty or undertaking by the [Company]. The [Contractor] shall be entitled to withhold any sum due under the Agreement to the [Company] in respect of any sum claimed under this indemnity by the [Contractor] until the matter is resolved.

1.086

The [Company] and the [Distributor] mutually undertake to indemnify the other against all liabilities, claims, demands, actions, costs, damages or loss directly arising out of any breach by them of any of the terms of this Agreement. In the event of an action, claim, dispute, writ or proceedings arising out of the performance of this Agreement, the [Company] and the [Distributor] agree to provide full details to the other party at the earliest opportunity and shall not settle any such matter without first consulting the other party.

1.087

In the event that there is an allegation that the use of the [Item] infringes any third party rights. The party against whom the claim is made shall defend it and shall be entitled at its sole discretion to join the other party or take third party proceedings for a contribution, indemnity damages or otherwise.

I.088

The [Company's] total liability (except for death or personal injury) for any one claim or for a total of claims arising out of one incident whether as a result of the negligence of the [Company] or not shall not exceed [figure/currency].

I.089

The [Assignor] and the [Assignee] mutually undertake to indemnify the other against all liabilities, claims, demands, actions, costs, damages or loss arising out of any breach by either of them of the terms of this Agreement. In the event of any claim, dispute, action, writ or summons the [Assignor] and the [Assignee] agree to provide full details to the other party at the earliest opportunity and shall not settle any such matter without first consulting the other party.

I.090

The indemnity shall only be provided in respect of any matter notified during the term of the Agreement which arise from [country] and shall be limited to [figure/currency].

I.091

The [Assignor] shall not be liable to and/or indemnify the [Assignee] in respect of any of the following matters:

1.1 Where the [Assignee] has adapted and/or changed the [Work] and/or added and/or deleted material which has materially and significantly changed the content to such an extent that over [number] per cent is different from the original.

1.2 For any sums due to a third party from the [Assignee] for copyright and/or other payments due for the use, adaptation and/or exploitation of the [Work].

1.3 For any sums due outside [specify countries].

I.092

The indemnity by the [Assignor] to the [Assignee] shall cease on [date]. The [Assignor] shall only be liable for any notified claims under the indemnity made by that date. Thereafter all liability by the [Assignor] to the [Assignee] shall cease and no further claims for any reason for any sums may be made by the [Assignee] under the indemnity. The [Assignee] agrees and undertakes to bear all the risk and to be responsible for the cost of all allegations and/or claims by third parties after [date].

I.093

The [Consortium] members agree and undertake that they shall all equally and jointly and be liable for any sums that may arise under any indemnity provided to any third party in respect of the [Project] in respect of agreements that may arise provided that:

1.1   No member of the [Consortium] authorises and/or concludes any agreement which is not approved by the Board and/or its legal advisors.

1.2   No contribution shall be sought from other members of the [Consortium] where it could be paid under an insurance claim through the policy paid for and taken out by the [Consortium] in respect of the [Project].

1.3   No more than [number] years have expired since the end of the [Project] and/or the expiry and/or termination of all the agreements.

1.4   Where a member no longer exists, then any successor and/or assignee of the member shall still be held liable for any sums due.

1.5   Where any sum claimed relates to a civil and/or criminal action and/or proceedings then any member shall be entitled to be provided with access to and/or copies of all material of any nature subject to payment of the administrative costs incurred to do so.

I.094
The [Distributor] agrees to indemnify [Name] in respect of the failure of any sub-agent, sub-licensee and/or other third party engaged by them to pay any sums due from the exploitation of the [Work] which are due to [Name] before [date].

Internet and Websites

I.095
No indemnity is provided to any person, company, business or entity which uses, accesses, downloads, reproduces, distributes and/or supplies and/or purchases any material, articles, products, services, data, software, film, DVDs, images, databases, logos, trade marks, service marks, merchandising, sound recordings, music, ringtones, computer-generated material, graphics, artwork or otherwise from this [Website]. Your arrangement, contract, license and/or purchase is direct with a third party and no responsibility is accepted by the [Company] for their failure, delay, errors, omissions, breach of agreement or otherwise and you agree that you shall not make any claim against the [Company].

I.096
The total indemnity by the [Company] shall be limited to the value of the [Product/Service/other] and no responsibility can be accepted for any other loss, damage, costs, expenses, destruction of data, delay in delivery, interruption, suspension, or other consequences which may arise whether direct and/or indirect at any time.

I.097

No person, company, entity and/or otherwise who uses this [Website] is provided with any undertakings and/or indemnity of any nature. Any use and/or reliance upon information, research and data and/or any film, sound recordings, text, images, music and/or any other material and/or media is entirely at your own risk and cost. No assurances are provided as to:

1.1 Ownership of material; copyright ownership and notices.

1.2 Compliance with any codes, practices, legislation, regulations, directives and cases.

1.3 That there are no viruses, defects and/or errors which could cause harm and/or damage.

1.4 That the content has been checked for errors, omissions, defamatory and/or offensive material and/or is threatened by and/or the subject of legal proceedings.

I.098

The [User] undertakes to indemnify the [Company] in respect of the total sum incurred by the [Company] and/or any legal advisors, [agents and/or consultants] for any allegation and/or settlement, legal proceedings and/or damages, losses and/or other costs for infringement of copyright, trade mark infringement, defamation, breach of database rights, infringement of computer software rights, breach of contract, and/or any other intellectual property rights and/or any other rights and/or interest by a third party in respect of any material uploaded by the [User] to the [Website] whether text, images, film, photographs, sound recordings, music, lyrics, trade marks, service marks, community marks, logo and/or any other material in any medium and any format at any time in any part of the world.

I.099

The indemnity in Clause [–] shall not apply:

1.1 To any issue which relates to any third party outside [country].

1.2 After [date].

1.3 Where the [Licensor] has already been paid [figure/currency] in total which is the maximum liability of the [Company]. shall only be provided in respect of any matter notified during the term of the Agreement which arise from [country] and shall be limited to [figure/currency].

I.100

The [Contributor] is not providing any indemnity to the [Company] in respect of any claim, liabilities, demands, actions, costs, damages and/or other losses arising out of any breach of the terms of this Agreement by the [Contributor].

I.101

The [Distributor] does not provide any undertakings and/or indemnity in respect of the supply and/or reproduction of the [Sound Recordings] in the form of [Discs] and/or downloads. There is no right to make copies and/or to transfer the material to third parties and/or to store the material as part of a storage and/or retrieval system on any equipment.

I.102

[Name] agrees to indemnify the [Distributor] in respect of any claim, action, losses, damages, costs and expenses which may arise from the exercise of the rights granted by [Name] under this Agreement before [date]. Provided that the indemnity shall not cover any sums paid by the [Distributor] to any employee, director, consultant and/or agent and no sum shall be paid and/or incurred in respect of a third party without prior consultation with [Name]. In any event the total indemnity shall be limited to [number/currency] and shall only be in respect of a claim and/or action in [country] and not any other part of the world.

I.103

The indemnity provided by [Name] to the [Distributor] shall only be in respect of any sums which are paid by the [Distributor] relating to allegations of breach of copyright, privacy, contract, defamation and/or infringement of trade marks in respect of the [Work] in [country] before [date]. The [Distributor] agrees to bear the cost and liability of all other matters of any nature that may arise which may result in payments by the [Distributor] and shall not offset and/or recoup these from any sums due to [Name].

Merchandising

I.104

The [Licensee] shall indemnify the [Proprietor] and their respective assignees and licensees and hold each of them harmless and shall be responsible for all liability, costs and expenses including legal fees on a full indemnity basis, arising out of or by reason of any breach by the [Licensee] of any of the representations, warranties or agreements made by it hereunder or arising as a result of the production, manufacture, use, reproduction, distribution, sale and supply by or for the [Licensee] of the [Licensed Articles].

I.105

The [Licensee] agrees to indemnify the [Licensor] and the [Agent] (and their respective assigns) against all actions, claims, costs, demands and expenses which it or any of them may suffer or sustain in respect of the exploitation of the rights granted by the [Licensee] under this Agreement.

I.106

The [Originator] will indemnify and at all times keep the [Company] fully indemnified against all actions, proceedings, claims, costs and damages whatsoever made against or incurred by the [Company] in consequence of any breach or non-performance by the [Originator] of any of the representations, warrantees or obligations contained in this Agreement.

I.107

The [Licensee] agrees to indemnify the [Licensor] and bear the total cost of all actions, demands, claims, settlements, criminal and/or civil proceedings of any nature at any time that are made against, and/or incurred by the [Licensor] as a result of any breach and/or alleged breach by the [Licensee] of any of the terms of this Agreement and/or any other agreement made for or on behalf of the [Licensee] with any third party including, but not limited to any sub-distributor, agent, sub-licensee, exhibitor or others in respect of the exploitation of the rights granted under this Agreement.

I.108

[Licensee] undertakes to the [Licensor] that they shall keep each other indemnified for the duration of the [Licence Period] against all actions, costs, proceedings, claims, demands and expenses that may be brought against or incurred by the [Licensee] or the [Licensor] in consequence of any breach or alleged breach of any undertaking in this Agreement by the other party.

Both parties agree to provide full details to the other party within a reasonable period of being aware of the matter and shall consult with each other as to the best course of action.

Both parties agree that the liability of the [Licensor] shall not be limited except that it shall only relate to matters arising within the Licence Period. The [Licensee's] total liability shall be limited to [–].

I.109

The [Distributor] agrees to indemnify the [Licensor] for any damages, losses, costs, expenses, legal fees, and/or loss of profit and/or royalties and/or rights whether direct or indirectly arising from the breach and/or alleged breach of the terms of this Agreement by the [Distributor] and/or any third party appointed or engaged by the [Distributor] including but not limited to:

1.1   Failure to by a third party to account or transfer any sums due.

1.2   The recall of the [Product] for health and safety reasons, and/or quality control reasons.

1.3   The delay, cancellation and/or alteration of the proposed launch date.

1.4   Any personal injury, death, or other matter relating to the use, and fitness for purpose of the [Product] its content and packaging and any other product liability or compliance required under any legislation, directive, regulation, policy or code in any country.

I.110
There shall be no general indemnity under this Agreement and the total liability of [Name] to the [Company] shall be limited to [figure/currency] under this Agreement for any breach of Clause [–].

I.111
The indemnity in Clause [–] shall not apply after the expiry of the licence and/or [date] whichever is the earlier. The indemnity shall continue to apply after the termination by the [Licensor] of the Agreement.

I.112
The indemnity under Clause [–] shall be limited to the [Licensee] and shall not apply to any sub-licensee under this Agreement. Nor shall the indemnity apply where the exploitation by the [Licensee] is in respect of any text which is a translation of the original.

I.113
The indemnity in Clause [–] by the [Author] shall not apply and no sum shall be due and/or paid to the [Distributor] where:

1.1   Any allegation and/or claim by a third party is made which is not proved to be correct by a court of law and/or is not agreed to as a settlement by the [Author].

1.2   To any issue which arises outside [specify countries].

1.3   After the expiry of a period of [one] year from the end of the Agreement.

1.4   Where the [Author] has already paid the [Distributor] [figure/currency] under the indemnity then that shall be the maximum liability of any nature of the [Author].

I.114
[Name] agrees to indemnify the [Distributor/Agent] in respect any sums which may be incurred which arise from the failure of [Name] to assist in the marketing and promotion of the [Product] as set out in clause [–] up to a maximum of [number/currency].

I.115

1.1 The [Consortium] agrees to indemnify the [Company] with a payment of no more than [number/currency] if circumstances require that the [Event] be delayed, cancelled and/or materially changed as to its content and the [Company] is able to provide evidence of any loss and/or damage as a direct result which cannot be recouped from a third party.

1.2 The [Company] agrees that the indemnity shall be limited as set out in 1.1 whether or not the [Company] has and/or will incur greater costs and/or expenses and/or created and/or developed and/or booked advertising based on the [Event]. The [Company] waives any claim in respect of any sum above that set out in 1.1 which may arise directly and/or indirectly for any reason.

1.3 The [Company] agrees that the indemnity shall not be due and/or payable where the [Company] agrees to any delay, cancellation and/or change in content and suffers no loss and/or damage and/or costs and/or expenses.

I.116

The [Distributor] agrees and undertakes to indemnify [Name] in respect of any costs, expenses, damages, losses including travel, loss of future work and fees, and damage to his/her reputation which are suffered and/or incurred by [Name] as a result of any allegation, claim, civil and/or criminal action and/or proceedings and/or any investigation against the [Distributor] and any sub-licensee at any time in any country to any part of their business and/or their manufacturers.

Publishing

I.117

The [Author] undertakes to indemnify and keep indemnified the [Publisher] and any other party whom the [Publisher] shall in the ordinary course of their business agree to indemnify against loss, injury or damage (including any legal costs or expenses and any compensation costs and disbursements paid by the [Publishers] on the advice of professional legal advisors to compromise or settle any claim) occasioned to the [Publishers] in consequence of any breach of this warranty or arising out of any claim alleging that the [Work] constitutes an infringement of copyright or contains anything obscene, blasphemous, indecent, defamatory, scandalous, objectionable or otherwise unlawful matter.

I.118

The [Author] shall indemnify the [Company] against any loss, injury or damage resulting from any breach by the [Author] of all warranties, undertakings and terms in this Agreement and against any legal costs and expenses and any compensation, damages, costs or disbursements (including any legal costs or expenses properly incurred) incurred or suffered by the [Company] as a direct consequence of any breach of any of the terms by the [Author] under this Agreement. The [Company] will consult the Author (if available) before concluding any compromise with a third party on any claim in respect of which the [Company] might seek to be indemnified by the [Author] hereunder.

I.119

The [Author] agrees to indemnify the [Publishers] in respect of any third party claims, losses, damages, settlements, legal costs and expenses which may be paid to such third parties as a result of any matter in the [Work] in respect of the exercise by the [Publishers] of the rights granted by the [Author] in this Agreement provided that in all cases the Publisher shall:

1.1 Notify the [Author] as soon as possible of the detail of any claim, loss or damage.

1.2 Consult with the [Author] as to the best course of action in dealing with such matter.

1.3 Not agree to pay any third party any sum for any reason arising from such claim, loss or damage without the prior approval of the [Author].

Where the [Publisher] fails to adhere to 1.1 to 1.3 above, then the [Author] shall not be liable for the sums paid by the [Publisher]. The [Publisher] shall agree a repayment schedule with the [Author] in respect of those sums which fall within this indemnity provision.

I.120

The [Author] shall indemnify the [Publishers] against any loss, injury or expense arising out of any breach or alleged breach of this warranty. The [Publishers] reserve the right to alter or insist that the [Author] alter the text of the [Work] in such a way as appears to them appropriate for the purpose of removing or amending any passage which, on the advice of the [Publishers'] legal advisers, may be considered objectionable or likely to be cause for action at law by a third party. The indemnity by the [Author] shall continue after the expiry or termination of this Agreement. The [Author's] liability in respect of any passage not removed or amended shall not be affected.

I.121

The [Author] agrees to indemnify the [Publisher] against any action, claim, proceedings, demands, loss, damage and/or injury and any costs or reasonable legal expenses incurred by the [Publisher] as a result of any breach or alleged breach of this Agreement by the [Author]. Provided that the [Author] shall have been consulted in advance on the details of the breach and provided with an opportunity to present his/her case in each instance. This indemnity shall end on [date].

I.122

The [Author] shall only indemnify the [Publisher] in respect of any loss or damages or settlement in excess of [figure/currency] and shall only be liable for a total sum of [figure/currency] in respect of any breach or alleged breach of any of the terms in Clauses [–] set out in this Agreement. In the event that the [Publisher] wishes to rely on this indemnity it must notify the [Author] immediately of any claim, action, proceedings or threat by notice in writing providing full details of the matter. The [Publisher] shall keep the [Author] fully informed and provide the [Author] with the opportunity to refute or deny the allegations in each case. The [Author] shall also be entitled to take responsibility for the case (except where the Publisher is cited as a party to the action) provided that he/she is willing to provide an indemnity to the [Publisher] that they shall not bear any cost and/or expenses and/or be responsible for any loss and/or damages that may result.

I.123

The [Publisher] agrees to indemnify the [Author] against any claim, action, proceedings, demands, loss, damage or injury and any costs or reasonable legal expenses incurred by the [Author] including any matter settled on the advice of a legal advisor by the [Author] as a result of a breach or alleged breach by the [Publisher] of its obligations under this Agreement.

I.124

The [Author] agrees to indemnify the [Publisher] against any action, claim, proceedings, demands, loss, damage or injury and any costs or reasonable legal expenses incurred. This shall include any matter settled on the advice of the legal advisors by the [Publisher] as a result of any breach or alleged breach by the [Author] of his/her obligations under this Agreement subject to a maximum limit of [–] and compliance with the following procedure:

1.1 Promptly notify the [Author] of any claim or legal proceedings which have arisen and make no admission or offer of settlement at that stage.

1.2 Provide the [Author] with the opportunity to be fully consulted as regards any proposed steps to be taken and any settlement of the matter.

1.3 The [Publisher] shall not have the right to deduct any sums owed by the [Author] under the indemnity from sums due under the Agreement to the [Author] unless there is written consent in each case from the [Author].

I.125
The [Artist] agrees to indemnify the [Music Publishers] and its licensees and assigns against all claims, actions, demands, costs, damages and expenses arising in any form from the use of the [Recordings] by the [Music Publishers] and/or its licensees and assigns in accordance with this Agreement. Except that the [Artist] shall not be liable in respect of claims for which the [Music Publishers] are responsible, including, but not limited to, the clearance of rights, consents, and/or payments under this Agreement.

I.126
The [Assignor] hereby indemnifies the [Music Publishers] from and against all costs, claims, demands, proceedings and damages including the [Publisher's] own legal costs on an indemnity basis howsoever arising in respect of any breach of this warranty.

I.127
The [Company] agrees that it shall not have the right to seek any sums from the [Name] in respect of this Agreement provided that he/she fulfils the obligation to deliver the [Work] by [date]. All responsibility for any legal liability or proceedings which may arise from the use of the [Work] and any other material collected, obtained or provided under this Agreement shall be at the sole risk, cost and expense of the [Company].

I.128
The [Publisher] shall carry out the following steps for all allegations, threats and actions against the [Work] and if it does not do so shall not be able to seek to be indemnified by the [Author]:

1.1 Notify the [Author/Agent] of the detail of any loss, damage, injury or other claim within [seven days] of receiving any letter, writ, complaint or otherwise.

1.2 The [Publisher] shall consult with the [Author] as to the best course of action to be adopted and the steps to be taken in dealing with the matter including the legal costs to be incurred.

1.3 The [Publisher] shall keep the [Author] regularly updated and provided with the opportunity to put their view of the allegations, claims or complaint.

1.4 The [Publishers] shall allow the [Author] to inspect all the material within the possession or control of the [Publisher] and/or their legal advisors relating to any claim, action, allegation or complaint including any legal reports and opinions.

1.5 In the event that the [Publishers] fail to adhere to these conditions then the [Author] shall not be liable to pay any sums of any nature.

1.6   The total liability of the [Author] under this indemnity shall be limited to [figure/currency].

1.7   The [Publisher] shall not seek to claim any indemnity for its own acts, omissions, failures or breaches of this Agreement nor for any third party whether a sub-licensee, sub-agent and/or distributor and/or in respect of any of the following material [specify].

1.8   This clause shall continue in force after the expiry or termination of this Agreement for [specify duration] from the date of termination and/or expiry in respect of exploitation of the [Work] before that date.

I.129
The [Publisher] shall not seek to be indemnified by the [Author] except under Clause [–] as to the originality of the [Work] supplied by the [Author]. All other claims, actions, complaints to the [Publisher] and/or any third party agent, distributor or otherwise shall be dealt with at the [Publishers] cost and expense and no sums shall be claimed from the [Author] and/or deducted from any advance and/or royalties.

I.130
The indemnity provision shall only apply to matters notified and claimed from the [Author] before [date].

I.131
The indemnity only applies to exploitation of the [Work] in [country], all other reproduction, publication, distribution and exploitation is at the [Publishers] risk and cost.

I.132
The indemnity only applies to any matter arising from the publication of the first edition of the [Book] in [country] by the [Publisher] before [date] which is related to the work of the [Author] and not to any other rights, person, agent, company, distributor at any time.

I.133
The [Publisher] agrees that the following matters are not covered by the indemnity in Clause [–] and shall not seek to be paid any costs, damages, losses, and/or expenses for these excluded items:

1.1   The index.

1.2   The title and the cover.

1.3   The accompanying promotional product and/or disc.

1.4 Liabilities which arise due to the errors, omissions, negligence and/or failures of the [Publisher], agents, distributors, printers, newspapers, magazines, and/or websites.

I.134
All claims under the indemnity Clause [–] must be received by the [Company] by [date] [time]. Thereafter the indemnity shall no longer apply. The [Publishers] waives all rights and agrees not to make any further claims against the [Company] after that date.

I.135
The [Software Company] agree to indemnify the [Company] and to pay all costs, expenses, losses and damages which may be substantiated in respect of the following failures by the [Software Company]:

1.1 The loss, destruction and/or damage to the [Master Copy] fixed at a maximum of [figure/currency].

1.2 The failure by the [Software Company] to restrict access to and keep confidential the [Master Copy] [while it is in its possession fixed at a maximum of [figure/currency].

1.3 The failure to prevent a copy of the [Master Copy] being made by an unauthorised third party fixed at a maximum of [figure/currency].

1.4 The corruption and/or addition of other material including viruses fixed at a maximum fee of [figure/currency].

I.136
[Name] agrees and undertakes to indemnify the [Publisher] and any [Distributor] and sub-licensee if it is proved and/or discovered at a later date that they have suffered any loss and/or damage and/or costs and/or expenses due to the fact that [Name] is not the copyright owner of the [Work] and/or has used and adapted material belonging to a third party without consent and/or has failed to clear and/or pay the fees due for any material in the [Work] and/or has failed to disclose an existing agreement with a third party which effects the terms of this Agreement and/or has already disposed of and/or assigned all and/or some of the rights granted and/or assigned under this Agreement to a third party. This indemnity shall end on [date] and no sums shall be due and/or paid which have not be demanded by that date.

Purchase and Supply of Products

I.137
The [Buyer] will hold harmless and indemnify the [Seller] for any breach of the terms of this letter of confidentiality for any reasonable and direct loss

suffered by the [Seller] as a result of any breach by the [Buyer] of the terms of this Agreement.

I.138

The [Buyer] shall fully indemnify the [Company] against all claims which may be made against the [Company] for loss or damage caused by, or arising from, or in connection with, any breach by the [Buyer] of the provisions in relation to the delivery or storage of the [Company's] products and against all costs and expenses incurred including the cost of investigating and defending such claims.

I.139

Where the material supplied is on hire to the [Customer] then the [Customer] shall indemnify the [Company] against the full cost of replacement or repair of the material whether or not such replacement or repair of the material is occasioned by loss, damage or destruction occurring as a result of the negligence of the [Customer], its servants, agents or otherwise.

I.140

The [Customer] agrees to indemnify the [Supplier] in respect of any claim or damages or any loss or costs which arise for any reason from the use of the [Material] without having first obtained the necessary consent, licences and authorisations from any person who may or does hold rights of any nature in such [Material].

I.141

The [Agent] agrees to indemnify the [Company] against any action, claim, proceedings, loss, damage or injury and any costs or reasonable legal expenses incurred, including any matter settled on the advice of expert legal advisers by the [Company], as a result of any breach or alleged breach by the [Agent] of its obligations under this Agreement.

I.142

The [Seller] shall indemnify the [Purchaser] from any and all claims, liabilities, damage and/or expenses incurred or sustained by the [Purchaser] including any consequential loss and/or damage as follows:

1.1 In respect of any alleged or actual infringement of any intellectual property rights, copyright, trade and/or service mark, patent, design rights or any other rights of any third party.

1.2 Any loss and/or damage sustained by the [Purchaser] and/or for which the [Purchaser] may be liable as a result of the failure of the [Seller] to perform its obligations to the [Purchaser].

1.3   In respect of any death and/or personal injury caused to an employee of the [Purchaser], its agents and/or sub-contractors and/or to any other person on the premises of the [Purchaser] and/or any loss and/or damage to any property of the [Purchaser] and/or any third party.

I.143

The [Seller] shall indemnify the [Purchaser] against liability, loss, damages, claims, costs and expenses as a result of any claim in respect of any rights in the [Product] of any nature and/or any personal injury and/or death and/or damage to property.

I.144

The [Supplier] and the [Seller] mutually undertake to indemnify the other against all claims, liabilities, demands, actions, costs, damages or reasonable foreseeable loss and expenses arising directly out of any breach by the defaulting party under the terms of this Agreement. The total maximum liability of either party in total for the duration of the agreement shall be [figure/currency] [in each of the following countries] [aggregate liability] excluding any liability for death and/or personal injury which shall not be limited.

I.145

1.1   The [Licensee] agrees to indemnify the [Licensor] against all actions, claims, costs, demands, losses and expenses which may arise out of the alleged breach or otherwise of any of the terms of this Agreement by the [Licensee] or any other matter arising from the exploitation of the [Licensee's] Product including death or injury. This indemnity shall continue to apply after the expiry or termination of this agreement.

1.2   The [Licensor] agrees to indemnify the [Licensee] against all actions, claims, costs, demands, losses and expenses which may arise out of the alleged breach or otherwise of any of the terms of this Agreement by the [Licensor] relating to the [Licensor's] Logo. This indemnity shall cease upon the expiry or termination of this Agreement.

I.146

1.1   The [Publisher] and the [Author] do not accept any responsibility for any type of use of the [Article/disc] by the [Purchaser], any business in which the [Purchaser] may be involved and/or third party to which the [Purchaser] may provide advice or material for any reason for any direct and/or indirect damages, losses, costs, expenses, actions, claims or otherwise.

1.2   The [Purchaser] shall use the [Article/disc] entirely at the [Purchaser's] sole risk and expense and the [Purchaser] shall be liable for its own costs and expenses or otherwise that may rise from any type of use.

1.147

In the event of any claim, demand, actions or otherwise by the [Purchaser] and/or any business for any reason arising from the use of the [Article/disc] and/or data and/or information. The [Publisher] and the [Author] shall only be liable in total to repay the full purchase price of the [Article/disc] to the [Purchaser]. The [Purchaser] agrees that it is the [Purchaser's] responsibility to arrange and bear the cost of insurance cover for the benefit of the [Purchaser], any business and third party for the use of the [Article/disc] by the [Purchaser]. That the [Publisher] and [Author] shall not bear any responsibility and/or liability for any direct or indirect use of any type of the [Article/disc] by the [Purchaser], any business, third party or otherwise at any time.

I.148

The [Distributor] agrees that the indemnity in Clause [–] shall end on [date] and that all rights to make a claim in respect of any other matters shall be waived after that date. All such matters shall be at the total risk and cost of the [Distributor].

I.149

The indemnity in Clause [–] shall not apply if:

1.1   The damage, loss, cost and/or expense is caused by the [Purchaser].

1.2   The [Product] has not been used in accordance with the instructions.

1.3   The [Purchaser] has not notified the [Distributor] and made a claim within [two] years of purchase.

I.150

The [Company] agrees and undertakes that it shall indemnify [Name] and his/her distributors, customers, agents and any other third party related to [Name] involved in the supply, sale and marketing of the [Products] in respect of all sums which they may reasonably demand and seek to claim in respect of losses, damages, legal and administrative, advertising, freight, customs duties, tests, health and safety reports and assessments, loss of orders and damage to reputation and any other costs and expenses of any nature which are reasonably incurred in any part of the world at any time whether during and/or after the termination and/or cancellation of this Agreement in the event that:

1.1   The [Company] and/or any manufacturer authorised and/or engaged by it uses and/or includes any ingredients in the reproduction of the

[Products] which are toxic and/or not suitable and likely to cause an allergic reaction and/or are not pure and/or the source, content and supplier cannot be verified.

1.2　The [Company] and/or any manufacturer authorised and/or engaged by it uses any premises which are unfit for purpose and pose a risk to health and safety of the employees and/or casual staff according to the international standards set by [specify] and/or has used persons under [number] age as workers.

1.3　The [Company] and/or any manufacturer authorised and/or engaged by it have not disclosed the fact that they do not hold a licence and/or certificate to carry out this type of work and do have suitably qualified management and/or craftsmen and/or machinery and/or software and/or facilities to complete the necessary techniques for the [Products].

1.4　The [Company] and/or any manufacturer authorised and/or engaged by it fails in whole and/or part to take such reasonable precautions as set out by [specify body] to protect the local environment and wildlife and community from any harm that may arise from any waste material that may be stored, discharged and/or released into any rivers, sea, sub-terrain, land and/or air at any time.

Services

1.151

The [Consultant] agrees that it will indemnify the [Company] on demand against any liability, assessment or claim for taxation whatsoever including (without limitation) any liability for personal income tax and/or for national insurance contributions where such liability, assessment or claim arises out of, or is made in connection with the performance of the services of the [Consultant] under this Agreement. The [Consultant] also agrees to indemnify the [Company] against all reasonable costs and expenses and any penalty, fine or interest accrued or payable by the [Company] in connection with or in consequence of any such liability, assessment or claim. The [Company] may at its option satisfy such indemnity (in whole or in part) by way of deduction from payments to be made by the [Company] under this Agreement to the [Consultant].

1.152

In the event that the [Manager] shall cause financial loss to the [Company] through any reckless or criminal activity resulting in damage to the property of the [Company] then the [Company] shall be entitled to deduct such loss from the salary payable to the [Manager] under Clause [–] above.

I.153

The [Presenter] shall not be bound to provide any indemnity to the [Television Company] for any reason [except for any claim for tax or national insurance arising out of the Presenter's services under this Agreement].

I.154

The [Television Company] acknowledges that it shall be entirely and solely responsible for the cost of all loss, damage, claims, legal actions, complaint or allegation arising out of, or in connection with, the provision of the [Presenter's] services whilst the [Presenter] is at the studios, on company business or presenting any material for the [Television Company]. Further the [Television Company] shall reimburse the [Presenter] with all reasonable expenses and costs which he/she may incur in assisting the [Television Company] with any matter.

I.155

The [Customer] shall be liable for and agrees to indemnify the [Company] in full against all damage to the facilities and equipment within the premises and plant and all assets of the [Company] and any third party where the act or omission is caused by the [Customer] and/or its officers, agents and/or employees who are acting as agents for the [Customer].

I.156

The [Contractor] agrees to fully defend, indemnify and hold harmless this [Company] and the [Group] from and against all losses, damages, claims, demands, proceedings, costs, charges and expenses (including legal fees and expenses) in respect of loss or damage to third parties which are caused by the [Contractor], the [Contractor's] personnel and/or sub-contractors whether personal injury, death and/or damage to property arising directly or indirectly from the performance of the work and/or the fulfilment of this Contract.

I.157

The provisions of the Clause [–] above shall not entitle the [Company] to disclaim all liability to third parties. The [Company] shall continue to be liable to third parties in respect of all losses, damages, demands, proceedings, costs, charges and expenses which arise directly or indirectly as a result of the negligence, default, omission or non-performance by the [Company], its directors, offices, agents or otherwise.

I.158

The [Contractor] shall be solely responsible for and indemnify the [Company] and the [Group] and its employees and/or agents against all losses, damages, claims, demands, proceedings, cost charges and expenses in respect of the injury or death of any person in the employment of the [Contractor] and/ or its sub-contractors whether or not the negligence, default, breach of duty or otherwise of the [Company] and/or Group and/or any employee and/or agent has caused or contributed in any way.

I.159

The [Contractor] shall bear the full cost and indemnify the [Company] in full in respect of all losses, damages, claims, demands, civil or criminal proceedings, costs or expenses incurred or suffered by the [Company] and/or its officers, employees or agents in respect of loss or damage to all facilities, tools, equipment, aircraft, ships, oil rigs, hovercraft, plant or personal belongings owned, hired or used by the [Contractor], its personnel or any sub-contractor. This indemnity shall not apply in the event that the incident was caused by, contributed to or due to instructions by the [Company].

I.160

The [Contributor] undertakes to indemnify the [Company] against all claims, liabilities, demands, actions, costs and damages or reasonable foreseeable loss arising directly out of any breach by the [Contributor] of the terms of this Agreement.

I.161

1.1 The [Name] agrees to indemnify the [Company] against all liabilities, claims, actions, costs, damages or loss arising out of any breach or alleged breach by the [Name] of any of the terms of this Agreement up to a maximum liability of [figure/currency].

1.2 The [Company] undertakes to indemnify the [Name] against all liabilities, claims, actions, costs, damages or losses arising out of any breach or alleged breach by the [Company] of this Agreement.

1.3 The [Name] and the [Company] agree that in order to seek an indemnity from the other in any case they must comply with the following conditions:

1.3.1 Notify the other party of the full details of the allegations which have been made and supply copies of relevant documentation;

1.3.2 Consult with the other party as to the best course of action in dealing with such matter;

1.3.3 Not incur significant legal costs or pay any third party any sum for any reason to resolve or settle the matter without the prior written approval of the other party which shall not be unreasonably withheld or delayed.

1.4 The indemnity of the [Company] shall continue after the expiry or termination of this Agreement. The indemnity of the [Name] shall end at the expiry or termination of this Agreement.

I.162

1.1 The [Author] and the [Agent] mutually undertake to indemnify each other against all liabilities, claims, demands, actions, costs, damages or loss arising out of any breach by either party of the terms of this Agreement.

1.2 In the event that either party shall seek to rely on 1.1 above they must first provide full details to the other party from whom they seek an indemnity at the earliest opportunity and not settle any matter without prior consultation.

I.163

The [Company] acknowledges that there are no indemnity provisions from [Name] to the [Company] and the [Company] shall not seek to make any claim, demand or otherwise against [Name] whether there is a breach of this Agreement or not.

I.164

The [Company] agrees that the [Presenter] shall only be liable for any breach of the undertakings in Clauses [–]. In the event that the [Company] is to seek an indemnity from the [Presenter] it agrees that it must promptly notify any claim by the [Company] or legal proceedings by a third party and make no admission or settlement. In either case the [Presenter] shall be provided with all the available information and given the opportunity to respond.

I.165

The [Company] agrees that the indemnity in Clause [–] to [Name] shall continue after the expiry and/termination of this Agreement.

I.166

The [Company] agrees that any undertakings and the indemnity in Clause [–] shall not apply in the following circumstances:

1.1 Where the claim, cost, expenses, damages, losses and/or liability has arisen as a result of the [Company] using and/or exploiting any material produced under this Agreement beyond the stated purposes.

1.2 The matter has arisen due to the negligence, error, omission and/or delay of the [Company] and/or any agent, sub-licensee, distributor and/or other third party authorised by the [Company].

1.3 The matter has arisen due to the delay, adaptation, editing, and/or alteration of the original material by the [Company] and/or any agent, sub-licensee, distributor and/or other third party authorised by the [Company].

I.167

The [Company] agrees that no indemnity is provided by the [Agency] in respect of the persons which it recruits for positions at the [Company]. That any final decision regarding appointments is at the sole discretion of the [Company]. Further that no indemnity and/or undertakings are provided by the [Agency] as to be references, personal backgrounds and/or criminal records of any person. That data and information and reports supplied for the [Company] are for guidance only and cannot be relied upon as verified facts for which an indemnity is provided.

I.168

The [Agency] undertakes to indemnify the [Company] in respect of any costs, expenses, losses and damages which may be incurred and/or suffered by the [Company] in respect of any candidate vetted and proposed by the [Agency] during the course of this Agreement. The indemnity shall cease to apply at the time of appointment and/or refusal of any candidate proposed and in any event no later than [date].

Sponsorship

I.169

The [Sponsor] undertakes to indemnify the [Sportsperson] against all liabilities, claims, demands, actions, costs, damages or loss arising out of any breach or alleged breach by the [Sponsor] of any of the terms of this Agreement.

I.170

1.1 The [Sponsor] indemnifies the [Television Company] against all liabilities, claims, costs, actions, damages, expenses including legal fees, expert witnesses and reports reasonably and properly incurred by the [Television Company] arising out of any breach or alleged breach of this Agreement up to a maximum total of [figure/currency] per year during the Sponsorship Period.

1.2 The [Television Company] indemnifies the [Sponsor] against all liabilities, claims, costs, actions, damages, expenses including legal fees, expert witnesses and reports reasonably and properly incurred by the [Sponsor] arising out of any breach or alleged breach of this agreement by the [Television Company] up to a maximum of [figure/

currency] whether during the existence of the Sponsorship Period or not.

1.3 In order to claim under the indemnity provisions the [Sponsor] and/or the [Television Company] must promptly notify the party from whom they seek the indemnity of any claim or legal proceedings and make no settlement or admission at that stage. The party who will pay the indemnity must be provided with an opportunity to participate in or control any settlement or proceedings as appropriate.

I.171

1.1 The [Company] shall keep the [Distributor] indemnified from and against all liabilities, actions, claims, proceedings, damages and losses suffered or incurred directly but not indirectly by the [Distributor], or awarded against the [Distributor] or any compensation or settlement agreed in consequence of alleged breach or actual breach by the [Company] [including/excluding] any third party appointed by them under this Agreement.

1.2 The [Distributor] agrees to indemnify the [Company] in respect of all liabilities, actions, claims, proceedings, damages and losses suffered or incurred directly but not indirectly by the [Company] or awarded against the [Company] or any compensation or settlement agreed in consequence of any breach or alleged breach of this Agreement by the [Distributor] [including/excluding] any third party appointed by them under this Agreement.

I.172

1.1 The [Sponsor] and the [Production Company] mutually undertake to indemnify each other against all liabilities, claims, demands, actions, costs, damages or loss arising out of any breach by the [Sponsor] or the [Production Company] of any of the terms of this Agreement.

1.2 In the event that either party shall seek to rely on this indemnity then they must provide full details to the other party, within a reasonable time, of the matter arising and allow the other party to be fully involved in the case at their own cost.

I.173

1.1 The [Sponsor] and the [Association] mutually undertake to indemnify the other against all liabilities, claims, demands, actions, costs, damages or loss arising out of any breach by either party of any of the terms of this Agreement. In the event that either party shall seek to rely on the indemnity then they shall provide full details to the other party at the earliest opportunity and shall seek their views before settling any matter. Each party shall bear its own legal costs but may later seek to reclaim them on an indemnity basis.

1.2   It is agreed that the maximum liability for any reason of each of the parties under this Agreement shall be fixed at:

1.2.1   [figure/currency] in total however many cases for the [Association].

1.2.2   [figure/currency] in total however many cases for the [Sponsor].

This limit shall include all costs, expenses, compensation, damages, losses or otherwise.

I.174
The [Sponsor] agrees that it shall not seek to be indemnified by the [Company] for any financial loss, expense, damage to reputation, changes to an advertising campaign, merchandising and/or other direct and/or indirect consequences which arise due to the following matters:

1.1   Cancellation, delay, alteration of the content of the scheduled [Film/Work/Event], artistes and/or the location.

1.2   Changes in any title, players, outfits to be worn, banners, flags, official brochures, television and media coverage.

I.175
The [Company] shall not provide any indemnity to the [Sponsor] for any reason under this Agreement. The [Sponsor] enters this Agreement at its own risk and cost.

I.176
The following matters shall not be covered by the indemnity in clause [–] and the [Company] agrees that there shall be no right to claim any sums and that all such rights are waived where:

1.1   Any sums which can be claimed and are paid under an existing insurance policy for the [Event].

1.2   Any sums due which arise as a result of the negligence, omission, error, delay and/or failure of a third party.

1.3   Any sums which are not notified and the reason provided by [date].

I.177
The [Athlete] acknowledges and agrees that the [Sponsor] does not provide any indemnity to him/her and his/her agent and/or coach and/or family and/or agree to meet any losses, damages, costs and expenses which may arise

in respect of the attendance of the [Athlete] at any event, race, presentation, interview, film and/or otherwise which he/she may attend, participate in and/or contribute to at any time.

I.178

The [Sponsor] agrees and undertakes to indemnify the [Athlete] in respect of any expenditure which may be due and/or incurred by him/her which arises directly to the provision of the services of the [Athlete] under this Agreement and/or the conduct of his/her training and/or contact with his business agent, coach and family including without limitation:

1.1　All mobile, WiFi and internet and telephone costs and charges in any part of the world.

1.2　All five star hotel, food, drink, hospitality, gym and spa costs including any additional services and costs charged during the stay.

1.3　All first class travel by aeroplane, train, chauffeur car, helicopter and/or any other means required.

1.4　All training and fitness equipment, sports clothes and shoes, membership, access and location fees.

Provided that the total monthly payment by the [Sponsor] to the [Athlete] shall be limited to [number/currency] and any additional sums due shall be held over until the next month until paid in full. Subject to the supply of a statement invoice and further receipts and/or payment records if requested.

University, Library and Educational

I.179

The [Company] shall be solely responsible for and shall indemnify the [Institute] and/or the [Enterprise] and its officers, employees and/or agents against all direct and/or indirect liabilities, losses, damages, actions, losses, damages, injury, damage to equipment and/or facilities, claims, demands, civil and/or criminal proceedings, administrative costs, charges, interest, court fees and legal expenses incurred by the [Institute] and/or the [Enterprise] including any matter settled on the advice of a legal advisor by the [Institute] and/or the [Enterprise] as a result of a breach or alleged breach by the [Company] of its obligations under this Agreement.

I.180

1.1　The [Institute] agrees and undertakes to indemnify the [Company] against all liabilities, claims, demands, actions, costs, damages or loss arising out of any breach and/or alleged breach by the [Institute] of the terms of this Agreement [up to a maximum of [figure/currency] [words]]. This indemnity shall continue until [date] and shall only apply to matters notified before that date.

1.2 The [Company] agrees and undertakes to indemnify the [Institute] against all liabilities, claims, demands, actions, costs, damages or loss arising out of any breach and/or alleged breach by the [Company] of the terms of this Agreement [up to a maximum of [figure/currency] [words]]. This indemnity shall continue until [date] and shall only apply to matters notified before that date.

1.3 In the event that either party shall seek to rely on the indemnity provided by the other party. Then they must first provide full details to at the earliest opportunity and allow them the opportunity to refute the allegations and/or claim and shall not settle any matter without prior consultation with the party.

I.181

The [Institute] and the [Company] mutually undertake to indemnify each other against all liabilities, claims, demands, actions, costs, damages or loss arising out of any breach by the [Institute] and/or the [Company] of any of the terms of this Agreement. In the event that either party shall seek to rely on this indemnity then they must provide full details to the other party, within [three months] of the matter arising and allow the other party to be consulted at all stages of the case at their own cost.

I.182

The [Contributor] shall indemnify the [Institute] against all liabilities, claims, demands, actions, costs, damages or loss arising out of any breach and/or alleged breach of the terms of this Agreement by the [Contributor]. The [Institute] shall have the right to change, alter, adapt and amend any material provided by the [Contributor] which in the opinion of the [Institute] is likely to cause offence, be defamatory and/or result in a civil and/or criminal proceedings. The indemnity by the [Contributor] shall continue after the expiry or termination of this Agreement until [date].

I.183

Both parties agree and undertake to arrange and bear the cost of suitable insurance cover for their own benefit for the [Project]. Neither party agrees nor undertakes to indemnify the other and each shall bear its own risks and costs which may arise. This clause shall not exempt any claim, action and/or costs which may be sought in the course of a civil and/or criminal against either party by the other.

I.184

The total indemnity by the [Institute] to the [Company] shall be limited to [figure/currency] [words] which is the value of the [Product/Service/other].

No responsibility can be accepted by the [Institute] for any other losses, damages, costs, expenses, destruction of data, delay in delivery, interruption of facilities and/or services, non-availability of key personnel, inaccuracies, errors, defects, failure to account and/or pay any sums due whether directly and/or indirectly arising from reliance on this Agreement by the [Company].

I.185
The indemnity in Clause [–] by the [Contributor/Institute] shall not apply in respect of the following matters [specify].

I.186
The [Consortium] agrees that no party to this agreement shall provide any indemnity to the other members of the [Consortium] at any time and that each party shall bear its own costs and expenses of any losses, damages and/or sums that may fall due and/or be claimed by any third party and/or any student, employee, consultant and/or otherwise.

I.187
It is agreed that where any sum falls due and is paid by any party due to the negligence, dishonesty, fraud, malice, death and/or civil and /or criminal proceedings relating to a member of the [Consortium] and/or a person and/or business they engaged for the [Project]. Then where a claim is paid and/or settled then a indemnity contribution of [number] per cent of the total sum paid and incurred in legal and other costs may be sought from all other members.

INDEX

General Business and Commercial

I.188
If the [Author] and the [Publishing Company] agree that an index is required but the [Author] does not wish to undertake the task the [Publishing Company] shall engage a competent indexer to compile one and the costs shall be shared equally between the [Publishing Company] and the [Author]. The [Author's] share shall be deducted by agreement between the parties or in default of such agreement at the [Publishing Company's] discretion either from part of the [Author's] Advance due on publication or from the [Author's] Royalties.

I.189
The [Author] shall provide the [Publishing Company] with a detailed index for the [Work] at his/her sole cost and expense by [date].

I.190

If in the opinion of the [Publishers] it is desirable that an index be included in the [Work] the [Publishers] shall prepare an index at their own expense. The [Publishers] agree to provide the [Author] with a copy of the index for approval at the earliest opportunity.

I.191

If in the opinion of the [Publisher] and the [Author] it is decided that an index bibliography or preface should be included in the Work, then the [Author] agrees at his/her sole cost to prepare, write and deliver such material to the [Publisher].

I.192

The [Author] undertakes to prepare an index for the [Work]. In the event that the [Publisher] prepares an index due to the [Author's] inability or unwillingness to do so then the reasonable cost of such an index prepared by an editor appointed by the [Publisher] shall be deducted from any sums due to the [Author]. The copyright in the index shall belong to [Author/Publisher].

I.193

The [Author] undertakes to prepare an index for the [Work]. In the event that circumstances change and this is done by the [Publisher] then the [Publisher] shall bear the cost.

I.194

The index for the [Work] shall be the responsibility of the [Publisher]. The index shall be subject to the prior approval of the [Author].

I.195

No index or other material shall be added to the [Work] by the [Publisher] unless written and supplied by the [Author]. The [Publisher] shall not amend, delete or revise the index without the [Author's] prior written consent.

I.196

1.1 [Author] shall create, compile and develop and index for the [Work] after delivery of the proofs by the [Company].

1.2 [Company] agrees that the copyright and ownership of the index and its taxonomy shall belong exclusively to the [Author].

1.3 That the [Company] shall not have any right to edit, adapt, amend and/or delete from the index without the prior written consent of the [Author].

1.4   Nor shall the [Company] have the right to supply, licence and/or distribute the index and taxonomy to any internet and/or website business and/or any other third party without the prior written consent of the [Author].

1.5   That the [Author] shall be entitled to the following copyright notice [specify] on each and every copy of the index and taxonomy reproduced, supplied and/or distributed by the [Company] in any format and in any media at any time.

I.197

That the index shall be compiled by a nominated person to be agreed between the parties. That the parties shall ensure that the copyright and taxonomy shall be assigned to both parties to be held jointly and equally. Neither party shall be entitled to amend, adapt, delete and/or develop the index and taxonomy without the prior written consent of the other party. All sums received from any exploitation shall be shared equally between the parties.

I.198

The [Company] shall not use the index and/or contents list of the [Work] in any manner without acknowledging the title of the [Work], the ISBN and the name of the [Author] and displaying the copyright notice on each occasion.

I.199

Where the [Company] sub-licences the [Work] to be translated into another language other than [specify]. Then the [Author] shall have the right to [approve/be consulted] concerning the translation of the title, contents list, headings, full text and images and the index. A complete copy should be provided to the [Author] at the [Licensees,] cost and expense prior to production, printing and distribution for the [Authors'] [approval/comments].

I.200

The [Company] agrees that the [Author] is the copyright owner of the title, logo, contents list, headings, text, graphics, illustrations, maps, layout and index and taxonomy of the [Work]. The [Company] shall not attempt nor register any such rights and/or interest in any media whether as a trade mark, domain name, with a collecting society, and/or as the owner of the rights.

I.201

The data, personal information, thematic subject headings, order of the text, images and logos and all indexes, key words, links, lists and databases belong to [Name] and there is no right to reproduce, adapt and/or exploit them in any form and/or by any means whether educational, for charity and/or commercial purposes unless the prior written agreement of [Name] has been obtained and a licence granted for any such use.

I.202

1.1   [Name] agrees to create a database and index for the [Company] for use in conjunction with their website, business, marketing and promotion.

1.2   In consideration of the payment of a fee of [number/currency] [Name] shall waive all rights of any nature including moral rights and a right to a credit and/or copyright and/or other acknowledgement to all material supplied to the [Company] under 1.1. [Name] assigns to the [Company] all present and future copyright, database, trade mark, service mark, computer software and any other intellectual property rights and/or other rights of exploitation in any form whether they exist now and/or are developed and/or created in the future through new legislation, technology and/or otherwise throughout the land, sea, air of the planet earth and through time and space without limit including the full period of copyright and the full period of database rights and any further periods which may arise and/or be created.

INSOLVENCY

General Business and Commercial

I.203

In the event of the [Management Contractor] making a composition of its debts or arrangement with its creditors, or having a proposal for a voluntary arrangement for a composition of its debts, or having an application made to the court for the appointment of an administrator, or having a winding up order made (except for the purposes of amalgamation or reconstruction), or a resolution for voluntary winding up is passed, or having an administrator, liquidator, receiver or manager appointed or having possession taken on behalf of the holders of any debentures or holders secured by a floating charge, the employment of the [Management Contractor] under this Contract shall be forthwith automatically terminated.

I.204

Without prejudice to any rights or remedies of either party at law if either party shall become insolvent and unable to make payments to its creditors as and when payment for such sums become due, then the other party who is not in that position shall have the right, but not the obligation to terminate this Agreement at its discretion.

I.205

'Insolvent' shall mean that the company, business or partnership is unable to fulfil to pay their debts as they fall due and an insolvency petition is likely to be and/or has been presented to a court.

I.206

If the [Company] delays in paying its sums due to the [Institute] as it has financial difficulties and/or is threatened with insolvency. Then the [Institute] shall have the right at its sole discretion to cancel and/or terminate and/or suspend and/or take such action as its thinks fit in the circumstances to protect the interests and rights of the [Institute].

I.207

It is agreed between the parties that where for any reason any member of the [Consortium] becomes insolvent and/or unable due to a reduction in funding contributions from a third party to continue with the [Project]. That all assets of the [Project] held by that member shall continue to belong to that member and not the [Consortium]. That the [Consortium] shall be provided with the option by the member to purchase the assets they hold relating to the [Project] for a value to be agreed between the parties. That where no purchase takes place the member may sell and/or licence the assets to a third party who is not part of the [Consortium].

I.208

It is agreed between the [Company] and the [Artist/Athlete] that where the [Managing director/Chief executive] has been advised by the Board of directors that the [Company] is to undergo restructuring and/or insolvency and/or disposal of the section of the business which relates to the [Artist/Athlete]. That the [Artist/Athlete] shall be notified at an early stage of this fact to enable them to seek full payment of their services under this Agreement and to obtain the return of all material which they own and/or to purchase any other material which they may wish to seek to exploit.

INSPECTION OF ACCOUNTS AND RECORDS

General Business and Commercial

I.209

The [Administrator] may issue instructions requiring the [Contractor] to arrange for the inspection of any work whether covered up or secured, and order tests of any materials or goods or of any work in relation to the [Project]. All costs paid for shall be at no cost to the [Contractor] if the inspection or test shows that the work, materials or goods are not in accordance with this Contract.

I.210

The [Author] shall at all times be allowed to inspect the accounts of the [Publisher] or to authorise a suitably qualified person to do so on his/her behalf. Provided that reasonable notice is given to the [Publisher] in order to verify the sums due to the [Author] and the [Author] pays for such inspection. If such inspection reveals an error in the [Publisher's] favour of [10%] [ten per cent] or more the cost shall be paid in full by the [Publisher]. In any event the [Publisher] shall only be obliged to allow such inspection [once] in any given accounting period.

I.211

The [Licensee] shall keep and maintain in accordance with professional and current accounting practices true and complete and accurate books of account and records of its exploitation of [DVDs/videos/other] of the [Film] and its receipts. The [Licensor] shall be entitled at its own expense to inspect, examine and make copies of such books and records. Such inspection shall be made at the offices of the [Licensee] during office hours by the [Licensor] itself and/or a qualified accountant and/or an authorised representative of the [Licensor]. [28 days'] written notice is required by the [Licensor] to the [Licensee] and shall occur not more than once in any period of [12 months] during the Term of this Agreement. If any such inspection shall reveal an error in excess of [5%] [five per cent] of monies due to the [Licensor], then the [Licensee] shall pay for the inspection in that case and interest on all sums shown to be due.

I.212

The [Company] agrees that the [Agent] shall be entitled to request copies of the invoices relating to the orders obtained by the [Agent]. In order to verify the sums due to the [Agent] under this Agreement for the [Garments] for which payment has been received. The [Agent] shall at its sole cost be entitled to arrange for one audit during the Term of the Agreement to inspect and make copies of the [Company's] accounts and records relating to orders obtained by the [Agent] in order to verify the sums paid or due to the [Agent]. Such audit shall be at such times and dates as may reasonably be agreed between the [Company] and the [Agent].

I.213

The [Contractor] agrees to maintain books and records in accordance with generally accepted accounting principles and to retain all such material for a period of not less than [2 years] after the completion of such services. The [Operator] and its authorised representatives shall have access at all reasonable times to the books and records maintained by the [Contractor] relating to any work or services performed under the Contract. The [Operator] and its authorised representatives shall have the right to audit such books and records at any reasonable time or for up to the end of the [2 year] period for the purpose of establishing that the correct sums were charged to the [Operator] and that the terms of the Contract were adhered to by the [Contractor]. The [Contractor] shall promptly pay to the [Operator] any sums which may be due as a result of such audit. The [Contractor] shall have the right to exclude any confidential information and data, databases, formulas or processes from such inspection or audit by the [Operator].

I.214

The [Company] shall be entitled at all reasonable times by its servants or agents to inspect the books of the [Licensor] relating to the exploitation of the rights granted in this Agreement. The [Company] may exercise a right of audit and inspection of the books only once in each year during the Term of this Agreement.

I.215

Where the sum due which has not been paid is more than [figure/currency] of the total sum to that party. The defaulting party who underpaid the sums due to the other shall also promptly pay the total costs and expenses paid or due to the accountancy firm or other professional advisor and/or representative who carried out the inspection and/or audit together with such sums as may be due.

I.216

The [Licensee] agrees to permit the [Licensor] or their authorised accountant at all reasonable times to inspect and audit and take copies or extracts from the relevant records and accounts. The [Licensee] further agrees to give any additional information reasonably required to enable the amount of the royalties due to the [Licensor] to be verified. In the event of an inspection revealing an error in excess of [specify percentage] of the royalties accrued due during the period for which such inspection and audit was made, the [Licensee] shall pay to the [Licensor] all the costs of such audit and inspection upon receipt of an appropriate invoice justifying the costs. The [Licensee] shall pay to the [Licensor] any sums shown to be due together with interest thereon at [4%] per annum above the base lending rate of [Bank]. In addition the [Licensee] agrees to preserve all relevant invoices records, letters and accounts relating to this Agreement for a period of not less than [–] years after the end of this Agreement.

I.217

The [Company] may at its sole cost through a firm of independent auditors up to [24 months] after the end of the Contract carry out an audit of the records of the [Contractor] and its sub-contractor in respect of the payments, costs and charges under this Contract. When the audit is completed the [Company] or the [Contractor] as appropriate shall pay any compensation due to the other party as shown by the audit.

I.218
The [Company] agrees and undertake to fully cooperate, and provide access to premises, warehouses, offices, data, documents, records, databases, discs, order forms and sales receipts, invoices, stock and any other material in any medium in order for [Name] to carry out a thorough and comprehensive inspection and audit in respect of [specify subject]. Any material which is relevant which the [Company] does not intend to allow access to for any reason should be listed in an inventory to be provided by the [Company] with a statement as to the grounds for non-co-operation.

I.219
Prior to the inspection of any records, accounts or other material the [Company] and their legal advisors and accountants shall sign a confidentiality agreement which undertakes that they shall not disclose to any third party any information which is not in the public domain except for legal or accounting purposes and strictly relating to the [Company].

I.220
The [Distributor] shall allow inspection of the [premises/goods/records/software/accounts] by the [Company] or any nominated person at any time by verbal notice from a senior officer of the [Company]. Inspection shall not be limited by time, frequency or material under this Agreement and unrestricted access shall be permitted so that the [Licensor] may examine any matter which relates or potentially relates to this Agreement.

I.221
All contracts executed by the [Licensee] shall permit the [Licensor] to inspect and verify for itself the sums due to the [Licensee] and/or the [Licensor]. A direct authorisation shall be sent to the [Licensor] on each occasion.

I.222
Each party agrees to make available to the other a copy of any inspection and/or audit upon request without charge.

I.223
The [Publisher] undertakes to the [Author] that a professional, comprehensive and complete history of the [Work] being exploited by the [Publisher] will be kept and recorded so that an accurate audit can be carried out by all parties.

I.224

Where after inspection and/or audit it is clear that the [Agent] has not fulfilled the terms of this Agreement and a serious error of more than [figure/currency] has occurred, then the [Agent] shall pay the sum due in full together with interest at [figure per cent] and damages on each occasion of [figure/currency] together with all legal and accountancy costs and expenses of the [Artist] which have been incurred.

I.225

The [Manager] shall upon request at no charge provide the [Sportsperson] with a copy of any contract, letter, document, data, database, accounts, software relating to the [Sportsperson] in the possession or under the control of the [Manager] and/or any sub-agent, sub-licensee, or related company.

I.226

The right of inspection shall not apply to any parent, associate or affiliate company in the [Group].

1.227

The [Company] shall not be obliged to bear the cost of any photocopying, telephone calls, electricity, catering or other facilities which may be required for the purposes of the inspection and audit which shall be arranged and paid for [Name].

I.228

1.1 The parties agree that the [Enterprise] shall keep the following list of documents and software as a record of the [Work/Products/Services] reproduced, supplied, distributed, licensed and/or sold under the terms of this Agreement [specify].

1.2 The documents and software listed in 1.1 shall be copied and supplied to the [Licensor] at the [Licensees'] cost at the end of each [three calendar month] period.

1.3 In addition the [Licensor] shall have the right to visit the premises and offices of the [Licensee] once in each calendar year for no more than [one week] to carry out an audit and inspection at the [Licensors] cost.

I.229

The [Institute] shall have the right to carry out a full and comprehensive inspection and audit of the software, records, documents, accounts, bank accounts, emails, film, sound recordings, images, corporate records and minutes of the [Company] and any associated business. The [Company] shall have the right to exercise this clause no more than twice in any year during the Term of this Agreement. The [Institute] shall have the right to appoint such legal and professional advisors to carry out the inspection and audit on its behalf as may be required in the circumstances.

I.230

There shall be no right to inspect and/or audit the accounts and records of the [Institute] by the [Company]. The [Institute] shall provide copies of such information as may reasonably be requested relating to the fulfilment of the Agreement, but reserve the right to refuse any request.

I.231

The [Company] shall have the right to arrange for a professional computer expert and financial advisor to visit the premises of the [Distributor] and to view and make copies of all relevant accounts, records and documents held on the hard drive of any computers, laptops, and/or any other gadgets and on any storage devices together with any discs and manual records that may be relevant in respect of the exercise of the rights granted under this Agreement, the collection of any sums from the exploitation of the rights and the calculation of the sums due to the [Company].

I.232

The [Distributor] agrees and undertakes to ensure that the [Licensor] shall have complete access to the computer and manual accounts and any documents and records and that it shall be a condition of all such agreements with any sub-licensee, agent, and/or other third party engaged by the [Distributor] who is exploiting the rights.

I.233

The [Distributor] shall make available to the [Licensor] a full set of audited accounts each year together with an itemised statement of the sums due to the [Licensor] at the [Distributors'] sole cost. The statement shall be clear as to the gross sums received and any sums deducted. No sums shall be withheld and/or not disclosed.

I.234

The [Sub-Licensee] agrees and undertakes to provide the [Company] with copies of all receipts for any expenditure which is claimed by the [Sub-Licensee] under this Agreement. The [Sub-Licensee] agrees to make available to the [Company] the following material and records in any format and/or medium including printed format, stored on a hard drive on a computer and/or laptop at the [Sub-Licensees'] offices at [address] in [country] in respect of the exploitation of the [Work] under this Agreement:

1.1   Warehouse and stock records.

1.2 Records of supply, sale, distribution, destruction, disposal without charge and any other method.

1.3 The latest audited accounts.

1.4 A list of all the methods by which the records are held in any format and/or medium.

1.5 A list of all locations at which stock is held.

1.6 A list of all parties who are authorised by the [Sub-Licensee] to deal in the stock.

I.235

1.1 The [Company] agrees to provide [Name] with a detailed statement of the sums due from the affiliation programme to [Name] during the term of the Agreement and/or before termination and/or expiry for any reason.

1.2 [Name] agrees that the [Company] shall not be required and/or obliged to supply personal information names, residential and business addresses, email addresses, mobile telephone numbers and bank details of any person and/or entity to [Name] and that information shall remain confidential to the [Company] and shall not be disclosed.

1.3 The Company agrees to provide in any statement information which shall include the date of any relevant transactions, the total value of the sale exclusive of any taxes and other charges received and not returned and the calculation of the sum due to [Name].

1.4 The parties agree that the statement shall be sent at the end of each calendar month but the schedule for delivery may be varied at the [Company's] discretion provided that it shall not exceed [six months].

1.5 The parties agree that where there is a dispute and [Name] wishes to seek to verify the sums paid and/or due and the stock sold and returned. That the [Company] shall arrange for [Name] to have a meeting with the [Finance Director] of the [Company] to be shown such part of the computer software and other records as may be available. That where the dispute involves a sum of less than [number/currency] the parties may agree to appoint a third party to provide a form of dispute resolution and that both parties agree to be bound by that decision. The cost of the dispute resolution to be paid by the [Company].

I.236

1.1 The [Agent] agrees and undertakes that no sums received by the [Agent] shall be held in any account except [specify] at [specify] bank. That the [Athlete] shall be entitled to receive copies of all bank statements and other documents that may be issued in relation to that account.

1.2 Further the [Agent] agrees that where any costs, expenses and other sums are attributed and deducted from any sums due to the [Athlete] that the [Athlete] shall be entitled to inspect and/or receive copies of all emails, documents and any other material which deal with the matter in any form. That where deductions have not been justified that the sum shall be paid to the [Athlete] in addition to a [number] per cent additional payment to recover the cost of the administration by the [Athlete].

1.3 The [Agent] agrees and undertakes that the [Athlete] shall be entitled to be provided with a copy of all material in any media which relate to the provision of his/her services to any third party at any time which is held, controlled and/or in the possession of the [Agent] and/or his advisors and/or consultants.

I.237

[Name] acknowledges that all records, data and information relating to access to, downloading and/or use of the [Apps/Links/Website/Blog] are carried out electronically and by computer software and telecommunications and supplied, delivered and processed by a variety of suppliers for the [Company]. [Name] agrees that a report by email in the form of a pdf and/or excel and/or other format shall be sufficient evidence supplied by the [Founder] as to the payments due and no paper and/or other records and/or documents need be provided.

I.238

There shall be no right of inspection of any corporate, advertising, promotional and/or sponsorship agreements by [Name] of the [Company] and any right shall be limited to the supply of the internal report entitled [specify] from [date to [date] during the existence of this Agreement.

INSURANCE

Building

I.239

The [Employer] undertakes to effect and maintain an [All Risks Insurance Policy] which provides cover against any physical loss or damage in respect of the [Project] but excluding the cost which is due to wear and tear.

I.240

The [Contractor] warrants that it has arranged and paid for professional indemnity insurance covering negligent design and specification under this contract with a limit of indemnity of not less than [figure/currency] for any occurrences arising out of each and every event for the benefit of [specify]. The [Contractor] undertakes to maintain such insurance at all times until [twelve years] after the practical completion of the [Project]. Such insurance will be maintained on commercially acceptable terms, having regard to the premium demanded, the policy conditions and the duties undertaken by the [Contractor] in relation to the Project and otherwise.

I.241

Employee's Liability including maritime employees with a limit of not less than [figure/currency] per occurrence.

1.1   Endorsement for liability by the [Contractor] for any employee which is on loan or working with the [Operator].

1.2   Comprehensive General Liability insurance or similar coverage with contractual liability for the work of not less than [–] in each case whether personal injury, death and/or damage to property including endorsements for all premises, operations, independent contractors, assumed liabilities, explosion, collapse, (whether above or below ground) and property damage.

1.3   All aircraft, vehicles, ships, machinery and equipment owned hired and/or used by the [Contractor] in respect of the performance of this Contract should be comprehensively insured for all risks, for not less than [–] per occurrence for injury, death, loss or damage, whether to employees of the Contractor, the [Operator] and/or any third party and/or the general public.

1.4   Insurance cover for environmental pollution and public health and safety risks arising from the performance of the work by the [Contractor], and the cover for the cost of any loss, damages, claim and the cost of rectifying the position.

I.242

The [Company] shall insure the Delivery Materials comprehensively for the benefit of the [Supplier] against all risks during any period when the Delivery Materials are in the possession of the [Company].

I.243

It shall be the responsibility of [Name] to arrange and pay for an insurance policy with [specify] to cover [specify] for the [Land/Building] at [address] registered as [reference] by [body] from [date] until [date] for not less than [number/currency] for the benefit of [specify].

DVD, Video and Discs

I.244

The [Distributor] shall arrange at its sole cost comprehensive insurance cover in respect of the exercise of the rights by the [Distributor] under this Agreement for the benefit of the [Distributor/Licensor] of not less than [figure/currency] in respect of any claim, damages, loss, liability and/or legal costs which shall be in effect from [date] to [date] and cover all the following countries [specify].

I.245

The [Distributor] shall ensure that it is a condition of the agreement with any sub-licensee, agent and/or other third party that they are insured for no less than [figure/number] in respect of any damage, loss, claim and/or other liability that may arise in respect of the [Work] for the duration of the Agreement.

I.246

The [Company] shall arrange and pay for insurance cover for the benefit of [Name] whilst the [Sound Recordings are in the possession and/or control of the [Company]. The [Company] shall at all times ensure that there is an exact copy kept in a secure place and kept in conditions which will not result in the deterioration of the material. The [Company] shall ensure that all persons involved in the production of the [Discs] from the [Sound Recordings] shall adhere to any conditions of the insurance policy.

I.247

It is agreed between the parties that the following matters be specifically excluded and shall not be covered by an insurance policy in respect of the [Project] and that each party shall bear such matters at their own risk and cost [specify].

I.248

[Name] agrees and accepts that the [DVDs/CDs/Discs] are not insured while stored at [address] and in the event of their destruction and/or damage for any reason agrees that payment to [Name] shall not exceed [number/currency].

I.249

The [Distributor] confirms that has no insured for the [DVDs/CDs/Discs] whilst they are in transit after they have left the [production company] and/or thereafter at any time. That in the event that any [DVDs/CDs/Discs] are lost, damaged and/or destroyed then all costs incurred shall be the responsibility of the [Distributor] but no additional sums shall be due and/or paid to [Name] in lieu of sales and/or as any claim at any time.

Employment

I.250

The [Company] confirms that there will be in existence during the Term of this Agreement adequate public and employer's liability insurance.

I.251

Subject to any limits set by any government agency or legislation the [Company] agrees to provide life assurance cover entirely for the benefit of the [Executive] and his family at rates and conditions acceptable to the [Company]. The [Company] shall make arrangement for life assurance [four times basic salary] and shall provide a copy of the policy to the [Executive].

I.252

Where at a later date it becomes clear and there is evidence that a person has not disclosed a pre-existing medical condition to the [Company] and/or the insurer at the time that a policy was arranged. The insurance policy may not provide cover for any such condition and in such circumstances no claim shall be paid by the [Company] and/or the insurer.

I.253

The [Company] agrees and undertakes that it shall arrange and pay for first class life insurance of not less than [number/currency] with [specify] and first class medical insurance to cover death, disability, cancer, allergic reactions, any operations and associated treatment and medical interventions that may be required in [country/worldwide] for [Name]. The cover shall be for all periods whether [Name] is at work and/or on holiday and/or other leave from [date] and shall continue until [Name] is no longer under a contract of employment with the [Company]. [Name] shall be specified on all policy documents and have the right to make any claim and not be limited to make any request through the [Company].

I.254

In the event that the [Company] fails to ensure that additional insurance and medical protection cover is in place at any time so that [Name] is insured for any work which is dangerous, high risk and/or outside the normal policy of the [Company]. Then the [Company] agrees that it shall be liable and pay for any sums due to the family and [Name] on the basis that there had been a policy at the [Company's] cost.

Film and Television

I.255

The [Producer] shall, in any event, effect and maintain throughout the duration of this Agreement, an Errors and Omissions Insurance Policy in respect of the [Programmes] in its own name and the cost of such Insurance Policy shall be paid for by the [Producer] and such cost shall [not] form part of the Budget. The [Producer] shall provide a copy of the policy to the [Commissioning Company].

I.256

The [Commissioning Company] acknowledges that the [Producer's] Errors and Omissions Policy referred to in Clause [–] below is for the benefit of [the Commissioning Company/the Producer] to [figure/currency] per single claim and [figure/currency] for any series of claims in aggregate in any single year.

I.257

The [Production Company] shall at all material times maintain effective insurance cover with a reputable company which shall be subject to the prior approval of the [Commissioning Company]. The insurance policies shall be in respect of the [Production Company] and the [Commissioning Company].

I.258

The [Production Company] shall observe and adhere to all the conditions of the insurance policies and agrees that it shall not do or must do anything which may invalidate the insurance cover. The [Production Company] shall ensure that all premiums are paid when they fall due and that the policies shall be maintained in full fare and effect until [date].

I.259

During the Term of this Agreement the [Company] will arrange and put in place at its own cost sufficient errors and omissions insurance with a reputable insurance company in respect of the transmission of the [Programmes] for the benefit of [Name]. The cover shall be at least [figure/currency] for each case with an annual total of [figure/currency], in respect of any claims relating to the [Programmes]. The insurance cover shall be fully comprehensive and shall not entitle the insurers and/or the underwriters to seek a contribution to the sums by any third party involved with the [Programmes] [unless caused by the negligence of that party].

I.260

The parties agree that the following matters are specifically excluded and shall not be covered by any insurance policy and each party shall be responsible for their own risk, liability, cost and expenses that may arise in respect of the production of the [Film/Programme] [specify excluded issues].

877

I.261

1.1   The [Company] agree that [number/currency] of the [Budget] shall be allocated to insurance in respect of the cast, equipment, locations, third party and public liability and that the policy shall be for no less than [number/currency] and apply in [country/worldwide] for the benefit of [specify].

1.2   That the [Company] shall also ensure that in the event that any person has a medical condition that this is notified to the insurers and that where additional payments are required that it be arranged.

1.3   That where there are additional risks and hazards and insurance cannot be arranged due to the high cost. That a risk assessment will take place in each case and if the health and safety advisor does not provide consent that the event will be cancelled.

General Business and Commercial

I.262

The failure to secure the insurance cover and/or to fully comply with any of the provisions of the insurance conditions of this Contract and/or the policies and/or to secure endorsements of the policies shall not in any way relieve the [Contractor] of its obligations under this Contract. In any event, where any loss, damage or injury is rejected by the insurers in whole and/or part for any reason and/or if the [Contractor] fails to maintain the required insurance and/or for any other reason, the insurance cover will not result in the [Company] receiving the sums it is owed. The [Contractor] agrees that it shall indemnify the [Company], its subsidiaries and affiliates, agents, employees, directors, officers, vessels and insurers against all claims, demands and actions of any nature including all costs, expenses, legal fees of counsel and solicitors, investigation agencies, and any other litigation expenses and/or liabilities which would otherwise be covered by the insurance that was agreed between the parties pursuant to this Contract.

I.263

The [Company] agrees that it shall at its sole cost arrange insurance against the [Event] not taking place for any reason for the benefit of the [Company] and the [Name] in the sum of [figure/currency] so that the cost of [specify] may be recouped in such case by the [Name]. The [Company] agrees to provide the [Name] with validated copies of such insurance policies upon request. The [Company] agree that they shall not do, omit to do or permit any act which would result in the insurance policies being declared invalid or which would result in them not being in force. The [Company] agree to notify the [Name] in the event of any circumstances which may arise which may result in a claim under the insurance policies and shall not settle any such claim without the prior written approval of the [Name]. Any sums paid by the insurers to the [Company] which is for the benefit of the [Name] shall be immediately paid without delay.

1.264

The [Company] shall promptly provide the [Licensee] with proof of adequate insurance upon request. If the [Company] fails to provide the [Licensee] with proof of such insurance within [7 days] of the request. Then the [Licensee] may either suspend payments to the [Company] until proof of such insurance is provided or arrange insurance on behalf of the [Company] and credit any premiums against sums due to the [Company] under this Agreement.

1.265

All insurance policies required of the [Company] under this contract shall contain endorsements that the underwriters will have no rights to sue, recover, claim and/or subrogate any loss and/or damages of any nature for any reason against the [Distributor], its subsidiary affiliated companies or their agents, directors, officers and employees.

1.266

During the Term of the Agreement the [Company] shall procure and maintain at the [Company's] sole expense, in the manner and amounts set out in the Schedule [–] insurance on an occurrence (not claims made) basis with insurance companies reasonably acceptable to the [Agent].

1.267

Any and all deductibles in the insurance policies arranged by the [Company] shall be at the [Company's] sole risk and cost.

1.268

All the insurance policies must specify that no cancellation or material charges in the cover shall become effective unless [20 days'] written notice has been provided to the [Agent].

1.269

The insurance cover must not contain any geographical and/or jurisdiction exclusion and/or limitation.

1.270

Where insurance is arranged in the joint names of the parties the party arranging the insurance shall ensure that the subrogation rights of the insurers are waived against the other party. Both parties shall be entitled to claim and/or act upon the terms of any policy.

I.271

In the event that the [Company] shall not arrange and/or maintain the agreed insurance cover the [Contractor] may arrange such insurance and pay the premiums and shall be entitled to deduct such sums from any monies due to the [Company] and/or pursue an action for recovery of the debt.

I.272

The [Distributor] shall ensure that it maintains adequate insurance cover at all times to meet its obligations to pay the sums due under this Agreement. The [Distributor] shall upon request provide evidence of such insurance and that the [Company's] interest is specified.

I.273

There are a number of areas which will not be covered by any insurance policy and these excluded areas are specified as follows [List]. It is agreed between the parties that all matters on the excluded list shall be carried out, performed and/or adhered to at each persons own risk and cost. There are no undertakings to indemnify the other party nor to make any contribution to any cost, expenses, damages and/or loss that may be incurred and/or arise as a result.

I.274

The [Consortium] agrees that each party may arrange and pay for its own insurance cover in respect of the [Project] and that in addition a further policy in the name of [specify] for the sum of [number/currency] shall be arranged with [specify] for the duration of the [Project] and for up to [number] years thereafter to cover claims by the persons engaged to work on the [Project] in any capacity and/or any trials and/or any products and/or data and/or records which may be supplied, reproduced, sold and/or exploited at any time. The cost to be met from [specify fund] for the [Project].

I.275

Where any party to this Agreement fails to have insurance cover for public and third party liability of no less than [number/currency] which is valid at all times and for which all the premiums are paid. Then such failure shall be deemed a breach of this Agreement and shall entitle the other party to terminate the Agreement without notice and to not be liable for any further payments that may fall due thereafter.

Internet and Websites

I.276

The [Company] shall not be obliged to provide any insurance cover for the benefit of the [Purchaser] in respect of the [Services/Product/other] and this must be itemised as a separate additional request and payment on the order form.

I.277

An additional sum must be paid to provide insurance against loss, theft, damage and/or destruction of any material ordered from this [Website]. No liability can be accepted by the [Website] for the failure to arrange insurance and/or any direct and/or indirect consequences which may arise from the use of this [Website].

I.278

The [Company] agrees and undertakes that it shall arrange and pay for comprehensive insurance cover with a reputable company for the value per claim of [figure/currency] which shall cover defamation, legal proceedings, and/or claims for losses and/or damages by any third party and/or employees, directors, officers and/or investors of the [Company] in [countries]. The [Company] shall send a draft copy of the insurance policy to [Name] for approval prior to finalising the policy. The [Company] shall also ensure that all the directors, officers, and/or investors are sufficiently protected by the insurance policy from a personal exposure to a claim arising from the actions and/or errors of the [Company] at any time.

I.279

The parties agree that neither the [Website] nor the [Company] is covered by a comprehensive insurance policy for all the countries in the world. It is agreed that where the insurance policy does not cover and/or the insurer refuses to meet the liability. Then the parties shall split the cost and expense of all liabilities according to the list in Schedule [–].

I.280

Any material which is sent by normal post in [country] is limited to a total value of [number/currency] regardless of the value of the actual contents. If you wish to have full insurance cover and protection then you must arrange to pay for a courier service and pay the additional costs. The [Company] cannot bear the cost of insurance and is only liable if you suffer any loss and/or damage and/or costs and/or death and/or disability and/or otherwise which have a direct causal connection to some serious failure by the [Company] and/or the products and/or the services and is not due to your own negligence and/or fault.

1.281

No undertakings are provided as to insurance cover by [Name] and/or the [Company] in respect of the [Blog/App/Website] and each party shall take all necessary precautions to minimise the threat of any allegations, claim, enforcement and/or civil and/or criminal action against either and/or both of them in [country] and in any other country of the world for any reason. Both parties agree that where there is an matter which arises that they shall notify the other and share the knowledge and assist in resolving the matter swiftly with the intention of reducing liability and costs regardless of whether the allegation and/or claim and/or otherwise has merit or not.

Merchandising

I.282
The [Company] agrees that it shall at its sole cost arrange insurance cover for the exercise and exploitation of the rights granted in this Agreement in respect of the [Product/Work]. This shall include product liability insurance of [figure/number] per claim by any third party. The [Company] agrees to provide the [Licensor] with a complete copy of the insurance policy for each year of the Agreement upon request.

I.283
The [Licensor] agrees that there is no requirement for the [Licensee] to arrange and/or pay for insurance cover in respect of the exercise of the rights granted under this Agreement.

I.284
During the Term of this Agreement the [Licensee] shall ensure that it has arranged and paid for insurance cover with a reputable insurance company for the production, reproduction and distribution of the [Work] and/or any adaptation for the benefit of the [Licensee and Name]. The cover shall be no less than [figure/currency] for each claim. The [Licensee] shall be entitled to deduct the insurance payments from any sums due to the [Licensor] under this Agreement.

I.285
The [Licensee] shall ensure that any sub-licensee, agent, distributor and/or other authorised third party shall be covered by public liability insurance to the value of [figure/currency] in [countries] for any period in which they are authorised to exercise and/or exploit the rights granted in this Agreement. The [Licensee] shall make available to the [Licensor] copies of the policies upon request together with evidence of the payment of the premiums. Where there is no insurance cover in place then the [Licensee] shall be obliged to notify the [Sub-Licensee] that the sub-licence is terminated.

I.286
The [Licensee] shall not be required to arrange additional insurance cover for the stock which the [Licensee] holds of the [Work/Articles] which are

created under this Agreement provided that it is covered by an existing policy for no less than [number/currency]. In the event that additional insurance cover is required the [Licensor] agrees that the [Licensee] may deduct [number] per cent of the premiums paid from any sums due to the [Licensor]. Provided that the [Licensor] and [Licensee] are both named on the policy and a copy is supplied to the [Licensor].

I.287
Where material which belongs to [Name] is destroyed, damaged, lost, stolen and/or otherwise not returned to [Name] for any reason after the end of this Agreement. Then the sum to be paid by the [Company] shall be limited to the cost of replacement and/or the market value whichever is the higher.

Purchase and Supply of Products

I.288
The [Customer] must ensure that each [Item] is returned to the [Supplier] by any method which can provide proof of delivery and that the [Item] is insured for not less than [figure/currency].

I.289
The [Owner] shall be liable to insure the [Data] in transit, whilst it is on deposit and upon its release. The [Escrow Agent] shall be liable for any loss, damage, cost or expense which may arise as a result of the [Owner's] failure to arrange suitable insurance cover.

I.290
The [Purchaser] will insure any goods, tools, materials and any other property provided by the [Seller] to the [Purchaser] for their full value whilst they are in the [Purchaser's] possession.

I.291
The [Company] shall take out adequate insurance for the benefit of the [Purchaser] in respect of any death, injury, loss or damage which may be caused by your servants and/or aspects whilst on the premises of the [Purchaser].

I.292
The [Licensee] confirms that:

1.1 A comprehensive public and product liability insurance policy is and will be in force covering any claims, actions or damages which may arise as a direct result or the indirect result of the use by the public of the [Product] and/or any associated packaging, promotional material and/or advertising together with all other products or services owned or controlled by the [Licensee] which the public would reasonably associate with the [Licensee].

1.2 Further the [Licensee] shall arrange and pay for insurance cover for the benefit of the [Licensor] to cover any failure to pay sums which arise from insolvency, bankruptcy, fraud, corruption, financial and accounting irregularities and/or non-payment by the [Licensee], and any agent, sub-distributor and/or sub-licensee.

1.3 [The [Licensee] agrees to provide the [Licensor] with a copy of the relevant insurance policies upon request.

I.293

The [Consortium] agrees that it shall arrange for such insurance cover at the [Consortiums] cost as may be necessary to ensure that the neither the Board, nor any individual Executive and Non-Executive Directors members are personally liable and/or have insufficient access to legal support and advice and insurance to deal with any matter which may arise relating to the [Products] and their development, production, licensing and exploitation and use and to meet all the costs, expenses and sums due.

I.294

1.1 The [Licensee] shall arrange individual product liability insurance for no less than [number/currency] for each type of [Product] by [date] and ensure that each such policy applies in [specify countries] which shall be for no less than [number] years.

1.2 The [Licensee] agrees that it shall ensure that where any [Product] has failed to pass any test and/or trial for any reason that it is not reproduced and/or distributed in that form and that a new text and/or trial must be carried out for the new version.

1.3 That the [Licensee] shall monitor and report on to the [Licensor] all cases where a product is recalled and/or withdrawn from production and/or exploitation.

Services

I.295

The [Presenter] will effect and maintain in force a policy of insurance against liability which he/she may incur for any damage, loss, costs, expenses or injury to any person or property which may arise in the course of providing his/her services under this Agreement.

I.296

[Name] agrees and undertakes that:

1.1 He/she is not now nor has at any time been subject to or suffering from any illness or injury which will in any way prevent him/her from providing their services and that the [Director] will at all times do all that is reasonably necessary to attain and maintain such a sound state of health as will enable him/her fully to perform his/her services and will not undertake any hazardous pursuits.

1.2 He/she will comply with the usual requirements necessary to enable the [Company] to obtain such insurance prior to the commencement of the [Film] as the [Company] may require.

1.3 He/she will attend a medical examination (including an HIV, blood, hair, skin, and urine test) as the [Company] shall require. The Director may have his own medical advisers present at such medical examination if he so wishes.

I.297

The [Company] may arrange, in its own name, for its own benefit and at its own cost and expense, life insurance, accident insurance or health insurance and any other insurance required by the [Company] in respect of the [Composer] (whether alone or together with others). The [Composer] agrees that he/she shall not have any right, title or interest in or to any such insurance policy or any money payable pursuant to any such insurance policies.

I.298

The [Composer] agrees to submit to the usual and customary medical examination required by the [Company] by any insurers. Such examinations shall be conducted in the presence of the [Composer's] own doctor if requested by the [Composer].

I.299

The [Composer] shall co-operate in the completion of all proposal forms and execute any other documents from time to time required by the [Company] in order to arrange for any policy of insurance or make any claim upon any such policy.

I.300

The [Person] agrees not to be involved in any hazardous pursuit or activity, nor take any risk at any time which would result in the insurance policy on his/her life or health which is likely to result in any claim being rejected by the insurers.

I.301

Without limiting the [Company's] liability under Clause [–] the [Company] undertakes that insurance is arranged and maintained to comply with its employer's liability and other relevant legislation in respect of the performance of the [Services].

I.302

The Contractor shall arrange and bear the cost of third party liability insurance of not less than [–] in any one case.

I.303

The [Company] shall ensure that suitable insurance cover is arranged for [Name] and his/her personal property in respect of the services provided under and during the Term of this Agreement. The [Company] shall provide [Name] with a copy of the insurance policy upon request. The [Company] confirms that the [Name's] personal life insurance for the benefit of his/her estate shall not be less than [–].

I.304

The [Company] shall not be entitled to insist that [Name] completes a full medical assessment in order for the [Company] to arrange insurance cover. A summary of the health and medical condition of [Name] by [Name's] own medical practitioner will be considered sufficient background information and no further information, data or assessments need to be provided and/or disclosed whether requested by the insurers or not.

I.305

The [Company] is not responsible for arranging and/or paying for any insurance cover for the [Consultant] during the term of the engagement of his/her services. The services of the [Consultant] are excluded from the [Company's] general insurance policy except to the extent of public liability insurance.

I.306

Where the [Athlete/Artist] is unable to provide his/her services for any period under this Agreement for any event and/or performance and no substitution can be made. Then it is agreed that the [Athlete/Artist] shall not be liable for any sums that may arise from any third party and/or the [Distributor] whether or not the matter is covered by insurance protection or not and all sums due shall be paid for by the [Distributor].

I.307

This service is not covered by any insurance policy and the [Company] operates and monitors the service at its own risk and cost. You use this service on the basis that liability for any reason is limited to [number/currency] and that you must bear the first [number/currency] of any costs.

Sponsorship

I.308
Irrespective of any insurance cover provided by the [Sponsor] the [Association] confirms that at its sole cost and expense it will take out comprehensive insurance policy for the [Event] for the benefit of the [Association] including adequate public liability for injury or death of any competitors or spectators and shall provide a copy of the policy to [Name] for inspection.

I.309
The [Sponsor] confirms that it shall arrange a comprehensive insurance policy at its sole cost for the following dates and benefits:

1.1 From [date] to [date].

1.2 Public liability at the [premises] at the [Event] in respect of the [Sponsor's] Product and any other materials, owned or controlled by the [Sponsor], or any personnel, agents or other persons authorised by the [Sponsor] to attend and/or carry out work which shall be not less than [–] for any one claim.

1.3 Loss, theft or damage in respect of [–].

1.4 To cover any loss, damage or claim directly or indirectly arising from the use by the public and the [Company] of the specific products and goods given away or promoted by the [Sponsor].

I.310
Neither party shall be required to take out insurance cover in respect of the [Project] and both parties agree to bear the risk, cost, losses and damages which may arise due to a claim, action or complaint relating to their own products, personnel, equipment, transport, material, or publications which they provide under this Agreement.

I.311
These excluded areas in Schedule [–] are not covered by any insurance policy. The [Sponsor] and the [Institute] shall each bear their own risk, cost and expense in respect of any liability that may arise as a result of the preparation, development, performance, completion and/or clearing up after the [Event]. Neither party shall be obliged to contribute and/or pay any of the liabilities that may arise which are caused by and/or incurred by the other party.

for product liability insurance at the [Consortiums] cost before any sample developments and/or products are placed in any trial, test and/or marketed to the public in any country.

I.320

The [Institute] does not accept any liability for any loss and/or damage to the equipment and/or resources and/or data and/or any viruses and/or scams against and/or to any person who uses the facilities of the [Institute] for their research at any time. Please ensure that you have suitable personal insurance cover and do not disclose any personal details such as passwords, pin codes and/or other information to any person who may contact you as this information is never requested by the [Institute].

INTEREST

General Business and Commercial

I.321

The [Guarantor] agrees to pay interest to the [Creditor] at the rate of interest [number per cent] on all sums which are actually due under this Guarantee. The interest shall be payable from the date of the [Creditor's] demand under this Guarantee provided that the [Creditor] has provided full details of the breakdown of the sums due whether damages, losses, costs or expenses. All such interest shall accrue on a day-to-day basis and be calculated by the [Creditor] on the basis of 365 days a year and interest shall be compounded in accordance with the usual practice of the [Creditor].

I.322

The [Creditor] shall [not] be entitled to recover any amount in respect of interest at any time whether under this [Guarantee Facility Documents] in respect of any failure to pay any sums which may fall due.

I.323

'Interest Rate' means [figure] per cent [–]%.

I.324

The [Company] shall pay to the [Stockholders] interest (after deduction of any tax duty or charge) on the principal amount of the [Stock] outstanding in the manner provided in the [Document] until the [Stock] is redeemed.

I.325

Without prejudice to any of its rights hereunder the [Company] reserves the right to charge interest on the outstanding balance of all overdue sums at the rate of the greater of either [2%] [two per cent] per annum above the current base rate at [specify Bank] or the maximum interest rate permitted by law.

I.326

The [Company] shall be entitled to charge interest on any sum payable by the [Licensee] under this Agreement which is not paid on or before the due date at the rate of [–]% above the base rate of [Bank plc] from the due date until the date upon which the payment is received.

I.327

If the independent chartered accountant appointed by a party under Clause [–] decides that the other party has not received all the sums due under this Agreement. The defaulting party shall immediately pay the sums due to the other party together with interest thereon at the rate of [–]% over the base rate of [Bank] at that time from the date when the payment should have been paid to the date when the payment was actually received.

I.328

The [Company] shall pay to the [Financier] interest on the aggregate of all the sums advanced which are from time to time outstanding at the annual rate of [number per cent] above the base rate for lending of [specify Bank].

I.329

The [Company] reserves the right to charge interest on the amount of any delayed payment at the rate of [–]% per calendar month or part thereof on the outstanding amount until payment has been made in full.

I.330

The [Company] reserves the right to charge interest at the rate of [–]% per annum on all amounts outstanding beyond the payment date(s) shown on its invoices.

I.331

The [Publisher] reserves the right to impose a surcharge of [–]% per month on overdue amounts.

I.332

The [Company] reserves the right to seek to recover interest on any sum which is not paid on time whether under subscription, purchase price, licence fee, and/or access fee and/or usage fee. The rate of interest shall be entirely at the sole discretion of the [Company] depending on the circumstances of the case and company policy.

I.333

The interest rate to be charged by the [Company] under Clause [–] shall not be more than [number]% [words] per cent in total at any time.

I.334

The total amount of interest which can be charged by the [Company] under Clause [–] shall not be more than [figure/currency] [words]. The [Institute] shall not be obliged to pay any additional sum.

I.335

Where the sums held by the [Licensee] accrue interest then the interest shall be added to the total funds before the calculation of the royalties due to the [Licensor].

I.336

Where the [Sponsor] delays and/withholds monies due to the [Company] under this Agreement for more than [number] days. Then all such sums shall be subject to an interest charge of [number] per cent which shall arise from the date the money is due to the day it is actually paid. The interest charge shall be paid at the same time as all the other money.

I.337

It is agreed by the parties that no interest will be charged and/or due provided that no payment is delayed beyond [number] [days/months].

I.338

The interest rates to be charged shall vary according to the daily rates of [specify]. The interest shall be charged on the total sum due that day. The interest rate may increase and/or decrease. Where no rate is available then the rate of the previous day shall be used.

INTERPRETATION

General Business and Commercial

I.339

Words which are singular shall include the plural number and vice versa. Words which are the masculine gender only shall include the feminine gender. Words importing persons shall include corporations. Wherever in this Agreement reference is made to a period of time and the last day of that period falls on a Saturday, Sunday, Public or Bank Holiday the period of time shall be deemed to be extended until the end of the next following working day.

I.340

In the case of any inconsistency between these Special Conditions and any other term of this contract the Special Conditions shall prevail.

I.341

Clause headings or titles do not form part of this contract and shall not affect its interpretation.

I.342

Headings are for convenience only and do not constitute part of this Agreement.

I.343

Headings are for convenience only and shall have no effect on the interpretation of the document.

I.344

Words imparting the singular number only shall include the plural and vice versa. A reference to any gender includes a reference to all other genders.

I.345

The headings in this Agreement are for convenience only and are not intended to affect the interpretation of this Agreement.

I.346

This Contract is signed on [date] and is complied in [Language] and [Language] with two copies existing in each language. Each party keeps one copy of this Contract in both languages and the text of both languages are of equal status.

I.347

Words and phrases under this licence will be construed in accordance with any legislation in [Country].

I.348

Unless otherwise stated references to clauses, sub-clauses, paragraphs, sub-paragraphs, schedules, annexes and exhibits all form part of this Agreement.

I.349

Headings, clauses or other parts are for reference only and are not to be construed as part of this Contract.

I.350

The interpretation of this contract shall be governed by [specify] language and the laws of [country]. Where there are issues which are ambiguous and/ or which conflict then both parties agree that the matter shall be resolved first by one of the following procedures [mediation/alternative disputes resolution/other] prior to any legal action being taken

I.351

The interpretation of this Agreement shall be in the [specify language] and using the [specify] dictionary. Where there are conflicts of meaning then no part shall take precedence over another. Any dispute shall be subject to resolution by mediation which shall be paid for by both parties agreeing to the fee in advance with the mediator. Where mediation is not successful then the parties shall be entitled to issue legal proceedings.

I.352

This Agreement and the attached schedules are in [language] and subject to the laws of [country] as has been specifically agreed between the parties. Both parties agree that any legal proceedings shall not be commenced in [country] where the parent company of the [Assignor] is based and/or [country] where the parent country of the [Assignee] is based.

INVALIDITY

General Business and Commercial

I.353

In the event that the [Employee] becomes incapable of performing his/ her duties under this Agreement in circumstances outside the [Employer's] Insurance Policy and to the extent that the [Employee] is deemed by a duly qualified medical practitioner to be suffering from a permanent disability. The [Employer] shall have the right to terminate this Agreement subject to the [Employee's] statutory rights and Severance Payments under Clause [–] of this Agreement.

I.354

The [Company] shall have the right to postpone the commencement of any period or to suspend the engagement of the [Presenter's] services for the

[Programme] if the [Presenter] is unable to devote the whole of the [Presenter's] time, attention and normal ability to rendering his/her services hereunder for any reason including illness or inability. If the [Company] has postponed or suspended the engagement of the [Presenter's] services it may:

1.1 Withhold payment of any sum otherwise due to the [Presenter] hereunder in respect of the period of postponement or suspension.

1.2 Either enter into an agreement with the [Presenter] to increase the period of engagement by the duration of the suspension or postponement prior to commencement of the services. If the illness or disability shall continue for a period of at least [two months] the [Company] shall be entitled to give notice of termination of the Agreement to the [Presenter]. In such circumstances the [Company] shall not be liable for any sums to the [Presenter] for the services which have not been performed or any sum in respect of loss of reputation or enhancement.

I.355
The [Company] has commissioned the [Writer] to write [a column/series of features/other] under this Agreement. If the [Writer] in the reasonable opinion of the [Company] is prevented by illness, injury or other mental or physical incapacity from fulfilling any of his/her commissions. The Company may at its sole discretion and shall have the right if it so chooses to send written notice to the [Writer] to terminate his/her engagement. In such circumstances the [Company] shall only be liable to pay for such work as has already been delivered to that date but without prejudice to the vesting of the rights in such work in the [Company].

I.356
The [Sponsor] acknowledges that the Sponsorship Fee shall be paid to the [Sportsperson] notwithstanding that the [Sportsperson] may be unable to provide his/her services under this Agreement due to illness or injury which is supported by a medical certificate from a qualified doctor.

I.357
The [Director] shall use his/her best endeavours to maintain a state of health which will enable him/her to provide their services under this Agreement and for the [Company] to arrange insurance cover for the loss of their services. The [Director] agrees to a medical examination for the purpose of obtaining insurance cover and agrees to provide any such medical, personal or other details that may reasonably be required by the [Company] and/or the insurers for that purpose.

I.358
If the [Writer] is prevented by illness, mental or physical incapacity, bereavement, family circumstances, or otherwise unavailable or unable

to write and deliver the [Commissioned Works]. The [Company] shall be entitled by written notice to the [Writer] to terminate his/her engagement under this Agreement and shall be entitled to engage another writer to write and deliver the [Commissioned Works] using the same, title, topic and research material. No sums shall be due to the [Writer] and all material delivered on loan from the [Company] shall be returned. The [Company] shall at all times be the copyright owner of the [Commissioned Works].

I.359

The [Company] shall pay the [Manager] in respect of absence by reason of incapacity as follows provided that he/she has complied with the required procedures for payment:

1.1   Less than [3 months'] service full salary for one week and [1/2] salary for the next one week only.

1.2   [3] to [12] months' service full salary for [2 weeks] and [1/2] of salary for the next [2 weeks].

1.3   [1] to [2] years' service full salary for [4 weeks] and [1/2] salary for the next [4 weeks].

1.4   The payments should be adjusted accordingly depending on the length of service subject to a maximum entitlement of [26 weeks] at full pay and [26 weeks] at half pay in any one year or period of absence due to incapacity.

I.360

The [Company] shall be entitled to deduct from sick pay or be reimbursed for any sums which are received by the [Employee] such as sickness or invalidity benefit, damages for loss of earnings.

I.361

If the [Employee] is absent from work due to sickness or incapacity for [60 days] in any one year (whether continuous or not) then the [Company] reserves the right to terminate the contract at once by notice in writing.

I.362

If the [Employee] receives sick pay to which he/she is not entitled the [Company] shall be entitled to deduct such sums from his/her subsequent salary.

I.363

1.1   Where an [Employee] is absent from work the [Employee] must notify his/her manager as soon as possible.

1.2   The [Employee] agrees to provide the [Company] with as much notice as possible in the event that the Employee is unable (whether as a result of sickness or otherwise) to perform any of his/her obligations under this Agreement.

1.3   The [Employee] agrees to provide a medical certificate for periods of sickness or injury of more than one week, and thereafter at weekly intervals and a final certificate before resuming normal duties.

1.4   The [Employee] shall not be entitled to payment by the Company for sickness or injury benefit after the date on which the employment has ended either by notice of termination or by expiry.

1.5   If the [Employee] is sick or injured on a Bank or Public Holiday, the Company will not grant additional leave. However, such days will not be set against paid sick leave entitlement. If the [Employee] is sick or injured whilst on annual holiday he/she will be entitled to take holiday at a later date within the holiday year provided a medical certificate for the period of sickness has been provided.

I.364
If the [Employee] is absent from duty without permission and without a reason acceptable to the [Company] the [Company] reserves the right to withhold payment or deduct from salary a day's pay for each day of unauthorised absence.

I.365
The [Company] reserves the right to set off against payment made to the [Employee] any statutory sick pay benefits received.

I.366
The [Company] shall not have the right to deduct from any salary, fees, costs and expenses due to [Name] any sums which the [Company] wishes to recoup for absence, incapacity, illness, or otherwise at any time unless agreed with [name] in advance.

I.367
Where the [Athlete] is unable or unwilling to participate in any event, filming, race, appearance due to injury, incapacity, training, a conflict of schedules or any other reason. The [Sponsor] shall not have the right to cancel, withdraw, terminate or alter this Agreement unless it agrees to pay all the sums due under the Agreement in full to the [Athlete].

I.368
Where a [Participant/Contributor] has misled and/or deceived the [Company] as to their identity and/or background. Then the [Company] reserves the

right to cancel and/or terminate the Agreement and to seek repayment of all funds paid under the Agreement.

1.369

If at a later date [Name] is discovered to have represented that they have a curriculum vitae and/or qualifications and/or work experience which is/are untrue and which would materially affect their ability to fulfil the work required by the [Company]. Then the [Company] shall be entitled to terminate the Agreement but shall not seek to reclaim any sums paid under the agreement.

INVENTIONS

General Business and Commercial

1.370

'Invention' shall mean a new invention involving an inventive step which is capable of industrial application and is otherwise capable of registration [under the Patents Act 1977 or any subsequent amending or repealing legislation].

1.371

Any inventions made by the [Contractor] during the performance of the Contract shall be the property of and owned by [Name] who may use them as they see fit, subject to any industrial, intellectual property or other rights which already exist.

1.372

All rights and the right to apply for statutory protection (such as patent protection) for any improvement to the [Technical Information] made by the [Company] shall be vested solely in the [Company].

1.373

Any invention or improvement made or discovered by an [Employee] alone or jointly with others during the course of being employed by the [Company], whilst involved in [Company] business of any nature, shall [subject to the Patents Act 1977 as amended] belong to the [Company].

1.374

The [Employee] agrees at the request and expense of the [Company] at any time to assist the [Company] to apply for, register and protect its rights in any invention, patent, copyright, development, variation, adaptation or improvement. The [Employee] shall provide an affidavit of the circumstances, sign any document and form and appear in person as required provided that the [Company] shall meet all incidental expenses and costs that may arise.

1.375

All inventions, patents, computer software, trade marks, service marks, logo, intellectual property rights, copyright, database rights, design rights, future design rights, domain names, formats, title, film, sound recordings, graphics, images, music, sounds and ringtones, slogans and any other rights of any nature in any material in any media created by the [Employee] in the course of his/her employment shall belong to the [Employer] and the [Employee] shall have no claim to or interest therein of any nature at any time.

1.376

The [Employer] agrees that in the event that the [Employee] creates any inventions, patents, computer software, trade marks, service marks, logo, intellectual property rights, copyright, database rights, design rights, future design rights, domain names, formats, title, film, sound recordings, graphics, images, music, sounds and ringtones, slogans and any other rights of any nature in any material in any media for which there is a distinct commercial value to the [Employer] [which is not in the normal course of the [Employee's] duties/whether or not it is in consequence of the [Employee's] routine duties]. The [Employee] shall be entitled to receive a substantial and equitable sum from such monies received by the [Employer] which shall be on terms to be agreed between the parties.

1.377

The [Consortium] agrees and undertakes that any new website, app, game, computer software, hardware, mobile telephone and/or telecommunication systems, processes, method and/or any other intellectual property rights and/or any inventions, patents, trade marks and/or any other creations and/or developments which arise directly and/or indirectly from the [Project/Work] and/or whether and/or not based and/or derived on material owned and/or controlled by any member which has been contributed to the [Project/work] shall be held and owned and controlled by the [Consortium] and all sums received therefrom shared in equal proportions. No member shall have a greater claim to any rights and/or sums than any other party.

1.378

[Name] has created and developed [Work/Project] and agrees to enter into an agreement with the [Agent] in order to create a commercial product which can be exploited. [Name] and the [Agent] agree that:

899

INVENTIONS

1.1 [Name] shall remain the sole and exclusive owner of all rights of any nature in the [Work/Project] and any commercial product including copyright, intellectual property rights, patents, trademarks, design rights, computer software and hardware rights, telecommunication, television, film and all media in any formats which may arise and/or exist and/or be recognised in the future in any part of the world at any time.

1.2 That the [Agent] agrees, accepts and undertakes that he/she shall not acquire any of the rights in 1.1 and/or any sums that may be derived from the exploitation in any form at any time. That the total sum due to the [Agent] for any contribution, work and/or services shall be a fee of [number] per month up to a maximum of [number]. All fees due shall be paid by [Name] at the end of each calendar month subject to invoice. The [Agent] agrees and undertakes that [Name] may terminate the Agreement at any time by one months notice in advance.

JURISDICTION

General Business and Commercial

J.001
The [Guarantor] irrevocably agrees for the [exclusive] benefit of the [Creditor] that the Courts of England shall have jurisdiction to hear and determine any suit, action or proceeding, and to settle any dispute, which may arise out of or in connection with this Guarantee and for such purposes hereby irrevocably submits to the jurisdiction of such Courts.

J.002
Nothing contained in this Clause shall limit the right of the [Creditor] to take proceedings against the Guarantor in any other Court of competent jurisdiction, nor shall the taking of any such proceedings in one or more jurisdictions preclude the taking of proceedings in any other jurisdiction, whether concurrently or not (unless precluded by applicable law).

J.003
The [Guarantor] irrevocably waives any objection which it may have now or in the future to the Courts of England being nominated for the purpose of this Clause on the ground of venue or otherwise and agrees not to claim that any such Court is not a convenient or appropriate forum.

J.004
The [Guarantor] hereby authorises and appoints [Name] (or such other solicitors as may from time to time be substituted by notice to the [Creditor]) to accept service of all legal proceedings arising out of or connected with this Guarantee. Service on such solicitors or such substitutes shall be deemed to be service on the [Guarantor].

J.005
Failing an amicable settlement, the [Court of Justice of the European Union] shall, in the absence of provision to the contrary in the Contract, have exclusive jurisdiction in any dispute relating to the performance or interpretation of the Contract.

J.006

Both parties to this Agreement acknowledge and confirm that any dispute, litigation, interpretation, damages or loss which arises directly or indirectly as a result of this Agreement shall be subject to the laws of [Country] and no other jurisdiction shall be applicable.

J.007

This Agreement shall be interpreted and construed in accordance with [specify] law and the parties hereby agree to submit to the jurisdiction of the [country/court]. Provided that nothing shall prevent either party from seeking redress in any other jurisdiction if it shall so think fit.

J.008

This Agreement is made in [England] and the proper law of this Agreement is [English] Law and any proceedings in relation hereto shall be brought in the [High Court of Justice] in [London] for which purpose the parties hereto submit to the jurisdiction of the [English] Courts.

J.009

This Agreement shall be governed and construed solely by the Laws of [Scotland].

J.010

This Agreement shall be governed by and construed in accordance with the Law of [Scotland] and the parties submit to the [non-]exclusive jurisdiction of the [Scottish] Courts.

J.011

This Agreement shall be subject to the Laws of [England].

J.012

This Agreement shall be governed and construed in accordance with the Laws of [England] and any dispute concerning it or its interpretation shall be adjudicated in that jurisdiction.

J.013

Regardless of its place of execution, the provisions of this Agreement relating to the performance or obligations of the [Author] shall in all respects be construed according to, and be governed by, the [Law of the State of New York]. However, the provisions of this Agreement relating to the performance or obligations of the [Publisher] shall in all respects be construed according to, and be governed by, the [Law of England], and be within the [non-] exclusive jurisdiction of the [English Courts].

J.014

Whatever the nationality, residence or domicile of the [Employer], the [Management Contractor], any [Works Contractor] or supplier or the Arbitrator, and wherever the [Project] or any part thereof is situated, the Law of [England] shall be the proper law of this Contract and shall apply to any arbitration under this Contract wherever it shall be conducted.

J.015

This Agreement is to be governed by and construed in accordance with [English] Law and the parties hereto submit to the exclusive jurisdiction of the [English] Courts in respect of any dispute and/or legal proceedings in respect of this Agreement and any matter arising thereunder.

J.016

This Agreement shall be subject to the Laws of [England] and any dispute concerning it or its interpretation shall be issued and adjudicated in that jurisdiction.

J.017

This Agreement shall be construed in accordance with the Laws of [England] and shall be subject to the exclusive jurisdiction of the [High Court of Justice in England].

J.018

This Agreement has been entered into in the State of [Name] and its validity, construction, interpretation and legal effect shall be governed by the State of [Name] applicable to contracts entered into and performed entirely within the State of [Name].

J.019

This Agreement shall be interpreted and construed in accordance with [Name] Law and the parties agree to submit to the jurisdiction of the [Name] Courts.

J.020

This contract shall be governed and construed in accordance with [English Law], and any regulations, directives, of the European Union and the judgments of the European Court of Justice.

J.021

Both parties agree and acknowledge and confirm that any interpretation, dispute, litigation, damages or losses which arise directly or indirectly as a result of this Agreement shall be subject to the Laws of [specify country/area/court] and no other jurisdiction shall be applicable.

J.022

This licence shall be governed and construed in accordance with the Laws of [England] in respect of any dispute relating to the performance or interpretation of this Agreement.

J.023

Any dispute, litigation or issues of construction shall be subject to the exclusive jurisdiction of [country/law].

J.024

This Licence shall be governed and interpreted by the laws of [country] and any claim, action, or legal proceedings shall only be commenced in that jurisdiction and any hearing, dispute, any Court, tribunal, whether this [disc/data/other] is supplied/and/or used in the [country] and/or any other part of the universe.

J.025

This Agreement shall be interpreted and fall within the jurisdiction of any country in which either party has their main business or in which the material is delivered, sold or otherwise exploited.

J.026

Both parties agree that this Agreement shall as far as possible be resolved first by mediation through [Name] and legal proceedings shall be instituted in [Name] as a final resort.

J.027

From [date] to [date] the parties agree that either may issue proceedings in any of the following countries [Name] and no others. After the expiry of [date] then either party may choose any jurisdiction which they believe is applicable in the circumstances.

J.028

The forum agreed for the governing law of this Agreement and in which either party may choose to institute or commence proceedings is limited to the following countries [in which the parties have their head office, the company is registered or incorporated or their main assets are held or in which most services or products are delivered or transactions take place] [specify].

J.029

All parties agree and undertake that all mediations, alternative dispute resolutions, arbitrations, resolution of disputes, applications for injunctions, institution of legal proceedings and/or claim for any breach, loss, damage, failure to deliver, non-performance, product liability, injury, death or otherwise which arises directly or indirectly from this Agreement shall be subject only to the laws, directives, regulations, standards and codes of [country]. That all parties agree and undertake that they have decided not to nominate or subject this Agreement to any other country, forum or jurisdiction.

J.030
The [Name] and the [Company] agree and undertake that this Agreement shall be subject to the jurisdiction of any Court in [state/country] for the purpose of commencing any legal proceedings and/or resolving any dispute by any method.

J.031
The [Employee] agrees that this contract shall be subject to the jurisdiction of the laws of the [state/country]. That for the purpose of resolving any dispute and/or taking legal action and/or seeking any remedy that this Agreement shall be governed by and construed under the law of [state/country].

J.032
This [document/contract/agreement/licence/assignment] shall be [governed/construed/interpreted/subject to] the laws of the State of [specify] in the [country]. You consent and agree to submit to the exclusive jurisdiction of the Courts of [specify] in [specify county] in the State of [specify].

J.033
This Agreement is governed by [English/French/Spanish/Indian/Chinese] Law and the parties submit to the exclusive jurisdiction of the Courts of [City/other] [country].

J.034
This Agreement is governed by [country/nationality] and any disputes arising directly and/or indirectly in connection with this Agreement shall be settled by the [country/nationality] Courts unless both parties agree in writing to amend this Agreement and change to a different governing law and to a different forum.

J.035
The [Company] reserves the right to choose the forum and/or place for any legal proceedings against the [Licensee] from any of the following at any time:

1.1   [country] where the parent company [specify] is based at [address].

1.2   [country] where the [Products] are manufactured at [address].

1.3 [country] where the [Supplier] is based at [address].

1.4 [country] where the website known as [specify] which markets the [Products] is based at [address].

1.5 [country] where the [Company] is based at [address].

1.6 [country] where the main office of the legal advisors of the [Company] are based at [address].

J.036

1.1 The [Athlete] agrees that the jurisdiction of this Agreement shall be [country] and subject to the laws of [country].

1.2 That the [Athlete] and/or the [Sponsor] shall use all reasonable means to mediate and/or resolve any matters without litigation.

1.3 That the [Athlete] and/or the [Sponsor] shall set out in writing the full detail of any claim and/or allegations and the remedy they seek and supply it to the other party prior to the commencement of any action and/or civil and/or criminal proceedings.

J.037

The use and/or supply and/or distribution of the [App/Blog/Website] is worldwide but any disputes, claims, actions and /or other matters which arise are subject to the legislation, policies and jurisdiction of [country] where [Name/Distributor] is based at [address]. You are not authorised by [Name/Distributor] to access, download, use and/or supply and/or distribute the content in any form unless you have agreed to this fundamental term.

K

KNOW-HOW

General Business and Commercial

K.001
The [Company] and the [Distributor] accept and acknowledge that the development of the [Software] will require the skills of the [Originator], therefore, even though the [Software] will be developed exclusively for the [Company] and the [Distributor], it is agreed that the [Originator] shall retain the right to use the algorithms, know-how, ideas, techniques, and concepts created by it in developing the [Software].

K.002
'Know-how' shall mean any industrial information and techniques likely to assist in the manufacture or processing of goods or materials, the working of a mine, oil-well or other source of mineral deposited (including the searching for, discovery or testing of deposits or the gaining of access thereto), or in the carrying out of any agricultural, forestry or fishing operations.

K.003
The [Licensor] and [Licensee] acknowledge that all know-how in the [Product] shall remain and/or belong entirely and exclusively in the [Licensor] and that the [Licensee] shall not acquire any rights, interest or otherwise of any nature therein as a result of this Agreement.

K.004
'The know-how' shall mean the confidential knowledge, method, processes and applications of the [Company] in respect of [any machines, products, materials, goods, services, processes] which are not in the public domain which were developed, created, or devised by the [Company].

K.005
Through the use of [specify] and inspection of [data/material/records] a list of which is set out in [–], you may/will have access to confidential information, price or market-sensitive data, news or developments or know-how or any

other material of any nature which is not in the public domain. You agree that access is only granted for the purpose of [specify] and that you will not disclose, publish, release, copy, transmit or benefit from any material of any nature except to the advisors [Name] at [address] who may provide confidential advice to your [Company] to senior executives from [date] to [date].

K.006

All rights in any know-how, design rights, future design rights, inventions, patents, copyright, trade marks, service marks, domain names, database rights, data, confidential information, shape, pattern, configuration, articles, machines, products, processes, method, delivery, retrieval or storage method, and any content, labels, packaging, marketing and any advertising material together with any goodwill and any right to apply and hold any registration in respect of the development, production, manufacture, reproduction, supply, sale and distribution or other exploitation in any media and/or material shall rest solely with [Name] and belong to [Name].

K.007

The [Company] agrees and undertakes that it shall not be entitled to apply for, register or represent that the [Company] or any part of their [Group] control or own any rights in any know-how, design rights, future design rights, inventions, patents, copyright, trade marks, service marks, domain names, database rights, data, confidential information, shape, pattern, configuration, articles, machines, products, processes, method, delivery, retrieval or storage method, and any content, labels, packaging, marketing and any advertising material together with any goodwill and any right to apply and hold any registration in respect of the development, production, manufacture, reproduction, supply, sale and distribution or other exploitation in any media and/or material shall rest solely with [Name] and belong to [Name].

K.008

The [Company] undertakes and agrees that it will enter into a confidentiality agreement with [Name] in respect of the [general subject] which he/she has created. That no disclosure shall be made by the [Company] to any parent, affiliate, associate or subsidiary company or any third party or any other officer, employee, or consultant of the [Company] of the [proposal/subject/invention] by [Name] to the [Company] and the information shall be limited to the following named persons [specify] and the legal advisors [specify]. In the event that no confidentiality agreement is concluded and details are disclosed by the [Company] outside the agreed circle of people. Then the [Company] shall be obliged and shall indemnify [Name] in respect of any damages, losses, loss of profit and commercial benefit and gain, and rights that he/she shall suffer, incur or shall arise directly or indirectly from the breach of this clause and there shall be no limitation on the liability.

K.009

The [Company] and the [institute] are working in partnership to develop the [Project]. It is agreed between the parties that all inventions, patents, copyright, design rights, future design rights, intellectual property rights, trade marks, service marks, domain names, database rights, data, confidential information, shape, pattern, configuration, articles, machines, products, processes, method, delivery, retrieval or storage method, and any material in any medium, or content, labels, packaging, marketing. Together with any know-how, confidential knowledge, methods, processes and applications in respect of any machines, products, materials, goods, services, ideas, concepts and techniques and software which are not in the public domain which were developed, created, or devised by the [Company] and/or the [Institute] for the [Project] shall be owned, controlled, registered and exploited jointly and equally between the [Company] and the [Institute]. That both parties shall require the prior written approval of the other party in order to take any steps to protect, licence, assign, transfer, exploit and/or use the rights and know-how they jointly own and control.

K.010

The [Consultant] agrees and undertakes all intellectual property rights, inventions, patents, copyright, design rights, future design rights, trade marks and know how of any nature including but not limited to confidential information, methods, processes, and/or applications in respect of any machines, products, materials, goods, services, processes which exist and/or are developed as a result of the [Project] are the sole and exclusive property of the [Company]. That the [Consultant] shall not have any claim and/or interest to any rights even if he/she has contributed to and/or worked on the [Project], attended meetings and/or made reports.

K.011

All data, records and material relating to the creation, development and exploitation of the [Project/Work] including know how, confidential information, recipes, techniques and processes, computer software records, documents and reports, test results, prototypes, tools, computer generated material and drawings, risk assessments, personnel records, laboratory analysis, film, sound recordings, images, text and/or otherwise shall be archived at [location] by [Name] for the [Consortium] and not destroyed and/or removed without prior [six] months prior notice to all members of the [Consortium].

L

LABORATORY ACCESS

General Business and Commercial

L.001
The [Company] undertakes to provide to the [Assignee] a complete written list of where and with whom all material of any nature in any medium and any copies, packaging, advertising, promotional and other material are stored or held of which they are aware whether or not they are in the possession or control of the [Company].

L.002
The [Production Company] shall obtain from the [Reproduction/Editing/Processing/Archive Company] a laboratory access letter in a form approved by the [Commissioning Company] signed by the [Production Company] and the [Reproduction/Editing/Processing/Archive Company] where all [original master material/other] relating to the [Series/Film/footage/outtakes/Sound Recordings/other] is deposited. The letter is to list all the material of any nature which is stored, the format, duration, language and to transfer the sole rights of access to the [Commissioning Company].

L.003
The [Production Company] shall authorise the [specify source] to grant [exclusive/non-exclusive] access to the [Commissioning Company] to request and make copies for the purposes of this Agreement at the [Commissioning Company's] sole cost and risk.

L.004
The [Production Company] shall procure a laboratory letter in the form specified under Schedule [–] to this Agreement addressed to the [Commissioning Company] and signed by both an authorised representative of the laboratory and the [Production Company].

L.005
The [Distributor] shall provide the [Company] with a laboratory access letter [in customary/agreed form] giving the [Company] the irrevocable right to

911

order copies of the [Film] and/or parts at the [Company's] sole cost direct from the original negatives or other material in the following formats [–]. The letter must contain irrevocable instructions that the negatives of the [Film] and/or parts must not be destroyed or transferred from the possession of the Laboratory prior to [date] without the prior written consent of the [Company].

L.006

The [Laboratory] are authorised and instructed by the [Company] to accept and honour any orders for laboratory services from:

[Company/Distributor] of [address] by [Officer] with respect to the [Film] entitled [Title] reference code [–] format [–]. This authorisation is effective from [date] until [further notice/date].

L.007

All costs, charges and expenses arising from any order placed by the [Distributor] shall be at the [Distributor's] cost and shall not be the responsibility of the [Company]. In the event that the [Distributor] shall fail to pay for the [Laboratory's] services then the [Laboratory] agrees and undertakes not to place any lien or charge or other claim over the material of the [Film/other] and/or to refuse to release copies to other third parties.

L.008

All laboratory services ordered by the [Distributor] will be at their sole cost and liability and on such terms as [Licensor] shall agree with the [Laboratory]. In the event of any default of payment by the [Distributor] no lien or charge shall ensue in respect any part of the master material and/or the negatives.

L.009

The parties agree that no original [master material/negatives/footage/outtakes/sound recordings/adaptations] of the [Film] and/or parts in any format held and/or controlled by either party shall be destroyed or erased at any time and/or any material removed from the [Laboratory] premises at [address] for any reason without the prior written consent of the [Company] and [Name] whether during the Term of this Agreement or thereafter.

L.010

The [Company] agrees that the [Distributor] shall be entitled to arrange for and bear the cost of obtaining [one full-length copy] of the [Film] which is held at the [facilities house] at [address] Party [Name] Address [registered or business address].

Provided that such consent by the [Company] is upon agreement to the following terms as follows by the [Distributor]:

1.1　They shall be responsible for and pay the [facilities house] the agreed cost of making the copy in the following format [–].

1.2　They shall not be entitled to delete any part of the [Film] and shall ensure that all the credits, copyright notices, trade marks, service marks, disclaimers and [other] are reproduced accurately.

1.3　In the event that the master material is damaged as a result of making the copy which they have ordered they agree to bear the full cost of a replacement for the master up to a maximum of [figure/currency].

1.4　They shall arrange for the copy of the [Film] before [date].

L.011

The [Company] shall not be entitled to access at any time to the [footage/master material/negatives/archive material] under the control of or in the possession of the [Company]. The [Purchaser] shall be required to request any copies of the [Work/other] from the [Company] direct. The [Company] shall be entitled to decide at its sole discretion whether it will fulfil such a request. In the event that the [Company] shall decide to provide any copies it shall be entitled to charge the [Purchaser] for the full cost of making the copies, freight and packaging, administration fee, and such additional fees as it may deem appropriate in the circumstances. The [Purchaser] shall pay total sums to the [Company] upon invoice which shall be due prior to the delivery of any copies.

L.012

Where a person and company is granted access to the [Master Material] of the [Work] at the facilities of the [Copyright Owner/Distributor] it is on the following grounds:

1.1　That there is no right to remove, damage, erase and/or otherwise alter the [Master Material].

1.2　Any use and/or exploitation of any material is subject to the conclusion of a written licence agreement between the parties.

1.3　That there shall be a charge for the costs of reproduction, administration and any freight costs which shall be paid [in advance/upon delivery].

1.4　That all credits, copyright notices and other notified contractual obligations shall be adhered to and shall be displayed in a reasonably prominent position at the end of the [Programme/Film/Disc].

L.013

1.1　The [Institute] agrees that [Name] and his/her research partners may have access to and use the following facilities on a non-exclusive basis at [location] [specify facilities from [date] to [date] from [specify start time] to [specify end time] for the [Project] details of which are attached in appendix [–] and form part of this Agreement.

1.2   The [Institute] agrees to pay all costs of electricity, light, water rates, security and any materials and equipment which may be required provided that the cost of any new materials shall not exceed [number/currency].

1.3   [Name] agrees and undertakes that neither he/she nor any of their research partners shall use, develop and/or adapt any material which would pose a serious risk to human health and/or pose a fire risk and/or is likely to result in the evacuation of the premises and/or involves any illegal action and/or process and/or method and/or intentionally commit any criminal offence and/or otherwise.

1.4   [Name] agrees that the [Institute] shall be acknowledged as a contributor to the [Project] and provided with the following acknowledgement in any future report and/or marketing: Research laboratory facilities at [specify] [image/logo/web reference].

1.5   [Name] agrees that if at any time the [Institute] refuses and/or delays access to the facilities in 1.1. That [Name] shall not be entitled to make any claim for any loss and/or damage and/or expenses that may occur and that [Name] shall bear all the sums.

1.6   [Name] agrees and undertakes that in the event that the persons involved in the research work cause any losses, damages, expenses and/or any other sums to be incurred by the [Institute] due to their acts, omissions and/or errors.

1.7   Name] agrees that neither he/she nor any research partners shall be entitled to remove, delete, erase, destroy, borrow, lend and/or otherwise dispose of and/or supply to any third party any data, information, records and/or equipment and/or material in any medium of any nature owned, controlled and/or purchased by the [Institute] at any time.

L.014

1.1   The [Institute] agrees that [Name] may use the following equipment [specify at [location] in order to develop and create a new website, app and game provisionally entitled:[specify].

1.2   [Name] agrees and undertakes to adhere to and abide by all the guidelines, policies and regulations of the [Institute].

1.3   [Name] agrees and undertakes to pay such sums and expenses as are set out in [specify document] for the access granted in 1.1.

1.4   Name] agrees that the [Institute] may refuse access and/or withdraw their agreement at any time without reason without advance notice.

1.5   [Name] agrees that he shall not use, access and/or download any material to any equipment which is likely to effect the reputation and/or create a negative marketing impact on the [Institute] and/or any other students and/or any third party in partnership with the [Institute].

1.6   [Name] agrees that he/she must not damage, remove, delete, adapt, vary and/or remove any data, records, equipment, computer software, computer hardware, furniture, fixture and fittings and/or any other material owned, controlled and/or possessed by the [Institute] and/or any other third party.

1.7   That [Name] agrees to a request to have their clothes and shoes and bag searched and to be subject to a body scan if required before entering and leaving the building by a person of the same gender who is a senior security officer. Provided that [Name] shall have the right on each occasion to refuse the request and may therefore be refused entry.

LANGUAGE

General Business and Commercial

L.015
All notices, demands or communications under or in connection with this [Guarantee/Agreement] shall be in [English].

L.016
The Contract is set out in both [Language] and [English] and in the event of a dispute as to the meaning of the words the [English/other] language shall prevail.

L.017
Where the language of the contract becomes out of date due to developments in technology, equipment, media, communication, storage, translation, adaptation or otherwise it is agreed between the parties that there should be a presumption that all such rights that are not directly covered shall be reserved by and belong to [Name].

L.018

Where the language of the contract becomes out of date due to developments in law, technology, equipment, media, communication, storage, translation, adaptation or otherwise it is agreed between the parties that there should be a presumption that all such rights that are not directly covered shall be owned and controlled by [Name].

L.019

The [Project/Film/Article] shall be in [English/German/Spanish/French/Mandarin/ Italian/other] and no other language shall be used. No new title, logo, text, dialogue, images, film, sound recordings, translation, sub-titles, dubbing, packaging and marketing shall be developed, reproduced, supplied and/or distributed without the prior written approval and consent of the [Company] in each case.

L.020

The [Sub-Licensee] shall be entitled to arrange for the translation of the [Work] in the following languages [specify languages].

L.021

The [Sub-Licensee] shall arrange for a translation of the title, text, index and images of the [Work] at the [Sub-Licensee's] cost. When it is completed the [Sub-Licensee] shall send a complete draft copy to the [Licensor] for approval. The [Sub-License] shall be obliged to make such changes to the translation as may be required by the [Licensor]. The [Sub-Licensee] shall not be entitled to proceed with the translated work without the prior written approval of the [Licensor] of the proposed draft version of the complete work.

L.022

The [Sub-Licensee] shall ensure that it is a condition of their contract with any third party that such third party shall not acquire any copyright and/or intellectual property rights, trade marks, database rights and/or any other rights and/or interest in the [Work] and/or any translation. The [Sub-Licensee] shall provide a draft copy of any proposed contract with such third parties to the [Licensor]. The [Sub-Licensee] shall be obliged to make such changes to the proposed contract as may be required by the [Licensor]. The [Sub-Licensee] shall not be entitled to proceed with the proposed contract without the prior written approval of the [Licensor].

L.023

The [Licensor] shall pay and arrange for any translations of the [Film/Work/Sound Recordings] at the [Licensors'] cost. The [Licensor] may also change the title, text and images of the [Film/Work/Sound Recordings] in order to meet the requirements of the market and/or the differences in meaning and/or culture.

L.024

The [Licensor] agrees that the [Licensee] and/or distributor and/or any other third party involved in the exploitation of the [Work] may in the process of any agreed adaptation and/or translation substitute any part of the [Work] including the main title, chapter headings, character names and any text, image and logo provided it is necessary due to differences in culture, religion and/or translation and interpretation. Further that the[Licensee] and/or any distributor and/or any third party must agree in advance to assign all copyright, intellectual property rights and trade marks in such new versions to the [Licensor] in consideration of the payment of [one/currency] and will agree to sign the documents supplied by the [Licensor] to effect any such assignment.

L.025

There shall be no right granted under this Agreement to exploit the [Work] in any other language except [specify language] with the regional accent for [specify]. No right exists to change, edit, adapt, vary the title, character and place names, quotes and/or any text, image, logo, film, sound recording, music, lyrics and/or any part of the [Work] and any associated packaging, marketing and/or promotional material.

L.026

Where any material is translated into computer generated material, computer software and/or hardware, website, apps, blogs and/or any other form of electronic and/or digital and/or internet and/or telecommunications including landlines, mobiles, television, radio and/or any other medium in any format whether in existence now and/or which comes in to existence at a later date. Where the material has authorised passwords and/or is in a code, algorithm, numeric system, software and/or other language which enables the process, mechanism and/or system to be developed, accessed, used, reproduced and/or changed at any time. Then it is agreed that all members of the [Consortium] shall be permitted to be provided with a complete copy of all such material in any form upon request.

LEGAL PROCEEDINGS

DVD, Video and Discs

L.027

In the event of any action, claim, dispute, writ or proceedings arising out of this Agreement the [Assignor] and the [Assignee] agree to provide full details to the other party at the earliest opportunity. No offer, settlement or disclosure shall be made to the other party [unless required by order of a court of law] until both parties have agreed the best course of action and/or taken legal advice. Each party shall bear its own costs and expenses unless the problem is directly attributable to one party, in which case the defaulting party shall bear all costs and expenses.

L.028

In the event that any complaint, claim, allegation and/or legal proceedings are made against and/or threatened or issued by any third party against the [Distributor] in respect of the [DVD/Disc] of the [Film] and/or any associated packaging, marketing or promotion. Then the [Distributor] shall immediately notify the [Licensor] of the nature of the claim, allegation, action or complaint and shall provide copies of all documents and shall provide all such assistance as may reasonably be required in order to deal with, refute, settle or defend such case. The [Distributor] agrees to follow the instructions and guidance of the [Licensor] and will permit the [Licensor] to assume control of the matter. The [Licensor] shall only reimburse and/or indemnify the legal costs and expenses incurred by the [Distributor] where the [Licensor] is in breach of this Agreement and its undertakings to the [Distributor].

L.029

In the event of the [Distributor] becoming aware of any infringement or breach by any third party of any copyright, or any other intellectual property rights or any other legal rights of any nature which may relate to the [DVD/Disc] of the [Film] and/or any associated marketing or material. The [Distributor] shall advise the [Licensor], but the [Distributor] shall be entitled a exclusive licensee to take legal action against any company or person who reproduces, sells, supplies and/or distributes copies of the [DVD/Disc]. The [Distributor] shall bear all the costs and expenses relating to any legal action it may decide to take and shall retain all sums recovered for losses, damages, legal costs or otherwise by the [Distributor].

L.030

Where any legal proceedings are issued against the [Licensor] and/or the [Licensee] in respect of the [Sound Recordings] and/or the [Disc]. The

918

parties agree to cooperate with each other in order to settle and/or defend any such claim. Each party shall bear their own legal costs and shall only seek to rely on any indemnity under this Agreement where they have fully disclosed all the details of the claim and consulted with the other party.

L.031

The [Distributor] agrees and undertakes that it shall not threaten and/or take any action to commence legal proceedings against any third party in respect of the [CD/Disc/other] of the [Film/Work] unless it has completed all the following steps and tasks:

1.1   Informed the [Licensor] of the details of the case and provided details of any supporting information.

1.2   The [Distributor] has verified the facts of the case and assessed the potential loss and/or damage to the [Distributor] and the [Licensor].

1.3   The [Distributor] has received the approval of the [Licensor] to proceed and to take such action as it thinks fit.

1.4   The [Distributor] is capable of funding all costs and expenses without any contribution from the [Licensor].

1.5   That the [Distributor] has carried out an assessment of the full potential liability if any action should fail.

1.6   he [Distributor] agrees that no costs and/or expenses shall be deducted from any sums due to the [Licensor] under this Agreement at any time.

1.7   In the event that the [Distributor] loses any legal proceedings it will still be capable of operating as a fully functional business and to meet all its liabilities and to pay all the sums due to the [Licensor].

L.032

The [Company] shall not be obliged to consult with [Name] in the event that the [Company] and/or any agent, licensee and/or distributor should decide to take any legal action of any nature to register, protect and/or defend any rights to the [DVD/Disc/CD] of the [Project].

Film and Television

L.033

If at any time in the future the [Distributor] becomes aware of any facts or information indicating that any third party is or may be infringing the [Licensor's] copyright in the [Films], the [Distributor] shall promptly inform the [Licensor] of such facts or information. If the [Licensor] in its sole discretion determines that it shall institute legal or other action then the [Distributor]

919

shall co-operate fully and the [Distributor] shall have the right to institute an action in its own name. The [Distributor] shall not institute any such legal action without the prior written consent of the [Licensor], such consent not to be unreasonably withheld or delayed.

L.034

1.1 In the event that any legal proceedings are commenced by any third party against either the [Commissioning Company] or [the Producer] in respect of the [Series] and/or any associated marketing or material. Then written notice of such a claim or threat shall immediately be given to the other party (as the case may be) who shall provide all such assistance as may reasonably be required in order to settle or defend such case. Each party shall bear its own legal costs and expenses.

1.2 In the event of either the [Commissioning Company] or [the Producer] becoming aware of any infringement or breach by any third party of any copyright, or any other intellectual property rights or any other legal rights of any nature which may relate to the [Series] and/or any associated marketing or material. Then written notice shall immediately be given to the other party (as the case may be) who shall provide all such assistance as may reasonably be required by the other party including joining in any legal or other proceedings against such third party. Each party shall bear its own legal costs and expenses.

L.035

The [Company] agrees and undertakes that it shall be responsible for, and bear the cost of, all complaints, allegations, claims and legal proceedings which may arise in respect of the development, production, exploitation, merchandising and marketing of the [Film] and/or parts and/or any sound recording and/or any adaptation, translation or otherwise. That no such sums, costs and expenses shall be deducted from any advance, royalties or other sums due to [Name] under this Agreement.

L.036

The [Company] shall not be entitled to deduct the legal costs and expenses from the Budget, Distribution Income or any other sums allocated to and/or received in respect of the [Film].

L.037

No settlement shall be made of any claim of any third party unless such claim is settled on reasonable grounds and in good faith taking into account the opinion and recommendation of the legal advisors of the [Company]. In the event that the parties cannot agree upon the terms in which to settle the matter, then it is agreed that the advice or opinion of a legal specialist shall be sought at the [Company's] cost but shall not be considered binding.

L.038
In the event that there is any allegation, claim, and/or legal proceedings against the [Author] or the [Company] in respect of the [Work] and/or the [Film] for infringement of copyright, breach of contract or otherwise. Then each party shall bear its own costs and expenses which may arise in order to defend, settle and/or contest the claim and shall act in its own best commercial and personal interests and shall not be obliged to take in to account the views of the other party as to how to deal with the matter. Such right of choice as to how to conduct, settle or defend the case shall be without prejudice to the right of either party to take proceedings against the other and/or seek any indemnity from the other for legal costs, damages, losses, or otherwise in respect of any matter arising out of this Agreement.

L.039
The [Licensor] and the [Distributor] agree that all complaints, allegations, legal proceedings, disputes, and taking of legal action in respect of the [Film], the soundtrack, the excerpts, and any packaging, advertising and marketing of the [Film] shall be passed to and controlled by the [Licensor]. The [Licensor] shall consult with the [Distributor] in any matter.

L.040
The [Licensee] must arrange suitable insurance cover for the benefit of the [Licensor] and the [Licensee] as part of the cost of the Budget with a reputable company to provide comprehensive cover for the threat of any legal proceedings, complaint, dispute, allegation, breach of contract, defamation, infringement of copyright, unauthorised use of material against either party or any authorised third party in respect of the [Film] and/or parts and/or any exploitation in any form from [date] to [date].

L.041
In the event that legal proceedings are threatened or some claim, action or breach is made by any third party in respect of the [Series] against the [Licensor] or the [Licensee], then either party shall promptly notify the other accordingly. The [Licensor] shall assume all responsibility for all such matters upon behalf of both parties and bear all costs and expenses. The [Licensee] shall provide such material, documents and other evidence as may be requested and generally co-operate fully with the reasonable requests of the [Licensor].

L.042
Where legal proceedings are instituted and/or any claim is made by a third party in respect of the [Film] based on the [Work] and/or any other adaptation

by the [Distributor]. The [Distributor] agrees and undertakes to pay for all the professional and legal costs of the [Author] that may be incurred by the [Author] and/or the [Agent].

L.043

[Name] agrees that the [Distributor] may at its discretion institute any legal proceedings and/or take such steps as may be necessary to protect its rights in the [Film/Sound Recording] of [Name]. That [Name] provides his/her consent to be named as a party to any such legal proceedings and/or steps provided that the [Distributor] shall pay of the legal costs, and any other expenses, interest and any other sums including losses, damages and third party legal costs that [Name] may incur and/or be advised and/or ordered to pay by mediator and/or court.

L.044

The [Distributor] agrees that in the event that it should take any legal actions and/or make any allegations against a third party in respect of the [Programme]. That [Name] shall not be obliged to assist and/or support and/or contribute in any form at any time and shall be entitled not to be joined as a party to any application and/or action in any other form. Nor shall the [Distributor] be entitled and/or authorised to represent to any third party that [Name] endorses and/or supports any legal proceedings.

L.045

The [Company] agrees and undertakes that it shall not be entitled to deduct any sums incurred as legal costs and expenses and/or losses, damages, interest and administrative costs in respect of the [Programme] from any gross receipts which maybe received nor from any sums due to be paid to [Name]. That the [Distributor] must be responsible and bear the liability for all such sums.

General Business and Commercial

L.046

1.1   The [Assignee] shall from [date] have the right entirely at its own discretion to litigate and proceed with any actions, proceedings, claims or demands against any third party who have or may have infringed or breached any rights held by the [Assignee] in the [Work] and/or [Work Material].

1.2   The [Assignor] agrees that after [date] all damages, costs, expenses and any other sums due or arising from the [Work] and/or [Work Material] shall belong to the [Assignee].

1.3   Where necessary the [Assignor] agrees to be a party to the action in name but all co-operation and assistance shall be subject to agreement as to the costs and expenses and the conclusion of an indemnity.

L.047

In the event that there is any allegation, complaint, report, or legal action that alleges and/or states the use of this [Product/Work/Services] infringes any third party rights. Then the party to this Agreement, against whom the claim is made, shall be entitled to defend it, without prejudice to the right of that party to take third party proceedings or any other action against the other parties to this Agreement whether under a claim for indemnity, loss or damages.

L.048

In the event of any claim, dispute, action, writ or summons arising out of the performance of this Agreement [Name] and [Name] agree to provide full details to the other party at the earliest opportunity and shall not settle any matter without first consulting the other party.

L.049

In the event that any infringement of any rights in the [Product/Work/Service] owned or controlled by the [Licensor] shall come to the attention of the other party, then such party shall promptly inform the other and the [Licensor] and [Licensee] shall accordingly take such action as each party shall decide at its own expense.

L.050

Each person agrees that they shall notify all the others immediately of any claim, demand or action that they may each or all become aware of, or be served upon them by any third party arising out of, or as a result of, any work performed pursuant to this Contract. Each person shall afford such other persons the full opportunity to be consulted as to the nature of the defence of such claim, demand or action.

L.051

The [Agent] agrees to advise the [Company] of any potential infringement of rights in the Territory relating to the [Samples], the [Product/Service/other] and the [Company's] Logo including copyright, trade mark, service mark, design rights or any other rights which have been brought to the attention of the [Agent]. Further the [Agent] agrees to provide assistance, expert evidence and affidavit if required with respect to any legal or other proceedings provided that an agreement is reached as to the basis upon which the time and effort of the [Agent] is to be paid for by the [Company].

L.052

During the Term of this Agreement both the [Licensor] and the [Licensee] agree that they shall co-operate in respect of any legal proceedings by third parties which arise in respect of this Agreement. The [Licensee] shall notify the [Licensor] as soon as reasonably possible in the event that any of the following matters should be brought to their attention:

1.1 Pirate copies of the [Product/Work/other] are manufactured, reproduced, distributed, supplied or sold by any third party in [any country in the world/other].

1.2 Copies of the [Product/Work/other] are marketed by unauthorised agents, distributors, retailers, wholesalers, or websites.

1.3 The [Product/Work] or copies are manufactured, reproduced, sold, supplied, distributed or otherwise exploited in circumstances which give rise to the suspicion that they are illegal copies and/or inferior quality.

1.4 The [Product/Work] or copies are being used in a derogatory, offensive or other prejudicial manner in any advertisement, periodical, newspaper or in any medium.

1.5 A third party has complained, threatened or commenced legal or other proceedings in respect of the [Product/Work], the soundtrack, music, the logos, trademarks, service marks, design rights, product liability, packaging, advertising, or any associated material.

1.6 A trade or consumer body or a retailer has complained of any matter including defects in relation to the [Product/Work].

1.7 A purchaser of the [Product/Work] has complained or notified any aspect which is defective, dangerous, or likely to cause harm.

1.8 The [Product/Work] have not complied with any product liability, censorship, law, regulation or standards and practice which apply.

L.053

The parties agree that they shall not be obliged to notify the other party of any threatened or the institution of any legal or other proceedings against them or a third party to the other party to this Agreement. They shall each be entitled to settle, defend, or institute any legal or other proceedings as they think fit entirely at their own discretion. Further each party agrees that in the event of any such legal or other proceedings of any nature they shall be entirely responsible for their own legal costs and shall not seek to be indemnified or compensated by the other party to this Agreement [whether they are entitled to do so or not].

L.054

1.1   In the event that the [Licensor] and/or the [Licensee] become aware of any infringement of any copyright and/or other rights and/or or contractual obligations and/or any other acts by a third party in respect of the [Product/Work]. Then the [Licensor] and the [Licensee] shall keep each other informed on a regular basis and keep the other party informed of any steps they have taken to resolve the situation.

1.2   Both the [Licensor] and the [Licensee] agree that they shall provide sufficient funds to pursue vigorously all third parties who infringement any copyright and/or other rights and/or or contractual obligations and/or any other acts by a third party in respect of the [Product/Work] and/or circumstances which have brought a breach or alleged breach of this Agreement.

1.3   Both the [Licensor] and the [Licensee] agree to co-operate in any legal proceedings and/or action that may be required. Where the parties have taken legal proceedings together and jointly shared the legal and administrative costs, then any sums received shall be shared equally. Where only one party institutes or commences the legal proceedings and pays all the legal costs and other expenditure incurred and the other is joined as a party, but make no contribution to the legal costs. Then the party which bears the legal costs shall be entitled to retain all sums received as damages, costs, for losses or otherwise.

L.055

The [Company] hereby authorises the [Licensee] to institute, prosecute and defend such proceedings and to do such acts as the [Licensee] may consider necessary to protect the rights granted under this Agreement or any part of them and to seek and claim damages, penalties or any other remedy for any infringement of such rights. The [Company] authorises the [Licensee] in so far as may be necessary to use the name of the [Company] for such purposes and the [Company] shall provide such assistance as the [Licensee] may reasonably require in proving or defending such rights and shall join with the [Licensee] as co-plaintiff if requested by the [Licensee] to do so. In such event the [Licensee] shall fully indemnify the [Company] against any costs, expenses and charges including counsel, solicitors', and agents' fees incurred by the [Company] relating to such proceedings.

L.056

The [Licensee] shall at its sole cost and expense take all necessary action and legal proceedings against third parties who infringe the copyright or any other rights in any media in the [Product/Work/Service] anywhere in the Territory which have been granted to the [Licensee] under this Agreement.

The parties mutually undertake to assist one another in their investigations and claims for any infringement or unauthorised use. The [Licensee] shall keep the [Licensor] informed of the progress of any legal proceedings. The [Licensee] agrees that as its sole discretion and cost the [Licensor] shall be entitled to institute its own enquiries and legal proceedings or to join any claim, demand or proceedings commenced by the [Licensee].

L.057

The parties agree to notify the other party as soon as reasonably practicable of such details as are known of any infringement of the copyright in the [Work/other] or the [Licensor's] or the [Licensee's] or any sub-licensee's rights or interest in the [Work/other]. The [Licensor] will at its own cost [and without any claim at a later date for a contribution by the [Licensee]] do all such acts and things necessary to protect the copyright, rights and interest of any nature including, but not limited to taking legal action and/or other steps that may be required against any person, firm or company and shall advise the [Licensee] of all such cases as they arise. The [Licensee] agrees to assist the [Licensor] at the [Licensor's] expense in any steps or action that need to be taken and if requested shall agree to be joined in any proceedings or action. Provided that the [Licensor] shall arrange for full disclosure to the [Licensee] of all legal documents relating to any case including any opinion of Counsel and expert witnesses, so that if necessary the [Licensee] can seek its own independent legal advice and give a full indemnity in relation to any legal costs. The [Licensor] accepts that the [Licensee] shall still be entitled if it should wish to do so to act and institute legal proceedings to protect its own rights and interest which shall be at the [Licensee's] sole cost and expense. In such instance the [Licensor] shall upon request agree to be joined to the proceedings or action subject to full disclosure to the [Licensor] of all legal documents relating to that case including the opinion of Counsel and any expert witnesses provided that the [Licensee] agrees to give a full indemnity to the [Licensor] for any legal costs.

L.058

In the event of any claim by any third party against either the [Contractor] or the [Company] in respect of any part of the obligations, services or products under this Agreement written notice of such claim shall be given immediately to the other party (as the case may be) who shall provide all such assistance as may reasonably be required including joining in any legal or other proceedings where appropriate.

L.059

In the event of the [Company] wishing to take proceedings in respect of any unauthorised use of the [Property/Work] or to defend any claim by a third party, the [Licensee] will to the best of its ability provide full assistance to the [Company] by providing information and obtaining such relevant evidence as may be within its power. Provided that the [Company] shall not be obliged to take any such proceedings or to defend any such claim and shall not be liable to the [Licensee] in any way for the failure on its part to do so.

L.060
Each party agrees that in the event of any legal proceedings they shall each bear their own legal costs and shall not be indemnified except under any insurance policy.

L.061
There shall be no obligation on the [Company] to take civil and/or criminal legal action nor to pursue all parties who infringe the copyright in the [Product/Work] and/or keep the [Licensee] advised as to the progress in any case. The [Company] shall be entitled at its sole discretion to decide whether to take any steps, actions or otherwise and may decide on the grounds of commercial judgment and costs that the matter should be pursued by criminal proceedings through the police or other authority and/or not to take any further action of any nature despite the loss or damage and effect on the reputation of the [Company], the [Licensee] or any agent, distributor or authorised third party.

L.062
The [Company] agrees that it shall not incur any legal costs and/or instruct any legal advisor to institute any legal proceedings of any nature unless it has been authorised in advance by the more than [number] Directors of the [Company] and a provisional statement of the issue, the proposed remedy and estimated costs and risk considered prior to any documents being issued to third parties.

L.063
No employee, consultant, agent, supplier and/or distributor and/or any other person engaged by and/or supplying services to the [Company] shall have the right to make any public statement and/or release any data and/or information and/or supply and/or distribute and/or publish any material in any medium regarding any investigation, enquiry, report, civil and/or criminal proceedings and/or any other allegations which are made against and/or by the [Company] against a third party at any time. Any breach of this clause shall be deemed a breach of this Agreement and entitle the [Company] to end the Agreement.

Internet and Websites

L.064

In the event that the [Company] is obliged to take legal action and/or any other steps against [Name] due to a breach of the user access licence, infringement of copyright, and/or any other rights owned or controlled by the [Company] on this [Website] and/or any action against the [Company] by a third party due to [Name] and/or any material and/or content which belongs to a third party or relates to a third party of any nature. The [Company] shall seek to recover from [Name] all legal costs, losses, loss of profit, damage to reputation, third party payments of any nature and any other sums which arise directly or indirectly from the conduct, acts, behaviour, communications, or otherwise to the [Company], the [Website], any third party connected, associated with and/or related to the [Website] including any supplier, distributor, bank, manufacturer, advertiser, product, service or other contributor.

L.065

It is not the policy of this [Website] to take legal action, or seek an indemnity of any nature from it users and we maintain a comprehensive insurance policy for that purpose. We reserve the right at all times to take such steps, disclose such information which we have in our possession to maintain a secure site, prevent criminal acts and activities, protect public interest and safety, and any other activity which we decide is or might be in our sole discretion wrong, inappropriate, or unlawful. We will advise the police, security investigators, and any other body or authority or person we decide should be informed and you accept that the [Company] shall not be liable to you for any consequence that may arise whether direct or indirect and you shall not be entitled to make any claim of any nature against the [Company].

L.066

The [Company] shall have the right to edit, delete, amend, vary and/or destroy any material of any nature whether text, film, sound recordings, music, logos, images and photographs added and/or reproduced on this [Website] by any third party. The [Company] may institute legal proceedings against any such person, company, business and/or entity which causes the [Company] to be the subject of a claim, action, injunction, dispute, writ, summons, fine, loss and/or damage arising out of the actions and/or conduct and/or material supplied by the person, company, business and/or entity.

L.067

Where any legal proceedings are issued and/or any claim made against the [Company] arising from your contribution of any material of any nature to the [Website]. Then the [Company] shall seek to reclaim all the administrative, management and legal costs and expenses, and any damages, losses and settlement payments that may be incurred by taking legal action against you without further notice.

L.068
Where a civil and/or criminal action is taken by an individual, company, the police and/or a government agency arising from text, images, photographs, sound recordings, music, lyrics and/or any other material that you have uploaded and/or sent to the [Website] whether open to the public and/or in a secure area. The [Company] may at its sole discretion provide full cooperation to such third party in pursuance of such matter and you accept that you shall have no right to a claim and/or action against the [Company].

L.069
All material which is uploaded and/or sent to the [Company] whether on public display and/or sent to a limited group which contains material of any nature which in the view of the [Company] is illegal will be reported to the relevant authorities who may decide to take criminal and/or civil proceedings against you.

L.070
The [Company] shall not be responsible for, nor make any payment towards, any legal costs and/or other expenses, damages and/or fines that any [Contributor] to the [Website] may incur as a result of their sending any material to the [Website]. Any [Contributor] must pay all their own costs and expenses of any legal proceedings.

L.071
In the event [Name] and/or the [Blog/App] and any text, image and/or any associated material and content are threatened with and/or subjected to legal proceedings by a third party for breach of contract, infringement of copyright, and/or any other allegation of infringement of intellectual property rights, data, privacy, defamation and/or otherwise of any nature. Then the [Company] reserves the right to remove and delete all reference to the [Blog/App] without consultation with [Name] in order to reduce the risk of any threat and/or legal proceedings against the [Company] at any time and [Name] agrees and accepts that the [Company] shall be entitled to do so without stating any specific reason.

L.072
The [Company] is not liable for the cost and expenses of any legal action and/or proceedings whether civil and/or criminal, claim, summons, investigation, enquiry and/or commission which relates to the actions and conduct of any person, director, officer and/or employee during their time at the [Company] after their term of employment and/or office has ended.

L.073

The [Company] shall accept responsibility and pay for any legal costs and expenses incurred by [Name] up to [number/currency] in total where the legal proceedings and/or any investigation, enquiry, royal commission and/or health and safety and/or other inspection is and/or are commenced in [country] and relate to his/her role as [specify] during the term of their employment and/or the supply of their services to the [Company] whether or not such matter arises after the expiry and/or termination provided it is within [number] years of the end date.

Merchandising

L.074

The [Licensee] shall be solely responsible for paying any costs, damages and expenses arising from any claim, action or liability arising from the production, manufacture, sale, distribution or other exploitation of the [Licensed Articles] [excluding the Character].

L.075

In the event that any legal proceedings are commenced by any third party against either the [Licensor] and/or the [Licensee] in respect of the [Character] and/or the [Licensed Articles] they shall ensure that written notice of such claims shall immediately be given to the other party. Where the allegation or claim relates to the infringement or breach of third party rights then either party shall be entitled to defend itself without prejudice to the right of that party to take third party proceedings or other steps or action.

L.076

If there is any dispute of any nature by any third party relating to the [Licensor's] rights to the [Licensor's] Logo, the use of it by the [Licensee] or the [Licensee's] Product at any time during the Licence Period or during the sell off period. The party against whom the allegation is made or who receives the complaint shall provide full details to the other within [seven days] and their response to the allegations or complaint within [one month]. Both parties shall assist each other as far as possible to settle or defend the matter. Each party shall bear its own legal costs but may seek to recoup them later on an indemnity basis under this Agreement.

L.077

Each party agrees that in the event of any complaint, threat, legal action or allegation of infringement of copyright, trade mark, service, mark, logo, slogan, domain name, words or images. That each party shall be entitled to deal with the matter without consulting the other and decide what to do based on their own commercial interests provided that they do not intend to seek to be reimbursed for any legal costs under any indemnity clause in this Agreement.

L.078

The [Licensee] shall at its sole cost and expense take all necessary action and legal proceedings against third parties who infringe the copyright or any other rights in any media in the [Product/Work/Service] anywhere in the Territory which have been granted to the [Licensee] under this Agreement. The parties mutually undertake to assist one another in their investigations and claims for any infringement or unauthorised use. The [Licensee] shall keep the [Licensor] informed of the progress of any legal proceedings. The [Licensee] agrees that as its sole discretion and cost the [Licensor] shall be entitled to institute its own enquiries and legal proceedings or to join any claim, demand or proceedings commenced by the [Licensee]. Where the [Licensee] intends to seek to be indemnified by the [Licensor] under this Agreement. Then the [Licensor] should be informed of the matter as soon as possible, be regularly consulted and allowed to refute the allegations, and kept informed of progress and advised of any proposed settlement.

L.079

In the event that any complaint, claim, allegation and/or legal proceedings are made against and/or threatened or issued by any third party against the [Distributor] in respect of the [Product/Article/Character] and/or any associated packaging, marketing or promotion. Then the [Distributor] shall immediately notify the [Licensor] of the nature of the claim, allegation, action or complaint and shall provide copies of all documents and shall provide all such assistance as may reasonably be required in order to deal with, refute, settle or defend such case. The [Distributor] agrees to follow the instructions and guidance of the [Licensor] and will permit the [Licensor] to assume control of the matter. The [Licensor] shall only reimburse and/or indemnify the legal costs and expenses incurred by the [Distributor] where the [Licensor] is in breach of this Agreement and its undertakings to the [Distributor].

L.080

The [Sub-Licensee] shall not be entitled to threaten and/or commence any legal proceedings against third parties who infringe the copyright or any other rights in the [Product] anywhere in the Territory without the prior written approval and agreement of the [Licensor] and the [Licensee]. The [Sub-Licensee] shall provide full details to the [Licensor] and the [Licensee] for their consideration and shall make a recommendation as to the steps to be taken. Where the [Licensor] and the [Licensee] provide consent all legal costs and expenses shall be at the [Sub-Licenses] risk and cost unless agreed otherwise. The [Sub-Licensee] shall keep the [Licensor] and the [Licensee] informed of the progress of any legal proceedings. The [Sub-Licensee] shall be entitled to keep all damages and costs awarded to the [Sub-Licensee].

L.081

The [Sub-Licensee] shall not require the consent of the [Licensee] in order to threaten and/or commence any legal proceedings against a third party who has breached and/or infringed the rights held and/or controlled by the [Sub-Licensee] in respect of the [Work/Film/Product]. The [Licensee] agrees to provide such cooperation as may be required subject to the proviso that the [Licensee] shall not be required to incur any additional costs. The [Sub-Licensee] shall keep the [Licensee] informed and provide copies of all documentation upon request. The [Sub-Licensee] shall be entitled to keep all costs awarded to the [Sub-Licensee], but all damages and other payments shall be included in the accounting reports to the [Licensee] and share [number] % to the [Licensee] and [number] % to the [Sub-Licensee].

L.082

The [Licensor] agrees and undertakes to cooperate and assist the [Licensee] in any legal proceedings by supplying authorised copies of any original documents that may be required in order to prove copyright ownership in respect of the rights granted to the [Licensee].

L.083

1.1   The [Agent/Distributor] shall inform and supply copies of any emails, attachments and documents to [Name] at the [Licensor] in respect of the [Work/Project] in the event that the [Licensee] is either contacted by any third party alleging personal injury, death, infringement of copyright and/or any other intellectual property rights and/or breach of contract, breach of product liability and/or any other health and safety legislation and/or policies and/or any other matter which may potentially give rise to a claim to a civil and/or criminal action and/or a fine and/or otherwise against the [Licensor] and/or the [Licensee].

1.2   That the [Agent/Distributor] agrees that where the [Licensor] wishes to take control of the response and any subsequent legal proceedings. That the [Agent/Distributor] shall agree provided that the [Licensor] agrees and undertakes to bear all legal costs and expenses for the [Agent/Distributor] and shall require that any legal advisor shall consult with the [Agent/Distributor]. In such case the [Agent/Distributor] agrees that the [Licensor] may use the same legal advisor for the [Licensor] and the [Licensee] in any case.

L.084

The [Licensee] agrees and accepts that where any dispute, legal proceedings and/or other claim and/or allegation is made against the [Licensor] in respect of any logo, image, text and/or content in respect of any of the [Products] set out in Schedule [–] in this Agreement. That the [Licensor] may withdraw any such item from the list and market and substitute another which is of comparable status and type where the [Licensor] has decided that such item should be withdrawn from the consumer market in any part of the world.

Publishing

L.085

1.1 If the [Publisher] shall, after professional legal advice, consider that the copyright in the [Work] has been infringed by a third party, then they shall be entitled to take such action as they may deem necessary including, but not limited to legal proceedings, settlement or otherwise.

1.2 In the event that the [Publisher] wishes to name the [Author] as a party to the proceedings they shall only be entitled to do so if they provide a written undertaking to the [Author] that the [Publisher] shall bear all costs and expenses and fully indemnify the [Author]. The [Author] shall bear no liability or responsibility for any sums of any nature that may fall due.

1.3 The [Publisher] shall, after deducting all legal costs and expenses not recovered from a third party, pay to the [Author] [fifty per cent] of any sums, profits damages or benefits including stock which may be recovered in respect of any matter.

L.086

The [Publishers] agree that the [Author] shall be consulted in relation to any proposed settlement or compromise of any matter. Further that the Author shall be entitled to a full account of costs and expenses, profits, damages and any other sums or benefits.

L.087

1.1 If during the Term of this Agreement either the [Author] or the [Publisher] consider the copyright or some other right is being infringed or injured by the act of another. The [Author] and/or the [Publisher] shall have the right to take legal proceedings and shall give written notice to the other party of its intention to do so. The [Publisher] shall be entitled to require the [Author] to take part in such proceedings and if it does so it shall pay all costs and expenses incurred in such proceedings by both the [Publisher] and the [Author].

1.2   Any monies which shall be recovered in respect of any such infringement as a result of proceedings in which both the [Author] and the [Publisher] have participated shall after deduction of all costs and expenses be divided equally between the [Author] and the [Publisher]. If no agreement is reached for joint action either party may proceed as it shall see fit bearing all costs incidental thereto and enjoying all of the benefits arising there from.

L.088

1.1   The [Writer] authorises the [Company] in any country of the world to institute, commence and defend such criminal and civil proceedings and to do such acts as the [Company] may deem fit to protect the rights assigned under this Agreement and to seek such damages, copies and other benefits.

1.2   The [Writer] authorises the [Company] to use his/her name as the author of the [Work] for such purposes provided that all costs and expenses shall be paid for by the [Company] and the [Company] shall keep the [Author] fully informed and supply copies of all documents relating to any proceedings or action.

1.3   The [Writer] agrees to provide his/her reasonable assistance in any action whether to prove or defend the rights assigned to the [Company].

1.4   The [Company] agrees to pay the [Writer's] and his/her agent's reasonable legal costs and expenses, accommodation, telephone, photocopying, and transport in providing such assistance.

L.089

The [Publisher] undertakes at its own discretion to instigate and proceed with any necessary actions, proceedings, claims and demands against any company, firm, or person who may infringe the copyright in the [Work]. The [Publishers] agree that any damages [and other benefits] recovered by the [Publishers] shall [after deduction of reasonable legal costs and expenses] be divided [allocate percentage] between the [Publishers] and the [Writer].

L.090

The [Company] shall not seek to take legal action against the [Author] for any reason for the use by the [Company] of the [Work] on the website whether sued or threatened by any third party.

L.091

The [Author] agrees that the [Publisher] may use the [Author's] name as a party to take legal action against any third party for copyright infringement in respect of the [Work] provided that:

1.1 The [Author] is kept fully advised of the details of the action.

1.2 The [Publisher] gives a full detailed indemnity to the [Author] agreeing to pay all costs, expenses, and losses in respect of the action incurred by the [Publisher] and the [Author].

1.3 That in the event that any profits, damages, awards or other sums or benefits or stock are recovered in respect of the [Work]. The [Publisher] shall share such sums or otherwise equally with the [Author] after the deduction of all reasonable costs and expenses of the [Publisher] which are not recovered.

L.092

The [Publisher] and/or any agent, distributor, supplier or otherwise shall not have the right or be entitled to take any legal actions or proceedings whether civil or criminal, report any matter to the authorities and/or take any steps against a person, company or business, make any applications, register any objections and/or defend any matter in the name of and/or on behalf of the [Author] without the prior written consent and authority of the [Author].

L.093

The [Publisher] shall notify the [Author/Illustrator] of the detail of the threat of any legal proceedings against the [Publisher] and any action, claim, demand for defamation, breach of copyright, infringement of trade mark and/or service mark, threat of injunction, loss, damage and/or injury and/or any other matter relating to the [Work/Artwork/Photographs] as soon as reasonably possible. The [Publisher] agrees and undertakes to provide copies of any documents relating to the case to the [Author/Illustrator] and/or their legal advisor and to consult with the [Author/Illustrator] where the [Publisher] intends to seek to be indemnified by the [Author/Illustrator] under this Agreement. Then the [Author/Illustrator] should be informed of the matter as soon as possible, be regularly consulted and allowed to refute the allegations, and kept informed of progress and advised of any proposed settlement.

L.094

The [Licensee] agrees and undertakes to cooperate and assist the [Sub-Licensee] in the issue of and/or defence of any legal proceedings in respect of the rights granted in respect of the [Work] under this Agreement. The [Licensee] shall provide at their sole cost authorised copies of any original documents that may be required in order to prove copyright ownership in respect of the rights granted to the [Sub-Licensee]. The [Licensee] shall not be liable for any costs, expenses, damages and/or losses the [Sub-Licensee] may incur under the indemnity in clause [–] which do not directly arise from the [Work].

L.095

The [Company] reserves the right at any time not to publish and/or to recall at its sole discretion any copies and/or to cease printing and/or to cancel and/or terminate any licence agreements and/or to remove, delete and/or to cease marketing any [Work] and/or any part where allegations and/or the threat of legal proceedings have been made by a third party which are established to be likely to be true and show that the content of the [Work] has resulted in the defamation of any person who is not deceased and/or a substantial part of the [Work] is based on and/or derived from the original copyright material of a third party and is not original to [Name].

L.096

Where there are any allegations and/or threats and/or claims and/or legal proceedings made against the [Company] and/or the [Work] and/or [Name] to the [Company]. In such event the [Company] shall provide evidence of the allegations and facts to [Name] and provide them with an opportunity to refute the allegations at a meeting at the offices of the [Company] with a senior executive and a legal advisor of the [Company].

L.097

Where as a result of the investigations, research and product of the work of [Name] the [Company] reproduces, supplies, sells and distributes and publishes an article and/or image and/or allegations against a third party. Then the [Company] agrees to pay for all personal and legal costs and expenses that may arise from any response, threat, claim, enquiry, police and/or government investigation, commission and/or civil and/or legal proceedings including any individual, estate, corporation and/or otherwise from any third party whether or not [Name] is no longer associated with the [Company]. This agreement shall not apply after [date].

Purchase and Supply of Products

L.098

The [Trade Mark User] shall immediately bring to the attention of the [Proprietor] any improper or wrongful use of the Trade Marks which comes to its notice [during the Term of the Agreement].

L.099

The [Agent] agrees to advise the [Company] on any potential infringement of rights in the Territory relating to the [Samples] and the [Products] including copyright, design rights, trade marks or any other rights which have been brought to the attention of the [Agent]. Further the [Agent] agrees to provide assistance in any legal proceedings at the [Company's] cost whether relating to non-payment, copyright, design rights, trade marks, or any other rights of the [Company] in the [Samples], the [Products] and/or the [Company] Logo.

L.100

The [Agent] shall immediately advise the [Company] of any complaint it may receive as to defects in the [Products] or of any infringements or threat of infringement of the [Company's] rights, designs, trademarks or names or any facts or actions that may be prejudicial to the [Company].

L.101

If there is any claim, demand or action by any third party against the [Supplier] and/or the [Seller] in respect of the supply to the public of the [Product] on the [Seller's] website and/or the [Supplier's] Logo each party shall notify the other immediately of the nature and detail of any such matter of which they have knowledge. In the event that any party seeks to be indemnified from the other for legal costs or damages then it is under an obligation to allow the other party to have the opportunity to [assist in/control] the defence of or settlement of such case.

L.102

If circumstances arise which give reasonable cause for action to be taken against any third party by virtue of a breach of either parties' intellectual property or contractual rights of any kind, the parties agree to provide reasonable co-operation to each other as is required to protect such rights. As a general principle all costs and monies recovered shall be shared equally provided that both parties are named in the action and equally share the legal costs.

L.103

The [Distributor], and/or any agent, supplier, website company, retailer, wholesaler or otherwise shall not have the right or be entitled to take any legal actions or proceedings whether civil or criminal, report any matter to the authorities and/or take any steps against a person, company or business, make any applications, register any objections and/or defend any matter in the name of and/or on behalf of [Name] without the prior written consent and authority of [Name]. [Name] agrees not to unreasonably withhold and/or delay their consent provided that there is full disclosure of the facts in each case to [Name] and the matter does not prejudice the commercial interests of [Name] and/or Name] has been advised by its own professional and legal advisors not to provide authority and/or consent.

L.104

Where a third party has made a complaint and/or threatened legal proceedings and/or started a legal action. Then the [Company] shall keep a complete log of all emails, calls and documents. Where the matter is not resolved and/or settled within [number] months. Then the [Company] agrees to follow the following procedure [specify].

L.105

The [Supplier] agrees that it shall pay to the [Distributor] upon invoice all the administrative, freight and legal costs and expenses and losses and damages which the [Distributor] may incur and/or which arise due to any personal injury, death, allergic reaction and/or ill health including short term and long term illness which is found by any investigation by an independent expert and/or government department and/or body and/or as a result of civil and/or legal proceedings to be connected with and/or result from the contents and/or packaging of the [Product] and/or any ingredients and/or other material used by the [Supplier] in developing, creating, producing and distributing the [Product] in any country at any time to the [Distributor] and/or any member of the public and/or other third party supplied by the [Distributor].

L.106

1.1 It is agreed that each party to this Agreement shall bear its own expenses and costs in the event that it decides to take advice, threaten, commence and/or defend any legal proceedings and/or object to any registration and/or defend and/or register any domain name, trade mark, service mark and/or other intellectual property rights and/or register as a controller of any data and/or any other matter.

1.2 That no party shall have the right to seek to deduct payments due to the other under this Agreement to set off any administration, legal costs and expenses.

1.3 That where the co-operation and assistance of any other party is required that terms shall be agreed as to the basis of the contribution and who is to pay the costs and who is to receive and/or pay any settlement and/or who is to retain sums received which may be awarded.

L.107

1.1 [Name] agrees and confirms to the [Company] that there are currently as at [date] no threats and/or pending and/or actual legal proceedings against the [Product] and/or [Name] in [country].

1.2 [Name] agrees that the failure to disclose to the [Company] the fact that there has been a threat of legal action by a competitor, member of the public and/or any other third party in [country] in respect of the

[Product] and the nature of the complaint shall be a breach of this Agreement for any matter before [date].

1.3 [Name] agrees that where there is a breach as set out in 1.2 above that the [Company] shall be entitled to terminate the Agreement and seek repayment of all sums paid under this Agreement to [Name].

Services

L.108

1.1 In the event that legal proceedings are commenced by any third party against either the [Designer] and/or the [Company] in respect of the [Proposal/Website] or some other matter relating to this Agreement. Then both parties shall be kept fully informed and provide each other with assistance to resolve or defend the matter. Each party shall bear its own legal costs and expenses and consult with each other prior to any settlement.

1.2 Where any action relates to work requested by the [Company] for the [Website] then the [Company] agrees to act on behalf of both parties and shall pay the [Designer's] legal costs and expenses provided that he/she agrees to be represented by the same legal advisors as the [Company]. The [Designer] agrees to execute such legal documents as may be reasonably required.

L.109

The [Company] accepts and agrees that it shall be solely responsible for the legal consequences and liabilities that may arise in respect of the content and exploitation of the [Event/Services/Series/other]. That where any legal proceedings, actions, claims, complaints and/or allegations are made the [Company] undertakes to fully indemnify the [Presenter] and his/her agent for the cost of separate and independent legal representation and advice, and/or any other costs, losses, expenses and sums that may be incurred or arise as a consequence.

L.110

The [Consultant] shall send copies of any complaints, and/or disciplinary and/or legal actions which are threatened and/or commenced against the [Consultant] and/or [Company] in respect of the services by the [Consultant] provided under this Agreement to the [Company] and/or third parties. The [Company] shall not be responsible for any legal costs and expenses incurred by the [Consultant] in defending any disciplinary and/or legal action.

L.111

[Name] and the [Company] agree that in the event of any complaint, threat, claim, legal action, disciplinary proceedings and/or other allegation in respect of any matter. That [Name] and/or the [Company] shall not be obliged to consult with and/or seek the approval of the other prior to reaching any settlement, defending the action and/or taking any other steps that may be necessary. This shall not prevent either party relying on clause and/or any indemnity in this Agreement to recover any costs and/or expenses that may have been incurred.

L.112

Both parties agree that where a third party takes legal action against both parties that they shall first try to resolve and settle the matter without incurring legal costs. That if that fails they shall agree the total budget for the legal costs and the [Company] shall pay [number] % and the [Distributor] shall pay [number]%.

L.113

[Name] has not authorised and/or provided any consent for the [Agent] to threaten any third party with legal proceedings by [Name] and/or to take any legal advice at [Names'] cost and expense and/or to instruct any person and/or company to register, take action, defend and/or settle any matter on behalf of [Name].

L.114

[Name] agrees that he/she authorises the [Agent/Company] to take such steps as may be necessary to seek advice and take legal action in order to develop, protect, register and defend the brand of [Name] and any associated trade mark, domain name, logo, images and slogan. Provided that where the proposed costs and expenses are likely to exceed [number/ currency] in any one case that the prior written approval of [Name] must be obtained. In such instance the [Agent/Company] must provide [Name] with a detailed breakdown of the total projected sums.

L.115

[Name] shall not be obliged to sign any documents, swear any affidavit and/ or commence any legal proceedings and/or be joined as a party to any legal action by the [Company] in respect of any matter which may arise directly and/or indirectly from the provision of the services of [Name] and his/her original material to the [Company].

Sponsorship

L.116
If any legal proceedings are commenced or threatened by any third party against the [Sponsor] and/or the [Television Company] in respect of the [Sponsor's Logo] and/or the [Films]. Within [seven days] of receipt the party who has received notice should inform the other of the problem. Each party shall be responsible for dealing with its own legal problems and bear its own legal costs. This does not, however, prevent a later claim for indemnity, legal costs, damages or otherwise against the party which is at fault, and has been in breach of this Agreement.

L.117
The [Sponsor] accepts and agrees that it shall be solely responsible for the legal consequences and liabilities that may arise in respect of the content and exploitation of the [Sponsors Logo] and the [Sponsors Product] by the [Athlete] and the [Company] under this Agreement. That the [Sponsor] shall not have any right to use the name of the [Athlete] and/or [Company] in relation to any matter without their prior consent in each case. Where any legal proceedings, actions, claims, complaints and/or allegations are made the [Sponsor] undertakes to fully indemnify the [Athlete] and his/her agent and the [Company] for the cost of separate and independent legal representation and advice, and/or any other costs, losses, expenses and sums that may be incurred or arise as a consequence.

L.118
If there is any threat, complaint, claim, and/or legal action by any third party against the [Sponsor] and/or the [Company] in respect of the [Event] and/or the services and/or products supplied by the [Sponsor] under this Agreement. Each party agrees and undertakes to notify the other within [number] days by email and in writing of the nature and detail of any such matter of which they have knowledge together with copies of any documents. In the event that the [Company] and/or the [Sponsor] seeks to be indemnified from the other for legal costs, expenses, damages and/or other costs. Then the party seeking to rely on any indemnity is under an obligation to allow the other party to have the opportunity to [assist in/control] the defence of and/or settlement of any such case.

L.119
Where any allegation is made and/or a complaint and/or a claim is made and/or any legal proceedings are commenced by any third party against either the [Sponsor] and/or the [Company] in respect of any matter directly and/or indirectly arising from the terms of this Agreement. Then both the [Sponsor] and the [Company] agree that where they shall seek to rely on

941

any indemnity from the other party to recoup the costs. That they shall be obliged to notify the other party as the earliest opportunity and to keep that other party fully informed. That no indemnity shall be relied upon under this Agreement if the party seeking the indemnity contributed to the legal problem as a result of their actions, error, omission and/or failure.

L.120

The [Athlete] agrees and undertakes to:

1.1 Notify the [Sponsor] by telephone and then in writing of any civil and/ or criminal proceedings which are threatened, commenced and/or pending against the [Athlete] during the Term of this Agreement.

1.2 Notify the [Sponsor] by telephone and then in writing of any disciplinary proceedings by any of the following organisations against the [Athlete] which arise during the Term of this Agreement [specify bodies].

1.3 Notify the [Sponsor] by telephone and then in writing of any failure by the [Athlete] to attend random tests required by any sporting organisation and/or failure of any test which arise during the Term of this Agreement.

1.4 Supply copies of any documents which relate to the above matters in confidence to the [Sponsors] upon request during the Term of this Agreement:

1.5 Cooperate in the drafting of and distribution of any press release and to be available at such press conferences as may be necessary during the Term of this Agreement:

L.121

The [Company] shall not be required to bear the cost of and/or contribute to the expenses and/or any damages, interest and/or losses incurred by the [Sponsor] as a result of legal proceedings by a third party against the [Sponsor] in respect of the [Event].

L.122

The [Sponsor] agrees that in the event that any third party shall make any threats, allegations, derogatory and/or offensive statements and/or institute any legal proceedings in any country of the world in respect of [Name] and/or the [Sponsor] in respect of any advertising campaign, promotion, appearance and/or trade marks, logos, images, films , sound recordings, interviews, blogs, websites, text and/or products and/or events and/or the personal life of Name] in connection with the work of [Name] and the material created under this Agreement. That the [Sponsor] agrees to pay all the costs and sums that may be incurred by [Name] and/or his/her professional advisors to deal with the matter including legal, travel, accommodation, pr and marketing and any payments, settlements and fees, losses and damages.

L.123
The [Sponsor] agrees that where the [Company] has received a claim for less than [number/currency] and has decided to settle the matter without any admission of liability in respect of allegation which relates to the [Company] and/or the [Sponsor] at the [Event]. That the [Sponsor] will pay [number] per cent the settlement sum to the [Company] and not dispute the cost.

University, Library and Educational

L.124
The [Institute] shall have the sole discretion as to whether to take any steps, actions and/or commence any legal proceedings for any civil and/or criminal matter. The [Institute] shall not be obliged to keep the [Company] informed as to the progress in any case. The [Institute] shall not be obliged to consult with the [Company] as to the terms of any settlement and/or claim. The [Institute] shall be entitled to keep all damages, costs, interest and any other sums received as a result of any such legal proceedings and the [Company] shall have no right to any part.

L.125
In the event that any threats, allegations, claim, demand, damages, losses, and/or legal proceedings are made against the [Institute] and/or the [Licensee] in respect of the [Work/Artwork/Product]. Then the [Institute] and/or the [Licensee] shall immediately notify the other party of the details and provide copies of any documents. The party against whom the allegation is made or who receives the complaint shall provide full details to the other within [seven days] at the latest. Both parties shall assist each other as far as possible to settle or defend the matter. Each party shall bear its own legal costs but may seek to recoup them later on an indemnity basis under this Agreement.

L.126
The [Institute] and/or the [Company] shall both have the discretion to take such legal, commercial and practical steps as may be required in order to claim ownership of, protect and/or defend their rights and interest in the [Project/Work/Product]. Both parties shall have the choice whether to issue any legal proceedings, make any claim, demand, defend any action and/or whether to settle any matter and/or register any domain name, patent, copyright and any other rights and interest. Where both parties decide to take any legal proceedings they shall agree in advance the basis upon

which any costs are to be split and any damages and other losses awarded are to be shared.

L.127

In the event that legal proceedings are commenced by any third party against either the [Institute] and/or the [Company] in respect of the [Project/Work/Event] or some other matter relating to this Agreement. Then both parties agree and undertake to inform the other party of any such allegation and where necessary provide each other with assistance to resolve or defend the matter. Each party shall bear its own legal costs and expenses and consult with each other prior to any settlement. This clause shall not prevent either party seeking to be repaid any sum under the indemnity provisions in this Agreement.

L.128

The [Institute] shall have the right to defend, settle and/or resolve any threat and/or start of legal proceedings, any allegations and/or breach of any code of conduct and/or policy guidelines as it thinks fit and in the best interests of the [Institute]. The [Institute] may settle a matter without any admission of liability in order to save costs and/or publicity. The [Institute] shall not be obliged to consult with any person prior to any final decision as to the best course of action.

L.129

The [University] agrees and undertakes that it shall not be entitled to take any legal action and/or commence any legal proceedings and/or instruct any debt collection agency against any person who has attended a [course/conference/other] organised and managed by the [University] unless [number] months has expired since the sum due has been owed and/or the [University] has offered to accept payment in monthly instalments over a [twelve-]month period and that offer has been refused.

L.130

1.1 The [College] and the board of [trustees/governors] reserve the right and shall be entitled to take such action, steps and seek legal advice and/or institute any legal proceedings, security and/or police presence and/or exclude any person and/or parents and/or family members and/or friends from the [College] as may be necessary to protect the health and safety of all the students, staff and other third parties at any time.

1.2 The [College] reserve the right to cancel and/or delete and/or terminate any right of access to the [College] website and resources for any reason where they have reason to believe that there is a security risk, virus and/or threat to safety and/or infringement of copyright and/or for any other reason.

1.3 That where the [College] has a security system in place to check the content of [bags/other] on site in order to vet entry and/or exit that where a person refuses to co-operate and permit a search that access may be refused.

1.4 The [College] agrees that no physical body searches shall take place at any time.

1.5 The [College] maintains constant filming through [CCTV] in locations throughout the site. These recordings are for the purpose of security and safety and the [College] reserves the right to use and/or supply any material taken whilst you are on the site to any third party without a court order including legal advisors and the police in order to assess and/or conduct and/or to supply evidence in support of any civil and/or criminal proceedings at any time.

LIABILITY

Buildings

L.131
We agree to make good any damage to the premises [name and address] arising directly out of our use thereof subject to any damage being the direct result of and caused by the negligence on the part of the [Company].

L.132
In the event that any error or alteration in the allotment of [Space/Stand] at the Exhibition by the [Company] or in the quoted exhibition times given to any client, it is specifically agreed that the [Company] shall not be responsible in respect of any loss or damage which may arise therefrom and shall bear no liability. In such cases the [Company] will endeavour without prejudice to make a substitute arrangement, but shall not be bound or obligated to do so. The [Company] is also specifically entitled to change the position allotted to a client should circumstances render it necessary. The [Company] may at any time cancel the arrangement and return the sums paid.

L.133
The total liability of [Name] for the use and hire of the premises at [location] shall be limited to [number/currency]. The [Company] agrees that any

additional losses, damages and/or sums due to the [Company] which may arise from the actions and/or behaviour of any guests at the [Event] shall be paid for by a claim against the insurance policy for which the premiums have been paid for by [Name]. Where any sums cannot be claimed then the [Company] may not seek to be reimbursed by [Name].

DVD, Video and Discs

L.134

The [Assignor] confirms that all sums due in respect of the production of the [Film] have been paid and that the [Assignee] is not and will not be liable for any such sums.

L.135

The [Licensor] shall not35e responsible or liable for any loss or damages of any nature whether direct or indirect including any loss of profits or any consequential damages suffered or incurred by the [Distributor] for whatever reason. In the event that the [Distributor] is prevented from manufacturing, reproducing, supplying and/or distributing the [DVD/Disc] of the [Film] in any country for any reason whether due to the fault of the [Licensor] or not. The [Licensor] shall be entitled to cancel or terminate the Agreement in respect of that country and return any sum paid in advance to the [Distributor]. The [Distributor] agrees that it shall not be entitled to seek to be indemnified, or claim any costs, expenses, or damages or any other sums which may have arise or be due directly or indirectly.

L.136

The [Licensee] agrees that no additional payments shall be due in compensation if the [Licensor] does not provide any option on any rights, first right of refusal and/or chooses not to renew and/or extend the term of this Agreement after it has expired and/or in respect of any sequel.

L.137

The [Distributor] shall be liable for any loss and/or damage to the master material of the [Sound Recordings] and any photographs and other material of [Name] whilst it is in transit to and/or from and/or at any location organised by the [Distributor] for the production of the [DVD/Disc]. The [Distributor] shall ensure that there is insurance cover in place to the value of [figure/currency] per claim and shall indemnify [Name] for the full replacement value at current market value in [country].

L.138

Where for any reason the [DVD/Disc] is not produced and/or is cancelled and/or is withdrawn from the market. The [Distributor] shall not be liable to

[Name] for any sum for damage to reputation, loss of publicity and/or any other reason and shall only be liable for the sums due in clause [–].

L.139
The total aggregate liability of each of the parties under this Agreement shall end on [date] and shall be limited as follows:

1.1   The [Licensor] to the [Distributor] shall be limited to [figure/currency].

1.2   The [Distributor] to the [Licensor] shall be limited to [figure/currency].

L.140
The [Licensee] agrees and undertakes to the [Licensor] that the [Licensee] shall be responsible and held liable for all the acts, errors, omissions and/ or failures of any sub-licensees, sub-agents, distributors and/or any other third parties engaged by the [Licensee] pursuant to this Agreement. That the [Licensee] shall be obliged to pay any sums due to the [Licensor] which should have been paid by such third parties.

L.041

1.1   The [Distributor] agrees and undertakes that [Name] shall not be liable and/or asked to contribute to any sums which may arise and/or be incurred by the [Distributor] and/or any other associated third party either during the term of this Agreement and/or thereafter whether losses, damages, legal costs and expenses, loss of revenue, loss of reputation and goodwill and /or any other matter as a result of the appearance and contribution of [Name] to the [Film/Sound Recording] for the [DVD/Disc/CD/other].

1.2   The [Distributor] agrees and undertakes that 1.1 shall apply even if the subsequent behaviour, acts and/or omissions of [Name] result in publicity which affects the marketing and sales of the [DVD/Disc/CD/ other] and/or causes the [Distributor] to cancel, delay and withdraw the proposed [DVD/Disc/CD/other].

1.3   The [Distributor] agrees and undertakes that provided that [Name] completes the scheduled work for the [Film/Sound Recording] that regardless of the circumstances which may arise in the future that the [Distributor] shall have no grounds to seek repayment of any fees and/ or expenses from [Name].

L.142
The [Licensee] agrees that in the event that the [Licensee] does not exploit and sell more than [number] copies of the [DVD/CD/other] before [date] that the [Licensor] shall have the right to serve written notice to the [Licensee]

to terminate the Agreement within [number] months. In such event the [Licensor] shall not be liable for any reproduction and development costs, marketing and promotional expenses, losses and/or payments associated with the [Licensee] and/or any third parties and/or any other sums which the [Licensee] may have to pay and/or incur. Nor shall the [Licensor] be liable to repay to the [Licensee] any advance payments against royalties which have not been recouped by the [Licensee].

L.143

Where the date of release and/or launch of any [DVD/CD/other] is delayed for any reason. The [Licensee] shall not be liable to the [Licensor] for any loss of royalties for that period.

Employment

L.144

The [Employer] shall not be liable to the [Employee] or to his/her personal representatives for:

1.1 Any loss or damage whatsoever caused to the [Employee] and/or his/ her property sustained at or whilst in transit to and/or from where the [Employee] provides his/her services except to such extent as the [Employee] is able to enforce a claim under the insurance policies held by the [Employer] for the benefit of the employees.

1.2 This shall not apply to personal injury or death caused by the negligence or deliberate default of the [Company].

L.145

The [Company] agrees and undertakes that it shall be liable to the [Employee] for all direct and indirect damages, loss, costs, expenses, injury, anguish, distress and any other identifiable and recognised condition and/ or compensation that may arise out of this Agreement to the [Employee] in [country] during the existence of this Agreement and thereafter.

L.146

The [Company] shall ensure that there is a suitable insurance policy arranged and that the premiums are up to date to cover any personal injury, emotional distress, damage, loss, costs and/or expenses due to [Name] which may arise as a direct and/or indirect result of the performance of the terms of this Agreement.

L.147

The [Employee] shall follow all reasonable directions, instructions, guidelines and policies and to complete any records that may be required by the

948

[Employer] which are in place in order to comply with existing and/or future health and safety legislation and/or any other legal requirements. Failure to do so may result in the [Employee] being in breach of this contract. Where the [Employee] acts recklessly and without regard to the safety of others then the [Employer] shall not be liable to the [Employee] for any personal injury, emotional distress, damage, loss, costs and/or expenses that may arise unless caused by the negligence of the [Employer].

L.148

The [Company] agrees and undertakes that [Name] shall not at any time be held liable by the [Company] for any sums that may fall due and/or be lost and/or be incurred as a result of the work of [Name] at the [Company].

L.149

1.1 [Name] agrees that where he/she uses the facilities and services of the [Company] and/or orders and/or commits the [Company] for a matter which is for his/her own personal use and not connected to their work and/or for the benefit of the [Company]. That the [Company] may seek to charge [Name] for such sums and [Name] will be obliged to pay.

1.2 The [Company] agrees that provided payment is made in 1.1 the [Company] shall not be entitled to use these grounds to terminate the terms and agreement of employment with [Name].

Film and Television

L.150

The [Company] reserves the right at its absolute discretion to do any act or thing in respect of the transmission of any advertisement or part thereof (including the fading, editing or cutting thereof) which is found to contain unsuitable advertisement copy. The [Company] shall not incur any liability to the [Agency] or the [Advertiser] who shall have no claim whatsoever for damages or otherwise in respect of the failure to transmit the advertisement or any part thereof. The [Agency] and the [Advertiser] shall remain liable to the [Company] for the charges payable under this Agreement.

L.151

The [Company] shall accept no liability for any failure to transmit any or all of the [Advertisement/Film] for any reason or for any error in any [Advertisement/Film] transmitted. Except that if a total failure to transmit shall be entirely due to the fault of the [Company] then the [Advertisement/Film] shall not be charged for by the [Company].

L.152

Any booking may be cancelled by either party without liability provided that notice in writing is received and acknowledged by the [Company] or the [Advertiser] as the case may be more than [number] working days before [the scheduled transmission date].

L.153

In respect of the [Film] all due care has been taken to ensure that no person copying, repeating or performing the physical exercises and/or movements and/or following any of the advice, information or directions will suffer any injury or other damage.

L.154

The [Licensee] agrees that there is no obligation on the [Licensor] to grant any option on any rights and/or provide any first right of refusal and/or to extend and/or to renew the term of this Agreement and/or to grant any rights in respect of any sequel and/or any adaptation.

L.155

The [Licensee] shall be liable for all sums due to the [Licensor] for all acts, errors, omissions, failures and non-payment by any of the [Licensee's] sub-licensees, sub-agents and any other authorised third parties engaged by the [Licensee] pursuant to this Agreement.

L.156

In addition to any sums due under the Agreement the [Licensee] shall pay for all the [Licensor's] legal and professional costs for auditing, accounting together with all administration and other costs such as reproduction, telephone calls, travel, accommodation, agents fees, translation charges and interest. Provided that sufficient proof of expenditure can be supplied.

L.157

1.1 The [Distributor] shall bear all liability and be responsible for any medical and legal costs and expenses, financial losses relating to future work, loss of insurance cover, and any payments due to the estate and beneficiaries of [Name] for death, disability, personal injury or otherwise of any nature that [Name] may incur as a direct result of his/her contribution and filming for [Film] in the capacity of [sport/activity].

1.2 The [Distributor] and [Name] agree that although an insurance policy is being arranged with [specify] for [cover] for [currency/number] from [date] to [date] at the [Distributors'] cost. That any exclusions within that policy shall not apply to the liability of the [Distributor] under 1.1.

L.158
The [Licensee] shall be liable for all payments due and/or that may arise related to obtaining clearance of any copyright and/or intellectual property rights relating to the reproduction, broadcast, transmission, performance and exploitation of all lyrics, words, music, sound recordings, films and any exploitation in any format at any time and any agency and administration costs. The [Licensee] shall not be entitled to recoup and/or set off any of these sums from payments due to the [Licensor].

L.159
The [Company] agrees that [Name] may take images and film the [Event] on [date] at [location] provided that [Name] agrees that no liability is accepted by the [Company] for any costs, expenses, damages and/or loss that may arise either directly and/or indirectly to [Name] and/or any transport, computer, photography and film equipment and/or otherwise unless caused by the negligence of the [Company] and results in personal injury which causes permanent damage and/or death. In any event [Name] agrees that the total liability of the [Company] is limited for all other matters to [currency/number].

General Business and Commercial

L.160
While every reasonable care will be taken in respect of [films/recordings/goods/equipment] the [Company] cannot accept liability for the delay in delivery, loss or damage whether on the [premises] or in transit or whether or not such [Items] are supplied by the Company.

L.161
While the [Supplier] takes all reasonable care in the performance of this Agreement, generally the [Supplier] shall not be liable for any loss or damage suffered by the client or any third party arising from use or reproduction of any [Picture] or its associated title, text, graphics or otherwise.

L.162
The [Company] reserves the right at its absolute discretion to refuse at any stage to carry out and/or perform this Agreement without giving any reason. The [Agent] or the [Client] shall not have the right to any legal action or claim against the [Company] provided that all sums paid are refunded promptly.

L.163
The total aggregate liability of the [Licensor] to the [Distributor] shall be limited to [figure/currency] and all liability shall end on [date] and all claims must be notified by that date. The liability of the [Distributor] shall be limited

L.175
The Company shall not be under any liability to [Name] in respect of any claim for loss of publicity or opportunity to enhance the [Name's] reputation whether or not the [Company] stops production or exploitation of the [Work/ Services] and/or the use of [Name] have been announced publicly or advertised.

L.176
The [Company] shall not be under any liability in respect of any loss or damage to the [Agent's] property whilst it is in transit to or from or whilst at places where the [Agent] renders services hereunder, nor for any personal injury or death arising out of or in the course of the [Agent's] engagement hereunder except to such extent as the [Company] may be able to claim for indemnity against a third party or under a policy of insurance by a third party or the [Company].

L.177
Any failure to renew or extend the terms of this Agreement following its expiry shall not constitute grounds for any claim or payments whatsoever. The [Agent] agrees that it shall not be entitled to any sum(s) nor shall the [Person] for any failure to renew or extend the Term of this Agreement.

L.178
The [Customer] confirms and agrees that the [Company] is only able to provide the service at the fees set out in this Agreement on the basis that the [Company] is under no liability whatsoever. The [Customer] agrees that the [Company] is under no liability to it whatsoever for any indirect, incidental or consequential damages, loss, whether by the [Customer] or a third party making a claim on the [Customer] in respect of any interruptions, delays, inaccuracies, errors, omissions or failures at any time in respect of the [Service]. The [Customer] undertakes to indemnify the [Company] in respect of any such claim by a third party through and/or against the Customer. The terms of this Clause shall survive any termination of this Agreement and shall continue in full force and effect.

L.179
The liability of the [Company] shall be limited to [figure/currency] in any one instant. The Client agrees that any additional sums that may fall due are to be waived and are not recoverable.

L.180
The total liability of the [Company] to the [Customer/Retailer/Distributor/ other] shall be limited to [figure/currency].

L.181

The liability of the [Company] shall be limited to [figure/currency] in respect of each and every claim. The total aggregate liability for the duration of this Agreement or thereafter shall be limited to [figure/currency].

L.182

The total liability of the [Company] to the [Customer/Retailer/Distributor/other] shall be limited to the [contract price/sale price].

L.183

The total liability of the [Company] to the [Customer/Retailer/Distributor/other] shall be limited to the [number] per cent]] of [specify].

L.184

If for any reason the [Company] reaches the decision that any person and/or property is likely to and/or has caused any costs, expenses, damages and losses and/or interfered with the operation of and/or acted in a manner which is to the detriment of other people at the [Event/other].Then the [Company] shall be entitled to exclude such person and/or property from the [venue/land/property]. In such circumstances the [Company] shall not be liable for any subsequent sums that the person may have to incur and/or their failure to attend the [Event/other].

L.185

In the event that the [Company] terminates this Agreement due to the failure of [Name] to fulfil the terms as set out in clause [–]. Then [Name] agrees that the [Company] shall not be liable for any related and/or associated agreements that [Name] may have agreed and/or concluded in reliance upon this Agreement

L.186

The liability of the [Company] shall be limited to [number/currency] in the event that it shall be obliged to delay and/or cancel and/or alter the content of the material for the [Exhibition/Conference]. No additional sums shall be paid for any travel, accommodation and/or other costs you may have booked and/or incurred which relate to your attendance at the [Exhibition/Conference].

Internet and Websites

L.187

You agree and undertake and waive all claims and rights and agree that the [Company] shall not be liable to you [and/or any third party] for the use of any content on this [Website] and/or any disc, CD-Rom, software, downloads, the instructions and directions of the [Company] in respect of the development and creation and reproduction of the [Images/ photographs/logos].

1.3 The [Company] accepts and agrees that it is the responsibility and liability of the [Company] to assess whether there is any similar material and/or conflict with any existing trade mark use in the market in any country and/or whether the material is capable of being registered as a trade mark. The [Company] agrees that [Name] shall not bear any liability and/or responsibility for any sums that may become due as a result of any litigation and/or legal proceedings.

1.4 That if at any future date the [Company] requires the assistance and co-operation of [Name] that the [Company] shall agree payment terms for any such work.

Merchandising

L.197

The [Distributor] agrees to arrange and pay for insurance cover for the [Work] whilst it is in the possession of [Name] from [date] to [date] for the value of [figure/currency] per claim in [Country].

L.198

The [Distributor] shall be liable for any loss, damage, costs and expense of any [Master Material] loaned by the [Licensor] [Distributor] from the date of delivery until it is returned to the [Licensor]. The total insurance replacement value shall be in accordance with Schedule [–] which set out the material and the sum to be paid. All sums due shall be paid within [number] days of a notified claim unless written reasons have been provided for rejection of the claim.

L.199

The total liability of the [Distributor] to the [Licensor] shall not be limited. The [Distributor] shall not be held liable for the acts, errors, omissions and/or failures of any sub-licensees, sub-agents, sub-distributors and/or any other third parties engaged by the [Distributor] pursuant to this Agreement. Nor shall the [Distributor] shall be obliged to pay any sums due to the [Licensor] which should have been paid by such third parties which are not received by the [Distributor].

L.200

The total liability of the [Licensor] to the [Distributor] under this Agreement shall be limited to [figure/currency]. No further sums shall be due for any reason.

L.201

The [Licensee] agrees that where any sums are not received from any third party in respect of the exploitation of the rights. That the [Licensee] shall be held responsible and shall be obliged to pay any sums owed to the [Licensor] out of their own funds.

L.202

The [Agent] agrees that he/she shall be held liable for any losses, damages, costs and expenses and interest and charges which [Name] may have failed to be paid and/or which [Name] has suffered and/or incurred which are attributed to the negligence, failure and/or fraud by the [Agent] and/or any of its accountancy, bank, legal and/or professional advisors and/or employees and/or consultants.

L.203

1.1 The [Distributor] must ensure that it has sufficient funds available held in [country] in order to meet the payments and liabilities due to [Name] under this Agreement.

1.2 Where the parent company of the [Distributor] changes its location and is based outside [Country] then the [Distributor] agrees and undertakes to open a bank account for the deposit of a minimum of [number/currency] in [Country].

1.3 That the [Distributor] agrees and undertakes that where a sub-licensee fails to make the necessary payments to [Name] that the [Distributor] shall be obliged to make the payment to [Name].

1.4 That the [Distributor] agrees that no currency conversion and/or bank charges for the transfer of any funds in any form shall be paid by [Name] and the [Distributor] shall pay any such costs.

Publishing

L.204

The [Author] acknowledges that the [Publishers] are not insurers of the [Book/Manuscript/Drawings/Photographs] placed in their possession by the [Author] and shall not be liable for any damage, destruction or loss thereof [unless caused by the negligence of an employee or agent of the Publisher].

L.205

The [Publisher] agrees that it shall be solely responsible for any damage, loss or copying of the manuscript once it has been delivered by the [Author]. In the event that the manuscript is lost or damaged the [Author] shall be entitled to the following sum(s) in compensation. Total loss [figure/currency]. Damage [figure/currency].

L.217

In consideration of the [Work] by the [Contributor] the [Company] shall pay a fee of [figure/currency] by [date] in [cash/cheque/other] to the [Contributor] which shall be in full and final settlement. No further sums of any nature for any reason shall be due to the [Contributor] for the provision of his/her services or the exploitation of the material in any media at any time. Nor shall any additional sums be due to the [Contributor] for any reason for any failure to provide a credit and no consent shall be required to add, delete, amend, translate, adapt and/or otherwise alter all and/or any part of the [Work] in any context at any time.

L.218

The [Company] agrees that the [Presenter] shall only be liable for any direct breach of the undertakings in this Agreement in Clauses [–] from [date] to [date] and the total liability of the [Presenter] to the [Company] shall be limited to [–] at any time. In the event that there is no claim by the [Company] before [date] then any liability by the [presenter] under this Agreement shall end and no sums shall be due and/or claimed by the [Company] whether caused by the [Presenter] or not.

L.219

The [Company] agrees and accepts that it shall be entirely responsible for the legal consequences and liabilities that may arise in respect of the production, transmission, content, marketing and exploitation of the [Series] and any other associated material. That where any claim, action, demand or complaint results in the [Presenter] incurring any costs, expenses, damages, losses or other sums of any nature including legal, accountant, agent or otherwise. The [Company] shall reimburse the [Presenter] and also agree an additional sum in compensation for the [Presenter's] assistance in each case.

L.220

[Name] is not providing any indemnity to the [Company] under this Agreement and the [Company] shall not seek any sums from the [Name] for any consequence arising directly or indirectly as a result of this Agreement, whether the matter arises from a breach by [Name] or not. All liability, risk, costs, damages and expenses are the entire and sole responsibility of the [Company] at all times and not [Name].

L.221

The [Company] accepts that it shall not be entitled to seek any sums from [Name] in respect of this Agreement provided that he/she fulfils to carry out the services by [date]. All responsibility for any legal liability or proceedings which may arise from the use of any material collected, obtained or provided under this Agreement and in the product of the services shall be at the sole cost, risk and expense of the [Company].

L.222

No liability shall be attributed to [Name] in the event that there is an error, omission or other inaccuracy and/or any allegation, claim, legal proceedings, complaint and/or objection in respect of the content, clearance and/or any intellectual property rights and/or any other rights, obligations or otherwise in any media of any nature in respect of the development, production, transmission, distribution, supply, licensing, and/or exploitation of the [Work/Service] in any country at any time.

L.223

Where for any reason the [Supplier] has to vary, cease and/or interrupt the services provided to the [Company] due to a change in circumstances of the availability of [material/other] for the [Supplier] which would affect its ability to fulfil the service as required. Then the [Company] agrees that the [Supplier] shall not be liable for any losses, damages and expenses and costs that may arise and the [Company] accepts the risk and liability at its own cost.

L.224

In the event that the service under this Agreement is terminated by the [Supplier] and the [Company] is unable to arrange a suitable substitute at short notice and is therefore forced to cancel the [Event/Exhibition/Festival]. Then the [Supplier] shall be liable to pay for all the expenses and costs of all sums relating to and associated the cancellation of that [Event/Exhibition/Festival] and rescheduling a new one including the cost of administration and advertising by the [Company] and third party agreements.

Sponsorship

L.225

1.1 The [Licensee] shall be fully liable to the [Licensor] for all acts, omissions, errors, and failures with respect to any third party engaged or appointed by the [Licensee] in respect of the [Licensor's Logo] and the [Licensor's Product].

1.2 The [Licensor] agrees and undertakes that the details of the content and the materials of the [Licensor's Logo] and the [Licensor's Product] delivered to the [Licensee] shall be complete and accurate. The [Licensee] shall not be liable to the [Licensor] under 1.1 provided that either are used in a manner and detail authorised by the [Licensor].

1.5 [–] upon first release of the [DVD/Disc] to the public in [country].

1.6 [–] upon the [DVD/Disc] achieving sales figures of [number] units in [country].

1.7 [–] upon the [DVD/Disc] winning the [specify] award.

1.8 [–] upon the [Licensee] receiving gross receipts from the exploitation of the [DVD/Disc] of [figure/currency] at any time and from any country.

L.257

'The Licence Fee' shall mean the sum of [figure/currency] which is a total sum payable by the [Licensee] as follows:

1.1 [–] upon signature by both parties to this Agreement.

1.2 [–] upon delivery and acceptance of the [Master Material].

1.3 [–] on or before [date] subject to the completion of the production of the master of the [Disc].

L.258

The 'Licence Fee' the sum of [figure/currency] which shall be paid by the [Licensee] to the [Licensor]. The [Licensee] may not set this sum off against any future royalties that may fall due nor shall it be returned by the [Licensor] if the [Project] does not proceed for any reason.

L.259

1.1 The [Distributor] shall pay a fee of [number/currency] to [Name] for the attendance at the filming and/or sound recording and/or photography for the [DVD/Disc/other] in accordance with the Work Schedule in Appendix [–].

1.2 The [Distributor] shall in addition pay the [Agent] [number/currency] subject to the completion of work by [Name] in 1.1

1.3 The fees paid in 1.1 and 1.2 shall not be repaid under any circumstances and may not be recouped by the [Distributor] from any other sums due to [Name] and/or the [Agent] under this Agreement.

L.260

1.1 The [Distributor] shall pay [Name] a fee of [number/currency] on [date] subject to the completion of the sound recordings by [Name] at [location] on [dates].

1.2 Where additional sessions for editing and adapting any material are required then the [Distributor] agrees to pay an additional fee of [number/currency] for each [number] hours completed by [Name] at the [Distributors'] request. All fees shall be paid monthly in arrears.

Film and Television

L.261

In consideration of the rights granted the [Company] shall pay the [Television Company] a royalty fee of [figure/currency] per item or part thereof actually broadcast by the [Company]. Such sums shall be paid in arrears at the end of each calendar month.

L.262

'The Licence Fee' means the fee of [figure/currency] payable by the [Licensee] to the [Licensor] in respect of the rights licensed by the [Licensor] to the [Licensee] under clause [–]. The Fee consists of [figure/currency] in respect of [specify rights] and [figure/currency] in respect of all other media. The fee is payable as a royalty advance which the [Licensee] shall be entitled to recoup under clause [–].

L.263

In consideration of all the services rendered by [Performer/Guest] hereunder the [Company] shall pay [Performer/Guest] the sum of [figure/currency] within [specify period] of the date of signing this letter [subject to the provision of the services and satisfactory completion of the work].

L.264

'The Licence Fee' shall mean the sum of [figure/currency] which is a total sum payable as follows:

1.1　[–] upon signature by both parties to this Agreement.

1.2　[–] upon approval of the Delivery Items as specified under Clause [–] to this Agreement.

L.265

In consideration of the rights granted in this Agreement the [Licensee] shall pay to the [Licensor] a fee of [figure/currency] which shall be payable as follows:

1.1　[–] on full execution of this Agreement and subject to approval of the full outline.

1.2　[–] subject to approval by the [Licensee] of [the rough cut of the [Film].

1.3　[–] on acceptance by the [Licensee] of the [Film Material].

1.4　[–] on or by [date] subject to completion of 1.1 to 1.3.

L.277

The [Company] agrees that it shall not be entitled to any advance licence fee from [Name] and that all payments by [Name] to the [Company] shall be subject to exploitation of the material and receipt of payments by [Name] in [country].

L.278

Where the [Company] fails to pay the Licence Fee by [date] then this Agreement shall end and all rights granted by [Name] shall be revoked and the [Company] shall not have any copyright and/or intellectual property rights under their control relating to the [Project/Work].

Internet and Websites

L.279

The licence fees for the use and/or exploitation of any [Material] to be downloaded and/or supplied from this [Website] must be agreed and paid in advance prior to the supply, transfer, downloading, reproduction and/or distribution of any [Material].

L.280

The total fee per [Unit] shall be [figure/currency] [words] which shall be payable when the [Unit] has been downloaded and the sum paid to the [Company].

L.281

The [Contributor] shall receive [number]% [words] per cent of the total [Usage Access Fee] per [Unit] shall be [figure/currency] [words] which shall be payable when the [Unit] has been accessed and clicked on by a member of the public and the sum received by and not returned by the [Company]. All fees shall be paid to the [Contributor] at the end of each [one month calendar] period and an accounting statement provided.

L.282

The [Customer] shall pay the [Company] a fixed fee of [figure/currency] per unit download on the [Website] to make [number] copy on their [specify equipment].

L.283

Where any licence fee and/or other fee charged by the [Company] is not paid by a [Customer] and/or payment is rejected at a later date by a bank. Then the [Company] shall be entitled to charge an additional administration fee for the costs incurred in collecting the sum due.

L.284
'The Contributor's Fee' shall be the sum of [figure/currency].

L.285

1.1 The [Company] charges a supply licence fee of [number/currency] per copy to access and download the complete copy of the [Work] per person for your own personal use at home for educational purposes for school and/or college and/or university.

1.2 It does not include supply to third parties and any such occurrence will result in the issue of additional fees, charges and costs.

1.3 It does not include any undertaking that any copyright and/or other intellectual property rights are owned and/or controlled by the [Company].

Merchandising

L.286
'The Non-Returnable Advance' shall be the sum of [figure/currency] payable by the [Distributor] to the [Licensor].

L.287
'The Licence Fee' shall be the sum of [figure/currency] payable to the [Licensor] which can be recouped against the royalties due to the [Licensor] until it has been paid back to the [Licensee].

L.288
No advance under this Agreement may be set off against any sums due under any other agreement between the parties at any time.

L.289
In consideration of the rights granted in this Agreement the [Licensee] shall pay to the [Licensor] a licence fee of [figure/currency] which shall be payable as follows:

1.1 [–] upon signature of both parties of this Agreement.

1.2 [–] subject to the acceptance by the [Licensee] of a copy of the [Master Material].

1.3 [–] upon approval of the [final version] by the [Licensor].

1.4 [–] upon first release to the public of the [Work] in [specify format] in [country].

L.290

The Licence Fee shall be repaid to the [Licensee] where the [Master Material] is not delivered by the date specified and/or the technical quality is not of sufficiently high quality for its intended purpose and so it has been rejected.

L.291

The [Distributor] agrees to pay the [Company] a licence fee as follows:

1.1 [Number/currency] upon delivery to and acceptance by the [Distributor] of copies of master material in clause [–].

1.2 [Number/currency] after approval by the [Company] of the sample prototype of the [Product].

1.3 [Number/currency] after the first date of release of the [Products] to the public in [country].

1.4 [Number/currency] after the first release of the [Products] in [language]. The [Distributor] shall be entitled to recoup these sums due in 1.1 to 1.4 from any future payments due to the [Company] under this Agreement.

Publishing

L.292

The [Publisher] shall pay the [Author] the following advance [figure/currency] which shall be on account and set off against all sums that may become due to the [Author] under this Agreement as follows:

1.1 [–] on signature of this Agreement by both parties hereto; and

1.2 [–] on [date] subject to delivery and approval of written evidence of sufficient progress such as outline of chapters and draft chapters; and

1.3 [–] on [date] subject to delivery and approval of the complete manuscript and photographs; and

1.4 [–] on [United Kingdom] hardcover publication of the [Work] by the [Publishers] [but in any event no later than [date] whichever is the earliest.

L.293

The [Publisher] shall pay to the [Agent] on behalf of the [Author] the following advance [figure/currency] which the [Publisher] shall not under any circumstances be entitled to recover except for failure to deliver the [Work] nor shall the [Publisher] be entitled to set the advance off against future royalties:

1.1 [–] on signature by both of this Agreement.

1.2 [–] on [date] subject to approval of [draft chapters/other].

1.3 [–] on [date] subject to delivery and approval of the [manuscript and disc].

1.4 [–] on first publication of the hardback of the [Work] by the [Publishers] or by [date], whichever is the earlier.

1.5 [–] on first publication of the paperback of the [Work] by the [Publishers] or by [date], whichever is the earlier.

1.6 [–] upon the hardback of the [Work] achieving [sales] figures of [number] units in [country] according to [specify source].

1.7 [–] upon a [DVD] based on the [Work] winning the [specify] award.

1.8 [–] upon the [Publisher] receiving gross receipts from the exploitation of the [Work] from any source in any country in excess of [figure/ currency].

L.294

The [Publishers] agree to pay the sum of [figure/currency] to the [Author] as a recoupable advance against royalties which may become due to the [Author] under this Agreement [which shall only apply to the first edition] and be paid as follows:

1.1 The sum of [figure/currency] on signature of this Agreement.

1.2 The sum of [figure/currency] on the receipt and approval by the [Publishers] of the copies of the manuscript and disc of the [Book] as set out in Clause [–].

1.3 The sum of [figure/currency] on or before [date].

1.4 The sum of [figure/currency] upon first publication of the [Work] of a hardback of the in [country].

1.5 The sum of [figure/currency] upon first publication of the [Work] of a paperback of the [Book] in [ountry].

All the sums specified in 1.1 to 1.5 shall be recoupable by the [Publisher] from the royalties due to the [Author]. In the event that for any reason there are insufficient royalties to recoup 1.1 to 1.5 the [Publisher] shall not be entitled to reclaim such sums directly from the [Author].

L.295

The [Publishers'] agree to pay the [Author] the following sums:

1.1 [–] within [7 days] of signature of this Agreement by both parties which shall be as non-recoupable advance and not to be offset against any royalties.

977

1.2 [–] within [10 days] of delivery of the first [number] pages of the manuscript.

1.3 [–] within [7 days] of acceptance by the [Publishers] of the [Work].

1.4 [–] on delivery of the marked up proofs to the Publisher.

1.5 [–] upon publication of the hardback of the [Work] but in any event not later than [date].

1.6 [–] upon publication of the paperback of the [Work] but in any event not later than [date].

1.7 [–] upon general release to the public of the [audiocassette/other] but in any event not later than [date].

L.296

The [Publishers] agree to pay the [Author] in advance and on account of all sums payable under this Agreement the sum of [figure/currency]. One third on signature of this Agreement, one third on delivery of complete copy and one third on first publication.

For the avoidance of doubt the advance payments set out above payable to the [Author] under this Agreement shall be repaid to the [Publishers] if there remains any unrecouped balance on the [Author's] account upon termination or expiry of this Agreement. Any unrecouped balance shall be repaid to the [Publishers] upon service of written notice on the [Author] to that effect [and without prejudice the Publishers agree to negotiate a repayment schedule with the [Author] over a one year period].

L.297

The [Author] agrees that if the [Publisher] refuses to accept and have valid reasons for rejecting the manuscript of the [Work]. That the [Author] shall repay all and/or such proportion of the advance as may be requested by the [Publisher], in regular instalments over a period of not more than [one year].

L.298

The [Publisher] agrees that as the [Author] has used and/or spent the advance on research, travel and/or other material relating to the [Work] prior to delivery as originally envisaged. The advance shall not be repayable by the [Author] even if the [Work] is not published by the [Company] for any reason.

L.299

The [Publisher] agrees that no part of the advance shall be reclaimed by the [Publisher] from the [Author] for any reason once the manuscript has been accepted and the [Publisher] may only offset it against future royalties.

L.300

In consideration of the permission granted by the [Licensor] for the use of the [Character/book] as a strip cartoon in the [specify magazine] for a period of [specify weeks] for publication in the [specify] language in [countries] by the [Licensee]. The [Licensee] shall pay the [Licensor] a fee of [figure/currency] for each picture strip published in the magazine each week. Such sums shall be payable immediately upon invoice. For the avoidance of doubt it is agreed that this sum is not related to the circulation figures of the magazine.

L.301

The [Publisher] shall be entitled to offset and recoup the advance for the [Work] against future royalties received from the publication of the [hardback/paperback] of the [Work] and any other sums received from the exploitation of the [Work]. In the event that for any reason there are insufficient royalties to recoup the advance the [Publisher] shall not be entitled to reclaim such sums directly from the [Author] and/or his agent.

L.302

The [Publisher] shall only be entitled to offset the [Licence fee/Advance] in clause [–] against royalties received for the [Book] in [hardback/paperback] in [Country].

L.303

The [Publisher] shall not be entitled to offset and/or claim back any unrecouped advance from the [Work] against any other work, book, option, licence, contract or otherwise that the [Publisher] may have with the [Author] at any time.

L.304

The [Distributor] shall not be obliged to pay any licence fee and/or other payment to [Name] for contributing to and supplying the [Blog] on the [Website]. [Name] agrees that no fee shall be due and that the [Distributor] may exploit, supply and distribute the [Blog] and/or any part as it thinks fit provided that [Name] is credited and any use is not defamatory, mocking and/or likely to adversely affect the reputation of [Name].

Services

L.305

The total licence fee due to the [Agent] for the supply of the services of [Name] shall be [number /currency] which shall be in addition to any fees and payments due to [Name].

L.306

The [Company] shall not be entitled to add and/or charge any additional copyright clearance payments, insurance costs, planning, licence fees and/or any other sums in addition to the cost of the service.

L.307

The licence fee charged by [Name] is for a fixed period of [number] months. Any additional use will incur an additional licence fee payment. The [Company] reserves the right to increase the fee and shall not be obliged to charge the same rate and/or provide the same service.

Sponsorship

L.308

'The Sponsorship Fee' shall be the sum of [figure/currency].

L.309

In consideration of the services of [Name] the [Sponsor] shall pay [Name] the Sponsorship Fee as follows [figure/currency] upon full signature of this Agreement and [figure/currency] by [date] subject to the completion of the work by [Name].

L.310

The [Sponsor] agrees that the Sponsorship Fee shall be paid despite the fact that [Name] may be unable to provide his services under this Agreement due to illness or ill-health provided that it is supported by a medical certificate from a qualified doctor or consultant.

L.311

In the event that the [Company] does not wish to use the [Sponsor's] Logo and/or products due to adverse publicity and/or other allegations regarding the [Sponsor], its officers, directors and/or products. The [Company] shall be entitled to terminate this Agreement without any further liability provided that it repays the [Sponsorship Fee] to the [Sponsor].

L.312

'The Placement Fee' shall be the sum of [figure/currency].

L.313

1.1   The [Sponsor] shall pay the [Company] a fee of [number/currency] by [date] as a payment for access to and use of the following facilities by persons who work at the [Sponsor] [specify].

1.2 The [Sponsor] agrees that this Agreement is not exclusive and that the [Company] may also be funded by any other sponsor and/or third party that it thinks fit including a competitor in the same market.

University, Library and Educational

L.314
The [Contributors] Fee shall be the sum of [Figure/currency] [words] which shall be paid to the [Contributor] as follows:

1.1 [–] within [twenty-one] days of the signature of this Agreement by the [Contributor] and the [Institute].

1.2 [–] upon delivery and acceptance of the [Work/Report/Service] by the [Institute].

1.3 [–] on and/or by [date] provided that 1.1 and 1.2 have been completed.

L.315
'The Licence Fee' shall mean the non-returnable sum of [figure/currency] [words] payable by the [Company] to the [Institute] under this Agreement. This sum cannot be offset and/or recouped against any other payment due to the [Institute].

L.316
In consideration of the rights granted by the [Institute] to the [Company], the [Company] shall pay the [Institute] the Licence Fee as follows:

1.1 [–] upon signature of this Agreement by both parties.

1.2 [–] on or before [date] subject to the delivery and acceptance of the material in Clause [–] to the [Company].

1.3 [–] upon publication of the hardback of the [Work] but in any event not later than [date].

1.4 [–] upon publication of the paperback of the [Work] but in any event not later than [date].

1.5 [–] upon general release to the public of the [CD/DVD/Disc].

1.6 [–] upon the [CD/DVD/Disc] achieving sales figures of [number] units in [country/worldwide].

L.317
The [Institute] agrees to pay the [Author] the following sums:

1.1 [–] within [twenty-eight] days of signature of this Agreement by both parties which shall be a recoupable advance which can be offset against future royalties.

1.2 [–] within [twenty-one] days of the acceptance by the [Institute of the [Work].

1.3 [–] upon publication of the [Work] in [format] by the [Institute] and/or any licensee.

L.318

The [Author] agrees that the Licence Fee shall be reclaimed by the [Institute] in the event that the [Author] fails to deliver the material specified in Clause [–] and/or the material is rejected on reasonable grounds and the [Author] has had the opportunity to remedy the matter and failed to do so.

L.319

The Licence Fee set out above payable to the [Author] under this Agreement shall be repaid to the [Institute] if there remains any unrecouped balance on the [Author's] royalty account upon termination or expiry of this Agreement. Any unrecouped balance shall be repaid to the [Institute] upon service of written notice on the [Author] to that effect and without prejudice to any repayment schedule which may be agreed with the [Author].

L.320

The [Institute] shall be entitled to offset and recoup the Licence Fee paid to the [Author] for the [Work] against future royalties due to the [Author] received from the exploitation of the [Work] in any media at any time. In the event that, for any reason, there are insufficient royalties to recoup the Licence Fee. The [Institute] shall not be entitled to reclaim such sums directly from the [Author] and/or his agent. Nor shall the [Institute] be entitled to offset and/or claim back any unrecouped Licence Fee from the [Work] against any other work, book, option, licence, contract or otherwise that the [Institute] may have with the [Author] at any time.

L.321

Where a fee is charged by the [Institute] for access, reproduction and/or other use of the facilities at [address]. These fees are not confirmation and/or supply of copyright clearance and use of the material for which an additional licence fee and other royalties will be charged subject to the conclusion of a licence agreement.

LICENCE PERIOD

General Business and Commercial

L.322
The [Company] hereby grants to the [Acquirer] an option to extend the Licence Period for a further period of [specify length] (or such other period as is specified in schedule) exercisable at any time prior to the expiry of the Licence Period and upon payment to the Company of a fee set out below [–].

L.323
'The Licence Period' shall commence upon the date of this Agreement and shall continue until [date/event/the completion of all transmissions].

L.324
The Licence Period shall commence as from the full execution of this Agreement and shall continue for a period of [two years] unless terminated at a prior date.

L.325
The Licence Period shall commence on the date the Agreement is signed by both parties and shall continue for a period of not less than [one year]. Thereafter it shall continue until such time as terminated by either party in accordance with Clauses [–] below. The [Licensee] shall always be liable to the [Licensor] for any and all proceeds from the commercial exploitation of the [Licence Articles] whether within the Licence Period or not.

L.326
The Licence Period shall be subject to:

1.1   The exercise of any Option under Clause [–].

1.2   The extension of the Licence Period by reason of force majeure under Clause [–] and other specific circumstances under Clause [–].

1.3   The payments due to the [Licensor] after the expiry of the Licence Period as set out in Clauses [–].

1.4   The undertakings and indemnity provisions under Clauses [–].

L.327
The Licence Period shall mean the period commencing from the first theatrical release of the [Film] in the [Territory] which shall not be later than [date] and shall continue for a period of [ten years] from that date.

L.328

The Licence Period shall commence on [date] and continue to (but not including) [date]. The Company shall supply the [Service] to the [Licensee] on such dates and at such times as specified in Schedule [–].

L.329

'The Licence Period' shall commence on the date of this Agreement and shall continue for a period of [seven years] from the date of acceptance by the [Licensee] of the [Film Material] set out in Clause [–].

L.330

The present licence agreement commences on [date] and terminates automatically on [date].

L.331

The Licence Period shall commence on the date of this Agreement and continue for a period of [ten] years from the date of first publication of the [hardback/paperback] of the [Work].

L.332

'Licence Period' Start Date [–] End Date [–].

L.333

'The Licence Period' in respect of the [Product] shall commence on the earlier of the acceptance of the [Material] by the Company and [date] and continue until the expiry of a period of [specify duration] from [date].

L.334

'Licence Period' shall commence on the date of this Agreement and shall continue for a period of [specify length] unless terminated earlier or extended in accordance with the terms of this Agreement.

L.335

The Licence Period shall commence on [date] and continue for a [three-month period] provided that payment is made in advance for each period and neither party serves notice to bring the Agreement to an end at the next expiry date.

L.336

The Licence Period shall commence on the [date] of this Agreement and continue for a period of [five years] from the [date] of first release to the general public of the [Licensed Article] in [country].

L.337

The [Company] agrees that there is no right of renewal, extension and/or variation of the Licence Period.

L.338

There is no option to extend the Licence Period.

L.339

'The Sponsorship Period' shall commence on [date] and continue until [date].

L.340

The Licence Period shall begin on [date] and continue for a period of [number] years and expire on [date].

L.341

The Licence Period shall be for the duration of the [Event] and shall begin on [date] at [time] and end on [date] at [time].

L.342

The licence period granted is for a period of [number] hours from the time of the completion of the download.

L.343

The [Licensee] shall not have any right to have the agreement renewed nor shall the [Licensee] have any right of first refusal in respect of any sequel and/or other adaptation and/or development.

L.344

1.1   The licence shall be held by the [Company] and shall not be transferable to any third party.

1.2   The licence shall commence on [date] and end on [time] on [date] on the last day of the [Event/Festival].

1.3   The licence shall be terminated by [Name] if any of the requirements set out in the document known as [specify] as attached as Appendix [–] are not complied with at all times.

L.345

1.1   The licence period shall commence on the date of the confirmation by the [Company] of [Name] in the [sport] team for the [Company] which shall be no later than [date] and shall continue thereafter for [one] year.

1.2   There shall be no automatic right of renewal, extension and/or any option for a further period.

1.3   The licence period shall continue for the full period even if [Name] is removed from the team by the [Company], suspended and/or suffers ill health, disability and/or dies at any time.

L.346

The parties in the [Consortium] shall all be granted the same licence period for the [Work] which shall commence on the date of this Agreement and continue for a period of [number] years. After that period no party shall be entitled to exploit the [Work] unless all the parties agree new terms and conditions.

L.347

The licence period in respect of your use of the [App/Game] shall commence on the date that you access, download and are supplied the use of the material by the [Company] and end at the end of a period of [six] months. The access code will no longer work after that period has expired.

LINKS

Internet and Websites

L.348

The database rights and taxonomy in the Links are owned by the [Company].

L.349

The [Company] is not responsible and/or liable for any links that you may follow from this [Website]. There is no assurance as to whether they are genuine or not and/or whether their contents and/or any cookies and/or viruses will cause damages, losses, loss of personal data, and/or any other problem. The [Company] does not monitor the links and does not endorse and/or make any recommendation in respect of the links which are used at your own risk and cost.

L.350

The [Company] reserves the right to remove any link from the [Website] at any time as it thinks fit without any reason.

L.351

No charge is made by the [Company] for the link to its [Website] by any third party. The listing as a link does not permit the third party to use the trade mark, logo and/or name of the [Company] and/or to represent that the parties are a joint venture and/or partners in business and/or otherwise.

L.352

Any third party who has a link on this [Website] shall not be entitled to represent that the [Company] is endorsing their website and/or business and/or is in any form engaged in business with the third party.

L.353

Any such third party with a link shall pay the [Company] a fee of [figure/currency] per [month] to be listed on the [Website] in the following format [specify].

L.354

Any links created by the [Company] which are attached to and/or displayed and/or connected to this [Website] may be deleted, edited, varied, blocked and/or added to at any time.

L.355

Where any person posts a link and/or reference to other material available on another website and/or through any business. The [Company] reserves the right to edit and delete any such reference at any time without notice. There is no right to promote and/or market any third party whether charitable, educational and/or commercial.

L.356

In the event that any person and/or company should post comments, images, films, sound recordings, links and/or any other material in any medium and any format on the [Website/App/Forum/other] which in the view of the [Distributor] are likely to cause offence, incite violence, corrupt any software and/or hardware, be connected to a political campaign and/or be obscene, invade the privacy of any individual and/or affect the reputation of the [Distributor] and/or for any other reason. Then any such material shall be removed without notice and the account blocked and no sums shall be paid by the [Distributor] to any person for the cancellation and/or termination of the account, access and/or otherwise.

987

LOAN OUT

General Business and Commercial

L.357

The term 'Loan Out' shall refer to a contract in writing between [Name] and the [Company] to which [Name] has agreed to provide his or her services.

L.358

In consideration of the payments made under this Agreement by the [Company] to the [Employer], the [Employer] undertakes to procure that the [Employee] will forward an Inducement Letter signed by the [Employee] and addressed to the [Company] which incorporates the terms and obligations of the Loan Out Agreement between the [Company] and the [Employer].

L.359

The [Company] agrees and undertakes that there shall be no transfer, loan, hire and/or request that the [Employee] be required and/or obliged to provide his/her services to any other parent company, subsidiary, firm, business and/or other venture under this Agreement.

LOCATION ACCESS

General Business and Commercial

L.360

The [Company] confirms the arrangements made and terms of agreement by the [Owner] to grant filming facilities to the [Company] to be used in the [Film] [brief description].

L.361

That the [Owner] owns and controls the freehold land and property [reference land registry/other] and there are no reasons why the [Owner] does not have the absolute right to grant the [Company] access to and use of the land and property for the purpose of rehearsals, filming and storage of equipment for the [Film] [title/brief description] on the following dates and times [specify].

L.362

That in consideration of the filming facilities the [Company] shall pay a fee of [figure/currency] exclusive of any value added tax due on or before [date].

L.363

That the fee is in full and final settlement and that no further sums shall be due to the [Owner] for the use of the material in any form.

L.364

That the [Owner] is entitled to grant access to and use of the filming facilities and no further releases, consents, rights of way, and/or other permissions are necessary except [specify local authority/other].

L.365

That there is no obligation to provide an on-screen credit in the [Film] to the [Owner].

L.366

The [Company] agrees and under takes that it shall be responsible for any electricity, utility, water, telephone and other bills and charges that may be incurred by the [Company] and/or the [Owner] whilst the [Company] is in occupation from [date] to [date] together with any loss and/or damage and/or expenses arising from the use of the land, property and storage by the [Company].

L.367

The [Company] undertakes to arrange and pay for comprehensive public liability insurance of not less than [figure/currency] per claim for the benefit of [specify parties].

L.368

The [Company] agrees and under takes that it shall ensure that the [location] is left in good order after use, and clear all rubbish, repair all damage and reimburse the [Owner] for any losses, damage and wear and tear up to a maximum of [figure/currency].

L.369

The [Company] undertakes that the material filmed on [location] and any marketing, advertising and promotional material for the [Film] will not be used by the [Company] in any manner which will bring the [Owner] into disrepute or is defamatory to the [Owner] and/or which is obscene, defamatory, offensive and/or prejudicial to the value of the [Owner's] [land and property].

L.370

The [Company] shall indemnify the [Owner] in respect of any financial loss, costs, expenses, loss of goodwill, damage, wear and tear by the [Owner] and/or any claim, complaint, demand, action or otherwise arising from the use, storage, access and filming and exploitation of the [Film] at any time from [date] to [date] up to a maximum limit of [figure/currency].

L.371

The [Owner] agrees and undertakes that they shall not be entitled to any additional sums and the [Company] shall only be obliged to pay the [Location Access Fee]. Any electricity, telephone, utility, rates and/or any financial loss, costs, expenses, loss of goodwill, damage, wear and tear and/or any claim, complaint, demand, action or otherwise arising from the use, storage, access and filming and exploitation of the [Film] at any time relating to the [Owner] and/or the land and/property shall be at the [Owner's] sole cost and risk.

L.372

Where a location is to be used for filming of material for the advertisement and marketing of a [Product]. Then the [Company] shall ensure:

1.1   That the [Product] has been approved by the [Owner].

1.2   That the material to be filmed is suitable for an audience on [television] at [time].

1.3   That the name and address of the location will not be made available in any press release.

1.4   That any additional filming and photo shoots shall be for an additional fee and subject to a separate agreement.

L.373

The [Company] shall ensure that the location is left in the same condition as when they started. Where any damage and/or losses are caused by the [Company]. The [Owner] shall arrange for [two] quotes to replace and/or repair the damage and agree the cost in advance with the [Company]. Where the [Owner] repairs the damage then a rate of [fee] per hour may be charged in addition to the material costs. Where the parties are unable to agree then the parties shall agree on an independent mediator paid for by the [Company].

L.374

The [Company] shall not have the right to use and/or adapt the name of the [house/location] and/or business of the [Owner] and/or to use any associated logo, trade mark, service mark and/or otherwise. There is no licence and/or grant of intellectual property rights under this Agreement to the [Company].

L.375

1.1   Where any person is permitted access for any reason you must comply with the reasonable directions and instructions of the [Company] and any security staff.

1.2   There is no right to access any area of the venue which is marked restricted, private and/or locked.

1.3   There is no right to take any images and/or film any area of the venue including by mobile phone.

1.4   There is no right to record any voice and/or interview and/or conversation with any personnel.

1.5   There is no right to dispose of any material at the venue and/or to cause any damage and/or to remove any material.

1.6   In the event that you are requested to leave the venue and refuse the [Company] shall use its security guards and film you as well as summon the police for assistance.

1.7   There is no right to use and/or access any telecommunication system, equipment, electricity, gas, water and/or other resource unless consent is provided by a member of staff.

LOGO

DVD, Video and Discs

L.376
The [Licensor] agrees to pay for the cost of supplying a master copy of the [Licensor's Logo] for reproduction by the [Distributor] in the [DVD/Disc].

L.377
The [Distributor] agrees and undertakes to put the following trademark, logo, text, image and credits to the [Licensor] on the content of the disc, the label, the outside of the Disc, the cover and in all press releases, posters, publicity, promotional, advertising and packaging material in respect of the [Disc] of the [Film/Work] as set out in Appendix [–] which forms part of this Agreement [specify size, shape, position on each type of material].

L.378
The [Distributor] agrees and undertakes to reproduce and display the [Licensors'] master material of the logo, trade mark, images, text and shapes in the exact size and colour that they are supplied. The [Distributor] shall not change, alter and/or vary any part without the prior approval of the [Licensor].

L.379

The [Distributor] agrees and undertakes that it shall not acquire any copyright, trade mark and/or other intellectual property rights in the master material owned and/or controlled by the [Licensor] including but not limited to any logo, trade mark, images, text and shapes.

L.380

The [Distributor] agrees that no part of this Agreement is intended to transfer any copyright, design rights, future design rights, domain name, trade mark, service mark, community mark, business name, trading name, invention, patent including any developments or variations in the master material of the [Licensors'] logo, trade mark, images, text and shapes to the [Distributor]. The [Distributor] agrees that all such rights in relation to such material are the sole and exclusive property of the [Licensor].

L.381

1.1 The [Designer] has created and developed a computer generated three dimensional moving image of the [Logo] which has been commissioned by the [Company] which is in different colours and formats as described in Schedule [–] entitled the [New Logo].

1.2 The [Designer] agrees to assign all copyright, intellectual property rights, computer software and design rights and any other rights and/or interest in the [New Logo] to the [Company] throughout the world and universe for the full period of copyright and all other period of intellectual property rights and any additional terms forever and without limit and in respect of all new rights and/or developments created at any time in the future in return for the payment of the [Commission/Fee] and [Budget] attached in Schedule [–].

1.3 The [Designer] agrees to provide all original and copies of all preparatory and development material to the [Company] which he/she may have in his/her possession at the [Company's] cost. The [Designer] agrees that he/she shall not retain any material except [specify].

1.4 The [Designer] agrees that he/she shall not receive any additional payment for the work and/or any registration of the [New Logo] and/or any exploitation and/or adaptation in any form at any time.

Employment

L.382

Where any [Employee] whether temporary, permanent and/or otherwise contributes to and/or designs and/or creates any new logo, slogan, lyric, image, photograph, film, sound recording, title, recipe, blog, website, app, invention, patent, trade mark and/or any other computer software, hardware, new technology, process and/or method of telecommunication which is entirely original and/or based and/or derived from other work by the [Company]. The [Employee] shall not own and/or control any copyright, intellectual property and/or any other rights of any nature in any such material and shall not be entitled to receive any sums from any form of exploitation, registration and/or sale at any time.

L.383
The [Company] acknowledges that the [Employee] owns and controls the following rights and material set out in Schedule [–] prior to the date of this Agreement.

L.384
The [Company] agrees that where the [Employee] designs, creates and/or invents a new logo, product and/or patent and/or any other new material which is original and which the [Company] wishes to produce and/or exploit. That the [Company] shall be obliged to negotiate a licence agreement with the [Employee] and the [Employee] agrees that the [Company] shall receive not less than [number] per cent of the sums received from the exploitation.

Film and Television

L.385
During the course of the [Programme] the [Television Company] undertakes that the [Sponsor's Logo] will appear on screen for not less than [number seconds] or not less than [number] separate occasions and further that the [Sponsor's Logo] will appear in the course of the [Programme] in the following circumstances and background to view [specify].

L.386
The [Television Company] agrees to ensure that the broadcast or transmission of the [Sponsor's Logo] and [Products] will not infringe any sponsorship, product placement or advertising codes, standards, rules, directives or statutes concerning the [Sponsor's Logo] and/or products including its size, shape, colour, wording, on-screen position or general nature and in particular those in existence issued by the following bodies and organisations [specify].

L.387
The [Production Company] agrees to provide the following trademark, logo and credits to the [Sponsor] in any publicity, promotional, advertising and packaging material in respect of the marketing and distribution of the [Film] [specify size, shape, position on each type of material].

L.388

The [Licensee] agrees that it shall be solely responsible for all costs and expenses incurred in respect of reproducing and incorporating the [Licensee's Logo] in the [Film/Product].

L.389

The [Licensor] agrees that the [Licensee] may use and/or reproduce the [Logo/Trade Mark/Image] in respect of an archive and/or on demand television and computer service known as [specify] in [country] by means of satellite, cable, terrestrial, WiFi and other forms of telecommunication and for viewing on computers, laptops and other portable gadgets from [date] to [date].

L.390

The [Licensor] agrees that the [Licensee] may use and/or reproduce the [Logo/Trade Mark/Image] in conjunction with its [Film Festival] in [year] at [location] to promote, market and endorse the proposed programme and catalogue.

General Business and Commercial

L.391

The [Licensee] warrants that:

1.1 All uses of the [Logo] upon the [Products] will be in accordance with the terms of this Agreement and no modification may be made to any part of the [Logo] which shall always be used in the format set out in the Schedule hereto.

1.2 It shall not make any challenge against the rights of the [Licensor] in the [Logo] or its validity in any way provided that the [Licensor] shall not be in breach of any of its warranties in relation to the [Logo].

1.3 If the [Licensee] becomes aware of any unauthorised use of the [Logo] within the Territory it will promptly notify the [Licensor] with appropriate details.

1.4 No other logo, image or wording will be used on any of the [Products] together with the [Logo] except with the prior written approval of the [Licensor].

L.392

The [Agent] may use the trade names, service marks, logos and icons set out in Appendix [–] or as otherwise specified by the [Company] in writing solely in the promotion and/or sales of the [Products] during the Term of this Agreement. The [Agent] acknowledges that all rights in relation to such material are the sole and exclusive property of the [Company] and that this Agreement is not intended to vest or transfer any interest to the [Agent].

L.393
The [Agent] acknowledges that it shall not acquire any title in the [Product Samples], the [Product], or the [Company] Logo. The [Agent] confirms that all goodwill and reputation created in the [Company] Logo shall remain the sole and exclusive property of the [Company] and that no part of this Agreement is intended to transfer any copyright, design rights, domain name, trade mark, service mark or any other rights in the [Company] Logo, the [Product Samples] or the [Product] to the [Agent] including any developments or variations.

L.394
'Logo' shall mean a two-dimensional graphic representation capable of registration as a trademark [under the Trade Marks Act 1994 as amended].

L.395
The [Company] Logo shall be the following trademark, design or logo together with any associated words briefly described as follows [specify]. A two-dimensional copy of the [Company] Logo is attached to, and forms part of, this Agreement.

L.396
The [Promoter's] Logo shall be the design, logo and trademark together with any accompanying words of the [Promoter] to be used for all promotion, advertising and marketing of the [Festival]. A copy of the [Promoter's] Logo is attached to, and forms part of, this Agreement.

L.397
The [Licensee] agrees to ensure that all third parties to be contracted by the [Licensee] under this Agreement will agree that all copyright and any other rights concerning the [Licensor's] Logo shall remain the sole and exclusive property of the [Licensor]. That the [Licensee] and all such third parties shall not acquire, nor represent that they own and/or control and/or attempt to register any rights, interest and/or goodwill in any the [Licensor's] Logo nor any trademark, logo, service marks, title, text, slogan, catchphrase, image, artwork or otherwise or any developments, variations or adaptations in any language at any time which is based on, derived from and/or associated with it.

L.398
The [Licensor] confirms and undertakes:

1.1 That it is the sole owner of or controls all intellectual property rights, trade marks, service marks, and any other rights in the [Licensor's] Logo throughout the [country] which is attached to and forms part of this Agreement in Schedule [–].

1.2 That the [Licensor's] Logo is registered with the following [authorities/ organisations] as follows [specify registration reference].

1.3 That the [Licensor] is not aware of any claim, allegation, complaint and/ or threat of legal action by any third party relating to the [Licensor's] Logo.

L.399

The [Licensee] acknowledge that all copyright, trademarks, service marks, design rights and any other rights in the [Licensee's] Logo together with any goodwill shall belong to and remain the sole property of the Licensor. The [Licensee] shall not acquire any rights or interests in the [Licensor's] Logo or in any trademark, design, title, artwork, in any medium including any developments or variations whether provided by the [Licensee] or a third party.

L.400

The [Company] agrees that the prior written approval of the [Manufacturer] shall be required in the event that the [Company] intends to promote, market or exploit the [Product] or the [Manufacturer's] Logo by any of the following means: publicity, advertising, promotional material, fashion shows, television, radio, newspaper, magazine features or articles and any other material or event or on any other method.

L.401

The [Company] confirms that it is the sole owner of or controls all copyright and any other rights in the [Company's] Logo and that the use of the [Company's] Logo under this Agreement will not expose the [Licensee] to any criminal or civil proceedings and that the [Licensee] shall not acquire any rights or interest in the [Company's] Logo including any developments or variations.

L.402

1.1 The [Consortium] acknowledge and agree that the trade marks, logos, images and slogans are owned and controlled by the following parties as set out in Schedule [–] which form part of this Agreement.

1.2 That this Agreement is not intended to transfer, assign and/.or licence any of the trademarks, logos, images and slogans in Schedule [–] to any other member of the [Consortium] and/or to entitle them to claim any revenue and/or sums from any exploitation and/or registration.

Internet and Websites

L.403

All trademarks, logos, brands, trade names, titles, names, products, slogans, catchphrases, ringtones, sound and domain names which are displayed and exhibited on this [Website] belong to a person, firm and/or company who own and control the rights. You need to contact them directly in order to copy, reproduce, transfer, attach, distribute and/or otherwise exploit their material. We have not provided any authorisation for you to use their material for your own personal use and/or for any commercial project. We cannot be liable to you for any claim they may make against you for any unauthorised use of their material.

L.404

The [Company] own and control the Logo known as [specify detail] which you may download in conjunction with the material relating to it on this [Website] for your own personal use at home whether in printed format, on a disc or onto the hard drive of your computer. There is no authorisation and/or consent to any reproduction for commercial purposes, but you may refer to this [Website] and the Logo and the associated material for criticism and/or review in the media and/or educational reasons by pupils, students and/or higher education establishments.

L.405

The [Customer] shall not delete, erase, change, alter and/or vary the [Company's] logo, trade mark, images, text and shapes which are on any services and/or products supplied by and/or downloaded from the [Website] by the [Customer].

L.406

No person and/or company who uses this [Website] shall have the right to reproduce on their own website and/or for any other purpose a copy of the [Company's] trade mark and logo [specify]. No person and/or company is entitled to represent that they own, control, have been authorised under a licence and/or shall attempt to register any interest with a third party and/or otherwise use the trade mark and logo.

L.407

There is no authority granted to reproduce, exploit and/.or distribute any logo and/or trade mark on this [App] to any third party except in the exact form, colour, words, shape and position in which it appears in conjunction with the material on this [App].

L.408

The [Licensor] agrees that you may make [one] copy of the [Product/App/Material] for your own personal use but not for school and university and other educational establishments, charitable and/or commercial purposes provided that no credits, acknowledgements, trademarks and logos are removed, deleted and/or adapted and no additional copies are made and/or distributed to any third party.

Merchandising

L.409

The [Licensor] agrees to supply at its cost and expense such exact master copies of the trade mark and/or logo and/or any other credit required by the [Licensee] in respect of all publicity, advertising, packaging, marketing, distribution and exploitation of the [Licensed Articles] by the [Licensee].

L.410

1.1 The [Licensee] agrees and shall ensure that any sub-licensee agrees to provide the following credit, copyright notice, trade mark and logo to the [Licensor] in respect of the [Licensed Articles] and the packaging in the positions and size specified in the attached Appendix [–] which is attached to and forms part of this Agreement.

1.2 The [Licensee] agrees that the [Licensor] shall be entitled to approve an exact sample of the [Licensed Articles] and packaging prior to reproduction for the public. The [Licensor] shall provide written approval or rejection of the sample within [number] days of delivery. Failure by the [Licensor] to reply within that period shall be deemed approval of the sample.

L.411

The [Licensor] shall not have a right of approval over all material for publicity, advertising, marketing, distribution of the [Licensed Articles] by the [Licensee]. The [Licensee] agrees to consult with the [Licensor] and where there is a trademark, logo and/or credit to the [Licensee] also include one to the [Licensor] in the same size and location.

L.412

The [Distributor] agrees and undertakes that all copyright, design rights, future design rights, computer software rights and intellectual property rights in the [Character/Product] together with any trade marks, service marks, community marks, logos and associated domain names and goodwill and any developments and/or adaptations are and/or shall be owned and controlled by the [Licensor].

L.413
'The Company's Logos' shall mean the designs and the associated texts, images and colours. A two-dimensional copy of the Company's Logos is attached to and form part of this Agreement.

L.414
Where during the course of this Agreement [Name] develops, creates and/ or registers a new logo and/or trade mark and/or any other marketing and/ or promotional material associated with his/her personal name and/or public name and/or sport activity which is/are owned by [Name] and/or any holding company. Then in the event that the [Company] wish to use any of the new material in any form the [Company] shall be required to enter into a new licence agreement with [Name] as that new material does not form part of this Agreement.

Publishing

L.415
The title of the [Work] shall belong to the [Authors] and the [Publisher] agrees and undertakes that it shall not have any right to claim ownership and/or register and/or apply for any trade mark, logo and/or to register as the copyright owner in that exact form and/or any variation and/or adaptation of words, shapes and/or colour.

L.416
In the event that the [Publisher] commissions a designer and/or requests an employee and/or consultant to create any artwork, photographs, images, typography, index, titles, character names and/or cover and/or slogan. The [Publisher] agrees that all such material shall be owned jointly by the [Author] and the [Publisher] and that no material shall be used, adapted and exploited without the prior written approval of the [Author] in each case and that the [Author] shall be entitled to [number] per cent of any sums received by the [Publisher] in such case.

L.417
The [Publisher] agrees that it may not add any new logos, trademarks and/ or other credits to the [Work] and/or any adaptation without the prior written approval of the [Author] of the exact proposed sample.

Services

L.418

There is no right granted by the [Consultant] for the [Company] to use the personal name and/or business name and/or logo of the [Consultant] in relation to any corporate document, application and/or marketing unless the [Consultant] has viewed and approved the material and provided his/her consent in each case.

L.419

The [Agent] does not own and/or control the personal name, stage name and/or slogans, logos, scripts, films and/or marketing material of [Name]. No rights are granted by the [Agent] to any third party and all material must be cleared with [Name] directly by email to [specify].

Sponsorship

L.420

The [Sponsor] confirms that it is the sole owner of or controls all copyright, trade marks and any other intellectual property rights throughout the world in the [Sponsor's] Logo. The [Sponsor] confirms that the [Sponsor's] Logo does not infringe the copyright or any other rights of any third party throughout the world.

L.421

The [Sponsor] agrees to bear all costs of creating the [Sponsor's] Logo and of supplying the [Sponsor's] Logo in a form acceptable to the [Company] for incorporation in its [brochure/programme].

L.422

The [Company] confirms that the [Sponsor's] Logo will be reasonably, prominently and clearly identifiable in the [brochure/programme] and in any event will not be less than the following dimensions [specify].

L.423

The [Sponsor] agrees to provide to the [Organisers], at the [Sponsor's] sole cost and expense, all suitable artwork of the [Sponsor's] Logo in order for it to be reproduced in all printed material under the control of the [Organisers] by the following date [–].

L.424

The [Organisers] confirm that the design, artwork, and wording of the [Sponsor's] Logo shall be at the sole discretion of the [Sponsor] subject to prior consultation with the [Organisers].

L.425

The [Organisers] confirm that whenever possible they will ensure that the [Sponsor's] Logo will be present in accordance with this Agreement and that the [Promoter] has undertaken to the [Organisers] to use its best endeavours to ensure that the [Sponsor's] Logo is incorporated in all promotional, advertising and publicity material.

University, Library and Educational

L.426

No person, company and/or supplier is entitled to reproduce the logo, shield and/or trade mark of the [Institute] in any form without prior consent of the [Institute] and/or to represent that they have their endorsement, support and/or represent their interests and/or associated with them by reproducing the name, logo, shield and/or trade mark on any business card, website, app, blog and/or otherwise.

LOSS

General Business and Commercial

L.427

'Loss' shall include all loss of whatever nature, including goodwill.

L.428

'Loss' shall mean direct and indirect financial loss but shall not include any payments which might otherwise be due in respect of personal injury or death.

L.429

Notwithstanding anything in this Agreement to the contrary, it is agreed that neither the [Contractor] nor the [Company] shall be held liable to the other party for loss of production, loss of profit, loss of use, or any other indirect or consequential damage or loss of any kind.

L.430

The [Company] agrees that it shall accept any order obtained by the [Agent] entirely at its sole risk and that the [Agent] shall not be liable for the failure of any [retail store or retail outlet] to pay any sums that may be due to the [Company] as a result of [shipment/delivery] of any such order.

L.431

The [Agent] agrees that it shall only be entitled to the [Agent's] Commission and the fee for the Term of the Agreement subject to the continuance of the Agreement and shall not be entitled to any other sums, garments, compensation, cancellation fee or otherwise from the [Company].

L.432

The [Agent] agrees that it shall be solely responsible and the [Company] shall not be liable for the costs and expenses incurred by the [Agent] in the provision of its services under this Agreement including, but not limited to, travel, accommodation, entertainment, meals, equipment, telephone, publicity and promotional material, insurance, freight, rent.

L.433

Notwithstanding any advertisement or announcement which shall have been made the [Company] shall be under no obligation to make use of the [Work] or to include the same or any parts in any [Film] or [Programme] and the failure of the [Company] to do so shall not give rise to any claim by the [Writer] whatsoever including, but not limited to, any claim for loss of opportunity to enhance his/her reputation or loss of publicity or damage to his/her reputation or otherwise.

L.434

Both parties agree that in the event that any of the [Work/Licensed Articles] should be destroyed as a result of fire, flood, marine peril or any other circumstances beyond the control of the Company no royalties shall be due or paid on any of the [Work/Licensed Articles] which are destroyed.

L.435

The [Company] is under no liability whatsoever for any damages or loss of profit claimed by the [Customer] in respect of any interruptions, delays, inaccuracies, errors, omissions or failure to transmit.

L.436

In the event any property of the [Contractor] is lost or damaged in the course of transportation by aircraft or vessel to [specify] then the [Contractor] shall be entitled to compensation from [Name/address].

L.437

The [Customer] is responsible for loss or damage to the [Product] occurring between the time the [Product] is delivered to the [Customer] and the time it is returned to the [Company].

L.438

The [Company] does not operate an insurance scheme for the [Product]. The [Customer] is responsible for safety and care of the [Product] and any that are lost or returned damaged will be charged to the [Customer] at [figure/currency] per [Product] plus value added tax.

L.439
If the [Licensee] fails to or delays the return of any [Item] to the [Licensor] or fails to forward or delays the forwarding of such [Item] to any other person as directed by the [Licensor], then the [Licensee] agrees to pay the [Licensor] the amount of any loss or damage so caused to the [Licensor].

L.440
If any [Item] is lost, stolen, destroyed, damaged or disappears between the time of delivery thereof by the [Licensor] and the return by the [Licensee]. The [Licensee] shall immediately notify the [Licensor] in writing and shall pay the [Licensor] the cost of replacement thereof. Any property which is damaged when delivered by the [Licensee] to the [Licensor] shall be deemed to have been damaged by the [Licensee] unless the [Licensee] has previously notified the [Licensor] that the property was damaged when delivered to the [Licensee].

L.441
Each party shall immediately give notice to the other of any loss or theft of any [Item] licensed to it hereunder and if so requested shall deliver an affidavit sworn by a person having personal knowledge of the facts setting out the information in detail.

L.442
Risk and responsibility for [Item] passes to the [Client] from the time that they are received until their safe return. The [Client] shall inform the [Supplier] in writing of any loss, damage, or other harm to the [Item] while in the [Client's] possession or control. If the [Item] is not returned within [specify length] of the date upon which it is due to be returned to the [Supplier], then the [Supplier] shall be entitled to deem that the [Item] has been lost or otherwise disposed of. The [Client] shall be liable to pay compensation to the [Supplier] in respect of each [Item] which is lost or damaged or otherwise harmed as follows [specify]. The [Client] agrees that the payment of compensation does not entitle the [Client] to any rights or interest in the [Item]. An [Item] which is subsequently returned when compensation has already been paid shall entitle the [Client] to a [fifty] per cent refund of the compensation.

L.443
'Loss' shall mean any damage and/or sum incurred, derived from, or otherwise arising whether direct and/or indirect and/or howsoever caused as a result of the failure by the [Contractor] to fulfil the terms of this Agreement to the [Company]. Loss shall include but not be limited to design, supply,

delivery, testing, breakdowns of power supply, interruption of service, increase production, manufacture and/or supply of material costs, loss of profits, damage to other equipment, alteration of personnel.

L.444

The [Contractor] shall not be liable for any of the following categories of losses which may arise and/or be incurred by the [Company] under this Agreement:

1.1 Any loss and/or damage which does not directly arise from the services of the [Contractor].

1.2 Design faults due to the nature of the material and/or any request by the [Company].

1.3 Delays in delivery due to changes in the original specification by the [Company] and/or force majeure.

1.4 Testing and compliance with legislation which results in the delay of the [Project].

1.5 Breakdowns and interruptions of equipment, power and service.

1.6 Loss of profit by the [Company].

1.7 Damage to equipment, data and property of the [Company] and any officer and/or employee and/or any other third party involved with the [Project].

1.8 Increase production, manufacture and/or supply of material costs.

1.9 Cancellation of any contracts, publicity, advertising and/or lapse of any consents, permissions and/or grants, funds and/or facilities.

L.445

Where a publisher and/or distributor suffers a loss as a result of the failure of a ghostwriter to deliver a {Work}. Then the total liability of the [Licensor] shall be limited to the total sum of the advance paid to date. No sums shall be due to compensate the publisher and/or distributor for loss of sales, withdrawal of marketing material and/or any other costs that may have been incurred.

L.446

If the weather conditions result in the cancellation of the [Event]. Then the [Company] shall not be obliged to repay the [Sponsorship Fee] to the [Sponsor]. Nor shall the [Company] be obliged to pay the [Sponsor] for any losses, costs and/or expenses that it may incur directly and/or indirectly as a result of the cancellation.

L.447

Where a sub-licensee fails to pay any funds due and/or ceases to operate and/or does not fulfil the terms of the sub-licence. Then any such losses, expenses, damages and costs that may be incurred by either party to resolve the matter shall be at their own cost. Further the [Licensee] shall not be liable to pay a royalty to the [Licensor] in respect of any sums it has not received from the [Sub-Licensee].

L.448

In the event that a product recall of the [Licensed Articles] results in losses, damages, fines and/or other costs and expenses to the [Licensee]. Then these sums shall be the [Licensees'] responsibility and not attributed to and/or shared by the [Licensor].

L.449

In the event that any person suffers any loss of data and/or damage to their software, laptop, gadgets, mobile and/or in any other form and/or suffers any other malfunction due to a virus and/or interruption to the service as a result of the use of the telecommunication service including WiFi supplied by the [Company] at [location]. Then the total liability of the [Company] shall be limited to [number/currency] which shall be supplied in the form of a voucher for future use at [location] and no financial payment shall be made at any time.

L.450

The location is not secure and members of the public use these premises and the [Company] cannot accept liability for any loss of equipment including laptops and/or mobile phones and/or headphones and/or other personal and/or business material which may be left on the floor, tables, in lockers and/or in any other manner on the site. You use this location at your own risk and shall bear the cost and responsibility of any loss and costs and expenses that may arise whether due to theft, accidental damage and/or otherwise.

L.451

There is a real risk that this investment may make a loss as well as make a gain and it is entered into by you at your own risk with the knowledge that you may lose all the fund supplied to the [Company] and not receive any payments.

MARKETING

Building

M.001
The [Contractor] agrees and undertakes that it shall not nor shall it permit and/or authorise any sub-contractor, employee, or other person engaged by the [Contractor] to release, supply, distribute and/or publish material, data and/or information of any nature relating to this contract or its contents or the [Project] without the prior [written] approval of the [Company]. The [Contractor], its sub-contractors, employees and other persons engaged by the [Contractor] shall be permitted to release their own personal and corporate data, information and material to professional advisors or government bodies for the purpose of legal, tax, health, safety or accounting reports, compliance and payments.

M.002
The [Contractor] agrees that it shall not be entitled to arrange and/or permit any advertising, promotional marketing and/or other material to be displayed, exhibited and/or reproduced on the hoardings, exterior walls, buildings, or otherwise of the [Land] and/or equipment and/or structure. That the [Company] shall have the sole right to exploit and retain any revenue from advertising, promotional material, sponsorship, marketing or public relations. and/or any other material to be displayed, exhibited and/or reproduced on the hoardings, exterior walls, buildings, land, equipment, structure or otherwise at any time.

M.003
Neither the [Project] nor any clothing, structure, land, equipment owned or operated by the [Company] or any marketing material, exhibition, promotional [DVD/Film] may be used by the [Contractor] or sub-contractors with regard to any marketing, promotions, advertising or publicity by them and/or any other person without the prior written consent of the [Company].

M.004

The [Contractor] agrees that it shall send to the [Company] at its sole cost copies of all material which it would like to use for publicity, marketing or promotional purposes whether website material, printed or in any other media which bear any name, logo, slogan, image, trade mark, quote or text relating to the [Company] and/or the [Project] or any of its clients. The [Company] shall then be entitled to reject or approve any such material which the [Contractor] agrees to delete or amend as requested.

DVD, Video and Discs

M.005

The [Assignor] acknowledges that the [Assignee] shall have the sole discretion as to the manner and method to be used in marketing, promoting, publicising and advertising in respect of the [DVD/Video/Disc] Rights assigned under this Agreement.

M.006

The [Company] undertakes to arrange for the development, production and release of at least [number] promotional [DVDs/Videos/Discs] at its sole cost and expense featuring the [Artist/Group] which shall be available for marketing purposes at the same time as the commercial release of any [recording/single/album/website material which can be downloaded] in [country] as follows:

1.1   DVD [minimum duration/location/budget/language/other].

1.2   [Video/Disc] [minimum duration/location/budget/language/other].

M.007

The [Company] agrees and undertakes not to place any advertisements, promotions and other material relating to the following groups and persons [specify] on the [DVD/Disc] and/or any material of any nature which is to be released and/or distributed to the media, public and/or displayed, exhibited and/or reproduced which relates to [Name].

M.008

The [Company] shall submit to the [Licensor] for approval in advance prior to production, publication, distribution, or release all sales literature, advertising material, brochures, catalogues, posters, labels, packaging, shop display material, promotional extracts and website material of the [DVD/Disc] in any shape, form or media. The [Company] shall take into account all changes and amendments made by the [Licensor] and shall then resubmit any such material for approval by the [Licensor]. No material shall be released unless it has been approved by the [Licensor].

M.009

The [Licensor] agrees to provide the [Licensee] upon request [at the Licensor's sole cost/on loan] the following promotional material and artwork for use in the creation of the packaging of [DVDs/Disc] of the [Film] and associated advertising and marketing:

1.1 Press cutting books, photographs, transparencies, artwork, designs, stills, and biographies of the principal artists, characters, author, writers, director, composer and musicians.

1.2 Sales literature, brochures, catalogues, posters, labels, packaging, shop display material, promotional extracts and website material.

1.3 The brand and style book of the [Licensor] together with accurate and precise copies of all copyright notices, trade marks, service marks, logos, and images.

1.4 A comprehensive full list and order of priority of the copyright notices, trade marks, service marks, logos, images, credits, disclaimers, copyright warnings, and any other contractual obligations.

M.010

The [Distributor] shall at all times have the right at their sole discretion to decide upon the production schedule, the release dates, the supply, subscription, sale, rental, and distribution prices, discounts, and price reduction strategy and promotional offers and the marketing of the [DVDs/Discs].

M.011

The [Assignee] confirms that it shall use its best endeavours to exploit the [DVD/Video/Disc] Rights assigned under this Agreement and to achieve as far as possible the maximum Gross Receipts.

M.012

The [Licensor] agrees to supply to the [Distributor] promptly upon request on loan at the at the [Licensors] request:

1.1 Samples of any advertising and promotional material held by the [Licensor] including photographs, biographies of the presenter and other contributors in connection with the [Film].

1.2 Such photographic negatives, transparencies, packaging, labels and other material as may be available for use in the promotion and advertising of the [DVDs/Discs] distributed hereunder.

M.013

The [Licensor] shall provide the [Distributor] with written instructions of any restrictions in respect of the use of any material, details of any copyright or other usage fees that may be due, and details of who owns the material. The [Distributor] shall only be permitted to use any material in respect of the distribution, sale, subscription and rental of [DVDs/Discs] under this Agreement which shall include any packaging, publicity material, or catalogues. The [Licensor] shall invoice the [Distributor] and the [Distributor] shall pay the full cost of the supply of such material including reproduction costs, delivery, customs and other incidental charges.

M.014

The [Distributor] shall be entitled to use the name, photograph, image and brief biography of the [Writer] in any commercial exploitation of any film and/ or DVD [and/or Disc] in respect of which the [Writer] has provided his/her services under this Agreement.

M.015

The [Distributor] shall be under no obligation to produce, manufacture, distribute and/or exploit any film or DVD in respect of which the [Writer] has rendered his/her services under this Agreement. In the event that there is any advertising, publicity or announcements by the [Distributor] or another party this shall make no difference and the [Writer] shall not have any right to a claim for loss of publicity, reputation, damage or otherwise from any failure to exploit or any cancellation.

M.016

The [Assignee] agrees upon request to provide the [Assignor] at the [Assignees] sole cost with copies and samples of all material created, reproduced, commissioned, issued, distributed and released by the [Assignee] to market, advertise, and promote the [DVDs] of the [Film] including but not limited to: press releases, publicity, packaging material, labels, CD-Roms, website material, banners, competitions, merchandising.

M.017

The [Assignee] confirms that it shall be responsible for any sums due in respect of the distribution, marketing and exploitation of the [DVD/other] Rights in the [Film] and any parts including any payments due in respect of the performing rights in any music and any sums due in respect of the mechanical reproduction of the [Film].

M.018

1.1   The [Licensee] undertakes that throughout the Term of this Agreement it will diligently and conscientiously manufacture, distribute, sell, rent, make available for hire by subscription and promote [DVDs/Discs] of the [Films] in the Territory.

1.2   The [Licensee] shall use its best efforts to ensure that copies are available in all markets in the Territory.

1.3   The [Licensee] shall have the final decision in respect of all aspects of the manufacture, distribution, price, sale, rental, subscription price and marketing of [DVDs/Discs] of the [Films].

M.019

The [Licensor] grants to the [Distributor] the right to use and publish in respect of the [Characters/Artists] whose performances are reproduced in the [Programmes] or any other person concerned in the making of the [Programmes], their legal and professional names, photographs and likenesses for cataloguing and exploiting the Videograms under this Agreement.

M.020

The [Distributor] may use and permit the use of excerpts of up to [three minutes] duration from the [Films] for the purposes of promotion, advertising and/or trade and in-store demonstrations.

M.021

The [Company] may without further payment use and permit the use of excerpts from the [Film] and/or soundtrack and/or images and/or text on television, radio, computer, video, telephone and any other media for the purpose of programme announcement trailing, criticism, and review, promotion and advertising, provided that the aggregate total of excerpts shall not exceed [five minutes] in total [of the same material]. There is no limit on the usage which shall be unlimited provided it is within the Licence Period and not for the purpose of sponsorship and/or endorsement of a product, article, film, person or business. This right shall be in addition to those rights set out in Clause [–].

M.022

The [Company] may incorporate extracts of other films provided that they are in the same type of market and rating as the [Film] on any copies reproduced under this Agreement for the purpose of promoting that film which is also in the catalogue of the [Company].

M.023

The [Company] shall have the right to authorise others to transmit/broadcast a short extract of the [Film] which shall be agreed with the [Licensor] and shall not exceed [two minutes].

M.024

The [Distributor] shall not have any merchandising, licensing, endorsement or sponsorship rights of the [Film] and/or any material created under this

Agreement not the right to appoint any sub-agent and/or sub-distributor, and/or any other person and/or company.

M.025

The [Licensee] may design, manufacture and create, at its own expense and cost, advertising, promotional and packaging material for the exploitation of the rights in the [Film] granted under this Agreement. The [Licensee] shall ensure that the material conforms in all respect with the contractual and moral obligations of the [Licensor] and all notified copyright notices, credits, trade marks and logos. All samples of every item shall be supplied in advance of distribution to the public and manufacture so that the [Licensor] may approve the details. The cost of the samples and freight shall be at the [Licensee's] cost to be deducted from the receipts.

M.026

All material of any nature in any media which is to be used on the DVD and/or in association with the [Film] for the exploitation of the [DVD/Disc] Rights shall be submitted to the [Licensor] for their prior written approval. The [Licensee] shall abide by all requirements of the [Licensor] as to colour, layout, title, copyright notices, credits, trade marks, logos and any other text, images and content.

M.027

The [Licensee] agrees and undertakes not to use any website, telecommunication system and/or mobile and landline telephone to sale, rent, and/or hire the copies of the [DVDs/Discs] which has not been agreed in advance with the [Licensor].

M.028

The [Licensee] agrees and undertakes that it shall not market, exploit and/or sell, hire, supply, and/or make available the [DVDs/Discs] in the following countries, and on aeroplanes, ships, vessels, oil rigs and/or other structures on the sea, in the air and/or transport [specify].

M.029

The [Licensee] shall not be entitled to licence and/or authorise the downloading, display and/or use of the [Film] in any form by means of the internet and/or a website. The [Licensee] shall only be entitled to a promotional film of [number] seconds supplied by the [Licensor] at the [Licensees] cost for the purpose of a banner advertisement for the [DVD/Disc] from [date] to [date].

M.030

The [Licensee] agrees that it shall not have the right to market any sound recording, title, character, and/or other part of the [Film] separately at any time and/or to authorise any third party to do so.

M.031

The [Licensee] agrees that it shall not be entitled to reproduce, create, develop, sell, supply, market, promote and/or exploit the [DVD/Disc/CD] of the [Film/Programme] in any of the following formats and/or mediums and/or countries and/or languages:

1.1 That there is no permission and/or consent and/or right to supply, rent, lend, sell and/or exploit the [Film/Programme] and/or [DVD/Disc/CD] in an electronic and/or digital format by any means as an ebook, download and/or another method of supply whether for free and/or at a commercial rate over the internet and/or any telecommunication and/or delivery system from any website, mobile and/or gadget in whole and/or in part at any time.

1.2 That there is no permission and/or consent and/or right to promote and/or market and/or use any part of the [Film/Programme] and [DVD/Disc/CD] in any advertisements on television and/or websites, links, television programmes whether terrestrial, cable and/or satellite and/or any exhibition and/or event whether educational, for charity and/or otherwise except those specified [–].

1.3 That there is no permission and/or consent and/or right to sub-licence and/or authorise the use by any third party of any part of the [Film/Programme] and/or [DVD/Disc/CD] except by a member of the public purchasing a copy for their own personal use at home only.

1.4 The [Licensee] acknowledges that the following countries are excluded from this Agreement [specify].

1.5 The [Licensee] acknowledges that the following languages are excluded from this Agreement [specify].

1.6 The [Licensee] acknowledges that there are no associated merchandising rights granted under this Agreement and the [Licensee] is not authorised to reproduce and/or supply any posters, stickers, confectionary, T shirts and/or any other products of any nature whether sold at a price and/or given away for free to promote the [DVD/Disc/CD].

1.7 The [Licensee] acknowledges that there are no right to authorise and/or produce any computer game, computer software and/or blog and/or app and/or to register with any collecting society and/or government

1013

and/or regulatory body any title, character name, place name, logo, image and/or slogan and/or text which forms part of and/or is associated with the [Film/Programme] and/or any work on which it is based at any time.

Film and Television

M.032

The [Licensor] shall provide to the [Company] without extra charge, any promotion and publicity material, stills, photographs and any commercially produced trailers for the [Film] as may be available.

M.033

The [Licensee] agrees to provide the following credit, copyright notice, trade mark, logo, slogan and image to the [Licensor] in the [Series] and in any advertising, publicity, promotional or packaging material in respect of the marketing and distribution of the [Series] which is set out in Schedule [–] and forms part of this Agreement. The size, position and location of such information shall be as clear and prominent as that for the [Licensee] in each case, and shall be legible and visible to the public.

M.034

1.1   The [Licensor] agrees to provide to the [Licensee] on loan any artwork, stills, photographs, biographies of the principal persons or other material that may assist the [Licensee] to exploit the rights granted under this Agreement.

1.2   The [Licensor] agrees that the [Licensee] shall be entitled to arrange for copies to be made of such material at the [Licensee's] cost so that the original material may be returned to the [Licensor] by an agreed date.

1.3   The [Licensee] agrees that any material shall only be used for the purpose of the promotion, marketing and commercial exploitation of the [Series] and that any other use shall be subject to the prior written consent of the [Licensor].

1.4   The [Licensee] agrees to be bound by any restrictions, credit or obligations that the [Licensor] may at any time specify which are required by the [Licensor] and/or any third parties in respect of such material.

1.5   The [Licensee] shall not be entitled to sub-licence, exploit and/or transfer rights in the material to any third party for any purpose who must contact the [Licensor] direct.

M.035

In respect of all publicity and promotional material for the [Film] it is agreed that no other party shall appear in vision more frequently, or prominently, than the [Artist] in any promotional extracts of the [Film], advertisements, stills, photographs, posters, likenesses, artwork, labels, catalogues, merchandising and packaging.

M.036

It is the intention of the [Company] to designate a distributor for the [Film] and to negotiate such terms with the distributor so as to ensure that [Production Company] will be entitled to not less than [forty-five per cent] of the Distribution Income [without further deduction of any costs relating to marketing, promotion and/or advertising].

M.037

The [Licensor] acknowledges that the [Licensee] shall have the sole discretion as to the manner and method to be used in marketing, promoting and advertising the [Film] and/or parts in respect of the rights granted under this Agreement.

M.038

The [Licensee] confirms that it shall use its best endeavours to exploit the rights granted under this Agreement and to achieve as far as possible the maximum Gross Receipts.

M.039

The [Licensee] agrees to provide to the [Licensor] at the [Licensee's] cost and expense copies and samples of any labels, packaging material, brochures, DVDs, CD-Roms, Discs, newspaper, magazine and television advertising, publicity, promotional, merchandising, sponsorship, endorsements and reviews in respect of the marketing and distribution of the [Film] and/or parts and any associated material of any nature every [two months] in the first year and at the end of each calendar year thereafter.

M.040

The [Licensee] confirms that it shall be solely responsible for any sums due in respect of the exploitation of the [Film] and/or parts and that the [Licensor] shall not be liable for any such payments.

M.041

The [Licensee] shall be entitled to use, license and permit the use of excerpts of the [Film] and/or parts for [advertising/publicity/marketing/sponsorship/endorsement] purposes only of the [Film/Company/Sequel/Products] for [television/radio/video/DVD/Discs/CDs/websites] provided that the total aggregate duration shall not exceed [number] [minutes] of the [Film].

M.042

The [Company] shall have the non-exclusive right in the Territory during the Term of this Agreement to use and broadcast and/or transmit excerpts of the [Film] on [television/radio] of not more than [three minutes] each for the purpose of any advertising, publicity, promotion or review of the [Film] and/or any sequel, the [Company] and/or any selection of films which includes the [Film].

M.043

The [Company] shall have the non-exclusive right in the Territory during the Term of this Agreement for the purposes of advertisement, publicity, promotion and/or review to reproduce and publish in any language a synopsis, or summary of not more than [number] words from the script of the [Film] in any printed format whether newspapers, magazines, trade journals, posters or otherwise and/or to a website company on the internet and/or a telephone company and/or a television or radio or news agency company and/or any other media and/or to authorise others to do so. Provided that at all times all parties agree and undertake to be the following associated credits, copyright notices and acknowledgement [specify].

M.044

The [Company] shall have the non-exclusive right in the Territory during the Term of this Agreement for the purposes of advertisement, publicity, marketing, and review only to use and to permit third parties to use in sound and/or vision the name, physical likeness, voice and biography of any actor, writer, director, or contributor to the [Film]. Provided that such use shall not constitute either an implied or direct endorsement of any product and/or services of any kind, merchandising or other activities other than the [Film] alone.

M.045

The [Television Company] shall have the right to use promotional excerpts from and make trailers of the completed [Series] as it sees fit to promote the [Series] and shall have access to any set or location during the course of production for the making thereof and/or shall be entitled to require the [Production Company] to produce trailers or to make available materials for this purpose.

M.046

Neither the [Licensor] nor the [Distributor] shall grant nor permit the exercise of the rights granted to the [Television Company] by any other person, company or body. Nor shall the [Licensor] or the [Distributor] execute any document or do anything in derogation from the rights granted under this Agreement. The [Licensor] and the [Distributor] shall have the non-exclusive right to permit any cable, satellite, terrestrial, or digital television company in the [United Kingdom/Europe/other] to transmit and/or broadcast excerpts from the [Film] of up to [three minutes] in total on any one occasion in programmes for the purpose of review, criticism, or promotion of the [Film]. The same excerpt of the [Film] shall be used on each occasion.

M.047

The parties agree that the advertising, marketing, publicity and promotion of the [Film] shall be the responsibility of the [Company]. Any matter relating thereto shall be passed to them to deal with whatever the nature of the issue. Failure to adhere to Clause [–] shall be considered by both parties as a significant breach of this Agreement. All personnel, artists, agents, writers, advisors, financiers, composers and musicians and other persons involved in the [Film] shall be advised accordingly in writing of this stipulation.

M.048

The [Licensor] shall make available at no extra cost and/or charge any trailers, promotion and publicity material and stills that may be available which shall be retained by the [Licensee] on loan for the duration of this Agreement. In the event that trailers of any of the [Films] are not available then the [Licensee] may transmit and/or broadcast short sequences of not more than [two minutes] from each of the [Films] for the purpose of programme announcement and trailing. The [Licensee] shall bear the cost of any damage caused to the [Films] by reason of the extraction of short sequences for such purposes.

M.049

The [Licensee] shall be entitled to broadcast and/or transmit short extracts of parts of the [Films] in sound and/or vision and/or image and/or text and to authorise others to do so whether on its own channel, radio, video, DVD, CD, CD-Rom, on the internet, by mobile and/or landline telephone, promotional goods, publication in written form for advertising, promotion and marketing purposes only. Provided that such use shall not total more than [five minutes in duration] of the [Film], shall abide by the credit, copyright notices and moral rights obligations in Clause [–] and shall be the same parts used in each format. That a full and detailed report shall be sent to the [Licensor] detailing the type, nature, frequency and exact use.

M.050

No use of any material shall be permitted which would be derogatory, demeaning, offensive, or prejudicial to the commercial or financial success of the [Film].

M.051

The [Distributor] shall be entitled to publicise, advertise, market and promote the [Films] in [country/Territory] and to appoint any sub-licensee or other authorised agent to do so during the Term of this Agreement.

M.052

1.1 The [Licensee] shall have the right to create a promotional extract in the following format [specify] incorporating not more than [number minutes] of the [Film] which shall be used only for promotional, marketing and review purposes.

1.2 The [Licensor] shall not have the right of approval of 1.1, but nothing shall be done which shall be derogatory or offensive to the [Film] or anyone associated with any part in vision, sound or otherwise.

1.3 The [Licensee] shall not have the right to license the promotional extract to any third party or any other programme or film transmitted by the [Licensee].

1.4 The [Licensee] shall provide the [Licensor] with one free copy of each promotional extract which may be created.

M.053

1.1 The [Production Company] undertakes that it shall be solely responsible for all costs incurred and sums due in respect of the development, production, distribution, marketing and exploitation of the [Film] and parts in any form. That the [Author] is not and will not be liable for any such payments and that the [Production Company] shall not be entitled to deduct them from the Gross Receipts.

1.2 The [Production Company] agrees to provide copies and samples at its own cost of any publicity, promotional, advertising and packaging material in respect of the marketing and commercial exploitation of the [Film] when requested to do so by the [Author].

1.3 The [Production Company] agrees to keep the [Author] informed of the progress of the production and exploitation in any media. The [Author] shall be advised of all proposed release dates in any media at any time in the Territory.

M.054

The [Author] accepts that the editorial and artistic control of the marketing shall be entirely at the [Company's] discretion.

M.055

No third party shall be entitled to be added as a sponsor or contributor to the funds for the [Film] and/or have its logo, trade mark, service mark, design, product, image, slogan, character, and/or music and/or sound recording associated with or incorporated in the introduction trailer or end credits or any marketing material at any time.

M.056
In the event that the [Licensee] cannot broadcast/transmit and/or market the [Film] then no compensation shall be due to the [Licensor] and the maximum liability of the [Licensee] under this Agreement shall be [–].

M.057
The [Assignee] agrees that it shall consult with the [Assignor] where it is proposed to use the [Film] and/or parts for the purpose of sponsorship, product endorsement or advertising of other services.

M.058
The [Licensor] shall ensure that the consent and agreement is obtained from all parties involved in the creation and supply of the publicity, promotion, advertising and marketing material. The cost of payment of any expenses and fees shall be paid for by the [Licensor/Licensee].

M.059
The [Licensee] shall be entitled to use, license and permit the use of excerpts of the [Film] and/or parts for advertising, publicity, marketing, sponsorship/ and/or endorsement purposes only of the [Film] and/or the [Company] and/ or the [Sequel] and/or the [Products] for newspapers, magazines, television, radio, video, DVD, CD-Roms, CDs, Discs, games, banner advertisements on websites and/or downloads from the internet to a mobile and/or landline telephone, television, computer and/or some other gadget. Provided that the total aggregate duration shall not exceed [number] [minutes] of the [Film] and it shall be the same extracts used across all the media.

M.060
The [Licensor] agrees that the [Licensee] shall entitled to use and to authorise others to transmit, play, and/or make available an agreed extract of the sound recording of the [Film] of no more than [number] minutes for the purpose of the promoting and marketing the [Film] on radio, the internet, mobiles and/or any other gadget and/or form of exploitation. The [Licensee] shall not be required to pay any additional copyright fee for such use and any right to use the sound recording in this manner shall end on [date].

M.061
The [Licensor] agrees that the [Licensee] may market and promote up to [number] minutes of the same extract of the [Film/Programme] which is agreed with the [Licensor] in advance in the form of banner links, pop ups,

advertisements, content on any websites, apps and/or blogs for viewing on any computer, television, laptop, gadget, mobile telephone and/or otherwise provided that the sole purpose is the promotion and marketing of the [Film/Programme] on [channel] in respect of the rights granted by the [Licensor] to the [Licensee].

M.062

The [Licensee] agrees and undertakes that it and/or any third party shall not be entitled to exploit, supply, sell, distribute and/or offer as a download and/or in electronic and/or digital format and/or by any method and/or means over the internet and/or any telecommunication system the [Film/Programme] and/or any parts to be viewed and/or received and/or stored by any business, educational body and/or for home use by the public in any marketing and/or promotional and/or advertising material at any time.

M.063

1.1 The [Licensor] agrees that the [Licensee] may use a sequence of [images/film] with added sound recordings and music supplied by the [Licensor] at its cost in [format] which are to be used in that exact form by the [Licensee] for marketing, advertising and promoting the [Film/Programme] on channel [specify] and on the website [specify] and in the [newsletter/feed] known as [specify] during the term of this Agreement.

1.2 The [Licensee] agrees that all other use of the material in 1.1 must be approved and agreed with the [Licensor] in advance in each case and may be refused at the sole discretion of the [Licensor].

M.064

[Name] agrees that the [Distributor] may use his/her personal and stage name, image, caricature, photographs, sound recordings and any part of their performance in the [Film/Programme] in any format and/or medium and/or language at any time provided that it is to promote and market the [Film/Programme] and [Name] receives and annual payment of [number/currency] by the [Distributor].

M.065

It is agreed between the parties that all costs of reproduction of material, editing, copyright and music clearances and payments, and payments due to collecting societies in any part of the world, freight, insurance, contract payments, commission, discounts, currency conversion and bank charges, development of marketing and promotional material, cost of advertisements, banner links, apps, blogs, newsfeeds and websites shall be at the [Licensees] sole cost.

General Business and Commercial

M.066
No reference is to be made to the terms and conditions of this Agreement by either party in any marketing, advertising or publicity material without the prior written consent of the other party.

M.067
The contributions [including any exhibits] provided by you shall not contain any advertisement, product placement, endorsement or anything of an advertising or promotional nature whether for payment or otherwise.

M.068
Nothing contained in this Agreement shall prevent or restrict the [Distributor/ Company] at any time developing or otherwise acquiring rights in or marketing or exploiting any other [DVD/Product] whether or not it is similar to the [DVD/Product].

M.069
The [Sub-Publisher] shall use its best endeavours to maximise the commercial exploitation of the [Compositions] in the Territory during the Term and shall use its best endeavours to recover all sums due.

M.070
The [Record Company] agrees that the minimum marketing budget with respect to each [Album] shall not be less than [figure/currency].

M.071
Neither the [Project/other] nor any facilities, vessels or other material owned or operated by the [Company] or its affiliated companies may be used by the [Contractor] or sub-contractors with regard to advertising or public relations without the prior written consent of the [Company].

M.072
Neither the [Contractor] nor its sub-contractor shall publish material relating to this Contract without the prior approval of the [Company]. The [Company] shall have the sole right to use the [Project/other] in respect of marketing, advertising and public relations.

M.073
The [Assignor] acknowledges that the [Assignee] shall have the sole discretion as to the manner and method to be used in marketing, promoting, advertising and distributing the [Product/Work/Services] in respect of the rights assigned under this Agreement.

M.074

The [Distributor] agrees to use its reasonable endeavours to exploit the [Records] commercially. The [Distributor] undertakes to ensure the distribution for retail sale within [twelve months] of the date of this Agreement not less than [singles/LPs/cassettes/compact discs/other].

M.075

The [Distributor] undertakes to arrange and pay for the production and release of a promotional [Disc/DVD/Film] featuring the [Performers] in conjunction with each of the singles, and/or albums from the Records which are commercially released for sale to the public.

M.076

The [Distributor] undertakes to provide the [Licensor] with a minimum of [number] free copies in each and every medium and/or format that the [Records] and/or any part(s) are released to the public or otherwise commercially exploited.

M.077

The [Licensee] acknowledges that it shall not be entitled to exploit in any manner any sound recordings of the [Musical Work] without the prior written consent of the [Licensor].

M.078

The [Licensee] agrees that it shall not be entitled to register any domain name, trade mark, character, title, logo, image and/or slogan associated with the [Work/Film] and that all such rights and material set out in Schedule [–] are the subject of existing and/or pending applications by the [Licensor].

M.079

[Name] agrees that the [Company] may use the material [filmed/recorded/ photographed] on [date] as it thinks fit and in any manner and /or by any means and/or medium at any time. Provided that the [Company] does not licence the material to any third party and/or edit, adapt and/or vary the material so that it mocks, demeans and/or represents [Name] in a derogatory and/or offensive manner.

Internet and Websites

M.080

Any material in any format which is supplied to the [Company] for display and exhibition on a webpage on this [Website] which is available to the public [and any user of this [Website] which is not protected by a password, code and/or encryption] may be quoted, referred to, and/or reproduced in any marketing, advertising and publicity material for the [Website] without payment whether by the [Company] directly and/or through a third party provided that there are suitable acknowledgements as to the source and/or any copyright notice and/or credit.

M.081
The [Distributor] undertakes to feature the [Work/Product] on the [Website] reference [specify] under the category listing [specify], together with the summary and an image for not less than [specify period]. No additional cost and/or charge shall be made to the [Company] for such advertising and promotion.

M.082
No contributor, blogger, company, member of the public and/or any other person and/or entity has the right to use this [Website] and/or any content and/or the name of the [Company] and/or any trade mark, service mark, logo, image and slogan for the purpose of promoting, advertising, endorsing and/or to assist their own business, products, services, website and/or those of a third party and/or otherwise whether for financial gain or not. If you wish to use any part of this [Website] the prior written consent of the [Company] will be required. Failure to do could result in the commencement of a legal action against you for infringing the rights and/or causing loss and/or damage to the [Company].

M.083
Users of this [Website] are permitted to assist the [Company] in the marketing, promotion and advertising of the [Website] to the public and may download short extracts of parts of the [Website] of not more than [three minutes] in duration in film, DVD, and/or moving images and/or number [words] in text and/or [three minutes] in duration in sound and supply it to other friends without charge provided that:

1.1   It is not for financial gain and/or any other benefit.

1.2   No credit, copyright notice, trade mark and/or copyright warning is deleted and/or edited and/or amended.

1.3   No use shall be permitted which would be derogatory, demeaning, offensive, or prejudicial to the material and/or the copyright owner and/or the [Company].

1.4   That the following credit is made to the [Company] and the [Website] [specify details].

M.084
The [Company] shall be entitled promote, market and/or exploit the product of the [Contributors] work and/or any part on the [Website] in any media

including but not limited to advertisements, television, radio, mobiles, the internet, blogs, downloads, merchandising, books, magazines and newspapers without any further payment.

M.085

The [Company] agrees and undertakes that:

1.1 It shall not market and/or promote the [Contributor] in any format and/ or media outside the [Website] without the prior written consent and approval of [Name].

1.2 It shall not seek to register a domain name in the [Contributor] personal and/or stage name.

1.3 That it has no authority and/or right to authorise any third party to use the name of the [Contributor] to endorse, market and/or promote any other website, service, product and/or any other matter.

M.086

The [Company] shall be entitled to market and promote the [Product] on its [Website] and on any banner advertisements, in any catalogue, printed adverts in magazines and newspapers, on flyers, by electronic attachments via emails, by text to mobile phones, through a regular newsletter and at events associated with [specify].

M.087

1.1 The [Company] agrees that it shall only use the trade mark, logo and name of the [Product] specified in Schedule [–] in conjunction with the [advertisement/banner] link in any blog, article and/or promotion on the website [specify].

1.2 That the [Company] shall not authorise any third party including any media to use any such material in 1.1.

1.3 That the [Company] agrees that it shall remove and delete all material referred to in 1.1 at any time when requested to do so by the [Supplier].

M.088

[Name] agrees that the [Company] may display, adapt, reproduce and supply to third parties in any form at no cost the [Image/Photograph/Sound Recordings] in order to promote and market the [Event/Festival] before [date].

M.089

The [Company] agrees that in the event that [Name] wants any marketing, promotional and/or advertising material amended, adapted, deleted and/

or removed for any reason from the website of the [Company] and/or any other material. Then the [Company] agrees that it shall make such changes and take such actions as may be required in order to meet the demands of [Name]. Provided that alternative material is agreed and substituted and the cost in total does not exceed [number/currency].

Merchandising

M.090
The [Licensor] agrees to provide on loan copies of the artwork of the [Character] and any trade mark, logo, copyright notice, image or other credit as may be required by the [Licensee] for the purposes of this Agreement.

M.091
The [Designer] agrees to be responsible for all packaging, publicity, advertising, promotions and sales of the [Licensed Articles] and confirms that all such costs shall be at the [Designer's] cost and shall not be offset in any manner in the calculation of the Net Receipts.

M.092
The [Licensee] shall ensure that the [Licensed Articles] together with all wrappings, containers, contents, labels, packaging, displays, articles, marketing, publicity or advertising materials and the like conform in all respects with the samples approved pursuant to Clause [–].

M.093
The [Licensee] acknowledges that it shall be solely responsible for all costs incurred in the commercial exploitation of the [Licensed Articles] including its production, manufacture, distribution, selling, advertising and promotion.

M.094
'Marketing' shall [be defined in accordance with the Copyright, Designs and Patents Act 1988 as amended] and shall mean in relation to the [Articles] that it is being sold, let for hire, or offered or exposed for sale or hire, in the course of the business.

M.095
The [Licensee] undertakers that the minimum retail selling price for each of the [Licensed Articles] shall be not less than [figure/currency].

M.096
The [Licensee] undertakes to use and apply the [Character] and any trade mark, logo, slogan, image, text, computer-generated material, graphics, icon, recording and music for the sole purpose of producing, manufacturing, selling, supplying, distributing and marketing the [Licensed Articles].

M.097

The [Licensee] undertakes that it shall use its best endeavours to exploit the rights granted under this Agreement and as far as possible to achieve a level of Gross Receipts of not less than [figure/currency] with a marketing budget for the first calendar year of not less than [figure/currency].

M.098

The [Company] undertakes that it shall be solely responsible and bear the cost of all sums incurred in respect of the development, production, manufacture, distribution, marketing, promotion, advertising and exploitation of the [Licensed Articles] and that such sums shall not be offset against the [Licensor's] Royalties at any time.

M.099

The Company undertakes that not less than [number] units of the [Licensed Articles] shall be manufactured within [twelve months] of [the delivery of the Prototype/approval of the Samples] of the [Licensed Articles].

M.100

The [Licensee] shall provide a regular marketing, advertising and sales report to the [Licensor] and supply examples of all material which has been distributed at the [Licensees] cost.

M.101

The [Licensee] shall be entitled to market and promote the [Product] [in language] as follows:

1.1 On the [Licensee's] [Website] and those of any agent, distributor and sub-licensee by means of a summary on a webpage, by promotional material as electronic attachments via emails, by text to mobile phones, through a regular newsletter and banner advertisements. The [Product] should always feature as a separate item and not combined with another service and/or item.

1.2 In any catalogue, printed adverts in magazines, newspapers, journals, and flyers in [countries].

1.3 At trade shows for [specify] in [countries].

M.102

The [Licensee] shall not be entitled to promote, market and/or exploit the [Product] by means of any form of podcasts, television, radio, merchandising, books, endorsement, film, plays, DVDs, discs, videos, and any other form of mechanical reproduction in any format and/or in hotels, aeroplanes and/or educational establishments.

1026

M.103

The [Licensor] agrees that the [Licensor] may market, promote and advertise the availability of the [Licensed Products] in newspapers, over the internet and on websites in articles, advertisements, banner links and in the form of prizes for competitions.

M.104

The [Licensee] agrees and undertakes that it shall not be entitled use and/or adapt any part of the [Licensed Products] and/or any associated trade, name, character, logo and/or image and/or storyline from the [Work] as a computer software game, toy, app, board game, household utensil and/or clothing, stationary and/or by any other form of adaptation except the exact form in which it is licensed and specified in Schedule [–].

Publishing

M.105

The [Publisher] agrees that the [Author] shall be entitled to be consulted in relation to the layout, size, colour, photographs, illustrations, artwork, typography, binding, index and copyright notices and corporate information of the [Work] and the design, text and blurb on the jacket or cover. In addition, the [Publisher] agrees to take account of the views of the [Author] in respect of the price, format and marketing of the [Work]. The [Author] acknowledges that the [Publisher] shall have the final decision in respect of the [Work] in all matters except [specify]. The [Publisher] shall use its reasonable endeavours to ensure that the following conditions in respect of the [Work] are fulfilled:

1.1　That the [Work] is accurately and adequately described and set out in each of its catalogues, brochures and other marketing and advertising material.

1.2　That sufficient copies of the [Work] are available for distribution and sale to the public by the publication date and the first print run in [country] shall not be less than [number].

1.3　That the cover of the [Work] and the text and artwork shall be of a high professional standard suitable for the nature of the [Work] and feature the name of the [Author] on the front and spine of the [Work].

1.4　That all quotes and use of statements from third parties in respect of the [Work] to be used in respect of any marketing, advertising, promotional material or the cover shall be subject to the prior written approval of the [Author].

1.5 That a total marketing and promotion budget of not less than [figure/currency] shall be allocated and used in respect of the [Work] in [country].

1.6 That review copies of the [Work] shall be sent to all persons specified by the Author up to [number] in total.

1.7 That the marketing and promotion of the [Work] shall include newspapers, television, radio, websites, book signing sessions, advertisements, posters, CD-Roms, features at Literary Festivals, Book Fairs and other events where reasonably possible.

1.8 That the [Publisher] shall pay to the [Author] all reasonable expenses and costs incurred in respect of the attendance of the [Author] and his/her agent at any marketing and/or promotion of the [Work].

1.9 The [Publisher] agrees to provide the [Author] with copies of all marketing, advertising or other material associated with the [Work] upon request.

M.106
The [Publishers] shall, unless prevented by circumstances beyond their control produce, print, reproduce and publish the [Work] in [Country]:

1.1 In [hardback] not less than [number] copies within [twelve months] of delivery and approval of the [Work]; and

1.2 In [paperback] not less than [number] copies within [twelve months] of the date of publication in [hardback].

M.107
The [Publisher] shall consult with the [Author] regarding the layout, design, binding and marketing of the [Work]. The editorial decisions, production, publication, promotion, pricing, reprinting, exploitation and sale of the [Work] shall be at the [Publisher's] sole discretion.

M.108
The [Publishers] shall (subject to force majeure) at their own risk and expense, produce, publish and market the [Work].

M.109
The [Publishers] agree to publish the [Work] not later than [twelve months] from the [delivery/acceptance] of the [Work].

M.110
The [Publisher] agrees that it shall be solely responsible for all costs incurred in developing, printing, binding, publishing, distributing, advertising,

promoting, marketing and exploiting the [Work] including all associated material and that no sums shall be deducted from the payments due to the [Author] under this Agreement.

M.111

1.1 At the date of this Agreement the proposed first print run of the Work is [number] copies in [format/country]. The [Publisher] agrees to inform the [Author] as soon as possible after publication of the actual number of copies printed and of the persons to whom complimentary copies have been promised on publication.

1.2 All details as to production, printing, publication, typography, cover design, price and terms of sale, advertisement and promotion of the [Work] both in the United Kingdom and overseas and the number and destination of free copies shall be at the discretion of the [Publisher] which shall bear all costs and expenses.

1.3 The [Publisher] will consult the [Author] on all matters regarding copy-editing, blurb, catalogue and type of illustrations, jacket design and publication date of the [Work] but the [Publisher] shall have the final decision.

M.112

1.1 The [Publishers] will have the entire control of the format, paper, binding, typography, layout and design of the [Work] and its jacket. All decisions as to the production, publication, distribution, advertising, price and terms of sale of the [Work] will be made by the [Publishers] at their sole discretion including the location of any images, names, titles, notices or credits.

1.2 The [Publishers] shall send a copy of the proposed jacket, biographical material and any marketing quotes to the [Author] in advance of publication of the [Work] for the purpose of consulting with the [Author].

M.113

The [Author] shall make himself/herself available as reasonably required by the [Publisher] for the promotion of the [Work] for the following periods:

1.1 [ten appearances/interviews] up to [four months] after the date of publication of the hardback.

1.2 [ten appearances/interviews] up to [two months] after the date of publication of the paperback.

The [Author] shall attend such events at no extra cost provided that the [Publisher] shall bear the cost of any reasonable expenses. The [Publisher] shall pay the [Author] a fee to be agreed in advance on each occasion for any additional appearances.

M.114

At the date of this Agreement the proposed first print run of the [Work] is [number] copies. The [Publisher] agrees to inform the [Author] as soon as possible after publication of the actual number of copies printed in each format. The [Publisher] shall also provide the [Author] with a list of persons who have received complimentary copies.

M.115

All details as to the manner of production, publication, advertisement and promotion of the [Work] in the Territory and the number and destination of free copies shall be at the discretion of the [Publisher] which shall be responsible for all such costs and expenses. The [Publisher] undertakes to produce and market the [Work] to a high standard.

M.116

The [Publisher] shall consult with the [Author] on all matters regarding copy-editing, blurb, labels, leaflets, posters, catalogue, copy, number and type of illustrations, text, jacket designs, new editions, publication dates of the [Work] but the [Publisher] shall have the final decision in each case.

M.117

The [Publisher] shall use its reasonable endeavours to market the [Work] effectively as follows:

1.1 Distribute a leaflet to a database of at least [number] companies/ persons who work in the field of [–].

1.2 Describe the [Work] accurately both in its brochure, marketing material and catalogue and when supplying information to third parties.

1.3 Despatch review or promotional copies to at least [–] companies/ persons.

1.4 Arrange for advertisements in the following [magazines/newspapers/ other].

1.5 For the first year of publication the [Work] will be featured on the [Publisher's] stands at all exhibitions and in any major promotions of books of a similar type.

1.6 Sufficient copies are printed for distribution and sale to the public by the publication date and in any event not less than [number].

1.7 The cover of the [Work], text and artwork shall be of a high professional standard.

1.8 All quotes and uses of statements from third parties by the [Publisher] of the [Work] shall be subject to the approval of the [Author].

1.9 The total marketing budget is not less than [–].

1.10 Review copies will be sent to [number] persons recommended by the [Author].

1.11 The marketing of the [Work] shall cover the following media [–].

1.12 The [Publisher] shall, unless prevented by force majeure or delay by the [Author], try to aim for these release dates in each format [hardback/paperback/film/DVD/merchandising dates].

M.118
The [Publisher] confirms that the recommended retail price of the [Work] in hardback shall be [figure/currency] per copy on first publication but the [Publisher] and/or any distributor or outlet shall have the sole discretion to alter the recommended retail price from time to time.

M.119
The [Company] shall be permitted to use extracts of the [Author's Work] on other books or publications up to a limit of [number] words without payment to the [Author]. Provided that the extracts are used solely for the purpose of advertising, promotion and publicity of the [Author] and/or the [Author's Work].

M.120
The [Company] shall regularly send the [Author] copies of all publicity, advertising and promotional material for the [Work]. Where the [Author] reports an inaccuracy and/or error then the [Company] agrees that it shall ensure that it is not repeated. Further the [Company] will be willing to arrange meetings for the [Author] with the marketing personnel prior to the preparation of the marketing material and launch of the [Work] so that the [Author] is given the opportunity of being consulted as to the proposed strategy.

M.121
The [Company] shall advise the [Author] of the advertising and marketing budget for the [Project] and shall fully disclose all intended expenditure. The [Author] shall be given the opportunity to comment on and recommend factors to be considered. The [Company] shall have the final decision in any marketing.

M.122

The [Company] agrees that it shall provide a budget of [figure/currency] for the marketing of the first edition of the [Work] in hardback/paperback in the [country].

M.123

Where the [Author] is required to attend any event in respect of the marketing of the [Work] in any form, then the [Company] agrees that it shall arrange for and bear the cost and expense of all [first class] accommodation, travel, meals, telephone, secretarial assistance and stationery incurred by the [Author] and/or his/her agent as a direct result of any such event.

M.124

The [Author] agrees that the [Publisher] shall be entitled to use and permit the use of an agreed style and material for his/her name, photograph, biography and image but not signature in respect of the publication and commercial exploitation of the [Work].

M.125

The [Author] agrees that the manner and method of producing, distributing and marketing the [Work] including the cover designs, selling price and terms of sale of the [Work] shall be at the [Publisher's] sole discretion subject to clauses [copyright notice, credits and moral rights].

M.126

1.1 The [Publisher] shall consult with the [Author] in respect of the appointment of any third party to exploit the [Work].

1.2 The [Publisher] shall provide the [Author] with details of the proposed release dates in respect of the exploitation of the [Work].

1.3 The [Publisher] agrees to provide the [Author] with not less than [number] copies of the [Work] in each and every form in which it is made available to the public free of charge to the [Author].

M.127

The [Company] shall not insert anywhere within the [Work] or on its cover or dust jacket or label or packaging any advertisement, promotion, sponsorship or marketing for any other company, business, person, book, product and/or article other than for the [Author's] own [Work] without the prior written consent of the [Author].

M.128

The [Agent] agrees to ensure as far as reasonably possible that the [Author] shall be entitled to approve or be consulted in respect of all proposed copies, and other material in respect of the [Work] including book covers, dump bins, posters, blurb, together with any publicity, promotional advertising or packaging material in respect of the marketing and exploitation of the [Work] throughout the world at any time.

M.129

The [Publisher] shall not be entitled nor shall it permit any third party to edit, adapt, alter and/or change the text, photographs and/or title in any way whether for the purpose of marketing the [Work] or not.

M.130

The [Publishers] agree and undertake to consult and work with the [Author] in respect of all aspects of the production, printing, publication, promotion, sale, display, price, advertising, marketing and exploitation of the [Work]. That the [Author] shall be forwarded:

1.1   Samples of the font for the text, and title.

1.2   Draft layout of the book.

1.3   A mock up cover and choose the colour of the cover from a selection available.

1.4   Draft advertising, catalogue extracts, flyers, and website and electronic promotional material.

M.131

The [Author] and the [Publisher] agree that they shall jointly own, control and hold the rights in the domain name and any other similar names which may be registered in respect of the title, characters and themes related to the [Work] which shall be registered at the [Publisher's] sole cost. That all rights, interest and sums received from any sale, exploitation and/or otherwise related to any such registration shall also be shared equally between the parties.

M.132

The [Author] and [Publisher] agree that where any App, website, blog , webinars, films, sound recordings, computer games, competitions, banner links, advertisements, covers and/or other material is created, developed and/or adapted from the [Work] and paid for by the [Publisher]. That the [Author] and the [Publisher] shall jointly own, control and hold all rights, intellectual property rights and interest and equally share any sums that may be received at any time.

M.133

The [Publisher] agrees that the [Author] shall be provided once a year with a detailed breakdown of the number of copies and formats of the [Work] supplied and/or sold in any country and details of and copies of all associated marketing including catalogues, flyers, email attachments and electronic versions.

Purchase and Supply of Products

M.134

1.1 The [Agent] agrees to promote, market and obtain orders for the [Products] based on the [Samples] at the prices and on the terms and conditions specified at any time by the [Licensor].

1.2 The [Agent] agrees to inform any retail store or outlet or website company that wishes to order the [Product] that they must pay the total sum in [dollars] of the [ex-factory] price of any item plus freight and insurance to the requested destination and shall be responsible for all customs clearance, storage duty and taxes that may be incurred.

1.3 Title in any [Products] ordered shall remain with the [Licensor] until full payment of the invoice has been received by the [Licensor].

M.135

The [Supplier] agrees that the [Seller] may:

1.1 Market, promote and sell the [Product] at any price it deems fit on the [Seller's website/other] provided that [price per unit] shall be paid for each unit supplied and not returned.

1.2 Display and market the [Product] and any image, text, endorsement in any shape and form as it thinks fit provided that there is no offensive or derogatory treatment of the [Product], the [Supplier] or any third party.

M.136

1.1 The [Distributor] shall at its own expense vigorously direct its activities to sell the [Products] supplied by the [Company] under the [Company's] name and trade marks.

1.2 The [Distributor] shall send to the [Company] as much market information as may be available in order to develop and manufacture other similar products which are more competitive.

1.3 Both parties shall co-operate with each other in good faith and in the event that there are any technical or marketing problems concerning the [Products] the parties shall endeavour to reach a solution based on a long-term working relationship for the benefit of both parties.

M.137

The [Distributor] shall submit to the [Company] for prior approval in writing all sales literature and advertising matter prepared by it or any third party in connection with the [Product]. The [Distributor] shall amend any material to the satisfaction and standard required by the [Company] which is not approved and shall re-submit it for approval.

M.138

The [Company] agrees that it shall arrange at the [Company's] cost in [country] for:

1.1 A major launch of the [Product] with a budget of not less than [figure/ currency].

1.2 [National/international] television, radio, magazine, newspaper and newswire coverage.

1.3 That there shall be distribution in a leading magazine [specify] of [number] flyers/brochures before [date].

1.4 Advertising webpage on [site] together with banner advertising on [number] leading websites for at least [three months].

1.5 Premium telephone line prize/promotion game.

1.6 A review report shall be made available for discussion with detailed data and information by [date].

1.7 An advertising and/or review podcast and/or banner advertisement on the following websites [–].

M.139

The [Company] shall advertise the [Seller's] [Products] on the website of [name/reference] as follows:

1.1 The [Seller] shall be the main display advertiser and the [Products] shall feature on all the main webpages [specify].

1.2 No other advertiser shall have the right to be displayed where there is a direct conflict of interest resulting from the same type of products or same market namely [specify].

1.3 That where there is associated publicity, advertising or promotional literature that the [Seller] and its [Products] shall be given due credit and recognition as the main advertiser on the website with the following text, trade mark and image [specify].

1.4 In any flotation of the [Website] or any stock market documents that may be issued by the [Company] then the [Seller] shall feature in the documentation.

1.5 The [Company] shall have the final editorial decision in respect of the position and size of the [Products] and the name of the [Seller] and any commentary. Provided that it shall represent a true and accurate image, trade mark, text and information of the [Product] and the [Seller].

M.140

The [Company] agrees that the [Product] shall only be sold in the following outlet and method [specify].

M.141

The [Seller] agrees that it shall not issue any statement to the media regarding the [Product] and/or the [Supplier] without the prior consultation with the press office of the [Supplier]. The [Seller] agrees that it shall not knowingly and with malice deliberately bring the [Supplier] or its [Product] into disrepute or act in a derogatory or offensive manner or cause loss, damage to their business or reputation.

M.142

The [Distributor] agrees and undertakes that [Name] shall not be liable for any of the costs and expenses associated with the development, production and /or exploitation of the [Work] in the form of the [Product] and all packaging, marketing, advertising, product liability and/or any competitions and/or associated promotions through the [Distributor] and/or any parent company, licensee and/or third party at any time.

M.143

The [Distributor] agrees that the domain names and the trademarks and the associated slogans, text, images and logo set out in Schedule [–] are owned by [Name]. That the [Distributor] agrees not to try to register any other material which may be created under this Agreement which is derived from and/or based on any concepts, contribution, work and/or other material supplied by [Name]. That any new domain names, trade marks and associated material which may be created in relation to the [Products] and capable of being registered shall be registered by [Name] in his/her sole name and interest. And at his/her cost.

Services

M.144

The [Manager] shall use his/her best endeavours to promote and publicise the [Group] in all forms of the media including television, radio, press, reviews, musical engagements, appearances, merchandising, CDs, commercial recordings and the internet. The [Manager] shall advertise the [Group] in [magazine] on no less than [number] occasions; display their details on the website [specify] and issue press releases relating to their services.

M.145

Subject to prior consultation the [Presenter] agrees that the [Company] shall be entitled to use his/her name, biography, photograph, likeness, signature and image in respect of the promotion and advertising of the [Company] and the [Programmes]. Provided that any commercial exploitation relating to the [Presenter] shall be subject to the prior written consent of the [Presenter] and upon the condition that the terms and payment offered are acceptable to the [Presenter].

M.146

The [Company] shall have the right and license to use and reproduce the [Artist's] name, signature, biographical material and likenesses for the purposes of this Agreement including labelling, cataloguing and exploiting the [Records] [DVDs] and website subscription service. The [Company] agrees to supply the proposed sample of any cover, packaging and/or web site material to the [Artist] for his/her appraisal. Provided that the [Artist] provides a written or verbal reaction to the [Company] within [ten days] then the [Company] agrees to incorporate all reasonable charges made by the [Artist].

M.147

The [Agent] undertakes not to disclose any material nor make nor repeat any statement, whether true or not, concerning the [Artist's] private life and social life, political and personal views to any media (including newspapers, television, radio and on the internet and/or any telecommunication system which is available to the public) at any time without the prior written consent of the [Artist].

M.148

The [Agent] agrees not to promote, market or advertise the [Actor] in anyway which may impugn the reputation or embarrass the [Actor]. As far as possible the [Agent] shall provide samples of all material and agrees to adhere to any changes requested by the [Actor]. The [Agent] agrees it shall be entirely responsible for the cost and no sums shall be deducted from any sums due to the [Actor].

M.149

The [Presenter] and the [Company] mutually agree and undertake that each of them shall not, during the Term of this Agreement, publish in writing or otherwise make known to the public or the media and/or act in any way likely to result in publication of any matter concerning the business affairs of each other at any time which are not publicly available without the prior written consent of the party to whom any such data, information and/or material may relate or effect.

M.150

The [Company] agrees to consult with the [Actor] and the Agent in respect of all proposed scripts, credits, labels, packaging, advertising, promotional, publicity and marketing material prior to the production, manufacture and distribution of the material by the [Company].

M.151

The [Company] acknowledges that the [Actor] shall be entitled upon request to be provided at the [Company's] sole cost with a copy of any publicity, advertising, promotional and marketing material in the possession or under the control of the [Company] featuring or relating to the [Actor].

M.152

The [Agent] agrees to ensure that the [Author] shall be entitled to be consulted with respect to all proposed copies, samples and other material of the [Work] including book covers together with any publicity, promotional, advertising or packaging material in respect of the marketing and exploitation of the [Work].

M.153

The [Manager] shall use his/her reasonable business endeavours to obtain work for the services of the [Sportsperson] and to promote and publicise the [Sportsperson] in all forms of the media in [country] including:

1.1 Programmes, films, DVDs, CDs, CD-Roms, discs, corporate videos, sound recordings, voice-overs, guest appearances, interviews, game shows and presentations.

1.2 Advertisements and commercials for all forms of terrestrial, cable, satellite, digital television and radio, telephone networks and telecommunication systems, websites and the internet, podcasts, blogs, advertisements, banner advertisements, newspapers, magazines and books.

1.3 Merchandising, theatre, biography, articles and features in newspapers, magazines and books.

1.4 Corporate events, public appearances, sponsorship, endorsement of products, services and their brands.

M.154

The [Company] agrees that all corporate, advertising, publicity, packaging, labels and promotional material shall be provided to the [Presenter] in the exact form in which it is intended that it should be used by the [Company]. The prior written approval of the [Agent/Presenter] shall be required and if refused the material of any nature shall not be used.

M.155

The [Presenter] gives all necessary consents to the [Company] under the [Copyright, Designs and Patents Act 1988 as amended] and shall assist in any necessary documentation:

1.1 To take, make or arrange and to use, authorise and reproduce such material for photographs, films, sound recordings whether for digital, cable, satellite, terrestrial or other form of television, video, DVD, internet, telephone or otherwise. This shall include a direct image or voice or digitised image or voice or an interactive one of the [Presenter].

1.2 To take, make and arrange for and to use, authorise and/or reproduce the [Presenters] name, nickname, signature, slogan, image, physical likeness, short form biography of the [Presenter] in whole or part.

1.3 All material is only to be used for the purpose of the advertisement, publicity, exhibition and commercial exploitation of the [Programme/ Product/Event] and no other reason. Nor is any use to directly or indirectly demean, be offensive or derogatory of the [Presenter] or any third party.

1.4 There shall be no endorsement or promotion of other services or products or any undisclosed use of any material of any kind.

M.156

The [Company] shall engage the services of the [Name] who agrees to be available on the terms and conditions in consideration of the payment terms in Clause [–]:

1.1 To appear in [number] advertisements to be transmitted on [national satellite, digital, cable and terrestrial television/cinemas/exhibitions/ videos/DVDs/discs/posters] in [country] from [date] to [date]. There may be unlimited use in any of these areas during the specified dates. There shall be no right to exploit any of this material after this date or in any format or media not stipulated nor to authorise others to do so without the prior written approval of [Name] and the negotiation of a new agreement.

1.2 The [Name] shall be available for [number] [eight hour] recording days for filming, voice-overs and photographs. Additional days shall be paid at [specify rate].

1.3 The [Name] shall not be obliged to fulfil any request which he/she decides is unsuitable to their image, career or reputation.

1.4 There is no obligation to attend award ceremonies, corporate or director events or to otherwise promote the [Company] and/or its products in any other circumstances, nor any restriction on the use or promotion of rival products by name at any time.

M.157

The [Company] shall agree in advance and pay for the cost and expenses and an additional fee for the services of [Name] at all marketing and promotional events, meetings, exhibitions [Name] is asked to attend.

M.158

The [Company] shall have the right and license to use and publish the [Contributor's] name, signature, biographical material, photographs and likeness for labelling, cataloguing, packaging and exploiting the [Product/Service/Material]. The [Company] agrees to send a proof of any sample material which contains and/or refers to the [Contributor's] name, signature, biographical material, photograph or likeness. The [Contributor] shall within [one week] provide details to the Company of any objections and comments to be considered.

M.159

Subject to prior consultation the [Presenter] agrees that the [Company] shall be entitled to use his/her name, biographical details, photographs, image, and stage name in respect of the promotion, advertising and marketing of the [Company] and the [Programme]. The [Company] agrees that any commercial exploitation or product endorsement shall be subject to prior written agreement between the parties.

M.160

The [Company] agrees at its own cost and expense to provide copies and samples of any proposed publicity, promotional, advertising and packaging material in respect of the [Product/Work/Services] upon request by the [Agent/Artist].

M.161

The [Agent] agrees to provide a regular report on [type] technical business and market trends and developments in the Territory which would assist the [Company] or could indicate factors that might be detrimental to its business.

M.162

The [Agent] agrees that the prior written approval of the [Company] shall be required in the event that the [Agent] intends to promote, market or exploit the [Collection Samples], the [Garments] or the [Company] Logo by any of the following means: publicity, advertising, promotional material, fashion and trade shows, radio, internet, video, DVD, discs, television, telephones and any telecommunications system, CD-Roms; appearances, newspaper and magazine articles, or features and any media in any country.

M.163
The [Agent] shall provide its services to the best of its skill and ability and shall perform all duties diligently to maximise the sales of the [Product] under this Agreement to retail stores, wholesalers and mail order outlets throughout the Territory.

M.164
The [Agent] agrees that it shall use its best endeavours to promote, market and obtain orders for the [Product] based on the [Samples] throughout the Territory for the Term of this Agreement.

M.165
The [Agent] shall keep the [Licensor] fully informed on a regular basis as regards negotiations with any third party pursuant to this Agreement and shall provide a written report by email [at the end of each three month period] during the Term of this Agreement.

M.166
The [Licensor] agrees to engage the [non] -exclusive services of the [Agent] for the Term of this Agreement throughout the Territory for the purpose of promoting, marketing and obtaining orders for the purchase of the [Product] based on the [Samples] from retail stores and retail outlets.

M.167
The [Agent] acknowledges that the [Licensor] shall be entitled to deal with, sell, loan or hire or supply or otherwise exploit the [Samples] [Product] and any other products to any third party at any time in the same Territory and/or to authorize and licence other to do so.

M.168
The [Management] agrees that it shall promote and advertise each date for the appearance of the [Group] at the [Venue] at the [Management's] sole cost in the following manner:

1.1   Billboards at [locations].

1.2   Advertisements of size [specify] in the following magazines and newspapers [specify].

1.3   A press release to be issued to no less than [number] media companies in [country].

M.169

The [Licensee] agrees that during the Licence Period it will or shall arrange that a sub-licensee will at its own cost and expense use its best endeavours to supply, distribute, market, advertise and otherwise exploit the [Product/ Work/Services] in [country].

M.170

The [Assignee] shall be entitled to use the [Assignor's] name, likeness and biography in connection with the exploitation of the rights assigned hereunder. Provided that no use shall at any time express or imply an endorsement by the [Assignor] of any product, or other material other than the subject matter of this Agreement.

M.171

[Name] shall not without the prior [written] approval of the [Company] inform any other person or company other than his/her agent, legal advisers, accountant, financiers and family about any advertising, marketing or publicity plans by the [Company] which are disclosed before and/or during the course of this Agreement. [Name] agrees not to release and/or disclose any details prior to any launch by the [Company which would damage or be prejudicial to the impact of the campaign.

M.172

[Name] agrees that the [Company] may use the name, logo and image of [Name] set out in Schedule [–] and all his/her contributions in person and by means of sound recordings and film at the [Event/Project] in the following manner:

1.1 On the website known as [specify] and by means of a news feed from the [Company] and/or a third party to other businesses and consumers worldwide.

1.2 Through on line webinars in sound and/or vision which are edited from the sound recordings and/or film.

1.3 Through magazine and newspaper articles, blogs and press releases by the [Company].

1.4 Through sub-licensing parts of the film and/or sound recordings for use in news, current affairs and reviews and/or future programmes for broadcast and/or transmission on television and/or any other format and/or media at any time in any part of the world.

1.5 Through the sale and assignment of all copyright, intellectual property rights and any other interest to a third party of the sound recordings and the film of the [Event/Project].

M.173

The services to be supplied by the [Consultant/Name] do not entitle the [Company] to expect and/or be provided with mobile, online and/or other contact with the [Company] by [Consultant/Name] outside of these times and days of the week [specify].

M.174

Where the [Consultant] is required to provide additional work, material and/or other support to the [Company] which is not listed in Schedule [–]. The [Company] agrees that additional fees and payments shall be due of not less than [number/currency] per hour.

Sponsorship

M.175

The [Organisers] confirm and agree that an official printed programme shall be made available to the general public at the [Festival/Event] at a price decided by the [Organisers]. The [Organisers] agree that the brochure shall include:

1.1 The [Sponsor's] Logo on the front cover.

1.2 A statement from the [Sponsor] of [500] words on page [–].

1.3 A full page advertisement of the [Sponsor's Product] on the inside back cover.

M.176

The [Organisers] agree that the [Sponsor] shall be entitled to create its own advertising and publicity material in respect of the [Sponsor's] association with the [Festival/Event] and that the [Organisers] shall not have the right of approval of such material issued by the [Sponsor].

M.177

The [Radio Station] confirms that no products, services or other material of any nature shall be advertised, promoted or in any way discussed or raised during the course of the [Programme] which is in direct competition with the [Sponsor's Product] for the duration of the Sponsorship Period. This clause shall also apply to any material in a commercial break.

M.178

The [Company] shall be entitled to have the advertising of any third party to be displayed at the Venue during the course of the [Event] in any form removed if the third party product directly conflicts with the following products of the [Sponsor] [specify products] and is used for [state purpose].

M.179

The [Sponsor] acknowledges that the [Association] shall be entitled to license, authorise or permit third parties to advertise or promote their products or services during the [Event] including advertisements, and displays for all types of products of any nature except the following category of products and/or services in the following markets [–].

M.180

The [Sponsor] agrees to provide at its sole cost the following minimum number of give-away products for the [Event] for the [Association] to distribute to competitors, press, and for hospitality [number/item].

M.181

The [Sponsor] agrees that the [Association] shall be entitled to retain all sums received from the exploitation of the [Event] in any form including ticket sales, programmes, television coverage, DVDs, CDs, sound recordings and music, merchandising, advertising, telephones and the internet.

M.182

The [Company] shall try to ensure that all marketing, promotional and publicity material released by the [Company] and/or a business and/or person appointed by the [Company] in respect of the [Event] shall ensure that the Title [specify] of the [Sponsor] shall be used on all printed material including the [Guide/brochure] and on all sound recordings, music, film, DVDs, advertisements for radio, television and any website material. This clause shall not apply to any merchandising products.

M.183

The [Sponsor] shall have the right at its own cost to market, publicise and promote the [Event] and all associated participants and content. The [Organisation] shall be required by the sponsor to include the use of the [Sponsor's Products].

M.184

1.1 The [Organisation] acknowledges that the purpose of the funding of the [Event/Work/other] by the [Sponsor] is to obtain the maximum amount of promotion for the [Sponsor] and its [Products/Work/business/other].

1.2 The [Sponsor] shall be entitled to publicise and promote the names, photographs, pictures, or other material relating to the [Event/Work/other] within the possession or control of the [Organisation].

1.3 The [Organisation] shall request that each participant in the [Event/Work/other] shall co-operate with the [Sponsor] in any public relations that may reasonably be required by the [Sponsor] during the Term of this Agreement.

1.4 The [Organisation] shall request that all participants use, eat, drink or wear as appropriate items supplied by the [Sponsors] including the [Products/clothing/other] at [location] from [date] to [date].

1.5 The [Sponsor] shall be able, subject to the prior consent of any individual, to use any such material for a period of [one year] after the [Event/Work/other] for the purpose of publicity and promotion of [–].

M.185
Where any participants and/or competitors refuse to use, endorse and/or wear the [Sponsors] products and/or clothing. The [Sponsor] agrees that the [Company] shall not be in breach of this Agreement provided that the majority have cooperated.

M.186
The [Company] shall be permitted throughout the [Event] to distribute, free of charge to spectators and others at the venue, free samples of such other products, samples and articles as the [Company] may decide.

M.187
The [Sponsor] agrees that the [Sportsperson's] name, images and endorsement shall not be used for any other purpose other than the promotion and endorsement of the [Sponsor's Product]. The [Sponsor] agrees to provide the [Sportsperson] with exact samples of all materials in any medium in which it is intended to use the name, image or endorsement of the [Sportsperson]. Such material whether for promotional, advertising, publicity or packaging shall be supplied at the [Sponsor's] cost to the [Sportsperson] prior to the production or distribution of such material. In the event that the [Sportsperson] requests alterations or changes relating to any references to the [Sportsperson] in any form, then the [Sponsor] agrees to be bound by these requests.

M.188
The [Sponsor] acknowledges that this Agreement does not oblige the [Sportsperson] to perform or appear in any films, radio programmes, videos, sound recordings, DVDs, CD-Roms, or CDs for the [Sponsor]. All such matters shall be the subject of a separate agreement on each occasion, and require the [Sponsor] to pay the [Sportsperson] further sums.

M.189
The [Sportsperson] agrees to attend and participate in all the events and occasions specified in the [Events Schedule] and to perform to the best

of his/her physical and mental skill and ability, and to have prepared with sufficient training and preparation subject to illness, injury and/or some other valid reason.

M.190
The [Sportsperson] undertakes not to enter into any agreement to endorse, promote or advertise the products or services of the following companies for the duration of the Sponsorship Period [specify rivals names] nor any services or products in any of the following markets [–].

M.191
The [Sponsor] agrees and undertakes not to engage any other person as the public image and promoter of the [Sponsor's] products, business and/or services from [date] to [date].

M.192
The [Sponsor] agrees to provide the [Sportsperson] at the [Sponsor's] cost with a sample of each and every product item, leaflet or other material in which the [Sponsor] uses the name, likeness, image, photograph or endorsement of the [Sportsperson] under this Agreement whether for promotional, advertising, publicity, packaging or marketing purposes.

M.193
The [Sportsperson] agrees to wear the clothing and use the equipment and car provided by the [Sponsor] under this Agreement as far as reasonably possible and appropriate at all competitions, events, press calls, and television interviews throughout the Sponsorship Period in the Territory and not to wear or use the sponsored goods of any third party unless provided by the [Organisers] of any event for all participants.

M.194
The [Sponsor] warrants that the name, nickname, images, photographs, films, recordings, merchandise, signature, comments and interviews and endorsement of the [Sponsor's] Products by the [Sportsperson] shall not be used for any purpose other than the promotion and endorsement of the [Sponsor's] Products and the [Sponsor's] business in general for the duration of the Term of the Agreement.

M.195
The [Sponsor] agrees that all material produced by them shall be of a high professional standard and the [Sportsperson] shall be consulted and have a right of approval over all material in any media which directly relates to them under this Agreement including promotional, publicity, advertising, packaging, brochures and press releases, photographs, illustrations,

artwork, typography, design and layout, biographical details, image, text, or otherwise.

M.196

The [Sponsor] agrees and undertakes not to attempt to register any interest, right and/or claim in respect of the name, nickname, abbreviation or initials, image, likeness, catchphrase, slogan, caricature version, logo, trademark, domain name and/or any other material derived from and/or based on the career, life, person and/or name of the [Athlete] which is supplied, created and/or developed for the purposes of this Agreement.

M.197

The [Sponsor] shall not be entitled to use the name, image and/or details of any [Participant] to market, promote and advertise the [Event] without the prior written and/or authority consent of that [Participant] and/or their parent and/or guardian. No authority and/or consent is provided by the [Company] in respect of any one individual and/or group.

M.198

The [Sponsor] shall be entitled to promote, market and advertise its funding of the [Event] as it thinks fit provided that it does not represent that:

1.1   It is paying any individual directly.

1.2   The funding is for political purposes.

1.3   It has any control over the content of the [Programme] and/or operation of the [Event].

1.4   It has the right to authorise, license, sub-license and/or exploit the [Programme] and/or [Event] to any third party in any media.

M.199

The [Sponsor] shall be entitled to use promote and market its connection with the [Event/Project] in any manner it thinks fit provided that any material developed and/or created is not offensive and/or derogatory and/or does not and/or will not permit and/or make any comments on the competitors, the teams and/or the [Company] which are not positive at any time.

M.200

1.1   The [Company] agrees that the [Sponsor] may arrange for its own film crew at the [Event/Project] in order to make such sound recordings and/or films as it may wish and to use such material for future advertisements and/or promotions both online over the internet and through radio, television, cinema and in any other format and/or media.

1.2 Provided that the [Sponsor] shall not be entitled to record and/or film [specify] and shall be obliged to ask any member of the public who may be interviewed by them to provided their written consent and shall be liable for all fees, costs and copyright, intellectual property rights and interest, contract and royalty payments, recording, performance and broadcast and transmission fees that may become and/or fall due as a result of 1.1.

University, Library and Educational

M.201

1.1 The [Institute] shall have the right and licence to use and publish the [Contributor's] name, biographical material, photographs, image and likeness for the cover, catalogue, website, flyers, packaging, marketing, advertising and exploiting the [Product/Service/Work] and to authorise others to do so.

1.2 The [Institute] agrees to send a draft sample of any material which contains and/or refers to the [Contributor's] name, biographical material, photograph, image or likeness for approval by the [Contributor]. The [Institute] agrees at its own cost to provide two copies of any material in respect of the [Product/Service/Work] in which the [Contributor] appears and/or is mentioned upon request by the [Contributor].

M.202

1.1 The [Institute] agrees to consult with the [Contributor] in respect of all proposed copies, credits, labels, samples, packaging, advertising, promotional, publicity and marketing material prior to the production, manufacture, distribution and exploitation of the material by the [Institute]. The editorial control and the decision of the [Institute] in respect of any matter shall be final and the [Institute] shall not be obliged to adhere to the views and/or proposals of the [Contributor].

1.2 The [Institute] shall at the [Institute's] sole cost deliver to the [Contributor] a copy of any products, packaging, publicity, advertising, promotional and marketing material in the possession or under the control of the [Institute] featuring or relating to the [Contributor].

M.203

At the date of this Agreement the proposed first print run of the [Work] is [number] copies. The [Publisher] agrees to inform the [Author] as soon as possible after publication of the actual number of copies printed in each format. The [Publisher] shall also provide the [Author] with a list of persons who have received complimentary copies.

M.204

The [Contributor agrees that the [Institute] shall at the [Institutes] sole cost have the entire control and discretion as to the management, production, budget, development and design, publication, launch date, advertisement and promotion of the [Work/Service/Event].

M.205

[Name] agrees that the [Institute] shall be entitled to reproduce, display and distribute the [Work] in the following circumstances:

1.1 As a three-dimensional moving image on the [Institutes'] website, and in any associated banner link and/or advertisement on any third party site and/or in the form of an app which can be accessed and/or downloaded by the public without charge.

1.2 In any printed material including any catalogue, brochure, marketing flyer, banner, flag and/or other merchandise in any form.

M.206

The [Consortium] agrees that it shall be liable for the cost and expenses of any marketing and promotion and administration and copyright and contractual and intellectual property rights clearances and payments which may arise in respect of the [Conference] which are incurred by the [Institute].

MATERIAL

Building

M.207

Designs, drawings, specifications, computer generated graphics, data and information and other work or material developed under this Agreement shall be the exclusive property of the [Company]. The [Contractor] agrees that none may be released or reused by the [Contractor] without the prior written consent of the [Company]. All original material shall be saved by the [Contractor] and shall be delivered to the [Company] upon completion or termination of this Agreement or at the request at any time of the [Company] at any time. No material shall be destroyed by the [Contractor] unless instructed to do so by the [Company].

M.208

'Building' shall [be defined the Copyright, Designs and Patents Act 1988 as amended] include a fixed structure and a part of a building or fixed structure.

DVD, Video and Discs

M.209

The [Company] engages the [Writer] and the [Writer] agrees to make his/her services available to the [Company] to produce a treatment for [number] [Programmes] not exceeding [duration] each on the subject of [description] provisionally entitled [title] along the lines discussed between the [Company] and the [Writer]. The treatment shall include information on the ownership of any existing film of any nature, the details of any music to be used (including composer, musicians and copyright owner). The [Writer] shall deliver this treatment to the [Company] not later than [date].

M.210

The [Licensee] undertakes not to supply, sell, hire, rent, transfer and/or distribute to any third party any of the material supplied in accordance with this Agreement. Neither shall the [Licensee] reproduce or exploit and/or authorize any third party to do so except as specified in this Agreement.

M.211

The [Author] agrees to provide the [Company] with a list of the source of the [Material] supplied by the [Author] for the [Programme] and confirms that the [Material] shall be cleared in respect of the rights granted by the [Author]. The [Company] shall be responsible for the payment of the sums due for the use of the [Material] in respect of the exercise of the rights under this Agreement.

M.212

The [Licensor] shall provide the [Company] with one copy of any consents, releases, documents, licences and contracts which provide evidence of the ownership of the material supplied by the [Licensor].

M.213

If and when requested by the [Licensee] the [Licensor] shall supply at the [Licensee's] cost copies of such stills, logos, trade marks, labels, packaging, advertising, publicity and other materials that the [Licensor] may have in its possession which are suitable to be adapted by the [Licensee] for the purpose of this Agreement.

M.214

The [Licensor] will provide the [Licensee] with a letter of access to enable the [Licensee] to order all such stills and other materials directly at the [Licensee's] cost and expense from [specify location] to be used for the purposes of this Agreement.

M.215
The [Company] shall promptly supply on request by the [Licensee] such Masters of the [Films] together with [scripts/running orders] in the [English/other] language and music cue sheets. Subject to acceptance of the Masters by the [Licensee], the [Licensee] shall upon delivery of the invoices pay to the [Company] the cost of supplying and reproducing the Masters including freight, any taxes, insurance and other charges.

M.216
'Master' shall mean a best quality [one inch 'C' format PAL videotape] or (at the [Licensee's] option) [1 35mm positive print in colour on low contrast stock] from the best complete original of the [Film] reasonably available together with a separate synchronous magnetic English Language soundtrack fully coated and Dolby encoded in two-track stereophonic sound, technically suitable for transfer on to [specify] for use in the manufacture of [DVDs/Discs] reproducing the [Film]. The [Licensee] shall be entitled for the purposes and the duration of this Agreement to retain possession of and have the sole right of access to the Master supplied by the [Licensor] hereunder and all derivatives of such Master made by or for the [Licensee] shall be and remain the property of the [Licensor].

M.217
'Master' shall mean a one-inch type 'C' broadcast standard videotape recording in 625-line PAL fully edited in colour (unless the [Film] is stated to be black and white only) technically suitable for use in the manufacture of [DVDs/Discs] reproducing the [Film(s)].

M.218
'Master' shall mean a fully edited, pristine, digitised [format] recording of broadcast standard incorporating fully synchronous music, voice, text and sound effects, technically suitable for use in the manufacture of [DVDs/Discs].

M.219
'Master' shall mean the edited Master of each of the [Programmes] reproduced as a Digital [Format] Copy Master.

M.220
'The Treatment' shall be the synopsis of the [DVD/Video/Disc]. A copy of which is attached to and forms part of this Agreement.

M.221
'The [DVD/Video/Disc] 'shall be the following film and any associated sound recording based on the Treatment entitled [–] which shall be [–] minutes in duration and briefly described as follows [–].

M.222

'The [DVD/Video/Disc] 'shall be the promotional film and any associated sound recording for the [Musical Work] to be performed by the [Artiste]. A full description of which is set out below:

1.1   Budget [figure/currency].

1.2   Completion date of the final edited version [date].

1.3   Director, production company, contributors, artists, musicians and compose [specify].

1.4   Duration [specify].

1.5   Language [specify].

1.6   Format of the final edited version to be supplied [specify].

M.223

'The Artistic Concept' shall be the brief narrative description of the [Film] which includes images, locations and the technical format. A copy of the Artistic Concept is attached to and forms part of this Agreement as Schedule [–].

M.224

The [Assignor] confirms that the [Video/DVD/Disc] shall be produced so that it appears on screen in colour in the English Language and that the musical work, voices, text and sound effects will be synchronised with the visual images and will be delivered in the following digitised format [–].

M.225

The [Assignor] confirms that the film shall not contain any other music, sound recordings, recordings or sound effects other than the [Musical Work] unless there is prior written consent by the [Assignee].

M.226

'The Material' shall be the following material of the [Film]:

1.1   Technical material suitable for [purpose] comprising of [–].

1.2   Laboratory access letter.

1.3   Typed final script.

1.4   Typed running order.

1.5   Music cue sheet.

1.6   Labels, packaging, any master material of trademarks, service marks, images of artists, stills, slogans, and any advertising, promotional, publicity and marketing material.

1.7 A full and comprehensive statement [with extracts of supporting documents if required] setting out all contractual obligations, copyright, consents, releases, moral right assertions and waivers, trade marks, service marks, logos, credits, images, copyright notices, copyright warnings and disclaimers in relation to the [Film] and any other material to be supplied, produced or created including packaging, publicity and advertising. The detail must include a description, image, duration, position, colour, context and background.

M.227

'The [DVD/Video/Disc] Package' shall be the following material of the [Film]:

1.1 Technical material of first class quality comprising [–].

1.2 [Specify] copies of the [Film] in the following digitised format [–].

1.3 A complete list of the laboratories and any other locations at which any material relating to the [Film] is held together with access letters giving the [Assignee] irrevocable authority to obtain the material and make copies for use at its sole discretion.

1.4 The original copies of the insurance policies arranged for the benefit of the [Assignee].

M.228

'The Master Material' shall be the following material of the [Film/Work] :

1.1 Technical material of first class quality [–].

1.2 Not less than [number/format] copies.

1.3 A complete list of the technical and master material and any copies in any format, gauge including rushes, outtakes, videotapes, discs, sound recordings, music and effects, tracks, title and subtitle tracks, viewing copies in the possession or under the control of the [Assignor].

1.4 A complete list of the laboratories and any other locations at which any material relating to the [Film/Work] is held together with access letters giving the [Assignee] irrevocable authority to have access to, make copies and remove the material at its sole discretion.

1.5 Typed final script and running order.

1.6 Music cue sheet listing each musical work with the name of the composer, author and publisher, the duration of each musical work and the description of use in each case.

1.7 A detailed statement and copies of all records of the contractual obligations, copyright, music and performing rights and mechanical

1053

reproduction clearance and payments, all moral rights asserted and waived, trade marks, service marks and any other rights and obligations which apply and/or have been agreed to in respect of the [Film/Work].

M.229

'The Film Material' shall be all the physical material of the [Film] and/or parts in the possession or under the control of the [Assignor] including:

1.1 All technical and master material and any copies in any format and in any gauge including, but not limited to, negatives, rushes, outtakes, videotapes, prints, sound recordings, music and effects, tracks, DVDs, CD-Roms, CDs, discs, trailers, promotional clips, banners, viewing copies, and website material and any material used on any telecommunication system at any time.

1.2 A complete list of all premises, locations and laboratories in the possession or under the control of the [Assignor] or any third party at which any material of any nature relating to the [Film] and/or parts is held together with access letters giving the [Assignee] irrevocable authority to obtain, remove and make copies as it thinks fit.

1.3 All originals and all copies of all records, documents and other data, text, information, images, graphics, computer generated material or storage system or otherwise in any form including scripts, music cue sheets, publicity, photographs, stills, negatives, posters, catalogues, packaging, labels, advertising, and promotional material. Contracts, copyright, credit and moral right clearances, domain names, trade marks, service marks, logos, icons, telephone numbers, and any obligations and commitments, any other intellectual property, and any consents, licences, releases or insurance.

M.230

'The Master Material' shall be all the sound recordings, documents, contracts and material stored on a storage and retrieval system and/or a computer hard drive and/or in other physical and/or other form in any medium in the possession and/or under the control of the [Assignor] in respect of [Name] in respect of any song, music and/or lyrics and in particular the material set out in Appendix [–] which is attached to and forms part of this Agreement.

M.231

1.1 The [Images/Photographs/Maps] supplied by [Name] on loan for inclusion in the [Film/Programme] on the day of the interview will not be retained and shall be returned immediately to [Name].

1.2 [Name] agrees that no additional payment and/or fee shall be charged for any use in the [Film/Programme] [DVD/Disc/CD] except that paid under clause [–].

1.3 In the event that the [Distributor] wishes to sib-license the [Film/Programme] and exploit the [Images/Photographs/Maps] reproduced in the [Film/Programme] in any other manner then an additional agreement shall be required and [Name] shall be entitled to refuse consent.

M.232

1.1 The [Licensee] agrees and undertakes that it shall not be entitled to exploit the [Sound Recordings/Film/Photographs] of the interview by [Name] on [date] except for the purpose of exhibition at the [Event] to be held on [date] at [location] organised by [specify].

1.2 No other form of exploitation and/or reproduction is permitted in any form and the [Sound Recordings/Film/Photographs] may not be licensed, sold, reproduced and/or supplied to any third party and/or made available on television, the internet and/or otherwise.

1.3 That in the event it is proposed to exploit the material in any other form that the prior written consent of [Name] and/or his/her estate shall be required and a new agreement concluded in which [Name] and/or his/her estate shall receive an advance of not less than [number/currency] and no less than [number] per cent of all the gross sums received from any form of exploitation.

Film and Television

M.233

The [Production Company] agrees to provide the [Distributor/Sponsor] with the following material at its sole cost upon request:

1.1 Copies and samples of all reviews, publicity, promotional, advertising and packaging material in respect of the [Programme].

1.2 [Number] free copies of all of the [Programme] in each format that it shall be either exploited or made available to the general public.

1.3 Other [–].

M.234

The [Licensor] shall deliver to the [Licensee] a first-class [specify format] of the English Language version in stereo. The print shall be first-class, unused, composite print, splice-free and free from scratches, fully edited and assembled, main and end titles and with such proper colour and shading intensity as is customarily required for television. The soundtracks shall be unused, splice-free and in perfect synchronisation with the visual images. The cost of such material shall be paid for by the [Licensee].

M.235

The 'Delivery Items' shall mean the following material to be supplied by the [Licensor] at the [Television Company's] cost and expense:

1.1 New and first-class technically acceptable 35mm transmission print of the full-length version with all commercial breaks removed of the [Film] in the English Language complete with the main and end titles and all credits on which the sound shall be fully synchronised with the picture.

1.2 Laboratory access letter in customary form giving the [Television Company] the irrevocable right to order prints of the [Film] at its sole expense direct from the original negatives held at the laboratories and containing irrevocable instructions that negatives may not be destroyed or transferred from the possession of said laboratories prior to the expiry of the Licence Period without the prior consent of the [Television Company].

1.3 Two clean typed copies of detailed final dialogue and action continuity for the [Film].

1.4 Two copies of a timed music cue sheet in customary form listing each musical work included therein, the name of the composer, author and publisher, the timing of each item and description of use for the [Film].

1.5 A statement of the on screen credit, copyright notice, trade mark, logo, and other contractual obligations for the [Film].

1.6 Such publicity material and still photographs and any trailers of the [Film] as are available.

M.236

The [Licensor] shall supply on loan [specify format of master] of the [Film] from which the [Company] shall be entitled to make at its cost a [specify format] for the purposes of this Agreement. The Licensor shall also supply to the [Company] neutral title backgrounds and title list.

M.237

The [Licensor] shall supply on loan [a digitised format] of the [Film] from which the [Company] shall be entitled to make at its cost [a master copy] for the purposes of this Agreement.

M.238

'The Delivery Items' shall mean:

1.1 One new first-class [35mm colour print/format] of the [Film] in the English Language complete with main and end titles and all credits which the sound shall be fully synchronised with the picture, the cost of which shall be paid for by the [Company].

1.2 One copy of a music cue sheet in the usual form listing each musical work, the name of the composer, author and publisher, the duration of each item and the description of use.

1.3 Samples of any available advertising and promotional material including posters, press books, photographs, trailers, which shall be supplied either on loan or at the [Company's] cost.

M.239

It is agreed that written [21 days] of the execution of the Agreement the [Company] shall arrange for the provision of [Number] rolls of [type of stock] in ratio [–] at the [Company's] cost to the [Licensor]. The [Licensor] shall then deliver the unprocessed film stock to the [Company]. The [Company] shall arrange for and bear the cost of processing and the [Licensor] shall collect the film stock for printing which shall be at the [Licensor's] cost.

M.240

All [digitised formats/DVDs/Prints/Videotapes/Discs] of the [Film] provided by the [Company] shall be in first-class condition and shall be to such technical standard as the [Licensee] may require for its programme material. After the expiry of the Licence Period the [Licensee] shall destroy all original master material of the [Film] in its possession or if the [Company] so requests shall return all such material to the [Company] at the [Company's] expense.

M.241

The [Licensee] shall be responsible for the safekeeping of the negative during the production of the [Series] and at all other times until the delivery to the [Licensee] of a master of the [Series]. Each party shall then be responsible whilst the master is in its possession for any loss or damage. Ownership of the negative shall at all times remain with the [Licensee] or the [Licensor] in accordance with Clause [–].

M.242

The [Film Package] shall be the following material of the [Film] supplied at the [Licensors/Licensees] sole cost including freight, taxes, duties, insurance and packaging:

1.1 Technical material of first-class quality comprising of [format].

1.2 Laboratory access letter.

1.3 Typed transcript of the final [script/dialogue].

1.4 Typed copy of [running order/action continuity/shot list].

1.5 Music cue sheet listing each musical work with the name of the composer, author and publisher including the duration of each musical work and the description of use in each case.

1.6 Statement of credits, copyright notices, trade marks, service marks, logos, moral rights, waivers or assertions or disclaimers, product placement, sponsorship and any other contractual obligations in the [Film], preview material, commercials, and trailers, publicity, advertising, promotional or any other material [in words, description and images].

1.7 Samples of such publicity and promotional material, trade marks, service marks, logos, preview material, commercials, and trailers, advertising, promotional or any other material as may be available including posters, photographs and stills.

M.243

The [Licensee] agrees to reimburse the [Licensor] in respect of all the reproduction and delivery costs incurred in providing an acceptable [Film Package] subject to satisfactory receipts being provided upon request.

M.244

The [Series Package] shall be the following first-class quality material of the [Series] comprising:

1.1 [number] [format] copies.

1.2 Typed synopsis of each episode.

1.3 Music cue sheet listing full details of each musical work.

1.4 Statement of all credit, contractual and moral obligations.

1.5 A detailed statement of the copyright consents and other clearances obtained and due in relation to all artists, music and any other material in the [Series] and the [Series Package].

M.245

'The Film Package' shall be the following material of the [Film]:

1.1 Technical material [–].

1.2 Script, music cue sheet and running order.

1.3   Statement of credit, copyright notices and other moral and contractual obligations.

1.4   Copies of such advertising and publicity material as may be available.

M.246
'The Programme' shall be the film and any associated sound recording to be produced by the [Company] provisionally entitled [–].

M.247
'The Series' shall be the series of films and any associated sound recordings based on the format entitled [–] comprising of [number] episodes each of which shall be [–] minutes in duration.

M.248
'Programmes' shall mean the programmes set out in the Schedule and such other programmes as may be added to the Schedule from time to time by written agreement between the parties.

M.249
'Programme' shall include all literary, dramatic, artistic and musical material, computer generated material, graphics, images, text, film, commentary, soundtrack, recordings and the source material and all third party material incorporated into, synchronised with or otherwise forming part of such programme. It shall also include all material produced for the purposes of the programme, negative, tapes, films, DVDs, discs-recordings, outtakes and sound recordings, however commissioned, ordered or otherwise.

M.250
'The Film' means a feature length cinematograph film entitled [Title] based on [Work] of which the following are brief particulars:

* Screenwriter [–] Individual Producer [–] Director [–]

* Composer(s) [–] Principal Artist [–]

* Running Time [–] [Colour Process/Gauge/Format] [–]. colons OK here

M.251
'The Programme' shall be the film and any associated sound recording entitled [Title] which shall be [–] minutes] in duration in [colour/black and white] in the [English] language.

M.252
The [Assignor] shall provide a detailed statement to the [Assignee] on or before [date] of the following matters in relation to the [Series] in the possession or under the control of the [Assignor]:

MATERIAL

1.1 All technical and master material, any copies in any format or gauge including, but not limited to, negatives, prints, rushes, out-takes, videotapes, DVDs, discs, recordings, music and effect tracks, title and sub-title tracks, trailers, promos, viewing copies.

1.2 A complete list of the laboratories, warehouses and other locations at which any material is held together with access letters giving the [Assignee] irrevocable authority to obtain material and/or copies at its sole discretion.

1.3 A complete list of all material held by any third party.

1.4 Copies of all documents, records, data in any form, registrations including, but not limited to, contracts, licences, consents, waivers, facility or other agreements, dialogue lists, scripts, music cue sheets, publicity, promotional, advertising material, computer software, premium telephone lines, domain names.

1.5 All on-screen publicity, advertising and promotional obligations in any media.

1.6 Publicity and marketing material, photographs, negatives, stills, posters, catalogues, and merchandising.

1.7 All copyright, copyright notices, trade mark, service marks, logos, design rights, moral rights, waivers, assertions, disclaimers and other intellectual property rights or contractual obligations including music, consents, clearances, fees and payments set out in full stating the party, personal details, the obligations, payments, and rights.

M.253

'The Format' shall be the novel idea for and structure of a [Series of Films] created by the [Licensor] details of which are attached to and form part of this Agreement in Schedule [–].

M.254

'The Format Package' shall be all the material of the [Format] in the possession or under the control of the [Assignor] including copies of all contracts, licences, copyright clearances and permissions and other data in any form and a complete list of all material relating to the [Format] held by any third party.

M.255

'The Format' shall be the original concept and novel idea for the structure of a series of films which are briefly described as follows [–]. Full details of which are attached to and form part of this Agreement in Appendix [–]. [Title, script, characters, plot, storyline, location, intellectual property rights, running order, sequence, design and layout of set, presentation of questions and answers, score system, prizes, slogans, graphics, costumes, telephone line recordings, website material and text messaging material and icons].

M.256
'The Treatment' shall be the summary of the contents and structure of the [Programme]. A copy of the treatment is attached to and forms part of this Agreement.

M.257
'The Treatment' shall mean the existing treatment by the [Writer] for the [Film] based on the novel referred to above. A copy of the Treatment has been delivered by the [Writer] to the [Company].

M.258
'The Treatment' shall be the summary of the [Pilot] which is based on the Format. Details of the Treatment are attached to and form part of this Agreement.

M.259
'The Treatment' shall be the summary of each of the episodes of the [Series]. A copy of the Treatment is attached to and forms part of this Agreement.

M.260
'The Treatment' shall be the summary of the [Film] based on [Work]. A copy of the Treatment is attached to and forms part of this Agreement.

M.261
'The Treatment' shall be the summary of the storylines prepared by the [Scriptwriter] based on the [Author's Work].

M.262
'The Scripts' shall be the draft and final scripts based on the Treatment to be prepared by the [Writer].

M.263
'The Scripts' shall be all draft and final scripts to be prepared by the [screenplay writers] based on the [Author's] Work.

M.264
'The Work' shall mean the fully developed screenplay of the [Work] based on the novel published under the title [–] by [Name] for the Film which is provisionally entitled [–] and shall further include all drafts, redrafts and

developments made during the course of pre-production and preparation and development of the [Work].

M.265

'The Work' shall mean all the Treatments and Scripts prepared or written by the [Author] including all drafts, redrafts, revisions, arrangements, translations, sub-titled versions, adaptations, or other developments including, but not limited to the titles, characters, plots, tones, dialogues, sequences, situations, and incidents arising from the provision of the [Author's] services pursuant to this Agreement.

M.266

The [Author] agrees and undertakes that he/she shall not have the right to create, develop, adapt and/or produce any sequel, strikingly similar work or material and/or subsequent film, mini-series, DVD, storyline, publication, or otherwise in any media at any time based on the whole and/or part of the [Work].

M.267

'The Footage' shall be the following parts from the [Film] [Reference/maximum duration/format].

M.268

'Actor's Performance' shall mean the reproduction into electronic form of the movements and gestures of the actor in synchronisation with the voice using the [Unit] so as to produce movements in the representation of the [Character].

M.269

'The Film' shall be the feature length cinematic film and any associated sound recordings to be produced by the [Production Company] based on and adapted from the [Author's Work] entitled [–] which shall be [–] minutes in duration in the [–] language.

M.270

The [Production Company] agrees that the [Author] shall be permitted to view the rushes of the [Film], the edited versions and the final version upon request.

M.271

The [Company] agrees and undertakes not to use, reproduce, licence, exploit and/or display and/or distribute the [Work/Film] by any method, manner or in conjunction with any other material which would be offensive, derogatory, defamatory, or otherwise prejudicial to the [Author].

M.272

The [Company] agrees that where new material is created and/or developed by them and/or any licensee whether in the [specify] language and/or any other adaptation which includes the name, image and/or character played by [Name] in the [Programme]. That the [Company] will consider of any comments which [Name] and his/her agent may make in respect of any draft and/or final version and shall ensure that all such new material does not represent [Name] and/or his/her character in any offensive and/or derogatory manner. That the [Company] acknowledges and recognises that [Name] and all material associated with him/her must be suitable for children.

M.273

1.1   [Name] agrees that the [Company] may create, develop and adapt such material as it thinks fit at any time to promote the [Film] and/or any part and/or any associated exploitation which may include the personal name, caricature, a three dimensional representation of [Name] and/or his/her image and/or his/her character which shall include but not be limited to any trailers, posters, product endorsement, merchandising and sub-licensing and distribution, blogs, apps, computer software and games, advertising, sponsorship and promotional material.

1.2   That where the [Company] is to receive any payments from a third party from 1.1 that the [Company] shall pay [Name] [number] per cent of all [gross/net] sums received at any time such payments to be made in [country] in [currency] within [number] months of receipt by the [Company].

General Business and Commercial

M.274

'The Designs' shall be the original concept and two-dimensional designs for a range of items described as follows [–]. Full details of the Designs are attached to and form part of this Agreement in Schedule [–].

M.275

'The Programme' shall be the [sound recordings] whether live or pre-recorded, broadcast or transmitted by [Radio Station] entitled [–] [length] [description].

M.276

'Artistic Work' shall [be defined in accordance with the Copyright Designs and Patents Act 1988 as amended] and shall mean:

1.1   A graphic work, photograph, sculpture or collage irrespective of artistic quality.

1.2   A work of architecture being a building or a model for a building.

1.3   A work of artistic craftsmanship.

M.277
'Graphic Work' shall include any painting, drawing, diagram, map, chart or plan and any engraving, etching, lithograph, woodcut or similar work,

M.278
'Sculpture' shall include a cast or model made for the purposes of the sculpture.

M.279
'The Artwork' shall mean any photographs, drawings, sketches, pictures, diagrams, maps or any other illustrations or visual images which are intended to be included as part of the [Work].

M.280
'Property' shall include all chattels, estates, real and personal, and all choses in action.

M.281
'Photographs' shall mean the physical and intellectual property rights in the negatives, stills, transparencies, images and prints howsoever stored, reproduced or supplied [which is not a film.]

M.282
'Photograph' shall [have the same interpretation the Copyright, Designs and Patents Act 1988 as amended] and mean a recording of light or other radiation on any medium on which an image is produced or from which an image may by any means be produced, and which is not part of a film.

M.283
'The Photographs' shall mean any photographs or drawings, sketches, pictures, diagrams or any other illustration which are intended to be included as part of the [Article].

M.284
'The Photographs' shall mean all recordings of light or other radiation on any medium on which an image is reproduced or from which an image may by any means be reproduced and which is not part of a film commissioned by the [person] or the [Company] or taken by them directly and shall include any negatives or prints howsoever stored or reproduced.

M.285

The [Company] reserves the exclusive right to take or arrange for the taking of photographs on the stands or at the [Exhibition]. The [Exhibitor] shall require the prior written consent of the [Company] in such circumstances and shall be required to pay a reasonable fee.

M.286

'The Stills' shall mean the following photographs: Reference Code [–] Title and Description [–] Source Material [–] to be reproduced and supplied by the [Licensor] to the [Licensee] at the [Licensee's] cost and risk.

M.287

'The Photographic Package' shall be the following material of the [Work] :

1.1 Number of developed prints [–] which shall be of the following dimensions [–] in [colour/black and white].

1.2 All technical and master material and any copies in any format including negatives and prints in the possession or under the control of the [Photographer].

M.288

'The Commissioned Work' shall be the following services or stills based on the summary to be created, produced, developed, printed and delivered by the [Photographer] to the [Assignee].

M.289

'The Stills' shall be the following photographs [reference code/title/ description/source material] in which the copyright is owned by [Name] and the physical material is owned by [Name].

M.290

'The Stills Material' shall be the following material owned or controlled by the [Licensor] to be reproduced and supplied to the [Licensee] at the [Licensee's] cost and risk [Description/Delivery Date/Address].

M.291

Subject to prior consultation the [Licensor] agrees that the [Licensee] shall be entitled to use his/her name, biography, and photograph, but not representational image, caricature or the name [specify] in respect of the exercise of the rights granted under this Agreement.

M.292

'The Records' shall be the reproduction of the master tape in whole or in part in any material form whether manufactured by any method for release to the general public or supplied or licensed to any third party with or without visual images.

M.293

'The Master Tape' shall be the sound recording of the performers which is in the following digitised format [–].

M.294

'Material' shall mean any and all materials of any nature whether comprising of:

1.1 Hardback and paperback books, newspapers, magazines, comics, stationery, cards, posters, stickers, calendars.

1.2 Images, graphics, photographs, drawings, illustrations, plans, sketches, electronically generated material, design rights, background tables, images, maps, computer generated art, maps.

1.3 Sounds, sound effects, sound recordings, music, ringtones, CDs, audio material.

1.4 Logos, trade marks, icons, characters, domain names, trading names, slogans, catchphrases.

1.5 Banners, bookmarks, borders, captions, clip art, links, blogs, website and internet material, and any material to be downloaded.

1.6 Terrestrial, cable, digital and satellite television, films, cartoons, videocassettes, discs and lasers, DVD, CD-Rom, games, films, advertisements, infomercials, mini-films, and landline and mobile telephone and any telecommunication system material, adaptations, and translations.

1.7 All products, articles, toys, merchandising, sponsorship, endorsement and product placement material.

1.8 All forms of electronic and digital and other method of supply, distribution, storage, and retrieval and mechanical reproduction.

1.9 Any combination of any and all such elements in 1.1 to 1.8, computer software, storage and retrieval system and any other media of any nature whether in existence now or created in the future.

M.295

'The Artwork' shall mean any photographs, plans, visual images, drawings, sketches, pictures, diagrams, maps, image maps or other illustrations or electronically generated material, logos, trade marks, design rights, character, clip art, computer generated art, domain name which are intended to be included as part of the [Work].

M.296

'The Work Material' shall mean all the material of the [Work] in the possession or under the control of the [Assignor] including:

1.1 All copies of any master material in any format and of any duration.

1.2 A list of locations at which any material is held together with access letters giving irrevocable authority for the [Assignee] to remove such material.

1.3 All documents, records, data in any form, contracts, licences, consents, waivers, lists, proofs, scripts, publicity, advertising material, computer software, photographs, advertisements, banners, negatives, posters, catalogues, and any other material in any medium.

M.297

The [Assignor] agrees that it shall not retain any right and/or interest in the [Work] and/or the [Work Material].

M.298

The [Assignor] agrees that it has fully disclosed any right or interest of third parties in the [Work Material].

M.299

1.1 [Name] agrees and undertakes that all material supplied by the [Company] for the purpose of reproduction for creating [Films/Printed Material/Websites] shall be held by [Name] is a secure and safe location and shall not be released and/or supplied to a third party at any time.

1.2 That when all the work required by the [Company] has been completed that [Name] shall return to the [Company] all material supplied by the [Company] and all copies held by [Name] at the [Company's] sole cost.

1.3 That in addition [Name] shall confirm in writing the existence and location of all other copies of the material that may be held and also any [Films/Printed Material/Websites] that may have been created.

1.4 [Name] acknowledges that it not the intention of this Agreement that [Name] shall be transferred any copyright, acquire any domain names and/or any computer software and/or data and/or any other intellectual property rights at any time. That in the event new rights and/or ownership are created and/or developed by [Name] based on work commissioned by the [Company] that [Name] shall transfer and assign all such rights to the [Company] in consideration of the payment of [one pound sterling/other]. That the [Company] shall arrange for such documents as may be necessary to be created and [Name] agrees to sign the documents to affect such transfer to [Name].

M.300

The [Company] does authorise and/or grant any consent for any material, data, trade mark and copyright notices and logos which are supplied under this Agreement to be edited, adapted and/or changed and/or registered by a third party at any time.

Internet and Websites

M.301

'The Website Material' shall mean the domain name and website reference [specify] and all the content, databases, downloads and links, but not any other website.

M.302

'The Website Material' shall mean the domain name and website reference [specify] and all the content, databases, downloads and associated material, but not any other website. The material shall include text, scripts, titles, index, data, footnotes, headings, publications, images, graphics, photographs, drawings, illustrations, plans, sketches, computer generated material, design rights, background, tables, maps, sounds, sounds, sound recordings, music, ringtones, icons, logos, trade marks, icons, characters, trading names, slogans, catchphrases, banners, bookmarks, borders, captions, clip art, and any advertising, promotional and publicity material and associated computer software, discs, CD-Roms and other methods of storage and retrieval of the material held, owned and/or controlled by [Name].

M.303

'The Digital File' shall mean the digitised record of the text of the [Work] which is held in electronic form for use on a website and/or the internet in any format.

M.304

'The Audio Digital File' shall mean the digitised record of the sound recordings which is held in electronic form for use on a website and/or the internet in any format.

M.305

'The Electronic Digital File' shall mean the digitised [and compressed] record of the words, text, sounds, music, logos, images, graphics, film, recordings and sound recordings which can be conveyed, transferred, supplied and/or distributed by electric, magnetic, electro-magnetic, electro-chemical, electro-mechanical means through any method or material and/or any telecommunication system and/or by any other means in electronic form [whether in existence now and/or created in the future]. This shall include but not be limited to use, display, exhibit, supply, license, reproduce, distribute and exploit in any medium and material in relation to the internet, websites, computers, telephones, mobiles, and any other gadgets and devices in any shape, form, process and method.

M.306

'The Contributor's Work' shall mean the audiovisual interview with the [Contributor] on the subject of [specify] which shall be filmed, recorded and edited for a Podcast for the [Company]. A summary of which is attached and forms part of this Agreement in Schedule [–].

M.307

'The Podcast' shall be the final version of the film and sound recordings of the [Contributor's Work] produced and developed by the [Company] and/or an authorised third party engaged for that purpose.

M.308

Where any material is submitted and/or provided and/or posted by a member of the public either on the [Website] and/or as part of a survey and/or through a competition and/or otherwise. The [Company] reserves the right to edit, adapt and/or delete any material where in its view it is offensive and/or likely to lead to a claim for defamation and/or civil and/or criminal proceedings and/or the [Company] has been notified and/or suspects that it is an infringement of copyright held by a third party and/or any other intellectual property, domain names, trade marks, service marks, design rights and/or otherwise. In such event the [Company] may exclude entry by that person to any account, online forum or competition and notify them that are not entitled to access any website and/or material owned and/or controlled by the [Company].

M.309

1.1 [Name] agrees that he/she has created and developed the [Computer Software/App/Blog/Website] for the [Distributor] based on an original idea and concept and/or brief summary of required work by the [Distributor].

1.2 That [Name] has agreed to payment of a fee of [number/currency] for all the work that he/she does and all the material which is supplied under this Agreement for the [Distributor] and that no additional payments, fees and/or expenses and/or royalties shall be paid and/or due.

1.3 That [Name] agrees and undertakes to assign all copyright and computer software rights and intellectual property rights and codes, passwords and master source material and copies to the [Distributor] upon request both in the form of the assignment of all such rights and the physical and stored material in any format and/or medium whether this Agreement is terminated early or not before all the work is completed.

M.310
'The Blog' shall mean the online internet series of pages hosted on [specify] which are written and composed by [Name] as a series of articles, images, photographs and links.

M.311
'The Blog' is on the [website/platform] known as [specify] owned by [specify] and controlled by [specify]. The Blog is entitled [specify] and written by [Name] and/or a member of his/her staff and edited by [specify].

M.312
'The App' is entitled [specify] and features [specify] and is available to the public as a free download and/or accessible from [website] on [specify].

M.313
'The App' entitled [specify] is supplied by [specify] from [source] to members of the public through [source] at a cost of [number/currency] for use in conjunction with [specify] for a period of up to [number] days.

M.314
'The Banner Link' shall mean the advertisement and promotional film and sound recording supplied and owned by the [Company] which features [Product] entitled [specify].

Merchandising

M.315
The [Owner] agrees that the [Goods] shall conform to the quality and description stated and shall be fit for their intended purpose and free from all defects.

M.316
All specification, drawings and any other material or information provided to the [Owner] by the [Company] shall remain the property of the [Company].

M.317

Any further material that the [Licensee] may require in the exercise of the rights hereunder may be obtained at the Licensee's cost from [Name/Address].

M.318

The [Agent] agrees that it shall not be entitled to permit or authorise the use, reproduction, copying, drawing, taking photographs, filming or exploitation in any form or medium of the [Items] or the [Company] Logo at any time without the prior written consent of the [Company].

M.319

The [Licensee] shall make available a copy of the [Items] specified in the Agreement for inspection and retention by the [Licensor] upon request at the [Licensee's] cost.

M.320

'The Prototype' shall be the three-dimensional reproduction of the [Board Game] created and reproduced by the [Licensor].

M.321

'The Licensed Articles' shall be the three-dimensional reproductions based on the prototype to be manufactured and distributed by the [Company].

M.322

The [Licensor] agrees to provide the [Company] upon request with access to all such materials of the [Product] and the [Prototype] as may be available to assist in the production and manufacture of the [Licensed Articles].

M.323

The [Licensor] shall supply such basic reference drawings and specifications of the [Characters] comprised in the [Product] as are available. All further artwork and designs involving the [Product] shall be based on the material and shall be carried out at the cost of the [Licensee]. All such artwork must be approved in all cases pursuant to Clause [–] provided that the [Licensee] shall have the right to commission a third party to prepare and produce any such artwork subject to the terms of this Agreement.

M.324

The [Product] shall be the original concept and novel idea for a [Product] created by the [Licensor] which is briefly described as follows Title [–]. Brief Description [–]. A copy of the full two-dimensional illustrative and written details of the [Product], including the colour, dimensions and materials of each of the components and a complete list of rules and instructions are attached to and form part of this Agreement.

M.325

'The Character' shall be the original concept and novel idea for a character which is briefly described as follows [Name/Trade Mark/Logo]. Full details of the character are attached to and form part of this Agreement.

M.326

'The Characters' shall be the original concept and novel idea for a series of characters which are briefly described as follows [Names] based on [specify source and copyright owner] with the identifying and original features [specify].

Full details of the characters are attached to and form part of this Agreement in Schedule [–]. [Copyright and other intellectual property rights, design rights, trade marks, logos, plot, storyline, artwork, colour, signs, scoreboard, equipment, catchphrase, slogan, costumes, outfits, scripts, 2D, 3D drawings].

M.327

'The Licensed Article' shall be the licensed product to be produced and distributed by the [Licensee] which shall be based on or derived from the [Character] and which is described as follows [–]. Full details of the [Licensed Article] are attached to and form part of this Agreement in Schedule [Colour, size, name, design, material, accessories].

M.328

The [Licensee] agrees that the [Licensor] shall be entitled to approve the [Licensed Articles] prior to manufacture and distribution. The [Licensee] undertakes to supply such samples of the [Licensed Articles] in the exact form and material in which the [Licensee] proposes to manufacture, distribute, market, advertise, promote and sell the [Licensed Articles] at the [Licensee's] sole cost. The [Licensee] acknowledges that such approval must be in writing from the [Licensor].

M.329

The [Licensee] agrees to provide the [Licensor] with not less than [number] [Licensed Articles] in each and every form in which they are released and/ or sold to the general public at the [Licensee's] cost.

M.330

'The Licensed Articles' shall be any licensed product based on or derived from the [Character] to be produced and distributed under agreements to be instigated, negotiated and concluded by the [Agent] [or any sub-agent or sub-licensee].

M.331

It is agreed that all merchandising, designs and formats shall be subject to the approval of the [Company] and such approval shall not be unreasonably withheld. The designs and formats shall be approved by the [Company] within [21 days] of delivery. In the event that there is no reply, then approval shall be deemed to have been given after the expiry of [21 days] following delivery.

M.332

The [Company] shall supply such basic reference drawings and specifications of the [Character] as are available. All further artwork and designs based on the [Character] for the [Products] shall be at the [Licensee's] cost and shall not be manufactured or distributed to any third party until the prior written approval of the [Company] has been provided. It is agreed that a third party may be engaged by the [Licensee] for the purpose of creating the artwork and designs.

M.333

The [Company] shall submit to the [Licensor] for written approval samples of the [Licensed Articles] and any contents or other articles to be sold or used including wrappings, containers, display materials, advertisements and publicity. The [Company] shall not distribute any [Licensed Articles] or publish any material unless prior written approval shall have been obtained.

M.334

The [Agent] agrees to ensure that all third parties to be licensed by the [Licensor] under this Agreement shall agree that the prior written approval of the [Licensor] shall be required to approve such samples of the [Licensed Articles] in the exact form and material in which such third party proposes to manufacture, distribute, supply and/or sell any of the [Licensed Articles].

M.335

'The Format' shall mean, but not be limited to, all the goodwill and reputation, the title, the basic idea and concept, the original script, character, plot, storyline, location, running order, design, layout, colour, signs, scoreboards, studio equipment, the rules, procedures, catchphrases, questions, answers, slogans, costumes, outfits, all written material, graphics, artwork and computer-generated graphics, all intellectual property rights, design rights, trade marks, service marks, logos, musical, literary, dramatic, artistic and other works which are described in detail in Appendix [1] and shall form part of this Agreement.

M.336

'The Format Package' shall mean all the material of the [Format] in the possession or under the control of the [Assignor] including copies of all documents, records and other data and material in any form and a complete list of all material relating to the [Format] held by any third party.

M.337

'The Board Game' shall be the original concept and novel idea for a board game created by the [Licensor] which is briefly described as follows [Title] [brief description]. A copy of the full two-dimensional illustrative and written details of the [Board Game] including colour, dimensions and materials of each of the components and a complete list of the rules and instructions are attached to and form part of this Agreement as Schedule [1].

M.338

'The Designs' shall be the original concept and two-dimensional designs, sketches, drawings and patterns for an individual piece of clothing described as follows [–].

M.339

'The Designs' shall be the original concept and two-dimensional designs for a range of [–] and other products to be created and provided by the [Designer]. The Design shall include all such designs which are set out in the attached Schedule [–] and form part of this Agreement together with such other designs as are created by the [Designer] in accordance with the terms of this Agreement.

M.340

'The Garment' shall be the three-dimensional reproduction of the Designs to be created and supplied by the [Designer] which shall principally be of the following material [–] and in the following colours [–].

M.341

'The Prototype' shall be the three-dimensional reproductions of the Designs which are the final products upon which the manufacture of the [Licensed Articles] are to be based.

M.342

'The Prototype' shall be the three-dimensional reproduction of the [Board Game] created and produced by the [Licensee].

M.343

'The Licensed Articles' shall be the three-dimensional reproductions based on the [Prototype] to be produced, manufactured and distributed by the [Licensor].

M.344

'The Licensed Articles' shall be the three-dimensional reproductions and adaptations of the Designs to be manufactured by the [Licensee].

M.345

The [Licensee] shall not be entitled to reproduce, distribute and supply copies of the [Licensed Article] based on the [Character] until the [Licensor] has provided written approval of the sample, the finished article, the packaging and the promotional material.

M.346

The [Sub-Licensee] shall not be entitled to edit, adapt and/or alter the marketing material supplied by the [Licensee] for the [Product] without the prior written approval of the [Licensee] in each case.

M.347

The [Licensee] agrees that it shall not be entitled to register as a domain name, trade mark and/or with any collecting society and/or government and/or international organisation any title, chapter headings and/or other any fictional character names, places names, catch phrases and/or any other images, text and/or themes associated with the [Work] and/or any part either in its original form and/or as adapted under this Agreement including any translation in any language.

M.348

[Name] and the [Licensee] agree that where any new material is created and/or developed under this Agreement by the [Licensee] at the [Licensees'] sole cost. That the parties shall be joint owners of all copyright, intellectual property rights and any other interest and in any media and format and other form of exploitation. Such joint ownership shall include new domain names, trade marks, websites, merchandising and publication material in any part of the world at any time.

M.349

'The Licensed Product' shall mean a [specify item] which bear the name, logo and image of [Name] in the exact form agreed in Schedule [–] and for which the sample for manufacture has been approved by [Name].

Publishing

M.350

'The Synopsis' shall mean the summary of the [Work] which sets out the chapter outlines, structure and general content of the [Work]. A copy of the synopsis is attached to and forms part of this Agreement.

M.351

The [Author] shall deliver [two] copies of the complete typescript of the [Work] consisting of approximately [Number] words ready for setting by the printer together with any artwork, photographs or illustrations [at the [Authors] cost and expense].

M.352

'The Author's Work' shall mean the original work of the [Author] including the Artwork entitled [–] published by [–] ISBN reference [–].

M.353

'The Work' shall be the following book including the artwork based on the synopsis provisionally entitled [–] which shall consist of approximately [number] typed A4 pages.

M.354

'The Synopsis' shall mean the brief summary of the [Work] which sets out the main elements of the storyline, the principal characters, chapter headings, structure and intended general content of the [Work]. A copy of the synopsis is attached to but does not form part of this Agreement.

M.355

'The Artwork' shall mean any photographs, drawings, sketches, pictures and diagrams, maps or other illustrations supplied by [Name] which are intended to be included as part of the Article.

M.356

'The Artwork' shall mean any photograph, drawing, sketch, picture, diagram, map, chart, plans, graphic work or any other illustration or any engraving, lithograph, woodcut or similar work and any other material listed [–] which forms part of or is attached to the [Work].

M.357

The [Licensee] undertakes not to permit, authorise, license or transfer the right to publish the Extracts or part(s) of the [Work] in any other newspaper, periodical or magazine owned or controlled by any third party or any other media throughout the Territory for the duration of the Licence Period except for the purposes of review, criticism or other fair dealing.

M.358

'The Periodical' shall mean the following publication owned or controlled by the [Licensee] in which the [Work] is to be serialised [–].

M.359

'The Extracts' shall mean the following parts of the [Work]: Written text hardback edition ISBN [reference] pages [–]. Illustrations on pages [–].

M.360

The [Publisher] shall send the [Author] two complete sets of proofs of the [hardback and paperback Book] and proofs of the illustrations, captions and notes on the jacket, the copyright notices and any other material to be included in or on the Book. The [Author] shall correct and return the proofs to the [Publisher] within [specify period]. The [Author] shall bear the cost of the proof corrections other than the printers or the [Publisher's] error in excess of [specify percentage] of the cost of the composition. The [Author] shall be notified in writing of such costs which shall be set out in detail. The [Publisher] shall then be entitled to deduct such sum from the royalties which shall become due to the [Author] after publication from the sale of the [Work] in the subsequent accounting period. In the event the [Work] is not published for any reason then this sum shall be the sole responsibility of the [Publisher] and the Author shall not be liable for such sum.

M.361

The [Publisher] agrees to send a copy of the final edited proof to the [Author] at least [specify period] before it is sent to the printers.

M.362

The [Author] will read and correct the proofs of the [Book] and will return them to the [Publisher] within [three weeks] of receipt. In the event that the proofs are not corrected and returned by the [Author] the [Publisher] shall be entitled to arrange for the proofs to be read and corrected (at the [Author's] cost) and shall be entitled to print and publish the [Work].

M.363

The [Author] shall correct and return the printed proofs to the [Publisher] within [twenty-eight] days of receipt. In the event that the cost of the [Author's] corrections amount to more than [ten per cent] of the cost of the composition then the amount in excess of [ten per cent] shall be payable by the [Author].

M.364

The [Publisher] shall be entitled to deduct from any sums due to the [Author] under this Agreement all costs of alterations and changes arising from any request by the [Author] which are incurred by the [Publisher] (but specifically excluding artists, editors, printer's errors, and errors and omissions by the [Publisher]). The [Author] shall bear the following costs:

1.1 The cost of such alterations to original or printed artwork or photography in excess of [five per cent] of the origination costs and artist's or photographer's fees.

1.2 Proofs of the [Work] in excess of [ten per cent] of the cost of the composition.

M.365
The [Publisher] agrees and undertakes that the [Author] shall not be liable and the [Publisher] shall pay all the costs and expenses of preparing the proofs, all alterations and changes to the proofs, artwork, photographs, index, mistakes by the printers, alterations due to legal problems and any other matters that may arise. The [Author] shall only bear the cost of the delivery of the manuscript.

M.366
The [Publisher] agrees and undertakes that the [Publisher] shall pay for the cost of the following matters in respect of the writing and preparation of the [Book], the proofs, the cover and/or jacket and any photographs, illustrations, maps, artwork, graphics, index, or other material that may be necessary for inclusion in the [Work]:

1.1 Where the [Author] requires access to additional material for research purposes for the text and/or artwork and/or photographs, to obtain copies and/or for the reproduction of any material. Then the [Publisher] agrees to pay the cost up to a maximum limit of [figure/currency]. This sum shall be paid upon request in advance subject to confirmation of the material required or upon receipt of an invoice for the expenditure.

1.2 There shall be no charges of any nature for any reason made by the [Publisher] to the [Author] for alteration, correction and changes made to the proofs and/or any later version of the [Book] whether due to requests by the [Publisher], [Author] and/or due to legal advice and/or any allegation and/or legal action at any time.

1.3 Where the index is prepared by the [Publisher] no deduction and/or charge shall be made to the [Author] either directly and/or by the deduction of any sums from the advance and/or royalties.

1.4 The cost of the design and artwork for the cover and/or jacket and any advertising, promotional and marketing material shall be entirely at the [Publishers] cost. No cost for any changes requested by the [Author] shall be claimed from and/or deducted from any sums due to the [Author].

M.367
'Typeface' includes an ornamental motif used in printing.

M.368

'Writing' includes any form of notation or code whether by hand or otherwise and regardless of the method by which or the medium in or on which it is recorded, and 'written' shall be constructed accordingly.

M.369

On first publication the [Author] will receive [Number] presentation copies of the [Work] and shall be entitled to purchase further copies for personal use but not for resale at a [number per cent] discount.

M.370

The [Authors] shall be entitled to receive on first publication [twelve] presentation copies each of the [Book] [in each and every format in which it is published]. The [Authors] shall also be entitled to purchase further copies for personal use at a discount on the published price [twenty-five per cent].

M.371

The [Author] shall be entitled to receive [number] free copies of the first and any subsequent editions of the [Work] and shall be entitled to purchase further copies at cost price for personal use, but not for resale.

M.372

The [Publisher] agrees at its sole cost to provide the [Author] with not less than [24] copies of the work in each and every form in which it is made available to the public in the Territory.

M.373

The [Author] undertakes that the [Work] will be of a standard and quality suitable for commercial exploitation and in any event shall consist of not less than [number] A4 typed pages together with a sufficient number of [black and white/colour] photographs to make [number] pages of illustration.

M.374

The [Publishers] agree and undertake that they shall not be entitled to add to, delete from and/or alter and/or adapt any part of the [Work] as delivered by the [Author]. The Editorial Director who edits the manuscript must advice the [Author] of all proposed changes they wish to make for the [Author's] approval. The only exception to this is where changes need to be made as a result of a libel report and/or other legal advice by the [Publisher's] legal advisors and they have recommended that there be some alterations in order to avoid potential legal actions by third parties.

M.375

The [Publishers] shall not have the right to engage any third party to contribute to the [Work].

M.376

The [Publishers] shall not have the right to publish the [Work] or any part in conjunction with any other work in any medium.

M.377

The [Publishers] shall not have the right to exploit, license, adapt, translate or create any new version in any media or country other than those specifically set out in this Agreement. Any other format or country requires a separate agreement.

M.378

The [Publishers] shall not include any material in any format in any medium of the [Work] which has not been provided by the [Authors] or for which the [Authors] have not provided their written consent in advance on each occasion.

M.379

The [Publishers] shall not without the [Authors'] prior written consent show the [Work] and/or disclose it contents to any other author before publication.

M.380

The [Publishers] shall publish the [Work] in [hardback/paperback/in print] no later than [twelve months] from acceptance of the [Work].

M.381

'The Artwork' shall mean the non-text elements of the Work including but not limited to the cover, artwork, illustrations, graphs, maps, drawings and photographs.

M.382

'The Logo and Title' shall mean the words and shapes and registrations set out in appendix [–] which are owned and/or have been registered as a trade mark and domain name and any other similar and/or distinct variations and which form part of this Agreement.

M.383

'The Project' shall be the website, app, blog and associated educational published works to be created, developed and developed by the [Distributor] based on the original concept and work of [Author].

Purchase and Supply of Products

M.384

All specifications, drawings, sketches, models, samples, tools, designs, technical information or data and other information written, oral or otherwise furnished to the [Buyer/Hirer] by the [Company] shall remain the property of the [Company] and shall be promptly returned on the [Company's] request. Such information shall be treated as strictly confidential and shall be kept safely and not used or disclosed by the [Buyer/Hirer] except as required for the performance of this order.

M.385

The description of [Goods] stated in this contract, invoice, order form, descriptive material, specifications, catalogue, brochure, or advertising material published or issued by the [Company] is for identification only and not intended as a sale by description. The [Goods] are available for inspection prior to any purchase order being made by the [Client].

M.386

It is a condition of the contract between the [Seller] and the [Company] for the supply of [Goods] that the [Goods] shall conform with the quality and description and other particulars stated in the purchase order. The [Goods] shall conform to all samples, drawings, descriptions and specifications furnished, shall be suitable for their intended purposes and free from all defects. These conditions shall survive any inspection, acceptance of delivery or payment and shall also include any replacement, repaired or substituted [Goods] by the [Seller] to the [Company].

M.387

'The Product' shall mean such items, goods or products including any packaging and instructions as are specified in Schedule [–] which is attached to and forms part of this Agreement. Together with such products which may be added by agreement and amendment in writing by both parties. Reference to the Product shall include the plural where the context so determines.

M.388

The [Seller] shall ensure that each [Product] is supplied with suitable packaging and supporting literature which clearly sets out the purpose for which each unit of the [Product] is suitable and the steps and precautions that should be taken to ensure that the [Product] is safe and will not put the public at risk.

M.389

'The Company's Products' shall mean the products and services of the [Company] which is briefly described as follows [–].

A two dimensional copy of the [Company's Products] is attached to and forms part of this Agreement in Schedule [–] setting out all intellectual property rights and where they should be displayed or located including copyright, trade marks, service marks, logos, designs, slogans, text, artwork, recordings, scripts, music, photographs, artistes, graphics, computer generated material, all consents, releases, moral rights, contractual obligations, clearances and releases and any sums owed and due.

M.390

'The Licensor's Logo' shall be the following trade mark, service mark, design or logo, slogan, text, graphics or other material. A two-dimensional copy of the [Licensor's Logo] is attached to and forms part of this Agreement in Schedule [–].

M.391

'The Licensee's Product' shall be the following product which is produced, manufactured and distributed by or on behalf of the [Licensee]. A two-dimensional copy of the [Licensee's Product] is attached to and forms part of this Agreement in Schedule [–].

M.392

'The Product Package' shall mean all material associated with the [Licensee's Product] including any labels, advertising, promotion and publicity material, films, videos, television and radio commercials and any other visual or sound recordings, photographs, computer generated graphics, scripts, artwork, music, DVDs, CD-Roms, CDs, discs, computer software, and material for the internet, mobile phones, premium rate telephone lines, domain names, trade marks, service marks, logos, slogans, and merchandising.

M.393

The [Licensee] agrees and undertakes not to use the [Material] supplied under this Agreement in any manner which could prejudice and/or damage the [Licensors] business and/or bring the [Licensor] into disrepute and/or create bad publicity and/or reduce sales of the [Licensors] products and/or services in any country.

M.394

The [Licensee] agrees and undertakes that the [Material] supplied under this Agreement is not to be reproduced and supplied to any third party, but is solely to be used for the purpose of the creating and developing the [Product].

M.395

1.1 [Name] agrees that [Name] shall not be entitled to access and/or be supplied with the master copies of the material created by the

[Company] to produce and manufacture the [Product/Article] and that these shall be retained by the [Company] in its archive for future use in respect of any order by [Name].

1.2 The [Company] agrees and undertakes that it shall not supply, use, adapt, and/or reproduce and/or permit any third party access to the master copies of the material created by the [Company] for [Name] at any time except with the prior written permission of [Name].

M.396

Where in the process of the development and manufacture of the [Product] by the [Company] based on a concept and idea supplied by [Name] material and/or copyright and/or intellectual property rights are created which are owned and/or controlled by the [Company]. Then the [Company] agrees and undertakes that it shall assign and transfer all such material and copyright and intellectual property rights to [Name] provided that the sums due for the work are paid and there are no additional fees and/or expenses due.

M.397

'The Template' shall be the master copy which has been approved by [Name] for the purpose of reproduction by the [Company] in the exact form, shape, material and packaging. A copy of which is set out in Appendix [–] and forms part of this Agreement.

Services

M.398

The [Company] agrees that it shall at its sole cost and expense provide the [Presenter] with a copy of any of the following material in its possession or control which is produced or created at any time:

1.1 Any photograph, illustrations, films, DVDs, discs, videos, sound recordings, computer generated material, website and internet material and/or other recordings of the [Presenter].

1.2 Any material used by the [Company] in relation to any advertisement, publicity, exhibition, corporate or commercial exploitation of the [Presenter] in which the [Presenter's] name, image, autograph, biography, performance or appearance is used in any form.

M.399

The [Director] shall at the end of the Term of this Agreement return and/or deliver to the [Company] all material prepared by him/her or in his/her possession or control relating to the [Company] or the services provided by the [Director]. The [Director] may only retain a copy of the script and such other material as the [Company] may agree that he/she can retain for his/her own personal use or references.

M.400

At the end of the Term of this Agreement the [Consultant] shall provide and/or return to the [Company]:

1.1 All originals and copies of all material in any format in any medium supplied by the [Company]. Where you wish to retain any material please supply a list for approval by the [Company].

1.2 All website material, domain name registration forms, databases, text, scripts, titles, index, data, publications, images, graphics, photographs, drawings, illustrations, plans, sketches, pictures, diagrams, computer generated material, tables, maps, sound recordings, music, logos, trade marks, characters, trading names, slogans, catchphrases, banners, and any advertising, promotional and publicity material, computer software, discs, CD-Roms and other methods of storage and retrieval of the material in the possession or under the control of the [Consultant] which are owned by or based on work for the [Company].

M.401

It is agreed that both parties shall be obliged to return to the other party all material which is owned and/or controlled by the other party which has been supplied on loan during the term of this Agreement.

M.402

1.1 The [Company] agrees that [Name] shall be entitled to retain and keep for his/her own personal reference and use copies of any documents, records, data and information in any media and format which have been supplied by the [Company] and/or obtained by [Name] from a third party during the course of this Agreement.

1.2 [Name] agrees that the material in 1.1 shall not be used for the purposes of publication and/or a television programme and/or distribution over the internet and/or any telecommunication system and/or exploitation in any media in any form at any time without the prior written consent of the [Company].

Sponsorship

M.403

The [Sponsor] agrees to provide the following items and benefits to the [Sportsperson] at the [Sponsor's] sole cost and expense for the duration of this Agreement [Sponsor's Product/Clothing/Equipment/Facilities/Medical Benefits/Other].

M.404

The [Sponsor] agrees that it shall provide the [Sportsperson] with a new car bearing the Sponsor's Logo for his personal and professional use throughout the Term of the Agreement which shall be comprehensively insured, taxed and serviced entirely at the [Sponsor's] expense and shall remain the property of the Sponsor. The car shall be [Description].

M.405

Any material which is provided by the [Sponsor] to the [Company] for distribution to the public at the [Event] may be retained and used by the [Company] after the [Event].

M.406

The [Sponsor] shall be entitled to request that any material donated by the [Sponsor] for the [Event] is destroyed and/or returned after the [Event] at the [Sponsor's] cost.

M.407

'The Marketing Material' supplied by the [Sponsor] shall comprise: the annual report and accounts; a recent newsletter; a three dimensional and two dimensional representation of [Sponsor's] name, logo and slogan; [number] banners; [number] flags; [number] [clothing]; [number] stationary; [number] wristbands]; and a short film highlighting [specify] which shall be supplied at the [Sponsor's] cost.

M.408

Where the [Company] has to incur additional costs and expenses in order to reproduce, adapt and/or display, exhibit and promote and market the [Sponsor] at the [Event/Festival]. Then the [Sponsor] shall be obliged to pay for all such additional costs and expenses in advance upon request by the [Company]. The [Sponsor] agrees and accepts that these additional costs may include flyers, brochure, posters, transport, labour, equipment, security, hire of staff, reproduction and manufacture costs, freight, insurance and administration.

University, Library and Educational

M.409

'The Consortium Project' shall mean the aims, work, targets, personnel, budget and proposals set out in the Schedule [–] which is attached to and forms part of this Agreement.

M.410

'The Contributors Work' shall mean the original work of the [Contributor] including the preface, artwork, photographs, index and headings based on the synopsis provisionally entitled [–] which shall consist of approximately [number] typed A4 pages. A copy of the synopsis is attached to and forms part of this Agreement

M.411

'The Work' shall mean the original document held by the [Institute] in its [archive/depository] entitled [specify] reference [specify] the physical copy of which is controlled by the [Institute] which is dated [year] [and is no longer in copyright].

M.412

'The Manuscript' shall be the draft document written and created by [Name] based on [specify] an original idea and concept by [specify] in [format].

MEDIATION

General Business and Commercial

M.413

If any dispute or difference of any nature between the parties shall arise pursuant to this Agreement then such dispute or difference shall:

1.1 At first be referred to a single mediator to be appointed in accordance with the mediation procedures of Media Dispute Resolution [–] or such other organisation which provides mediation services. The mediator shall be agreed upon by the parties but failing such agreement within [twenty-eight days] of one party requesting the appointment of a mediator the mediator shall be appointed by the [President of the Law Society] of [country] at that time.

1.2 If not resolved by the procedure in 1.1 such dispute or difference shall be referred to a single arbitrator under the [Rules of the Chartered Institute of Arbitrators/other] in [country] for resolution.

1.3 If not resolved by the procedures in 1.1 or 1.2 then either party shall be at liberty to pursue such action and remedies as it shall, at its sole discretion, decide in the circumstances subject to the terms of this Agreement.

M.414

The [Licensor] and [Licensee] agree that in the event that any dispute arises pursuant to this Agreement which cannot be resolved by negotiation between the parties they shall endeavour to agree the appointment of a third person to assist in the resolution of the matter. The cost of the services of such person to resolve the dispute shall be shared equally between the parties.

M.415

Without prejudice to any rights or remedies of either party to this Agreement, the [Manager] and the [Sportsperson] agree that prior to the commencement of any legal proceedings in the event of a dispute, difference or other problems which arise pursuant to this Agreement which cannot be resolved by negotiation between the parties they shall endeavour to agree the appointment of a third party to assist in the resolution of the matter. The cost of such mediator shall be shared equally between the parties, irrespective of the eventual outcome of the dispute.

M.416

If any dispute or difference of any nature shall occur which cannot be resolved by negotiation between the parties. Then prior to the start of any legal proceedings the parties shall consider whether they can agree the appointment, on a shared cost basis, of a mediator who will review the facts and advise upon a basis on which to settle the dispute. Neither party is bound to use a mediator nor are they bound by any recommendation or decision.

M.417

The [Company] and the [Distributor] agree that in the event of any dispute, difference or problem that may arise under this Agreement which cannot be resolved by negotiation between the parties. Without prejudice to any legal claim or remedy, the parties shall use their reasonable efforts and resources to agree the appointment of a third party to act as mediator between the parties on terms to be agreed.

M.418

There shall be no provision as to arbitration, mediation, complaints procedure, appeal, code of practice or other method of resolution of any disputes or problems under this Agreement.

M.419

Prior to taking any legal action the parties agree that they shall first use one of the following processes and methods to try to reach a resolution of the dispute:

1.1 Arbitration.

1.2 Mediation.

1.3 Alternative Dispute Resolution.

1.4 Appointment of a third party who is independent and a legal expert to provide a written opinion. Both parties will have the opportunity to provide the written arguments of their case, and a conference prior to any report and/or decision.

M.420

The parties agree that in the event of any dispute, threat of legal action, threat of termination of the agreement and/or failure to deliver and/or adhere to the terms of this Agreement. Then as the first option both parties agree that they shall avoid litigation and opt instead for mediation through [specify organisation]. In the event that either party refuses to cooperate with the mediation process in good faith and/or matter is not resolved to the satisfaction of either party. Then either party shall have the right to take legal action against the other at its sole discretion.

M.421

The [Licensee] and the [Sub-Licensee] agree that where they are in dispute in respect of any matter under this Agreement that [Name] of [organisation] shall be appointed as a mediator at [cost] which shall be paid by each party in equal shares.

M.422

The [Sponsor] and the [Company] agree and undertakes that where there is a dispute between the parties. That the parties shall endeavour to reach terms for the appointment of a mediator to resolve the matter in [country]. That if they are unable to agree terms and/or the mediation is unsuccessful then either party may issue legal proceedings.

M.423

Where the [Licensee] is in dispute with a sub-licensee in respect of the exploitation of the [Character]. The [Licensee] shall keep the [Licensor] fully informed and provided copies of all documents and/or legal advice that may be obtained at the [Licensees'] cost.

M.424

It is agreed between the parties that both parties shall consider the process of mediation and/or arbitration and/or alternative dispute resolution and/or some other method of resolving the issue which may have caused the dispute for a period of [number] months after the dispute arises prior to the commencement of any legal proceedings in order to avoid unnecessary legal costs.

M.425

1.1   The parties to this Agreement have agreed that if a dispute should arise that they will refer the matter to [Name] who shall endeavour to act as a mediator and resolve the matter. The cost of [Name] shall be paid for by both parties from [specify fund].

1.2   In the event that [Name] cannot resolve the matter to the satisfaction of both parties then either party may seek to find another forum for resolution of the dispute and/or take legal action in any court in [country].

1.3   Either party may use the information, data and/or material disclosed in 1.1 in any subsequent legal action.

MEDICAL REPORT

General Business and Commercial

M.426
This Agreement is conditional upon [Name] undergoing a medical examination at the expense of the [Company] and the receipt by the Company on or before [date] of a medical report on [Name] satisfactory to the [Company] confirming that [Name] is in good health and able to perform the services hereunder.

M.427
The [Director] agrees to submit to any reasonable and professional medical examination required by the [Company's] insurers in order to provide suitable insurance cover for the [Director] throughout the Term of this Agreement.

M.428
The [Employee] agrees to undergo a medical examination by a competent and qualified doctor of the [Company's] request and at the [Company's] cost for insurance cover purposes only.

M.429
In the event that the [Company] should require a medical report for any reason in respect of the [Presenter] then the [Presenter] shall only agree upon the terms:

1.1 That the Doctor or Consultant should be specified by the [Presenter].

1.2 That the full cost of the medical report is paid by the [Company].

1.3 That an additional fee is to be agreed in advance with the [Presenter] together with all reasonable expenses.

1.4 That a copy of the medical report is to be sent to the [Presenter] for written approval before it is sent to the [Company].

1.5 That the medical report will only be used for the purpose specified in writing in advance by the Company and will only be sent to the named personnel.

1.6 That in the event this Agreement is terminated or when it expires all records relating to the medical report shall be returned to the [Presenter] or an undertaking given that they have been destroyed.

M.430

The [Presenter] agrees to be the subject of a medical examination and report relating to his/her general health once in each year during the Term of this Agreement. The medical shall only be carried out by a qualified doctor who is acceptable to the [Presenter] and shall be only for the purpose of obtaining or continuing insurance over for the benefit of the [Presenter] by the [Company].

M.431

The [Sponsor] acknowledges that the sponsorship fee shall be paid to the [Sportsperson] notwithstanding that the [Sportsperson] may be unable to provide his/her services under this Agreement due to illness or injury which is supported by a medical report from a qualified doctor.

M.432

The [Executive] is eligible for the annual medical screening at the [Company's] cost by a qualified medical practitioner specified by the [Company]. The [Executive] agrees to a medical examination [including a drug, blood, urine, hair and HIV test] at the request and expense of the [Company] at any time during the continuance of his/her appointment provided that it shall not exceed one review in any twelve-month period. The [Executive] authorises [the Chief Executive/Head of Personnel] to view and read any such report made by the medical practitioner provided that they agree that it is private and confidential. There is no obligation by the [Executive] to permit access or authorise copies of any other medical records held by any other general practitioner or consultant at any time.

M.433

The [Executive] is eligible for the annual health screening at the [Company's] cost by a qualified medical practitioner specified by the [Executive]. The

[Executive] agrees to a general medical examination, but shall not be required to provide any drug, blood, urine, hair, HIV and/or other tests]. There is no obligation on the [Executive] to permit access or authorise the release of copies of any medical records at any time relating to the [Executive] and/or his family.

M.434

The [Sportsperson] agrees to submit to [one] medical examination by a private medical Consultant in order for the [Manager] to arrange suitable insurance cover throughout the Term of this Agreement. Provided that the following conditions are applied:

1.1   The [Sportsperson] should agree the choice of Consultant.

1.2   The full cost of the medical report is to be paid by the [Manager].

1.3   The [Manager] is to pay the [Sportsperson's] reasonable expenses.

1.4   That there shall be no obligation to undergo any internal examination, X-rays, drug test, hepatitis, HIV or other blood, urine, hair test, psychometric tests and/or counselling.

1.5   That a draft copy of the medical report will be sent to the [Sportsperson] for their comments by the Consultant. The final report shall then only be read by [Names] on a strictly confidential and private basis and all copies shall be held by [Name] at [premises]. No additional copies shall be made and at the end of this Agreement the Consultant's medical file and all reports shall be returned to the [Sportsperson].

M.435

The [Company] agrees that [Name] is not to provide personal medical details or to agree to any medical examination for the purpose of this Agreement. All insurance shall be arranged without the supply of any such information by [Name].

M.436

It is specifically agreed that [Name] shall not be required and/or requested to have any medical and/or health review and/or provide any personal details concerning themselves or their family other than those required by the [Company] under any legislation, regulation, directive and/or code in [country].

M.437

The [Participant] shall be obliged to adhere to the [Company's] [Drug Testing and Health] [Policy/Code of Practice]. Failure by the [Participant] to comply for any reason shall result in automatic disqualification from the [Event] and/

or removal of any prize, bonus, title and/or other benefit that may have been awarded.

M.438

[Name] shall be entitled to be absent for up to [number] days without any medical evidence as to the cause of the absence. After that period a medical certificate shall be required from a doctor who has seen [Name] in person.

M.439

The [Company] shall have no right to require a medical report in respect of any personnel involved in the [Project]. The personnel shall be requested by the [Company] to complete a medical questionnaire for insurance purposes, but may refuse to do so and arrange their own insurance cover.

M.440

Where a person fails to attend a drug test and/or medical for any reason. They shall be provided with the opportunity to attend a later date within the next [week/month]. Where they fail to attend on a second occasion then the [Company] shall be entitled to deem that they have refused to be subject to a test and/or medical.

M.441

[Name] shall not be required to agree to a personal medical examination by any medical practitioner appointed by the [Company] for any reason nor shall he/she be obliged to disclose any medical data which he/she would prefer not to supply to the [Company].

M.442

[Name] agrees that where he/she becomes ill with any virus, infection and/ or disease which his /her doctor has advised them is contagious, infectious and/or easily transmitted that they shall not attend work at the [Company] until they are no longer a risk to any other person with whom they may come into contact whilst at work.

MONITORING

General Business and Commercial

M.443

The [Employee] acknowledges and agrees that the [Company] and any third party appointed by them shall have the right under this Agreement to monitor, record and store copies of all emails, telephone calls, faxes, texts, downloads, data, and material which is sent, received and/or transmitted in any format in any media using equipment, and/or facilities and/or on premises owned and/or controlled by the [Company] and/or incurring costs at the [Company's] expense.

M.444

The [Company] shall not have the right to monitor, record or store copies of emails, telephone calls, faxes, texts, downloads, data, and material which are sent, received and/or distributed by the [Executive] without first notifying the [Executive] of their intention to do so.

M.445

The [Company] agrees that the [Executive] shall be allowed to use the equipment, and facilities at the [Company's] cost and expense for personal and non-company matters including emails, text messages, landline and mobile telephone, taxis, petrol and other transport [provided that it does not interfere with the [Executive's] duties.

M.446

The [Employee] recognises and accepts that there is a strict ban of the use of [Company] equipment and facilities which are not for [Company] business such as emails, texts, telephone calls, and/or other benefits without the express permission of a line manager.

M.447

The [Company] may record and store this [telephone call/email] and use it to review its services, marketing and sales, and exchange such information with other companies within the [Group], but for no other purpose.

M.448

The [Consultant] agrees that the [Company] shall be entitled to monitor and carry out surveillance at the [Premises] of the [Consultants'] presence at the [Premises] and work for the [Company] and/or any other personal matters that are conducted on the premises including but not limited to emails, blogs, faxes, documents, mobile calls, telephone calls, CCTV cameras, and any other sound and/or recording system.

M.449

The [Consultant] agrees to complete and return such questionnaires, surveys and assessments that the [Company] may require in order to monitor, assess, evaluate and compile reports in respect of the [Project].

M.450

The [Consultant] only agrees to comply with any request by the [Company] to agree to monitoring, surveillance, questionnaires and/or other requests to that the extent that the [Company] complying with the law in [country].

M.451

[Name] does not provide any consent to the [Company] to access, intercept and/or monitor his/her mobile telephone calls which are made on the equipment supplied by the [Company].

MORAL RIGHTS

Employment

M.452

The [Employee] waives [asserts] all moral rights in respect of the services provided under this Agreement [under the Copyright, Designs and Patents Act 1988 as amended].

M.453

The [Employee] acknowledges that all copyright, design rights, future design rights, property rights and any other rights in the [Series] shall remain the sole and exclusive property of the [Company]. This Agreement does not purport to grant, assign or transfer any rights in the services to the [Employee].

M.454

The [Employee] may not reproduce any [Work] created in the course of his/her employment or at the [Company's] request (whether published or not) without the prior written consent of a Director of the [Company].

M.455

The [Employee] acknowledges that there are no moral rights in works produced by the [Employee] in the course of his/her employment under this Agreement. The [Employee] acknowledges that when a literary, dramatic, musical or artistic work is made by the [Employee] in the course of his/her employment the [Company] shall be the first owner of any copyright in the work.

M.456

The [Employee] acknowledges and agrees that the right to object to derogatory treatment shall not apply to work created by the [Employee] in the course of his/her employment under this Agreement. In the event that the right does apply to the [Employee] then the [Employee] agrees that the right shall not be infringed if there is a sufficient disclaimer.

M.457
The [Employee] waives all right to subject to derogatory treatment of his/her work created in the course of his/her employment under this Agreement by the [Company] at any time provided that he/she is not identified in relation to the work.

M.458
The [Company] agrees and supports the fact that [Name] asserts his/her rights to be credited as the creator of the original concept and idea [specify] to be exploited by the [Company] which was not developed and/or commissioned under his/her contract of employment.

M.459
The [Company] agrees and undertakes that where an employee make a suggestion, creates an idea and/or proposes changes and/or develops a product and/or invention which significantly benefits the [Company] by more than [number/currency] in any financial accounting year. That the [Company] shall acknowledge the contribution by an award of a payment to the employee of [number/currency] for every such year up to [number] years.

M.460
The [Finance Director/Company Secretary] are the authors of the annual report and accounts which is and/or has been approved by the [Board of Directors/Trustees] and issued by the [Company] endorsed by the [Chairman].

General Business and Commercial

M.461
The [Author] declares his/her moral right to be recognised and acknowledged as the original [creator/author/other] of the [Work] and to be clearly, identifiably and prominently brought to the attention of the public to be known as [–] on all copies of any material distributed or exploited by the [Company] based on, referring to and/or copies of the [Work].

M.462
The [Author] declares his/her right to object to derogatory treatment of the [Work] unless the [Author] has given his/her prior written approval to the [Company] in which case there shall be a conditional waiver. No waiver shall be applicable to any other matter.

M.463

The [Company] acknowledges the moral rights in Clauses [–] and agrees to be bound by them and to ensure that all third parties and successors in title are given notice of them and agree to accept such contractual conditions.

M.464

A sufficient disclaimer of a work in respect of an act capable of infringing the right [under the Copyright, Designs and Patents Act 1988 as amended] to object to derogatory treatment of a work. Where a work has been subject to derogatory treatment then the disclaimer will only be sufficient if it be a clear and reasonably prominent indication that the [Work] has been subjected to treatment to which the [Author or Director] has not consented. That if there is a identification of the [Author or Director], along with that identification should be a clear and reasonably prominent indication that the [Work] has been subjected to treatment to which the [Author or Director] has not consented.

M.465

In consideration of the payments made and due to be made under this Agreement the [Author] waives all moral rights [under the Copyright, Designs and Patents Act 1988 as amended] except to the extent that the [Author] shall be given the credit as detailed under Clause [–].

M.466

1.1 The [Author] of the copyright of the film, literary, dramatic, musical or artistic work entitled [–] has the right to be identified as the [Author] of the work [under the Copyright, Designs and Patents Act 1988 as amended] and the identification must in each case be clear and reasonably prominent.

1.2 The [Author] therefore hereby asserts the right to be identified in relation to the work entitled [Title/ISBN] at all times in the following form [Name/Pseudonym/Initials].

1.3 The [Author] asserts this right to be identified in relation to the work entitled [Title/ISBN] at all times in the following form [Name/Pseudonym/Initials] generally whether in relation to the original work or any subsequent adaptation or copies of the original or any adaptation.

M.467

For the avoidance of doubt any adaptation shall include merchandising, audio material, film, DVD, video, CD, any edited website and internet version, stage play, or otherwise which is based on or derived from the original work in any format in any media or country.

M.468

The [Author] of the musical work and/or literary work consisting of words intended to be sung or spoken with music entitled [–] duration [–] [Brief Description] asserts the right to be clearly and reasonably prominently identified as the [Author] by the following form of identification [Name/Pseudonym/Initials/Other] whenever:

1.1 The work is published commercially.

1.2 Copies of a sound recording of the work are issued to the public.

1.3 A film of which the soundtrack includes the work is shown in public or copies of such a film are issued to the public.

That right shall include the right to be identified whenever any of those events occur in relation to an adaptation of the work as the [Author] of the work from which the adaptation was made or any copies of the original or adaptation. The [Licensee] shall be obliged to notify all third parties who acquire a licence or interest in the work or any adaptation thereof of this assertion by the [Author] and shall ensure that the [Author] is identified on each copy in a clear and reasonably prominent manner likely to bring the identity of the [Author] to the attention of the public.

M.469

The [Author] of an artistic work entitled [–] [Brief Description] has the right [under the Copyright, Designs and Patents Act 1988 as amended] to be identified whenever:

1.1 The work is published commercially or exhibited in public or a visual image of it is broadcast or included in a cable programme service.

1.2 A film including a visual image of the work is shown in public or copies of such a film are issued to the public.

1.3 In the case of a work of architecture in the form of a building or a model for a building, a sculpture or a work of artistic craftsmanship, copies of a graphic work representing it, or of a photograph of it, are issued to the public.

1.4 The [Author] of a work of architecture in the form of a building also has the right to be identified on the building as constructed or where more than one building is constructed to the design, on the first to be constructed.

The [Author] asserts the right generally and in relation to each of the acts above to be identified as follows [–]. Further in relation to the public exhibition of the artistic work, the [Author] confirms that he/she has identified himself/herself on the original on the [frame/mount/other] as follows [–].

M.470

The [Licensee] shall not remove or obscure the identification of the [Author] and shall ensure that all copies bear the same identification.

M.471

The [Author] of the [Computer Programme/Computer Generated Work] acknowledges that there are no moral rights in the [Work] in [Country].

M.472

The [Company] recognises that the [Author] of a copyright, literary, dramatic, musical or artistic work has the right [under the Copyright, Designs and Patents Act 1988 as amended] to object and not to have the [Work] entitled [–] [description] subjected to derogatory treatment. The treatment of a work shall mean any addition to, deletion from, alteration to or adaptation of work other than:

1.1   A translation of a literary or dramatic work.

1.2   An arrangement or transcription of a musical work involving no more than a change of key or register.

The treatment of a work is derogatory if it amounts to a distortion or mutilation of the work or is otherwise prejudicial to the honour or reputation of the [Author]. In the case of a literary, dramatic or musical work the right is infringed by a person who:

1.1   Publishes commercially, performs in public, broadcasts or includes in a cable programme service a derogatory treatment of the work; or

1.2   Issues to the public copies of a film or sound recording which include a derogatory treatment of the work.

This right extends to the treatment of parts of a work resulting from a previous treatment by a person other than the [Author] if those parts are attributed to or likely to be regarded as the work of the [Author].

M.473

The [Company] recognises that the [Author] of the artistic work entitled [–] has the right to object to and not have his/her work subjected to derogatory treatment. Treatment of a work means any addition to, deletion from, alteration to or adaptation of the work. The treatment of a work is derogatory if it amounts to distortion or mutilation of the work or is otherwise prejudicial to the honour or reputation of the [Author]. In the case of an artistic work the right is infringed by the [Company] or any third party authorised by the [Company] who:

1098

1.1 Publishes commercially or exhibits in public a derogatory treatment of the work or broadcasts or includes in a cable programme service a visual image derogatory of the work.

1.2 Shows in public a film including a visual image of a derogatory treatment of the work or issues to the public copies of such a film; or

1.3 In the case of a work of architecture, in the form of a building, a sculpture or a work of artistic craftsmanship, issues to the public copies of a graphic work representing or a photograph of a derogatory treatment of the work.

M.474

The [Author] acknowledges that in relation to the [Computer Programme/ Any Computer Generated Work] that there is no right to object to derogatory treatment of the work in [Country].

M.475

The [Author] acknowledges that the right to object to derogatory treatment is not infringed by anything done for the purpose of:

1.1 Avoiding the commission of an offence.

1.2 Complying with a duty imposed by or under any enactment; or

1.3 In the case of the British Broadcasting Corporation, avoiding the inclusion in a programme broadcast by them of anything which offends against good taste or decency, which is likely to encourage or incite to crime or to lead to disorder or to be offensive to public feeling.

Provided where the [Author] is identified at the time of the relevant act or has previously been identified in or on published copies of the work that there is a sufficient disclaimer.

M.476

The [Author] waives all moral rights [under the Copyright, Designs and Patents Act 1988 as amended] in the [Work] entitled [–] [Brief Description]. The waiver shall apply to:

1.1 The right to be identified as the author.

1.2 The right to object to derogatory treatment of the work.

1.3 The waiver shall apply to the [Company] and any licensees, or other parties who may acquire an interest or right in the exploitation of the [Work] as well as all successors in title and assignees of the [Company].

1.4 The waiver in this clause is conditional upon the full payment of all sums due to the [Author] being made under the terms of this Agreement. In the event that all or part of the sums are not paid or accounted for in full then the [Author] shall be entitled to revoke the waiver by notice in writing to that effect to the [Company] at any time up to [five] years from the date of this Agreement.

M.477

The [Author] waives the right to be identified as the [Author] in respect of the [Work] upon the following terms:

1.1 That the [Company] pays the [Author] the sum of [figure/currency] in consideration of this waiver by [date].

1.2 That no other person is identified as the author of the [Work].

1.3 That this waiver shall only apply to the use of the [Work] by the [Company] for the purposes of [–].

1.4 That the waiver shall not apply to any other act by the [Company] or any third party.

1.5 That the [Author] shall be entitled to revoke the waiver if these conditions are not fulfilled by notice in writing to the [Company] at any time.

1.6 That in the event a further waiver is required by the [Company] from the [Author] at any time for some other act then an additional fee shall be negotiated between the parties.

1.7 That this waiver shall only be applicable from [date] to [date].

M.478

1.1 The [Artist] is the creator and original designer of the [Work/Logo] which was commissioned by [Name] at the [Company] for the [Event/Festival] at [location] between [date] and [date].

1.2 [Name] and the [Company] have been agreed that the [Artist] shall retain all copyright and/or intellectual property rights in the [Work/Logo].

1.3 The [Artist] has granted the [Company] an exclusive licence to use the [Work/Logo] for the [Event/Festival] in all marketing and promotional material in any media and format. Provided that the [Company] shall not be entitled to sub-licence and/or authorise any other use and/or adaptation of the [Work/Logo] and the [Artist] is at all times credited with a copyright notice as follows [specify] in all material in any media and/or format.

M.479

The [Researcher] acknowledges that he/she shall have no right to be credited and/or acknowledged as the person who created, developed and/or edited and/or annotated and/or indexed the [Material/Database] which was commissioned by [Name]. That for the avoidance of doubt the [Researcher] waives all moral rights of any nature and agrees that [Name] may exploit, adapt and sub-licence the [Material/Database] as he/she thinks fit at any time and no further payments shall be due.

Internet and Websites

M.480

The [Company] acknowledges that the [Author] asserts his/her moral rights generally in respect of the [Work] under the [Copyright, Designs and Patents Act 1988 as amended] and in particular to be reasonably, prominently and clearly identified as follows [–] on the [Website] by the [Company] at all times and on any downloads, copies and/or adaptations.

M.481

The [Author] waives the right to be identified as the [Author] in respect of the [Work] supplied to the [Company] for the [Website] [reference] upon the following terms:

1.1 That the [Company] pays the [Author] the sum of [figure/currency] in consideration of this waiver.

1.2 That the [Company] may be identified as the author of the [Work] and the copyright owner.

1.3 That there is no limitation on the use, reproduction, supply, transfer, assignment, distribution, adaptation, registration of the [Work] by the [Company] at any time and no further sums or payments shall be due to the [Author].

1.4 That the [Author] shall not be entitled to revoke the waiver and/or object to any derogatory treatment.

1.5 That the [Author] shall authorise a full assignment of all rights in all media of any nature whether in existence now or created in the future in the [Work] forever to the [Company].

M.482

The [Contributor] asserts her moral rights in respect of her original work for the [Website] which is [specify material/title/location]. The [Contributor] asserts her right to the [Company] that operates the [Website] and any third parties who may use it that she should at all times be credited and acknowledged as author of and copyright owner as follows [specify name/title of work/copyright notice].

M.483

1.1 The [Development Team] assert their moral right to be acknowledged in the following manner in respect of the content of the text, images, sound recordings, film and other material on the [Website/App] [specify].

1.2 The [Development Team] accept that such acknowledgement may either be at the bottom of a page and/or on the corporate section.

1.3 The [Development Team] accept that there may be variations in the form of acknowledgement due to lack of space and/or layout.

Merchandising

M.484

The [Author] asserts his/her moral rights in respect of the [Artwork/Text] to be credited as the copyright owner of the [Artwork/Text] in respect of all copies of any adaptations produced, reproduced, sold, supplied and/or distributed by the [Licensee] on both the article itself and any packaging under this Agreement in the following manner: © [year] [Name] [The original Artwork and Text of Title].

M.485

The [Licensee] agrees and undertakes to notify any sub-licensee, agent, distributor and all other third parties who acquire a licence or interest in the work or any adaptation thereof of this assertion of moral rights by the [Author].

M.486

The [Licensee] shall ensure that it is condition of any contract and/or licence with any [Sub-Licensee] that they agree that the [Author] has asserted his/her moral rights in respect of the [Artwork/Text] to be credited as the copyright owner of the [Artwork/Text] in respect of all copies of any adaptations produced, reproduced, sold, supplied and/or distributed by the [Sub-Licensee] in the following manner © [year] [Name] [Title].

M.487

That the [Sub-Licensee] agrees that it shall ensure that the [Author] is identified on each copy and on all packaging in a clear and reasonably prominent manner likely to bring the identity of the [Author] to the attention of the public.

M.488

The [Company] agrees that in the event that any [Products] which are produced do not bear the relevant copyright, credits and trade mark notices specified by the [Licensor] on all items and on all packaging and marketing and promotional material. That the [Company] shall be obliged to withdraw such material at its own cost and expense and shall be obliged to destroy and verify the disposal of all such items and material to the [Licensor].

M.489

1.1 [Name] asserts his/her moral rights to be identified as the author of the [Work] and all the characters, artwork and storylines entitled [specify] and any adaptation which may be developed and/or created based on that [Work] in any language at any time in any country.

1.2 [Name] shall be entitled to approve all proposed copyright notices, trade mark notices and other credits for [Name] and any third party in respect of the [Work] in any media and/or format at any time. In the event that [Name] does not approve and provide written consent then the proposal cannot proceed and must be cancelled.

Publishing

M.490
The [Ghostwriter] agrees that he/she shall not be entitled to any credit or acknowledgment in respect of the exploitation of the [Work] by individual or any third party in any media at any time. Accordingly, the [Ghostwriter] unconditionally waives all moral rights [under the Copyright, Designs and Patents Act 1988 as amended] in respect of the [Work] and all the product of his services to [Name] pursuant to this Agreement.

M.491
[Name] agrees that the [Ghostwriter] shall be entitled for biographical purposes only to state that the [Work] was written by [Name] with the research assistance of the [Ghostwriter].

M.492
In consideration of the Assignment Fee the [Author] agrees that he/she shall unconditionally waive all moral rights in the [Work] and the artwork which he/she may have [under the Copyright, Designs and Patents Act 1988 as amended] including the right to be identified as the original [Author] of the [Work] and the artwork.

M.493
The [Author] hereby asserts [as required under the Copyright, Designs and Patents Act 1988 as amended] his/her right to be identified as [Author] of the [Work] and further asserts the right not to have his/her [Work] subject to derogatory treatment and/or to have any other work falsely attributed to him as [Author].

1103

M.494

The [Author] further asserts the right not to have the [Work] subject to derogatory treatment and/or to have any other work falsely attributed to him/her. The [Company] acknowledges this assertion and agrees to advise and make it a condition of any contract with third parties.

M.495

The [Company] acknowledges that the [Author] asserts his/her moral rights generally in respect of the [Work] under the [Copyright, Designs and Patents Act 1988 as amended] and in particular to be reasonably, prominently and clearly identified as follows [–].

M.496

The [Author] asserts all his/her moral rights [under the Copyright, Designs and Patents Act 1988 as amended] generally in respect of the [Work] and in particular his/her right to be identified as [–] on all copies of the [Work] in all media.

M.497

The [Publisher] agrees to make it a condition of any contract with any third parties that the [Author] must be identified in relation to the [Work] in all packaging, publicity, advertising, marketing, promotional and website, internet and telecommunication system material.

M.498

The [Company] acknowledges that the [Author] has asserted his/her moral rights under this Agreement in relation to the [Work]. In addition the [Company] agrees to identify the [Author] as such on all publicity, promotional and marketing material.

M.499

The [Author] hereby asserts his/her moral rights under the Copyright, Designs and Patents Act 1988 [as amended].

M.500

The [Author] asserts his/her moral rights and in particular, but not limited to, the right to be identified as [Author] of the [Work] as specified in Clause [–].

M.501

1.1 The Company accepts that the [Author] of the literary work or dramatic work entitled [title, description, code] (other than words intended to be sung or spoken with music) has the right and asserts the right to be identified in each case clearly and reasonably prominent whenever the work is published commercially, performed in public, broadcast or included in a cable programme service, or copies of a film or sound recording including the work are to be issued to the public.

1.2 The right shall include the right to be identified whenever any of those events occur to an adaptation of the work of the [Author] or in each case in respect of copies of the original or any adaptation.

1.3 The [Author] asserts the right to be identified as follows [–].

1.4 This assertion shall bind both the [Licensee] and any other third party who acquires any interest or rights in the literary work or dramatic work at any time.

1.5 The [Licensee] shall be obliged to notify all other third parties of this assertion by the [Author].

M.502

1.1 The parties to this Agreement recognise and accept that the [Author] of the [Work] entitled [–] [Brief Description] has the right to object to derogatory treatment of his/her [Work].

1.2 Treatment shall mean any addition to, deletion from, alteration to or adaptation of the [Work] other than a translation of the literary or dramatic work. The treatment shall be deemed to be derogatory if it amounts to a distortion or mutilation of the [Work] or is otherwise prejudicial to the honour or reputation of the [Author].

1.3 The [Author] acknowledges that the right to object to derogatory treatment is not infringed where anything is done for the purpose of avoiding the commission of an offence or complying with a duty imposed by or under any enactment provided that the [Author] is identified at the time of the relevant act or has been previously identified in or on published copies of the work and there is a sufficient disclaimer.

M.503

The [Author] waives all moral rights [under the Copyright, Designs and Patents Act 1988 as amended] in respect of the [Work] entitled [Description] to the [Company] and any licensees but not any successors in title upon the following terms:

1.1 That in consideration of the waiver the [Company] shall pay the [Author] the sum of [–] by [date] which should not be added to the advance and/or recouped from the royalties due to the [Author].

1.2 The [Company] agrees and undertakes to identify the [Author] as the author of the [Work] in a suitable and reasonably prominent position on the [cover, binding, inside front pages] of the [Work] on all copies that it may publish and/or distribute.

1.3 That the [Author] shall be identified in all marketing, publicity and advertising material as the author of the [Work] by the [Company].

1.4 That the [Author] shall be identified as follows [–].

1.5 That the [Author] shall have the right to be identified as the author of the [Work] in any translation, adaptation, serialisation or other exploitation of the rights granted in this Agreement by the [Company] or any third party licensee appointed by the [Company].

1.6 That any changes of any nature of the original [Work] by the [Company] or any third party licensee appointed by the [Company] shall be subject to the prior approval of the [Author] who shall be provided with full details of the proposed changes in each case.

1.7 The [Company] shall endeavour to ensure that there is no derogatory treatment of the [Work] which is prejudicial to the honour or reputation of the [Author] by the [Company] or any third party which it licenses or appoints in respect of the [Work]. In the event that there is clear evidence of derogatory treatment the [Company] shall arrange for all copies to be destroyed and publicly apologise to the [Author] in [–].

1.8 The [Publisher] shall not license, permit or otherwise consent to any other person being identified as the author of the [Work] in its original form, or any translation, adaptation or otherwise.

M.504

The [Publisher] acknowledges that the [Author] asserts his/her moral rights generally in respect of the [Work] [under the Copyright, Designs and Patents Act 1988 as amended] and in particular to be reasonably, prominently and clearly identified as follows [–] in all references to the [Work] and/or parts including the title by the [Publisher].

M.505

The [Publisher] undertakes to respect the moral rights of the [Author] and to ensure that where part or all of the [Work] is supplied, distributed or sold that the following copyright notice will be displayed on the [Work] or any part on each occasion [–].

M.506

The [Licensor] agrees that he/she has viewed the [Work] in [format] and does not object to any such treatment.

M.507

[Name] agrees that it has viewed the proposal for the adaptation of the [Work] in [language] and agrees that the [Publisher] may sub-licence the [Work] and authorise the sub-licensee to develop the translation which will not be an exact copy of the existing [Work].

M.508

The [Contributor] acknowledges and agrees that he/she shall only be credited as [Editor] for the [number] edition and that his/her name shall not appear in future editions where they are not the main editor.

Services

M.509

The [Company] acknowledges that:

1.1 [Name] asserts his/her moral rights generally in respect of the product of his/her services under this Agreement as set out in the [Work Plan] including any documents, artwork and other material and in particular to be identified in a clear, prominent and reasonable manner on all copies in any media as [name/author/copyright owner/creator/other].

1.2 [Name] asserts the right to object to derogatory treatment of his/her work under this Agreement whether addition to, deletion from, alteration or adaptation which is a distortion or mutilation or is otherwise prejudicial to the honour and reputation of the [Name] [which is not a direct translation].

M.510

The [Director] asserts all moral rights in the product of his/her services with respect to the [Film] and/or parts.

M.511

The [Company] affirms that the [Director] of the [Film] has the right [under the Copyright, Designs and Patents Act 1988 as amended] to be identified as the [Director] of the work in the following circumstances:

1.1 Whenever the [Film] is shown in public, broadcast or included in a cable programme service.

1.2 Copies of the [Film] are issued to the public.

The [Director] asserts his right generally and in relation to each of the above acts to be identified in the following form [–].

M.512

The parties to this Agreement recognise and accept that the [Director] of the [Film] has the right to object to and not to have his work subject to derogatory treatment. The treatment of a work means any addition to, deletion from, alteration to or adaptation of the work. The treatment of a work is derogatory if it amounts to distortion or mutilation of the work or is otherwise prejudicial to the honour or reputation of the [Director]. The [Director] is the author of the [Film] entitled [–] [duration] [description]. In the case of the [Film] the right is infringed by a person who:

1.1 Shows in public, broadcasts or includes in a cable programme service a derogatory treatment of the [Film]; or

1.2 Issues to the public copies of a derogatory treatment of the [Film]; or

1.3 Along with the [Film] plays in public, broadcasts or includes in a cable programme service or issues to the public a derogatory treatment of the soundtrack of the [Film].

This right extends to the treatment of parts of the [Film] and/or soundtrack resulting from a previous treatment by a person other than the [Director]. If those parts are attributed to or are likely to be regarded as the work of the [Director].

The [Director] acknowledges that the right is not infringed by anything done for the purpose of:

1.1 Avoiding the commission of an offence; or

1.2 Complying with a duty imposed by or under any enactment; or

1.3 In the case of the BBC, avoiding the inclusion in a programme broadcast by them of anything which offends against good taste or decency, or which is likely to encourage or incite crime or to lead to disorder, or to be offensive to public feeling.

Provided where the [Director] is identified at the time of the relevant act or has previously been identified in or on published copies of the [Film] that there is a sufficient disclaimer.

M.513

The [Director] acknowledges that the [Company] is the person to be treated as the author of the [Film] [by virtue of the Copyright, Designs and Patents Act 1988 as amended]. The right to object to derogatory treatment of the [Film] shall not apply to anything done in relation to such a work by or with the consent of the [Company] unless the [Director] is identified at the time of the relevant act or has previously been identified in or on publishes copies of the [Film]. In such a case the right does apply but the [Director] acknowledges that the right is not infringed if there is a sufficient disclaimer.

M.514

The [Director] waives all rights to object to derogatory treatment of the [Film] at any time by the [Company] and/or any licensees, distributors or otherwise.

This waiver shall be unconditional and shall extend to all third parties who acquire an interest on rights in the [Film] and/or soundtrack and/or parts and shall include any successors in title of the [Company].

M.515

The [Record Company] acknowledges that the [Artist] asserts his/her moral rights generally in respect of the [Sound Recordings] [under the Copyright, Designs and Patent Act 1988 as amended] and in particular to be identified as follows [–].

M.516

The [Company] agrees that [Name] is asserting his/her moral rights in general in respect of the services to be provided under this Agreement. The [Name] shall be reasonably, prominently and clearly identified at all times in the following [style/manner/format] and in particular by the following [Name] whether in any original material created and exploited under this Agreement, supplied by the [Celebrity] or issued in supporting press releases or otherwise.

M.517

The [Presenter] asserts his/her moral rights generally in respect of the [Programme] and the product of their services and any other contributions in sound, text or vision that may be created by the [Presenter] under this Agreement. The [Presenter] shall be identified as [Name] [size/location/colour/order] [media].

M.518

The [Presenter] asserts the moral right not to have any work which he/she has contributed to or created treated in a derogatory manner at any time.

M.519

The [Presenter] asserts all his/her moral rights to the [Company] and any third parties or successors in title in respect of the [Series]. The [Presenter] asserts that he/she must be identified in the form and style [–] in respect of the [Series], on all copies and any adaptations thereof whether during the Term of this Agreement or not. The identification must be clear and sufficiently prominent for him/her to be brought to the attention of the public.

M.520

The [Company] acknowledges that [Name] asserts his/her moral rights generally in respect of the [Programme] and/or parts [under all relevant sections of the Copyright, Designs and Patents Act 1988 as amended] to be identified as [Name/Initials/Other] and to object to derogatory treatment of his/her work.

M.521

The [Company] shall observe and respect the moral rights of [Name] to be reasonably, prominently and clearly identified as the [Author] of the [Work].That the [Work] shall not be treated in a derogatory or demeaning manner which would impugn on the reputation of the [Author] or the [Work].

M.522

The [Designer] waives all moral rights in respect of Clause [–] both to the [Company] and any licensees and in respect of any successors in title. The [Designer] agrees that it shall not be entitled to any credit, copyright notice, acknowledgement or otherwise in respect of the [Website] and any subsequent development thereof.

M.523

[Name] agrees that the [Company] may license and/or exploit all and/or any part of the [Programme] without any credit to [Name] and that his/her appearance and/or contribution may be edited out, adapted, changed and/or a new sound and/or voice over recording added with a new person. That no such alterations shall be a breach of the moral rights of [Name] and no additional payments shall be due.

M.524

[Name] agrees that he/she shall not be entitled to any personal credit in the [Report/Work] which has been commissioned by the [Company]. That the [Company] shall be entitled to claim copyright ownership and to display a copyright notice and to register any interest with a third party without any reference to [Name].

Sponsorship

M.525

The [Sponsor] agrees that it is not aware of and has not received any assertion of any moral rights by any person in respect of any material supplied by the [Sponsor] under this Agreement.

M.526

The [Sponsor] notifies the [Company] that the following credit and copyright notice in due to the [Designer] on all copies of the [specify material] which is reproduced and/or adapted by the [Company].

M.527

The [Company] shall not be entitled to subject the [Work] to derogatory treatment in the form of distortion and/or mutilation and/or to do anything which is prejudicial to the reputation and/or honour of the [Designer] without the prior written consent of the [Sponsor] and the [Designer].

M.528
The [Sponsor] has and/or will obtain waivers of all moral rights in respect of the material and products supplied by the [Sponsor] to the [Company] under this Agreement. These waivers shall not apply to any third parties and/or any successors in title of the [Company].

M.529
The [Sponsor] agrees that it shall not be entitled to any reductions in the payment of any fees as a result of any failure by the [Company] to reproduce, display, supply and/or exhibit and/or transmit the name, image and logo of the [Sponsor] in the exact form in Schedule [–].

University, Library and Educational

M.530
The [Institute] acknowledges that the [Author] asserts her/his moral right in respect of the [Work] to be reasonably, prominently and clearly identified as follows [–] on all copies of the [Work] to be distributed to the public during the Term of this Agreement.

M.531
The [Contributor] as the original author asserts all her moral rights to the [Institute] and any third parties or successors in title in respect of the [Work/Project]. The [Contributor] asserts that she must be clearly identified as follows [–] in respect of the [Work/Project] and on all copies and any adaptations thereof whether during the Term of this Agreement or not. In addition the [Contributor] asserts her right to object to derogatory treatment of the [Work/Project].

M.532
The [Consortium] agrees that as a matter of policy only the lead person on any project shall be acknowledged and credited in any summary report to be published by the [Consortium].

M.533
The [Consortium] agrees that where any individual project has originated by a third party which is funded by the [Consortium] in whole and/or in part that the [Consortium] shall be credited and acknowledged with the following names, logos and images and web references set out in appendix [–] a copy of which is attached and forms part of this Agreement.

MULTIPLE OCCUPATION

General Business and Commercial

M.534

'Multiple Occupation' shall mean any premises (other than a private residential home) establishment or location (whether operated for commercial profit or otherwise) containing rooms or any other units which are made available as temporary or permanent accommodation for more than one guest or household or as office or business premises including, without limitation, hotels, motels, inns, guest houses, boarding houses, hospitals, nursing homes, schools, or other places of multiple occupation.

M.535

For the purpose of this Agreement the multiple occupation shall be [address] in [country] which comprises of [number] units which are occupied by [number] student as a halls of residence at [specify] [college/university] which is owned by [specify] and controlled by [specify].

MUSIC CUE SHEETS

General Business and Commercial

M.536

The [Licensor] shall furnish the [Company] with [one] copy of a full music cue sheet for the [Series] listing each music work included therein, the name of each composer, author and publisher, the duration and description of use thereof (vocal, feature, background).

M.537

The [Licensor] shall provide the [Licensee] with a copy of the music cue sheet for the [Film] which shall list the following details for each separate section of music.

1.1   Title of music.

1.2   Performer(s).

1.3   Composer/Arranger.

1.4   Publisher.

1.5   Record Label and Number.

1.6   Duration of the music.

1.7   Description of use of the music (background, featured, vocal, instrumental).

M.538
The [Company] shall furnish the [Licensee] where available and on request with a list of titles, composers, and publishers of all music used in the [Material/Sound Recordings/other].

M.539
[Name] agrees to supply details of the information required for the music cue sheets for all the musical works that he/she performs, sings, plays and/or accompanies at the [Event] for the [Company] at no additional cost.

MUSICAL WORK

General Business and Commercial

M.540
'Music' means such incidental background music, featured music songs, themes and other musical works and lyrics written by the [Composer] as may be required by the [Company] and sufficient in the sole discretion of the Company for inclusion in the [Film] and all trailers of the [Film].

M.541
'Musical Work' shall [be defined in accordance with the Copyright, Designs and Patents Act 1988 as amended and shall] mean a work consisting of music exclusive of any words or action intended to be sung, spoken or performed with the music. The musical work shall be recorded in writing or otherwise.

M.542
'The Musical Work' shall be the musical composition and recording entitled [Name] [Duration].

M.543
'The Work' shall be the following original musical work including any associated works, lyrics or arrangement entitled [–].

M.544

'The Work' shall mean any and all lyrics and/or musical compositions and/or other musical, literary or dramatic works, whether written, generated or stored electronically, mechanically, graphically or by any other means whatsoever and whether wholly or partly directly or indirectly owned, controlled, written, composed, orchestrated or arranged by the [Composer] whether alone or in collaboration with others.

M.545

1.1 [Name] has a new [Musical Work] in [format] which he/she has developed and created with [specify] to the [Company].

1.2 [Name] has agreed that the [Musical Work] was based on a concept and theme decided by the [Company] to be used in conjunction with a future media marketing and promotional campaign for [subject].

1.3 That [Name] agrees that he/she and the [Company] shall jointly hold all the copyright and intellectual property rights in the [Musical Work] and any sound recordings, film and/or other material which are as follows [specify].

1.4 That [Name] and the [Company] shall share any sums received from any collecting societies in any part of the world equally and any other sums from the exploitation of the [Musical Work] and any sound recordings, film and/or other material in 1.3 above. That all the parties in 1.3 must be named in and sign any agreement to sub-licence any rights to a third party.

1.5 That where the parties cannot agree on any form of exploitation that they shall endeavour to avoid litigation and appoint a third party to assist with the resolution of the matter prior to taking any legal action for any reason.

1.6 That if any party wishes to buyout all the rights from the other the payment shall not be less than [number/currency] but no party shall be obliged to dispose of their share of the rights in any form.

NET RECEIPTS

DVD, Video and Discs

N.001
Where [DVDs/Videos/Discs] are sold, rented, supplied and/or distributed by the [Distributor] under any arrangement, but which are then subsequently deleted, altered and/or changed to a lower price than the published dealer price from the catalogues and/or websites as old stock, reduced price, or a special promotion. Then the royalty payable will be calculated upon the sums received exclusive of sales tax by the [Distributor] instead of the published dealer price.

N.002
No sums shall be withheld by the [Licensee] for any reason which is not disclosed to the [Licensor].

N.003
The [Licensee] agrees that the Advance under Clause [–] shall not be returnable nor offset against the Net Receipts or the Royalties and that this is not contingent in any way on the sales under this Agreement.

N.004
'Net Receipts' shall mean the total proceeds of the exploitation of the [DVD/Video/Disc] Rights in the [Film] and/or part(s) actually received by the [Licensee] after there shall have been deducted or paid from such sums all reasonable costs, expenses, commission, charges, insurance, freight, taxes, duties and other sums which may be incurred and/or arise by the [Licensee] and/or any sub-agent and/or sub-distributor and/or sub-licensee including any sums paid under any indemnity provision.

N.005
'The Net Receipts' shall mean the aggregate of the proceeds of exploitation of the [DVD/Video/Disc] Rights in the [Film] received by the [Company]

(or its nominated distributor, agent or other authorised third party) in freely convertible currency after there shall have been paid or deducted from such proceeds all costs and expenses of and relating to the production, reproduction, distribution, sale or other exploitation of the [DVD] of the [Film] and/or parts up to a maximum limit of [figure/currency] [in total during the Agreement/in any accounting period/in any one calendar year].

N.006

'Net Receipts' under this Agreement shall mean all the sums received by and or credited to the [Distributor] in respect of the reproduction, supply, sale, rental, subscription, and distribution of the [DVDs/ Videos/Discs] of the [Film] in the [Territory] [and/or any other country] whether during the Term of this Agreement or thereafter after the deduction of the [Distributors] Commission which shall be fixed at [number per cent]. No other sums, costs, commission, expenses, charges, freight, insurance or otherwise of any nature shall be deducted.

N.007

The [Licensor] agrees and undertakes that the [Distributor] shall be entitled to offset the Advance to the [Licensor] in Clause [–] against the Net Receipts due to the [Licensor] until such time as the Advance has been recouped in full.

N.008

The [Distributor] agrees and undertakes that it shall not offset the Advance to the [Licensor] in Clause [–] against the Net Receipts and/or any sums due to the [Licensor].

N.009

'The Net Receipts' shall be the total proceeds of any sums received by the [Distributor] from the exploitation of any of the rights granted under this Agreement less the following reasonable commission costs and expenses:

1.1   Distribution Fee to the Distributor of [specify percentage in words and figures] of the total sums received.

1.2   A commission of no more than [–]% [number per cent] due to any authorised third party who is in the control of the [Distributor] and/ or with whom the [Distributor] have concluded an arrangement or agreement. Together with a maximum limit of [figure/currency] [in any accounting period/during the Term of the Agreement].

1.3   No sums shall be deducted for publicity, promotion, advertising, marketing, merchandising, packaging, storage, currency conversion costs and charges, brochures, catalogues, website and internet material, mobile, telephone and telecommunication system material, competitions, trade fairs, exhibitions for any reason.

1.4   The [Distributor] shall try to ensure that the reproduction and freight costs are paid for by any licensee and the material returned at the end of the agreement. Where costs are paid for by the [Distributor] there shall be a total maximum limit of all such sums which can be deducted of [figure/currency] which shall be spread in equal instalments over the duration of the Agreement and shall not be exceeded for any reason.

N.010

'Net Receipts' shall mean all the monies received by and/or credited to the [Company] in respect of the reproduction, supply, sale, licence, rental, subscription, downloading, distribution and/or any other exploitation of the [Sound Recordings] by means of Disc and/or any other form of mechanical reproduction and/or over the internet and/or to mobile phones and/or any other form of transmission by any telecommunication system and/or by any form of television and/or radio in the [Territory] whether during the Term of this Agreement and/or received thereafter after the deduction of the [Distributors] Commission which shall be fixed at [number per cent].

N.011

'Net Receipts' shall be defined as all sums received by the [Licensee] from the exploitation of the rights granted under this Agreement after the deduction of the following agreed expenses and commission in each accounting period:

1.1   Commission to the [Licensee] of [number] %.

1.2   All costs of reproduction, freight, packaging and insurance to supply and deliver material to third parties.

1.3   Marketing costs up to a total maximum of [figure/currency].

N.012

'The Net Receipts' shall be all sums in any currency received by and/or credited to the [Company] and/or any parent and/or subsidiary company less the following permitted deductions during the Term of the Agreement as follows:

1.1   [figure/currency] maximum in total for reproduction costs for the [Sound Recordings].

1.2   [number] per cent commission to the [Company].

1.3   A commission of no more than [number] per cent to any agency.

1.4   [figure/currency] maximum in total for marketing, promotion and advertising of the [Sound Recordings] by the [Company].

N.013

'The Net Receipts' shall be all the sums actually received by [Name] after conversion from any other currency from the exploitation of the [Disc] by [Name] and/pr any third party at any time in any part of the world after the deduction of the following costs:

1.1 Bank charges and costs arising from the transfer and/or conversion of currency.

1.2 Commission, fees and other costs and expenses incurred by [Name] required to promote, exploit and/or market the [Disc] including travel, accommodation, mobile telephone charges, insurance and hospitality, entertainment, food and drink.

1.4 Administration and office costs and expenses and all costs of reproduction and supply of any material.

1.5 Translation, design and artwork, computer generated material and banner link costs, manufacture, packaging and freight, marketing and advertising costs and expenses.

N.014

'Net Receipts' shall mean all sums and/or benefits received by [Name] and/or any associated company in any country in the world at any time from the exploitation of the [Work] and/or any part and/or any image, word, text and/or other matter associated with the [Work] including any sequel, option, character, title, trade mark, domain name and/or merchandising and/or any other form of exploitation, licensing and/or transfer of assets and/or rights and/or interest less commission to [Name] of [number] per cent [–]% and without deduction of any other sums except taxes which are legally charged on the transfer of good and/or services by any government.

Film and Television

N.015

'Net Receipts' shall be the Gross Receipts less the Distribution Expenses.

N.016

'Net Receipts' shall mean the balance of the Gross Receipts after the deduction of the Distribution Expenses and all Programme Overheads.

N.017

'Net Receipts' shall mean the Gross Receipts after the deduction therefrom of all Distribution Fees and Distribution Expenses.

1118

N.018

'Net Receipts' shall be the Gross Receipts less the Approved Budget and the Distribution Expenses.

N.019

'Net Receipts' shall be the Gross Receipts less the Production Costs and the Distribution Expenses.

N.020

'The Distribution Income' shall mean the aggregate of the proceeds of exploitation of [specify type of rights] in the [Film] and/or parts actually received by the [Television Company] (or its nominated distributor, agent or other authorised third party) in freely convertible currency after there shall have been paid or deducted from such proceeds all costs and expenses of and relating to production, reproduction, distribution, sale or other exploitation of the [Film] and/or parts including, but not limited to, all distribution charges, commissions and all other deduction and expenses which such distributors are entitled to make, which they suffer or in respect of which they are entitled to reimbursement, recoupment or indemnity under their Agreements with the [Television Company].

N.021

'The Net Receipts' shall mean the balance of the proceeds from the distribution and exploitation of the [Film] received by all means and in all media throughout the world which is remaining after the following sums shall have been paid or deducted from the gross sums:

1.1 All costs and expenses relating to the distribution, sale or other exploitation of the [Film] including charges, commissions and all other sums which any third party, sub-licensee, distributor, representative or agent are entitled to make or in respect of which they are entitled to be reimbursed or any indemnity under their agreements with the [Company].

1.2 The cost of the production of the [Film] and any interest thereon and any amounts retained by the Distributors of the [Film] to recoup the cost of any changes.

1.3 All completion guarantee costs and expenses.

1.4 The aggregate cost of any sums not included in the certified cost of the production which are payable at a later date for any reason or any sum due as a percentage of Gross Receipts to any person who provided finance, facilities or services or otherwise in connection with the [Film].

N.022

'Distribution Income' means the total proceeds of the exploitation of the rights in the [Film] and/or part(s) in any media actually received by the [Licensor] and/or any appointed third party after there shall have been deducted or paid from such sums all reasonable costs and expenses relating to the distribution and exploitation of the [Film] and/or parts which are not recouped from some other party.

N.023

'The Net Receipts' shall be the total proceeds of any sums received by the [Distributor] from the exploitation of any of the rights granted under this Agreement less the following reasonable commission costs and expenses:

1.1   A Distribution Fee to the Distributor of [specify percentage in words and figures] of the total sums received.

1.2   The actual cost of supply, distribution, promotion, advertising and marketing including, but not limited to processing, reproduction costs, material, merchandising, packaging, storage, customs, freight, insurance, currency conversion costs and charges, brochures, catalogues, website and internet material, mobile, telephone and telecommunication system material, competitions, promotions, trade fairs, exhibitions, advertising, publicity and promotion, clearances, copyright and consents payments that may be due in respect of any material, stills, graphics, artists, director, contributor, music, computer generated material, sound recording, voice-over, the performance and/or mechanical reproduction and/or reproduction and/or transmission and/or exploitation.

1.3   The balance of the sum after such deduction shall be split equally between the parties. The [Distributor] shall then receive [specify percentage] of the balance of the sum, and the remaining sum shall be the Net Receipts due to the [Licensor].

N.024

'The Net Receipts' shall be the total amount of all monies received by the [Distributor] from the exploitation of the rights granted pursuant to this Agreement [at any time/during the Term of this Agreement] less the following sums which the [Distributor] shall be entitled to deduct provided that they are reasonable and full details are provided justifying the costs and expenses:

1.1   The Distributor's Commission which shall be [specify percentage] of the total amount of all monies from all [Television Rights] and [percentage] of the total amount of all monies from all [Video/DVD/Disc] Rights.

1.2 There shall be no deduction for any sub-agent, sub-distributor or other third party or associated, subsidiary or parent company at any time.

1.3 The direct cost of the supply and distribution of the materials of the [Film] such as reproduction charges, freight, customs duties, insurance.

1.4 Any royalties, fees, residuals or other payments arising from the clearances, copyright and consents payments, usage, reproduction, performance and/or transmission and/or mechanical reproduction of any part of the [Film] and/or associated material including music, sound recordings, voice-overs, artists, stills, computer generated material or otherwise which may be due to any person or company or collecting society which are not recovered or paid for by a third party.

1.5 There shall be no deduction for publicity, promotion, advertising, marketing, merchandising, packaging, storage, currency conversion costs and charges, brochures, catalogues, website and internet material, mobile, telephone and telecommunication system material, competitions, trade fairs, exhibitions.

1.6 The Net Receipts shall be the total balance of monies after the deduction under 1.1 and 1.3 and 1.4 above which shall then be allocated in accordance with Clause [–].

N.025

In consideration of the Licence granted hereunder the [Licensee] agrees to pay to the [Licensor] royalties as follows:

1.1 [–]% [number per cent] of the Gross Receipts after the deduction of the Distribution Expenses from the exhibition of the [Film].

1.2 [–]% [number per cent] of all other Gross Receipts after deduction of Distribution Expenses.

N.026

The [Company] agrees that it shall be solely responsible for any sums due in respect of the production, reproduction, supply, performance, mechanical reproduction, broadcast, transmission, advertising, promotion, marketing, distribution and exploitation of the [Film] and/or parts in respect of the rights granted under this Agreement and that the [Licensor] shall not be liable for any such sums.

N.027

The [Assignee] agrees that it shall not offset the Budget against the Gross Receipts only the Distribution Expenses.

N.028

'The Net Receipts' shall be all sums in any currency in any part of the world at any time received by or credited to the [Distributor] and/or any authorised third party who is in their control and/or with whom they have concluded an arrangement or agreement in respect of the [Film]. The only deductions that are permitted before the transfer of the total sum on [date] and [date] each year to the [Licensor] shall be as follows:

1.1 In any one year a maximum of [figure/currency] for material reproduction costs for the supply of the [Film] and/or parts together with freight and custom duties.

1.2 After the deduction of 1.1 then the [Distributor] may allocate and receive [number per cent] for their commission.

1.3 No sums are to be deducted for costs and expenses of the [Distributor] and/or any authorised third party who is in their control and/or with whom they have concluded an arrangement or agreement of any nature.

1.4 No sums are to be deducted for the marketing, promotion and advertising by the [Distributor].

1.5 The [Distributor] shall endeavour to ensure that as far as possible that any authorised third party shall either receive material on loan or pay the reproduction and freight costs in advance and then return material at the end of the agreement.

1.6 The cost of any commission or other sum due to any authorised third party who is in the control of the [Distributor] and/or with whom the [Distributor] have concluded an arrangement or agreement of any nature shall be paid for by and at the [Distributor's] sole cost.

N.029

'The Net Receipts' shall be the total proceeds of any sums received by the [Distributor] from the exploitation of any of the rights granted under this Agreement less the following reasonable commission costs and expenses:

1.1 A Distribution Fee to the Distributor of [specify percentage in words and figures] of the total sums received.

1.2 A commission of no more than [–]% [number per cent] due to any authorised third party who is in the control of the [Distributor] and/ or with whom the [Distributor] have concluded an arrangement or agreement. Together with a maximum limit of [number/currency] in any accounting period.

1.3 Any sums paid for publicity, promotion, advertising, marketing, merchandising, packaging, storage, currency conversion costs and charges, brochures, catalogues, website and internet material, mobile, telephone and telecommunication system material, competitions, trade fairs, exhibitions with a total maximum limit of all such sums which can be deducted of [figure/currency] which shall be spread in equal instalments over the duration of the Agreement and shall not be exceeded for any reason.

1.4 The [Distributor] shall try to ensure that material is either supplied on loan for a short period or that the reproduction and freight costs are paid for by any licensee and the material returned at the end of the agreement. Where costs are paid for by the [Distributor] with a total maximum limit of all such sums which can be deducted of [number/currency] which shall be spread in equal instalments over the duration of the Agreement and shall not be exceeded for any reason.

N.030
It is agreed between the parties that neither party shall seek to be paid for the following matters either from the other party and/or from the gross receipts:

1.1 Administration, travel, accommodation, food and drink and mobile and wifi and technology charges and costs for any personal staff and/or other third party engaged directly by them.

1.2 Clothing, hair, spa and hospitality and entertainment costs.

1.3 Personal insurance and promotion and marketing and social media monitoring.

1.4 Personal legal costs and expenses, agency, management and security costs, fees, commission and expenses.

General Business and Commercial

N.031
'Net Receipts' shall mean all the Gross Receipts less any agreed Expenses.

N.032
'Net Receipts' shall mean the Gross Receipts less the following [specify Items/costs/limit].

N.033
'Net Profits' shall mean the Gross Receipts after deduction therefrom of all Distribution Fees and Expenses, any percentage participation, all the production costs, and any deferments, but without deduction of any share of profits payable or retainable by any party.

N.034

'Net Royalties' shall mean the gross royalties and gross fees earned from the exploitation of the [Work] after the deduction of value added tax or any other taxes and all proper charges of any collection agency.

N.035

'The Net Receipts' shall be the total sums received from any third party by the [Licensee] pursuant to the exploitation of the rights granted in this Agreement at any time (whether during the Term of this Agreement or not) including, but not limited to, compensation, damages, advances, royalties, or otherwise. The [Licensee] shall not be entitled to deduct any costs or expenses from the sum.

N.036

'The Net Receipts' shall be the Gross Receipts received by the [Company] for the supply and distribution of the [Work/Service/Item] less the following agreed costs:

1.1   The fixed cost of producing each unit of [figure/currency].

1.2   The fixed cost of supply, distribution, packaging, insurance of each unit of [figure/currency].

N.037

No sums shall be deducted, retained and/or withheld and/or not disclosed by the [Distributor] of any nature relating to the [Work/Service/Item].

N.038

All sums deducted from the Gross Receipts shall be supported by copies of relevant invoices with the accounting statements.

N.039

All sums due shall continue to be paid and accounted for under clauses [–] after the end of the Term of this Agreement.

N.040

'Net Receipts shall mean all sums received by, credited to or transferred to the [Company] in respect of the [Project/Product/Service] in any currency after the deduction of the following costs and expenses:

1.1   Development, production, manufacture, reproduction, supply, distribution, packaging, freight and sales costs [up to a total maximum of [figure/currency].

1.2   Advertising, marketing, merchandising, promotions, competitions, telephone service [up to a total maximum of [figure/currency].

1.3 [Project/Product/Service] liability, legal proceedings, actions and costs, refunds, compensation, indemnity payments, fines, cancellations, and disputes [up to a total maximum of [figure/currency].

N.041

The [Company] shall not be entitled to deduct the following costs and expenses from the sums received prior to the calculation of the Net Receipts:

1.1 Staff, personnel and administrative costs, and related transport, accommodation, catering, entertainment and benefits costs.

1.2 Currency conversion costs and charges, taxes, duties, national insurance, insurance, health and safety compliance, environmental compliance.

N.042

'Net Receipts' shall be the total of all sums received by [Name] from the sale of tickets, sponsorship and other forms of exploitation of the [Event] less any expenses and costs incurred by [Name] of any nature which have been paid and/or are due to any third party from the [Event] which are supported by receipts and invoices before [date].

N.043

'Net Receipts' shall be the sums retained by the [Company] after it has deducted all the costs and expenses of organising, producing and promoting the [Event].

Internet and Websites

N.044

'The Net Receipts' shall be the total sums received by the [Company] in respect of the [Item/other] less:

1.1 The [Company's] Commission of [number] per cent.

1.2 Insurance, packaging, freight, duties, taxes and any other delivery costs which are not reimbursed to the [Company].

1.3 Refunds, cost of replacements, currency conversion costs and charges, health and safety compliance, environmental compliance, banking and trading compliance, product liability and repayment under indemnity provisions, and legal costs.

N.045

'The Net Receipts' shall be the total sum of all monies received by the [Company] in [currency] at any time when [specify subject] is sold, made available, disposed of, or transferred to any third party by the [Company] whether for a fixed price, discount, fee and/or under subscription less the [Company's] Commission of [number] per cent.

N.046

The [Company] agrees that if within [twelve months] of the date of this Agreement the Net Receipts paid to [Name] are less than [figure/currency], then [Name] shall have the right to terminate this Agreement by notice in writing to the [Company].

N.047

'The Net Receipts' shall be the total sum of all monies received by the [Company] from [the payment processing company] in [currency] at any time when [specify subject] is made available under any subscription service to be downloaded by the general public and/or any third party less the [Company's] Commission of [number] per cent.

N.048

'The Net Receipts' shall be the actual sums received by the [Company] in respect of the [Work/Product/Service] less any deductions for any of the following expenses and costs:

1.1 Commission and any agency fees due to any sub-agent, sub-distributor or other third party.

1.2 Reproduction and conversion costs and charges, freight, customs duties, packaging, insurance and payments arising from the clearance of and exercise of any copyright, intellectual property rights, and/or any other interest.

1.3 Any sums due to any collecting society.

1.4 Any sum due for advertising, marketing, merchandising, trade fairs, and exhibitions.

1.5 Taxes due to any government which form a distinct element of the price and are not recoverable.

1.6 Discounts, refunds, rebates and/or any payments due to loss and/or damage.

1.7 Legal and accountancy costs and expenses.

1.8 The cost of any legal proceedings whether to sue and/or to defend and/or the cost of any settlement.

1.9 The cost of currency conversion costs and bank charges.

N.049

'The Net Receipts' shall be all the sums received in any currency by the [Company] and/or held by any associated and/or parent company and/or third party connected with the [Company] from any form of exploitation and/or benefit derived from the [App] and/or any part of the name, logo and/or content at any time from any part of the world at any time and which has been developed and licensed by [Name] after the deduction of the following sums:

1.1 Currency and administrative conversion charges made by any third party bank.

1.2 [Number] per cent commission to the [Company].

N.050

The [Company] agrees and undertakes that it shall not be entitled to deduct any design, development and/o production and/or computer software and/or marketing, promotional and/or advertising costs and expenses and/or agency and/or distributor and/or copyright clearance payments and other intellectual property payments and/or any costs and expenses due to collecting societies and/or for any music and/or other contribution and/or any legal and/or other advisors and/or consultants and/or any other matter from the sums received except those set out in clause [–] in respect of the [App/Download/other].

N.051

'The Net Receipts' shall be the sums paid to the [Distributor] which are retained and not returned to any third party which are received from the exploitation of the [App] and/or any part on [website] and/or by any other means and/or telecommunication system, website and/or other form in any medium in any format during [the term of this Agreement/at any time] less the following costs and expenses:

1.1 Sums paid for the development, production, design, artwork and computer software up to a maximum of [number/currency].

1.2 Sums paid to register any domain name, trade mark, design and/or to engage the services of third party legal and other advisors in the creation, development and/or licensing of the [App] up to a maximum of [number currency].

1.3 Sums paid for copyright and intellectual property and computer software clearance payments and any other collecting society payments up to a maximum of [number/currency].

1.4 Sums paid in commission, agency fees and other payments for affiliations and/or links up to a maximum of [currency/number].

1.5   Sums paid for advertising, promotion and marketing up to a maximum of [currency/number].

N.052

'The Net Receipts' shall be the sum paid by any person and/or other third party to the [Company] to acquire and purchase [one] print of the [Image/Work/Photograph] at [price] which is owned by [Name] less the following agreed deductions:

1.1   Total reproduction costs of the limited edition which shall less than [number/currency].

1.2   A fixed fee per sale of [number/currency] to the [Company].

Merchandising

N.053

'The Net Receipts' shall be the Gross Receipts less the [Distributor's/Agent's] Commission.

N.054

The [Agent] acknowledges that he/she is solely responsible for all costs and expenses he/she may incur in respect of their services under this Agreement and that they are not to be deducted from the Gross Receipts.

N.055

The [Licensor] agrees that all sums due under any licence agreement shall be paid direct to the [Agent].

N.056

The [Licensee] acknowledges that the Licence Fee shall not be offset against the Gross Receipts, the Net Receipts and/or the [Licensor's] Royalties.

N.057

'The Net Receipts' shall be the Gross Receipts less:

1.1   The cost of all raw materials incurred by the [Licensee] during the course of making the [Licensed Articles].

1.2   The reasonable costs of engaging specialist services in the making of the [Licensed Articles] including but not limited to [–].

1.3   All additional insurance costs incurred by the [Licensee] in relation to use of business premises, the designs, the [Licensed Articles] and the raw material used or obtained for the purpose of producing the [Licensed Articles].

1.4   Any other costs [–].

N.058

'The Net Receipts' shall be the total monies [in sterling] actually received and paid to the [Company] at any time from third parties in the Territory during the Term of this Agreement after deductions of any sums incurred due to exchanges of currency alterations, rejections, discounts or any other reduction in the ex-factory price excluding freight, additional insurance (not covered in the ex-factory price) and any taxes or duties arising from Orders obtained by the [Agent] under this Agreement.

N.059

'The Net Merchandising Receipts' shall be the balance of the total monies [in sterling] received by the [Distributor] from exercise of Merchandising Rights granted under this Agreement less the following sums below:

1.1   Distribution Fee to [Distributor] of [–] % [number per cent].

1.2   The cost of reproducing, marketing, distribution and exploitation including catalogues, tapes, photographs, artwork, graphics, leaflets, packaging, trademarks and logos, customs duties, freight, insurance, publicity and promotional expenses, copyright clearance and payments, contractual obligations, consents and fees, clearance and payments of any sums to collecting societies for recordings, transmission or otherwise of any nature that may be due to any third party in respect of this Agreement.

N.060

'Net Receipts of the [Company]' shall mean Gross Receipts less the [Company's] commission, agreed Launch Costs, trade mark registration and search fees and legal costs.

N.061

'The Net Receipts' shall be the Gross Receipts less:

1.1   The cost of all the raw materials incurred by the [Licensee] during the course of making the [Licensed Articles].

1.2   All additional insurance costs incurred by the [Licensor] in relation to the business premises, the designs, the [Licensed Articles] and raw materials used or obtained for the purpose of producing the [Licensed Articles].

1.3   All reasonable additional security costs incurred by the [Licensee].

N.062

The [Distributor] agrees that it shall be solely responsible in respect of all costs incurred in the development, production, manufacture, distribution, marketing, promotion, advertising, sales and exploitation of the [Licensed Articles] and that such sums shall not be offset against any sums under this Agreement.

N.063

'The Net Receipts' shall be the total proceeds of any sums received by the [Distributor] from the exploitation of any of the rights granted under this Agreement less the following reasonable commission costs and expenses:

1.1   A Distribution Fee to the Distributor of [–]% [number/currency] of the total sums received.

1.2   A commission of no more than [–] % [number] per cent due to any authorised third party sub-agent and/or sub-distributor with whom the [Distributor] have concluded an arrangement or agreement. Together with a maximum limit of [number/currency] in any accounting period.

N.064

The [Distributor] agrees and undertakes that any other sums not specified as authorised to be deducted under this Agreement shall be at the cost and expense of the [Distributor] including but not limited to:

1.1   Advertising, marketing, merchandising, brochures, catalogues, distribution and exploitation including catalogues, photographs, artwork, graphics, leaflets, packaging, trade marks and logos, customs duties, freight, insurance, publicity and promotional expenses, website and internet material, mobile, telephone and telecommunication system material, competitions, trade fairs, exhibitions.

1.2   The cost of development, materials, production, manufacture, security, copyright clearance and payments, contractual obligations, consents and fees, clearance and payments of any sums to collecting societies or storage, currency conversion costs and charges or otherwise of any nature that may be due to any third party in respect of this Agreement.

N.065

The [Distributor] agrees that if the [Distributor] does not achieve and pay the following minimum targets under the Net Receipts to the [Licensor]. Then the [Licensor] shall have the right to terminate this Agreement by notice in writing as soon as the payments have not been achieved and/or paid by the due date:

1.1   From the date of this Agreement to [date] the [Company] to achieve Net Receipts of [figure/currency] for that period which shall be paid to the [Licensor] on [date].

1.2   From [date] to [date] the [Company] to achieve Net Receipts of [figure/currency] for that period which shall be paid to the [Licensor] on [date].

1.3   From [date] to [date] the [Company] to achieve Net Receipts of [figure/currency] for that period which shall be paid to the [Licensor] on [date].

N.066

'The Net Receipts' shall be the sums received by and/or held by the [Licensee] during the term of this Agreement and/or thereafter which relate to the supply, rental, sale, disposal and/or exploitation of the [Game/Product/Work] to any third party including any parent company and/or associated business and/or any other person and/or company and/or entity after the deduction of the following costs and expenses:

1.1   The actual wholesale cost and/or manufacture costs which have been paid by the [Licensee] to a manufacturer and/or other production company to supply the [Game/Product/Work] in a form with packaging suitable for marketing.

1.2   The actual cost paid by the [Licensee] for a short advertising campaign on [specify].

1.3   A commission to the [Licensee] of [currency/number] for every [number/currency] which is to be paid to the [Licensor].

N.067

'The Net Receipts' shall be the sums received by the [Agent] from the exploitation of any products, services, endorsements, product placement and/or other forms of exploitation and/or licensing in any part of the world in any medium which relate to the [Brand Name] and/or [Logo] and/or [Image] and/or [Trade Mark] and/or [Domain Name] and/or any associated material owned and/or controlled by [Name] from [date] to [date] less commission to the [Agent] of [number] per cent of any sums received before payment is made to [Name].

N.068

After [date] the [Agent] shall not any have right to receive and/or retain any sums from the rights granted in clause [–] by [Name]. The [Agent] agrees and accepts that all payments thereafter under any agreements and/or licences concluded and/or arranged by the [Agent] shall be made direct to [Name] and that the [Agent] shall not be due and/or paid any commission on any sums after [date].

Publishing

N.069
'Net Royalties' and 'Net Fees' shall mean the gross royalties and gross fees earned from the exploitation of the [Work] by the [Publisher] after deduction of Value Added Tax or other similar tax and the bona fide commission charges of any agency and discounts given to any third parties.

N.070
'The Net Receipts' shall be the total proceeds from the distribution and exploitation of the [Work] whether by retail, sale, hire, license or otherwise throughout the Territory at any time received by or credited to the [Publisher] or its sub-agents or its sub-licensees after the deduction of any value added tax, sales tax and any commission fees of any collection agencies.

N.071
The [Publishers] undertakes to pay the [Author] the following percentages of the net sums received by the [Publishers] less any fees for the reproduction of copyright material from the sale of such rights [category] [percentage].

N.072
'The Net Receipts' shall mean the sums actually received by the [Publishers] from the exploitation of the [specify] Rights in the [Work] [at any time/during the Term of this Agreement] from all countries outside [specify territory].

N.073
The [Distributor] agrees that if the [Distributor] does not achieve and pay the following minimum targets under the Net Receipts to the [Licensor]. Then the [Licensor] shall have the right to terminate this Agreement by notice in writing as soon as the payments have not been achieved and/or paid by the due date:

1.1 From the date of this Agreement to [date] the [Company] to achieve Net Receipts of [figure/currency] for that period which shall be paid to the [Licensor] on [date].

1.2 From [date] to [date] the [Company] to achieve Net Receipts of [figure/currency] for that period which shall be paid to the [Licensor] on [date].

1.3 That by [date] the total aggregate Net Receipts shall be no less than [figure/currency] and the total aggregate Net Receipts paid to the [Licensor] shall be not less than [figure/currency].

N.074
'The Net Receipts' shall be the total sum of all monies received by the [Company] in [currency] at any time when [specify subject] is sold, made

available, disposed of, or transferred to any third party by the [Company] whether for a fixed price, discount, fee and/or under subscription less the [Company's] Commission of [number] per cent.

N.075

The [Company] agrees that if within [twelve months] of the date of this Agreement the Net Receipts paid to [Name] are less than [figure/currency], then [Name] shall have the right to terminate this Agreement by notice in writing to the [Company].

N.076

The [Distributor] shall not be entitled to deduct the following costs and expenses from the sums received either from the published price, whole sale price and/or any other sums received from any form of exploitation of the [Work]:

1.1 The cost and expenses relating to the operation and administration at the [Company] and the appointment of any legal and/or accountancy and/or trade mark advisors, consultants, recruitment and/or marketing agencies and/or any third party agreements for development of computer software and/or technology.

1.2 The cost and expenses relating to development of designs, artwork, covers, labels, competitions, newsletters and/or any creation of any format and/or reproduction of any samples and/or prototypes and/or any website and/or app and/or blog.

1.3 Any losses, damages and/or other sums incurred due to destruction and/or withdrawal of stock and/or delays in publication and/or translation of the [Work] and/or the creation of an audio and/or braille edition at any time.

N.077

'The Net Receipts' shall be the sums received by the [Distributor] from the supply and licence of the [Work] to the [Sub-Licensee] [in [specify format]/ to be adapted] to be downloaded and/or accessed from [specify website] to any member of the public, commercial and/or charitable and/or educational enterprise at any time for a fee of not less than [number/currency] for complete [Work] by the [Author].

N.078

The [Author] agrees that the [Sub-Licensee] in clause [–] shall be entitled to a fixed commission of [number] per cent of all sums received by the [Sub-Licensee] in respect of copies of the [Work] in [format] from the [specify website].

N.079

The [Author] agrees that the [Sub-Licensee] in clause [–] shall be entitled to a fixed fee of [number/currency] in respect of each complete copy of the [Work] in [format] which is sold and/or supplied and for which a fee of [number/currency] is received by the [Sub-Licensee] from the [specify website].

N.080

'The Net Receipts' shall be defined as the sums which are paid to the [Company] from third parties for the use and/or adaptation of the [Sound Recording] of [Name] reading the [Work] for [Programme] entitled [specify] on [radio/television/webinar] in [country] in the [specify] language at any time from the date of production until [date].

N.081

[Name] agrees that he/she shall not be entitled to any payments from the Net Receipts after [date] and/or any other form of exploitation and/or adaptation after that date. That all obligations to account, report and make payments by the [Company] to [Name] shall end and there shall be no further liability to [Name] and/or sums due.

Services

N.082

The [Record Company] shall pay the [Artiste] a royalty of [number per cent] of the retail price (less all taxes) in respect of [90]%[ninety per cent] of [Records] manufactured and sold in the Territory from recordings made pursuant to this Agreement [less the cost of packaging]. When the recording from the [Artiste's] recordings only form part of an entire Record the royalty payable shall be limited to an equitable proportion relative to the extent of the [Artiste's] recordings to the whole Record.

N.083

'The Net Receipts' shall be [–]% [number] per cent of the total proceeds from the distribution and exploitation of the Records (including promotional material) whether by retail, sale, hire, license or otherwise throughout the Territory at any time received by or credited to the [Company] and its sub-agents, sub-licensees and sub-distributors after deduction of any value added tax and any sales tax which may from time to time be in force paid by the [Company].

N.084

The [Company] shall pay you a royalty of [–]% (number per cent) of the retail price (less all taxes) in respect of [90%] (ninety per cent) of the records manufactured and sold in the [United Kingdom and United States of America] from recordings made under this Agreement.

N.085
The [Company] shall pay to the [Artist] the royalties on [Records] sold by the [Company] or its agents calculated on [85]% [eighty-five per cent] of the price to the general public after deducting an allowance for packaging and any taxes levied as part of the selling price.

N.086
'The Net Receipts' shall be [100]% [one hundred] per cent of the total proceeds from the distribution and exploitation of the [Records] whether by retail, sale, hire, license or otherwise throughout the Territory at any time received by or credited to the [Record Company] or its sub-agents or its sub-licenses after the deduction of the following reasonable costs and expenses:

1.1 Value added tax and any other taxes which form a distinct element of the price and are not recoverable.

1.2 The Production Costs of the recordings which shall not exceed [figure/currency].

1.3 The cost of the artwork, label and ancillary packaging for the Records but excluding any below line costs or marketing and publicity up to a maximum of [figure/currency].

N.087
'Net Receipts' shall mean all income received directly or indirectly by the [Manager] as a result of the performance of the obligations of both parties to this Agreement less the [Manager's] Expenses.

N.088
'Net Receipts' shall mean the Gross Receipts less the [Agent's] Commission and the [Agent's] Expenses.

N.089
'The Net Receipts' shall be the Gross Receipts less the Agent's Commission.

N.090
'The Net Receipts' shall be the Gross Receipts less the Authorised Expenses.

N.091
'The Manager's Commission' shall be the following percentage of the Net Receipts [–].

N.092

'The Sportsperson's Fees' shall be the Net Receipts less the Manager's Commission.

N.093

The [Agent] agrees that if within [twelve months] of the date of this Agreement the Net Receipts paid to the [Artist] are less than [figure/currency], then the [Artist] shall have the right to terminate this Agreement by notice in writing.

N.094

The [Agent] and the [Artist] agree that in the normal course of business all third party contracts shall be directly with the [Artist] and signed by the [Artist]. The [Artist] undertakes and agrees that in each third party contract negotiated by the [Agent] under this Agreement the [Agent] shall be entitled to a clause which authorises the third party to make all payments under the Agreement to the [Agent]. However both parties shall have the right to audit and inspect any accounts and records.

N.095

The [Company] agrees that if the [Company] does not achieve the following minimum targets for sales and/or meet the target payments under the Net Receipts to [Name]. Then [Name] shall have the right to terminate this Agreement by notice in writing as soon as the targets for sales and/or payments have not been achieved and/or paid by the due date:

1.1 From the date of this Agreement to [date] the [Company] to achieve Net Receipts of [figure/currency] for that period which shall be paid to [Name] on [date].

1.2 That by [date] the total aggregate Net Receipts shall be no less than [figure/currency] and the total aggregate Net Receipts paid to the [Licensor] shall be not less than [figure/currency].

1.3 To achieve [sales/other] of [number] units of [specify product/format/service] in [country] by [date].

1.4 To achieve total aggregate [sales/other] of [number] units of [specify product/format/service] by [date].

N.096

'The Net Receipts' shall be the total sum of all monies received by the [Company] converted into [currency] at any time from any country and any type of exploitation in respect of the [Recordings/Film/Work] of the product of the services of [Name] which is made available by any method by the [Company] whether for a fixed price, discount, licence fee and/or under subscription service, rental, hire, or other payment less the [Company's] Commission of [number] per cent.

N.097
'Net Receipts' shall be the sums received by the [Agent] from any distributor, licensee and/or other third party with whom the [Agent] has concluded an agreement for the use of the services, image, logo and/or personal name of [Name] at any time after the conversion from the currency in which it is paid to [sterling/dollars/euros/other] and the deduction of the following sums:

1.1 The [Agents'] commission fee of [number] per cent for the first [number/currency] and thereafter the commission shall be reduced to [number/currency] on all further sums in that financial year. The financial year shall start on [date and end [date].

1.2 The cost and expenses which the [Agent] has paid, advanced and/or contributed to [Name] for travel, accommodation, equipment and technology, security, hospitality, clothes, accessories and styling and related costs and charges for his/her family members up to a maximum of [number/currency] in total in any one financial year. Any sums in excess of that sum shall be paid for by the [Agent].

N.098
All sums received by the [Agent] in respect of the Net Receipts due to [Name] must be held in a separate bank account in the name of [specify] at [bank]. Such funds must not be used by the [Agent] in any form and/or any lien and/or charged created for his/her business and/or expended and/or transferred to any third party.

University, Library and Educational

N.099
'The Net Receipts' shall be the total sum of all monies received by and/or credited to the [Institute] which has been cleared and retained by the [Institute] in [currency] at any time from the exploitation of the [Work/Service/Product] after the deduction of:

1.1 Value Added Tax or other similar taxes which form a distinct element of the price and are not recoverable.

1.2 Commission charges and expenses of any agency, licensees and distributors.

1.3 Discounts, refunds, or rebates to any third parties.

1.4 The cost of development, materials, production, publication, packaging, distribution, and exploitation.

1.5   Legal and accountancy costs and expenses.

1.6   The cost of registration of any rights, domain names, trade marks, computer software and/or patent and any legal or agents fees and costs.

1.7   The cost of advertising, marketing, merchandising, brochures, photographs, artwork, graphics, leaflets, packaging, trade marks and logos, publicity and promotional expenses, website and internet material, mobile, telephone and telecommunication system material, competitions, trade fairs, exhibitions.

1.8   The cost of customs duties, freight, storage and insurance.

1.9   The cost of copyright clearance and payments, contractual obligations, consents and fees, clearance and payments of any sums to collecting societies.

1.10 The cost of currency conversion costs and bank charges.

1.11 The cost of any legal settlement or litigation with a third party relating to any matter regarding the [Work/Service/Product].

N.100

'Net Receipts' shall mean the Gross Receipts less the [Distributor's] Commission and the [Distributors] Expenses. The [Distributor's] Expenses shall be limited to [figure/currency] in any one year.

N.101

The [Distributor] agrees that it shall be solely responsible in respect of all costs incurred in the development, production, manufacture, distribution, marketing, promotion, advertising, sales and exploitation of the [Work/Service/Product] and that such sums shall not be offset against any Net Receipts due to the [Institute] under this Agreement.

N.102

The [Enterprise] agrees that if within [twelve months] of the date of this Agreement the Net Receipts paid to the [Institute] are less than [figure/currency], then the [Institute] shall have the right to terminate this Agreement by notice in writing. In such case all rights granted and/or acquired under this Agreement by the [Enterprise] shall revert to the [Institute]. The [Enterprise] agrees that it shall account for and pay any sums that may be due. The [Enterprise] agrees and undertakes that it shall sign any such documents as may be required to revert all rights to the [Institute] at the [Institutes'] cost.

N.103

The [Company] agrees that the [Institute] shall have the right to terminate this Agreement] by notice in writing if the [Company] does not achieve and/

or provided evidence of and/or does not pay any of the sums due to the [Institute]:

1.1 That by [date] the [Company] will have provided a financial statement and paid to the [Institute] the sum of [figure/currency] which shall be the [Institutes'] percentage of the Net Receipts.

1.2 That by [date] the total aggregate Net Receipts shall be no less than [figure/currency] and the total sum paid to the [Institute] shall be not less than [figure/currency].

1.3 That the [Company] shall have sold and been paid for not less than [number] units of the [Work] by [date].

N.104

'The Net Receipts' shall be the balance which is available for distribution by the [Licensee] to the [Consortium] after the deductions of all sums incurred and paid for by the [Licensee] in respect of the [Project] in the development and testing, registration and compliance procedures and processes, production, manufacture, promotion, marketing, advertising and legal and administrative costs and expenses associated with any advisors, consultants, agents and/or government and/or international bodies.

N.105

Where no Net Receipts are available for distribution to the [Consortium] and the [Licensee] has incurred a loss. The [Licensee] agrees that the [Consortium] shall not be liable to make any contribution to such losses and all such costs and expenses shall be the responsibility of the [Licensee].

NEW EDITIONS

DVD, Video and Discs

N.106

The [Distributor] confirms that it will not edit, adapt, alter or add to the [Master Tape] without the prior written approval of the [Licensor] and that any such changes shall be entirely at the [Distributor's] cost.

N.107

There shall be no obligation on the [Licensor] to provide any consent and/or grant any new licence for an updated version, sequel and/or new edition of the [DVD/Video/Disc]. Nor shall the [Licensee] have any option and/or first right of refusal on any subsequent [DVD/Video/Disc] of the [Film].

N.108

The [Company] shall be entitled to modify, revise, enhance, develop, adapt, update, and re-issue the [DVD/Video/Disc] of the [Film] and any associated material such as instructions, packaging or brochures in any way that the [Company] may decide without further payment to the [Licensor] provided that it is in accordance with the terms of this Agreement and during the Licence Period.

N.109

1.1 Where the [Company] wishes to make a sequel and/or other adaptation and/or animation and computer generated version and/or any other new and/or subsequent version and/or sequel and/or translation and/or audio and/or sound recording of the [Film/Programme] and/or [DVD/Disc/CD/other]. The [Distributor] agrees and accept that it shall have no right and/or option and/or any interest in any such new material which the [Company] may decide to create, develop, distribute, market and sell whether during the term of the existing Agreement with the [Distributor] or not.

1.2 In addition the [Distributor] agrees that it shall have no right to any payment of any nature in respect of 1.1.

N.110

The [Artist/Presenter] agrees that where at a future date a new adaptation and/or sequel of the [Film/Programme] and/or [DVD/CD/Disc] and/or any sound recordings is to be created by the [Company] and/or any third party. That there is no contractual obligation to use the [Artist/Presenter] by the [Company] and that the [Company] may choose such person as they shall decide at their own discretion.

General Business and Commercial

N.111

The [Publisher] shall not have the right to make and publish new adaptations or arrangements of the [Work], or to make additions in and to the music, or to provide a new lyric without the prior written consent of the [Writer].

N.112

The [Publisher] shall procure that the copyright in any new adaptations or arrangements of the [Work], or additions or alterations in or to the music, or any new lyric, shall vest in the [Publisher]. The [Publisher] assigns to the

[Composer] and the [Author] the music and/or words or lyrics respectively to each in all media for the full period of copyright and any extensions or renewals throughout the world. Provided that all parties agree that the terms of this Agreement shall apply to such new material.

N.113
Where the [Company] wishes to order a variation of the [Works] then the [Company] shall give the [Contractor] reasonable notice and shall bear the full cost of any charges that may arise. The alterations shall not be carried out by the [Contractor] until the parties have settled the cost and price which will be paid to the [Contractor].

N.114
The [Company] shall have the right to modify, revise, develop, enhance, adapt, update, exploit and re-issue the [Work] and any associated material such as instructions, packaging, or brochures in anyway that the [Company] may decide without further payment to the [Licensor].

N.115
The [Distributor] agrees and undertakes that it has no right and/or authority to develop, create and/or licence and/or supply any new edition, sequel, adaptation and/or variation of the [Work/Product] by the [Author] and that it is only permitted to exploit the rights granted under this Agreement in [specify] language and in the exact form and with the exact copyright notice, disclaimer, moral rights notice and content, layout, design and format specified in schedule [–] which is part of this Agreement.

Publishing

N.116
The [Author] shall, if requested by the [Publisher] and without charge to the [Publisher], edit and revise the [Work]. In the event that the [Author] shall neglect or be unable for any reason to edit or revise the [Work] to the reasonable satisfaction of the [Publisher]. The [Publisher] shall be entitled to engage some other competent person to carry out such work and any fee or other payment made to such person shall be deducted from the royalties for the [Work] due to the [Author]. Provided that the choice of such person and the fee to be paid to such person shall be subject to the [Author's] prior written approval, not to be unreasonably withheld or delayed.

N.117
The [Work] shall not be edited, revised, re-issued, altered or changed in any manner without prior written consent of the [Author]. If the [Author] and the [Company] agree that the [Author] shall undertake revisions or provide

new material for a new edition, this work shall be undertaken subject to an agreed additional advance against Royalties being paid to the [Author]. No third party shall be engaged to revise or add to the work without the prior written consent of the [Author]. The cost of the services of the third party shall be paid for by the [Company] in full. The engagement of any third party by the [Company] shall be subject to the prior written approval of the [Author]. The [Company] shall bear all liability in respect of any loss or damages arising from the work of the third party and agrees to indemnify the [Author] in full in respect of any claim including all legal costs. Any such third party shall not be entitled to a credit as the author of the [Work] at any time or to claim any right or interest therein. The [Company] shall ensure that all copyright in the work of the third party is transferred to the [Author] and the [Author] agrees to grant a licence to the [Company] upon the same terms as set out in this Agreement in consideration of the sum of [figure/currency].

N.118

Prior to the publication of a new edition the [Publishers] shall send a written request to the [Author] requiring the [Author] to update the [Work] with all necessary changes, alterations and deletions within a reasonable period. In the event that the [Author] shall fail to deliver a new edition or refuse to revise or write a new edition within [two years] of such notice, then the [Publishers] shall be entitled to engage a competent and qualified third party to revise the [Work] at the [Publisher's] sole expense. The Author shall be entitled to receive the royalties set out in this Agreement in respect of such new editions and agrees the third party who updates the work shall be entitled to a suitable credit, but shall not be entitled to acquire any copyright or interest in or royalties from the [Work].

N.119

In order to keep the [Work] up to date the [Authors] will, when mutually agreed between the parties, prepare new editions of the [Work] during the continuance of this Agreement. The [Authors] shall supply such new material, and amend, or alter the [Work] as may be necessary. In the event that the [Authors] are unwilling or unable by reason of death or otherwise to edit or revise the [Work] the [Publishers] shall not have the right to ask any third party to do so.

N.120

The [Publishers] shall have the right to make alterations in, deletions from and additions to the [Work] at the sole discretion of the [Publishers]. The [Publishers] shall also be entitled to arrange for translations, new lyrics, additional and new music and to authorise others to do so. All such new material, developments or variations shall belong to the [Publishers].

N.121

The [Publishers] shall not be entitled to alter, change, amend or develop the [Work] and/or any part(s) including the music, words, images, title or otherwise at any time. The [Publishers] shall only be entitled to exploit the [Work] in the exact form that it is supplied by the [Author] under this Agreement. In the event that the [Publisher] would like to make any variations or developments then the [Publisher] shall propose them in writing to the [Author]. Subject to the payment of a reasonable fee on each occasion the [Author] may agree to carry out such work. The [Author] shall not be obliged to provide any changes and/or new material and may refuse his/her written consent. The [Publishers] shall be bound by the final decision of the [Author] and shall not be entitled to make any changes, or variations of any nature without the prior written consent of the [Author]. The copyright in any such material shall be vested in and/or assigned to the [Author] by the [Publisher] [subject to the terms of this Agreement].

N.122

In the event that the [Publishers] decide to issue a new edition of the [Work], then the [Publishers] shall make a written request to the [Author] to bring the [Work] up to date by a specified date [which shall not be unreasonable in the circumstances and in any event not less than [one year]. In the event that the [Author] shall fail or refuse to write a new edition, then the [Publishers] shall be entitled to engage a third party to update the [Work] upon such terms as shall be agreed in advance on each occasion with the [Author].

N.123

The [Author] agrees to edit and revise the [Work] upon request once every [five years] so that there are necessary changes to update the material which would involve less than [number] pages being altered. Where it is clear that the work would substantially require more than the number of pages stated then this is considered a new book and not an update and requires a new advance and agreement for publication. The [Publishers] shall pay the [Author] an update fee for each revised work of [figure/currency] together with all reasonable expenses on each occasion up to a maximum of [figure/currency].

N.124

The [Publisher] shall not have the right to any updated, revised or new editions of the [Work] by the [Author] or to engage any third party to do so during the Term of this Agreement. The agreement is for the single edition and no further updated, revised or new editions which shall be the subject of a separate and new publishing agreement on each occasion. Nor shall the [Author] be bound to enter into any new agreement on the same terms as this Agreement. The [Author] shall have the right during the Term of this Agreement to offer any third party the right to publish an updated, revised and/or new edition of the [Work] upon expiry or termination of the Agreement.

N.125

Where there are escalating royalty provisions the publication of a new edition shall not permit the [Publisher] to treat the print run as if it has begun at zero and is effectively a new book. Where the advance and royalties relate to the same Agreement then the print run for the new edition shall be added to the previous print run figures.

N.126

The [Distributor] agrees and accepts that:

1.1   A new edition and/or any development of a digital and/or e book and/or translation and/or other adaptation of the [Work] shall be the subject of a new agreement between the parties.

1.2   There shall be no obligation on the [Author] to update, revise and/or develop new material of any nature in any part of the [Work] after the publication of the [Work] in [country].

1.3   That any new material created by the [Author] including marketing and promotional material at the [Company's] request which is agreed shall be the subject of separate agreements and payments by the [Distributor].

N.127

Where the [Publisher] fails to commission anew edition of the [Work] [from the [Author] within [number] years from the date of publication of the last edition. Then the [Author] shall have the right to offer the new edition to any third party and the [Publisher] agrees that it shall not have the right to object if it has failed to commission a new [Work].

N.128

1.1   That in consideration of the payment of an additional fee of [number/currency] It is agreed that the [Publisher] shall be entitled to have first option to commission a new edition in respect of the [Work] which shall be the subject of a new Agreement. The option shall start on [date] and end on [date].

1.2   That if the [Publisher] and the [Author] fail to conclude a new Agreement for any reason that the fee paid in 1.1 shall not be paid back by the [Author]. After [date] the [Author] may offer the new edition of the

[Work] in any format and any medium to any third party including a competitor of the [Publisher].

1.3   Where the [Author] concludes an agreement with a third party for a new edition then the [Publisher] agrees to conclude a document to release the [Author] and confirm the rights are available to be licensed to the third party at no additional cost to the [Author].

University, Library and Educational

N.129

1.1   The [Institute] shall have the right to update, revise and/or create a new edition and/or sequel and/or adaptation of the [Work/Service/Product] by the [Contributor] and/or to engage any third party to do so whether during the Term of this Agreement or thereafter.

1.2   This Agreement is for the single edition and the [Contributor] shall have no right, interest, option and/or claim to any future editions, update, revisions, new editions and/or adaptations.

1.3   There shall be no royalties, advances and/or any other sums due to the [Contributor] in respect of any other to any future editions, update, revisions, new editions and/or adaptations.

1.4   The [Contributor] shall not be entitled to any credit, copyright notice and/or acknowledgement in respect of any other future editions, update, revisions, new editions and/or adaptations.

N.130

The [Institute] agrees that it shall not have the right to develop, produce, publish and exploit any future new editions, updates, revisions, sequels and/or adaptations without the prior written consent of the [Author]. The parties shall enter into negotiations for a new agreement on each occasion. In the event that the [Author] is unwilling or unable by reason of death or otherwise to edit, revise, develop and/or adapt the [Work] the [Publishers] shall not have the right to ask any third party to do so without the prior written consent of the [Author] or an executor and/or trustee of their estate and a new agreement has been concluded as to the terms.

N.131

The [Institute] shall be entitled to edit, adapt and delete and vary contributions by any person to any [Work] which it may wish to supply, distribute and reproduce and exploit at any time. Any such person whose contribution is then not included shall not be entitled to receive any sums from the subsequent version and/or edition of the [Work].

NOTICES

Employment

N.132

Any notice shall be duly served hereunder if in the case of the [Company] it is handed to a Director of the [Company] (other than the Manager) or sent by recorded or first class post to the [Company] at its registered office for the time being which is at [Address] and if in the case of the Manager it is handed to him/her or sent by recorded or first class post to him/her at his/her address specified in this Agreement or such other address as he/she may notify to the [Company]. A notice sent by first class post shall be deemed served on the day following the posting.

N.133

Without prejudice to the right to serve notices by any other means any notice served under this Agreement shall be in writing. Any notice which has been sent by first class pre-paid post shall be deemed to be received [48 hours] thereafter (excluding Saturdays, Sundays and Public Holidays). For the purpose of this Agreement all notices shall be sent to the following addresses:

The Employee [Address].

The Company [Address].

N.134

In the event that there are any material changes to these particulars and/ or service of any notice is required then the parties will send material to the addresses set out in this letter or as otherwise advised.

N.135

1.1 Notices pursuant to this Agreement shall be in writing by first class recorded delivery to the following parties:

[Name] [address] in respect of service on the [Executive].

[Name] [address] in respect of service on the [Company].

1.2 No service shall be in person at the work place of the [Executive].

1.3 Any change or alteration of any address in 1.1 must be in writing and confirmed as agreed by the other party. No amendment may be made to 1.2.

1.4   No other methoof service and/or notification whether by fax, email, in person or otherse shall be accepted as notice under this Agreement.

N.136

Notices pursuant to is Agreement may be by any method provided that it is in writing and in [lnguage] to the [Executive] or the [Company] whether by fax, text, email, pst, courier or hand delivered. Provided that no method and circumstance shll be chosen to embarrass, humiliate and/or prejudice the career prospect of the [Executive] and/or cause distress in front of other personnel of th [Company].

N.137

The [Company] sha provide not less than [three calendar] months of the reduction of the woing hours of the [Employee] under the terms of this Agreement.

N.138

The [Company] resrves the right to serve notice to any person and/or company as follows:

1.1   By pre-recorde and registered post and/or first and/or second class post in the forn of a letter.

1.2   By email and txt message to the last known email address and/or mobile telephoe number.

1.3   Through an announcement on the sound system at the premises.

1.4   In person through a delegated person directly employed by the [Company] and/or engaged through a third party.

General Business and Commercial

N.139

1.1   All notices and accounting which the [Licensee] is required or may desire to give to the [Licensor] hereunder shall be in writing and shall be sent by pre-paid postal service and/or by a delivery service to [Address] with a copy of all notices and accounting to [Address] or to such other address or addresses as [Licensor] may designate from time to time by written notice to the [Licensee].

1.2   All notices which the [Licensor] is required or may desire to give to the [Licensee] hereunder shall be in writing and shall be sent by pre-paid postal service and/or by a delivery service to the [Licensee] at [Address] or to such other address as the [Licensee] may designate from time to time by written notice to the Licensor.

N.140

Without prejudice to the right to serve notices by any other means any notice required to be served hereunder shall be deeed sufficiently served [specify hours/days] (Saturdays, Sundays, and Pub Holidays excluded) after it has been sent first class pre-paid post to the gistered office or last known address of the party on whom it is desired to rve it.

N.141

1.1 Any notice given under the provisions of this greement shall be in writing and sent to the address of the party to b served set out at the head of this Agreement or to such other addres of which notice has been given.

1.2 Any notice to the [Licensee] shall be marked fr the attention of the following person [Name] and a copy thereof sha be sent to [Name] at the same address.

1.3 All notices shall be delivered by hand or set by facsimile or by registered or recorded delivery letter. All notice shall be deemed to have been received when delivered by hand or on the date on which they would be received in the normal course o posting if posted or when the proper answer code is received back by the sender if sent by facsimile.

N.142

Any notice to be served under this Agreement shall be sent by one of the following methods:

1.1 Pre-paid recorded delivery or registered post which shall be deemed to be received within [seven days] of posting provided that the notice is sent to the following addresses in respect of each party [Name of Party] [Address] [Name of Party] [Address].

1.2 By facsimile machine or email which shall be deemed to be received within [twenty-four hours] provided that notice is sent to the other party using the following codes [Name of Party] [Facsimile Code] [email address] for each party.

1.3 Neither party shall be entitled to alter the details for service of notice in this Agreement unless notice is served in accordance with the Clause [–].

N.143

Except as otherwise provided in this Agreement all notices shall be in writing and sent by registered post or air mail and addressed to the principal office of the parties as set out herein or to such address as either party may later provide in writing to the other party. All notices shall be deemed to have been made on the date of dispatch.

N.144

Notices pursuant to this Agreement shall be in writing by first class post addressed as follows:

The [Company] [Name] [Address]

The [Customer] [Name] [Address]

N.145

Any notice to be served hereunder shall be in writing and may be served personally or by registered post. In respect of notice to the [Company] at its registered office and in the case of the [Customer] at its last known address or at its registered office. Any notice shall be effective on the day it is received.

N.146

All notices required to be given pursuant to this Agreement shall be in writing and sent by first class post. At the same time a copy of the notice shall be sent by fax or email to the business address of the party to be served as set out above or may be delivered by hand. Any notice shall be deemed to have been delivered by post in the ordinary course of delivery by posting, or if by fax or email on the day of transmission, or if by hand on the day of delivery.

N.147

Any notice or other document to be given pursuant to this Agreement shall be in writing in the [English Language] signed by the [Managing Director] of the party and in a legible written form. Notices shall be sent to the registered office and last known address of the relevant party. Any notice shall not be deemed received unless there is sufficient evidence that it was properly served.

N.148

Any notice under these conditions shall be given in writing. Any such notice shall be deemed to have been properly served if it is either delivered to a prominent part of the Exhibition Stand of the Exhibitor, handed personally to the [Exhibitor] and/or any employee and/or sent to the last known registered office or business address by any method.

N.149

Any notice or direction to be given by the [Company] to the [Contractor] under this Agreement shall be made on behalf of the [Company] by any person(s) holding the position of [Managing Director] and/or [Company

Secretary]. Any notice to be given by either party shall be in writing and shall be sent pre-paid recorded delivery addressed in the case of the [Company] to its principal address at [–] and in the case of the [Contractor] to its registered office. [Any such notice if sent by pre-paid recorded delivery shall be deemed to have been served on the day after the date of posting unless returned for any reason.]

N.150
Notices must be served under this Agreement in writing and sent by first class pre-paid post or air mail to the last known business address of the party. All notices shall be deemed served when received at the business address.

N.151
Any notice, communication or demand to be given or made pursuant to this Agreement shall be given or made in writing and sent by pre-paid first class mail and/or by personal delivery to the address stated above and addressed to the Managing Director/Company Secretary or to such other address as may have been duly notified to the other party in writing. Any notice if given by post shall be deemed to have been received at the expiry of [three] business days from such dispatch, or if by personal delivery at the time the notice was served.

N.152
Any notice to be given by any one party to the other in this Agreement may be given by any reasonable method provided that it is in writing. A notice shall be deemed properly served if it is in writing and sent pre-paid first class post or courier or personally delivered to the registered office or the business address set out in this Agreement. Any such notice must be signed by any one of the Secretary, Directors, or Chairman and be on official letterhead paper of the party. Provided such conditions are fulfilled it shall be accepted as proof of authority and service by the party giving the notice.

N.153
Unless otherwise stated every notice and other communications shall be sent by post addressed in the case of the [Licensor] to its Agent [Name] [Address]. In the case of the [Licensee] to its registered office for the time being and shall be deemed to have been received upon the date which in the ordinary course of the first class post it would have reached its destination [Name] [Address].

N.154
Any notice sent under this Agreement shall be by pre-paid first class post to the address of the other parties as stated above. [Any notice shall be deemed to have been served [forty-eight] hours after posting.]

N.155

Any notice given under the provisions of this Agreement shall be in writing and be sent to the address of the party to be served as above written or to such other address of notice has been previously given. All notices shall be delivered by hand or sent by first class registered or recorded delivery letter within the [United Kingdom] and by registered air mail letter outside the [United Kingdom]. All notices shall be deemed to have been received when delivered by hand or [two working days] after posting thereof if within the [United Kingdom] and [eight working days] after posting thereof if outside the [United Kingdom] respectively.

N.156

All notices hereunder shall be in writing and shall be given either personally or by first class pre-paid letter post to the address of the [Company] or [Presenter]. Any notice given by post shall be deemed to have been received on the business day immediately following the date of dispatch.

N.157

Any notices to or from parties shall be in writing and shall be deemed to have been given when delivered by hand, posted by recorded delivery or sent by fax to the party as follows:

[Agent] [Contract] [Fax] [Address]

[Licensee] [Contract] [Fax] [Address]

These details may be changed by confirmation in writing to the other party. Notices received by personal delivery or fax shall be deemed received the first working day following the date of transmission or delivery. Notices sent by recorded delivery shall be deemed received [–] working days after posting.

N.158

Any notice made under this Agreement may be served upon the [Artist] by posting the notice to the last known address or to his Agent (if any) with whom this Agreement was negotiated.

N.159

Any notice given pursuant to this Agreement shall be writing and be sent to the address of the party to be served as set out in this Agreement or to such other address of which notice has been given. Any notice given to the [Distributor] shall be marked for the attention of the Managing Director and a copy thereof shall be sent to the [Contracts Manager] at the same address. All notices shall be delivered by hand or by registered or recorded delivery letter.

N.160

1.1 Unless otherwise specifically stated in this Agreement, all notices, approvals, payments or accounting which the [Licensee] is required to deliver to the [Licensor] shall be in writing and shall be personally delivered or posted for which the postage/or cost shall be pre-paid and sent to the [Licensor] [Name] [Address] or to such other address as the [Licensor] may subsequently notify.

1.2 All notices, approvals, documents and other materials which the [Licensor] is required to deliver to the [Licensee] shall be in writing and shall be personally delivered or posted for which the postage or cost shall be pre-paid and sent to the Licensee [Name] [Address] or to such other address as the [Licensee] may subsequently notify.

1.3 Courtesy copies of all notices to the [Licensee] shall also be sent to the [Licensee] at the above address to the attention of the [Department].

1.4 Notices shall not be deemed served unless there is clear evidence that the notice was received by the other party.

N.161

The parties agree to serve notices to each other by first class post, fax or by email. Irrespective of the manner used to serve notice, the notice will be deemed to have been served by the end of the following business day on which the notice was sent.

Notice to the [Company] shall be to [Name] [details].

Notice to the [Designer] shall be to [Name] [details].

N.162

The parties agree that they may serve notice under this Agreement by any method, post, in person, email, fax, text messaging, cable, telephone, videophone or otherwise. There is no requirement that notice must be served in writing.

N.163

Notices served under this Agreement shall be in writing whether by letter, fax, email in [English] and set out all the words and details and cannot be in the form of text messaging, videophone or [specify]. [Names and details of each party.]

N.164

Any notice under this Agreement shall be in writing and either by recorded delivery post and/or courier which is then signed for upon delivery by an authorised officer of the [Licensor] at [Address] and/or an authorised officer of the [Licensee] at [Address]. Notice is received when it is signed for by the recipient.

N.165

Any notice given under this Agreement may be in any method provided it is in [English] and legible. It will only be accepted as received if there is sufficient and clear evidence that it was properly served and received by the party.

N.166

Any notice under this Agreement shall be given personally to the party or sent by recorded or first class post.

N.167

Any notice shall be served personally on the [Managing Director] of the [Company] or [Name] by hand or shall be by first class recorded delivery post marked private and confidential to [specify details]. No other method shall be accepted as proper service.

N.168

Any notice or direction given by the [Company] to [Name] shall be made by only the following person or his/her substitute [Managing Director/Company Secretary/Director] or other person of comparable position in charge of the [Project]. Any formal notice shall be in writing and may be sent by any method to the other party. Every effort should be made to verify that notice has been received.

N.169

Notices pursuant to this Agreement shall be in [writing/text/graphics/film/icons/text messaging/other] and may be sent by the following methods [specify]. Any notice shall be sent to the other party to the last known address or other details of which there is sufficient evidence as well as the address stated on this Agreement. Any notice shall only be effective once it is received and the other party has knowledge of its contents.

N.170

Any notice must be in writing and the sender must be able to prove that it was actually received.

N.171

All notices under this Agreement must be in writing and delivered by courier, hand delivered or first class or recorded post. Service by fax, email or text messages or otherwise will not be accepted by either party as proper service under this Agreement.

N.172

All notices must be in writing and by letter by recorded or registered delivery whether by post or courier. Copies may be sent by fax, email, or texted, but shall not constitute sufficient notice.

N.173

Notices may be sent by any method provided they are legible and the sender can provide evidence of their receipt. [State length] must be given on each occasion to allow a breach to be remedied. Where notice is to terminate or suspend the Agreement then notice must be by courier or recorded delivery. The parties' details are as follows unless otherwise amended [specify].

N.174

Notices shall be in writing by recorded delivery whether post or courier as follows [Title/Name/Address] of each party. Information may also be sent by other means but will not constitute service of notice.

N.175

All notices must be in writing under this Agreement and delivered by courier, hand delivered, first class, recorded and/or registered post. Service by fax, email or text messages or otherwise will not be accepted by either party as proper service under this Agreement. Service shall be made to the parties as follows:

[Institute] [Name] [Chief Executive] Address [–]

[Enterprise] [Name] [Chief Executive] Address [–]

N.176

Where a party has attempted to serve notice and it has been wrong for some reason. They may serve a subsequent valid notice in respect of the same matter.

N.177

It is agreed between the parties that no notice and/or amendment to this Agreement may be made by voicemail, email, text and/or some other electronic method. That the only valid and recognised process is in writing on paper in the [specify] language.

N.178

[Name] agrees that for the purposes of this Agreement where [Name] is not available for any reason that any notice may be served on [specify] their Agent and/or their [specify] their legal advisor.

N.179
The parties agree that any notice and/or any amendment to this Agreement may be made by email, text, voicemail, fax, letter and/or by any other method and/or process provided that it is in the [specify] language and clear as to the content.

N.180

1.1   It is agreed between the parties that the [Company] may notify the [Customer] of changes and amendments to this Agreement by publishing notices on the [Company] website and through text and email messages to the registered mobile number and email account for the [Customer].

1.2   the [Company] agrees that where the notice relates to a price increase that the [Customer] may terminate the Agreement provided that he/she pays for [number months] of the service thereafter at the current price.

NOVATION

General Business and Commercial

N.181
The [Television Company] shall be entitled to assign the whole or any part of the benefit of this Agreement to a third party. The [Television Company] shall give the [Publisher] notice in writing of any proposed assignment and the [Publisher] agrees that it shall co-operate with the novation of this Agreement and enter into an Agreement on the same terms with the third party. Provided that the [Television Company] and the third party can provide sufficient evidence that the third party can and will fulfil all the terms of the original Agreement and that there shall be no detriment to the [Publisher] from such action.

N.182
The [Company] may assign all of its right, liabilities and obligations under this Agreement to any person to whom it assigns the Licence. In the event of such assignment the [Company] shall remain jointly and severally liable to the [Licensor] with its assignees for the performance of its obligations. The [Company] shall not be entitled to make or consent to any other or further assignments without prior written consent of the [Licensor]. Full details of the proposed assignment and any other agreement with any third party in respect of the material covered by this Agreement shall be provided to the

[Licensor] [except for any confidential company information] at least [one month] prior to the execution of any such assignments. The [Company] shall in any event be bound to make the payments due to the [Licensor] in the event that the third party is unable or unwilling to do so for any reason.

N.183

The parties to this Agreement acknowledge that any successors in title to the [Company] shall be entitled to the benefit and burden of the terms of this Agreement without the prior consent of the parties.

N.184

1.1 [Name] agrees to novate the Agreement dated [–] between the [Company] and the [Name]. The [Company] shall be under no obligations of any nature to the [Name] nor shall the [Company] have any interest in or entitlement to any rights of any kind in the [Work] under this Agreement.

1.2 [Name] agrees that the [Company] shall be entitled to assign the benefits and obligations of this Agreement in respect of the [Work] to the [Third Party] who shall assume all rights and obligations to the [Name].

1.3 [Name] agrees to 1.1 and 1.2 subject to the [Third Party] entering into an agreement directly with the [Name] on the same terms and conditions set out in this Agreement. Except that the third party agreement shall be on the condition that the [Third Party] shall not seek to recoup or set off at any time any sums which have been paid to the [Name] by the [Company] which shall include any advances.

N.185

The [Author] agrees to the novation of the Publishing Agreement dated [–] by the [Publisher] to the [Company] on the following terms and conditions:

1.1 In consideration of the payment of the sum of [figure/currency] by the [Publisher] to the [Author] upon signature of this document by the [Author]. The [Author] agrees to novate, relinquish and release the [Publisher] from its contractual obligations to the [Author]. Further the [Author] agrees that the [Publisher] may assign the Publishing Agreement to the [Company].

1.2 The [Publisher] shall not be released from its contractual obligations to the [Author] unless and until it pays the consideration set out in 1.1 above, pays all sums due under the existing agreement and sends [free of charge] all existing stock which is in its control to the [Author] and transfers title to the [Author].

1.3   The [Publisher] shall confirm to the [Author] in writing that it has no further claim to or interest in the Publishing Agreement and/or the [Work].

1.4   The [Publisher] shall provide the [Author] with a detailed account of the royalties due and/or payable by the [Publisher] to the [Author] and shall pay all sums due upon signature by the [Author] of this document.

1.5   In addition the [Publisher] shall undertake to continue to account to the [Author] in respect of all sums received and/or in respect of the [Work] after the date of this document. The [Publisher] shall provide a full breakdown of any such future sums specifying the payments due in detail and providing copies of all agreements.

1.6   The [Publisher] agrees to arrange with the [Company] that any advances against royalties previously paid by the [Publisher] shall not be offset against royalties due to the [Author] from the [Company].

1.7   The [Company] shall provide a new Publishing Agreement to the [Author] signed by the [Company] setting out its rights and obligations to the [Author].

1.8   The [Publisher] agrees that all existing material including the cover in any published work of the [Author] is respect of the [Work] shall be [assigned/licensed] to the [Company].

1.9   Despite the fact that the [Publisher] is no longer contractually bound to the [Author] and has no rights, interest or obligations. In the event that the [Company] is unable or unwilling to publish the [Work] within [–] year of the date of this document and/or is made bankrupt, put into receivership and/or an administrator is appointed, then the [Publisher] shall pay to the [Author] the sum of [figure/currency].

N.186

There are no rights of novation by the [Company] under this Agreement, either to a different company or a related body whether there is a change of policy, ownership or control or otherwise. The Agreement is only with the [Company] for the particular imprint agreed namely [–].

N.187

Where the parent company and a subsidiary changes control and is sold to a third party then the [Author] agrees to the transfer to the successor in title provided that the interests of the [Author] are not prejudiced and there is no reduction in the marketing and promotion of the [Author's] Work.

N.188

Where the ownership of a parent company changes to a third party. The [Author] shall have the option to terminate the agreement with the parent company and/or the subsidiary with immediate effect and to notify the [Company] that he/she wants a full reversion of all rights with immediate effect. Provided that the [Author] shall repay [number] per cent of any advance royalty payments after the conclusion of a publishing agreement with another party.

N.189

The [Company] agrees and undertakes that any successors in title to the [Sponsor] shall be entitled to the benefit and burden of the terms of this Agreement and shall not require the prior consent of the [Company].

N.190

Where there is a change of control and/or ownership of the [Licensee]. Then the [Licensee] shall be entitled to such event to notify the [Sub-Licensee] of the novation of the Agreement. In such event the parties shall agree a novation agreement either for the reversion of all the rights to the [Licensee] and/or transfer to a third party.

N.191

The [Author] agrees to the novation of the Merchandising Agreement dated [–] by the [Distributor] to the [Company] on the following terms and conditions:

1.1 In consideration of the payment of the sum of [figure/currency] by the [Distributor] to the [Author] upon signature of this document by the [Author]. The [Author] agrees to novate, relinquish and release the [Distributor] from its agreement with the [Author and shall assign the Merchandising Agreement to the [Company].

1.2 The [Distributor] shall confirm to the [Author] in writing that it has no further claim to and/or interest in the Merchandising Agreement and/or the [Work] and that all sums due to the [Author] have and/or will be paid by [date].

N.192

Where either party wishes to novate and/or transfer the benefits and liabilities of this Agreement to a third party in respect of the [Service/Work/Project]. Then a new agreement must be drawn up between the parties setting out:

1.1 The sums to be paid to any party.

1.2 The date on which the novation and/or transfer takes effect.

1.3 The ownership of all physical and intellectual property and copyright material which may exist

1.4 The accounting process for outstanding sums due if any.

1.5 The transfer of any registrations with any collecting society and/ or government body and/or international organisation in respect of domain names, trade marks, service marks and/or otherwise.

1.6 The supply of documents relating to any continuing payments and/or obligations to third parties.

1.7 The supply of documents relating to the buyout and/or assignment of any rights.

1.8 The supply of documents relating to any active legal and/or contractual and/or other claims, actions and/or investigations by third parties.

O

OBSCENITY

DVD, Video and Discs

O.001
The [Assignor] undertakes that the [DVD/Video/Disc] shall not contain any obscene, offensive, defamatory or derogatory material and will not expose the [Assignee] to civil or criminal proceedings unless it is agreed in advance in writing between the parties or set out as part of the [Artistic Concept] or is part of the performance by the [Artist] or the sound recording or lyrics of the [Musical Work].

O.002
The [Licensor] undertakes that the [Film] and/or parts, its title and contents, any sound, text, vision, music, lyrics and/or sound recording in respect of the exploitation of the [DVD/Video/Disc] Rights granted to the [Distributor] will not expose the [Distributor] to civil or criminal proceedings or infringe or breach the copyright, contract, trade mark, service mark, logo, design, literary, dramatic, musical, artistic or other rights of any third party [in [country] during the Term of this Agreement.]

O.003
This clause shall only apply to the [original master material/other] and not apply to any material of any nature added to the [Film] and/or any text of a sub-titled version and/or sound recording of a translated version which is supplied and added by the [Licensee].

O.004
The [Licensor] confirms that the [Film] does not contain any obscene or defamatory material and will not expose the [Licensee] to civil or criminal proceedings. Provided that the liability of the [Licensor] under this clause shall be a maximum of [figure/currency] in total.

O.005
The [Licensor] agrees and undertakes that the [DVDs/Discs] of the [Film] and/or parts and the exercise of the rights by the [Distributor] in accordance

with the term of this Agreement shall and will not expose the [Distributor] to the threat of civil or criminal proceedings in [country] in respect of obscenity, copyright infringement or defamation during the Term of this Agreement.

O.006
Where the [Licensee] has added sub-titles and/or a sound track which has not been arranged and/or paid for by the [Licensor]. Then the indemnity in clause [–] shall not apply to any such material and the [Licensee] shall be bear all the liability, cost and expense of any allegation, claim, fine and/or civil and/or criminal proceedings that may arise.

O.007
The [Licensee] agrees and undertakes to the [Sub-Licensee] that the copies of the master material of the [Sound Recordings] reproduced on the [Disc] which shall be supplied to the [Licensee] under this Agreement shall not contain any lyrics, words and/or title which is obscene, defamatory and/or will expose the [Sub-Licensee] to civil and/or criminal proceedings in [country] from [date] to [date].

O.008
1.1 The [Distributor] agrees and undertakes not to promote, market and/or advertise the [DVD/Disc/CD] and/or any associated material on any websites, blogs, apps and/or in any magazine and/or other periodical and/or on television and/or through any telecommunication system in any form which is classified [as adult material only] and/or contains obscene and/or graphic images which members of the public are likely to find offensive and/or images and/or text which [Name] would not want to be associated with at any time.

1.2 The [Distributor] agrees that where [Name] notifies them under 1.1 that there is material posted and/or displayed and/or distributed which [Name] finds offensive and/or falls within 1.1 that the [Distributor] will take action and endeavour to remove all such material as soon as possible.

Film and Television

O.009
The [Licensor] and the [Distributor] undertake to the [Licensee] that there are no acts, words, text, images, products or computer-generated material in the [Film] including the soundtrack and any other material supplied under this Agreement which are or may be construed as obscene and/or defamatory in [country] whether under any law, statute, regulation, directive, guidelines, standards or code relating to the exercise by the [Licensee] of the rights granted in this Agreement.

O.010

Unless a copy of the [Film] supplied by the [Company] pursuant to Clause [–] is rejected on the grounds of quality and/or fitness for purpose and/or that the performances, words, text, images or soundtrack are obscene and/or defamatory within [thirty days] of delivery, then the [Distributor] shall be deemed to have accepted the [Film] and the material.

O.011

In the event that the [Film] is considered by the [Licensee] to be obscene and/or indecent in law and/or to contravene any codes of practice in any part of the Territory. The [Licensor] shall use its best endeavours to enable the [Licensee] to obtain, alter, amend, edit and otherwise change the offending part(s). In the event that the [Film] cannot be edited to an acceptable standard then the [Licensee] shall be entitled to request an immediate refund of all sums paid to the [Licensor] by the [Licensee] in respect of that [Film].

O.012

The [Licensor] confirms that the [Films] do not and will not contain any material of any nature whether in sound, vision, or text which is obscene or defamatory or will expose the [Distributor] to civil and/or criminal proceedings in respect of the exercise of the rights granted to the [Distributor] under this Agreement. The [Licensor] confirms and undertakes that the version of the [Film] supplied to the [Distributor] will be that which has already been approved or rated by the relevant censorship authority in the Territory.

O.013

The [Company] confirms and undertakes that the [Film] contains no obscene or defamatory matter [in sound, image or text] and will not expose the [Licensee] to civil and/or criminal proceedings.

O.014

The [Company] agrees and undertakes to ensure that the [Series] will not contain any act, performance, image, words, text, lyrics, article, or sound recording which is obscene, defamatory or would prevent the sale of the [Film] in the following countries [specify] or would result in the [Film] not obtaining a classification as [rating] with [specify organisation].

O.015

The [Licensee] agrees and undertakes to the [Licensor] that it shall bear responsibility for any legal and/or other proceedings including any costs, expenses, damages, losses, penalties and settlement which arise as a result of the exploitation of the [Film] by the [Licensee] under this Agreement. This shall include but not be limited to any allegation of obscenity, defamation, a fine by a regulatory body, an allegation of breach of confidence and/or privacy, infringement of copyright and/or otherwise.

O.016

[Name] agrees and accepts that the interview by the [Presenter] with [Name] may include questions, jokes, caricatures, film , sound recordings and other material which is rude, vulgar, obscene, derogatory and offensive.

O.017

[Name] agrees and undertakes to conduct him/herself in a respectable manner at all times at the [Location] for the filming of the [Programme] and shall not make any obscene gestures, swear, wear any clothing which displays offensive words and/or images and/or cause offence and/or cause the [Distributor] to be in breach of the Code of Practice relating to [specify] and/or the terms of its licence issued by [specify].

General Business and Commercial

O.018

In the event that an [Exhibitor] or his representative or an employee shall conduct himself on the premises of the exhibition in a manner considered by the [Organisers] to be objectionable for any reason including, but not limited to, obscene behaviour, drunkenness, obstruction, use of drugs or other illegal activities. The [Organiser's] at their sole discretion and decision shall have the right to request that any such person leave the premises immediately under escort. In the event that they fail to comply with the request then the [Exhibitor] agrees that the person may be removed by security staff from the premises.

O.019

[Name] warrants and undertakes that his/her performance shall not contain anything obscene and/or defamatory and/or anything calculated to bring the [Company] into disrepute and that it shall not contain any advertisement or promotion of any company, service, product and/or person.

O.020

To the best of the [Company's] knowledge and belief nothing in the [Work] shall be defamatory, seditious, blasphemous or obscene, or commit a tort in breach of any right of privacy or other personal rights, or be in breach of any contract or duty of confidence or data or official secrets or in contempt of court or in breach of any statute, directive or regulation in force or an infringement of copyright, design right, moral rights, trade or service mark, performance right, right of mechanical reproduction, patent, computer software, registered design or other intellectual property right including passing off [in the Territory during the Term of this Agreement].

O.021
The [Licensor] agrees and undertakes that the version of the [Work] supplied to the [Licensee] shall be in the form and content approved by the censorship authority. The [Licensee] shall be entitled to make such changes, cuts or alterations as may be required by such censorship authority prior to the distribution of the [Work].

O.022
The [Licensee] undertakes to use all reasonable endeavours to obtain approval from the relevant censorship authorities in the Territory for the commercial exploitation of the [Work].

O.023
The [Licensor] agrees and undertakes that the [Work] is not obscene, defamatory and/or does not contravene any standards, practices or codes in any of the following countries in [specify] and shall not expose the [Licensee] to civil or criminal proceedings in those countries.

O.024
The [Licensor] agrees and confirms that to the best of its knowledge and belief the [Work] does not contain any material which is obscene, defamatory, libellous, offensive or likely to incite violence or [specify issue] in the jurisdiction of [countries]. The [Film] has not been cleared for each country in the world.

O.025
The [Assignee] agrees that it has [examined/viewed] the [Work] and does not rely on any undertaking by the [Assignor] as to any threat of civil or criminal proceedings that may arise nor as to whether any of its content are legally in contravention or breach of any laws in any country in any respect including obscenity, defamation or otherwise. The [Assignee] agrees that it shall bear its own cost and expenses and seek its own independent advice.

O.026
The [Licensor] confirms that its own legal advisors do not believe the [Work] to be obscene, offensive or defamatory but no such undertaking is given to the [Licensee]. The [Licensee] have examined and viewed the [Work] and has agreed to take its own independent advice. The [Licensee] must arrange suitable insurance cover for the [Licensor] and the [Licensee] to adequately cover the threat of legal proceedings of any type from the exploitation of the [Work].

O.027
The [Licensee] agrees that the [Licensor] shall only be liable in respect of a claim for expenses, damages, costs and losses arising from material in the [Film] which is agreed as part of a settlement to be and/or found by a court and/or a regulatory body to be obscene, offensive, defamatory and/or derogatory up to [figure/currency] in total.

O.028
The [Company] shall be entitled to dismiss for gross misconduct any person who makes an obscene gesture and/or is abusive and/or makes offensive and derogatory remarks in person and/or via any social media and/or by text and/or image and/or film and/or sound recording to any senior manager and/or other member of staff at the [Company] whether during their hours of employment and/or at any other time when not at work at the [Company].

Internet and Websites

O.029
The [Company] regularly checks and monitors the [Website], but we cannot be responsible for any obscene, defamatory, offensive, derogatory and/or other material which is posted and/or submitted by members of the public. We will try to:

1.1   Remove material brought to our attention within [specify period].

1.2   To block all material which we consider is not rated suitable for [specify].

1.3   To ban and/or serve notice on any member of the public who posts obscene, defamatory, offensive, derogatory and/or other material which we consider unsuitable that they will be personally liable for any damages, losses and costs arising from their contributions to the material on the [Website].

O.030
[Name] acknowledges and agrees that the [Company] cannot be responsible for any obscene, defamatory, offensive, derogatory and/or other material which is posted and/or submitted by members of the public. That [Name] will be personally liable for any damages, arising from [Name's] contributions to the material on the [Website].

O.031
The [Contributor/Client] agrees and undertakes to the [Company] that:

1.1   All the material whether text, images, photographs, graphics, logos, film, sound recordings and/or any other format and/or medium shall be the original work of the [Contributor/Client].

1.2 That all the material in 1.1 will not infringe the copyright or any other rights of any person.

1.3 That all the material in 1.1 will not contain any defamatory, libellous, blasphemous, obscene, indecent material or any matter which would tend to deprave or corrupt any persons who may have access to the material and/or is otherwise unlawful.

1.4 That all the material in 1.1 will not make the [Company] and/or its licensees, agents and representatives and/or any parent and/or associated business liable to civil or criminal proceedings.

O.032

Where as a result of an email, text, image, slogan, photograph, film and/or any other material being sent to any part of the [Website] by a member of the public and/or any other registered user of this [Website]. The [Company] receives an allegation of obscenity and/or indecent material from any person and/or is the subject of civil and/or criminal proceedings. The [Company] will supply the details of the sender of such material to the police and such other government authorities as it thinks fit in the circumstances without any liability whatsoever to the sender of the material. Where the [Company] is also the subject of legal proceedings it shall be entitled to seek a full indemnity against the sender of the material including all legal costs.

O.033

All subscribers who submit material which is obscene, defamatory, spam, hoaxes, contains viruses and/or other damaging content shall have all their material deleted and their access blocked from all websites associated with the [Company] without any liability. Legal proceedings may be commenced without notice and a claim made by the [Company] for damages, losses and legal costs.

O.034

The [Supplier] agrees and undertakes that the [Service/Banner/other] to be delivered by the [Supplier] shall not contain any content which is obscene and/or illegal and/or an infringement of copyright and/or trade mark and/or likely to lead to a claim by a third party against the [Supplier] and/or the [Company] and/or action by the police and/or any other civil and/or criminal proceedings in [country] from [date] to date].

O.035

The [Company] agrees that any material of any nature which is included in the [Website] and/or app to be developed by the [Company] for [Name] shall not contain:

1.1 Any images, text, sound recordings, film, logos, artwork, signs, trade marks, service marks, designs, music, lyrics and/or other content which belongs to a third party which has not been cleared and/or paid for and/or acquired for use by [Name].

1.2 No content of the [Website] and/or app shall be unsuitable for [specify group and age].

Merchandising

O.036

The [Licensor agrees and undertakes to the [Distributor] that the [Work/Product] is the original work of the [Licensor] and will not infringe the copyright or any other rights of any person in respect of the rights and Territory granted to the [Distributor]. Nor does the [Work/Product] contain any material which is and/or could be construed as defamatory, obscene, and/or is likely to resulting civil and/or criminal proceedings in [country].

O.037

The [Distributor] agrees and undertakes to the [Licensor] that it shall not alter, edit, change and/or add any material whether text, images, and/or sound recordings to the [Work/Product] which is alleged to be defamatory, could be construed as obscene, is offensive and/or not directed at the [specify] market.

O.038

The [Distributor] agrees and undertakes to the [Licensor] that all the titles, packaging, advertising, marketing, brochures, flyers and posters shall be designed and directed at the [specify age group] market. That no content shall be rude, swearing, alleged to be defamatory, alleged to be obscene and/or contain any text, images and/or innuendos which are not appropriate and could bring the [Licensor] into disrepute.

O.039

There are no undertaking and/or assurance by the [Author] that the content of the [Work] to be adapted to develop the [Product] is free from any legal claim in respect of an allegation of defamation, and/or obscenity and/or other unsuitable material. The onus is on the [Distributor] to take legal advice for each country as required and to change the [Product] as required to avoid litigation.

O.040

1.1 The [Licensee] shall be entitled to delete, amend, substitute and/or vary any words and images in the [Work] which would be deemed obscene, offensive and/or inaccurate as a result of the translation of the [Work] in to another language.

1.2   The [Licensee] agrees and undertakes to make such changes at its sole cost but shall not be entitled to reproduce and distribute the new version in 1.1 until the draft [proofs/sample] has been approved by the [Licensor] in each case.

O.041

The [Licensee] agrees that the packaging, marketing, advertising and/or promotional material for the [Work/Product] shall not involve any person and/or material and/or design which would not be suitable for [children] under [age] years.

Publishing

O.042

The [Author] confirms that nothing in the [Work] contains any obscene or indecent material or any matter which would tend to deprave or corrupt any persons who may have access to the [Work] and will not render the [Publisher] liable to proceedings of any nature in respect thereof.

O.043

The [Author] warrants to the [Publishers] that all statements contained in the [Work] which are facts are true and that the [Work] contains nothing which is obscene, libellous, defamatory, blasphemous or otherwise unlawful.

O.044

The [Company] warrants that the [Works] shall be the original work of the [Writer] except where the [Work] is based on or incorporates material supplied by the [Distributor] or any third party at the request of the [Distributor], and will not infringe the copyright or any other rights of any person. The [Company] shall carry out reasonable investigations and research to establish whether the [Works] contain any material which is defamatory or obscene. The [Company] shall ensure that the [Works] will not contain any material which is defamatory or obscene or will expose the [Distributor] or its licensees to civil or criminal proceedings.

O.045

The [Publishing Company] warrants to the [Author] that the [Publishing Company] will not incorporate into the [Work] prior to publication anything which is libellous, obscene or the publication of which is an infringement of copyright of any third party. The [Publishing Company] shall indemnify the [Author] in respect of any damages, loss, expenses and costs arising suffered and/or incurred by the [Author] directly as a result of the unauthorised material added by the [Publishing Company].

O.046

The [Publisher] reserves the right in its absolute discretion to cancel any contract or to omit or suspend any advertisement for any reason including but not limited to the advertisement and/or the product and/or service it promotes is defamatory, obscene, offensive, pornographic, and/or for any reason unsuitable for the publication.

O.047

That the [Writer] will make or cause to be made all reasonable searches and enquiries to establish whether or not the [Works] contain any matter of a defamatory or obscene nature. The [Writer] undertakes that the [Works] will not contain any material which is obscene, offensive, defamatory or will expose the [Company] to civil or criminal proceedings in the Territory.

O.048

The [Author] confirms that the [Work] does not and will not contain any obscene, offensive, defamatory, or racially prejudiced material and will not expose the [Publisher] to civil or criminal proceedings for the duration of the Licence Period in the following specify countries [–].

O.049

The [Author] agrees and undertakes that the [Work] supplied by the [Author] shall not contain any obscene, offensive, defamatory, or racially prejudiced material and will not expose the [Publisher] to civil or criminal proceedings in respect of the publication of the [Work] in the [hardback and paperback] in the [United Kingdom/other] during the Term of this Agreement. In the event that there is any claim by the [Publisher] against the [Author] under this clause the total liability of the [Author] shall be limited to [figure/currency].

O.050

The [Author] agrees and undertakes that the [Work] supplied by the [Author] shall not contain any obscene, offensive, or defamatory material.

O.051

The [Author] understands and agrees that the [Publisher] shall be entitled to delete, add to, vary and/or amend any minor part of the [Work] which its legal advisors have requested should be made in respect of the publication of the [Work] in the [hardback and paperback] in the [United Kingdom/

other] during the Term of this Agreement. Where major changes are to be made then the prior consent of the [Author] shall be required.

O.052
The [Publisher] agrees that the [Author] shall not be under any obligation to the [Publisher] in respect of any legal problems that may arise from the publication of the [Work] and that the [Publisher] exercises the rights granted under this Agreement at its own cost and risk. Nor shall the [Publisher] seek to claim any indemnity and/or offset and/or recoup any sums from the advances and/or royalties due under this Agreement. That the [Publisher] shall commission at its own cost a pre-publication libel and risk-assessment report of the accuracy, sources, copyright infringement, and potential civil and criminal proceedings that may arise.

O.053
[Name] shall have the right to refuse to have any contribution which he/she has created, developed and/or written to be combined with other material in a compilation for publication which in the opinion of [Name] is obscene and/or not suitable for the [specify] market and/or likely to have a negative impact on the reputation of [Name] and/or effect the ability of [Name] to carry out his/her work as [specify role].

Purchase and Supply of Products

O.054
The [Seller] agrees and undertakes that the [Seller's] Website does not contain and will not contain any sound recordings, music, lyrics, literature, slogans, text, images, logos, articles, products or other material which are or may reasonably be construed as being defamatory, offensive, obscene or bring the [Supplier] or its products into disrepute or lower their reputation or cause loss or damage to their business.

O.055
The [Licensee] undertakes that the [Licensee's Product] and the [Product Package] will not be offensive or obscene in any nature or derogatory of any third party and will not expose the [Licensor] to any civil or criminal proceedings [in respect of the exercise of the rights granted under this Agreement.]

O.056
The [Licensee] agrees and undertakes to the [Licensor] that the [Product/Work] shall not be sold in conjunction with any other product and/or service which is obscene, lewd and/or offensive and/or may lead to criminal proceedings.

O.057

The [Licensee] agrees that it shall make it a condition of supply to any third party that the [Product/Work] is not suitable for sale to anyone under the age of [number] years.

Services

O.058

The [Presenter] undertakes that all the product of his/her services under this Agreement shall not contain any defamatory, obscene or illegal act or anything of an advertising nature and will not expose the [Company] to legal proceedings in [Territory]. Except that the [Presenter] shall not be held responsible in anyway where material of any type is included at the request or direction of the [Company].

O.059

The total liability of the [Presenter] under this clause shall be limited to [figure/currency].

O.060

This clause shall not apply to any use and/or exploitation by the [Company] and/or any authorised third party outside the [country].

O.061

This clause shall not apply to any use and/or exploitation by the [Company] and/or any authorised third party after [date].

O.062

[Name] acknowledges and undertakes that [Name] shall have the right not to be subjected to or at any time required to use any material, present any script and/or make any recording, film, or carry out any work which [Name] considers is obscene, racist, offensive, demeaning, defamatory, rude or which mocks, ridicules or might prejudice the career of [Name].

O.063

The [Company] undertakes that no material of any nature concerning [Name] shall be used by the [Company] or licensed and/or supplied to any third party which is to be used in any offensive, obscene, derogatory, defamatory or demeaning manner and/or might result in the risk of civil and/or criminal proceedings against the [Company] and/or [Name].

O.064

The [Company] acknowledges and agrees that no part of the services to be supplied to the [Enterprise] are intended to include any person, material and/or performance and/or display which features anything which is likely to offend religious organisations, those with disabilities and/or families with children and/or create any negative reaction and/or response from the local community.

Sponsorship

O.065
The [Sponsor] undertakes that it will not do anything or permit any third party to do anything or require the performance under this contract of any action, word, text, sound or image, recording, film, appearance or otherwise which is likely to be derogatory, detrimental or damaging to the reputation of the [Sportsperson]. In the event that the [Sportsperson] advises the [Company] of any such material it shall be withdrawn from the public and destroyed. The [Company] shall then negotiate in good faith to agree compensation for the loss and/or damages together with any costs incurred.

O.066
The [Company] confirms that the [Products] and the [Company's Logo] do not contain any obscene, defamatory or other derogatory or demeaning material and will not expose [Name] to any civil or criminal proceedings.

O.067
The [Sponsor] agrees and undertakes not use the name, image, photograph, details and/or representation of any official, competitor, and/or any other person in association with the [Event] in any advertising, promotion, packaging and/or marketing which could be construed as offensive, derogatory, obscene, defamatory, ridiculing, mocking, and/or in any manner and/or style in conjunction with other material which impugns their reputation.

O.068
The [Company] shall not be liable for any content, material, services, products and/or other material supplied by the [Sponsor] which results in civil and/or criminal proceedings including but not limited to allegations of defamation, obscenity, product liability, errors and/or omissions.

O.069
[Name] agrees and acknowledges that he/she must at all times during the course of their training and participation in [sport] events during the course of this sponsorship agreement conduct themselves as an ambassador for the [Sponsor] and avoid any gestures, words, behaviour and/or innuendos which might be construed in any language in [country] as obscene and/or vulgar and/or expose the [Sponsor] to ridicule and/or adverse publicity.

University, Library and Educational

O.070

The [Institute] agrees and confirms that to the best of its knowledge and belief the [Work/Service] does not contain any material which is obscene and/or defamatory in [specify country]. No undertakings are given as regard any other country in the world and no responsibility can be accepted. The [Institute] cannot accept responsibility for third parties who use the [Work/Service]. The [Institute] does not accept responsibility for compliance with any standards, practices and/or codes. This clause shall only apply from [start date] to [end date]. The [Company] agrees and accepts that any matters arising from this clause must be notified in writing to the [Institute] within [three months] of the [end date].

O.071

The [Contributor] agrees and undertakes to the [Institute] that the [Work/Service] supplied by the [Contributor] shall not contain any obscene, offensive, defamatory and/or any other material of any nature which exposes the [Institute] to the threat of and/or does expose and/or makes the [Institute] liable to criminal and/or civil proceedings in [countries/Territory/world].

O.072

The [Contributor] agrees that the [Institute] shall be entitled to delete, add to, vary and/or amend all and/or any part of the [Work/Service] at the [Institutes'] sole discretion. If in the opinion of the management of the [Institute] the content of the [Work/Service] creates a risk of civil and/or criminal proceedings being commence by a third party against the [Institute].

O.073

The [Institute] confirms that the [Work/Service] does not contain any obscene or defamatory material and will not expose the [Distributor] to civil and/or criminal proceedings. The [Distributor] agrees and accepts that the maximum liability of the [Institute] under this clause shall be limited to [figure/currency] in total in respect of all matters arising under this clause.

O.074

The [Institute] reserves the right to ban any person from the site of the premises and offices and to prevent their participation in an event, course and/or workshop. Where that person has threatened,, abused and/or made obscene gestures to any member of security, staff and/or another student at any time. The ban will continue indefinitely and may be invoked by the [Institute] at any time [specify]. The ban will only be lifted if the [Institute] is satisfied that any person no longer poses a threat to others on the site and/or has agreed to adhere to any conditions imposed by the [Institute].

OMISSION

General Business and Commercial

O.075

Any act or omission which, if it were an act or omission by the [Licensee] would be a breach of this Agreement, shall be deemed to be an act or omission for which the [Licensee] is responsible if done or omitted by any associate, affiliate, subsidiary, parent company, sub-agent, sub-licensee or other person, firm and/or business who has been engaged, instructed or appointed by the [Licensee].

O.076

The term 'act or omission' shall include all acts or omissions whether there is a legal duty to act or not.

O.077

The [Purchaser] shall be responsible for errors, omissions or discrepancies in drawings and written information supplied by the [Purchaser] or his representative. The [Purchaser] shall, at his own expense, carry out any alterations or remedial work which may arise directly or indirectly from such defects.

O.078

The [Company] shall be responsible for and shall indemnify the [Service Company] against all costs, claims and damages arising by reason of the acts and/or omissions of the [Company's] Agents.

O.079

In the event that any error should arise from the allotment of space at the Exhibition or in the quoted exhibition time provided to the [Client] by the [Organisers]. The [Organiser] will endeavour to provide a substitute arrangement, but are not bound to do so. The [Organisers] also reserve the right to change the position allotted to the [Client] should it be necessary. The [Organisers] shall not be liable for any damages which may arise from the allotment of space or the quoted exhibition 'time' and reserve the right to alter the arrangements at any time.

O.080

The [Publisher] shall take reasonable care in inserting the advertisement in the position form and date agreed with the [Advertiser]. In the event that the advertisement is not published or there is any other error or omission of any nature whether on the part of the [Publisher] or any third party the

[Advertiser] agrees that the maximum liability of the [Publisher] shall be the total cost of the payment for the advertisement. The [Publisher] shall not be liable for any direct or indirect consequential loss or damage incurred of any nature for any reason. The [Advertiser] shall notify the [Publisher] within [21 days] of the intended date of the advertisement in writing specifying in detail the grounds of complaint. Thereafter the [Advertiser] shall be deemed to have waived any claim of any kind against the [Publisher].

O.081

Where there is an error, omission, and/or other inaccuracy which occurs in respect of the [Work/Film/Product] which is not deliberate and/or malicious. Then the defaulting party shall be provided with the opportunity to correct the mistake and to rectify the position. Where the error, omission, and/or other inaccuracy is of such a nature that the other non-defaulting party has suffered damage to their reputation and/or incurred losses. Then the defaulting party shall be obliged to indemnify the non-defaulting party for all such costs and expenses.

O.082

The [Licensee] agrees and undertakes that it shall be responsible for all the acts, errors, omissions, inaccuracies, negligence and/or breaches by any agent, distributor, sub-licensee, bank and/or any other person engaged by the [Licensee] in respect of the exploitation of the [Work] under this Agreement.

O.083

The maximum liability of the [Licensor/Licensee] in respect of any errors, omissions, delays, inaccuracies and/or interruptions of the [Service] shall be [figure/currency] in total to [Name].

O.084

[Name] agrees and accepts that in the event his/her performance is not included in the [Film/Programme] for the [DVD/Disc/other] after the material has been edited by the [Distributor]. That [Name] shall not be entitled to any further payments from the exploitation of the [DVD/Disc/other].

O.085

The [Distributor] agrees and undertakes that it shall not have the right to omit any part of the [Film] and/or credits and copyright notices from the transmission of the [Film] on [channel]. That the failure to transmit the [Film] in its complete state as it is delivered and/or the omission of any part shall be a serious breach of this Agreement and the [Distributor] shall be obliged to pay the [Licensor] an additional fee of [number/currency] per minute of material that is not transmitted.

O.086

Any omissions, errors, delays and misrepresentations which occur which are not deliberate by either party shall not be grounds for termination of this Agreement provided that any such matter is resolved within [one] month of the date that the matter first arises.

O.087

[Name] agrees that he/she shall not be entitled to any refund and/or repayment for failure to deliver the [Service] where the delay, error and/or omission is for less than [number] hours in any week.

O.088

The [Company] does not accept any liability where errors, omissions and/.or other inaccuracies on the website, app and/or data service provide information which is misleading and/or not reliable. The information is for guidance and may change at any time before the information can be updated and you are advised to verify the information with your own research and professional advice.

University, Library and Educational

O.089

The [Institute] shall not be responsible for and/or liable to the [Distributor] for any omissions, errors, delays, costs, amendments, corrections, and/or substitutions which may arise under this Agreement at any time. Nor shall the [Institute] provide any indemnity to the [Distributor].The [Distributor] agrees and undertakes that it shall bear its own costs and expenses, arrange suitable insurance and not seek to rely on any indemnity from the [Institute].

O.090

The [Institute] shall be responsible for the acts, omissions, and errors of any associate, affiliate, subsidiary, and/or parent company, agent, licensee and/or any other person, company, and/or business who has been engaged, instructed, appointed and/or authorised by the [Institute] to carry out any work and/or services under this Agreement.

O.091

The [Institute] shall be responsible for any errors, omissions, and inaccuracies which it shall endeavour to rectify as it thinks fit within [two months] of complaint by the [Licensee]. The [Licensee] agrees that the maximum liability of the [Institute] shall be the total cost of the payment for the [Work/Service] paid by the [Licensee] and that no additional sums for any direct and/or indirect damage, and/or loss shall be due and/or payable.

O.092

The [Consortium] agrees that the omission by one party to fulfil the terms of this Agreement in accordance with the timeline in Schedule [-] shall entitle the other parties to serve notice to terminate the continuance of the [Project] with that party.

OPTION

DVD, Video and Discs

O.093

The [Licensor] hereby agrees to grant to the [Distributor] an Option to extend the Licence Period by a further [two years] under the existing Agreement provided that the Agreement has not been cancelled, expired and/or terminated. The Option can be exercised at any time during the Licence Period before [date] by written notice to the [Licensor] to that effect and the payment of the option fee [figure/currency] by the [Distributor] to the [Licensor]. This option fee shall not be recouped and/or offset against any advance, royalties and/or otherwise by the [Distributor]. In the event that the Option is exercised the Agreement shall end on [date] and there shall be no further option and/or right of extension of the Licence Period.

O.094

The [Company] grants to the [Licensee] three separate sole exclusive and irrevocable Options in consideration of an initial payment [–] as follows:

1.1   The first Option is to acquire the [DVD/Mechanical Reproduction Rights] in the [Film] in [country] on terms to be agreed between the parties subject to an additional payment of [–].

1.2   The second Option is to acquire the [Interactive Game Rights] in the [Film] in [country] on terms to be agreed between the parties subject to an additional payment of [–].

1.3   The third Option is to acquire the [Internet, Worldwide web, Telecommunication system and Landline and Mobile Telephone Rights] in the [Film] in [country] on terms to be agreed between the parties subject to an additional payment of [–].

The [Licensee] shall be entitled to exercise the options at any time between [date] and [date] by notice in writing in respect of each option to the [Company] and the payment of the second option instalment in each case. The [Licensee] shall then have a period of [three calendar months] to negotiate and conclude an agreement for the acquisition and exercise of the rights in each case with the [Company]. No payments for the Options shall be refunded by the [Company] nor shall the payments be offset against any other sums relating to the grant and/or exercise of the rights under the new agreements.

O.095

1.1   In consideration of the Option Fee of [figure/currency] [Name] grants to the [Company] the sole and exclusive right to exercise an option to produce a [Film] based on the [Work] and to exercise and exploit the [DVD/Video/Disc] Rights in [country] from [date to [date].

1.2   The right to exercise the Option shall commence [date/date of this Agreement] and end [date]. Notice must be in writing and an additional sum paid of [figure/currency] to [Name] in order to exercise the Option.

1.3   In the event that the [Company] exercises the Option and has made the second payment, then [Name] and the [Company] agree to enter into an [exclusive licence/other agreement] with the following main terms [specify].

1.4   The [Company] acknowledges that if the parties fail to agree terms and conclude an agreement or the [Company] does not exercise the Option and/or pay the sums due the [Company] shall have no further rights in the [Work].

O.096

In consideration of the payment of [figure/currency] the [Author] grants the [Company] the sole and exclusive Option to acquire an exclusive licence for [all media rights] in the [Sound Recordings] in accordance with the draft Licence set out in Appendix [–] which forms part of this Agreement. The Option shall start on [date] and end on [date]. During that period the [Company] may exercise the Option by the payment of [figure/currency] and written notice that they wish to conclude the Licence.

O.097

There is no option and/or first right of refusal granted in respect of any subsequent [Work/Sound Recording/Film] which is based on and/or associated with the [Work/Sound Recording/Film] by the [Licensor].

O.098

The [Licensee] shall not be obliged to offer and/or provide the [Sub-Licensee] with a first option to purchase the [Work] for any country. The [Sub-Licensee] shall not have any rights and/or interest and/or option over any sequel, new series and/or any other development.

O.099

1.1   The [Company] agrees that in the vent it decides to make another [Film/Programme] for the [DVD/CD/Disc] market that it shall first offer the role of main [Presenter/Consultant] to [Name] upon the same terms and conditions as set out under this Agreement.

1.2   [Name] agrees that if he/she has not accepted the offer within [seven] days then the [Company] shall appoint a third party and the offer shall lapse and end.

O.100

In consideration of the payment of [number/currency] by direct to the bank account of [Name] by [date]. [Name] grants the [Distributor] an exclusive option which shall start on [date] and end on [date] to acquire the sole and exclusive right to distribute and sell the [Format] of the [Work] in [country]. If the parties have not concluded the agreement for the acquisition of the rights by [date] then the option shall end and [Name] shall retain all sums paid to that date. [Name] shall then be able to exploit, sell and offer an option to a third party and the [Distributor] shall no longer have any option to exercise.

Film and Television

O.101

The [Licensor] hereby agrees to grant to the [Media Company] an option to make a further repeat broadcast of the [Film] such option to be exercised in writing before [date]. In the event the [Licensee] does exercise this option the Licence Period shall be extended and will expire on [date]. An additional Licence Fee of [figure/currency] shall be payable upon the exercise of the option by the [Media Company] to the [Licensor].

O.102

The [Production Company] agrees and undertakes that it shall not be permitted to arrange or carry out any development or any other work in respect of the treatment, scripts or other material relating to the [Author's Work] unless it has exercised the option granted under this Agreement and the exclusive licence agreement has been concluded between the parties.

O.103

The [Company] grants to the [Distributor] an exclusive option to acquire the same rights in respect of any further [Programme] which the [Company] commissions or produces upon the same terms and conditions except that the financial terms shall be subject to separate negotiation. The [Company] shall notify the [Distributor] of any [Programme] when it is completed and available. The [Distributor] shall have [one calendar month] from the date of notice in which it shall be entitled to reject or negotiate for the acquisition of the [Programme]. In the event that there is no response from the [Distributor] the [Company] shall be entitled to deem the [Programme] rejected and to offer the [Programme] to any third party.

O.104

The [Licensor] shall have the option to acquire all copies or derivatives of the [Film] within the possession or control of the [Licensee]. The option period shall be the period of [6 months] prior to the date of expiry of this Agreement. The [Licensor] shall provide the [Licensee] with written notice of that intention to acquire such material and enter into negotiations for the settlement of the sum due and the detail of the material available. In the event that no such notice is received by the [Licensee] or the [Licensor] does not wish to acquire such material, then the [Licensee] shall destroy all such material at the end of the date of the Agreement and provide a statement to the [Licensor] to that effect.

O.105

In consideration of [figure/currency] the [Company] grants to the [Licensee] two separate sole exclusive and irrevocable options as follows:

1.1 The first option is to acquire the Television Rights in the [Film] as defined in Clause [–] of the draft Licence set out in Schedule [–].

1.2 The second option is to acquire a share of the profits from the [Film] as defined in Clause [–] of the draft Licence set out in Schedule [–].

The [Licensee] shall be entitled to exercise each of the options from [date] to [date] by notice in writing to the [Company]. Within [7 days] of the exercise of the option in respect of the Television Rights the [Licensee] shall deliver to the [Company] a signed copy of the Licence in Schedule [–] and pay the sum of [figure/currency].

Within [7 days] of the exercise of the option in respect of the profit share, the [Licensee] shall deliver to the [Company] the Licence in the Schedule [–] duly signed and the sum of [figure/currency].

O.106

In consideration of the Option Fee the [Author] grants to the [Production Company] the sole and exclusive right to exercise an option to produce the [Series] based on the [Author's Work]. The right to exercise the option shall be for the duration of the Option Period.

O.107

'The Option Period' shall mean the period commencing [date/date of this Agreement] and ending [date].

O.108

In the event that the [Production Company] exercises the option, then the [Author] and the [Production Company] agree to sign the exclusive licence agreement which is attached to and forms part of this Agreement.

O.109

The [Production Company] acknowledges that after the expiry of the Option Period the [Production Company] shall have no further rights in the [Author's Work] and shall not be entitled to produce the [Series].

O.110

The [Author] undertakes that he/she shall not grant an option nor authorise, license or permit any third party to produce a film [or recordings] based on the [Author's Work] or any adaptation, variation or development during the Option Period without the prior written consent of the [Production Company].

O.111

In the event that the option is not exercised then all copyright, intellectual property rights, computer software and all other rights in the [Work], title, format, and any associated material shall remain vested in and belong to the [Author].

O.112

Any failure to renew or extend the Option Period following the expiry shall not be grounds for any claim or payments for any reason. The [Author] and the [Production Company] agree they shall not be entitled to any claim or sums for failure to renew, extend, or negotiate a further period.

O.113

The [Company] agrees and undertakes that in the event it decides to create, develop and produce a new series of the [Programme] that it shall offer [Name] the role of [specify] if it continues as a character in the script. If the character is not in the new [Programme] then there shall be no obligation to make any offer of another role.

O.114

The [Company] agrees and undertakes to grant the [Distributor] an exclusive option to acquire the [interactive online game and betting rights] to be used in conjunction with the [Distributors] website [specify] and its business [specify] provided that the following terms are fulfilled:

1.1   The [Distributor] pays a non-returnable option fee of [number/currency] by [date] to the [Company].

1.2   The [Distributor] concludes an exclusive licence agreement with the [Company] by [date] which has a non-returnable advance of not less than [number/currency] and is for a fixed term of [number] [months/years].

1.3   At the time of the conclusion of the agreement in 1.2 the [Distributor] is solvent and not the subject of any investigation and/or action and/or civil and/or legal proceedings by any government and/or regulatory body.

1.4   The [Distributor] agrees and undertakes that it shall assign all copyright and all intellectual property and computer software rights in any new material and rights created and/or commissioned by the [Distributor] in respect of the exercise of the rights granted under 1.2.

General Business and Commercial

O.115
'The Option Fee' shall be the sum of [figure/currency] which shall be payable upon signature of this Agreement by the [Licensee]. This sum (which shall be an additional sum to any other payments due under this Agreement) shall be non- returnable and not offset against any future payments to which the [Licensor] may be entitled.

O.116
The [Company] warrants that it has not assigned, licensed, charged or in any way dealt with the copyright or any other rights in the [Synopsis/Work/other] and will not do so until the expiry of the Option on [date].

O.117
'The Option Period' shall mean [12 calendar months] from the date of this Agreement and shall not include any further option periods without the prior written agreement of both parties.

O.118
'The Option Period' means the period commencing on [date] and ending on [date].

O.119
'The Option' shall mean the sole and exclusive option and right to acquire the [specify Rights] during the period [date] to [date] by the [specify party] by notice of the exercise of the rights and the payment of the [Option Fee].

O.120

The [Company] warrants that it shall not grant or purport to grant the [specify Rights] for any part of the Territory to any other person unless the [Distributor] fails to exercise the option during the Option Period.

O.121

The Option shall be exercised (if at all) by the [Distributor] giving to the [Company] written notice of exercise of the option at any time during the Option Period.

O.122

In the event that the [Company] decides to appoint another agent in the Territory during the Term of the Agreement. The [Company] agrees to give the [Agent] the opportunity to match or better the terms offered, but the [Company] shall not be bound or obligated to accept any such proposal by the [Agent].

O.123

The [Company] agrees that until the expiration of the Option Period it will not assign, license or in any way dispose of or subject to a lien or charge the copyright, intellectual property rights or any other rights in respect of the [Work] in any manner which would or might impair the grant by the Company of the [Rights].

O.124

The [Company] agrees that it will not do or permit anything which would or might in any way impair the [Rights] or the ability of the [Company] to make the representations and give the warranties contained in the Licence.

O.125

The [Company] warrants that it is the sole and absolute owner of, or to the extent that the [Property] has not yet been made the prospective owner of, the entire copyright and all other rights of any nature in the [Property] and of all rights in all material incorporated and to be incorporated in the [Property] as are or may be required to permit the [Property] to be produced and exploited by all means and by all media. Such rights are or will, prior to the start of the Option Period, be vested in the Company or its successors absolutely free from encumbrances.

O.126

The [Company] shall be entitled to renew this Licence for a further period of [specify duration] at their sole option by notice in writing before the expiry of the Agreement. If the option is not exercised or received until the day after the date of expiry then there shall be no further period as the right to extend had lapsed.

O.127
[Name] agrees and accepts that he/she has no right of first refusal, option and/or any other preferential claim and/or right to a reduced and/or discounted rate in respect of the [Work].

Internet and Websites

O.128
The [Company] grants the [Consultant] the non-exclusive option to extend the Agreement for a further period of [number] months. The [Consultant] shall notify the [Company] by [email] in order to exercise the option before [date]. After that [date] the option shall not apply and the Agreement cannot be extended.

O.129
The [Company] grants [Enterprise] the exclusive option to exploit the [specify] Rights in respect of the Website. The [Enterprise] shall pay the Option Fee by [date] and may only exercise the option from [date to [date]. In the event that the option is exercised then the parties shall conclude an exclusive licence agreement with an advance of not less than [figure/currency].

O.130
The [Distributor] shall pay to the [Company] an option payment of [figure/currency] by [date]. The [Company] grants the [Distributor] the exclusive option to acquire the [Distribution] Rights for the [Product] in accordance with the terms and conditions set out in the Licence in Appendix [–] which forms part of this Agreement.

O.131
No person, business and/or third party shall be entitled to any priority, option, renewal and/or extension of any Agreement with the [Company]. Nor shall they be entitled to any sums for loss of reputation, investment, projected sales, commission, and/or any other losses and/or damages, costs and expenses.

O.132
[Name] agrees to grant the [Distributor] an exclusive option to enter into an agreement to be licenced the next [number] original apps that he/she shall create, develop and produce subject to the following terms:

1.1 The [Distributor] pays [Name] an option fee of [number/currency] within [number] days and/or by [date] at the latest.

1.2 If the option fee is paid in 1.1 then the [Distributor] shall have a period of [number] months where [Name] agrees not to enter into agreement with any third party for the next [number] original apps he/she will create. This shall not prevent [Name] from having discussions with third parties.

1.3   During the option period if the [Distributor] and [Name] do not agree and conclude an agreement then [Name] shall not be obliged to repay the option fee. If the parties do conclude an agreement then the option fee shall not form any part of that agreement.

Merchandising

O.133

The [Company] shall have the exclusive and sole option to be the exclusive [Supplier/Distributor] of products for [market/type] at all the Venues including stadium, press centres and any other facilities or premises over which the [Organisers] and/or the [Television Company] have control or authority in [country]. In the event that the [Company] decides to exercise that Option then they shall serve written notice on the [Organisers] before [date] and pay [figure/currency] which shall be an advance against the sums to be paid to the [Organisers] under the agreement to be concluded between the parties.

O.134

The [Company] shall have the option to be exercised by notice in writing for a period of [28 days] prior to the expiry date of the Licence to renew the Licence for a further period of [duration]. Such renewal shall be on the same terms and conditions as set out in the initial Licence, except that there shall be no option to renew for a further period thereafter. Upon exercising the option the [Company] shall pay the [Originator] the sum of [figure/currency] and such sum shall not be included within or offset against any sums due under the new further Licence.

O.135

In consideration of the Option Fee, the [Author] grants to the [Company] the sole and exclusive right to exercise an option to produce products, articles and/or other manufactured goods, based on the [Author's Work] and any [Film] derived from it and any associated character, name, title, trade mark, logo, design, image or words. The Option must be exercised by notice in writing to the [Author] during the period from [date] to [date] and the agreement shall an exclusive licence for [number] years summarised in the attached Schedule [–].

O.136

The [Author] grants to the [Distributor] an exclusive option to acquire the [Merchandising] Rights in respect of any further [Work] which the [Author] writes based on the [Characters] from [date] to [date]. The exclusive licence shall be as set out in Schedule [–] except that the financial terms shall be subject to separate negotiation at that time. The [Distributor] agrees to pay the [Author] the sum of [figure/currency] upon full signature of both parties of the exclusive option. The [Distributor] shall exercise the option by notice in writing after [date] and before [date] to the [Author] setting out their intentions. The option shall not entitle the [Distributor] to have any other rights and/or interest and/or first right of refusal once the option period has ended.

O.137

1.1 The [Company] agrees that the [Distributor] shall have an exclusive option to acquire the merchandising rights for the [specify] market in all its [Works] provided that it pays an annual fee to the [Company] of [number/currency] payable by [date] in each year. This exclusive option shall start on [date] and end on [date].

1.2 The [Company] shall offer any [Work] to the [Distributor] and if the parties cannot agree terms and conclude an agreement and/or if the [Distributor] refuses the offer. Then the [Company] may offer that particular [Work] to a third party whether within the period of the exclusive option or not.

1.3 In the event that the [Distributor] fails to pay any advance and/or royalties due to the [Company] and/or any person in the [Work] at any time. Then the [Company] shall have the right to terminate the exclusive option in its entirety and all agreements which have been concluded with the [Distributor] connected with it. In such event the [distributor] agrees that it shall not have the right to be repaid any sums paid prior to termination.

Publishing

O.138
Unless otherwise stated nothing herein is to be taken as granting or implying the grant of an option to the [Publisher] over any of the [Author's] future works.

O.139
In the event that the [Company] exercises the option then the [Author] and the [Company] both agree to sign the exclusive licence agreement which is attached to this Agreement and negotiate a Development and Production Agreement in good faith on terms to be agreed.

O.140
The [Company] acknowledges that after expiry of the Option Period the [Company] shall have no further rights in the [Work] and shall not be entitled,

unless terms are agreed in writing between the parties thereto, to produce or further exploit the [Series].

O.141

The [Author] undertakes that he will not grant an option nor authorise, license or permit any third party to produce a film based on the [Work] or any adaptation or variation during the Option Period without the prior written approval of the [Company]. Except that the [Author] shall not be obliged to take any legal proceedings in order to comply with this clause. The [Author] does agree to co-operate fully with the [Company] in the event that the [Company] wishes to take action provided that the [Company] agrees to indemnify the [Author] in respect of all costs and expenses that he may incur including the provision of independent legal advice and representation.

O.142

The [Author] agrees to give the [Publisher] the first option to publish [in volume form] the next full-length work by the [Author] on such reasonable and fair terms to be agreed between the parties for the purpose of granting the same Rights and Territories as have been agreed for the [Work]. The Advance and Royalties are not to be less than those set out in this Agreement, but in any event are subject to such sums being agreed between the parties. The [Publisher] agrees that such option shall only last for a period of [specify duration] from the date that the [Author] delivers the next full-length work to the [Publisher]. In the event that the parties fail to agree terms then the [Publisher] shall return all copies of the [Work] to the [Author] at the [Publisher's] expense.

O.143

In consideration of the sum of [figure/currency] paid to the [Author] on the date of this Agreement receipt of which the Author acknowledges. The [Author] grants to the [Publishers] first right of refusal of the [Author's] next full-length work which he/she may write which shall be on such fair and reasonable terms as shall be agreed between the parties. The right of first refusal shall include the first opportunity to read the work and consider it for publication.

O.144

The [Author] undertakes that he/she will not grant an option nor authorise, license or permit any third party to produce a film, video, DVD, television programme or series or other visual moving image, sound recordings, and/or produce for and/or distribute on the internet, any telecommunication system, telephone, computer, gadget, or storage and retrieval system, computer generated material whether in sound, vision or text any version in any language based on the [Author's Work] and any associated character, name, title, trade mark, logo, design, lyrics, music, image or words or any adaptation or variation during the Option Period without the prior written consent of the [Company].

O.145

The [Author] agrees that he/she shall not grant a licence, authorise or permit the use of the [Work] in any form in [country] from [date] to [date]. This restriction shall include exploitation in film, recordings, text, text messaging, sound, sound effects, music, computer generated material, advertisements, sponsorship or advertisements.

O.146

The [Author] grants to the [Publisher] the exclusive option to negotiate terms for the publication of the next full-length work in the field of [subject] by the [Author]. The [Author] shall deliver the synopsis of the work to the [Publisher] for their consideration. The [Publishers] shall then have a period of [4 weeks] to negotiate terms which are acceptable to the [Author] which shall be no less than those set out in this Agreement. In the event that the [Publisher] is not in a position to make an offer, or rejects it or the parties cannot agrees terms, then at the expiry of the [4 week] period the [Author] shall be entitled to offer the work to any other third party and the option shall be at an end. If the [Publishers] wish to extend the Option Period then they shall be obliged to pay the sum of [figure/currency] to the [Author] for a further [4 week] Option Period.

O.147

If the [Assignor] should write or permit to be written a sequel to the [Work] before [date], the [Assignor] shall deliver a copy thereof to the [Assignee] as soon as it is completed and ready for submission to publishers. The [Assignor] agrees not to exercise or grant to any third party any rights in such sequel which in respect of the [Work] are granted to the Assignee unless the following stages have been completed. During the period [state duration] following such delivery the [Assignee] shall be exclusively entitled to negotiate for such rights. If at the end of such period the [Assignee] has not agreed to acquire such rights, the [Assignor] shall not exercise or grant such rights to any third party unless the [Assignor] shall first make a written offer to the [Assignee] to grant the relevant rights in the sequel to the [Assignee] on terms the [Assignor] proposes granting such rights to a third party. The [Assignee] shall have a period of [state duration] to accept or reject such a proposal and unless the [Assignee] agrees to such terms the [Assignor] shall be entitled to grant such rights to any third party.

O.148

The [Publishers] acknowledge and agree that this Agreement is solely limited to the first edition of the [Work] in [format]. The [Publishers] shall have no right of first refusal, option, or prior claim to any further work of the [Author] and or any sequel and/or subsequent edition and/or any version for any film, DVD, and/or sound recording or any other media whether based on, derived from and or adapted from the [Work] or not including any character, plot, storyline, name, words, images, illustrations or otherwise.

O.149

1.1 [Name] agrees to consider and may offer the [Distributor] the opportunity to purchase future editions of the [Work] and/or other material created and developed by [Name].

1.2 The [Distributor] agrees that there is obligation for [Name] to make an offer in 1.1 and that the [Distributor] has no right to develop, adapt and/or vary the [Work] in any manner to create new versions for exploitation at a later date.

University, Library and Educational

O.150

The [Institute] does not grant any option and/or rights to the [Company] which can be exercised in respect of the [Work/Service] and/or any sequel, adaptation, new edition, development and/or subsequent version of the [Work/Service] or any part.

O.151

The [Institute] shall have the exclusive option to extend this licence for [twelve months] and/or to enter into a further licence on the same terms and conditions for [two years]. The [Institute] must exercise the option by notice in writing to the [Company] by [notice date]. If the option is not exercised and/or notice received then this Agreement shall expire on [end date].

O.152

1.1 The [Contributor/Author] agrees that the [Institute] shall have the first right of refusal to any sequel and/or subsequent edition and/or any other version and/or development of the [Work]. This right of refusal shall not apply to any other books, articles, work and/or subjects written by and/or developed by the [Contributor/Author] at any time.

1.2 The [Contributor/Author] shall deliver the outline of the sequel and/or subsequent edition and/or any other version and/or development of the [Work] to the [Institute]. The [Institute] shall then have a period of [two calendar months] to negotiate terms which are acceptable to the [Contributor/Author] and conclude a new agreement or to reject the outline. At the end of the [two calendar month] period the [Contributor/

Author] shall be entitled to offer the outline of the sequel and/or subsequent edition and/or any other version and/or development of the [Work] to any other third party and the first right of refusal shall be at an end.

O.153
The [Institute] agrees that it has no prior claim and/or option over the work of the [Researcher] and that he/she may offer their analysis, data, records, information and reports to any third party for publication and/or exploitation in any form.

ORDER

DVD, Video and Discs

O.154
Any order for [DVDs/Videos/Discs] shall be in writing stating the title, duration, reference code, wholesale price [excluding vat] and the requested method and date of delivery and cost. Payment of the price and cost of delivery shall be made in advance and delivery shall not be arranged until all sums have been received.

O.155
Delivery by the [Company] of [DVDs/Discs/other] shall be free for any purchase in excess of [number/currency] between [date] and [date] in [country].

General Business and Commercial

O.156
The Company shall proceed with the [Works] in accordance with the decisions, instructions and orders given by [Name] in accordance with the Contract.

O.157
All orders are only accepted when [approved/authorised] by [Name].

O.158
The [Company] shall be under no liability in respect of orders for the service placed by or on behalf of the [Customer] until the [Company] shall have accepted such orders in writing.

O.159

The [Contractor] undertakes to provide the [Company] with any information it may request for the management of the Contract.

O.160

All initial orders and repeat orders for the manufacture of [Product] shall be placed by the [Company] in writing.

O.161

All orders are accepted subject to the acceptance of the copy by the [Publisher]. The [Advertiser] shall supply all details of any special offer, merchandising or competition or any other material which is associated with the [Product] for the advertisement at the time that the copy is submitted to the [Publisher].

O.162

All orders are subject to all conditions being accepted as stated on the published rate card by the [Company] at the time that the copy is submitted.

O.163

The [Company] shall supply the [Material] in accordance with the written orders supplied by the [Customer] and/or its agents. The [Company] shall be under no liability in respect of such orders until the [Company] shall have accepted the order in each case [in writing/by allocation of an invoice number]. The orders are placed on the express understanding that acceptance by the [Company] shall be governed by the terms of this Agreement.

O.064

1.1 The [Company] reserves the right to cancel, vary, amend and/or substitute an order at any time with the [Supplier] based on the requirements of its business.

1.2 The [Supplier] agrees to 1.1 provided that the minimum order in any one financial year shall be [number/currency].

1.3 The parties agree that where the order has been delivered then 1.1 shall not apply.

Purchase and Supply of Products

O.165

All orders accepted by the [Company] from the [Buyer] are accepted on the terms herein contained. No other term of any nature whatsoever shall be added unless expressed in writing and signed by an authorised officer of the [Company]. No servant or agent of the [Company] has authority to agree to any oral variation or modification of or addition to these terms in any circumstances whatsoever. Except as otherwise herein provided all conditions and warranties, express or implied, statutory or otherwise, relating to the [Company's] products or to any container or package are hereby excluded in so far as may be permitted by law.

O.166

No formal acknowledgment of orders for material sold will be given unless requested by the [Customer] in writing. Formal acknowledgment of orders for material supplied on hire will be given for all orders which are received by the [Company] more than [8 days] (exclusive of Saturdays, Sundays and statutory holidays) prior to the commencement of the hire.

O.167

The [Supplier] shall be responsible for all export duties, taxes or other expenses, charges and costs that may be incurred until the [Product] is delivered to the [Company]. All property, rights, risks and liabilities shall remain with the [Supplier] until delivery.

O.168

The [Supplier] agrees to deliver the [Product] to the [Seller] on a non-exclusive basis for the duration of the Agreement in consideration of the payments stated under this Agreement.

O.169

The [Supplier] shall deliver the [Product] in accordance with the delivery dates and quantities specified in accordance with Schedule [–]. Thereafter the [Supplier] shall provide each unit of the [Product] in accordance with a written request.

O.170

It is a condition of this order that the [Goods] comply and will continue to comply with all provisions relating to the designs, manufacture, supply and use of the [Goods] of any statute, regulation, order, directive or other legislation in force at the time of delivery in the [United Kingdom/Territory].

O.171

The [Goods] and all supporting literature and material will conform with all descriptions and not be in breach of the statute, law, directive, regulation, guidelines or code in [country] from [[date] to [date]/at any time/during the existence of this Agreement].

O.172

The [Seller] will supply at the [delivery date/installation/by date] of the [Goods] all instruction manuals, spare part lists, and other relevant information in respect of the [Goods]. In particular the [Seller] shall ensure that there is supporting literature which clearly sets out the purpose for which the [Goods] are suitable, and the steps and precautions that should be taken to ensure that the use of the [Goods] will be safe and not put the [public] at risk.

O.173

The conditions of this Purchase Order shall be incorporated in the contract between the [Seller] and the [Company] for the supply of goods specified in the purchase order and shall prevail over any inconsistent terms or conditions contained in or referred to in the seller's quotation or acceptance of order or otherwise or implied by trade or custom. No addition to or variation of these conditions shall be binding upon the [Company] unless in writing and signed by a duly authorised representative of the [Company].

O.174

The [Purchaser] agrees that when placing a firm order for the [Goods] from the [Company] that it shall pay a deposit of [one-third] of the total price. The [Purchaser] shall ensure that all details and measurements on the order form are correct. The [Company] shall not be responsible for any incorrect details or measurements. In any event, the Purchaser agrees that the order cannot be rectified once work has commenced [two days] after the order form date.

O.175

The [Company] shall place an order with the [Manufacturer] for the [Products] in the form of a purchase order or similar document specifying the product name, model number, description, quantity price, payment terms, production month and destination of the [Products]. The [Company] shall place the purchase order at least [4 months] before the order is intended to be manufactured. The [Company] agrees that the failure of any purchase order to arrive at the [Manufacturer] shall delay production and shipment. The [Manufacturer] shall not be in any way responsible for any direct or indirect consequential losses arising from the delay or otherwise of the purchase order.

O.176

Such purchase orders shall be deemed to be offers by the [Company] to the [Manufacturer] to purchase the [Products] on the terms set out therein. If the [Manufacturer] accepts the order it will send on acknowledgment form of a separate sales contract.

O.177

The [Company] shall provide the following goods, materials, machinery equipment or facilities and the [Buyer/Hirer] shall purchase or hire the same as specified for delivery or use on the date(s) specified and in accordance with the payment terms.

O.178

These conditions shall be incorporated in the contract between the person to whom the sales order is addressed the [Buyer/Hirer] and the [Company]. These conditions shall prevail over any other contracted terms or otherwise contained in or referred to the [Buyer's/Hirer's] request form or otherwise or implied by trade custom.

O.179

The signature and return of the copy of the sales order by the [Buyer/Hirer] or the [Company's] signature of the sales order or the start of the work or the delivery of the order shall constitute acceptance of the terms of the sales order by the [Buyer/Hirer], provided that the terms have been drawn to the attention of the [Buyer/Hirer].

O.180

All terms contained in this sales order shall apply to the sale of the [Goods/Products/Articles] by the [Company] to the [Buyer]. No terms stipulated by the [Buyer] shall be included in this order unless set out in writing by the [Company]. There shall be no binding agreement until the [Company], its employee or agent has notified the [Buyer] in writing that the order is accepted.

O.181

The [Company's] catalogues, price list and/or advertising material are for information and guidance only.

O.182

Where, within [one] month after delivery, an Order is found to be incomplete and/or some items are defective and/or not of the standard of the sample shown to the representative of the [Company]. Then the [Supplier] agrees to deliver the missing items and/or substitute others of suitable standard which are acceptable to the [Company] within [number] days of notification by the [Company].

O.183

The [Company] agrees that where it has placed an order with the [Supplier] for delivery of [Products] and the weather conditions means that the [Products] may not sell as expected. That the [Company] shall not have any right to cancel the order and/or delay delivery which has been placed once the payment for the complete order has been made to the [Supplier].

Services

O.184

The [Agent] agrees that the [Company] shall be entitled to accept or reject any order obtained by the [Agent] for any reason including poor credit rating of client, bad payment record, the failure to obtain suitable textiles, conflict of interest with existing client, potential or threatened legal proceedings.

O.185

The [Company] agrees that where the [Agent] has obtained orders from any retail store or retail outlet in the Territory introduced by the [Agent], accepted by the [Company], the [Company] agrees not to sell any of the [Products] based on the [Samples] to such retail store or retail outlet for that relevant [season] without arranging the order through the [Agent].

O.186

The [Agent] agrees to use the order forms provided by the [Company] and acknowledges that it is not permitted to offer any discount or other reductions in the ex-factory price or vary any other terms and conditions without the prior written consent of the [Company].

O.187

The [Agent] agrees that all existing customers in the Territory notified by the [Company] shall not be contacted by the [Agent] for the purpose of obtaining orders for the [Products]. A copy of the list of existing customers is attached to and forms part of this Agreement.

O.188

The [Agent] agrees not to contact for the purpose of obtaining orders for the [Products] any persons or companies with whom the Company has business dealings at any time which it may notify to the [Agent] and which the [Company] wishes to exclude from the Agreement. It is acknowledged by the [Company] that this clause shall not apply to introductions made by the [Agent].

O.189

It is agreed that the [Agent] shall be entitled to deal with existing clients or excluded clients provided that the [Company] has provided prior written consent. In such event where an order is placed as a result of the [Agent] which is accepted by the [Company], then the [Agent] shall be entitled to [50%] [fifty per cent] of the [Agent's] Commission in respect of such Order, but not for any subsequent orders not dealt with by the [Agent].

O.190

The [Company] agrees to send to the [Agent] at its expense order forms to be used by the [Agent]. The Company agrees that it shall accept any order obtained by the [Agent] entirely at its own risk and that the [Agent] shall not be liable for the failure of any retail store or outlet to pay any sums that may be due to the [Company] as the result of the shipment of any such order.

O.191

The [Company] agrees to advise the [Agent] with the reason for rejecting any particular order requested by the [Agent].

O.192

The [Company] agrees to inform the [Agent] in writing as soon as possible of any changes in the prices or terms and conditions required by the [Company] for orders for the [Products].

O.193

The [Agent] agrees that the title in any [Products] ordered shall remain with the [Company] until full payment of the invoice has been received by the [Company].

O.194

The [Agent] shall offer the [Products] for sale only at the prices and upon the terms and conditions of delivery and sale set by the [Principal] from time to time. The [Principal] shall supply the [Agent] with order forms to be used by the [Agent]. The [Agent] shall immediately fax all orders received for the [Products] to the [Principal] for the [Principal's] acceptance or rejection. Any order not rejected within [–] days shall be deemed to have been accepted.

O.195

The [Agent] shall not deviate from the [Company's] price list and terms of business in respect of the [Products]. The Agent shall not be entitled to offer any discount, credit, delay in payment or any other inducements of any nature without the prior written consent of the [Company].

O.196

The [Agent] shall as far as possible keep the [Company] informed on a regular basis as regard any negotiations with any third party pursuant to this Agreement.

O.197

The [Agent] agrees to promote, market and obtain orders for the [Garments] based on the [Collection Samples] at the prices and on the terms and conditions specified at any time by the [Company]. The [Agent] acknowledges and agrees to inform any retail store or outlet that wishes to order the [Garments] that they must pay the total sum in [dollars] of the ex-factory price of any item plus freight and insurance to the requested destination. Further that the [Purchaser] shall be responsible for all customs clearance, storage duty, and taxes that may be incurred. Further that the title in the [Garments] shall remain with the [Company] until full payment of the invoice has been received by the [Company].

O.198

The [Ghostwriter] shall carry out his duties at such times, dates and locations as the [Company] may reasonably require and observe all reasonable instructions by the [Company].

O.199

It shall comply with all reasonable directions given to him/her in connection with the services to be performed hereunder.

O.200

The [Contractor] shall perform all services under this Contract as an independent Contractor. Except as specified in this contract the [Company] shall not exercise any control over the employees, agents, or sub-contractors of the [Contractor] in the performance of such [Work] or services.

O.201

The [Writer] shall provide his services conscientiously and to the best of his skill and ability in accordance with the directions from time to time given by the [Company]. The [Writer] agrees that he shall work in collaboration with such person(s) as the [Company] may reasonably specify to the [Writer]. The [Writer] agrees to attend such meetings and conferences at the [Company] or elsewhere as the [Company] may reasonably require for instructions and consultations in respect of the [Work].

O.202

The [Writer] agrees that during the continuance of the engagement under this Agreement that the [Writer] shall carry out his obligations to the best of his skill and ability. The [Writer] agrees to observe all directions and restrictions as may be reasonably given to him by or on behalf of the [Company] for the purpose of this engagement.

O.203

The [Company] shall be entitled to cancel and/or terminate the order for the [Services] at any time by notice in writing and shall only be liable to pay the sums due to the end date specified in any such notice.

University, Library and Educational

O.204

The [Distributor] agrees that it shall not without the prior written consent of the [Institute]:

1.1 Reproduce, manufacture, supply and distribute [Work/Products], packaging, and/or marketing which have not been approved by the [Institute].

1.2 Deviate from the price list and terms of business in respect of the [Work/Products] which has been approved by the [Institute].

1.3 Offer any discount, credit, delay in payment or any other inducements of any nature.

O.205

The [Company] shall ensure that all its employees, directors and contractors adhere to the [Work Plan] and the [Work Schedule] and any instructions and orders given by [Name] as the representative of the [Institute]. The [Company] agrees that at all times its personnel shall take account of the health and safety of the public and employees at the [Institute] and shall abide by all codes, practices, regulations and legislation that may be applicable.

O.206

1.1 Where the [Institute] makes an order for any service, product and/or other material it must be in accordance with its tender and procurement policy [specify] and authorised by [department] with a requisition number.

1.2 The [Institute] does not accept responsibility for any orders placed by anyone purporting to represent the [Institute] where 1.1 has not been followed for the order to be completed and paid for by the [Institute].

ORIGIN

General Business and Commercial

O.207

The [Company] confirms and undertakes that the [Product/Material] was [grown/produced/manufactured/reproduced] in [country].

O.208

The [Supplier] undertakes that all materials for any products or goods supplied to the [Company] will be traceable from its original source where it was grown and/or created. That the [Supplier] shall keep accurate and comprehensive records so that any defects and/or impurities can be traced by the [Company].

O.209

In the event that the [Supplier] finds that any person and/or company has misled the [Supplier] as regard the origin of the materials for any products or goods supplied to the [Company]. The [Supplier] shall immediately notify the [Company] and provide full details.

O.210

The [Supplier] agrees and undertakes to disclose the true origins and source of the ingredients of the [Products] which it provides to the [Company] under this Agreement prior to production in [country].

O.211

The [Company] is unable to verify all the origin of the sources of the material for the order and ingredients may have been blended, added, mixed and/or packaged in different countries.

ORIGINALITY

Employment

O.212

The [Employee] warrants that all contributions supplied by the [Employee] to the [Employer] shall to the best of his/her knowledge and belief be original, shall not contain anything which is an infringement of copyright or other like right or is defamatory and shall not contain any advertisement or anything of an advertising nature where the work or material is purported to be the sole creation and work of the [Employee]. Where any work or material is requested by the [Employer], based or derived from material supplied or referred to by the [Employer], then this clause shall not apply.

O.213

Any commercial or non-commercial exploitation of any material or work created by the [Employee] during the course of this employment shall be entirely at the risk and cost of the [Employer] and the [Employer] shall not be entitled to make any claim of any nature against the [Employee].

O.214

The [Executive] shall not authorise the reproduction for commercial exploitation or self-promotion of any work or material created during the course of this Agreement without the prior consent of [Name/Title].

O.215

The [Executive] provides no undertaking as to the originality, copyright or content of the material or work which is to be created by him/her or others under his/her authority during the existence of this Agreement. All material and work is used and exploited at the sole risk and cost of the [Company] and shall only bear the name and status of the [Executive] at any time if he/she approves the item in advance and provides his consent. No material or work shall be used by the [Company] at any time in a manner which demeans the reputation of the [Executive], is derogatory of the [Executive] or others. Nor shall the [Company] be entitled to attribute the material and work of the [Executive] to some other person and substitute their name as author and/or the creator of the work or material.

O.216

The [Employee] provides no undertaking as to the originality of their work, material and/or otherwise at any time during the course of their employment. The [Company] agrees and undertakes that it uses any such work and material entirely at its own cost and risk and waives any right and agrees it shall have no right to seek an indemnity, claim, costs, expenses or otherwise against the [Employee].

O.217

The [Company] agrees and acknowledges that where the [Employee] creates, develops, invents and/or designs a new and original work, service and/or product and/or process and/or method and/or means of exploitation in any media outside of work hours at the [Company]. That the [Company] shall have no claim and/or right to any part unless it has been derived and/or based on access by the [employee] to materials, confidential information, reports and data held and/or stored and/or owned and/or controlled by the [Company].

DVD, Video and Discs

O.218

The [Author] agrees and undertakes that the [Book] entitled [specify] ISBN [–] published by [Publisher] is the sole and original work of the [Author].

That the [DVD/other] Rights are held and controlled by the [Author] and that no option, licence, assignment, transfer and/or charge has been and/or is due to be made to the [Publisher] and/or a third party. That the [Author] hold the free and unencumbered [DVD/other] Rights in the [Book] in [country].

O.219

The [Company] agrees and undertakes that the [Film] entitled [specify] transmitted on [date] and distributed by [Distributor] is owned and controlled by the [Company]. That the [DVD/other] Rights are held and controlled by the [Company] and that no option, licence, assignment, transfer and/or charge has been and/or is due and that copyright ownership is held by [specify] and the original material was created by [specify]. That the [Company] hold the free and unencumbered [DVD/other] Rights in the [Film] throughout the [world/universe].

O.220

The [Licensor] confirms that the [Sound Recordings] are based on music by [specify] and lyrics by [specify] and were produced by [Name]. The [Licensor] confirms and undertakes that the [Sound Recordings] are an adaptation and not original. The [Licensor] controls all rights in the [Sound Recordings] and is entitled to grant the rights specified in clause [–] of this Agreement.

O.221

[Name] confirms and undertakes that he has designed, created and produced the artwork and computer generated version images of which are set out in Schedule [-] and that it is original and not based on the work in any form of a third party.

Film and Television

O.222

The [Assignor] confirms that the [Format] is an original idea created solely by the [Assignor] and has not been previously exploited in any form and is not in the public domain.

O.223

The [Producer] warrants that the [Script] is and will be original in the [Writer] and that the [Writer] was (during the period the Script was written) resident in [country] and paid taxes in [country] and will remain so until the [Writer] has completed rendering the [Writer's] services in connection with the [Series].

O.224

The [Author] agrees that the [Script] shall be the original work of the [Author] and shall not contain any other published material by the [Author] unless agreed in advance by the [Company].

O.225

The [Author] agrees and undertakes that the [Book] entitled [specify] ISBN [–] published by [Publisher] is the sole and original work of the [Author]. That the [Cable, Satellite, Digital, Terrestrial Television] Rights are held and controlled by the [Author] and that no option, licence, assignment, transfer and/or charge has been and/or is due to be made to the [Publisher] and/or a third party. That the [Author] hold the free and unencumbered [Cable, Satellite, Digital, Terrestrial Television] Rights in the [Book] in [country].

O.226

The [Company] agrees and undertakes that the [Film] entitled [specify] transmitted on [date] is owned and controlled by the [Company] under an [exclusive licence] from [Name] who is the copyright owner of the original material. That the [Cable, Satellite, Digital, Terrestrial Television] Rights, the [DVD/Video] Rights and [other rights] are held and controlled by the [Company] and that no option, licence, assignment, transfer and/or charge has been and/or is due in respect of the [Film] and/or part and/or any adaptation.

O.227

[Name] agrees and undertakes that the [Script/Work/Speech] is has supplied to the [Company] is his/her original work and that no part is based on real life characters and/or plagiarised from any book, sound recording, film and/or other material whether stored in an archive and/or out of copyright or not and/or copied from any other resource of any nature in any country of the world.

General Business and Commercial

O.228

The [Originator] warrants for the benefit of the [Company] that the [Concept] is original and confidential to the [Originator] and has not been disclosed to any other party.

O.229

The [Originator] warrants that he is the original creator and sole owner of or controls all copyright, design rights and any other rights in the product of his services to the [Company] under this Agreement, excluding any information or material supplied by or included at the request of the [Company].

O.230

The [Work] is original to the [Assignor] and nothing therein infringes or violates the copyright or any other rights of any third party.

O.231

The [Author] warrants that the [Work] is an original work or arrangement and that the [Author] is the owner of the copyright therein. The [Author] has not granted, transferred or assigned any rights assigned in this Agreement or any part thereof to any third party.

O.232

The [Assignor] warrants that he is ordinarily resident in the [United Kingdom] and that the [Software] is original to the [Assignor].

O.233

The design shall not be treated as original in respect of the design right in original designs if it is a commonplace in the design field in question at the time of its creation.

O.234

The [Company] can provide copies of the original agreements with the persons who created and developed the [Work] to the [Licensee] in the event that the [Licensee] is subject to any claim and/or action by a third party in respect of the originality of the [Work] and infringement of copyright in [country].

Internet and Websites

O.235

The [Designer] warrants that the entire product of its services shall be original and that the performance of the obligations by the [Designer] under this Agreement shall not contravene any rights of any third party and that where the [Material] to be included in the website is not the original work of the [Designer] that it shall be set out in detail in the report specifying the type of material, the name of the company, the nature of their rights and the expected cost of the use of their material and any credit or other conditions.

O.236

[Name] undertakes that all the product of his/her services under this Agreement shall be original and will not infringe the copyright or any other rights of any third party except where the work is based on or incorporates material of any third party which is included at the [Company's] request or with their knowledge or is in the public domain.

O.237

There is no provision as to the originality of material on this [Website] and you must use your own endeavours to ensure that you do not infringe the copyright, designs, graphics, trademarks, service marks, logo, moral rights, or any other rights of any person, company and/or business. There is no automatic right to copy, adapt and/or exploit material due to the fact it is displayed on this [Website].

O.238

All the product of the work of the [Designer] for the [Website] is based upon and/or derived from ideas and concepts provided by the [Client] and is not the original idea of the [Designer].

O.239

Where you are sending original material to the [Website] you are strongly advised to appreciate that the [Company] cannot be liable for any infringement of copyright and/or any other intellectual property rights that may arise from your use of the [Website] and/or the actions of third parties.

O.240

1.1   [Name] created, designed and developed the [App] based on the content and background material supplied by the [Company] and the software known as [specify].

1.2   [Name] commissioned artwork, graphics and computer generated moving images, sound recording and film from [specify].

1.3   [Name] has delivered the completed [App] in [format] to the [Company].

1.4   Both [Name] and [specify] agree to assign all copyright, computer software rights and/or any other intellectual property rights in each and every part of the material and data they have created in 1.1 and 1.2 to the [Company] in consideration of payment for the completion of their work.

1.5   [Name] and [specify] provide no undertakings as to originality to the [Company].

Merchandising

O.241

The [Company] confirms and undertakes that:

1.1   [Name] was the original creator of [Product and Character] and by an assignment dated [date] assigned all rights in all media throughout the world to the [Company] which now owns and controls all intellectual property rights, design rights, trade mark, logo, image in the [Product and Character], the domain name [specify] and all the packaging, material and property associated with and/or based upon it.

1.2   That no option, licence, assignment, transfer and/or charge has been and/or is due to be made and that the [Company] holds the free and unencumbered all rights in all media in the [Product and Character], the domain name [specify] and all the packaging, material and property associated with and/or based upon it throughout the [world/universe].

O.242

The [Originator] warrants to the [Company] that the [Concept] is original and confidential to the [Originator] only and has not been disclosed to any other third party except to the [Company] and its advisers. Further, that the [Concept] has not been previously licensed, assigned, or exploited in any form in any part of the world and is not in the public domain and that the [Concept] was created by [Name] and that all rights therein rest in the [Originator].

O.243

The [Assignor] undertakes and agrees that it is the original creator and sole owner of all copyright and any other rights in the [Work] which are [assigned/ granted] under this Agreement.

O.244

The [Licensor] confirms that he/she is the original creator and sole owner of or controls all copyright, design rights and any other rights in the [Board Game] and the [Prototype] which are granted to the [Company] under this Agreement.

O.245

The [Sub-Licensee] shall not be entitled to any claim, damages, losses, costs and/or expenses against the [Licensor] and/or the [Licensee] in the event that it is found that the material for the [Work/Product] is not original at any time.

O.246

[Name] owns and controls all rights in the material of the [Work] but is not the author. No assurances and/or undertakings can be provided as to the origin and/or originality of the [Work].

O.247

The [Manufacturer] agrees and undertakes not to include and/or reproduce any material in the [Products], packaging and other marketing for the

[Distributor] which it knows is not original and/or belongs to third party and has not been licensed for reproduction and authorised by the [Distributor].

Publishing

O.248

The [Author] warrants that the [Work] is the [Author's] own original material created by his/her own skill and effort except for material in the public domain and such excerpts from the other bodies that may be included with the written permission of the copyright owners as stated in the manuscript.

O.249

The [Writer] warrants that he has not granted and will not purport to grant or assign any rights in the [Work] inconsistent with or likely to impair the exercise by the Company of its rights hereunder. The [Writer] further warrants that the [Work] (except to the extent that it incorporates material supplied by the [Company] or any third party at the [Company's] request or direction) shall be the original [Work] of the [Writer].

O.250

The [Author] warrants that the [Work] shall be the original work of the [Author] and does not and will not infringe the copyright or any other rights of any third party in respect of the rights granted under this Agreement.

O.251

The [Author] warrants that the [Work] has not been previously published or otherwise exploited in any form in the Territory.

O.252

The [Author] warrants to the [Publisher] that he has full power to enter into this Agreement and that the [Work] is an original work that has not been published in volume or other form within the territories in which the [Publisher] has been granted exclusive rights under the terms of this Agreement.

O.253

The [Assignor] agrees and undertakes that the [Work] is his own unpublished original [Work].

O.254

The Author confirms that the [Work] is the [Author's] own work except for such material as in the public domain and such extracts from other material for which the written consent of the copyright owner has been provided to the [Author] for inclusion in the [Work].

O.255

The [Works] shall be original to the [Writer] except where it incorporates any material supplied or requested by the [Company].

O.256

The [Author] confirms that the Synopsis and the [Work] are and shall be the original work of the [Author] and do not and will not infringe the copyright or any other rights of any third party in respect of the rights granted under this Agreement.

O.257

The [Author] confirms that to the best of his knowledge and belief that all statements purporting to be facts are true and that any instructions, recipes, games, questions, advice or recommendations have been tested and assessed as safe by the [Author] and that they are accurate and not likely to cause any loss, damage or injury.

O.258

The [Author] confirms that the [Synopsis] and the [Work] shall be the original work of the [Author] and does not and will not infringe the copyright, design right, moral rights, trade or service mark, logo or other intellectual property rights of any third party in respect of the rights granted by the [Author] under this Agreement.

O.259

The [Author] confirms that the [Work] is the original creation of the skill and effort of the [Author] and does not infringe the copyright or any other right of any third party in the following countries [specify]. Except the following material which is owned or controlled by a third party which has been included in the [Work] and for which the following consent has been obtained [specify material/consent/cost]. A copy of the relevant document is attached as Appendix [1] and forms part of this Agreement.

O.260

Where the [Publisher] arranges for a cover and/or other design to be created and/or developed by an employee and/or consultant for the [Work]. The [Publisher] agrees that any material submitted for approval by the [author] shall be original and new and that the copyright shall be assigned to the [Publisher/Author].

Services

O.261

The [Contributor] confirms that he/she is and will be the sole owner and originator of the product of his/her services performed under this Agreement unless based on or incorporating material specifically included at the request of the [Company].

O.262
[Name] shall provide his services to [Company] at [address] from [date] to [date] in accordance with the following description [specify]. There is no undertaking or confirmation that the duties provided or any work created are original, new or otherwise.

O.263
The [Actor] agrees that the product of his/her services shall be original and will not infringe the copyright or any other rights of any third party throughout the Territory except where any material or information is used which is supplied by the [Agent] or any third party.

O.264
The [Sportsperson] confirms that all the product of his/her services shall be original except where work is based on or incorporates material of any third party which is supplied by a third party under an agreement concluded by the [Manager] or is included at the request of the [Manager].

O.265
[Name] provides no undertaking as to the originality of the work under this Agreement and the [Company] shall use any material at its own cost, risk and expense and shall not be entitled to seek to be indemnified by [Name]. In the event that for any reason [Name] is held liable there shall be a limit of [figure/currency] in total under this Agreement.

O.266
The [Consultant] undertakes that:

1.1 All information, advice and material provided to the [Company] by the [Consultant] shall to the best of his knowledge and belief be true and accurate, and original. Where material is not original the source will be clearly identified and credited in any report.

1.2 Where requested by the [Company] and/or its legal advisors the [Consultant] will assist in providing supporting documentation to support the matters upon which the [Consultant] has advised.

O.267
[Name] undertakes that all the product of his/her services under this Agreement shall be original and will not infringe the intellectual property rights, domain name, trade mark, service mark, logo, computer software, database rights, confidential information, patent, or any other rights of any

third party except where the work is based on or incorporates material of any third party which is included at the [Company's] request or with their knowledge or is in the public domain.

O.268

The [Company] acknowledges that the [Distributor] is not the original creator of the [Service/Work].

O.269

1.1 [Name] confirms that he/she inherited the estate of [specify] under a will for which probate was granted on [date] in [country]. That [Deceased] was the original creator of the [Work/Service] and that it is now owned and/or controlled by [Name].

1.2 That the [Work/Service] has been adapted and developed and translated and that there the main contributors to new original material for the [Work/Service] are [specify].

1.3 That no undertakings are provided to the [Company] by [Name] in respect of originality and/or risk of any civil and/or criminal proceedings in 1.1 and 1.2 above.

Sponsorship

O.270

The [Sponsor] agrees and undertakes to the [Company] all trade marks, logos, slogans, artwork, products, services and other material provided by the [Sponsor] under this Agreement shall be owned and/or controlled by the [Sponsor]. That if required by the [Company] the [Sponsor] shall be able to prove the originality and authorship of any part of such material at the [Sponsors'] cost and expense.

O.271

The [Sponsor] agrees and undertakes to the [Company] that as at [date] there are no pending legal proceedings and/or disputes in respect of the originality and/or content and/or packaging of the material specified in Schedule [–] which is to be supplied by the [Sponsor] to the [Company] under this Agreement.

O.272

The [Company] shall ensure that they own and/or control and/or are licensed to use any material which is to be printed in the [Brochure] and/or displayed on the [Website] and/or are reproduced in respect of any merchandising. No claim shall be made as to copyright ownership by the [Company] of material which originated from any third party unless there is a written agreement to support that assertion.

O.273
The [Sponsor] undertakes that the [Logo] is the original work of [Name] and that all rights in all media in all countries have been assigned to the [Sponsor].

O.274
The [Sponsor] confirms that all products, services, names, logos, images, film, advertisements, banners and other material to be distributed and/ or displayed at the [Event] by the [Sponsor] and/or any agent acting on its behalf shall either be original material owned by the [Sponsor] and/or supplied by a third party under an existing licence agreement. In any event all such material must be approved in advance by the [Company] and the [Sponsor] must submit exact samples for inspection at the [Sponsors'] cost.

University, Library and Educational

O.275
The [Contributor/Author] agrees and undertakes that:

1.1 The [Contributor/Author] is a national of [country] and resides in [country].

1.2 The [Contributor/Author] is the original author and developed, devised, wrote and designed the [Work] and owns all the rights and interest.

1.3 The [Contributor/Author] agrees and undertakes that the [Work] has not and will not infringe the copyright, design rights, future design rights, computer software rights, trade marks, database rights, confidential information, patents and/or any other intellectual property rights of [any third party/the company] at any time in [any country/throughout the world].

O.276
The [Consultant] confirms that all the product of her services shall be original except where work is based on or incorporates material of any third party and/or is supplied by the [Institute] and/or is in the public domain. Where material is not original the [Consultant] agrees that the source will be clearly identified and acknowledged in any report.

O.277
The [Author] agrees and undertakes that the [Work/Film] are and shall be the original work of the [Author] and do not and will not infringe the copyright

or any other rights of any third party in respect of the rights granted under this Agreement to the [Institute].

OUTER SPACE

General Business and Commercial

O.278
The [Licensee] confirms that all necessary licences, consent and authority has or will be obtained from any national, government, military, space, peacekeeping, international or European body that may be necessary or required to provide the license in respect of [Outer Space] and that the [Licensee] shall not be threatened or subject to any criminal or civil proceedings at any time in respect of the authority provided under this Agreement.

O.279
'The Territory' shall mean the world and Outer Space.

O.280
'The Territory' shall include all geostationary orbits, howsoever positioned in relation to the earth.

O.281
'The Territory' shall include all land, man-made islands, sea, sky, beneath the land and below the sea, and throughout the universe, outer space and the galaxy without limit of time and/or space.

O.282

1.1 This Agreement shall not apply to any to any planet other than Earth and all other planets, moons and outer space which form part of the universe shall be excluded.

1.2 The planet Earth shall include the sea, land, sub-terrain and air and up to a distance of [number] metres above the Earth and shall also include oil rigs, satellites, aeroplanes, helicopters but not rockets and/ or space stations for transportation and/or orbit.

PARTIES TO AGREEMENT

General Business and Commercial

P.001

AN AGREEMENT made the [–] day of [–] 20 [–]

BETWEEN:

[full registered Name] whose registered office is situated at [address] in [country] (hereinafter called the 'Company') which expression shall include all assigns, assignees, licensees and successors in title of the Company; and

[full registered Name] whose address is situated at [address] in [country] (hereinafter called the 'Employee').

P.002

THIS AGREEMENT is made on this [–] day of [–] 20 [–]

BETWEEN:

[Name] a Company incorporated in [country] under number [specify] having its registered office at [address] hereinafter referred to as the [–] and

[Name] a Company incorporated in [country] under number [specify] having its registered office at [address] hereinafter referred to as the [–].

P.003

THIS AGREEMENT is made the [–] day of [–] 20 [–]

BETWEEN:

1.1 [Name] registered in [country] [no] whose principal place of business is at [address] (hereinafter called 'The Company'); and

1.2 The Contributors whose names and addresses are set out in the first column of Schedule [–] hereto (hereinafter called 'The [Contributors]').

P.004
AGREEMENT DATED [–]

PARTIES:

[–] (The Company) [address]

[–] (The Licensee) [address]

DEFINITIONS: In this Agreement the following expressions shall, unless the contract otherwise requires, have the following meaning [specify].

P.005
TITLE OF AGREEMENT [–]

AN AGREEMENT made this [–] day of [–] 20 [–]

BETWEEN:

1   [–] of [–] (To be known as the Licensor in this Agreement); and

2   [–] of [–] (To be known as the Licensee in this Agreement).

P.006
AN AGREEMENT dated [–] BETWEEN:

1   [Name] of [Address] (To be known as the Licensor in this Agreement); and

2.   [Name] [Address] (To be known as the Distributor in this Agreement).

IT IS AGREED as follows [specify].

P.007
The expression 'Organiser' shall be [Name].

'The Exhibitor' shall mean the company, partnership or business in whose name the application form has been signed.

P.008
AN AGREEMENT made [date]

PARTIES:

1   [Company] of [address] ('the Company'); and

2   [Writer] care of [Agent's Name] of [address] ('the Writer' which expression includes his successors in title and assignees).

P.009
AN AGREEMENT dated [–].

1214

BETWEEN:

1   Web Designer [Company Name] ('the Designer') of [address of business or registered office] and

2   Commissioning Company [Name] ('the Company') of [address of business or registered office].

WHEREAS [Preamble]

P.010

AN AGREEMENT dated [–].

BETWEEN:

1   [Name] registered in [country/address] whose principal place of business is at [address] (to be known as the Supplier); and

2.   [Name] registered in [country/address] whose principal place of business is at [address] (to be known as the Seller).

P.011

TITLE OF AGREEMENT [–]

BETWEEN:

1   [–] ('the Company') of [registered and business address]; and

2   [–] ('the Contributor') of [address].

P.012

MEMORANDUM OF AGREEMENT made this [–] day of [–] 20 [–] BETWEEN:

[Name of Authors] [addresses] (hereinafter called 'The Authors') of the one part [and shall include the [Authors] executors, personal representatives, administrators and assignees].

and

[Name of Company] [address] (hereinafter called 'The Publishers' of the other part) for themselves, and their respective executors, administrators and assigns or successors in business as the case may be.

P.013

PUBLISHING AGREEMENT made this [–] day of [–] [year]

[Name of the Author] of [address] (who shall be referred to as the Author throughout this Agreement) which shall be defined to include the Authors' executors, personal representatives, administrators and assignees of the one part

AND

[Name of the Company] registered number [reference] in [county/country] under the [specify] whose registered office is [address] (which shall be referred to as the Publishers throughout this Agreement) which shall be defined to include the following agreed assignees who form part of the [Name Group] [registered number] of [address]: the parent company [name], the subsidiary company [name], the affiliate company [name].

P.014
Agreement dated [date].

[Full Name] who writes under the pseudonym of [specify] of [address] (who shall be referred to as the Author) which shall be defined to include the Author's executors, personal representatives, and administrators of the one part, but excluding all other assignees.

AND

[Registered Name] [registered reference] registered in [county/country] whose registered office is at [address] which trades under the name [specify Trading Name] (which shall be referred to as the Publishers throughout this Agreement) excluding all other assignees, successors in business, parent, subsidiary, associate, affiliate or joint venture partners.

P.015
The [Publishers] shall not have the right to assign, transfer and/or licence and/or delegate the whole of the Agreement [and/or parts], the rights and/or obligations under this Agreement to any other company, body and person within the [Group], consortium, joint venture partner or any other third party of any nature except the named companies above who are the agreed assignees of the [Publishers].

P.016
THIS AGREEMENT is dated [date] and between [Name of Group] a corporation of [region/county/area] and its successors (the 'Company') and [Name] a person who resides at [address/state/country] (the 'Employee').

P.017
Name of parties:

[Name] (the Employee)

The [Officer] of the State for [Government Department/Agency] referred to as (the 'Department/Agency') as the authorised signatory and representative of the Government of [specify] in [country].

P.018

[Agreement/Contract] Reference [–]

The [Name] (the 'Name') represented by the [specify representative person/company] which has authorised the [specify the office/title of person] [specify name of person] to sign this [Agreement/Contract] of the one part

And

[Name of Consortium] (the 'Consortium') which has been set up in [address/ state/country] represented by [Name of advisors] who act as [purpose] advisors on behalf of the Consortium and are authorised to sign this Agreement on their behalf.

P.019

[Subject] Agreement dated [–].

Between the following parties:

1.   [Full Name of Institute] whose main address is [address]

      and

2.   [Full Name of Contributor] who resides at [address].

P.020

THIS AGREEMENT is made [date]

BETWEEN:

      [Seller] a UK private limited company registered with [Companies House/other]. Company Registration No. [–] having its registered office at [address] and its place of business at [address] (hereinafter called 'The Seller').

AND

      [Purchaser] of [address] (hereinafter called 'The Purchaser').

P.021

AN AGREEMENT made the [–] day of 20 [–]

BETWEEN:

(1)   [Name] of [address] (hereinafter referred to as 'Member A')

(2)   [Name] of [address] (hereinafter referred to as 'Member B')

(3)   [Name] of [address] (hereinafter referred to as 'Member C').

P.022

AN AGREEMENT made the [–] day of 20 [–]

BETWEEN:

[–] a private limited company registered under the Laws of [England/other], Company Registration No. [–] having its registered office at [address] (hereinafter referred to as "the Licensor'), on behalf of themselves, their successors in business and title on the one part,

AND

[–] of [address] ('the Licensee').

P.023

AGREEMENT dated [date]

THE CONTRACTING PARTIES TO THIS AGREEMENT ARE AS FOLLOWS:

1   [Name] of [address] (referred to as 'the Actor')

AND

2.   [Company] registered office at [address] and main place of business [address] (referred to as 'the Agent').

P.024

AN AGREEMENT made the [–] day of 20 [–]

BETWEEN:

[Name] of [address] (to be known as 'the Author')

AND

[Company] of [address] a company registered under the Laws of [specify] (to be known as 'the Publisher') in this Agreement such expressions to include the Publishers' successors in business and title).

P.025

PUBLISHING AGREEMENT made this [–] day of [month] [year]

BETWEEN:

[Name] and [Name] both of [address] (hereinafter jointly and severally called 'the Authors' which shall include the Author's executors, personal representatives, administrators and assigns) of the one part

AND

[Company] incorporated in [specify] Registration No. [specify] whose registered office is at [address] (hereinafter called 'the Publishers' which expression shall include the Publishers' permitted assignees as defined below at clause [–]) on the other part on behalf of the parent company [Parent Company] incorporated in [specify] Registration No. [–] whose registered office is at [address].

P.026
Agreement date [specify].

This Agreement is between the following parties and no other and does not apply to any estate, beneficiary, assignee, administrators and/or other third parties:

[Personal Name] currently living at [address] in [country] and also known as [professional name] and

[The Agent] which operates under the trading name [specify] and is registered as a company in [country] under the name [specify] of [address].

P.027
Terms of proposed Agreement subject to contract dated [–]

Party 1. [The Charity] otherwise known as [specify] which is registered with the [specify organisation] as reference [specify] whose head office is based at [address].

Party 2. [The Sponsor] which trades under the [Brand Name] and is registered as an [incorporated company] in [specify name] in [country] registration reference [specify].

Party 3. [The Artist] who is not a signatory to this Agreement and is represented by the [Agent] whose address is [specify] in [country] and operates under licence from [specify] and is registered as a business with [specify] as [specify] reference [specify].

P.028
These terms and conditions which are proposed are for discussion only and may be changed by [Name] at any time. It is not intended that there should be any binding pre-contract and/or verbal terms and conditions and all matters are subject to a final written agreement. If no agreement is concluded then [Name] has made no commitment and you should not rely on pre-contract discussions to incur costs and expenses and/or to make any commitment to a third party.

PARTNERSHIP

General Business and Commercial

P.029

The [Partners] each agree and undertake that they shall:

1.1 Use their best endeavours towards the successful operating of the Partnership and at all times shall conduct themselves in a fair and proper manner.

1.2 That in all transactions and/or business dealings of any nature effecting the Partnership, all [Partners] shall disclose to the other [Partners] any matter which may prejudice or conflict with the rights, interests or business of the Partnership.

P.030

'The Partnership' shall mean the partnership created by this Deed dated [–].

P.031

No other partners may be added to this Partnership without the express prior written approval of all the current Partners listed under Schedule [–].

P.032

This Agreement shall not constitute or to be deemed to imply a partnership between the parties and neither party shall be or be deemed to be an agent of the other for any purpose whatsoever and neither party shall have any authority or power to bind the other in any way.

P.033

Nothing herein contained shall be deemed to constitute a partnership between the parties.

P.034

This Agreement has not and will not create any relationship or connection or association between the parties which is or might be deemed to be a partnership, joint venture, agency, fiduciary or employment relationship between the parties. No such relationship between the parties was intended by this Agreement either between themselves and/or in respect of the [Film/Recordings/Work/Services].

P.035

Nothing in this Agreement shall be deemed to create any joint venture, partnership or principal/agent relationship between any of the parties hereto and none of them shall hold itself out in its advertising material or activities or otherwise in any manner which would indicate or imply any such relationship with the other.

P.036
This Agreement shall not be deemed to constitute a partnership or joint venture or contract of employment between the parties.

P.037
This Agreement shall not be deemed to create any partnership or employment relationship between the parties.

P.038
No Partner shall have any personal financial interest in the [Film/Services/other] apart from those sums declared on [date] unless the prior written approval of all partners is obtained in advance.

P.039
This Agreement shall not be deemed to create any partnership, joint venture, agency, fiduciary or employment relationship between the parties. Neither party shall hold itself out as the agent or partner of the other.

P.040
This Agreement shall not be deemed to create any partnership or employment relationship between the parties. Nor shall it create any relationship which allows a third party to enforce the terms of this agreement without the consent of both parties.

P.041
This Agreement is only intended to be [purpose] and does not constitute a partnership, employment, agency or other relationship of any kind except those specified. This Agreement is not intended to affect any acquisition or transfer of rights except those explicitly specified. No third party may join, rely on, endorse and/or assume any rights and/or obligations under this Agreement without the prior written consent of both parties.

P.042
This Agreement shall not constitute or imply a partnership, employment or other relationship between the parties. Neither party shall be deemed to be an agent of the other for any purpose whatsoever. Neither party shall have any authority or power to bind the other in anyway.

P.043
This Agreement shall not be deemed to create any partnership, employment or agency relationship between the parties. Nor shall it entitle either party to

commit or enter into any agreement with any third party on their behalf nor to inform a third party that they may rely on the Agreement.

P.044
Neither party to this Agreement has any authority to act on behalf of the other, or comment, commit nor pledge any matter on behalf of the other [unless set out in the Business Plan and agreed in advance].

P.045
This Agreement is a [type] agreement between the particular named parties. There is no intention by either party to create any terms, conditions and/or relationship between the parties other than that set out in this Agreement. There is no agency, partnership, employment, joint venture, and/or other legal and/or trust and/or contractual relationship except [specify].

P.046
No party shall be entitled to hold themselves out as representing the other to any third party, any company within their Group, any government agency and/or body and/or to commit, pledge, consent, undertake and/or enter into any contract, licence, or other agreement on their behalf as they are not entitled and/or authorised to do so at any time.

P.047
The [Institute], the [Company] and all the parties in engaged in this [Project] shall remain at all times, separate legal entities. There is no intention to create any partnership, employment, agency, joint venture and/or other relationship. No party shall be entitled to authorise, commit and/or sign any documents and/or incur any costs, fees and/or pledge to pay any sums on behalf of any other party.

P.048
Both parties agree and undertake that it shall require the consent and agreement of both parties in order to sub-licence, novate, sell, transfer, assign, licence, endorse, sponsor and/or otherwise exploit any of the rights and interests owned and controlled by both parties under this Agreement.

P.049
Where the [Company] engages third party consultants to work and collaborate on the [Project] at any time. It is not intended that any such collaboration shall be construed as forming any partnership with the [Company]. The [Company] is commissioning work from such third party consultants and shall make payment in return for the assignment and transfer and waiver of all the copyright, intellectual property rights, computer software and data

rights and moral rights and any other rights and/or interest in the product of any of the third party consultants work including all drafts, samples and finished versions which may be created and/or developed in any medium and/or format at any time. It is not intended that any consultant should retain any rights and/or interest.

P.050

In the event that no formal [deed/document] of partnership is drawn up between [Name] and the [Creator]. Then it is agreed that the parties shall not be entitled to exploit and rights and/or interest held by the other party without prior written consent and agreement in the form of a licence.

P.051

1.1   In the event that one of the partners wishes to retire, leave and/or sale his share of the [Company/Partnership]. Then it is agreed that an independent valuation shall be sought from a third party to assess and validate the total value in [currency] of the whole [Company/Partnership] including land and other assets which shall be paid for by the [Company/Partnership].

1.2   The partner may sell his share to existing partners and/or any third party provided that the third party is acceptable to the existing partners.

PATENT

General Business and Commercial

P.052

The term 'Patent' shall mean all patents granted or applied for [under the Patents Acts 1977 and/or Patents Act 2004 and/or the Copyright, Designs and Patents Act 1988 and any amendments or revisions].

P.053

All rights and the right to apply for statutory protection including, but not limited to, patent protection for any improvement to the [Product] made by the [Company] or [–] shall vest and be retained solely in the [Company].

P.054

The [Manager] agrees that he/she shall promptly communicate to the [Company] all inventions, modifications, improvements, processes, formulae, materials, know-how, designs, models, photocopies, sketches, drawings, plans or other original matter (whether or not they are capable of protection) which he/she may create or discover during the performance of his/her employment with the [Company].

P.055

The [Manager] shall while employed by the [Company] or thereafter at the direction and expense of the [Company] apply for and do all acts and things necessary to obtain industrial property protection in respect of such industrial property [which by virtue of this clause and/or the Patents Acts 1977 and 2004 as amended] belong to the [Company] in any part of the world as the [Company] may require. The [Manager] shall vest any and all industrial property in the [Company] or as the [Company] may direct and grant to the [Company] the right to use the [Manager's] name to obtain such industrial property protection. The [Manager] will not do anything to imperil the validity of any industrial property protection and at the request and expense of the [Company] will provide assistance to obtain and maintain such protection.

P.056

The [Company] agrees and undertakes that where the [Executive] during the course of his employment creates, develops, and/or discovers on his own at the [Company's] expense and/or with others as part of a team inventions, modifications, improvements, processes, formulae, materials, know-how, designs, trade marks, logos or other original matter (whether or not they are capable of protection) which the [Company] intends to register, use, exploit, licence, sell or market and/or use in any research project and/or development joint venture. That all rights shall be shared [jointly/percentage share] and registered in both names in any part of the world whether for industrial property protection or otherwise. The parties shall share any sums received from the rights in equal proportions. The [Company] agrees and undertakes to bear all the costs and expense of registration and protection which it shall not be entitled to recoup from any sums due to the [Executive]. Further the [Company] waives any right to dispute this clause and any claim under the provision relating to the [Patents Acts 1977 and 2004 as amended] and any other legislation, directive, and regulation that the employer is the owner of material created during the course of employment.

P.057

The [Company] agrees and undertakes to assign to the [Institute] all rights and interest of any nature in any medium and any format that may be created, developed, discovered and/or originated by the [Company] and/or any employee and/or consultant engaged by the [Company] during the course of the [Work/Project] [and at any time thereafter] which arise directly [and/or indirectly] as a result of the [Work/Project]. The rights and interest owned and/or controlled by the [Company] shall include but not be limited to all patents, inventions, modifications, improvements, processes, formulae, materials, know-how, design rights, and future design rights, all copyright in any text, images, photographs, film, DVDs, sound recordings, music, and all rights in any database, index and taxonomy rights and the right to register any trade marks, service marks, logos, computer software, source codes, passwords, formats, domain names and any other original material whether or not defined and/or capable of protection under existing legislation, regulations, directives and/or codes of practice.

P.058
The [Company] and the [Institute] agree that they shall both ensure that all third parties who are licensed and/or involved in the adaptation and exploitation of the [Work/Project] shall not acquire any rights and/or interest in the [Work/Project] whether in existence now and/or created in the future including any patent, copyright, trade mark, service mark, computer software, design rights, future design rights, and all any other intellectual property rights and/or other interest at any time.

P.059
The [Supplier] agrees and accepts that if it assists with the design, development and creation of a new generation of products based on work, instructions, guidance and/or ideas provided by the [Company]. That the [Supplier] agrees that in the event that any new computer software and/or other patents and/or intellectual property rights are designed, developed and/or owned and/or controlled by the [Supplier] as a result that the [Supplier] shall transfer all such rights to the [Company] and shall not be entitled to register any interest and/or receive any sums from the exploitation in any form.

PAYMENT

Building

P.060
In the event of the Total Price being exceeded by up to [–]% [–] per cent then the [Company] agrees to pay such additional costs provided that the [Contractor] informs the [Company] in advance and provides upon request a statement of costs incurred to date and details of the additional costs.

P.061

In the event of the [Agreed Cost] being exceeded by more than [number per cent] the [Company] agrees to pay such additional costs provided it has given prior written approval of the expenditure to the [Contractor].

P.062

1.1 The [Contractor] agrees that its total financial entitlement under this contract (excluding any entitlement to any sums and/or remedies which may arise and are recoverable at law) shall be the sum of [figure/currency] (the Guaranteed Price) plus value added tax.

1.2 In the event that the [Contractor] is issued with further instructions requiring Project Changes or Works Contract Variations under Clause [–] resulting in additional costs to the [Contractor]. The [Contractor] shall be entitled to decline to carry out the work unless it is agreed between the parties to increase the [Contractor's] total financial entitlement hereunder above the Guaranteed Price plus value added tax and the increase is confirmed in writing by all parties.

P.063

All payments shall be made in the following currency [–] to the address on the invoice. The rates stated in the Contract Order shall not be subject to any increase unless the [Company] has received notice of such increase not less than [30 days] prior to the effective date of the increased rate. The rates or payment shall not however be increased in respect of any specific part of the work which the [Contractor] has already accepted, unless otherwise specifically agreed.

P.064

No overtime shall be payable unless specifically approved by the [Company].

P.065

The [Contractor] shall invoice the [Company] each month in a form acceptable to the [Company]. All time sheets shall be subject to the approval of the [Company] and each invoice shall refer to the relevant Contract Order together with details to support the charges and original receipts. The [Company] shall pay the invoice within [specify period] of receipt of the invoices. In the event that the [Company] disputes any item on an invoice it shall notify the [Contractor] and payment may be withheld until the matter is resolved. Delayed payment of disputed items shall accrue interest at [number per cent] from the due date. Costs which are not invoiced by [date] will not be reimbursed. All bank charges, transfer costs and currency exchanges shall be at the [Company's] expense in respect of payment unless the [Contractor] requests payment into an account not specified in this Agreement. Additional bank charges shall be at the [Contractor's] cost.

Employment

P.066

Subject to the provisions herein contained and to the due compliance by the [Employee] with its obligations hereunder. The [Company] shall as inclusive remuneration and as full consideration for all services rendered and for all rights granted to the [Company] hereunder pay to the [Employee] the remuneration specified and subject to the receipt of satisfactory references the remuneration set out in Clause [–].

P.067

The [Employer] agrees and undertakes that all remuneration payable hereunder shall be paid to the [Employee's] bank account specified in the Special Conditions each [25th] day of each calendar month. Where such date falls on a weekend or Bank Holiday the payment shall be made on the following weekday.

P.068

The [Employee's] rate of pay will be [figure/currency] payable every two weeks in arrears. This equates to an annual salary of [figure/currency] and includes [specify financial benefits] and [specify type] allowance. The [Employee] will receive increments in accordance with the union agreement [specify]. Payment to the [Employee] by the [Company] will be made by credit transfer direct to his/her bank account. The [Employee's] salary will be received on [date].

P.069

The [Company] agrees to pay the [Employee's] remuneration by credit transfer to the [Employee's] personal bank or building society account on the last Thursday of each month. In the event that a Bank Holiday falls on a Thursday the [Company] shall be entitled to make payment to the [Employee] on the next working day unless some other arrangement is made between the parties.

P.070

The [Employee] shall during the continuance of this Agreement receive a fee at the rate of [figure/currency] per annum during the first [eight] calendar months, and a fee of [figure/currency] during the balance of the term. The fees shall be paid in calendar monthly instalments in arrears on the last day of each month. The first payment shall be made on [date].

P.071

The fee of [figure/currency] shall be paid by the [Company] by equal four-weekly payments of [specify] in arrears throughout the period of this Agreement. Each instalment shall be paid upon presentation of invoice at least one week in advance of the notified pay dates.

P.072

The [Employee's] rate of pay will be [–] payable every four weeks in arrears. This is an annual salary of [–] including [–]. The [Employee's] salary shall be reviewed each year on [date]. All payments shall be made to the [Employee] by credit transfer.

P.073

The [Employee] shall receive increments in accordance with the main agreement between [specify parties, agreement and date] [a copy of which is attached and forms part of this Agreement].

P.074

The [Company] agrees that the [Employee's] pay shall be reviewed on [date] each year. There is no obligation on the part of the [Company] to increase payments but in any event it shall not exceed [number per cent].

P.075

'Executive's Basic Remuneration' shall mean the annual sum of [figure/currency] which shall be the gross sum payable by the [Company] to the [Executive] in accordance with the terms of this Agreement.

P.076

1.1   The [Company] agrees to pay the Executive's Remuneration by credit transfer to the [Executive's] personal bank account on the [last Thursday] of each month. In the event that there is a Bank Holiday then the payment shall be made on the [earlier/next] working day unless some other arrangement is made between the parties.

1.2   The [Company] agrees to make all payments required under this Agreement to the [Executive] personally by [specify method] and shall not be authorised to alter or change this arrangement without written instructions from him/her.

P.077

'Additional Remuneration' shall mean such financial or benefit in kind to which the [Executive] may be entitled including any annual bonus of [specify] in the event the [Company] achieves specified turnover, profit and/ or cashflow targets as set out in the Executive's Bonus Scheme attached as

Appendix [–]. Such additional remuneration shall also include the benefit of any Executive Share Scheme details of which are attached in Appendix [–].

P.078

The basic salary shall be paid to the [Employee] by the [Company] from [date] at regular intervals per [week/month] [in arrears/in advance] and shall be paid by [direct debit/cheque/other].

P.079

1.1   The [Company] shall pay [Name] at the rate of [currency/number] per hour for every full half hour of completed work as [specify] at the [Company] from [date].

1.2   Payment shall be at the end of each calendar month by direct debit to your nominated account subject to supply of the following documents [specify].

1.3   If you are late no payment shall be made for that time.

1.4   If you do not attend then no payment shall be made.

1.5   No payment shall be made for ill health whether or not a medical certificate is available.

1.6   If you do not pass the first probationary day of work then you shall be paid for that day only.

1.7   If you do not wear the required uniform and hair protection then you may be refused work even if you attend.

DVD, Video and Discs

P.080

The [Company] shall be entitled to charge for any material ordered at the price published by the [Company] in its price list current at the date of despatch. This shall apply whether or not there shall have been an increase after the date when the order in respect of the material was received and whether or not the price(s) charged correspond(s) to any price list or quotation relied upon when such order was placed.

P.081

Payment for [DVDs/Videos/Discs] sold by the [Distributor] hereunder shall be due [30 days] after the date of invoice.

P.082

'The Wholesale Selling Price' shall be the selling price of a single [Video/DVD/Disc] charged by the [Assignee] to any third party including dealers and distributors whether for sale, rental or otherwise to the public including any premiums and surcharges or other additional charges imposed by the [Assignee] in respect of the [Videos/DVDs/Discs] supplied excluding any discounts or deductions given by the [Assignee] and excluding any value added tax and any sales tax from time to time in force.

P.083

In consideration of the rights and obligations imposed upon the [Assignor] and the [Assignee] under the terms of this Agreement the [Assignee] shall pay to the [Assignor] the Assignment Fee as follows:

1.1 [figure/currency] upon full signature of this Agreement by both parties.

1.2 [figure/currency] upon delivery and acceptance of the [Master Material of the [Film] by the [Assignee].

1.3 [figure/currency] upon delivery and acceptance of all the promotional, advertising and marketing material by the [Assignee].

1.4 [figure/currency] upon first public release of the [DVDs/Discs] of the [Film] by [date] in [country] but in any event no later than [date].

P.084

The [Company] agrees to pay [Individual] the total fee of [figure/currency] which shall be paid in two stages, half on signature of this Agreement and half on completion of all the work required in clause [–] in this Agreement.

P.085

'The Total Cost' shall mean the sum of [figure/currency] which is agreed to represent the fixed price sum (exclusive of VAT) of the entire cost of developing, making, producing and delivering the master of the [Film] which can be reproduced to make [DVDs/Discs] in accordance with the terms of this Agreement.

P.086

'The Licence Fee' shall be the sum of [figure/currency].
In consideration of the rights granted under this Agreement the [Distributor] shall pay to [Name] the Licence Fee as follows:

1.1 [–] upon signature of this Agreement.

1.2 [–] on or before [date].

1.3 [–] upon first [DVD/Disc] release of the [Film] to the public in [country].

1.4 [–] which shall be paid once only upon the conclusion of a subscription service arrangement for the supply, rental and/or sale of the [DVD/Disc] with a major retailer through a website or other means.

1.5   The [Distributor] agrees that the Licence Fee shall not be returnable by [Name] and shall not be offset and/or recouped against any royalties due to [Name].

P.087
The [Company] shall open a separate bank account designated as an account for all sums received and/or credited to the [Company] under this Agreement in respect of the exploitation of the [DVDs/Discs] of the [Film].

P.088
'The Advance' means the payment to the [Company] by the [Distributor] of the sum of [–] upon full signature of this Agreement. This advance shall be recouped by the [Distributor] from the [Company's] share of the Distribution Income under Clause [–].

P.089

1.1   The [Licensee] shall pay to the [Licensor] a non-returnable Advance.

1.2   The [Licensee] may recoup the non-returnable Advance against the [Licensor's] share of the Gross Receipts as they arise.

1.3   No payment shall be due to the [Licensor] until the Advance sum shall be recovered by the [Licensee] in full.

P.090
The [Distributor] shall pay the [Company] a non-returnable advance of [figure/currency] on [date] subject to [specify signature/delivery/other]. The [Distributor] shall have the right to offset the advance against any royalties due under this Agreement to the [Company]. In the event that the receipts are insufficient for the [Distributor] to recoup all of the advance then the [Distributor] shall not have the right to recover any such sum from the [Company].

P.091
'The Licence Fee' shall the sum of [figure/currency] which may be set off against the [Author's] Royalties. In consideration of the rights granted under this Agreement the [Company] shall pay the [Author] the Licence Fee as follows:

1.1   [–] upon signature by both parties to this Agreement.

1.2   [–] on or before [date] subject to [–].

1.3   [–] upon acceptance by the [Author] of the final script.

1.4   [–] upon first [release to the public/exhibition] of the [DVD/Disc] in the [United Kingdom/other] but no later than [date].

P.092

In consideration of the rights granted by the [Licensor] to the [Licensee] under this Agreement in respect of the [Sound Recordings]. The [Licensee] agrees to pay the [Licensor] in [currency] as follows:

1.1   [figure/currency] [words] upon signature of this Agreement.

1.2   [figure/currency] [words] on or before [date] subject to delivery and acceptance by the [Licensee] of a copy of the master material of the [Sound Recordings].

1.3   [figure/currency] [words] upon approval by the [Licensor] of the final version of the [Sound Recordings] to be reproduced and exploited by the [Licensee].

The [Licensee] agrees that the sums set out above shall not be set off against any royalties due to the [Licensor] nor shall they be recouped by any other means.

P.093

The [Licensee] agrees to ensure that all sums received from the exploitation of the [Sound Recordings/Disc] in any currency are converted at the most favourable exchange rate in existence at that time. That any conversion costs shall be paid for by the [Licensee].

P.094

The [Licensee] agrees to ensure that all [Sub-Licensees] shall keep any sums received from the exploitation of [the Sound Recordings/Disc] in a separate bank account and shall not mix such sums with those of the rest of the business and/or create any lien, charge and/or other claim over the sums by a third party.

P.095

[Name] agrees to pay the [Artist/Performer] a fixed fee of [number/currency] which shall be paid as follows:

1.1   [Number/currency] subject to completion of the work for the [Film/Project] on [dates].

1.2   [Number/currency] subject to completion of any photographs and images for the marketing.

1.3   [Number/currency] for attendance at the launch of the [DVD/Disc/other] of the [Film/Project] and a short speech and presentation and [number] press interviews at the event.

P.096

The [Company] shall pay [Name] a fee of [number/currency] by direct debit to a nominated account the day after completion of the filming for the [Project] at [location] on [date] which has been agreed with the [Company]. Any payment shall be accompanied by any additional payment required for [value added tax] purposes if an invoice is provided in advance supported by a [value added tax number].

Film and Television

P.097

In consideration of the rights and obligations imposed upon the [Assignor] and the [Assignee] under the terms of this Agreement the [Assignee] shall pay to the [Assignor] the Assignment Fee as follows:

1.1   [–] upon full signature of this Agreement by both parties; and

1.2   [–] upon delivery of the final approved script; and

1.3   [–] upon commencement of principal photography; and

1.4   [–] upon first public release of the [Film] by [specify] anywhere in the Territory.

1.5   In the event that the contingencies envisaged under Sub-Clauses 1.2 and 1.3 above are not fulfilled, the [Assignee] shall pay to the [Assignor] in lieu thereof the sum of [–] not later than the following date [–].

P.098

The [Company] agrees to pay [Name] the total fee as follows:

1.1   [–] upon signature of this Agreement by both parties, such sum to be deemed a Non-Returnable Advance.

1.2   [–] in accordance with the Budget and cashflow in Clause [–].

P.099

The Fixed Price Budget shall mean the sum of [–] which is agreed to represent the fixed price sum (exclusive of VAT) of the entire cost of developing, making, producing and delivering the [Programmes] in accordance with the terms of this Agreement. The Fixed Price Budget shall only be varied in exceptional circumstances and in any event only in accordance with the specific circumstances and procedures mentioned in Clauses [–] to this Agreement.

P.100

'The Option Fee' shall be the sum of [–].

In consideration of the [Author] granting to the [Company] the option rights under this Agreement, the [Company] agrees that it shall pay to the [Author] the Option Fee within [28 days] of both parties signing this Agreement.

P.101

In consideration of your agreement to the filming facilities we agree to pay you a fee exclusive of any value added tax of [figure/currency] for each period of [specify hours] each day. The sums shall be paid by [figure/currency] upon signature of this Agreement and the balance on completion of filming. The fee is in full and final settlement and no further sums shall be due to you in respect of our use of the material in any form.

P.102

'The Sponsorship Fee' shall be the sum of [figure/currency]. The [Sponsor] agrees to pay to the [Television Company] the Sponsorship Fee as follows:

1.1   [–] upon full signature of this Agreement by the parties.

1.2   [–] within [7 days] of the first broadcast/transmission of the first episode of the [Series].

1.3   [–] on or before [date] subject to the completion of 1.1 and 1.2.

P.103

'The Transmission Fee' shall be the following amount due to be paid by the [Agent] to the [Television Company] in consideration for the transmission or broadcast of the Advertising Copy [–].

The [Agent] agrees to pay to the [Television Company] the Transmission Fee after deducting the Agent's Commission on or before [date].

P.104

'The Repeat Fees' shall be the sums to be paid by the [Company] to [Name] in addition to the Basic Fee on each occasion when any of the following types of advertisements or any part which include the performance or voice-over of [Name] are broadcast and/or transmitted at any time throughout the Territory:

1.1   Standard Television Commercial on each of the following channels [specify channel and fee].

1.2   Cable Television Commercial on each of the following channels [–].

1.3   Satellite Television Commercial on each of the following channels [–].

1.4   Digital Television Commercial on each of the following channels [–].

1.5 Cable, satellite, digital and terrestrial Radio Commercial on each of the following stations [–].

1.6 All other forms of exploitation and/or use not set out in this Agreement are subject to the payment to be agreed in advance between the parties in each case.

P.105

'The Licence Fee' shall be the sum of [figure/currency].

In consideration of the rights granted under this Agreement the [Production Company] shall pay to the [Author] the Licence Fee as follows:

1.1 [–] upon signature of this Agreement.

1.2 [–] on or before [date].

1.3 [–] upon first video release of the [Film] to the public in [country] but in any event no later than [date].

1.4 [–] upon first DVD release of the [Film] anywhere throughout the Territory but in any event no later than [date].

1.5 [–] upon first broadcast or transmission of the [Film] on television in any form whether terrestrial, cable, satellite or digital anywhere throughout the Territory but in any event no later than [date].

1.6 The [Production Company] agrees that the Licence Fee shall not be returnable by the [Author] and shall be due on the specified dates at the latest irrespective of whether the [Film] is not completed and/or it is delayed for any reason or otherwise.

P.106

The amount of [figure/currency] shall be paid in full within [21 days] of broadcast/transmission of the [Film].

P.107

The [Production Company] shall open a separate bank account designated as a trust account under the name of the [Production Company] and the [Film]. The [Production Company] shall credit all sums paid by the [Television Company] under this Agreement to such account. The sums held on trust shall only be used for the purpose of the production of the [Film].

P.108

'The Production Advance' shall be the sum to be advanced by the [Television Company] towards the cost of the production and delivery of the [Films]. This sum shall not exceed the amount set out in the [Budget].

P.109

'The Royalty Advance' shall mean the payment to the [Company] by the [Cable Distributor] of the sum of [figure/currency] which shall be paid as follows:

1.1 [figure/currency] upon full signature of this Agreement.

1.2 [figure/currency] subject to acceptance of the [Material] of the [Film] by the [Cable Distributor].

1.3 [figure/currency] upon first transmission of the [Film] on cable television in [country] but in any event no later than [date].

P.110

1.1 The [Licensee] shall pay to the [Licensor] a non-returnable Advance.

1.2 The [Licensee] may recoup the non-returnable Advance against the [Licensor's] share of the Gross Receipts as they arise.

1.3 No payment shall be due to the [Licensor] until the Advance sum shall be recovered by the [Licensee] in full.

1.4 The [Licensee] shall pay to the [Licensor] the sum of [–] for the [Material] within [ten days] following completion of this Agreement and subject to acceptance of the [Material].

P.111

1.1 The [Distributor] shall pay the [Company] an advance of [figure/currency] which shall be in addition to the royalties.

1.2 The [Distributor] shall have the right to offset the advance against any royalties due under this Agreement to the [Company]. In the event that the receipts are insufficient for the [Distributor] to recoup all the advance then the [Distributor] shall have a claim against the [Company] for any unrecovered sum.

P.112

1.1 It is agreed that the [Licensee] shall pay the [Licensor] an unrefundable minimum guarantee on the sums to be received by the [Licensee] as an Advance of [sum] payable as follows [–].

1.2 It is expressly agreed that the [Licensee] may recoup this Advance by withholding sums due from the [Licensor's] share of the receipts. When the [Licensee] shall have fully recouped such sum then the [Licensor's] share of the receipts will be paid according to the terms of this Agreement.

1.3   If there are not enough receipts to allow the [Licensee] to recover the Advance, then the [Licensee] shall not have the right to claim the amount from the [Licensor]. The Advance is a non-refundable minimum guarantee and shall remain the property of the [Licensor].

P.113

The [Licensor] shall pay to the [Company] a non-returnable advance of [figure/currency] plus [VAT] on [date] subject to [specify signature/delivery/other]. Such sum shall not be contingent on any further matters and cannot be repaid at a later date.

P.114

The [Production Company] agrees that the [Licence Fee] shall not be returnable by the [Author] and shall be due in its entirety on or before the specified dates irrespective of whether the production or exploitation of the [Film] is cancelled, delayed or altered.

P.115

'The Licence Fee' shall be the non-returnable and recoupable advance against the [Author's] Royalties which is the sum of [–].

The Author agrees that the Licence Fee can be offset against the [Author's] Royalties.

In consideration of the rights granted under this Agreement the [Company] shall pay the [Author] the Licence Fee as follows:

1.1   [–] upon signature by both parties to this Agreement.

1.2   [–] on or before [date] subject to [–].

1.3   [–] upon acceptance by the [Author] of the final script.

1.4   [–] upon first [television/video/DVD/other] [transmission/release to the public/exhibition] in the [United Kingdom] but no later than [date].

P.116

The fixed sum of [figure/currency] shall be paid by the [Licensee] to the [Licensor] in respect of each [Customer] which books and pays for the [Film/Event/Match/other] under the television service operated by the [Licensee] in [country/area/premises] regardless of the method of payment including subscription, a package deal, pay per view, whether direct dial booking, remote controlled or otherwise. Customers whose package or service includes the [Film/Event/Match/other] will be deemed to have booked and paid.

P.117

The fixed sum of [figure/currency] shall be paid by the [Licensee] to the [Licensor] in respect of each [Customer] which books and pays for the [Film/Event/Match/other] under the pay per view television service operated by the [Licensee] in [country/area/premises] with direct dial booking, and/or remote controlled booking.

P.118

The [Distributor] agrees that an additional payment of [number/currency] shall be made to the [Licensor] for the right of the [Distributor] to make available the [Film] to the public for a period of [number] days through its [VOD/player/archive] for personal home use only on any television set, laptop and/or other gadget including mobile telephones and tablets.

P.119

It is agreed between the parties that where completion of work by any person is delayed due to force majeure which are beyond the control of the [Distributor] that no payments shall be due.

General Business and Commercial

P.120

Nothing herein contained shall be deemed to mean that any monies due or payable to the [Licensor] hereunder are held in trust by the [Licensee] for the [Licensor]. It is the intention that the [Licensee] shall be entitled to mix any part or portion of the [Licensor's] share of Gross Receipts which may be received by the [Licensee] with any of the [Licensee's] own monies.

P.121

All payments by the [Licensee] to the [Licensor] under this Agreement shall be made without any deduction or withholding any monies, unless required by law. In the event that monies are deducted or withheld the [Licensee] shall promptly pay the amount withheld to the appropriate authority and shall provide the [Licensor] with the original receipt issued by that authority or other sufficient evidence of payment.

P.122

In the event that the [Company] or any associated Company or subsidiary shall enter into agreement for the fulfilment of the terms of this Agreement in accordance with Clauses [–] in the Territory. The [Licensee] shall ensure that the sub-licensee shall either account directly to the [Licensee] or the [Licensor] in the same terms as agreed hereto between the [Licensee] and the [Licensor]. The [Licensee] nevertheless shall at all times remain fully liable to the [Licensor] under the terms of this Agreement.

P.123

The [Licensee] agrees to reimburse the [Licensor] in respect of all reproduction, insurance and delivery costs and charges incurred in providing acceptable [Material] subject to satisfactory receipts being provided upon request.

P.124

Written confirmation by the [Managing Director] of the prices for the purposes of Clause [–] and any variation shall be conclusive evidence of the price(s) agreed between the parties.

P.125

The [Licensor] agrees that all sums due under any licence agreements pursuant to this Agreement shall be paid direct to the [Agent] until the expiry or termination of this Agreement. Thereafter all sums shall be paid direct to the [Licensor].

P.126

All monies payable by the [Licensee] to the [Company] under this Agreement shall be paid to the following representatives of the [Company] as follows:

1.1   [number per cent] thereof to [Name] of [address] or at such other address as may be notified to the [Licensee] in writing by the [Company]; and

1.2   [number per cent] thereof to [Bank] of [address] for the credit of the account in the names of [–] or such other account as may be notified in writing to the [Licensee] by the [Company].

1.3   The receipt of the monies by the parties in 1.1 and 1.2 shall be good and sufficient discharge to the [Company] of the sums paid.

P.127

Notwithstanding the provisions of this Agreement any sums to be paid to the [Company] shall not be paid until the [Assignee] has received a release in writing executed by each of the persons entitled to the benefit of the Charge created by the [Company] described in Clause [–] in a form and manner acceptable to the [Assignee].

P.128

The Assignment Fee shall be the sum of [figure/currency].

In consideration of the rights assigned by the [Assignor] the [Assignee] shall pay to the [Assignor] the Assignment Fee as follows:

1.1   [–] upon signature of this Agreement.

1.2   [–] on or before [date].

P.129

Payment of the deposit and the balance shall be made on or before the date(s) specified in the form and time of payment shall be of the essence. Cheques shall be made payable to the [Company]. In the event that payment has not been received and/or any cheques have not been cleared [14 days] prior to the start of the exhibition the [Company] shall be entitled to reallocate the stand, without prejudice to any claim for damages by the [Company] or otherwise and to retain the deposit.

P.130

The [Company] reserves the right to withhold delivery to the [Licensee] of any material if payments due under this or other agreements have not been received by the [Company]. In addition the [Company] shall charge interest at the rate of [20]% [number per cent] per annum on all amounts outstanding beyond the payment date(s) shown on its invoices. The Agreement shall not take effect until the Agreement has been signed and returned to the [Company] and the Licence Fee (unless otherwise agreed) has been paid in full.

P.131

The [Company] shall open an account in the name of [Bank] of [address] entitled [specify Name]. It is agreed that it shall be a condition of the account that all withdrawals shall be made on cheques countersigned by a representative of the [Licensor] and that the instructions to each bank shall not be altered without the prior written consent of the [Licensor].

P.132

All payments made under this Agreement shall be in [currency] and by company [cheque/direct debit/other].

P.133

All payments are made via bank transfer and all charges are at the [Customers] sole cost.

P.134

It is agreed between the parties that where payment under this agreement is delayed and/or prevented by force majeure for any reason. That such non-payment shall not be deemed a breach of this Agreement provided that payment is made within [number months]. Thereafter the other party who has not been paid shall have the right to terminate this Agreement and to seek payment of the sums due together with interest and legal and administrative costs incurred.

P.135

Where the [Company] has paid any sum in advance for delivery of services and/or products by [Name]. Then in the event that [Name] fails to deliver the [Company] reserves the right and [Name] agrees that the [Company] may remove alternative stock to the value of the payment without notice.

Internet and Websites

P.136

All fees due for the use of the subscription service must be paid on the due date monthly in advance otherwise the [Company] reserves the right to cancel your access to and use of the service.

P.137

You may download one [unit/song/film] upon the terms of the Licence set out below provided that you have paid the Access Licence Fee and agree to be bound by the terms and conditions of the Licence.

P.138

No fees shall be charged for you to read, view and make one copy for your own personal use at home and for non-commercial purposes of the contents of this [Website] provided that there is sufficient acknowledgement of the source and copyright ownership. There is however no waiver of the right to demand fees, royalties and charges for any other use that you may make of the contents in any language, in any medium at any time. There is no licence granted to supply, distribute, transfer and/or reproduce the material to any third party at any time whether by copying, scanning, or otherwise.

P.139

1.1   The [Company/Distributor] shall pay the [Supplier] the fixed sum of [figure/currency] as a Usage Fee for every [Film/Sound Recording/ Unit] provided by the [Supplier] which is used on the [Website] and which is clicked on and for which the correct sums are received and retained by the [Company/Distributor].

1.2   The [Company/Distributor] shall provide a statement to the [Supplier] in arrears [each month/every three months] from [date] which sets out the name of the [[Film/Sound Recording/Unit], the date upon which the click through and payment was made and the sum received by the [Company/Distributor].

1.3   The [Company/Distributor] shall pay the [Supplier] all sums due in respect of the Usage Fees in arrears [each month/every three months] from [date].

P.140

The [Company] agrees and undertakes to keep accurate records of the orders from the public and shall meet such requests promptly and shall pay the [Supplier] for all the [Units/Service] for which payment is received by the [Company].

P.141

'Unit Price' shall mean the fixed sum for each item of the [Products] that the [Distributor] shall pay to the [Supplier]. A copy of the Unit Price for each item of the [Products] is set out in the attached Schedule [–] and forms part of this Agreement.

P.142

'The Contributors Fee' shall mean the sum of [figure/currency] per [hour/day/week].

P.143

The [Company] shall pay the [Contributors'] Fee by [cheque/direct debit/cash] in arrears within [twenty-eight days/one week] of receipt of an invoice setting out the sum due and subject to signature by the [Contributor] of this Agreement.

P.144

'The Basic Fee' shall mean the sum of [figure/currency].

P.145

The [Company] shall pay the Basic Fee in equal monthly instalments one month [in advance/arrears] the first payment to be made within [three days] of the signature of this Agreement by both parties. Payment shall be made directly into the [Contributors'] bank account by direct debit.

P.146

'The Bonus Fee' shall mean a one off payment of [figure/currency] which is separate and additional to the Basic Fee and any expenses which shall be payable by the [Company] in the event that the number of [email/clicks/premium line calls] exceeds [number] from [date] to [date].

P.147

The [Company] shall provide the [Contributor] with a report by [date] which sets out the number of [email/clicks/premium line calls] exceeds [number] from [date] to [date]. The [Company] shall then pay any sums due to the [Contributor] within [seven days] of receipt of an invoice.

P.148

The [Company] shall pay the [Contributor] a fee of [figure/currency] for the completion of the interview and filming for the [Podcast]. No payment shall be due if the work is not completed and/or the [Contributor] is not available on the agreed date.

P.149

The [Company] shall not be obliged to pay any fee, royalty and/or other payment to any member of the public, subscriber and/or other person who has submitted text, images and/or other material to the [Website] for the use of such material in any advertising, promotion and/or marketing material at any time and/or the sub-licensing of such material to a third party.

P.150

All financial transactions and payments in respect of this [Website] are made through [specify payment company] which is an independent and separate legal entity and not part of the [Website Company]. No order shall be sent until confirmation of payment has been received from the [payment company]. No responsibility can be accepted by the [Website Company] for any problems that may arise from the use of the [payment company] and/or any loss, damage, costs and/or expenses that may be incurred.

P.151

The [Company] may at any time substitute an alternative [Film/App/Event] which [Name] has paid for provided that [Name] is permitted to refuse the offer and receive a full refund.

P.152

1.1 No refunds will be made at any time by the [Company] where the [Service/Download/other] which [Name] has paid for has been interrupted, delayed and/or has been without sound and/or vision and/or text and/or images for any reason.

1.2 A [voucher code] will be offered where it is deemed that [Name] has not received a reasonable standard in the circumstances.

P.153

1.1 Payment must be made in full in advance by a [specify] card held in your own name which you are authorised to use through [specify company].

1.2 Payment cannot be accepted by any other method.

1.3 Any bank charges to be incurred shall be at your own cost.

1.4   Part payment will not be accepted nor payment by instalments.

1.5   Where there is evidence of fraud, misrepresentation of age and/or the payment is rejected by the bank then no ticket shall be supplied for the [Event].

Merchandising

P.154

'The Licence Fee' shall mean the sum of [figure/currency] which shall be payable by the [Licensee] to the [Licensor] as follows:

1.1   [–] upon signature to this Agreement by both parties.

1.2   [–] upon acceptance by the [Licensee] of the Delivery Material.

1.3   [–] upon acceptance of the prototype of the Licensed Articles.

1.4   [–] upon release of the Licensed Articles to the general public.

P.155

In the event that the cost of the development of the [Article/Product] exceeds the sum of [–] the payment of any overspend shall be at the entire discretion of the [Company] on terms to be agreed. In any event no overspend shall be paid for by the [Company] unless a revised [Budget] is provided to the [Company].

P.156

The [Designer] agrees to consult with the [Licensee] with respect to the prices at which the [Licensed Articles] are to be sold, whether by retail, wholesale or at a discounted price.

P.157

The [Company] undertakes that the minimum wholesale selling price for each unit of the [Licensed Articles] throughout the Territory shall not be less than [retail/wholesale/per unit/per stock run/other].

P.158

In consideration of the rights granted under this Agreement the [Licensee] shall pay to the [Licensor] the Licence Fee as follows:

1.1   [–] upon signature of this Agreement.

1.2   [–] on or before [date].

1.3   [–] upon the first release of the [Licensed Articles] to the distributors in [country].

1.4 The [Licensee] acknowledges that the Licence Fee is not returnable and is not to be offset against the [Licensee's] Royalties and is not contingent on the sales of the [Licensed Articles].

P.159

The minimum sum for each unit of the [Licensed Articles] on which the [Licensor's] Royalties shall be calculated shall be [–] if the sum received for any reason is lower the accounts shall be carried out as if this is the deemed receipt. The difference shall be entirely at the [Licensee's] cost.

P.160

'The Assignment Fee' shall be the sum of [figure/currency].

In consideration of the rights assigned under this Agreement the [Assignee] agrees to pay the [Assignor] the Assignment Fee as follows:

1.1 [–] upon full signature of this Agreement by both parties.

1.2 On or before [–].

1.3 [–] subject to satisfactory collection of the [Work Material].

P.161

In consideration of the rights granted under this Agreement the [Distributor] shall pay to the [Licensor] the Licence Fee as follows:

1.1 [figure/currency] upon signature of this Agreement.

1.2 [figure/currency] on or before [date] subject to acceptance of the [Material].

1.3 [figure/currency] upon approval of the sample of the [Licensed Articles] by the [Licensor].

1.4 [figure/currency] upon approval of the labels, packaging and advertising of the [Licensed Articles] by the [Licensor].

1.5 [figure/currency] upon first availability of the [Licensed Articles] by the [Licensor] to the general public anywhere in the world.

P.162

'The Licence Fee' shall be the non-returnable and recoupable advance against the [Authors'/Licensors'] royalties which is the sum of [figure/currency] [words].

P.163

In consideration of the rights granted under this Agreement the [Company] shall pay the Licence Fee to the [Authors/Licensor] as follows:

1.1   [figure/currency] upon full signature of this Agreement by both parties.

1.2   [figure/currency] on or before date [date] subject to 1.1 has been completed.

1.3   [figure/currency] upon acceptance by the [Author] of the final version of the Script, but in any event no later than [date].

1.4   [figure/currency] upon first television release in [country], but no later than [date].

1.5   [figure/currency] upon first DVD release in [country], but no later than [date].

1.6   [figure/currency] upon first release of the [Computer Game/Product] in [country], [but no later than date].

P.164

[Name] agrees to pay the [Artist] a fee of [number/currency for the creation, development, assignment of rights and delivery of the [Image and Logo]. Payment shall be in three stages:

1.1   [Number/currency] on signature of this Agreement for the services of the [Artist].

1.2   [Number/currency] on delivery to [Name] of the following material: all draft copies of the [Image and Logo] and the master copy of the computer generated [animated] film and sound recording together with music and music cue sheets.

1.3   [Number/currency] on signature by the [Artist] of the assignment document supplied by [Name].

Publishing

P.165

The [Author] acknowledges that the selling price of the [Work] shall be within the sole and exclusive discretion of the [Publisher]. The [Publisher] shall consult with the [Author] prior to making a final decision on the recommended retail price.

P.166

Any payments due to the [Author] under this Agreement shall be satisfied by making payment to the [Author's] agreed representative [Company] whose address for these purposes is [address] unless written notification and instruction to the contrary is received by the [Publisher] from the [Author]. In the event that the [Agent] fails to transfer payment to the [Author] and is found to be fraudulent and/or negligent and/or misappropriates the sums paid in any form the [Publisher] shall not be held liable. Further if the [Author] instructs the [Publisher] to make payment direct to the [Author] then the [Publisher] shall be bound to follow the instructions of the [Author] and shall not be liable to the [Agent] for any reason.

P.167
The [Publisher] shall pay the [Author] the Advance against Royalties as follows:

1.1 [–] on signature of this Agreement.

1.2 [–] on delivery of an acceptable manuscript.

1.3 [–] on first publication of the [Work].

P.168
The [Writer] confirms that the [Company] shall be entitled to retain all sums received from the exploitation of the [Work] in any media throughout the Territory at any time and the [Writer] shall not be entitled to any such sums.

P.169
'The Serialisation Fee' shall be the sum of [figure/currency].

The [Licensee] agrees to pay the Serialisation Fee to the [Author] as follows:

1.1 [–] upon signature of all the parties to this Agreement.

1.2 [–] on or before [date] subject to publication of the [Extracts].

P.170
'The Writer's Fee' shall be the following sum [figure/currency].

In consideration of the services provided by the [Ghostwriter] under this Agreement and the rights assigned, the [Originator] shall pay to the [Ghostwriter] the [Ghostwriter's] Fee as follows:

1.1 [figure/currency] upon signature of both parties to this Agreement.

1.2 [figure/currency] on or before [date] subject to delivery and approval of written evidence of sufficient progress such as outlines of chapters and draft chapters.

1.3 [figure/currency] subject to delivery and acceptance of the [Work] and the artwork by the [Originator].

1.4 [figure/currency] on or before [date].

1.5 [figure/currency] on publication of the [hardback] in [country].

1.6 [figure/currency] on publication of [paperback] in [country].

P.171

The [Company] shall pay to the [Writer] the total fee of [–] (exclusive of value added tax) as follows:

1.1 [–] on the full signature of this document.

1.2 [–] upon [the receipt/acceptance/approval] of the Treatment by the [Company].

1.3 [–] upon [the receipt/acceptance/approval] of the Script by the [Company].

P.172

As full consideration for the rights in and to the [Works] the [Publisher] shall pay to the [Writer] the total sum of [figure/currency] (exclusive of value added tax). The sum shall be paid [number per cent] due on execution hereof and the balance upon receipt to the [Publisher's] satisfaction of the [manuscript/treatment].

P.173

The [Publisher] shall pay the [Author] the sum of [–] in advance. Such payment to be on account of any sums that may become due to the [Author] under this Agreement in respect of the first edition as follows:

1.1 The sum of [–] on signature of this agreement; and

1.2 The sum of [–] on receipt and approval by the [Publishers] of the [manuscript/transcript/disc/recordings].

P.174

The [Publisher] agrees to pay the [Author] the Advance Royalty payment as follows:

1.1 [–] upon full signature of this Agreement.

1.2 [–] upon delivery of the first [number pages/chapters].

1.3 [–] upon delivery of an acceptable manuscript [and disc] of the [Work].

1.4 [–] upon delivery of the proofs.

1.5 [–] on or before [date].

1.6 [–] upon first publication of the [Work] in hardback.

1.7 [–] upon first publication of the [Work] in paperback.

1.8 [–] upon first distribution of any related merchandising.

1.9 [–] upon first serialisation.

1.10 [–] as a bonus in the event that sales of the [hardback/paperback book] exceed [number] in total in [the first year of publication].

1.11 [–] upon first [Video] release of a [Film] adaptation of the [Work] to the public in [country].

1.12 [–] upon first [DVD/Disc] release of a [Film] adaptation of the [Work] anywhere throughout the Territory.

1.13 [–] upon first broadcast or transmission of all the [Film] on television in any form whether terrestrial, cable, satellite or digital anywhere throughout the Territory.

1.14 [–] upon first [Computer Game/Merchandising] release based on the [Work] or in conjunction with a [Film] adaptation of the [Work] anywhere throughout the Territory.

P.175

The [Publisher] agrees that no part of the Advance Royalty payment shall be returned by the [Author] once the [Publisher] has accepted the manuscript of the [Work].

P.176

Rates may be increased at any time upon [3 months'] written notice prior to the publication date. Orders are subject to all conditions stated on the latest published rate and in addition to the advertisement rates the [Customer] is responsible for the cost of artwork, sketches, layout and photography. All advertisements accepted for publication are subject to the standard conditions of the [–]. Payment shall be required within [30 days] of the first publication date of the magazine.

P.177

The [Publisher] shall be entitled to offset the Advance against future royalties due to the [Author] under this Agreement, but not against any other agreement that the [Author] may have with the [Publisher].

P.178

The [Publisher] agrees and undertakes that it is not entitled to claim any unearned advance back from the [Author] which is not recouped against royalties nor can the unearned advance be offset against royalties due to the [Author] under any other agreement which the [Author] has with the [Publisher].

P.179

The [Publisher] shall be entitled to offset the Advance against future royalties due to the [Author] under this Agreement and against any other agreement that the [Author] may have with the [Publisher]. The [Author] agrees that the [Publisher] shall be entitled to claim any unearned advance back from the [Author] which is not recouped against royalties due under this Agreement and/or which cannot be offset against royalties due to the [Author] under any other agreement which the [Author] has with the [Publisher].

P.180

The [Publishers] shall not recoup and/or offset any sums due from one agreement against another without notifying the [Author] in writing and explaining the reasons. The [Author] shall be provided with the opportunity to dispute and to set out in writing the reasons as to why this is not acceptable.

P.181

The [Licensor] shall pay to the [Company] a non-returnable advance of [figure/currency] plus [VAT] on [date] subject to [specify signature/delivery/other]. Such sum shall not be contingent on any further matters and cannot be repaid at a later date.

P.182

The [Publisher] agrees that it shall not be entitled to recoup and/or offset any sums due under this Agreement with [Name] against any other previous and/or future agreement without the prior written consent of [Name].

P.183

The [Author] shall not receive any additional payment for contributions to promotion, development and/or marketing of the [Work] which is less than [number] hours. Thereafter the [Distributor] agrees to pay the [Author] a daily rate of [number/currency] for [number] hours per day such sums to be paid within [number] days subject to invoice.

Purchase and Supply of Products

P.184

Payment shall be made by the [Buyer] at the time of delivery. The [Company] shall however be entitled to demand payment by banker's draft or alternatively by direct debit at the time of delivery. Interest shall accrue to overdue payments at the rate of [number] per cent per annum above the Base Rate] from time to time of [Bank plc] in the event that payment is not received within [specify period] of delivery.

P.185

Unless otherwise stated in the sales order, payment of invoices shall be made by the 15th of the month, following the month in which the goods are received, and time is of the essence. The [Company] reserves the right to deduct from any monies due or becoming due to the [Buyer/Hirer] from the [Company] those sums which are due to the [Company].

P.186
Save as may be set out in this Agreement, payments shall be made upon receipt of an invoice in sterling within [60] [sixty days] after receipt of the invoice. Payments on account shall not prejudice the existence or amount of the [Company's] obligation. Such payments shall be recorded in the final total sum. Any delay due to a dispute concerning an invoice shall extend the time limit for payment accordingly.

P.187
Terms of payment are strictly within [30] [thirty days] from the date the material is sent by the [Company]. Thereafter interest will be charged at an annual rate of [–]% above the Base Rate charged from time to time by [specify Bank]. In the case of rental plans the [Company] shall not be obliged to supply any material until such time as payment in full has been received. No title to material sold shall pass to the [Customer] until payment has been received in full.

P.188
The price of the [Products] shall be paid in [currency]. The Company shall establish with a reputable bank satisfactory to the [Seller] an irrevocable letter of credit representing the full amount of the purchase price in [currency] under the contract in favour of the [Seller] to be drawn on or by [date].

P.189
The price to be paid by the [Buyer] for the [Company's] Products shall in all cases be the relevant price contained in the [Company's] Wholesale Price Lists in force at the date of delivery. Where the [Company's] Products are delivered in returnable packages the [Buyer] shall pay the appropriate deposit charged by the [Company] thereon.

P.190
The [Hirer] agrees to match the competitive prices which the [Buyer] can show are available for equipment and/or personnel hire to operate hardware and/or produce software to achieve the following purpose [specify].

P.191
'Wholesale Selling Price' shall be the sum actually paid by each retail sales outlet for the purchase of each [Item].

P.192

These conditions shall be incorporated in the Contract between the person to whom the sales order is addressed the [Buyer] and the [Company] for the supply of the goods, material, machinery or equipment or facilities to the Goods specified in the sales order. These conditions shall prevail over any inconsistent terms or conditions contained in or referred to in the [Buyer's] request for the Goods or elsewhere or implied by trade custom or otherwise. No addition to or variation of any of these conditions shall be binding on the [Company] unless in writing and signed by an authorised representative of the [Company].

P.193

The prices shall be stated in the Sales Order for the [Goods/Products] unless otherwise agreed in writing by the [Company].

P.194

The price which is stated in the quotation provided by the [Company] shall only be held for a maximum [twenty-eight days]. The price may be changed by the [Company] at its entire discretion at any time within that period if there is a major change of circumstances which effects the quoted price including but not limited to cost increases in petrol, oil, transport, taxes, exchange rates, or supply of materials. The price which is agreed to by the [Company] shall be the price in the order form acknowledgement with the order reference confirmed.

P.195

'Firm Sale' shall mean that the [Seller] shall pay the [Supplier] for all the [Product] supplied and the [Seller] shall have no right to return the [Product] to the [Supplier] unless it is rejected for one of the reasons set out in this Agreement.

P.196

1.1 'Dealer Price' shall mean the price per unit of each [Product] which the [Seller] shall pay to the [Supplier] with respect to each unit of the [Product] supplied to the [Seller].

1.2 The [Seller] agrees to pay the [Supplier] the Dealer Price in respect of the [Product] upon demand by the [Supplier] subject to completion of delivery and any such sum shall be made within the Accounting Period.

P.197

'The E price' shall be the recommended price at which the [Work] is sold to the public over the internet excluding freight, packaging, insurance and administrative costs which shall be [figure/currency].

1252

P.198

The [Agent] acknowledges that it is not permitted to offer any discount or other reduction in this ex-factory price or offer any other special terms, promotions and/or discounts without the prior written consent of the [Company].

P.199

In consideration of the [Goods] the [Company] agrees to pay the [Distributor] the following fee/rates [–]. Payment shall be made in full subject to satisfactory [Goods] within [30] days of receipt of invoice.

P.200

Prices are inclusive of value added tax subject to any changes in the rate before the [Client] paid the price in full. Prices are in pounds sterling. The [Client] shall reimburse the [Company] on demand for any expense incurred on the conversion of foreign currencies, bank charges, presenting and/or processing of any payment or otherwise which arose from converting the sums to sterling. Payment is not actually made until the sums in sterling have been received by the [Company].

P.201

A deposit of [–]% of the total price must be sent to the [Company] with the application form. The balance of the price is due [–] days before the provision of the [Goods]. Time of payment shall be of the essence of the contract.

P.202

The [Agent] shall follow the [Company's] price lists, sale instructions and conditions. The [Agent] shall not under any circumstances have the right to change, vary or alter the conditions of sale or prices of the [Products]. The [Agent] shall not grant or accept discounts, allowances, deferments in payment nor issue receipts, accept [Products] or transfer [Products] from one customer to another without the prior written approval of the [Company].

P.203

All orders are subject to payment on receipt of invoice, unless otherwise agreed in writing by a Director of the [Company]. All accounts must be settled by the agreed due date. Failure to do so will entitle the [Company] to withdraw such facilities. All charges involved in the collection of overdue accounts will be payable by the [Customer].

P.204

The [Company] shall provide the [Agent] with a list each season of the prices in [US$ dollars] of the cost of ordering the [Garments] based on the collection samples which shall be the ex-factory price together with the estimated freight and insurance costs to destination which shall each be itemised. The price list shall not include custom clearance, storage duty and taxes which shall be the responsibility of the [Customer]. The [Agent] agrees to promote, market and obtain orders for the [Garments] at the prices and on the conditions specified by the [Company]. The [Agent] acknowledges that title to any garments ordered shall remain with the [Company] until full payment of the invoice has been received by the [Company].

P.205

The payment terms shall be in full upon receipt of invoice. Interest shall be charged at [number per cent] on accounts not paid within [–] days of the invoice date. The prices shall be as stated in the Sales Order unless otherwise agreed in writing by the [Company].

P.206

Unless otherwise stated in the Sales Order the payment of invoices shall be made by the [15th] of the month following the month in which the [Goods] were received. The [Company] reserves the right to deduct from any monies due to the [Buyer] any monies due from the [Buyer] to the [Company].

P.207

1.1 The [Company] shall pay [Name] the sum of [figure/currency] as an advance against royalties that may be earned from the sale of the [Product].

1.2 The [Company] agrees that it shall not seek to reclaim the advance from [Name] and that it can only recoup such sum from the allocated future royalty payments to [Name].

1.3 In the event that the sales of the [Product] exceed [number] in the first six months, then the [Company] agrees that it shall pay [Name] an additional advance of [figure/currency].

P.208

Where the [Company] has paid the sums due for the [Products] to the [Supplier] and subsequently discovers after delivery that the [Supplier] has misled and/or provided inaccurate information to the [Company] as to the country of origin of the content. The [Supplier] agrees that the [Supplier] shall pay for the cost of shipment of the [Products] back to the [Supplier] and/or arrange for collection. In addition the [Supplier] shall refund all payments made for the [Products] by the [Company] plus an additional penalty of [number/currency] to cover administrative costs incurred. Such payment to be made by the [Supplier] within [number] days of notification by the [Company] as to the facts.

P.209

If payment is delayed then the [Supplier] shall be entitled to cancel the order by [Name] and to offer the [Products] to a third party whether the material was specially commissioned or not.

Services

P.210

The [Photographer] acknowledges and agrees that the [Assignee] shall be entitled to commercially exploit the [Work] in any form without further payment to the [Photographer].

P.211

In consideration of [Contributor's] services the [Company] agrees to pay the Contributor's Fee as follows:

1.1 [–] upon signature by all parties of this Agreement.

1.2 [–] on or before [date] subject to the completion of the services and work set out in clause [–].

1.3 [–] on or before [date] subject to the return to the [Company] of all material supplied on loan and the assignment of all copyright in the material created by the [Contributor] under this Agreement.

P.212

The [Company] agrees to pay the [Celebrity] the Repeat Fees within [–] days of each of the dates upon which a repeat broadcast and/or transmission is made throughout the Territory at any time. Any other matters not dealt with in this Agreement shall be the subject of separate notification in each case by the [Company] to agree an additional payment for that use. The [Company] agrees that no payment shall be less than [figure/currency].

P.213

'Payment Schedule' shall mean Schedule [–] which specifies the payments by the [Company to the [Designer] and the conditions to be fulfilled by the [Designer].

The [Company] shall make such payments as are agreed under this Agreement in accordance with the Payment Schedule subject to completion of the required work to a satisfactory standard to the [Designer] within [28 days] of receipt of a VAT invoice. Further the [Company] agrees to make such payments to the [Designer] as may be agreed in accordance with the Support Services under Schedule [–].

P.214

1.1   The [Company] shall pay the [Artist] a fee of [figure/currency] as an advance against future royalties and earnings relating to the [Artist] and the [Group]. This sum shall be paid on [date].

1.2   The [Artist] agrees that the [Company] shall have the right to recover the fee from the royalties and earnings due to the [Artist] under this Agreement. That if by [date] the [Company] has not recouped the fee that the [Company] shall have the right to seek that the [Artist] repay the sum due provided that the [Company] have commercially released the [Recordings] by [date].

1.3   That the [Company] agrees not to issue any legal proceedings against the [Artist] provided that it is agreed that the sum due will be repaid within [twelve months] of the demand for payment.

P.215

The [Company] shall pay the [Artist] a fee of [figure/currency] as a non-returnable Advance against future royalties relating to the services of [Artist] provided under this Agreement as follows:

1.1   [–] upon full signature of this Agreement.

1.2   [–] upon delivery and acceptance of the [Lyrics/compositions of the Music Works] set out in Schedule [–].

1.3   [–] upon [date] subject to the successful completion of [duration] hours of sound recordings and filming set out in Schedule [–].

1.4   [–] upon first release to the public of the [CD/Album/Disc] in [country].

1.5   [–] in the event that the [CD/Album/Recordings] are made available by the [Company] either under a subscription service and/or per download payment to the public via the internet, worldwide web and/or to any other gadget, computer, telephone, television and/or other method of listening to and/or watching the words in any language.

1.6   [–] upon first distribution of any related merchandising.

1.7   [–] as a bonus in the event that [unit] sales of the [CD/Album/other] exceed [number] in total anywhere in the world.

P.216

The [Company] agrees and undertakes that it is not entitled to claim any unearned advance back from the [Artist] which is not recouped against royalties nor can the unearned advance be offset against royalties due to the [Artist] under any other agreement which the [Artist] has with the [Company].

P.217

The [Artist] agrees that the [Company] shall have the right to recover the Advance from the royalties and earnings due to the [Artist] under this Agreement. That if by [the expiry date] the [Company] has not recouped the Advance that the [Company] shall have the right to seek that the [Artist] repay the sum due provided that the [Company] have commercially released the [CD/Album/other] by that [expiry date]. The [Company] agrees not to issue any legal proceedings and/or to seek to be entitled to legal costs against the [Artist] provided that the sum due shall be repaid within [twelve months] of the demand for payment.

P.218

The [Company] shall be entitled to offset the Advance against future royalties due to the [Artist] under this Agreement and against any other agreement that the [Artist] may have with the [Company]. The [Artist] agrees that the [Company] shall be entitled to claim any unearned advance back from the [Artist] which is not recouped against royalties due under this Agreement and/or which cannot be offset against royalties due to the [Artist] under any other agreement which the [Artist] has with the [Company].

P.219

The [Company] shall not recoup and/or offset any sums due from one agreement against another without notifying the [Artist] in writing and explaining the reasons. The [Artist] shall be provided with the opportunity to dispute and to set out in writing the reasons as to why this is not acceptable.

P.220

The [Consultant] shall in consideration of the services to be provided hereunder be paid a fee of [figure/currency per hour/half day/day]. Such sums shall be payable in arrears on the last day of each such four-week period and the first of such payments shall be made on the [date]. The fee shall be subject to review on [date] and annually thereafter.

P.221

In consideration of the services to be rendered to the [Company] the [Presenter] shall receive a fee of [figure/currency] per [four-week period/ calendar month] payable in [advance/arrears] upon production of an invoice to the [Company]. The fees stated are exclusive of [VAT] but the [Company] agrees to pay [VAT] on such fees upon submission of a [VAT] invoice.

P.222

'The Presenter's Fee' shall be the following sums:

    [–] for the first twelve calendar months.

[–] for the following twelve calendar months.

[–] thereafter until [date].

In consideration of the [Presenter's] services the [Company] agrees to pay the [Presenter's] Fee in equal instalments throughout the Term of the Agreement on the last day of each calendar month. The first instalment shall be due on [date].

P.223

The [Company] shall during the continuance of this Agreement receive a fee at the rate of [figure/currency] per annum during the first [8 calendar months] and a fee of [–] during the balance of the Term of Agreement. The fees shall be paid by equal calendar month instalments in arrears on the last day of each month and the first payment shall be on [date].

P.224

1.1   The [Contributor's] Fee shall be the sum of [–] payable in equal monthly instalments one month in advance, such sum to be in addition to the Expenses as defined in Clause [–] to this Agreement and exclusive of any [VAT]. The first payment shall be made immediately following the signing of this Agreement by both parties. Payment shall be made directly into the [Contributor's] bank account by electronic transfer.

1.2   The [Contributor] confirms that he/she shall be liable for the arrangement for and payment of his/her [National Insurance Contributions] and any other sums which are or may be payable to the [Inland Revenue] as a result of the payments made under this Agreement.

P.225

The [Company] shall pay to the [Director]:

1.1   [–] exclusive of [value added tax] of which [–] has been paid by the [Company] to the [Director] prior to the date hereof and the balance of which shall be paid [date].

1.2   [–] on the commencement of principal photography of the [Film] but not in any event later than [date].

1.3   [–] on the last day of the third week of principal photography.

1.4   [–] on completion of the final cut of the [Film].

1.5   [–] on the expiry of the Production Period.

The fee shall be inclusive of all additional payments including payments by reason of late working or weekend working, holiday pay and sick pay to which the Director may be entitled in accordance with the relevant union agreement.

P.226

The [Celebrity] confirms that all sums due to the [Celebrity] shall be paid directly to the [Agent] until such time as the [Celebrity] may otherwise supply different instructions. Any payments due to the [Celebrity] under this Agreement shall have been met and fulfilled by the [Company] by payment to the instructed representative. In the event that the [Agent] fails to transfer payment to the [Celebrity] then the [Celebrity] agrees and undertakes that it shall not be the fault and/or responsibility of the [Company]. If the [Celebrity] instructs the [Company] to make payment direct to the [Celebrity] then the [Company] shall be bound to follow the instructions of the [Celebrity] and shall not be liable to the [Agent] for any reason. Payment to the [Agent] at the direction of the [Celebrity] does not make the [Agent] a party to this Agreement and/or provide any legal obligation to the [Agent] from the [Company].

P.227

In consideration of the services provided by the [Contributor] and the rights assigned to the [Company] under this Agreement. The [Company] shall pay to the [Contributor] the fee of [–] on or by [date]. In the event that the [Contributor] is requested by the [Company] to provide services over and above those set out in paragraphs [–], then the [Company] undertakes to agree with the [Contributor] the payment of an additional fee.

P.228

In consideration of the services provided by the [Researcher] and the rights assigned under this Agreement, the [Company] shall pay the [Researcher] a daily fee of [–]. The [Researcher] acknowledges that the above daily fee shall be for an [8 hour day] and pro rata payments may be made where appropriate. No overtime or additional fees shall be due unless specifically agreed between the parties in advance.

P.229

The [Company] agrees to pay the [Researcher's] Fee within [–] days of the end of each working week following receipt of an invoice setting out the hours and days worked by the [Researcher] and the details of all such work.

P.230

In consideration of the services/work/contribution [specify] by [Name] the [Company] is to pay the fee of [–] by [date] in [cash/cheque/other] to the [Name] in full and final settlement. No further sums of any nature shall be due to [Name] for the provision of his/her services/work/contribution or the exploitation of the material in any media at any time.

P.231

The charges for the service are specified in Schedule [–] provided that the [Company] may at any time for each calendar year increase the charges once or more subject to a maximum aggregate increase of [number per cent/sum] in any one year.

P.232

The [Customer] shall be entitled to an [annual dollar volume discount] for all services purchased under this Agreement. The discount shall be calculated by the [Company] within [60 days] of each year end. The [Customer] may elect to receive discount in payment or in a credit to future billing. The discount shall only apply if all invoices for services during the year have been properly paid in full and by the specified date.

P.233

The charges for the service are those specified in Schedule [–], provided that the [Company] reserve the right to increase the charges at any time. All charges are exclusive of tax and must be paid without any deduction. Where appropriate value added tax, sales tax, or any other taxes on the service shall be paid by the [Customer] in addition to the charges.

P.234

'The Repeat Fees' shall be the following sums to be paid by the [Company] to the [Celebrity] in addition to the Celebrity Fee. These sums shall be due to the [Celebrity] on each occasion any material in whole or part produced under this Agreement is exploited and/or reproduced and/or licensed in any medium at any time except for the transmissions specified in Schedule [–] including but not limited advertisements, performances, recordings, films, photographs, image, voice-over or otherwise. The payment for each type of use shall be in a accordance with the Schedule [–] and all payments made [within [28 days] of the material being licensed for use by the [Company]/ the material is used by the sub-licensee].

P.235

In consideration of the services of [Name] the [Company agrees and undertakes to pay [Names] fee as follows:

[–] within [10 days] of both parties signing this Agreement.

[–] on or before [–] subject to completion of [specify work/services].

P.236

[Name] agrees that if he/she does not pay for the [Service/Work] by [date] at the end of each calendar month. That the [Company] shall have the right to terminate the Agreement within [number] days after a final warning by [email/letter].

P.237
The [Company] agrees that it shall accept payments by instalments spread over [number] months provided that an additional cost is paid of [number/currency].

Sponsorship

P.238
In consideration of the rights assigned under this Agreement the [Sponsor] agrees to pay to the [Association] the Sponsorship Fee as follows:

1.1   [–] upon signature of this Agreement.

1.2   [–] on or before [date].

1.3   [–] within [14] days of the completion of [–].

P.239
In addition to the Sponsorship Fee the [Sponsor] agrees that it shall be responsible for the payment of all the prize money to be paid to the successful competitors at the presentation ceremony in accordance with the [Prize Money Schedule] which is attached to and forms part of this Agreement. The [Sponsor] confirms that the total prize money amounts to not less than [figure/trust].

P.240
The [Sponsor] agrees that it shall not be entitled to authorise any third parties to assist in the funding of the event without the prior written consent of the [Association].

P.241
'The Performance Related Fee' shall be the sums to be paid by the [Sponsor] to the [Sportsperson] in the event that the [Sportsperson] wins or achieves any of the events, records or other matters set out in the Performance Related Schedule which is attached to and forms part of this Agreement.

In consideration of the services provided under this Agreement the [Sponsor] shall pay to the [Sportsperson] the Sponsorship Fee as follows:

1.1   [–] upon signature of this Agreement by all the parties.

1.2   [–] on or before [date].

1.3   [–] on or before [date] subject to the completion of the work specified in clause [–].

The [Sponsor] agrees to pay to the [Sportsperson] the Performance Related Fee subject to fulfilling any of the Performance Related Schedule. Payment shall be made by the [Sponsor] within [7 days] of receipt of notice of the event or occasion on which the [Sportsperson] achieves or wins in each case. The [Sponsor] acknowledges that more than one sum may become due for any one event or occasion.

P.242

The [Sponsor] acknowledges that the Sponsorship Fee shall be paid to the [Sportsperson] notwithstanding that the [Sportsperson] may be unable to provide his services under this Agreement due to illness or injury which is supported by a medical certificate from a qualified doctor.

P.243

'The Annual Sponsorship Fee' shall be the sum of [figure/currency] to be paid by the [Sponsor] to the [Athlete] during the continuance of this Agreement until the end of the Term of the Agreement. The sum shall be paid each year in equal monthly instalments one month in advance, such sum to be in addition to the Expenses as defined in Clause [–] to this Agreement and exclusive of any [VAT]. The first payment shall be made immediately following the signing of this Agreement by both parties. Payment shall be made directly into the [Athlete's] bank account by electronic transfer.

P.244

The [Athlete] agrees and undertakes that he/she shall be liable for the arrangement for and payment of his/her [National Insurance Contributions] and any other sums may be payable in taxes or otherwise in respect of the sums received by the [Athlete].

P.245

The [Athlete] accepts that where the contract and/or the [Athlete] has instructed the [Sponsor] to make any payments under the contract to the [Agent], a family member, a parent or guardian. That once payment has been made by the [Sponsor] as instructed that the [Sponsor] has fulfilled its contractual obligations in that respect and is no longer liable to the [Athlete] for that sum.

P.246

The [Sponsor] shall not be entitled to withhold and/or not pay all and/or any part of the Sponsorship Fee due a change of venue, artists, programme, television and radio coverage, weather conditions and/or rescheduling of the date of the [Event].

P.247

The [Sponsor] agrees to make additional payments to the [Artist/Athlete] in respect of the achievement of the following events:

1.1 [Number/currency] if the [Artist] wins [specify] personality of the year at any time in each case during the term of this Agreement.

1.2 [Number/currency] if the [Artist/Athlete] wins race entitled [specify] at [specify event] in [year].

1.3 [Number/currency] if the [Artist/Athlete] writes and/or commission an authorised biography which mentions the [Sponsor] on the book cover in [country].

1.4 [Number/currency] if the [Artist/Athlete] attends more than [number] promotional events on behalf of the [Sponsor] in [year].

University, Library and Educational

P.248

The [Institute] shall pay the [Company] the total sum of [figure/currency] (exclusive of value added tax) for the [Work/Service/Product]. The sum shall be paid in four equal instalments:

1.1 [figure/currency] upon acceptance and confirmation of the order by the [Company].

1.2 [figure/currency] upon approval of the [draft/sample/pilot/prototype] by the [Institute].

1.3 [figure/currency] upon delivery and approval of the completed [Work/Service] by the [Institute].

1.4 [figure/currency] by [date] provided that the [Work/Product] has been in operation for [one month] without any failure, defects and/or errors effecting the [Work/Service/Product].

P.249

The [Institute] agrees to pay the Contributor's Fee of [figure/currency] in four stages:

1.1 [figure/currency] upon signature by all parties of this Agreement.

1.2 [figure/currency] on or before [date] subject to the completion of the [Work/Project] set out in clause [–].

1.3   [figure/currency] on or before [date] subject to delivery and acceptance by the [Institute] of the [Report/Prototype/Film/Website].

P.250

1.1   The [Licensee] shall pay the [Institute] a Licence Fee of [figure/currency] which shall be paid in advance before delivery of a copy of the [Work/Artwork/Photograph].

1.2   The [Licensee] agrees and undertakes to report to the [Institute] the number of copies, format and use of the [Work/Artwork/Photograph] and to pay the fees for such exploitation which are set out in the attached Price List a copy of which is attached to and forms part of this Agreement.

P.251

In consideration of the rights assigned under this Agreement the [Company] agrees to pay to the [Institute] the Licence Fee as follows:

1.1   [figure/currency] upon signature of this Agreement.

1.2   [figure/currency] on or before [date].

1.3   [figure/currency] within [–] days of delivery and acceptance of the sample [Work/Product] by the [Company].

1.4   [figure/currency] within [–] days of first general release to the public of the [Work/Product] anywhere in the world by the [Company].

1.5   [figure/currency] as a bonus payment in the event that sales of the [Work/Product] exceed [number] in total in [country/world].

P.252

The [Company] agrees and undertakes that it shall not be entitled to authorise and/or permit any third parties and/or to change its shareholding and/or corporate structure so that any other person and/or company is able to assist in, support and/or donate to the financing of the [Project/Work] without the prior written consent of the [Institute].

P.253

The [Consortium] agree that no one party to this Agreement shall be entitled to make and/or authorise any payments from the funds held at [specify] on behalf of the [Consortium] unless the payment has been disclosed to the Board in advance and approved as within the agreed [Budget].

P.254

The [Consortium] agree that the [Finance/Managing] Director of [specify] shall monitor and report on and make payments required to third parties on behalf of the [Consortium] from [date] until [date] from the funds held by [specify] provided that he/she shall not be entitled to authorise payments in excess of [number/currency] in total.

PENALTY

General Business and Commercial

P.255
The parties agree and undertake to mitigate any losses, damages and/or other consequences that they may suffer and agree and undertake that neither party shall seek to claim more than [figure/currency] in total including legal costs for any breach of this Agreement from the other at any time.

P.256
Both parties agree and undertake to quantify the loss and/or damage they may suffer for the non-performance of the other of this Agreement. The [Company] shall be limited to a single claim in total of [figure/currency] or less for Non-Delivery of the [Work/Products]. The [Supplier] shall be limited to a single claim of [figure/currency] or less for non-payment for the [Work/Products].

P.257
In the event that the [Distributor] commits a fundamental breach of this Agreement and fails to [specify] then a penalty of [figure/currency] shall be paid to the [Company] within [specify period]. If the penalty is not paid then the [Company] shall have the right to terminate the Agreement by notice in writing with immediate effect and shall no longer be liable to the [Distributor] under the Agreement and shall be entitled to a reversion of all rights, return of all material and repayment of all sums paid under this Agreement within [specify period]. If the penalty is not paid within the time limit there shall be no right to make the payment later and remedy the fundamental breach.

P.258
No penalty and/or additional charge will be imposed by the [Company] for a delay of up to [number] days of any payment under this Agreement.

P.259
The [Company] shall charge a daily rate of [number/currency] as a penalty for non-payment of the sum due up to a maximum of [number/currency] in any one calendar month.

PENSION

General Business and Commercial

P.260

The [Executive] shall be eligible to be a member of the [Company's] Pension Scheme upon the terms and conditions from time to time applicable under the Scheme and the [Company's] pension policy. Company contributions in respect of the [Executive] shall at all times be subject to the applicable [Tax Authority/Inland Revenue] limits.

P.261

If the [Executive] chooses not to be member of the [Company's] Pension Scheme the basis upon which the [Company shall contribute to a personal pension taken out by the [Executive] shall be subject to agreement with the [Company]. The contribution by the [Company] shall in any event not be less than [number]% [words] per cent of the [Executives'] Basic Remuneration.

P.262

The [Contributor/Consultant] undertakes to bear the cost of his own pension and pension contributions and agrees that no right and/or interest is acquired by the [Contributor/Consultant] under this Agreement to any pension run, operated and/or administered by the [Company] and/or any associated business.

P.263

There is no pension, life assurance, medical cover and/or other expenses provided under the terms of this Agreement to [Name].

P.264

[Name] agrees and accepts that he/she shall not have any right to a pension from the [Company] unless he/she has been employed by the [Company] for more than [number] months. Thereafter [Name] shall have the right and choice as to whether to join the [Company] pension fund or not and to make such contributions as may be required to acquire the range of benefits.

PERFORMANCE BOND

General Business and Commercial

P.265

The [Guarantor] covenants with the [Employer] and any permitted successors in title and assigns that:

1.1 During the course of this Agreement the [Contractor] shall observe and perform all the terms of this Agreement. If at any time the [Contractor] shall make any default in observing or performing any of the terms of this Agreement the [Guarantor] will be held liable and bear responsibility to the full extent of the terms of the obligations and duties of the [Contractor] for which the [Contractor] is unable or unwilling or otherwise in default.

1.2 The [Guarantor] shall indemnify the [Employer] against all losses, damages, costs and expenses arising or incurred by the [Employer] as a direct result of such default by the [Contractor] in 1.1 which are not remedied.

1.3 The Guarantee shall not be affected by any variation to this Agreement or allowance of time or waiver or compromise, and this Guarantee shall apply to such amendments.

1.4 If at any time during the course of this Agreement the [Contractor] shall enter into liquidation and the liquidator shall disclaim this Agreement, the [Guarantor] shall within [30] days of written notice of such disclaimer assume the full responsibilities, obligations and liabilities of the [Contractor] under this Agreement.

P.266

'Performance Bond' shall mean a written arrangement executed under Deed between the [Contractor] and the [Guarantor], the beneficiary of which is the [Employer], which has the effect of guaranteeing the performance of the terms of this Agreement without any additional payments by the [Employer].

P.267

The [Company] shall procure and be responsible to the [Contractor] for the performance and observance by the sub-licensee or sub-contractor of the terms and undertakings contained in such sub-licence or sub-contract and on its part to be observed and performed.

P.268

The [Contractor] shall at the [Contractor's] sole cost provide the [Purchaser] with a bond or guarantee for the performance of the Contract by a reputable and established insurance company, bank or verifiable individual in [country]. The bond shall be provided within [number day of [the date of this Agreement] and shall contain the following minimum conditions:

1.1 Amount of the bond [figure/currency].

1.2 Period for which it is in force from [date] to [date] or subject to completion of [specify], whichever is the earlier.

1.3 Procedure for inspection.

1.4 Arrangements for release of bond.

1.5 In the event that the bond is not in place by [date] then the [Purchaser] shall have the right to bring the contract to an end and shall be repaid all sums that the [Purchaser] has paid under this Agreement.

P.269

Notwithstanding inspection, the [Contractor] shall at its sole cost guarantee for [one year] from the date of acceptance of the [Goods] by the [Customer] to replace and repair the [Goods]. If any [Goods] are found to be defective, then a further guarantee period of [one year] shall run from the date the repair [Goods] or a suitable replacement are returned to the [Customer]. The [Contractor] shall not be liable where any [Goods] were used in a manner other than for their intended purpose, or repairs or charges have been carried out without the consent of the [Contractor] by the [Purchaser].

P.270

There are no additional guarantees, performance bonds and/or other undertakings provided by the [Company] to the [Customer] except those required by law in [country]. Where additional provision is required then the [Customer] will have to pay an additional sum for insurance protection and/or other policy and/or scheme with a third party.

PERFORMERS

General Business and Commercial

P.271

'Performers' shall mean actors, singers, musicians, dancers, mime artistes and other persons who act, sing, deliver, play in or otherwise perform literary or artistic works.

P.272

'Performances' shall include acting, mime, dance, speech, singing, playing a musical instrument or conducting, either alone or with other persons.

P.273

'Performance' shall [be defined in accordance the Copyright, Designs and Patents Act 1988 as amended] mean:

1.1   A dramatic performance (which includes dance and mime).

1.2   A musical performance.

1.3   A reading or recitation of a literary work; or

1.4   A performance of a variety act or any similar presentation which is or so far as it is a live performance given by one or more individuals.

P.274

1.1   [Name] agrees to read his/her poetry from [specify title] at [location] on [date] as a free event for the [Company]. [Name] agrees that no fee shall be due and/or paid to [Name].

1.2   [Name] agrees that the [Company] may take photographs and film the performance and event for the purpose of marketing and promotion in newspapers, magazines and to post on sites on the internet. Provided that a link and credit is provided to [specify].

1.3   The [Company] agrees to display the [specify title] in the front window at [location] for [one] week between [date and [date].

1.4   The [Company] agrees that it shall not have any authority to authorise and/or to reproduce extracts of the [specify title] in any marketing and promotional material without the prior approval and consent of [Name].

P.275

'The Recitals' shall mean the musical performance by [Name] playing the [instrument] at [location] on [dates] with the music by the composers set out in Appendix 1 which forms part of this Agreement as part of the [specify] season by the [Company].

PHONOGRAM

General Business and Commercial

P.276
'Phonogram' shall mean any exclusively aural fixation of sounds of a performance or of other sounds.

PIRATED GOODS

General Business and Commercial

P.277
'Pirated Goods' shall mean goods which are or contain copies of protected works, performances or designs made without the consent of the holder of the copyright or related rights or of the owner or holder of a design right whether registered under national law or not, or of a person duly authorised by him/her in the country of production in cases where the making of those copies would have amounted to an infringement of the right in question under Community Law or the Law of the Member State in which the application for action by the Customs authorities is made.

P.278
'Illicit recording' in relation to a performance [shall be defined in accordance with the Copyright, Designs and Patents Act 1988 as amended] shall mean that for the purpose of a performer's rights, a recording of the whole or any substantial part of a performance of his/her is an illicit recording if it is made otherwise than for private purposes without his/her consent. For the purposes of the rights of a person having recording rights a recording of the whole or any substantial part of a performance subject to the exclusive recording contract is an illicit recording if it is made otherwise than for private purposes without his/her consent or that of the performer.

PODCAST

General Business and Commercial

P.279
'The Podcast' shall mean the final edited version of the film and sound recording of the [Contributors' Work] produced and developed by the [Company] and/or an authorised third party engaged by the [Company] for that purpose.

P.280
'The Contributors' Work' shall mean the audiovisual interview with the Contributor on the subject of [specify in detail] which shall be filmed, recorded and edited for a Podcast by the [Company] and/or an authorised third party. A summary of which is attached to and forms part of this Agreement in Appendix [–].

P.281
The [Company] agrees to engage the non-exclusive services of the Contributor for the purpose of conducting, recording, filming and editing an interview with the Contributor for the Contributors Work.

P.282
In consideration of the Contributors Work and the rights assigned in this Agreement to the [Company]. The [Company] agrees to pay the [Contributor] the [Contributors' Fee] as follows:

1.1   [figure/currency] upon full signature of this Agreement by both parties.

1.2   [figure/currency] subject to the completion of all the [Contributors' Work].

P.283
The [Company agrees and undertakes that it makes the arrangements, films, records and edits the interview of the [Contributor] at its own risk and cost. That the [Contributor] shall not be liable for any such costs. That no indemnity is provided by the [Contributor] to the [Company] in respect of any claim, liabilities, demands, actions, costs, damages and/or losses arising out of any breach by the [Contributor] of any part of this Agreement. The total liability of the [Contributor] if any shall be limited to [figure/currency].

P.284
In consideration of the [Contributors'] Fee the [Contributor] assigns to the [Company] all copyright, intellectual property rights and any other rights in

the product of the [Contributors' Work] and the product of the [Contributors] services and the Podcast to the [Company] in all medium and all media whether in existence now and/or created in the future for the full period of copyright and any other rights and any extensions and renewals and in perpetuity throughout the world and universe. This shall include the right to transmit, broadcast, display, licence, supply, distribute and/or exploit the [Contributors' Work] and/or the Podcast and/or any parts on the internet, television, radio, in print, mobiles and/or as any form of electronic dissemination.

P.285

The [Company] and/or any third party shall be entitled to develop, adapt, amend, alter and/or add to the [Contributors' Work] and/or the product of his/her services and/or the Podcast provided that the original material is still credited to the [Contributor] in the following manner [specify]. In addition the changes must not result in the [Contributor] being associated with material which is obscene, illegal, offensive, and/or is otherwise likely to impugn and/or damage the reputation of the [Contributor]. In such event the [Contributor] shall be entitled to have all the original material removed from such new work.

P.286

1.1 In consideration of the payment of a fee of [number/currency] for each webinar delivered to the [Company] by [Name]. [Name] agrees to appear and perform as sole presenter and to write the content for a series of short webinars to be transmitted and displayed on a website to be set up by the [Company] for the [Work] and/or on the main [Company] website [specify].

1.2 The [Company] agrees to pay the fees due for each webinar in 1.1 within [seven] days of completion of each webinar by [Name] and delivery of the material to the [Company].

1.3 The [Company] agrees that it shall not edit, adapt and/or vary the content of any webinar without prior approval and consultation with [Name]. That where [Name] objects to any changes and the parties cannot agree that the webinar shall not be transmitted and/or displayed.

1.4 It is agreed that the purpose of the webinars in the marketing and promotion of the [Work] and the [Company] has no authority to sub-licence the webinars and/or to sell them as part an educational and/or commercial service to a third party at any time.

1.5 That in the event that the [Company] ceases to sell, promote and/or supply the [Work] that the [Company] shall remove and delete the webinars at the request of [Name].

1.6　It is agreed between the parties that where [Name] has written and filmed the webinars that all copyright and intellectual property rights and any other rights and interest in the webinars shall belong to [Name].

POLICIES

General Business and Commercial

P.287

This [title] Policy is for guidance only and is a summary of the existing legislation which relates to [subject]. All persons at the [Company] are expected to adhere to the Policy. Any issues which arise relating to the Policy should be raised with [Name] who is [specify].

P.288

The following Policies [Health and Safety/Data Protection/ Freedom of Information/Child Protection Policy/Equality/Energy Conservation/Travel and Parking/Expenses/Recycling/Internet and Emails/Telephone and Mobiles/ Drugs/Alcohol/Complaints/other] have been issued by the Board of Directors of the [Company] for the purpose of following existing legislation and/or to provide a clear and coherent procedure and acceptable practice across the [Company] to all officers and staff.

P.289

The officer for the [subject] Policy is [Name] who will advise any member of staff on any questions that may arise from the Policy in the future. No other person in the [Company] is entitled to deal with, contact, advise, and/or report on any matter arising from the content and/or fulfilment of the Policy with any third party. All queries from the media and/or the public should be directed to [Name].

P.290

Where a person is reported for a breach and/or failure to adhere to any Policy of the [Company] for any reason. Then the person against whom the allegation has been made shall be provided with an opportunity to explain the matter to the relevant nominated officer of that Policy. The person may be required to follow a further training programme of the Policy, but any breach shall not be deemed a breach of their contract with the [Company] unless they are shown to have acted ultra vires of their authority and position at the [Company] and/or caused significant loss and/or damage to the [Company].

P.291

The Policies specified in Schedule [–] [List title of all Policies and attach actual Policy] are attached to and form part of this Agreement. The [Name] agrees and undertakes to adhere to the procedures and/or conditions set out in the Policies during the Term of this Agreement at the [Company].

P.292

The [Company] agrees that the [Staff handbook] and the [Policies] of the [Company] are for guidance only and may be changed without notice to [Name]. The [Company] agrees that any breach by [Name] of the [Staff Handbook] and/or [Policies] shall not be a breach of this Agreement and/or deemed a disciplinary offence and/or the subject of any other internal inquiry and/or investigation. All such matters shall be dealt between [Name] and [specify].

P.293

This Agreement shall not include any policies, company handbook and/or any other guidelines that the [Company] shall issue to its staff and/or otherwise. It is specifically agreed that all such documents shall not apply to [Name] and are excluded from the terms of this Agreement. That any such document may only be added to this Agreement by an amendment document referring to the additional material which is signed by both parties.

P.294

1.1 This Licence reference number [–] has been awarded to the [Company] by the [Organisation] on [date] and continues for a period of [number] years.

1.2 During that period of the Licence the [Company] shall be subject to all the policies, guidelines and Codes of conduct which may be issued by the [Organisation] whether in existence at the time the Licence is awarded and/or created and/or developed at any time thereafter either by the [Organisation] and/or any other body and/or institute which takes over the governance and control of the [specify] market in [country].

1.3 It is a requirement of this Licence that the [Company] at all times adheres to all matters in 1.2 and the laws of [country]. Failure to do so may result in the suspension, withdrawal, amendment and/or termination of the Licence by the [Organisation].

POWER OF ATTORNEY

General Business and Commercial

P.295

This Power of Attorney given on this [–] day of [–] 20 [–] by me [Name] of [address] witnessed by [Name of witness] as follows:

1.1   I appoint [Name] of [address] to be my attorney for the purposes of the [Trustees Act 1925 as amended and/or the Mental Capacity Act 2005 as amended [and the Code of Practice/other] with authority to execute or exercise on my behalf all the trust, powers and discretions vested in me as [Trustee of the Trust] created by the [Will/Deed] dated the [–] day of [–] 20 [–].

1.2   This Power of Attorney shall operate from the [date] and shall continue until a written notice of replacement is served.

1.3   I hereby confirm that I have given notice of this Power of Attorney to my co-Trustees.

1.4   This Power of Attorney is executed and delivered as a Deed.

IN WITNESS WHEREOF I have hereunto set my hand this [–] day of [–] 20 [–].

Signed by the Donor [–]

Witnessed by [title and name] of [address]

whose date of birth [date] and occupation is [specify title and work address].

P.296

BY THIS POWER OF ATTORNEY

I [Name] of [address] being a Director, Employee or person who works full time for the [Company]

HEREBY APPOINT [Name] of [address]

to be my Attorney and in my name or otherwise and on my behalf and as my act and deed to apply for the aggregate of [Number] Ordinary Shares of [–] each in the [Company] pursuant to the Prospectus dated [–].

AND I HEREBY undertake to ratify everything which the Attorney shall do or purport to do by virtue of this Power of Attorney. IN WITNESS whereof I set my hand and seal the [–] day of [–] 20 [–].

Signed, sealed and delivered by [–]

In the presence of [name/signature]

P.297

The [Company] shall deliver to the [Licensee] a Power of Attorney in favour of the [Licensee] duly executed either by the author of the copyright of the [Film] or his/her exclusive licensee appointing the [Licensee] his/her Attorney. The [Licensee] shall be entitled by the Power of Attorney to institute, prosecute and defend legal proceedings and to do such acts as may be advisable to protect the rights granted by the Licence Agreement and for the recovery of costs, losses, damages and penalties. The [Licensee] agrees to provide an indemnity to the [Company] against any costs and expenses in respect of such legal proceedings that the [Company] may incur as a result of any legal action.

P.298

DATED [–]

PARTIES:

[Name] of [address] ('the Copyright Owner')

[Name] of [address] ('the Company')

1.1 The [Copyright Owner] hereby appoints the [Company] to be its attorney and in its name on its behalf and as its acts and deed to institute, prosecute and defend such proceedings and do all such acts as the [Company] may consider advisable to protect the rights granted to the [Company] pursuant to the Agreement dated [–] with and made between [–] and [–].

1.2 The [Copyright Owner] hereby undertakes to ratify everything which the [Company] shall do or purport to do in pursuit of this Deed and declares that this appointment shall have effect as a power coupled with an interest and shall be irrevocable.

1.3 This Deed shall be governed and interpreted in accordance with [English/other] Law and any dispute arising hereunder shall be referred to the [High Court of Justice in England/other].

IN WITNESS whereof the Copyright Owner has caused its Common Seal to be applied hereto on the date set out above.

The Common Seal of the [Copyright Owner] affixed in the presence of:

DIRECTOR [–] of the [Copyright Owner]

COMPANY SECRETARY [–] of the [Copyright Owner]

P.299

The [Company] shall deliver to the [Distributor] a power of attorney in favour of the [Distributor] duly executed either by the copyright owner and/or the exclusive licensee of the [Work]. The power of attorney shall appoint the [Distributor] to institute, prosecute and defend proceedings and to do such acts as the [Distributor] may consider advisable to protect the rights granted by the Licence Agreement.

P.300
Each [Partner] undertakes to execute on becoming a partner, a power of attorney in a form approved by the [Board] appointing the Senior Partner as his/her attorney to execute on his/her behalf such documents as are required to be executed by him/her as relate to the ordinary course of the firms business from time to time.

P.301
[Name] of [address] being of sound mind [and not subject to any incapacity, disability and/or a mental health order which would restrict their ability to reach this decision] wishes to appoint [specify] of [address] to manage and deal with their legal, financial, medical and other affairs and to act in [Names'] best interest and on their behalf including their freehold house at [address] and bank account at [location] held in the name of [specify] and private pension held at [specify] and state pension [reference] and all other sums held and/or received from any source. That [Name] has and/or will execute a power of attorney to [specify] in the form attached to this document in Schedule [–].

PREAMBLE

General Business and Commercial

P.302
WHEREAS:

The [Employer] is entitled to the exclusive services of the [Director] and to make available such services and to grant and assign all rights in the products thereof to others so far as is necessary for the purposes of this Agreement.

P.303
WHEREBY:

1.1 [The Author] owns and controls all copyright and all other intellectual property rights in the [Work] which is intended to be adapted for television.

1.2 [The Production Company] wishes to procure a commission from a [Commissioning Television Company] the Network Centre to produce the [Programme].

1.3 Subject to [The Production Company] securing a commission to produce the [Programme] from a [The Production Company] the parties hereto have agreed to co-produce the [Programme] on the terms and conditions set out herein.

P.304
WHEREAS:

The [Company] intends (but does not undertake) to make the proposed [Film] more specifically described in the Special Conditions. In order so to do the [Company] wishes to retain the services of the [Name] as Director.

P.305
WHEREBY IT IS AGREED THAT:

Upon the terms and conditions attached hereto and in consideration of the Licence Fee hereinafter appearing the [Licensor] hereby grants to the [Licensee] the exclusive rights specified in Schedule A in the [Film] throughout the Territory.

P.306
The [Licensor] is the owner of the Copyright and Technical Information and has the sole and exclusive right to make the [Product] in the Territory.

The [Licensee] wishes to receive and the [Licensor] is willing to grant a Licence in the Territory on the terms and conditions set out in this Agreement to use the Copyright and Technical Information in order to manufacture, use and sell the [Product].

P.307
WHEREBY it is mutually agreed as follows concerning the [Work] provisionally entitled [–] (hereinafter called The Work), that the [Authors] undertake to write, compile or edit this [Work] and to provide necessary copy ready for printing written by the [Authors] in accordance with the terms of this Agreement.

P.308
The [Lender] warrants that the facts set out in the preamble are correct and that neither the [Lender] nor the [Presenter] has or will enter into any commitment with any third party which might in any way detract from the rights granted in this Agreement or the [Presenter's] ability to perform the services set out herein.

P.309

1.1 The [Designer] has experience in developing, designing and creating websites for marketing, promotional and commercial purposes.

1.2 The [Company] wishes to engage the services of the [Designer] to develop, design, create and deliver a fully functional website suitable for the [Company's] business.

P.310

1.1 The [Institute] is creating a website and wishes to engage the freelance services of the [Contributor] to assist in the construction of the website.

1.2 The [Contributor] has experience and expertise in website design, development and software and agrees to provide his services to the [Institute] to assist in the construction of the [Institutes'] new website.

P.311

1.1 The [Illustrator] and the [Author] intend to enter into a publishing agreement with [Publisher] concerning a series of books provisionally entitled [title] ['the Work/Books'].

1.2 The [Illustrator] and the [Author] wish to enter into an agreement to clarify their legal positions and to agree the ownership of the material and the allocation of royalties in respect of the exploitation of the [Work/Books] and any future sequels, adaptations, licences and merchandising in any media and/or format at any time throughout the [world/universe].

P.312

1.1 The [Distributor] wishes to acquire for valuable consideration such rights, obligations, liabilities, and benefits as exist between the [Publisher] and [Author] under the written agreement dated [date].

1.2 The [Publisher] wishes to be released from the agreement with the full knowledge and consent of the [Author] from such rights, obligations, liabilities, and benefits as exist between the [Author] and the [Publisher].

1.3 The [Author] wishes to release the [Publisher] from such rights, obligations, liabilities, and benefits as exist between the [Author] and the [Publisher] and for the [Publisher] to assign all such rights, obligations, liabilities, and benefits to the [Distributor].

P.313

Whereas the [Employee] was employed by the [Company] on a full-time basis under a contract of employment dated [date] ('the Employment

Contract'). The [Employee's] employment came to an end at [time] [date] ('the Termination Date') by reason of redundancy.

P.314

1.1   The Purchaser and the Seller (collectively 'the parties') entered into a [Heads of Agreement/Memorandum of Understanding] dated [date] for the sale and purchase of the Assets of the Seller.

1.2   The Seller wishes to sell a specific publishing list, existing stock and current work in progress as specified in this Agreement.

1.3   The Purchaser wishes to purchase and the Seller wishes to sell the Purchaser the Assets on the terms and conditions as agreed and defined below [specify].

P.315

[Name] and the [Company] wish to enter into an agreement for the commissioning and creation of a new website and app for the [Company] based on the description and summary for the [Project] set out in Schedule [–] which forms part of the terms of this Agreement.

PREMISES

General Business and Commercial

P.316

'The Premises' shall [include/exclude] any boarding house, hotel, inn, tavern, guest house and lodging house.

P.317

'The Work Premises' shall mean all offices, studios and locations owned or controlled by the [Company].

P.318

'Premises' shall be construed to include land, buildings, fixed or moveable structures, vehicles, vessels, aircraft and hovercraft.

P.319

'The Proprietor' is the following owner of the Venue [Name/Company] whose registered office is at [address] and whose [main place of business/trades at] [address].

P.320

The [Company] confirms and undertakes that it shall be responsible for and bear the total cost of the organisation and staging of the [Event/other] at the premises in accordance with the [Event/other] Schedule.

P.321

1.1 The [Association] confirms and undertakes that it has or will enter into a bona fide written agreement for the use of the premises with the Proprietor and that all administrative, safety, health, security and financial arrangements necessary for the smooth running of the [Event/Festival], including the hiring of the Premises, health and safety, the police, fire regulations, planning, licensing and music permission, consents and compliance, and any other statutory and local authority consents, regulations and/or requirements have been or will be arranged.

1.2 That a copy of any documents relating to the above matters will be provided at no charge to the [Sponsor] upon request. That the [Sponsor] shall have the right to appoint any third party to carry out inspections of the premises and documents to ensure compliance under this Agreement.

P.322

'The Premises' shall be the house, outbuildings, land, access roads, electricity, gas, water, drainage and sewage arrangements and facilities specified on the attached map in Schedule [–] which is attached to and forms part of this Agreement.

P.323

[Name] shall not be responsible for all the charges and costs associated with the premises for the [dates] except: hospitality, WiFi and internet, parking, housekeeping and cleaning, repairs, replacement of items lost and/or damaged. An itemised statement shall be provided within [number] days and the sum recouped from the advance deposit.

PREMIUM RATE PHONE LINES

General Business and Commercial

P.324

The Competition starts on [date] and ends on [date]. All entries must be received by time on [date]. All entries received and/or made after that time shall not be eligible to be entered in the Competition and shall be disqualified. There may be a charge incurred even though the entry is not accepted as valid. [There is no entry cost to the competition/The entry cost to the Competition is [figure/currency.] All cost which you may incur in entering the Competition are your personal responsibility. There are no refunds for any entries which are disqualified and/or received after the deadline.

P.325

Telephone entries by telephone may be by landline, mobile and/or the internet by telephone call to [number]. Then follow the instructions provided which shall be in the [specify] language. Speak clearly and leave your personal details that are requested and the answer. Failure to follow the instructions accurately may result in your disqualification from the Competition. [There is no limit to the number of entries you may make to the Competition/only [number] calls will be eligible from each telephone number.]

P.326

All entries must be completed by the deadline. Calls from mobiles and/or other networks and/or by any other method may be charged at a higher rate than landlines. All persons who enter must be age [number] and over by [date] and you must obtain the permission of the person in whose name the telephone and/or mobile is held and/or pays the bill. No acknowledgement of entry shall be provided by the [Company].

P.327

All entries by text shall be to [telephone number]. All entries by text shall receive a text confirming entry. The [Company] shall not be liable for any texts not received for any reason and/or any interruption, suspension, fault and/or delay in the service which may cause the entrants text not to be delivered, delayed and/or to contain errors.

P.328

No responsibility and/or liability shall be accepted by the [Company] for any entries which are disqualified as a result of being inaudible, incomplete, delayed, abusive, and/or otherwise not acceptable.

P.329

No responsibility and/or liability shall be accepted by the [Company] for any costs, charges and/or other expenses incurred by any person who enters the Competition at any time.

P.330

It is a condition of entry that you agree to assign all the copyright, intellectual property rights and all rights in all media in your [Answer/Competition Entry] to the [Company]. You agree to complete and sign such a document if so requested to do so by the [Company].

P.331
This is a commercial service and calls to this premium rate line [specify] are charged by the [Company] at [number/currency] for every minute. Less than a minute is charged as a full minute. No refunds are provided where this service is used by mistake and a competition has ended and/or by any person under [age] and/or otherwise. The complaints procedure can be used on [specify].

PRIVACY

General Business and Commercial

P.332
The [Photographer] hereby acknowledges that the [photographs/images/computer generated material] have been commissioned for private and domestic purposes and the [Commissioning Party] has therefore a right to privacy [within the Copyright, Designs and Patents Act 1988 as amended].

P.333
It is hereby agreed that the use of the [Photographs] shall be used solely for the purposes defined under Clause [–] to the Agreement and the [Photographer] shall not be entitled to use the negatives, prints, computer generated material or any other copies in any format nor to authorise or provide any material to any third party for any other purpose without the prior written consent of the [Commissioning Party].

P.334
[Name] confirms that the [Photographs/Film] was not taken pursuant to a private commissioning arrangement with any third party and that the publication of the [Photographs/Film] will not infringe the privacy rights of any third party [under the Copyright, Designs and Patents Act 1988 as amended].

P.335
'Privacy' shall mean the right to privacy in relation to the [Photographs and Films] and shall be defined [in accordance the Copyright, Designs and Patents Act 1988 as amended] that where a person who for private and

domestic purposes commissions the taking of a photograph or the making of a film where copyright subsists in the resulting work, that person shall have the right not to have copies of the work issued to the public; the work exhibited or shown in public; or the work broadcast or included in a cable programme service.

P.336

[Name] and [person] agree that the following terms and conditions shall apply to the [Event/Ceremony]:

1.1   That this is a private [Event/Ceremony] which is by invitation only and not open to the public.

1.2   That everyone involved in the [Event/Ceremony] has been informed or provided written consent that they agree that they are only permitted to attend and/or contribute to and/or participate on the condition that they are not entitled to take any recordings, sound recordings, photographs, images, films whether using a camera, mobile phone or any other gadget or method in any format for any reason and undertakes not to bring any equipment or devices for that purpose.

1.3   That they will advise the [Name] immediately of any knowledge of an intended or actual breach of the requirement by others of 1.1 and/or 1.2.

1.4   That they recognise that the only published material of the [Event/Ceremony] will or may be that authorised by [Name]. That they shall not be entitled to any fee and/or payment of any nature for such exploitation or use at any time.

1.5   That they agree not to bring and/or use a mobile phone and/or other recording device and/or gadget and shall not attempt to film, record and/or take any pictures of the [Event/Ceremony].

1.6   That they shall not release and/or distribute and/or make available to the public and/or the media and private arrangements and/or details of the [Event/Ceremony] and/or any company and/or business who has been engaged to provide their services.

P.337

This is the stated privacy policy of this [Website/business] which is provided by [Company]:

1.1   Your personal details, name, address, age, employment, occupation, nationality, email, telephone, internet access dialling code, access codes, bank account, credit card, charge are accepted by us as your private information and data.

1.2 These details in 1.1 will only be transferred and used by us for the express purpose stated on the [Website].

1.3 Any transfer of information and/or details to third parties will require your prior consent by responding to a request on this [Website]. This shall not apply where the [Company] is required by Court Order under criminal or civil proceedings to provide such information and data to a Court of Law for any reason.

1.4 We shall have the right to extract information and data which does not release private and personal details which provides generic and statistical analysis and shall have the right to provide such marketing and promotional material to third parties without any further consent from you. This shall include type of usage of site, number and type of purchases, method of payment, age group, financial category, ethnic origins and any other materials which does not reveal your specific details.

1.5 Information and data is constantly collected on this [website] by the use of 'cookies' and other mechanisms which is then stored, analysed and reproduced in different formats. If you do not wish to have this system applied when you are using the [website] then follow the following steps [–].

1.6 Where you provide updated, altered, amended or varied information and data then we will try but cannot undertake that it will be changed as requested. The previous details may however still be kept on file in the system either through error, historical records or otherwise.

1.7 We cannot ensure that a third party will not unlawfully access private details, and we advise you to take all the precautions we suggest and do not permit others access to your codes.

1.8 Neither indemnity nor acceptance of liability of any nature is provided to you and you accept the inherent risks of using this [Website].

1.9 In the event that there are any legal proceedings then the jurisdiction shall be at the discretion of the [Company].

P.338

The [Company] agree to be bound by any prevailing law, judgement, directive, regulation and/or statutory instrument that imposes on the [Company] restrictions regarding the use in any manner of confidential information supplied to the [Company] by the [Client]. This shall include credit and debit card details, bank details, username, passwords and any other personal and financial details [which are not in the public domain].

P.339

The [Company] reserves the right to trade, supply and/or disclose with any third party details relating to the date of purchase, the nature of the [Product/Service] purchased, the method of payment and the cost.

P.340

The use of and access to this [Website] is conditional on your agreement to the use of cookies to be stored on your web browser that enables the [Company] to monitor your movements and provide restricted and limited data as to the use of the [Website]. If you wish to check the details held by the [Company] are accurate then contact [email address]. To remove the cookies please complete the following steps [detail process].

P.341

Any emails on laptops, computers and gadgets, telephone calls on mobiles, landlines and/or otherwise which are owned and/or controlled by the [Company] shall be monitored and shall not be private and/or confidential.

P.342

The [Company] shall not be in breach of any clauses relating to confidentiality, privacy and/or data protection where disclosure is made as a result of an order of a court, tribunal and/or as a result of any civil and/or criminal proceedings.

P.343

After the expiry and/or termination of this Agreement neither party shall disclose any information, financial details, reports, business plans and/or discussions to any third party which are not in the public domain and were provided in confidence and/or in a private meeting.

P.344

The [medical/health/financial] report to be provided by [Name] shall only be disclosed and copied to the following persons [specify] for [specify period]. The [Company] agrees to ensure that such persons provide an undertaking not to disclose the information in the report to any third party and that they return all copies which shall then be destroyed.

P.345

[Name] agrees and undertakes that he/she shall not at any time whether during the term of this Agreement and/or thereafter for a period of [number] months:

1.1 Take any images and/or film on their mobile phone, camera and/or any other gadget and device while at the [location] of any person, object, room and/or view and/or any other material and/or matter in respect of the [Project].

1286

1.2 Make any recording and/or allow another person to listen to a conversation and/or discussion at the [location] and/or any other matter in respect of the [Project].

1.3 Enter into any arrangement with a third party to be supplied news, images and/or any other material relating to [location] and/or any other matter in respect of the [Project].

1.4 Provide details of conversations, discussions and exchanges with [specify] to any media including radio, television, websites, magazines and/or newspapers and/or post any comments and/or criticism and/or complaint on any part of the internet and/over any telecommunication system by text, image and/or otherwise.

PROBATIONARY PERIOD

General Business and Commercial

P.346
The first [three months] of the [Employee's] service will be a probationary period. During this period, either party may terminate the contract by giving [one week's] notice in writing to the other.

P.347
The [Company] agrees that the period from [date] to [date] inclusive shall be treated as a trial period during which the [Licensee] shall have the right to terminate this Agreement, if the [Product Package] does not meet reasonable operational requirements.

P.348
The [Employee] acknowledges that throughout the probationary period the [Company] shall be entitled to terminate this contact with [one week's] notice or [one week's] pay in lieu.

P.349
'The Probationary Period' shall commence from the date of this Agreement and shall continue for a period of [three/six] months thereafter.

P.350
The [Consultant] shall be required to complete an initial [number] months probationary period which ends on [date]. In the event that the

[Company] decides during the probationary period that it does not wish to continue to use the services of the [Consultant] then there shall be no obligation for the [Company] to extend the engagement of the services of the [Consultant] and/or to enter into an extended contract for his/her services after [date].

P.351

It is agreed between the parties that there is no probationary and/or other periods during which the suitability of [Name] for the role of [specify] are to be assessed and reviewed.

PRODUCT

General Business and Commercial

P.352

'Product' shall mean any industrial or handicraft item including parts intended to be assembled into a complete item, sets or compositions of items, packaging, get-ups, graphic symbols and typographic typefaces but excluding a computer programme or semi-conductor products.

P.353

'The Product' shall be the subject-matter of the advertising copy which is briefly described as follows [–].

P.354

'The Sponsor's Product' shall be the following [Item/Goods/Services] [–].

P.355

'The Company's Products' shall mean the products and services of the 'Company' including instructions, labels, packaging, trade or service marks, designs, logos and any associated words and slogans which are briefly described as follows [–]. A two-dimensional copy of the Company's Products is attached to and forms part of this Agreement.

P.356

'The Licensee's Product' shall be the following product which is produced, manufactured and distributed by or on behalf of the [Licensee] [–]. A two-dimensional copy of the Licensee's Product is attached to and forms part of this Agreement in Appendix [–].

P.357

'The Company's Products' shall mean the products and services of the [Company] which are briefly described as follows:

A two-dimensional copy of the Company's Products is attached and forms part of this Agreement in Schedule [–] setting out all intellectual property rights, patents, contractual and moral right obligations, consents, releases obtained paid for and/or due and the relevance to the products including copyright, trade marks, service marks, logos, designs, slogans, text, artwork, title, recordings, films, scripts, text, images, artwork, music, photographs, computer generated material and artists and any other persons.

P.358

'Product Specification' shall mean the detailed technical, commercial and marketing requirements of the [Company] in respect of the [Website] as set out in attached Schedule [–] which is attached to and forms part of this Agreement.

P.359

'The Products' shall mean [Title/ISBN/author].

P.360

'The Product' shall be the computer software and fully functional material for an [App] to be created, developed and delivered by [Name] based on the idea and concept supplied by the [Company] described in Appendix [–] and as adapted through the process of development, tests and production. The products shall include all stages of the process of development including draft drawings, computer generated material, artwork, images, text, sound recordings, film, music, passwords and codes and access data and any material of any nature in any format and/or medium.

PRODUCT LIABILITY

General Business and Commercial

P.361

1.1　The [Licensor] confirms that the [Product] conforms with all legislation, byelaws, product liability, regulations, statutory instruments and EU Council Directives relating to product liability including but not limited to, the [EU Council Directive 85/374] and any amendments, variations and modifications thereof.

1.2　The [Licensor] confirms that a fully comprehensive insurance policy is and will remain in force with respect to any claims, actions, demands, suits, proceedings (whether civil or criminal) with respect to all product liability throughout the Territory until [date].

P.362
The [Licensee] undertakes that it will ensure that all the [Licensed Articles] comply in all respect with statutes, legislation, directives, guidelines, standards, practices or otherwise imposed or set out by any governmental or other competent authority from time to time in the Territory. The [Licensee] undertakes to the [Licensor] that all the [Licensed Articles] are and will be safe for use by the public and in particular suitable for children.

P.363
[The Licensee] agrees that prior to the sale of the [Licensed Articles] it will produce at its own expense satisfactory insurance on behalf of the [Licensee] and the [Licensor] in respect of liability to the public and in respect of the exploitation of the [Licensed Articles]. The extent of such insurance shall be at the discretion of the [Licensee] but in any event shall not be less than [figure/currency] for any one claim. The [Licensee] shall ensure that the interest of the [Licensor] is endorsed on the policy and at the request of the [Licensor] shall produce a copy of the policy and evidence of payments of the premiums.

P.364
The [Company] shall at all material times be covered by a comprehensive product liability insurance policy until [date]. That the [Company's] Product and all other products owned or controlled by the [Company] shall be safe and fit for their intended use and comply with all necessary [legislation/ statutes/codes/regulations/directives] in respect of the [material/components/ packaging/electrical components/instructions/safety/health/children] that [may be in force at the time/are in existence now/at any time].

P.365
The [Agent] agrees to ensure that all third parties to be licensed by the [Licensor] under this Agreement shall undertake that all the [Licensed Articles] and any associated packaging, advertising and promotional material shall be safe for their intended use and shall comply with all statutes, regulations, directives, standards and any other relevant legislation or guidelines in force at any time in the individual Member States of the Territory. In any event comprehensive public liability insurance cover for the benefit of the [Licensor] to cover the legal obligations of the [Licensor] and any acts, omissions and/or errors by any licensee shall be in existence with a reputable company and underwriter and paid for by the [Licensor] of not

less than [figure/currency] for each claim prior to the release to the general public or media of the [Licensed Articles].

P.366

The [Sponsor] undertakes that the [Sponsor's Product] shall be safe for its intended use, namely [specify details of use] and shall comply with all statutes, regulations, directives, codes and any other legislation or guidelines in force in the [specify countries] at any time. The [Sportsperson] shall not be liable at any time in respect of any civil or criminal proceedings that may arise indirectly or directly from the use by the public of [Sponsor's Product].

P.367

The [Sponsor] confirms that a comprehensive public liability insurance policy will be in force during the Sponsorship Period covering any writ, action, claim, or damages, or loss that may arise as a direct or indirect result of the use by the public of the specific product or services being promoted under this Agreement, together with all other products or services owned or controlled by the [Sponsor] which the public could associate with the [Sponsor's Logo] and [Product]. The [Sponsor] shall provide a copy of such policies and evidence of payment of premiums upon request.

P.368

The [Licensee] acknowledges that the [Company] is not competent to determine whether the [Licensed Articles] are safe for sale to the public and any approval by the [Company] shall not detract from the [Licensee's] product liability under this Agreement.

P.369

The [Seller] agrees that the [Product] shall comply and continue to comply with all provisions relating to design, content, material, manufacture, supply, use and packaging of any part of the [Product] relating to any statute, regulation, order, directive or other governing law in force at the time of delivery to the [Seller] in [countries/Europe/world].

P.370

That the [Seller] shall ensure that each [Product] is supplied with suitable packaging and supporting literature which clearly sets out the purpose for which each part of the [Product] is safe and suitable and any safety features or risks and any warnings of potential dangers from use.

P.371

That the [Supplier] agrees that it shall take out adequate insurance for the benefit of itself and the [Seller] in respect of any death, injury, loss, damage or other liability that may occur in respect of the [Product] and any associated material as a result of this Agreement.

P.372

The [Supplier] agrees that a comprehensive public and product liability insurance policy for the benefit of the [parties] is and will be in force covering any claims, actions, damages or loss that may arise as a direct or indirect result of the use by the public of the [Product]. A copy of such policy with evidence of payment of the premiums shall be provided to the [Seller]. Both parties shall be named on the policy, the minimum value per claim shall be [–] and both parties shall share any cost.

P.373

The [Seller] confirms that the selling process and dealings with the public shall conform with any relevant legislation, regulations, directives and standards of conduct in any part of the [Territory].

P.374

The [Company] agrees that all costs, expenses and liability incurred in respect of the development, production, distribution and exploitation of the [Company's] Product and any advertising, promotional events and any other material shall be at the [Company's] sole cost and risk and the [Celebrity] shall not be liable for any such sums.

P.375

The [Company] confirms that there exists comprehensive public and product liability insurance which shall remain in force at all material times covering any claims, actions, demands, loss or damages which may arise as a result of any direct or indirect use by anyone including the public of the [Company's] Product. Such insurance will extend to all other products or services owned or controlled by the [Company] which the public would reasonably associate with the [Company]. The [Company] agrees to provide the [Celebrity] with a copy upon request of the policy and in addition to insure the [Celebrity] in the sum of [–] against any civil or criminal proceedings arising directly or indirectly from this Agreement at any time.

P.376

The [Licensee] agrees that a disclaimer shall appear on the packaging relating to the [Licensor] and that the [Licensed Product] shall be tested by a trial of [–].

P.377

The [Licensee] shall provide copies and details to the [Licensor] of any alleged incidents, faults or consumer complaints of the [Product] at the end of each calendar month.

P.378

The [Licensee] agrees that the approval of samples and/or [Licensed Articles] by the [Licensor] does not detract or waive any duty by the [Licensee] to ensure that the [Product] is safe for its intended purpose and generally. Further that it does not contain any material, chemical or parts which are toxic, dangerous or likely to result in injury or death particularly to children.

P.379

That the [Licensee] shall be solely responsible for any costs, damages or losses from any action, claim, or liability arising from the production, manufacture, sale and distribution of the [Licensed Articles]. In the event that the [Licensor] is joined or sued then the [Licensee] agrees to repay all consequential liability, costs, expenses and losses incurred by the [Licensor].

P.380

The [Licensee] shall ensure that each [Licensed Article] shall conform in all respects to the quality, design, packaging and materials of the [Sample/Prototype] submitted to and approved by the [Licensor]. That the workmanship or materials shall not be defective, of poor quality, contaminated with undeclared substances or unable to be used for the intended purpose without a significant degree of wear and tear at an early stage which result in the loss of attachments which might pose a risk.

P.381

1.1 The [Licensee] agrees that the [Licensor] shall be entitled to approve a sample of the [Licensed Article] and any associated label, attachments, merchandise, leaflets, packaging and marketing material prior to the production, manufacture, supply, distribution and/or marketing.

1.2 The [Licensee] undertakes to provide the each and every sample in the exact form in which it is proposed it should be sold, displayed, and/or distributed to the public.

1.3 The [Licensee] agrees that no production and/or manufacture of the [Licensed Articles] should commence until the prior written approval of each of the samples has been provided by the [Licensor].

P.382

The [Company] agrees that the [Licensor] shall be entitled to approve the appointment of any third party to be used in respect of the production, manufacture, distribution, sale and supply of the [Licensed Articles].

P.383

The [Company] agrees to provide the [Licensor] at the [Company's] cost with not less than [number] units of the [Licensed Articles] in the form in which they are distributed to the general public.

P.384

The [Licensor] agrees to provide written approval or reject the samples and/or the [Licensed] Articles within [specify period] of receipt.

P.385

Where for any reason there is a dispute over product liability under this Agreement. Then the parties agree to refer the matter to an independent person agreed between both parties. Such person must be a member of [specify] and will endeavour to resolve the matter prior to litigation. Each party shall provide written arguments of their case and then be able to make representations.

P.386

1.1 Approval by the sample and/or prototype by the [Distributor] from the [Supplier] shall result in the fact that the [Supplier] shall not be responsible for the content and/or use and/or sale of the [Product] except where it causes injury and/or death.

1.2 The [Distributor] agrees to bear all liability and cost and expenses for any losses and/or damages and/or claims that may arise from the specially commissioned [Product] and shall pay for a insurance policy at the [Distributors] cost to also cover a death and/or serious injury claim against the [Supplier] in 1.1.

P.387

Where any party to this Agreement engages third parties consultants, companies, contractors and/or suppliers. Then that party shall continue to be liable for the third party errors, omissions, delays, insolvency, administration and/or product and/or other content liability to all the other parties under this Agreement and pay for all costs and expenses, losses, damages, claims, actions and/or settlements and legal costs which may arise.

PROXIES

General Business and Commercial

P.388

The instrument appointing a proxy shall be in writing and signed by the [Appointor] or his Attorney duly authorised in writing or if the [Appointor] is a corporation, either duly executed according to law or signed by an Attorney or officer so authorised. The [Company] may, but shall not be bound to, require evidence of the authority of any such Attorney or officer.

P.389

A person appointed to act as proxy need not be a [stockbroker]. The Chairman of the meeting may be designated as a proxy in an instrument of proxy without being named.

P.390

An instrument of proxy may be in the usual common form or in any other form which the [Company] may approve and such proxy shall be deemed to confer the authority to demand or join in demanding a poll.

P.391

An instrument of proxy shall be valid for any adjournment of the meeting to which it relates unless the contrary is stated on it.

P.392

The instrument appointing a proxy and the Power of Attorney under which it is signed or a copy certified by a notary of such Power of Attorney shall be deposited at the [Company's] registered office or at such place as may be specified in the notice convening the meeting or any document accompanying such notice not less than twenty-four hours before the time appointed for holding the meeting or adjourned meeting or for the taking of the poll to which such instrument relates. Any instrument of proxy not deposited shall be invalid.

P.393

An instrument appointing a proxy shall be invalid on the expiration of [twelve months] from the date of execution.

P.394

A vote given in accordance with the terms of an instrument appointing a proxy shall be valid notwithstanding the previous death or insanity of the principal or revocation of the proxy or of the authority under which the proxy is given. Unless notification in writing shall have been received at the registered office of the [Company] prior to the commencement of the meeting or adjourned meeting or the taking of the poll at which the vote is given.

PUBLICITY

General Business and Commercial

P.395

The [Employee] is not permitted to publish any letters, articles, books or other material in any media or format which purport to represent the views of or report how the [Company] conducts its business and the conversations of the [Executives], its business, its products, its personnel or directors without the prior consent in writing of the [Managing Director].

P.396

The [Employee] must not contact or communicate with any member of the press or media or anyone connected with it relating to any matter concerning the business of the [Company] without the prior written consent of [Name].

P.397

The [Licensee] shall not make any statement to the press or any other media concerning any aspect of the [Company] without obtaining permission from the [Company's] press office or the [Managing Director].

P.398

[Name] undertakes that he/she have not and will not during the continuance of this Agreement publish, supply material or act in any way in which publication is likely relating to any matter concerning the internal affairs of the [Company] without the prior written approval of the [Company].

P.399

The [Director] agrees and undertakes that he/she shall not except at the request of the [Company] or with its written consent directly or indirectly authorise, make or provide any statement, photograph, image, email, text and/or information relating to this Agreement and/or the services to be rendered by the [Director] hereunder and/or to the [Film] and/or the affairs of the [Company] to any person in circumstances in which such statement, photograph, image, email, text or information may reasonably be anticipated to be published and/or used in any media.

P.400

No reference is to be made to the terms of this Agreement by either party in any advertising, publicity or promotional material without the prior consent of the other party.

P.401

The [Artist] shall not issue any statement in public or to the media (including the press, radio, television, on the worldwide web or through any telecommunication system) concerning any confidential business or future plans of the [Company].

P.402

The [Group] agrees not to issue any statement to the press during the Term of the Agreement concerning the future plans of the [Group] or the [Manager] without the prior consent of the [Manager].

P.403

The [Artist] agrees that all publicity shall be the sole responsibility of the [Agent] and that the [Artist] shall not issue, release or respond to any request of any third party in the media concerning the personal or professional life of the [Artist] without the prior approval of the [Agent].

P.404

The [Agent] undertakes not to disclose any material or make any statement (whether true or not) concerning the [Artist's] private and social life, political and personal views to the media including newspapers, television, radio, internet or any telecommunication system at any time without the prior written consent of the [Artist].

P.405

The [Artist] agrees not to issue any statement to the media at any time concerning any confidential business or future plans of the [Agent] or details of any negotiations, or the terms of any agreements in progress or concluded by the [Agent] without the prior consent of the [Agent].

P.406

The [Celebrity] agrees not to participate in any dangerous sport, political controversy, take any illegal substances, or act in any manner which could be capable of being a criminal act or other activities which would prejudice the goodwill and reputation of the [Company] and the Company's Products during the Term of the Agreement and generate negative publicity surrounding the engagement of the services of the [Celebrity].

P.407

The [Author] shall not make any statement whether in writing or otherwise to the press or in public to any media concerning the [Film] and/or the business of the [Production Company] without the prior written consent of the [Production Company] whether or not this Agreement has been terminated and/or the [Film] has been completed and/or the [Author] and the [Production Company] are in dispute for any reason.

P.408
The [Writer] undertakes not to disclose any material of any nature nor make any statement whether true or not concerning the private or public life or otherwise of the [Originator] or any third party interviewed or researched for the purposes of the preparation and writing of the [Work] to any third party at any time without the prior written consent of the [Originator] or unless requested to do so by the [Originator] or his [Agent].

P.409
The [Company] shall not without the written approval of the [Television Company] inform any person other than its professional advisers and persons with whom it negotiates the financing of the production of the [Film] about or issue any advertising or publicity in respect of any part of this Agreement.

P.410
The [Company] shall not make any statement to the press or any other media concerning any aspect of the [Licensor] without obtaining permission from the [Licensor's] press office, or its Managing Director.

P.411
[Name] is not permitted to make any arrangement with a third party for the publication, release, distribution or supply of information, data, products or services relating to the [Company] unless prior permission is obtained in writing from [specify position/office]. Failure to comply with this permission may, if the circumstances are considered appropriate, be regarded as gross misconduct for which the [Employee] may be liable to summary dismissal.

P.412
[Name] must not contact, communicate or supply documents, recordings, films or data in any form to any member of the press or media or anyone so connected on behalf of the [Company] unless prior permission has been obtained from [name/position/office].

P.413
The [Agent] undertakes not to disclose any material nor make any statement whether true or not concerning the [Actor's] private and sexual life, politics and personal views to the media at any time without the prior specific approval of the [Artist] in each case.

P.414

1.1 The [Company] agrees that the [Presenter's] name, image, signature and endorsement shall not be used for any purpose other than the marketing of the [Product/Film] unless agreed in advance in each case.

1.2 The [Company] agrees to provide the [Presenter] with the exact samples of all materials in any medium in which it is intended to use material relating to the [Presenter].

1.3 All reasonable requests for changes by the [Presenter] shall be incorporated at the [Company's] cost.

A separate fee shall be paid for each case and shall be negotiated in good faith dependant on the circumstances.

P.415
The [Supplier] agrees and undertakes that it shall not issue and/or make any statement to the media, press and/or trade journals concerning the agreement with the [Company, the products which it supplies and/or any health and safety issue relating to them without first clearing it in advance with the head of the [specify] department of the [Company].

P.416
The [Institute] agrees that in any associated publicity, advertising, promotional material, emails mailshots, and marketing. The [Company's] name, trade mark and image as set out in Schedule [–] shall be given equal prominence and position with the [Institute].

P.417
The [Company] agrees that no other person, company, products, services, information and/or data shall appear in any publicity associated with the [Event] which conflicts with and/or damages the reputation of the [Institute], and/or its products and/or services.

P.418
The [Institute] agrees and undertakes that the product of the [Contributors'] services, and his name, image and support of the [Event/Project] shall not be used for any purpose other than [specify purpose].

P.419
The [Company] agrees and undertakes that the [Work/Material] provided by the [Institute] shall not be used and/or licensed for any purpose except those set out in this Agreement. That the [Company] does not have the right to use any [Work/Material] and/or any part and/or the name, trademark and/

or logo of the [Institute] in any publicity, advertising, brochures, and/or on any website without the prior written approval of the [Institute].

P.420

The [Company] agrees and undertakes that it shall not publish any letters, provide any interviews, issue any statements and/or contact and/or communicate with any person and/or company purporting to represent the views of the [Institute] unless prior consent is provided under this Agreement and/or the prior approval of the [Chief Executive] of the [Institute] has been obtained.

P.421

The [Sub-Licensee] agrees and undertakes not to issue and/or distribute any press release, marketing and/or other promotional material without the prior approval of the [Licensee] of the content of the material.

P.422

The [Sub-Licensee] shall use and adapt the press releases, data, promotional and marketing material supplied by the [Licensee] in respect of the [Film/Work/Disc]. The [Sub-Licensee] shall not have the right to create, develop and reproduce other material based on the [Film/Work/Disc] for the purpose of marketing and exploiting the rights granted under this Agreement.

P.423

The [Company] agrees to display the trade mark and logo of the [Company] on the [Product/Disc/Work] which is set out in the attached Schedule [–] on all copies of any material in any format which display and/or reproduce the image of the [Product/Disc/Work].

P.424

[Name] agrees that the [Company] may promote, advertise and market the [Work/Product] in any of the followings ways:

1.1 Over the internet on websites, on apps, banner links and online competitions in conjunction with digital newspapers, magazines, newsletters, direct email marketing, media news and other service and/or social media and mobile and other telecommunications but not call centre direct marketing to landline and mobile numbers.

1.2 Advertisements and free promotions in printed newspapers, journals, magazines, puzzle books, comics, event and conference brochures and in flyers and free merchandise.

1.3 Funded character promotional events, exhibitions and at galleries, museums and festivals.

QUALIFICATION

General Business and Commercial

Q.001
The [Author] confirms that he is a [British] subject or a national of the following Member State of the European Union [specify country] and will remain so during the Term of this Agreement.

Q.002
The [Author] confirms that he is a qualifying person [as defined by the Copyright, Designs and Patents Act 1988 as amended] and shall remain so during the Term of this Agreement.

Q.003
The [Author] confirms that he holds as passport in the name of [specify] [passport reference] issued by the authorities of [country] that he is a [specify] national of the following [country] and entitled to reside in [country] and will remain so during the Term of this Agreement.

Q.004
'Qualifying Revenue' shall mean, in relation to any accounting period of the [Licensee], the aggregate of:

1.1 All sums received by or which are due to the [Licensee] or any connected person in respect of the inclusion in the Licensed Service of advertisements or other programmes and any charges, costs, fees or other sums in respect of the reception of programmes included in the Licensed Service for that period by the [Licensee]; and

1.2 The total amount of any direct or indirect financial benefit derived by the [Licensee] or any connected person from payments made by any person by way of sponsorship, product placement or of any other nature for the purpose of defraying or contributing towards costs incurred or to be incurred in connection with any programmes included in the Licensed Service.

Q.005

The [Person] confirms that he is a bona fide and paid up member of [Equity/ Musicians/other Union] and will continue to be so during the Term of this Agreement.

Q.006

The [Writer] confirms and undertakes that he is a [British] subject ordinarily resident in the [United Kingdom] and that he shall remain so for the duration of his engagement pursuant to this Agreement.

Q.007

The [Consultant] confirms that he is a qualified [Profession] and an expert in the field of [Subject] and a member of the following bodies [specify] and that he is a competent, skilled and professional person and is a well recognised authority and in a position to provide detailed accurate and correct information and reports to the [Company].

Q.008

The [Designer] shall perform its obligations under this Agreement to the best of its skill and ability and shall maintain such high standards as are reasonably expected by the [Company] for [state purpose] under this Agreement.

Q.009

The [Designer] shall at all times employ suitably qualified and experienced [staff/consultants] who are reliable, skilled in their field and able to contribute to the success of the [Project].

Q.010

The [Contractor] confirms and undertakes that it is able to provide the service stated in the Schedule [–] to the standard, quality and level stipulated by the [Company] and that:

1.1 All the [Company's] personnel who will work on the [Project] as [specify] hold professional qualifications of not less than [specify grade/qualification/level of expertise/years of experience] and are members of [specify organisation].

1.2 That the [Company] is able to provide and/or source material for the [Project] which are not inferior to the samples displayed [as part of the presentation].

1.3 That the facilities to be provided by the [Company] to process, design and develop the [Project] shall included the following [specify equipment].

1.4 That no temporary, unqualified, inexperience and/or unsuitable personnel and/or any person with a criminal record, and/or a record of alcohol and/or drug abuse will be used and/or supplied by the [Contractor] for the [Project].

Q.011

The [Contributor/Consultant] confirms and undertakes that he/she holds the following professional qualifications [List details] and holds a [first/second/third] class degree from [Name of University]. That he/she has practised as a [specify profession] continuously for the last [number] years. That there is no pending disciplinary proceedings and/or criminal action against the [Contributor/Consultant]. That there are no facts of which the [Author/Consultant] is aware which would effect the decision of the [Institute] to appoint the [Contributor/Consultant].

Q.012

The [Company] agrees and undertakes that all the personnel which it provides under this Agreement to fulfil the tasks set out in Clause [–] shall hold the following qualifications [specify] and that there shall be no pending and/or threatened disciplinary and/or other legal proceedings against them in respect of their services and/or work by any government agency, professional body and/or any other party.

Q.013

The [Company] agrees and undertakes that all persons supplied by the [Company] under this Agreement shall have had the following checks carried out and they have passed:

1.1 That they are entitled to work in [country] and have met all the legal requirements that must be met.

1.2 That they have a valid [national insurance number].

1.3 That there is no medical reason and/or any other ill health which would make them unsuitable and/or prevent them performing their work.

Q.014

1.1 The failure by the [Supplier] to provide personnel who hold the relevant qualifications in [country] to fulfil the terms of the Agreement and provide the [Service] as required shall entitle the [Company] to terminate the Agreement with immediate effect.

1.2 The [Supplier] agrees that in the event of termination in 1.1 that the [Company] shall have the right to be repaid all sums paid after the date of the failure and that the [Company] shall not be liable to pay any further sums due to the [Supplier] throughout the term of the Agreement.

QUALITY CONTROL

Building

Q.015
All materials and goods shall be of the quality and standard described in the [Project Specification] or as may be set out in any subsequent specification in any [Works Contract]. In any event all materials and goods shall be subject to the prior written approval of the [Architect/Contract Administrator] in each case either as set out in the [Project Specification and/or the Works Contract]. There must be no changes or developments as to style, content, colour, quality, source or otherwise which are not given written approval in advance.

Q.016
All workmanship shall be of the standard described in the [Project Specification] or as may be set out in any subsequent specifications or bills of quantities in any [Works Contract]. If there is no standard specified then workmanship shall be professional and competent and subject to the approval of the [Architect/Contract Administrator].

Q.017
The [Company] shall upon the request of the [Architect/Contract Administrator] provide full details, documents and evidence to prove that the materials and goods comply with the standards, quality and quantity required for the fulfilment of the contract.

Q.018
The [Contractor] shall employ or otherwise engage the Personnel listed in the Schedule [–] on site and for the completion of the [Project]. The prior written consent of the [Architect/Contract Administrator] shall be required for any replacement, addition or deletion of any such Personnel or their functions, but such consent shall not be unreasonably withheld or delayed.

Q.019
The [Contractor] agrees and undertakes that the [Company] shall be provided with access to all documentation, records, databases, plans, drawings, tables, graphic, designs, computer generated material, computer

software, discs, patents, models or other material, data and/or information in the control or possession of the [Contractor] or any associated company, partnership, entity, director or senior executive of any nature in any media relating to the [Project] within [seven days] of receipt of a written request. The [Contractor] agrees and undertakes that the [Company] shall be entitled to unlimited access during the [Project] by any parties who are employed by them and/or act as their professional advisors and shall be entitled to inspect and take copies as required. The [Contractor] shall provide the facilities for inspection and copying at the [Contractor's] cost and shall not make any charge to the [Company].

Q.020

The [Contractor] undertakes to perform and carry out the [Project] in accordance with the highest professional standards and to ensure that all health and safety measures are carried out to safeguard the employees of the [Contractor] and members of the public. In the performance of the Contract, the [Contractor] is required to use only its own highly qualified professional staff.

Q.021

1.1 The [Contractor] shall at all times supervise, control and be responsible for the work, acts and conduct of its personnel, sub-contractors, consultants, agents, suppliers and others that it engages and/or employs for any matter connected with the [Project].

1.2 The [Contractors] agrees and undertakes that it shall immediately remove and replace any person, sub-contractor, consultant and/ or supplier which the [Company] notifies that it considers to be not qualified, unsuitable and/or whose work, conduct and/or acts have been such that they effect the quality, schedule and/or compliance with any health and safety and/or other legislation, standards and practice for the [Project].

Q.022

The [Contractor] shall employ a sufficient number of qualified personnel for the proper execution of the [Work]. The [Contractor] shall provide the [Company] upon request with detailed documentary evidence that those personnel comply with any requirements for such work as may be required by law [whether by statutes, regulations, directives, code of practice or trade guidelines] in the Territory.

Q.023

Prior to the date upon which the [Work] commences the [Contractor] shall provide the [Company] with the following details:

1.1 Name, address and telephone number of the person responsible for work on the [Site/Project] [and his deputy].

1.2 Names of all delegated staff on the [Site/Project] and their areas of responsibility.

Q.024

The [Company] shall advise the [Contractor] of all the names and telephone numbers of the [Company's] personnel delegated the responsibility of monitoring the performance of the work on the [Site/Project], adherence to the terms and specifications of the Contract, and materials and equipment used. The [Contractor] shall ensure that the [Company's] authorised personnel (including safety inspectors, architect, lawyers and accountants) shall be provided access to the site for assessment, review and inspection purposes. The [Contractor] shall provide such administration equipment and technical facilities that the authorised personnel may require on site to assess, review and inspect the work at no extra cost.

Q.025

The [Company] and its delegated officers (whether notified or not) shall have the right to order both verbally and/or in writing that all or part of the work on the [Site/Project] be stopped at once or some other specified date if it is not, in their opinion, carried out in accordance with the conditions of the Contract. The [Company] shall set out the terms on which work may continue in writing to the [Contractor].

Q.026

The [Contractor] shall remain solely liable for the performance of the work and adherence to the terms of the Contract. The supervision, review, monitoring and access to the [Site/Project] by the [Company] shall not be deemed to constitute a waiver of any of the terms of the Contract nor reduce or vary the liability of the [Contractor].

Q.027

The [Contractor] shall be independent and solely responsible for the performance of the [Project] under the Contract. The [Contractor] shall be responsible for, bear the cost of and be liable for the actions of all its employees, agents, sub-contractors, consultants and any other third parties required by the [Contractor] to carry out any work on the [Project]. The [Contractor] shall ensure that all such persons adhere to the standard and quality of work required by the [Company] at all times.

DVD, Video and Discs

Q.028
The [Assignor] confirms that the [DVD/Video/Disc] shall not contain any other music, lyrics, text, sound recordings, sound effects, persons, background material, trade marks, service marks, logos, products and/or other articles than [specify] unless there is prior written consent in advance from [Name].

Q.029
The [Company] confirms that the [DVD/Disc] will be of first-class technical quality according to standards set by [specify] in [country] and will conform to the specifications set out in Schedule [–].

Q.030
The [Company] undertakes that it will produce the [Film] for the [DVD/Disc] using the Key Personnel, Artists and Material as follows:

1.1 The Director [–]

1.2 The [Presenter/Voice-over] [–]

1.3 The [Writer/Choreographer] [–]

1.4 The Senior Cameraman [–]

1.5 The Editor [–]

1.6 The Artist(s) [–]

1.7 The [Musical Works/Sound Recordings/other] [–]

1.8 The [Stills/Photographs/Archive/Film] [–]

1.9 The [Products/Articles/clothes] [–]

1.10 The [Computer Generated Material] [–].

Q.031
The [Distributor] confirms that a representative of the [Company] shall be entitled to attend the filming and editing of the [Film/Disc] at any stage prior to its completion.

Q.032
The [Distributor] agrees and undertakes that it will ensure that the [Film/Work] and the [DVD/Disc] shall conform to all statutes, regulations, directives, guidelines and Codes of Practice in relation to [DVD/Disc] in [country] and issued by [body/organisation].

Q.033
The [Licensee] agrees and undertakes that:

1.1 It shall produce an adaptation of the [Sound Recordings] which is of a professional standard suitable for the [specify] market and release to the public.

1.2 No existing material of a third party which has already been released to the public shall be added to the finished version.

1.3 That the following persons shall be engaged to produce, record and play the music; [specify].

Q.034
The parties agree that the [Film/Footage/Recording] is for reproduction in the form of a [specify] for exhibition for free by the [Charity] at events, workshops and is not intended to be sufficient quality for use for transmission on television and/or reproduced on the website except as still images.

Q.035
The parties agree that the [Project] shall be recorded by [Name] on [specify equipment] and that copies shall be supplied in [format] to all the parties for use and adaptation in any manner they think fit at each parties cost and expense.

Film and Television

Q.036
The [Company] shall at all times employ, contract or engage personnel of suitable experience and technical ability in relation to their intended services and to use such suitable equipment as may be required to ensure compliance with the detailed requirements of the terms of this Agreement.

Q.037
The [Company] confirms that the [Programme] will be of first-class editorial quality and will conform to the technical standards and specifications set out in Schedule [–].

Q.038
'The Key Personnel' shall be as follows:

1.1 The Producer [–]

1.2 The Director [–]

1.3 The Presenter [–]

1.4   The Writer [–]

1.5   The Narrator [–]

1.6   The Senior Cameraman [–]

1.7   The Editor [–].

The [Assignor] undertakes that it will produce the [Film] using the Key Personnel.

Q.039
The [Production Company] agrees that the prior approval of the [Commissioning Company] shall be required for the [Advertisement/Film] in respect of:

1.1   The Artist(s) and voice-overs.

1.2   The music, whether original musical works or existing soundtracks.

1.3   Any stills or photographs.

1.4   Any archive film footage.

1.5   All copyright notices, credits and acknowledgments on the label and any packaging.

Q.040
The [Production Company] confirms that a representative of the [Commissioning Company] shall be entitled to attend the filming and editing of the [Advertisement/Film] at all times prior to the completion of the final version. The [Production Company] shall keep the [Commissioning Company] fully informed as to all locations, dates and times that work on the [Advertisement/Film] is being carried out.

Q.041
The [Production Company] agrees and undertakes that it will ensure that the [Advertisement/Film] shall conform to all statutes, directives, regulations, standards and practice in respect of any intended use by the [Commissioning Company] of [Advertisement/Film] in the [Territory] including those issued by [specify].

Q.042
The [Producer] warrants that it has exercised and shall exercise in the performance of its duties and obligations under this Agreement the skill, care and diligence reasonably expected of a [television franchise holder/other] holding itself out as having the competence, experience and resources

necessary for the performance of such duties and obligations required for the competent fulfilment of the terms of this Agreement.

Q.043

The [Company] agrees that the prior [written/verbal] approval of [Name] at the [Agent] shall be required in respect of the [Advertisement] in respect of the inclusion of any [Artists/music/voice-overs/stills/film/slogans/text/images/products/other].

Q.044

[Name] agrees and undertakes not to wear any jewellery, clothes, make up and/or use any mobile telephone, tablets and/or laptops and/or any other gadgets and/or any other material and/or equipment whether for free and/or for payment and/or display any logos, products names and/or words and/or images and/or mention, write and/or make reference to any company, product and/or service which is either a sponsor of [Name] and/or some other third party. [Name] agrees and accepts that it is a condition of this Agreement that sponsorship agreements, free products and product placement are not permitted by the [Company] for all persons appearing in the [Programme].

Q.045

[Name] agrees that the decision as to which music and/or sound recording to add to the [Programme] shall be entirely at the [Company's] discretion. [Name] accepts and agrees that the [Company] may use a different person, dialect and/or language for the sound recording and voice for [Name] in the [Programme] provided that this is made clear in the credits at the end.

General Business and Commercial

Q.046

The [Company] agrees that it shall not have the right to exploit in any media the [Article/Film/recordings/photographs/other work] other than for the purpose of [specify limited use] without the prior written consent of [Name] and payment of a sum and/or royalties in each case.

Q.047

The parties agree that all approvals shall operate to allow each party [seven weekdays] to respond to any request.

Q.048

The [Company] agrees that it shall not be entitled to edit and/or alter the [Work] in any way without the prior [written] consent of the [Distributor].

1310

Q.049

No authority is given to the [Company] to sign or authorise contacts on behalf of [Name]. All offers, proposals and contracts should be supplied to [Name] who shall then be entitled to agree or reject any matter as he/she thinks fit.

Q.050

The [Company] shall provide the following service [specify] which shall be according to the standards set by [specify organisation].

Q.051

The [Distributor] undertakes to meet the following [performance targets/ level of service] [specify]. In the event that the [Distributor] fails to meet any of these targets then the [Company] shall have the right to terminate this Agreement by notice in writing to end the Agreement by [four weeks'] notice.

Q.052

The [Company] may alter, change and amend any part of the supply of the service and/or products and/or substitute any material, content, packaging, product, or other matter in respect of this Agreement. The [Company] shall not be obliged to notify you in advance, but you shall have the right to reject any substitute which either is materially different and/or which does not fulfil the same function. If you do not accept substitution you should make this clear in advance of signing this Agreement.

Q.053

It is a condition of this Agreement that the [Supplier] must be able to produce evidence of the following matters when requested to do so by the [Company]:

1.1 Date and time of manufacture and production.

1.2 Source of supply of all content.

1.3 Health and safety and hygiene compliance in accordance with the standards set in [country].

1.4 Source of supply of any water.

1.5 Verification as to the method and location of production.

1.6 Materials rejected and/or destroyed as not of suitable standard.

1.7 Manufacture and production data and supply to shipping agent.

1.8 Any claims and/or complaints by those working at the factory in respect of injuries, disability and/or death and/or working conditions recorded and/or made by any person.

1.9 Evidence of waste disposal and recycling procedure and compliance.

Internet and Websites

Q.054

The [Contributor] undertakes that to the best of his/her knowledge and belief that the facts and information contained in the [Work] are true and accurate except where any material is supplied by or specifically included at the request of the [Company].

Q.055

The [Contributor] agrees that the [Company] shall have absolute discretion as to the suitability of the content of the [Work] for the [Website] and shall be entitled to request any amendment and/or changes to the [Work] as the [Company] may require.

Q.056

Where there are any failures, suspension, delays and/or faults which are due to the [Company]. The [Company] shall try to remedy the problem as quickly as possible and shall not be liable to repay any sums and/or any compensation, losses and/or damages of any nature for any failure which shall be less than [seven days]. Thereafter the [Customer] shall be entitled to cancel the [Service/Order] and be repaid [all sums paid under the Agreement/all sums paid for after the end date].

Q.057

In the event that the [Company] fails to achieve the expected performance, sales and advertising targets set out in Schedule [–] for the [Website]. The [Licensor/Contributor/other] shall be entitled to terminate this Agreement by [three months] written notice and all the rights granted and all the material created and/or supplied under this Agreement shall revert and be transferred back to the [Licensor/Contributor/other].

Q.058

The [Company] has a number of policy guidelines regarding the use and access to the material on the [Website] which are part of the terms and conditions of the Agreement for the [Subscriber] to use the [Website]. These policies may be amended by the [Company] without notice. The policies are:

1.1   Privacy.

1.2   Copyright Notices, Credits and Trade Marks.

1.3   Data Protection.

1.4   Downloading and use of Material.

1.5   Cookies.

1.6   Age requirements and parental consent.

1.7   Uploading and clearance and use of material.

Q.059

The [Contributor] agrees and undertakes that all material of any nature in any format supplied by the [Contributor] to the [Website] as content whether text, images, film, video, sound recordings, music, lyrics, computer generated material, photographs, trade marks, logos, slogans or otherwise shall comply as follows:

1.1   That it shall not be in breach of any contract and/or an infringement of copyright and/or any trade marks and/or intellectual property rights and/or any data protection and/or any other interest of any person and/or company.

1.2   That no material shall be permitted which is likely to cause offense and/or could be considered defamatory, derogatory and/or demeaning and/or could be evidence of a criminal act and/or involves behaviour which causes distress to another person and/or or promotes violence and/or anything of a sexual nature and/or is pornographic.

Q.060

Where any material submitted contains the image, name and/or other details regarding any child and/or other person age [number] years or under. The prior written consent of the parent and/or guardian has to have been obtained to permit the material to be displayed on the [Website]. The [Company] shall have an absolute discretion to refuse to display and/or to delete any material which it decides should not be on the [Website].

Q.061

The [Company] agrees and undertakes that it have the professional knowledge and expertise to create, develop and deliver a fully functional website with moving film images, banner links and all the other specifications made by [Name] which is easily updated in accordance with the [Synopsis] in Schedule [–] and the [Budget] in Schedule and in accordance with the stages set out in the [Delivery and Completion Schedule [–] all which form part of this Agreement.

Q.062

The [Company] agrees and accepts that [Name] may wish to make changes in the layout, design and functions of the website and agrees that these

1313

changes are included in the price which has been agreed between the parties.

Q.063

1.1   In the event that [Name] decides at any stage that the quality of the work delivered by the [Company] is not of the standard expected by [Name] and/or the website cannot fulfil the functions which were requested under this Agreement. Then [Name] shall have the right to terminate the Agreement and to be delivered all computer software, codes, passwords and all master material and copies completed to date by the [Company] provided that [Name] agrees to pay for all work completed prior to the date of termination.

1.2   The [Company] agrees that it shall not have any right to be paid the remaining fee after the date of termination and/or to charge for supply of the computer software and/or master material to [Name] except the cost of delivery.

Merchandising

Q.064
The [Licensee] undertakes that each and every part of the [Products] shall:

1.1   Conform in all respects to the quality, design, packaging and materials of the samples submitted to and approved by the [Licensor] and will abide by and not contravene any statutes, laws, regulations, directives, codes, standards and guidelines whether in respect of design, safety, health, advertising, or any other matter within the [Territory/country/world/universe].

1.2   The [Licensee] will supply at the [Licensee's] cost the Licensor with [number] samples of each of the finished [Products] and any associated material including packaging, leaflets, any other attached or enclosed feature or article, advertisements, publicity and any other material for approval by the [Licensor].

1.3   Not breach any third party intellectual property rights or any other rights of any nature.

1.4   Not be defective in workmanship or materials and shall not be made of dangerous materials or those which are not suitable for the [Product] in relation to its intended or reasonably anticipated use.

1.5   The [Licensee] shall ensure that the [Products] which are intended for purchase or supply to the public shall be suitable and safe for their intended purpose and shall not pose a risk to the health and safety of the public.

1.6 The [Licensee] shall take out sufficient and adequate insurance cover in respect of any product liability which may arise from any claim by the public or any third party.

1.7 The [Licensee] shall indemnify the Licensor from any claim, loss, damage, expense or liability arising from any claim from the public or any third party in respect of any defect or flaw in the [Products] or any injury damage or loss which arises directly or indirectly from the use of the Products.

1.8 The [Licensee] shall bear responsibility for and bear the cost of any default, failure, loss or error by any distributor, sub-licensee or other third party engaged or contracted by the [Licensee] which affects or detracts from this Agreement.

Q.065

1.1 The [Licensee] shall submit to the [Licensor] for prior written approval samples of the [Licensed Articles] and any contents or articles to be sold therewith, including proposed trade marks, copyright, design or other acknowledgments, logos or credits, together with samples of all wrappings, containers, display materials, advertisements, publicity and any other material which it is intended to be used with the [Licensed Articles].

1.2 The [Licensee] shall refrain from the supply, distribution, sale or publication of any of the [Licensed Articles] and/or any associated materials until the approval in writing has been provided by the [Licensor].

1.3 The [Licensee] shall ensure that once approval has been given all the [Licensed Articles] and associated material shall adhere exactly in all respects with the approved samples.

Q.066

The exact shape, size and position of the [Logo/other] on the [Licensed Article] and in all packaging, advertising and marketing material shall be agreed between the [Designer] and the [Licensee] before the production of any of the [Licensed Articles] under this Agreement.

Q.067

The [Designer] confirms that the [Licensee] shall have the right to reject any of the [Designs] on the grounds that in the reasonable opinion of the

[Licensee] the Design is too vague or is generally of insufficient quality to be developed or manufactured as a [Licensed Article].

Q.068

The [Licensee] confirms that all the manufacturing of the [Licensed Articles] under this Agreement shall be at the business premises [address] except where in the opinion of the [Licensee] specialist services in the development, production and manufacturing of the [Licensed Articles] are required.

Q.069

The [Licensee] agrees that the [Licensor] shall be entitled to approve or reject the following material:

1.1　An exact sample of the [Licensed Articles].

1.2　A list of the proposed copyright notices, trade marks, design or other acknowledgments, logos or credits.

1.3　An exact sample of all labels, wrappings, containers and any other article to be given away and/or attached to the [Licensed Article].

1.4　Display materials, advertisements including any slogan, music, artist and/or sound recording, publicity, brochures and any other material which it is intended to be used with the [Licensed Articles].

The [Licensee] acknowledges that such approval must be in writing in each case and that no production can commence until it has been agreed unless authorised by the [Licensor].

Q.070

The [Licensee] agrees to provide the [Licensor] with copies of all artwork, packaging, promotional and advertising material in relation to the supply, sale and distribution of the [Licensed Articles] which shall be subject to the prior approval of the [Licensor] in each case before they are used in association with the [Licensed Articles].

Q.071

The [Licensor] agrees that the final decision as to the content, quality, dimension, colour, and marketing of the [Product] shall be entirely at the [Licensees] sole choice and discretion and that no consultation and/or approval from the [Licensor] shall be required.

Q.072

The [Licensee] undertakes and shall ensure that the [Character/Image] is reproduced and supplied by the [Licensee] on any product and/or article in the exact form, shape and colour and with the words in the same style, layout and position as set out the Schedule [–]. The [Licensee] accepts and agrees that it is not authorised to make any changes, variations and/or developments nor to use the [Character/Image] in any manner which would be detrimental and/or damaging to its goodwill, use and/or value to the [Licensor].

Q.073

In the event that the [Licensor] discovers that the [Licensee] is creating, developing and reproducing and supplying any service and/or products and/or sub-licensing any rights and/or providing any unauthorised endorsement which are not licensed under this Agreement in respect of the [Work/Logo]. Then the [Licensor] shall be entitled to notify the [Licensee] of the allegations and permit them [one] week to reply and to provide a response. If the [Licensor] does not accept the reasons and/or the [Licensee] doe not respond the [Licensor] shall in any event be entitled to terminate the Agreement with [one] weeks' notice and all rights granted under the Agreement shall revert to the [Licensor].

Q.074

The [Licensee] agrees and accepts that:

1.1 It must follow the exact template for the [Image/Logo/Name] for reproduction on the [Articles] provided by the [Licensor].

1.2 It shall not reproduce and/or develop and/or register any adaptation, variation and/or any different colour version.

1.3 It shall not create and develop a computer generated version of the [Image/Logo/Name].

1.4 It must not grant any sub-licence to any third party in any country at any time.

1.5 It shall not supply any [Articles] for inclusion on advertisements, competitions, banner links, features on websites and in magazines and newspapers without notifying the [Licensor] in advance.

1.6 It shall not make any press and media statement which would lead to ridicule and/or damage the reputation of the [Licensor] and/or the [Image/Logo/Name] and/or issue any sales figures and/or details of complaints and/or allegations by members of the public.

Publishing

Q.075

The [Author] shall deliver not later than [date] [two] legible typed copies of the manuscript of the [Work] and in disc form using the software [–]. The

[Work] shall comply in every way with the specifications set out below and shall be written in a competent manner and be of a sufficient standard for publication.

Q.076

The [Ghostwriter] agrees to deliver [two] typed copies of the [Work] and the Artwork to the [Name] on or before the [target date]. The content shall be of a standard and quality that is suitable for publication [with only minor editing] by a reputable publisher.

Q.077

The [Author] agrees to write and deliver [two] copies of the [Work] to the [Agent] based on the [Synopsis] on or before [date]. The [Work] shall be of a standard suitable for commercial publication and shall be not less than [figure] words.

Q.078

The [Company] shall try to ensure that the [Writer] during the continuance of the engagement, shall carry out the obligations under this Agreement to the best of his/her skill and ability. That the [Writer] shall observe all directions, restrictions and requests given by an authorised representative of the [Distributor] which are reasonable and relevant in the circumstances to the [Company] or the [Writer].

Q.079

The [Company] shall use its best endeavours to ensure that the screenplay is written in such a way that it is likely to attract finance for the production of the [Film] based on the [Book]. Further that all steps are taken by way of preparation of a budget, shooting schedule, actors and lead roles or otherwise as may be necessary to enable potential investors to consider whether to contribute to the production costs.

Q.080

The [Interviewer] and the [Publisher] agree that they shall not be entitled to exploit in any media the [Article] and/or the [Recordings] and/or the [Photographs] for any purpose other than publication in the magazine [Name] on [date] without the prior written consent and agreement of both parties.

Q.081

The [Name] and the [Publisher] agree that the [Name] shall be entitled to:

1.1 Approve the [Article] prior to publication in the exact form, words, photographs and headlines or other text or images and on the page in which it is intended that it should be published in the magazine.

1.2   Veto the Article in the event that any requested changes or alterations are not incorporated.

1.3   Prior approval of the final version of the Article.

1.4   The Article shall not be published without the prior receipt by the [Publisher] of the written consent of the [Name] that it is acceptable and that the [Name] wishes it to be published.

Q.082
The [Publisher] agrees that the subject-matter of the [Article] shall mainly cover [specify] and that the [Name] shall have the right to decline to answer questions of any nature and in particular those outside the specified subject area.

Q.083
The [Name] agrees that to the best of his knowledge and belief that the facts and information which he provided to the [Company] are true and accurate. Where the [Company] seeks to rely on such information and facts in the [specify use] they do so at their own risk and shall be liable for any actions or claims that may arise. The [Company] are advised to seek to verify the details of any such material from independent research and investigation.

Q.084
The [Author] confirms that he has sought to verify and check all statements, text and images in the [Work] which he purports to be true and is able to provide documentary evidence in support. Further that where there are instructions, directions, recipes, formulae or advice to be acted upon or copied by the public that all such material has been verified and it is certain that there is no risk to the health and safety of the public, especially children. The [Author] undertakes that there is no risk of loss, damage or injury arising from any contents of this [Work].

Q.085
The [Writer] agrees that to his/her knowledge and belief that the facts and information contained in the [Work] is true and accurate except where any material is supplied by or specifically included at the request of the [Company].

Q.086
The [Company] agrees that any loss, damage or injury arising from the contents or use of this [Work] shall be entirely the responsibility of the [Company] who shall bear all costs and expenses and expenditure of the [Company] and the [Author] which may arise as a result of any subsequent consequence.

1319

Q.087

The [Author] agrees to amend, alter, edit or change such parts of the [Work] as the [Publisher] may request in the event that the [Publisher's] legal advisors consider that there is a risk that the [Work] contains material which may result in legal proceedings against the [Publisher].

Q.088

The [Publisher] agrees that it shall not be permitted to adapt, amend, add to or detract from the manuscript or approved proofs of the [Work] prior to publication or at any time thereafter without the prior [express/written] approval of the [Author] in each case.

Q.089

The [Name] confirms that:

1.1 The [Commissioned Work] shall be of first class technical quality;

1.2 The [Commissioned Work] shall comply with the standards and requirements of [–]; and

1.3 The [Commissioned Work] shall not contain anything of an advertising, promotional, sponsorship or product placement nature unless specifically requested by the [Company].

Q.090

The [Agent] acknowledges that it shall not be allowed nor be authorised to permit others to adapt, alter, edit, add to or delete from or in any way change the [Work] without the prior [written] consent of the [Author].

Q.091

The [Distributor] agrees and undertakes that it must ensure that:

1.1 There is a suitable copyright notice, moral rights notice and credit as set out in the master copy of the [Work] in all copies reproduced.

1.2 No third party in [country] reproduces extracts of the [Work] in any promotional, marketing and advertising material of more than [number] words using the pages [number] to [number] only of the [Work].

1.3 No translations and/or adaptations are permitted and/or authorised at any time except with the prior written consent and approval and subject to a new licence with the [Licensor].

Purchase and Supply of Products

Q.092

The [Supplier] agrees that it shall provide the [Seller] with a full list of the details of:

1.1 The Product.

1.2 The number, dimensions, weight content and description.

1.3 Method of transport together with shipment and/or carriage costs.

1.4 Import/export taxes and duties.

1.5 Value including dealer price and retail price.

1.6 Insurance policy cost.

Q.093
The [Goods] shall be of merchantable quality, fit for their intended purpose and the description and other particulars of the [Goods] stated or referred to in the sales order shall conform to all samples, drawings, descriptions and specifications provided by the [Company].

Q.094
The [Supplier] confirms that:

1.1 The [Product] is safe and satisfactory for its intended purpose if used properly according to the accompanying instructions.

1.2 The [Product] conforms with the quality and description and other particulars stated in [document] and is free from all defects.

Q.095
The [Company] shall take every care to ensure that the best results are as far as possible obtained where materials or equipment are supplied by the [Customer], but the [Company] will not accept responsibility for or be liable for any imperfect work caused by defects in or unsuitability of such materials or equipment.

Q.096
If after the date of this Agreement the health, safety and quality of standards is changed, modified or altered which are applicable to the [Products] under any laws, regulations, directives, codes, guidelines or other relevant material in the Territory. The [Distributor] shall provide such information to the [Company] and the [Distributor] shall bear all the cost and expenses arising from the modification of the specifications of the [Products] and all costs and expenses of passing the health and safety and quality standards in force at that time.

Q.097
If within a [twelve-month] period after shipment from the [Company] of the [Products] any of the products or their component parts exhibit defects of the same kind and nature or at a frequency of more than [five percent] [5]%

of the total quantity [sold/shipped in one year] by the [Company] and if such defects are attributable to faulty workmanship by the [Company] the [Company] agrees [at its discretion] to:

1.1   Supply at no cost, freight pre-paid replacement component parts.

1.2   Provide technical assistance at no cost to repair any such defects.

Subject to the [Purchaser] complying with the following conditions in respect of the defective [Products]:

1.1   Provide written details of the defective [Products] within [specify duration] of the discovery or receipt of notice of any defect in each case.

1.2   The defect shall be subject to confirmation by the [Company].

1.3   The [Purchaser] shall not dispose of any such defective products unless directed to do so.

Q.098

The [Supplier] agrees that the [Goods/Services] shall conform with the quality and description stated and shall be of a quality, design, material and standard that is suitable and safe for use by the public for the [Goods/Services] intended use and that they are and shall be free from defects, damage, faults or any other flaws of any nature.

Q.099

No products shall be sent by the [Company] unless they have passed the safety and quality standards set out in Clause [–] unless the [Purchaser] has provided a written request for the [Company] to do so, without any liability on the part of the [Company].

Q.100

It is a condition of the contract between the [Seller] and the [Company] for the supply of [Goods] that:

1.1   The [Goods] shall conform with the quality, description, performance specifications and other particulars of the [Goods] stated or referred to in the Purchase Order;

1.2   The [Goods] shall conform to all samples, drawings, descriptions and specifications provided;

1.3   The [Goods] shall be of merchantable quality;

1.4   The [Goods] shall be fit for their intended purpose and use;

1.5   The [Goods] shall be free from all defects; and

1.6 The [Goods] shall comply with any standards, laws, regulations, codes, guidelines and any other requirements applicable in the trade, industry or intended markets or countries in respect of goods of that nature.

These conditions shall apply after delivery and inspection, acceptance or payment pursuant to the Purchase Order and shall extend to any replaced, repaired or substituted or repaired [Goods] provided by the [Seller] to the [Company].

Q.101

If the [Products] are found to be damaged, defective or not in conformity with the Order by the [Purchaser] upon delivery. Then a report shall be made to the [Seller] by the [Purchaser]. The [Products] will not be accepted by the [Purchaser] unless the repairs or replacements are satisfactory. The [Purchaser] shall have the right to reject the [Products] and to request that they be collected by the [Seller].

Q.102

1.1 The [Licensee] agrees and undertakes to carry out regular quality control tests of the [Products] to ensure that the content and/or any attachments and/or any associated packaging do not pose a risk to health and safety of the public.

1.2 Where the [Licensee] identifies any problem in 1.1 then the [Licensee] agrees to inform the [Licensor] and to also advise the [Licensor] as to how the matter is to be resolved.

1.3 In the event that any matter poses a serious risk then it is agreed between the parties that production of the [Products/Work] should cease until such time as a satisfactory solution can be obtained. In such event the [Licensee] shall not be entitled to any extension of the licence period under this Agreement.

Q.103

The [Supplier] agrees that a representative of the [Distributor] may visit the premises of the manufacturer of the [Products] without notice to carry out an inspection and review and to report on conditions at the manufacturer for the workers and the hygiene, health and safety and production of the [Products] to the [Distributor]. The [Supplier] accepts that the failure to admit the representative shall be deemed a serious breach of this Agreement.

Services

Q.104

The [Agent] acknowledges that he/she is not entitled to negotiate or promote in any manner or form the commercial interests of the [Character/Product/

Artists] outside the Territory unless specifically agreed in advance in each case with the [Company].

Q.105

The [Company] shall at all times engage or contract personnel with professional experience and technical ability in relation to their intended services and to use such equipment and materials as may be required to ensure compliance with the detailed requirements of the terms of this Agreement.

Q.106

The [Company] agrees and undertakes that:

1.1   The [Presenter] shall render his/her services to the best of the [Presenter's] skill and ability.

1.2   That the [Presenter] will comply with all reasonable directions given to the [Presenter] in connection with the services to be provided by him/her hereunder.

1.3   That the [Presenter] shall not engage in any hazardous or dangerous activities without the prior consent of the [Company].

Q.107

The [Agent] shall endeavour to ensure that the [Presenter] shall whilst performing his services under this Agreement comply with all directions and instructions of the [Company] in so far as they are reasonable and practicable. The [Presenter] shall provide his non-exclusive services to the Company in a professional manner and use his best endeavours to promote the interests of the [Company] [and its associates].

Q.108

The [Manager] shall provide his services to a level of competence and professionalism which can reasonably be expected and shall perform all services diligently to ensure that the [Group] is regularly engaged by third parties on the best terms which can be achieved in each case.

Q.109

The [Director] shall provide his services to the best of his technical and artistic skill and ability and shall perform his services diligently and expeditiously to ensure the completion of the [Series]. The [Director] agrees not to make any public statement at any stage which might reasonably be construed as defamatory, derogatory, offensive to or critical of the [Series].

Q.110

The [Promoter] shall perform all services under this Agreement conscientiously to ensure that the [Event] is promoted, marketed and advertised cost-effectively throughout the Territory for the duration of the Promotion Period.

Q.111
The [Designer] shall perform its obligations under this Agreement in accordance with the recognised standards of a professional [Website/other] designer in the industry. The level of work shall be skilled, accurate, and consistent in order to create a fully functional website for the [Company] on or before [launch date].

Q.112
That where necessary any personnel employed or engaged by the [Designer] shall be suitably qualified, experienced, fit and capable of contributing to the success of the [Project] and agree to sign a confidentiality document with the [Company].

Q.113
The [Designer] confirms and undertakes that the [Website/other] shall be fully operational and consistent with the [Project Specification] in Schedule [–] and the [Payment Schedule].

Q.114
The [Agent] shall use his best endeavours to promote, publicise and advertise the [Actor] generally and in particular to do the following [specify].

Q.115
The [Agent] shall provide his/her services in a competent and professional manner, and in each case advise, negotiate and conclude the most advantageous terms for the [Actor]. The [Agent] shall endeavour to ensure that the [Actor] is regularly engaged by third parties in respect of appearances and performances [in all media] throughout the Territory for the Term of this Agreement.

Q.116
The [Agent] shall as far as possible keep the [Actor] fully informed on a regular basis as regards any offers, negotiations or other business with third parties relating to the [Actor]. The [Agent] agrees that he shall not be entitled to conclude or sign any agreement without the prior consent of the [Actor].

Q.117
The [Agent] confirms that [Name] shall have the final decisions to conclude and sign any agreement, contract or other document relating to the exploitation of the services of [Name] and that no authority is granted under this Agreement for the [Agent] to sign on behalf of [Name].

Q.118

The [Agent] agrees that the [Actor] shall be entitled upon request, either orally or in writing, to be provided with a copy of any contract, record, document, invoices or any other material in any medium in the possession or under the control of the [Agent] relating to the [Actor] at any time during the Term of this Agreement. Thereafter all requests must be in writing and the [Agent] shall only be obliged to keep such material for a period of [number] years.

Q.119

The [Agent] shall provide his services to the [Author] in a professional, competent and thorough manner and shall perform his duties with regard to the career of the [Author] to achieve the following target. The [Agent] agrees that by [date] he shall have approached several leading publishing companies in [country] and tried his best to negotiate and conclude an agreement for the publication of the [Work] by a reputable [Company] with an advance of not less than [figure/currency].

Q.120

The [Consultant] undertakes that all the information, advice and material provided to the [Company] by the [Consultant] shall be true, accurate and that work which is attributed as original has not been derived from some other source. The [Consultant] shall observe all rules and regulations in force at any location where he/she may be required to provide his/her services and shall carry out and observe all directions as may reasonably be given to him/her on behalf of the [Company].

Q.121

'The Services' shall mean the product of the services of the [Executive] to be provided to the [Company] under this Agreement which are described in the attached Appendix [–].

Q.122

In the event that the service provided by [Name] for the [Event/Project] is not as represented by [Name] in the brochure entitled [specify]. Then [Name] agrees that the [Consortium] shall be entitled to a refund of [number] per cent of the total budget paid to [Name].

Q.123

The [Company] agrees and undertakes to provide a professional and first class service as a [recruitment/publicity] agent to [Name] and shall ensure that:

1.1   All matters advised by the directors and officers and any other person at [Name] are treated by the personnel of the [Company] as confidential and private unless advised otherwise.

1.2   No statements, media and press release and/or social media and/ or other text, image and email exchanges shall be released and/or distributed to the general public without the prior consent of [specify] at [Name].

1.3   No commitment, representation and/or contractual liability shall be made and/or incurred on behalf of [Name] without prior authority.

Sponsorship

Q.124
The [Sportsperson] agrees to provide his/her exclusive services to the best of his/her skill and ability as far as reasonably possible in the circumstances and shall perform his/her duties under this Agreement at such times, dates [excluding bank holidays and weekends] and locations [except those designated dangerous] as may be agreed with the [Manager] in each case including the attendance at and participation in events, competitions, promotions, press calls, appearances, meetings and recordings as specified in the Work Schedule.

Q.125
The [Sportsperson] agrees to conduct himself/herself in his/her family, public and in his/her sport in a manner which will not result in a criminal record, allegations of drug misuse, scandal or otherwise detract from the reputation of the [Company]. The [Sportsperson] agrees that other than due to ill-health or injury that he/she shall maintain the training schedule and keep fit and act at all times when outside his/her home in a proper and professional manner during the Term of the Agreement and will abide by the rules and regulations of the following bodies [specify].

Q.126
The [Sportsperson] agrees to provide his/her services to the best of his/ her skill and ability to ensure the fulfilment of his/her obligations under this Agreement. The [Sportsperson] agrees to act in their public life in a fit and proper manner and agrees not to engage in any public activities which are detrimental, derogatory or offensive to the [Sponsor] or the [Sponsor's Product].

Q.127
The [Sponsor] agrees to provide the [Sportsperson] with samples of all proposed promotional, advertising, publicity, packaging and other material

in which it is intended to use the name, image, voice, trade mark, slogan, and/or endorsement of the [Sportsperson] under this Agreement.

Q.128

The [Sponsor] agrees that the name, image and endorsement of the [Sportsperson] shall not be used for any purpose other than the promotion and endorsement of the [Sponsor's Product] for the duration of the Sponsorship Period and that the [Sponsor] shall not be entitled to do so in any form at any time thereafter.

Q.129

The [Company] undertakes that as far as reasonably possible all personnel [specify categories] involved in the [Project] shall be members of recognised craft, trade or other professional bodies.

Q.130

The [Promoter] shall provide its services under this Agreement to the best of its skill and ability and agrees to use its reasonable endeavours to perform the following duties in respect of the Event [specify responsibility].

Q.131

The [Promoter] shall provide its services under this Agreement to the level and standard which could reasonably be expected of a competent business within the budget which has been allocated under this Agreement.

Q.132

The [Company] agrees that the [Celebrity] shall be entitled upon request to be provided at the [Company's] sole cost with an exact sample of any article, packaging, publicity, advertising, promotional and marketing material in the possession or under the control of the [Company] featuring or relating to the [Celebrity].

Q.133

The [Celebrity] agrees not to participate in any dangerous sport, political controversies or other activities which would prejudice the goodwill and reputation of the [Company] and the [Company's Product] during the Term of the Agreement.

Q.134

The [Sponsor] agrees that it shall not have the right to use, exploit or promote the title of the [Film/Work] or any script, artist, presenter, music, slogan or other parts of any nature whether in conjunction with the [Sponsor's Products] or any other products or services of the [Sponsor] under any circumstances. This Agreement is solely related to the placement of the [Sponsor's Product] in the [Film/Work] and not a sub-licence or other transfer of authority to the [Sponsor] to use any material and/or exploit any rights of any nature.

Q.135
The [Sponsor] agrees that the [Company] may in respect of the [Image/Logo/Name] supplied by the [Sponsor]:

1.1   Adapt the size, colour and layout to suit the new marketing material created with the [Event/Programme].

1.2   Create and develop a computer generated version as part of the animated introduction for transmission on screen at the [Event/Programme].

1.3   Reproduce the [Image/Logo/Name] on all merchandise and material on which the name of the [Company] appears in connection with the [Event/Programme].

University, Library and Educational

Q.136
The [Institute] shall be entitled to display, exhibit, publish, reproduce, exploit and/or cease to use the [Work/Service] in any manner at its sole discretion as it thinks fit. There are no assurances as the method, timescale, quality, quantity, packaging and/or marketing nor shall any licensees be subject to the approval of the [Licensor].

Q.137
The [Licensee] agrees that it shall not supply to any third party the same and/or substantially similar [Work/Products] that it has supplied to the [Institute] without the prior written approval of the [Institute].

Q.138

1.1   The [Institute] agrees and undertakes that it will not authorise any third party to test, appraise and/or repair the [Work] without the prior written approval of the [Company].

1.2   That all the material which shall be created and developed by such third party in respect of the [Work] shall be returned to the [Institute] and ownership of the material and copyright and all other intellectual property rights and interest assigned to the [Company].

Q.139
The [Institute] confirms that to the best of the knowledge and belief of its officers in [specify department] that the facts, information, data, and material are a true and accurate representation of [Project] at that time.

Q.140

1.1 The [Institute] does not confirm the accuracy, originality, copyright, and/ or legal ownership of the material of the [Work] which is provided to the [Company]. All use of the [Work] shall be entirely at the [Company's] risk and cost and no responsibility shall be accepted by the [Institute].

1.2 The [Company] shall acknowledge the [Institute] as the source of the material of the [Work] on all copies reproduced, supplied and/ or distributed by the [Company] and all associated packaging, promotional and marketing.

1.3 The [Company] agrees that the quality and content of the [Work] shall be of a high standard suitable for the [specify] market and shall comply with all legislation, directives, regulations and codes of practice which may exist in respect of the [Work] and the [specify] market.

Q.141

The [Author] agrees that where in the opinion of the management of the [Institute] and/or their legal advisors the content, title and/or marketing of the [Work/Product/Service] should be edited, delayed, cancelled and/or recalled due to the threat of legal action by a third party, and/or there is a serious defect and/or fault and/or there are significant inaccuracies. Then the [Author] agrees that the [Institute] shall be entitled to take such action as may be necessary and the [Author] and the [Institute] shall enter into negotiations to resolve the matter. The [Author] agrees that he shall not be entitled to any sums for loss of reputation, royalties and/or an advance which is delayed and/or not paid where the [Author] was liable for the matter.

Q.142

1.1 The [Company] agrees and undertakes that the [Work/Product/ Service] shall not contain any text, images, photographs, music, sound recordings, film, trade marks, logos, slogans and/or any other material in any medium which has not been approved by the [Institute].

1.2 The [Company] agrees and undertakes that the [Work/Product/ Service] shall not be adapted, altered, edited, nor shall any material be added to and/or deleted from it and/or changed without the prior written consent of the [Institute] in each case.

Q.143

1.1 The [Consortium] agree that [Name] shall be responsible for monitoring and reporting on the [Project] and compliance with the [Budget], [Completion Dates] and the overall quality of the services provided by the [Supplier].

1.2   That [Name] shall provide a written report to the [Consortium] at the end of each calendar month which highlights the work completed and any failures and the payments made and raises any concerns which may have arisen.

1.3   The [Consortium] agrees that [Name] shall have delegated authority by the [Consortium] to issue both verbal warnings and written letters to the [Supplier] on behalf of the [Consortium].

R

RATES OF EXCHANGE

General Business and Commercial

R.001

The [Company] and the [Agent] understand and agree that there shall be no fixed rate of exchange and the correct rate shall be such as may be obtained from a reputable bank on the day that any such currency may be converted. Further, both parties accept that the rate of exchange may rise or fall to the benefit or loss of either party.

R.002

Where any sum is to be paid by the [Company] in [currency] then the [Company] shall (subject to Bank of England consent) be entitled to pay to the [Licensor] the equivalent in sterling calculated using the [specify reference source] on the working day prior to payment.

R.003

The [Creditor] may convert or translate all or any part of such credit balance into another currency applying a rate which in the [Creditor's] reasonable opinion fairly reflects prevailing rates of exchange.

R.004

The rate of exchange shall be [specify] and shall be fixed at that rate for all conversions of currency from [specify] to [specify] for the period of the Term of the Agreement.

R.005

The [Licensee] shall not be obliged to justify the rate of exchange used to convert any currency under this Agreement provided that it is conducted through an established bank in the [United Kingdom] and receipts can be produced. Commission charges shall be deducted from the sums by the bank prior to payment of any sums to the [Licensor].

R.006

The [Licensee] shall use the best rate of exchange available at the time from any reputable bank for the conversion of any sums prior to payment to the [Licensor] in [currency]. The [Licensee] shall as far as possible not incur additional charges and/or commission costs for the conversion of any currency, but if they do arise shall be entitled to deduct them from any sums due to the [Licensor].

R.007

The [Institute] shall be entitled to choose the most appropriate rate of exchange which in its opinion is most suitable to convert the currency to [specify]. The [Institute] is not obliged to choose the best rate available on the market, but that which is most convenient and cost effective in the circumstances.

R.008

Where the [Sub-Licensee] has to arrange for the conversion of any currency in respect of this Agreement. The [Sub-Licensee] shall use the most favourable rates available and keep all costs to a minimum. The [Sub-Licensee] shall provide written evidence of the conversion rate and costs on each occasion to the [Licensor] in respect of each accounting period.

R.009

All payments by the [Sponsor] under this Agreement shall be in [sterling/dollars/euros/other]. Where the [Sponsor] is requested to make payment in any other currency, then the expenses and charges associated with the conversion of the sum shall be at the [Company's] cost. The [Company] agrees that the [Sponsor] shall be entitled to deduct such expenses and charges from the payment due to the [Company] provided that the deduction is agreed in advance.

R.010

Where the [Agent] and/or [Distributor] incurs any bank charges and costs relating to the conversion of any currency and/or sums due to [Name] under this Agreement. There shall be no right to deduct and/or set off any such sums to those payments due to [Name] under this Agreement.

RECORDINGS

General Business and Commercial

R.011
'The Recordings' shall mean any visual and/or sound recordings of the [Event/Film/other] in any medium, including electronic or chemical forms of reproduction, whether in existence now or created in the future.

R.012
The [Company] confirms that it shall provide to the [Distributor] such sound recordings of the [Musical Work] as may be available at the [Company's] sole discretion and cost for the purpose of production, reproduction, supply and distribution of the [Video/DVD/Disc].

R.013
'The Sound Recordings' shall be all sound recordings of the performances of the [Artiste] for and on behalf of the [Record Company] made during the Term of this Agreement regardless of the medium in which the sound recording is made or the method by which the sounds are produced or reproduced.

R.014
'The Records' shall be the reproduction of the Sound Recordings in whole or part in any material form, whether manufactured by any method for release to the general public or supplied or licensed to any third party with or without visual images.

R.015
'The Recordings' shall mean all sound recordings made of the [Interviewee] for the purpose of the Article, regardless of the medium on which the sound recording is made or the method by which the sounds are produced or reproduced.

R.016
'Recording' in relation to a [Performer's] rights in a performance shall mean a film and/or sound recording made:

1.1 Directly from the live performance; or

1.2 From a broadcast of a cable programme including the performance; or

1.3 Directly or indirectly from another recording of the performance.

[as defined in the Copyright, Designs and Patents Act 1988 as amended].

R.017

'The Recordings' shall mean:

1.1   The right to make a recording of the whole and/or part of the [Event] in any medium from which a moving image may by any means be produced and/or reproduced by any method whether in existence now or created in the future.

1.2   The right to make a sound recording of the whole and/or part of the [Event] in any medium and the production and/or reproduction by any method of the sounds whether in existence now or created in the future.

1.3   The right to make the [Film] and/or soundtrack of the [Event].

R.018

'The Recording Rights' shall mean the right to exercise and make the Recordings of the [Event] and/or parts and to reproduce, supply, and distribute all material arising from the Recordings and to authorise others to do so.

R.019

The [Sponsor] acknowledges that the [Association] has no editorial control in respect of the times, dates, duration and content of the broadcast, transmission or supply of the [Recordings/Film] by the [Television Company]. Nor will the [Sponsor] seek to receive any compensation, refund, damages or other sum from the alteration, disruption or delay or failure to [use/broadcast/transmit] the [Recordings/Film].

R.020

1.1   The [Association] agrees that in the event that the [Production Company] does not produce or deliver the [Recordings] of the [Event] for any reason [number per cent/amount] of the Sponsorship Fee shall be repaid to the [Sponsor] by the [Association].

1.2   The [Association] agrees that in the event that the [Television Company] does not broadcast, transmit or supply the [Recordings] for any reason, then the [amount] of the Sponsorship Fee will immediately become repayable to the [Sponsor] by the [Association].

1.3   The [Sponsor] agrees that no sums shall be repaid provided that the [Television Company] had broadcast or transmitted not less than [number minutes] before [date].

1.4   The [Association] agrees that the [Sponsor] shall not be liable for any costs, expenses or otherwise in respect of the arrangements for and/or making of the [Recordings] or the Recording Rights except [–].

R.021

Subject to prior consultation the [Presenter] agrees that the [Company] shall have the right to use his/her name, biography, image and recordings in any commercial exploitation of the [Series] under this Agreement.

R.022

'The Series' shall be the series of films and any associated sound recordings or recordings based on the Treatment and the Scripts with the provisional title [–] number of episodes [–] each of duration [–].

R.023

'The Exclusive Recording Rights' in relation to [Event/Festival/Performance/ Artists] shall mean:

1.1   The sole and exclusive right in respect of [Artists] to make film and/or sound recordings directly from the live performances and/or

1.2   The sole and exclusive right in respect of [Artists] to make film and/ or sound recordings directly made from any broadcast of a cable programme including the performances and/or

1.3   The sole and exclusive right in respect of [Artists] to make film or sound recordings directly or indirectly from any other recordings of the performances.

1.4   The sole and exclusive right to make any recording of the whole and/or part of the [Event] in any medium from which a moving image may by any means be produced and/or reproduced by any method whether in existence now or created in the future.

1.5   The sole and exclusive right to make any sound recording of the whole and/or part of the [Event] in any medium and the production and/or reproduction by any method of the sounds whether in existence now or created in the future.

1.6   The sole and exclusive right to make any [Film] and/or soundtrack of the [Event].

1.7   The sole and exclusive right to reproduce, supply, and/or distribute any material and/or rights arising from 1.1 to 1.6 and the right to authorise, licence, assign and/or transfer such rights to any third party.

R.024

1.1   The [Advertiser/Sponsor] has contributed to the funding of the [Event/Film/Programme] and shall be entitled to an equal share with the [Company] of all sums received from the exploitation of the [Recordings] and/or any parts made by the [Company].

1.2 The [Recordings] shall mean any visual and/or sound recordings of the [Event/Film/Programme] in any medium, including electronic or chemical forms of reproduction, whether in existence now or created in the future. This shall include but not be limited to television, film, computer downloads, mobile downloads, DVDs, audiocassettes.

1.3 The [Advertiser/Sponsor] agrees that it shall not be entitled to any sums received by the [Company] at the [Event/Film/Programme] from ticket sales, merchandising, refreshments, brochures and/or other printed material.

R.025

The [Advertiser/Sponsor] agrees that it has not and will not:

1.1 Acquire any exclusive and/or non-exclusive rights to any recordings, film, and/or sound recordings in relation to the [Event/Programme].

1.2 Make any recordings, film and/or sound recordings either directly from the live performances and/or any broadcast and/or transmission of a cable, satellite, terrestrial, mobile, computer and/or other gadget programme including the performances.

1.3 Make any recordings, film and/or sound recordings directly or indirectly from any other recordings, film and/or sound recordings of the performances and/or of the whole and/or part of the [Event/Programme] in any medium from which a moving image and/or sound and/or music may by any means be produced and/or reproduced by any method whether in existence now or created in the future.

1.4 Represent that it has the right to authorise any third party to do 1.1, 1.2 or 1.3. Nor shall the [Advertiser] purport to licence, assign and/or transfer such rights to any third party.

1.5 Have any editorial control and/or rights of consultation in respect of the times, dates, duration and content of the broadcast, transmission or supply of the recordings, film and/or sound recordings by the [Institute].

1.6 Have any right to seek to claim any compensation, refund, damages or other sums if there is any alteration, disruption, delay, failure to use, broadcast, and/or transmit any of the recordings, film and/or sound recordings at any time and/or the [Event/Programme] is cancelled for any reason.

R.026

The [Advertiser/Sponsor] and the [Institute] agree that the [Advertiser/Sponsor] and the [Institute] shall hold the joint copyright, and joint intellectual property rights and interest in the [Event/Programme]:

1.1 The title of the [Event/Programme]. A copy of which is attached in Appendix 1 and forms part of this Agreement.

1.2 The trademarks, logos and images of the [Event/Programme]. A copy of which are attached in Appendix 2 and forms part of this Agreement.

1.3 That the agreement of both parties shall be required to exercise, grant and/or authorise the sole and exclusive right to make, reproduce, supply, distribute and/or exploit any recordings, film, and/or sound recordings either directly from the live performances and/or any broadcast and/or transmission of a cable, satellite, terrestrial, mobile, computer and/or other gadget including the performances and/or of the whole and/or part of the [Event/Programme] in any medium from which a moving image and/or sound and/or music may by any means be produced and/or reproduced by any method whether in existence now or created in the future.

1.4 That the agreement of both parties shall be required to exercise, grant and/or authorise any third party and/or to licence, assign and/or transfer any rights to any third party.

1.5 That the agreement of both parties shall be required to apply for, register, and/or defend and/or to issue legal proceedings in respect of the joint copyright, and joint intellectual property rights and interest in the [Event/Programme] held by [Advertiser/Sponsor] and the [Institute].

1.6 That both parties shall have the equal right of editorial control and must both agree before any decisions are made in respect of the content, time, date, duration, alteration, disruption, delay, failure to use, broadcast, and/or transmit, translation, cancellation, licensing and/or exploitation in any medium and/or format.

R.027

The [Licensor] agrees and undertakes not to authorise, license and/or permit the reproduction and/or exploitation of the rights in the [Recordings] and/or any material to any other third party from [date] to [date].

R.028

The [Archive] agrees and undertakes that:

1.1 It shall keep the physical material of the [Recordings] at [location].

1.2 It has only been granted the right to permit access by the public for private viewing for research purposes only to a copy of the [Recordings] and not for any commercial exploitation and/or reproduction in any form.

1.3 That all copyright and any other rights in the [Recordings] are owned by [Name]. That the [Archive] will acknowledge and credit [Name] as the copyright owner on any database and in any other reference to the [Recordings] in any electronic, printed and/or marketing material.

1.4 That the [Archive] has no right to register any copyright ownership with any collecting and/or other society and/or to receive any fees and/or other sums from such exploitation.

1.5 That the [Archive] has no right to license, and/or authorise the reproduction of the [Recordings] and/or any adaptation by any third party at any time.

R.029

The [Recordings] by the [Group] shall be jointly owned by all the following members [specify]. All sums received from the exploitation of the [Recordings] in all media in any format and/or medium shall be shared equally between the parties regardless of the actual contribution that each member made to the [Recordings] whether lyrics, music, singing, computer generated material and/or otherwise. Each member agrees that all parties should be registered as joint copyright owners with all collecting societies for all parts of the [Recordings] throughout the world and that all sums received should be spilt equally between the parties.

R.030

1.1 The [Company] acknowledges and agrees that [Name] shall be entitled to retain and shall own the copyright and all intellectual property rights and interest in any film, recording and/or other image of the [Event] in which [Name] performs which he/she may wish to make with any third party.

1.2 That the [Company] shall not be entitled to film, record and/or make any sound recording of the [Event] and/or authorise and/or sub-license any third party to do so while [Name] is performing and/or appears in the [Event].

R.031

1.1 [Name] agrees that he/she shall not make any arrangement and/or conclude an agreement with any third party to record, film and/or otherwise exploit the performance of [Name] at the [Event].

1.2 [Name] agrees that the [Company] shall hold and does control all forms of commercial and non-commercial exploitation including radio, television, sponsorship and merchandising and supply of services and extracts and that [Name] may not licence such rights at any time.

1.3   That the [Company] agrees it shall conclude an agreement for the reproduction of any music, lyrics and sound recordings and/or transmission in conjunction with any film with [Name] directly and/or any collecting society who may hold the rights.

REJECTION

DVD, Video and Discs

R.032
The hiring of a [DVD/Video/Disc] may not be cancelled except by notice to the [Company] not less than [five days] prior to the commencement of the hire (excluding Saturdays, Sundays and Bank Holidays). Cancellation includes any alteration to the contents of the hire and/or change in the location to which material supplied on hire is delivered and/or any substitute order in lieu of any previous order.

R.033
In the event that the [DVD/Video/Disc] is not of suitable [broadcast/technical quality] the [Company] shall be responsible for providing an acceptable replacement at its sole cost within [7 days] of receipt of notice of rejection by any of the following methods [email/customer care line/in writing]. If there is no acceptable replacement provided then all sums shall be repaid by the [Company].

R.034
All [DVDs/Discs] of the [Film] supplied by the [Distributor] to the [Company] shall be in first class condition and shall be to such technical standards and quality as customarily required for the general public in [country] and packaged in sealed wrappers. If any [DVD/Disc] of the [Film] is returned by anyone on the grounds of unsatisfactory technical quality and/or any other reason then the [Distributor] shall at its sole cost provide an acceptable replacement.

R.035
The [Company] shall have the right to reject the [Material] of the [Film] supplied by the [Distributor] for the [DVD/Disc] on the grounds that:

1.1   The [Material] is of poor quality and is not suitable for the reproduction of [DVDs/Discs] for sale to the public and/or

1.2   That the [Material] is the wrong duration and/or

1.3   That the sound track is of poor quality and/or

1.4   That the [Material] is for the wrong film and/or sound recording.

1.5   That the [Film] is not in the [specify] language.

1.6   The [Material] is not fit for its intended purpose.

In the event of any rejection of the [Film] and/or Material by the [Company] and the [Licensor] is unable to supply an acceptable replacement within [one month]. Then the [Company] shall be entitled to terminate this Agreement and the [Licensor] shall immediately repay to the [Company] any sums received by them under this Agreement in respect of the [Film] and/or [Material].

R.036
The [Licensee] shall have the right to reject the master material of the [Sound Recordings] supplied by the [Licensor] on the grounds that the technical quality is of a low standard and is not suitable for reproduction without additional cost and expense being incurred. In the event of that the [Licensee] rejects the master material and the [Licensor] is either unable to supply acceptable material and/or refuses to meet the cost and expense of the additional work required. Then the [Licensee] shall be entitled to terminate this Agreement and the [Licensor] shall immediately repay to the [Licensee] all sums received under this Agreement.

R.037
The [Sub-Licensee] agrees and accepts that the reproduction of the master material to be supplied to the [Sub-Licensee] by the [Licensee] is not of first rate quality and contains defects, flaws and other errors which need to be remedied. The [Sub-Licensee] agrees to pay the cost of any additional work that may be required to bring the copy up to suitable standard for reproduction in order to exercise of the rights granted under this Agreement.

R.038
Where material is rejected for any reason by the [Company] and the rejection is accepted by the [Distributor]. Then the [Distributor] shall not be entitled to substitute an alternative [Work/Film] and/or offer a voucher and/or credit note. The [Company] shall be entitled to a full refund of the payment made to the [Distributor]

Film and Television

R.039
All prints of the [Film] supplied by the [Company] to the [Television Company] shall be in first class condition and shall be to such technical standards as customarily required for programme material under the [Ofcom Technical Performance Code/other]. If any print of the [Film] is rejected on the grounds of unsatisfactory technical quality then the [Company] shall use its best endeavours to provide an acceptable replacement print as required at the sole cost of the [Company].

R.040
The [Company] shall retain the right to terminate this Agreement in the event that the [Film] is not produced in accordance with the agreed proposal and/or the [Company] does not approve the rough cut of the [Film] and/or the [Film] does not conform to the [Company's] normal technical standards or the delivery of the [Film] is not made on or by [date]. In the event of such termination the [Company] shall be under no further liability or obligation to the [Licensor] and shall not be liable to pay the [Licensor] any further sums hereunder. The [Company] shall not exercise this right of termination unreasonably or without obvious course.

R.041
The [Company] shall have the right to reject the [Film Material] supplied hereunder on the grounds of quality and/or fitness of purpose which shall not be exercised without reasonable cause. In the event of the rejection of the [Film Material] by the [Company] and in the event that the [Licensor] is unable to supply acceptable material. The [Company] shall be entitled to terminate this Agreement and the [Licensor] shall immediately repay to the [Company] any sums received by them in respect of the Licence Fee.

R.042
The [Company] shall have the right to reject any of the [Films] if the content of such [Films] is in the opinion of either the [Company] and/or [Ofcom/other] or such other regulatory body within the [United Kingdom/country] unsuitable for its film purposes. This right of rejection shall not be exercised unreasonably or without obvious cause. In the event of such rejection the [Company] may elect to accept substitute films in place of each [Film] rejected. Such substitution to be mutually agreed in good faith between the [Licensor] and the [Company]. Failing such substitution the total Licence Fee payable hereunder shall be reduced by an amount representing the Licence Fee due in respect of each [Film] so rejected.

R.043

The [Licensor] reserves the right at any time to change the titles of any episode of the [Series]. The [Licensor] also reserves the right to withdraw any episode because of litigation or threatened litigation. In the event an episode is withdrawn the [Company] shall receive a proportionate credit of the Licence Fee for the withdrawn episodes.

R.044

In pursuance of the [Author's] right of approval under Clause [–] the [Author] agrees to either accept or provide written reasons for the rejection of the Treatment and/or Scripts in each case for the [Film] within [28 days] of delivery and undertakes that such approval shall not be unreasonably withheld or delayed.

R.045

The [Licensee] agrees to either accept or provide written reasons for its rejection of the [Film Package] within [21 days] of delivery.

R.046

In the event that the [Film] is not of suitable technical quality and the [Licensor] cannot deliver an acceptable replacement within [30 days], then the [Licensee] shall be entitled to terminate this Agreement and the [Licensor] shall repay all sums paid to it within [28 days].

R.047

The [Company] agrees to either accept or provide written reasons for their rejection of the [scripts/storyboard/Advertisement Material] within [7 working days] of delivery in each case. The [Company] agrees that any rejection shall be on reasonable grounds and in good faith.

R.048

The [Production Company] agrees that it shall use its reasonable endeavours to comply with the following conditions:

1.1 That [Name] shall be provided with a reasonable opportunity to review and comment on the draft and final script, the key personnel and the production schedule and locations together with any major or significant changes that may occur.

1.2 That [Name] shall have the right to approve the final script prior to production of the [Film] and shall be consulted on all changes except minor editing.

1.3 That the [Name] shall be provided with and approve a sample of each and every type of proposed form of exploitation in each form of the media.

1.4   That the [Name] shall be entitled to revoke the moral rights waiver under Clause [–] by notice in writing if these conditions are not fulfilled at any time.

R.049

[Name] shall have the right to reject any material under this Agreement on the grounds that:

1.1   It is not of a high professional standard and workmanship.

1.2   It has not been produced using the key personnel and/or artists set out in Clause [–].

1.3   The music and/or soundtrack is inaccurate, substandard and/or does not correlate to the [Film].

1.4   The [Film] is too [long/short].

1.5   The [dialogue/storyline/computer graphics/costumes] are poor quality and/or do not represent the features agreed in the [Treatment/Script].

1.6   The material has been delivered too late and not in accordance with the stipulated date schedules.

1.7   The material is offensive, obscene, or generally not suitable for the age category or market for which it was intended.

1.8   Not all the material has been properly cleared for use by [Name].

1.9   A third party has served legal proceedings or a Court Order on [Name] concerning the material and/or the [Film].

R.050

The [Company] agrees that it has viewed the [Film] and shall not reject the [Film] on the grounds of content. The [Company] shall only be entitled to terminate this Agreement on the grounds that the [Licensor] has failed to delivery of an acceptable a copy of the master in [format] suitable for reproduction and broadcast and/or transmission.

General Business and Commercial

R.051

The [Work] shall not be rejected by the [Company] except in good faith and on reasonable grounds. In any event the [Work] shall not be rejected solely on the grounds of change in company policy or any change or economic circumstances affecting the [Company].

R.052

The [Company] shall have the right to reject any [Material/Work/Service] under this Agreement on the grounds that:

1.1   It is not of merchantable quality and/or fit for its intended purpose.

1.2   That it is not of a professional standard.

1.3   The workmanship is of poor quality and substandard.

1.4   The content is not as specified in the contract.

1.5   The content is not in accordance with the approved sample and/or presentation.

1.6   It is defective.

1.7   It does not operate as intended.

1.8   There are key elements which are missing.

1.9   There are serious errors in the content.

1.10 The dimensions [size/volume/weight/length/height] are inaccurate.

1.11 It has not been delivered by the delivery date.

1.12 The [title/label/content/artwork/words] is wrong, offensive, obscene, or generally not suitable for the age category or market for which it was intended.

1.13 A third party has threatened legal action and/or made claims of ownership and/or allegations of infringement and/or breach of contract.

1.14 A government agency has raised concerns relating to product liability, breach of any quotas and/or breach of any laws, regulations, directives and/or standards.

R.053

[Name] agrees that the [Company] shall have a period of [number] days after delivery to assess the quality and content of the [Products/Work] and to decide whether to accept them. After that expiry of that period if the [Company] has not rejected the [Products/Work] then the [Company] shall be deemed to have accepted delivery.

Internet and Websites

R.054

The [Service] may be cancelled by the [Company] at any time at the end of each [four-week period] where payment has not been cleared by the due date for the next subscription period.

R.055

If the [Supplier] does not deliver the [Product] by the Delivery Date, then the [Customer] shall be entitled to reject the [Product] and return it to the [Supplier] and request a full refund of all sums paid including delivery costs.

R.056

If the [Supplier] does not deliver the [Product] by the Delivery Date, then the [Customer] agrees that the [Supplier] shall have the opportunity within the next [seven days] after the Delivery Date to rectify and remedy the problem. After that time the [Customer] shall be entitled to refuse to accept delivery and to reject the [Product] and if it subsequently arrives to return it to the [Supplier] and request a full refund of all sums paid including delivery costs.

R.057

The [Company] shall not be entitled to deliver substituted [Goods/Products] and undertakes that all [Goods/Products/other] shall conform to the description as to content, the packaging, dimensions, weight, colour and be safe for their intended and advertised purpose. The image on the screen is intended for guidance only. The [Customer] may reject the [Goods/Products] for any reason up to [specify period] after delivery. After that time rejection must be on the grounds that there is a defect, failure and/or fault which is not due to incorrect use and/or the work of a third party.

R.058

The [Company] shall be entitled to deliver substituted [Goods/Products] which are similar. The [Company] cannot ensure that all [Goods/Products/other] will conform to the description as to content, the packaging, dimensions, weight, colour. The image on the screen is intended for guidance only. The [Customer] may reject the [Goods/Products] for any reason up to [specify period] after delivery. After that time rejection must be on the grounds that there is a defect, failure and/or fault which is not due to incorrect use and/or the work of a third party and which is within the [specify period] of the date of purchase.

R.059

The [Company] reserves the right to reject the [Work] if it is clear that the contents of the [Work] do not conform to the style, form and content stipulated by the [Company]. In the event that the [Company] rejects the [Work] the [Author] shall be obliged to repay to the [Company] all sums previously paid to the [Author] as an Advance against Royalties.

R.060

The [Company] shall have the right to reject any [Material/Work/Service] under this Agreement on the grounds that:

1.1 It is defective and has serious errors and does not fulfil the intended function. It is not of merchantable quality and/or fit for its intended purpose.

1.2 That it is not of a professional quality and does not comply with the standards of [specify organisation].

1.3 That it has not been delivered in the required materials and with the [content/sample] specified in the contract.

1.4 That there has been a failure to clear copyright, acquire consents and/or any other rights from third parties.

R.061

The [Company] shall be entitled to reject the [Website Design] on the grounds:

1.1 That the layout, colour, function and operation of the [Website] is not in accordance with the agreed instructions and/or the [Website Summary].

1.2 That the [Website Design] is not the original of the [Designer] and has been copied from a third party and/or infringes the rights of a third party.

1.3 That the [Website Design] is not of a professional standard and quality suitable for the purpose set out in the [Website Summary] and is not capable of dealing with the volume of traffic which was stated in the [Website Summary].

R.062

[Name] accepts that the [Company] may reject the [Website/App] and request that [Name] vary and/or change the layout, design, function and/or colour in the event that:

1.1 The [Website/App] does not function and fulfil the tasks and/or contain the content agreed with the [Company] set out in the schedule [–] as the specification.

1.2 The [Website/App] is not compatible with the existing system and/or technology of the [Company] as required in clause [–].

1.3 The [Website/App] has been delivered in a format which does not conform to the standard [specify].

1.4 The [Website/App] is incomplete and/or missing material and/or functions.

Merchandising

R.063
The [Licensee] confirms that the [Prototypes] shall not be rejected by the [Licensee] except on reasonable grounds and in good faith. In the event the [Licensee] rejects the [prototypes] such rejection shall be made in writing within [twenty-eight days] of delivery to the [Licensee].

R.064
The [Licensee] confirms that in the event the [Prototypes] are not accepted by the [Licensee] all sums paid or due to be paid to the [Licensor] under this Agreement including the Prototype Fee and the [Licensor's] Consultancy Fee shall be paid back by the [Licensee] to the [Licensor].

R.065
The [Company] agrees that the [Licensor] shall have the right to approve all aspects of the [Licensed Articles] and any associated material prior to their production, manufacture, supply and distribution. The [Company] shall supply at its cost to the [Licensor] such copies, samples and packaging of the [Licensed Articles] in the exact form and material in which it is intended that they should be exhibited, distributed or sold at any time. In the event that the [Licensor] does not in each case provide written approval then the [Company] must not proceed with production until the reasons for the rejection have been resolved and written approval provided.

R.066
The [Licensee] undertakes that the [Products/Articles] and all samples, artwork, posters, packaging, catalogue, website, advertising, marketing and publicity material shall not be produced and/or manufactured by the [Licensee] and/or supplied and/or distributed and/or sold to any third party and/or the public until they have each in turn been inspected, assessed and written approval provided in each case by the [Licensor]. The [Licensor] shall have the right to reject any matter on grounds of artistic quality, size, colour, shape, safety, risks to health, legal, copyright, product liability, packaging or any other reason.

R.067
The [Sub-Licensee] agrees that it shall not reject any copies of any master material supplied on technical grounds provided that it is capable of upgraded to a suitable standard. The [Sub-Licensee] shall carry out such additional work as may be required at its sole cost to remedy any problem up to [figure/currency]. Where the work exceeds this sum the [Licensee] agrees to pay any additional costs provided that the [Sub-Licensee] agrees the cost in advance with the [Licensee].

R.068

Where the [Company] has commissioned, designs, artwork, photographs and/or other images. It is agreed that the [Company] shall not be entitled to reject them in the event they are no longer needed and there has been a change of strategy in relation to the marketing. The [Company] agrees to pay [Name] subject to delivery of the [Work] by the stated deadline.

Publishing

R.069

1.1 The [Publisher] reserves the right to reject the [Work] if it is clear that the contents of the [Work] do not conform to the style, form and synopsis agreed in writing with the [Author] or the standard reasonably expected of the [Author] by the [Publisher].

1.2 In the event that the [Publisher] rejects the [Work] or for any other reason under this Agreement, the [Author] shall be obliged to repay to the [Publisher] all sums previously paid to the [Author] as an Advance against Royalties.

R.070

The [Publisher] shall not reject the [Work] under Clause [–] above unless the [Author] has been given a reasonable opportunity to resubmit the [Work] having been notified in writing of the reasons for the rejection of the [Work] by the [Publishers].

R.071

If the [Work] has been completed and delivered by the [Author] in good faith and with proper care, then the [Publisher] agrees to abide by the [Publishers' Association Code of Practice/other]. In such event if the [Publishers] shall reject the [Work] it shall not seek to reclaim any sums paid in advance to the [Author].

R.072

The [Publisher] agrees that it shall only be entitled to reject the manuscript of the [Work] on reasonable and valid grounds which cannot be remedied by additional further amendments by the [Author] or by the editing process prior to publication. Provided that the [Author] has completed the [Work] in the style, form and content agreed in writing and has maintained a sufficiently competent standard of writing. Then the [Publisher] agrees that it shall be obliged to accept the [Work]. In the event the [Work] is rejected the [Publisher] shall provide detailed reasons for such rejection and provide the [Author] with sufficient time to remedy the alleged defects. Where the [Work] is further rejected then the [Publisher] agrees not to seek to recoup the sums paid in advance against royalties from the [Author] whether or not the [Work] is subsequently published elsewhere. The rejection of the [Work] by the [Publisher] shall terminate this Agreement and all rights provided to the [Publisher] by the [Author] shall immediately revert to the [Author]. The [Publisher] agrees to confirm the reversion of rights to the [Author] in writing and that the [Author] is permitted to arrange for the publication of the [Work] with another publisher.

R.073

The [Publisher] shall be entitled within a period of [six months] of the [date of this assignment] to decide whether to retain or reject the [Work] under this Agreement. In the event that the [Publisher] decides to reject the [Work] written notice shall be given to the [Assignor] and the [Publisher] shall assign all rights and interest it has acquired in the [Work] to the [Assignor]. The [Assignor] shall not be obliged to repay to the [Publisher] any sums that it has received from the Publisher in respect of the [Work] at any time. The [Publisher] shall not be liable to pay the [Assignor] any sums which may become due under this Agreement in respect of the [Work] from the [date of notice/date of reversion of the rights to the Assignor] which have not accrued to the [Assignor] before that date.

R.074

1.1 The [Publisher] agrees either to accept or provide written reasons for its rejection of the [Work] within [one month] of delivery.

1.2 The [Publisher] agrees that it shall provide the [Author] with a [three month] period in which to remedy the reasons for the rejection of the [Work] and that the [Author] may then resubmit the [Work] for consideration.

1.3 The [Author] agrees that in the event that the [Publisher] shall refuse to accept the manuscript of the [Work] on reasonable grounds and in good faith and has provided substantial written reasons for the rejection of the manuscript and/or after it has been resubmitted, then the [Author] shall be obliged to repay the [Publisher] the following sum [figure/currency] by [date/method/other].

R.075

The [Publishers] shall notify the [Author] within [number] days of the delivery of the [manuscript and the discs] whether they have accepted and/or rejected the [Work] in the form, content and style in which it has been delivered. The [Publishers] may reject the [Work] and/or require further changes before it can be resubmitted and in either case shall provide the details for their actions.

R.076

The [Publisher] agrees that it has read and assessed the [manuscript/treatment/synopsis] by the [Author] and accepted that the standard and quality of work by the [Author] is suitable for publication by the [Publisher]. There shall be no right of rejection under this Agreement and no right to reclaim sums paid on that basis. In the event that the [Publishers] express the view that the work by the [Author] requires further attention for any reason then an in-house editor shall be appointed to work with and advise the [Author] at the [Company's] cost.

R.077

1.1 The [Publisher] agrees that [Name] shall have the right to be consulted regarding the accuracy and detail of the [Articles] prior to publication in the form in which it is intended to be published in the [newspaper/magazine] including [headings, photographs, front cover, full article, surrounding material] and any associated promotion and advertising.

1.2 If the [Name] is not satisfied that any part of the material in 1.1 is accurate and correct and the [Publisher] is not willing to make the proposed changes, alterations or amendments. Then the [Publisher] agrees not to publish any of the material and to cancel the [Articles] provided that [Name] repays all sums paid to him/her under this Agreement within [ten days].

R.078

The [Publisher] agrees that the subject-matter of the [Article] shall principally cover [specify] and the interview will be conducted by [Name]. The [Publisher] agrees that the [Interviewee] shall have the right to decline to answer questions and statements outside the parameters of this area and/or to refuse to participate in an interview with any other person except [Name].

R.079

There shall be no right to reject the manuscript and demand a refund of the advance under this Agreement by the [Publisher]. The [Publisher] agrees and undertakes that, in the event that the material submitted is not suitable and/or to the standard expected, the parties shall work together to improve, develop and edit the [Work].

R.080

The [Company] agrees that it shall not be entitled to reject the [Work] and/or terminate the Agreement on the grounds of non-delivery where the [Author] delivers the [Work] within [one] month of the delivery date.

R.081

The [Distributor] agrees to accept and not reject the written material submitted by [Name] for the series of articles on the [Website] on the topic of [subject] provided that the articles:

1.1   Shall meet the length set by the [Distributor] in each case of [number] words.

1.2   Shall not contain any product placement and/or endorsement and/or mention any other website and/or competing brand to [specify].

Purchase and Supply of Products

R.082

The [Buyer/Hirer] shall carefully inspect and test the [Goods] immediately upon delivery to ensure that they comply with the requirements of the [Sales Order]. If requested by the [Company] reasonable notice shall be given of any such tests at which the [Company] shall be entitled to be represented. In the event that the [Goods] are rejected they shall be returned at [Buyer/Hirer's] risk and expense within [–] to the [Company] and no use whatsoever shall be made of such [Goods] so rejected.

R.083

If the [Goods] do not comply with the [Order] or any of the conditions are not complied with by the [Seller]. The [Buyer] shall at its sole discretion be entitled to reject the [Goods] and the [Order]. The [Buyer] shall return the rejected [Goods] to the [Seller] at the [Seller's] risk and expense or notify the [Seller] to collect the [Goods]. The [Buyer] may use its discretion to request the [Seller] to replace the [Goods] according to the [Order] or refund any monies paid.

R.084

Cancellation of this Agreement shall be subject to Clause [–]. Where written notice of cancellation has been received by the [Supplier] not less than [28] days prior to the Delivery Date, then no payment shall be due by the [Customer] to the [Supplier] for the [Goods] but the [Customer] shall not be entitled to a refund of the deposit if any.

R.085

1.1   The [Seller] agrees to advise the [Supplier] in writing with the reasons for rejecting any order within [a reasonable period/ten days] of delivery in each case.

1353

1.2 The [Seller] agrees that the order for the [Product] is on a firm sale basis and is not returnable unless faulty, defective or not fit for the intended purpose.

R.086

The [Company] agrees to advise the [Supplier] in writing with the reasons for rejecting any order in writing within [seven] working days of delivery in each case.

R.087

The [Company] reserves the right not to fulfil the terms of any Purchase Order and/or a request for specific goods and/or services at any time for any reason including but not limited to non-availability of material, goods and/or failure of facilities and/or suspension of manufacturing. In the event of the rejection of an order and/or request and/or cancellation at a later time. The [Company] agree to reimburse the [Client] in respect of any advance payment that has already been made.

R.088

The [Client] shall be entitled to reject the [Products] if the [Products] are not the type specified in your order (whether written and/or emailed) and/or the [Products] are not in a condition when they arrive which is of merchantable quality and/or fit for their intended purpose. The [Company] shall be provided with the opportunity to verify the condition and nature of the [Products] before the [Company] accepts the rejection of the [Products] which shall be no more than [twenty-eight days] after rejection by the [Client]. No subsequent delivery, insurance and freight charges and costs are accepted by the [Company] unless agreed in writing in advance.

R.089

The [Company] agrees that it shall not be entitled to reject the [Products] due to the non-delivery of [number] of the items in total per order.

R.090

The [Company] shall not be liable to the [Client] for any reason for any consequential loss and/or damages and costs suffered and/or incurred as a result of the rejection of the [Products] unless agreed in advance in writing by the [Company].

R.091

The [Purchaser] reserves the right to reject any [Products] supplied under this Order if in the opinion of the [Purchaser] they do not conform to the exact written specifications provided by the [Purchaser].

R.092

The [Purchaser] may at its sole discretion accept the [Products] without further payment where the number of units supplied by the [Company] exceeds the original Order. The [Purchaser] reserves the right to reject the [Products] if the number of units delivered is less than the original Order.

R.093

In the event that the [Purchaser] rejects the [Products] then the [Company] shall be responsible for all consequential administration, delivery, freight and insurance costs that may be incurred by the [Company].

R.094

The [Company] agrees that signature for acceptance of delivery of the [Products] at the designated address shall not constitute formal acceptance of the number, content and condition and shall not prevent the [Purchaser] rejecting the items at a later stage.

R.095

The [Company] reserves the right to take up to [number] weeks to decide whether to reject any service and/or products delivered by its suppliers and/or other third parties. Where a service and/or delivery of products is found to be below the standard required by the [Company]. Then the supplier and/or other third party shall be notified and permitted [number] days to remedy the problem. No payments are made until the problem has been resolved to the standard required by the [Company].

Services

R.096

The [Licensor] agrees to advise the [Agent] with the reason for rejecting any particular order requested by the [Agent].

R.097

If the [Agent] is unable and/or unwilling to provide [–] then the [Company] shall not be obliged to [provide the service/work]. In such case the [Company] shall have the right to retain [sum] and shall repay the balance to the [Agent].

R.098

Where the [Agent] and/or the [Company] give notice to the [Distributor] to cancel the Agreement, then the [Distributor] shall be have the right to keep the following percentages of the [Fee] prior to returning the balance to the [Agent]:

1.1   Where the [Distributor] receives written notice of cancellation [duration] prior to the [date] [number per cent].

1.2   Where the [Distributor] receives written notice of cancellation [duration] prior to the [date] [number per cent].

R.099
The [Company] shall have the right to reject the provision of the services by the [Enterprise] and to terminate this Agreement with [one] months notice where:

1.1   [Enterprise] is the subject of criminal proceedings and/or civil proceedings and/or other allegations which have received extensive negative media coverage and to which they have admitted their guilt and/or not defended the matter.

1.2   [Name/Enterprise] has provided a service which has been regularly interrupted, suspended, withdrawn, unavailable, defective, inaccurate and/or otherwise not to a suitable professional and technical standard for its intended purpose.

R.100
The services provided by [Name] to the [Company] may be rejected and the Agreement terminated in the event that:

1.1   The qualified personnel are not available at the times and dates required and/or are late and/or not equipped to complete the work.

1.2   The standard to which the work is carried out by the personnel poses a risk to the public and/or raises security and/or health and safety issues to the detriment of the [Company].

R.101
Where after the signature of this Agreement the [Performer/Presenter] suffers ill health and/or some other incapacity and/or disability which means that he/she cannot fulfil the terms of this Agreement. The [Company] agrees to delay the start of the Agreement for a period of [one] year. If after that time the [Performer/Presenter] is still unable and/or unwilling to fulfil the terms then he/she accepts that the [Company] may decide to cancel and/or terminate the Agreement and that the [Performer] shall not be entitled to any sums and/or payment.

Sponsorship

R.102
The [Contributor] confirms that his final decision as to whether to provide consent to the conclusion of any agreement negotiated by the [Company] shall not be unreasonably withheld and/or delayed.

R.103

The [Company] agrees that the [Contributor] shall be entitled to refuse to carry out any work and/or provide any endorsement of any matter which in the opinion of the [Contributor] would detrimentally effect his name, image, reputation, career prospects, and/or would contravene his status with any organisation of which he is a member and/or is likely to cause physical harm and/or injury at any time.

R.104

The [Sponsor] shall have the right to approve and/or reject any material upon which its name, logo and/or trade mark shall appear at the [Event] and/or in any merchandising, marketing and advertising and/or any other material. The [Company] shall supply a sample copy at the [Company's] cost on each occasion of any such material. The [Sponsor] agrees to approve and/or reject the material within [number] days. If the [Sponsor] rejects the material they shall specify the reason and make a recommendation as to the solution required to gain approval. The [Sponsor] agrees that they shall not be entitled to terminate the Agreement on the grounds that the [Company] did not seek approval for any material provided that it was a genuine error.

R.105

The [Club] shall be entitled to reject any material and/or products supplied by the [Sponsor] on the following grounds:

1.1 Health and safety and failure to comply with current legislation as to labels, content and/or product liability.

1.2 That the material and/or products are associated with a political organisation.

1.3 That the material and/or products are damaged, defective, flawed and/or not fit for their intended purpose.

R.106

The [Sponsor] shall not have any rights of approval and/or rejection over the advertising, marketing and promotion of the [Event]. The [Sponsor] shall not be entitled to refuse to pay the fees in clause [–] because it does not approve of the content of the catalogue, posters, banners and/or any other material. Provided that the [Sponsor's] [Logo/Name/Image] has been reproduced accurately and in the correct form and format agreed between the parties.

University, Library and Educational

R.107

1.1 The [Institute] agrees to provide details of the reasons for any rejection of the [Work/Project] in writing to the [Company] within [specify duration] of delivery and/or the operation of the [Work/Project].

1.2 The [Institute] shall not be obliged to provide the [Company] with an opportunity to remedy any defect, fault, error, omission and/or lack of compliance with the original specifications.

1.3 In the event that the [Institute] rejects the [Work/Project] on reasonable grounds and in good faith it shall be entitled to repayment of all the sums paid by the [Institute] to the [Company] prior to the date of delivery. Together with all direct consequential losses, damages, costs and expenses.

R.108

In the event that the [Work/Project] delivered to the [Institute] is not of satisfactory quality and/or does not comply with the [Synopsis]. Then the [Institute] shall provide the [Author/Contributor] with a reasonable opportunity to amend the [Work/Project] and specify the changes required. If the amended [Work/Project] is still not of sufficient quality and/or content then the [Institute] shall be entitled to give the [|Author/Contributor] written notice of rejection. The [Institute] shall be entitled to seek repayment of any advance against royalties which have been made to the [Author/Contributor].

R.109

There can be no presumption of acceptance of delivery of a [Work] by the [Institute]. A [Work] may be rejected at any time after delivery and acceptance can only be confirmed by notice in writing with the appropriate reference and confirmation allocated.

R.110

If there is a delay in delivery for any reason of the [Work/Products] to the [Institute] of more than [seven days] then the [Institute] shall be entitled to reject the delivery and shall not be liable to pay any sums for the [Work/Products].

R.111

If the [Work/Project] is damaged, destroyed, unfit for its intended purpose, not in accordance with agreed specifications as to size, shape, colour, use, and/or is technically defective, and/or unable to function and/or requires additional materials not originally disclosed by the [Company]. Then the

[Institute] shall be entitled without prejudice to any claim to reject the [Work/Project] by notice in writing to the [Company].

R.112

The [Institute] shall reject any manuscript submitted by any Contributor which:

1.1   Contains material in text and/or images from a third party which has been reproduced without sufficient credit and/ort acknowledgement and/or source reference.

1.2   Contains material which the [Institute] does not wish to publish as it would associate the [Institute] with a political and/or religious and/or other campaign.

1.3   Contains material which is potentially defamatory and/or could pose a risk of contempt of court and/or may lead to criminal and/or civil proceedings against any person named and/or the [Institute].

1.4   May lead to a negative media reaction against the [Institute].

REMAINDERS

General Business and Commercial

R.113

The parties agree that no [Product/Material] under this Agreement shall be sold off or disposed of except in strict accordance with the terms of this Agreement. Where either party wishes to remainder, destroy, sell off or otherwise depart from this Agreement then it shall be subject to the prior written agreement of the parties in each case. Failure to do so shall result in the party being bound to pay the full royalty rate under this Agreement in Clause [–].

R.114

All surplus stock which remains following the termination of fulfilment of this Agreement shall be disposed of at the complete discretion of the [Seller].

R.115

After the fulfilment or termination of this Agreement any stock surplus to requirements shall be returned immediately to [Name/address].

R.116

If not less than [two years] after the date of first [distribution/manufacture/ other] hereunder the [Company] wishes to sell off, dispose of and/or supply copies at a reduced price and/or as remainder and/or to destroy surplus copies. The [Company] shall notify [Name] and the parties shall negotiate a fixed unit cost payment per copy to be paid to [Name] on terms to be agreed.

R.117

Where the [Sub-Licensee] has stock remaining at the expiry of this Agreement. The [Sub-Licensee] agrees and undertakes that there is no right to sell, supply, distribute and/or otherwise exploit such material. The [Sub-Licensee] agrees and undertakes to arrange for the destruction of all such stock at a location and date agreed with the [Licensor]. The [Sub-Licensee] shall pay for all the costs of the destruction. Where stock is returned to the [Sub-Licensee] by third parties after the date of destruction then the [Sub-Licensee] shall ensure the safe disposal and destruction of all such material.

R.118

It is agreed between the parties that at the end of this Agreement the [Licensee] shall not be able to sell off any remaining stock and it must all be destroyed and verification provided to [Name] to that effect.

R.119

It is agreed between the parties that stock held by the [Distributor] on [date] the last day of the Agreement may be sold at a reduced price to a third party. Provided that [Name] is paid [number] per cent of the sum received by the [Distributor] within [number] days of receipt of payment for the stock. Further that evidence is provided of the disposal and total payment to the [Distributor] upon request by [Name].

Publishing

R.120

If not less than [two years] after the date of first publication hereunder the [Publisher] wishes to sell off copies at a reduced price or a remainder or to destroy surplus copies, the [Publisher] shall notify the [Author]. If the copies are sold the [Publisher] shall pay the [Author] [10]% (ten per cent) of its net receipts provided the copies are sold at or above cost price. If the copies are sold below cost price no royalty is payable. The [Author] shall be given [twenty-eight] days to purchase copies at the remainder price for his/her personal use. The [Author] shall not resell the copies without written permission of the [Publisher]. In the event of the [Publisher] deciding to destroy surplus copies the [Author] shall have the right to obtain all copies free of charge within [twenty-eight] days of notification provided that they are for personal use and/or for promotional purposes only and not for resale.

R.121

The [Publisher] shall not sell off copies of the [Work] as remainders within the expiry of [18 months] from the date of first publication without the prior written consent of the [Author]. In the event of copies of the [Work] being sold off as remainders at more than cost price the [Publishers] shall pay the Author [ten per cent of the net receipts from such sales/a fixed unit cost per copy of [figure/currency]]. The [Publishers] shall notify the [Author] in writing of their intention to remainder such of the [Work] at any time and shall allow the [Author] the opportunity to acquire the stock at the remainder price. After notification in each case if the [Author] has not offered to purchase the stock at remainder prices the [Publisher] shall be entitled to remainder such copies but shall provide the [Author] free of charge with [12] additional copies of the [Work].

R.122

The [Publisher] shall not be entitled to destroy, pulp, remainder or sell off any stock of the [Work] unless notice has been sent to the [Author] of their intentions and the Author offered the opportunity to acquire the stock. In any event the [Author] shall be sent [6] copies of the [Work] on each occasion free of charge.

R.123

If not less that [two years] after the date of first publication the [Company] wishes to destroy surplus copies it shall notify the [Author]. The [Author] shall have the right to obtain copies free of charge within [28 days] of notification. The [Author] shall not resell surplus stock copies without the prior written consent of the [Company].

R.124

The [Publishers] will not destroy all stock or sell them off as pulp without first providing written notice to the [Author] of their intention and sending the [Author] [12] copies for personal use.

R.125

The [Publishers] agree that it shall not remainder, destroy or pulp any copies of the [Work] which are of sufficient quality for sale to the public for a period of [12 months] from the date of first publication of the [Work] in hardback and [12 months] from the date of first publication of the [Work] in paperback. In the event that the [Publishers] decide to remainder the [Work] then the [Author] shall be entitled to receive [50%] of the receipts therefrom, whether above or below cost. If the [Publishers] shall decide to pulp or destroy copies of the [Work] then they shall provide written notification to the [Author] to that effect and the [Author] shall be entitled to negotiate a reasonable sum to purchase all such copies at cost price or less which the [Author] may resell at the [Author's] discretion. In the event that the [Author] does not wish to purchase the copies then the [Publishers] may destroy such copies provided that [30] are provided to the [Author] at no cost for the [Author's] personal use but not for resale.

R.126
Within [28 days] of the last day of [June/December] in each year the [Publisher] shall provide a detailed report to the [Author] with a full breakdown of the exploitation of the [Work] setting out the total sales including the number of copies for review or publicity purposes and the number of copies lost through damage or theft, destroyed, pulped, remaindered or for any other reason for which no royalty has been paid to the [Author].

R.127
The [Publishers] shall be entitled at their absolute discretion to remainder, pulp, destroy and/or sell off at a reduced price copies of the [Work] in any format where it is clear that there is not a demand, and/or there is too much stock and/or it has been reprinted and/or it is out of date and/or there is a legal problem and/or printing error and/or the [Work] is damaged and/or any other reason.

R.128
The [Publishers] shall be entitled at their absolute discretion to remainder, pulp, destroy and/or sell off at a reduced price copies of the [Work] in any format at any time. The [Publishers] agrees to pay the [Author] the minimum fixed unit price of [figure/currency] on all copies disposed off below [figure/currency].

R.129
If at any time the [Institute] shall decide that in their view there is no longer a demand for the [Work] and the [Institute] wishes to cease the production, publication, distribution and/or exploitation of the [Work] or of any edition and/or part of a series. Then the [Institute] agree and undertake to notify the [Author] of their intention and to provide the opportunity for the [Author] to purchase the remaining stock [at a low price at or below cost] and for all the rights to revert to the [Author]. In the event that the parties fail to reach agreement within [six months] from the date of notice then the [Institute] may destroy the stock.

RESIDENTIAL SUBSCRIBER

General Business and Commercial

R.130

'Residential Subscriber' shall mean a private residential home or dwelling unit other than a room including, but not limited to, a residential apartment building or complex which is entitled to receive the [Channel] by virtue of a contract with an Operator.

R.131

'Residential Subscriber' shall mean a private residence of any type whether rented, freehold and/or leasehold which is not classed as a business for tax purposes by which the person who is responsible for the household bills has entered into an agreement for the supply of the [Service] through a [Service Provider] through [method and equipment] and agreed to pay monthly instalments for such [Service].

RESTRAINT OF TRADE

Employment

R.132

The [Employee] is not allowed without prior written consent of the [Company] to undertake any other employment outside working hours whether paid or not, nor is he/she permitted to have any interest in business or connections with any similar or competing business to the [Company].

R.133

The [Employee] confirms that he/she shall not during the course of this Agreement supply services of the same or similar nature to the services provided under this Agreement to any third party without the prior written consent of the [Company].

R.134

Except with written consent of the [Company] the [Employee] shall not be engaged directly or indirectly in any other activity which conflicts with the interests and/or operation of the [Company]. During working hours the [Employee's] duties to the [Company] shall have first priority.

R.135

The [Manager] shall not without the prior written consent of the [Chairman] of the [Company] during the period of [one year] after the termination of his/her employment either alone, jointly, as agent, director, consultant or otherwise of any other person, firm or company directly or indirectly in competition with any business or activities of the [Company]:

1.1 Solicit the services, work or contribution of any person, firm or corporation who or which at any time during the last year of the [Manager's] employment with the [Company] shall have been a supplier, agent or distributor or customer of the [Company].

1.2 Endeavour to entice away from the [Company] any person who at any time is an employee, director [or consultant].

1.3 Deal with any person, firm or corporation who at any time in the last year of the [Manager's] employment with the [Company] shall have been in the habit of dealing under contract with the [Company].

R.136

The [Employee] may not reproduce any work created in the course of his/her employment or at the [Company's] request (whether published or not) without the [Company's] prior written consent.

R.137

Each [Partner] agrees that upon his/her departure from the [Firm] he/she shall not without the prior written approval of the [Firm] for a period of [two years] from the date of [departure/termination/resignation] either alone or in conjunction with any other third party do any of the following matters which would prejudice the business interests of the [Firm]:

1.1 Provide legal advice in any capacity within [a radius of one mile/the area of [–] of the [Firm].

1.2 Solicit or entice away any existing employee, partner or otherwise of the [Firm].

1.3 Approach, solicit, contract or seek to obtain the custom of any client of the [Firm] who was a client at the date of the [Partner's] departure particularly those persons who were advised by the [Partner] while at the [Firm] [but excluding [Names] who were brought to the [Firm] by the [Partner].

1.4 The [Partner] shall not use any confidential information about the clients or business interests of the [Firm] for his/her own benefit or another to either obtain their custom or for the benefit of a competing person or company.

R.138

The [Employee] confirms that he/she shall not during the course of this Agreement supply services of the same or similar nature to any third party without the prior consent of the [Company].

R.139

The [Employee] agrees and undertakes that he/she shall not during a period of [number months/years] after the expiry or termination of this Agreement deliberately approach, contact and pursue any person, firm, company or business with whom the [Company] had a regular business relationship or a large contract at the time of the departure of the [Employee] of which the [Employee] was aware or with whom the [Employee] dealt with on behalf of the [Company].

This Clause shall not apply where:

1.1 The [Employee] is approached or contacted by the person, firm or company, and the [Employee] shall have the right to take up an offer of employment to be with them.

1.2 The [Employee] was provided with written consent in advance by the [Company].

1.3 The [Employee] was or is alleging that he/she was unfairly dismissed or is suing the [Company] for breach of contract.

1.4 The person, firm or company was first introduced to the [Company] by the [Employee] due to a prior business relationship with the [Employee].

1.5 The [Company] is not trading or is insolvent or is bankrupt.

1.6 The [Company] moves premises to another area, totally changes the market which it targets, totally changes the [products/services] which it sells.

R.140

The [Employee] undertakes that he/she shall not for a period of [six months/ one year] after the expiry or termination of this Agreement induce or seek to induce any employee of the [Company] to leave its service.

R.141

The [Company] agrees that it shall have no right to restrict and/or prevent [Name] from applying for a new job at a competitor and/or to restrict the ability of [Name] to be employed and/or work as a consultant for any such competitor whether or not that involves making pitches and presentations to the same clients.

Film and Television

R.142
The [Company] agrees that the [Television Company] is entitled to arrange for other companies to sponsor, endorse, advertise or promote their products, services, designs, trade mark and/or logos in the [Programme]. Provided that no third party shall be entitled to have its products, services, logo, trade mark or designs incorporated in the [Programme] which directly competed with the [Sales/Market] of [specify] of the [Company's Product].

R.143
The [Company] agrees and undertakes that it will not with immediate effect assign, license, charge or in any other way deal with any rights in any media assigned hereunder including, but not limited to the following [specify areas of rights] in respect of the Film(s) and/or any part(s) of them in any part of the Territory until the expiry of the [Assignment Period/Term of this Agreement].

R.144
The [Sponsor] of the [Film/Work/Event] agrees that it shall have no right to prevent and/or restrict the contribution and/or participation by third parties to the [Film/Work/Event] on any grounds and/or in any other way to interfere with the editorial decisions.

General Business and Commercial

R.145
Both parties confirm and declare that the provisions of this Agreement are fair and reasonable and both parties having taken independent legal advice and declare that this Agreement is not against public policy either on the grounds of inequality or bargaining power or on the general grounds of restraint of trade.

R.146
The [Radio Station] confirms that no products, services or other material belonging to any third party which would reasonably be construed as being in direct competition with the [Sponsor's Product] shall be promoted on the [Programme] for the duration of the Sponsorship Period. This clause shall apply only to the [Programme] itself and not to any advertisements broadcast or transmitted during a commercial break in the [Programme].

Internet and Websites

R.147
The [Company] does not have any right to restrict the services or work of the [Contributor] at any time either now or in the future or to acquire any interest,

1366

option or rights over any future services or work other than those specifically set out in this Agreement.

R.148
The [Company] agrees that [Name] shall be entitled during the Term of this Agreement to provide his/her services to any third party provided that it is not for the advertisement, promotion and/or endorsement of a product or service in the category of [specify type] from [date] to [date] in the following media [specify].

R.149
The [Contributor] agrees and undertakes that he/she shall not provide his/her services to any other website and/or internet related business during the term of this Agreement without the prior written consent of the [Company].

R.150
It is agreed between all parties that the [Website] is only to be used for the promotion of [subject] by the [Consortium] and not for any purpose connected with [specify].

Merchandising

R.151
In consideration of the payment of the [Fee] the [Company] agrees and undertakes not to license, authorise and/or endorse the reproduction and/or adaptation of the image of [specify] reference [specify] on the following products and/or services from [date] to [date] in [country].

R.152
The [Distributor] agrees and undertakes that it shall release any directly competing product on its catalogue on the subject of [specify] at the same time and/or within [number] weeks of the [Licensed Article].

R.153
The [Licensee] agrees and undertakes not to enter into an agreement with any other person and/or business with a directly competing product on the subject of [specify] from [date] to [date].

R.154
The [Company] agrees that it shall not be entitled to use, exploit, promote, advertise and/or market the title of the [Programme/Work] and/or any script, artist, music, slogan and/or any other parts in conjunction with the [Company's] products and/or any other services and/or products of the [Company]. This Agreement is solely related to the placement of the

1367

[Company's] Product on the [Programme/Work] and not a licence, sub-licence and/or any other authority to the [Company] to exercise and/or exploit any rights and/or interest.

R.155

The [Licensee] agrees and undertakes that it shall not be entitled to engage, employ and/or permit any manufacturer to use persons who are:

1.1   Under [number] year of age.

1.2   Paid less than the minimum wage of [number/currency] per hour.

1.3   Work for more than [number] hours in each week.

Publishing

R.156

The [Copyright Owner] warrants that prior to this Agreement he/she has not assigned, transferred or licensed and will not during the Licence Period, assign, transfer or license any of the rights or title to the [Concept] for the Territory.

R.157

The [Copyright Owner] warrants that during the period of the Licence set out in Clause [–] no third party shall exercise the following rights [specify] in the Territory in the [Concept] or any development or variation in any form under licence or with the authority of the [Copyright Owner].

R.158

The [Author] shall not without prior consent of the [Publishers] write, supply, publish, authorise and/or permit the publication of any other work in [printed form/in any media] on the topic of [–]. Nor shall the [Author] contribute to or collaborate in the [preparation/publication] of a work in [printed form/in any media] on the same or similar subject as set out in this Agreement which may reasonably be regarded as likely to compete with or prejudice the sale of the [Work] in the Territory during the Term of this Agreement.

R.159

The [Author] shall not without the written consent of the [Publishers] (which shall not be reasonably withheld or delayed) arrange the publication of any other work by the [Author] which because of its content is likely to have a prejudicial or damaging effect on the sale of the [Work].

R.160

The [Author] shall not throughout the Territory for the duration of the Licence Period publish or authorise the publication of any other work in any printed form for sale to the public on the same subject as the [Work] which is likely or intended to compete with or prejudice or injure the sales of the [Work] without prior written consent of the [Publishers]. Such consent not to be unreasonably withheld or delayed.

R.161
The [Author] shall not prepare, except for the [Publishers] in the Territory covered by this Agreement, any work which is identical or substantially similar in title, content or form to the [Work] under this Agreement.

R.162
The [Company] agrees not to authorise or permit or enter into any agreement with any third party to write, research or produce any other book or publication based on the synopsis or any development or variation at any time during the Term of the Agreement throughout the Territory.

R.163
The [Publisher] agrees that the [Author] shall not be restricted as to the type of future work that he/she may write and/or any third party that they may wish to enter an agreement with by the terms of this Agreement whether the future work directly competes with this [Work] or not and whether or not it may prejudice sales. That this Agreement is limited to the licence only of the [number] edition of the [Work]. The [Author] may enter into a new agreement with a third party for any new edition, revised version, sequel and/or development of any nature whether based on this [Work] or not at any time after the expiry of [one] from the date of this Agreement.

R.164
[Name] agrees and undertakes that from the date of this Agreement until the expiry of [30 days] from the last day of the Publication Date(s) he/she will not give any interview, disclose any information, agree to be filmed and/or in a sound recording and/or appear in any photographs and/or engage in any telephone conversation with any person, firm, company and/or business in the media including but not limited to newspapers, radio, television, news agencies, website companies or otherwise. Nor shall [Name] grant, consent or provide permission for the supplying, taking and/or reproduction of [Photographs/Stills/other] to any third party in the Territory. The [Publisher] agrees that after the expiry of [30 days] from the last day of the Publication Date(s) that [Name] shall be entitled to exploit the information and/or [Photographs] as he/she thinks fit.

R.165
The [Publisher] agrees that it has no rights to:

1.1 Any subsequent work by the [Author] whether based on the same subject or not including any new edition.

1.2 Prevent and/or restrict the [Author] being employed, engaged as a consultant and/or commissioned by any other publisher and/or distributor in any country.

Purchase and Supply of Products

R.166

The [Seller] agrees that the [Supplier] shall be entitled to deal with, sell, loan or hire or otherwise exploit the [Product] at any time to any third parties whether on the internet or otherwise.

R.167

Where the [Supplier] intends to supply the [Product] to a direct competitor of the [Seller] whether a website business, mail order, distributor, manufacturer, supplier and/or otherwise. The [Supplier] shall notify the [Seller] of its intentions and the [Seller] shall have the right to cancel the Agreement and/or only be liable to pay for any sums due to the date of cancellation.

R.168

The [Distributor] is not to use the information obtained under this Agreement concerning the products and/or the market and/or the business and/or staff of the [Company] to entice, poach or solicit employees or customers of the [Company] nor shall the [Distributor] disclose any such information and/or or data to any third party who competes in the same market which is not available to members of the public.

R.169

The [Supplier] agrees and undertakes not to supply and/or distribute the [Product] to retail shops and supermarkets and/or wholesale outlets in the town of [specify] until after [date].

Services

R.170

The [Manager] shall not without the prior written consent of the [Company] for a period of [one year] after the termination of this Agreement carry on or be engaged, concerned or interested in any business which is directly competitive to that carried out by the [Company]. This restriction shall apply to any premises within [number mile radius] of any premises listed below [specify].

R.171

The [Contractor] undertakes that he/she will not during the period of the Agreement without the prior written consent of the [Company]:

1.1 Undertake any activity which is likely to associate him/her in any way with commercial advertising on [television, radio, telephones, products, services, internet, computer software, DVDs, CDs, CD-Roms, discs, games] nor permit himself/herself to be so associated.

1.2 Offer for publication or speak in public about or assist in the making of a sound recording about and/or distribute any statement about the [Company's] business affairs, directors, or personnel. Written consent shall only be withheld if there is a reasonable likelihood of damage to the interests of the [Company].

R.172

The [Artist] undertakes that he/she will not [record/enter into a contract with/release a musical product with] any other party within [one year] from the termination or expiry of this Agreement or [six months] from the deletion of the [Record/CD/other] from the [Company's] current catalogue, whichever period is the shorter, any composition recorded by the [Artist] for the [Company] at any time. If such recorded composition has not been commercially released by the [Company] within [twelve] months after the termination or expiry of this Agreement then this prohibition shall not apply thereafter to any such composition.

R.173

The [Artist] agrees that he/she shall not be entitled to record for the purpose of commercial exploitation throughout the Territory with any third party any material recorded by or on behalf of the [Record Company] for a period of [specify period] from the date of expiry or termination of this Agreement.

R.174

The [Artist] warrants that for a period of [duration] from the date upon which a particular [Record/CD/other] which includes a performance by the [Artist] is first released to the general public, the [Artist] shall not either alone or with a third party perform any of the songs, lyrics, compositions, or musical works performed on that [Record/CD/other] whether in the Territory or not and whether during the License Period or not.

R.175

The [Presenter] agrees not to provide services for any other [television/ radio/internet telephone/advertisement/publishing/other media] business] other than of a charitable nature and purpose throughout the Term of this Agreement [in country] without the prior written consent of the [Company].

R.176

The [Presenter] agrees that he/she shall not engage in any hazardous or dangerous pursuit or voluntarily take any risks the taking of which might result in the [Presenter] being prevented from providing his/her services pursuant to this Agreement.

R.177

The [Presenter] shall not at any time either on his/her own account or jointly with or for any other person, firm or company solicit, interfere with or endeavour to entice away from the [Company] any person, firm, company who at any time during the Term of this Agreement [or after termination] were contractors, employees, licensees, suppliers, advertisers with and/or agents of and/or had business dealings with the [Company] or any subsidiary or associated company.

R.178

The [Consultant] undertakes to the [Company] that he/she shall not during the Term of this Agreement knowingly engage in any activities or otherwise act in a manner conflicting with or contrary to the requirements of [Name] or any code guidelines or other instructions made or issued by the [Company] at any time.

R.179

The [Presenter] agrees that he/she shall not at any time during the continuance of this Agreement or for a period of [–] after the termination or expiry of this Agreement solicit, interfere with or endeavour to entice away from the [Company] any person, firm or company who at any time during the preceding year or at the date of the end this Agreement were licensors, licensees, agents, distributors, consultants, advisors, advertisers, sponsors, or any other person, firm and/or business of which the [Presenter] was aware had agreements with and/or provide services and/or goods and/or paid the [Company].

R.180

During the Term of this Agreement the [Artist] undertakes not to contribute to or make any sound recordings or other recordings or supply any musical work created by the [Artist] for any third party in any form for commercial exploitation without the prior written consent of the [Record Company].

R.181

The [Record Company] confirms that the [Artist] is entitled to make contributions of a charitable nature to any third party. Provided that the [Artist] gives the [Record Company] reasonable notice of the event, and that no such engagement shall take precedence over obligations of the [Artist] under this Agreement.

R.182

The [Artist] agrees that for a period of [–] he/she will not engage himself/herself in anyway to any third party for the production of a record, CD or other sound recording or other recording which copies, replicates or uses any musical work, sounds, sound effects or performance by the [Artist] which has already been recorded and performed by the [Artist] for the [Company] in [reference/title/detailed description] without first obtaining the prior permission of the Company. This restriction shall not apply after [date].

R.183

The [Company] agrees that the [Person] is already committed and entitled to carry out the following work during the Term of this Agreement [specify]

R.184

The [Company] agrees that the [Person] shall be entitled during the Term of this Agreement to provide his/her services to any third party for work (in addition to that set out in Clause [–]) provided that it is not for the advertisement, promotion and endorsement of a product or service [specify type].

R.185

The [Company] acknowledges that the [Contributor] shall be entitled to offer his/her services in any other media [except any website and/or internet related business] during the term of this engagement to third parties.

R.186

The [Agent] agrees that this Agreement relates exclusively to the [Work] and that the [Agent] does not have the right to exploit any other material including any books created by the [Author] whether prior to the date of this Agreement during the Term of this Agreement or at any time thereafter without the prior written consent of the [Author].

Sponsorship

R.187

The [Sportsperson] undertakes that he/she will not enter any other [sponsorship, endorsement or promotion agreement] with any third party concerning the [same/similar items/market] in respect of the [Sponsor's] Product for the duration of the Sponsorship Period without the prior written consent of the [Sponsor].

R.188

The [Sportsperson] undertakes not to enter into agreement to promote or endorse the products of the following companies for the duration of the Sponsorship Period [specify]

R.189

The [Person] undertakes not to provide his/her services to any third party for the advertisement or promotion of a product or service of any type whether it directly competes with the [Company's] product or not other than services of a charitable nature throughout the Term of this Agreement without the prior written consign of the [Company].

R.190

This Agreement shall not entitled the [Sponsor] to prevent, restrict and/or interfere with the [Athlete] entering into a contract with any other firm, person and/or business and/or to be sponsored by and/or to endorse any goods and/or services of any nature in any country at any time.

R.191

The [Company] agrees and undertakes not to enter into any contract with and/or to authorise the sale, supply, and/or distribution of another product which is a [specify type] at the [Event]. This clause shall not apply after [date].

R.192

The [Company] agrees and undertakes not to authorise, permit and/or enter into any agreement for any product which is in the field of [–] to be used in any advertisements, promotions, signs, banners, sound recordings and/or any other material at the [Event] and/or in any marketing, merchandising and/or other forms of exploitation controlled by the [Company]. This clause shall not apply after [date].

University, Library and Educational

R.193

The [Company] agrees that it shall not produce, publish, supply, market, promote, distribute and/or exploit any work and/or product and/or service in any format and/or medium which is based upon and/or derives from the [Project] and/or any part including the title at any time. The [Company] agrees if it does so that this shall be considered a breach of this Agreement and the [Company] shall be liable to pay the [Institute] the sum of [figure/currency] [without prejudice to any other rights and claims of the [Institute].]

R.194

The [Contributor] agrees and undertakes to the [Institute] that she will not without the prior written consent of the [Institute] for a period of [six months] after the expiry and/or termination of this Agreement enter into an agreement with and/or be employed by the following directly competitive businesses [specify companies].

R.195

The [Institute] agrees and undertakes that this Agreement does not confer any right on the [Institute] to restrict, prohibit and/or prevent the [Company] carrying out any work and/or services for any other person, company or otherwise. This shall also apply to third parties in the same [specify] market, and/or directly competing works and/or services and/or parts.

R.196

1.1 The [Institute] acknowledges and agrees that the [Contributor] shall be entitled during the Term of this Agreement to provide her services to any third party except the following directly competing companies [specify].

1.2 That the [Contributor] will not arrange her commitments so that those to a third party shall take precedence over the obligations of the [Contributor] to the [Institute] under this Agreement.

1.3 The [Institute] acknowledges that the [Contributor] is already committed and entitled to carry out the following work during the Term of this Agreement [specify]

RIGHTS

Employment

R.197

The [Executive] acknowledges, agrees and undertakes that all intellectual property rights including copyright, design rights, computer software rights, inventions, patents, modifications and improvements, processes, formulae, know-how, computer generated material, rights to data and databases, trade marks, service marks, logo, domain names, character, title, slogan, sound recordings, films, photographs, downloads, banners and any other rights and material of any nature whether in existence now and/or created in the future in the product of the services under this Agreement shall remain the sole and exclusive property of the [Company]. This Agreement does not purport to transfer, assign, licence or provide consent to the use and/or registration by the [Executive] of any rights and/or material.

R.198

The [Executive] agrees and undertakes that all intellectual property rights including but not limited to copyright, design rights, trade marks, service marks, patents, rights to data and databases, and computer software which arise as a result of the provision of the [Executives'] services to the [Company] shall entirely belong to the [Company]. The [Executive] shall not have any rights and/or interest and/or be entitled to receive any sums from the exploitation of any material in any medium at any time.

R.199

The [Company] agrees and undertakes that the [Company] shall not be entitled to any material and/or rights in any work, research, project, and/or publication on the subject of [specify] which is created and/or developed by [Name].

R.200

The [Company] shall be entitled to own, control and represent that it is the copyright owner of all material and/or rights which are created during the course of the [Employees] work for the [Company].

R.201

Where the [Executive] during the course of the services and/or work for the [Company] creates and/or develops any new material and/or rights and/or computer software rights, inventions, patents, modifications and improvements, processes, formulae, know-how, trade mark, logo, domain name, character or otherwise of any nature whether in existence now and/or created in the future. The [Company] agrees and undertakes to enter in to a separate agreement for such rights and/or material with an advance and royalties paid to the [Executive] for the use, registration and exploitation by the [Company] at any time. Both parties shall hold the rights and/or material as [joint owners].

R.202

[Name] agrees that in consideration of the fees by the [Company] that he/she shall assign to the [Company] all copyright, intellectual property rights, computer software rights, inventions, patents, trade marks, logos, slogans, computer generated material, documents, data, emails, text messages, recordings, films, photographs, images and any other material in any medium and/or format which he/she creates, develops, sends, receives and/or produces at any time during the course of his/her engagement and work at the [Company] whether during normal office hours and/or thereafter using equipment owned and/or controlled and/or supplied by the [Company].

R.203

The [Company] agrees and accepts that:

1.1   It shall have no right to access and/or use and/or reproduce the private emails of [Name] whether sent during hours of employment or not.

1.2   It shall not have any right to supply the personnel file of [Name] at the [Company] to any third party which includes any confidential medical report and records.

1.3   That the [Company] may not disclose all the contents of a personnel file of [Name] to any third party except a professional qualified legal advisor to the [Company] and then any disclosure shall be limited to documents and emails as may be directly relevant.

1.4   It shall have no right to distribute, release and/or use and/or reproduce and/or supply the image of [Name] on his/her security pass and/or any other taken by the [Company] in any material and/or to a third party without the prior written consent of [Name].

DVD, Video and Discs

R.204

'The DVD and Video Rights' shall mean the right to transfer, manufacture, duplicate, supply, distribute, sale, rent, make available under a subscription service or otherwise exploit the [Film] by means of electronic reproduction in the form of a disk or magnetic tape (including, but not limited to cassettes, cartridges, reel to reel) which consists of a sequence of visual images (with or without sound) capable of being shown as a moving picture via a television and DVD/video player and/or some other portable device and/or a computer and/or other product, but excluding the internet and any website and/or any telecommunication system, transmission and/or broadcast of any nature. The right is only applicable for use in a private domestic residence, and/or private domestic car by members of the public and not for any educational, commercial, religious, promotional and/or non-domestic use.

R.205

'The Videogram Rights' shall mean the right to transfer, manufacture and duplicate the [Series] by means of electronic reproduction in the form of any disk or magnetic tape [including, but not limited to, cassettes, cartridges and reel to reel or otherwise] which consists of a sequence of visual images with or without sound and/or subtitles capable of being shown as a moving picture and to sell, rent, supply, distribute and have distributed the [Series] in any such form for private home use only by the public.

R.206

'The DVD and Video Rights' shall mean:

1.1   The right to transfer, manufacture, reproduce, supply, distribute, rent and sell the [Film] by means of electronic reproduction in the form of any disk or magnetic tape which consists of a sequence of visual images with or without sound capable of being viewed as a moving picture by means of a playback device which is either separate from but used in conjunction with or is in fact an integral part of the television set, computer, or portable product, but the [Film] is displayed on the screen for private home use only by the public and

1.2   The right to authorise any third party to carry out and do the things set out in 1.1 provided that the party authorising the work is responsible and liable for all their acts and omissions.

R.207

'The DVD and Disc Rights' shall mean the sole and exclusive right in the Territory during the Licence Period to manufacture, reproduce, supply, distribute, rent and/or sell the complete [Film] in the form of discs and DVDs by means of electronic reproduction in the form of any disc which consists of a sequence of visual images with sound capable of being viewed on a screen as a moving picture by means of a playback device in conjunction with a television set, computer, and/or portable gadget for private home use only by the public.

R.208

'The Video, DVD and Disc Rights' shall mean the right to transfer, manufacture, duplicate, reproduce, sell, rent, supply, distribute and have distributed the [Film] whether for home use only and/or by educational, cultural, religious and/or social groups and/or otherwise and to commercial companies and businesses including hotels, airlines, ships by means of electronic and/or mechanical reproduction [whether in existence now or created in the future] in any form of disk, magnetic tape or other method so that the [Film] is shown as a moving image (with or without sound but not sound on its own) intended for reproduction on copies which are inserted in or used in conjunction with a machine or other apparatus to be played on a television, computer or other visual screen by a video recorder, DVD player or some other machine whether the two are distinct or one item including a videocassette, disc, disk, laser, reel to reel, DVD, CD-Rom. This shall not include the internet and websites or any electronic communication, delivery by mobile telephone or any telecommunication system, item or article.

R.209

'The Non-Theatric Rights' shall mean the right to permit or license, sale or hire the exhibition of the [Film/DVD] to non-paying audiences in all formats in business and commercial industries and organisations of an educational, cultural, religious, charitable and social nature including, but not limited to, schools, churches, evening institutions, museums, hospitals, prisons, summer camps, drama groups, film societies, professional associations, public libraries, colleges and universities, hotels and private clubs [and aeroplanes].

R.210

'The Non-Theatric Rights' shall mean the right to exhibit the [Film] in the Territory during the Licence Period to non-theatric audiences who are not making any specific payment to view or hear the film including, but not limited to, the following categories of audiences:

1.1 Educational institutions such as schools, universities, colleges.

1.2 Educational classes and meetings held by companies or other non-educational bodies.

1.3 Clubs or other organisations of an educational, cultural, charitable or social nature including film libraries and societies.

1.4 Closed circuit television, an enclosed wired system which is relayed to an audience in a confined area such as hotels, oil rigs, ships, aeroplanes.

R.211

'The Non-Theatric Rights' hereby granted means the sole and exclusive right in the Territory during the Licence Period to permit or license the exhibition of the [Film(s)] and to authorise others to do any of such things: sale, hire, lease or licensing in all formats and by means of all technologies now in existence or hereafter invented or discovered for the exhibition of the [Film(s)] and/or parts to non-paying audiences in all educational institutions, schools, public libraries, colleges, universities, dormitories and residence halls, churches, evening institutions, museums, hospitals, prisons, summer camps, business and industry hotels, clubs and other organisations of any educational, cultural, religious, charitable or social nature, drama groups, film societies and professional associations, instructional television and to all other entities and all other places except for the exclusive showing in private theatres to which the general public is customarily invited and admitted upon payment of an admission fee.

R.212

'The Non-Theatric Rights' shall mean the right to exhibit the [Film] to non-paying audiences in all business and commercial industries and organisations of an educational, cultural, religious, charitable and social nature including, but not limited to, schools, churches, educational and social institutions, museums, hospitals, prisons, summer camps, drama and film groups, professional bodies, libraries, colleges, universities, hotels and private clubs.

R.213

The [Licensee] is not being granted the electronic communication and/or telecommunication rights in the [Film] and/or parts, nor any right to transmit or receive the [Film] and/or parts by any electronic communication or telecommunication system whether by use of mobile telephones, terrestrial landline or cable telephones, or on the worldwide web or internet otherwise. All rights not specifically granted are reserved by and belong to the [Licensor].

R.214

The [Licensor] hereby grants the [Licensee] the exclusive and irrevocable right [in perpetuity/for the Term of the Agreement] to manufacture and have manufactured [Videos/DVDs/Discs] containing the [Programme] and to sell, lease, license, sub-license, distribute, advertise and otherwise market and exhibit such [Videos/DVDs/Discs] and to license, sub-license, and otherwise authorise others to do so. The rights granted do not include the right to authorise the use of such [Videos/DVDs/Discs] for viewing in any place where an admission fee is charged, or for viewing over a television broadcast, satellite, digital or cable system, whether free or pay per view or otherwise, or for theatrical exhibition. The [Licensee] shall also have the right to use the [Programme] or portions thereof for the purposes of advertising, publicity and otherwise promoting and testing and demonstrating [Videos/DVDs/Discs] containing the [Programme] and the [Videos/DVD/Discs] system or devices, and to exhibit excerpts thereof for such purposes.

R.215

In consideration of the Advance and the [Licensor's] Royalties, the [Licensor] grants to the [Licensee] the sole and exclusive [Video, DVD and Disc Rights] in the [Film] [and/or parts] throughout the Territory for the duration of the Licence Period.

R.216

In consideration of the Assignment Fee the [Assignor] assigns to the [Assignee] all present [Video, DVD and the Non-Theatic Rights] in the [Film] and/or parts throughout the Territory for the full period of the copyright and any extensions or renewals.

R.217

In consideration of the Assignment Fee the [Assignor] assigns to the [Assignee] all present and future copyright and any other rights in all media whether in existence now or created in the future, including, but not limited to, [specify rights] in the [Video/DVD] and/or part(s) throughout the [Territory/ world] for all the period of copyright and any extensions and renewals.

R.218

In consideration of the Licence Fee and the [Licensor's] Royalties the [Licensor] grants to the [Licensee] the sole and exclusive [Videogram Rights and Non-Theatric Rights] in the [Film] and to authorise any third party to exercise such rights throughout the Territory for the duration of the Licence Period.

R.219

Subject to Clause [–] below the [Assignor] and the [Assignee] both agree that they shall hold joint present and future copyright and all other rights in the [Series] and parts in all media whether in existence now or created in the future throughout the Territory for the full period of copyright and any extensions or renewals.

R.220

In consideration of the Budget the [Assignor] assigns to the [Assignee] the sole and exclusive [Video, DVD and Disc Rights] in the [Series] and part(s) throughout the Territory for the full period of copyright and any extensions or renewals.

R.221

The [Assignee] shall be entitled to use and permit the use of the [Film] for the purpose of trade and in demonstrations to promote and advertise the [DVD/Video/Disc] of the [Film].

R.222

1.1   The [Licensor] grants by way of license to the [Licensee] the sole and exclusive right to manufacture, sell, rent, supply and distribute, whether by wholesale, retail, mail order, subscription or direct marketing and to authorise others to do so in the Territory during the Term of this Agreement [DVDs/Videos/Discs] reproducing the [Film] in respect of the exercise of the [DVD/Video/Disc Rights].

1.2   The [Licensee] may incorporate [one or two extracts] of less than [–] of the [Film] with any other films reproduced on DVDs or videos or discs or as a trailer or advertisement before or after other films. Provided that the other DVDs, videos, discs or films appeal to a similar market in terms of age and content and the extracts are only used to promote and advertise the [Film]. No royalties shall be due to the [Licensor] in respect of reproduction of the parts of the [Film] for the purpose of trailers, advertising and promotion of [Film].

1.3 The Licensee shall have the right at its sole discretion, to commission and produce dubbed and/or sub-titled versions of the [Film] for exploitation of the DVDs, videos and discs in non-English speaking countries of the Territory. The [Licensee] shall bear the cost of all such work [but shall be entitled to deduct the cost in full from royalties due to the [Licensor] under this Agreement subject to providing details of the full costs and supporting documentation]. The [Licensee] shall provide on request copies of the sub-titled and dubbed versions for use by the [Licensor] at the [Licensor's] cost and expense.

R.223

The material is supplied to the [Customer] on the terms that:

1.1 It shall be used by the [Customer] only for private and/or domestic use or for exhibition to the [Customer's] own staff only without charge of an entrance fee.

1.2 The [Customer] will not exploit, copy, reproduce or part with physical possession of the material or part thereof to any other third party.

1.3 No fee shall be charged by the [Customer] for any private exhibition of any film material or video cassette or slides and no such exhibition details shall be advertised, be released in publicity material or distributed except to the [Customer's] own staff.

R.224

All contracts for the exploitation by the [Company] of the [DVD/Video/Disc Rights] shall be subject to the prior written approval of the [Licensor], such approval shall not be unreasonably withheld or delayed.

R.225

The [Licensor] grants a licence to the [Licensee] to record the [Musical Works] in synchronisation with the soundtrack of the [Film] and to manufacture, distribute, sell and supply [Videos/DVDs/Discs] reproducing the [Musical Works] synchronised with the [Film] throughout the Territory for the Term of this Agreement.

R.226

The [Distributor] grants the [Exhibitor] a licence for the non-commercial exhibition of the [Film] on [date] [one showing] during the period of the Licence at the [venue] provided that:

1.1 The [Film] may not be exhibited to the general public.

1.2 The exhibitions may not be advertised to the general public.

1.3 No admission charges or other consideration may be requested of the members of the audience whether or not such charge or consideration relates to the exhibitions of the [Film].

1.4 The [Film] must be exhibited in full as supplied including copyright notices, credits, titles, trade marks, and soundtrack.

1.5 The [Exhibitor] shall ensure that any licence for the performance of the [Film] is obtained from the [Performing Rights Society/other] and shall be paid for by the [Exhibitor].

1.6 The Exhibitor shall pay all [Distributor's] charges and costs set out in clause [–].

R.227

The [Licensee] shall be entitled to use and permit the use of not more than [five minutes] of the [Film] in each case for the purpose of trade and in-store demonstrations to promote and advertise the [Film].

R.228

The [Licensee] shall be entitled to incorporate not more than [specify duration] of the [Film] in each case on videograms reproducing other films for the purpose of promoting and advertising the [Film], provided that the other films shall not be offensive, obscene, or not in the same classification viewing bracket as the content of the [Film].

R.229

The [Licensee] agrees that all other rights including [specify rights or areas] are specifically excluded from this Agreement and retained by the [Licensor].

R.230

This Agreement does not cover future developments which may be created after the date of this Agreement for the purpose of viewing films, or sound recordings at home, businesses or others. Any new apparatus or method of reproduction shall enable the [Licensor] to grant a new licence to any third party regardless of whether the new apparatus or method of reproduction directly competes with the market covered by this licence.

R.231

This [Licence/Agreement] does not grant any right to use and/or exploit in the [Film] and/or parts by means of transmission, broadcast and/or supply by means of cable, digital, satellite, and terrestrial television; by means of any telecommunication system, mobile telephone, landline and/or cable telephone and/or any electronic communication, the internet and/or any website.

R.232

'The DVD and Disc Rights' shall mean the right to reproduce, manufacture, supply, hire, rent, distribute, sub-licence, and/or to authorise any third party to do any of those things in respect of the [Film/Work/Sound Recordings] in the form of DVDs, CD-Roms, discs and any other form of mechanical reproduction which involves the replication of the material on a disc which is slotted into a machine and/or equipment of any type to be used in conjunction with a playback device so that the moving image and/or audio recording is played on the screen. This shall include a television, computer, laptop and portable gadget. It shall not include any form of telecommunication, the internet and websites, and/or any electronic method and/or any storage and/or retrieval system.

R.233

'Video on Demand' shall be defined as the right of the [Company] to supply on a non-exclusive basis copies of the [Films] to members of the public for a fixed fee to be viewed on any television, laptop, mobile telephone and/or any other device which is supplied by the [Company] from its website [specify] and through which is accessed the archive library of [Films].

R.234

1.1 It is accepted by the [Licensor] that the public purchasing the [Films] may be located in any country in the world.

1.2 The [Company] agrees and accepts that there are no rights to edit the [Films] and/or sub-licence any rights to any commercial, charitable and/or educational establishments including universities, care homes or clubs in any country for viewing by groups of people except in private homes.

R.235

[Name] grants the [Company] the non-exclusive right to reproduce a copy of the [Image/Logo/Artwork] on the cover of the [DVD/Disc] of the [Film] as part of the packaging for supply, sales and distribution in [country] from [date] to [date]. Provided that the [Company] does not distort and/or mutilate the [Image/Logo/Artwork] and provides a proof sample for approval and pays the sum of [number/currency] by [date]. Together with a payment in advance thereafter of [number/currency] for every six month period that the [Company] wishes to exploit the rights on the cover of the [DVD/Disc].

Film and Television

R.236
'The Standard Television Rights' shall mean the right to broadcast the [Film] on conventional VHF and UHF broadcast television transmitted by means of over the standard television signals (including [multiplex services], pay per view, subscription, licence, rental and on demand) for general reception excluding cable television, digital and satellite television, any telecommunication system and/or electronic communication and/or the internet.

R.237
'The Standard Television Rights' shall mean the right to broadcast the [Film] and/or parts over the air signals from terrestrially based transmitters in digital or analogue form for general reception by the public by television [whether or not the reception has been adapted] regardless of whether it is free, subscription, rental, license or on demand or otherwise, encrypted or not but excluding cable or satellite delivery and any other method of viewing whether computer, telephone or other device.

R.238
'The Standard Television Rights' shall mean the sole and exclusive right in the Territory during the Licence Period to broadcast or transmit whether by digital or analogue systems, the [Film(s)] by way of conventional free terrestrial television [excluding purchase of reception box], transmitted by means of over-the-air television signals and to authorise others to do any such things but will exclude [cable, satellite and other distribution and transmission systems].

R.239
'The Standard Television Rights' shall mean the right to broadcast the [Musical Work] and sound recording in synchronisation with the [Series] on conventional VHF and UHF broadcast television transmitted by means of over-the-air standard television signals (including free, pay per view, subscription, licence and rental) for general reception excluding Cable, Digital and Satellite Television Rights.

R.240
'The Television Rights' shall mean the transmission of sound and/or visual images capable of reception by the public whether such signals are encrypted or scrambled or not and shall include all means of transmission whether by over the air, UHF, VHF, signals from terrestrially based transmitters or by means of a satellite and shall further include the transmission and re-transmission by all forms of cable distribution and redistribution and

all forms of wireless telegraphy and telecommunication systems and any digitised information and data conveyed in electronic form through a telecommunication system.

R.241

'Broadcasting' means the broadcast or transmission or relay by cable or by satellite or by any other means whatsoever of sound, data, text and/or visual images.

R.242

'The Cable Television Rights' shall mean the right to transmit or deliver the [Series] throughout the Territory for the duration of the Licence Period by way of basic cable or pay cable (including free, pay per view, subscription, licence, rental and on-demand) [or by way of any other cable medium whether in existence now or created in the future].

R.243

'The Cable Television Rights' shall mean the right to transmit the [Film] and/or parts by means of a cable system or similar technology whether in existence now or created in the future regardless of the method of charging, payment or whether it is free and whether or not it is encoded or otherwise distorted.

R.244

'Non-Standard Television Rights' shall mean the sole and exclusive right in the Territory during the Licence Period to sell, hire, lease or otherwise exploit the [Film] and/or any parts by way of basic or pay cable or by way of any other cable medium hereinafter invented or discovered whereby payment is made to the cable operator or company in respect of the reception of programmes and to authorise others to do any of such things and for the avoidance of doubts such rights shall exclude the Digital and Satellite Television Rights.

R.245

'The Satellite Television Rights' shall mean the right to transmit the [Film] by means of a satellite whether encrypted or not and regardless of whether it is free or some other method of payment.

R.246

'The Satellite Television Rights' means the sole and exclusive right in the Territory during the Licence Period to broadcast and/or transmit the [Film] or any parts by means of a satellite and the signals transmitted by the satellite are intended mainly for reception within the Territory including distribution by means of any direct subscription or other services for payment or not and shall include the right to authorise others to exercise and sub-license such rights.

R.247
'The Satellite Transmission Rights' means the sole and exclusive right to transmit the [Film] and/or parts by means of a satellite so that the footprint of the satellite transmission is principally aimed at the Territory.

R.248
'The Satellite Rights' shall mean the right to transmit the [Film] and/or parts by means of a satellite and the signals transmitted by a satellite which creates a footprint [or similar technology] whether in existence now or created in the future regardless of the method of charging, payment or whether the service is free and whether the service is encrypted, scrambled or otherwise distorted to avoid illegal reception. The method of reception and viewing may be via any apparatus, machine or equipment including landline and mobile telephone, television, watch, game, car and computer systems.

R.249
'The Satellite Television Rights' shall mean the right to broadcast or transmit the [Film] by means of a satellite (including free, pay per view, subscription, licence, rental and on demand) whether encrypted or not including [specify].

R.250
'The Satellite Television Rights' shall mean the right to broadcast in digitised form or otherwise, or transmit the [Musical Work] and any sound recording in synchronisation with the [Series] by means of a satellite (including free, pay per view, subscription, licence and rental) whether encrypted or not including [specify].

R.251
'The Satellite Rights' shall mean the right to broadcast or transmit the [Film] by means of a satellite including pay per view, subscription, licence and rental, on demand or otherwise whether encrypted or not.

R.252
'The Television Rights' shall mean the right to broadcast, transmit, deliver and supply the [Films] on all forms of television in existence now or created in the future whatever the method of supply of sound and vision including but not limited to cable, satellite, digital, over the air and/or whatever method of payment required or not as the case may be such as rental, subscription, free, pay per view or otherwise. The equipment to receive the [Films] shall be limited to [specify] and shall not include [specify].

R.253

'The Television Rights' shall mean the right to broadcast, transmit or otherwise exploit the [Film] by all forms of reception provide that it is displayed and viewed in conjunction with a television, including digital, satellite, cable, terrestrial, whatever the method of payment whether it is free and whatever the method of delivery whether in existence now or created in the future.

R.254

'The Digital Television Rights' shall mean the right to convert the [Film] into a digitised format and to transmit the [Film] using digital means and further the right for viewers to interact with the on-screen display of the [Film] in a manner consistent with the enabling technology now known or invented in the future.

R.255

'The Digital Programme Service Rights' shall mean the [exclusive/non-exclusive] right to broadcast in digital form by means of multiplex service the [Programme] on the following Digital Programme Service:

1.1 [Name]

1.2 [Hours] [Days of Week]

1.3 [Coverage Area specified by attached map, transmitter sites, grid references, frequencies, transmitter power and polarisation]

1.4 Digital Capacity for the Term of this Agreement.

R.256

The Digital Additional Services Rights' shall mean the [exclusive/non-exclusive] right to broadcast in digital form by means of a multiplex system the [Teletext Services/Electronic Programme Guides/Data Services] on the following Digital Programme Service [specify] and Multiplex System [specify] for the following period [Start/End Date].

R.257

'Theatric Rights' shall mean the sole and exclusive right in the Territory during the Term of the Agreement to produce and distribute a feature film of or based on the [Programme] intended primarily for exhibition in cinemas and/or the right to exhibit the [Programme] in cinemas and in both cases to authorise others to do so.

R.258

'The Theatric Rights' mean the sole and exclusive right in the Territory during the Licence Period to distribute the [Films] for exhibition to audiences where a charge for admission is made including by way of example cinemas, theatres, concert halls [and other public places] and to authorise others to do any of such things.

R.259
'The Theatric Rights' shall mean the right to exhibit the [Film] to audiences where a charge for admission is made including, but not limited to, public and private cinemas, concert and lecture halls and arenas.

R.260
'The Off-Air Recording Rights' shall mean the right to include the [Programme] in a Licensing Scheme [under the Copyright, Designs and Patents Act 1988 as amended] whereby licences are granted to enable the [Programme] to be recorded by or on behalf of educational establishments from any broadcast or cable programme service including the [Programme] or any of them when such recording is for the educational purposes of such establishment.

R.261
'The Recording Rights' shall mean the right to make any visual and/or sound recordings of the [Event] or any part in any medium including all electronic forms of reproduction whether in existence now or created in the future.

R.262
'The Primary Rights' shall mean those rights which are the principal rights granted under this Agreement and shall mean the sole and exclusive right to transmit the [Series] on standard television for the duration of the Licence Period throughout the Territory in accordance with the terms of this Agreement.

R.263

1.1 In consideration of the Licence Fee the [Licensor] grants to the [Licensee] the sole and exclusive [Standard Television Rights] throughout the Territory for the duration of the Licence Period in the [Film] and/or part(s).

1.2 The [Licensee] shall be entitled to [number] broadcasts/transmissions of the [Film] within [the Licence Period/two years from the date of the first broadcast/transmission].

1.3 The [Licensee] shall have the right to transmit no more than [number] minutes of the [Film] for the purpose of programme announcement, trailing and post transmission comment or review in each case without further payment.

R.264

The [Licensor] undertakes that the [Film] will not be transmitted or broadcast on [satellite television or cable television] until the expiry of a period of [specify period] from the date of this Agreement.

R.265

In consideration of the Licence Fee the [Licensor] grants to the [Licensee] the sole and exclusive Satellite Television Rights throughout the Territory for the Licence Period whether such transmission is capable of being received by individuals or by cable operators (which have a written licensing agreement with the [Licensee] at the date of this Agreement.

R.266

1.1 In consideration of the Licence Fee the [Licensor] grants to the [Licensee] the sole and exclusive Satellite Television Rights throughout the Territory for the Licence Period.

1.2 The [Licensee] shall only be entitled to [number] transmissions of the full length of the [Film].

1.3 The [Licensee] shall be entitled to transmit excerpts of any part of the [Film] for the purpose of programme announcement, trailing without further payment on any channels owned or controlled by them including [specify] without further payment. Provided that the total aggregate shall not exceed [number] minutes.

1.4 The [Licensor] agrees that where in the Territory the service is provided by the [Licensor] is supplied by cable operators for that purpose only. Then the [Licensee] shall be permitted to authorise the exercise of the non-exclusive cable rights in the [Film] and/or parts provided it is shown simultaneously with the transmission by the [Licensee] and payment is made to the relevant collecting society for any such usage. Nor shall any parts of the [Film] be supplied to the cable operator for any promotion or trailers.

R.267

In consideration of the Licence Fee the [Licensor] grants to the [Licensee] the non-exclusive [Cable Television Rights] in the [Film] throughout the Territory for the Term of this Agreement.

R.268

In consideration of the Licence Fee the [Licensor] grants to the [Licensee] the sole and exclusive right to exercise the Digital Programme Service Rights, Standard Television Rights, the Digital Television Rights, the Cable Television Rights and the Satellite Television Rights throughout the Territory for the duration of the Licence Period in the [Musical Work] and any sound recording in synchronisation with the [Series].

R.269
The [Licensee] agrees that it shall not be entitled to exploit in any manner any sound recordings of the [Musical Work] without the prior consent of the [Licensor] except as specified under the terms of this Agreement.

R.270
The [Licensor] undertakes not to license any third party to broadcast or transmit the [Musical Work] in synchronisation with any film for use on television in any form throughout the Territory for the duration of the Licence Period without the prior written consent of the [Licensee].

R.271
In consideration of the Licence Fee the [Author] grants to the [Company] the sole and exclusive right to produce the [Film] based on the [Author's Work] for the duration of the Licence Period throughout the Territory.

R.272
In consideration of the [Author's] Royalties the [Author] grants to the [Company] the sole and exclusive right to exercise the [Standard Television Rights, the Digital Television Rights, the Cable Television Rights, the Satellite Television Rights, the Video, DVD and Non-Theatric Rights and the Theatric Rights] in the [Film] and/or parts based on the [Author's Work] throughout the Territory for the full period of copyright and any extensions and renewals.

R.273
The [Company] agrees that after the end of the Licence Period the [Company] shall have no rights in the [Author's Work] and shall not be entitled to exploit the [Film] which has been produced during the Licence Period without further Agreement with the [Author].

R.274
The [Author] agrees that he/she will not license, authorise or permit any third party to produce any other [Film], recording, sound recording, video, DVD, CD Rom, disc, or any other moving visual image and/or animation and/or any adaptation based on the main characters and plot of the storyline for an animated version and/or any sound recording and/or audio material based on the [Author's Work] during the Licence Period.

R.275

In consideration of the Approved Budget the Assignor assigns the [Assignee] all present and future copyright in respect of the [specify rights] in the [Film] and part(s) throughout the Territory for the duration of the Assignment Period.

R.276

The [Assignee] agrees that after the expiry of the Assignment Period, the [Assignee] shall have no rights in the [Film] and/or part(s) and that all rights assigned under this Agreement shall revert to and be vested in the [Assignor].

R.277

The [Assignor] and the [Assignee] agree that Clause [–] is subject to the following existing agreements [specify date/title/subject] and the [specify] agreement shall prevail in the event of conflicting clauses. Copies of the Agreements are attached and form part of this Agreement.

R.278

In consideration of the Approved Budget the [Assignor] assigns to the [Assignee] all present and future copyright and any other rights in all media whether in existence now or created in the future including, but not limited to, the Television Rights, the DVD, Video and Disc Rights, the Theatric Rights and the Non-Theatric Rights in the [Series] and parts throughout the Territory for the full period of copyright and any extensions and renewals.

R.279

The [Licensor] hereby grants to the [Licensee]:

1.1 The sole and exclusive right to broadcast, transmit and/or exploit the [Film] and/or part(s) on television whether cable, digital, satellite, terrestrial and/or any combination in vision and/or sound.

1.2 The sole and exclusive right to produce any other film, recording, sound recording, video, DVD, CD Rom, disc or any other moving visual image and/or animation and/or any sequel, and/or adaptation based on the main characters and plot of the storyline of the [Film] for an animated version for television and/or any sound recording and/or audio material based on the [Film] during the Licence Period.

1.3 The sole and exclusive right during the Licence Period to distribute the [Film] for exhibition to audiences where a charge for admission is made including by way of example cinemas, theatres, concert halls and other public places and to authorise others to do any of such things.

1.4 The sole and exclusive right to convert the [Film] into a digitised format and to transmit the [Film] using digital means and further the right for viewers to interact with the on-screen display of the [Film] in a manner consistent with the enabling technology now known or invented in the future.

1.5 The sole and exclusive right to commission and produce dubbed and/or sub-titled versions of the [Film] for exploitation in non-English speaking countries during the Licence Period.

1.6 The sole and exclusive right to manufacture, sell, rent, supply and distribute, whether by wholesale, retail, mail order, subscription or direct marketing and to authorise others to do so [DVDs/Videos] reproducing the [Film] during the Licence Period.

1.7 The sole and exclusive right to operate and charge for access to a premium rate telephone line in respect of the [Film] and/or parts.

R.280
The [Company] may broadcast by television and in sound only on radio short sequences of not more than [three] minutes duration from the [Film] for the purpose of programme announcement, trailing and post-transmission comment or review without further payment and such broadcasts shall be without prejudice to the number of broadcasts specified in Clause [–].

R.281
The [Licensor] hereby grants to the [Licensee] the sole and exclusive right to broadcast the [Work] on [Channel] in [country] throughout the Territory for the duration of the Licence Period without limitation on the number of transmissions.

R.282
The [Licensor] hereby grants to the [Licensee] the sole and exclusive right to broadcast the [Work] throughout the Territory for the duration of the Licence Period. The [Licensee] shall only be entitled to a maximum of [number] transmissions of the [Work].

R.283
The [Licensor] grants to the [Licensee] the sole and exclusive right to broadcast the [Film] by means of [specify rights or type of television] throughout the United Kingdom of Great Britain, Northern Ireland, the Channel Islands and the Isle of Man for the duration of the Licence Period the following number of broadcasts [specify].

R.284
Notwithstanding anything contained in this Agreement the [Licensor] agrees that there is no obligation on the part of the [Television Company] to broadcast the [Film] and/or excerpts from any part of the [Film].

R.285

Nothing contained in this Agreement shall be construed to imply an obligation on the [Company] to broadcast the [Film] but in the event the [Company] decides not to broadcast the [Film] then the Licence Fee shall nevertheless be retained by the [Licensor].

R.286

Neither the [Company] nor [Name] shall assign, grant, transfer or otherwise exploit the rights granted to the [Licensee] nor shall either of them execute any document or do anything in derogation from the grant. Provided that the [Company] shall have the non-exclusive right to permit any [Channel 3/ Channel 5 Licensee/Satellite Company/Cable Operator/other] the right to broadcast or transmit up to [three minutes] in total of the same excerpt of the [Film] for inclusion in programmes for the purpose of review or criticism at any time.

R.287

The [Licensee] shall not exercise the rights granted hereunder so as to make more than [Number] broadcasts/transmissions of the [Film] which shall only be on the [Licensee's] national channels for the broadcast/transmission throughout the [United Kingdom/other].

R.288

In the event that the [Licensor's] rights in the [Film] are extended after [Date] the [Licensee] shall be entitled to the benefit of such extension up to a maximum of [number] years from the beginning of the Licence Period at no extra cost.

R.289

The [Licensee] and its sub-licensees may make dubbed and/or sub-titled versions of the [Series] and/or the Excess Footage in such languages as may be necessary for the exploitation thereof in non-English speaking countries.

R.290

The [Assignee] shall be entitled to broadcast or authorise the broadcast of and retain payment for the following number of broadcasts of the [Series] on [terrestrial/cable/digital/satellite television] in the United Kingdom of Great Britain and Northern Ireland, the Republic of Ireland, the Channel Islands and the Isle of Man [specify].

R.291

The [Company] undertakes and agrees that it shall not broadcast the [Film] and/or parts before [date].

R.292

The [Company] will not broadcast, authorise and/or permit the broadcast and/or transmission and/or supply by television of the [Film] from or to [country] until after the [Film] has first been broadcast by the [Licensee] pursuant to this Agreement.

R.293

The [Licensee] agrees to use all reasonable endeavours to ensure that the [Film] is broadcast/transmitted within [six months] of the date of this Agreement.

R.294

The [Licensor] undertakes that the [Film] will not be broadcast or transmitted on satellite or cable television until the expiry of a period of [one year] from [date].

R.295

The [Licensor] warrants that the [Film] will not be broadcast or transmitted on television and [computer/mobile/other gadget] in any country of the Territory until the expiry of the following periods from the date of first release of [Videos/DVDs/Discs] of the [Film] to the public and [date] whichever is the earlier in each such country:

1.1 Satellite Television Rights [–].

1.2 Cable Television Rights [–].

1.3 Terrestrial Television Rights [–].

1.4 Digital Television Rights [–].

R.296

The [Television Company] undertakes to broadcast or transmit the [Programme] in accordance with the Programme Schedule set out below throughout the Territory during the Term of this Agreement [Television channel/dates/times].

R.297

In consideration of the non-returnable Advance and the [Licensor's] Royalties, the [Licensor] grants to the [Licensee] the sole and exclusive [Cable Television Rights and Satellite Television Rights] in the [Film] and/or part(s) throughout the Territory for the Term of this Agreement and the right to authorise third parties to exercise such rights provided it is in accordance with the terms of this Agreement.

R.298

The [Licensee] acknowledges that all other rights including the right to sub-licence, the Publishing Rights, Merchandising, Endorsement, Sponsorship and Product Placement, Video, DVD and Disc Rights, Theatric and Non-Theatric Rights are not granted under this Agreement and are specifically retained by the [Licensor].

R.299

The [Assignee] acknowledges and agrees that all other rights in the [Film] not specifically assigned under this Agreement shall remain vested in the Assignor including, but not limited to, any merchandising and publication rights.

R.300

In consideration of the payments made and due to be made by the [Licensee] to the [Licensor], the [Licensor] hereby grants to the [Licensee] all Distribution Rights in the [Series] throughout the Territory for the duration of the Licence Period. The [Licensee] shall not be allowed to appoint any sub-distributors or agents or sub-licensees without the prior written approval of the [Licensor], such approval not to be unreasonably withheld or delayed.

R.301

During the Licence Period the [Television Company] shall have the right to undertake the distribution of the [Film] in respect of the rights granted hereunder and to appoint agent(s) to undertake such distribution. The [Television Company] shall be entitled to retain all income derived from the exercise of the rights granted hereunder.

R.302

The simultaneous relay of any broadcast/transmission of the [Film(s)] or any parts of them outside the Territory which is under authority of international treaty or regulation and for which a system for making copyright payments to copyright owners through a collection agency is in existence shall not be a breach of this Agreement.

R.303

1.1   In consideration of the Licence Fee and the [Author's] Royalties the [Author] grants to the [Company] the sole and exclusive right to exploit All Media Rights in the [Film] based on the [Author's Work] for the duration of the Licence Period throughout the Territory.

1.2   The [Author] agrees that he/she shall not from the date of this Agreement until the expiry of the Licence Period or termination of this Agreement exercise and/or license and/or authorise and/or suffer the exercise in the Territory in any media of a film of any type based on the [Author's Work].

1.3 The [Author] agrees not to license or otherwise exploit any media of any nature based on the [Author's Work] until the expiry or termination of this Agreement.

R.304

'The Performers Rights in a Performance' shall mean the rights of a [Performer] and a person having recording rights in relation to a performance made without his/her consent or of that [Performer].

R.305

'Performers Rights' shall mean those rights which are held by performers [under the Copyright, Designs and Patents Act 1988 as amended] and performance(s) and performer(s) shall be construed accordingly.

R.306

'Performance' shall mean a dramatic performance including dance and mime, a musical performance, a reading or recitation of a literary work or a performance of a variety or a similar presentation, which is or so far as it is a live performance given by one or more individuals.

R.307

'The Performer(s)' shall be the following [Group/Artiste] [–].

R.308

'Performances' shall include acting, mime, dance, speech, singing, playing an instrument or conducting, either alone or with others.

R.309

'Performance' shall [have the same meaning as afforded the Copyright, Designs and Patents Act 1988 as amended and] mean a performance of the [Work] being a work protected by copyright as a literary dramatic or musical work in public which would otherwise be a restricted act including delivery in the case of lectures, addresses, speeches, sermons and includes in general any mode of visual or acoustic presentation, including presentation by means of a sound recording, film, broadcast or cable programme of the [Work].

R.310

The parties acknowledge that the playing or showing of the [Work] in public is an act restricted by the copyright in a sound recording, film, broadcast or cable programme.

R.311

The [Company] agrees that the [Artist] shall be entitled to a minimum of [number] performances to be recorded by the [Company] during each year of this Agreement.

R.312

'The Radio and Stage Rights' shall mean the right to broadcast by means of radio or perform in public on a stage the [Script] and/or the [Programme] and to authorise others to do so and shall include all drafts and/or material incorporated in such [Scripts].

R.313

'Rental and Lending Rights' shall mean those rights bestowed upon Authors, Performers, Phonogram Producers, Film Producers and Film Directors [under EU Council Directive 2006/115/EC and as subsequently incorporated under legislation].

R.314

'Rental Rights' shall mean any arrangement under which a copy of a [Work] is made available for payment in money or money's worth or in the course of a business as part of services or for which payment is made on terms that it will or may be returned.

R.315

'The Performing Rights' shall include those rights administered by the [Performing Rights Society] and any society affiliated to it, including the right to perform the [Work] in public (whether a live performance or recorded) and to broadcast the [Work] known as grand rights such as ballets, operas and musicals unless otherwise agreed with the [Performing Rights Society].

R.316

In consideration of the payment of the Placement Fee the [Television Company] grants to the [Company] the non-exclusive right to have the [Product] in the [Programme]. The [Television Company] agrees and undertakes to incorporate the [Company's] Product and the [Company's] Logo in the [Programme] in accordance with the summary set out in Schedule [–] which is attached to and forms part of this Agreement.

R.317

The [Company] agrees that the [Television] Company] shall be entitled to have other third parties sponsor, advertise, promote and/or include their products and/or services in the [Programme] and that no approval and/or consultation shall be required with the [Company].

R.318

The [Television Company] agrees and undertakes not to advertise, promote and/or place a product, service and/or other material in the [Programme] which directly competes with the sales of [Product] in the [specify] market.

R.319

'The Advertising, Sponsorship and Product Placement Rights' shall the sole and exclusive right of the [Supplier] to:

1.1   Advertise and promote products and/or services in the [thirty] minutes before the transmission, and/or broadcast of the [Programme] on channel [specify].

1.2   Advertise and promote products and/or services in the [thirty] minutes after the transmission, and/or broadcast of the [Programme] on channel [specify].

1.3   Appear and/or be credited as the only sponsor of the [Programme].

1.4   To supply up to [number] copies of the [Product] to be used by the [Company] in the [Programme] in visible setting to suit the circumstances of the script. Attached is a copy of the proposed running order and script with markings for the use of the [Product] which is attached to and forms part of this Agreement.

All the above rights shall apply to the transmission and/or broadcast of the [Programme] from [date] to [date] by the [Company] on channel [specify] throughout the Territory.

R.320

1.1   In consideration of the Licence Fee in clause [–] the [Licensor] grants the [Distributor] the non-exclusive right to transmit and/or broadcast the [Series] on [specify channel] for delivery members of the public to view on television in [specify countries] including through the exercise of the Satellite Rights, Cable Rights and Terrestrial Television Rights for the Licence Period.

1.2   The [Licensor] agrees that the [Distributor] may supply and transmit the [Series] no more than [number] in total.

1.3   The [Licensor] accepts that the transmission and/or broadcast may be supplied by a combination of satellite and cable and may in parts be outside the agreed countries.

1.4   The [Distributor] agrees that no right is granted to supply the [Series] as part of an archive and/or on demand playback and/or record service.

1.5 The [Distributor] accepts that the [Licensor] may sell the [Series] to a competing business in the same countries at any time.

R.321

The [Licensor] agrees to grant the [Company] the following rights provided that the [Company] pays the Licence Fee by [date].

1.1 The exclusive right to transmit and/or broadcast and/or deliver the [Film] in the Territory by the exercise and means of the Satellite, Cable, and Terrestrial Television Rights and/or the Telecommunication Rights and/or the right to receive and/or download the [Film] through a delivery and/or archive service associated with the [Company] whether it is free and/or paid for on demand where reception is through a television, laptop, mobile telephone, tablet and/or some other form of software and/or device for the Licence Period.

1.2 There are only [number] broadcasts and/or transmissions allowed from [date] to [date] by satellite, cable and terrestrial television by the [Company].

1.3 There is no right granted to create and/or license associated merchandising and/or to authorise third parties to use, adapt and/or exploit the [Film].

1.4 The only permitted promotional extracts of the [Film] which may be used on the [Company] website and/or on the channel on which the [Company] operates are those specifically supplied by the [Company] as approved marketing extracts. There is no right to use any other extracts from the [Film] and/or images, music and/or sound tracks.

General Business and Commercial

R.322

'Third Party Rights' shall mean the right of any third party who is not a signatory to this Agreement. The parties to this Agreement agree that the third party [Name] shall be allowed to enforce the following rights directly against the parties to this Agreement [specify].

R.323

No rights are to be conferred on any third party and all rights are limited to those parties which have signed this Agreement. Any third party rights which may exist are specifically excluded from this Agreement.

R.324

The [Copyright Owner] owns and controls all intellectual property rights and any other rights throughout the [country/world/universe] in the [Work/Service/Product/other] and the material including but not limited to:

1.1 Television: local, national, analogue, UHF, VHF, terrestrial, digital, cable, satellite television, teletext, interactive and via any computer and/or gadget and/or telephone.

1.2 Radio; analogue, over the air, digital, interactive and in combination via any television, computer, gadget and/or telephone.

1.3 Telecommunication systems and Telephones: mobile, cell phones, land-line, via the internet, services, interactive, clips, games, screensavers, ringtones, sounds, noises, images, animations, mobile comics.

1.4 Film, cartoons, animations, stage play, performance, sound recordings, recordings, computer generated material, stills, photographs, visual images, sound, voice, data, text, audio material.

1.5 Designs, design rights, future design rights, models, sculptures, graphics, drawings, sketches, illustrations, artwork, two-and three-dimensional representations, plans, tables, maps, colour, shape, noise and smell.

1.6 Computer hardware, software, data, databases, material and information; CDs, CD-Roms, discs and any other method of storage, retrieval, supply and distribution. Internet and worldwide web, telecommunication systems, electronic, digital, electromagnetic, electrochemical and/or any other form of reproduction, supply and distribution by any method and/or process.

1.7 All music, lyrics and adaptation and exploitation including performing rights and mechanical reproduction, downloads from any website, publishing and synchronization.

1.8 Merchandising; toys and games, interactive games for computers, portable gadgets and consoles, licensing of characters, title, names, plot, format, posters, calendars, kits, sports and out doors, clothing, badges, household goods, stationary, magnets, bags, theme parks, gambling, betting, lottery, festivals, competitions, sculptures and 3D shows and costumes.

1.9 Brand, trade marks, service marks, logos, words, phrases, domain names, business name and trading name and the right to register any interest.

1.10 Confidential information, moral rights, trade secrets, know-how, goodwill, inventions, patents, modifications, improvements, formulae and processes.

1.11 Publications; hardback, paperback, picture books, co-editions, large print, foreign editions, magazines, periodicals, digests, comics, colouring books, educational books, serialisation, newspapers, quotations, anthologies.

1.12 Free or payment whether rental, subscription, licence, mail order, entrance fee, pay per view, on demand, scrambled, encrypted, or other charges.

1.13 The right to appoint a supplier, distributor, agent, or other third party; to reproduce, supply, distribute, adapt, develop, translate, arrange a sequel, and to exploit the rights and material any manner through third parties.

1.14 Advertising, publicity, promotion, wrappings, containers, labels, packaging, display materials, exhibitions, conferences, courses, webinars and/or training, licensing of extracts, sponsorship, endorsement, product placement and/or other form of sub-licensing and/or use of any rights.

1.15 Any other combination, use, device, method, system, process, transfer, supply whether in existence now or created at any time in the future.

R.325

'All Media Rights' shall mean all intellectual property rights and any other rights and interest of whatever nature in the [Work/Project/Product] and any parts including without limitation all copyright, trade marks, service marks, design rights, patents, computer software, digital and electronic files, trade secrets, moral rights and confidential information, domain names and the sole and exclusive right to adapt, use, copy, license, authorise, print, transmit, disseminate, store, retrieve, display, process, record, playback, rent, lend, supply or sale, promote or otherwise exploit by any method, medium or process whether created in the future or in existence now of any nature and any developments or variations or adaptations whether text, visual images, photographs, drawings, plans, sketches, electronically generated material, sounds, sound effects, music or any combination, software and information, logos, background, banner, bookmark, border, table, caption, character, clip art, cartoons, computer generated artmap image, map link, common gateway interface, script, data, domain names, footnotes, headings, hypertext, video or computer generated graphics or any combination or interactive or digitised including but not limited to:

1.1 All forms of television whether analogue or digital including terrestrial, UHF, VHF, cable, satellite.

1.2 All forms of radio whether by direct reception, via television, personal computer telephone or in digitised form.

1.3 All forms of telecommunication systems including telephones, mobile telephones, pagers and other machinery and apparatus.

1.4 All forms of mechanical reproduction including videodiscs, videocassettes, lasers, DVDs, CDs.

1.5   All forms of non-theatric audiences whether for business or commercial use, educational, cultural, religious or social, schools, museums, readings, plays, speeches, addresses or lectures.

1.6   All forms of theatric exploitation including cinemas.

1.7   All forms of publication and/or dissemination of information by any electronic method and process.

1.8   All forms of computer software and interactive multi-media such as compact discs, CD-Roms, computer games including all circumstances where there is an element of interactivity and/or there is any combination of sound, text, vision, graphics, music or otherwise.

1.9   All forms of merchandising, toys, cloths, mugs, costumes, household goods, stationery, games, product endorsement, sponsorship, product placement and any two or three representation of any part of the [Work].

1.10 Theatre, stage plays, festivals, theme parks and gambling.

1.11 Commercial advertisements, promotional items and giveaways, format and character exploitation in any form.

1.12 All forms of exploitation in respect of the internet, websites, links, apps, blogs, text, images, recordings in any form and/or other medium.

R.326

'All Media Rights' shall mean the right to exploit the [Work] [and parts] throughout the [Territory/world] for the duration of the [Assignment/Licence Period/the full period of copyright including any extensions or renewals as far as possible in perpetuity] in all media whether in existence now or created in the future including but not limited to:

1.1   All forms of exploitation through the medium of television and radio including transmission and reception by standard UHF and VHF, over-the-air analogue signals or digital for general reception with or without payment of any nature, all forms of satellite distribution irrespective of the footprint of the satellite and irrespective of whether the signals are encrypted or scrambled.

1.2   All forms of cable distribution and re-transmission irrespective of technical method by which the sound and vision is transmitted and all other forms of transmission including wireless telegraphy and all other manner of telecommunications systems.

1.3   All forms of exploitation through the medium of [Videos and DVDs] or some other format which is capable or being recorded, stored or replayed by any form of cassette, disc or laser and irrespective of whether it is distributed on a sale-through, rental, closed-user or on-demand basis to the general public or to hotels, aircraft or otherwise.

1.4 All forms of non-theatric audiences including, but not limited to, business and commercial use, educational, cultural, religious and social establishments of any kind, schools, churches, prisons, hospitals, summer camps, drama groups, workshops, film societies, professional and trade bodies, private and public libraries, colleges, universities, hotels and clubs, irrespective of any payment in kind made by one party or another.

1.5 All forms of theatric exploitation including all kinds of indoor and outdoor cinemas and screenings where a charge is made for entry.

1.6 All forms of publishing whether in printed form or electronic form.

1.7 All forms of electronic communication, internet, worldwide web and multi-media exploitation and all other methods of interactivity, sound, vision, text or graphics of any nature and any method of access, storeage and retrieval including apps, blogs and domain names.

1.8 All forms of merchandising whether based on character, logo or image or otherwise including commercial exploitation through any item of any nature such as toys, clothing and accessories, cutlery, badges, sweets and food, souvenirs, stickers, posters, cards, electronic devices, stationery, memorabilia and/or festivals, sports events, sponsorship, product placement, theme parks, lottery, betting, gambling and 3D versions in any medium and/or format.

1.9 All other forms of adaptations, variations and developments of the [Work] of any nature whether by title, theme, character and/or text and/or image.

R.327

'All Media' shall mean all media whether in existence now or created in the future including, but not limited to:

1.1 All forms of television including terrestrial, digital, cable and satellite.

1.2 All forms of radio including terrestrial, digital, cable and satellite.

1.3 All forms of mechanical reproduction of the images and/or sound including DVD, videos, cassettes, discs, lasers.

1.4 All forms of publishing, hardbacks, paperbacks, newspapers, magazines, comics, serialisation, packaging and co-editions.

1.5 All theatre, plays, readings, films, advertisements, performances and exhibitions.

1.6   All forms of merchandising and adaptation and sub-licensing of the title, character, storyline, logo, image, film, computer generated material, photographs, text, interactive and/or multi-media, theme parks and 3D formats.

1.7   All forms of electronic communication and/or mechanical reproduction, storage, retrieval, supply, reproduction and distribution of information, data, sound, vision, graphics, interactive, multi-media including, but not limited to the worldwide web.

R.328
'All Rights' shall mean all intellectual property rights of whatever nature including without limitation all copyright, trade marks, service marks, design rights, trade secrets, computer software, digital and electronic files, moral rights and confidential information in existence now [and created in the future].

R.329
'All Media Rights' shall mean the sole and exclusive right to produce, manufacture, supply, sell, rent, distribute, license, market and exploit the [Work] and any part(s) including the artwork and any adaptations or developments whether in existence now or created in the future in all forms of the media including but not limited to:

1.1   All forms of publication including hardback, paperback, digests, serialisation, newspapers magazines, periodicals, quotations, anthologies, translations including exploitation of the title, index and taxonomy.

1.2   All forms of radio, television, video, and mechanical and/or electronic forms of reproduction and/or storage and retrieval and/or playback including videos, disks, DVDs, CD-Roms, cassettes, lasers.

1.3   All forms of theatric and non-theatric exploitation including theatre, readings, plays, exhibitions.

1.4   All forms of merchandising and promotion including computer games, toys, clothing, mugs, stationery, sponsorship, endorsement, product placement.

1.5   All forms of telecommunication systems, electronic communication, internet, intranet and interactive multi-media exploitation, and any method of reproduction, storage, access, retrieval and supply, including landline and mobile telephones, mobile telephones and pagers, watches and games, computer software, digital and electronic files.

1.6 Any technical method and/or process of reproduction, supply, communication, storage, access, retrieval, delivery, reception and use shall apply to this Clause [–].

1.7 Any method of payment, no charge or participation conditions including subscription, rental, charging, one-off payment shall apply to this Clause [–].

1.8 Any development, variation or combination of sound, vision, smell, text, icons, images, graphics, film, sound recordings, and/or photographs shall apply to this Clause [–].

1.9 The right to licence, authorise and/or permit third parties to exploit any of the rights and/or to assign, transfer, and/or charge any of the rights and interest in this Clause [–].

R.330
'All Media Rights' shall mean the sole and exclusive right to produce, manufacture, supply, rent, distribute, license, market, adapt and exploit the [Work] and any parts in all forms of the media whether in existence now or created in the future including, but not limited to, all forms of publication; hardback, paperback; all forms of television, radio, video, sound recordings, films and recordings; cable; satellite; digital; cassettes; laser; disks; any technical method of delivery; any method of payment, charging, subscription, rental, lease and free; all forms of telecommunication systems; sound; sound effects; vision; graphics; text; icons; images or any combination; all forms of theatric and non-theatric exploitation; all forms of mechanical and electronic reproduction, dissemination or otherwise, internet, intranet and multi-media exploitation; CD-Roms, CDs, DVDs; all methods of merchandising; all patents, computer software, digital and electronic files and any method or process of storage, retrieval, supply and distribution and any developments, variations or adaptations of any nature.

R.331
The [Contributor] acknowledges and agrees that all present and future copyright and any other rights in the [Company's] [Work/Products/website] shall be and remain the property of the [Company]. That the [Contributor] shall not acquire any rights or interest by virtue of this Agreement to any copyright or any other rights in the [Company's] [Work/Products/Website]. At the end of the agreement the [Contributor] shall sign and document or do anything which is reasonably required by the [Company's] legal advisors to confirm or transfer any rights which may have been acquired by the [Contributor] by reason of this Agreement.

R.332
The [Assignor] agrees that it shall not retain any rights in the [Work] and/or the [Work Material].

R.333

The [Assignor] also transfers and [grants/assigns] to the [Assignee] all media rights in the [Work] and the Work Material in respect of the following matters which may be part of the [Work] and/or the [Work Material] except those owned and controlled by a third party [trade marks/design rights/ service marks/logos/domain name/trade secrets].

R.334

In consideration of the Assignment Fee the [Name] assigns all present and future copyright and All Media Rights and any other rights of any nature whether in existence now or created in the future in the [Work] and any parts including the artwork and the material in Schedule [–] throughout the world, universe and outer space for the full period of copyright and any extensions, renewals and variations and [in perpetuity/continuing indefinitely and without limitation].

R.335

The [Licensor] hereby grants to the [Licensee] during the continuance of this Agreement a sole and exclusive licence to use the [Technical Information] and all copyright and other rights in respect of all drawings, documents and other items bearing or embodying any part of the Technical Information and required to be delivered to the [Licensee] under Clause [–] to develop, manufacture, use and exhibit the [Product] in the territory, including a non-exclusive licence to use the [Trade mark] in the Territory as a trade mark in relation to the [Product]. The Licensee may sub-license or sub-contract the rights licensed hereunder in accordance with Clause [–]. Nothing in this Agreement shall confer any right upon the [Licensee] in respect of the [Trade mark] other than to use the [Trade mark] in relation to the [Product].

R.336

All rights not specifically and expressly granted to the [Licensee] by this Agreement are reserved to the [Licensor].

R.337

For the avoidance of doubt, the rights granted are those specifically listed under Clause [–] hereto and the rights in all media other than those expressly licensed are hereby reserved by [Name].

R.338

The rights assigned are for the Assignment Period only after which time all rights under this Agreement shall revert to the [Assignor].

R.339

1.1 In consideration of the Non-Returnable Advance and the Licensor's Royalties the [Licensor] grants to the [Licensee] the sole and exclusive [specify rights granted] throughout the Territory for the duration of the Licence Period and the right to authorise third parties to exercise such [specify rights]

1.2 The [Licensee] acknowledges that all other rights including but not limited to the [specify rights not given] are specifically excluded from this Agreement.

R.340

The [Author] agrees to execute any document or do any reasonable act as may reasonably be required by the [Company] for the purpose of confirming the rights assigned under this Agreement, provided that the [Company] shall agree to bear the cost of all expenses incurred by the [Author] in so doing, including any legal fees.

R.341

1.1 The [Company] agrees that there is no transfer of copyright and/or any intellectual property rights and/or computer software rights in the [Artwork] and/or the computer generated material and/or software programme designed and created by the [Licensor] to the [Company] under this Agreement.

1.2 That the [Licensor] has authorised the [Company] to use, display and exhibit the [Artwork] as an installation at [location] for the [Festival/ Event] from [date] to [date].

1.3 That the [Licensor] has authorised the reproduction in the official programme and on the website [reference] the image and credits of the [Artwork] supplied by the [Licensor].

1.4 The [Company] agrees that no other image and/or photograph shall be used in association with the [Artwork] other than that supplied under 1.3

Internet and Websites

R.342

'Internet Rights' shall mean the right of the [Company] to make available by whatever means (whether in existence now or created in the future) the [Work] on the internet via the worldwide web for promotional purposes only in accordance with Clause [–] of the Agreement.

R.343

'Internet Rights' shall mean the non-exclusive right to disseminate electronically for financial and commercial gain the [Work] in whole or in part including in combination with associated text, sound, music, music effects, stills and moving images on any and all online services and networks irrespective of the platform or software and whether referred to as 'Internet', 'Intranet', 'Extranet' or otherwise and whether made available through any system of collation and distribution known as a website or otherwise.

In such circumstances the [Company] and the [Author] agree that the Author will receive such remuneration as is fair and equitable taking account of the Author's involvement in the commercial exploitation of the Work in such manner but in any event not less than [number per cent] of sums received by the Company from such exploitation.

R.344

'The Internet Rights' shall mean the right to transfer, distribute, supply, sell, dispose of or otherwise exploit the [Work] in whole or in part whether for free, financial or other consideration electronically throughout the world on any online services or networks irrespective of the nature of the method of delivery or reception whether internet, intranet, worldwide web, television, telephone or some other product whether in existence now or created in the future. This shall include the right to exploit and use the [Work] and any part in any media and in any format electronically including, but not limited to, text, visual images, photographs, drawings, plans, sketches, electronically generated material, sounds, sound effects, music, background, banners, bookmarks, border, captions, characters, clip art, cartoon, computer generated art, maps, links, footnotes, headings, hypertext, film, video, DVD, CD-Rom, recordings and any other method of conveying any material from that source.

R.345

The [Licensor] agrees that for the duration of the Licence Period the [Licensor] shall not directly or indirectly license, sub-license, promote, distribute or make available the [Work] and/or parts by any method and/or means which would breach the grant of the Internet Rights. Nor shall the [Licensor] license or permit or authorise any third party to copy, produce, manufacture, develop, distribute any development, variation or altered version on the worldwide web either directly or indirectly. [Except that the [Licensor] shall not be responsible for the actions of unknown third parties].

R.346

1.1   [Name] understands and accepts that the following [Work/other] is to be displayed on the internet at the [Website] location and address [–] under the Domain Name [–] which is held on behalf of the [Company] which is registered in [country] as [details] and which trades [–].

1.2   The duration of the licence is for [specify period] and may be renewed thereafter for any further period by consent in writing and payment of the fee specified. The consent may be withdrawn at any time at the end of any period by notice in writing or email to the [Company].

1.3　The fee for the consent is [specify] which shall be due at the start of each [three month] period.

1.4　[Name] agrees that the [Work] once on the worldwide web may be copied, distributed, supplied and transmitted by others in different forms over which the [Company] has no control. That the [Website] is linked to other sites and the [Company] has no means of monitoring or controlling the number of websites on which the [Work] may appear nor to ensure that the [Names] moral rights are observed.

1.5　That even when the [Work] is no longer on the [Company's] website there will be other sources on the internet.

R.347

The use of the content, data and information on this [Website] is available at no charge for non-commercial use only. You are permitted to download any part of the [Website] and to retain a copy on your hard drive and/or on a disc for your own personal non-commercial use, but not for any financial gain. You may not make any further copies and/or reproduce the material in any format in sound, text, images or otherwise and/or distribute, transfer, transmit and/or exploit the [Website] without our prior written consent.

R.348

'The Theme Park Rights' shall mean the right to build, develop and create [one] commercial enterprise in [country] which is based on the [Work] and the [Characters] for which for which a charge is made for entry by the public. Such commercial enterprise to contain buildings, retail shops, restaurants and fairground attractions and other two and three dimensional representations based on and/or derived from the [Work] and [Characters].

R.349

'Translation of the Computer Programme' shall mean [under the Copyright, Designs and Patents Act 1988 as amended] a version of the [Programme] in which it is converted into or out of a computer language or code or into a different computer language or code or otherwise than incidentally in the course of running the [Programme].

R.350

1.1　The [Purchaser] is granted a non-exclusive and non-transferable licence to use the [Disc] information and data for the purpose for which it is intended in conjunction with the [Work/Product/Service] in the normal course of business, namely to [specify steps, actions and purpose that may be taken].

1.2 The [Purchaser] shall not acquire any rights and/or interest in the [Work] [Disc] and/or content and/or any part in any media of any nature at any time. All rights which are not specifically granted are reserved.

R.351

This right is personal to the [Purchaser] and shall also permit the [Purchaser] to copy files from the [Disc] of the [Work] to their hard drive and also to make one security copy of the [Disc]. There is no right to make additional copies of the [Work] and/or [Disc] and/or data for any reason except the stated purpose in Clause [–].above.

R.352

The [Purchaser] shall not have the right to make any additional copies and/or permit, authorise, sub-license, assign, transfer and/or otherwise exploit the [Work] and/or [Disc] and/or information in any form whether for commercial purposes or otherwise.

R.353

There is no right granted to copy the [Work], [Disc] and/or data by word processing, photocopying and/or scanning more than [number] words in total and/or copying the [Work], [Disc] and/or data on the computer and/or other gadget or device more [number] words in total and sending it by electronic means to any third party.

R.354

There is no right granted to use the [Work] [Disc], data and any content to create, edit, adapt and/or develop a taxonomy, index, and/or any other format and/or medium which shall be displayed and/or supplied on the internet and/or any website and/or in a directory, database and/or any computer software and/or by any other form of telecommunication including mobiles.

R.355

There is no right granted to exploit, adapt, licence, translate, create a new format based on the [Work] and/or develop a new version based on the [Work] for use on the internet and/or to use the [Work] as part of any storage and retrieval system and/or process whether electronic, digital or otherwise in any media.

R.356

There is no right granted to permit, authorise, sub-licence, assign, transfer, and/or otherwise exploit the [Work], [Disc], data and any content and/or any parts in any form in any medium and by any method, process and/or system whether for commercial, educational, charitable and/or non-commercial purposes or otherwise whether in existence now and/or created in the future.

R.357

There is no right granted to permit the [Purchaser] to represent that the [Work] [Disc] and/or parts are owned and controlled by the [Purchaser] as the copyright owner and the owner of all other intellectual property rights.

R.358

The [Work] and [Disc] are an excluded work from the [Copyright Licensing Agency] and there is no licence granted to scan, photocopy, create a digital and/or electronic version and/or to reproduce, supply, distribute and/or licence the [Work] and/or [Disc] and any content and/or any part for reference, search, index and/or taxonomy purposes on the internet and/or a website and/or for educational purposes for school and universities.

R.359

'The Digitised Format Rights' shall mean the right to convert the [Film/Work] into a digitised format enabling the [Film/Work] to be stored onto a disk known as a digital visual display device or otherwise and the right for the disk to be played on an enabling device including, but not limited to, personal computer, television, or other equipment, apparatus designed or created for the purpose of retrieving and displaying the information, data, sound and vision.

R.360

The use of the [Directory] on this [Website] is available at no charge for non-commercial use only by those persons who have registered online for a period of [one year]. You may search, copy, download and store on your hard drive and/or on a disc and/or USB and/or other storage device up to [number] details from the database in total for your own personal non-commercial use for research, educational, and personal use only, but not for any commercial [and/or charitable reason]. You may not make any further copies and/or reproduce the [Directory] and any data, database, index and/or taxonomy in any form and/or medium and/or distribute, transfer, transmit and/or exploit the [Directory] without the prior written consent of the [Company].

R.361

'The Digital Rights' shall mean the right to exploit the [Work/] commercially by digital means only but including the right to scan, copy, digitise, reproduce, adapt, promote, advertise, market, supply, distribute and sell the [Work] for electronic dissemination by whatever means whether in existence now and/

or created in the future throughout the [Territory/world and universe] as a complete entity and/or part as a complete text and/or an adaptation and/or an abridged electronic file in conjunction with and/or without other electronic files including audio files, sounds, music, text, data and/or visual images and the right to authorise and/or sub-license third parties to exercise such rights.

R.362
'The Digital Rights' shall mean the exclusive right to reproduce, scan, copy, digitise, adapt, licence, supply, distribute, market, advertise, promote and exploit the [Work/Artwork/Photograph/Sound Recordings] in whole and/or part whether for educational, charitable, non-commercial and/or commercial purposes in digital and electronic format by means of electronic dissemination over the internet and world wide web for use by means of any laptop, computer, telephone and mobile, and/or other gadget and/or portal which is capable of permitting access to the material by the public, and/or any limited group and/or any person which is in existence now and/or created during this Agreement throughout the [Territory/world and universe]. This shall include the right to add, delete, change, vary, alter and/or reproduce in different languages, colours and/or in conjunction with any other material.

R.363
In consideration of the [Fee] the [Licensor] grants [Name] the non-exclusive right to digitise and reproduce in electronic form the [Image/Text] for reproduction on the [Website] reference [specify] from [date] to [date]. Provided that:

1.1 There shall appear at al times a copyright notice and credit to the [Licensor].

1.2 The copyright in the digitised electronic file shall be assigned to the [Licensor].

1.3 No copy shall be supplied to the public by the [Licensee] and/or sub-licensed to any third party.

1.4 A copy of the digitised file shall be delivered to the [Licensor] at the [Licensees'] sole cost on or by [date].

1.5 That by [date] all copies of the digitised file shall be erased provided that the [Licensee] has fulfilled 1.4 above.

1.6 That by [date] all copies in any format and/or storage and retrieval system of the [Image/text] and/or the digitised file held by the [Licensee] shall be erased and/or destroyed.

R.364

In consideration of the Asset Transfer Fee of [number/currency] to be paid by the [Company] to [Name] on [date] to his/her personal bank account in [country]. [Name] grants and assigns to the [Company] the sole and exclusive rights and all copyright, intellectual property rights, domain name rights, trade mark rights, computer software and password and code rights, data, films, sound recordings, advertising, promotional and merchandising material, artwork and images, text, slogans and music, lyrics and all rights of exploitation in any form and in any medium whether in existence now and/or created at a later date for the full period of copyright and for the full term of all other rights which may exist and thereafter in perpetuity through the world and the universe in the following:

1.1   The website known as [specify] [reference] which trades under the name [specify] registered in [country] as [specify].

1.2   Al the content of 1.1 and all material in draft and final form including master copies which was created to develop 1.1.

1.3   The domain names [specify] [reference].

1.4   The trade marks [specify] [reference].

1.5   All corporate documents, financial reports, agreements, licences, music cue sheets, registration forms, photographs, and any other material held by [Name] which relate to 1.1 to 1.4.

R.365

1.1   The [Contributor] agrees that he/she shall not acquire any rights and/ or copyright and/or intellectual property and/or domain name and/or trade marks rights in the content of the [Blog] and/or the title and/or any image and/or logo whether or not the [Blog] was created by the [Company] specifically for [Name] and his/her contributions or not.

1.2   That the [Contributor] agrees that he/she shall not be entitled to receive any payment for the [Blog] except a writer's fee of [number/ currency] each week subject to delivery of the material for the [Blog]. That the [Company] shall be entitled to assign, transfer, remove and/ or delete the [Blog] at any time and/or to terminate and/or cancel the arrangement with [Name] for the supply of material.

1.3   The [Contributor] assigns all copyright and intellectual property rights in the written material which he/she delivers for the [Blog] for the full period of copyright and any extensions and/or renewals throughout the world in all media in any format which may exist now and/or be developed and/or come into existence at a later date.

R.366

1.1   The [Company] agrees that no part of this Agreement is intended to assign and/or transfer the personal and/or business name of the [Contributor] to the [Company] and/or the right to register it as a trade mark and/or to exploit it in any other form.

1.2   The [company] agrees that if after the [contributor] has ceased to supply material for [Blog] to the [Company]. The [Contributor] requests that the [company] remove his/her name from the [Blog] and/or website [reference] and/or any other material distributed and/or supplied by the [Company]. Then the [Company] agrees to remove and/or delete all reference to the [Contributor] as requested.

R.367

1.1   The [Company] has designed and developed and created the [App] known as [specify] which is described in Schedule [–].

1.2   The [Company] agrees to licence the [App] to the [Distributor] on a non-exclusive basis to be downloaded from [their website/archive storage facility/shop] [specify] from [date] to [date] for [free/a fee] by the public to be used to [calculate/find] [specify subject].

1.3   The [Company] agrees that the licence for the [App] is for the world as it may be accessed and downloaded in any country for use by individuals, commercial companies, educational establishments and/or other third parties by a variety of methods including mobiles, laptops, tablets, computers and other gadgets and telecommunications systems and over the internet.

1.4   The [Distributor] agrees to pay the [Company] a fee of [number/currency] for each person that [downloads/accesses/clicks on] the [App]. Any sums due to the [Company] shall be paid one month in arrears at the end of each calendar month direct to the bank account of the [Company].

1.5   The [Distributor] shall pay for all costs and expenses of adapting its [website/archive storage facility/shop] to incorporate the facility of access to the [App].

1.6   Where the [Distributor] fails to report and/or pay any sums due to the [Company] then the [Company] shall have the right to terminate this Agreement by email with immediate effect.

R.368

1.1   The [Licensor] grants [Name] the non-exclusive right to reproduce the [Sound Recordings] in conjunction with the [Film] for the banner link which they have [produced/commissioned] to market and promote their [Work/Products/Service].

1.2 The [Licensor] agrees that [Name] may authorise the use and reproduction of the banner link with the [Sound Recording] on its own website, search engines and any other telecommunication system including the internet and mobiles for access through television, laptops and other computers and gadgets for the period in 1.4.

1.3 The [Licensor] agrees that no credit and/or copyright notice is required on the banner link with the [Sound Recording].

1.4 The Licence shall start on [date and end on [date] and shall only come into existence and continue until the end date if [Name] has paid the fees due for the Licence as follows [specify].

Merchandising

R.369

'The Merchandising Rights' shall be the right to reproduce, manufacture, sale and supply goods including comic strips and printed matter of all kinds other than books reproducing and depicting or decorated with characters, scenes and incidents of or articles appearing in the [Novel] or in such films or programmes based on the [Novel].

R.370

'The Merchandising Rights' shall be the right to reproduce, manufacture, sale, supply and distribute [and to authorise others to do so] the following:

1.1 All printed material which is in the form of comic strips, comics, calendars, stationery, posters, cards, stickers.

1.2 Three-dimensional products such as mugs, toys, puppets, T-shirts, bags, slippers and [–] bearing the [Character(s)] [Logo] [Depicting scenes] and or other material based upon the [Book/Film/Character] full details of which are set out below [Name, Title, Publisher, Production].

R.371

'The Merchandising Rights' shall mean the sole and exclusive right to exploit the [Character] through the manufacture, production, distribution, promotion, supply and sale of articles of any type based on or derived from the [Character] including, but not limited to, posters, toys, games, computer software, stationery, clothes, models, food, drinks, goods, comics, publications, give-aways and promotions throughout the Territory for the duration of the Licence Period.

'The Character' shall be the original concept and novel idea for a Character which is briefly described as follows:

Name of Character [–] Trade mark/Logo [–]

Full details of the Character are attached to and form part of this Agreement.

R.372
'The Licensed Article' shall be the licensed product to be produced and distributed by the [Licensee] which shall be based on or derived from [Character] and which is described as follows [–]. Full details of the [Licensed Article] are attached to and form part of this Agreement.

R.373
'The Format' shall be the original concept and novel idea which is briefly described as follows [–]. Full details are attached to and form part of this Agreement.

R.374
'The Licensed Articles' shall be any licensed product based on or derived from [Character] to be produced and distributed under agreements to be concluded by the [Agent] or any sub-agent or sub-licensee.

R.375
In consideration of the Licence Fee the [Licensor] grants to the [Licensee] the sole and exclusive right to produce, manufacture, distribute and sell the [Licensed Article] based on the [Character] throughout the Territory for the duration of the Licence Period.

R.376
The [Licensor] shall have the sole and exclusive right to grant licences for the manufacture, marketing, distribution, promotion, publication or performance of any article or other matter whatsoever based upon or derived from [Characters] or any other matter relating to the [Property] described in Schedule [–].

R.377
In consideration of the Licence Fee and the [Licensor's] Royalties the [Licensor] grants to the [Licensee] the sole and exclusive right to produce, manufacture, distribute, sell and exploit the [Licensed Articles] based on the [Character] throughout the Territory during the Licence Period.

R.378
In consideration of the payment of the Licence Fee and the Royalties, the [Licensor] shall grant the [Licensee] the sole and exclusive right to exercise

and exploit all film, video, electronic and mechanical reproduction rights in the [Characters] in the [Films/Work] and in all other media whether in existence now or created in the future, but not the publication and merchandising rights which shall be retained by the [Licensor]. For the avoidance of doubt the [Licensee] shall be granted the following rights [specify]. The [Licensee] shall retain rights to [specify].

R.379

The [Licensee] agrees that no film or commercial featuring the [Property] or the [Licensed Articles] shall be made without the prior consultation with and written consent of the [Licensor].

R.380

1.1 The [Licensee] undertakes that he/she will not license any third party to produce the [Licensed Article] based on the [Character] or any development or variation in the Territory during the Licence Period.

1.2 Nor shall the [Licensee] authorise, permit or license any other products based in [–] field which are to be derived from or incorporate the [Character] or any part before [date].

R.381

The [Company] grants to the [Contractor] the right to exhibit the [Character] to non-paying audiences for non-commercial exhibitions throughout the Territory for the duration of the Licence Period. It is specifically agreed that no authority or licence is granted to the [Contractor] to permit, authorise, or exercise this right by any third party, agent, or sub-licensee or otherwise.

R.382

The [Licensee] agrees that it is only being licensed to produce the specified product and that it may not sub-license, sub-distribute or otherwise produce any other item based on the [Character] or engage any third party to exploit the [Licensed Articles].

R.383

The [Agent] agrees that it shall not be entitled to permit or authorise the use, reproduction, copying, drawing, taking photographs, filming or exploitation in any form or medium of the [Samples], the [Product], or the [Company] Logo at any time without the prior written consent of the [Company].

R.384

The [Agent] agrees not to issue any requests for payment on behalf of the [Company] and not to pledge or commit the [Company] to pay any sums or perform any acts for any reason without the prior consent of the [Company].

R.385

The [Licensor] shall have and retain the sole and exclusive right as against the [Licensee] to license any third party to use the [property] in connection with any articles including the [Licensed Articles] in connection with any premium give-aways or promotions.

R.386

The [Licensee] shall not sell, dispose or supply the [Licensed Articles] to any person or body or other entity for use either by itself or in association with any other products, goods or services for promotional, publicity, advertising, premium or give-away purposes. The [Licensee] shall forward details of all such requests to the [Licensor].

R.387

The [Company] undertakes that it will not license or permit or authorise any third party to copy, produce, manufacture or distribute the [Character] or any development or variation in the Territory during the Licence Period except as agreed under this Agreement.

R.388

The [Company] appoints the [Distributor] to be the [Company's] sole and exclusive agent to distribute and have distributed and to sell, rent and supply the [Licensed Articles] in the Territory during the Term of this Agreement in respect of the Merchandising and Multi-Media Rights reproducing the [Programmes] based on the [Work] subject to the following terms:

1.1 The [Distributor] shall not advertise, publicise or promote the [Licensed Articles] reproducing the [Programmes] at any time outside the Territory. Unless otherwise agreed in writing between the parties the [Distributor] shall not sell, supply, rent or distribute any similar articles to the [Licensed Articles] reproducing the [Programmes] in any other country outside the Territory.

1.2 The [Distributor] shall be entitled to use excerpts from the [Programmes] of up to [three minutes] duration in any one case. The excerpts may be used for demonstration and promotional purposes at trade fairs and exhibitions outside the Territory for the purpose of obtaining sales inside the Territory.

1.3 The [Company] shall retain all rights not specifically granted under this Agreement including, but not limited to, non-theatric exploitation of the [Work] and the [Programmes].

1.4 The [Distributor] undertakes during the Term of this Agreement to use its best endeavours consistent with reasonable commercial practice to obtain orders for and to promote the sale, rental and supply in the Territory of the [Licensed Articles] reproducing the [Programmes].

1.5   The [Distributor] shall at all times during the Term of this Agreement endeavour to maintain a stock of the [Licensed Articles] reproducing the [Programmes] sufficient to meet dealer requirements in the Territory.

R.389

In consideration of the Licence Fee the [Licensor] grants the [Licensee] the sole and exclusive right to produce, manufacture, distribute and sell the [Licensed Article] based on the [Character] throughout the Territory for the duration of the Licence Period.

R.390

The [Licensee] agrees and undertakes that it shall not, except with the prior written consent of the [Agent] or [Licensor], reproduce, use or exploit the [Licensor] or the [Agent's] name in connection with the [Licensed Articles]. The [Licensee] shall not represent itself in any manner as the agent or representative of the [Licensor] or the [Agent] at any time.

R.391

The [Agent] agrees and undertakes not to negotiate, promote, or distribute in any manner or form the Character or [Licensed Articles] outside the Territory. Provided that it is agreed that the Agent shall attend the following exhibitions/fairs [specify].

R.392

The [Licensee] agrees that it shall not acquire any interest, goodwill or right in the name of the [Character] or any associated slogan, words, image, text or any trade mark, logo or otherwise under this Agreement except to manufacture and distribute the [Licensed Article] and undertake not to attempt to register any such rights or interest.

R.393

'Image Rights' shall mean such right to license, reproduce and exploit in the form of advertising, products and other products and methods whether for direct financial gain or to enhance sales, business or otherwise the name, nickname, image, appearance, photograph, still, caricature, voice, slogan, goodwill, reputation, career [and family background] of the [Name].

R.394

'Image Rights' shall mean the right to exploit commercially the image and reputation of [Name] which shall be licensed by the [Name] to some third party. The right shall include the right to exploit commercially the image and reputation in all forms of commercial activities outside [specify main profession/contract]. Provided that it is outside this stated main role the commercial activities are unlimited and may include modelling, sponsorship, promotions, merchandising, electronic games, digitised image representation in all forms of [moving and still] visual images.

R.395
'The Image Rights' shall mean the exclusive right to reproduce the still or moving image and likeness, mannerisms, gestures, body language, catch phrases and voice likeness of the [Actor/Sportsperson] in all formats and in all media whether in existence now and/or created in the future throughout the [Territory/country/world] for the [Term of the Agreement/Licence Period/ other]. This shall include but not be limited to all forms of animation, film, electronic digitisation, telecommunication systems, digital photography, two and three dimensional reproductions, sounds and electronically generated voice likeness.

R.396
'The Image Rights' shall mean the exclusive right to reproduce the still and/ or moving image and likeness, mannerisms, gestures, body language, catch phrases, imitation, voice likeness and/or other representations of [Name] in all formats and in all media without limitation to all forms of animation and film, audio and sound recordings, electronic digitisation and dissemination, telecommunication systems, mobiles and telephones, two and three dimensional reproductions, toys, accessories, stationery, clothing, bags, calendars, advertisements, promotions and marketing throughout the [Territory/other] for the duration of the Term of this Agreement.

R.397
The [Licensor] agrees that the [Licensee] shall have the right to sub-licence the rights set out in clause [–] to any third party. Provided that the [Licensee] shall not be relieved from any terms of this Agreement and undertakes to bear all responsibilities for the acts and/or omissions and/or work of the [Sub-Licensee]. Further the [Licensee] shall bear the cost and pay for all sums due to the [Licensor] which are not paid to the [Licensee] by the [Sub-Licensee].

R.398
The [Actor/Sportsperson] expressly reserves the book publication, personal appearances and interviews, professional [specify] which are managed by the [Agent] and do not form part of this Agreement.

R.399
The [Company] agrees and undertakes that [Name] shall retain all past, present and future copyright, trade mark and intellectual property rights he

owns and/or may own with respect to the Image Rights and any other rights of any nature. That this Agreement is not intended to transfer, grant, vest and/or assign any rights of any nature to the [Company].

R.400

'Secondary Rights' shall mean all rights generated as a direct result of the production of the [Programme] but which are not in themselves rights in the [Programme] such as music, publishing and merchandising rights.

R.401

In consideration of the Assignment Fee the [Assignor] assigns to the [Assignee] all present and future copyright and all other rights in all media in the [Work/Format] whether in existence now or created in the future throughout the Territory for the full period of copyright and any extensions and renewals including but not limited to:

1.1 All forms of television, terrestrial, digital, cable, satellite and archive retrieval.

1.2 All forms of DVD, video cassettes, discs, lasers, USBs and other portable storage devices.

1.3 All forms of theatric, non-theatric, educational, charitable and fundraising exploitation.

1.4 All forms of merchandising, sponsorship, endorsement and product placement, festivals, sports and other outdoor events, lotteries, betting, theme parks.

1.5 All forms of publication including hardback, paperback, newspapers, magazines and comics.

1.6 All forms of electronic dissemination of information and mechanical reproduction and any method of access, storage and retrieval.

R.402

'The Music Publishing Rights' shall mean the right to publish the musical compositions commissioned for the [Programme] including the signature tune (if any) and to authorise others to do so.

R.403

'The Music Publishing Rights' shall mean the following rights in respect of the title, words and music of the composition entitled [–] the [Work]:

1.1 To publish, print, sell and distribute the [Work] whether in the form of ordinary sheet music edition or as part of a folio or album or in any other printed form and to sub-license third parties to exercise such rights.

1.2 To reproduce the [Work] by means of mechanical reproduction by way of a record, disk, tape or other means of conveying sound and/or visual images (excluding television, video and film) whether in existence now or created in the future and the right to authorise others to do so.

1.3 The right to grant the Licences for the synchronisation of the [Work] with any feature film, film for television, advertisement or other visual moving images.

1.4 The right to make and publish translations of the lyric in the [Work] in any languages.

R.404

1.1 The [Licensee] grants the [Sub-Licensee] the non-exclusive right to reproduce, manufacture, distribute, supply and sell the [Character/Logo] on all copies of [specify article] from [date] to [date] anywhere in the world and over the internet through websites.

1.2 The [Sub-Licensee] shall not have the right to sub-licence the rights and/or authorise any third party to reproduce, manufacture, distribute, supply and/or sell copies of the [Character/Logo] and/or any articles, products and/or services bearing the [Character/Logo] at any time.

R.405

The [Sub-Licensee] agrees and undertakes not to:

1.1 Sub-licence the rights and/or authorise any third party to reproduce, manufacture, distribute, supply and/or sell copies of the [Character/Logo].

1.2 Sub-licence the rights and/or authorise any third party to reproduce, manufacture, distribute, supply and/or sell any articles, products and/or services bearing the [Character/Logo] at any time.

1.3 Reproduce and/or manufacture any article, product and/or service bearing the [Character/Logo] except the authorised article in accordance with the approved [sample/prototype].

R.406

The [Licensee] agrees and accepts that it shall not acquire any right to register a domain name, trade mark and/or any other copyright and/or intellectual property rights of any nature in the [Work/Project/Product] and/or any logo, image, character name, title, slogan, text, words and/or other content and/or packaging and/or marketing material whether it is supplied by the [Licensor] and/or created and developed for the purpose of this Agreement.

R.407

The [Licensee] agrees and undertakes not to:

1.1   Change any part of the layout, design, copyright notice, content and packaging for the [Product] for which the sample has been approved by the [Licensor].

1.2   Market and/or promote the [Product] in association with any person, location and/or event which would affect the reputation of the [Product] and/or business of the [Licensor] in a detrimental manner.

1.3   Make representations and/or claims in any marketing and promotional material which cannot be verified by supporting data and evidence.

1.4   Breach any guidelines, policies and codes of practice in any part of the world which relate to health and safety, product safety, advertising and/or customs, taxes and/or transfer and supply of products.

Publishing

R.408

'Electronic Publication Rights' shall mean the right to make available, facilitate, disseminate electronically the disposal, sale or otherwise of the [Work] in whole or in part whether for financial gain to members of the public including in combination with text, sound, music, music effects, stills, moving images on any and all online services and networks irrespective of the method, internet, intranet, extranet or otherwise from a website or platform via the worldwide web which is owned or controlled by the [Publishers] or some third party who has acquired such material via a link.

R.409

'Book Publishing Rights' shall mean the right to publish in printed form the [Scripts] or any adaptation thereof or other literary work(s) based on or deriving from [Programme] and to authorise others to do so.

R.410

'The Publication Rights' shall mean the right to adapt the [Script] of the [Programme] in volume and/or electronic form and/or an edited and/or adapted version of the [Script/Work] for a [Book] based on the [Script/Work] whether described as a 'tie-in' book or otherwise.

R.411

'Volume Form' means the publication of the [Work] in book form, whether packaged as a hardback or paperback.

R.412
'The Serialisation Rights' shall mean the right to publish the [Extracts] in the Periodical.

R.413
The [Author] reserves the right to publish the [Work] in volume form and all other rights in all media are specifically reserved in Clause [–].

R.414
The [Author] grants to the [Publisher] the sole and exclusive right and licence for a period of [twenty years] from the date of this Agreement or delivery of the typescript (whichever is the later) to print, publish and sell the [Work] in volume form, and to sub-license the rights in all languages throughout the World. If the [Work] is in print at the end of the Agreement the [Company] shall have the right to request the [Author] to negotiate in good faith with the intention of concluding an agreement for a further period upon revised terms.

R.415
The Author hereby grants to the Publisher [for the legal term of copyright and any extensions and renewals thereof/for a period of ten years] the sole and exclusive right to print, publish, produce, distribute and sell the Work in volume form throughout the Territory as specified in Schedule [–] and the non-exclusive rights in the rest of the world outside the Territory.

R.416
In consideration of the [Author's] Royalties and the Advance Royalty Payment the [Author] grants to the [Publisher] the sole and exclusive right to publish, exploit and license the [Work] and any part(s) in all media including, but not limited to, all methods of publication, electronic and mechanical reproduction and communication and performances including hardback, paperback, serialisation, translations, anthologies, quotations, radio, theatre, film, television, computer software, merchandising and the internet throughout the Territory for the duration of the Licence Period.

R.417
In consideration of the Advance and the Royalties the [Author] grants the [Publisher] the following: specify rights in the [Work] in the Territory from [date] to [date]:

1.1 Hardback, reprint, large print, new editions, digest book condensation, book club editions, educational editions and sub-licensing.

1.2 Paperback, reprint, large print, new editions, digest book condensation and book club editions, educational editions and sub-licensing.

1.3   Soft cover baby books and sub-licensing.

1.4   Cassette, CD, DVD, disc and interactive talking books.

1.5   Readings and associated electronic presentations, liturgical text for talks, exhibitions, television, radio, religious meetings and occasions which are not dramatised versions.

1.6   Anthologies, quotations, taxonomy of subject and index.

1.7   Theme parks, 2D and 3D adaptations, retail shops and restaurants, gambling, bingo, lottery, competitions based on characters, title or subject matter of the [work].

1.8   First, second and any subsequent serialisation, both exclusive and/or non-exclusive both before and after publication in newspapers, periodicals, magazines, journals, and on the internet.

1.9   One shot digest of hardback or paperback or any later version as an abridgement in any newspaper and periodical.

1.10 Dramatic adaptations of any type whether for television, radio, video, DVD, film, theatre, exhibition, or other performance.

1.11 Computer software, CD Rom, any method of access, storage and retrieval.

1.12 The internet, websites, Wi-Fi, domain names and trade marks.

1.13 Terrestrial, cable, satellite and other telecommunication systems such as telephones, mobiles, pagers.

1.14 Sponsorship, endorsement, product placement, cross-promotion, merchandising, fundraising.

1.15 Cartoons or picture representation in newspapers, magazines, film or other.

1.16 Any licensing, sub-licensing, translations, subtitles, Braille or other development or variation of any of the above.

1.17 Any other rights in any form of the media of any nature not set out above.

R.418

In consideration of the payments set out in this Agreement the [Author] grants to the [Publishers] the sole and exclusive right and licence to produce, publish and distribute the [Work] in volume form in [English language/all languages] for the full period of copyright and any extensions or renewals throughout the [British Commonwealth, the United States of America, its territories and dependencies, the Philippine Islands and Canada] together with the non-exclusive right throughout the rest of the world.

R.419

In consideration of the payments set out in this Agreement the [Author] grants to the [Publishers] the sole and exclusive right and licence to produce and publish, broadcast and perform the [Work], any abridgement, adaptation or part(s) in all editions, languages and forms throughout the rest of the world for the [legal/full] term of copyright and any extensions or renewals.

R.420

The [Publishers] shall be entitled to use the title of the feature film, television or other dramatic version of the [Work] for their editions of the [Work]. The [Author] agrees to inform the [Publisher] of any proposed release dates.

R.421

1.1 In consideration of the Serialisation Fee the [Licensor] grants the [Licensee] the sole and exclusive Serialisation Rights throughout the Territory for the duration of the Licence Period.

1.2 The [Licensee] undertakes not to permit, license or transfer any of the Serialisation Rights to any third party without the prior written consent of the [Licensor].

1.3 The [Licensor] undertakes not to permit, license or transfer the right to publish the [Extracts] or any other parts of the [Work] in any other newspaper, periodical, magazine owned or controlled by the [Licensee] or any other third party throughout the Territory for the duration of the Licence Period [except for the purpose of review, criticism or other fair dealing].

R.422

The [Publisher] confirms that it has granted a non-exclusive licence to the [Copyright Licensing Agency] to reproduce literary works published by the [Publisher] which shall include the [Work] by photocopying and other reprographic means. The [Copyright Licensing Agency] shall divide the proceeds from the reprographic rights equally between the [Author] and the [Publisher]. The [Author] shall receive the [Author's] share of the proceeds through the [Author's Licensing and Collecting Society] in accordance with their standard terms and conditions.

R.423

The [Publisher] confirms that the [Copyright Licensing Agency] have been or will be authorised to grant non-exclusive licences to reproduce the [Work] and other literary works published by the [Publisher] by photocopying and other reprographic means. The [Work] shall be included with the others and the [Copyright Licensing Agency] shall divide the proceeds from the [Work] [specify percentage] between the [Publisher] and the [Author]. The [Author's] share of the proceeds shall be paid [specify].

R.424

The [Author] does not grant the [Publisher] any reprographic rights in the [Work] whether by photocopying or any other means. All sums due in respect of the exercise of those rights shall belong to the [Author] and the [Publisher] shall not be entitled to any sum at any time.

R.425

The [Writer] will procure the renewal or extension of the copyright in the [Work] under the laws of all the countries that afford such rights and will [assign/grant] to the [Company] such renewal or extension in respect of the rights set out in this Agreement.

R.426

The [Publisher] shall not be entitled to arrange to give away copies of the [Work] as premiums in connection with any other products without the prior written consent of the [Author] and the agreement with the [Author] in respect of the royalty and/or advance to be paid.

R.427

No licence is granted in respect of the [Work] except to the [Publisher] and all further sub-licensing is strictly prohibited.

R.428

The [Publisher] agrees that the [Author] shall remain the copyright owner of the [Work] and that the [Author] has not granted any rights to the [Publisher] outside the Territory. There is no transfer of rights in respect of outer space or the universe.

R.429

For the avoidance of doubt this Agreement does not purport to grant to the [Publishers] the right to display the [Work] to the public in a way which does not involve the purchase and/or right to read and financial gain to the [Publisher] and the [Author] for the [Work]. The [Publisher] may display no more than [number] pages of the [Work] in total in a manner that does not require payment by a third party.

R.430

The [Publishers] have no interest in or control of the [film, television, video, disc and DVD rights] in the [Work] and/or parts. The [Publishers] agree that a third party acquiring such rights shall have the right to print and publish for advertising and promotional purposes only including quotations and a film synopsis of not more than [number] words for use anywhere in the Territory.

R.431

The right to reproduce the typography and design of the [Work] is reserved by the [Publishers].

R.432

The title, design of the cover, layout, format and design of the content, and index shall belong to [specify party].

R.433

The [Publisher] shall not have the right to employ, engage and/or authorise any person, company and/or business to edit, adapt, add to, delete from and/or change the title, disclaimer, content, typography, index, copyright notices, acknowledgements, credits, layout, format of the [Work] and/or any material supplied with it without the prior written consent of the [Author].

R.434

The [Publisher] shall not have the right to publish and/or market the [Work] and/or any part as part of some other service, work or product.

R.435

All rights not specifically granted to the [Company] are reserved by the [Author] for exploitation by the [Author] and/or any third party at any time. [The [Author] agrees to inform the [Company] of the licence, sale or otherwise of any such rights to a third party but not the details of the Agreement.]

R.436

The [Company] shall not have the right to exploit, adapt, licence, develop and/or authorise the use of the [Work] as a whole or in part and/or based on and/or derived from any part on the internet and/or any website and/or for any storage and retrieval system and/or computer software programmes and/or use in any format or by any method, system and/or process to be supplied, distributed, or reproduced whether in electronic, digitized, scanned, mechanical reproduction, by loading and playing a disc, or downloading the material or any other media of any nature in text, computer generated material, computer language and whether free, subscription, pay on demand or otherwise except that specified in clause [–].

R.437

The [Work] shall be listed as an excluded [Work] with the [Copyright Licensing Agency/Author Lending Copyright Society/other] and the [Author] shall be entitled to be responsible for the grant of any rights for copying, scanning, digitization or other proposed method of reproduction and adaptation [and to retain all sums that may arise/to split the sums received on terms to be agreed with the [Author].

R.438

In consideration of the [Fee/Fixed Unit Price] the [Author] grants the [Company] the non-exclusive right to photocopy and/or scan [number] pages of the [Work] and to send part and/or all of such copies over the internal computer system and intranet at [address] to [number] persons who are employees of the [Company] from [date] to [date].

R.439

In consideration of the [Fee/Fixed Unit Price] the [Author] grants the [Company] the non-exclusive right to photocopy and/or scan [number] pages of the [Work] and to store it in electronic and/or digital format on the internal database system for its staff and employees only at [specify] from [date] to [date]. The [Company] shall have the right to send part and/or all of such copies over the internal computer system and intranet at [address] to [number] persons who are employees of the [Company] from [date] to [date]. No right is granted to email, distribute and/or display any part of the [Work] on the internet and/or any website including the website of the [Company]. After the expiry of the licence then all copies of the [Work] shall be deleted from the internal database system.

R.440

1.1 The [Company] agrees and undertakes that it shall at all times ensure that the digital copy stored in the database and/or any other copies of the extracts of the [Work] distributed by the [Company] shall have a clear prominent copyright notice and credit to the [Author] and specifically make reference to the limitations of the rights granted to the [Company].

1.2 The [Company] agrees to ensure no copies of the [Work] are displayed any website by the [Company] and/or sent by electronic attachment and/or any other means to third parties. Nor shall the [Company] authorise any publication in a brochure, journal and/or other printed format and/or reproduction in any format in any media.

1.3 The [Company] agrees and undertakes to assign all rights in all media in the digital copy to the [Author] and/or any other material adapted from the [Authors'] Work. The [Company] agrees to supply a copy of the digital version to the [Author] at the [Company's] cost.

R.441

There is no right granted by the [Author] for the [Company] to engage a third party to carry out the development of the digital copy. In the event that the [Company] wishes to outsource the project to a third party then the prior written consent of the [Author] shall be required and the conclusion of an agreement between the [Author] and the third party.

R.442

In consideration of the payment of the [Fee] and the [Royalties] the [Author] grants the [Company] the non-exclusive right to make a digital copy of the [Extract/Article/Work] and to store it on a database and/or storage and retrieval system on a computer at [address] from [date] to [date]. The [Author] grants the [Company] the right to reproduce, supply, distribute and make available copies in electronic and/or printed format from its address and on its website to the public and/or any other third party anywhere in the world from [date] to [date] for personal use and private research only and not for any commercial, educational and/or any adaptation.

R.443

The [Company] shall pay the [Author] a fixed rate royalty of [figure/currency] for every copy of the [Extract/Article/Work] which is made available by the [Company] to any third party at any time.

R.444

No right is granted by the [Author] to the [Company] to engage any agent and/or distributor and/or to sub-licence any part of the [Extract/Article/Work] to any other third party at any time. Nor shall the [Company] have the right to authorise any third party to include the [Extract/Article/Work] in any journal, book, course work and/or to make any adaptation.

R.445

In consideration of the Fee the [Author] grants the [Licensee] the non-exclusive right to reproduce the following original [Poem/Report/Extract] entitled [specify] in the journal entitled [specify] for publication and distribution in the [month] issue and publication by [date]. The [Licensee] shall be entitled to sell and distribute the journal anywhere in the world. The [Licensee] shall also be entitled to reproduce the [Poem/Report/Extract] on the website reference [specify] for a period of [figure] months from the date of publication of the journal. No right is granted to syndicate, license and/or otherwise exploit the [Poem/Report/Extract].

R.446

In consideration of the Fee and Royalty the [Author] grants the [Company] the non-exclusive right to reproduce, print, distribute and sell the [Article/

Essay/Coursework] throughout the world for the Licence Period in a [Book/ Journal] and/or as a download as a file on a website for which a charge is made. The [Company] agrees and undertakes that the [Article/Essay/ Coursework] shall only be grouped with articles, essays and/or course work by other persons on the subject of [specify].

R.447

The [Company] agrees and undertakes not to sub-licence, adapt, alter and/or amend the [Article/Essay/Coursework] at any time without the prior consent of the [Author].

R.448

The [Company] agrees and undertakes not to:

1.1 Register any interest and/or rights with any collecting society and/or copyright organisation.

1.2 Attribute any other person as the Author.

1.3 Delete, erase and/or amend the copyright notice.

1.4 Arrange for and use a translation which has not been approved by the [Author].

R.449

The [Licensee] agrees that no part of this Agreement is intended and it does not permit the [Licensee] to:

1.1 Register the name of the author and/or the title of the [Work] and/or any similar words as a trade mark, service mark, domain name, company name and/or otherwise.

1.2 Register with any collecting society and/or copyright organisation to receive sums from the exploitation of the [Work] except:[specify].

1.3 Grant and/or authorise any third party to use the [Work] in any media as product placement and/or to be reproduced in an advertisement associated with some other product and/or service and/or to be reproduced as postcards, greetings cards and/or any other merchandise in any form except as set out in clause [–].

1.4 Destroy the master copy which is used to reproduce the [Work] by the [Licensee] without first offering the material at no additional cost to the [Licensor] at the end of the Agreement.

R.450

1.1 [Name] grants the [Distributor] the non-exclusive right to reproduce and supply copies of the [Artwork/Logo/Work/Sample] in the form of [greetings cards/T shirts/covers for mobile telephones] from [date] to date] for supply, distribution and sale in [country].

1.2 In consideration of 1.1 the [Distributor] shall pay [Name] a fixed payment of [number/currency] for every copy of the [Artwork/Logo/Work] in any format reproduced by the [Distributor] in each calendar month and such sums due to be paid within [number] days together with a detailed statement of account.

1.3 The [Distributor] agrees that payment to [Name] is not linked to sales and/or receipt of sums from third parties.

Services

R.451

1.1 [Company] [name/address/email/telephone/other].

1.2 [Contributor] [name/address/email/mobile/other].

1.3 The [Company] has [filmed/recorded/photographed/interviewed] the [Contributor] on the subject of [specify] and the [Contributor] has carried out the following [work/service/other].

1.4 In consideration of 1.3 the [Company] is to pay the sum of [fee] by [date] in [cash/cheque/other] to the [Contributor] in full and final settlement. No further sums of any nature for any reason shall be due for the provision of the work or the exploitation of the material in any media at any time.

1.5 The [Contributor] assigns to the [Company] all present and future copyright and any other rights in all media in the work and any material created, produced or provided under this Agreement throughout the world, outer space and the universe for the full period of copyright and any extensions and renewals. All media shall include any developments and variations and include, but not be limited to, film, television, video, DVD, radio, publishing, internet, merchandising.

1.6 The [Company] shall have the right to assign, license and transfer any rights to any third party at any time without further payment of any type.

R.452

The [Contributor] assigns to the [Company] all present and future copyright and any other rights in the product of the services of the [Contributor] made under this Agreement throughout the world for the full period of copyright and any extensions or renewals.

1433

R.453

In consideration of the [Presenter's] Fee and the [Presenter's] Royalties, the [Presenter] assigns to the [Company] the [Television Rights, the Video and DVD Rights, the Theatric Rights and the Non-Theatric Rights] in the product of his/her services in the [Series] including the script and sound recordings under this Agreement throughout the Territory for the full period of the copyright and any extensions and renewals.

R.454

The [Company] agrees that the [Presenter] reserves all rights not specifically assigned to the [Company] in Clause [–]. The [Presenter] also owned and/or controls the rights in the following [Books/CDs/Work] which are in existence at the time of this Agreement and no rights and/or interest are transferred to the [Company] under this Agreement.

R.455

The [Agent] agrees that she is not entitled to negotiate or promote in any manner or form the commercial interests of the [Artiste] outside the Territory unless specifically approved in advance in writing with the [Artiste].

R.456

In consideration of the Assignment Fee the [Presenter] assigns all present and future copyright and any other rights in all media throughout the world [and universe and outer space] in the product of his/her services and any other material created for the purpose of this Agreement by, with or in connection with the [Presenter] in any format for the full period of copyright and any extensions and renewals including, but not limited to, [photographs, press releases, films, sound recordings, recordings, advertisements, promotions, scripts, website material].

R.457

The [Presenter] acknowledges that any intellectual property of any kind including but limited to copyright, design rights, service marks, trade marks, logos, inventions, titles, slogans, property rights in the associated material and any other rights held by the [Company] or which are created or developed in conjunction with the services of the [Presenter] under this Agreement shall be the sole and exclusive property of the [Company]. The [Presenter] shall not acquire any rights or interest nor does this Agreement purport to transfer, grant, assign any such rights in or derived from the product of the services to the [Presenter].

R.458

The [Company] agrees that it shall not have the right to use, exploit or license any of the material produced or created for the purposes of this

1434

Agreement in which the [Celebrity] appears in sound or vision or by any other reference for any purpose at any time other than the endorsement, promotion or advertising of the [Company's Product] during the Term of the Agreement. Where the [Company] wishes to use any such material at any time for any purpose or to license a third party then it is clear that the prior written consent of the [Celebrity] is required and the negotiation and settlement of a new agreement to the satisfaction of both parties.

R.459

The [Promoter] assigns to the [Company] all present and future copyright, design rights and any other rights in the product of its services in respect of the [Company] and the [Company's Products] within its possession or control throughout the world for the full period of copyright and any extensions, renewals as far as possible to perpetuity.

R.460

In consideration of the Fee and Repeat Fees the [Celebrity] assigns to the [Company] all present and future copyright and any other rights in all media throughout the Territory in the product of his/her services and any other material created for the purpose of this Agreement for the full period of copyright and any extensions, renewals or otherwise. For the avoidance of doubt all media shall include, but not be limited to television, internet, telephone, radio, video, DVD, computer software, music, publishing and merchandising.

R.461

1.1　In consideration of the [Presenter's] Fee and the [Presenter's] Royalties the [Presenter] assigns to the [Company] the following rights [specify] in the product of his/her services in the [Films] including the [films, scripts and sound recordings] under this Agreement throughout the Territory for the [Assignment Period/for the full period of copyright and any extensions and renewals.

1.2　The [Company] agrees that all rights not specifically assigned to the [Company] in Clause [–] are reserved by the [Presenter].

R.462

The [Company] agrees and undertakes that it shall not be entitled to use, exploit or license any of the material produced or created for the purpose of this Agreement in which the [Celebrity] appears in sound or vision or by any other reference for any purpose at any time after the promotion or advertising of the [Company's] Products during the Term of this Agreement without prior written consent of the [Celebrity].

R.463

The [Company] agrees that all copyright, design rights and any other rights in the [Celebrity's] name, image, slogan, trade mark, logo, associated jingle or music or any other rights supplied by the [Celebrity] under this Agreement shall be the sole and exclusive property of the [Celebrity] and the [Company] shall not acquire any rights or interest or in any development or variation pursuant to this Agreement.

R.464

The [Agent] agrees that this Agreement relates only to the [Work] and that the [Agent] does and has not acquired any rights, interest, option, or right to exploit any other works or other original creations of the [Author] whether in existence prior to the date of this Agreement or created at any time in the future. All other material shall be the subject of separate negotiation and agreement between the [Agent] and the [Author].

R.465

The [Agent] acknowledges that the name of the [Actor] and any goodwill and reputation created in respect of any trade mark, business name, logo or otherwise shall remain the sole and exclusive property of the [Actor] whether in existence now or created during the Term of this Agreement. No part of this Agreement is intended to transfer any copyright or any other rights vested in the [Actor] to the [Agent].

R.466

The [Agent] shall use his/her reasonable endeavours to protect the copyright and any other rights of the [Actor] which may be created or developed under any contract with a third party. As far as reasonably possible the [Agent] shall ensure that the copyright and any other rights in any photographs, images, or other material commissioned for the [Actor's] portfolio and marketing shall be transferred to the [Actor].

R.467

The [Manager] agrees that he/she is not acquiring any copyright or any other rights in any name, logo, trade mark, image or any other material owned or controlled by [Name].

R.468

In consideration of the non-returnable Advance and the [Author's] Royalties, the [Author] grants to the [Publisher] the sole and exclusive right to exploit the [Work] in the form of sheet music and any songbook throughout the Territory for the duration of the Licence Period.

R.469

In consideration of the [Assignment Fee] and the [Artiste's] Royalties, the [Artiste] assigns to the [Record Company] all present and future copyright and any other rights in all media whether in existence now or created in the future in the [Sound Recordings/Recordings/Film] made during the Term of this Agreement by the [Artiste] and the [Record Company] throughout the world for the full period of the copyright and any extensions or renewals.

R.470

In consideration of the Licence Fee and the [Licensor's] Royalties, the [Licensor] grants to the [Record Distributor] the sole and exclusive right to exploit the [Performing Rights/the Music Publishing Rights/the Recording Rights] in the Master Tape throughout the Territory for the duration of the Licence Period.

R.471

The [Record Distributor] agrees that the [Master Tape] remains the property of the [Licensor] and that the [Licensee] is not acquiring any copyright in any [Musical Work] in the [Master Tape] or any associated lyrics, composition or arrangement.

R.472

In consideration of the Assignment Fee and the Royalties the [Author] assigns to the [Company] all present and future copyright and any other rights in all media whether in existence now or created in the future in the [Work] and parts throughout the Territory for the Assignment Period.

R.473

The [Author] confirms that he/she is a member of the [Performing Rights Society/other]. The [Publisher] agrees that the Performing Rights in the [Work] are held by the [Performing Rights Society/other]. The [Author] and the [Publisher] agree that during the Assignment Period any sums due from the Performing Rights in the [Work] shall be divided between them in accordance with the following percentages: Author [number per cent] Publisher [number per cent].

R.474

The [Licensee] shall be responsible for all payments due in respect of the Performing Rights in any music as are controlled by the [Performing Rights Society/other] or a society affiliated to it in respect of the rights granted under this Agreement.

R.475

The [Author] confirms that he/she is a member of the [Performing Rights Society] and the [Publisher] acknowledges that the Performing Rights in the

[Work] are held by the [Performing Rights Society] and that all sums received by them shall be paid directly to the [Author] and that the [Publisher] shall have no right or claim to any such sums.

R.476
The [Management] agrees to be responsible for any payments due to the [Performing Rights Society/other] arising from this Agreement.

R.477
The [Composer] agrees to sign such additional documents and agreements as the [Publishers] may reasonably request to facilitate the collection of royalties in respect of the [Compositions]. In particular the [Composer] agrees to sign the division of fees form of the [Performing Rights Society] or any other affiliated organisation.

R.478
The [Composer] is or shall become and remain a member of the [Performing Rights Society] and agrees that this Agreement shall be regarded as a document authorising the [Performing Rights Society/other] to treat the [Publisher] as exploiting the [Compositions] otherwise than by publishing for the benefit of the persons interested in them and in addition an agreement to vary the division of fees.

R.479
[Name] agrees that this Agreement is for a fixed term and ends on [date]. There is no right granted by the [Company] to renew, extend and/or otherwise continue the Agreement beyond that date.

R.480
Where the [Company] agrees to any changes to the provision of services by the [Artist/Distributor] under this Agreement whether temporarily and/or permanently. The [Company] shall not be obliged to pay any additional costs and/or expenses unless they are agreed in advance in writing between the parties.

R.481
In consideration of the [Fee] the [Contributor] assigns to the [Company] all copyright, intellectual property rights and any other rights in the product of the services of the [Contributor] for the [Podcast/Film/Work] which are described in Schedule [–] which is attached to and forms part of this Agreement in all medium and in any media whether in existence now and/or created in the future for the full period of copyright and any extensions and renewals and in perpetuity throughout the world and universe. The [Contributor] shall not retain any rights in the product of his/her services under this Agreement nor

be entitled to any sums except those set out in Clause [–]. No additional payments shall be made for any form of exploitation by the [Company] and/or any registration, sub-licence, transfer and/or assignment of the rights to a third party.

R.482
The [Company] agrees that:

1.1 The [Supplier] shall be entitled to substitute any other suitably qualified person to carry out the task required under this Agreement without notice to the [Company] in the event that any of the persons listed in the [Project] are not available for any reason.

1.2 The [Company] shall not have any right to terminate the Agreement due to the fact that [specify] is at any time not involved in the [Project] and/or leaves the [Supplier].

1.3 The [Supplier] may make changes to improve and develop the [Project] and make minor adaptations provided that the cost is not increased and there are no differences in the final planned result.

1.4 The [Supplier] shall be entitled to add additional costs to the [Project] where it is discovered at a later date that the technology and/or software and/or security systems at the [Company] are not compatible and/or do not function effectively with the proposed [Project].

R.483
The [Company] agrees that the services to be provided by [Name] to develop and create an integrated software system for the delivery of [specify] which is fully operational as set out in the specifications document in Appendix [–] does not include any future updates, tests and/or maintenance once the system has been installed and approved by the [Company].

Sponsorship

R.484
In consideration of the Sponsorship Fee the [Company] acknowledges and agrees:

1.1 The [Company] grants to the [Sponsor] the exclusive right to sponsor the [Programme] and to have the [Sponsor's] Logo incorporated in the [Programme] for the duration of the Term of this Agreement throughout the Territory.

1.2 The [Company] grants the [Sponsor] the non-exclusive right in the Territory for the Term of this Agreement to exhibit the [Programme] at conferences, trade fairs and exhibitions without further payment.

R.485

'The Title Rights' shall mean the exclusive right to have the [Event] for all commercial promotion and other purposes including the broadcast and/or transmission of the [Event] on all forms of television referred to as follows [specify].

R.486

In consideration of the Sponsorship Fee the [Association] grants to the [Sponsor] the following rights in respect of the [Event] for the duration of the Licence Period throughout the world:

1.1 'The Title Rights' which shall be the exclusive right to have the [Event] referred to for all commercial and promotional purposes including, but not limited to, any broadcast and/or transmission of the [Event] on television in any form (whether by terrestrial, satellite, cable, digital, BBC, Channel 3, Channel 5 or otherwise) as follows [The [Sponsors] Event].

1.2 The non-exclusive right to have [Sponsor's] Logo displayed on any promotional material (flysheets, national and local events, press, posters, tickets, stationery) and any publicity under control of the [Association].

1.3 The exclusive right to have the [Sponsor's] Logo displayed on each competitors' clothing during the course of the [Event] and on the clothing of all stewards, staff and personnel employed by the [Association] on public duty as follows [–].

1.4 The non-exclusive right to have the [Sponsor's] Logo displayed on banners, scoreboards, electronic display systems, fencing, advertising boards within the venue in accordance with the display schedule which is attached to and forms part of this Agreement.

1.5 The exclusive right of representation of the [Sponsor] to award the championship trophy.

R.487

1.1 In consideration of the Sponsorship Fee the [Company] grants to the [Sponsor] the non-exclusive right to have the [Sponsor's Logo] and the [Sponsor's Product] incorporated in the [Programme] for the duration of the Sponsorship Period.

1.2 The [Company] agrees that the [Company] has the right at its sole discretion to arrange sponsorship with other third parties whether it directly competes with the [Sponsor's] Product or not.

R.488

1.1 The [Sponsor] agrees that all intellectual property rights including copyright, trade marks, designs, logos, slogans, text, artwork, title, recordings and sound recordings, music, scripts, photographs, graphics and computer generated material and all other material in the [Programme] and any associated material and/or merchandise shall be the sole property of the [Company]. The [Sponsor] shall have no rights in the [Programme] and any associated material and/or merchandise in respect of the exploitation in any media except for those specified in Clause 1.2 and shall not receive any royalties, sums or other payments.

1.2 The [Company] acknowledges that the [Sponsor's] Logo and the [Sponsor's] Product shall remain the sole and exclusive property of the [Sponsor] and the [Company] shall not acquire any right or interest in the [Sponsor's] Logo and/or [Product] including any developments and variations.

R.489
The [Sponsor] agrees and undertakes that it shall not have the right to sub-licence, adapt, authorise and/or otherwise exploit any part of the [Event/Programme/Performers] at any time.

R.490
The [Sponsor] shall not have any option, first right of refusal, and/or any other interest in any subsequent [Programme/Event/Festival].

R.491
The [Company] assigns to the [Sponsor] all copyright, intellectual property rights and any other rights in any material (which has and/or will be created) which is an adaptation of the [Sponsor's] trade mark, logo and/or any other material of any nature which is owned and/or controlled by the [Sponsor] and has been supplied to the [Company] under this Agreement in all medium and in any media for the full period of copyright and any extensions and renewals and in perpetuity throughout the world and universe.

R.492
The [Athlete] agrees that he/she is not acquiring any copyright and/or any other rights and/or interest in any name, logo, trade mark, image, text, products, services and/or any other material supplied by the [Sponsor] which is owned and/or controlled by the [Sponsor].

R.493
The [Sponsor] shall not have the right to approve any other sponsors who may contribute to the [Project]. In the event that the [Sponsor] decides to

withdraw from the [Event/Programme] due to the contribution of another sponsor. Then the [Sponsor] shall be obliged to pay all sums due under this Agreement and to pay an equivalent value in [sterling] for any products and/ or services that the [Sponsor] would have contributed under this Agreement.

R.494

Where after the conclusion of this Agreement the [Company] concludes another agreement with a third party for the [Event/Programme]. In the event that the [Sponsor] decides that the third party is suitable for any reason. Then the [Sponsor] shall have the right to notify the [Company] that it wishes to be excluded from all further material to do with the [Event/Programme] and the [Sponsor] shall only be obliged to pay the sums set out in clause [–].

R.495

[Name] shall have the right to cancel and/or terminate the Agreement with the [Sponsor] at any time without providing a reason provided he/she provides [number] months notice to the [Sponsor] to that effect by [email/ written letter].

R.496

The [Sponsor] agrees and undertakes that it shall not:

1.1   Reproduce and/or create any caricature of [Name].

1.2   Register any domain name, trade mark and/or any other rights and/or interest which is for the personal name and/or any pen name and/or any other reference, word, action, image and/or sound used by [Name].

1.3   Provide interviews to any unauthorised biographer and/or access to material concerning [Name] held by the [Sponsor] without the prior written consent of [Name].

1.4   Represent that it has the authority to act as an agent for [Name] and/ or to provide any consents and/or approvals on his/her behalf at any time.

1.5   Create, develop and/or authorise any app, blog and/or website and/or advertisement which features [Name] and/or his/her name, image and/ or representation as if he/she is endorsing, promoting and selling the services and/or products except [specify].

University, Library and Educational

R.497

'The Non-Theatric Rights' shall mean the right to permit or license, sale or hire the exhibition of the [Film/DVD] to non-paying audiences in all formats in business and commercial industries and organisations of an educational, cultural, religious, charitable and social nature including, but not limited to schools, churches, evening institutions, museums, hospitals, prisons, summer camps, drama groups, film societies, professional associations, public libraries, colleges and universities, hotels and private clubs [and aeroplanes].

R.498

'The Non-Theatric Rights' shall mean the right to exhibit the [Film] in the Territory during the Licence Period to non-theatric audiences who are not making any specific payment to view or hear the film including, but not limited to, the following categories of audiences:

1.1   Educational institutions such as schools, universities, colleges.

1.2   Educational classes and meetings held by companies or other non-educational bodies.

1.3   Clubs or other organisations of an educational, cultural, charitable or social nature including film libraries and societies.

1.4   Closed circuit television, an enclosed wired system which is relayed to an audience in a confined area such as hotels, oil rigs, ships, aeroplanes.

R.499

'The Non-Theatric Rights' hereby granted means the sole and exclusive right in the Territory during the Licence Period to permit or license the exhibition of the [Film(s)] and to authorise others to do any of such things: sale, hire, lease or licensing in all formats and by means of all technologies now in existence or hereafter invented or discovered for the exhibition of the [Film(s)] and/or parts to non-paying audiences in all educational institutions, schools, public libraries, colleges, universities, dormitories and residence halls, churches, evening institutions, museums, hospitals, prisons, summer camps, business and industry hotels, clubs and other organisations of any educational, cultural, religious, charitable or social nature, drama groups, film societies and professional associations, instructional television and to all other entities and all other places except for the exclusive showing in private theatres to which the general public is customarily invited and admitted upon payment of an admission fee.

R.500

'The Non-Theatric Rights' shall mean the right to exhibit the [Film] to non-paying audiences in all business and commercial industries and organisations of an educational, cultural, religious, charitable and social nature including, but not limited to, schools, churches, educational and social institutions, museums, hospitals, prisons, summer camps, drama and film groups, professional bodies, libraries, colleges, universities, hotels and private clubs.

R.501

'The Reprographic Rights' shall [be defined the Copyright, Designs and Patents Act 1988 as amended] mean the reprographic copying by means of a reprographic process. Reprographic process means a process for making facsimile copies or involving the use of an appliance for making multiple copies and includes in relation to a [Work] held in electronic form any copying by electronic means but not a film or a sound recording.

R.502

'The Reprographic Rights' shall mean the right to reproduce the [Work] by photocopying and other reprographic means for which non-exclusive licences are granted by the [Copyright Licensing Agency] in the [United Kingdom and payments to the [Author] are made through the [Authors' Licensing and Collection Society/other] in accordance with their standard terms.

R.503

'The Reprographic Rights' shall mean the right to reproduce the [Work] by photocopying and the reprographic means whether laser, photo images or otherwise so that a mirror image copy of the text words, [illustrations, drawings or other material] in the [Work] is exactly copied on to another two-dimensional format.

R.504

The [Company] confirms that it has granted a non-exclusive licence to the [Copyright Licensing Agency/other] to reproduce literary works published by the [Company] which shall include the [Work] by photocopying and other reprographic means. The [Copyright Licensing Agency/other] shall divide the proceeds from the reprographic rights equally between the [Author] and the [Company]. The [Author] shall receive the [Author's] share of the proceeds through the [Author's Licensing and Collecting Society/other] in accordance with their standard terms and conditions.

R.505

The [Company] confirms that the [Copyright Licensing Agency/other] have been or will be authorised to grant non-exclusive licences to reproduce the [Work] and other literary works published by the [Publisher] by photocopying and other reprographic means. The [Work] shall be included with the others and the [Copyright Licensing Agency/other] shall divide the proceeds from the [Work] [specify percentage] between the [Company] and the [Author]. The [Author's] share of the proceeds shall be paid [specify].

R.506

The [Author] does not grant the [Company] any reprographic rights in the [Work] whether by photocopying or any other means. All sums due in respect of the exercise of those rights shall belong to the [Author] and the [Company] shall not be entitled to any sum at any time.

R.507

In consideration of the [Fee] and [Royalties] the [Contributor] assigns to the [Institute] all present and future copyright and intellectual property rights and any other rights in all media in the [Work/Service] as a whole and in part whether in existence now or created in the future throughout the world and universe for the full period of copyright and any extensions and renewals including but not limited to:

1.1   The right to assign, transfer, licence, exploit, adapt, develop and/or authorise any third party to reproduce, register and/or protect any part in any medium in any language.

1.2   To transmit and exploit the [Work/Service] by means of terrestrial, digital, cable and satellite television, DVD, video, audiocassettes, CDs, disks, lasers, radio, gadgets and other portable equipment.

1.3   To exploit the [Work/Service] by means of theatric and non-theatric exploitation, merchandising, sponsorship, endorsement, product placement, publication including hardback, paperback, newspapers, magazines, comics, educational, heritage and charity conferences, events, exhibitions and marketing.

1.4   To exploit the [Work/Service] by means of all forms of electronic dissemination and/or any method of access, storage and retrieval and/or on the internet and/or any website and/or computer software programmes and/or use in any format or by any method, system and/or process to be supplied, distributed, or reproduced whether in electronic and/or digital, scanned, or by mechanical reproduction, or any other media of any nature whether free, subscription, pay on demand or otherwise.

R.508

'The Off-Air Recording Rights' shall mean the right to include the [Programme] in a Licensing Scheme [under the Copyright, Designs and Patents Act 1988 as amended] whereby licences are granted to enable the [Programme] to be recorded by or on behalf of educational establishments from any broadcast or cable programme service including the [Programme] or any of them when such recording is for the educational purposes of such establishment.

R.509

'The Theatric Rights' shall mean the right to exhibit the [Film] to audiences where a charge for admission is made including, but not limited to, public and private cinemas, concert and lecture halls and arenas.

R.510

'Performance' shall mean a performance of the [Work] being a work protected by copyright as a literary dramatic or musical work in public which would otherwise be a restricted act including delivery in the case of lectures, addresses, speeches, sermons and includes in general any mode of visual or acoustic presentation, including presentation by means of a sound recording, film, broadcast or cable programme of the [Work].

R.511

The [Institute] grants a non-exclusive licence of its [Name/Image/Logo] a description and drawing of which is specified in Schedule [–] to the [Company] for the purpose of reproduction on the [Articles] throughout the Territory for the duration of the Licence Period.

R.512

[Name] grants the [Institute] the non-exclusive right to store the [Essay/Article] on a storage and retrieval system and database on a computer at [location] from [date] to [date]. [Name] grants the [Institute] the non-exclusive to reproduce copies to be distributed at no cost to be read by other students at the [Institute] for personal and private study and not for any commercial purpose. No right is granted by [Name] for the [Institute] to register any rights and/or interest at any copyright and/or collecting society, make copies available on the [Institute] website, sell, and/or distribute copies to the public, to sub-licence, edit, adapt and/or alter the [Essay/Article] at any time and/or to arrange and/or authorise any translation.

R.513

The [Institute] agrees that it shall not have any right to exploit and/or reproduce and/or licence images and/or films and/or sound recordings which it and/or any members of its staff and/or students have made of the contribution and appearance of the [Contributor/Presenter] at the [Event] for commercial purposes in any format in any part of the world unless the [Contributor/Presenter] has concluded a commercial licence exploitation agreement with the [Institute].

RISK

General Business and Commercial

R.514

The risk in the [Company's] [Products] shall pass on delivery to the [Buyer] or his/her agent.

R.515

The risk in respect of the material sold hereunder shall pass to the [Customer] on delivery of the material by the [Company] (or its agents) to the [Customer] at the place specified by the [Customer] for delivery.

R.516

The entire risk in respect of the [Work/Products] shall remain with the [Supplier] and shall not pass to the [Buyer] until they have inspected and approved the [Work/Products].

R.517

[Name] agrees that they enter the [premises] and perform the [activity] entirely at their own discretion, choice, risk and liability. That they accept that there is an inherent danger and risk of injury due to the very nature of the [activity]. That whilst the [Company] will endeavour to take all reasonable safety and health precautions that there shall be no claim against the [Company] unless caused by the [Company's] negligence and recoverable on that ground.

R.518

All risk in the [Products] shall remain with the [Supplier] in transit until such time as the [Company] shall accept delivery.

R.519

The risk in respect of storage and delivery shall be the [Clients] responsibility and not the [Company's].

R.520

1.1   The [Sub-Licensee] agrees and accepts that it shall be responsible for its own costs, expenses, liabilities and risks and shall not seek to be indemnified by the [Licensee] and/or the [Licensor].

1.2   That the [Sub-Licensee] shall arrange and pay for its own insurance to adequately cover any claims by the public and/or any other third party [and/or the Licensee and Licensor].

1.3 That the [Sub-Licensee] shall carry out such risk assessments as may be required in accordance with any guidelines and/or code of practice which may be in existence at that time. That where the [Sub-Licensee] finds a serious failing as a result of any risk assessment then action should be taken to reduce the risk to the public immediately.

R.521

You access, download, store and/or retrieve, contribute to, view the [Website] and/or banner advertisements, enter the competitions, and/or allow communications, cookies, and/or exchanges of text, images, sound recordings, photographs, film, and/or services with this [Enterprise] and/or any authorised agency and/or any other person and/or company on this [Website] entirely at your own risk and cost.

R.522

Where the [Company] carries out a risk assessment and identifies a serious risk to the public in respect of the [Programme/Event]. Then the [Company] agrees to notify the [Sponsor] of the matter together with a recommendation as to the action it intends to take to resolve the problem. Where it is clear that the problem cannot be resolved by the start date of the [Programme/Event] then the parties are agreed that it should be rescheduled to start on later date. The parties agree that such a delay shall not be a breach of this Agreement provided the delay is for longer than [number] days in total.

R.523

1.1 The parties agree that this is a high risk [Project] and that each shall bear its own liability, costs and expenses and arrange such insurance as it thinks fit in the circumstances.

1.2 The parties accept that the [Project] may be cancelled at any time due to weather conditions and/or failure of any risk assessment which has been carried out prior to the commencement of the [Project].

1.3 That each party agrees to ensure that all equipment, services and personnel to be provided by them to the [Project] are of the highest standard for the conditions in [country] and have been subject to all the necessary tests, protocols and reviews specified by [organisation].

1.4 That each party shall notify the others in the event that there are any risks which are identified as of concern and/or failures, omission, errors and/or any other matters which may effect the successful conclusion of the [Project].

ROYALTIES

DVD, Video and Discs

R.524

In consideration of the rights granted to the [Licensee] the [Licensor] shall be entitled to the following sums:

1.1 [number]% calculated on the Published Dealer Price (inclusive of any rental surcharge, premium, or licence fee) (after deduction of sales tax) in respect of all videograms of the [Musical Work] synchronised with the [Film].

1.2 No royalty shall be paid in respect of promotional copies distributed free of charge.

1.3 Where the [Musical Work] synchronised with the [Film] is on a videogram with other works, then the royalty due shall be proportionately reduced by the proportion of the duration of the [Musical Work] to the total duration.

1.4 Where videograms are remaindered or deleted from the catalogue the royalty payable shall be calculated on the sums received (exclusive of sales tax).

R.525

Rental Income shall mean either:

1.1 Where the retailer accounts to the [Company] for a royalty on each rental transaction, the amounts (exclusive of taxes) payable to the [Company] (over and above the supply price) in respect of the rental of such videograms; or

1.2 In the case of videograms supplied on a wholesale basis to dealers or distributors for either sale and/or rental where the price includes a distinct premium surcharge or fee for rental, then that distinct sum (less taxes and [number]% for single videograms.

R.526

'Rental Surcharge' shall mean the sum actually applied to the Wholesale Selling Price of each Videogram sold for rental purposes.

R.527

'[Rental/Hire] Price' shall mean the price (exclusive of sales tax) at which each videogram) is supplied by the [Company] to dealers or distributors which account to the [Company] by payment of a royalty on each [rental/hire] transaction.

R.528

'The [Licensor's/Assignors] Royalties' shall be the following percentage of the Gross Receipts [–]%.

R.529

'The [Licensor's] Royalties' shall be the Net Receipts after the deduction of the [Licensee's] Commission.

R.530

The [Assignee] agrees that the [Assignor] shall have the right to be paid the [Assignor's] Royalties in respect of the exploitation of the [Video/DVD/Disc/Non-Theatric] Rights. There shall be no royalty due where the [Assignee] uses and/or permits the use of copies of [Videos/DVDs/Disc] of the [Film] for exhibition, display or transmission for the purpose of trade exhibitions, in-store demonstrations or conferences where the sole purpose is promotion and advertising to achieve sales.

R.531

1.1 The [Distributor] shall pay to the [Company] a fixed sum of [figure/currency] per [Video/DVD/Disc] of the [Film] sold, disposed and/or distributed by the [Distributor] to any third party during the Licence Period.

1.2 In addition the [Distributor] shall pay the [Television Company] [number per cent] of all income (exclusive of sales tax) received by the [Distributor] from the rental, hire, lease, subscription or other loan of [Videos/DVDs/Discs] of the [Film] to dealers or other third parties during the Licence Period.

1.3 The [Distributor] agrees that the Published Dealer Price in the first six months shall be [figure/currency] per [Video/DVD/Disc].

R.532

'The Contributor's Royalties' shall be the Net Receipts less the [Licensee's] Commission

R.533

'The Licensor's Royalties' shall be the following percentage of the Gross Receipts [number per cent].

R.534

'The Licensors Royalties' shall be [number] per cent of the sums actually received by [and/or credited] to the [Distributor] from the sale, supply, distribution, sub-licence and exploitation of the [Sound Recordings] and/

or [Discs] in any part of the world. Together with all sums received from any collecting societies and/or other organisations for the transmission, broadcast, reproduction and/or other exploitation of the [Discs] and/or [Sound Recordings] in any part of the world.

R.535
The [Distributor] shall not be entitled to deduct any costs of production, manufacture, distribution, sales, marketing, advertising and/or promotion from the sums actually received prior to the payment of the Licensors Royalties.

R.536

1.1 The royalties to be paid by the [Licensee] shall be based on the numbers of copies of the [DVD/Disc/other] which are manufactured and produced by the [Licensee] and/or its appointed manufacturer which incorporate the [Image/Logo] on the cover and/or on the [Film] in [country] from [date] to [date].

1.2 The [Licensee] shall pay the [Licensor] a fixed fee of [number/ currency] per unit manufactured and produced in 1.1. Payment shall be at the end of each calendar month direct to the bank account of the [Licensor]. Payment is not based on sales and/or distribution of any stock.

R.537
The [Licensor] shall not be paid for any units which are:

1.1 Destroyed during the production and/or manufacture process provided they are not sold to a third party.

1.2 Provided for free for display, exhibition, promotional, marketing and/or advertising purposes up to a maximum of [number] copies.

1.3 Sold and/or disposed of below cost price for charitable purposes.

Film and Television

R.538
The [Licensee] agrees to pay the [Licensor's] Royalties subject to the terms and conditions set out below:

1.1 [number per cent] of the Gross Receipts (after deduction of Distribution Expenses) from the exhibition of the Film at [–] Cinema.

1.2 [number per cent] of all other Gross Receipts (after deduction of Distribution Expenses).

R.539

'Film Rental' shall mean an amount equal to the aggregate of the monies received [or accrued] before [date] from exhibitions by the [Distributor] of the [Film] for the [Company] in respect of the exhibition of the [Film] to the public in cinemas and theatres in the Territory excluding any value added tax and any advances (to the extent that they are not recouped) on account of such sums.

R.540

'The Licensor's Royalties' shall be the Net Receipts received by the [Company] in [currency] in [country] less the [Company's] Commission.

R.541

'The Author's Royalties' shall be the following percentage of the Gross Receipts [number] per cent.

R.542

The [Licensor] agrees that in the event that any merchandising, publishing or other income shall become due or payable to the [Licensor] which is not covered under the terms of this Agreement, the [Licensor] shall pay the [Licensee] not less than [10]% (ten) per cent of such income received which shall be accounted for on a quarterly basis.

R.543

'The Assignor's Royalties' shall be the following percentage of the Net Receipts [number per cent] [number]%.

R.544

The [Author] agrees that the non-returnable Advance shall be offset against the [Author's] Royalties.

R.545

The [Author] agrees that no royalties will be due from promotional copies of the [Work] for which no payment is received by the [Company].

R.546

The [Assignor] agrees that no royalties shall be due from promotional, review, free or other exploitation of the [Film] and/or parts for which no sums are received by or credited to the [Assignee].

R.547

No copies shall be paid to the [Assignor] in respect of copies of the [Film] and/or parts which are destroyed in transit, by fire, water, remaindered, sold at cost or on stock transfer provided that no income, benefit or credit is received of any nature from such disposal, loss or damage.

R.548

In consideration of the assignment of the rights the [Assignee] agrees to pay the [Assignor's] Royalties to the [Assignor] in respect of the exploitation of the [Film] or any parts in [currency] in accordance with clause [–].

R.549

The [Licensor] agrees that no royalties shall be due for the use of any part of the [Film/Programme] for promotional and advertising purposes on the [Company's] website reference [specify].

R.550

The [Company] shall have the option to buyout all the other rights of [Name] in the [Film/Programme] for a single royalty payment of [figure/currency] which must be exercised by the [Company] by [date]. Where it is not exercised and the sum paid in full to [Name] by that [date] then the option shall not exist.

R.551

All royalties shall be paid in [sterling/euro/other] and where any other payment is required then the [Licensor] shall pay for all the costs and charges of any conversion to the requested currency. Where necessary an advance payment of the costs and charges may be requested by the [Licensee].

R.552

Where for any reason the [Distributor] is owed any sums by the [Company] then the [Distributor] may withhold any royalties and set them off against the other sums owed and/or due. Provided that the [Distributor] confirms the reason and amount in the royalty statement.

R.553

1.1 The [Company] shall pay any royalties and fees due to the [Artists] for their performances on the [Films/Programmes] within [one] calendar month after completion of the work and thereafter at [three] month intervals in respect of the exploitation of the rights granted to the [Company]. No royalties shall be withheld and/or set off against any other [Film/Programme].

1.2 Where any [Artist] dies then all payments shall be made to their named beneficiary and/or held on account until claimed by the estate. The [Company] shall not require confirmation of probate and agrees to accept a personal letter from a family member.

General Business and Commercial

R.554

The [Licensee] agrees that no sums shall be withheld from the [Licensor] which are not disclosed.

R.555

The [Licensor] agrees that the [Advance/Royalties] may be requested to be returned if the terms of this Agreement are not fulfilled.

R.556

Where under this Agreement there is any doubt as to the royalty percentage to be applied to any exploitation of the rights, then the highest rate in this Agreement shall apply if the right is specified. If there is no right specified because it is new then the royalty rate to apply shall be subject to separate negotiation and agreement.

R.557

Where no royalty rate is stated in the Agreement and/or the rights and/or method of exploitation did not exist at the time of the conclusion of this Agreement. Then it is agreed that the rights and/or method of exploitation shall still belong to the [Licensor]. The [Licensee] shall have the first right of refusal, but in the event that the parties cannot agree terms within [number] months then the [Licensor] shall be entitled to exploit the rights and/or method of exploitation with a third party.

R.558

The parties agree that where no rights and/or technology existed at the time of this Agreement that a new royalty rate shall be set by agreement at a later date for any new form of exploitation. That there is no presumption under this Agreement that the later development and/or creation of rights have been passed to the [Licensee].

Internet and Websites

R.559

No royalties, fees, expenses, costs and/or other sums shall be paid to you by the [Company] for your contribution and work. The [Company] and others who use the [Website] shall be able to reproduce the material for their own personal use and/or for other purposes provided that they provide a credit and/or copyright notice as appropriate.

R.560

The [Company shall pay [Name] a fixed unit payment of [figure/currency] for each completed transaction where funds are received and cleared in respect of any authorised completed download of your [Material] from the [Website]. Payment and a statement shall be made every [three/six months] to [Name] or a nominated representative.

R.561

'The Licensors' Royalty' shall be the fixed sum of [figure/currency] which shall be paid by the [Licensee] to the [Artist] each time that a copy of the [Artwork/Image/text] is downloaded from the [Website] in any part of the world at any time.

R.562

The [Licensee] shall pay the [Licensors'] Royalty to the [Licensor] at the end of each calendar month in arrears by electronic bank transfer in [currency]. The [Licensor] shall also supply by means of an email attachment a full statement of the details of the access and downloading of the [Artwork/Image/text] from the [Website]..

R.563

The [Company] agrees to pay [Name] a fee of [number/currency] for every copy of the [Image/App/Work] sold by the [Company] either directly through its website and/or services and/or through a third party for which the [Company] receives payment. The [Company] shall pay [Name] any sums due every two calendar months from the commencement of the supply, reproduction and sale of the [Image/App/Work] by electronic transfer at the [Company's] cost to a nominated bank account. A short summary report shall also be sent by email to [Name] to explain the sales and payment.

R.564

The [Distributor] shall pay [Name] a fee of [number/currency] which shall be [number] per cent of the total [gross/net] revenue received by and/or credited to the [Distributor] from subscribers to the [Service] through its internet, website and mobile telephone and telecommunication service throughout the world either directly by the [Distributor] and/or any associated, connected and/or parent company and/or any sub-agent and/or sub-distributor and/or any authorised and/or unauthorised third party at any time.

Merchandising

R.565

The [Licensee] agrees to pay the [Licensor] [number] % of the Net Receipts of the [Licensee] with respect to any revenue generated through the merchandising of the [Character] throughout the Territory for the duration of the Licence Period.

R.566

The [Licensor's] Royalties shall be the following percentage of the recommended retail selling price for each [Licensed Articles] [number] %.

R.567

The [Licensee] agrees that the Licence Fee is not returnable and is not to be offset against the [Licensor's] Royalties and is not contingent upon the sales of the [Licensed Articles].

R.568

'The [Licensor's] Royalties' shall be the following percentages of the recommended retail selling price or any other sums at any time received by or credited to the [Company] in respect of the exploitation of the [Licensed Articles]:

1.1 In respect of units sold within the United Kingdom of Great Britain, Northern Ireland, the Republic of Ireland, the Channel Isles and the Isle of Man:

   1.1.1 [number]% for the first [number] units of the [Licensed Articles];

   1.1.2 [number]% for the following [number] units of the [Licensed Articles]; and

   1.1.3 [number]% for the following units thereafter.

1.2 In respect of units sold throughout the Territory excluding the United Kingdom of Great Britain, Northern Ireland, the Republic of Ireland, the Channel Islands and the Isle of Man.

   1.2.1 [number]% for the first [number] units of the [Licensed Articles];

   1.2.2 [number]% for the following [number] units of the [Licensed Articles]; and

   1.2.3 [number]% for the following units thereafter.

R.569

The [Licensor] agrees that the Advance is to be offset against the [Licensor's] Royalties but it is not returnable or contingent upon any sales figures of the [Licensed Articles].

R.570

The [Contributor's] share of the profits shall be the agreed percentage of the [Net/Gross] Profits.

R.571

The [Contributor's] share of the profits shall be the agreed percentage(s) of the selling price of the [Licensed Articles].

R.572

No royalties shall be due for any stock disposed of without charge as donations to educational and/or community projects, lost, damaged, recalled as faulty, defective, destroyed, and/or for which no sums are received from any sub-licensee, agent and/or distributor. Provided that all such stock is declared to the [Licensor] and the reason stated for the non-payment.

R.573

The [Licensee] agrees to pay the [Licensor] a royalty of [number] per cent on all sums received by the [Licensee] after the deduction of [number] per cent of the production, packaging, marketing and advertising costs up to a maximum limit in total of [figure/currency] from the exploitation of the Rights granted in the [Work].

R.574

The [Sub-Licensee] shall not be entitled to continue to exploit and exercise the rights granted under this Agreement where the [Sub-Licensee] has failed to pay any sums due and/or supply any royalty statements at any time during the term of this Agreement.

R.575

The [Licensee] must pay all royalties directly to [Name] and not any agent and/or management company.

R.576

Delay in paying any royalties due shall incur a penalty fee of [number/currency] per day including weekends. Such sum to be added to any royalty payment due at that time.

R.577

Royalties must be paid on all units of the [Work/Product] supplied to a third party by the [Distributor] whether or not they have been disposed of for free, below cost and/or payment is not received by the [Distributor] due to the collapse and/or failure of the third party business.

Publishing

R.578

'The Author's Royalties' shall mean [figure/currency] for each unit of the [Work] sold, disposed of, transferred, copied supplied or otherwise distributed whether for free or consideration. This figure applies up to [number] units thereafter a higher figure per unit shall be applicable of [figure/currency].

R.579

The [Author] acknowledges that the Advance Royalty Payment shall be offset against the [Author's] Royalties.

R.580

The [Publisher] agrees to pay to the [Author] the Advance Royalty Payment as follows:

1.1   [–] upon signature of this agreement by both parties.

1.2   [–] upon delivery of an acceptable manuscript of the [Work].

1.3   [–] on or before [date].

1.4   [–] upon the first [display/marketing/pages] of the [Work] on the [Publisher's] website.

R.581

The [Publisher] agrees that no part of the advance or the royalties already paid shall be returned by the [Author] once the manuscript has been accepted by the [Publisher].

R.582

The [Publisher] agrees to pay the [Author's] Royalty on all copies of the [Work] or any part sold, disposed of, transferred, copied, supplied or otherwise distributed whether for free or for any other price or consideration. Payment shall be linked to the unit of the [Work] and/or part and not the financial consideration. It is also to be applied to all copies supplied to the press, television, radio, magazines, video or any other form of promotion, marketing or review or criticism throughout the Territory.

R.583

The [Publishers] shall pay to the [Author] the following royalties in respect of the Primary Rights granted under this Agreement:

1.1   [number]% on the first [number] copies then [number] % on the next [number] copies, then [number] % thereafter all copies sold of the hardcover edition of the [Work] in the United Kingdom and Republic of Ireland, calculated on the recommended published price.

1.2   [number]% on the first [number] copies then [number] % on the next [number] copies, then [number] % thereafter, on all copies sold of the hardcover edition of the [Work] sold throughout the world (excluding the United Kingdom of Great Britain, the Republic of Ireland and the

United States of America) calculated on the sums received by the [Publishers].

1.3 In the event that editions of the [Work] are sold in non-traditional trade outlets including, but not limited to, mail order, supermarkets, premiums, subscriptions and direct selling, the Author shall be entitled to [number]% of the sums received by the Publisher.

1.4 [number]% on the first [number] copies, then [number]% on the next [number] and thereafter [number] % on all copies sold of the paperback edition of the [Work] in the United Kingdom and Republic of Ireland on the recommended published price.

1.5 [number]% on the first [number] then [number]% on the next [number] and thereafter [number] % on all copies sold of the paperback edition of the [Work] throughout the World (but excluding the United Kingdom of Great Britain, the Republic of Ireland and the United States of America) calculated on the sums received by the Publisher.

1.6 In the event that the [Publishers] publish a reprint of the Work of [number] copies or less the royalties due to the [Author] shall be [number]% for hardback editions and [number]% for paperback.

1.7 Where editions of the Work are sold at a discount of over [50]% up to and including [62.5]% the [Author] shall be paid [number]% on the prevailing royalty.

1.8 When editions of the Work are sold at a discount over [62.5]% the [Author] shall be paid [60]% on the prevailing royalty.

R.584

The [Publishers] agree to pay to the [Author] the following royalties on the monies received by the [Publishers] (excluding value added tax) in respect of the printed copies of the [Work] sold anywhere in the World:

1.1 [10] %(ten per cent) on the first 500 copies.

1.2 [12.5]% (twelve-and-a-half per cent) on the next 1,000 copies.

1.3 [15] %(fifteen per cent) thereafter.

[For the Term of this Agreement/for the duration of the legal period of copyright and any extensions or renewals.]

R.585

The [Publishers] agree to pay the [Author] the following royalties on all sums received by the [Publishers] (excluding value added tax) in respect of all copies of the [Work] on [compact disk or tape form] sold anywhere in the World:

1.1 [5]% on the first 500 copies.

1.2 [6]%on the next 1,000 copies.

1.3 [7.5]% thereafter for the duration of this Agreement.

R.586
The [Publishing Company] shall pay to the [Author] a royalty in respect of all sales and disposals of the [Work] at the rate of [figure/currency] per copy on the first [1,000] copies of the [Work] and at the rate of [figure/currency] per copy for any further sales or disposals of the work.

R.587
The [Publishing Company] shall pay to the [Author] a royalty in respect of all sales and disposals of the [Work] at the rate of [number]% of the Recommended Retail Price (without any deduction being made in respect of the cost of discounts, distribution, promotion, commissions, copyright fees or otherwise) of the [Work] to the public [on first publication] for the first [number] copies of the [Work] and thereafter at [number]% per copy of the Work sold or disposed of as if deemed sold at the Recommended Retail Price (without any deduction of any kind).

R.588
The [Publishing Company] shall sell and dispose of the [Work] at the best price as may reasonably be obtained at the time of the sale or disposal.

R.589
The [Publishing Company] shall sell and dispose of the [Work] for retail sale to the public at [figure/currency] per copy.

R.590
The [Publishers] shall pay to the [Author] a royalty of [20]% (twenty) per cent of the sums received by the [Publishers] on all copies of the [Work] sold by the [Publishers] at any time. The sums received shall mean the amount received by the [Publishers] after deduction of any discounts, commissions, sales or other taxes, duties or costs incurred in respect of the sales of the copies of the [Work].

R.591
In the event that the [Work] is reprinted and the number of copies of the reprint is [500] or less (which shall not include a new edition) then the royalty payable to the [Author] shall be [number]% of the sums received by the [Publishers].

R.592

'The Authors Royalties' shall mean the following percentages [in respect of all sums received and credited to the [Publisher]] in respect of the [Work]:

1.1   The Home Market

Hardback copies of the [Work] sold in the United Kingdom of Great Britain and Northern Ireland, the Republic of Ireland, the Channel Islands and the Isle of Man:

In respect of the first 2,000 copies [number]%

In respect of the next 3,000 copies [number]%

In respect of the next 10,000 copies [number]%

Thereafter [number]%

Such percentages are to be calculated on the United Kingdom recommended retail price except where copies of the [Work] are sold for export including sales to the [Publisher's] branches and subsidiaries overseas in which case the percentages shall be based on the net amounts received or credited to the [Publisher].

1.2   Paperback copies of the [Work] sold in the United Kingdom of Great Britain and Northern Ireland, the Republic of Ireland, the Channel Islands and the Isle of Man:

In respect of the first 5,000 copies [number]%

In respect of the next 10,000 copies [number]%

In respect of the next 15,000 copies [number]%

Thereafter [number]%

Such percentages to be calculated on the United Kingdom recommended retail price except where copies of the [Work] are sold for export including sales to the [Publisher's] branches and subsidiaries overseas in which case the percentages shall be based on the net amounts received by or credited to the [Publisher].

United States of America and Canada

1.3   Hardback copies of the [Work] sold throughout the United States of America and Canada and their respective territories and dependants and the Philippine Islands:

In respect of the first 2,000 copies [number]%

In respect of the next 3,000 copies [number]%

In respect of the next 10,000 copies [number]%

Thereafter [number]%

Such percentages to be calculated on the net amount received by or credited to the [Publisher].

1.4 Paperback copies of the [Work] sold throughout the United States of America and Canada, its territories and dependants, the Philippine Islands:

In respect of the first 5,000 [number]%

In respect of the next 10,000 copies [number]%

In respect of the next 15,000 copies [number]%

Thereafter [number]%

Such percentages to be calculated on the net amount received by or credited to the [Publisher].

The Overseas Market excluding the United States and Canada

1.5 Hardback copies of the [Work] sold throughout the Territory excluding the United Kingdom of Great Britain and Northern Ireland, the Republic of Ireland, the Channel Islands, the Isle of Man, the United States of America and Canada and their respective territories and dependants, the Philippine Islands:

In respect of the first 2,000 copies [number]%

In respect of the next 3,000 copies [number]%

In respect of the next 10,000 copies [number]%

Thereafter [number]%

Such percentages to be calculated on the net receipts received by or credited to the [Publisher].

1.6 Paperback copies of the [Work] sold throughout the Territory excluding the United Kingdom of Great Britain and Northern Ireland, the Republic of Ireland, the Channel Islands, the Isle of Man, the United States of America and Canada and their respective territories and dependants, the Philippine Islands:

In respect of the first 5,000 copies [number]%

In respect of the next 10,000 copies [number]%

In respect of the next 15,000 copies [number]%

Thereafter [number]%

Such percentages to be calculated on the net amount received by or credited to the [Publisher].

Remainder, Discounted and Reduced Hardback and Paperback copies

1.7 Where the [Publisher] disposes of copies of the [Work] throughout the United Kingdom of Great Britain and Northern Ireland, the Republic of Ireland, the Channel Islands and the Isle of Man at a discount, reduced price, remainder or overstock. The [Author] agrees that he/she shall only be entitled to receive [number]% in respect of all sums actually received by or credited to the [Publisher] where the [Work] is sold at less than [number]% of the recommended retail price.

1.8 Where the [Publisher] disposes of copies of the [Work] throughout the Territory excluding the United Kingdom of Great Britain and Northern Ireland, the Republic of Ireland, the Channel Islands and the Isle of Man at a discount, reduced price, remainder or overstock, the [Author] agrees that he/she shall only be entitled to receive [number]% in respect of all the sums actually received by the [Publisher] where the [Work] is sold at less than [number]% of the recommended retail price.

Mail Order

1.9 Where the [Publisher] sells copies of the [Work] throughout the United Kingdom of Great Britain and Northern Ireland, the Republic of Ireland, the Channel Islands and the Isle of Man through mail order or other direct selling method, the [Author] agrees that he/she shall only be entitled to receive [number]% of the price of the [Work] by mail order or other direct selling method.

1.10 Where the [Publisher] sells copies of the [Work] throughout the Territory excluding the United Kingdom of Great Britain and Northern Ireland, the Republic of Ireland, the Channel Islands and the Isle of Man through mail order or other direct selling method, the [Author] agrees that he/she shall only be entitled to receive the following [number]% of the price of the [Work] by mail order or other direct selling method.

Premium Offers, Book Club, Educational Editions and Subscriptions

1.11 Where the [Publisher] disposes of copies of the [Work] throughout the United Kingdom of Great Britain and Northern Ireland, the Republic of Ireland, the Channel Islands and the Isle of Man as a premium offer, book club or educational editions or subscriptions, then the [Author] agrees that he/she shall only be entitled to receive [number]% in respect of all sums received by or credited to the [Publisher] where the [Work] is sold at less than [figure]% of the recommended price.

1.12 Where the [Publisher] disposes of copies of the [Work] throughout the Territory excluding the United Kingdom of Great Britain and Northern Ireland, the Republic of Ireland, the Channel Islands and the Isle of Man as a premium offer, book club or educational editions or subscriptions, then the [Author] agrees he/she shall only be entitled to receive [number]% in respect of all sums actually received by or credited to the [Publisher] where the [Work] is sold at less than [number]% of the recommended retail price.

Small Reprints

1.13 Where the [Work] is reprinted in hardback for sale in the United Kingdom of Great Britain and Northern Ireland, the Republic of Ireland, the Channel Islands and the Isle of Man in quantity of [number] copies or less [number], then in respect to those small reprint hardback copies the [Author] shall only be entitled to [number]% of the recommended retail price of the [Work].

1.14 Where the [Work] is reprinted in paperback for sale in the United Kingdom of Great Britain and Northern Ireland, the Republic of Ireland, the Channel Islands and the Isle of Man in the quantity of [number] copies or less, then in respect of those small reprint paperback copies the [Author] shall only be entitled to the [number]% of the recommended retail price of the [Work].

Subsidiary Rights

1.15 The [Author] shall be entitled to receive the following percentages of the net sums received by the [Publisher] in respect of the exploitation of the following rights in the [Work] throughout the Territory:

1.16 Anthology and Quotation Rights [number]%.

1.17 Translation Rights [number]%.

1.18 Audiotape Rights/Cassette or talking books [number]%.

1.19 Straight non-dramatic radio and television readings [number]%.

1.20 Dramatic adaptations for all forms of television, radio, film and theatre excluding video and DVD market [number]%.

1.21 Dramatic and non-dramatic Video Rights [number]%.

1.22 Dramatic and non-dramatic DVD Rights [number]%.

1.23 Computer Software and CD-Rom Rights [–].

1.24 First Serialisation published prior to publication in hardback [number]%.

1.25 Second and subsequent Serialisation after publication in hardback [number]%.

1.26 One-shot digest to publish an abridgement of the [Work] in a periodical or newspaper [number]%.

1.27 Digest book condensation in volume form [number]%.

1.28 Any electronic and mechanical reproduction in information, data, images, text, music or otherwise, storage and retrieval systems excluding the [worldwide web/internet/domain name rights] and [DVD/Disc] [and interactive and multi media] [number]%.

1.29 Three Dimensional, Theme Park, Festivals, Sports and Events and all Merchandising, Character and Image Rights [number]%.

1.30 Product Placement [number]%.

1.31 Sponsorship/endorsement/cross promotion/advertising [number]%.

1.32 Hardback Reprint Rights licensed to another publisher [number]%.

1.33 Paperback Reprint Rights licensed to another publisher [number]%.

1.34 Book Club Editions licensed to another publisher on a separate royalty basis [number]%.

1.35 Internet/Worldwide web/Domain Name Rights [number]%.

1.36 Lotteries, betting, gambling, bingo, premium phone lines, competitions and other associated rights [–]%.

1.37 Strip cartoons and picture form [number]%.

1.38 Photocopying and other Reprographic Rights administered by the [Copyright Licensing Agency/other copyright and collecting agencies/Author/Publisher] [–]% [such sum to be collected through the [Authors Lending and Collecting Society/other].

1.39 All other rights and methods of exploitation shall be subject to agreement between the parties whether they are in existence now and/or created and/or developed in the future.

R.593

The [Author] grants the [Publishers] the sole and exclusive right for the Term of this Agreement to exploit the subsidiary rights in the [Work] which shall include any title, name, character set out below in the Territory and to authorise others to do so. The [Publishers] shall pay the [Author] the following percentages of the net sums received by the [Publishers] less any fees for the reproduction of copyright material paid to third parties from the sale of the [Work].

1.1 Translation [80]%.

1.2 Anthology and Quotation [50]% (the right to reproduce extracts from the [Work] in books, periodicals, maps, plans or other illustrations provided by the [Author]).

1.3 Digest Book Condensation in volume form [50]% (the right to publish an abridgement of the [Work] in volume form).

1.4 Digest Periodical Rights [50]% (the right to publish a condensation or digest of the [Work] including maps, plans, or illustrations or any abridgements in a journal, periodical or newspaper either before or after the first publication of the [Work]).

1.5 Single issue or One Shot Newspaper or Periodical Rights [50]% (the right to publish the complete [Work] in one or more issues of a periodical or newspaper).

1.6 Dramatisation and documentary rights on stage, film, radio, television, including digital, cable, satellite or other medium [80]%.

1.7 Sound broadcasting and Television Rights [80]% (single voice or straight reading of the text or illustrations of the [Work]).

1.8 Merchandising Theme Park, Competitions, Trade Mark, Domain Name, Product Placement, Promotion and Endorsement rights [80]%.

1.9 First Serial Rights [90]% (the right to publish one or more extracts from the [Work] in successive issues of a newspaper, periodical or magazine before publication of the work in hardback).

1.10 Second and subsequent Serial Rights [80]% (after first publication of the [Work] in hardback).

1.11 Strip cartoon or picturisation rights [50]%.

1.12 Hardcover reprint rights [50]% (licensed to another publisher).

1.13 Book Club Editions [50]% (licensed to another publisher).

1.14 Book Club Editions [10]% of the net receipts (sold to another publisher on a royalty inclusive basis).

1.15 United States Rights [80]%.

1.16 Paperback Rights (licensed to another publisher) [50]%.

1.17 Large Print and educational editions [50]%.

1.18 Mechanical Electromagnetic, Electronic Facsimile Reproduction Rights [50%] (including the right to store, retrieve, print out, reprographic reproduction or laser or other means of copying whether in existence now or created in the future. The right to use and license the [Work] in information storage and retrieval systems whether by mechanical, electronic or electromagnetic means whether in existence now or created in the future (except for commercial film, video, television, digital, cable and satellite) including any system of text data, sound and image including, but not limited to, sound recordings, records, tapes, video, software).

R.594

In the event that the [Work] is sold or licensed in the United States of America in volume form, the [Publishers] shall pay the [Author] [80]% of all sums received by them from such sales or licences. Where the [Publishers] sell copies of the [Work] to a publisher in the United States of America for a price by a subsidiary, holding or associated company of the [Publisher] [or by], then the [Publishers] shall pay the [Author] the following royalties on the copies sold in the United States of America:

1.1 Hardcover edition [10]% (ten per cent) on the first [5,000] (five thousand) copies, then [12.5]%(twelve-and-a-half per cent) on the next [5,000] (five thousand) copies, then [15]% (fifteen per cent) thereafter. In respect of all copies of the [Work] sold in the United States of America calculated on [the Suggested Customer Price] in the USA, where there are small reprints of [2,000] (two thousand) copies or less, the royalty to be paid to the [Author] shall revert to the lowest percentage rate above for that reprint only.

1.2 Paperback edition [6]% (six per cent) of the first [25,000] (twenty five thousand), then [8]% (eight per cent) thereafter, on all copies of the [Work] sold in the United States of America calculated on [the Suggested Customer Price in the USA/UK] [all sums received by the [Publisher].

Where there are small reprints of [6,000] or less then the royalty to be paid to the [Author] shall revert to the lowest percentage above calculated on the [USA Suggested Customer Price] for the reprint only.

R.595

The [Publisher] shall pay the [Author] [50]% (fifty per cent) of the sums actually received by the [Publisher] from the sale and/or licence of the:

1.1 Translation Rights.

1.2 Reprographic and Scanning Rights.

1.3 Document Delivery Service Rights

1.4 Any other Rights (except non-print Media Rights).

Sums received by the [Publishers] from the sale of the non-print Media Rights in the [Work] shall be divided in a proportion to be agreed between the [Author] and the [Publisher].

R.596
All other rights not specified in this Agreement or which may be in existence now or developed in the future in respect of the [Work] may not be exploited by the [Publisher] at any time without the prior written approval of the [Author and the Author's Agent] and agreement in respect of the payment terms.

R.597
'The [Author's] Royalties' shall mean the following percentages in respect of all sums received by or credited to the [Publisher] in respect of the [Work] [number per cent] [rights/area] [countries].

R.598
The [Company] shall be entitled to authorise free of charge the reproduction of the [Work] in Braille. No royalties shall become due to the [Author]. The [Company] shall not authorise the recording of the [Work] as a talking book without the prior consent and agreement of the [Author].

R.599
The [Publishers] shall have the right to grant permission for Braille and charitable recordings or tapes to be made of the [Work] for the sole use of the blind and handicapped, provided that no charge or copyright fee is made by the [Publisher] and in which case no royalty shall be due to the [Author].

R.600
The [Publishers] shall be entitled to authorise free of charge transcription of the [Work] into Braille and/or recordings of the [Work] as a talking book for the blind. No royalty payment in respect of these copies of the [Work] shall be due to the Author unless a fee is payable to the [Publisher].

R.601
Should any copies of the [Work] be destroyed as a result of fire, flood, marine peril or any other circumstances beyond the control of the [Publisher] no royalties shall be paid on any of the copies destroyed.

R.602
No royalty shall be payable on any copies of the [Work]:

1.1   Destroyed, damaged, lost, stolen and/or otherwise not in a good condition suitable for sale and not offered for sale.

1.2   Distributed for promotional and/or review purposes [and/or for marketing at trade exhibitions].

1.3   Provided free of charge to the [Author].

1.4   Sold at a discount to the [Author] under Clause [–].

1.5   Deposited at a library, university and/or institute as part of the legal scheme in the [United Kingdom] and [country/worldwide].

1.6   Disposed of at below cost under Clause [–].

R.603

No royalty shall be paid on copies of the [Work] destroyed by fire or water in transit or otherwise or on copies of the [Work] provided as review or promotional copies to the press, media or otherwise at no charge, or remaindered, or otherwise sold or disposed of at a cost or on stock transfers between subsidiary companies.

R.604

In the event that the [Author] receives royalties on copies of the [Work] sold by the [Publisher] and then returned or not paid for, the [Publishers] shall be entitled to recoup the sum from any other sums due to the [Author] under this Agreement.

R.605

The [Publishers] shall have the right to reserve against returns of the [Work] [10%] (ten per cent) of the royalties due to the [Author] in respect of the hardback edition and [20%] (twenty per cent) in respect of the paperback edition of the royalties due to the [Author]. The [Publishers] shall be entitled to withhold such sums up to and including the [third] royalty statement. All monies withheld shall then be paid in full to the [Author] on the [fourth] royalty statement.

R.606

During the first year of publication of the [Work] the [Publishers] may withhold up to [10%] (ten per cent) of the royalties on home sales as a reserve against returns. At the next accounting period this reserve will be added to the [Author's] royalties less any deductions for returned copies. Thereafter the [Publishers] shall be entirely responsible for the cost of any monies paid or incurred in respect of returns of the [Work].

R.607

The [Publishers] agree that at no time shall they be entitled to withhold any sums due to the [Author] as a reserve against returns.

R.608
After publication of the [Work] and provided that the Advance has been recouped [and provision made for returns] and the [Author] does not owe the [Publishers] any sums, then the [Author] may request the [Publisher] to pay any sums in excess of [figure/currency] being held by the [Publisher] on the [Author's] account in respect of subsidiary rights to the [Author] at the end of the calendar month in which such sums were received. [The Publishers shall not be requested to make more than [number] such payments in any one year.]

R.609
The [Publisher] may suspend payment of royalties to the [Author] in the event of any breach or alleged breach of the warranties and undertakings in Clause [–] until such time as such claims are resolved, or settled and the Publisher may deduct from the royalties held or which may become due any sums owed by the Author in respect of Clause [–].

R.610
The [Author] agrees that the Advance shall be offset against the [Author's] Royalty. The [Publisher] agrees that no part of the Advance shall be returnable by the [Author] once the [Publisher] has accepted the manuscript of the [Work].

R.611
The [Publisher] and the [Author] agree that the [Work] shall be listed with the [Copyright Licensing Agency and the Authors Licensing Collection Society] as an excluded work. Any licence for photocopying, scanning, reproduction in the form of electronic and/or digital files shall be the subject of a separate agreement between the [Author] and the [Publisher].

R.612
The [Publisher] shall not be entitled to exercise any of the subsidiary rights without prior consultation and the consent of the [Author] in each case.

R.613
[Name] shall not receive any royalties from the [Publisher] where no sums are received for the supply of the [Work] provided that the transfer is not to an associated and/or parent company and/or a distribution content service with whom the [Publisher] has concluded an agreement. In such case the transfer value shall be the retail price in the [country] which supplies the original version of the [Work].

Purchase and Supply of Products

R.614

The [Licensee] shall pay to the [Licensor] [number] per cent of the [Wholesale Selling Price] in respect of each Product sold in the Territory by the [Licensee], any member of the [Licensee's] Group and/or any sub-licensee. The [Wholesale Selling Price] shall be defined as the price invoiced to the [Customer] for the product less value added tax, sales taxes, duties, transport and insurance charges, allowances, discounts, rebates and returns.

A consignment of the Product shall be deemed sold on the first to occur of the following:

1.1 The date of actual delivery of that consignment to the [Customer].

1.2 The date of the invoice to the [Customer] in respect of that consignment.

1.3 The date that the consignment is mixed by the relevant company with another ingredient or product.

R.615

The [Licensee] shall pay to the [Licensor] [figure/currency] per unit in respect of each Product [reproduced, supplied, distributed and] sold anywhere in the world by any means through retail and wholesale outlets, over the internet, shopping television channels, mail order and/or otherwise where the sums are received and/or credited to the [Licensee]. No deduction shall be made by the [Licensee] for any costs and expenses, taxes, duties, freight, insurance charges, advertising and/or other sums incurred.

R.616

Any delay in payment of any royalties shall result in an additional charge of [number/currency] per cent of the sum due being added to the payment due to the [Licensor].

Services

R.617

The [Company] will pay the [Artist] the following Royalties on [Records] sold by the [Company] and/or its sub-licensees calculated on [90%] [ninety per cent] of the recommended retail price to the general public (after deducting any tax or taxes levied on the selling price), and in respect of [Records, Cassettes and Cartridges or other formats] less an allowance for packaging as follows:

1.1 Not more than [6.5]% (six-and-a-half per cent) in respect of disk records.

1.2　Not more than [7.5] % (seven-and-a-half per cent) in respect of tape records [provided that Royalties payable on tape records shall be calculated in the same selling price to the general public as for a disk record containing the same material].

A Record shall be defined as consisting of a number of tracks, each track containing one musical composition. It is agreed by the [Artist] that where a Record contains tracks by other artists to whom royalties are payable by the [Company] then the percentage royalties due shall be reduced pro rata to the number of tracks by the [Artist] as compared to the total number of tracks in the Record. It is agreed that where the [Artist] is performing at the same time on a track with other artists to whom royalties are payable then the percentage of royalties from the track shall be reduced pro rata based on the total number of artists performing on the track to who royalties are due.

R.618
The [Company] shall pay to the [Artist] the following royalty on all [Records] sold outside the United Kingdom except for those sold under any record club, direct mail or similar operation [number]%.

R.619
The [Company] shall pay to the [Artist] the following royalty on all Records sold outside the United Kingdom in the Territory (except for those sold under any record club, direct mail or similar operation) [number] %.

R.620
The [Company] shall pay to the [Artist] [50%] of the royalties in Clause [–] in respect of the Territory on all [Records] sold throughout the following methods:

1.1　Record club, direct mail order, or similar operation excluding free or give-away or promotional Records.

1.2　Low prices service provided that in any event the [Artist] shall receive royalties in respect of [50]% of the quantity of [Records] distributed through 1.1 whether free, sold or otherwise.

R.621
The Royalty shall be paid for the term of this Agreement and for [50/70] years thereafter.

R.622
It is agreed that the [Company] shall be entitled to recoup all the production costs of the [Record] and any other recordings of the [Artist] against the Royalties due to the [Artist] under this Agreement.

R.623

The [Company] shall only be obliged to pay the royalties on sums received in respect of those countries in which currency restrictions are in force.

R.624

'The [Artist's] Royalties' shall be:

1.1 [number]% of the Net Receipts in respect of all [Records] sold, hired, licensed or otherwise commercially exploited in the United Kingdom of Great Britain, Northern Ireland, the Republic of Ireland, the Channel Islands and the Isle of Man.

1.2 [number]% of the Net Receipts in respect of all the [Records] sold, hired, licensed or otherwise commercially exploited in all countries of the Territory excluding those countries specified in 1.1 above.

1.3 [number]% of the Net Receipts of all [Records] sold, hired or licensed or otherwise commercially exploited at a reduced price or as a low budget line or through a record club, mail order scheme or similar method.

1.4 In the event that any of the [Records] feature other artists who also receive royalty payments from the [Company] in respect of their performances, then the [Artist's] Royalties shall be reduced by the same proportion as the number of performances by the [Artiste] to the total of other artistes performances and the [Artist] combined in each such case. [For example if a long playing record featuring 10 songs, two of which are by the [Artist], then the [Artist's] Royalties shall be 1/5 of the Net Receipts in the case.]

R.625

The [Licensor] agrees that the Licence Fee shall be offset against the [Licensor's] Royalties.

R.626

'The [Author's] Royalties' shall be:

1.1 [number]% of the retail selling price in respect of the [sheet music] sold in the United Kingdom of Great Britain and Northern Ireland, the Republic of Ireland, the Channel Islands and the Isle of Man.

1.2 [number]% of the retail selling price in respect of [sheet music] sold throughout the Territory excluding those specified in 1.1 above.

1.3 A pro rata payment shall be made to the [Author] where the [Work] appears with the work of a third party entitled to a royalty payment which is included in any song book, folio or other printed format other than in any newspaper, periodical or book.

1.4 [number]% of the Net Receipts in respect of the use of the [Work] including any sound recordings in synchronisation with any visual images in connection with any film, video, or television programme in any medium (whether pre-recorded or not) throughout the Territory.

1.5 [number]% of the Net Receipts in respect of the publication of the [Work] in any newspaper, periodical, or both sold throughout the Territory.

1.6 [number]% of the Net Receipts in respect of the internet and downloading of material, DVDs, CD-Roms and any method of storage and/or retrieval and/or dissemination and any other rights not listed above.

1.7 [number]% by all other means in any other medium and/or format.

R.627

In consideration of the assignment of the rights in respect of the [Work] the [Publishers] shall pay the [Assignor] the following royalties in respect of the [Work]:

1.1 Sheet music royalties [10]% [ten] per cent of the retail selling price of each pianoforte copy (the orchestration and arrangement) of the [Work] sold by the [Publishers] in the United Kingdom and the Republic of Ireland which is paid to the [Publishers].

1.2 A pro rata amount of the retail selling price in respect of all copies of any songbook, printed album or folio which includes the [Work] sold by the [Publishers] in the United Kingdom and the Republic of Ireland which is paid to the [Publishers].

1.3 Mechanical Royalties [50]% [fifty] per cent of all royalties received by the [Publisher] in the United Kingdom and the Republic of Ireland (after deduction of any collection charges made by the [Publishers] or any mechanical collecting society) for the reproduction of the [Work] in the manufacture of sound recordings, records, tapes, piano works and all other mechanical reproductions of the [Work] whether sound alone or in conjunction with visual images.

1.4 Film Synchronisation Fees [50]% [fifty] per cent of all sums received by the [Publishers] in the United Kingdom and the Republic of Ireland (after deduction of any mechanical collecting society charges) in respect of the right to record the work on soundtracks for use with the Film, Television, Video, or other visual images.

1.5 Foreign Royalties [50]% (fifty per cent) of the net royalties received by the [Publishers] from affiliated or associated companies of the [Publishers] and/or from collecting societies and/or from companies or persons sub-licensed by the [Publisher] to exploit the [Work] outside the United Kingdom and the Republic of Ireland (excluding performing rights and/or performance fees and broadcast and/or transmission fees).

1.6 Other Fees [50]% [fifty] per cent of all monies received by the [Publishers] from any other source in respect of the [Work] including newspapers, periodicals, books and sub-licence and/or other exploitation of the [Work] and/or any parts.

R.628

The [Author] and the [Publisher] agree that during the Assignment Period any sums due from the [Performing Rights] [or a society affiliated to it] in the [Work] shall be divided between them in accordance with the [Performing Rights Society] rules in force at any time. In any event the [Author's] share shall not be less than [50]% [fifty] per cent of all fees distributed in respect of the performance of the [Work].

R.629

The [Publishers] are members of the [Performing Rights Society Limited/ other and/or any society affiliated to it] and fees are collected by PRS and distributed in accordance with the conditions of [PRS/other]. The [Assignor] agrees that the [PRS] shall be entitled by virtue of this Agreement to pay all fees collected by them to [the Publisher/the Author]. The Assignor shall receive [50]% [fifty] per cent of all fees distributed by the [PRS] in respect of the performances of the [Work] which shall be paid direct to the [Assignor] by the PRS provided that the [Assignor] is a member. In the event that the [Assignor] is not a member of the [PRS] all fees shall be paid direct in full to the Publisher, who shall then pay the Assignor [50]% [fifty] per cent of all fees received by them in respect of all rights administered by the [PRS].

R.630

No royalty payment shall be made to the [Assignor] in respect of any copies of the [Work] in any form which are distributed to the trades, profession, media or otherwise for the purpose of promoting and publicising the [Work] provided that no payment is received by the [Publishers].

R.631

If the [Assignor] of the [Work] consists of two or more Composers and/or Authors then the payments to the [Assignor] shall be apportioned between them as follows [Name] [number per cent] [Name] [number] per cent.

R.632

Prior to collaborating with any third party in the writing, composition or creation of any musical material, the [Composer] shall advise the third party that the [Composer] is under exclusive contract to the [Publisher] and that the third party must grant to the [Publisher] the same rights in any [Composition] produced as the Composer grants under this Agreement and that the third party must agree to accept in full consideration for his/her work a proportion of the Royalties for any joint composition payable by the [Publisher] to the [Composer] under Clause [–].

R.633

The proportion of Royalties for joint [Composition] shall be either equally divided between the [Composer] and all third party contributors or alternatively such other proportion as may be agreed and notified to the [Publisher].

R.634

The total Royalties payable by the [Publisher] in respect of [Compositions] jointly written with third parties shall not exceed the royalties payable by the [Publisher] under Clause [–].

R.635

The [Composer] shall procure that each third party contributor enters into a publishing agreement with the [Publisher] in respect of their contribution to the joint [Composition].

R.636

'The Presenter's Royalties' shall be [number] per cent of the [Gross Receipts/ Net Receipts].

R.637

All royalties under this Agreement shall continue to be paid by the [Company] to the [Presenter] for such period as the rights shall be exploited and sums due to the [Presenter] whether or not this Agreement shall terminate or expire.

R.638

Payment of any royalties under this Agreement due to the [Presenter] shall not be offset or withheld against any claim under any legal proceedings at any time against the [Presenter] and/or a third party.

R.639

All other rights not specifically granted under this Agreement to the [Company] and/or which may not be in existence now or which are developed in the future in respect of the product of the services of [Name] may not be exploited by the [Company] at any time without the prior written approval of [Name] and the conclusion of a further agreement for the acquisition and/exploitation of any such rights which are owned by [Name].

R.640

Where the [Licensee] fails to declare royalties and/or payments due at any time over [number/currency] and they are accounted for and paid in any subsequent statement then a late fee of [number/currency] shall be paid as compensation for the delay.

R.641

All royalties and payments due under this Agreement must be made in [country] by electronic transfer to the nominated account on the date that they fall due. Any statement may be sent to the [Licensor] by email and [pdf/excel] attachment. Where required for the purpose of verification the [Licensor] may request access to the documents, data, agreements and reports on which the royalty payments are based which shall be supplied at the [specify party] cost.

Sponsorship

R.642

The [Sponsor] agrees that it shall not be entitled to any royalties and/or other sum from the [Company] from any payments received by the [Company] for the sub-licensing, assignment and/or transfer of any rights and/or any other form of exploitation of the [Event/Programme] at any time.

R.643

The [Company] agrees that the [Sponsor] shall be entitled to receive a royalty payment of [number] % of all sums received by the [Company] before [date] from the sub-licensing of the merchandising rights to a third party for the [Event] after the [Company] has recovered all its costs and expenses for the [Event] and any associated advertising, marketing and promotional material.

R.644

The [Licensee] agrees that the [Sponsor] shall be paid [number] % of the Net Receipts received by the [Licensee] from the premium rate line entitled [specify] from [date to [date].

R.645

The [Sponsor] shall not be entitled to any payment, royalty and/or other sum from the [Company's] website, the organised events, any merchandising and/or licensing of rights, television and/or radio and/or media coverage and fees, funding from grants, government and/or individuals and/or any other financial contribution to the [Company].

R.646

The [Sponsor] agrees to pay [Name] an additional fee of [number/currency] in arrears at the end of each calendar month for the exploitation of the [Image/Name/Logo] of [Name] on free corporate merchandising material for the [Sponsor] to be given away at events, conference and exhibitions during the Term of this Agreement.

University, Library and Educational

R.647

The [Author] shall be entitled to receive [number]% [words] from the Net Receipts received by the [Institute] from the exploitation of the [Work] at any time. The payments shall be made to the [Author] by [date] in each year in [currency] and shall be supported by a detailed statement of accounts which sets out the calculation for the payment.

R.648

No royalty payments shall be made to the [Contributor] in respect of any copies of the [Work] in any form which are:

1.1 Distributed to the trade, media or otherwise for the purpose of reviewing, promoting and publicising the [Work] provided that no payment is received by the [Institute].

1.2 Destroyed and/or damaged by fire, water, chemicals and/or otherwise whilst in transit or in the warehouse or the premises of the [Institute].

1.3 Sold or disposed of at a cost under Clause [–].

1.4 Stolen and/or otherwise not in a good condition suitable for sale and not offered for sale.

1.5 Provided free of charge to the [Contributor].

1.6 Sold at a discount to the [Author] under Clause [–].

1.7 Deposited at a library, university and/or institute as part of the legal scheme in the [United Kingdom] and [country/worldwide].

R.649

The [Contributor] agrees that the [Institute] may offset the Licence Fee offset against the Royalties due the [Contributor] under this Agreement, but not any other agreement which the [Contributor] may have with the [Institute].

R.650

The [Institute] agrees to pay the [Author] the [number]% [words] on all sums received by the [Publishers] (excluding value added tax) in respect of all copies of the [Work] sold in [specify format] sold anywhere in the world.

R.651

The [Institute] agrees and undertakes to pay the [Author] a royalty in respect of all sales and disposals of copies of the [Work] in [specify format] to the public at the rate of [number]% of the Recommended Retail Price (without any deduction being made in respect of the cost of discounts, distribution, promotion, commissions, copyright fees or otherwise).

R.652

The [Institute] agrees to pay the [Author] at the rate of [figure/currency] per copy on all copies of the [Work] in [Format] sold in [country] during the [Licence Period] and for which the sums are received and retained by the [Institute].

R.653

Where there are no royalties stated in the Agreement for the exercise of specific rights due to the fact that the technology and/or method has not been discovered and/or developed then all such rights are reserved to and retained by the [Author] and not granted to the [Institute] under this Agreement.

S

SALES TAX

General Business and Commercial

S.001

'Sales Tax' shall mean any sales tax, value added tax or other tax or taxes levied on sales or supplies of the goods or services which form a precise and calculable element in the price and which are recovered directly or indirectly as part of the selling or supply price.

S.002

'The Sales Tax' shall mean any sales or other taxes levied by the European Union, any of its member states, any other authority anywhere in the world on the sale, supply, rental, purchase or subscription of the [Film] which form a distinct element on the price and which are recovered as part of the price directly or indirectly by the [Licensee].

S.003

'The Sales Tax' shall be any taxes levied by the European Union, United Kingdom or foreign authorities on the sale or supply of the [Records/ Products/Articles] which form a distinct element and which are recovered as part of the [retail] selling price directly or indirectly by the [Company/ Distributor].

S.004

'The Sales Tax' shall mean any sales or other taxes levied by the member states of the European Union or British authorities on the sale, rental, supply or purchase of [Videos/DVDs/CD-Roms] which form a distinct element in the wholesale selling price and which are recovered as part of the wholesale selling price by the [Licensee].

S.005

'Sales Taxes' shall mean any sales or other taxes levied on sales or supply of goods which form a recognisable distinct element of the price and which are recovered directly or indirectly as part of the selling or supply price and all other taxes, levies, duties or government charges on [Videos/DVDs/Discs] from manufacture, production, supply, distribution, sale, lending, rental and subscription.

S.006
All payments and charges are exclusive of taxes, levies, charges, duties that may arise and/or be due on the production, sale, supply, transfer, licence, distribution or otherwise of the [Character] in any format under this Agreement, provided that the sums are charged and then paid to any government agency by any party and not retained. Such sums do not have to be specified in the accounts.

S.007
All sums payable under this Agreement are exclusive of any sales tax, value added tax and any other sum charged on the sale and supply of [Services/ Products/other]. Each party shall be responsible for its own personal, corporate taxes and insurance.

S.008
All sums are exclusive of tax whether value added tax, sales tax or other tax levied on the goods or services and it is deducted or added for any reason and must be disclosed in the accounts. Each party shall bear the cost of its own taxes of any nature unless required by law to pass the charge or cost to the other party.

S.009
The [Dealer Price] is exclusive of tax and must be paid without any deduction whatsoever. Where relevant Value Added Tax, Sales Tax and any other tax shall be paid by the [Seller]. Value Added Tax shall only be paid where an invoice bearing the correct registered number is provided.

S.010
All charges and payments are not inclusive of tax and must be paid as far as legally possible without any deduction including Value Added Tax, Sales Tax and any other tax, levy or assessment. Each party shall be responsible for any national insurance, income tax or otherwise levied on their receipt of the sums.

S.011
All sums payable under this Agreement are exclusive of any taxes to be paid and/or due to be paid by either party including any tax on sales and/or supply of [Products].

S.012

All sums to be paid by the [Sub-Licensee] to the [Licensor] shall be exclusive of any sales taxes due to any government for the sale and/or supply of any material and/or services under this Agreement.

S.013

Where any taxes are imposed and/or charged to any person and/or company on the supply of goods and/or services which any party wishes to claim. Then proof of registration for that tax shall be necessary by the supply of a legitimate reference and also an appropriate invoice specifying the tax and the goods and/or service to which it applies.

SCRIPTS

General Business and Commercial

S.014

'The Scripts' shall mean the full text whether typed or handwritten including all preparatory notes, drafts, revisions and all other written material arrangements, dramatisations, adaptations or any other variations including, but not limited to the title, characters, plots, themes, dialogues, episode titles and all sound recordings, recordings and any other material of any nature in respect of the [Writer's] services hereunder.

S.015

'The Scripts' shall be the typed draft and final scripts based on the Treatment to be prepared by the [Writer/Licensor].

S.016

The [Assignor/Licensor] shall deliver the scripts to the [Assignee/Licensee] for approval on or before the following dates:

Draft script [date/stages] Final script [date]

S.017

'The Script' shall mean the typed copy of the final script of the [Advertising Copy].

S.018

'The Script' shall be all draft and final scripts to be prepared by the [Screenplay Writer] based on the [Author's Work].

S.019

The [Production Company] agrees that the [Author] shall be entitled to approve the Scripts and shall deliver the Scripts to the [Author] on or before the following dates [Draft/Final Script].

S.020

The agreed script material with the [Contractor] shall be subject to incidental amendments which may arise from the production of the [Work].

S.021

The [Production Company] shall deliver the scripts and storyboard of the [Advertisement] to the [Commissioning Company] for approval on or before:

1.1   Draft scripts [date]

1.2   Final scripts [date]

1.3   The storyboard [date].

S.022

The [Company] agrees that except for minor alterations the final script shall be used for the [Series] unless there is a material alteration in the circumstances which demand changes in which case the [Author] shall be consulted for his/her approval.

S.023

[Name] shall return all copies of the [Script] to the [Company] at the end of the production period and/or by [date] whichever is the later and shall not be entitled to keep a copy for personal reference.

S.024

The [Author] shall either accept and/or provide written reasons for the rejection of the [Script] within [one calendar month] of delivery. Provided that the [Author] agrees not to unreasonably withhold and/or delay his consent.

S.025

1.1   The [Company] shall be provided with a reasonable opportunity to comment on the draft script, the key personnel, the production schedule together with any significant changes that occur at a later date.

1.2   The [Company] shall be entitled to approve the final script prior to production of the [Film] and shall be consulted on all changes except minor editing.

S.026

The [Production Company] shall not permit and/or allow any editorial control by [Name] in respect of the [Film], but shall agree that the [Author] shall be consulted about the draft and final script.

S.027

All drafts, documents, scripts, brochures and/or other material developed and//or created for the [Project] by the [Company] shall belong to and be the property of the [Company]. No rights are granted to any person to reproduce, license and/or exploit the material at any time.

S.028

'The Manuscripts' shall be all the diaries, draft notes, documents, drawings and other material prepared, written and/or drawn by [Name] which are owned and controlled by the [specify] Estate details of which are described in the attached appendix [–] which forms part of this Agreement.

S.029

The copies of the scripts for the [Film] must not be supplied, released, distributed, copied and/or reproduced to any third party and must be returned to the [Production Company] upon request and/or at the end of each day of completed filming for that script.

SECURITY

General Business and Commercial

S.030

1.1 The [Company] agrees to ensure that the original and all reproductions of the [Material/Work] shall be kept in a secure and safe location at [address] in a [safety deposit box/vault/warehouse] which shall be fireproof and where there is [twenty-four] security guards at the [Company's] cost and expense.

1.2 The [Company] agrees and undertakes that no copies shall be released, distributed and/or supplied to the press, media and/or any third party except for the purposes of printing and storing the [Material/ Work] until the launch date.

S.031

The [Company] agrees to arrange at its own cost security software for the [Website] which shall prevent and/or scan for viruses, hackers, trojans and/or any other losses, damages and/or interference with the data, emails and/or content of the [Website].

S.032

The security for the payment of any sums shall be at your own risk and cost through [specify company]. No liability can be accepted by the [Distributor] any charges, costs, fraud, losses and/or any other consequence that may arise as a result of using that payment method.

S.033

The [Company] does not accept any responsibility for any failure of the security, and/or any loss and/or damage to personal valuables, cars and/or other portable items at the [Event].

S.034

The [Sponsor] agrees to arrange at its cost personal security for [Name] for the Term of this Agreement which shall be subject to the approval of [Name].

S.035

Any safety measures and/or security and/or restrictions on access which need to be arranged and/or provided by the [Company] at the [Event/Exhibition] shall be at the [Company's] sole cost and shall not be charged to [Name].

S.036

The [Company] can only ensure that the [App/Blog/Website] is secure to the extent that it will operate the [specify/programme] system to scan the material submitted by the public.

SELL-OFF PERIOD

General Business and Commercial

S.037

1.1   The [Assignee] shall be entitled to sell off on a non-exclusive basis, licensed material and stocks previously manufactured under this

Agreement for the purpose of commercial sale for a period of [twelve months] from the date of expiry or termination.

1.2   This clause shall only apply as long as the [Assignee] is not in breach and adheres to all the terms of this Agreement.

S.038

After expiry or termination or completion of the sell-off period then the [Assignor] shall be entitled to instruct the [Assignee] to return or destroy all master material, licensed material and any copies and any derivatives or associated material of any nature in the possession or under the control of the [Assignee] pursuant to this Agreement.

S.039

1.1   Provided that the [Licensee] has not manufactured or arranged for the manufacture of the [Licensed Articles] in numbers exceeding those that the [Licensee] can reasonably be expected to sell prior to expiry or termination and there are no unresolved allegations of breach or alleged breach of this Agreement. The [Licensee] shall be entitled to sell off and distribute on a non-exclusive basis for a period of [three months] the [Licensed Articles] which are already held in stock.

1.2   The [Licensee] shall not be entitled to manufacture and/or produce any more [Licensed Articles] after the expiry or termination of the Agreement.

1.3   The [Licensee] must ensure that the Royalties are accounted for to the [Licensor].

1.4   The [Licensee] must ensure that the price charged by the [Licensee] for each [Licensed Article] is not less than the price charged prior to the sell-off period.

1.5   After the [three month] period the [Licensee] shall cease to sell the [Licensed Articles] and shall provide the [Licensor] with an inventory of stock at that date which shall at the request of the [Licensor] be verified by an independent chartered accountant at the [Licensee's] cost.

1.6   The [Licensee] shall either destroy the remaining stock at the instruction of the [Licensor] or agree a reduced price for the purchase by the [Licensor].

S.040

1.1   At the expiry of the sell-off period the [Licensee] will at the request of the [Licensor] and its own expense destroy all remaining stocks of the [Licensed Articles] and all moulds, patterns, screens and/or other material and apparatus used to produce the [Licensed Articles].

1.2   The [Licensee] shall within [14] days of such destruction supply to the [Licensor] an affidavit of destruction detailing items which have been destroyed and confirming that no material of any kind relating to the [Licensed Articles] is in the possession or control of the [Licensee].

S.041

It is specifically agreed between the parties that there shall be no sell-off period and/or right to dispose of stock and/or the right to retain any stock and/or any other additional licence period and/or rights after the expiry or termination of this Agreement.

S.042

Upon expiry of the Term of this Agreement the [Licensee] shall immediately cease any further manufacture or production of the [Videos/DVDs/Discs]. The [Licensee] shall have the non-exclusive right to sell off existing stocks manufactured hereunder for a period of [six weeks] from the last day of the Term of this Agreement. The [Licensee] shall not be entitled to reproduce and/or authorise any new stock. At the completion of such a sell-off period the [Licensee] shall destroy or erase all remaining stocks in the possession or under the control of the [Licensee]. If so requested by the [Licensor] the [Licensee] shall supply a statement of that fact from the [Managing Director] at the [Licensee].

S.043

Upon the expiry of this Agreement the [Licensee] shall be permitted on a non-exclusive basis to sell the [Licensed Articles] already manufactured under this Agreement at a reduced price but in any event not less than [cost] until [date]. The royalty rate payment due shall not be reduced. Thereafter the [Licensee] shall return all master material, licensed articles, artwork stock, publicity and any other material of any nature in the possession or under the control of the [Licensee], and any agents, sub-licensees, or other third parties who have been authorised by the [Licensee] to hold any such material. All collection, freight and other costs shall be at the [Licensee's] sole cost.

S.044

The [Licensee] and any sub-licensee shall have the non-exclusive right after the expiry, but not the termination of this Agreement to dispose and sell off old stock whether at a reduced price, discounted or otherwise for a period of [three/six/twelve] months from the date of expiry. The [Licensee] shall pay the [Licensor] a [fixed price/royalty] on all such old stock of not less than [figure/currency]/[number] per cent.

S.045

There shall be no right under this Agreement to any sell-off period and/or to dispose of any old stock and/or material after the expiry date and/or in respect of any earlier termination. The ownership of the stock and all other material shall be transferred to the [Licensor] and returned to the [Licensor] and/or destroyed as directed by the [Licensor]. No payment of any kind shall be due to the [Licensee] for the stock and/or material and/or the transfer of rights nor shall any sums be set-off by the [Licensee] against under sums due under this Agreement to the [Licensor].

S.046

Where the [Supplier] terminates the Agreement with the [Company] it is agreed that [Company] shall still be entitled to list the [Products] on their stock database and on their [Website] for up to [three] months thereafter and to sell and dispose of the [Products] to the public. Provided that the [Company] makes no claim to be an exclusive distributor and/or takes any orders from the public which do not relate to existing stock within its possession.

S.047

The [Licensee] and/or any sub-licensee shall not have the right to dispose of, sell and/or otherwise supply, distribute and/or exploit the [Work] after [date] and/or the termination of this Agreement whichever is the earlier. The [Licensee] and/or any sub-licensee shall provide a comprehensive list of all the copies which are in their possession and/or control. The [Licensor] shall then have the option to either notify the [Licensee] and/or any sub-licensee to destroy the stock and/or dispose of it to a third party on specific terms and/or deliver the stock to the [Licensor] at the [Licensor's] cost.

S.048

After [date] the [Licensee] shall have no right to sell, supply, reproduce and/or exploit any copies of the [Image/Logo/Name] on any material and/or to supply, sell, distribute and offer for sale and/or promote and/or advertise any [Products] which are in stock in any part of the world. All stock held by the [Licensee] as at [date] must be delivered on that date to the [Licensor] at the [Licensee's] cost. The [Licensor] may then either destroy the stock and/or sell it to a third party and retain all the sums paid.

S.049

The [Licensee] shall not have any additional period under this Agreement for the disposal of stock held at the end of the Licence. All stock must be disposed of in the form of recycling and/or pulp at a source which can verify the materials delivered to the [Licensor] directly.

SET-OFF

General Business and Commercial

S.050
The [Creditor] may at any time, apply any of the monies referred to in Clause [–] in or towards satisfaction of any of the monies, obligations and liabilities which are the subject of this Guarantee as the [Creditor] in its sole discretion may from time to time decide.

S.051
The [Creditor] may without notice to the [Guarantor] withdraw and apply any credit balance which is at any time held by any office or branch of the [Creditor] in an account of the [Guarantor] in order to settle and pay any sum then due and payable from the [Guarantor] under this Guarantee.

S.052
The [Licensor] acknowledges that the Licence Fee shall be set-off against the [Licensor's] Royalties.

S.053
The [Designer] agrees to be responsible for all packaging, containers, labels, advertising, promotions and sales of the [Licensed Articles] and confirms that such costs shall be at his/her sole cost and expense and shall not be offset in any manner in the calculation of the Net Receipts.

S.054
The [Company] acknowledges that the non-returnable Advance is to be set-off against the [Licensor's] Royalties but that it is not returnable nor contingent on sales figures of the [Licensed Articles].

S.055
Without waiver or limitation of any rights or remedies the [Company] shall be entitled to deduct from any amounts due or owing by the [Company] to the [Contractor] in connection with this Contract all amounts due or owing at any time by the [Contractor] to the [Company].

S.056
Neither the [Licensee] nor the [Licensor] shall be entitled to set-off any sums in any manner from payments due or sums received in respect of any claim under this Agreement or any other agreement at any time.

S.057
The [Licensee] shall be entitled to set-off any and all monies owed by the [Licensee] to the [Licensor] against any and all monies owed by the [Licensor] to the [Licensee].

S.058
The [Creditor] may place to the credit of a suspense account any monies received under or in connection with this Guarantee in order to preserve the rights of the [Creditor] in relation to its claim against the [Debtor] or any other person.

S.059
Notwithstanding any instructions to the contrary from the [Customer], the [Company] may set-off, retain or hold on to any payments by the [Customer] in or towards the discharge and/or payment of any sum(s) owed by the [Customer] to the [Company] at any time at the sole discretion of the [Company].

S.060
Any overpayment by the [Publishers] to the [Author] in respect of the [Work] may be deducted from any sums subsequently due to the [Author] from the [Publishers] for the [Work].

S.061
Each party shall pay to the other in full and without set-off or deduction all sums payable in respect of each accounting period.

S.062
The [Licensee] shall be entitled to set-off the sum of [figure/currency] per annum against any income prior to the distribution of the receipts which shall be considered remuneration as a fixed cost for expenses and costs. No other sums of any nature may be deducted prior to payment to the [Licensor].

S.063
The [Company] shall have the right to recoup, recover, set-off and/or deduct any sums which it is owed by the [Licensee] against any sums the [Company] may owe the [Licensee] against any contract, agreement, licence and/or other business dealing of any nature.

S.064
No sums shall be set-off, deducted and or recovered by the [Company] under this Agreement which are not fully disclosed in the accounts provided to the [Assignor].

S.065

Where at any time the [Company] assigns and/or transfers this Agreement to a third party then the rights of set-off in clause [–] shall cease and the [Company] agrees that no sums due by [Name] to the [Company] shall be transferred to the assignee and/or purchaser of the Agreement.

S.066

The right to set-off any sums in clause [–] shall start on [date] and end on [date] and shall only apply to those Agreements where the [Company] has published and/or distributed and sold the [Work] to the public and made it widely commercially available.

SETTLEMENT

General Business and Commercial

S.067

In consideration of the payment of the [Settlement Price] by the [Distributor] to the [Company], the [Company] agrees from the [Settlement Date] to accept all such rights, obligations, liabilities, and benefits as exist between the [Name] and the [Distributor] under the agreement dated [specify] entitled [–]. A copy of which is attached and forms part of this Agreement.

S.068

[Name] confirms that he is fully aware of the content and consequences of this Agreement and accepts and agrees to the transfer and assignment to the [Company] of all the rights, obligations, liabilities, and benefits as exist between the [Name] and the [Distributor] under the agreement dated [specify] entitled [–].

S.069

The following claims, outstanding costs and other matters are disclosed by the [Distributor] and are now accepted by the [Company] as their responsibility and liability from [date].

S.070

[Name] agrees to accept the sum of [figure/currency] [words] in full and final settlement of any and all claims, actions, and/or allegations against the [Company] and in particular to the [specify subject].

S.071

However nothing in this Agreement shall prohibit and/or undermine the [Names'] residual legal rights against the [Company] relating to pension entitlement and/or claims with respect to personal injury.

S.072

'The Settlement Fee' shall be the sum of [figure/currency] [words] payable by the [Company to the [Employee].

S.073

The [Company] agrees to pay the [Settlement Fee] within [seven days] of the signature of this Agreement by the [Company] and the [Employee].

S.074

Both [Name] and the [Company] agree to keep the terms of this Agreement private and confidential. Disclosure shall not be a breach of this Agreement where disclosure is made to a court of law, under a court order, to a government department and/or to accountancy, legal and other professional financial advisors.

S.075

[Name] agrees to return the following items [car/mobile/keys/security pass/ uniform] and all other the property, reports, products, documents and other material in any format and/or medium to the [Company] by [date] at [Names'] cost except for [specify] which may be kept for personal reference only.

S.076

The [Company] agrees and undertakes to provide the following reference in response to any future request for a reference by a third party. A copy of the wording of the reference is set out in Schedule [–] and is attached to and forms part of this Agreement.

S.077

The parties agree that the following agreements between the parties [date/ title/summary] are summarily terminated. The parties agree that the following Clauses shall survive the termination and be binding on the parties until the end date set out below in each case [Specify clause/agreement/end date].

S.078

This settlement shall not prevent [Name] from making a claim against the [Company] at a later date for defamation and/or any other legal action where an officer and/or director of the [Company] has made reference to [Name] and impugned and/or damaged his/her reputation and made allegations and/or statements which are untrue and/or an incorrect account of the terms of this settlement.

S.079

The [Licensee] agrees that it shall not settle any claim with a third party in respect of the [Service/Work/Product] unless it has consulted with the [Licensor] and received their approval as to the terms of the proposed settlement. The [Licensor] agrees that it shall not unreasonably withhold approval where the settlement is based on no admission of liability.

SEVERANCE

General Business and Commercial

S.080

If any provision of this Agreement shall be prohibited by or judged by a court to be unlawful, void or unenforceable then such provision shall be severed from this Agreement. The remaining provisions of this Agreement shall not as far as possible be changed or modified and all other terms and conditions not so severed shall continue in full force and effect.

S.081

The parties agree that in the event of one or more of the provisions of this Agreement being subsequently declared invalid or unenforceable by a court or other binding authority then such invalidity or unenforceability shall not in any way affect the validity or enforceability of any other provisions.

S.082

In the event that any (or any part) of these terms, conditions or provisions shall be declared invalid, unlawful or unenforceable such terms (or parts), conditions or provisions shall be severed. The remaining terms (or parts), conditions or provisions shall continue to be valid and enforceable to the fullest extent permitted by law.

S.083

If any portion of this contract is held to be invalid or unenforceable for any reason by a court or government authority of competent jurisdiction, then such terms and conditions will be deemed to be removed from the contract and the remainder of this contract shall continue in full force and effect.

S.084

Any unenforceable or invalid provision contained in this Agreement shall be deleted. The remaining provisions shall remain in full force and effect, except that where the unenforceable or invalid provisions are at the core of this Agreement and their deletion makes the Agreement so incomplete or it cannot be fulfilled or is unworkable, then the Agreement as a whole shall be brought to an end on terms to be agreed between the parties.

S.085

The parties agree that in the event of one or more clauses of this Agreement being subsequently declared invalid or unenforceable by a court or other authority with jurisdiction, the invalidity or unenforceability of any clauses shall not in any way affect the validity or enforceability of any other clauses except those which comprise an integral part of it or are otherwise clearly inseparable.

S.086

Any unenforceable or invalid provision or portion contained herein shall be deemed severed from the valid provisions which shall remain in full force and effect.

S.087

Each clause and sub-clause of this Agreement shall be separate and severable from each other. In the event that any of the clauses or sub-clauses are deemed invalid or unenforceable this shall not affect the validity or enforceability of the other clauses or sub-clauses. In the event that any right, obligation, exclusion, restriction or other matter is held to be invalid, unenforceable or ineffective but would be if some part of it were deleted or modified then it shall be deleted or modified to the extent that may be necessary to make it valid, enforceable or effective.

S.088

In the event that any part of any clause of this Agreement is decided by a competent court of law to be unenforceable, illegal, invalid or otherwise wrong in law, then no part of this Agreement may be severed and the whole Agreement shall come to an end on the date of that judgment.

S.089

In the event that any clause and/or any part of this Agreement is declared by any judgment in any court to be unenforceable, invalid, and/or wrong in law then no part of this Agreement may be severed and the whole Agreement shall come to an end on the date of that judgment. All sums due and/or owed prior to that date shall be paid and the parties shall enter into negotiations to resolve all outstanding issues, payments and transfer of any rights.

S.090

In the event of severance of any clauses by a competent court then this Agreement shall only continue if the clauses [specify reference] are not affected. If these clauses are affected then this Agreement shall immediately come to an end. The parties shall enter into discussions to resolve any matters which are not decided by the court.

S.091

Where any term of this Agreement is deleted, erased, severed and/or otherwise removed from this Agreement for any reason. Then it is agreed between the parties that unless it relates to clauses [specify] then the Agreement shall continue in existence. Where clauses [specify] are effected in whole and/or part then the Agreement shall be terminated immediately. The parties enter into negotiations to reach a final settlement relating to the payments due and/or work completed and/or ownership of any rights under the Agreement.

SIGNATURE

General Business and Commercial

S.092

IN WITNESS OF THEIR AGREEMENT each party has caused its authorised representative to execute this instrument effective as of the date first above written:

[Contractor] [–] [Operator] [–]

By [–] By [–]

Title [–] Title [–]

Date [–] Date [–]

S.093

AGREED by the parties through their authorised signatures on the date of this Agreement:

Signed for and on behalf of [Company]

Signed [–]

Name [–]

Title [–]

1496

Date [–]

Signed for and on behalf of [Company]

Signed [–]

Name [–]

Title [–]

Date [–]

S.094

The [Agent] and the [Owner] warrant to the [Licensee] that they have tested and are entirely satisfied as to the [accuracy/quality/safety] of the [Property] on date [–].

Signed by Authorised Signatory [–] on behalf of the [Agent].

Signed by Authorised Signatory [–] on behalf of the [Owner].

S.095

AS WITNESS the duly authorised representatives of the parties the day and year first above written

Signed by [–]

On behalf of [Company]

In the presence of [–] and year hereinbefore written.

Executed and Delivered as Deed by [–]

Signed Director [–]

Director/Company Secretary [–]

Executed and Delivered as a Deed by [–]

Signed by: Individual [–] Witness

S.096

Signed by [–] Date [–]

FOR AND ON BEHALF OF [–]

In the presence of [–] Date [–]

Signed by [–] Date [–]

FOR AND ON BEHALF OF [–]

In the presence of [–] Date [–]

Signed by [–] Date [–]

S.097

Signed by [–] Date [–]

For and on behalf of the Company.

Signed by [–] Date [–]

For and on behalf of the Designer.

S.098

Name of [Author] [–] Signature [–]

Address [–] Date [–]

Name of [Company] [–] Signature [–]

Address [–] Date [–]

S.099

Name and Title [–]

Signed by [–] The Assignor Date [–]

Name and Title [–]

Signed by [–] The Assignee Date [–]

S.100

Executed and delivered as a deed by [–]

Signed by [–] Witness

Signed by [–] Company Secretary

S.101

Signed by [–]

For and on behalf of the Artist.

[Print Name/date]

Signed by [–]

For and on behalf of the Agent

[Print Name/date]

S.102

Agreement dated [–]

1498

[signature] [Title/Name]

[Sponsor]

[signature] [Title/Name]

[Sportsperson]

S.103

Signed by the Presenter [–]

[Print Name in full]

Signed by the [Company] [–]

[Print Name in full]

Agreement dated [–]

S.104

If [person] is under eighteen years signed by parent/guardian [–]

S.105

For and on behalf of the [Sponsor] [–]

For and on behalf of the [Association] [–]

S.106

Date of the Agreement [–]

Signed by:

Website Company [–]

Advertiser [–]

S.107

Name [–]

Designation [–]

Signed by [–] [date]

For and on behalf of the Company.

Name [–]

Designation [–]

Signed by [–] [date]

For and on behalf of the Executive.

S.108

In the event that this Agreement is not executed by the [Licensee] within [forty-five days] of dispatch by the [Licensor], then the [Licensor] shall have the right at its sole discretion to withdraw the offer set out in this by written notice to the [Licensee].

S.109

In the event that the [Author] in this Agreement is more than one person then all such persons confirm that they will be jointly and severally bound by the terms of this Agreement and that any part of this Agreement in the singular shall apply to each person separately.

S.110

Each member of the [Group] acknowledges that he/she is jointly and individually bound by the terms of this Agreement.

S.111

All members of the [Group] confirm that they are [18/21] years of age or older at the date of signing this Agreement. Any member who is not [18] years of age must have this Agreement signed by a parent or guardian.

S.112

The [Author] confirms that he/she has taken specialist legal advice and fully understands the consequences of signing this document.

S.113

The [Operator] shall upon request provide the [Contractor] with a copy of every counterpart of this Agreement or substantially similar agreement which is executed by another [Signatory] pertaining to the [Operations].

S.114

This Agreement shall become binding on the [Contractor] and the [Signatories] on the date of execution by the [Contractor] or the execution of the counterpart of this Agreement by all the [Signatories].

S.115

[Name] agrees that they are authorised to sign this Agreement on behalf of the [Company] and have the approval of the Board of the Directors.

S.116

[Name] confirms that there is no mental and/or legal reason why they are not capable of signing this Agreement. [Name] confirms that they have read all the terms and be advised to seek independent legal advice.

S.117

Signed by [Name] as the representative and on behalf of the [Charity] [–]
Signed by Chair of the [Sponsor] [–].
Date executed by both parties [–].

SOFTWARE

General Business and Commercial

S.118

'The Software' shall mean the source code of the computer and the binary
code the machine readable coded programme [excluding the server] known
as [specify name].

S.119

The [Company] agrees to supply at no additional cost any modifications,
additions, amendments, adjustments and/or error corrections at its sole cost
to the [Licensee] for that edition of the [Software], but not a copy of any later
edition.

S.120

The [Licensee] is granted a non-exclusive non-transferable licence by
the [Company] to use the [Software] [and data] for the purpose which it is
intended [indefinitely/until date]

S.121

The [Licensee] agrees that no right is granted by the [Company] to the
[Licensee]:

1.1 To make additional copies [except for one back up copy].

1.2 To reproduce, exploit, adapt, license, translate, develop the [Software]
and/or any content for any reason.

1.3 To sub-license, permit, authorise, assign and/or transfer any rights of
any nature in the [Software] to any third party.

1.4 To make any digital and/or electronic files of the [Software] available
over the internet and/or to sell, supply, distribute, upload and/or make
available the [Software] and/or any part to any other persons and/or
websites.

S.122

The [Company] does not accept any responsibility for any errors, defects, omissions, failures, losses, damages and/or other liability arising directly and/or indirectly from the installation, use and/or any modifications, additions, amendments, adjustments and/or error corrections supplied by the [Company] at any time and/or any other matters of any nature arising from the [Software]. The [Licensee] must install and use the [Software] and any other material entirely at its own risk and cost and the [Company] shall be liable for any costs of any nature that may arise unless personal injury and/or death directly caused by the negligence of the [Company].

S.123

The [Licensee] agrees that it shall not acquire any rights in any copyright, intellectual property rights and/or computer programme rights and/or database rights in the [Software] and/or any data and/or the source code and/or the title. The [Licensee] agrees not to erase, delete and/or alter any copyright notices and/or warnings on any part of the [Software] and any additional material at any time.

S.124

The [Supplier] is not providing any copyright and/or ownership of the computer software programme which is owned by [specify]. The [Supplier] is developing and adapting the software programme to suit the requirements of the [Company] and to assist in the upgrade of the computer software in accordance with the specification in appendix [–] which forms part of this Agreement.

S.125

The [Supplier] agrees that the [Company] must be able to test and approve the capacity and functionality of the computer software prior to the payment of the instalment due on completion of the [Project]. That in the event that the system does not function as expected and there are unresolved problems. Then the final payment must be delayed until the [Company] has approved all the work.

S.126

The [Supplier] confirms that maintenance and later upgrades are not part of this Agreement and required additional payments and agreements to be concluded.

S.127

Where the [Company] wishes to add features, functions, tools and/or development to the computer software and system which were not part of the original specification agreed at the start. Then the [Supplier] shall be entitled to charge and be paid additional sums for any extra work.

SOUND RECORDINGS

General Business and Commercial

S.128

'The Sound Recordings' shall be the sound recordings of the performance by the [Artist] for and on behalf of the [Record Company] made during the Term of this Agreement regardless of the medium on which the sound recording is made or the method by which the sounds are produced or reproduced.

S.129

'Sound Recording' shall mean the sound recording of [specify subject] which has and/or will be made by [Name] regardless of the medium on which the sound recording is made or the method by which the sounds are produced or reproduced, but does not include a film soundtrack when accompanying a film.

S.130

'The Master Recordings' shall mean all sound recordings of the [Interviewee] made by or for the [Interviewer] for the purpose of the [Article/Work] regardless of the medium on which the sound recording is made or the method by which the sounds are produced or reproduced.

S.131

'The Sound Recording' shall [be defined in accordance with of the Copyright, Designs and Patents Act 1988 as amended and shall] mean:

1.1　A recording of sounds from which sounds may be reproduced; or

1.2　A recording of the whole or any part of a literary, dramatic or musical work from which sounds reproducing the work may be produced.

This applies regardless of the medium on which the recording is made or the methods by which the sounds are reproduced or produced.

S.132

The [Licensor] agrees to attend at such times, dates and locations as the [Licensee] may reasonably require to assist in the sound recordings of the [Work] and the dubbing of the sound recording for the [Series], subject to reasonable notice.

S.133

The [Company] agrees and undertakes that it shall not use the sound recordings and/or any part and/or licence, transfer and/or authorise the use and/or adaptation by others of the sound recordings for any purpose except [specify authorised purpose]. Any other use and/or exploitation shall require the prior written consent of the [Licensor].

S.134

At the end of the Licence Period all copies of the [Sound Recordings/Film/ Stills/other] in any format and any medium shall be returned to the [Licensor] at the [Licensees] cost and expense and confirmation in writing provided by the [Licensee] that neither it nor any third party that it has engaged to work on the [Project] have in their possession and/or control any material.

S.135

'The Sound Recordings' shall mean all the sound recordings of the discussions and interviews between [Name] and the [Presenter] on behalf of the [Company] regardless of the medium on which the recording is made and/or the methods by which the sounds are produced and/or reproduced.

S.136

'The Exclusive [Sound Recording] Rights' shall mean the sole and exclusive right to exercise, license, and/or authorise any third party [to the exclusion of all others and the copyright owner] the right to reproduce, supply, distribute and/or exploit the [Sound Recordings] of the [Work].

S.137

The [Licensor] agrees that the [Licensee] shall be entitled to sub-license the [Sound Recordings] reproduced in the [Disc] to third parties for the purpose of the sound and music being reproduced for advertisements and/or other use on television, radio, banner advertisements, ringtones, storage and retrieval systems for supply of music to the public, podcasts, films, plays, conferences and shopping centres.

S.138

The [Licensee] shall not have the right to advertise, promote, display, package, distribute and/or reproduce the [Sound Recordings] in the [Disc] in association with any sponsorship, merchandising, marketing and/or promotion by a third party without the prior written consent of the [Licensor].

S.139

The [Licensee] grants the [Sub-Licensee] the non-exclusive right to play the [Sound Recording] in conjunction with the [Podcast] of [Name] on the [Website] from [date] to [date] for viewing by the public over the internet. The [Sub-Licensee] shall not be entitled to make the [Sound Recording] available as a download and/or digital and/or electronic file and/or to authorise and/ or permit the public to make copies and/or otherwise reproduce the [Sound Recordings].

S.140

The [Sound Recordings] of the [Event] which are made by [Name] on behalf of the [Sponsor] may be used in conjunction with any promotional banner link and/or advertisement by the [Sponsor] for a period of [number] months from the date of the [Event]. Provided that the [Sponsor] pays the [Charity] the sum of [number/currency] by [date].

S.141

[Name] grants the [Company] the non-exclusive right to transmit and/or reproduce the [Sound Recordings] from a large screen and/or white board and/or other device as part of an [Exhibition/Conference] in conjunction with the [Products/Artworks]. Provided that a credit and trade and logo is provided on screen at all times as follows [specify] and an advance fee of [number/currency] is paid to [Name] before that date.

STATUTORY PROVISIONS

General Business and Commercial

S.142

Any reference to any statutory provision shall be deemed to include a reference to any statutory modification or re-enactment of the same.

S.143

References herein to any statute or regulation shall be deemed to extend to any statute or regulation passed in substitution thereof or amending substantially, re-enacting or consolidating the same.

S.144

[The Interpretation Act 1978 as amended] shall apply for the purpose of interpreting the conditions of this Agreement subject to any judgment, directive, regulation and/or other legislation which may be applicable.

S.145

Reference to any statute or any statutory provision shall include reference to any statute provisions which amends, extends, consolidates or replaces the same and to any other regulation, instrument or other subordinate legislation made under the statute.

S.146

All statutory rights of the [Buyer/Hirer] are reserved.

S.147

The [Contractor] shall ensure compliance with, and give all notices required by, any Act of Parliament, any instrument, rule or order made under any Act of Parliament or any regulation or byelaw of any local authority or of any statutory body which has any jurisdiction with regard to the [Project].

S.148

The [Contractor] shall be entitled to do such things and order such materials for the [Project] as may be necessary in order to comply with any statutory provisions in order to avoid exposure of the [Contractor] and/ or the [Company] to civil or criminal proceedings. The [Contractor] shall immediately provide written notice of the circumstances to the [Company]. The [Company] agrees to bear the cost of compliance provided that it is reasonable and necessary in each case.

S.149

The [Contractor] shall not be liable for the failure to comply with any statutory provisions in the event that he/she has been instructed by an officer of the [Company] either orally or in writing not to do so. The [Company] agrees to bear full responsibility for such direction and any consequences which may arise from such failure to comply with any statutory provisions.

S.150

You will in relation to the [Goods/Services] comply and it is a condition of this order that the [Goods/Services] comply and will continue to comply with the provisions applicable to the design, manufacture, production, content, durability, packaging, supply and use of the [Goods/Services] (whether express or implied) of any statute, regulation, rule, directive, or order in force at the time of delivery.

S.151

The [Work/Goods/Services] shall be performed and delivered in accordance with any statutes, directives, regulations, codes, industry practice which shall exist either at the time of signature of this Agreement or may come into force at any time thereafter until the expiry or termination of this Agreement in [countries].

S.152

Each party under this Agreement shall be responsible for ensuring its own compliance with any statutes, directives, regulations, policies, standards, codes of any nature including but not limited to the reproduction, supply, distribution, packaging, product liability, advertising, sponsorship, product placement, health, safety, environmental, recycling or otherwise. Further each such party shall bear the cost of any fines, damages, losses and/or other liability and/or expenses that may arise and shall not be entitled to offset them against any sums due under this Agreement to the other party.

S.153

This Agreement shall be subject to legislation, directives, Codes of Practice, guidelines and policies which apply in [country]. Where there is any reference to any legislation it shall also include subsequent amendments and/or repeals relating to that subject

SUB-LICENCE

General Business and Commercial

S.154

1.1 The [Company] reserves the right and shall be entitled to assign, sub-license, sub-contract, transfer and/or appoint any subsidiary, affiliate, associate, and/or parent company and/or third party to fulfil the terms, condition, rights and/or obligations to [Name] without notice at any time.

1.2 In the event of 1.1 [and the subsequent agreement by [Name] the [Company] shall be under no further obligation to [Name] and shall be relieved of its rights or obligations under this Agreement. Nor shall the [Company] be responsible and/or liable for any acts, omissions and failures of any party in 1.1.

S.155

The [Company] shall notify [Name] of the appointment of any third party who have been engaged to provide [Services/Work/Goods] in order to assist the [Company] in the fulfilment in the terms of this Agreement. The [Company] shall only be required to provide a copy of the sub-licence or other document to [Name] where the payment is in excess of [figure/currency] per annum and it is intended to claim this sum as part of the Expenses.

S.156

The [Licensee] may sub-license any of its rights and benefits in whole or part to any person, firm or company who shall then be entitled to the same rights and benefits with regard to the [Property] as the [Licensee] has under this Agreement including the right to sub-licence.

S.157

Where in this Agreement the [Company] acquires any rights or licence or undertakes any liability or obligation, the [Company] shall be entitled to grant such right or licence or to delegate such liability or obligation to [any third party/any associates] provided that the [Company] shall continue to ensure fulfilment of the terms of this Agreement to the [Licensor].

S.158

Unless otherwise stated, sub-contracting shall be permitted.

S.159

Both parties to this Agreement shall be entitled to sub-license or sub-contract any of the terms or conditions of this Agreement. Provided that they shall each remain bound by all its terms and conditions and shall ensure that they are fulfilled in the event that the sub-licensee or sub-contractor should not perform, breach or default in any circumstances.

S.160

The [Contractor] shall be liable for the acts, defaults, and neglects of any sub-contractor, his/her servants, workforce and agents as if they were deemed to be the acts, defaults, or neglect of the [Contractor].

S.161

The [Distributor] may sub-license or sub-contract the manufacture of the [Product] to a wholly owned subsidiary of the [Distributor] for so long as it is a wholly owned subsidiary in respect of the rights granted in Clause [–]. The [Distributor] shall remain responsible and liable for all acts or omissions of such sub-licensees or sub-contractors as though they were by the [Distributor].

S.162

The [Distributor] shall immediately notify the [Company] of any sub-licence or sub-contract granted and provide details of the parties.

S.163

Except for Clause [–] above the [Distributor] may not grant any sub-license or sub-contract in respect of the [Product] without the prior written consent of the [Company].

S.164

In the event that the [Company] provides written consent to the appointment of any third party to perform any part of this Agreement on behalf of the

[Distributor]. The [Distributor] undertakes and agrees that it shall be a condition of such consent by the [Company] that the [Distributor] shall grant any sub-licence or sub-contract on the same terms and conditions as are set out in this Agreement including in particular Clauses [–]. The only exception shall be that any sub-licence or sub-contract shall expire or terminate automatically upon the expiry or termination of this Agreement. Where in this Agreement the consent or approval of the [Company] is required or there is any right of inspection, audit or otherwise, then the [Distributor] will ensure that the same provisions giving such rights directly to the [Company] shall be set out in any sub-licence or sub-contract. The [Distributor] shall be responsible for and liable to the [Company] for the performance and adherence to any such sub-licence or sub-contract.

S.165

For the avoidance of doubt this Agreement contains the full rights and obligations conferred upon the parties to this Agreement and shall not be construed as conferring upon the [Licensee] or its assignees or successors in title any franchising, sub-contracting, or sub-licensing rights of any nature.

S.166

The [Licensee] agrees that no sub-contracting arrangement or sub-licence (whether referred to as a franchise agreement or otherwise) of any nature will be entered into with any third party without the prior written approval of the [Licensor].

S.167

All Franchise Rights exercised by the [Licensee] under this Agreement shall only be exercised in accordance with the detailed terms of this Agreement. This Agreement does not permit and is not intended in any way to confer any greater rights upon any third party which are any way greater than those granted to the [Licensee] under this Agreement, including but not by way of limitation to the [specify particular clauses].

S.168

Any rights granted by any sub-licence by the [Licensee] shall be subject and restricted to the terms of this Agreement and shall not provide or purport to provide any greater rights to the sub-licensee than the [Licensor] has granted to the [Licensee].

S.169

The [Licensee] shall at all times be responsible for all acts, omissions and other matters arising directly or indirectly from any sub-licences and any sub-licensees as set out under the terms of this Agreement including without limitation to all accounting provisions under Clauses [–] and all indemnity provisions under Clauses [–].

S.170

Where the [Company] authorises the [Contractor] to sub-contract all or part of the Work to third parties, the [Company] shall remain bound by its obligations to the [Company] under the contract.

S.171

The [Contractor] shall be required to include in any contracts signed with third parties for all or part of the [Work] terms and conditions enabling the [Company] to have the same rights and guarantees in relation to the third parties as in relation to the [Contractor] itself. The [Contractor] shall be bound to ensure that there are such contractual obligations to the [Company] unless the [Company] provides written consent that they need not apply.

S.172

The [Company] may not grant any sub-licence under this Agreement nor may the [Company] sub-contract the work of developing, manufacturing, supplying and/or distributing and/or advertising and/or marketing the [Product/Service] without the prior written consent of the [Licensor].

S.173

If the [Licensor] consents to any third party being appointed as a sub-licensee or otherwise the [Company] undertakes it shall be a condition of such consent that:

1.1   Such appointment shall be by a written sub-licence subject to the same undertakings as set out in Clauses [–] and shall be brought to an end either by termination or expiry on the same date as this Agreement.

1.2   The [Company] shall ensure and be responsible to the [Licensor] for the performance, observance and liabilities of the sub-licensee or any other third party so appointed.

S.174

The [Licensee] shall not assign the benefit of the Licence which is purely personal in nature and shall not grant any sub-licence under this Agreement.

S.175

[Name] agrees that the [Company] may sub-license the rights granted in the [Work] to a third party provided the prior written consent of [Name] is provided and the sub-licence is limited to the rights granted to the [Company]. The sub-licence shall not release the [Company] from the obligations to [Name] and all reports, statements and payments shall be made direct from the [Company] to [Name].

Internet and Websites

S.176
In consideration of the payment of the Fees and Royalties the [Licensor] grants the [Licensee] the right to sub-license the [Work] reproduced in the [Disc/Sound Recording] to third parties for the purpose of the sound, music and lyrics being reproduced for advertisements and/or other use on television, radio, banner advertisements, ringtones, storage and retrieval systems for supply of music to the public, podcasts, films, plays, conferences and exhibitions, shopping centres, airports and any other form of commercial exploitation.

S.177
In consideration of the Fee the [Licensor] grants the [Licensee] the right to sub-license the [Work] reproduced in the [Disc/Sound Recording] to third parties to advertise, promote, display, package, distribute and/or reproduce the [Work] reproduced in the [Disc/Sound Recording] in association with any sponsorship, merchandising, marketing and/or promotion by such third party.

S.178
In consideration of [figure/currency] the [Licensor] grants the [Licensee] the non-exclusive right to play the [Disc/Sound Recording/Work] in conjunction with the opening credits of the [Podcasts] of different persons developed by the [Licensee] on the [Website] for the duration of the Licence period. The [Licensee] shall be entitled to permit the [Disc/Sound Recording/Work] in conjunction with the opening credits of the [Podcasts] to be viewed by the public over the internet and/or from any mobile and/or other gadget with and/or without any payment. The [Licensee] shall be entitled to make the [Disc/Sound Recording/Work] in conjunction with the opening credits of the [Podcasts] available as a download and/or digital and/or electronic file and/or to authorise and/or permit the public to store the [Disc/Sound Recording/Work] in conjunction with the opening credits of the [Podcasts] for a period of [one] month after which it must be deleted.

S.179

1.1 [Name] agrees and accepts that the [Distributor] may grant multiple non-exclusive and/or exclusive sub-licences to third parties and/or affiliates to exploit, market and promote the [Work] and/or parts at any time.

1.2   [Name] agrees and accepts that payments due may be directly from the [Distributor] and/or any sub-licensee through a payment agency [specify].

Merchandising

S.180

The [Licensor] undertakes that it shall not license nor permit any third party to produce, manufacture, supply and/or distribute the [Game] and/or the Prototype including any developments or variations throughout the Territory for the duration of the Licence Period.

S.181

The [Licensee] shall be fully liable for all acts, omissions and failures to pay of any sub-distributor, sub-agent or sub-licensee.

S.182

The [Licensee] shall ensure that its sub-agents and sub-licensees shall keep full and accurate accounting records, contract and payment systems to which the [Licensor] shall be granted regular access for inspection, accounting and stock purposes.

S.183

The [Company] agrees that the [Licensor] shall be entitled to approve the appointment of any sub-agent, sub-licensee, distributor and any other third party in respect of the development, production, manufacture, distribution, marketing and exploitation of the [Licensed Articles] under this Agreement.

S.184

The [Licensee] shall have no right to discharge his/her obligations under this Agreement through any sub-agent or sub-licensee without prior written approval of the [Licensor] such approval not to be unreasonably withheld or delayed.

S.185

'Sub-Licensee' shall mean any person, firm or company appointed by the [Licensee] in accordance with Clause [–].

S.186

The [Company] may sub-license or sub-contract the manufacture of the [Product] to a wholly owned subsidiary of the [Company] (as long as it remains so) provided that the [Company] shall remain responsible for all acts or omissions of such sub-licensees or sub-contractors as though they were by the [Company].

S.187

1.1   It is hereby acknowledged that the rights of the [Licensee] hereunder are strictly personal to the [Licensee] who shall not wholly or partially assign the licence nor grant any sub-licence relating to the [Property] or any part to any other person, firm or company.

1.2   However the [Licensee] may arrange for a third party to manufacture for the [Licensee's] own benefit and purpose alone the [Licensed Articles] subject to the prior written consent of the [Licensor] and upon condition that the third party signs a written agreement not to supply the [Licensed Articles] to any person or company other than the [Licensee].

1.3   The [Licensee] agrees that he shall not charge nor grant any rights under the licence or in the [Property] or any part nor in any way part with the control of the licence or its rights hereunder.

S.188
The [Licensee] acknowledges and agrees that the [Licensor] shall have and retain the sole and exclusive right as against the [Licensee] to license any third party to use the [Property] in connection with any articles other than the [Licensed Articles].

S.189
The [Licensee] shall ensure that its sub-agents and sub-licensees shall keep full and accurate accounting records, contract and payment systems to which the [Licensor] shall be granted regular access for inspection, accounting and stock purposes.

S.190
The [Company] agrees that the [Distributor] shall be entitled to sub-license the [Work] in whole and/or in part to reputable sub-licensees provided that they have been in business for at least [three] years and the [Distributor] undertakes:

1.1   That any such sub-licence shall be subject to the prior written approval of the [Company].

1.2   That any such sub-licence shall not adversely effect the obligations of the [Distributor] to the [Company] and

1.3   The [Distributor] undertakes to be liable to the [Company] for the acts, omissions, errors and default of any sub-licensee.

1.4   That the [Distributor] shall indemnify the [Company] against any loss, damage and/or claim and/or allegation caused directly and/or indirectly by any sub-licensee.

S.191

The [Licensee] agrees that the [Sub-Licensee] shall be entitled to sub-license and/or authorise the [Work/Product] to third parties for the purpose of being reproduced and/or used in advertisements, product placement and/or other use on television, radio, websites, mobiles, ringtones, films, plays, conferences and shopping centres.

S.192

The [Licensee] shall not have the right to advertise, promote, display, package, distribute and/or reproduce the [Work/Product] in association with any sales, sponsorship, merchandising, marketing and/or promotion by a third party without the prior written consent of the [Licensor].

S.193

The [Licensee] grants the [Sub-Licensee] the non-exclusive right to reproduce the [Work/Product] in the form of a [specify article] in conjunction with [Name] from [date] to [date] for the charitable purpose of [specify].

S.194

The [Licensee] agrees to provide a complete copy of all sub-licences and sub-distribution agreements to the [Licensor].

Publishing

S.195

The [Publishing Company] shall not be entitled to assign any of the rights hereunder nor grant a sub-licence without prior written consent of the [Licensor].

S.196

The [Publisher] shall consult in good faith with the [Author] in respect of the appointment of any third party to exploit the [Work].

S.197

The [Publisher] agrees to consult with the [Author] as to the terms and conditions for sub-licensing the rights to a third party and shall ensure that no agreement shall be concluded with a third party which is likely to go into administration and/or insolvency.

Purchase and Supply of Products

S.198

This Agreement is personal to the [Customer] who may not assign, sub-license or sub-contract in whole or part.

S.199
You shall not at any time assign, transfer, sub-contract or sub-license the [Order] to any third party.

S.200
The [Supplier] shall under all circumstances be solely and exclusively liable to the [Company] and to third parties for the performance of the contract.

S.201
Except where otherwise provided the [Contractor] shall not sub-contract any part of the [Work] without the prior consent of the [Company].

S.202
The [Contractor] shall be entitled to sub-contract any part of the [Work] which is only minor in nature, or for the purchase of materials or for any manufacturer or supplier named in the Contract.

S.203
The [Company] reserves the right to assign, transfer, sub-license, sub-contract or otherwise any of its rights and/or obligations to the [Customer] without notice. Provided that no such assignment, sub-licence or sub-contract shall, unless the parties otherwise agree, relieve the [Company] of its rights or obligations under this Agreement.

S.204
The [Company] reserves the right to sub-contract the performance of the Contract or any part thereof.

S.205
The [Distributor] shall not be entitled to sub-license any copyright and/or other intellectual property rights in the [Work] reproduced in the [Product] and/or to authorise any reproduction and/or exploitation by a third party.

S.206
It is agreed between parties that no sub-licence shall be granted to any third party which cannot produce three sets of certified accounts for the last three financial period prior to the proposed date of any agreement.

SUBSIDIARY

General Business and Commercial

S.207

'Subsidiary Company' shall mean [as afforded under the Companies Act 1985 as amended, revised, modified and/or extended] a Company shall be deemed to be a subsidiary of another if (but only if) that other is either a member of it and controls the composition of its Board of Directors, or holds more than half in nominal value of its equity share capital, or is a subsidiary of any company which is that other's subsidiary.

S.208

For the purposes of this Agreement a company is deemed to be another's holding company if (but only if) the other is a subsidiary, and a company is deemed the wholly owned subsidiary of another if it has no members except that other and that other's wholly owned subsidiaries and its or their nominees.

S.209

'Subsidiary Company' shall mean a company and/or body corporate which shall be deemed to be a subsidiary if [51]%[fifty-one] per cent of another body corporate holds, controls, or owns its ordinary share capital directly or indirectly through another body corporate or other bodies corporate or partly directly and partly through another body corporate or otherwise.

SUSPENSION

General Business and Commercial

S.210

The [Publisher] shall be entitled by notice to suspend the engagement of the [Composer's] services in the event that:

1.1 The [Composer] does not observe and abide by or fails to perform any of the services or obligations, undertakings or warranties or is otherwise in breach of this Agreement.

1.2 The [Composer] shall have been prevented from performing the services by injury, illness, mental or physical disability or otherwise or shall be in the opinion of the [Publisher] incapable of performing the services for any reason.

1.3   The Composer shall have died or ceased to work as a composer.

1.4   Any force majeure circumstance which shall prevent the [Composer] from making use of or exploiting the [Work]. Fulfilling the terms of this Agreement for more than [one] week,

1.5   The Period of such suspension shall continue indefinitely until notice of resumption of service is given by the [Publisher]. During any period of suspension the [Publisher] shall not be obliged to pay the [Composer] any remuneration and the dates of any further payment obligations shall be extended by a period equivalent to the length of the suspension as shall the length of the engagement.

1.6   Throughout the period of suspension the [Composer] shall continue to comply with all of the obligations on the part of the [Composer] in this Agreement and the Composer undertakes not to enter into any agreement relating to the services of the [Composer] with any other person without the prior consent of the [Publisher].

1.7   The [Publisher] will remain entitled to all rights granted or assigned to the [Publisher] by the Composer.

1.8   Suspension by the [Publisher] shall be in addition to and without prejudice to any of the other rights or remedies of the [Publisher].

S.211

The Company shall be entitled to suspend the engagement of the [Director] in the event that:

1.1   The [Project] is prevented, delayed, interfered with or interrupted by any cause beyond the control of the [Company] (including without limitation fire, accident, war, civil disturbance, Act of God, lockout, strike, labour disturbance, illness or injury of key personnel); or

1.2   The [Director] shall refuse or neglect to render any of his/her services hereunder; or

1.3   The [Employer] shall be in breach of any of its material obligations hereunder; or

1.4   The [Director] shall be or become unable by reason of mental or physical incapacity to render his/her services hereunder.

In the event that the services of the [Director] are suspended the [Employer] shall not be obliged to make the [Director's] services available hereunder but shall continue to comply with the provisions of Clauses [–] and shall not bind the [Director] to any contractual obligation which might conflict with the obligations hereunder at the end of the suspension. The Company shall remain entitled to all rights hereby granted in all services rendered by the [Director] and the [Products] thereof. The Company may extend the engagement for a period equal to the total period of suspension.

S.212

[Name] may be suspended by the [Company] on any of the following grounds provided that the [Company] shall continue to pay such sums as may be due to [Name] until such time as the suspension shall end or the Agreement is terminated:

1.1 [Name] shall fail to submit to a medical examination and/or drug test in any year.

1.2 The business of the [Company] is materially prejudiced by the conduct of the [Name].

1.3 The function or position of [Name] in the [Company] has ceased due to reorganisation.

1.4 The [Name] has committed an act of dishonesty, breach of confidentiality, or gross misconduct.

S.213

The [Company] shall not have the right to suspend the services of the [Consultant] for any reason whether with or without payment. Any suspension shall be deemed a termination of this Agreement by the [Company].

S.214

The [Distributor] shall have the right to suspend the [Name/Work/Service/ other] for a period not to exceed [three calendar months] in any one year in the following circumstances:

1.1 If the [Name/Company] is unable [fulfil the work/supply the products] required under this Agreement whether due to lack of time, lack of skilled labour, faulty equipment, illness or injury.

1.2 If the [Name/Company] enters into any agreement with a third party which conflicts with this Agreement.

1.3 If the [Name/Company] shall fail or neglect to perform any term of this Agreement and it is not remedied within [fourteen days] of notice to that effect from the [Distributor].

S.215

There shall be no right or consent of any nature under this Agreement to any form of suspension, delay without payment, gardening leave, holding the agreement in abeyance or requiring any of the terms to be removed or parties not to fulfil the terms as set out. This Agreement shall continue without interruption until it expires or is terminated.

S.216

In the event that the [Employee] is asked to leave the premises suddenly and without [seven days'] written notice or suspended or told to go on gardening leave and/or asked to be on paid leave which is to continue indefinitely, then the [Employee] shall be entitled to the sum of [figure/currency] which shall be in addition to any other rights and remedies that the [Employee] may have in law. This sum is intended to compensate the [Employee] for the failure of the Employer to act in good faith and the deliberate act of failing to provide the [Employee] with reasonable notice.

S.217

In the event that the [Website], any service, product, game, telephone care service, delivery, payment facility and/or other content and/or any associated company and/or any directly and/or indirectly related other matter is not available, suspended and/or withdrawn, recalled, cancelled and/or otherwise terminated. Then the [Company] shall not be responsible for, and/or liable for any costs, expenses, damages, losses which may be incurred and/or any acts, omissions, errors, failures and/or non-compliance by any agent, sub-licensee, distributor or otherwise and the total liability shall be limited to a refund of any sums paid by the [Customer] to the [Company] for any product, service and/or other work.

S.218

The [Service] may be suspended by the [Company] due to force majeure and/or loss of energy and/or power failure, floods, maintenance work and/or upgrade work and/or riots, war, acts of violence and/or delays in travel and/or any other reason. The [Company] shall post notices on its website with regular updates as to the expected time before it is resolved.

TAXES

General Business and Commercial

T.001
The [Contractor] shall promptly pay directly to the appropriate government or authority all taxes, levies, and assessments imposed on the [Contractor] and its personnel and agents by any government or authority having or claiming jurisdiction in the areas in which the operations under this Contract are carried out. The [Contractor] shall be solely liable for all sums due arising out of or in connection with the [Contractor's] performance under this Contract including, but not limited to, corporate and personal income taxes, employment taxes, sales taxes, customs and excise taxes, stamp tax, social insurance taxes, contractor licence or business privilege taxes or any other tax, levy or assessment.

T.002
Where the [Author] is resident outside [the United Kingdom] and he/she is liable under [English Law] to be charged income tax at the appropriate rate, then the [Publishers] shall be entitled to deduct such amounts from any sums due to the [Author] where there is a double taxation agreement between the [United Kingdom] and the country in which the [Author] resides and the [Author] has completed and returned the relevant documentation to the appropriate tax authorities in the [United Kingdom]. In the event that the [Author] provides sufficient proof to the [Publishers] that he/she is entitled to receive payment without any such deduction for tax the [Publishers] at their sole discretion may pay all the sums due to the [Author].

T.003
The [Company] shall be responsible for complying with the national and European Union taxes, levy, assessment, social insurance payment and currency laws, directives and regulations of any country which may be applicable in respect of the fulfilment of the terms of this Contract by the [Company].

T.004

The [Company] shall not be obliged to make any payment to [Name] in any case where by reason of taxes, levies, assessments, social insurance, currency or other controls by an overseas territory from which payment is due the monies due to the [Company] shall be withheld, reduced, or only become payable in the overseas territory. However the use of and access to such sums by the [Company] shall be deemed to be receipts by the [Company] and then payment shall become due to [Name].

T.005

All payments by either party to the other under or pursuant to this Agreement shall be made without any deduction or withholding of any sums unless the deductions or withholding is required by law. In such a case the party who is responsible shall pay the amount withheld promptly to the appropriate authority and shall provide the other party with a verified original document (or other reasonable evidence) issued by that authority on the receipt of the amount withheld.

T.006

All charges are exclusive of tax and must be paid without any deduction whatsoever and where relevant, value added tax, sales tax, or any other tax imposed or levied upon the service shall be paid by the [Customer] in addition to the charges.

T.007

The [Sportsperson] agrees that he/she shall be responsible for his/her own national insurance, personal tax and value added tax which shall be due in consequence of this Agreement.

T.008

The [Manager] agrees to assist [Name] in the financial management of all the [Name's] Fees and financial affairs generally including tax, expenses, value added tax, national insurance, pension, health contributions and personal insurance. [Name] shall seek the benefit of specialist professional advice where appropriate and shall not seek to rely on the [Manager] to arrange and pay for such matters.

T.009

[Name] acknowledges that although the [Manager] shall assist in the [Name's] financial affairs, [Name] shall be ultimately responsible for seeking expert professional advice and paying for such costs and expenses together with his/her own value added tax, national and personal insurance, pension and health contributions arising under this Agreement.

T.010

1.1 The Dealer Price is exclusive of tax and must be paid without any deduction whatsoever. Where relevant value added tax, sales tax or any other tax shall be paid by the [Seller]. Payment of any tax shall require a proper invoice with full details.

1.2 The [Seller] shall be responsible for complying with all national and international tax, import and export laws applicable to the fulfilment of this Agreement by the [Seller] and shall bear the cost of relevant expert advice that may be required and shall comply with payment deadlines.

T.011

The [Publisher] shall be responsible for complying with and payment of any national, European and/or international tax laws that may apply to the sums under this Agreement in respect of the [Company]. All sums due to the [Author] shall as far as possible be paid unless the [Company] is required by law to withhold them or pay a part to a government agency, European or international body. All sums withheld or paid to third parties shall be verified by supporting documentation. The [Author] shall be responsible for complying with any national, European and/or international tax laws that may apply to the sums paid to the [Author] by the [Company].

T.012

All charges and payments are not inclusive of taxes, levies or other sums of any kind that may be imposed by Law. Taxes may be deducted and/or added as required by Law depending on the circumstances but in each case shall be a separate itemised figure with appropriate reference to the type of tax, the rate and any codes or registration number, and whether it is deducted or added to the sum.

T.013

All [sums/prices/other] are exclusive of taxes of any kind unless otherwise stated. Any sales tax, value added tax or any other taxes or levies which are due to or imposed by any government or authority which are not included must be stated as a separate itemised section of the invoice, with the type of tax, the rate and relevant registration or other details.

T.014

All payments and charges are exclusive of tax. Any sums deducted and/or added for exchange rate or currency controls or tax purposes must be specified.

T.015

Each party shall be responsible for the cost and expense of their own [personal/corporate] tax and national insurance liability, payments and costs.

T.016

All charges, payments and sums shall be exclusive of sales tax, value added tax and any other sum due on the sale or supply of [Products] that may be payable by either party. There shall be a separate itemised charge or additional cost as appropriate on each relevant sales or payment document for any such taxes which shall be paid, withheld or transferred as appropriate.

T.017

The [Company] shall pay the [Settlement Fee] without deduction of tax and/or national insurance in accordance with the [Inland Revenue] policy document reference [–].

T.018

All refunds and/or rebates of any taxes due to be received by the [Company] shall be included in the calculation of the assets and value of the [Company] as at [date].

T.019

Each member of the [Consortium] shall be responsible for their own corporation taxes, insurance, customs and excise and other duties and taxes that may fall due under this Agreement.

TENDER

General Business and Commercial

T.020

1.1 The Tender may be awarded by the [Company] based on any number of factors which the [Company] may decide in its absolute discretion to be a significant criteria for the [Work/Services/other].

1.2 There shall be no obligation to award the contract to be lowest bidder in terms of cost, price or otherwise.

1.3 Nor shall the [Company] be obliged to justify and/or state reasons for the award and/or the rejection of any party who may apply.

T.021

The [Company] may vary, adapt and/or modify the terms, subject and conditions of the tender process and/or application format at any time and/

or withdraw the Tender. The [Company] shall not be responsible for and/ or liable to any party who may have incurred costs and/or expenses of any nature in respect of any application and tender for a contract at any time. All parties become part of the application process and award at their own cost, risk and expense whether guided by the terms and conditions set out by the [Company] or not.

T.022
The [Company] shall consider all the factors in any applicants submission for the contract and may at its absolute discretion request further information, data and/or evidence and/or fail to permit an applicant to proceed to the final selection due to an inadequate submission.

T.023
The [Company] shall not be bound to consider the [value/price] of the [quotation/tender] for the [Work/Service] to be the sole reason for the award of any contract and may attach due weight and consideration to any factors that it shall in its absolute discretion decide including but not limited to the following:

1.1 Disclosure of facts, financial details and credit history, health and safety records, corporate background, compliance with legislation, directives, standards and policies and any other matter which may arise from an assessment of the stability, track record, and suitability of the applicant.

1.2 Personal, bank and business references.

1.3 Details of suppliers of materials, quality of materials, samples, products, packaging, the condition of the premises, insurance, freight, delivery, returns policy.

1.4 Customer service policy, complaints procedure, efficiency and operational management.

T.024
The [Company] reserves the right to amend the Tender dates due to unforeseen circumstances for any reason including but not limited to the acknowledgement of proposed application, the delivery of the application documents, the award of the Tender, the conclusion of the Agreement and/ or the Tender terms and conditions and/or payment of funds. In the event that any dates are altered all the applicants who have notified their intention to bid will as far as possible be notified in advance.

T.025
If in the opinion of the [Trustees/Directors] of the Board of the [Institute] any part of any of the applications is unacceptable. Then the [Institute] shall have

the absolute right to refuse such an applicant and may also refuse to award the Tender. The grounds of refusal by the [Institute] are not limited but may include the lack of quality of the applications and/or the proposed use of personnel and/or the budgets and/or completion dates for work schedules and/or any other disclosure by the applicants.

T.026

There shall be no obligation on the [Institute] to award the Tender to any third party nor to justify the grounds of refusal to any applicant. The decision as to whether there shall be an award of the Tender, the terms upon which the Tender may be given and the payment of any sums that may be due shall be at the absolute discretion of the [Institute] at any time.

T.027

Any applicant accepts as a condition of entry to the Tender process that the applicant shall not have any right, claim and/or action against the [Institute] for any costs, expenses, fees, charges, administrative costs, legal, accounting and consultants costs or any other sums which may be incurred and/or due by the applicant as a result of the applicants decision to apply for the Tender.

T.028

The failure by any applicant to disclose some material fact about their business, products and/or service in the application process shall be grounds for termination and/or cancellation of the Tender Process by the [Institute]. Where the [Institute] has awarded the Tender to the applicant prior to the disclosure and/or discovery of the material fact which would have affected the decision of the [Institute] to award the Tender to the applicant. Then the [Institute] shall be entitled to cancel and/or terminate the award of the Tender to the applicant.

T.029

The applicant grants the [Company] to right to store the details of the application form on a storage and retrieval system and database on a computer at the [Company] for a period of [number] months for the purposes of the tender application and process. If the applicant is successful then this period shall be extended upon terms to be agreed between the parties.

T.030

The [Company] agrees to delete the details of the application form of the applicant which is stored on a storage and retrieval system and database on a computer at the [Company] after the expiry of a period of [number] months and/or within [number] weeks of the application being unsuccessful which ever is the sooner.

T.031

The initial Tender by the [Company] is for expressions of interest from third parties who may wish to be considered for the award of the contract. Each applicant must fill in the online form in all parts and submit it by the deadline. No applicants will be considered for the second part of the Tender application process who have not expressed an interest before the deadline.

T.032

The Tender requires that all applicants for the award of the Agreement must have:

1.1 Personnel to provide the service who speak fluent [specify language].

1.2 Expertise and experience in the field of [subject] and are able to provide evidence of delivery of such work and services over the last [number] years to a [local/national] body with a budget of not less than [specify].

1.3 A solvent company as the party to any tender on the application which has clear evidence of trading in [country] in the field of [subject] over the last [number] years.

1.4 The applicant must not be the subject of civil and/or criminal proceedings in [country] which are not disclosed to the [Company] which relate to personal injury, death, fraud, tax evasion, product liability and/or any other matter.

1.5 The applicant must disclose all material facts which would affect its ability to deliver the Tender as required.

T.033

The submission of an expression of interest is not binding on the [Company] and/or the applicant and either party may withdraw at any time. The [Company] reserves the right to end the Tender process at any time and it shall not be liable for any costs and expenses incurred by the applicant in reliance on the Tender process.

T.034

In the event that no applicant applies which the [Company] wishes to consider for the second part of the Tender procedure. Then the [Company] shall have the right to end the Tender and then begin a further process of advertising the Tender. Any applicant to the first Tender may apply to the new Tender.

TERM OF THE AGREEMENT

Employment

T.035

The [Employer] shall have the right to terminate this Agreement during the Probation Period by giving [one week's] notice in writing to the [Employee]. After the completion of the Probation Period then the procedures set out in Clauses [–] must be followed by both parties.

T.036

The employment thereunder shall be subject as hereinafter provided to be terminated by either party giving to the other not less than [three months'] notice in writing. The [Manager] shall in any event retire upon attaining [number] years of age.

T.037

This contract of employment supersedes all previous arrangements if any relating to the employment of the [Manager] by the [Company] which shall be deemed to have terminated by mutual consent and shall be effective from [date]. This Agreement shall commence on [date] and continue until the expiry of the Term subject to the provisions for termination in Clause [–].

T.038

'Term of the Agreement' shall commence on [date] and shall continue until terminated by either party in accordance with the terms of this Agreement.

T.039

'Continuous Employment' for legal purposes shall mean the period of continuous employment beginning on the commencement of this Agreement under Clause [–].

T.040

The first day of employment shall be [date]. The date for calculating continuous employment shall be [date]. We may bring this contract to an end by serving on you the following notice period [specify duration].

T.041

There shall be no regular and/or continuous employment between [Name] and the [Company] and all dates and hours shall be on a part time and short term basis and shall be subject to alteration and cancellation by the [Company] at any time.

Film and Television

T.042
The [Licensee] acknowledges that after the expiry of the Term of this Agreement that the [Licensee] shall have no rights in the [Format] and shall only be entitled to exploit the [Series] which has been produced.

T.043
The [Licensee] agrees that at the end of the Term of this Agreement it shall execute any documentation or anything required by the [Licensor] to vest all copyright and any other rights in any variations or developments of the [Format] in the [Licensor].

T.044
The [Company] agrees that it shall not be entitled to exploit the [Work/Film] in any form after the expiry of the Term of this Agreement without the prior written consent of the [Author].

T.045
The Term of this Agreement shall be for the period starting on [date] and ending on completion of the first or so called Director's cut of the [Film] which period is hereinafter called 'the Production Period'.

T.046
'The Term of the Agreement' shall commence on the date of this Agreement and continue until the expiry of [five years] from the date of the first [transmission/broadcast] or [date] whichever is the earlier.

T.047
'The Term of this Agreement' shall commence on [date] and continue for the full period of copyright and any extensions and renewals.

T.048
'The Term of this Agreement' shall commence on [date] and shall continue until [date].

T.049
'The Term of this Agreement' shall commence on [date] and shall expire on [date].

T.050
'The Term of this Agreement' shall begin on the date of this Agreement and shall continue until [date].

T.051

'The Term of this Agreement' shall begin on the date of this Agreement and shall continue for a period of [number] years.

T.052

'The Term of this Agreement' shall be for a period of [three] months] which shall start on [date] and expire on [date].

T.053

'The Term of the Agreement' shall begin upon acceptance of the [Material] and continue until the [Licensee] has completed all the transmissions set out in clause [–] but in any event shall end on [date].

T.054

'The Term of the Agreement' shall commence on [date] and continue for a period of [number] years and/or until the [Licensee] has completed all the transmissions of the [Series] if that is an earlier date.

T.055

The Term of this Agreement cannot be extended by the [Licensee] for any reason whether due to delay by the [Licensor], force majeure and/or otherwise.

General Business and Commercial

T.056

This Agreement shall continue in force for the duration of the Assignment Period after which time all rights granted to the [Assignee] shall revert to the [Assignor] subject to the Accounting Provisions contained within Clauses [–] and the Indemnity Clauses [–] under this Agreement which shall continue.

T.057

This Agreement shall operate for the full period of copyright including any extensions and renewals for as far as possible in perpetuity.

T.058

This Agreement shall be deemed to have commenced on [date] and shall endure for a period of [twelve months] and thereafter unless and until determined by [three months] prior written notice given by either party hereto.

T.059

This Agreement shall be for a fixed period of [three years] starting with the [Commencement Date].

T.060

This Agreement shall continue in force until terminated in writing in accordance with the termination provisions contained within Clauses [–] in this Agreement.

T.061

'Term of the Agreement' shall mean for the full period of copyright including any extensions and or renewals as far as possible in perpetuity and indefinitely and without limitation of time.

T.062

'The Term of the Agreement' shall mean the period of [five years] from the date of delivery of the [Material].

T.063

'The Term of this Agreement' shall commence on the date of this Agreement and shall continue until [date/event].

T.064

The [Company] authorises the [Distributor] to collect all sums due to the [Company] in respect of the [Work/Services/Products] from any source throughout the Territory from the exploitation of the rights granted under this Agreement both during the Term of this Agreement and thereafter provided that all sums are then accounted for to the [Company].

T.065

Any failure to renew or extend the Term of this Agreement shall not constitute grounds for any claim or payments for any reason to the [Company] and/or [Name].

T.066

'The Term of the Agreement' shall commence on [date] and unless terminated earlier in accordance with the provisions of this Agreement shall continue for [two years] up to and including [date]. This Agreement shall thereafter automatically be renewed for periods of [six months] unless either party shall give the other party [two months'] written notice that the Agreement is at an end either before the expiry of the initial or any renewed period.

T.067

'Term of the Agreement' shall commence on [date] and continue until [–].

T.068

The period of the engagement by the [Consultant] shall commence on [date] and continue until the completion of the [Work/Film/other], but in any event not later than [date].

T.069

The [Agent] acknowledges that he/she shall not be entitled to any commission in respect of work done or agreed to be done by the [Artist] prior to the date of this Agreement whether that work is performed during the Term of this Agreement or not.

T.070

The [Company] acknowledges that [the Celebrity] is already committed and entitled to carry out the following work for third parties during the Term of the Agreement as follows [specify].

T.071

The [Manager] agrees that he/she shall not be entitled to any commission in respect of any work done or agreed to be carried out by the [Sportsperson] prior to the date of this Agreement whether the work is performed during the Term of this Agreement or not and including the following additional specific matters [–].

T.072

The [Company] agrees that it shall not be entitled to exploit the [Work/Film/Sound Recordings] in any form after the expiry or termination of the Term of this Agreement whichever is the earliest without the prior written consent of [Name].

T.073

Any failure to renew or extend the Term of this Agreement following the expiry shall not be grounds for any claim or payments for any reason. The [Company] and the [Artists] both agree that neither party shall be entitled to make any claim for any sum for the failure to renew, extend and/or negotiate a further agreement.

T.074

The 'Option Period' shall commence on the date of this Agreement and continue until [date].

T.075

This Agreement shall commence on the date hereof and shall continue until the expiry of the Term subject to the provisions for termination contained in Clause [–].

T.076

This Agreement shall continue in force unless terminated in accordance with its provisions for the [specify duration] thereafter either party may give [six months'] notice of termination.

of years from the date of delivery and acceptance of the [Material] for the [Project/App/other] to [Name] and/or until at the latest the expiry of [number of years] from [date].

T.091

It is agreed that neither party shall have the right to continue the annual Agreement which starts on [date] and ends on [date] into the following year. A new agreement must be signed and agreed in each case.

TERMINATION

Employment

T.092

1.1 The [Executive] is required either to deliver to the [Company] or arrange for the [Company] to collect at the end of his/her employment (howsoever terminated) all papers, documents, keys, credit cards, security passes, pagers, mobiles, cars, and all other property belonging to the [Company] of any nature.

1.2 The [Executive] shall not be under any obligation to sign an undertaking that all such property has been returned.

1.3 The [Executive] shall have the right to retain all gifts, purchases or other material of which the [Company] is or was at some time aware which were acquired during the course of his/her employment or which are documents required for [tax, insurance or national insurance payments].

1.4 The [Executive] shall not be obliged to return any material and/or products which is in dispute as to ownership and he/she intends to use for the purpose of legal proceedings against the [Company] provided that they are commenced within [one year] of termination.

T.093

The [Employee's] appointment may be terminated forthwith by the [Company] without any period of notice and without payment in lieu if the [Employee] shall at any time:

1.1 Be guilty of serious misconduct or any other conduct which is likely to seriously adversely affect the interests of the [Company]; and/or

1.2 Becomes incapable of fulfilling his/her duties for more than [–] months due to mental health problems which he/she has confirmed cannot be resolved so that he/she may commence part-time work.

1.3 Becomes unable to attend the location for the performance of the duties required due to relocation to another country for more than [number] months.

Such termination shall be without prejudice to any other rights of the [Company] against the [Employee].

T.094

The [Company] shall not terminate this Agreement without any period of notice and/or payment unless the [Employee] has:

1.1 Committed a serious act of misconduct which could form the basis for a criminal charge and/or a civil prosecution in respect of his/her employment and/or personal life.

1.2 Disclosed confidential information and/or data to a journalist, newspaper and/or media which has resulted in adverse publicity which has seriously detrimentally affected the interests of the [Company].

1.3 Been diagnosed as mentally ill, with psychiatric problems, or is aggressive, threatening, or violent at work or tested positive for illegal drugs in a medical by the [Company].

1.4 Failed to carry out the duties required and/or is in serious and repeated breach under this Agreement. That despite formal warnings, and/or being the subject of a disciplinary hearing the problem has not been remedied and the breach or non-observance of this Agreement has continued.

Such termination shall be without prejudice to any other rights of the [Company] against the [Employee].

T.095

The [Company] may summarily terminate the [Manager's] employment without prior notice so that he/she shall have no claim for damages or otherwise against the [Company] if he/she shall:

1.1 Be guilty of any serious failure or neglect to carry out his/her duties or commit any repeated or serious breach of any of the terms of this Agreement; and/or

1.2 Become the subject of a bankruptcy order or be incapable of paying his creditors; and/or

1.3 Become a mental patient [for the purposes of the Mental Health Act 1983 as amended]; and/or

1.4 Be convicted of a serious criminal offence in any part of the world; and/or

1.5   Commits a serious act of misconduct and/or neglect whether or not in connection with his/her duties and/or commits any act which might seriously affect his/her ability to carry out his/her duties hereunder; and/or

1.6   Commits an act of dishonesty in respect of a claim for expenses and/or uses the [Company] credit card for an unauthorised purpose; and/or

1.7   Supplies, distributes, posts and/or reproduces any photo, image, text and/or film and/or sound recording on the internet and/or any website, app and/or blog.

T.096

The [Company] shall be entitled at the sole discretion of the [Company] to request that the [Manager] be on paid leave from the [Company] for a period of up to [one month] for the purpose of investigating allegations concerning the conduct of the [Manager].

T.097

Upon termination of his/her employment by the [Company] for whatever reason the [Manager] shall (without prejudice to any claim, for damages or other remedy which either party may have) immediately deliver or arrange for collection by the Company all [Company] documents, papers, property, photographs, and any other material in any medium belonging to the [Company], its associates or its customers in the possession or control of the [Manager] [whether prepared by the Manager or not]. The [Manager] shall not be entitled to retain any material of any nature in any format without the prior written consent of the [Company].

T.098

The [Employee] may terminate the employment by giving notice of termination as set out below:

1.1   If the [Employee] has less than [12 months'] consecutive service he/she shall provide [4 weeks'] notice.

1.2   If the [Employee] has more than [12 months] but less than [5 years'] consecutive service he/she shall provide [6 weeks'] notice.

1.3   If the [Employee] has more than [5 years'] service he/she shall provide [8 weeks'] notice.

Alternatively the [Employee] may terminate his/her employment by not receiving payment of any sum(s) in lieu of notice and terminate the employment immediately.

T.099

In the event of any serious misdemeanour on the part of the [Employee] the [Company] shall have the right to summarily terminate the employment without notice.

T.100

Either party may terminate the employment by giving notice of termination as specified in the [Union] Agreement.

T.101

This Agreement may be terminated by the [Executive] or the [Company] by giving [six months'] notice to the other party in the first year and [twelve months'] notice during the next five years, and [two years'] notice thereafter from [date].

Subject to the Grievance Procedure as set out in Schedule [–] the appointment may be terminated at once by the [Company] without prior notice and without pay in lieu if the [Executive] shall at any time:

1.1 Be guilty of serious misconduct or other conduct including criminal convictions likely to affect prejudicially the interests of the [Company];

1.2 Become of unsound mind or incapable of functioning normally due to psychiatric or mental problems;

1.3 Make a public statement which directly criticises the [Company] and/or exposes any failures and/or investigations at the [Company] without authority of the Board of the [Company];

1.4 Be guilty of any breach or non-observance of any of the provisions of this Agreement on his/her part to be performed or observed.

Such termination shall be without prejudice to any other rights claim and/or interest of the [Company].

T.102

In addition to any other rights and remedies at law and notwithstanding Clauses [–]. This Agreement may be terminated by the [Company], by giving written notice to the [Executive] where the [Executive] has failed to attend to his/her duties for a continuous period of [specify duration] or more. The [Company] undertakes not to invoke this procedure where medical certificates have been provided for the period by the [Executive].

T.103

The [Company] shall have the right to request the [Executive] be on paid leave from the [Company] for a total period not exceeding [one] month for the purpose of investigating any allegations concerning the conduct, actions or health of the [Executive].

T.104

Upon termination of this Agreement by the [Company] the [Executive] shall within [14 days] of receipt of a written request by the [Company] return or arrange for collection of all material of any nature in any medium in the possession or under the control of the [Executive] which belongs to the [Company]. Where any material is required by the [Executive] for the purpose of potential evidence in future legal proceedings against the [Company] then all such material shall not be returned but placed with his/her legal advisors.

T.105

The [Employee] shall only be obliged to return the following items in the event that this Agreement is terminated by the [Company] [specify]. At least [specify period] notice in writing must be given to terminate this Agreement without any additional payment. Where less notice is given then payment in lieu of the full notice period shall be made to the [Employee].

T.106

The [Executive] shall have the right at the end of his/her employment to keep a selection of personal items relating to their history at the [Company] including [business cards, minutes, papers, products, data and software] provided that they are for personal use and not for publication and remain confidential where appropriate.

T.107

The [Company] shall only have the right to terminate this Agreement if the [Employee] has significantly breached one of the terms of this Agreement or is unavailable permanently to carry out his/her work or is the subject of criminal proceedings for which imprisonment is likely or consistently refuses to follow reasonable requests at work and/or is repeatedly abusive, offensive or late at work.

T.108

There shall be no right under this Agreement for the [Company] to summarily dismiss and/or remove the [Executive] from the premises without notice under any circumstances at any time. Where the [Company] has a complaint about the conduct of the [Executive] and/or alleges that he/she is in breach of this Agreement then the [Company] shall set out all the reasons in writing to the [Executive] supported by the evidence. The [Executive] shall be provided with the opportunity to refute the alleged breach and/or allegations and an independent expert shall be appointed which shall be agreed between the parties to review all the arguments from both parties at the [Company's] cost. The decision of the independent expert who shall decide the case shall [not] be binding on both parties.

T.109

Where the [Company] wishes to terminate any Agreement with [Name] then it agrees to provide at least [number] months notice to [Name] in advance and to provide a reference to assist [Name] to seek a position at another [Company].

DVD, Video and Discs

T.110

The [Licensor] may in addition to all its other rights and remedies at law and at its option upon giving written notice to the [Distributor] to terminate this Agreement forthwith:

1.1 If the [Distributor] shall fail to make payments hereunder or shall fail to perform any other material obligation required of it hereunder and the [Distributor] shall not have cured or remedied such failure within [sixty days] of notification thereof to the satisfaction of the [Licensor] and in accordance with this Agreement.

1.2 If the [Distributor] shall make any assignment for the benefit of its creditors or make any composition with its creditors or if any actions or proceedings under any bankruptcy or insolvency law is taken against the [Distributor] and is not dismissed or if the [Distributor] shall effect a voluntary or compulsory liquidation of assets (other than for the purposes of reconstruction or amalgamation of which prior notice shall have been given to the [Licensor]).

T.111

The [Distributor] may in addition to all its other rights and remedies at law and at its option upon giving [ten days'] written notice to the [Licensor] terminate this Agreement if the [Licensor]:

1.1 Shall fail to perform any of its obligations required of it hereunder and the [Licensor] shall not in so far as is possible have cured or remedied such failure within [thirty days] of notification thereof to the satisfaction of the [Distributor].

1.2 Or shall make any assignment for the benefit of creditors or make any composition with creditors or if any action or proceeding under any bankruptcy or insolvency law is taken against the [Licensor] and is not dismissed or if the [Licensor] shall effect a voluntary or compulsory liquidation of assets (other than for the purposes of reconstruction or amalgamation).

T.112

Upon the expiry or termination of the Term of this Agreement stocks of the [Videos/DVDs/Discs] in the possession and/or under the control of the [Distributor] hereunder and in good condition shall be sent to such address as specified in the written notification by the [Licensor] at the [Distributor's] cost.

T.113

Upon the expiry or termination of the Term of this Agreement the [Distributor] shall be entitled to sell off existing stocks for a period of [six months] after the date of expiry or termination.

T.114

Upon the expiry or termination of the Term of this Agreement the [Distributor] shall within [one month] arrange to sell and/or dispose of existing stock to the [Licensor] at the manufacturing cost price. The [Distributor] shall not be entitled to sell off or dispose of the stocks to any other person unless directed to do so by the [Licensor] in writing. The [Distributor] shall reserve the right to offset the price of such stocks against any amount of money unpaid or becoming due from [the trading account of] the [Distributor] to the [Licensor] hereunder.

T.115

Termination of this Agreement for any cause whatsoever shall be without prejudice to the rights of either party then accrued or to the rights of either party in respect of the breach by the other party.

T.116

In the event of the termination or expiry of this Agreement for any reason the [Distributor] shall immediately cease to have any rights in respect of the [DVDs/Videos/Discs] and all rights and material, [data and records] shall be assigned, transferred to and belong to the [Licensor] including any new material which has been created and/or developed. The [Distributor] shall not have any claim, interest and/or rights nor shall the [Distributor] be due any sums from the [Licensor]. The [Licensor] shall arrange for and bear the cost of the collection of all material of any nature which relate to the [DVDs/Videos/Discs] including but not limited to the original material of the [Film], customer sales list, packaging, artwork, merchandising, press reviews and reports, advertising, posters, labels, discs, sub-licensee, agency and distribution arrangements, mechanical copyright clearances and payments, copies of all accounting and royalty records. The [Distributor] shall only be entitled to retain those business records which it requires for compliance with legislation for any government agency and a copy of any documents and financial records it requires for its business use.

T.117

1.1　Any order for [Videos/DVDs/Discs] accepted in writing by the [Distributor] prior to the date of termination shall be valid. In the event of any order being received after the date of termination or during the period of notice the [Licensor] shall have the right at its option to accept or reject such order provided that such action does not cause a breach of contract between the [Distributor] and its customers. If the [Licensor] accepts the order in writing the terms of this Agreement shall apply thereto.

1.2　After termination the [Distributor] shall supply and return at the [Licensor's] cost a complete list of all material of any nature of which the [Distributor] is aware which exists directly or indirectly related to the [Films/Videos/DVDs/Discs] whether held by the [Distributor] or a third party including, but not limited to, all master material, artwork, sales literature, posters, merchandising, publicity, copies, list of customers, sub-licensees and agents, all accounting and royalty records which do not need to be retained for tax purposes, any consents, releases and contracts.

1.3　The [Distributor] shall immediately cease any use of all trade marks, service marks and logos of the [Licensor].

1.4　The [Distributor] shall co-operate with the [Licensor] to effect the assignment of any rights which may have been acquired by the [Distributor] under this Agreement.

T.118

1.1　Upon the expiration of the Term of the Agreement the [Licensee] shall immediately cease to use for the manufacture of [Videos/DVDs] of the [Film] the Master supplied hereunder together with all materials derived therefrom.

1.2　At the option of the [Licensor] to be exercised by written notice within [sixty days] from the expiry of the Term of Agreement, the [Licensee] agrees to deliver possession and ownership to the [Licensor] in the Territory by such means as may be reasonably instructed the Master and other material which remains in the [Licensee's] possession or control. The [Licensor] shall pay the [Licensee] the full cost of the material together with all packaging and shipping charges in respect thereof.

T.132

The [Company] and the [Producer] agree that:

1.1 If either party shall commit a substantial breach of the Agreement which cannot be corrected; or

1.2 If either party shall commit a substantial breach of the Agreement which cannot be remedied within [14 days] of written notice notifying the breach and requesting that it be rectified; or

1.3 If either party shall go into liquidation (other than for amalgamation or reconstruction purposes) or become insolvent or have an administrator or receiver appointed over any of its assets or fail to satisfy any trial judgment within [7 days].

Then the other party shall be entitled without prejudice to its other remedies to terminate the Agreement by notice in writing to the party in breach. In the event of breach by the [Producer] the whole amount of all sums paid by the [Company] which have not been spent on items set out in the Budget shall immediately become repayable and the [Producer] shall pay such sums upon demand.

T.133

In addition to any other rights and remedies at law either party may by giving written notice to the other party terminate this Agreement on the grounds that:

1.1 The other party has failed to account or make payments as required under this Agreement;

1.2 The other party has committed a serious breach of is obligations and has not rectified the position within [period];

1.3 The other party has gone into voluntary or involuntary liquidation;

1.4 The other party has been declared insolvent and/or gone into administration;

1.5 The other party has not distributed and/or marketed and/or sold any copies of the [Work] for more than [number] months.

T.134

Each party shall be entitled to terminate this Agreement immediately by serving written notice on the other party if that other party shall:

1.1 Commit a breach of any of its major obligations under this Agreement which is not capable of being remedied or is not remedied with [seven days] of receipt of notice; or

1.2 Make an arrangement for the benefit of or make a composition or arrangement with its creditors or any action or proceedings in bankruptcy or insolvency is taken against it including appointment of a receiver, administrator, liquidator or other trustee (other than for the purpose of amalgamation or reconstruction of the business).

T.135

The [Licensee] shall have the right to terminate this Agreement at an earlier date where the [Licensor] has made allegations against the [Licensee] regarding the content, production, reproduction and/or exploitation of the [Film/Recording] which damage the reputation of the [Licensee] and/or effect the value of the shares, assets and/or goodwill of the [Licensee]. In such event the [Licensee] shall be entitled to serve notice of termination with the grounds and to seek to reach a settlement of the matter based upon the completion of the Agreement to that date.

T.136

The failure by the [Assignor] to supply the material and/or copyright clearance and other contractual agreements required in clause [–] to the [Assignee] by [date] shall entitle the [Assignor] to terminate this Agreement and not pay the sums due in clause [–].

General Business and Commercial

T.137

Each contracting party may at their own discretion and without being required to pay compensation terminate the contract by serving formal notice [two months] in advance. The [Contractor] shall only be entitled to payment for past performance of the contract in the event that the [Company] terminates the contract.

T.138

The [Company] may terminate the contract at any time during its performance subject to the payment of fair compensation with respect to the outstanding part [which shall not exceed the total value of the outstanding part].

T.139

The [Company] may terminate the contract in whole or in part without compensation as of right and without instituting legal proceedings:

1.1 In the event that the [Contractor] is made bankrupt, wound up, has ceased trading, has been wound up by a Court Order or is in any other comparable situation as a result of a similar procedure provided under the laws of the country of the [Contractor]; or

1.2 In the event that the [Contractor] is made the subject of proceedings for a declaration of bankruptcy, for a court winding up Order or for a composition or any other comparable proceeding provided by the laws of the country of the [Contractor].

T.140
The [Distributor] confirms that if within [two years] of the date of this Agreement that the [Licensee's] Royalties actually paid and received is less than [figure/currency] (including the Licence Fee). The [Licensor] shall have the right to terminate this Agreement by giving written notice to the [Distributor] and upon such notice being received by the [Distributor] all rights granted under this Agreement shall revert back to the [Licensor].

T.141
The [Distributor] acknowledges that the [Licensor] shall be entitled to retain all sums paid including the Licence Fee and to receive payment of all sums which may be due under this Agreement whether or not received by the [Distributor] at the date of termination.

T.142
This Agreement may be terminated by either party giving written notice to the defaulting party who has committed a material breach of the terms. Where the breach is capable of being remedied the defaulting party shall be permitted [thirty days] from receipt of the notice to remedy the breach. Unless the breach is remedied the Agreement shall be terminated at the end of that period.

T.143
After the expiry of the termination or the completion of the sell-off period the [Assignor] shall be entitled to instruct the [Assignee] to return or destroy all master material, licensed material, any copies of the licensed material and stock previously manufactured under this Agreement in the possession or under the control of the [Assignee] relating to the rights assigned under this Agreement.

T.144
In addition to any other rights and remedies at law of the [Licensor] or the [Licensee] either party may by giving written notice to the other party terminate this Agreement on the grounds that the other party has defaulted or breached this Agreement as follows:

1.1 That the other party has failed to account or make payments as required under this Agreement.

1549

1.2 That the other party has committed a serious breach of its obligations under this Agreement and has failed to rectify the position within a reasonable period.

1.3 That the other party has gone into liquidation, been declared insolvent, had a receiver or administrative receiver appointed over the whole or part(s) of its business.

T.145

After the expiry or termination of the Licence the [Licensor] shall be entitled to instruct the [Licensee] to return all the master material and any copies in the possession or under the control of the [Licensee] together with any other documents, contracts and material relating to the rights granted under this Agreement.

T.146

The [Licensee] agrees that in the event that [Licensor's] Royalties received by the [Licensor] by date [–] are less than [figure/currency], the [Licensor] shall have the right to terminate this Agreement by notice in writing to the [Licensee] to that effect at any time before [date].

T.147

If the Agreement is terminated by either party under Clause [–] it is agreed that [Name] shall be entitled to retain all sums already paid and to receive any future royalties which may fall due under this Agreement.

T.148

In the event that the Licence is revoked, terminated or withdrawn within the terms of this Agreement, the [Licensee] shall be obliged to immediately revoke, terminate or withdraw (as the case may be) all sub-licences which it may have granted.

T.149

This Agreement shall commence on the date hereof and shall continue for an initial period ending on the [second] anniversary of such date and shall subject to earlier termination in accordance with the Conditions in Document [–], thereafter continue:

1.1 Unless and until terminated by the [Company] giving to the [Licensee] [two months'] notice in writing to expire no earlier than the [second] anniversary; or

1.2 Unless and until terminated by the [Licensee] giving to the [Company] [two months'] notice in writing to expire no earlier than the [first] anniversary.

Any termination by or in respect of the [Licensee] pursuant to this Agreement will not affect the continuance of this Agreement with respect to any other licensee and any licences granted by the [Licensor].

The termination of this Agreement by the [Company] with respect to the Licensee shall immediately terminate at the same time all Sub-Licences granted by the [Licensee].

T.150
If the [Licensor] does not supply the services and/or is in breach of its obligations hereunder the [Licensor] acknowledges that the [Licensee] may elect either:

1.1 To receive from the [Licensor] as liquidated damages an amount which is equal to [double] the Licence Fees that the [Licensee] would reasonably have been anticipated to have paid to the [Licensor] hereunder either for the period of two years immediately following the supply ending or for the period of the remainder of the Licence Term whichever is the shorter period; or

1.2 Claim damages against the [Licensor] for the losses actually incurred by the [Licensee] as a consequence of the [Licensor] not continuing the supply of the Services.

T.151
The following clauses [–] shall survive the termination of this Agreement.

T.152
This Agreement shall continue until the expiration or termination of the [Patent Licence] whereupon this Agreement shall automatically terminate. Termination of this Agreement (howsoever arisen) shall be without prejudice to any other rights or claims of either of the parties against the other.

T.153
This Contract may be terminated by either party at any time by notice to the other.

T.154
In the event of termination by the [Contractor] the [Contractor] shall complete any Work which the [Contractor] has already accepted for which the [Contractor] shall be compensated as provided herein. In the event of termination by the [Company] the Work shall be discontinued as provided in the notice of termination and the [Company] shall pay the [Contractor] as provided herein for the Work carried out until the date of termination.

T.155

Either party shall be entitled to terminate this Agreement immediately by serving written notice on the other if that other party shall:

1.1 Commit a breach of any of its major obligations under this Agreement which is not capable of remedy or which is capable of remedy but is not rectified within [fourteen] days of receipt of notice; or

1.2 Make any arrangement for the benefit of or make any composition or arrangement with its creditors or any action or proceedings in bankruptcy or insolvency is taken including, but not limited to, the appointment of a receiver, administrator, liquidator or other trustee which is not dismissed or discharged within [sixty] days of the start of the action or if the other party shall go into liquidation (whether voluntary or compulsory) other than for the purpose of amalgamation or restructuring and/or consolidation of the business.

Termination under this Clause shall not prejudice the rights and remedies of the parties [prior to the date of such termination]. All terms and conditions set out in this Agreement which relate to the period after the expiry or termination of this Agreement shall continue in full force and effect.

T.156

The warranties and indemnities on the part of [Name] in this Agreement shall survive the termination of this Agreement.

T.157

Clauses [–] shall survive the termination and/or expiry of this Agreement and continue for [number] years from the [termination/expiry] date.

T.158

The [Company] shall have the right to terminate this Agreement before the expiry of the Agreement in the event that the [Enterprise] and/or any officer discloses confidential data and information to the media and/or any competitor at any time. In such event the [Company] may notify the [Enterprise] of termination with immediate effect of the Agreement. No further payments shall be made to the [Enterprise] and the [Company] shall be under no further liability to the [Enterprise] under this Agreement.

T.159

Where this Agreement is contingent upon the conclusion of another agreement by the [Company] to a third party. Then where this Agreement has been signed the [Company] shall have the right to terminate this Agreement at any time if the third party agreement is not concluded.

T.160

Where the [Company] is sold to any other third party. Then it is agreed between the parties that the successor in title shall have the right to terminate this Agreement by notice in writing within [number] months of the transfer of title to the successor.

T.161

Where the [Licensee] fails to comply with legislation relating to [Health and Safety/Product Liability/Company Law] and/or any other matter which results in a fine and/or penalty by a court of law and/or other body. Then the [Licensor] shall have the right to terminate the Agreement at an earlier date than the expiry date on those grounds.

T.162

The [Distributor] shall be entitled to terminate the Agreement with the [Sub-Licensee] in the event that the [Sub-Licensee] releases and/or supplies confidential business plans and/or product designs and/or other corporate information which is not available to the public to a third party.

Internet and Websites

T.163

This Agreement may be terminated by notice in writing at any stage by either party and any obligations, undertakings and payments due shall continue until and/or be made by the termination date.

T.164

The [Company] may at its absolute discretion cease to provide any service, supply any goods and/or distribute any other material without notice and/or reason. The [Company] shall only be liable to refund any sums paid for goods and/or services not supplied and not for any consequences that may arise either directly and/or indirectly.

T.165

Where a [Customer] has entered into a monthly subscription [Service/Supply] Agreement with the [Company]. The [Customer] may cancel and/or terminate the [Service/Supply] by notice in writing and/or by telephone to the [Company] prior to the next payment date. In the event that notice is not received before the payment date then the full months' payment shall be due and shall be paid.

T.166

The Agreement shall continue for periods of [one year] and may be terminated by notice in writing at any time before the end period of each year and the start date of the next. There shall be an obligation by the [Customer] to pay the full years payment and no sum shall be waived and/or reduced by the [Company] whether or not the [Customer] does not want to receive the [Service] and/or has served notice to cancel the Agreement.

T.167

The [Company] agrees and undertakes that the [Customer] shall be able at any time to terminate, cancel, withdraw from and/or amend the [service/ other]. That there shall be no additional charges, penalty and/or otherwise incurred as a result and no obligation to pay any sums which fall due after the end of the Agreement.

T.168

In addition to any rights and remedies this Agreement may be terminated by giving written notice to the defaulting party who has committed a material breach of this Agreement. The defaulting party shall be given not less than [ten] working days to remedy the alleged breach following formal notice from the other party and the Agreement shall be terminated if they have not complied.

T.169

1.1 In addition to any rights and remedies this Agreement may be terminated by giving immediate written notice to the defaulting party who has committed a material breach of this Agreement. Provided that the defaulting party has been given not less than [one calendar month] to remedy the alleged breach following formal notice.

1.2 Either party shall have the right, but not the obligation to terminate this Agreement immediately by notice in writing in the event that the other party becomes insolvent, enters into an arrangement with its creditors, a receiver or receiver/administrator is appointed over the business of the defaulting party and/or the directors and/or the shareholders of the [Company] pass a resolution to suspend trading, to wind up and/or dissolve the [Company] other than for the purpose of amalgamation and/or reconstruction.

T.170

1.1 In addition to any rights and remedies this Agreement may be terminated by giving immediate written notice to the [Contributor] if he commits a material breach of this Agreement subject to the payment of such sums as may have been due to the [Contributor] prior to the date of the notice of termination.

1.2 The [Company] shall have the right, but not the obligation to terminate this Agreement in the event that the [Contributor] becomes bankrupt, insolvent, enters into an agreement with his creditors, and/or a receiver and/or administrator is appointed over the [Contributors'] business.

1.3 Upon termination of this Agreement the [Contributor] will upon request return all material which is owned and/or controlled by the [Company] acquired by the [Contributor] and/or produced for the [Company] during the course of this Agreement including but not limited to computer software, reports, documents, laptop, car, security pass, mobile phones and any other gadgets.

T.171

In the event that the [Distributor] and/or the [Company] become aware and/or have reasonable grounds to believe that the [Purchaser] and/or its business, employees and/or associates are using the [Downloads/CD-Roms/Material] and/or any data, information and/or other content in a manner which contravenes the terms and condition of this Licence and/or is prejudicial to the financial, sales and/or other interest of the [Distributor] and/or [Publisher]. Then this Licence may be summarily terminated without any notice whatsoever. The [Purchaser] shall upon written request surrender all copies of any nature in any medium to the [Distributor] and [Company].

T.172

The [Company] agrees that it shall not terminate the Agreement with [Name] where delivery of the [App] by [date] is delayed due to additional requirements and/or specifications and/or changes requested by the [Company]. Provided that a new delivery date is agreed as a substitute.

T.173

The [Company] shall have the right to terminate the arrangement with [Name] to supply articles and information and images for blogs, articles and other content for the [Company] website and marketing and promotional material at any time. Provided that [Name] is paid for all work completed for the four weeks after notice of termination.

Merchandising

T.174

Upon or at any time after any of the following events shall occur the [Company] may by notice in writing to the [Licensee] forthwith terminate the sub-licence granted:

1.1 The [Licensee] shall have failed to manufacture and sell a minimum of [number] of the [Licensed Articles] within [six months] of the date of commencement of the sub-licence.

1.2   The [Licensee] shall have failed to make the best arrangements that can reasonably be secured for the distribution throughout the Territory and sale of the [Licensed Articles].

1.3   Any of the royalties due to the [Company] shall remain unpaid after they shall have become contractually due (whether or not they shall have been formally demanded).

1.4   The [Licensee] shall have failed to furnish statements provided for in Clause [–].

1.5   The [Licensee] shall commit or allow to be committed a breach of any of the undertakings on the part of the [Licensee] contained in this Agreement.

1.6   If in each year of the Term of this Agreement the [Licensee] shall fail to manufacture and sell a minimum of [number] units of any one category of the [Licensed Articles] in any particular country of the Territory as specified in this Agreement. The [Company] shall have the right at its discretion to terminate all of the rights sub-licensed to the [Licensee] in respect of that specific category of the [Licensed Articles] in that country. The [Company] shall from the date of termination have the right to grant licences to third parties in respect of those specific rights.

1.7   An order shall be made or resolution passed for the winding-up of the [Licensee] (other than for the purpose of reconstruction or amalgamation) or the [Licensee] shall make any arrangement with or for the benefit of its creditors or if a receiver shall be appointed in respect of any of the [Licensee's] assets.

Provided that any termination under this Clause [–] shall be without prejudice to any of the [Company] rights or remedies including the right to be paid the royalties which shall have been due or payable pursuant to this Agreement whether prior to the date of termination or thereafter.

T.175

Upon termination all rights in the [Character] shall immediately revert to the [Company] and all licences granted by the [Licensee] shall be transferred to the [Company].

T.176

Unless otherwise stated the [Licensed Products] shall be on sale to the public within [six months] from the date of this Agreement. If they are not available the [Licensor] shall have the right to notify the [Licensee] of the fact that the licence terminates in [six weeks] unless the situation is remedied.

T.177

Either the [Company] or the [Distributor] without prejudice to any other right or remedy available to it, may terminate this Agreement at any time by notice in writing to the other having immediate effect in any of the following circumstances:

1.1   If the other party commits any breach of any of the provisions of this Agreement which cannot be remedied or can be remedied but not within the terms of this Agreement. A breach shall be deemed capable of remedy if the party in breach can comply with the conditions in all respects within the time limits of this Agreement. Where the breach is capable of remedy then [specify period] written notice giving particulars of the breach and requiring it to be remedied should be given. In order for the termination not to apply the remedy must commence within the notice period and continue until it is complete.

1.2   If the other party is unable to pay its debts, is declared insolvent or is the subject of any legal proceedings which result in the party being unlikely to continue trading and meeting its commitments.

T.178

When this Agreement is terminated the [Distributor] shall cease all further manufacture of the [Products]. The [Distributor] may during the period of [three months] from the date of termination sell off on a non-exclusive basis existing stocks of [Products] manufactured prior to the date of termination and fulfil any contracts for the sale of the [Products] already concluded subject to the payment of the royalty due to the [Licensor] under Clause [–].

T.179

On termination of this Agreement the [Distributor] shall immediately return to the [Licensor] at the [Distributor's] cost all designs, drawings, specifications, data, material and any other information supplied by the [Licensor] under this Agreement or made or created by [Distributor] which contains the [Technical Information] and all copies thereof. The [Distributor] shall not be entitled to make any further use of such [Technical Information]. Upon termination, the [Distributor] shall refrain from any use of the Trade Mark or any trade name or mark of the [Licensor] on any of its products or advertising or promotional material or in any other manner.

T.180

All rights and obligations under this Agreement and all licences granted pursuant thereto shall automatically terminate with the following exceptions:

1.1 Such rights of action as shall have accrued prior to termination including, but not limited to, any claims for any breach of any term or undertaking contained in this Agreement.

1.2 All obligations of either party under this Agreement which are stated to continue and survive after its termination shall be in full force and effect thereafter.

1.3 Any licence granted by the [Distributor] to the [Licensor] in respect of improvements, variations, developments or enhancements.

T.181

Upon termination of this Agreement for any reason all rights in the [Character] shall immediately revert to the [Company].

T.182

The [Licensor] may terminate this Agreement by notice in writing in the event the [Licensee] shall:

1.1 Fail to have manufactured and/or distributed and sold to the public [number] units of the [Licensed Article] before [date].

1.2 Fail to pay the Licence Fee in full by date [–].

1.3 Fail to make payment of the [Licensor's] Royalties or report for any accounting period.

1.4 Commit a serious breach of this Agreement which is not remedied within [seven days].

1.5 Be unable to pay its debts and/or trade while insolvent or is wound up, put into receivership or liquidation or otherwise no longer a viable business.

T.183

The [Licensor] may terminate this Agreement by notice in writing in the event that the [Licensee] shall have failed to:

1.1 Provide a [Prototype/Sample] for approval by the [Licensor] and/or to reproduce the [Licensed Articles] in accordance with the approved [Prototype/Sample].

1.2 Manufacture, distribute and sale [number] of the [Licensed Articles] before [date].

1.3 Pay the Licence Fee by [date] and/or make payment of the [Licensor's] Royalties and/or provide any royalty statement and/or shall not allow the [Licensor] to carry out any audit of the accounts and records as set out in Clause [–].

1.4 Provide samples of the packaging, advertising, website material and/or publicity and/or labels for approval by the [Licensor].

1.5 The [Licensee] is unable to pay its suppliers and/or ceases to manufacture the [Licensed Articles] and/or is about to be wound up and/or declared insolvent and/or may cease trading.

Termination shall be without prejudice to any other rights and remedies that may be available to the [Licensor].

T.184

In the event of termination of the Agreement the following shall apply:

1.1 All sub-licensees, sub-agent and/or distributors shall immediately be notified by the [Licensee] and/or the [Licensor] that the rights have been revoked and that they must immediately cease exploiting the rights and that the rights have reverted to the [Licensor] and any outstanding payments must be made direct to the [Licensor].

1.2 The [Licensee] shall ensure that all master material and any other contracts, copyright clearances, documents, photographs, artwork, recordings, films or other material of any nature and/or format in the possession and/or under the control of the [Licensee] and/or any sub-licensees, sub-agent and/or distributors shall not be destroyed but returned at the [Licensors/Licensees] cost to the [Licensor].

1.3 No further sums shall be collected by the [Licensee] and/or rights exploited by the [Licensee] at any time.

T.185

In addition to any other rights and remedies at law this Agreement may be terminated by giving written notice to the other party who has breached this Agreement and/or defaulted in the following circumstances:

1.1 Where the [Company] has failed to account or make payments as required under this Agreement.

1.2 Where the other party has committed a serious breach of its obligations under this Agreement unless the defaulting party rectifies the position within [number] days.

1.3 Where the [Company] goes into voluntary and/or involuntary liquidation.

1.4 Where the [Company] is declared insolvent either in bankruptcy or other legal proceedings.

1.5 Where an agreement with creditors has been reached by the [Company] due to its failure or inability to pay its debts as they fall due.

1.6 Where a receiver or administrator is appointed over the whole or part of the [Company's] business.

1.7 Where [Name] is convicted of a serious criminal offence anywhere in the [Territory/country/world] including a drink driving offence which results in a driving ban and/or a drug offence.

1.8 Where [Name] is found to be in serious breach of the rules of the [specify organisation] of which he is a member and is found guilty of serious professional misconduct.

1.9 Where [Name] conducts himself in a persistently demeaning, derogatory and bad public manner that it prejudices and/or affects the business interests of the [Company].

T.186
Termination for any reason will not affect the responsibility of the [Company] to make payments as would otherwise be due under the terms of this Agreement. Such obligations as exist to make payments shall survive termination subject to completion of the work.

T.187
Termination of this Agreement for whatever reason shall require the [Company] to serve notice of termination upon all third party agreements concerning the use of the [Name/Image/Product/Work].

T.188
In the event of termination of the Agreement the following steps shall be taken:

1.1 All sub-licence and sub-agents rights shall be terminated and revoked.

1.2 All master material owned and/or controlled by the [Company] shall not be destroyed, but returned to the [Company] at the [Company's] cost.

1.3 All property of [Name] shall be returned.

Publishing

T.189
This Agreement may be terminated and the rights granted hereunder shall revert to the [Company] if:

1.1 The [Magazine] commits any breach or alleged breach of the provisions of the Agreement and does not take steps to remedy such breach or alleged breach within [28 days] of receiving written notice from the

[Company] to do so. Provided that if within that period the [Magazine] informs the [Company] that there is a valid dispute relating to such alleged breach this Agreement shall not be terminated. The parties in such event agree in good faith to use their best endeavours to resolve the dispute amicably.

1.2 If the conduct of the [Magazine] is in the opinion of the [Company] prejudicial to the interests of the [Company] any termination shall not cancel any indebtedness of the [Magazine] to the [Company].

T.190
In the event that the [Publishers] decide not to accept or publish the [Work] the [Publishers] shall immediately notify the [Author] of the reasons for their decision in writing.

T.191
The [Publisher] agrees and confirms that if within [two years] of the [date of this Agreement/date of first publication] the Author's Royalties paid are less than [figure/currency] [including/excluding] the Non-Returnable Advance. The [Author] shall have the right but not be obliged to terminate this Agreement by giving written notice to the [Publisher]. In such event upon receipt of notice for this reason the [Publisher] shall be obliged to ensure that all rights assigned under this Agreement shall revert back to the [Author]. For the avoidance of any doubt the Author's Royalties in this Clause shall mean the total Royalties paid to the [Author] (whether the [Author] is one or more persons).

T.192
Where the [Publisher] allows the [Work] to go out of print throughout all and/or part of the Territory and/or the [Work] is not available to the public through retail outlets and/or no new editions are issued. The [Author] shall be entitled to terminate this Agreement by giving the [Publisher] [one month's] written notice. In such circumstances all rights granted under this Agreement shall revert to and be vested in the [Author] at the end of the period of notice and this shall be without prejudice to any claim that the [Author] may have for monies due under this Agreement and/or any claim for breach of contract and/or damages or otherwise.

T.193
The [Publisher] agrees that if within [three years] of the [date of this Agreement/first publication of the Work in hardback] the Author's Royalties paid are less than [_] [including the Advance], the [Author] shall be entitled to terminate this Agreement by giving written notice to the [Publisher] that shall take effect upon receipt. The [Publisher] shall ensure that all rights

granted under this Agreement revert to the [Author] subject to existing agreements with third parties and without prejudice to any other claims or damages or otherwise of the [Author].

T.194

In the event that the [Author] shall fail or neglect to deliver the complete copy of the [Work] the [Publishers] may decide not to publish the [Work] in which case the Agreement shall be terminated by notice in writing to the [Author]. The termination shall be subject to the provision that the [Author] shall not be permitted to publish the Work elsewhere without first offering it to the [Publishers] upon the same terms. The Advance payments to the [Author] shall be immediately repaid to the [Publishers].

T.195

The [Publishers] confirm that if the [Work] is not accepted by the [Publishers] for any reason the [Author] shall be entitled to have the Work published by a third party and all rights granted to the [Publisher] under this Agreement shall revert to the [Author].

T.196

If the [Author] shall not deliver the typescript of the [Work] by the delivery date and in the form [style and content] set out in this Agreement, the [Publishers] may if they think fit decline to publish the [Work]. In which case the [Publishers] shall give notice to the [Author] and the Agreement shall be terminated upon receipt by the [Author]. All sums which have been paid to the [Author] under this Agreement shall upon such termination be immediately repayable to the [Publishers]. The [Author] shall not be entitled to arrange or enter into a contract for the publication of the [Work] [or any similar work] by another publisher at any time without first offering the work to the [Publishers].

T.197

If by date [–] which shall be of the essence of this Agreement the [Publishers] have not received the typescript of the [Work] or in the [Publisher's] opinion it is not of the standard, content, style, format or length which had been agreed or might reasonably be expected, the [Publishers] shall have the choice as to whether to publish the [Work]. If they decide to terminate the Agreement then the [Publishers] shall notify the [Author] in writing stating their reasons and the termination date. All sums paid under this Agreement to the [Author] shall immediately be repayable to the [Publishers]. Once such sums are received in full by the Publishers, the [Work], typescript and all rights granted under this Agreement shall revert to the [Author].

T.198

It is agreed that the [Publishers] shall be entitled to commission some third party to write a similar work provided that it is not based on or derived from the [Author's] Work.

T.199

The [Author] shall have the right to terminate this Agreement by [three months'] written notice setting out the reasons and the termination date if the [Work] is allowed to go out of print at any time in [country] and the [Publishers] shall fail to authorise a new edition or print and distribute at least [number] copies of the existing edition by the termination date. The only exception shall be where the [Publishers] notify the [Author] within [14] days of receipt of written notice that there are circumstances under the force majeure provisions which are applicable which are the reason for the failure by the [Publishers]. If there are no force majeure circumstances stated by the [Publisher] and no new copies or new edition then the Agreement shall terminate at the end of the notice period and the rights in the [Work] granted to the [Publishers] shall revert in full to the [Author]. The reversion of rights shall be subject to any third party agreements concluded by the [Publishers] prior to the receipt of the notice and without prejudice to any claim which the [Author] may have for sums due and/or damages and/or otherwise. In the event that there are force majeure circumstances the [Publishers] shall only be allowed a further period of [specify duration] from the date of receipt of notice to comply with the request and at the end of that period the Agreement shall be terminated and all rights shall revert to the [Author].

T.200

If after the expiry of [two years] from the date of first publication by the [Publishers] the [Work] is out of print and/or not available in any edition (licensed or published), the [Author] shall have the right to serve the [Publishers] with [two months'] notice of termination of the Agreement which shall take effect in the event that the situation is not remedied in that period. If the [Publishers] should refuse or fail to make the [Work] available to the public all the rights granted or assigned under this Agreement shall revert to the [Author] (without further notice). The [Publisher] shall be bound to grant or assign all rights subject to any existing third party agreements (excluding subsidiaries, associates or holding companies) to which the Publisher was contractually committed prior to the date of termination which shall revert to the [Author] as soon as possible in the circumstances.

T.201

1.1   In the event that the [Work] becomes out of print for any reason and the [Publishers] decline for any reason or are unable to reprint the

Work within [two months] of a written request by the [Authors], this Agreement shall be terminated at the end of the notice period.

1.2 Upon termination the [Publishers] shall if requested by the [Authors] in writing give and assign to the [Authors] without any charge or fee all rights in the [Work] including transferring and/or arranging for a novation of the rights in the [Work] which the [Publishers] have granted to third parties.

T.202

The [Authors] both confirm that if this Agreement is terminated for any reason [Author A] and [Author B] shall only hold the copyright in their individual contributions to the [Work] and shall be entitled to exploit their own individual contributions without the consent or any payment to the other author.

T.203

This Agreement may be terminated without notice in writing at any stage where the [Authors] both agree to do so.

T.204

The [warranties/conditions/representations] and indemnities on the part of the [Author] in this Agreement shall survive the termination of this Agreement.

T.205

The [Author] may terminate this Agreement by giving notice in writing to the [Publisher] in the following circumstances:

1.1 If the [Publisher] shall be in fundamental breach of the Agreement or if the [Publisher] shall go into liquidation or has a receiver appointed over its business and assets. The [Author] shall have the right to terminate the Agreement immediately upon service of notice.

1.2 In the event that all editions of the [Work] published in the [English] language are out of print (less than fifty copies remain in stock) and are not available through retail outlets generally to the public and the [Publisher] has not within [three months] of receipt of a written request from the [Author] reprinted at least [number] copies of any edition or has not within [nine months] of receipt of such a request issued a new edition of at least [number] copies. The Agreement shall terminate at the relevant period and all rights shall revert to the [Author]

1.3 Termination under 1.1 or 1.2 shall not affect the continuance of any sub-licences granted by the [Publisher] during the duration of the Agreement which shall end on their relevant expiry or termination date.

1.4 Termination shall be without prejudice to any claims which the [Author] may have for any monies due or owing and any claims which the [Author] may have against the [Publisher] in respect of breaches by the [Publisher] of the terms of this Agreement.

T.206

The [Licensor] may by written notice terminate this Agreement immediately:

1.1 If any royalty payable is in arrears and the [Publishing Company] fails to pay the sum within [seven days] of receipt of a notice in writing from the [Licensor] requesting payment.

1.2 If the [Publishing Company] has a receiver appointed over the whole or any substantial part of its assets or if an order is made or a resolution is passed for the winding up of the [Publishing Company] (except where such winding up is for the purposes of amalgamation or reconstruction and the company resulting, if a different legal entity, effectively agrees to be bound by or assumes the obligations of this Agreement, and the [Licensor] provides its consent).

1.3 If the [Publishing Company] shall be in default under or in breach of any of the terms of Clauses [–].

T.207

This Agreement shall be terminated at the discretion of the non-defaulting party if either party fails to perform or observe any of the terms set out herein on its part to be performed and observed, or is in breach of any of the warranties set out herein. Or if the defaulting party fails to remedy such failure or breach within [fourteen days] of receipt of a notice in writing from the other party such notice giving adequate particulars of the alleged default and of the intention of the party giving notice to terminate this Agreement. Or if the failure or breach is not remedied in the manner reasonably required by the party serving the notice or if a longer period is required but no steps have been taken and it is not being diligently pursued, then the party serving the notice may serve a further written notice of termination on the other party which shall have the effect of terminating this Agreement [seven days] after the date of receipt of such final notice of termination.

T.208

1.1 The parties agree that any termination of this Agreement shall be without prejudice to the rights of either party against the other which may have accrued up to the date of such termination.

1.2 That the [Licensee] shall ensure that all agreements with any sub-licensee, sub-agent and/or distributor shall contain a clause that the duration of the Agreement shall be subject to this Agreement. That the termination of this Agreement shall cause any other agreement and/or arrangement based and/or derived from it to automatically cease at the same date of termination.

1.3 That after the date of the termination of this Agreement the [Licensee] and/or sub-licensee, sub-agent and/or distributor shall not be entitled to sell, supply and/or dispose of (other than by authorised destruction) any unsold copies of the [Work].

1.4 Within [thirty days] after the date of termination of this Agreement the [Licensee] shall deliver to the [Agent] a statement showing full details of all matters necessary to enable the [Agent] to calculate the royalty due hereunder (including but not limited to the number and type of copies of the Work sold or disposed of, the gross prices, the payments made or which will become due to the [Company] and the date when such payment was actually made) for the period from the end of the last period in respect of which a statement confirmed by an auditor's certificate has already been delivered to the date of termination and any period thereafter. Such statement shall be accompanied by an auditor's certificate confirming it as true, and a cheque in respect of any sum owed or to become due to the [Agent] under this Agreement. Any payment due to the [Company] after the date of termination shall be deemed for the purposes of this Clause to fall due on the date of termination.

T.209

The delivery date of the [Work] shall be of the essence of this Agreement. If the [Author] shall fail for any reason to deliver the [Work] by the delivery date, the [Publisher] shall have the right to give the [Author] written notice to deliver the [Work] by a specific date which shall not be less than [three months]. If the [Author] still fails to deliver the [Work] then the [Publisher] may immediately terminate the Agreement by notice in writing. The [Publisher] shall revert all rights in the [Work] to the [Author] subject to the repayment by the [Author] of all sums already paid under this Agreement.

T.210

In addition to any other rights and remedies at law this Agreement may be terminated by written notice to the other party who has breached this Agreement in the following manner:

1.1 Where [Name] has failed to account or make payments as required under this Agreement.

1.2 Where the [Writer] has committed a serious breach of his/her obligations under this Agreement unless the [Writer] remedies the position within [–].

T.211

Either party may terminate this Agreement before [date] on any grounds. After that date either party shall have the right to terminate this Agreement by notice in writing if the other is unable to fulfil its obligations or commits a material breach or whose conduct or activities are considered seriously detrimental, derogatory of or offensive to the other party.

T.212

In the event that the [Author] shall fail to deliver the [Work] by the delivery date and/or the [Work] is not accepted by the [Publishers]. The [Publishers] shall have the right to refuse to publish the [Work] and/or require changes to comply with the content and form set out in the Agreement. The Advance against royalties shall not be due and/or paid by the [Publishers] until the [Work] has been delivered and/or accepted. In the event that the [Publishers] refuse to publish the [Work] and/or the changes are unacceptable to the [Author]. The Agreement shall be terminated and all rights shall revert entirely to the [Authors] as if this Agreement had never existed and the [Publishers] shall not be entitled to claim any rights, interest, option or otherwise in the [Work].

T.213

The [Author] shall have the right to terminate this Agreement by [one] calendar month's notice in writing in the event that:

1.1   The [Company] shall be trading while insolvent and/or unable to meet its debts.

1.2   The [Company] shall fail to publish the [Work] by [date].

1.3   The [Company] shall fail to promote, market and/or advertise the [Work] in [country].

1.4   The [Company] shall publish, adapt and/or exploit the [Work] without any credit and/or copyright notice to the [Author].

1.5   The [Company] shall subject the [Work] to derogatory treatment which prejudices the [Work] and/or [Author].

Purchase and Supply of Products

T.214

Without prejudice to any other rights or remedies to which the [Company] may be entitled it may terminate this [Sales Order] immediately and without liability in the event that:

1.1   The [Buyer/Hirer] concludes a debt settlement plan with creditors, or becomes bankrupt or goes into receivership or there is a court Order made or a resolution passed that it be wound up (other than solely for the purpose of amalgamation or reconstruction) or if the [Buyer/ Hirer] takes or suffers any similar action in consequence of debt, lien or charge; or

1.2   The [Buyer/Hirer] commits any breach of its obligations hereunder and fails to remedy such breach within [seven days] of receipt of written notice from the [Company].

T.215

In the event that the [Exhibitor] should fail to pay the [Distributor] the full price of the [Goods/Service] or is otherwise in breach of the terms and conditions of the booking or licence between the parties, the [Distributor] may at its sole discretion by written notice to the [Exhibitor] terminate the licence with immediate effect.

T.216

1.1   If the [Buyer] shall receive from the [Company] a notice to the effect that the [Buyer] has failed on the due date to pay the full purchase price for the [Company's] Products; or

1.2   If a receiver or other administrator or officer over the [Buyer] is appointed or if any action is taken for the dissolution or liquidation of the [Buyer]; or

1.3   If the [Buyer] shall cease to trade or appears to be unable to pay a debt or appears to have no reasonable prospect of being able to pay a debt (within the meaning of the Insolvency Act 1986 as amended) so as to entitle a creditor to bring a creditor's petition; or

1.4   If the [Buyer] shall sell or otherwise dispose of all or any part of the [Buyer's] interest in the land upon which the [Company's] Products are situated or if all or any part of the assets of the [Buyer] shall be attached or distrained upon.

The Buyer shall be deemed to have repudiated the contract for the purchase of any of the [Company's] Products in respect of which the property has not passed to the [Buyer] if any one of the matters set out above shall occur. The [Company] shall serve notice of termination and request that the [Buyer] immediately deliver the [Company's] Products in the possession or control of the [Buyer] to the [Company].

T.217

If you shall become bankrupt or be put into receivership or administration or shall make any composition or arrangement with or for the benefit of your creditors or shall purport to do so or shall have an action made against you for bankruptcy or any resolution is passed or an Order is made by a court to wind up the [Company] or a receiver or manager shall be appointed by any creditor or any act shall be done which would cause any such event to occur. The [Supplier] shall be entitled to terminate the [Purchase Order] by written notice to the [Company] but without prejudice to any other right or action which the [Supplier] may have at the date of such notice.

T.218

If the [Buyer] shall commit any breach of the contract or become insolvent or is unable to pay its debts or becomes bankrupt or being a company goes into liquidation (other than for the purposes of reconstruction or amalgamation) or has a receiver appointed over its assets or any part. The [Company] may without notice suspend or terminate the contract or any part which has not been fulfilled and stop any goods in transit without prejudice to any other right or remedy of the [Company].

T.219

If you do not comply with the requirements of this contract we can terminate it and recover the [Goods] by giving you written notice.

T.220

It is agreed that the [Company] shall have this right to terminate this contract if the [Hirer] is the subject of a bankruptcy or similar order or becomes insolvent or makes any arrangement or composition with or assignment for the benefit of creditors or if any assets are the subject of any form of seizure. If the [Hirer] is a company the [Company] shall have the right to terminate this contract if the [Hirer] goes into liquidation (either voluntary or compulsory) or if a receiver or administrator is appointed.

T.221

In addition to any other rights or remedies at law this Agreement may be terminated by giving immediate written notice to the defaulting party who has committed a material breach of this Agreement provided that the defaulting party has been given not less than [number] working days to remedy the matter following formal notice.

T.222

Either party shall have the right but not the obligation to terminate this Agreement immediately by notice in writing if:

1.1   The other party becomes insolvent;

1.2   Enters into an arrangement with its creditors;

1.3   A receiver or receivership administrator is appointed over the business of the defaulting party;

1.4   The director or its shareholders pass a resolution to suspend trading, wind up or dissolve the company other than for the purpose of amalgamation or restructuring.

T.223

If the [Company] and/or the [Distributors] become aware and/or have reasonable grounds to believe that the [Purchaser], business and/or third party is using the [disc/data] in a manner which was not set out in the licence document and which is prejudicial and/or detrimental to the business interests of the [Company] and/or the [Distributor] and/or is in breach of any intellectual property rights including copyright and/or trade marks of such parties. The [Company] and/or the [Distributor] shall have the right to terminate the licence with the [Purchaser] without prejudice to any other rights and remedies. The [Purchaser] shall be obliged on receipt of notice to surrender all copies of the [discs/data] held by the [Purchaser] and in their possession or control and/or to supply a list of all such copies supplied to third parties.

T.224

[Name] may terminate this contract for any one of the following reasons and shall be entitled to a full refund of all sums paid:

1.1   The [Goods] are not delivered by [date].

1.2   The [Goods] are not fully installed at the premises by [date] to a satisfactory standard whatever the reason for the delay provided it is not due to the fault of [name].

1.3   The [Goods] are defective, flawed, do not match, are of lower quality then the samples, are not fit for their intended purpose or the complete order is not delivered.

1.4   The [Company] has financial difficulties and is likely to cease trading.

1.5   There have been reports by a consumer body or government department which are detrimental to the [Goods].

T.225

The [Company] shall be entitled to terminate this Agreement early and with immediate effect where the [Distributor] has been the subject of an investigation by a local authority and/or other government agency and found guilty of any offence which relates to health and safety, product liability and/or content of its products.

Services

T.226
The [Agent] agrees that if within [six months] of [the date of this Agreement] the Company has not received as part of the Net Receipts full payment of the invoiced cost of [number] of the [Garments] ordered through the [Agent]. The [Company] shall have the right to terminate this Agreement by [twenty-one days'] written notice to the [Agent].

T.227
The [Agent] agrees that the [Company] shall be entitled to give notice to terminate the Agreement immediately in the event that [Name] is no longer actively involved in the business.

T.228
The [Agent] acknowledges and agrees that if within [six months] of the date of this Agreement the [Agent] has not negotiated an agreement with a reputable publisher for the publication of the [Work] the [Author] shall be entitled to terminate this Agreement immediately by notice in writing to the [Agent].

T.229
The [Writer] agrees to deliver to [Name] at [Name's] cost all documents, written material, recordings, photographs, tapes, masters and research discs, videos, DVDs, press cuttings, artwork and all other material of any nature relating to the [Work] and any parts, copies and/or adaptations, developments and/or variations in the possession or under the control of the [Writer] after the expiry or completion of this Agreement. The [Writer] shall provide a detailed inventory list of all the material, and confirm in writing that there is no further material of any kind in any medium in his/her possession or control.

T.230
The majority of the members of the [Group] may demand the departure of any member subject to a fair hearing on the following basis:

1.1 A meeting of all members of the [Group] shall be arranged to discuss the proposed departure.

1.2 Sufficient notice shall be given to all members of the time date and location of the meeting.

1.3 The grounds of complaint against any member who the other members want to depart shall be made known to that member prior to the meeting and in sufficient time to allow that member to answer any complaints.

1.4   Any member which the others intend to ask to leave the [Group] shall be given the opportunity to state his/her case in the presence of all members before any decision is made.

1.5   Any member who makes an allegation against the member who may be asked to leave shall be obliged to justify the complaint and may be questioned by any other member of the [Group].

1.6   No complaint shall be treated as valid unless it is of a serious nature.

T.231

The [Presenter] agrees that in the event that the [Company] decided for any reason to discontinue the production of the [Programme/Film/Series] and consequently wishes to dispense with the services of the [Presenter]. The [Company] shall only be liable for the [Presenter's] Fee [and the allowances] due for the outstanding period of the Term of the Agreement.

T.232

The [Presenter] shall on the expiry or termination of this Agreement deliver to the [Company] upon request all property of the [Company] which is in the possession or control of the [Presenter] including security pass, mobile phone, car, television, pager, documents, staff memorandum, films, books and photographs, laptops and other equipment, after deletion of the hard drive and all data which may be stored. The [Presenter] may retain such material as may be agreed with the [Company] for his/her own personal use but not for commercial publication and/or exploitation without the prior written consent of the [Company].

T.233

Each party shall have the right by summary notice in writing to the other to terminate this Agreement if the other party fails or neglects to perform or observe any material condition of this Agreement. Any failure or neglect by the [Presenter] or his/her agency may be used by the [Company] as a reason for this purpose. In the case of a failure or neglect which is capable of being remedied if the defaulting party does not correct the matter within [four days] the other party shall be entitled to terminate the Agreement.

T.234

The [Company] shall have the right by summary notice in writing to the [Presenter's] agency to terminate this Agreement if the [Presenter] shall for a period of [thirty] consecutive days on which the [Presenter] is required to provide his/her services to devote the whole of his/her attention, ability and work for any reason including illness and disability.

T.235

The [Agency] and the [Company] shall have the right by notice in writing to terminate this Agreement if that other party shall have passed a resolution or had an order made to wind up their business or a receiver is appointed over any part of the assets or an administrative officer is appointed.

T.236

The [Company] may terminate this Agreement without prior notice and with immediate effect and without prejudice to any other claim or remedy by the [Company] if the [Actor] shall:

1.1 Be in breach of his/her material obligations under this Agreement.

1.2 Become a mental patient or voluntarily enter a psychiatric ward for treatment for more than one month.

1.3 Be convicted of a serious criminal offence or any other serious act of misconduct or neglect whether or not in connection with the provision of his/her services which might bring or have brought him/herself and/ or the [Company] into disrepute or materially affect the performance of his/her services under the Agreement.

1.4 Become involved in any matter of public, political or social controversy in a manner which exposes the [Company] to unfavourable publicity by association.

1.5 Commit any act or neglect to anything which brings the [Company] into disrepute.

1.6 Make an admission in an interview in the media and/or on any social media that he/she has committed an act which is illegal in [country].

T.237

The [Manager] agrees that if within [twelve months] of the date of this Agreement the Fees received by the [Sportsperson] are less than [–], the [Sportsperson] shall have the right to terminate this Agreement with [seven days'] notice to the [Manager]. If this right of termination is exercised then the contracts already concluded shall continue in existence, but all sums shall be paid to the [Sportsperson] and no sums shall be paid and/or due to the [Manager].

T.238

When this Agreement expires or is terminated all rights granted to the [Company] in respect of the work done and the services provided prior to the end date shall remain the sole property of the [Company].

T.239

When this Agreement expires or is terminated the [Company] shall pay to the [Agent] the balance of any unpaid fees which have accrued and/or are due provided that these sums may be set off against any other which the [Company] claims are owed prior to payment.

T.240

After the expiry and/or termination of this Agreement any claim which either party may have against the other in respect of any alleged breach and/or non-performance shall not be prejudiced.

T.241

We shall have the right to terminate this Agreement without notice and with immediate effect and without liability in the event of misconduct, fraud or failure to carry out the services.

T.242

The [Company] shall be entitled at any time and without specifying any reason to give notice in writing to [Name] to terminate his/her engagement immediately. If so the [Company] agrees to pay [Name] and [Name] agrees to accept the sum of [figure/currency] which shall be in full and final settlement of any claim. [Name] agrees that he/she shall not be entitled to be paid any additional sums except those accrued prior to the date of this Agreement.

T.243

In addition to any other rights and remedies at law this Agreement may be terminated by giving written notice to the other party who is in breach or defaulted in the following circumstances:

1.1 Where the [Manager] has failed to account or make payments as required.

1.2 Where the [Manager] or [Sportsperson] has committed a serious breach of its obligations and the matter is not remedied within [one month] of written notice.

1.3 Where the [Manager] appears likely to go into voluntary or involuntary liquidation, be declared bankrupt or insolvent, or has his business assets or premises subject of a court Order due to debt, or have a receiver appointed.

1.4 Where the [Sportsperson] is likely to be convicted of a serious criminal offence including all drink driving related offences and/or illegal drugs and/or a breach of the rules of the professional sports association specified in Clause [–].

T.244

The [Presenter] shall have the right by notice in writing to end this Agreement if the production schedule is delayed, or the [Company] has financial problems concerning payment of its debts or has recently been associated in the media with negative publicity which involves in some controversy over a social, political or topical issue.

T.245

Either party shall be entitled to terminate this Agreement by serving notice in writing with a termination date on the other party if the other party shall:

1.1 Commit a breach of its obligations under this Agreement which is not capable of remedy or which is capable of remedy but is not completely resolved before the termination date.

1.2 Make any arrangement for the benefit of or with its creditors or any action or proceedings in bankruptcy or insolvency is taken including, but not limited to, the appointment of a receiver, administrator, liquidator (whether voluntary or compulsory) other than for the purpose of some form of restructuring or merger.

Termination shall not prejudice the rights and remedies of the parties. All terms and conditions set out in this Agreement which relate to the period after expiry or termination of this Agreement shall continue in full force and effect.

T.246

[Name] shall have the right to terminate the contract at any time on the following grounds which shall be accepted as constituting a breach of this Agreement by the [Company]:

1.1 The [Products] to be promoted or endorsed are found not to be safe and/or suitable for children and are withdrawn from the market.

1.2 The [Company] shall cease to manufacture and/or sell the [Products] before [date].

1.3 The [Company] shall be the subject of serious allegations of misconduct, fraud, breach of trading standards, price fixing or otherwise.

1.4 The [Company] is in serious financial difficulties.

[Name] shall have the right to be paid the full outstanding value of all fees in Clause [–] whether or not the work is completed or fulfilled and shall rank in priority over other creditors. Where no payment can be made due to lack of resources then some other material of equal value shall be agreed to be provided in lieu.

T.247

Without imposing on the [Company] any liability to the [Agent] for damages or otherwise or loss occasioned thereby and without prejudice to any rights, claim or interest of the [Company] hereunder. The [Company] shall have the right by notice to [Agent] forthwith to determine this Agreement:

1.1 If the [Agent] or [Name] fails or neglects to perform or observe any term or condition of this Agreement. In any case which is capable of remedy the [Agent] shall be given the opportunity to do so with [three days] of the Company notifying the [Agent].

1.2 If [Person] is unable to devote the whole of his/her time, attention and normal ability to performing the services to be provided hereunder for any reason including seriously incapacitating illness or disability.

Upon any expiry or determination of this Agreement:

1.1 All rights granted to the [Company] in respect of the work done and services rendered and the products thereof prior to such expiry or determination shall remain vested absolutely in the [Company].

1.2 The [Company] shall pay to [Agent] the balance (if any) outstanding and unpaid of the fees accrued due and payable to the date of such expiry or termination. Thereafter all liability of the [Company] to the [Agent] for the fees shall cease.

1.3 Any claim which either of the parties hereto shall have against the other for or in respect of any breach, non-observance or non-performance of any of the provisions hereof occurring prior to such expiry or termination or out of which such termination shall have arisen shall not be affected or prejudiced.

T.248

If within a period of [two years] from the date of the assignment to the [Music Publisher] one or more of the following forms of exploitation have not taken place the [Author] shall have the right to serve notice to terminate the Agreement:

1.1 The [Music Publisher] has released and/or distributed not less than [number] copies of the [DVD/CD/Download] of the [Sound Recordings] which are available for sale to the public;

1.2 The [Music Publisher] has published and/or distributed not less than [number] copies of a printed version of the [Sound Recordings] which are available for sale to the public;

1.3 The [Music Publisher] has licensed the synchronisation of the [Sound Recordings] for use for the soundtrack of a feature film with a reputable film company and/or distributor which is or will be available on general release;

1.4 The [Music Publisher] has authorised and/or licensed the public performance of the [Sound Recordings] on television and/or radio and/ or stage.

The [Author] shall have the right to terminate this Agreement by [one months'] notice in writing to the [Music Publisher] and all rights, sums received and material shall from the date of termination revert to and be paid to the [Author]. The [Music Publisher] shall be obliged to effect the assignment of any rights it may hold and any third party licence agreements and all material shall be returned to the [Author].

The [Author] agrees that it shall not have any further claim against the [Music Publisher] except for any royalties that may be due from the exploitation of the [Work].

Sponsorship

T.249

In addition to any other rights and remedies at law this Agreement may be terminated by the [Sponsor] or the [Sportsperson] by notice in writing to the party who is alleged to have breached or defaulted in the following circumstances:

1.1 Where the [Sponsor] has failed to account or make payments as required under this Agreement.

1.2 Where the [Sponsor] or [Sportsperson] has committed a serious breach of its obligations under this Agreement unless the defaulting party remedies the position within [10] days of receiving notice to that effect.

1.3 Where the [Sponsor] goes into voluntary or involuntary liquidation, been declared insolvent either in bankruptcy or other legal proceedings or has reached or is due to reach an agreement with creditors due to its failure or inability to pay its debts as they fall due or the [Sponsor's] business or part of it has been or is due to be placed in receivership.

1.4 Where the [Sportsperson] is convicted of a serious criminal offence including a drink/driving offence which results in a driving ban or a drug-related offence of any nature.

1.5 Where the [Sportsperson] has been found in breach of the rules of the [Sports Organisation] of which he/she is a member.

1.6 Where the conduct or activities of the [Sportsperson] are seriously detrimental, derogatory or offensive to the [Sponsor's] business or the [Sponsor's Products].

T.250

The [Sponsor] reserves the right to terminate this Agreement in the event that any subsequent legislation, directive, regulation, industry code or other guidelines shall restrict or prohibit sponsorship or endorsement of the [Event/Person/Product] under the agreed title or any other significant terms set out in this Agreement.

T.251

On termination of this Agreement the [User] shall immediately:

1.1 Cease all use of the Trade Marks, and any logo, image, text and/or any similar domain name.

1.2 Cease to have any right to use the Trade Marks and shall refrain from doing so. At the request of the [Proprietor] assist in the cancellation of the entry of the Register of Trade Marks of the [User] as a registered user.

1.3 Transfers any similar domain name to [Proprietor].

T.252

The [Sponsor] agrees that if for any reason it serves notice to terminate the Agreement it shall still be bound to pay the [Company] the minimum sum of [number/currency] in total under this Agreement.

University, Library and Educational

T.253

1.1 The [Institute] and the [Company] agree that any termination of this Agreement by either party shall be without prejudice to the rights and remedies of either party.

1.2 That the [Company] undertakes and agrees that all sub-licences, agency and/or distribution agreements based on and/or derived from this Agreement shall be terminated at the same time that this Agreement is terminated. That the [Company] shall ensure that all sub-licences, agency and/or distribution agreements shall contain a clause to that effect and further that none shall continue beyond the Term of this Agreement.

1.3 Within [seven] days of the date of termination of this Agreement the [Company] shall deliver to the [Institute] a statement showing full details of all sub-licensees, agents and/or distributors with which the [Company] has agreements based on and/or derived from this Agreement which have been terminated.

1.4 Within [twenty-one] days of the date of termination of this Agreement the [Company] shall deliver to the [Institute] a statement showing full details of the location, number and condition of all the stock, copies, marketing and/or other material held and/or controlled by all sub-licensees, agents and/or distributors with which the [Company] has sub-licences, agency and/or distribution and/or any other agreement based on and/or derived from this Agreement which have been terminated.

T.254

1.1 In addition to any other rights or remedies at law this Agreement may be terminated by either the [Institute] and/or the [Company] providing written notice to the other defaulting party which has committed and/or is alleged to have committed a material breach of this Agreement.

1.2 Both the [Institute] and the [Company] agree that the defaulting party shall be provided with the opportunity to remedy the breach within [one calendar month].

1.3 If the breach is not remedied then the non-defaulting party shall be entitled to termination of this Agreement on the first day after the calendar month if the breach has not been rectified without any further notice being required.

1.4 The [Institute] and/or the [Company] shall have the right but not the obligation to terminate this Agreement if the other party becomes insolvent, enters into an arrangement with its creditors for its debts, has a receiver or receivership administrator appointed over its business and/or the directors, trustees and/or its shareholders pass a resolution to suspend trading, wind up or dissolve the legal entity except where it is necessary for the purpose of amalgamation or restructuring.

T.255

1.1 The [Company] agrees that if within [twelve] months of the date of this Agreement the total sums received by the [Institute] from the [Company] under this Agreement are less than [figure/currency]. Then the [Institute] shall have the right and discretion to terminate this Agreement.

1.2 The [Institute] shall terminate the Agreement by formal notice in writing and shall specify the termination date. There shall be no right on the part of the [Company] to remedy the situation.

1.3 The [Institute] and the [Company] agree that If the [Institute] provides written notice of termination to the [Company] that the contracts already concluded by the [Company] on behalf of the [Institute] shall continue in existence. The [Company] agrees that all such contracts shall be transferred and assigned to the [Institute] by the [Company]. Further the [Company] shall not be entitled to receive any further sums at all under such contracts and all such sums shall be paid to the [Institute].

1.4 When this Agreement is terminated the [Company] shall pay to the [Institute] the balance of any unpaid sums which have accrued and/or are due. These unpaid sums held by the [Company] may not be used to set off against any claim, action and/or loss and/or damages and/or costs which the [Company] may have against the [Institute]

T.256

1.1 The [Institute] shall have the right by [seven] days written notice to the [Consultant] to terminate this Agreement without any reason and is not obliged to provide any grounds.

1.2 The [Consultant] shall not be entitled to any sum for loss of reputation, loss of fees, loss of publicity and/or credit for involvement in the [Project], damages, expenses and/or otherwise.

1.3 The [Institute] agrees to pay the [Consultant] for all work completed to the date of termination in accordance with the terms of this Agreement. Thereafter all liability of the [Institute] to the [Consultant] for the fees and any other sums shall cease.

1.4 The [Consultant] shall assign to the [Institute] all rights and/or interest acquired and/or created by the [Consultant] in respect of any work done and/or services provided to the [Institute] prior to the date of termination of the Agreement.

T.257

In addition to any other rights and remedies at law this Agreement may be terminated by the [Institute] or [Name] by notice in writing to the other party who is alleged to have breached or defaulted in the following circumstances:

1.1 Where the [Institute] has failed to account or make payments as required under this Agreement.

1.2 Where the [Institute] or [Name] has committed a serious breach of its obligations under this Agreement unless the defaulting party remedies the position within [one calendar month] of receiving notice to that effect.

1.3 Where the [Institute] and/or the [Name] goes into voluntary or involuntary liquidation, been declared insolvent either in bankruptcy or other legal proceedings or has reached or is due to reach an agreement with creditors due to its failure to pay its debts or the [Institute] or part of it has been or is due to be taken over by a third party as it is unable to operate and/or meet its debts as they fall due.

1.4 Where [Name] is convicted of a serious criminal offence including a drink/driving offence which results in a driving ban or a drug-related offence of any nature and/or is the subject of criminal and/or civil proceedings which have not yet been concluded which would jeopardise and/or have been decided and have affected detrimentally the reputation and/or standing of the [Institute] by attracting derogatory media attention and publicity.

1.5 Where [Name] has had a professional qualification removed by any organisation and/or where the conduct and/or activities of [Name] in his personal and/or professional life are not in the interests of the [Institute] and are likely to affect the support of [Institute] by the public, government bodies and/or sponsors.

TERRITORY

General Business and Commercial

T.258
'The Licensed Vessels' shall be the ships owned and controlled by the [Company] which are set out in appendix [–] and which are operational from [date] to [date].

T.259
'The Licensed Aeroplanes' shall be the fleet of aeroplanes owned and/or controlled by the [Company] which are shown on the existing schedule which sets out flight routes in appendix [–].

T.260
'The Licensed Area' shall mean the following countries [specify]. The land and territorial waters are marked on the attached map in Schedule [–] and form part of this Agreement.

T.261
'The Territory' shall mean throughout the universe.

T.262
'The Territory' shall mean throughout the world and outer space.

T.263
'The Territory' shall mean the world.

T.264
'The Territory' shall mean all countries, bases and locations throughout the world.

T.265
'The Territory' shall be all countries, areas, ships, aeroplanes, oil rigs, bases and any other locations throughout the world excluding [–].

T.266
'The Territory' shall be the following specified countries [–].

T.267
'The Territory' shall be the following [Licensed Area/countries] [–] and all ships, oil rigs, aircraft and military installations in that location.

T.268
'The Territory' shall be all countries, bases and locations both above and below the sea and land whether moveable or not throughout the planet Earth.

T.269
'The Territory' shall be the following countries marked on the attached map in Schedule [–] as follows; [–] and all surrounding territorial waters and any ships, airlines, vessels or other moving methods of transportation or property of companies which are registered in the relevant country.

T.270
'The Territory' shall mean the Licensed Areas listed in Schedule [–] or as subsequently agreed in writing between the [Licensor] and the [Licensee].

T.271
'The Territory' shall mean those countries listed in Schedule [–] attached hereto.

T.272
'The Territory' shall mean the following specific [English/French/Spanish/German/other] speaking countries [–].

T.273

'The Territory' shall mean outer space [as defined in the Outer Space Act 1986 as amended].

T.274

'The Continental Shelf' means the areas designated by order under [Continental Shelf Act 1964 as subsequently amended].

T.275

'The Territory' means the [country] and all oil rigs, military installations ships and aircraft wherever located of that country.

T.276

Set out below are the countries in which the [Work] may be exclusively published by the [Company] [–].

The countries in which the [Work] may be non-exclusively published by the [Company] [–].

The countries in which the [Work] may not be published by the [Company] [–].

T.277

'Territory' shall mean all countries, islands, sub-terrain, sea, airspace, bases, locations, sites and structures whether stationary, stable and/or moving including aeroplanes, ships, rigs, space vessels, throughout the world, outer space and the universe.

T.278

'The Territory' shall mean all countries, bases and locations throughout the world [the universe or otherwise without limitation of boundary including outer space].

T.279

The land and name shall be that which is recognised and acknowledged by [Organisation] [at the time of this Agreement/at any time during the Agreement.]

'The Territory' shall be defined as the following countries, their territorial waters and seas, airspace, mountains, under and below the land and any associated isles, islands and surrounding fragments of land as follows [specify countries].

T.280

'The Territory' shall be the area known as [specify] in [country] which is marked out on the attached map in Appendix [–] which is included as part of this Agreement.

T.281

'The Territory' shall mean all the countries listed below together with any sub-terrain below the land, and any area above in the sky, and the territorial waters and any area under the water and below the seabed and any islands which are developed and/or created by the country [specify list].

T.282

The Territory shall not include any aeroplanes, ships, oils rigs, vessels, tunnels, bridges and other objects which are not within the area specified even if they are registered as based in that country.

T.283

'The Territory' shall be defined as Algeria, Angola, Benin, Botswana, Burkina Faso, Burundi, Cameroon, Cape Verde, Central African Republic, Chad, Comoros, Congo (Brazzaville), Congo (Kinshasa), Ivory Coast, Djibouti, Egypt, Equatorial Guinea, Eritrea, Ethiopia, Gabon, Gambia, Ghana, Guinea, Guinea-Bissau, Kenya, Lesotho, Liberia, Libya, Madagascar, Mali, Mauritania, Mauritius, Morocco, Mozambique, Namibia, Niger, Nigeria, Rwanda, Sao Tome and Principe, Senegal, Seychelles, Sierra Leone, Somalia, South Africa, South Sudan, Sudan, Swaziland, Tanzania, Togo, Uganda, Zambia, Zimbabwe.

T.284

'The Territory' shall be Afghanistan, Bahrain, Bangladesh, Bhutan, Brunei, Cambodia, China, East Timor, India, Indonesia, Iran, Iraq, Israel, Japan, Jordan, Kazakhstan, Korea North, Korea South, Kuwait, Kgrgyzstan, Laos, Lebanon, Malaysia, Maldives, Mongolia, Myamar (Burma), Nepal, Oman, Pakistan, The Philippines, Qatar, Rusra, Saudia Arabia, Singapore, Sri Lanka, Syria, Taiwan, Tajikistan, Thailand, Turkey, Turkmenistan, United Arab Emirates, Uzbekistan, Vietnam, Yemen.

T.285

'The Territory' shall be the following countries and areas: Afghanistan, Bangladesh, Bhutan, China, Hong Kong SAR, India, Japan, Korea (North), Korea (South), Macao SAR, Mongolia, Maldives, Nepal, Pakistan, Sri Lanka, Taiwan.

T.286

'The Territory' shall be defined as Brunei Darussalam, Burma/Myanmar, Cambodia, East Timor, Indonesia, Laos, Malaysia, Philippines, Singapore, Thailand, Vietnam.

T.287

'The Territory' shall mean:

1.1   Australia, Fiji, Guam, New Zealand, Maldives, Pacific Islands, Solomon Islands, Samoa, Sri Lanka, Tonga, Vanuatu, South Africa, Africa.

1.2   Bangladesh, India, Pakistan.

1.3   Burma, Cambodia, China, Hong Kong, Indonesia, Laos, Macau, Malaysia, Myanmar, Nepal, Papua, New Guinea, Philippines, Singapore, Taiwan, Thailand, Vietnam.

1.4   Japan, Korea.

T.288

'The Territory' shall mean the following countries and islands: Australia, Fiji, Kiribati, Marshall Islands, Micronesia, Nauru, New Zealand, Palau, Papua New Guinea, Samoa, Solomon Islands, Tonga, Tuvalu, Vanuatu.

T.289

'The Territory' shall mean the following countries and islands: Australia, Tasmania, New Zealand.

T.290

'The Commonwealth' shall mean the following countries by region: Africa: Botswana, Cameroon, Ghana, Kenya, Lesotho, Malawi, Mauritius, Mozambique, Namibia, Nigeria, Rwanda, Seychelles, Sierra Leone, South Africa, Swaziland, Uganda, United Republic of Tanzania, Zambia.

Asia: Bangladesh, Brunei, Darussalan, India, Malaysia, Maldives, Pakistan, Singapore, Sri Lanka

Caribbean and Americas: Antigua and Bermuda, The Bahamas, Barbados, Belize, Canada, Dominica, Grenada, Guyana, Jamaica, St Kitts and Nevis, St Lucia, St Vincent and the Grenadines, Trinidad and Tobago.

Europe: Cyprus, Malta and the United Kingdom.

Pacific: Australia, Fiji, Karibati, Nauru, New Zealand, Papua New Guinea, Samoa, Solomon Islands, Tonga, Tuvalu, Vanuatu.

T.291

'The Commonwealth' shall mean the independent countries of the Commonwealth as at [date] as follows:

Antigua & Bermuda, Australia, The Bahamas, Bangladesh, Barbados, Belize, Botswana, Brunei, Canada, Cyprus, Dominica, Darussalam, Fiji Islands, The

Gambia, Ghana, Grenada, Guyana, India, Jamaica, Kenya, Kiribati, Lesotho, Malawi, Malaysia, Maldives, Malta, Mauritius, Mozambique, Namibia, Nauru, New Zealand, Nigeria, Pakistan, Papua New Guinea, St Kitts and Nevis, St Lucia, St Vincent, Samoa, Seychelles, Sierra Leone, Singapore, Solomon Islands, South Africa, Sri Lanka, Swaziland, Tanzania, Tonga, Trinidad and Tobago, Tuvalu, Uganda, United Kingdom, Vanuatu, Zambia, but shall not include Eire or Northern Ireland.

T.292
'The European Community' shall mean all the full and associate Member States of the European Union as at [date] set out below namely [–].

T.293
'The European Union countries' shall mean all full Member States of the European Union as at [date] and which shall be the following [–].

T.294
The Territory of this Agreement shall include 'Europe' which for the avoidance of doubt means those countries which are full members of the European Union as set out on europa.eu, the official website, as at the date of execution of this Agreement [and at any time thereafter] as specified in Schedule [–] to this Agreement but shall specifically exclude the countries specified as excluded under Schedule [–] whether such country becomes a full member of the European Union or not.

T.295
'The Territory' shall mean Austria, Belgium, Cyprus, Czech Republic, Denmark, Estonia, Finland, France, Germany, Greece, Hungary, Ireland, Italy, Latvia, Lithuania, Luxembourg, Malta, Poland, Portugal, Slovakia, Slovenia, Spain, Sweden, The Netherlands, United Kingdom, Bulgaria, Croatia, Romania, Turkey, Albania, Andorra, Belarus, Bosnia-Herzegovina, of Macedonia (former Yugoslav Republic), Iceland, Liechtenstein, Moldova, Monaco, Norway, Russia, San Marino, Serbia and Montenegro, Switzerland, Ukraine, Vatican City State, Georgia, Azerbaijan, Armenia.

T.296
'The Territory' shall be limited to the land, territorial waters and airspace of the following countries which are full members of the European Union at [date]: Austria, Belgium, Bulgaria, Croatia, Cyprus, Czech Republic, Denmark, Estonia, Finland, France, Germany, Greece, Hungary, Ireland, Italy, Latvia, Lithuania, Luxembourg, Malta, Poland, Portugal, Slovakia, Slovenia, Spain,

Sweden, The Netherlands, United Kingdom. It shall not include those which are candidate countries or potential candidates.

T.297
'The Territory' shall be Europe and shall be defined by the shaded areas of land, sea as set out in the attached map in Schedule [–] and cover a space below the sea of [distance] and above the land and sea of [distance]. The licensed area is defined by area rather than by the names of the countries which may change and it is not defined by reference to the European Union memberships.

T.298
'The Territory' shall be the following full member states of the European Union: Austria, Belgium, Bulgaria, Croatia, Cyprus, Czech Republic, Denmark, Estonia, Finland, France, Germany, Greece, Hungary, Ireland, Italy, Latvia, Lithuania, Luxembourg, Malta, Netherlands, Poland, Portugal, Romania, Slovakia, Slovenia, Spain, Sweden, United Kingdom the [29] full members and Iceland, Montenegro, Serbia and Turkey the [4] candidate countries Albania, Bosnia and Herzegovina and Kosovo are specifically not included.

T.299
'The Territory' shall mean all the following countries which are full members states of the European Union as at [date] their land and territorial waters: Belgium, Bulgaria, Croatia, Czech Republic, Denmark, Germany, Estonia, Ireland, Greece, Spain, France, Italy, Cyprus, Latvia, Lithuania, Luxembourg, Hungary, Malta, Netherlands, Austria, Poland, Portugal, Romania, Slovenia, Slovakia, Finland, Sweden, United Kingdom.

T.300
'The Territory' shall be the following countries of Eastern Europe and Central Asia: Albania, Armenia, Azerbaijan, Belarus, Bosnia and Herzegovina, Croatia, Georgia, Kosovo, Kazakhstan, Kyrgyz Republic, Macedonia (former Yugoslav Republic), Moldova, Montenegro, Russia, Serbia, Tajikistan, Turkmenistan, Ukraine, Uzbekistan.

T.301
'The Territory' shall be the following Western European countries; Andorra, Iceland, Liechtenstein, Monaco, Norway, San Marino, Switzerland, Vatican City.

T.302
'The Territory' shall be the Mediterranean and the Middle East which shall be defined as Algeria, Bahrain, Egypt, Iran, Iraq, Israel, Jordan, Kuwait,

Lebanon, Libya, Morocco, Oman, Palestinian Authority, Qatar, Saudi Arabia, Syria, Tunisia, Turkey, United Arab Emirates, Yemen.

T.303
'The Territory' shall mean Iraq, Iran, Israel, Jordan, Kuwait, Libya, Lebanon, Qatar, Saudi Arabia, Syria, United Arab Emirates.

T.304
'The Territory' shall mean the borough of [–] in the county of [–] in England.

T.305
'The Territory' shall mean the United Kingdom of Great Britain and Northern Ireland, the Republic of Ireland, the Channel Islands and the Isle of Man.

T.306
'The Territory' shall mean the United Kingdom, Northern Ireland, the Channel Islands and the Isle of Man and the following countries [–].

T.307
'The Territory' shall be the United Kingdom meaning the United Kingdom of Great Britain and Northern Ireland, the Channel Islands, the Isle of Man and the United Kingdom Continental Shelf.

T.308
'The United Kingdom' shall mean the United Kingdom of Great Britain which includes England, Wales, Scotland, Northern Ireland, and the Channel Islands, the Isle of Man, and the territorial waters of the United Kingdom shall be treated as part of the United Kingdom. It shall also include things done in the United Kingdom sector of the continental shelf on a structure or vessel which is present there for purposes directly connected with the exploration of the seabed or sub-soil or the exploration of their natural resources.

T.309
'The Territory' shall be the British Islands (which expression shall mean the United Kingdom of Great Britain and Northern Ireland, the Channel Islands and the Isle of Man, [the Republic of Ireland], Malta and Gibraltar). The Territory shall also include in respect of each country of the Territory all ships, oil rigs and aircraft of the nationality, flag or registry of such country and all camps, bases, installations and reservations of the armed forces of such country.

T.310
'The Territory' shall be limited to the land known as [address] as specified on the [map/chart/plan] a copy of which is attached and forms part of the

Agreement. No rights are specified in relation to the sub-terrain and/or the air space above except in relation to the actual dimensions of the buildings and structures on the land.

T.311
'The Territory' shall be the United States of America and Canada, Hawaii, Puerto Rico, Mexico, Alaska, Guam and the North Mariana Islands.

T.312
'The Territory' shall be Central America and the Caribbean which shall mean Antigua and Bermuda, Bahamas, Barbados, Belize, Costa Rica, Cuba, Dominica, Dominican Republic, El Salvador, Grenada, Guatemala, Guyana, Haiti, Honduras, Jamaica, Nicaragua, Panama, Saint-Kitts and Nevis, Saint-Lucia, Saint-Vincent, Suriname, Trinidad and Tobago.

T.313
'The Territory' shall mean Argentina, Bolivia, Brazil, Caribbean, Central America, Chile, Columbia, Ecuador, French Guiana, Guyana, Mexico, Paraguay, Peru, Suriname, Uruguay, Venezuela.

T.314
'The Territory' shall be North America which shall mean Canada, Mexico, and the United States of America.

T.315
'The Territory' shall be South America which shall be defined as Argentina, Bolivia, Brazil, Chile, Colombia, Ecuador, Paraguay, Peru, Uruguay, Venezuela.

T.316
'The Territory' shall be all the independent states in the world and the dependencies and areas of special sovereignty noted below:

Afghanistan, Albania, Algeria, Andorra, Angola, Antigua and Barbuda, Argentina, Armenia, Aruba, Australia, Austria, Azerbaijan, The Bahamas, Bahrain, Bangladesh, Barbados, Belarus, Belgium, Belize, Benin, Bhutan, Bolivia, Bosnia and Herzegovina, Botswana, Brazil, Brunei, Bulgaria, Burkina Faso, Burma, Barundi, Cambodia, Cameroon, Canada, Central African Republic, Chad, Chile, China, Columbia, Comoros, Democratic Republic of the Congo, Republic of the Congo, Costa Rica, Cote d' Ivoire, Croatia, Cuba, Cyprus, Czech Republic, Denmark, Djibouti, Dominica, Dominican Republic, Ecuador, Egypt, El Salvador, Equatorial Guinea, Eritrea, Estonia,

Ethiopia, Fiji, Finland, France, Gabon, The Gambia, Georgia, Germany, Ghana, Greece, Grenada, Guatemala, Guinea, Guinea-Bissau, Guyana, Haiiti, Holy See, Honduras, Hungary, Iceland, India, Indonesia, Iran, Iraq, Ireland, Israel, Italy, Jamaica, Japan, Jordan, Kazakhstan, Kenya, Kiribati, North Korea, South Korea, Kosovo, Kuwait, Kyrgyzstan, Laos, Latvia, Lebanon, Lesotho, Liberia, Libya, Liechtenstein, Lithuania, Luxembourg, Macedonia, Madagascar, Malawi, Malaysia, Maldives, Mali, Malta, Marshall Islands, Mauritania, Mauritius, Mexico, Micronesia, Moldova, Monaco, Mongolia, Montenegro, Morocco, Mozambique, Namibia, Nauru, Nepal, Netherlands, Netherland Antilles, New Zealand, Nicaragua, Niger, Nigeria, Norway, Oman, Pakistan, Palau, Panama, Papua New Guinea, Paraguay, Peru, Philippines, Poland, Portugal, Qatar, Romania, Russia, Rwanda, Saint Kitts and Nevis, Saint Lucia, Saint Vincent and the Grenadines, Samoa, San Marino, Sao Tome and Principe, Saudia Arabia, Senegal, Serbia, Seychelles, Sierra Leone, Singapore, Slovakia, Slovenia, Solomon Islands, Somalia, South Africa, South Sudan, Spain, Sri Lanka, Sudan, Suriname, Swaziland, Sweden, Switzerland, Syria, Taiwan, Tajikistan, Tanzania, Thailand, Timor-Leste, Togo, Tonga, Trinidad and Tobago, Tunisia, Turkey, Turkmenistan, Tuvalu, Uganda, Ukraine, United Arab Emirates, United Kingdom, United States, Uruguay, Uzbekistan, Vanuatu, Venezuela, Vietnam, Yemen, Zambia, Zimbabwe.

Akrotiri sovereignty of United Kingdom, American Samoa sovereignty of United States, Anguilla, sovereignty of United Kingdom, Antarctica, Aruba sovereignty of Netherlands, Ashmore and Cartier Islands, sovereignty of Australia, Baker Island sovereignty of United States, Bermuda sovereignty of United Kingdom, Bouvet Island sovereignty of Norway, British Indian Ocean Territory sovereignty of United Kingdom, Cayman Islands sovereignty of United Kingdom, Christmas Island sovereignty of Australia, Clipperton Island sovereignty of Frances Cocos (Keeling) Islands sovereignty of Australia, Cook Islands sovereignty of New Zealand, Coral Sea Islands sovereignty of Australia, Curacao sovereignty of Netherlands, Dhekelia sovereignty of United Kingdom, Falkland Islands sovereignty of United Kingdom, Faroe Islands sovereignty of Denmark, French Guiana, French Polynesia sovereignty of France, French Southern and Antarctic Lands sovereignty of France, Gibraltar sovereignty of United Kingdom, Greenland sovereignty of Denmark, Guadeloupe, Guam sovereignty of United States, Bailliwick of Guernsey British Crown Dependency, Heart Island and McDonald Islands sovereignty of Australia, Hong Kong sovereignty of China, Howland Island sovereignty of United States, Isle of Man, British Crown Dependency, Jan Mayern sovereignty of Norway, Jarva Island sovereignty of United States, Balliwicke of Jersey, British Crown Dependency, Johnston Atoll sovereignty of United States, Kingman Reef sovereignty of United States, Macau sovereignty of China, Martinique, Mayotte, Midway Islands sovereignty of United States, Montserratt sovereignty of United Kingdom, Navassa Island sovereignty of United States, New Caledonia sovereignty of France, Niue sovereignty of New Zealand, Norfolk Island sovereignty of Australia, North Mariana Islands sovereignty of United States, Palmyra Atoll sovereignty of United States, Paracel Islands, Pitcairn Islands sovereignty of United Kingdom, Puerto Rico sovereignty of United States, Keurin Reunion, Saint Barthelemy, sovereignty of France, Saint Helena sovereignty of United Kingdom, Saint Martin sovereignty of France, Saint Pierre and Miquelon sovereignty of France, Saint Maarten sovereignty of Netherlands, South Georgia and the South Sandwich Islands sovereignty of United Kingdom, Spratly Islands, Svalbard sovereignty of Norway, Tokelau sovereignty of New Zealand, Turks and Caicos Islands sovereignty of United Kingdom, Virgin Islands sovereignty of United States, Wake Island sovereignty of United States, Wallis and Futuna sovereignty of France, Western Sahara.

THIRD PARTY TRANSFER

General Business and Commercial

T.317
Either party shall be entitled to transfer, assign or charge the benefit or obligations under this Agreement provided that the rights granted under this Agreement to the other party are not adversely affected and the indemnity in Clause [–] shall continue in full force and effect.

T.318
The [Licensee] shall not assign the benefit of this Licence which is of a purely personal nature nor grant any sub-licence under this Agreement.

T.319
This Agreement is not assignable in whole or part by either party.

T.320
The [Company] may at any time assign, sub-let, or transfer any or all of its rights or obligations under this Contract subject to its first obtaining the consent of the [Contractor] (which shall not be reasonably withheld). The [Company] may at any time assign this Contract to members of the [Company's] Group.

T.321
The [Contractor] shall not assign, sub-let or transfer any or all of its obligations under the Contract without the prior consent of the [Company] such consent not to be unreasonably withheld or delayed.

T.322

The [Contractor] shall not without the prior and express approval of the [Company] assign the rights and obligations arising out of his/her contract in whole or in part nor sub-contract any part of the contract nor cause it to be carried out or performed by third parties. Even where the [Company] authorises the [Contractor] to sub-contract all or part of the Work to third parties the [Contractor] shall remain bound by its obligations to the [Company]. The [Contractor] shall also be required to include in all contracts with such third parties provisions that ensure that the [Company] shall have the same rights and undertakings in relation to the third parties as the [Contractor] itself.

T.323

1.1 The [Licensee] shall not assign the benefit of this Agreement in whole or in part or sub-license any of its rights hereunder without the prior written consent of the [Licensor] except that the [Licensee] may assign to a permitted assignee.

1.2 A permitted assignee shall mean a parent or subsidiary of the [Licensee] or a person, firm or corporation who acquires a substantial part of the assets of the [Licensee]. Every permitted assignee shall assume all of the obligations of the [Licensee] to be performed or accruing after the effective date of the assignment but no assignment shall relieve the [Licensee] of its obligations hereunder.

T.324

Subject to Clause [–] hereof neither party hereto shall assign, transfer, charge or make over this Agreement or any of its rights or obligations hereunder without the prior written consent of the other party.

T.325

Neither party hereto shall assign, transfer, charge or make over this Agreement or any of its rights or obligations hereunder without the written consent of the other party.

T.326

This Agreement cannot be assigned by either party hereto except by [Name] to [specify person].

T.327

Neither party shall assign, transfer or otherwise dispose of this Agreement in whole or part(s) or any right hereunder to any third party without the prior written consent of the other party.

T.328

Neither party shall transfer or assign this Agreement or any rights acquired or obligations undertaken hereunder to any person, firm or corporation without the prior consent in writing of the other party. Such consent may not be unreasonably withheld or delayed in the case of an associated company of the party seeking consent. Clause [–] above shall be without prejudice to the rights of either party to sub-license their respective distribution rights in the [Film/Product/Services].

T.329

1.1   The [Creditor] may disclose to any person related to the [Creditor] and/ or any person to whom it is proposing to transfer or assign or has transferred or assigned any of its rights under this Guarantee any information about any of the guarantors and any person connected or associated with it.

1.2   Each of the guarantors represents and warrants that it has and subject to any contrary requirements of law will maintain any necessary authority by or on behalf of any such person to agree to the provisions of this Clause.

T.330

This Guarantee is freely assignable or transferable by the [Creditor].

T.331

None of the [Guarantors] may assign any of its rights and may not transfer any of its obligations under this Guarantee or enter into any transaction which would result in any of those rights or obligations passing to another person.

T.332

The Licence is not transferable except with the prior consent in writing of the [Company]. Consent shall not be given unless the [Company] is satisfied that the person or persons to whom it is proposed to transfer the Licence would be in a position to comply with all the Conditions hereof throughout the remainder of the Licence Period.

T.333

You shall not without our written consent, assign, transfer or sub-contract the [Order] to any third party.

T.334

This Contract is personal as between the parties and the [Contractor] may not assign any rights or obligations under this Contract to any entity (other than an affiliated company) without the prior written consent of the [Operator]. Any assignee shall expressly assume the rights and obligations of this Contract. Subject to this clause this Contract shall continue and be binding on the transferee, successors and assigns of such party.

T.335

The [Company] acknowledges that the [Licensee] shall be entitled at any time and from time to time to dispose of any of its interests in whatever form in any Licensed Area. If such right is exercised then the only liability of the [Licensee] to the [Company] shall be to notify the [Company] that the [Licensee] has disposed of its interests to such third party. The [Licensee] shall no longer be entitled to receive and deliver the [Service/Work] in accordance with the terms of this Agreement. In such event the [Company] agrees that it shall enter into a new agreement on terms not materially less favourable than this Agreement with the person or persons to whom such disposal is made for the [Service/Work] in the Licensed Area.

T.336

The [Licensor] may assign this Agreement or any of its rights hereunder to any third party but any such assignment shall not relieve the [Licensor] of any of its obligations hereunder.

T.337

The [Licensor] and the [Licensee] may assign this Agreement or any of their respective rights, licences or interest hereunder to any person, firm, corporation or other entity. Provided that no such assignment shall relieve the [Licensor] or the [Licensee] of its obligations hereunder and they shall be responsible and bear the cost of all acts, omissions, breaches, failures and/or damages and losses arising from any assignee for which they are responsible. In no event shall the [Licensee] be obligated to make payments hereunder to more than one person or entity at any one time.

T.338

The [Licensor] shall be entitled to transfer, assign or charge the [Registered Trade Marks] in whole or parts including, but not limited to, the use of the trade mark for a particular service or goods or in a particular manner or country.

T.339

The assignment or other transfer of a registered certification mark is not effective without the consent of the Registrar [as set out in the Trade Marks Act 1994 as amended].

T.340

The [Licensor] shall have the right to assign the benefit of this Agreement provided:

1.1   That the rights and licences granted to the [Licensee] shall not be adversely affected by such assignment and,

1.2   The [Licensor] agrees to indemnify the [Licensee] against any loss, damage or claim that may arise in consequence of any such assignment.

T.341

The [Company] shall be entitled to assign or transfer the benefit of this Agreement or to grant sub-licences hereunder without the consent of [Name]. In each case the [Company] shall only be required to give written notice of such assignment, transfer or grant to [Name] within [one] month of the date of the Agreement in each case.

T.342

This Agreement shall bind and ensure to the benefit of the parties and the respective personal representatives, assigns or other successors in title.

T.343

This Agreement shall be binding upon the successors in business and/or title of the [Company/individual] and may in any event be transferred to any third party by the [Company/individual] provided that the person or company receiving the transfer agrees to be bound by the benefit and burden of this Agreement.

T.344

This Agreement is restricted to the contracting parties. Neither party may seek to assign, transfer, charge or otherwise dispose of at any time of any part of this Agreement to any third party. Nor shall either party grant any sub-licence of any part nor cause it to be carried out by third parties without the prior written approval of the other party. There is no obligation to provide any approval and even where consent is provided it shall not relieve either party of their undertakings and obligations under this Agreement.

T.345

This Agreement is personal to the contracting parties. Neither party may seek to transfer, charge or make over this Agreement to any third party without the consent in writing of the other party in each case [except to the extent that the benefit and burden of this Agreement shall be binding upon the successors in business and/or title of the [Assignor/Assignee].

T.346

After the launch date the [Designer] shall be limited to the provision of support services agreed between the parties. The [Company] shall be entitled either before or after the launch date to sell, transfer, charge or otherwise dispose of the Domain Name or website as it thinks fit. The consent and/or approval of the [Designer] is not required and the [Designer] waives any rights and/or interest provided that he/she is paid for the completion of the work set out in the [Proposal].

T.347

Anybody, corporate or otherwise, which is not a party to this Agreement shall have no right to enforce any obligation or right against the [Company] or the [Designer].

T.348

Neither party shall assign, charge, or make over this Agreement or any of its rights or obligations without the prior written consent of the other party. Such consent may not be unreasonably withheld or delayed in the case of a parent, subsidiary and/or associated company which requires consent. Any such consent shall be subject to the conclusion of a written undertaking to the effect that the assignee will fulfil all the rights, obligations and liabilities under the Agreement. However no such assignment to an assignment shall relieve the party of any obligations and liabilities under this Agreement.

Merchandising

T.349

The [Licensee] undertakes not to assign to any third party any rights acquired under the terms of this Agreement unless previously authorised in writing by the [Company] to do so.

T.350

The [Company] shall not be entitled to assign, transfer or otherwise encumber this Agreement or any of its benefits or obligations hereunder without the prior consent of the [Licensor] which consent shall not be unreasonably withheld.

T.351

The [Distributor] shall not assign the rights granted to it in the Agreement or the benefit thereof except as part of an internal restructuring of the [Distributor] without the [Company's] written consent such consent not to be unreasonably withheld or delayed.

T.352

The [Licensor] agrees that he shall not license or authorise any third party to produce any other [Property] based on the [Format] or any development or variation during the Licence Period.

T.353

The [Licensee] agrees that the [Licensor] shall be entitled to approve the appointment of any sub-agent, sub-licensee, or a third party in respect of the production, manufacture, supply, distribution, marketing or other exploitation of the [Licensed Article/Record/Work/Rights] under this Agreement.

T.354

The [Licensor] agrees that it shall not have the right to approve the appointment of any sub-agent, sub-licensee, distributor and any other third party in respect of the production, manufacture, supply, distribution, marketing and exploitation of the [Licensed Articles/other] under this Agreement.

T.355

Subject to Clause [–] neither party may assign, transfer, charge or make over this Agreement or any of its rights or obligations except that the [Distributor] may assign to a holding, subsidiary or associate company or a person, firm or company that owns or acquires more than [fifty per cent] of the [Distributor's] stock or assets. No assignment shall relieve the [Distributor] of any of its obligations under this Agreement.

T.356

1.1 Neither party shall assign, transfer, charge and/or make over this Agreement and/or any of its rights and/or obligations without the prior written consent of the other party.

1.2 This Agreement is not intended to confer any rights and/or obligations upon any third party which is not a signatory to this Agreement.

T.357

The [Licensee] shall not be entitled to assign, transfer, charge, makeover, sub-licence, sub-contract and/or otherwise delegate any part of this Agreement to any third party except for professional legal and accounting advisors who provide data, information, reports and payments pursuant to this Agreement on behalf of the [Licensee]. This shall not in any way absolve the [Licensee] from the obligations, duties and responsibilities set out in this Agreement nor shall any such advisors be party to this Agreement. No third party shall be entitled to rely on and/or enforce the terms of this Agreement which is only between the contracting parties.

Publishing

T.358

The term '[Publisher/Company]' in this Agreement shall be deemed to include the person or persons or company for the time being carrying on the business under the same registered name as the [Publisher/Company], whether they be heirs, executors, personal representatives, administrators or assignees.

T.359

This Agreement shall bind and ensure to the benefit of the parties and their respective personal representatives, assigns, licensees or other successors in title.

T.360

The [Publishers] may assign or grant the benefit of this Agreement or any of its rights or benefits in whole or in parts to any person, firm or company that is a subsidiary of or affiliated to the [Publishers] and such assignee or licensee shall be entitled to the same rights and benefits as stated in respect of the [Publisher] in this Agreement. The assignee or licensees shall assume the same undertakings and terms as the [Publisher] in respect of such rights as have been assigned or granted.

T.361

The [Company] shall be entitled to assign the benefit of this Agreement in whole or in part to any third party. The [Writer] agrees that in the event of such assignment he/she will fulfil his/her obligations hereunder and the [Company] shall remain liable for its obligations hereunder. In the event that the [Company] desires that the [Writer] shall render his/her services in whole or in part to any third party, the [Writer] agrees that if so requested by the [Company] he/she shall enter into an agreement with such third party in substitution for and on the same terms and conditions as set out in this Agreement. The [Company] agrees that it shall be bound to fulfil the obligations to the [Writer] in the event that the third party shall fail to fulfil its obligations thereunder.

T.362

The [Licensor] undertakes not to permit, license or transfer the right to publish the Extracts or any other part(s) of the [Work] in any other newspaper, periodical or magazine owned or controlled by any third party throughout the Territory for the duration of the Licence Period except for the purposes of review criticism or fair dealing.

T.363

[Name] agrees and undertakes not to engage or enter into any agreement with any third party to write, research or produce any other book or publication based on the [Synopsis/subject/other] or any development or variation at any time during the Term of the Agreement [throughout the Territory].

T.364

The [Company] shall consult with the [Author/Artist] in respect of the appointment of any third party to exploit the [Work].

T.365

The [Author] undertakes that he/she will not grant an option nor authorise, license or permit any third party to produce a [Film/Work] based on the [Author's Work] or any adaptation, variation or development during the [Option Period] without the prior written consent of the [Company].

T.366

The benefit and burden of this Agreement shall be binding upon the successors in title and/or business and/or part to [specify party].

Purchase and Supply of Products

T.367

Both parties shall have the right to assign, transfer, license and charge the benefit of this Agreement to any third party provided:

1.1   That it shall not relieve the [Seller] of any of the obligations under this Agreement. In the event of a breach by the company or person receiving any type of benefit which is not remedied then the [Seller] shall be liable as if it were a breach by the [Seller].

1.2   The third party receiving the benefit must undertake that the rights of the other party under this Agreement shall not be adversely affected by the [assignment/transfer/licence/charge] and must agree to indemnify the other party against any loss, damage or claim arising in consequence of such agreement with the third party.

T.368

You shall not assign, transfer or sub-contract the [Order/Work/Item] to any third party.

T.369

The [Company] may procure that this Agreement shall be performed by any parent, subsidiary or associated company of the [Company] or any third party, but no such procurement or assignment shall relieve the [Company] of any of its obligations to the [Buyer/Hirer].

T.370
The [Seller] shall not without the written consent of the [Company] assign, transfer or sub-contract any part or all of the [Purchase Order] or delegate any duties hereunder and any such purported assignment or delegation shall be void.

Services

T.371

1.1 This Agreement is between the [Agent] and the [Actor]. No third party shall be entitled to rely on the benefits and obligations under this Agreement.

1.2 Neither party shall assign, transfer, charge or make over this Agreement or any of its rights to any third party without the written consent of the other party.

T.372

1.1 This Agreement is purely personal between the [Actor] and the [Agent] and no third party may seek to benefit or enforce its obligations unless it has been agreed to by the [Actor] and the [Agent].

1.2 This Agreement may be terminated with immediate effect by notice in writing if either party is not available for a continuous period of [three months] (excluding weekends) to perform the obligations set out.

1.3 The [Agent] shall at all times be responsible for the acts and omissions and other matters arising directly or indirectly from any third parties whom the [Agent] has arranged and/or appointed to carry out any work on behalf of the [Agent] relating to the [Actor].

1.4 Neither party shall assign, transfer, charge or make over any part of this Agreement or any part of its rights and obligations without the prior written consent of the other party.

T.373
This Agreement is personal to the [Company] and [Name]. No third party shall have the right to seek to enforce or rely on the benefits or obligations set out in this Agreement.

T.374
The [Company] agrees that it shall not be entitled to use, exploit or license any of the material produced or created for the purposes of this Agreement

in which [Name] appears or performs in sound or vision or by any other reference for any purpose at any time other than the promotion or advertising of the [Company's Product] during the Term of the Agreement without the prior written consent of [Name].

T.375

The rights granted in this Agreement are personal to the [Client] and may not be assigned, transferred, sub-licensed, charged or otherwise disposed of at any time.

T.376

The [Exhibitor] has no right to transfer, share, assign, sub-let, sub-license or in any other manner use or allocate the (stand) with any other third party. The [Stand] is only for the personal use of the [Exhibitor] except that the [Exhibitor] may reach an arrangement with third parties for:

1.1 Sponsorship, endorsement and advertising purposes.

1.2 Sales of their products or services.

1.3 Commission or otherwise as agents.

T.377

The [Agent] undertakes that he/she shall not for the Term of this Agreement assign, transfer, or charge any of the rights or obligations in this Agreement to any third party without the prior written consent of the [Artist].

T.378

The [Company] shall be entitled to assign the benefit of this Agreement either in whole or in part or to lend the [Director's] services to any third party and the [Employer] undertakes to procure that the [Director] shall if and when and where required by the [Company] render his/her services hereunder for any such third party. Provided that the [Company] shall remain liable for all its obligations notwithstanding such assignment and that the [Company] shall within [ten days] of such assignment give the [Employer] written notice thereof including the name and address of the assignee.

T.379

The [Company] shall be entitled to assign the benefit of this Agreement or to make available the services of the [Presenter]:

1.1 To any associated company, affiliate, subsidiary, parent company, joint venture partner and/or any other related business, advertiser, sponsor and/or supplier and

1.2 To any third party pursuant to or in connection with any direction or recommendation or permission of the [–].

T.380

The [Company] may with the [Lender's] consent (such consent not to be unreasonably withheld) make available the [Artiste's] freelance services in whole or in part to any other person, firm, or company provided that the [Company] remains liable for the performance of all its obligations hereunder.

T.381

The [Music Publisher] shall not have the right to transfer or assign the benefit of this Agreement or any part(s) without the prior written consent of the [Author]. Any consent provided by the [Author] shall be subject to the transferee or assignee undertaking in writing to the [Author] to perform and fulfil all the terms and conditions of the [Music Publisher] in this Agreement.

T.382

The [Publisher] acknowledges and agrees that the [Author] shall be entitled to transfer, assign or bequeath the benefit of this Agreement provided that it is not to another person or company in the [music business/music publishers] and that due notice is given to the [Publishers] [seven days] prior to the transfer or assignment or otherwise.

T.383

The [Publisher] agrees that after the delivery and acceptance of the [Work] the [Author] shall have the right to assign, transfer, charge and/or dispose of the Agreement to any third party provided that the [Author] shall continue to fulfil the obligations set out in clauses [–].

Sponsorship

T.384

The [Association] agrees and undertakes that it has not and will not grant to any third party any rights, licences or consents which have, or will conflict with or derogate from the rights granted to the [Sponsor] under this Agreement.

T.385

The [Sponsor] agrees that it shall not be entitled to authorise any third parties to assist it on the funding of the [Event] without the prior written consent of the [Association].

T.386

Where there is a change of control and ownership of the [Sponsor] then the [Sponsor] shall not have the automatic right to transfer and/or assign this

Agreement to the successor in title. The prior written consent and authority of [Name] shall be required. [Name] is entitled to refuse consent and to serve notice of the termination of the Agreement due to the change of control and/ or ownership of the [Sponsor].

University, Library and Educational

T.387
The [Institute] shall be entitled to assign or transfer the benefit of this Agreement to other third parties and successors in business and to grant sub-licences for the [Work]. Provided that the [Institute] shall give written notice of such assignment, transfer or grant to the [Company] and that the person or company receiving the transfer, or assignment agrees to be bound by the benefit and burden of this Agreement. The [Institute] shall be bound to fulfil and/or bear the cost of any obligations not carried out by the person or company.

T.388
Neither the [Institute] nor [Name] shall assign, transfer, charge or make over any part of this Agreement or any part of its rights and obligations without the prior written consent of the other party [which shall not be unreasonably withheld or delayed.]

T.389
The [Institute] shall have the right to assign, transfer, license and charge the benefit of this Agreement to any third party provided that a formal novation agreement is signed and authorised by the [Institute] and [Name] and [Name] is provided with a one off payment of [figure/currency] by the [Institute] as a novation fee.

T.390
The [Company] shall not without the written consent of the [Institute] be entitled to assign, transfer, charge, make over, appoint a sub-contractor, appoint an agent and/or delegate any of the duties, responsibilities, work, obligations and liabilities in this Agreement without the prior written consent of the [Institute] on each occasion. The [Institute] shall be entitled to refuse all such requests. Any consent which is provided shall not absolve the [Company] from the terms of this Agreement at any time. No third party shall be entitled to rely on and/or enforce the terms of this Agreement which is only between the contracting parties.

TIME OF THE ESSENCE

General Business and Commercial

T.391
Both parties agree that all times and dates referred to in this Agreement shall be of the essence.

T.392
Both parties agree that all times and dates referred to in this Agreement shall be of the essence. In the event that the [Photographer] fails to deliver the [Photographic Package] by the Delivery Date the [Assignee] shall have the right to terminate this Agreement by notice in writing. The [Assignee] shall be entitled to be repaid all sums previously paid to the [Photographer] in respect of the [Photographer's Fee].

T.393
In the event that the [Author] fails to deliver the manuscript by the stipulated date [date] as it is agreed between the parties that time is of the essence the [Publishers] may at their sole discretion exercise their right to terminate this Agreement immediately. The [Author] shall be obliged upon such termination to repay all sums previously paid to him/her pursuant to this Agreement.

T.394
Both parties agree that the date(s) set out in this Agreement for the performance of the contract are for guidance only and are not of the essence of this Agreement and may be varied by mutual agreement between the parties. Neither party shall be entitled to terminate this Agreement due to the failure of the other to carry out their obligations by the dates unless they shall have failed to continuously do so for a period of [six months] thereafter in each case.

T.395
The delivery date of the [Work] shall be of the essence of this Agreement. If the [Author] shall fail to deliver the [Work] by the delivery date the [Publisher] shall give the [Author] [two months'] written notice to deliver the [Work] and may at its discretion extend this period. If the [Author] fails to deliver the [Work] by the notified delivery date then the [Publisher] shall be entitled to terminate the contract in which event the Advance shall [not] be returnable to the [Publisher].

T.396
The delivery date is not the essence of the contract, but the [Publisher] may give the [Author] [six months'] or longer written notice to deliver the Work

once the delivery date has passed and no manuscript has arrived. If the [Author] still fails to deliver the [Work] the [Publisher] shall have the right to terminate the Agreement and have all the advance repaid to the [Publisher].

T.397
It is agreed that the delivery of the [Product] by the specified date shall be of the essence of this Agreement. In the event that the [Production Company] fail to deliver the [Product] to the [Company] by the Delivery Date the [Company] shall be entitled to terminate the Agreement by notice in writing and/or the [Company] shall be entitled to reduce the amount of consideration due to the [Production Company] payable by the [Company] by [figure/currency] (exclusive of VAT and any other taxes or levies) for every day or part of a day by which delivery of the [Product] is delayed. Where the total deductions for later delivery exceed the total consideration due under this Agreement to the [Production Company] then the [Production Company] shall pay the [Company] the remaining sum which is owed for late delivery.

T.398
Both parties agree that all times, dates and deadlines referred to in this Agreement shall be the essence of this Agreement unless the parties agree otherwise.

T.399
Both parties agree that all delivery dates referred to in this Agreement shall be of the essence unless the parties agree in writing that they may be varied in any instance.

T.400
Where a date which is specified in this Agreement is waived, amended and/or varied this shall not mean that the party may not rely on the later agreed date to terminate the Agreement. Nor does it mean that the party shall be obliged to waive and/or alter other dates which are set out in the Agreement.

TITLE

Building

T.401
The [Management Contractor] agrees that the [Company] shall be entitled (upon paying a reasonable charge) to be supplied by the [Management

Contractor] with copies of all drawings, details, plans, specifications and calculations produced by the [Management Contractor] relating to the [Project] and the [Company] shall be entitled to use and copy the documents for any purpose relating to the construction, repair, maintenance, letting and sale of the [Project] only. The copyright and proprietary rights in all such material shall remain vested in the [Management Contractor].

DVD, Video and Discs

T.402

The supply to the [Distributor] of the Masters shall not imply a change of ownership in the [Films] therein and all such Masters shall be and remain the property of the [Company] and shall not be used for any other purpose other than the manufacture of Derivatives and/or Videograms as set out in this Agreement. It is agreed that in the event that the [Distributor] has paid for the cost of a copy of the Master that they shall be entitled to retain possession of it for their sole use for the Term of this Agreement. All Derivatives of the Masters made by or for the [Distributor] shall be and remain the property of the [Distributor]. The [Distributor] acknowledges that the [Films] contained in any such Derivatives shall be and remain the exclusive property of the [Company].

T.403

The [Distributor] agrees that the copyright in all promotional material and artwork provided by the [Company] and reproduced in whole or part by the [Distributor] shall be vested in the [Company]. The [Distributor] shall at the [Company's] request and cost execute all such documents as the [Company] may require to vest the copyright in the [Company].

T.404

The [Company] acknowledges that the copyright and all other rights of any nature whether in existence now or created in the future shall be the sole property of the [Distributor]. The [Company] agrees at the expense of the [Distributor] to do and execute all such documents as may be required by the [Distributor] to confirm its title to the rights. The [Company] as beneficial owner by way of assignment of present and future copyright assigns to the [Distributor] the [Works] and all copyright therein for the full period of copyright and all extensions and renewals throughout the universe. The [Distributor] shall be entitled to exploit the [Works] in whole and/or in part in all media by any means whether known now or created in the future.

T.405

The copyright in the material supplied is owned by the [Company]. No licence is granted to the [Customer] to make copies and/or to exhibit the material in public.

T.406

The [Assignor] confirms that it is the sole owner of or controls all copyright and any other rights in the [Video] which are assigned under this Agreement except in respect of the [Artist] and the [Musical Work].

T.407

In consideration of the rights granted under this Agreement the [Distributor] assigns all the copyright, intellectual property rights, and/or any other rights and/or interest in all medium and/or of any nature to the [Licensor] in respect of the [Sound Recordings] reproduced in the [Disc] by the [Distributor] whether in existence now and/or created in the future throughout the world and universe for the full period of copyright and any extensions and renewals.

Employment

T.408

The [Employee] acknowledges that all present and future copyright, design rights, property rights and any other rights in the services shall remain the sole and exclusive property of the [Company] and this Agreement does not purport to grant, assign or transfer any rights in the services to the [Employee].

T.409

The [Executive] acknowledges and agrees that all intellectual property rights including copyright, design rights, data and database rights, computer software rights, trade marks, patents, photographs, text, images, logos, film, sound recordings, documents, emails and reports and all other material created, developed, produced and/or authorised by the [Executive] during the course of his service shall belong to the [Company]. No rights or interest are acquired, transferred and/or assigned to the [Executive] under this Agreement.

Film and Television

T.410

'The Title Rights' shall mean the exclusive right to have the [Event] referred to for all commercial and promotional purposes including the broadcast or transmission of the [Recordings/Film] on television (whether terrestrial television, digital, satellite or cable or other medium) as follows [specify].

T.411

'The Title Rights' shall mean the sole and exclusive right to have the [Event] referred to in all forms of the media of any nature and in any format at any time during the Term of this Agreement as [specify words/logos/trade marks] in all forms of exploitation by the [Association/Company] and any agents, licensees, distributors and/or any third parties including but not limited to digital, satellite, cable terrestrial television, radio, DVDs, newspapers, magazines, mobiles, advertisements, display materials, brochure.

T.412

The [Licensor] undertakes and warrants that it has full power and authority to enter into and perform this Agreement. At the date of this Agreement there are not and during the full period of time during which the [Licensee] retains the rights granted hereunder there will not be any liens or encumbrances against the [Film] which will or might impair the exercise by the [Licensee] of its rights hereunder. The [Licensor] has not and will not grant any rights the exercise of which would derogate from or be inconsistent with the rights granted to the [Licensee] hereunder.

T.413

The [Company] warrants that it derives title to the right hereby granted from a person who is the sole and absolute owner of the copyright and all other rights in all material incorporated in the [Film] as are or may be required to permit the [Film] to be produced and exploited by all means and in all media except for such rights as are administered by [performing rights societies/mechanical copyright protection society/other] throughout the world and such rights are vested exclusively in the [Company] free from encumbrances.

T.414

The [Company] warrants that it has good title and full right and authority to grant the rights hereby granted and it is and will remain fully entitled to give the warranties, undertakings and representations in respect of the [Film] contained in this Agreement.

T.415

The [Company] agrees that the material shall remain the property of the [Licensor] and that at the end of the Licence Period the material will be returned to the [Licensor] at the [Licensor's] cost.

T.416

The manuscript or other programme material provided to the [Performer] by the [Company] is on loan to the [Performer] solely for the purpose of the performance set out in this Agreement. The [Company] are and shall remain the copyright owners of all such material and the [Performer] is not entitled to copy, exploit or use the material for any other purpose without the prior written consent of the [Company].

T.417

The [Company] shall be the sole and beneficial owner of all copyright subsisting in the [Work] including, but not limited to any broadcast, or transmission, or publication or any other means whether of visual images or sound, films or sound recordings which have been or will be developed in respect of all material created or produced during the Licence Period incorporated or based on the [Concept] or any development and the [Originator] shall have no claim or title.

T.418

The [Distribution Company] warrants that it is the sole owner of or will control all rights in the [Film] and/or part(s) (including all rights of copyright) which are granted to the [Television Company] for the purposes of this Agreement and that such rights are or will prior to the start of the Licence Period be vested in it free from any encumbrances except that the [Television Company] shall be responsible for any payment in respect of the performing rights in any music as are controlled by the [Performing Rights Society] or any society affiliated to it in respect of the exercise of the rights hereunder.

T.419

In consideration of the [Licensee] financing the [Pilot] the [Licensor] shall assign to the [Licensee] the joint, present and future copyright in the [Pilot] and the exclusive Option to conclude an agreement for the production and commercial exploitation of the [Series] in all media throughout the world including Terrestrial and Digital Television Rights, Cable Television Rights, Satellite Television Rights, Video and DVD Rights. The Option shall lapse if it is not exercised by the [Licensee] within [three months] of written notification by the [Licensor] of the completion of the [Pilot] and delivery of the [Pilot Material]. In the event of the Option not being exercised then all copyright, property and all other rights shall revert to and be vested solely in the [Licensor]. The [Licensee] undertakes to execute all such documents as may be required to effect such reversion of copyright and all other rights. The [Licensee] acknowledges that the [Licensor] shall be entitled to exploit the [Pilot] upon any such reversion without payment or liability to the [Licensee].

T.420

1.1 The [Production Company] agrees and undertakes that the copyright and all other intellectual property rights, trade marks, service marks, design rights, computer software rights, database rights and any other rights whether in existence now and/or created in the future and all extensions and renewals in the [country] and in any other part of the world in the [Film] and any part and any associated material including but not limited to any films, recordings, sound recordings, soundtrack, scripts, running orders, budgets, profiles, databases, images, photographs, characters, logos, advertisements, packaging, merchandising and any other material commissioned by or on behalf of the [Company] under or pursuant to this Agreement shall belong entirely to the [Company] and be assigned by the [Production Company] subject to the ownership of any material by third parties.

1.2 The [Production Company] agrees that it shall at the request and expense of the [Company] enter into any such agreements or do any such things as may reasonably be required or necessary to perfect or secure any of the [Company's'] rights and ownership of any material.

1.3 The [Production Company] acknowledges that for the purpose of copyright law in the United States of America and any other jurisdiction which does not recognise any assignment of future copyright the [Production Company] agrees to effect and transfer an assignment to the [Company] on completion of the work under this Agreement.

T.421
The [Licensor] confirms and undertakes that it is the sole owner of or controls all copyright and any other rights in respect of the [Film] and/or parts and the Film Material which are granted under this Agreement. That such rights are vested in the [Licensor] free from encumbrances and that the [Licensor] is not bound by any prior agreement which adversely affects or restricts its authority to enter into this Agreement.

T.422
The [Licensor] agrees and undertakes that it controls and is an exclusive distributor of the rights in the [Film] which are granted to the [Licensee] under this Agreement and that there is no third party except the copyright owner [–] who has a claim or controls the rights which have been granted.

General Business and Commercial

T.423
Nothing in this Agreement shall pass any intellectual or proprietary rights to the [Licensee].

T.424
The Agreement shall bind and ensure to the benefit of the parties and their respective personal representations, assigns, licensees or successors in title.

T.425
Nothing in this Agreement shall be interpreted as a transfer of any property rights and/or copyright ownership and/or intellectual rights and/or title and/

or control and/or possession of the [Work] to the [Licensee] except as set out in the Agreement. All rights not granted are reserved by the [Licensor].

T.426
The [Assignor] confirms that it has and will retain good title and authority to enter into this Agreement and is not bound by any previous agreement which adversely affects this Agreement except for those agreements specifically referred to in Clause [–].

T.427
The [Assignor] and the [Assignee] acknowledge and agree that the assignment in Clause [–] is subject to the following existing agreements [–].

T.428
The [Assignor] confirms that it has and will retain good title and authority to enter into this Agreement and is not bound by any previous agreement, commitment or undertaking which conflicts with, jeopardises or which adversely affects this Agreement.

T.429
The [Company] warrants that neither it nor its predecessors in title to the rights hereby granted has at any time prior to this Agreement assigned, licensed or charged or in any other way dealt with the [Treatment/Work/Material] or any rights which is inconsistent with the terms of this Agreement, and shall not to do so after the date of this Agreement until expiry or termination if earlier of this Agreement.

T.430
All registrations, contracts, licences, consents, waivers, documents, records, material and payments necessary to establish the [Company's] title to the [Works] and to grant the rights herein expressed to be granted, assigned or licensed shall be available for inspection by the [Licensee].

T.431
The [Licensor] confirms that the [Work] shall be the original creation of the [Licensor] and that he/she shall be the sole owner or control all copyright and any other rights in the [Work] which are granted under this Agreement. The [Licensee] acknowledges that all copyright and any other rights not specifically granted under this Agreement remain the sole property of the Licensor.

T.432
The [Assignor] agrees that he/she has full power to enter into this Agreement and is the sole owner of the copyright and any other rights in the [Work]

which are assigned under this Agreement. That the [Work] has not been exploited in any form except those matters set out in Schedule [–].

T.433
The [Assignor] agrees that it is the sole owner of all intellectual property rights and any other rights in the [Work] and parts and in which the [Assignor] is bound by and obliged to provide the following contractual obligations, credits and moral rights to third parties set out in Schedule [–]. The [Assignor] shall be responsible for all payments up to the day before the Agreement and the [Assignee] shall bear all costs and expenses owed to third parties from the date of the Agreement.

T.434
The [Assignor] confirms that the [Series] is based on an idea by [–] which is original and not copied from any third party. That the copyright and all other rights have been transferred and assigned by [Name] to the [Assignor].

T.435
All specifications, drawings, sketches, models, samples, tools, design, artwork, technical information, data, software, or any other material or information written or oral or otherwise provided by [Name] to the [Company] shall remain the property of [Name]. All material together with any copies shall be promptly returned to [Name] upon request and all confidential information shall be kept safe and not used or disclosed except as strictly required for the performance of this Agreement.

T.436
Designs, drawings, specifications and other work developed pursuant to this Agreement shall be the exclusive property of the [Company] in any way it so decides. Such material may not be released or reused by the [Distributor] without the prior consent of the [Company]. All material prepared hereunder and all copies shall be delivered to the [Company] upon request. The [Distributor] acknowledges that all information, data, databases and any other material in any medium obtained by the [Distributor], its employee's, agents and sub-contractors in performance of this contract is and shall be the property of the [Company].

T.437
The [Distributor] agrees that the [Master Tape] shall remain the property of the [Licensor] and that the [Distributor] is not acquiring any copyright in any musical work in the [Master Tape] or any associated lyrics, composition or arrangement or sound recording.

T.438

The Company shall recognise the [Stockholder] as the absolute owner of his/her [Stock] and as alone entitled to receive and give effectual discharges for the monies comprised therein. The [Company] shall not (except as ordered by a court of competent jurisdiction) be bound to take notice of, or to see to the execution of, any trust (whether express, implied or constructive) to which any [Stock] may be subject and shall not be affected by any notice it may have, whether express or constructive of the right title interest or claim of any other person to or in such [Stock] or monies. Nor shall the [Company] (except as by statute required or by an Order by a court of competent jurisdiction) enter in the Register notice of any trust (express, implied or constructive) in respect of any [Stock].

T.439

The receipt by the [Stockholder] or, in joint holdings, of any one of the registered joint holders of any monies payable in respect of such [Stock] shall be an effective discharge of liability by the [Company] notwithstanding any notice it may have received.

T.440

Each [Stockholder] shall be entitled to his/her stock free from any equity set-off or cross claim on the part of the [Company] against the original or any intermediate [Stockholder].

T.441

The [Company] shall recognise the executors or administrators of a sole registered holder of [Stock] as the only persons having any title to or interest in such [Stock] on the death of such Stockholder. In respect of joint registered holders of [Stock] the survivor or survivor(s) shall be recognised as the only person(s) having any title to or interest in such [Stock] on the death of one or more of such joint registered Stockholders.

T.442

[Name] agrees and confirms that this is their last will and testament and that all other wills and codicils which may exist are revoked and/or lapsed. That [Name] wishes to ensure and agrees that [Specify Beneficiary] shall be entitled upon the death of [Name] to receive all physical and intellectual property rights whether in existence now at the date of this document or created in the future owned and/or controlled by [Name] including but not limited to patents, copyright, design rights, future design rights, film, trade marks, domain names, logos, text, images, photographs, sound recordings, DVDs, CD-Roms, artwork, titles, music, lyrics, computer generated material, books, articles, posters, packaging and marketing material in the [Work] set out in the attached Schedule [–] which forms part of this will. That

[Name] assigns and leaves upon his death all such rights and interest to the [Beneficiary] in the [Work] for the full period of copyright and any extensions and renewals and in perpetuity.

T.443
The [Company] confirms and agrees that it holds the [Work/Material] which is no longer protected by copyright in its original form. No undertakings and/or agreement is provided by the [Company] as to who owns and/or any controls the intellectual property rights including copyright and/or whether any rights have been cleared and/or paid for in respect of any use by the [Licensee].

Internet and Websites

T.444
The [Customer] acknowledges that all copyright and any other rights in the [Website] and any trade mark, logo or associated goodwill shall remain the property of the [Company] and that the [Customer] shall not acquire any rights in the [Website] or any name, slogan, word, phrase, trade mark, logo, title, artwork, images, design, music, lyrics, stills, recordings, film, sound recordings or any developments or variations or any right to adapt and/or translate and/or exploit the [Website]. Nor does this Agreement purport to transfer, licence or assign any copyright ownership or any other rights to the [Customer].

T.445
The [Contributor] to the [Website] agrees and undertakes that to the best of his/her knowledge and belief the facts and information contained in the [Work] shall be original true and accurate and that where material is quoted and/or relied upon from third parties that sufficient acknowledgement shall be provided to the source material, title and copyright owner.

T.446
The [Company] is the copyright owner and owns and controls all rights on this [Website] unless stated otherwise. The right granted to use this [Website] is limited and personal to the [Client] and does not permit the [Client] to exploit the [Website] in any media of any nature at any time or to permit others to do so. The [Client] shall not acquire any rights or interest in the [Website] at any time which may be exploited by the [Client] and all rights are reserved by the [Company] and there is no permission, authorisation and/or rights granted by virtue of this Agreement.

T.447
The [Company] is the copyright owner and owns and controls all intellectual property rights, copyright, trade marks, service marks, computer software

rights, database rights and data, and electronic and digital rights in the electronic files on this [Website], in the computer programmes, the codes and the passwords. No rights are granted nor any permission or authorisation provided to allow the [Client] to exploit any material or any part of this [Website] in any media of any nature at any time or to permit others to do so. All rights are reserved by the [Company].

T.448

The website and associated content, trade marks and marketing material shall be held in the name of [specify] on behalf of all the parties which form the [Consortium]. Any sale, disposal, transfer, charge, lien and/or assignment shall require the prior approval of the [Consortium].

T.449

The [Company] agrees and confirms that the following parties hold all the copyright, intellectual property rights in the following material:

1.1 The artwork, designs, sketches, illustrations and drawings in appendix [–] are owned by [Name] and all use of any material must bear a copyright and/or trade mark notice as follows [specify].

1.2 The sound recordings in appendix [–] are owned by [Name] who requires the following copyright notice and credit; [specify].

1.3 The website and app and computer generated material and content are owned by [Name] and a copyright notice, trade mark notice and registered company notice are as follows [–].

Merchandising

T.450

'The Trading Name' in respect of the commercial exploitation of the [Licensed Articles] shall be under the following title [specify].

T.451

The [Licensee] acknowledges that all copyright, intellectual property rights, computer software rights, design rights and any other rights in the [Character], the name, the words and phrases, slogans, sounds, and any associated samples, models, images, artwork, graphics, sound recordings, computer generated material, articles, clothes or other material and any trade mark, logo, words, phrases or associated goodwill or any developments or variations shall remain the property of the [Licensor] and that the [Licensee] shall not acquire any such rights and/or interest and/or represent that they own and/or control them and/or attempt to register any interest.

T.452

The [Company] acknowledges and agrees that all present and future copyright and design rights in the [Product] (including the title) and the [Prototype] are and will remain the sole and exclusive property of the [Licensor] and that this Agreement does not in any way purport to transfer any copyright or design rights to the [Company].

T.453

The [Company] undertakes that at the end of the Licence Period it shall execute any document or do anything required by the [Licensor] to confirm that all copyright, design rights and any other rights in any developments or variations of the [Licensed Articles] are the sole property of the [Licensor].

T.454

The first owner of all copyright including any computer software required to be created for the creation and proper functioning of the [Character/Product] through the use of the [Licensor's Package] or otherwise shall be deemed to be vested in the [Licensee], but the copyright in the software used to create the [Hardware] and the [Package] shall be vested solely in the [Licensor].

T.455

The [Artist] agrees that he/she shall not be entitled to or acquire any rights in any character, title, pseudonym, design, logo or slogan provided by the [Company] for the purpose of this Agreement and that the [Artist] shall not be entitled to use any such material in any form except with the prior written consent of the Company except for personal references only.

T.456

The [Licensor] confirms that he/she is the original creator and sole owner of or controls all copyright and any other rights in the [Characters] which are granted under this Agreement.

T.457

The [Distributor] confirms that [Name] is the original creator and copyright owner of the [Board Game] and the Prototype and that the [Distributor] has been granted an exclusive distribution agreement and controls all the [specify] rights under licence in [country].

T.458

The [Licensee] acknowledges and agrees that all future copyright and design rights in the Designs, the [Licensed Articles], the Prototypes and the Complete Set are and shall remain the sole and exclusive property of the [Licensor] and that this Agreement does not in any way purport to transfer any copyright or design rights to the [Licensee].

T.459

The [Purchaser] agrees that it will not license or authorise any third party to copy, reproduce, manufacture, supply or distribute the [Garment] or the Designs including any development or variation at any time throughout the world.

T.460

The [Designer] agrees that all present and future copyright, design rights and any other property rights in the [Licensed Articles] manufactured during the Licence Period will be held jointly by the [Licensee] and the [Designer].

Publishing

T.461

The [Publisher] acknowledges that all copyright in the [Work] remains vested with the [Author] and that this Agreement does not purport to transfer or assign any copyright ownership to the [Publisher].

T.462

The [Author] confirms that no agreement which has been signed by or on behalf of the [Author] concerning the publication of the [Author's Work] prohibits or prevents the [Author] from granting the rights in the [Author's Work] to the [Production Company] pursuant to this Agreement.

T.463

The [Writer] agrees that to the best of his/her knowledge and belief the facts and information contained in the [Work] shall be true and accurate, including all references to source material and title except where any material is supplied by and specifically included at the request of the [Originator].

T.464

The [Publisher] whose publishing offices are at [address] intends to publish a book which the [Author] agrees [to write/has written] the title of which shall be [specify] or such other title as may be mutually agreed between the [author] and the [Publisher] (which book is called 'the Work').

T.465

In consideration of the Fee the [Interviewee] acknowledges that the [Publisher] owns all present and future copyright and all other rights in the [Article] and the [Recordings] in all media whether in existence now or created in the future throughout the Territory for the full period of copyright and any extensions and renewals.

T.466

The [Publisher] agrees that the photographs, documents, sound recordings and other material supplied by the [Interviewee] to the [Publisher] shall be on loan and that the copyright, property and all other rights in respect of all such photographs, documents, sound recordings and material are and shall remain the property of the [Interviewee].

T.467

The grant to the [Publishing Company] is by way of licence only and shall not transfer to the [Publishing Company] any right or interest in the Publishing Rights (except as stated in this Agreement) or copyright in the work, or in any literary or artistic works included in the work, or the script, illustrations, photographs, maps or diagrams supplied by the [Licensor]. All rights not specifically granted to the [Publishing Company] are vested in and belong to the [Licensor] including, but not limited to serialisation rights, one shot digest rights, digest book condensation rights, strip cartoon rights, film rights, merchandising rights, television and radio rights, anthology and quotation rights, Braille and talking book rights, the right to publish extracts in newspapers and magazines.

T.468

The [Author] confirms that he/she has and will retain good title and authority to enter into this Agreement and is not bound by any agreement which adversely affects this Agreement except [–].

T.469

The [Publisher] confirms that the publication Agreement with the [Author] entitled the [Publisher] to grant to the [Licensee] the Serialisation Rights under this Agreement.

T.470

The [Author] confirms that no Agreement has been signed by or on behalf of the [Author] concerning the [Work] which prohibit or restricts the grant of rights under this Agreement to the [Company].

T.471

1.1 [Name] confirms that he/she is the copyright owner of all intellectual property rights including copyright and any other rights in the [Artwork] and owns and controls the material that is to be supplied on loan under this Agreement due to [circumstances of ownership].

1.2 That neither the [Artwork] nor the material is subject to any prior or future claim, right, contractual obligation or other interest which would prevent, interfere with or be prejudicial to the publication in the [Magazine].

1.3 The [Publisher] agrees that it shall acquire no rights in the [Artwork] or the material except for the non-exclusive right to publish the [Artwork] in the [Magazine] in the following article [description/title/publication date/countries].

1.4 There are no rights granted to the [Publisher] to sub-license, syndicate or otherwise exploit the [Artwork] or material either to a parent, associated, subsidiary or third party. Any such action shall be considered a serious breach of this Agreement.

T.472

The [Authors] agree and undertake that:

1.1 That they are the copyright owners of the [Work] which they have created with their own skill and labour.

1.2 That the [Work] is not adapted from and/or based on any other work which is not disclosed in the [Synopsis/Manuscript].

1.3 That there is no agreement, licence, contractual obligation and/or undertaking in respect of the [Work] which has and/or will be concluded with any third party which would affect this Agreement.

T.473

There is no undertaking given by the [Author] in respect of the copyright and/or any other rights in the [Work]. The [Publisher] accepts the risk in respect of publication and agrees to bear all the costs in respect of any legal problems and/or litigation that may arise.

Purchase and Supply of Products

T.474

The [Commissioning Company] confirms that it is the sole owner of or controls all intellectual property rights including copyright and any other rights in the [Commissioning Company] and the [Product] in all media throughout the Territory including trade marks, logo, title, artwork, slogan, packaging and any developments or modifications.

T.475

The property in the [Goods] remains with the [Company] at all times in the case of a hire transaction and until payment in full is made in the case of the sale of [Goods].

T.476

The [Goods] shall remain the sole and absolute property of the [Company] as legal and equitable owner until such time as the [Buyer] shall have paid to the [Company] the agreed price. The [Company] may for the purpose of recovery of its [Goods] enter upon any premises where they are stored and may repossess the [Goods]. Until such time as the [Buyer] becomes the owner of the [Goods] he/she will store them on his/her premises separately from his/her own goods or those of any other person and in a manner which makes them readily identifiable as the [Goods] of the [Company].

T.477

The [Buyer] acknowledges that he/she is in possession of the [Goods] solely as a fiduciary for the [Company] until payment in full is made for the [Goods]. If the [Goods] are resold or otherwise disposed of by the [Buyer], the [Buyer] will ensure that the entire proceeds of the sale are held in trust for the [Company] and shall not be mixed with any other monies or paid into an overdrawn bank account and shall at all times be identifiable as monies belonging to the [Company].

T.478

Title in the [Goods] remains vested in the [Company] until such time as the [Goods] have been fully paid for. The Company may without prior notice or liability and without prejudice to any other legal remedy repossess any unpaid [Goods]. The [Goods] from the time of delivery or collection are at the [Customer's] risk.

T.479

The [Company] warrants that it holds full title to the [Products] which are to be conveyed to the [Purchaser] and that the transfer is lawful and that the [Products] are delivered free from any security, interest, or encumbrance except as agreed in advance in writing between the [Company] and the [Purchaser].

T.480

The property in the [Goods] shall pass to the [Company] on delivery without prejudice to any right of negation to which the [Company] may be entitled hereunder or otherwise.

T.481

All Goods supplied under this Agreement are supplied on a retention of title basis. Ownership of the Goods shall pass to the [Customer] as and when all monies (however arising) owed by the [Customer] to the [Supplier] have been paid in full.

T.482

The property in the [Company's Products] shall not pass to the [Buyer] until payment by the [Buyer] to the [Company] of the full purchase price for all [Products] which the [Buyer] has contracted to purchase from the [Company] whether under this contract or any other contract. Until such payment the [Buyer] shall hold the [Company's Products] in a fiduciary capacity as bailee thereof on behalf of the [Company] and shall deliver the same up to the [Company] upon demand and shall not deal with the [Company's Products] except in accordance with the written instructions of the [Company] provided that the [Company] hereby authorises any [Buyer] who is a Dealer or Authorised Distributor on behalf of and for the account of the [Company] to sell all or any part of the [Company's Products] at full market value at any time before the property therein shall have passed to the [Buyer] and to pass good title to the same the proceeds of any such sale to be held by the [Buyer] on trust and for the account of the [Company].

T.483

The [Company] warrants that title to the [Products] when transferred to the [Purchaser] is lawful, valid and correct, that the [Company] has the authority to transfer the title and that the [Products] are delivered free from any security interest or encumbrance [except as otherwise agreed upon in writing between the parties].

T.484

The property and risk in the [Goods] shall pass on delivery or if by instalments then in respect of those items delivered. Where all or part of the [Goods] are retained by the [Seller] but the [Purchaser] has paid the agreed price, the property in the [Goods] shall pass to the [Purchaser] on payment, but the risk in such Goods shall remain with the [Seller] until actual delivery.

T.485

The [Assignor] confirms that it is the sole owner of or controls all copyright and any other rights in the [Product] and any associated packaging which are being disposed of under this Agreement.

T.486

The [Agent] acknowledges that the [Company] shall have the right to deal with, sell, loan or hire or otherwise exploit the [Product] and any other products to any third party at any time.

T.487

The [Supplier] confirms that it is the sole owner of or controls all copyright, design rights, trade marks and service marks and any other rights in the

[Product] and the [Supplier's Logo] throughout the Territory except as otherwise disclosed in writing to the contrary to the [Seller].

T.488
The copyright owners of the [Disc/Work] are the [Author and the Illustrator]. The user licence and rights granted are personal to the [Purchaser] and only allow the [Disc/Work] to be used for non-commercial use by one person, and not for any internet business. The [Purchaser] is not entitled to exploit any rights in the [Disc/Work] in any media at any time or to permit others to do so and/or to supply copies to third parties. All rights are reserved by the [Author and the Illustrator] and the exclusive licensee, the [Company].

Services

T.489
The [Lender] warrants and undertakes that the facts set out in the preamble are correct and that neither the [Lender] nor the [Artiste] has or will enter any commitment with any third party which has or will detract from the rights granted in this Agreement or the [Artiste's] ability to perform the services hereunder, that neither the [Lender] nor the [Artiste] is under any disability restriction or contractual obligation or otherwise which affects the [Lender's] or the [Artiste's] ability to enter into this Agreement.

T.490
The [Presenter] confirms that he has full authority to enter into and perform this Agreement and that he is not bound by any previous agreement which adversely affects this Agreement.

T.491
The [Company] agrees that this Agreement only relates to the provision of the services by the [Contributor] for the engagement period. The [Company] shall only acquire copyright ownership of the product of the services and no right to any further services, rights, interest, option or other works of the [Contributor].

T.492
The [Contributor] acknowledges and agrees that all present and future copyright and any other rights in the [Company's] Website shall be and remain the property of the [Company] including any developments and variations subject to any interests of third parties. The [Contributor] shall not acquire any rights or interest by virtue of this Agreement to any copyright or any other rights in the Website or any associated material. At the end of the engagement period the [Contributor] shall sign an assignment document

to effect the assignment of any rights that may have been acquired by the [Contributor] in the provision of his/her services under this Agreement.

T.493
The [Agent] acknowledges that the name of the [Actor] and his/her image, slogan, text, logo and his/her family and any other material supplied, written, performed, filmed or recorded and any goodwill and reputation under this Agreement to the [Agent] shall remain the sole and exclusive property of the [Actor] whether in existence now or created in the future. No part of this Agreement is intended to transfer, assign or vest any copyright and/or any other intellectual property rights in the product of the [Actor's] services or any associated material in the [Agent] at any time. Where material is commissioned by the [Agent] the [Agent] agrees to sign whatever assignment of copyright documents may be required and requested by the [Actor's] legal advisors upon payment of a nominal sum to carry out the intention of this Agreement.

T.494
The [Agent] shall use his/her reasonable endeavours to protect the copyright and any other rights of the [Actor] which may be created or developed under any contract with a third party. As far as possible the [Agent] shall ensure that any material which is created belongs to the [Actor].

T.495
The [Photographer] confirms that he/she is the sole owner of and controls all copyright and any other rights in the [Commissioned Work] which are assigned under this Agreement.

T.496
All drawings, photographs, film, videos, DVDs, discs and other material supplied by [Name] shall remain the property of [Name].

Sponsorship

T.497
The [Sponsor] acknowledges that all intellectual property rights including copyright, trade marks, services marks, designs, logos, slogans, text, artwork, title, films, recordings, sound recording, scripts, photographs, business name, music, graphics, computer generated material and any other rights in the [Series] together with any associated advertising, promotions and marketing shall remain the sole property of the [Television Company] and that the [Sponsor] shall not acquire any rights in the [Programme] or any associated material or any developments or variations.

T.498

The [Television Company] acknowledges that all intellectual property rights including copyright, trade marks, service marks, designs, logos, slogans, text, artwork, name, music, lyrics, computer generated material and any other rights in the [Sponsor's Logo] and the [Sponsor's Product] shall remain the sole and exclusive property of the [Sponsor] together with any goodwill and the [Television Company] shall not acquire any rights including any developments or variations [nor shall they be able to exploit them].

T.499

The [Sponsor] acknowledges that the sponsorship of the [Programmes] does not give the [Sponsor] the right to use the name of the [Television Company], logo, programme title or other material owned by the [Television Company] in any promotion, advertising, marketing or product owned and controlled by the [Sponsor]. The [Television Company] agrees that the following use is permitted [specify each type and details of layout, colour, size].

T.500

The [Sponsor] agrees that the [Radio Company] shall have the right to advertise, promote and endorse any third party products in the [Programme] or in conjunction with it whether or not it directly competes with the [Sponsor's] business, market or products.

T.501

The [Sponsor] confirms that it is the sole owner of or controls all intellectual property rights including copyright and any other rights throughout the Territory in the [Sponsor's Logo] and the [Sponsor's Product]. The [Sponsor] undertakes that the [Sponsors Logo] and the [Sponsor's Product] do not and will not infringe the copyright and any other rights of any third party in the Territory.

T.502

The [Licensor] confirms that it is the sole owner of or controls all intellectual property rights including copyright, trade marks, service marks and any other rights in the [Licensor's Logo] throughout the Territory.

T.503

The [Licensee] acknowledges that the [Licensor] owns all rights in the [Licensor's Logo] and that with any goodwill created under this Agreement it shall remain the sole property of the [Licensor]. The [Licensee] shall not acquire any rights or interest in the [Licensor's Logo] or in any part of it or the material used to create or develop it under this Agreement nor shall the [Licensee] attempt to register such interest in its own name.

T.504

The Sponsor reserves the absolute right to veto advertising, sponsorship or endorsement of any third party intended to be displayed at the [Venue] and on any associated advertising, publicity and marketing material and merchandise in any form which in the reasonable opinion of the [Sponsor] is selling or promoting goods or services which directly conflicts with or competes with the following of the [Sponsor's] Products [specify].

T.505

The [Association] agrees that during the Term of the Agreement that the [Event] shall be called and referred to at all times as the [specify]. The [Association] shall ensure that the Promoter and all other third parties engaged by the [Association] shall be contractually bound to use their best endeavours to ensure that the [Event] in all marketing, promotional, publicity, brochures, guide, advertising, television, radio and media coverage shall use the title [specify] and none other.

T.506

The [Sportsperson] confirms that he/she has full title and authority to enter into this Agreement and that he/she is not bound by any previous agreement or professional rules and/or code of conduct [and/or medical report within the last six months] which adversely affects this Agreement.

T.507

The [Sportsperson] acknowledges that all copyright and any other rights in the [Sponsor's] Logo and the [Sponsor's Product] together with any goodwill shall belong to and remain the sole property of the [Sponsor] and that the [Sportsperson] shall not acquire any rights or interests in the [Sponsor's] Logo or the [Sponsor's Product] including any trade mark, design, image, title, words, phrases, artwork, articles, developments or variations.

University, Library and Educational

T.508

The [Contributor] agrees that all intellectual property rights, copyright, computer software rights, design rights and any other rights in the [Work], the name, the words and phrases, slogans, sounds, and any associated samples, models, images, artwork, graphics, sound recordings, computer generated material or other material and any associated trade mark, domain name, website, logo, words, phrases or associated goodwill or any developments or variations shall remain the property of the [Institute]. The [Contributor] shall not acquire any such rights and/or interest and shall not represent that he owns and/or controls them. Nor shall the [Contributor] attempt to register any such interest.

T.509

1.1 The [Company] agrees that the [Institute] owns all rights in the [Institute's] name, trade mark, logo and image and that any goodwill created under this Agreement shall remain the sole property of the [Institute].

1.2 The [Company] shall not acquire any rights or interest in the [Institute's] name, trade mark, logo and image or any part.

1.3 The [Company] shall not acquire any rights or interest in the material used or any developments or variations under this Agreement in the [Institute's] name, trade mark, logo and image.

The [Company] shall not attempt to register the [Institute's] name, trade mark, logo and image as belonging to the [Company] or a third party nor shall the [Company] try to exploit them.

T.510

1.1 The [Company] acknowledges and agrees that all intellectual property rights, copyright and any other rights in the [Work/Service/Product] and the physical material shall belong to and remain the sole property of the [Institute].

1.2 The [Company] agrees that the [Company] shall not acquire any rights or interest in the [Institutes'] name, trade mark, service mark, logo, image, slogan, brand or any developments or variations at any time.

TRADE MARKS

DVD, Video and Discs

T.511

The [Licensee] agrees to provide the following copyright notice, trade mark, and logo set out in the attached Appendix [–] to the [Licensor] on every copy of the label for the [Disc] of the adaptation of the [Sound Recordings] and on all covers, press releases, publicity, advertising, packaging, marketing, on any website and in any database.

T.512

The [Licensee] agrees and undertakes not to change, alter, adapt and/or vary the copyright notice, trade mark and logo of the [Licensor] without their prior written consent. The [Licensee] agrees that the copyright notice, trade mark and logo set out in Appendix [–] shall be and remain at all times the sole property of the [Licensor]. The [Licensee] agrees that it shall not have the authority to sub-license and/or authorise the reproductions of the copyright notice, trade mark and logo by a third party. The [Licensee] agrees not to attempt to register a trade mark and/or logo which is similar and/or an imitation and/or to register as the copyright owner of the [Work].

T.513
In consideration of [specify] the [Licensor] grants the [Licensee] the non-exclusive right to reproduce copies of the copyright notice, trade mark and logo set out in Appendix [–] on all copies of the [Work/Film] reproduced on the [Disc/DVD] for the Licence Period in the Territory.

T.514
The [Licensor] agrees to supply electronic copies of the digital files of the trade mark and logo for the purposes of this Agreement. At the termination and/or expiry of this Agreement the [Licensee] undertakes to ease and/or delete all copies of the digital files subject to any legal proceedings that may be pending between the parties.

Film and Television

T.515
The [Company] grants to the [Television Company] a non-exclusive licence to incorporate [the Company's Product] and the [Company's Trade Mark] in the [Programme] throughout the Territory for the Term of the Agreement in accordance with the terms set out in this Agreement.

T.516
The [Company] acknowledges that the [Television Company] is entitled to arrange for other companies or persons to sponsor, advertise or promote their products or services in the [Programme] provided that no third party shall be entitled to have its product, trade mark, logo, design, image and/or music incorporated in or around the [Programme] which directly competes with the sales of the [Company's Products] in the category of [specify].

T.517
The [Licensee] shall be entitled to release copies reproducing the [Programme] in the Territory bearing or incorporating the [Licensor's] Logo or such other trade or service marks as the [Licensee] and/or the [Licensee's] Associates may use from time to time in the following manner and on the following associated material [labels, catalogues, posters, advertisements,

promotions] [specify in each case words, logo, position, size, location and be specific].

T.518
The [Licensee] agrees to provide the following on-screen credit, copyright notice, trade mark, or logo to the [Licensor] in the [Series] and in any publicity, advertising, promotional or packaging material in respect of the marketing and distribution of the [Series] [–].

General Business and Commercial

T.519
It is agreed that this Agreement is not intended to contain and shall not be deemed to contain any trade mark licence.

T.520
The [Proprietor] shall join with the [User] at the [User's] expense in making an application to the Register of Trade Marks for the purpose of securing the registration of the [User] as a registered [User] of the Trade Marks [in accordance with the Trade Marks Act 1994 as amended].

T.521
Each party shall promptly, when so requested by the other, enter into a registered user agreement in respect of the use of the [Company's] Trade Mark.

T.522
The Trade Mark shall be and remain at all times the sole property of the [Company] and the [Licensee] shall not use the Trade Mark in any way except in the performance of this Agreement without the prior written approval of the Company. The [Licensee] shall not be entitled to any ownership of or claim in the Trade Mark, and shall not apply to register or cause to do so, anywhere in the world, the Trade Mark or any similar mark or imitation.

T.523
The [Licensee] shall not use the Trade Mark in any manner which might threaten or put at risk the validity of the registration.

T.524
The [Proprietor] authorises the [User] on a non-exclusive basis during the Term of this Agreement to use the Trade Marks in respect of the [Product/ Work] made by the [User] in accordance with all such conditions specified in the Agreement.

1628

T.525
'Trade Mark' shall mean any sign capable of being represented graphically which is capable of distinguishing goods or services of one undertaking from those of other undertakings. A trade mark may consist of words, designs, letters, numerals or the shape of goods or their packaging [in accordance with the Trade Marks Act 1994 as amended].

T.526
'A Collection Mark' shall mean a mark distinguishing the goods or services of members of the Association which is the [Proprietor] of the mark from those of other undertakings [as defined in the Trade Marks Act 1994 as amended].

T.527
'A Certification Mark' shall mean a mark indicating that the goods or services in connection with which it is used are certified by the [Proprietor] of the mark in respect of origin, material, make or manufacture of the goods or performance of services, quality, accuracy or other characteristics [as defined the Trade Marks Act 1994 as amended].

T.528
The assignment or other transmission of a registered certification mark is not effective without the consent of the Registrar [as specified under the Trade Marks Act 1994 as amended].

T.529
'Existing Registered Mark' shall mean a trade mark certification trade mark or service mark registered under the Trade Marks Act 1938 immediately before the commencement of the Trade Marks Act 1994 as amended.

T.530
'Community Trade Mark' shall be defined in accordance with Directive 2008/95/EC and Regulations (EC) No 207/2009 and (EC) No 2868/95 as defiined as at [date].

T.531
'Trade Marks and potential trade marks' shall be defined for the purpose of this Agreement to include any actual registered trade marks, community trade marks, international trade marks, and/or service marks and/or any other titles, images, text, words, designs, sign, packaging, letters, manuals or shapes including real and made up names of places, people and products capable of being represented graphically that may potentially or actually distinguish any product, service, work or other material in existence before and/or created during this Agreement.

T.532

'The Registered Trade Mark' shall mean such trade mark as defined in the Trade Mark Act 1994 as subsequently amended.

T.533

'Trade Marks' shall mean the registered and unregistered Trade Marks belonging to the [Company] relating to the [Goods] and/or used by the [Company] and/or its subsidiaries in connection with the [Goods] and/or which shall be notified by the [Company] to the [Distributor] from time to time.

T.534

It is agreed that the licence to use the Registered Trade Mark (whether in general or limited) shall be binding on the successor in title to the Assignor's interest [as specified under the Trade Marks Act 1994 as amended].

T.535

The Licence granted for the use of the Registered Trade Mark shall not be binding on the successor in title of the grantor of this Agreement and there is no right to make such a transfer at any time and/or provide authority to that effect.

T.536

The name of the [Group] whether registered as a trade mark or not shall belong to the parties to this Agreement, namely all members of the [Group]. In the event of the departure from the [Group] of any of its members the name shall only be used by the remaining majority. If the split results in there being no remaining majority of the parties to this Agreement then no one shall be entitled to use the name for any purpose without the prior written consent of all parties.

T.537

The [Contractor] warrants that it is the absolute and sole owner of all rights in the [software and hardware] including all copyright, title, computer software rights, trade marks, service marks and any other rights whatsoever therein.

T.538

The following Trade Marks are owned and/or controlled by third parties [specify] are [registered trade marks/community trade marks] of [full company name] in [country].

T.539

[specify trade mark] is the [registered/ unregistered] [trade mark other/of [Company].

T.540

[specify trade mark] is the registered Trade Mark of [Company]. All rights are reserved by [Company]. The use of the [Trade Mark] by a third party in any format and/or medium is not permitted without the written permission of [Company].

Merchandising

T.541

The [Licensor] agrees to supply copies of the artwork of the [Character] and any trade mark, logo or other credit at the [Licensor's] cost [on loan] which may be required by the [Licensee] to assist in the production, manufacture and distribution of the [Licensed Articles].

T.542

The [Licensee] undertakes to use and apply the [Character] and any trade mark and logo for the sole purpose of manufacturing, distributing, selling and marketing the [Licensed Article] and not for any other purpose. The [Licensee] agrees that no film, recording, sound recording or commercial featuring the [Character] for advertising and promotional purposes shall be made without the prior written approval of the [Licensor].

T.543

The [Licensee] agrees to provide the following credit, copyright, notice, trade mark and logo to the [Licensor] in respect of the [Licensed Article] and in all publicity, advertising, promotional and packaging material in respect of the marketing and distribution of the [Licensed Articles] [specify].

T.544

The [Licensee] agrees that the [Licensor] shall be entitled to approve an exact example of the [Licensed Articles] prior to manufacture and distribution. The [Licensee] undertakes to supply at the [Licensee's] cost to the [Licensor] such samples of the [Licensed Articles] and packaging in the exact form and material in which the [Licensee] proposes to manufacture and distribute the [Licensed Articles]. The [Licensor] shall provide written approval or rejection of the sample [Licensed Articles] within [one month] of receipt. Failure by the [Licensor] to reply within that period shall not be deemed acceptance or approval.

T.545

The [Licensee] agrees that the Licensor shall be entitled to approve in advance all publicity, promotional, advertising or packaging material in any proposed format which bears or incorporates the [Licensor's] trade mark, logo or credit, that no such material shall be distributed without prior written consent of the [Licensor].

T.546
The [Licensee] agrees and acknowledges that all copyright and any other rights or interest in the [Character], any trade mark or logo and domain name together with any goodwill are and shall remain the sole property of the [Licensor]. The [Licensee] shall not acquire any rights of any nature in the [Character] or any trade mark, logo, title, domain name, artwork or any developments or variations except for those specifically authorised uses for the purpose of this Agreement.

T.547
'The Company's Products' shall mean the products and services of the [Company] including packaging, trade marks, service marks, designs, logos, and any associated words, phrases, slogans which are as follows [–]. A two-dimensional copy of the Company's Products is attached to and forms part of this Agreement.

T.548
'The Company's Products' shall mean the products and services of the [Company] which is briefly described as follows [–]. A summary of the products is attached and forms part of this Agreement setting out all trade marks, service marks, logos, designs, images, text or other material associated with them as Appendix [–].

T.549
'The Character' shall be the original concept and novel idea for a character which is briefly described as follows [name/description]. Full details of the Character are attached to and form part of this Agreement including copyright, other intellectual property rights, domain name, design, trade mark and logo statement, representations and words, plot, storyline, artwork, colour, signs, equipment, slogans, clothes, scripts, drawings, films and sound recordings.

T.550
'The Character' shall be the original concept and idea for a character described as follows [name, image, words] together with the following trade marks, service marks and domain names registered and/or controlled as follows [–].

T.551
The [Commissioning Company] confirms that it is the sole owner of, or controls all copyright and any other rights in the [Product] in all media throughout the

[Territory] including any trade mark, design, logo, title, artwork, packaging, slogan and domain name or and any developments or variations provided by the [Commissioning Company] pursuant to this Agreement.

T.552

The [Commissioning Company] agrees to supply at its sole cost copies of such artwork and other material relating to the [Product] in its possession or control including any goods, packaging, trade mark, logo or other credit which are required by the [Production Company] for the purpose of this Agreement.

T.553

The Trade Mark or Marks to be used by the [Company] in the Territory for use as a trade mark on or in respect of the [Product] shall be those specified by the [Company] and approved or rejected by the [Distributor] in writing on or before [date] [and such approval not to be unreasonably withheld or delayed].

T.554

The [Company] shall provide the [Distributor] with a style book incorporating the manner, form, size, colour and position in which the copyright notice and Trade Marks are to be used. The [Distributor] agrees not to deviate from the style book and that the [Distributor] shall use the Trade Mark in the exact form and manner specified.

T.555

Nothing in this Agreement shall prevent or prohibit the [Distributor] from identifying itself as the manufacturer and distributor of the [Product] and the [Distributor] shall be entitled to use its own trade mark, design or logo in addition to the [Company's] Trade Mark.

T.556

The [Distributor] shall ensure that the Trade Mark is given suitable prominence on any packaging, trade literature, advertising or promotional material or website in respect of the [Product].

T.557

The [Distributor] and its associates shall be entitled to distribute the [Licensed Articles] in the Territory bearing the logo or such other trade marks as may be used by the [Distributor] and/or its associates from time to time.

T.558

The labels and inlay cards for the [Licensed Articles] distributed hereunder shall be subject to the approval of the [Licensor] and shall bear the name and trade mark designed by the [Licensor] (hereinafter together referred to as 'the Trade Mark') and the [Licensor] shall keep the [Licensee] fully and effectively indemnified against all costs, damages, expenses and claims which the [Licensee] may incur or sustain by reason of the use of the Trade Mark. The [Licensor] hereby warrants to the [Licensee] that the [Licensor] is authorised to use the Trade Mark and is empowered to authorise the [Licensee] to use the Trade Mark within the terms of this Agreement. The [Licensee] hereby acknowledges and recognises that the Trade Mark shall be free from any claim by the [Licensee] and undertakes not to register the Trade Mark on its own behalf. It is agreed that the [Licensee] shall not be deemed by virtue of this Agreement to have acquired any rights in or to the Trade Mark.

T.559

The [Licensee] shall ensure that the [Product] or its packaging sold or offered for sale or exhibited in the Territory, and all specifications and descriptive literature issued in the Territory in relation to the [Product] shall be marked in a form approved by the [Licensor] with the Trade Mark [–] with the notice that:

'The Trade Mark is manufactured under Licence from [Licensor] and the Trade Mark is the [registered] Trade Mark of [Licensor] and copyright in the Product and all rights therein are owned by the [Licensor] and reproduced under Licence.'

T.560

'The Licensor's Trade Mark' shall be the following trade mark, design, image and logo together with any associated words briefly described as follows [–].

A two-dimensional full colour copy of the [Licensor's] Trade Mark is attached to and forms part of this Agreement.

T.561

'The Licensor's Brand' shall be the following trade mark, service mark, design, logo, slogan, text, graphics or other material. A detailed list of two and three dimensional representations is set out in Schedule [–] and forms part of this Agreement.

T.562

'The Licensee's Product' shall be the following product, which is produced, manufactured and distributed by or on behalf of the [Licensee] [–].

T.563

'The Product Package' shall mean all material associated with the [Licensee's] Product including any packaging, labels, advertising, promotion, publicity, films, videos, links, banner advertisements, merchandising, television and radio commercials or CD-Roms, and any other material in any medium.

T.564

In any consideration of the Licence Fee the [Licensor] grants the [Licensee] the non-exclusive right to reproduce the [Licensor's] Trade Mark in each and every form of the [Product Package] throughout the Territory for the duration of the Licence Period in accordance with the terms of this Agreement.

T.565

The [Licensee] agrees that the [Licensor's] Trade Mark shall be incorporated in the [Product Package] in the following specific manner [–].

T.566

The [Licensee] agrees that the [Licensor] shall be entitled to approve in advance of production, manufacture, supply or distribution all material in respect of the [Licensee's Product] and the [Product Package]. The [Licensee] agrees that it shall not be entitled to use, manufacture, distribute or supply any material until the written approval in each case of the [Licensor] has been obtained.

T.567

The [Licensee] undertakes that it shall supply at its sole cost samples of the [Licensee's Product] and the [Product Package] in the exact form and material in which the [Licensee] proposes to manufacture, distribute, sell, market and advertise the [Licensee's Product] and the [Product Package].

T.568

The [Products] shall bear the trade name of the [Licensor] and the registered trade mark [–]. The [Licensor] agrees that any disputes or claims filed by any third party with respect to the trade name of the [Licensor] and/or the trade mark which are used as directed by the [Licensor] on the [Products] shall be dealt with at the [Licensor's] sole cost.

T.569

The [Licensor] agrees that where it is required by law in any country of the Territory to put the manufacturer's name on the [Products] the [Licensee] may place the name and/or symbol of the [Licensor] or any other necessary marks on the [Products].

T.570

The [Licensee] shall submit to the [Licensor] for written approval samples of the [Licensed Articles] and of any contents thereof including trade mark, copyright or design right acknowledgments together with samples of all wrappings, containers, display materials, advertisements, publicity, internet website material and banners and any other material intended to be used therewith and the [Licensee] shall refrain from distribution, sale or publication of any [Licensed Article] and production of advertisements, publicity and internet material until such approval shall have been given in writing by the [Licensor].

T.571

The [Licensee] shall ensure that the following words are set out on each and every item of the [Product Package]: 'The trade mark is manufactured and reproduced under licence from the [Licensor] and the trade mark is a registered trade mark of the [Licensor]'.

Services

T.572

The [Artist] agrees that the [Company] shall be entitled to the sole right of production, reproduction, sale (under such trade marks as it may select), use, performance and exploitation throughout the world by any means whatsoever of [Records] manufactured in pursuance of this Agreement.

T.573

The [Artist] warrants that he/she shall not at any time use the name of the [Company] or any trade mark, service mark, design, logo or other device in any manner likely to give the impression that any performance or other matter is authorised by or is endorsed by or associated with the [Company] unless the prior written consent of the [Company] has been provided in each case.

T.574

The [Agent] acknowledges that the name of the [Artist] and any goodwill and reputation created in respect of any image, icon, trade mark, business, personal name or logo shall remain the sole property of the [Artist] and that no part of this Agreement is intended to transfer any copyright, trade marks or other rights or interest to the [Agent].

Sponsorship

T.575

The [Company] warrants that it is the sole owner of or controls all rights of any nature throughout the world in the [Company's] Trade Mark and that the [Company's] Trade Mark does not infringe the copyright, trade mark, service or business mark or any other right of any third party throughout the Territory.

T.576

The [Company] agrees to provide to the [Association] at the [Company's] sole cost and expense all suitable artwork of the [Company's Logo] in order for it to be reproduced in all printed matter under the control of the [Association].

T.577

'The Association's Brand' shall mean the artwork, design, logo, service mark and trade mark and any associated words, slogan, text, image, sound effects or music to be used for the promotion, advertising and marketing of the [Event]. A package of samples of each of the types under this umbrella of brands are to be supplied as Schedule [–] which forms part of this Agreement.

T.578

The [Organisers] agree that all copyright, design rights and any other rights in the [Company's] trade mark, design and logo shall be the sole and exclusive property of the [Company's], together with any goodwill. The [Organiser] shall not acquire any rights or interest in the [Company's] trade mark, design and logo or any developments or variations [made or commissioned by the [Organisers] pursuant to this Agreement].

T.579

The [Company] confirms that it is the sole owner of or controls all copyright and any other rights in the [Company's Trade Mark] and that the use by the [Organisers] of the [Company's Trade Mark] under this Agreement will not expose the [Organisers] or the [Promoter] to any civil or criminal proceedings.

T.580

The [Company] undertakes that the specific products or services being promoted under this Agreement together with all other products or services owned or controlled by the [Company] which the public would reasonably associate with the [Company's Trade Mark] shall be fit and safe for the intended use and shall comply with all statutes, regulations, directives and codes in force [in the Territory].

T.581

The [Promoter] agrees to execute any document or do anything required by the [Company] to confirm that all copyright, design rights, artwork, trade marks, service marks and logos and any other rights in the products of its services provided under this Agreement shall belong to the [Company].

T.582

The [Sponsor] shall be the major sponsor of the event and shall be entitled to the following rights in respect of the Event during the Term of this Agreement:

1.1 The right to display banners and advertising boards bearing or incorporating the [Sponsor's] name, trade mark, logo, design, slogans and the [Sponsor's Products].

1.2 The right to reproduce the [Association's] trade mark, logo, slogan or design on the [Sponsor's Products] and in any publicity, promotional or marketing material relating to the [Sponsor's Products] or the Event.

1.3 One full page advertisement for the [Sponsor] in the official programme guide and one full page statement from the [Sponsor]. All such artwork, text and photographs to be supplied at the [Sponsor's] cost to the [Association].

1.4 The exclusive right to include the [Sponsor's] name and trade mark, logo or design on all competitor's numbers.

1.5 The right to use the words the Official Supplier of [–] together with a depiction of the [Association's] trade mark logo, or slogan to the Event in all publicity, advertising, promotional, and marketing material.

T.583

The [Sponsor] agrees to assist the [Association] in the legal protection of the ownership and goodwill in respect of the [Association's] trade mark, logo or design by ensuring the relevant trade mark or copyright notice is used in relation to all the material which it reproduces, distributes or supplies [during the Term of this Agreement/at any time].

T.584

The [Sponsor] agrees that it will not enter into joint promotions with third parties in respect of material or goods which bear or incorporate the [Association's] trade marks, name, logo or design at any time without the prior written approval of the [Association] except with the [Sponsor's] associate, subsidiary or holding companies.

T.585

The supply of articles, products and/or services under this Agreement which bear trade marks, service marks, images, logos and slogans does not imply and/or grant any right to reproduce and/or exploit such rights to the other party and/or to any purchaser.

U

UNION

General Business and Commercial

U.001
The [Company] recognises and acknowledges that the [Employee] shall be entitled to become a member of a trade union, trade organisation or other body and that this shall not prejudice or affect the [Employee's] employment of or future prospects at the [Company].

U.002
The [Company] agrees that it shall not prevent or deter the [Employee] from being actively involved in an independent trade union at any time and/or shall not penalise the [Employee] for such participation.

U.003
In the event that the [Employee] becomes a recognised official of an independent trade union the [Company] agrees to allow the [Employee] to take time off during working hours for the purpose of carrying out those official duties as a recognised official which are concerned with industrial relations between the [Company] and its employees. In addition the [Employee] shall be allowed to undergo training in aspects of industrial relations relevant to his/her duties as an official.

U.004
In determining the amount of time the [Employee] shall be entitled to take off for official duties and training, the [Company] shall take into account the specific purpose and any ad hoc conditions which may be agreed between the [Employee] and the [Company]. In any event the [Company] agrees to be reasonable, taking all the circumstances into account and shall have due regard to any relevant provisions of any policies, guidelines, standards or code of practice issued by: [government agency/union/other].

U.005
In the event that the [Company] and the trade union of which the [Employee] is a bona fide member of good standing enter into a formal Agreement

relating to: [specify] the [Company] undertakes that it shall incorporate the terms of such formal Agreement into the terms agreed with the [Employee].

U.006

The [Production Company] undertakes that [as far as reasonably possible] all production personnel, artistes, musicians and performers involved in the production of the [Advertisement] shall be members of recognised unions, craft or trade organisations.

U.007

[Name] confirms and undertakes that he/she is a bona fide member of [Equity/Musicians Union/other] in [country] and will continue to be so during the Term of this Agreement.

U.008

The [Sportsperson] confirms that he/she is a bona fide existing member of the following [professional/sports] organisation: [specify] and has been since [date].

U.009

The [Sportsperson] confirms and undertakes that he/she has full authority to enter into this Agreement and is not bound by any previous Agreement, arrangement, licence, professional rules, code of conduct or disciplinary decision or other criminal offence which is likely to adversely affects this Agreement.

U.010

[Name] is a fully paid up member of [Professional/Trade Organisation] in [country] and has been qualified as a [specify] position since [date]. There is no dispute, disciplinary hearing and/or other complaint and/or allegation against [Name] of which [Name] is aware which is pending and/or has been decided by that body since [date].

U.011

The [Company] acknowledges that [Name] is not a member of any trade and/or craft union and/or professional body and agrees that this is not required for the purposes of this Agreement.

U.012

The [Company/Distributor] agrees that it shall abide by all laws, regulations, directives, policies, codes and practices that may be in force at any time during the Term of this Agreement in respect of union, trade and international agreements which apply to any employee, premises, transport, health and safety, products, insurance, pensions, agents, suppliers, contractors, the use of resources, and the environment.

U.013

The [Consultant] agrees and undertakes that he/she is a qualified [profession/ other] and is a fully paid up member of [specify body/union]. That there is no conflict of interest and/or any other reason which would affect the ability of the [Consultant] to provide his services under this Agreement and/ or to provide independent, high quality and comprehensive advice to the [Company].

U.014

The [Consultant] is not providing any confirmation as to his professional background, nor is he/she required to have joined and/or be a member of any trade union and/or any other organisation for the purposes of this Agreement.

U.015

The [Company] adheres to the national terms and conditions set by [organisation] in respect of [specify] and all payments to [Name] shall be in accordance with the rates which may be applicable at the time of completion of the work by [Name].

V

VALUE ADDED TAX

General Business and Commercial

V.001
The Dealer Price is exclusive of tax and must be paid without any deduction whatsoever. Where relevant value added tax (VAT), sales tax, or any other tax shall be paid by the [Seller], VAT shall only be paid provided there is an invoice provided stating the registered VAT number of the party claiming payment.

V.002
All sums payable under this Agreement are exclusive of any value added tax that may be payable by either party.

V.003
It is agreed that all fees due and paid under this Agreement shall, unless otherwise stated, be exclusive of value added tax but the Company agrees to pay Value Added Tax on such fees at the appropriate rate upon submission of a VAT invoice.

V.004
All sums payable under this Agreement are exclusive of value added tax (VAT) that may be payable by either party. VAT shall not be paid unless a VAT invoice is sent with the VAT number of the relevant party.

V.005
The [Artiste] agrees that he/she is solely responsible for his/her national insurance, personal tax and VAT which may become due in consequence of this Agreement.

V.006
All fees are exclusive of VAT. The [Contributor] agrees to be responsible for his/her own national insurance and personal tax. The Company agrees

to make all payments required under this Agreement to the [Contributor] directly. The [Company] shall only be obliged to pay value added tax upon receipt of a formal invoice.

V.007

If the tax laws to which the Contractor is subject require the Contractor to charge [VAT/other] on fees received under the Contract the amount of [VAT/other] shall be included in the total sum payable by the Company in consideration of services rendered.

V.008

1.1 The [Company] confirms that it is registered with [specify government body] to pay [specify tax] and has the reference code [specify].

1.2 The [Company] confirms that it is up to date with all payments in respect of the tax in 1.1 and that none are currently overdue.

1.3 The [Company] confirms that it is not the subject of any legal action by any third party in respect of any taxes in [country].

1.4 The [Company] confirms that it has an accrual policy for tax received in 1.1 that may be due to be paid.

V.009

[Name] confirms that he/she is not registered for [specify tax] and that none shall be claimed and/or due from the [Company] in respect of any of the services supplied under this Agreement.

VARIATION

General Business and Commercial

V.010

Where the [Contractor] receives an instruction or order which requires a significant change or alteration of the [Project]. The [Contractor] shall within [14 days] of receiving such instruction prepare and submit to the [Contract Administrator] a written estimate specifying the total revised cost thereof (including any change to the Management Fee and any additional extension of schedule costs) together with the effect on the Completion Date.

V.011

The [Company] agrees that the detailed terms of the Production Schedule shall only be varied in exceptional circumstances but in any event shall not be varied without the prior written approval of the [Commissioning Company] as represented by [Name] or such other representative of the [Commissioning Company] as may be notified. Such approval must not be unreasonably withheld or delayed taking into account the contractual commitments in respect of the production.

V.012

The [Company] acknowledges that where such adaptations, variations, edits or developments of the [Programmes] as are permitted have the effect of creating a new copyright or any other intellectual property rights, then such adaptations, variations, edits or developments shall be outside the scope of the Producer's [Errors and Omission] insurance policy.

V.013

There shall be no variation, change, alteration, modification, development, creation of new material, deletion of existing material or destruction without the written agreement of [Name] and [Name].

V.014

No variation, amendment, changes, alteration or otherwise shall be allowed to the [Product/Film/Work] which are not set out in a document specifying the authorised variation and signed by representatives on behalf of both parties.

V.015

The parties agree that changes, developments, alterations, increase in costs, delivery dates, materials, manufacturers, agents, distributors, suppliers, advertising, packaging and any other matters may be varied at any time either by [verbal agreement/email] between the parties.

V.016

The [Company] agrees and undertakes that it shall not vary, amend and/or change any part of the [Work/Project/Order] without the prior consent and authority of [Name] at the [Institute].

V.017

The [Consultant] agrees that the [Company] may change any part of the [Project] at any time and the scope of the work that is to be completed by the [Consultant]. Provided no additional costs and/or expenses are to be incurred and/or more time is required to complete the work. Then the [Company] shall not be obliged to pay any additional sums in fees to the [Consultant].

V.018

It is agreed between the parties that if at any time the [Supplier] cannot deliver any part of the content of the [Service/Work] and/or shall not meet the criteria set out in Schedule [–] that there shall be no right to substitute an alternative person, material and/or other third party.

VENUE

General Business and Commercial

V.019

'The Venue' shall be the following premises at which the [Event/Festival/ Conference] is to take place [specify address/site], which is owned or controlled by the following Proprietor [Name] [Registered address] whose main place of business is at [address] in [country].

V.020

'The Venue' shall be the [land/site/house and grounds] which is known by the [Land Registry/other] as reference [specify] which is held in the name of [Name] as the freehold owner and on which [Name] has a lease for [number] years and has exclusive rights of occupation from [date] to [date].

V.021

The [Association] confirms that the [Sponsor] shall be provided with the following amenities, services and facilities:

1.1 A hospitality suite capable of accommodating not less than [–].

1.2 An administrative headquarters for the [Sponsor] which shall have available the following facilities [–].

1.3 Not less than [number] complimentary [tickets/brochures/other] together with [number] free parking spaces at the Venue.

V.022

The [Sponsor] agrees to reimburse the [Association] with the cost and expenses incurred in respect of [number percent/all] the telephone, security, marketing, food, drink and catering, licensing application, freight, postal services, cleaning services and any other matter which may arise as a result of the access and use by the [Sponsor] of any the amenities, services and facilities provided by the [Association].

V.023

The [Association] confirms that it has entered into a bona fide written Agreement for the use of the Venue with the [Proprietor] and that the [Association] has or will make all necessary administrative and financial arrangements necessary for the smooth running of the [Event] including the hiring of the Venue, any prior arrangements with the Proprietor, the local authority, fire brigade, the police and ensure that fire regulations and licensing laws have been or will be adhered to for the duration of the [Event].

V.024

The [Association] agrees that it shall make all necessary administration and financial arrangements for the [Event] between [date] and [date] which shall be of a suitable and reasonable standard at an appropriate venue. The [Sponsor] shall be entitled to approve the choice of the proposed venue by the [Association] prior to the [Association] entering into any contract for the [Event].

V.025

'The Venue' shall be the following site marked on the map in Schedule [–] at [address] the freehold of which is owned by [Name/address] and which is [leased/rented by] [Name/address].

V.026

The [Institute] shall provide the conference room on [date] from [hour] to [hour] and all necessary electricity, lighting and heating for normal use. The [Company] shall not install, connect and/or use any equipment without first obtaining prior consent from [Name]. The [Company] shall be liable for any damage, loss, expense, costs which may arise directly and/or indirectly as a result of the use of and access to the hired premises and any car parking facilities. The [Company] agrees to indemnify the [Institute] in full upon invoice for any sums that may fall due provided that the claim is itemised and justified by the [Institute].

V.027

[Name] agrees that the [Company] may hire of the [specify location and address] a summary of which is attached in Appendix [–] from [date] to [date]. The cost of hire shall be [figure/currency] which shall be paid by [date] by [method of payment]. The cost of hire does not include the cost of electricity, water, rates, broadband, insurance, gas, telephone rental and charges, cable and satellite television and the supply of and/or of any other material and/or facilities.

V.028

'The Venue' shall mean [address] and the access road and use of the following rooms, facilities and outside space; [specify] from [date] to [date].

This shall include all the cost of the use of the facilities such as light, heat, water, internet and WiFi, electricity, waste disposal and rubbish removal, insurance including accidental damage.

VERIFICATION

General Business and Commercial

V.029
The [Company] undertakes that the information, statistics, sales figures, product details and any other data and materials which it has provided to the [Distributor] are correct and there has been no intention to misrepresent, distort and/or withhold any fact which would materially affect the [Distributors] decision to enter into this Agreement.

V.030
The [Company] agrees and undertakes that it cannot rely on the facts, figures, documents, presentations, projections, accounts, databases, sales records and/or any other data provided by [Name] in respect of the [Project/Product/Business]. The [Company] agrees that it must carry out its own investigations, research, due diligence, assessments, valuations and projections at its own cost and enters into this Agreement entirely at its own risk.

V.031
All projections, estimates, forecasts, predicted sales and costs, valuations and any other information relating to the future of the [Company] is for guidance only and is not part of any undertaking and/or agreement by the [Company]. All parties agree that there shall be no right at a later date to seek to reclaim any losses, damages and/or fall in value based on any of those facts and data.

V.032
In the event that the [Company] decides to verify any fact relating to the Agreement which relates to the [Supplier] and/or the [Products] and any associated material. The [Supplier] undertakes to provide its full cooperation and to disclose any information, data, records, accounts, codes, reports, tests, samples and/or other material of any nature in any medium that may be requested at the [Company's] cost provided it is not confidential and/or is not in breach of its contractual obligations to a third party.

V.033

[Name] agrees and undertakes to provide the following documents to verify their identity and right of residence in [country] and current home address:

1.1 Original passport from [country].

1.2 Original birth certificate in [country].

1.3 [National/Medical] Insurance number [specify].

1.4 Bank statement held by [Name] which has been issued by bank in [country] which is dated [month/year].

1.5 Drivers Licence [full/provisional].

1.6 Student card [specify].

1.7 Credit card statement.

1.8 Reference from [specify].

1.9 Original visa issued by [country].

VISAS

General Business and Commercial

V.034

The [Contractor] shall at its own expense obtain all visas, permits, licences, registrations, certificates or other authorisations as may be required by any governmental authority which may be necessary or arise from the [Contractor's] performance of its obligations under this Agreement including, but not limited to, importation of equipment, the entry of personnel and/or the supply of services.

V.035

Where any persons who are used by the [Supplier] to carry out part of the service to the [Company] under this Agreement does not hold a valid visa and/or other documents to support a claim of a right to work in [country]. Then the [Company] shall have the right to prevent any such persons right of access to the premises of the [Company] and to terminate this Agreement in its entirety with the [Supplier] and shall not be obliged to pay any further sums to the [Supplier].

V.036

Where any person does not hold a [specify] passport which is valid in [country]. Then where the [Supplier] intends to use persons who hold passports from other countries to fulfil the terms of the service specified under this Agreement. Prior to the commencement of the provision of the service the [Supplier] must provide verified copies of all passports and visas and permission for the right to work in [country] for each of those persons.

VOLUNTARY DEPARTURE

General Business and Commercial

V.037
Any member who has decided to leave the [Group] shall inform all other members at the earliest opportunity of that decision. The departing member shall be obliged to fulfil his duties to which he/she is already committed for [three months] from the date on which the member who keeps the diary for the [Group] was so informed by the departing member.

V.038
In the event that [Name] is unable or unwilling to perform the obligations and/or provide the services under this Agreement, then both parties shall agree fair and reasonable terms to end the contract which shall include payment for the conditions fulfilled.

V.039
[Name] agrees to end the post of [specify] on [date] subject to:

1.1 The payment on that [date] of [currency/number] by the [Company].

1.2 The transfer of ownership of the following items to [Name] by the [Company].

1.3 The payment of [currency/number] in lieu of any pension.

1.4 An excellent reference to be supplied on [date] a draft copy of which is attached and forms part of this Agreement.

VOTING

General Business and Commercial

V.040
In the case of an equality of votes whether on a show of hands or on a poll the Chairman of the meeting (provided he is also a Stockholder or corporate

representative of a Stockholder) shall be entitled to a casting vote in addition to any vote or votes to which he may be entitled as a Stockholder or proxy or corporate representative.

V.041

On a show of hands, every Stockholder who being an individual is present in person or being a corporation is present by its authorised representative or proxy shall have one vote. On a poll, every Stockholder who is present in person or by proxy or, in the case of a corporation, by its authorised representative shall have one vote for every £[–] in nominal amount of Stock recorded in the Register.

V.042

A person entitled to more than one vote on a poll need not use all his votes or cast all the votes he uses in the same way.

V.043

In the case of joint Stockholders the vote of the first named person who tenders a vote, whether in person or by proxy, shall be accepted to the exclusion of the votes of the other joint holders and for this purpose the first named person shall be determined by the order in which the names stand in the Register in respect of such holding.

V.044

No objection shall be raised to the qualification of any person voting except at the meeting or adjourned meeting at which the vote objected to is tendered and every vote not disallowed at the meeting shall be valid. Any objection made in due time shall be referred to the Chairman whose decision shall be final and conclusive [unless the Memorandum and Articles of Association of the Company show good reason in those circumstances not to do so].

V.045

Any decision regarding the [Group] of any nature shall not be made without the consent of more than [fifty] per cent [50]% of the members. If the [Group] consists of two members then both must agree, if three then two members must agree, if four then three members must agree, if five then three members must agree, if six then four members must agree and so on.

WAIVER

Employment

W.001

This Agreement sets forth the entire agreement between the [Company] and [Employer] with respect to the subject-matter hereof. No modification, amendment, waiver, termination or discharge of this Agreement or any provision hereof shall be effective or binding unless it is in writing and signed by the Chairman or another duly authorised officer or Director of the [Company].

W.002

The [Employee] waives all moral rights in respect of the services provided and the work created under this Agreement under the [Copyright, Designs and Patents Act 1988 as amended].

DVD, Video and Discs

W.003

The [Author] conditionally waives his/her moral rights in respect of the [Film] and its exploitation in the form of a [DVD/Video] under this Agreement. Provided that the [Company] uses its reasonable endeavours to comply with the following conditions:

1.1 The [Author] shall be provided with the opportunity to review and comment on the draft script, the key production personnel, the music, and the artists.

1.2 The [Author] shall be entitled to approve the final script prior to production of the [Film] and shall be consulted on all changes except minor editing.

1.3 The [Author] shall be provided with an end credit on the [Film] and any catalogue, poster, packaging, advertising, marketing and website material as [specify credit].

1.4　The [Author] shall be provided with [number] free copies of the [DVD/Video].

1.5　The [Author] shall be entitled to revoke the waiver if these conditions are not fulfilled at any time by notice in writing to the [Company].

W.004

There is no waiver of any moral rights of any nature by [Name] and [Name] asserts their rights to be identified as [specify] in a clear and prominent position on all copies of the [Work] and any adaptation, development, translation, packaging, labels, marketing, advertising and other material of any nature based on and/or derived from the [Work].

W.005

Where the [Licensor] decides at any time to waive any clause of this Agreement in respect of any proposed action and/or act by the [Licensee]. It shall not constitute a waiver of all other later actions which may be a breach of any clause.

W.006

The [Licensor] and [Licensee] agrees that no waiver shall be binding on the [Licensor] and/or the [Licensee] unless it is authorised by the [Managing Director] of the relevant party.

Film and Television

W.007

The [Production Company] agrees to ensure as far as reasonably possible that the [Director] of the [Advertisement] will waive unconditionally and without additional payment all moral rights in the [Advertisement] [and any form of exploitation].

W.008

The [Author] conditionally waives his/her moral right to object to derogatory treatment of the [Film] and its exploitation in any media under this Agreement. Provided that the [Company] uses its reasonable endeavours to comply with the following conditions:

1.1　The [Author] shall be provided with a reasonable opportunity to review and comment on the draft script, the key personnel and the production schedule together with any later significant changes that may arise.

1.2　The [Author] shall be entitled to approve the final script prior to production of the [Film] and shall be consulted on all changes except minor editing.

1.3   The [Author] shall be provided with and approve a sample of each type of proposed form of exploitation in each form of the media.

1.4   The [Author] shall be entitled to revoke the waiver if these conditions are not fulfilled at any time by notice in writing to the [Company].

W.009
The [Author] has the right to object to derogatory treatment of the [Author's Work] on which the [Film] is based and does not waive any right to do so by approving the scripts. The [Author] accepts that the [Film] will not be an exact reproduction of the [Work].

W.010
The [Assignor] waives all moral rights in any media of any nature in respect of the [Format] at any time in any country.

W.011
In consideration of the payment of the [Waiver Fee] the [Author] agrees to unconditionally waive all rights to be identified and/or credited as a contributor to the [Script] for the [Film]. The [Author] agrees to waive all moral rights of any nature either to be identified as a contributor and/or to object to derogatory treatment of the contribution to the work by the [Author] to the [Script] for the [Film]. The [Author] agrees that no further payments and/or royalties shall be due to the [Author] and there shall be no right to object to any adaptation, assignment and/or other exploitation of the [Script] for the [Film].

General Business and Commercial

W.012
No waiver of any default or breach of this Agreement by either party shall be deemed to be a continuing waiver or a waiver of any other breach or default pertaining to this Agreement, no matter how similar.

W.013
No waiver of any breach shall be decreed a waiver of any preceding or succeeding breach whether the same or not. No delay or omission in exercising any right or remedy shall operate as a waiver. No waiver shall be binding for any purpose unless put in writing and signed by the party. Any written waiver shall only be effective for the purpose stated and no other.

W.014
No waiver whether express or implied by this [Company] or [Name] shall be deemed as waiver or consent to any subsequent or continuing breach of

this Agreement. Nor shall any failure to exercise and/or delay in exercising any right or remedy under this Agreement operate as a waiver of such right.

W.015
The [Name] irrevocably and unconditionally waives all rights relating to the [Services/Work/other] to which the [Name] is now or may in the future be entitled pursuant to the provisions of the [Copyright, Designs and Patents Act 1988 as amended] and any other moral rights to which the [Name] may be entitled under any legislation now existing or in future enacted in any part of the world.

W.016
No waiver of any breach of any term hereof shall be deemed a waiver of any preceding or succeeding breach of the same or any other term.

W.017
Waiver of a breach shall not be or deemed to be a waiver of any other breach or subsequent breach of this Agreement.

W.018
No delay or omission in exercising any right or remedy hereunder shall operate as a waiver hereof. No waiver shall be binding or effectual for any purpose unless set out in writing and signed by the party giving such waiver and such waiver shall only be effective in that specific case and for the purpose for which it is stated that the waiver is provided.

W.019
No waiver (whether express or implied) by the [Licensor] or the [Agent] of any breach by the [Licensee] of any of its obligations under this Agreement shall be deemed to be a waiver or consent to any subsequent or continuing breach by the [Licensee] of any obligations under this Agreement.

W.020
A waiver by a party hereto of any particular provision hereof shall not be deemed to be a waiver in the future of the same or any other provision of this Agreement.

W.021
Failure of either party to insist upon the performance by the other party of any provision of this contract or documents attached hereto shall in no way be deemed or construed to in any way affect the right of that party to require such performance.

W.022
No failure to exercise and/or delay in exercising by either party of any right or remedy pursuant to this Agreement shall operate as a waiver of such right.

W.023
Any failure by the [Licensor] to exercise any right hereunder or the waiving or condoning by the [Licensor] of any delay or failure by the [Licensee] to comply with any of the terms of this Agreement shall not be deemed to mean that the [Licensor] has waived any right to take legal action against the [Licensee]. The [Licensee] agrees that any acceptance by the [Licensor] of any delay or failure shall only be binding on the [Licensor] until such time as the [Licensor] shall serve notice on the [Licensee] that the failure or delay must be remedied by a specified date or the [Licensor] will be obliged to take appropriate action.

W.024
The [Assignor] unconditionally waives any and all moral rights under existing or future legislation and the [Assignor] shall not be entitled to any credit or acknowledgment with respect to the exploitation of the [Work] and the [Work Material] by any party in any media at any time.

W.025
The [Assignee] agrees that the waiver only applies to the [Assignor] individually and does not apply to any other third party who may be due a credit or other acknowledgment in respect of the [Work] or the [Work Material].

Internet and Websites

W.026
No waiver by the [Company] of any breach, acceptance of any delay, omission and/or error shall be binding on any subsequent breach, act, error and/or omission.

W.027
The [Author] unconditionally waives his/her moral rights and the right to object to derogatory treatment of the [Work] provided that the [Company] uses its reasonable endeavours to comply with the following conditions:

1.1 That all persons who access and copy the [Work] shall be requested to use the following credit and copyright notice in respect of their use of the [Work] [specify]

1.2 That no authorisation and/or consent shall be provided by the [Company] to alter, adapt, translate and/or exploit the [Work] except for private home use only and that all persons seeking some other use should contact the [Author] at [specify].

1.3   The [Author] shall be entitled to revoke the waiver if these conditions are not fulfilled at any time by notice in writing to the [Company].

W.028

The [Name] irrevocably and unconditionally waives to the [Company] and/or any licensees and/or other third party and/or any successors in title and/or business:

1.1   All rights relating to the [Services/Work/other] to which the [Name] is now or may in the future be entitled pursuant to the provisions of the [Copyright, Designs and Patents Act 1988 as amended]; and

1.2   Any other moral rights to which the [Name] may be entitled under any legislation now existing or in future enacted in any part of the world relating to the [Website].

1.3   The [Name] agrees that he/she shall no longer have the right to be identified as the author and/or the right to object to any derogatory treatment.

1.4   The waiver shall apply to [Name] and any publisher, licensees, assignees and any third party who may acquire any rights or interest.

1.5   [Name] agrees that the waiver cannot be revoked or otherwise altered at any time even after the death of [Name].

W.029

The [Designer] waives all moral rights both to the [Company] and/or any licensees and/or other third party and/or any successors in title. The [Designer] agrees that he/she shall not be entitled to any credit, acknowledgement, copyright notice or otherwise in respect of the [Website] or any subsequent development thereof at any time.

W.030

1.1   The [Company] agrees that the [Artist] has not waived any moral rights of any nature.

1.2   The [Company] agrees to credit the [Artist] on the website and in all apps, posters and marketing and promotional material and other forms of exploitation with the copyright notice (c) [year] [Artist] which shall be placed either on and/or very close to the [Artwork].

1.3   The [Company] shall not make any changes to the [Artwork] in any form and/or medium and/or add and/or delete any part unless the prior written consent of the [Artist] has been obtained.

1.4 Where the [Company] fails in any case to provide the copyright notice and credit in 1.2 it shall be obliged to pay the [Artist] an additional fee of [number/currency] in total in each case.

W.031

1.1 The [Developer] waives all moral rights to any part of the content of the [App/Blog] which he/she has created and delivered to the [Company]. No recognition and/or credit shall be made to the developer in any part of the [App/Blog].

1.2 The [Developer] accepts and agrees that the [Company] may make such changes and adaptations to the [App/Blog] as it wishes and any time and therefore waives all moral rights which he/she may hold in relation to changes in content and/or appearance and/or design and/or colour.

W.032

The [Contributor] to the making of the music, performance and singing at the [Event] which has been recorded by means of sound recording and film by [Name] waives his/her moral rights which may exist to be identified and/or receive any payment in respect of any future exploitation by [Name] of the material which [Name] has created.

Merchandising

W.033

Where the [Licensor] has waived any breach by the [Licensee] and/or sub-licensee and/or agent and set a new condition and/or date as a pre-condition of their consent to the waiver. Then such waiver shall not be deemed to be a waiver and/or consent to any subsequent breach by the [Licensee] and/or any sub-licensee and/or agent.

W.034

Where the [Licensee] has failed to perform any term of this Agreement by a specified date and the [Licensor] has agreed to a waiver for that breach of this Agreement. If the [Licensee] then fails to fulfil the conditions of the waiver by the subsequent date, then the [Licensee] shall not be entitled to rely on the waiver to avoid an allegation of breach of contract.

W.035

In consideration of the [Waiver Fee] the [Assignor] unconditionally waives all moral and/or legal and/or equitable rights in any part of the world in all media and in all medium to be credited and acknowledged and to have any copyright notice as the author of the original [Work] which has been assigned to the [Company].

W.036

In consideration of the [Waiver Fee] the [Assignor] unconditionally waives all moral and/or legal and/or equitable rights in any part of the world in all media and in all medium to object to derogatory treatment as the author of the original [Work] which has been assigned to the [Company]. The [Assignor] agrees that the [Company] shall be entitled to edit, adapt, delete from, add to and/or distort and/or otherwise change any part of the [Work] and/or exploit the [Work] in any manner it thinks fit at its sole discretion.

W.037

The [Author] has not provided any waiver in this Agreement and asserts all his/her moral rights and/or other legal and/or equitable rights which may exist now and/or be created in the future to be identified as the author of the original [Work] and to object to any derogatory treatment and/or distortion and/or adaptation in any form without the prior written consent of the [Author].

Publishing

W.038

The [Ghostwriter] unconditionally waives all moral rights in any of the material created under this Agreement and in the [Work]. The waiver shall apply to the right to be identified as the author and the right to object to any derogatory treatment of the [Work]. The waiver shall apply to the [Writer] and any publisher, licensees, assignees and any third party who may acquire any rights or interest. The [Ghostwriter] accepts that the waiver cannot be revoked or otherwise altered at any time even after the death of the [Writer].

W.039

The [Writer] agrees that the [Ghostwriter] shall be entitled for biographical purposes only to state that the [Work] was written by [Writer] with the research assistance of [Ghostwriter].

W.040

In consideration of the Assignment Fee the [Author] agrees:

1.1 That he shall waiver all moral rights in the [Work] and any parts including the [Artwork] and the material in Schedule [–].

1.2 That the [Author] shall not object to any failure to identify him as the author of the [Work] and/or the [Artwork] and/or the material.

1.3 The [Author] waives all right to object to derogatory treatment of the [Work] and/or [Artwork] and/or the material.

1.4   That all these waivers are unconditional and shall extend to all third parties and successors in title.

1.5   That he waives all right to a copyright notice in respect of the [Work] and the [Artwork] and/or the material in all media at any time in the [country/Territory].

Purchase and Supply of Products

W.041
Failure on the part of the [Company] to exercise any rights conferred by the [Sales Order] shall not be deemed to be a waiver of any such right nor operate so as to bar the exercise or enforcement thereof at any time.

W.042
No admission, act or omission made by the [Purchaser/Seller] during the continuance of this order shall constitute a waiver or release the [Purchaser/Seller] from any liability under any of its terms.

W.043
Failure on the part of the [Company] to exercise any rights conferred by the [Purchase Order] shall not be deemed to be a waiver of any such right nor operate so as to prohibit or prevent the exercise thereof at any time thereafter or any other legal rights available to the [Company].

Services

W.044
In consideration of the payments under this Agreement the [Contributor] waives all moral rights except to the extent that the [Contributor] shall be given the credit set out in Clause [–].

W.045
The [Contributor] waives any and all moral rights in the product of the [Contributor's Work] and in particular waives any right to be identified as the author and creator of the [Contributor's Work].

W.046
In consideration of the [Assignment Fee] the [Author/Composer/Musician/Artist] agrees to waive unconditionally all moral rights in the [Work] to which he may be entitled under the [Copyright, Designs and Patents Act 1988 as amended] in [country].

W.047

In consideration of the payments made under this Agreement the [Name] waives all moral rights under the [Copyright, Designs and Patents Act 1988 as amended] in the [Work] on the condition that the [Assignee] shall credit the [Name] as the [specify details] of the [Work] as specified under Clause [–] and the [Assignee] further agrees to use its reasonable endeavours to ensure that all third parties engaged or licensed or otherwise used to exploit the [Work] shall undertake to abide by this clause to the [Assignee].

W.048

In consideration of the payments made under this Agreement the [Name] waives all moral rights provided that the [Assignee] shall ensure that the [Work] is not subjected to derogatory treatment by the [Assignee] or any third party which it may engage or license.

W.049

In consideration of the payments made under this Agreement the [Composer/Musician] waives all moral rights under the [Copyright, Designs and Patents Act 1988 as amended] in the [Work] subject to the following condition. That the [Assignee] shall ensure that the [Work] is not distorted or mutilated or otherwise treated in a manner which is prejudicial to the honour and reputation of the [Composer/Musician] or otherwise may amount to derogatory treatment. The [Composer/Musician] agrees that an arrangement or transcription of the [Work] involving no more than a change of key or register will not amount to derogatory treatment.

Sponsorship

W.050

No waiver by the [Sponsor] of any breach, acceptance of any delay, omission and/or error and/or failure shall be binding on the [Sponsor] in respect of any subsequent breach, act, error, omission and/or failure by [Name].

W.051

The [Sponsor] agrees to waive any rights to rely on a breach of contract in respect of any of the following circumstances:

1.1   Where [Name] has been fined and/or suspended for less than [number] months by his/her professional body for a breach of the rules and/ regulations and/or for misconduct.

1.2   Where a fine has been imposed by a Court of Law provided it is not for [specify].

W.052
The [Company] agrees that there shall be no credit either on screen and/or in the catalogue and/or at the end of the [Event] in respect of any products which are supplied by the [Company] to be placed on the set and are agreed between the parties to be classified as product placement.

W.053
The [Sponsor] agrees to waive any credit in any material produced, distributed and supplied by the [Managers] of the [Project] provided that a suitable credit and mention is made of their contribution to the funding on the website [specify] and in any material distributed and/or supplied to the newspapers and media before [date].

University, Library and Educational

W.054
No waiver, failure to act and/or enforce the Agreement by the [Institute] against the [Company] shall mean that the [Institute] is bound and not able to take action at a later date if it is repeated.

W.055
The [Company] shall not be released from its liabilities under this Agreement by a verbal waiver from a representative of the [Institute]. All waivers and/or acceptance of breaches, failures and or errors must be in writing between the parties.

W.056
In consideration of the Fee the [Contributor] agrees to waive all moral rights in the [Work/Artwork/Article/Film] including the right to be identified as the author and to object to derogatory treatment. That the waiver and this term shall apply to any third party licensee and/or any successors in title to the [Institute].

W.057
In consideration of the [Assignment Fee] the [Author/Artist] agrees to waive unconditionally all moral rights in the [Work] to which he/she may be entitled under the [Copyright, Designs and Patents Act 1988 as amended].

W.058
The [Distributor] agrees to respect and adhere to the moral rights of the [Author] and shall endeavour to ensure that there is a clear and prominent display of the name of the [Author] and the copyright notice on all copies of the [Work] and any associated packaging and marketing material. The [Distributor] accepts that it shall not be entitled to waive the right of the

[Author] to be identified and/or the removal and/or failure to put such details on all copies.

WAR DAMAGE

General Business and Commercial

W.059

In the event that the [Structure] or any part thereof or any unfixed materials or goods sustain war damage as defined in Clause [–].
Then in such event the following terms shall apply:

1.1 The war damage shall not be taken into account in respect of the payments due to the [Contractor].

1.2 The [Administrator] shall issue such instructions as may be necessary to ensure that the damage is remedied and the [Project] made safe.

1.3 The parties shall agree a new Completion Date taking into account the additional work required due to war damage.

1.4 All such work requested in respect of war damage shall be treated as a variation to this contract and additional costs and payment shall be agreed between the parties.

W.060

'War Damage' shall mean any loss or damage caused by, or in repelling, enemy action, [excluding terrorist organisations] or by measures taken to avoid the spreading of the consequences of damages caused by or in repelling enemy action.

W.061

'War Damage' shall mean any damage and/or loss which may arise directly or indirectly as a result of hostile contention by means of armed forces whether between nations, states or rulers or between parties in the same state or nation or any other kind of active hostility or contention between armed forces provided that a state of war shall have been declared by the existing ruler, state, government or nation. Attacks by terrorist organisations and other acts of resurgence by any party group or individual are not included.

W.062

In the event that the government or state provides at any time a scheme for compensation for war damage then it is agreed that the [Company] shall be entitled to all such sums in respect of any war damage sustained or incurred by the [Project].

W.063

'War Damage' shall mean any loss or damage caused by, or in repelling, enemy action, acts of violence and work of terrorist organisations, hostility, attacks by armed forces with weapons, chemical, biological and/or other warfare, whether a state of war has been declared or not, and any measures taken to avoid attack, mitigate loss and damage and/or to repel enemy action.

WARRANTIES

General Business and Commercial

W.064

The [Company] warrants that the terms and conditions set out in this Agreement shall be complied with by the [Company].

W.065

The [Institute] shall be bound by the undertakings, warranties and terms of this Agreement until the end of the Term of the Agreement and/or the date of termination whichever is the sooner.

W.066

The following clauses which set out the warranties provided by the [Company] shall survive the end of the Licence Period and/or termination of this Agreement. Provided that all sums due under the Agreement by the [Institute] have been paid to the [Company].

W.067

The [Company] warrants that all material, data, documents, accounts, reports, contracts and information provided by the [Company to the [Purchaser], their auditors and/or professional advisors in any format and/or medium relating to the [Assets] of the [Company] are true, accurate and comprehensive as at [date].

W.068

The [Company] warrants to the [Purchaser] that no facts, data, information, record, documents, contract and/or other material has been withheld, not disclosed and/or not revealed which would have an impact on the assessment of the value of the [Assets] and/or the decision by the [Purchaser] to buy the [Assets].

W.069

The [Company] warrants that clauses [–] and all the documents attached in Schedule [–] are true, accurate and complete and that no material data, document and/or information has been withheld.

W.070

The [Company] warrants and confirms it is a company which is established and operates under the Laws of [specify]. That the [Company] has the power and authority to own its assets and operate and conduct its business and to enter into legally binding agreements. That this Agreement constitutes and sets out the legally binding obligations of the [Company] to the [Purchaser].

W.071

The [Company] warrants that it has at all times carried on its business in accordance with its [Memorandum and Articles of Association] in existence at that time and/or as subsequently amended.

W.072

The [Company] represents and warrants and undertakes to the [Purchaser] and its successors in title that to the best of the knowledge and belief of the [Company] the warranties in this Agreement are true and correct in all material respects.

W.073

The [Company] warrants that to the best of its knowledge and belief the [Company] has not manufactured and/or sold products which were and/or are and/or will become faulty and/or defective and/or which did not and/or do not comply with any warranties and/or representations expressly and/or impliedly made by the [Seller] and/or with all applicable laws, Treaties, Conventions, EU Council Directives, regulations, standards and Codes of Practice and/or Guidelines.

W.074

The [Company] warrants that it holds good title to the [Assets] which are free from any lien, charge, claim, interest of any kind of a legal and/or equitable nature and/or otherwise and in particular no part of the stock of the [Company]. Except for the disclosures made by the [Company] as to any part owned and/or controlled by a third party and/or in respect of which ownership has not yet passed, but will subject to payment.

W.075
The [Licensor] warrants that it has full title and authority to grant such rights to the [Publisher] in the [Work] and is not bound by any agreement with a third party which undermines and/or prohibits either expressly and/or by implication the right of the [Licensor] to enter into this Agreement.

W.076
The [Licensor] warrants that it has full title to the [Trade Mark] and shall upon request provide to the [Licensee] a true copy of the formal certificate of registration of the [Trade Mark].

W.077
The [Company] warrants that all past, present and future copyright and any other intellectual property rights of any nature in the [Work] including without limitation to such copyright and other legal rights as subsists now and/or in the future in the text, maps, illustrations, graphs, data, index, artwork, structure, font, electronic and digitised formats, format layout and livery, title, characters, typographical arrangement relating to the [work] vests solely and absolutely in the [Company/Enterprise].

W.078
This warranty is subject to the following restriction, reservation and disclosure [–].

W.079
[Name] confirms and undertakes that he/she has the original concept for the [Project] and that it was not based on any idea and/or work of a third party. That as a result of that concept [Name] designed, created and developed and original [Game/Search Facility/other] which he/she then adapted so that it could be made into an [App] by the [Development Company].

W.080
The [Company] confirms and undertakes that the facts and financial data in the annual report and accounts and in all the documents supplied to [Name] prior to the date of this Agreement on which the valuation for this agreement was based are facts true, accurate and not intended to mislead and/or hid any information and/or disclosure which would have a detrimental effect on the valuation of the [Company].

WAYLEAVE

General Business and Commercial

W.081

The [Company] warrants that it has obtained the necessary wayleave from [specify person/legislation]. For the purposes of this Agreement 'necessary wayleave' shall have the same meaning as defined in the relevant legislation and mean the consent for the [Licence Holder] to install and keep installed the electric line on, under or over the land and to have access to the land for the purpose of inspecting, maintaining, adjusting, repairing, altering, replacing or removing the line.

W.082

The [Purchaser] shall within the times stated in the Schedule or if not specified before the delivery of any part to the site obtain all consents, wayleaves and approvals in connection with the regulations and byelaws of any local authority, government body, electricity, gas, water or other company or person which shall be applicable to [Works] on the Site.

WEBSITE

General Business and Commercial

W.083

'The Website' shall mean the world wide web reference [specify] which is owned by the [Company] registered as a [business/corporation] in [country] trading under the name of [Trading Name] whose domain name is [specify] which is registered with [specify].

W.084

'The Website' shall mean the world wide web reference [specify] which is owned or controlled by the [Company] whose main business address is [specify].

W.085

The [Company] agrees and undertakes not to register any domain name, trade mark, patent, computer software and/or other rights and interest and/or set up any website in its own name and/or through any third party which is based on and/or derived from any knowledge, work and/or services provided by the [Institute] under this Agreement.

W.086

'The Online Business' shall mean all the websites owned and controlled by [Name] which are set out in the attached appendix [–] and all the associated registered domain names whether in use and/or similar which have been registered by [Name].

WORK

General Business and Commercial

W.087

'The Work' shall be the following book including the [artwork] based on the [Synopsis] entitled [–] which shall consist of approximately [–] A4 typed pages.

W.088

'The Work' shall mean the following:

Title [–] Author [–]

ISBN No. [–] Published by [name]

Pages [–] Description [–]

W.089

'The Work Schedule' shall mean such times, dates and locations at which the [Originator] has agreed to provide his services under this Agreement. A copy of the Work Schedule is attached to and forms part of this Agreement.

W.090

'The Work Plan' shall mean the detail of the nature of the services of the [Company] to be provided to the [Distributor] under this Agreement which are described as follows [–]. The [Distributor] agrees that no alteration shall be made to the Work Plan or the Work Schedule without the prior approval of the [Company].

W.091

'Working Day' means Monday to Friday inclusive in each week except any Bank or Public Holidays.

W.092

'Works' means all plant to be provided and work to be done by the [Contractor] under the Contract.

W.093

'The Work Plan' shall be the detail of the nature of the services of the [Name] to be provided to the [Company] under this Agreement which are described as follows [specify duties/location/times].

1.1 Research and arrange interviews and recordings of [–] on [subject].

1.2 To keep full and accurate records of all sources of information, documents, interview recordings.

1.3 To report on the existence, format and quality of any stills, photographs, newspaper cuttings, film, video, DVD material and sound recordings. Further, to provide a detailed statement of ownership of copyright, credits, moral rights, waivers and contractual obligations, the cost of reproduction, access, copyright and other clearance and intellectual property payments.

1.4 To obtain clearance of and arrange payment by the [Company] of such material as may be required.

1.5 To view, edit and comment on the final [–].

W.094

'The Company's Work/Services' shall mean the provision of a professional and expert service in accordance with the standards and code of practice expected of members of [specify governing or trade body] which shall be as follows [specify nature/manner to be provided/exactly what is expected].

W.095

'The Work' shall include all:

1.1 Text, Text messaging.

1.2 Images/graphics/artwork/stills/photographs/drawings/plans/sketches.

1.3 Electronic sound/sound effects/music/sound recordings/ringtones.

1.4 Logos/trade marks/service marks/icons/design rights.

1.5 Titles/formats/slogans/Characters.

1.6 Inventions, patents, formulae, processes, modifications and developments.

1.7 Films/recordings/advertisements.

1.8 Computer generated art and material/software/website and internet related/domain names/banners.

1.9 Data/maps/scripts/documents/flyers/marketing/labels/covers/packaging.

1.10 Computer software, source codes and passwords.

1.11 Designs, signs, made up names and words, shapes, colours and other text, images which are in the title, character, any illustration, index, or any other part of the Work.

W.096

'The Work Material' shall mean all the material of the [Work] in the possession or control of the [Assignor] including:

1.1 All copies of any master material in any form.

1.2 A list of locations at which any material is held together with access letters giving irrevocable authority for the [Assignee] to remove such material.

1.3 All documents, records, data in any form including contracts, licences, consents, waivers, lists, proofs, scripts, publicity, advertising material, computer software, photographs, negatives, posters, catalogues, drawings, plans, sketches, electronically generated material, sounds, sound effects, music combination software and information, tables, computer generated art, image map, video, film, DVD or otherwise.

W.097

'The Work' shall mean the text of the [Titles/Books] specified in Schedule [–] to this Agreement and shall also include any other material which may be later specifically agreed in writing.

W.098

In accordance with the Work Schedule the [Artist] agrees to provide the following specific services:

1.1 The presentation of and performance in not less than [specify number/frequency] advertisements of not more than [specify duration] on each occasion for the purpose of broadcast or transmission on television.

1.2 The presentation of the corporate video which shall be no more than [specify maximum length in minutes].

1.3 The attendance at no more than [specify events/official functions/meetings/other] [specify who is to pay cost and expenses].

1.4 Photographic sessions [–].

1.5 Radio appearances [–].

1.6 Sound recordings/other [–].

W.099

'The Work Schedule' shall mean the times, dates and locations of all competitions, events, promotions, appearances and meetings at which the [Sportsperson] is obliged to attend under this Agreement. A copy of the [Work Schedule] is attached to and forms part of this Agreement.

W.100

'The Events Schedule' shall mean all the competitions, sporting and promotional events and meetings which the [Sportsperson] agrees to attend and participate in during the Sponsorship Period. A copy of the Events Schedule setting out the names, dates and locations of all such events is attached to and forms part of this Agreement.

W.101

'The Work Proposal' shall be the written report of [Name] which gives accurate and specific information, data and other material of:

1.1 The exact technical nature of the work to be provided including completion dates and penalties for failure to complete.

1.2 A complete and exact replica model of the finished [Product] showing all components and functional image, text, sound and links.

1.3 A full breakdown of the cost and personnel involved including key executives.

1.4 The layout and functioning of the Homepage and other elements of the [website].

1.5 The Fees and payment schedule which shall be linked to completion of work.

1.6 Details of all copyright and all other rights of any other nature which must be cleared and/or paid for relating to the [website].

W.102

The [Executive] shall during the course of the appointment work for the [Company] on a full-time exclusive basis in a professional manner. He/she shall carry out the duties described in the [Executive's] job description as specified in Appendix [–].

W.103

It is agreed between the parties that the job description may be moderately varied but not entirely redesigned in order to accommodate developments within the [Company]. Any increase in responsibilities or duties shall result in an increase in pay which shall be agreed between the parties.

W.104

The [Executive] agrees to undertake such duties and exercise such powers in relation to the conduct and management of the [Company] or its associated bodies, businesses and affairs as the Board of the [Company] shall decide that he shall fulfil and carry out from time to time.

W.105

The [Company] agree to provide the services of [Name] on the following terms:

1.1   Nature of contribution [Research/scripts/on screen appearance/other].

1.2   Title of Film/episodes/duration/transmission date.

1.3   Dates [Rehearsals/recording/voice-overs/other].

W.106

The [Company] confirms that the [Consultant] is engaged to provide his/her services for the [Series] as follows:

1.1   Title [–].

1.2   Number of episodes [–] duration:[–].

1.3   Proposed transmission/release date [–].

W.107

In consideration of the [Fee] the [Consultant] agrees to provide his/her specialist advice and knowledge in respect of the [Series] to prepare background material and information, to review and report on the synopsis, scripts, stills and other content that may from time to time be requested by [Name]. The [Consultant] shall provide his assistance upon request to the [Writer] and/or [Director] and attend such meetings, recordings, filming, editing, marketing and other events as may be required up to a maximum of [number] days in total for all the work under this Agreement.

XEROGRAPHY

General Business and Commercial

X.001
'Xerography' shall mean the reproduction of the [Work] by a process of copying which does not involve liquids or chemicals in the developments of the images but shall include any electrical or other means now known or hereinafter invented.

XYLOGRAPHY

General Business and Commercial

X.002
For the purpose of this Agreement, Artistic Work shall include all works created by means of xylography and any other material created through xylographic methods.

Y

YEAR

General Business and Commercial

Y.001
For the purposes of this Agreement, 'Year' shall mean the period of twelve months commencing on [1st January] and ending on [31st December] and Yearly Interest shall be construed accordingly.

Y.002
For the purposes of this Agreement, 'Annual' shall mean the period of twelve months commencing on [1st April] and ending on [31st March] in each year and annual interest shall be construed in respect of each such period.

Y.003
The Agreement shall begin on [date] and continue for a period of one year until [date]. It shall not continue indefinitely and be renewed unless a new written agreement is concluded for the following period. Failure to conclude an agreement for any subsequent period after [date] shall mean that the [Institute] shall have the right to terminate the agreement at any time.

Y.004
This Agreement shall be terminated at the end of each year and end on [date]. There shall no automatic right of renewal and the Agreement may only be continued for another yearly period if written notice to that effect is received in writing by the [Supplier] from the [Company] by [date] in each year.

Y.005
The annual period of each year for the Agreement shall commence on [date] in each year and end on [date] in the following year thereafter.

Y.006
It is agreed between the parties that where any party wishes to change the start date and end date of any accounting period. That any such change shall be subject to prior written agreement with the other party.

Y.007

The [Company] reserves the right to change, amend and/or vary any payment, statement and invoice dates where new technology, software and/or procedures at the [Company] are adopted and implemented at any time.

Z

ZERO RATED

General Business and Commercial

Z.001
The [Supplier] and the [Purchaser] hereby acknowledge that all goods supplied under clause [–] and all services provided under clause [–] shall be treated as [zero-rated outputs] and will therefore not be subject to value added tax. In the event that any such goods or services should be subject to value added tax due to a change in the law or the nature of the classification of the goods or services or some other tax or some other additional payment to the government is introduced which directly relates to the supply or purchase of goods or services then these sums that fall due shall be paid by the [Supplier/Purchaser].

Z.002
The [Supplier] confirms receipt of the [Purchaser's] certificate confirming the [Purchaser's] [zero-rated VAT status] and the [Purchaser] confirms that such certificate is in the form specified by [government department/statute/legislation].

Z.003
The [Purchaser] undertakes to provide the [Supplier] with a zero-rated certificate confirming the [Purchaser's] [zero-rated VAT] status within [seven weekdays] from the date of this Agreement.

Z.004
The [Supplier] and [Purchaser] acknowledge that printed books supplied under this Agreement are zero-rated but 'E-books' will attract VAT [at the standard rate] in the [United Kingdom] and at various other rates throughout the countries in the [European Union] as at [date].

Practical key highlights of some of the main types of clauses in a contract and how they may be varied

This summary is only a general guide and is not intended to cover every aspect of drafting each type of clause in an agreement. It is really meant to highlight possible areas you should consider.

Pre-contract research

Before you even start to look at the contract first of all look at the wider picture of the actual set up and business of the parties involved. Are they a subsidiary? What do they actually produce and where? Do they make it themselves or is it produced by a third party? Where is their head office? Where are they incorporated? Are they new to the market or do they have a track record? What actual physical material steps are involved in creating your final product? Whether the contract is for a book, an app or a sponsorship agreement the same basic principle applies. The more you understand the parties, the easier it will be to create a document which will be successful and used to develop a long term relationship, rather than as a tool for litigation. Look at the last annual report and accounts, recent press releases, marketing reports and catalogues; ask to see samples and understand the creative process involved. The purpose of the agreement would in most cases would be a commercial one to make income and develop revenue and so it is important to also look at the financial stability and reliability of the company.

1   The nature of the work, material or services which are being assigned should be considered in two parts. The physical material and the actual rights both at the time of the agreement and later as the product is developed. The physical element would include the drawings for a logo, computer generated versions, text, sound recordings, film and other material which should all be viewed as completely separate elements. Similarly the rights would cover both the copyright in each physical element but also associated rights that may be registered such as trade marks, domain names and lyrics.

2   Whether the assignment is intended to cover both the physical material and rights developed or created in the future, either as an adaptation or because new technology has been developed.

3   The length of the assignment, which could be for the full period of copyright and in perpetuity, or for a fixed term. A shorter term allows the possibility of additional advances and new agreements as well as new form of exploitation.

4   The definitions which are applicable to the material and the rights which are being assigned. The rights can be drafted to be very narrow; this is done by being very specific as to the method of use and specifically excluding those which are not authorised so it is not ambiguous.

5   Whether the assignment relates just to copyright or extends to other intellectual property rights, trade marks, design rights, computer software, patents, database rights and domain names.

6   Any assignment must be in writing and requires consideration of some kind to be provided.

7   The assignment clause should specify the party which is assigning the rights and who is to receive them.

8   Most often the assignment is for the world, but it is possible to assign rights only for specified countries or territory.

9   It may be appropriate to make it clear that there is no right to register any further interest or to receive any more revenue.

Exclusive Licence

1   The possible conflict of existing agreements should be raised and an undertaking provided that there are none.

2   The exclusive licence must be linked to consideration, whether a fixed fee, royalties or an advance.

3   A licence may be exclusive for a fixed period, but the different rights may revert back to the licensor in stages as they have been used.

4   The definition of the rights is crucial and should be wide and extensive or as narrow as possible. Those rights which are not granted should be stated as reserved. This may also include rights which do not exist at the time of the agreement but which come into existence at a later date due to advances in technology.

5   Regard should be given to new material which will be created in the future – either commissioned, or developed – and that means not just the main service or product, but anything associated with it. It should be clear who will own the rights.

6   The term of the licence can vary and is often the term of copyright. The shorter a licence period is then the more opportunity there is to generate revenue and to exploit the rights effectively. A fixed licence period with start and end dates and no right of renewal should be considered. Where you want to prolong it there should be a commencement date and the start of the duration of a period of years can be linked to completion of work, a distribution date or use of the rights.

7   The circumstances in which you would want a situation to be deemed applicable under force majeure may be considered, such as failure in supplies, electrical fault or strikes. The period of any such suspension of the agreement would mean that the length of the agreement still available might be insufficient. Therefore consideration should be given to a clause to provide an extension in such circumstances.

8   There should be specific consent given for the licensee to sub-licence or authorise third parties to exploit any rights which are granted. Where it is not permitted then it should be stated that no consent is provided.

9   An undertaking may be required that the rights granted will not be licensed, or exploited during the licence period by the licensor or any third party. This may also apply to any development or adaptation.

10   The territory for which the exclusive licence is given should be quite clear and the countries listed in the definition. A general word such as 'Europe' should be avoided. Most countries refer to their land and territorial waters, which do not apply to ships, oil rigs and aeroplanes. With the advent of satellite and other moving objects revolving the earth, the extension of the grant of the area covered to 'throughout the world and universe' looks to future developments.

11   Where it is likely that there will be translations, sub-titling, use of material or rights in promoting a product or service then this should be agreed to in each case. The licence may be limited to one language and if translations are to be permitted a procedure for editorial control and consent of the adaptation may be necessary.

Amendments

1   Whether the only document which is to be considered binding is the contract, or whether there are any other catalogues, brochures or quotes which need to be included and which provide significant details. Have any important representations or disclosures been made which you have relied upon which are not in the agreement? Either make sure this is attached as part of the original agreement or ensure an enforceable amendment is made and signed by both parties.

2   The method by which the contract can be amended is usually in writing, but often this is forgotten and emails and telephones calls are not verified in writing by a formal amendment. The trail of exchanges is often only looked at when there is a dispute. So clarity of the terms and any amendments is needed.

Obligations and Undertakings of Each Party

Payments and Costs

1 Any sums should be specified in detail whether advances, royalties, budget, costs, fees, and the currency.

2 The items can be specified in detail preferably by means of a definition at the front of the contract.

3 There should be undertakings as to when each of these payments will be made, the method of such payments, how they will be accounted for and whether there are any rights of inspection.

4 The method by which any budget or costs can be increased should be agreed.

5 In order to protect your liability to costs for any project then a maximum figure which cannot be exceeded in any circumstances should be inserted and an undertaking given by the party not to exceed this sum.

6 The responsibility for the payment of clearance costs of material and rights should be set out in detail both for acquisition and exploitation.

7 An undertaking to bear all the costs and expenses for a project and agreement that the other party will not be liable for or bear the cost.

8 To address the issue of set-off, whether any sums can be recouped and when, and whether any sums owed under the contract can be set off against another by either party.

9 If payment is delayed – whether an additional payment or interest will be made and if so the rate at which it will be calculated and the period in which it will fall due.

Accounting and Inspection Provisions

1 The date of payment of the royalties in each year and how often this is to occur.

2 The currency in which any payment is to be paid and who is to pay the exchange rate and bank costs and charges.

3 The detail of the content of the accounting statement and how it is to be broken down.

4 To which companies do the accounting provisions apply.

5 The number of occasions that any accounting statement is to be provided in a year.

6   The basis upon which the figures involved are calculated. For example is it a percentage of net or gross receipts, or a fixed sum per unit.

7   The duration of the period after the expiry or termination of the agreement in which the accounting process should continue.

8   The sums that can be set off or deducted from the accounts – withheld stock, returns, remainders, advance, sums owed under other contracts.

9   The supply of any documentation with the accounts such as licences, invoices or contract summaries

10   The accounts procedure for sub-licensees, and sub-contractors.

11   The right to carry out an inspection and how often this can be done and at whose cost.

12   The extent of the documents, records, software, discs, and stored material that can be inspected, and whether they can be copied.

13   The length of time that documents, records, software, discs, and stored material should be kept and whether they can then be destroyed.

14   Which party pays the cost of the legal and accountancy fees for the audit if there are errors or omissions and whether any additional sums such as an additional payment or interest are due and how these will be calculated.

Credits, Copyright Notices and Moral Rights

1   The exact wording and shape of any credit or copyright notice to any person or company, the location and size of any accompanying logo, image or trade mark should be stated in the contract and specifically related to the format of material upon which it will appear.

2   In the event that the credit or copyright notice does not appear or is not displayed by the company as required under the agreement or a third party. There may be circumstances in which it may be possible to exclude liability for this failure.

3   It can be specifically stated where the credit will not appear, for example in posters, packaging, reviews, and merchandising.

4   The copyright notice or credit may appear more than once in any product or service.

5   An undertaking can be provided that any copies produced which have no credit or copyright notice will not be supplied or distributed, but destroyed.

6   Moral rights are not relevant to every situation. There is the right to be identified in a reasonably prominent position and the name should be set out in the contract.

7   The second part of the moral rights assertion is the right not to be subject to derogatory treatment and this should be asserted if relevant.

8   A complete waiver of any credit and moral rights would be applicable where all the material and rights are being bought out through an assignment.

9   A copyright warning may also be considered in order to alert users of a service to the fact that the misuse of the content of a service could result in legal action against them.

Copyright Ownership and Title

1   An undertaking that the company owns or controls the material and rights which are being granted or assigned.

2   That there is no conflict with a previous agreement or any charges or restrictions which apply.

3   That the rights and material will remain the property of the licensor and that the licensee does not become the copyright owner or have the right to register any such interest.

4   That the rights and the material are listed and specified in detail and defined.

5   That where rights or material is not cleared and there are prior agreements. That the material is then listed as excluded or accepted on that basis.

6   Where there is an assignment it needs to be clear if it applies to new material and rights as well as those that exist already.

7   Rights can be defined in many ways and can include and exclude, inter alia, copyright, intellectual property rights, satellite, cable and terrestrial television, DVDs, computer games, merchandising, publishing, computer software, database rights, patents, inventions, design rights, electronic rights, image rights, recordings, music, logos, photographs, artwork, models, and prototypes.

8   When the agreement expires or is terminated then it should be clear what happens to the material and rights and who owns them.

9   Clearance of material or rights should not be confused with payment and may be the responsibility of different parties. If it is expected that

there will be no sums due to pay then a clause should be included to that effect.

Editorial and Quality Control and Marketing

1   Specify which party has the final editorial decision.

2   There may be consultation or approval clauses and the obligation to provide samples or copies in every format; a number of the final products and copies of all marketing.

3   Written approval in relation to particular material such as samples, covers, flyers or products allows degree of control which is greater than consultation. There is no limit as to how or when this should be and increases your involvement in the project. Build in a concept for the supply of copies of drafts and for discussion even if you have no final editorial control.

4   Specify the detail of the content of the work, the standard and style expected, and the format in which it is to be delivered or distributed.

5   Where the product, service or film is to be edited, or parts deleted or adapted then prior written approval can be required. Where you do not want to have to do this then it is imperative that the right to make changes extensively is incorporated in the agreement.

6   Marketing, packaging and associated material should not be ignored nor should the use of any adapted logo, title or character name. It is vital that approval or consultation clauses are included in order to be able to express a view as to how your work is being exploited and promoted. This often also highlights the fact that a third party has created some new material which should be acquired and assigned.

7   In some cases approval of material allows errors to be corrected, copyright notices to be put in which have been forgotten and misuse of your work avoided.

Insurance

1   Whether insurance is required to protect both parties or an individual or a product it needs to be specified who is to bear the cost and who is to benefit from the policy.

2   Product liability, a hazardous activity, defamation, life insurance and public liability insurance on location are just some of the policies that are included in agreements.

3   Attention needs to be provided to those items which are excluded under the policy and who is to meet the shortfall of any claim which is not covered by the policy.

Indemnity, Liability and Legal Proceedings

1   Both parties or just one party may provide any indemnity. It can apply to the whole contract or just a selection of clauses.

2   The indemnity may apply to only certain work, services or rights and may be limited by duration, country and cost.

3   You need to examine which areas of the agreement create the most risk and assess the possibility of a claim under the indemnity. It may be an allegation of defamation, faulty products, or exceeding the budget.

4   It is perfectly acceptable to agree a maximum fixed cost liability under the indemnity although liability for death and personal injury may not be excluded.

5   A procedure for being notified of any potential claims, taking over control of a case or being consulted about any proposed settlement is necessary to be alerted at an early stage.

6   Each party may bear its own costs and risk and no indemnity be provided.

7   The length of time which the indemnity lasts is significant, and may only be for the life of the contract or extend many years thereafter. There may be a time limit by which a claim must be made under the indemnity by the other party in respect of specified areas.

8   If you are the party providing the indemnity it may be cost effective to take out insurance cover to cover that potential liability.

9   Legal proceedings may be about defending or taking legal action, but the question of responsibility for legal costs and whether this is covered by any indemnity or can be set off from any of the sums due under the agreement needs to be considered.

10   The right to join and use the name of the other party in any legal proceedings which may arise to protect the product may be agreed. There may be a specification that there is no responsibility for the administrative and legal costs and an undertaking to reimburse or pay in advance for any separate legal advice that may be required and to provide a full indemnity to cover all costs, expenses, damages and other sums.

Third Party Transfer, Termination and Governing Law

1   The right to be able to transfer, charge or make an agreement to a third party without consent is a valuable clause in an agreement. It allows a degree of flexibility to sell on the product or service without paying any additional sum.

2   A restriction prohibiting any such third party transfer allows you the opportunity to negotiate a fee to agree to the novation or sale. In addition you can choose the companies with which you do business. Often such contracts are assigned as part of a wider package.

3   The assignment or transfer may or may not affect the liability and obligations of the company which has made the assignment. It needs to be stated whether they are released from their responsibilities and if the new business fails whether they will still be liable for the consequences under the agreement.

4   There are many grounds of termination which can be included to end a contract and some should be directly relevant to the development and completion of the project.

5   There may be sell-off provisions to allow stock to be disposed of at cost or for an agreed fixed price. The payments should be connected to this late sale.

6   Whether it is the force majeure or terminations provisions which result in the end of the agreement. There should be steps included to try to avoid litigation as the next stage; such as mediation, arbitration or dispute resolution. These procedures may or may not be obligatory on the parties, but the issue of costs needs to be clear and whether any decision is binding.

7   The jurisdiction or governing law may affect the type of action that can be taken, the evidence required, the costs and the damages and losses that can be awarded. The conduct of litigation in a forum where the law is uncertain in relation to the rights or obligations of parties for a project could result in protracted and expensive litigation in which, even if you win, not all the costs are recouped.

Guide to the mistakes, omissions and errors to avoid in contract, licence and distribution agreements

There is plenty that can go wrong at any stage of a contract, but a great deal can be avoided by sufficient preparation at an early stage so that it is clearer as to what each party is actually expected to supply, create, undertake and expects to achieve.

Clarify your aim and optimum terms

The most important part of any contract or agreement starts well before the negotiation and drafting stage. It is important that you are clear about the aim of the project and the most advantageous terms you hope to achieve as the outcome in the contract. That means that you have to try to establish which terms and conditions you would optimistically like to achieve, which rights you want to own or licence, and how much revenue you would like to generate in each financial year. You need to try to plan through and map out how any rights you want to acquire may be used commercially, what material will be created and by whom, how will it be packaged, sold and marketed. If you don't have your own contractual targets and also a practical idea of the steps which will be taken to exploit any rights and material. Then not only will it be very much harder to negotiate a good agreement as you have no focus for what you want to achieve, but you are unlikely to cover all the issues effectively in the contract.

Create one contract document

Contract documents vary in extremes as to their depth and complexity, and may be just one or a series of documents. It is not uncommon these days for businesses to put their terms and conditions on the back of invoices and then seek to rely upon them to exclude some prior agreement, or for two parties to both seek to rely on their contrasting terms of business. Such conflict is best avoided by insisting that the other company accept that your terms and conditions apply and to get this confirmed in writing or to create a new agreement. Many general terms and conditions which are used for years do not spell out in sufficient detail what each party is meant to do and often avoid the issue of copyright ownership and intellectual property rights entirely.

Investigate the business of the other party

As a fundamental rule, even before you attempt to negotiate, draft or amend anything, you need to understand far more about the business of the parties to the contract. This is a very necessary step of negotiating and drafting a good contract. At an early stage get an idea of how they do business and understand how they operate. Obviously make the effort to look at their website, review corporate documents or an annual report and understand what their business actually does and how they do it. A better understanding of the key personnel, products, brands and trade marks, sales, markets and distribution methods of a company will enhance your ability to create a short, clear and useful contract. You need to consider the turnover and profit history and solvency of the company, and whether it in fact is an empty shell subsidiary. Where any company is newly created for a project or is an insignificant subsidiary then you should consider whether a 'comfort letter' agreeing to take responsibility, and bear the cost of all liability and indemnities should be sought from the parent company or an individual.

This type of background research is important and will help you understand not only what the company does well, but also their future plans and the products or services they do not exploit. That knowledge may give you the advantage to negotiate a far higher percentage royalty and a much greater advance. It may also mean that you may decide to retain a considerable number of rights or withhold countries or markets in which you know they have no experience.

Parties to the Agreement
It is essential to check that the party who purports to own the rights and grant them in that company name actually holds them. The trading name can be referred to, but the contracting party should be the name of the incorporated company or institute from which the revenue flows and for which there are annual reports otherwise it risks undermining the value of the contract. It is worth considering whether the parent company and the subsidiary should both be the contracting parties. Often at this point some parties try to put in additional words such as 'including assignees and successors in business'. If you don't want the other party to be allowed to sell you on then all these type of references should be deleted. A third party transfer clause which deals with the issue and sets out permitted assignees or bars them altogether unless there is consent is the preferable route. The signature of the agreement is equally important and that the person signing has both the authority and the capacity to do so. If it is a particularly large contract a finance director or chief executive should be the signatories.

Law and Contracts
There are two main areas of the law which are used when drafting contracts and clearing and using any type of material – intellectual property rights and contract law. Often the legal definitions in the legislation, case law and regulations merely form the background to what is actually in the agreement. This is particularly true of the latest technological developments of content downloads on mobiles, interactive television, and wireless

telecommunications. Quite often the law is far behind, or does not even recognise certain rights. This was true until relatively recently of the right to apply for a computer software patent and still applies to format rights for television programmes. The terms of a contract are not limited by the definitions which exist in law nor are the terms of a contract limited by the legislation of any country except to the extent that the terms in some way are illegal or contravene the law or are contrary to some case law or code of practice or policy.

Original Work and Copyright

Copyright is about the protection of an original work which has been created through skill and labour. The quality of the work is not the issue. In any contract where a person or company claims copyright in any material five basic questions should be raised.

1   Is it original or is it merely copied from someone else's work?

2   Who made the work and where did they make it or what is their nationality?

3   How did they, or will they, make the work?

4   Who has or will pay for the work and what type of agreement is required?

5   What materials already exist and what will be created?

In the United Kingdom the Copyright, Designs and Patents Act 1988 (as amended) groups materials in these categories: artistic work, photographs, sound recordings, literary works, computer-generated material, film, and soundtrack. Commissioned work is presumed to belong to the person who pays for it, but this is not always the case and so a signed assignment document is preferable to a dispute at later date.

Copyright clearance of material, work, services and rights which are either being contributed by third parties or which are only a small part of the main project should not be overlooked. The clearance and consent to use something is not the same as who bears the cost; these are two separate issues which often cause problems. Clearance should always be as wide as possible so that fixed fees are agreed in advance, but minimise the payments upfront so that payment is only linked to different types of actual use. This may be publication of a book, broadcast of a film, use of a service or operation of a website. As a rule any fees should not be linked to sales or net receipts and a one-off fee paid in stages for all media in any country is preferable. The aim should always be to acquire an assignment of all rights and actually become the copyright owner of the material and the rights. This makes it much easier when selling on your business to provide assurances in due diligence as to the ownership of your intellectual property rights.

Existing Material and Clearance Costs

It is important that you establish at an early stage which material, work or service is being used or supplied for the project and not to treat this as an administrative matter to be sorted out later. The first list to draw up is that of material which already exists which is being used for the project. For every different example of material on the list the question is who owns or controls it, in which format is it being supplied and at whose cost. It is important to obtain a full list of all the clearance costs and to identify the agreements that need to be concluded. There may be a copyright licence or an assignment of all rights in all media required. You also need to research whether you need a licence from any collecting societies for the performance, broadcast, transmission, mechanical reproduction, digitisation, reproduction or otherwise of any of the material and what sums will have to be paid for each type of use. Any licence or document providing consent should specify whether a copyright notice or credit is required and how it should be displayed and when. It is useful to include a clause that no credit will be provided rather than not address this issue.

New Material, Adaptations, and Developments

You need to find out whether the material, work or service is to be adapted or developed, and if so who is creating the new work, the method used and whether there is a prototype, sample or draft before the final product. It helps establish a clear list of the material which will be created, the production costs and what rights are likely to be created in relation to specific types of material. It is very difficult to draft an agreement without having addressed this issue and understood the cycle of the agreement in a practical sense as well as from the perspective of the different types of copyright and intellectual property rights that are created.

Draw up a list of all the material from the first drawings or computer software being created, to the finished product. Are any music, artwork, sound recordings, film, computer generated material or photographs used, or is the product a development of an earlier work? This will help when resolving copyright issues in the drafting. Is a third party being commissioned, or are they an employee? If so does their contract deal with this issue or would an assignment of copyright and all other rights be the safer option. Wherever you engage anyone, whether on a freelance basis, as a friend or pay to commission a company to create new material of any type – artwork, photographs, designs, three dimensional manufacturing models, text, logos, or music – it is vitally important that there is a complete and full assignment of all rights in all media and that the proper paperwork is completed. It is only when a project is successful that it is likely that contributors will then try to claim an interest or register a right and this is best avoided. So that it is unequivocal who owns the material and the rights. There have been a number of disputes which have arisen either because the question of who owns new material which has been created has not been stated or because the question of the creation of new rights has not been dealt with. The ownership of the material and the ownership of the copyright or intellectual property rights should never be presumed to be clear but always specified in the contract.

Editorial and Quality Control

The lists of existing material and that which is to be created in the future will allow you identify which clauses need to be incorporated in the agreement so that you can have the right to exercise the necessary degree of control over the project. This equally applies to the associated items such as labels, packaging, posters, advertising and marketing material. This can be dealt with by editorial control, quality control and title clauses. Even if the other party has final editorial control that does not prevent you from having rights of approval or consultation at each stage over the cover, binding, index, layout, colours, credits, copyright notices, disclaimers, type of content, and any additions or deletions which may be made. The essential aim is to impose undertakings to preserve the quality of the content or product at each stage. This equally applies to services and work. It is important that the personnel who carry out the project are suitably qualified and experienced.

Definitions

If you try to define a large number of factors at the front of the contract which are referred to in a number of clauses then it simplifies the drafting. Definitions at the front of the agreement help create a clearer contract and hopefully avoid repetition throughout which makes it even more difficult to read.

Failure to do this results in constantly repeating the descriptive narrative throughout which is often very confusing and in many cases inconsistent. You may list for example a definition of the work, service or product to be supplied under the agreement, the advance, the territory to be licensed, the fees to be charged, the delivery date, the website, the term of the agreement, the work schedule, or how each of the different types of rights which are to be granted in the agreement are defined. The list is unlimited and should be used by providing the best possible description that you can.

However attention needs to be made as to whether you are creating definitions which are not achievable and may result in the other party using it as an excuse to terminate the contract. Therefore when providing a description if the title, length, images or content is not yet certain state that it is only provisional and may be varied.

The use of definitions can affect the revenue which is received under an agreement, an advantageous definition of the distribution expenses, the net or gross receipts, or the royalties will clearly affect how much money a company is able to deduct before it is obliged to pay any royalties.

Assignment, Licence and Rights

There are five aspects to understanding rights and defining rights in an agreement.

1   The material, work or service which already exists in any medium and which is to be supplied or used.

2   The material, work or service which is to be created in the future.

3   Which parties are carrying out which work or providing services and the method by which this is to be done.

4   How the services, work and material fit in with the legal categorisation and definitions which exist.

5   Then fit all this into achieving the best terms possible in the agreement.

Ownership of the material is separate from copyright and the exploitation of the rights. The licensing of use of any copyright or the transfer of ownership must be done in writing and cannot be given in any verbal form unless it is a non-exclusive licence. An exchange by email and text may be deemed binding but would be based on the facts of the case. The key debate would be about the signature and whether the sender could be clearly identified and had consented or whether the exchange was merely negotiations and not intended to be binding. For clarity it is therefore useful to make any such exchange 'not binding and subject to final contract' to avoid ambiguity. In any event an original signed document is always better. An introductory letter for an interview does not amount to an assignment of all rights in all media. As a basic rule you should acquire widely and licence narrowly. There are broad categories of types of agreements as follows:

1   Assignment – Buyout – transfer of all rights in all media throughout the world and universe. This may be for a one off fee or a royalty percentage which varies according to the type of use. No rights are reserved.

2   Assignment – transfer all rights in all media but only for fixed period of time such as ten or twenty years and for a fixed sum not necessarily royalty and may only be for limited territory. All rights are to be assigned back to the assignor at the end of that period of assignment.

3   Assignment – transfer only limited rights such as publishing or film, for a fixed period for a one off fee or royalty. Either worldwide or for certain countries. Rights are reserved which are not assigned.

4   Exclusive licence of all rights in all media for the full period of copyright

and any extensions and renewals and in perpetuity for the world and universe. No rights are reserved.

5   Exclusive licence of all rights for fixed term such as five years. Rights revert back after the end date of the term of the agreement.

6   Exclusive licence of limited rights for full period of copyright, but only in a specific licensed area or territory.

7   Exclusive licence of limited rights for a fixed term in a country. The rights revert back after the end date of the licence period.

8   Non-Exclusive licences which can be varied as to the rights, the length of time for which it is granted, and the countries.

If you are granting or assigning rights the primary intention should always be to retain as many rights as possible, to hold as much control over the project as you can and to maximise the revenue in the smallest amount of territory that needs to be given. The licence period should not be longer than absolutely necessary and all rights in the project should revert back to you at the end. Many agreements which are concluded fail to fulfil all these criteria as insufficient effort is put into shortening every aspect of the terms to achieve this intended aim. Every single aspect of the grant or assignment clause is important from the definition of the rights to be granted or assigned, the term of the agreement or licence period, the territory and the material to which it applies.

The duration of the agreement could be crucial as to the financial liability and is too often included without any real thought as to the consequences. Establish whether it is in your interest to negotiate a very short licence period or term of the agreement. The drafting can be adapted to delay the start date or bring it forward so that it starts on the date of full signature of the agreement. It may be useful to link the duration to the meeting of financial targets and receipts of funds or to include a break clause. The concept of contracts which just roll on and are renewed without any consent without any real start and end date should avoided. Where the term of the agreement or payments are linked to completion of work or delivery or use of the rights then care should be taken to set out either a fixed date by which payment is triggered or by which the agreement will end.

The territory should be either as wide or as limited as possible. The widest would be throughout the world and universe, next the world or only a defined list of countries, a single country or just a small licensed area which is local to a community. The issue of seas outside territorial waters around land, the sky, aeroplanes, satellites, ships, oil rigs and other moving objects may not fall within the countries defined and have to be addressed separately.

Often there are all embracing exclusive licence clauses which are in effect buying everything because no effort has been made to spell out only limited rights and to negotiate a shorter licence period. Even three, ten or twenty years is better than agreeing to the full period of copyright. Where you are acquiring rights a comprehensive assignment with an extensive all media definition which covers all formats, all mediums and any use is always preferable to a licence, but an exclusive licence for the full period of copyright and in perpetuity throughout the world and universe is the next step down. Whether it is an assignment or a licence there is no reason to give more than needed in the circumstances and so you should as a rule licence or assign only give those specific rights which you have defined in the agreement individually and reserve everything else.

Especially those rights and technologies which are not in existence now and will be created in the future. It is important that the copyright and intellectual property rights in any new material are assigned back to the original copyright owner or business either during or at the end of the project.

There have been many agreements where new technologies such as videos, CDs, computer games which exist now were not referred to at all and in which all royalties were only linked to certain formats of products. The resulting effect is that the assignor or licensor has not received any royalties as they did not reserve these rights. The assignee or licensee have successfully argued that they had no right to additional royalties as no royalty was mentioned in the agreement in relation to those new rights or products. In other examples the assignment or licence was sufficiently ambiguous for it to be accepted that the definition covered these new products which did not exist at the time.

Sub-Licensees

It is also important to plan ahead and only to allow a project to be sub-licensed to those third parties which you have approved and which agree to be bound by the terms of the main agreement. Nor should the licensee be permitted to rely on the sub-licence to avoid responsibility and liability under the main agreement. Often no reference is made to the sub-licensing of rights and the licensor is unable to exert sufficient control over them or rights and material are created which are not assigned to the licensor. The steps required to deal with this are then unnecessarily expensive and protracted as it was not dealt with in enough detail in the contract. There is little benefit in granting rights to a company which they have no experience of exploiting or which will be sub-licensed to an unknown third party. The term of any sub-licence that can be granted should be limited to the duration of the main agreement and any sub-licence should end at the same time if possible.

Trade Marks, Logos, Slogans, and Domain Names

The ownership of trade marks, service marks, community marks, logos, slogans, and domain names should be clarified and stated in the agreement. This is often forgotten, but it is particularly important whether it is to protect your own brand or to establish who can share in any interest and revenue. Any trade marks, service marks, community marks, logos, slogans, and domain names should be defined and a copy attached if possible to the agreement. The agreement should state which party owns and controls it and who has the right to register any interest, reproduce it in different formats, licence third parties, commission new artwork and how it can be used. If there is no permission given to adapt or change the logo or trade mark then this should be clearly stated. A comprehensive list of material on which it may be used and the location may be drawn up and rights of approval incorporated which require written consent at each stage of development.

Credits, Copyright Notices and Moral Rights

It is often forgotten that moral rights consists of two categories: the first is the right to be identified; and the second the right not to be subjected to derogatory treatment which is quite different. That is, nothing is to be added, taken away, changed, or varied unless authorised in advance. In order to avoid any problems later it may be easier to draft a waiver of moral rights, but then include a consultation clause instead. The copyright notices and credits should be set out in the agreement including the location, size and whether it should really apply to all material or just the main product or service. There is often no mention of the requirements for packaging, associated marketing and websites. It is also useful to have a waiver or to state that no credit is required.

Costs, Expenses, and Insurance

The budget, costs, expenses, and allowances for hotels, telephones and travel should all be specified in the definitions and a maximum limit set out in order to control the expenditure from the outset. The responsibility of each party as to the budget, costs, expenses and allowances should be set out in detail. Where possible documents should be attached which set out each item and they should form part of the agreement. A procedure for any increase can then be set out which has to be formally approved in advance and what is to happen to any underspend. Failure to place any restrictions could result in an unexpected financial liability and the possibility of being sued for the balance. It is also worthwhile to include a clause that each party will bear its own administration, travel or other costs which are not specified and that they cannot be recovered under the agreement. Also consider whether insurance cover should be taken out for a project and to assess the impact this may have to minimise the liability and potential claims against each party.

Delivery, Rejection, Risk and Title

Delivery, target or distribution dates should be included in an agreement otherwise there is no focus for the payments to begin. The dates may relate to the completion of each stage of a project, delivery of a manuscript, proofs or index, the development of a final product, operation of a website or release to the public. If it is stated that time is of the essence in relation to these dates then failure to comply may result in the right to terminate the agreement. There should also be a risk clause which identifies the point at which ownership in the material which is being delivered passes. A retention of title clause will ensure that ownership of the rights in the material are retained until payment is received in full. If the service or product is not delivered by the date then there should be a right to cancel or terminate. Often there is no completion date and so it is harder to rely on this as a grounds of termination if it is delayed. It is helpful to try to set out the manner in which a party shall be entitled to reject a product or service and to require them to specify the grounds and to do so within a specified period of time.

Royalties, Advances, Accounts and Inspection

The royalties, advance and the stage at which payments can be made can all be varied according to each set of rights and forms of exploitation which exist. The most common mistake is apply the same royalty to too many rights instead of negotiating higher percentages for those which are worth the most money and retaining those which are not going to be exploited. It is also worthwhile including a clause where the royalties escalate either when basic costs have been recouped or if sales targets are achieved. There could even be a series of such increasing royalties linked to different markets. Targets can be either the total value of sums received, units sold, clicks on banner on a website, or the winning of a sporting event. Bonus and performance related sums may also be paid on sales or an event or the achievement of sales figure by a certain date.

Any references to money should include the currency and how the exchange rate is to be fixed and who pays the charges. The sum received from the royalty percentage is totally dependent on the definition of the sum from which it is derived. This may be a fixed unit cost, a percentage of gross receipts or a percentage of net receipts. Often the net receipts are drafted in such a manner that there is never any royalty payment actually received as there are no limits to the expenditure and marketing costs which a company can deduct. A lower percentage of gross receipts is often better than a larger percentage of net. The only exception may be where costs and deductions from net receipts are capped and are not unlimited or where the product would not be exploited at all as it would not be commercially viable.

All discounts, agent's commission or fees should be set out and limited in a contract and it made clear as to how and when they can be deducted.

An advance can be any type of staged payments and does not have to be in one thirds, it can be linked to dates or completion of work. The contract should state whether the advance is to be recouped against future royalties or if it is non-returnable. If the companies have other contracts then a clause should be added that sums due under the agreement either can or can't be set off against other agreements between the parties.

It is important that there are provisions regarding how the sums received are held or managed. The contract may require a new bank account with agreed signatories allowed access. It may be preferable to arrange for sums to be paid direct rather than allow a third party to receive it as an agent. The money remains within their control until it is handed over and unless it is clearly identifiable as separate falls within their business and is subject to the possibility of mismanagement and the business collapsing. The accounting provisions should be very clear as to what is required in a royalty statement and should be as frequent as possible. For a mobile phone or website company every month or two is not unreasonable, but once a year is at the other end of the scale. Inspection of accounts and records is needed in order to verify the sums stated as due, but the inspection provision needs to be drafted widely to allow access to as much material as possible. A clause can also be included which obliges the party who has made the error in the accounts to pay interest and both the legal and accounting professional costs of the audit. There may be a margin of error over which this provision comes into effect this could be a percentage or a fixed amount.

Defamation, Liability, and Indemnity

There should always be an undertaking that a party has not entered and will not enter into any other agreements or arrangements which would conflict with the present agreement. There may be one or more clauses which relate to the responsibility for checking the contents of any service or product and ensuring that it does not contain anything which is defamatory, obscene or offensive. These types of clauses need to be drafted very widely if you are seeking assurances and narrowly if it is your business providing the undertaking. Such undertakings would also be given for any consequential loss and damage arising from product liability and for compliance with any necessary legislation, tests, and codes of practice. The question is whether the clauses as drafted cover both direct and indirect losses and damages and is accompanied by an indemnity which is equally wide and unlimited. In the present climate of litigation it is commonsense to consider whether both parties would be protected more efficiently by insurance cover.

It is important to include a right to be able to edit, delete or amend material which in the view of the company's management or legal advisors is likely to result in litigation or adverse publicity. Where a company is going to rely on an indemnity provision for reimbursement of legal costs, losses and damages. Then there should be an additional clause relating to any potential right to be indemnified. The other party should be notified of any potential claims at an early stage by the company seeking to rely on the indemnity. The party should be consulted about the case and how it should be dealt with and provided with the opportunity to refute the allegations. Further that no settlement can be reached without prior consultation as to the terms of the proposed settlement.

Both indemnity and liability provisions can be subject to a fixed maximum limit under a contract to minimise the financial exposure of a company and this should always be considered for any contract. Liability can be limited in most areas but not for personal injury or death so it is possible to limit the clause by a fixed period of time, the type of loss and damages. Exclusion of liability is very common in insurance, health, and product policies or for computer software and equipment, but not so extensive in other agreements. It is possible to limit the life of indemnity, so that it ends with the agreement or only extends for a fixed number of years. Indemnity undertakings can also be limited to selected clauses in an agreement.

Jurisdiction, Legal Proceedings and Disputes

The legal system and law which both parties decide the agreement should fall within is often not seriously considered. It needs to be decided in conjunction with the other alternative methods of resolving a dispute that the parties would like to have such as arbitration, mediation and alternative dispute resolution if any. There are serious cost and legal implications dependent on the forum which is chosen. Where the issues at stake are not serious then the avoidance of litigation and the heavy costs involved if one loses make it valuable to have the opportunity if you so wish to seek some other method of resolving a matter without prejudice to any rights or claim.

Termination and Force Majeure

The termination clauses provide the chance to specify in detail the circumstances in which a party should have the right to terminate an agreement. It is possible to go well beyond the standard clauses to set out other grounds such as the failure to reach certain financial targets, complete stages of the project by certain dates, and get a product released to the public. Often it is forgotten that it should be stated what exactly is to happen if the agreement is terminated and whether any sums would be repaid, or rights revert or whether the parties would have to negotiate a settlement. The force majeure clause is also about suspending or terminating the agreement, but the circumstances which qualify within that category can be quite varied. It is possible to include specific types of situations than can be covered and exclude those that are agreed not to fall within this clause.

Third Party Transfer

Particularly where the contract is for the services or work of an individual with a company it is important to include a no third party transfer clause. This may also apply to a company in order to prevent the obligations, liabilities and benefits being transferred to a business which is far less solvent or with which you do not wish to be associated. A website company would want to make sure that it could be sold on without any delay and so the opposite approach would be taken and a clause included which specifically agrees that third party transfers are permitted and that no consent is required or any additional sums due in payment.

Sub-Licensing and Merchandising

It is stating the obvious, but often forgotten that before you negotiate or conclude any sub-licensing, or merchandising agreement or option you should look at the existing contracts and documents in your possession and try to get a complete picture as to who owns what material and rights. It is crucial that you make a clear and positive decision as to who actually owns those rights which you hope to exploit. No presumptions should be made that your company owns the rights. If the position is unclear or requires more research or clarification – now is the time to do so and not after the contract has been signed and the threat of litigation becomes an expensive mistake. It may be necessary to declare your hand to a potential claimant to state your view of the rights position and for them to confirm that you own such rights. Alternatively it may be that when the agreement was concluded that the technology or rights did not exist. This could be the case with many earlier agreements which did not envisage satellite television, mobile phones, websites and the internet. Sometimes there is merely ambiguity because at the time the contract was concluded merchandising and sub-licensing was not even considered. The whole issue is therefore reduced to the interpretation of the actual wording of the agreement and documents that were concluded.

You should carefully check the exact wording not only of the clauses relating to the rights which have been licensed or assigned to your company, but also whether there are other clauses in the agreement which restrict or prohibit your company's right to transfer, licence or assign the rights to a third party. There may be a no licence, transfer or assignment clause to a third party. Or any such new agreement may be subject to the prior approval or written consent of the original copyright owner.

It is important that some research is done as to whether any other agreement has been signed at any stage prior to this agreement which would either prevent or restrict the rights that could be granted. There may be for instance a distribution agreement or option or other licence or assignment which relates to another topic, but still deals with these ancillary rights. Quite often company records are incomplete and badly filed and not specific as to anything except the main subject of a contract. Therefore it is worth asking about the history as far as people recall – which will at least alert you to the fact that relevant documents may exist. Any document which potentially has already assigned or granted the rights must be examined to see whether that is in fact the case. It is also worth doing some basic research as to whether those rights and products have actually already been marketed in the specific country or area.

There is always a need prior to entering into negotiations with a third party to check out their track record, financial history and how and where they actually currently market their products or services. Do your homework on the proposed third party – are they a distributor or a manufacturer with agents overseas? Are they a new company or have they been trading for some time? Is it a subsidiary of a more substantial company? Do they manufacture products themselves or do they appoint a manufacturer? Who have they used in the past? What products do they actually sell and where? Have there been any health and safety problems? Look at their website, catalogue, marketing material. Find out what stages they do go through before they market the final product? What trade marks, service marks or other registrations have they worldwide?

Where are their main premises based, and where do they hold their bank accounts? It is not difficult to obtain copies of the accounts of a business. All this information helps you complete a more detailed picture of the operation and to assess the reliability of a third party.

As a basic principle you should licence rather than assign rights to a third party and should not and cannot grant more rights than you actually already own. Therefore where you are a company and have acquired rights which you wish to sub-licence the sub-licence should end on the same date as the rights acquired under the main agreement or earlier. The sub-licence cannot be granted for a longer term without the consent of the copyright or other rights owner.

There is no reason to conclude a document which is either clearly defined as an assignment or which purports to be a licence, but in effect is so wide as to be similar to an assignment. It is often argued by sub-licensees or merchandising companies that an assignment is required, but this is not the case. An assignment would transfer all copyright and ownership to the third party and would prevent the copyright owner or your company having any further right to exploit the rights.

The whole process should be to licence the rights and material as narrowly as possible for the shortest feasible period. There is no logical reason to licence rights which will not be exploited nor to allow the licensee to sub-licence rights further without any consultation or rights of approval. If a licensee wishes to acquire other rights then look at the detail of whom they licence, how the process is monitored and the reporting and accounting structures which are followed.

The definitions section at the front of the agreement is very important as it is here that the work, the material, the trade mark and logo, and the rights which are to be referred to in the licence are described in detail. A sub-licence or merchandising agreement may be exclusive or non-exclusive this

1704

is obviously reflected in the payment in terms of an advance or royalties. The term of the agreement can be any length, but should not be left open to being linked to a task that is never completed. So always put a start and end date to avoid ambiguity. When granting a licence the rights given should be specific and not wide and limited to the actual product that is to be marketed. There is no reason to grant all the other rights and these should be reserved. There may be an undertaking not to exploit all or some of those reserved rights until after a certain date. The point is that they are still owned by the licensor and not the licensee. It is very important to make quite clear what you are not granting. Quite often you will find that a contract makes no reference at all to rights which are not granted. However where new technology or rights are created at a later date, the reservation of rights may then permit the licensor to grant another licence to someone else. A grant of rights must also define the territory for which the rights have been granted. This can be as large as the world and the universe to as small as a specific commercial premises.

Where it is likely that the book, product or film is part of a series or set. Then it is important to address the issue as to whether there is any right of first refusal or an option granted over future editions or sequels. Unless there is some consideration for this in the payments then it is better to make it clear that there are no such rights There may also be clauses which are intended to prevent competing works being made available for a fixed period on the market before a specified date. These clauses should be drafted as narrowly as possible or even refused.

If a licensee wishes to acquire an exclusive option or a right of first refusal, then that should be clearly drafted as such and consideration given. There is no reason to at this stage to limit your negotiation position by agreeing to the same terms for the new material.

Delivery dates should be realistic as an agreement with a time of essence clause will then allow the licensee to terminate for non-delivery. Calculating the costs of the supply of material is important and the agreement should make clear who is paying and at which point the risk and ownership of the material passes.

Editorial Control and Quality Control clauses facilitate procedures to inspect, approve and also prevent others exploiting your material in an unacceptable manner. This would apply to master material, samples, prototypes, packaging, marketing, translations, change of name, and other adaptations and sub-licensing.

The essence of these types of agreements is to make money. This means that the accounting requirements should be clear and the detail of how and when the money is to be paid. It is better for you to sign the agreement, and to have the sums paid directly to you. If you provide authority under the contract for the agent to receive the sums and statements, then make sure that you can still personally have a right of inspection of the accounts and records. Discuss with your agent where and how your funds are to be kept and paid. Where the royalty is to be paid as a percentage of net receipts then it should be drafted to limit the amount of deductions that are permitted by the licensee. Failure to do so may mean that a very successful project results in no royalty payments to the licensor as the licensee literally deducts every penny of its costs before it makes any payment. A percentage of gross receipts is often better than a percentage of net receipts which is broad. An advance may be a one off non-returnable payment or recouped against future royalties. Escalating royalties linked to successful sales allow for the licensor to benefit from greater financial rewards once certain costs are recovered. You should also look at exchange rates and the cost of transfer of funds; how are funds held and where; accounting statements and the detail these will provide; audits and errors. As well as how long records, documents and invoices should be kept.

There are often clauses which prevent transfer or assignment of the rights to a third party without consent or those which relate to change of control of the business. The issue of product liability where an article or product is sold to the public is important and the arrangement of insurance is an integral part of these clauses. Where you are the licensor then you should endeavour to provide a limited indemnity in terms of the undertakings it covers and also one which is capped so that it is not an open ended financial risk. Try to limit your indemnity both by the length of time it operates; the amount, and the areas that it covers. The indemnity should be addressed at the same time as liability and legal proceedings. There should be a requirement that the licensor is kept advised of any threat of legal proceedings and that no legal costs are to be claimed unless the licensor has been kept informed. Further that if the licensor is required to join any legal action the licensee intends to take against a third party that both parties will agree the costs in advance.

In any sub-licence it is important to include clauses which cover copyright ownership, copyright notices, moral rights and credits from the viewpoint of the rights and the material which exists at the time of the agreement and those which will be created in the future.

The ownership of names, titles, trade marks and logos should be clear and who has the right to register them and exploit them at a later date. As a product is exploited in different forms new versions are often created and the ownership of these new adaptations should be stated. There have been a number of cases where consultants have designed new images and the rights have not been assigned to the company. It doesn't matter whether it is a new link logo design, on a marketing label or part of a new website, the ownership should be clarified. Merchandising can vary from toys, to DVDs, books, films, computer games, clothing and ringtones to a format for a quiz show. The material created these days is extensive from posters for stands at trade fairs, to banner advertisements, podcasts, flyers, brochures, packaging and television advertisements. Both during negotiations and at a later stage ask for a marketing plan and report which will set out estimated forecast of sales, formats and the marketing strategy in different countries.

It is likely that a licensee will use a range of third parties to create new material and care needs to be taken that all rights in any such material are assigned to the licensor. You should ensure that all work commissioned by the licensee or carried out by any third party results in assignment of the copyright and it is not left unresolved.

The termination provisions set out the basis upon which the agreement can be ended and so it makes sense to include grounds for termination for non-payment of any part of the advance or royalties. The failure to reach specified performance targets may also be grounds for termination.

The licensee will want any force majeure clause to be wide, but this is not in the interests of the licensor. Certain types of technical or other failure may actually be the licensee's fault. So you do not want the licensee to be able to rely on force majeure when the licensor would prefer to terminate the agreement. Look at the termination and force majeure from view of the licensee not printing your book or product, stopping selling it or going out of business. You need to make sure there are clauses that allow the licensor to have the rights transferred back to the licensor.

After the expiry of the licence there may be a sell-off period where the licensee is permitted to dispose of stock. This should preferably be non-exclusive and have a specified end date where material is destroyed or returned to the licensee at no charge or at cost. It is equally reasonable to not allow this, but insist that the end of the licence period is the final date and no further sales or distribution is allowed after that date.

At the end of the sub-licence there will be in existence a whole collection of material from master material and moulds, to software, packaging, brochures, flyers and digital files. It is therefore important to have addressed the ownership of this material in the contract and whether or not the licensor is entitled to have all copies delivered at the licensee's cost or whether it is to be destroyed or stored.

The governing law clause is important both in terms of legal costs, but also what legal rights you may have as this will obviously vary depending on the jurisdiction.

Understanding copyright and how it is used in contracts

It is always necessary in any agreement to think about whether there are any copyright, trade mark, or other intellectual property issues that need to be addressed in relation to both parties. This article is only concerned with copyright. There are two parts to this issue the rights and the material which exist at the time of the contract. Then the rights which may be created in the future and the material which will be developed. There may be different types of rights which all exist at the same time. Similarly there may be different types of material created at a variety of stages. It is crucial prior to drafting any contract to understand the practical issues of the format of the material required to be delivered or the methods by which it is to be produced, reproduced and exploited.

Copyright is about the protection or exploitation of someone's original work which they have created as a result of their skill and labour. We are not dealing with all the other criteria which may be necessary in order to qualify for copyright protection in this article which you would need to meet. The quality of the work is not the issue, merely whether the work is original, and by whom, where and how it is created and the type of material which forms the record of its existence. A person may be the original copyright owner or they may have licensed their work to a company under an exclusive or non-exclusive licence. Alternatively the work may have been assigned to a distributor and the rights bought out in return for an advance and a royalty. The potential scenarios are wide and varied, but the same basic questions apply. Who was the original copyright owner? When and how did they make it? Was it original or was it based on someone else's work? What materials were created? If the company or distributor has acquired the rights under a licence or assignment where is the contract? What rights did you acquire under the contract? and what does the contract actually authorise you to do? Are you entitled to sub-licence these rights to a third party?

The legal definitions in legislation and case law both in the UK, Europe and elsewhere merely form the background. Such terminology is not directly used in the terms of an agreement, but is changed to suit the circumstances. The whole aim when drafting a contract is to summarise the situation as far as possible so that the intention of the parties is most accurately and comprehensively described. Most legislation worldwide is far behind the advanced technological developments such as interactive television, downloading of material onto mobiles, websites and social networking. Some of the legislation has been drafted in broad terms to describe the method and medium, but without specifics and so would be unsuitable to use in a contract. Copyright is best envisaged as consisting of many slices of a cake and as technology develops new sections are created which did not exist before. It is crucial that the issue of rights of ownership of the copyright are dealt with as a separate one from the ownership of the material. A library may for instance own the physical copy of the work, yet not own or control the copyright in the work.

The motto 'license narrowly and acquire widely' is a good one as a starting point. The licensing of the use of copyright or the transfer of ownership of any material of any type must be done in writing, and cannot be given on the telephone, by voicemail or any verbal form unless it's a non-exclusive licence. Where the services of a third party are being engaged for a project then the question of copyright ownership of the rights and material should always be dealt with in order to avoid a dispute at a later date. An informal arrangement with a consultant, web designer or other contributor can be a very expensive mistake if a project later becomes successful. If someone is commissioned to design any artwork, create a logo, record some music or write a text. Then as a fundamental principle there should be a written document where consideration is provided to acquire some or all of the rights that you intend to exploit and to prevent the other person licensing third parties or registering the rights with a collecting society. In contrast it is also needed to protect the author and their work so that the rights of the creator are not exploited without consent or without remuneration. Where you intend to sell the business on at a later stage, then it makes sense to have a clear and consistent record of the acquisition of rights and to adhere to this policy so that it permeates all parts of the company. This applies to all departments of a business as due diligence will reveal any failures to acquire rights which everyone presumed were owned by a company. Marketing departments often create or commission new labels, logos and artwork without the necessary paperwork being concluded and it has only been when a company has tried to register a trade mark that they have discovered that they do not even own the rights and that they were never acquired at an early stage.

There is no reason to grant or assign rights for which you are receiving little financial gain or which the other party is not even going to exploit. Any licence which is to be granted should be as short as possible. There is no reason why an exclusive licence should be for 'the full period of copyright' when a period between one to five years will achieve the same financial result.

The Copyright, Designs and Patents Act 1988 as subsequently amended ('the CDPA') allocates material into groups which include Artistic Work, Photographs, Sound Recordings, Computer Generated Material, Film, Literary Work and Musical Work. There are others, but we are not dealing with all of them in this article. You will find many examples of different definitions in this book under the main headings Material and Rights as well as under other headings.

An Artistic Work is defined to include a graphic work, photograph, sculpture or other work of artistic craftsmanship. A Graphic Work is expressed as including any painting, drawing, diagram or map. Therefore in a contract which involves artwork one of the ways in which the material could be described in the definition section at the beginning of the agreement would be as follows:

'The Artwork' shall mean any photographs, drawings, sketches, pictures, diagrams or other illustrations or visual images which is intended to be included as part of the [Work].

Photographs is defined widely in the legislation, so that the photographs may be shot on any type of format. The description is of a recording of light or other radiation on any medium on which an image is produced or from which it may be reproduced. However it does not apply to one which forms part of a film. In a contract the photographs may simply be described as stills with a reference code as follows:

'The Stills' shall be the following photographs; [reference/code/title/ description/source material] in which the copyright is owned by [Name] and the physical material is owned by [specify].

Where the photographs are part of a commission then the following definition may be used:

'The Commissioned Work' shall be the following services and images to be created, developed, produced and delivered by the [Photographer] to the [Company] based on the summary which is set out in Schedule [–] which is attached to and forms part of this Agreement.

Sound Recordings is also very broadly defined to mean a recording of sounds from which sounds may be reproduced or the recording of the whole or any part of a literary, dramatic or musical work. This shall be the case regardless of the medium on which the recording is made or the method by which the sounds are reproduced. This does not apply to a film soundtrack accompanying a film which has a different definition. Therefore a recorded interview would be applicable if it was in sound only, but moving images would fall within film. When dealing with sound recordings there are separate issues of copyright relating to the words and lyrics as opposed to the music. It is an important issue to ensure in the agreement that there is an undertaking that both these rights have been cleared with the relevant copyright owner and/or collecting society and paid for and also to state who is to bear the cost of any future payments that may fall due.

The Sound Recordings may be defined in the agreement as follows:

'The Master Recording' shall mean all sound recordings of [Name] made by or for the [Interviewer] for the purpose of the [Article/Work] regardless of the medium on which the sound recording is made or the method by which the sounds are produced or reproduced.

Computer-Generated Material is stated to mean work or designs that are generated by a computer where there is no human author. The act of creating the work on a computer such as text or graphics which you feed into the machine which is your own work and labour is not a computer-generated work as it was put together by your skill, and not the machine.

Film is expressed very widely so that the moving image could be on a variety of formats. It is described as being a recording on any medium from which a moving image may by any means be reproduced. A cable programme and service have a different further definition. Examples include shooting material on your camcorder, in a studio or on location. It doesn't matter how long or short the recording is or what it is shot on and it can be in any format.

In an agreement the film may be referred to as a film, series, programme or pilot, but the aim is to be quite specific so the title, duration and other details would be listed.

'The Film' shall mean a feature length film and an accompanying soundtrack and musical score complying with the following particulars [Title/duration] Based on [Book/Script] created by [Name] [Producer/Director/Artists] [Material].

'The Series' shall be the series of films and any associated sound recording based on the [Pilot] which both parties may agree to produce, develop and exploit following satisfactory completion of the [Pilot].

Literary Works are defined as those in written form and cover text or others such as quotes. In an agreement reference would be made to the script, the book, the extract or the synopsis.

'The Synopsis' shall mean the summary of the [Work] which sets out the chapter outlines, structure and general content of the [Work]. A copy of which is attached and forms part of this Agreement.

Musical Work is described as meaning the music excluding any words which are to be sung or performed with the music. However in an agreement the definition at the front may be defined so that the lyrics are included.

'The Musical Work' shall be the original musical composition entitled [Title] [duration] created and written by [Name].

In relation to the internet and websites there is no reference to the word digital in the CDPA. Throughout the word electronic is used and is broadly defined to encompass both the internet and telecommunications and the use of mobiles, gadgets and computers. These rights can therefore be drafted very narrowly by reference to a specific website or to encompass future technology in a form that has not even been developed yet.

In reality there are often packages of material supplied under an agreement at different stages from one party to the other. Whether it is the supply of a copy of the master material or samples for approve of marketing, packaging and products. In order to protect your copyright position, quality control provisions play an important part as you are not only preserving the integrity of your brand, but vetting the new material. It is also important to address the issue as to who owns the material at the end of a contract.

It would seem obvious that before granting or sub-licensing rights that you should check that you own them. You cannot grant rights to a third party to exploit the copyright in a work which you don't own. There are many organisations today who try to do just that and forget the most basic principles. Often assumptions are made based on no research or evidence except details in a database that rights have been acquired in the past and no effort is made to verify the situation. It is crucial that good contract records are kept and if no record is available then the last known copyright owner contacted to clarify the issue. It is not acceptable to assume that because your business has the material on its premises that it has the right to exploit the material and license it to a third party. Nor is it possible to assume that you are entitled to exploit material or rights because the copyright owner has not notified you of their objections. It is totally wrong to assume that a copyright owner has an obligation to notify anyone of the fact that they wish to be excluded from a licensing scheme. The obligation is always on the person who is seeking to exploit work owned by someone else that they must seek prior consent.

Drafting a contract or licence which deals with copyright and intellectual property is best approached on a factual basis and not directly derived from the legal definitions which can be either too limiting or too wide. When drafting a contract it is important that there are clear and detailed definitions at the start of the agreement. These definitions are then woven in at a later stage to the grant or assignment of rights.

A short checklist of the areas in an agreement which are effected by the copyright issues include:

1   The definitions at the front.

2   The wording of the assignment or licence and the rights which are assigned or granted.

3   A reservation of rights which are not granted or assigned may avoid disputes and also allow you to retain rights which don't exist at the time of the agreement.

4   The undertakings by the copyright owner as to the originality and ownership of the rights in the work and the material; the fact there is no pre-existing agreements which conflict with the current one or any legal proceedings pending.

5   An indemnity which can be drafted narrowly and capped so that liability is not unlimited or drafted widely so that direct and indirect costs are recouped.

6   The issue of the degree of change which is allowed to any adaptation must be stated. This is best done by defining the proposed new version and attaching a summary, and also putting approval or consent mechanisms in place. An editorial control clause may be used to stipulate the degree of change that can be made to any new adapted material that is based on the original work. Also the copyright owner can put in place quality control provisions so that there are rights of approval or consultation over each stage of a project.

7   Credits and copyright notice clauses are important in an agreement. Your name and copyright notice should be displayed in a prominent position on every single copy in any format of your work. This can be achieved in different styles, but involves a copyright notice, the name of the copyright owner and the year of first publication or release to the public. The issue of credits should be stipulated in the contract as a separate issue and if required the size/position/prominence set out. This may be important where there are other contributors.

8   Moral rights may be asserted or waivered and fall into two parts. The right to be identified as the author and the right not to be subjected to derogatory treatment of a copyright, literary, dramatic, musical or artistic work.

A treatment of a work is defined to cover any addition to, deletion from, alteration to or adaptation of a work, but does not apply to an authorised translation. Where you get other people to carry out work for you such as photos, artwork or writing. The safest option is to make sure that there is a full and complete assignment of 'all rights in all media whether in existence now or created in the future for the full period of copyright and any extensions or renewals'.

Advertising, marketing and packaging is often an area which is not considered for copyright issues in agreements. However it is crucial to be able to insist on rights of approval or consultation. As well as basic copyright notices and credits appearing on all copies that may be reproduced or distributed. It is also important to maintain a consistency of brand and to ensure that any person who creates a new version based on your own does not acquire any rights.

Funding and sponsorship of an Event or Festival

Do you even need an agreement? Sponsorship in a wide variety of forms and shapes is now a very lucrative and desirable form of funding for the arts, culture, music, sports and festivals. It is a growing market where businesses are seeking to create an image and identity to align themselves to a very specific target audience and to feed into the social media as a tool for achieving sales. Organisations and individuals often rely for these arrangements on an exchange of emails which broadly sets out the amount of money to be paid and how the logo and name of the company is to be used in marketing and in the programme catalogue or on the entry tickets. Often these exchanges fail to clarify expenditure costs, liability and responsibilities and how the sponsor may use and promote its role as a sponsor or the material available to it from other third parties who are taking part or even who owns the new logos and other material which is created. Expectations may be high and planned television coverage and attendance may not be achieved due to bad weather or some other reason. It is in all the parties interest to set out the terms so that representations made in a meeting, on a website or by email are either set out as part of the document or recognised as promotional hype or useful background material but not binding.

Many festivals and events set out what they can offer a sponsor and the role expected to be fulfilled by a sponsor on their website. Some organisations have levels of sponsorship and funding from platinum to bronze with clearly defined benefits attached to the annual payment. The sponsors' details may be displayed in the form of their name and logo on the website; in a catalogue; on a venue wall and in any email marketing newsletter; and on associated marketing merchandise. The level of sponsorship may fund the right to have the corporate, product or individuals name listed as the title for a seasonal programme of events; or it may fund the right to have a venue such as a research or sports centre named in their honour with an associated logo.

Establish whether you are the sole funder of an event or if there is a tier of sponsors linked to sub-groups of a programme or categories such as food, drink, VIP hospitality, equipment, security, radio and television coverage, products, music, transport etc. Get a map or programme of previous years so that although the sponsors may not be the same. You have an actual example of the layout and use of the previous sponsors name, logo and products. Understand the operation and management of the event so that you can optimise displays and marketing material. Look at issues of the need for planning consent as well as health and safety factors relating to electrical supplies, adverse weather conditions and location access problems. You may not be sponsoring the event; just a display in a clearly defined sector or part of a programme of performances or you may be the sole sponsor and supplier in relation to a category of food, drinks or other products or services. There would therefore be a term in the contract that no other company, business or competitor would be allowed to have a stall, distribute or promote their products or take or contribute any funds or products in any part in the event or festival. In extreme cases this has meant that as people have entered a venue all drinks have been confiscated as a condition of entry.

The sponsorship agreement is often of combination of funds, products, services, staff and attendance by the sponsor. The payment of the funds by the sponsor may be in one payment in advance or subject to stage payments signature of the agreement, booking the venue, draft programme, first day of event and finally enabling all the banners, flags and promotional material to be displayed as required under the agreement. The first option is obviously preferable for the organisers and no access to the site is permitted if the advance payment has not been received. The arrangements may be as diverse as a literary festival where in return for non-exclusive sponsorship funds there may be:

1   An agreed number of complimentary tickets;

2   Credits of the name and logo of the sponsor on the programme, tickets and website.

3   Some banners permitted to be displayed supplied by the sponsor or the sponsor's logo and name included on the banner and other displays of the organisers but not necessarily in conjunction with the name of the event and title rights which may be held by someone else;

4   Branding on a hired or allocated stall, tent or other venue to be used by the sponsor which may either be supplied for free or incur an additional hire cost. Staff wearing branded outfits and promoting and selling products or services. The site of any location reserved should be specified in relation to a map of the site which is attached as part of the agreement. The traffic from those that attend may vary enormously based on the location.

5   The right to host a hospitality event at the sponsor's cost.

6   Membership of an organisation for a year as a listed sponsor and access to the use of their services.

7   A sponsored feature article in a newsletter or magazine distributed to members.

8   A promotional space on the website.

9   Banner links on the website.

10   Access to the site and the use of third party facilities such as electricity, water, light if any and how the costs associated with this right are to be paid. Combined with an indemnity to repair any damage caused by access to the site and use of the facilities.

11   The right to offer tickets in a competition for the public and how that may be promoted and marketed.

To a more green environmental or arts and cultural ethos which would automatically restrict the types of sponsors and would even involve a process of vetting their credentials in terms of international trade; waste; recycling and how their brand is perceived by the public. The organisers may offer opportunities subject to a policy of the products, services and contributions which would not be allowed. This may include:

1   Refusal to allow any perimeter advertising on the site or even any large banners, flags or electronic displays. This may be in order for the organisers to comply with their own occupation of the site; planning consent issues and on a more subjective level the overall appearance of the festival to maintain an environment which meets the organisers own criteria of their brand for that event.

2   There may be restrictions which ban leaflet distribution in total through the site or limit promotion to a hired location.

3   There may be restrictions as to the total number of categories of vendors and sponsors for food, drink and other goods being sold and distributed. Logos and names may also appear on litter bins and sponsors may be obliged to contribute to clean up costs related to the disposal process. In addition all glass may be banned on site as a safety measure.

4   An obligation for the sponsor to have minimum public liability insurance cover and supply copy of policy to the organisers with proof of payment of the premiums.

5   There are clear advantages for addressing each case on its facts and setting the roles and responsibilities for costs and budgets, liabilities and indemnities from either party to each other. This enables risk to be reduced and also for finances to be kept within reasonable accountable parameters.

6   The organiser would want to list a series of circumstances in which force majeure could be construed as applying including fire, evacuation due to smoke, floods, electrical or other power failure, ill health of major performers. To clarify how costs are to be met and how the event is to be rescheduled if at all. The circumstances in which the holding

company for the organisers goes into administration and who will then either have access to or own the material which has been created to date. Consequently clauses relating to the process of resolving disputes and claims by either party would assist in order to avoid delays.

7	There is a very common move for new marketing images and logos to be altered and adapted for each festival and events; with new banner link advertising, products and slogans to specifically appeal in style and content to the audience attending. This creation and adaptation means that new artwork and computer generated material, sound recording, film, photographs and text are commissioned, designed and delivered. It is vital that the issue of ownership is reviewed so that where there is payment there is also a reciprocal written assignment in all rights in all media in all formats. There may also be a waiver of any future credits or acknowledgement or agreement that the artists' role shall be acknowledged and the style and layout and location set out.

8	Where a sponsorship agreement is for a particular individual who is an athlete or sportsperson. Then standards of behaviour not being adhered to may be reasonably be set out as grounds of termination of the agreement. It is useful for all parties to refer to the sports body and any code of conduct which may exist, but also to be very clear as to behaviour which would be deemed unacceptable by the sponsor.

9	This also works in reverse the individual may want to be able to terminate the agreement in the event that company with which he or she is involved with gets into financial difficulties; is associated with a political campaign or is found to be distributing products which could cause harm. It is also important that an individual should be entitled to terminate an agreement with a sponsor where the sponsor becomes involved at a later date in promoting, selling or exploiting products or services which the individual finds offensive, derogatory or believes will damage their reputation and career. That may be acceptable to the sponsor and may mean there is no further liability to pay any further sums to the individual under the agreement or it may still be liable to pay all sums in full.

10	Sponsorship can also be limited by duration and/or territory; what is actually sponsored and covered and specifically be limited to the parties and not be transferable to any third party. Demands and duties may be set out on both sides to create a complete picture. Often what is most forgotten is the use of logos, names, slogans and products in promotion and marketing material on line and on site. There could be a process of approvals or consultation even if the organisers still retain complete editorial control.

11   It is useful to specify the date on which any rights to the sponsor in relation to the event cease and that the sponsor must not claim to be associated to a later event by implication. The sponsor may agree to remove all logos and titles and names relating to the event from its website, products and marketing.

12   Sponsorship of a charity or other organisation may also take the form of payments for branding on products to gain the factor of commercial advantage by association with a cause which is perceived as worthwhile. The payments may then linked to achievement of sales or completely unrelated and fixed.

13   It is quite common now for an event, whether it is a marathon or a car rally, to have numerous sponsors who fund and support the project in relation to the venue with flags, banners and electronic displays, equipment, products being distributed during or after the event, the programme, the agreed credits for the radio and television coverage as well as the participants' shoes, clothes, drinks, bags, accessories, technology and mobiles. Bonuses can be paid linked to success at competitions to an organisation and an individual.

14   Sponsorship is a growing form of promotion and the development of new and imaginative ways of collaborating necessarily mean that slogans, names, logos, images, music and other rights are created which need to be protected and controlled. Either by the organisers of the event or the sponsor's failure to address the issue only results in unnecessary disputes at a later date which could have been avoided.

15   The control and access to data of sales information, personal data of customers and expenditure and budget can also be dealt with. Many organisers will not release personal data or emails for marketing purposes unless specific consent has been provided by an individual due to their need to comply with legislation. If there is any requirement for a sponsor to contribute to any expenditure or budget then how is evidence of this to be substantiated. If the organisers only wish to supply an invoice without any other supporting documents then this should be agreed. A maximum amount may be set as a limit which must not be exceeded.

16   The liability of the sponsor to pay any sums that may be due to any collecting societies for any material performed, broadcast, reproduced or otherwise exploited which they use at any time.

Archive assets for the future. Do you know who owns the new material you commission?

It is very common these days for many different people within a company to be involved in the process of creating, developing and commissioning new material. Whether it the supply of new software and technology for your company, marketing and promotion, product design developers, editors, interns, researchers, executives, license managers or legal and business units. A failure to agree terms and for letter agreements or some other document to be signed often means that a company is not creating a useable archive of assets for the future. This avoidance is largely due to a perception that the creative process may be delayed or impeded or that any such process is unnecessary. If the only evidence of the arrangement is an exchange of emails then when in later years the question is asked who owns this material? Then the answer to the question could go either way and be based on a factual examination of the material which exists looking for copyright notices and other credits.

The importance of agreeing terms affects the livelihood of the designer, creator, artist, musician or songwriter or author and it is essential for them to consider whether they will want to retain ownership and control of the copyright and other rights in the original work and material as well as any subsequent adaptations. There has been numerous instances of material whether it be a design for a logo or a photograph or a contribution to a musical work or a sound recording or written work. Where parties have been involved in expensive litigation as a failure to clarify the nature and extent of their agreement at the time. If you are only agreeing for the work to be used in a specific manner for the payment then spell it out clearly and reserve all the other rights. Then additional rights can be licensed at a later date and payments can be negotiated for those specific uses if you so choose. If the work is only licensed for one language and translations are not permitted then it is important this these details are set out. The more specific areas that are covered then the less likely there is to be disputes.

The preferred route would be therefore to licence anything on a non-exclusive basis for a limited time period in a small area for a specific authorised purpose only. Everything else would be reserved and retained by the rights or copyright owner. This would effectively allow sales and exploitation elsewhere and increase advance payments over a period of time. The second choice would be to grant an exclusive licence for a small territory for a specific purpose for a fixed period. So that the licensee has a margin of exclusivity for those types of services or products in that zone but not for anything else. So the exclusivity might be limited to calendars but would not apply to household goods or other types of merchandise. Here it is very important to try to set out the exact nature of what is permitted and what is not in detail and to retain everything else whether those rights exist in a form you are aware of now or not. There have been many cases of older contracts not making any reference to new rights and technology and so performers and contributors have not been paid any additional royalties or payments when the material has been reproduced and exploited in that new medium. There have also in the past be disputes over whether a plastic children's book for the bath constitutes a book or whether it is a toy.

You would want to avoid exclusive arrangements which in effect transfer copyright and other rights in all media to another party for the full period of copyright and in perpetuity. Unless of course that is what you wanted to achieve because the financial remuneration which you are being paid is sufficient for that disposal in effect to be worthwhile. It does not matter whether you have a start up business and your friends are helping by doing some artwork and photographs or you have a successful company. In due diligence when a company is prepared for flotation for the stock market and all the representations are verified. The failure to have set up a library of documentation can affect both the final price and the speed at which matters can progress. It is a clear benefit to have a strategy to acquire, own and control either all or as many of the rights as feasible given the budget. As well as the actual material including the masters in everything you commission or exploit. This can be done by an assignment or buy out of all rights in all media in the title, content, prototype, any sample and the final product. Everything is handed over and stored for future use by the purchaser of all the rights. The agreement would also include resolving the issue of whether there would be a right to a credit or some other form of acknowledgement; and also whether moral rights were asserted or waivered. It is useful to have a clause that makes it clear that the purchaser of the rights can edit, delete from, vary and adapt any part of the material and also use a third party to work on it or make a contribution. That in such instance there would be no need to consult with the creator and that all editorial control and rights to adapt or vary the material rest with the owner of the rights. The reverse scenario would be for the creator and originator to hold on to the majority of the rights and material and only licence a very narrow section for a limited period. This would have the effect over a period of time of generating the most revenue.

Great care should be taken in deciding whether it in your interests to register your work with a collecting society. It is vital that you understand the authority that you have handed to these organisations to licence your work. The range of areas now covered means that unless you are on their excluded list at your request. That you may find that they have licensed material to a third party without any consultation with you despite the fact that you are not a registered member and have never asked them to deal with your work. Where you do authorise them to act on your behalf they are effectively acting as your authorised representative and will often not be required to consult with you regarding any request or to seek your specific consent. The collecting societies meet a demand and collect revenues which in many cases would not otherwise be paid.. So a strategy in relation to all collecting societies is important so that you do not find your work has been exploited in a manner which permits use by a third party in return for very little revenue. Collecting societies do not just licence and exploit by collecting sums for scanning, photocopying, reproduction, performance and broadcast and resale. They now cover extensive forms of exploitation. They serve a worthwhile function for many members but you need to understand the scope of what they do and look at each one separately.

It has not been unknown for a great deal of money to be spent on designing and developing websites, films or photographs which have subsequently been abandoned as a result of the work never being finished within budget or to the quality required. It is important to set out what in expected and to be achieved for the budget and costs and to link payment to completion of tasks and delivery. There have been numerous cases where web pages have not functioned properly; design quality has been poor and the budget has been exceeded. This then leads to additional requests for cost and the additional sums justified in terms of changes and alterations that were different from the original idea. Therefore scope for changes should have been factored into the original budget and seen as a predictable factor with a contingency. Many of these types of disputes have meant that some developers have refuse to hand over all the codes, software and rights to the unfinished site or to let any other third party work on it. Even if the developer has been paid all the original sums in the budget. So in a web design agreement the right to get someone else to work on the project and for the developer to hand over all the material and rights is a key term whether or not the website is completed.

Where the artist, photographer or other creator has licensed a logo, artwork or photograph for a book cover, label, website or marketing tool, but you know the company wishes to exploit it in other media. Then it is to your advantage to agree terms and prices at the start of the project. If the book or website is very successful either in terms of traffic or revenue the payments to be made for sub-licencing and merchandising will increase significantly. There is no reason however why a creator should not be entitled to share in the benefits of contributing to a project which is financially successful. This may be achieved in the form of a bonus or escalating royalties or fixed payments.

The streaming of material makes it important that rights been cleared or acquired across many types of medium. It is not acceptable to assume that as you have acquired the photograph for a book cover or contribution to a magazine that it may also be used by licensing it to a third party through a subscription service. Nor can it be adapted and the colours and medium changed to suit a promotional or marketing campaign if terms of use and payment have not be agreed. Consideration has to be given not only to copyright notices, credits, acknowledgement of sources as well as trade marks and domain names, but also to the different forms of moral rights which exist and can be asserted. There are two aspects to moral rights the right to be identified as the creator of the work in the form of a reasonably prominent and identifiable credit but also the right not to have a work changed and adapted so that it is distorted and represented in a completely different way from the original without consent. In an archive you are either trying to get such moral rights waived as a matter of policy and then agreeing credits and notices or moral rights in all forms are asserted in detail and the expected layout, design, wording and any logos specified.

An undertaking as to originality and the formats in which the work is to be delivered and at whose cost ensure that both parties are clear that material is not expected to be a copy or plagiarised from third parties. Where the work is expected to contain third party material then it helps if it is spelt out that all such material must be clearly identified and the extent of the information required ie title, author ISBN, publication date, page reference or format, where material is held and by whom together with contact details. The source reference in the delivered work may be less extensive then the additional list.

Where technology is changing at such a rapid rate one of the issues which arises is whether a party has the right to exploit something which did not even exist at the time of the agreement. This will depend on the terms of the agreement both parties concluded. This has resulted in artists and performers not receiving any payments for films being exploited on vhs, in animation form and by merchandising arrangements. This failure to receive any sums could have been avoided of the agreements had specifically reserved the rights or had an additional clause which may reference to future rights and developments and set a rate or fee to be paid.

Legal, Commercial and Business Development Directory

• The website references are grouped under broad headings and are not divided into countries. Obviously some cover more than one listed topic. This is a quick reference guide to other sources of information that we hope you will find helpful for background research and business development.

• The Authors and the Publisher cannot accept any responsibility for your use of any links and/or any reliance you may place on the information that you may obtain from any websites. We are not endorsing nor making any recommendations as to the quality and/or accuracy of any of the websites. You use the website references and resources entirely at your own risk. The Authors and the Publisher shall not be liable for any consequences of any nature whether direct and/or indirect that may arise as a result of your access to, use of and/or reliance upon on any website and/or its content.

Film, Television, Radio, DVD
Ofcom www.ofcom.org.uk
BBC www.bbc.co.uk
BBC Worldwide www.bbcworldwide.com
ITV www.itv.com
Channel 4 www.channel4.com
ITN News www.itn.co.uk
Channel 5 www.channel5.com
All3media www.all3media.com
STV www.stv.tv
Sky www.sky.com
Discovery Communications www.discovery.com
CNN www.cnn.com
Freeview www.freeview.co.uk
MGM www.mgm.com
Time Warner www.timewarner.com
Endemol www.endemol.com
Lion TV www.liontv.com
Tiger Aspect Productions www.tigeraspect.co.uk
Walt Disney Company www.thewaltdisneycompany.com
Warner Bros www.warnerbros.co.uk
Paramount www.paramount.com
RDF Television www.rdftelevision.com

Zodiak Media www.zodiakmedia.com
Artificial Eye www.artifical-eye.com
Capital Films www.capitol-films.com
Shine Group www.shinegroup.tv
Shine TV www.shine.tv
British Pathe www.britishpathe.com
Pathe UK www.pathe.co.uk
20th Century Fox International www.fox.co.uk
20th Century Fox www.foxmovies.com
Universal Pictures UK www.universalpictures.co.uk
Universal Pictures international www.universalpicturesinternational.com
Producers Alliance for Cinema and Television PACT www.pact.co.uk
British Film Institute www.bfi.org.uk
UK Film Council www.industry.bfi.org.uk
The British Academy www.britac.ac.uk
British Federation of Film Societies BFFS www.bffs.org.uk
British Video Association www.bva.org.uk
Video Performance Ltd www.vpl.co.uk
The Association for TV on Demand www.atvod.co.uk
University Film and Video Association www.ufva.org
British Universities Film and Video Council www.bufvc.ac.uk
Cinema Exhibitors Association www.cinemauk.org.uk
UK Screen Association www.ukscreenassociation.co.uk
Irish Film Board www.irishfilmboard.ie
European Broadcasting Union www.ebu.ch
European Conference of Postal and Telecommunications Administrations
CEPT www.cept.org
European Film Export Association EFEA www.efea.eu
Commonwealth Broadcasting Association www.cba.org.uk
International Federation of Film Producers Associations www.fiapf.org
International Association of Wildlife Filmmakers www.iawf.org.uk
British Film Commission www.britishfilmcommission.org.uk
Community Broadcasting Association of Australia www.cbaa.au
Australian Communications and Media Authority ACMA www.acma.gov.au
Beyond www.beyond.com.au
Hong Kong Office of the Communications Authority www.ofca.gov.hk
Hong Kong Digital Audio Broadcasting www.digitalradio.gov.hk
Digital TV www.digitaltv.hk
Gov HK www.gov.hk
Infosec www.infosec.gov.uk
Communications Association of Hong Kong www.cahk.hk
Hong Kong Television and Entertainment Licensing Authority www.tela.gov.hk
Motion Picture Licensing Corporation www.themplc.co.uk
Motion Picture Association of America www.mpaa.org

American Film Institute www.afi.com
Independent Film & Television Alliance www.ifta-online.org
IMDb www.imdb.com
Film Distributors Association www.launchingfilms.com
International Game Developers Association www.igda.org
Association of Film Commissioners International www.afci.org
Media Desk UK www.mediadeskuk.eu
European Children's Film Association www.ecfaweb.org
Film Producers Guild of Russia www.kinoproducer.ru
Spanish Association of Producers www.fapae.es
Swiss Film Producers Association www.swissfilmproducers.ch
Czech Film Commission www.filmcommission.cz
Nepal Film Producers Association www.nfpa.org.np
Screen Producers Association of Australia www.spaa.org.au
Canadian Media Production Association www.cmpa.ca
China Filmmakers Association www.sfs-cn.com
Danish Film Producers Association www.pro-f.dk
West Finland Film Commission www.wfci.fi
Association of Icelandic Film Producers www.producers.is
National Film Development Corporation of India www.nfdindia.com
Italian Film Producers ANICA www.anica.it
Motion Picture Association of Japan www.eiren.org
Netherland Filmproducenten www.speelfilmproducenten.nl
Screen Production and Development Association of New Zealand www.
spada.co.nz
RadioCentre www.radiocentre.org
Screen Digest www.screendigest.com
Screen Daily www.screendaily.com
Hollywood Reporter www.hollywoodreporter.com
Screen International www.screeninternational.com
Scriptwriter magazine www.scriptwritermagazine.com
Variety www.variety.com
Spotlight www.spotlight.com
The Stage www.thestage.co.uk
Equity www.equity.org.uk
British Equity Collecting Society BECS www.equitycollecting.org.uk
American Federation of TV and Radio Artists www.aftra.com
International Artists Managers Association IAMA www.iamaworld.com
Directors Guild of GB www.dggb.co.uk
Directors Guild of America www.dga.org
Guild of Location Managers www.golm.org.uk
European Producers Club www.europeanproducersclub.org
British Association of Picture Libraries and Agencies BAPLA www.bapla.
org.uk

Institute of Professional Sound www.ips.org.uk
British Video Association www.bva.org.uk
The Media Trust www.mediatrust.org
Satellite Industry Association SIA www.sia.org
European Satellite Operators Association ESOA www.esoa.net
ITN Source www.itvnsource.com
Sony Pictures www.sonypictures.com
Televisual www.televisual com
Society of Audiovisual Authors www.saa-authors.com
Association of Model Agents www.associationofmodelagents.org
Event Cinema Association www.eventcinemaassociation.org
Lion Television www.liontv.com
Century TV www.century-tv.co.uk
Maverick TV www.mavericktv.co.uk
Fremantlemedia www.fremantlemedia.com
Verve Productions www.verveproductions.co.uk
BAFTA British Academy of Film and Television Arts www.bafta.org
Videotel www.videotel.com
Avalon Entertainment www.avalonuk.com
M & C Saatchi Merlin mcsaachimerlin.com
Ray Knight www.rayknight.co.uk
Storm www.stormmodels.com

Writers, Publishers and Newspapers
The Society of Authors www.societyofauthors.org
International Federation of Journalists www.ifj.org
Authors Licensing and Collecting Society www.alcs.co.uk
Publishers Association www.publishers.org.uk
Independent Publishers Guild www.ipg.uk.com
The Professional Publishers Association www.ppa.co.uk
Institute of Practitioners in Advertising IPA www.ipa.co.uk
Association of Learned and Professional Society Publishers www.alpsp.org
Society of Editors www.societyofeditors.co.uk
The Writers Guild of Great Britain www.writersguild.org.uk
Chartered Institute of Journalists www.cij.co.uk
Writers Guild of America www.wga.org
The Association of American Publishers www.publishers.org
American Society of Journalists and Authors www.asja.org
The Council of Editors of Learned Journals www.celj.org
Periodical Publishers Association www.ppa.co.uk
The Bibliographical Society www.bibsoc.org.uk
Press Complaints Commission www.pcc.org.uk
Newspapers Society www.newspapersoc.org.uk
Newspaper Publishers Association www.n-p-a.org.uk

The Association of Newspaper and Magazine Wholesalers www.anmw.co.uk
World Association of Newspapers www.wan-press.org
National Newspaper Association www.nnaweb.org
National Newspapers Publishers Association www.nnpa.org
Press Association www.pressassociation.com
PR Newswire www.prnewswire.co.uk
Commonwealth Press Union www.cpu.org.uk
Bloomsbury Publishing www.bloomsbury.com
Bloomsbury Professional www.bloomsburyprofessional.com
Press Gazette www.pressgazette.co.uk
Nielsen Book Data www.nielsenbookdata.co.uk
Association of Authors' Agents www.agentassoc.co.uk
The Agent's Association GB www.agents-uk.com
Association of Subscription Agents www.subscription-agents.org
The Royal Society of Literature www.rslit.org
Journalism www.journalism.co.uk
The Bookseller www.thebookseller.com
Association of American Publishers www.publishers.org
Australian Publishers Association www.publishers.asn.au
Australian Booksellers Association www.aba.org.au
Australian Society of Authors www.asauthors.org
Association of Publishers in India www.publishers.org.in
Association of Czech Booksellers and Publishers www.sckn.cz
Society of Indexers www.indexers.org.uk
American Society for Indexing www.asindexing.org
Pearson www.pearson.com
Historical Writers Association www.thehwa.co.uk
National Association of Press Agencies www.napa.org.uk
National Press Photographers Association NPPA www.nppa.org
Gardners Books www.gardners.com
Bertram www.bertram.com
Barnes and Noble www.barnesandnoble.com
Amazon US www.amazon.com
Amazon UK www.amazon.co.uk
Publishers Weekly www.publishersweekly.com
Bowker www.bowker.co.uk www.bowker.com
The Royal Society www.royalsociety.org
Copyright Licensing Agency www.cla.co.uk
Canadian Copyright Licensing Agency www.accesscopyright.ca
SACD www.sacd.fr
SABAM Belgium Society of Authors, Composers and Publishers www.sabam.be
SGAE Spanish Society of Authors and Editors www.sgae.es
Australian Society of Authors www.asauthors.org

Society of Children's Book writers and Illustrators Australia and New Zealand www.scbwiaustralianz.com
UNESCO www.unesco.org
UNESCO Depository Libraries www.publishingunesco.org/depositories.aspx
UKSG www.uksg.org
BIC www.bic.org.uk
Legal Week www.legalweek.com
Evening Standard www.standard.co.uk
The Guardian www.theguardian.com
Telegraph www.telegraph.co.uk
Country Life www.countrylife.co.uk
The Scotsman www.thescotsman.com
Times Higher Education www.timeshighereducation.co.uk
International Press Institute www.freemedia.at
PLR Canada Council www.plr-dpp.ca/PLR
Alibris www.alibris.com

Internet, Telephones and Mobiles

Internet Corporation for Assigned Names and Numbers ICANN www.icann.org
Country Code Names Supporting Organisation www.ccnso.icann.org
Hong Kong Internet Service Providers www.hkispa.org.
Hong Kong Wireless Technology Industry Association www.hkwtia.org
The Society of External Telecommunication Service Providers www.hkets.org
Association of Online Publishers www.ukaop.org.uk
Online Publishers Association www.online-publishers.org
Content Marketing Association www.the-cma.com
Ebay www.ebay.co.uk
Amazon www.amazon.com
Ofcom www.ofcom.org.uk
Mobile Broadband Group www.mobilebroadbandgroup.com
ECTA European Competitive Telecommunications Association www.ectaportal.com
European Telecommunications Network Operators' Association www.etno.be
International Association of Internet Hotlines Inhope www.inhope.org
Internet Watch Foundation www.iwf.org.uk
European Commission – Telecoms and Internet www.ec.europa.eu/digital-agenda
Mobile Operators Association www.mobilemastinfo.com
Mobile Entertainment Forum www.mefmobile.org
Mobile Marketing Association www.mmaglobal.com
Phonepayplus www.phonepayplus.org.uk
Information Commissioners Office www.ico.org.uk
Scottish Information Commissioner www.itspublicknowledge.info

Mail Preference Service www.mpsonline.org.uk
Telephone Preference Service www.tpsonline.org.uk
Fax Preference Service www.fpsonline.org.uk
Commonwealth Telecommunications Organisation www.cto.int
ISPA Internet Service Providers Association www.ispa.org.uk
Nominet.uk www.nominet.org.uk
InterNIC The Internet's Network Information Centre www.internic.net
The Internet Society www.internetsociety.org
Uwhois www.uwhois.com
Verisign www.verisign.com
Unicode Consortium www.unicode.org
ISNN www.issn.org
Google www.google.com www.google.co.uk
Google App for Business google.com/enterprise/apps/business
Android Get Apps www.andorid.com/apps
Blackberry World appleworld.blackberry.com
Windows Phone Apps www.windowsphone.com/en-gb/store
Windows App Builder www.windows-appbuilder.co.uk
Twitter www.twitter.com
App Card Twitter Developer www.dev.twitter.com/docs/cards/types/app-card
Youtube www.youtube.com
Facebook www.facebook.com
Bing www.bing.com
Ask www.ask.com
Yahoo www.yahoo.com
Myspace www.myspace.com
EDRI European Digital Rights www.edri.org
Netflix www.netflix.com
Instagram www.instagram.com
PInterest www.pinterest.com
Apple www.apple.com
Itunes www.apple.com/uk/itunes
Tumblr www.tumblr.com
Delicious www.delicious.com
Criteo www.criteo.com
Survey Monkey www.surveymonkey.com
eBooks.com www.ebooks.com
ebooks on Amazon www.amzon.co.uk/kindle
Gardners – The Hive Network www.hive.co.uk
Kobo Books.com www.kobobooks.com
E reading Apps Kobo www.kobo.com/apps
ebooks for Sonyreader www.gb.readerstore.sony.com www.ebookstore.
sony.com
ebooks for Nook www.barnesandnoble.com/u/nook www.uk.nook.com

Whatsapp www.whatsapp.com
Apps Radioplayer www.radioplayer.co.uk/apps
Apps Data Gov UK www.data.gov.uk/apps
Paypal www.paypal.com
Reddit www.reddit.com
Vine Lab Inc www.vine.co www.itunes.apple.com/us/app/vine

Designers, Artists and Photographers

Design and Artists Copyright Society www.dacs.org.uk
Association of Illustrators www.theaoi.com
Society of Illustrators www.societyillustrators.org
Chartered Society of Designers www.csd.org.uk
The Society of British Theatre Designers www.theatredesign.org.uk
The Royal Photographic Society www.rps.org
National Photographic Society www.thenps.co.uk
Artists Collecting Society www.artistscollectingsociety.org
Institute of Art and Law www.ial.uk.com
National Portrait Gallery www.npg.org.uk
The British Postal Museum and Archive www.postalheritage.org.uk
Royal Academy of Arts www.royalacademy.org.uk
National Archives www.nationalarchives.gov.uk
Royal Collection Trust www.royalcollection.org.uk
British Film Designers Guild www.filmdesigners.co.uk
Creative England www.creativeengland.co.uk
Tate www.tate.org.uk
The Design Society www.designsociety.org
The Fine Art Society www.faslondon.com
Contemporary Art Society www.contemporaryartsociety.org
The Art Fund www.artfund.org
Design History Society www.designhistory.org
Arts Law Centre of Australia www.artslaw.com.au

Patents, Trade Marks and Copyright

The Patent Agency www.patent.gov.uk
British Copyright Council www.britishcopyright.org
Europa EU www.europa.eu
OHIM Office for Harmonization in the Internal Markets (Trade Marks and Designs) www.oami.europa.eu
Eur-Lex Official EU Law Portal old – www.eur-lex.europa.eu/en/index and new – www.new.eur-lex.europa.eu/homepage
Cordis www.cordis.europa.eu
EU Who is Who www.europa.eu/whoiswho/public/index
N Lex gateway to National Law eur-lex.europa.eu/n-lex/index
EU Ted Public Procurement www.ted.europa.eu/TED

Eurovoc eurovoc-europa.eu/drupal
FACT Federation against Copyright Theft www.fact-uk.org.uk
British Library Business and IP Centre www.bl.uk/bipc
EPO European Patent Office www.epo.org
European Community Trade Mark Association www.ecta.org
Australian Copyright Council www.copyright.org.au
Benelux Office for IP www.boip.int
Irish Patents Office www.patentsoffice.ie
Institute of Trade Mark Attorneys ITMA www.itma.org.uk
International Trade Mark Association INTA www.inta.org
European Patent Institute www.patentepi.com
International Intellectual Property Institute www.iipi.org
American Intellectual Property Law Association AIPLA www.aipla.org
Copyright Licensing Agency www.cla.co.uk
Copyright Clearance Centre www.copyright.com
World Intellectual Property Organisation www.wipo.int/portal
Worldwide list of IP offices www.wipo.int/directory
UK Intellectual Property Office www.ipo.gov.uk
Austrian Copyright Society www.akm.co.at
US Patent and Trade Mark Office www.uspto.gov
US Copyright Office www.copyright.gov
Legal Information Institute www.law.cornell.edu/topics/copyright
Munich Intellectual Property Law Centre MIPLC www.miplc.de
Japan Patent Office www.jpo.go.jp
Austrian Patent Office www.patentamt.at
Benelux Office for Intellectual Property www.bmb-bbm.org
Denmark IP Centre www.dkpto.dk
Finland Patent Office PRH www.prh.fi
French Patent Office INPI www.inpi.fr
German Patent Office DPMA www.dpma.de
Greek Patent Office www.gge.gr
Luxembourg Patent Office www.etat.lu.se
Netherlands Patent Office www.agentschapnl.nl
Spain Patent Office OEPM www.oepm.es
Sweden Patent Office PRV www.prv.se

Music, Lyrics, Performances and Sound Recordings
PRS for Music PRS –MCPS Alliance www.prsformusic.com
PPL www.ppluk.com
Musicians Union www.musiciansunion.org.uk
Incorporated Society of Musicians www.ism.org
Music Publishers Association www.mpaonline.org.uk
Music Producers Guild www.mpg.org.uk

Guild of International Songwriters and Composers www.songwriters-guild.co.uk
The British Academy www.britac.ac.uk
BPI – recorded music industry www.bpi.co.uk
UK Music www.ukmusic.org
Association of Independent Music www.musicindie.com
BASCA www.basca.org.uk
Music Managers Forum www.themmf.net
The Association of British Orchestras www.abo.org.uk
APRA/AMCOS www.apra-amcos.com.au
Australian Music Publishers Association AMPAL www.ampal.com.au
American Society of Composers, Authors and Publishers ASCAP www.ascap.com
Music Publishers Association of US MPA www.mpa.org
American Performing Rights Society for Songwriters and Publishers SESAC www. sesac.com
Recording Industry Association of America www.riaa.com
Canadian Music Publishers Association CMPA www.musicpublishercanada.ca
Canadian Musical Reproduction Rights Agency www.cmrra.ca
Norwegian Performing Right Society www.tono.no
Nordisk Copyright Bureau www.ncb.dk
Danish Music Publishers Association www.dmff.dk
Danish Collecting Society for Composers, Songwriters and Music Publishers www.koda.dk
Finnish Music Publishers Association www.musiikkikustantajat.fi
German Music Authors Society www.gema.de/en
International Bureau of Societies Administering Recording and Mechanical Reproduction Rights www.biem.org
International Federation of Societies for Authors and Composers www.cisac.org
International Confederation of Music Publishers www.icmp-iciem.org
National Music Publishers Association www.nmpa.org
Society of Composers Inc www.societyofcomposers.org
Music Week www.musicweek.com
Warner/Chappell Music www.warnerchappell.com
Universal Music Group www.universalmusic.com
Royal Opera House www.roh.org.uk

Legal
Laing & Co www.laingandco.co.uk
The Bar Council www.barcouncil.org.uk
The Honourable Society of Gray's Inn www.graysinn.org.uk
The Honourable Society of Inner Temple www.innertemple.org.uk

The Honourable Society of Middle Temple www.middletemple.org.uk
The Honourable Society of Lincoln's Inn www.lincolnsinn.org.uk
Ministry of Justice www.justice.gov.uk
American Bar Association www.americanbar.org
International Bar Association ibanet.org
International Federation of IP Attorneys www.ficpi.org
Institute of Chartered Patent Agents www.cipa.org.uk
The New York State Bar Association www.nysba.org
Hong Kong Bar Association www.hkba.org
Japan Federation of Bar Associations www.nichibenren.or.jp/en
Law Society www.lawsociety.org.uk
Law Society of Scotland www.lawscot.org.uk
Law Society of Northern Ireland www.lawsoc-ni.org
Law Society of New South Wales www.lawsociety.com.au
Law Society of New Zealand www.lawsociety.org.nz
Kwa-Zulu Natal Law Society www.lawsoc.co.za
The Institute of Brand and Innovation Law www.ucl.ac.uk.laws/ibil
Institute of Arbitrators www.arbitrators.org
Worshipful Company of Arbitrators www.arbitratorscompany.org
Licensing Executives Society www.lesi.org
Association of Pension Lawyers in Ireland www.apli.ie
Asia Pacific Legal Institute www.apli.org
Institute of Chartered Secretaries www.icsa.org.uk   www.icsaglobal.com
Institute of Directors www.iod.com
Companies House www.companieshouse.gov.uk
British and Irish Legal Information Institute www.bailii.org
British Institute of International and Comparative Law www.biicl.org
British and Irish Law, Education and Technology Association www.bileta.ac.uk
Scottish Law Agents Society www.scottishlawagents.org
ICLR (The Incorporated Council of Law Reporting) www.lawreports.co.uk
Scottish Council for Law Reports www.scottishlawreports.org.uk
Scottish Law Commission www.scotlaw.com
Law Commission www.lawcommission.justice.gov.uk
Judicial Appointments Commission www.jac.judiciary.gov.uk
International Association of Entertainment Lawyers www.iael.org
Commonwealth Lawyers Association www.commonwealthlawyers.com
Commonwealth Magistrates and Judges Association www.cmja.org
Commonwealth Association of Public Sector Lawyers www.capsl.org
Procurement Lawyers Association www.procurementlawyers.org
International Legal Technology Association www.iltnet.org
Commercial Law Association of Australia www.cla.org.au
Canadian Association of Legal Administrators www.alanet.org
Chartered Institute of Legal Executives www.cilex.org.uk

Institute of Paralegals www.theiop.org
National Association of Licensed Paralegals www.theiop.org
State Bar of California www.calbar.ca.gov
American Arbitration Association www.adr.org
American Law Institute www.ali.org
United Nations International Law www.un.org/en/law
Student Law Journal www.studentlawjournal.com
IPKat www.ipkitten.blogspot.com
Society for Computers and the Law www.scl.org
Institute of Advanced Legal Studies www.ials.sas.ac.uk
UK Environmental Law Association www.ukela.org
American Society of International Environmental Law www.asil.org
Centre for International Environmental Law www.ciel.org
Ecclesiastical Law Society www.ecclawsoc.org.uk
Charity Law Association www.charitylawassociation.org.uk
Sports Lawyers Association www.sportslaw.org
Australian and New Zealand Sports Law Association www.anzsla.com.au
Industrial Law Society www.industriallawsociety.org.uk
The Notaries Society www.the notariessociety.org.uk

Government and Agencies

Legislation gov uk www.legislation.gov.uk
Office of Public Sector Information www.opsi.org.uk
HM Courts and Tribunals Service www.justice.gov.uk/about/hmcts
Local Government Association www.local.gov.uk
Department for British Innovation and Skills www.gov.uk/government/organisations/department
Gov UK www.gov.uk
Justice Gov UK www.justice.gov.uk
Justice/Mediation www.justice.gov.uk/courts/mediation
Privy Council www.privycouncil.org.uk
Competition Commission www.competition-commission.org.uk
Gambling Commission www.gamblingcommission.gov.uk
Cabinet Office Gov UK www.gov.uk/government/organisations/cabinet-office
Commonwealth Parliamentary Association www.cpahq.org
Pensions Regulator www.thepensionsregulator.gov.uk
Pensions Ombudsman www.pensions-ombudsman.org.uk
Department for Works and Pensions www.dwp.gov.uk
Land Registry for England and Wales www.landregistry.gov.uk
Property Ombudsman www.tpos.co.uk
Health and Safety Executive www.hse.gov.uk
Scottish Government www.scotland.gov.uk
Welsh Government www.wales.gov.uk
Charity Commission www.charitycommission.gov.uk

Office of the Scottish Charity Regulator www.oscr.org.uk
Council of Europe www.hub.coe.int
Europa EU www.europa.eu
European Parliament www.europarl.europa.eu
Europolitics www.europolitics.info
US Department of State www.state.gov
US Environmental Protection Agency www.epa.gov
US Customs and Border Protection www.cbp.gov
Federal Communications Commission www.fcc.gov
European Network of Equality Bodies www.equineteurope.org
European Disability Forum www.edf-feph.org
European Police Office www.europol.europa.eu
European Centre for Development Policy Management www.ecdpm.org
Institute of Chartered Surveyors www.rics.org
Crown Estate www.thecrownestate.co.uk
United Nations www.unesco.org/culture

Trade, Advertising and Marketing
UK European Consumer Centre Trading Standards Institute www.ukecc.net
British Standards Institute www.bsi-global.com
Trading Standards Institute www.tradingstandards.gov.uk
National Association of Manufacturers www.nam.org
International Organization for Standardization www.iso.org
Office of Fair Trading www.oft.gov.uk
World Trade Organisation www.wto.org
Supply to Government www.supply2gov.net
Wired Gov www.wired-gov.net
Advertising Association www.adassoc.org.uk
Advertising Standards Authority ASA www.asa.org.uk
Clearcast Advertising Services www.clearcast.co.uk
Institute of Practitioners in Advertising www.ipa.co.uk
American Association of Advertising Agents 4 A's www.aaaa.org
Advertising Federation of Australia www.afa.org
Direct Marketing Association UK www.dma.org.uk
The Marketing Society www.marketingsociety.co.uk
Chartered Institute of Marketing CIM www.cim.co.uk
Advertisers Producers Association www.a-p-a.net
British Web Design and Marketing Association www.bwdma.org.uk
Direct Marketing Commission www.dmcommission.com
Country Land and Business Association www.cla.org.uk
Chartered Management Institute www.managers.org.uk
Chartered Institute of Personnel and Development www.cipd.co.uk
Institute of Sales and Marketing Management www.ismm.co.uk
International Chamber of Commerce www.iccwbo.org

British Chamber of Commerce www.britishchambers.org.uk
American Chamber of Commerce to EU www.amchameu.eu
Hong Kong Commerce and Development Bureau www.cedb.gov.uk
UK Trade and Investment www.ukti.gov.uk
British Toy and Hobby Association www.btha.co.uk
Chartered Institute of Purchasing and Supply CIPS www.cips.org
Institute for Supply Management www.ism.ws
Association of European Chambers of Commerce and Industry www.eurochambres.be
Austrade Australian Trade Commission www.austrade.gov.au
New Zealand Trade and Enterprise www.nzte.govt.nz
Italian Institute for Foreign Trade www.italtrade.com
Hong Kong Trade Development Council www.tdc.org.hk
The Royal Commonwealth Society www.rcsint.org
The Commonwealth Secretariat www.thecommonwealth.org
Commonwealth Foundation www.commonwealthfoundation.com
The Communications Council www.communicationscouncil.org.au
Legal Marketing Association www.legalmarketing.org
Branded Content Marketing Association www.thebcma.info
Chatham House Royal Institute of International Affairs www.chathamhouse.org.uk
United Nations www.un.org
US Department of State www.state.gov
The American Economic Association www.aeaweb.org
The Economist www.economist.com
Marketing Week www.marketingweek.co.uk
Marketing Magazine www.marketingmagazine.co.uk
Institute of Public Relations www.ipr.org.uk
PR Week www.prweek.com
Marketing Association of Australia and New Zealand www.marketing.org.au
Brand Republic www.brandrepublic.com
British Jewellers Association www.bja.org.uk
The Federation of European Employers www.fedee.com
ACAS www.acas.org.uk
Eures European Job Mobility Portal www.eures.europa.eu
Foreign Trade Association www.fta-eu.org www.foreigntradeassociation.com
European Brands Association www.aim.be
British Brands Group www.britishbrandsgroup.org.uk
Federation of International Trade Associations www.fita.org
Chartered Insurance Institute www.cii.co.uk
Society of Local Authority Chief Executives www.solace.org.uk
Institute of Economic Affairs www.iea.org.uk
Australian Institute of International Affairs www.aiia.asa.au
European Commission www.ec.europa.eu/eures/home

Finance and Accounts
Companies House www.companieshouse.gov.uk
Institute and Faculty of Actuaries www.actuaries.org.uk
Institute of Chartered Accountants in England and Wales www.icaew.com
Institute of Chartered Accountants Scotland www.icas.org.uk
International Federation of Accountants www.ifac.org
PrimeGlobal Association of Independent Accounting Firms www.primeglobal.net
International Group of Accounting Firms www.igaf.org
American Institute of Certified Public Accountants www.aicpa.org
American Finance Association www.afajof.org
World Bank Group www.worldbank.org
Bank of England www.bankofengland.co.uk
British Bankers Association www.bba.org.uk
European Accounting Association www.eaa-online.org
The London Stock Exchange www.londonstockexchange.com
Commercial Finance Association www.cfa.com
Financial Executives International www.fei.org
Financial Planning Association www.fpa.net
Financial Director www.financialdirector.co.uk
European Investment Bank www.eib.org
European Banking Authority www.eba.europa.eu
Federation of European Accountants www.fee.be
Audit Commission for England and Wales www.audit-commission.gov.uk
HM Revenue and Customs www.hmrc.gov.uk
Financial Reporting Council www.frc.org.uk
Financial Conduct Authority www.fca.org.uk
Accounts Commission for Scotland www.audit-scotland.gov.uk
National Audit Office www.nao.org.uk
International Council of Securities Association www.icsa.bz/index

Sports and Sponsorship
British Olympic Association Team GB www.teamgb.com
International Association of Athletics Federations www.iaaf.org
England Athletics www.englandathletics.org
British Athletics www.britishathletics.org.uk
London Athletics www.londonathletics.org
UK Sponsorship Database www.uksponsorship.com
Sports Management www.sports-sponsorship.co.uk
English Institute of Sport www.eis2win.co.uk
Sport England www.sportengland.org
Association of Professional Sports Agents www.apsa.org.uk
UK Sport www.uksport.gov.uk
European Commission - Sport www.ec.europa.eu/sport

Official Olympic site www.olympic.org
London Federation of Sports and Recreation www.london-fed-sport.org.uk
Federation of International Football www.fifa.com
Football Association www.thefa.com
Rugby Union Official www.rfu.com
Commonwealth Games Federation www.thecgf.com
Australian Sports Commission www.ausport.gov.au
American Sports Institute www.amersports.org
European Non-Governmental Sports Organisation www.engso.eu
Business in Sports and Leisure www.bisl.org
Sports Business Group www.sportsbusiness.com
Sportcal www.sportcal.com
Institute for Sports Parks and Leisure www.ispal.org.uk
European Sponsorship Association www.sponsorship.org
Chartered Institute for the Management of Sport and Physical Activity www.cimspa.co.uk
The Lawn Tennis Association www.lta.org.uk

Archives, Libraries, Museums and Universities
British Library www.bl.uk
Bodleian Library www.bodley.ox.ac.uk
Imperial War Museum www.iwm.org.uk
Royal Botanic Garden www.kew.org
National Library of New Zealand www.natlib.govt.nz
The National Archives www.nationalarchives.gov.uk
English Heritage www.english-heritage.org.uk
British Museum www.britishmuseum.org
American Association of Law Libraries www.aallnet.org
Library of Congress www.catalog.loc.gov
MyLoc gov (Library of Congress) www.myloc.gov
National Library Strasbourg www.bnus.u-strasbg.fr
Biblioteque National France www.bnf.fr
British and Irish Association of Law Librarians www.bialii.org.uk
National Museum of Photography, Film and Television www.nationalmedia musuem. org.uk
National Trust www.nationaltrust.org.uk
Historical Manuscripts Division www.hmc.gov.uk/archondirectory
Museum Association www.museumassociation.org
European Digital Libraries Programme www.ec.europa.eu/digital-agenda
European Bureau of Library, Information and Document Associations www.eblida.org
The European Library www.europeanlibrary.org
Association of College and Research Libraries www.ala.org/acrl
Association of Media Libraries www.aukml.org.uk

Chartered Institute of Library and Information Professionals www.cilip.org.uk
International Federation of Library Associations and Institutions www.ifla.org
American Library Association www.ala.org
American Association of Law Libraries www.aallnet.org
Archives and Records Association www.archives.org.uk
Association of Commonwealth Archivists and Record Managers www.acarm.org
Association of Research Libraries www.arl.org
Information and Records Management Society www.arms.org.uk
Commonwealth Association of Museums www.maltwood.uvic.ca/cam
Association of Commonwealth Universities www.acu.ac.uk
Association of University Research and Industry Links www.auril.org.uk
Special Libraries Association www.sla.org
Copac www.copac.ac.uk
University of Melbourne www.unimelb.edu.au
Ucas www.ucas.com

Exhibitions and Data
Association of Event Organisers www.aeo.org.uk
Legal IT Show www.legalitbizshow.com
E Commerce Expo www.ecommerceexpo.co.uk
Online Information www.online-information.co.uk
Midem www.midem.com
Publishing and Media Expo www.publishing-expo.co.uk
eCommerce Expo www.ecommerceexpo.co.uk
The London Book Fair www.londonbookfair.co.uk
Book Expo America www.bookexpoamerica.com
Cannes Film Festival Mipcom www.mipcom.com

Environmental and Recycling
European Climate Foundation www.europeanclimate.org
Friends of the Earth Europe www.foeeurope.org
International Union for Conservation of Nature www.iucn.org
European Environment Agency www.eea.europa.eu
European Maritime Safety Agency www.emsa.europa.eu

Festivals, Fundraising and Ideas
Institute of Fundraising www.institute-of-fundraising.org.uk
MediaDesk www.mediadeskuk.eu
Glastonbury www.glastonburyfestivals.co.uk
Glyndebourne www.glyndebourne.com
Netherlands Film Festival www.filmfestival.nl
Sheffield Doc/Fest www.sheffdocfest.com
Berlin Film Festival www.berlinale.de

Chelsea Flower Show www.rhs.org.uk/shows
Crowdfunding www.crowdfunding.co.uk
Ideastap www.ideastap.com
Ted www.ted.com/talks
Kickstarter www.kickstarter.com

Index

This index is compiled by reference to the alphabetical main clause headings and clause code numbers. * Indicates that there is no such main clause heading in the book and you will be referred to other relevant main clause headings.

Other content:

Six background supporting articles:
1. Practical key highlights of
   some of the main types of
   clauses in a contract and how
   they may be varied.
2. Guide to the mistakes,
   omissions and errors to avoid
   in contract, licence and
   distribution agreements.
3. Sub-Licensing and
   Merchandising.
4. Understanding copyright and
   how it is used in contracts.
5. Funding and sponsorship of
   an Event or Festival.
6. Archive assets for the future.
   Do you know who owns the
   new material you commission?

**Legal, Commercial and Business
Development Directory.**

Single End Licence Agreement for use of CD-Rom by purchaser of the book

The CD-Rom is only sold in conjunction with the book The A-Z of Contract Clauses Sixth Edition which is published under an exclusive licence by Bloomsbury Professional www.bloomsburyprofessional.com ('the Publishers'). The A-Z of Contract Clauses Sixth Edition is an original work written by Deborah Fosbrook and Adrian C Laing ('the Authors'). The Authors are the copyright owners of the book ('the work') and the disc, data and contents.

It is a condition and you are required to agree to the terms set out below in order to be permitted to use the work as reproduced in the CD-Rom whilst it is in the possession or under the control of the Purchaser. If you do not agree to these terms then no authority is provided to use any part of the disc, data and contents in any manner.

1   The Purchaser of the book and CD-Rom is granted a non-exclusive and non-transferable licence by the Authors and the Publishers to use the disc, data and contents for the purpose for which it is intended in conjunction with The A-Z of Contract Clauses Sixth Edition. That is to be able to edit, cut and paste the clauses to your own documents and/ or agreements and/or to add clauses to documents supplied to you by third parties in order to use them in your business transactions and/ or as part of your terms and condition of trading on your website. This right is personal to you as the Purchaser and shall also permit you to copy the files from the disc on to your personal hard drive and also to make one security copy.

2   It is accepted by the Publishers that lawyers and others in practice and/or the media and/or other industries may use the work, disc, data and contents to provide legal advice and/or services to individuals and companies. This does not permit the Purchaser to supply documents over the internet as a business using the work, disc, data and/or contents. There is no right to copy, reproduce and/or supply the work, disc, data and/or contents for supply by the Purchaser to such persons by photocopying or electronically supplying large sections of the work. Please advise your clients or company to purchase the work and disc for each person.

3   You shall not have the right to make any additional copies and/or to reproduce the work, disc, data and contents for any other reason and/ or to add the work, disc, data and/or contents to any central clause library for your business which is available to more than one person or any one else other than the Purchaser. You shall not have the right to use the work, disc, data and contents to create an index for clauses

and/or to develop and create any model clauses for use by your business and/or organisation which will be displayed, promoted and/or supplied on the internet and/or in a directory and/or to create and/or develop any contract software and/or any training resource and/or workshops. You shall not have the right to exploit, adapt, licence, translate and/or create a new format and/or create a version for use on the internet and/or as part of any storage and/or retrieval system in any form whether electronic, digital or otherwise in any media and/or to permit, authorise, sub-licence, assign, transfer and/or otherwise exploit the work, disc, data and contents in any form in any medium, whether for commercial purposes or otherwise and/or any other method whether in existence now or created in the future. For the avoidance of doubt unauthorised copying includes using the precedents in any manner (whether for commercial gain or not) other than for adapting the contents in the normal course of your personal business and you must not therefore make the contents available to the public in the form they appear in the disc, nor represent that the clauses individually or collectively are your property. Nor may you display the work, disc, data and contents on your website in whole and/or part in order to offer the contents to third parties at anytime.

4   The work, disc, data and contents are an excluded work from the Copyright Licensing Agency and all other collecting societies and there is no license granted to scan, photocopy and/or to create a digital version and/or provide the work, disc, data and contents as part of any service of any nature whether for educational purposes or not.

5   You shall not under any circumstances use the work, disc, data and/or its content in any manner that brings the Authors into disrepute or is otherwise used to the detriment of the Authors. The copyright owners shall claim damages for any breach by a third party and/or any unauthorised substantial copying, use, adaptation and/or other unauthorised exploitation of any nature which is in breach of the copyright and other rights held in this work, disc, data and contents.

6   The Purchaser shall not acquire any copyright, intellectual property and/or other rights and/or interest in the work, disc, data and/or contents and/or any adaptation derived from it in any form in any media of any nature at any time and/or represent to third parties that they are entitled to do so. All rights that are not specifically authorised and granted are expressly reserved.

7   The Publishers and the Authors do not accept any responsibility arising out of the use of the work, disc, data and contents by the Purchaser at any time for any purpose. Neither the Publishers nor the Authors shall be liable for any expenses, losses, damages and/or injury of any nature whether direct and/or indirect, consequential and/or otherwise that may arise in respect of the Purchaser and/or any business in which

the Purchaser is and/or may be involved and/or to which the Purchaser may supply material and/or advice for any reason and/or purpose. The Purchaser therefore uses the work, disc, data and contents entirely at the Purchaser's sole risk and cost and the Purchaser agrees that the Publishers and Authors shall not be liable for any reason.

8 Neither the Publishers nor the Authors accept any responsibility of any nature howsoever arising for any errors, omissions, viruses, defects, failures and/or any other matters of any nature in the work, disc, data and contents whether such fault is of a legal, technical or other nature. The Purchaser must use the disc and/or data entirely at its sole risk and cost and accept that the contract clauses are for reference and guidance only and are intended to be adapted and varied accordingly by each Purchaser to suit their particular circumstances.

9 In the event that there is a fault in the disc itself not directly or indirectly caused by the Purchaser, the Publishers agree to replace the disc within 30 days of purchase provided that the disc and/or the data has been treated with all due care and not mistreated in some manner and/or damaged by some other means after purchase. If the disc and/or the data is incompatible with the Purchaser's hardware and there is no alternative product available then there is no liability and/or responsibility on the part of the Publishers to provide any other disc and/or make any refund of any nature to the Purchaser.

10 In the event of any claim, action and/or demand of any nature being made against and/or by the Purchaser arising out of the use of the work, disc, data and contents in any circumstances. Any such claim against the Publishers and/or the Authors shall be limited to the purchase price of the work and disc.

11 The Purchaser agrees that it is the Purchasers' own responsibility to pay the cost of insurance cover for the benefit of the Purchaser, any business and/or third party for the use of work, disc, data and contents by the Purchaser. The Purchaser agrees that the Publisher and the Authors shall not bear any responsibility and/or liability for the use of the work, disc, data and contents by the Purchaser, any business, third party or otherwise which is supplied directly or indirectly by the Purchaser at any time.

12 The copyright owners of the work, disc, data and contents are the Authors who formally assert individually and jointly their moral rights which may exist now and/or may be created in the future and shall therefore at all times be prominently and reasonably identified as follows: © Deborah Fosbrook and Adrian C Laing 1996–2014.

The Publishers shall be identified where appropriate as Bloomsbury Professional.

13 In the event that the Purchaser has reasonable grounds to believe that the work, disc, data and contents is being used in any unlawful manner the Publishers and the Authors shall be informed in confidence without delay by the Purchaser.

14 In the event that the Publishers and/or the Authors become aware and/or have reasonable grounds to believe that the Purchaser, its business, employees and/or associates are using the work, disc, data and contents in a manner that contravenes the terms of these conditions and/or which is prejudicial is any manner to the Publishers and/or the Authors. Then this licence may be summarily terminated without notice. In such circumstances the Purchaser will be obliged upon written request to surrender all copies of the disc and/or to delete all copies held on any hard drive and/or otherwise.

15 The Purchaser shall not use the work, disc, data and/or contents in any manner inconsistent with the above terms and under no circumstances shall the Purchaser alter, remove, deface, erase and/or amend the copyright notice, trade marks, or details concerning the Publishers and/or the Authors displayed on any part of this disc and/or its packaging.

16 The licence is intended to be a legally binding agreement and shall be governed exclusively by the Laws of England and Wales.